THE Ultimate Book of Trees and Shrubs for New Zealand

THE Ultimate Book of Trees and Shrubs for New Zealand

Edited by Geoff Bryant

David Bateman
New Zealand

Publisher	Gordon Cheers
Managing editor	Sue Wagner
New Zealand editor	Geoff Bryant
Production manager	Margaret Olds
Introduction (pp 10–14) & feature panels (pp 10–47)	Geoff Bryant
The Cultivation of Trees & Shrubs (pp 14–47)	Roger Mann
Consultants	Tony Rodd
	Roger Mann
	Dr J. Gentilli
	Tony Pile
	Fabrice Rolando
Writers	Bettina Gollnow
	Allen Gilbert
	Sarah Guest
	Prof. Colin Johnson
	Julia Hancock
	Helen Moody
	Judy Moore
	Dalys Newman
	Adri Pienaar
Editors	Kate Etherington
	Lisa Foulis
	Heather Jackson
	Susan Page
	Marie-Louise Taylor
Art director	Stan Lamond
Page layout	Joy Eckermann
Picture sizing	Jean Burnard
Map	Stan Lamond
	Graham Keane
Picture research	Gordon Cheers

Sophora tetraptera, the North Island kowhai.

Published in New Zealand by
David Bateman Ltd
Albany Business Park
Bush Road,
Albany, Auckland, New Zealand

First published 1996

All rights reserved. No part of this book may be reproduced, stored in a retrieval system or transmitted in any form or by any means, electronic, mechanical, photocopying, recording or otherwise, without the prior written permission of the Publisher.

ISBN 186 9 533208

Type formatting: Deetype

Film separation:
  Pica Colour Separation Overseas Pte Ltd

Printed in *Hong Kong* by
  Dah Hua Printing Press Co. Ltd

Page 1: *Clianthus puniceus*, kaka beak.

Page 2: *Metrosideros umbellata*, southern rata.

Page 5: Trees and shrubs of varying sizes complement this gentle waterfall.

Contents

PART ONE
Introducing Trees & Shrubs 8

INTRODUCTION 10

NATIVE OR EXOTIC? 10

EVERGREEN OR DECIDUOUS? 13

FAST-GROWING OR SLOW-GROWING? 13

FLOWERS, FRUIT, FOLIAGE 13

SCULPTURAL EFFECTS 13

ATTRACTING BIRDS 14

THE CULTIVATION OF TREES & SHRUBS 14

The Environment 14

FORESTS 14

THE FOREST EDGE 15

THE IMPORTANCE OF CLIMATE 16

HARDINESS ZONE MAP 17

Planning the Garden 22

Choosing the Trees & Shrubs 23

The Uses of Trees & Shrubs 24

SHADE, SHELTER & PRIVACY 24

WINDBREAKS 25

Contents

Growing Trees & Shrubs 25

PLANTING 25

WATERING & FEEDING 27

PRUNING 28

TRANSPLANTING OR REMOVING TREES 34

PESTS & DISEASES 35

TREES & SHRUBS IN CONTAINERS 36

TREES & SHRUBS INDOORS 38

Propagating Trees & Shrubs 38

SEED 38

CUTTINGS 40

LAYERING 40

GRAFTING 41

Special Treatments of Trees & Shrubs 43

BONSAI 43

HEDGES 44

TOPIARY 44

ESPALIER 44

STANDARDS 46

STREET TREES 47

PART TWO

A–Z of Trees & Shrubs 48

PART THREE

Reference Table 448

INDEX 498

INTRODUCTION

Just about every garden has at least one or two trees, and of course many shrubs. These plants are fundamental to the structure of a garden. They can provide shade, shelter and privacy; be used as a windbreak or to define a particular area of the garden; or they can be planted in containers and placed indoors or outdoors.

The botanical distinction that trees have one main stem, shrubs several, is not always very helpful horticulturally, so we have followed the usual gardener's rule of thumb that a shrub grows less than about 15 or 18 ft (5 or 6 m) tall. But do note that some genera contain both trees and shrubs. We have excluded the plants the botanist calls 'subshrubs', which though bushy have no permanently woody stems. You won't, therefore, find such well-known garden plants as geraniums and marguerite daisies in this book. Nor will you find climbing plants, even though some do have woody stems. You will, however, find them in *The Ultimate New Zealand Gardening Book* and *The Ultimate Book of Flowers*.

Even so, the over 1,500 trees and shrubs in this book present the gardener—or indeed just the lover of plants—with an embarrassment of riches. Will the favoured species be natives or exotics; evergreen or deciduous; those with spectacular flowers; lovers of sun or shade; those that demand a starring role in the garden or those that take their place in the chorus? Which are the ones that appeal most, the ones you wish to live with—and your children and grandchildren too, for trees are the longest lived of all living things? And the choice is increasing all the time, for the world's trees and shrubs have not yet all been discovered, named and introduced to an admiring public.

Left: Wollemi pines in the remote mountains of New South Wales, seen from the air.
Below: New Zealand beeches in Craigieburn Forest Park, Canterbury.

One of the most remarkable botanical discoveries of this century happened as recently as 1994, when a new conifer genus, *Wollemia,* was found in eastern Australia only a short distance from Sydney, in a deep sandstone gorge in the Wollemi National Park. Now famous as the 'Wollemi pine', its significance lies in its status as the third known genus in the primitive family Araucariaceae after *Agathis* (the kauri pines) and *Araucaria* (Norfolk Island pine, monkey puzzle, etc.), and for the resemblance of its leaves to fossils from the Jurassic era, which ended about 180 million years ago; in addition its pollen matches a type that disappeared from the fossil record about 50 million years ago. As an event, its discovery was reminiscent of the discovery in China in 1945 of living *Metasequoia,* also a conifer genus, only a few years after it had been named from fossil specimens from the Cretaceous era collected in Japan and North America. Like *Metasequoia, Wollemia* holds promise for future ornamental and perhaps medicinal use, though its propagation is more difficult.

NATIVE OR EXOTIC?

Many gardeners do not really give much consideration to whether a plant is native or exotic. They buy and plant on the basis of appearance and performance, with origin being very much a secondary consideration. Yet there are those gardeners who insist on a policy of natives only or natives first. Are native plants really that important, do those native enthusiasts have a point? Yes, they do. Indeed, one of the important things to consider in planning your garden is the balance of exotic and native species you envisage.

The popularity of native plants waxes and wanes. There is a burst of interest in natives that sees thousands planted, often in the most unsuitable places, then gardeners yearn for something different and go back to the more widely accepted and recognized exotics.

New Zealand natives suffer from an unfortunate general perception that they are rather dull plants that lack colourful flowers and bright foliage. Well, to some extent that is true. We don't have many natives that can match the Australian banksias and grevilleas or the South African proteas and leucospermums. And we certainly don't have anything approaching a New Zealand equivalent of the rhododendrons, though residents of Taranaki and Dunedin could almost be forgiven for thinking rhododendrons were native, so successful are they in those districts.

No, in the main New Zealand plants do not offer huge flowers and masses of brilliant colour, but they provide us with a range of plants in all styles and sizes that are perfectly adapted to our climate. Not that all New Zealand natives will grow anywhere in the country; some are frost-tender and others have precise growing requirements, though most will grow quite happily outside their natural range. Remember that most of the 'native' plants sold in garden centres are really cultivated forms with larger flowers or more brightly coloured foliage that do not occur in the wild. To be certain of the maximum suitability for your climate you should choose plants endemic to your particular region and the best way to do that is to visit your local Department of Conservation nursery. They are now spread throughout the country and specialize in local plants.

Gardeners have an important role in the conservation of rare and endangered native plants, which in turn provides the right conditions for our endemic wildlife. While we can't hope to replace the millions of acres of native bush lost over the last 200 years, your contribution of a kowhai or a manuka will keep the local tuis, bellbirds and geckoes happy. Indeed the effect of just a few extra native plants is quite considerable. It is amazing how even a small concentration of natives can draw birds, especially fantails, bellbirds, grey warblers and tuis. Hybrid natives and those from outside your region will still attract native animals: they don't seem too concerned about whether the plants that feed them are natural species or garden cultivars. By planting a wide selection of nectar- and berry-bearing natives it should be possible to have something to offer the birds every day of the year. A stand of native plants in a garden can be a lifesaver for native birds, and if you provide supplementary feed, you may find that your garden takes on an exciting new dimension with regular visitors that may become permanent residents.

Some 80 per cent of our plants occur nowhere else and many of them have very restricted local distributions in areas that are under constant threat either through development or the possibility of natural catastrophes that could wipe out small populations. Although your garden may seem insignificant as a conservation zone, it all helps, and it is only through increased planting that a tree or shrub gains popularity. Once the demand is there, more specimens are propagated and the survival of the species, albeit 'in captivity', is assured. Endangered species of

trees and shrubs suggested as being suitable for much of the country include weeping tree broom (*Chordospartium stevensonii*), Bartlett's rata (*Metrosideros bartlettii*), *Pennantia baylisiana*, heart-leafed kohuhu (*Pittosporum obcordatum*), *Carmichaelia williamsii*, kaka beak (*Clianthus puniceus*), Kermadec Islands koromiko (*Hebe breviracemosa*), *Hebe cupressoides*, titirangi (*Hebe speciosa*), *Kunzea sinclairii* (syn. *Leptospermum sinclairii*), three kings kawakawa (*Macropiper melchior*) and shrubby tororaro (*Muehlenbeckia astonii*). Once again visit your local Department of Conservation nursery for information about the threatened plants that would do best in your garden. The Queen Elizabeth II National Trust also publishes guides on the topic.

Another aspect of protecting native plants is the control of exotics that have proven too successful. These plants, often grown as ornamentals, have been shown to have the potential to outgrow and smother native vegetation. A list of invasive plants has been published as part of a regional pest plant management strategy programme. This list, too extensive to print in full here, includes such popular plants as Chinese jasmine (*Jasminum polyanthum*), *Cotoneaster franchetii*, *Polygala myrtifolia* and *Buddleja davidii*. Not all are problems over all of the country, but the list does highlight the fact that we can't assume that simply because an exotic plant has a long and successful history of cultivation it is no threat to native plants.

It would be wrong, however, if in our enthusiasm for natives we ignored their drawbacks or the advantages of exotics. There will be times when native trees and shrubs will not be ideally suited to the purposes you have in mind. There are very few native deciduous trees for example, and those there are display little or no autumn colour. If you desire trees but want to let light into your garden in the winter, natives would not be a good choice.

While our trees, such as the pohutukawa, puriri and kowhai, can compete with any others, our shrubs are somewhat limited in the combination of flowers and foliage. Although we have many impressive foliage plants like the puka (*Meryta sinclairii*) and rangiora (*Brachyglottis repanda*), there are relatively few large-leafed shrubs with showy flowers in any colours other than yellow and white. Close examination will reveal that the deep red flowers of *Pittosporum crassifolium* are stunningly beautiful, but unfortunately they simply don't have the instant appeal of say, a fancy Indica azalea.

Cordyline australis

CABBAGE TREE (TI KOUKA)
Cordyline australis
Asteliaceae

If ever a plant could be said to be a New Zealand icon it is the cabbage tree. It is instantly recognizable and stands out from any plants growing nearby. It occurs all over the country from coastal areas to quite high in the mountains, and is also grown extensively overseas as a palm substitute in cool climates.

In recent years cabbage trees, especially those in the North Island, have suffered from a die-back problem that has killed many of them. Considered at first to perhaps be caused by increased ultra-violet light levels, it is now thought to be the result of a pathogen, possibly in combination with higher ultra-violet levels. Fortunately the problem appears to be lessening in severity.

The cabbage tree has many practical uses. Pre-European Maori ate both the tender shoots, said to taste like artichoke, and the starchy roots, which have a high sugar content. Early European settlers took advantage of the sugary roots for brewing. The long, sword-like leaves contain very tough, stringy fibres and like flax leaves they were an important source of material for weaving, rope-making, clothing and thatching. Infusions from the leaves were used to treat stomach disorders and leaf extracts were said to have styptic properties. The fibre pulp makes a high-grade paper.

The beauty of the cabbage tree lies as much in its huge panicles of fragrant flowers as in its form. The creamy white flowers are followed by white berries, a transition that involves little apparent colour change, so plants that appear to have been in flower for long periods have often simply moved imperceptibly from flowering to fruiting.

As well as being attractive garden plants, cabbage trees are very effective when grown in containers. For the brightest and most colourful effect try 'Albertii', a variegated cultivar with leaves striped cream, more pinkish on new growths.

Right: *The beautiful flowers of the New Zealand flax* (Phormium tenax).

Some natives are showy enough to stand alone in the garden and compete with the best exotics. The kaka beak, the new Wiri hebes and the best manuka (*Leptospermum*) cultivars are unrivalled for colour. However, as many gardeners know to their cost, the use of natives as specimen plants has a drawback. As much as our natives are well adapted to our climate, so the native plant pests are well adapted to the plants. When such plants are used in the background, foliage damage and the occasional incidence of disease can be ignored provided it is not too serious. But when planted in the foreground it can be hard to ignore the leaf-roller caterpillars on the hebes, the leaf miners tunnelling through the kaka beak and the sooty mould on the manukas. Plant importation restrictions mean that exotic plants are only rarely accompanied by exotic pests and often grow better in New Zealand than in their countries of origin. It is perhaps a paradox of conservation that in planting greater numbers of native species we may end up using more pesticides.

When establishing a balance of natives and exotics the best answer, as always, is to compromise. As mentioned earlier there are parts of the country where exotics, like those Taranaki and Dunedin rhododendrons or the poplars of Arrowtown, grow so well and are so loved that we would be silly to discard them. Fortunately such plants combine well with many natives and there is nothing to stop us using them together. Most of our larger botanic gardens show how

Left: Metrosideros excelsa 'Variegata'.

well such combinations can work. Probably the best example is the Pukeiti rhododendron garden near New Plymouth, where thousands of species and hybrid rhododendrons are protected and complemented by established native trees, shrubs and ferns. It is a perfect symbiosis where neither native nor exotic would be as beautiful or effective without the other. And of course native birds abound at Pukeiti.

While your garden is unlikely to be large enough for anything nearly as grand, similar blends of natives and exotics will work well in many situations, especially where our large range of small native trees is used as a backdrop or shelter for the more flamboyant exotics. We are so well endowed with large shrubs or small trees that are perfect for hedging and shelter belts—olearias, corokias, coprosmas and griselinias to name a few—that it would be ridiculous to ignore them. Not only are they very effective as shelter plants, they have evolved to cope with our variable and often fickle climate. They can withstand any amount of wind (and there are few places in New Zealand that don't get their share), most are very frost-hardy, and they adapt well to regular shearing.

The readiness with which many native shrubs can be trimmed to control shape and growth is of great benefit to the gardener and probably had some evolutionary advantages too. It is seen at its most extreme in a style of plant found more commonly in New Zealand than anywhere else: the divaricating shrub. These species have developed bushy growth with a dense mass of wiry twigs with little or no foliage on the outside of the plant. The leaves and flowers appear behind a protection of fine, overlapping outer branches and twigs.

There are several theories as to why species that are not otherwise closely related should develop such a similar growth-habit. Obviously it was due to some environmental stimulus, but what? One idea is that it was in response to heavy browsing by moas. Leaves and flowers that were inside the framework of the bush had a better chance of reaching maturity and so over a period of time the plants concentrated growth in these areas and developed their outer twigs into a protective layer. Another theory suggests that divarication is simply an adaptation to a very harsh, windy environment. Outer leaves and flowers would be desiccated by the wind or broken off under the weight of snow.

Coprosma robusta

COPROSMA
Coprosma spp.
Rubiaceae

Coprosmas occur in a range of species found all over New Zealand from the coast to high in the mountains. They are notable for their glossy leaves (at their best in the coastal species) and colourful berries. They range from minute alpines such as *C. atropurpurea* to large shrubs or small trees such as the karamu (*C. robusta*). A wide range of hybrids and selected forms are also grown. The flowers are generally insignificant but are often followed by the attractive (and poisonous) berries.

Taupata (*C. repens*) is a coastal species which is the parent of several variegated foliage cultivars and which is often used for seaside hedging and shelter. In the USA it is also known as the mirror bush because of its extremely glossy leaves which are covered with a salt- and desiccation-resistant cuticle. Several small-leafed, bronze-foliaged cultivars are available which are the result of seedlings collected around Wellington Harbour from a natural hybrid between *C. repens* and an unknown species.

Coprosma kirkii, which is often crossed with *C. acerosa*, is a wide-spreading groundcover. It has strong wiry stems clothed with tiny, glossy, deep olive-green leaves. It is an ideal bank cover that seems to be able to withstand just about any conditions. *Coprosma* 'Kiwi Gold' is a popular gold-variegated groundcover cultivar that is clearly related to *C. kirkii*. However, it requires sunlight to maintain the foliage colour.

Coprosmas bear male and female flowers on separate plants and both sexes are needed to produce berries, which are of course only present on female plants. Many of the garden forms are male clones that are grown for their foliage alone. The sand dune coprosma (*C. acerosa*) fruits well and has unusual bright blue berries. Despite the common name, the best fruiting forms of this species occur not in coastal sand dunes but in alpine areas.

When grown in good soil with shelter, regular feeding and watering, divaricating shrubs tend to look much like any other garden plant. Their true character only emerges under harsh conditions. If you have an area of your garden that seems to be exposed to wind from every direction and takes the full brunt of every passing storm, that's the place to grow your divaricating natives.

Understanding unusual natives like the divaricating plants will lessen any inhibitions you have about using them. Don't feel restricted in your use of natives, they fit in well in any garden design and are very adaptable with regard to climate, soil type and moisture levels. They can be used in the same ways as their exotic cousins and combine well with them.

Information on some of the popular New Zealand natives is provided in feature panels throughout this Part.

EVERGREEN OR DECIDUOUS?

Many new gardeners vow never to use anything but evergreens, thinking that year-round foliage equals year-round interest, but don't write off deciduous plants before considering all they have to offer. They are no less attractive or more demanding than evergreens and their constantly changing appearance actually adds vitality and interest. Besides, winter is winter however much you try to ignore it—even evergreens take on a winterish look after prolonged cold weather—and densely planted evergreens can make a garden awfully dark and damp in winter.

In many cases there will be no need for a conscious choice between evergreen and deciduous. If you want rhododendrons then most will be evergreen; hydrangeas, however, will largely be deciduous. On those few occasions when you are faced with a real choice, consider how the foliage retention will affect that part of your garden. Bulky evergreens take up considerable space and though they have leaves throughout the year they may flower only briefly. Deciduous plants may be just as large and as fleeting in their flowering but they have a more open feel and allow in more light in winter. If you need the bulk and foliage as a filler, a windbreak or to disguise something unattractive, opt for the rhododendron or camellia, otherwise don't forget the deciduous alternative—why not choose a deciduous azalea or a magnolia instead?

Although both evergreen and deciduous plants offer changing foliage colour in autumn, the effect is far more marked in deciduous plants. Few evergreens offer anything like the spectacular autumn foliage of maples, *Enkianthus* and *Liquidambar*. You may have to rake a few leaves but that's a small price, and think of all that compost.

Of course, not all deciduous plants lose their leaves as a response to cold. Many species of tropical origin are bare during the dry season when leaves are just too thirsty to keep. Under such conditions it is only sensible to use plants that are going to look after themselves rather than battle to keep evergreens alive.

FAST-GROWING OR SLOW-GROWING?

The question of how fast the species grows can be vitally important. It is all very well to say that we should be patient, but some people just aren't. And we don't stay in one place as long as our grandparents did; what is the use of planting a tree which will take thirty years to show its full beauty if we know that we may be moving house in five? The problem with fast growers is twofold. On the one hand, they may be short lived, like species that prepare the way for the climax forest. The kanuka (*Kunzea ericoides*) and pittosporums are cases in point, as is the silver birch in all but the coldest climates. The poplars are short lived too. If you are only planning to be there for a few years, the fact that your grandchildren won't see them won't bother you much, perhaps; but it is still a courtesy to the people who'll live in your house after you to plant a few more permanent species. On the other hand, the fast growers may be fast because they are in a hurry to get really big. The poplars and willows are the classic examples here, and so are the forest eucalypts. Often, this fast growth is supported by rampaging root systems that wreak havoc on any drains or foundations that get in their way. On a country place, plant these by all means, but think very carefully about them in a suburban garden. You might be gone before trouble arises; but it is anti-social to knowingly create problems for other people.

FLOWERS, FRUIT, FOLIAGE

While they tend to be the most spectacular feature, it is wrong to think in terms of flowers alone. The appeal of a plant rarely lies in just one part; it is the sum of many aspects and it pays to consider all a plant has to offer when making your selection.

Choosing a plant usually comes down to four main points: climatic suitability, size, colour and season. Having decided on your size requirements and determined the climatic limitations, think about colour and season. That means all sources of plant colour and all seasons. Flowers are just part of a process that offers colour at all stages. First there is the bud, then the flower followed by the fruit or seed pods, and finally the seeds. The leaves too are constantly changing: bright fresh growth darkens as it matures then changes colour and dries as it ages and falls. Then there are the selected variegated and coloured foliage forms that offer extra foliage colour.

Every plant offers varying combinations of flower, fruit and foliage with the changing seasons. Also, the effect varies depending on where the plant is grown. Sunny positions yield more flowers and fruit, and intense foliage colours, especially the yellow and red tones. Shade produces fewer flowers and fruit but larger leaves with the emphasis on lush greens. Why think of roses as just flowers when the brilliant red hips may be just as spectacular? Don't consider crab apples only for their fruit, they have magnificent spring flowers and some offer brilliant autumn foliage.

SCULPTURAL EFFECTS

Some plants provide greater design opportunities than others. The bold outlines of yuccas, tree-sized aloes, saguaro and other large succulents and cacti are solid enough to almost become part of any building they are growing near —they are truly architectural plants. Palms, billowing shrubs and grasses flex with the wind; their effect is softer, they mould to the garden and respond to the elements and are sculptural rather than architectural. Yet others are tactile and demand to be touched.

The use of textures and forms in a garden tends to be well down the priority list when planting. However, the careful selection of plants for these features can lead to an interesting garden even with just a few varieties. For example conifers, often considered boring, offer a huge range of textures and shapes —soft, billowy, stiff, arching, erect. Shape and texture combined with plant type go a long way towards creating the feeling of a certain location. Cacti and succulents say desert wherever they are planted, while Japan comes to mind when we see moss-covered rocks and evergreen azaleas. The effect is due as much to plant shapes— angular and sharp for the desert, rounded and soft for the Japanese effect—as any other aspect.

Right: *Apples, favourite fruit everywhere. The tree prefers a cool climate.*
Below: *Clipped hedges of* Prunus lusitanica *set off intricate compositions of coloured foliage.*

Blending is a key feature often missing from urban gardens, which can be a jumble of mismatched shrubs and trees. As much as any path, plants should lead you into the garden and create a harmonious feeling. Combining similar forms appropriately and knowing when to break up the lines brings out the sculptor in any gardener.

ATTRACTING BIRDS

Birds add life and vitality to a garden and though they make take a few seedlings and leave a few droppings, a garden without birds can be a very dull place. While the range of birds that will visit your garden varies greatly from place to place, the strategies used to attract them are much the same anywhere.

All birds need water for drinking and bathing. A small pond or a bird bath will guarantee a regular crowd of visitors. Keep the water level very shallow; most bird baths are gradually sloping bowls and birds feel comfortable with them. Ponds, however, can be too deep or move too sharply from shallow water to deep water. You might like to consider adding a few rocks and flat stones to make a shallow bath within the pond. Also, keep the bathing area clear of foliage because birds will not settle for long if they feel something may be lurking in wait for them.

Garden birds fall into two main categories: solid food feeders such as finches and robins, and nectar feeders like tuis and bellbirds. The solid food feeders are the easiest to attract. You simply put out food—bird seed, soft fruits and grain—and incorporate a few berrying shrubs in the garden. Nectar feeders are a little more difficult to cater for. A few will feed from drip feeders filled with honey water but most prefer natural nectar sources. Fast-growing New Zealand natives with plenty of nectar include the kowhai (*Sophora* species), the puriri (*Vitex lucens*) and the pohutukawa (*Metrosideros excelsa*). Most nectar-bearing exotics, such as proteas, banksias, buddlejas and *Cantua buxifolia,* will also attract native birds. Many plants with long tubular flowers that are obviously difficult for bees to access are pollinated by nectar feeding birds and will provide nectar in exchange for pollination.

Providing nesting sites will help to maintain a year-round bird population. Large, densely foliaged shrubs and trees offer plenty of natural nesting opportunities and you could also consider nest boxes or even a dovecote.

Left: *A native pigeon feeds on the flowers and leaves of tree lucerne.*
Below: *A collection of oaks at an arboretum in the USA, planted to simulate a natural forest.*

THE CULTIVATION OF TREES & SHRUBS

The Environment

FORESTS

Forests are one of the earth's most ancient features. For nearly as long as there has been life on land there have been forests. Over the millenia exactly where forests grew and the species they comprized have varied and developed under the influence of evolution and an ever-changing climate. Early forests of club mosses and tree ferns (which are very similar to our modern New Zealand tree ferns such as mamaku, *Cyathea medullaris,* and wheki, *Dicksonia squarrosa*) gave way to the primitive conifers such as *Ginkgo* and *Metasequoia* that in turn have largely been replaced by modern conifers and flowering trees.

Forests are vital to our existence. Without them all advanced life—including ourselves—could not exist. The oxygen we breathe is their creation and so, to a large extent, is the soil. Without trees to cushion the rain and filter it through their roots, the soil would be washed away.

The creation of a forest is a long process, which scientists call 'ecological succession'. As the process has yet to be documented entirely, there is argument about exactly what happens but there is general agreement along these lines. First there is bare rock, on which only lichens grow. These most primitive plants, half fungus, half seaweed-like alga, secrete acids that break up the rock, and gradually dust and dirt, as well as their own dead bits, accumulate around them to form pockets of shallow soil. In this small herbs (non-woody plants) such as grasses take root, and the soil-building process accelerates; although by human standards it still proceeds at a very slow pace. Then small shrubs can take root; then the toughest, fastest growing trees, and we have our first forest. But the process does not end there. In the shade of the tough trees, others can germinate and grow, so that over the millennia the forest changes. Eventually these new trees become dominant, and we have what is called the 'climax forest'.

All of these stages can be seen close together in many areas of the South Island, particularly in south Westland. Areas of scree soil laid bare by slips are colonized by mosses and ferns, then wiry scrub and small shrubby trees. Under this nursery cover larger trees such as the southern beeches (*Nothofagus* species) begin their development and quickly establish themselves as the predominant species.

At each stage, the web of life becomes more and more complex and finely tuned to the local conditions; and once the climax forest is established, it will, barring some catastrophe such as an ice age, persist forever.

No two climax forests—and they comprise most of the forests of the world—are alike, simply because no two places have quite the same climate and geology. The stands of Joshua trees of the High Desert of California; the great equatorial rainforests of the Amazon, perhaps the richest on earth; the coniferous forests of Oregon and British Columbia; the mixed hardwood forests of New England whose autumn colours are one of the wonders of the world; the mountain forests of Nepal whose trees are giant rhododendrons and magnolias; and of course our own podocarp and beech forests as well as the temperate rainforests of Fiordland and Westland: all, and many more besides these, are climax forests.

The softwood trees are the cone-bearing trees or conifers, most of which are instantly recognizable by their needle-like leaves and the familiar woody cones on the scales of which the seeds sit naked. There are only about 500 species, but they are of great importance; roughly one tree out of three in the world is a conifer. They include the pines, cypresses and firs, and our majestic native conifers: kauri, rimu, totara and kahikatea (which often produce fleshy berry-like drupes rather than cones). The ginkgo is usually classed with them too, though it is really all on its own, the sole survivor of a class of plants (even more ancient than the conifers) which

Hebe 'Pamela Joy'

HEBE
Hebe spp.
Scrophulariaceae

With around eighty native members, *Hebe* contains more species than any other local genus, and worldwide is probably the most widely grown New Zealand genus. As with so many natives, it is often more appreciated overseas than at home but many species and hybrids can be found in local gardens. Hebes range from minute groundcovers to small trees; from species with spectacular flowers to those that seldom bloom; from the very tough, conifer-like whipcords such as *H. ochracea* to the somewhat tender broad-leafed cultivars derived from *H. speciosa*.

Hebes fall into three broad categories: the lowland and coastal broad-leafed species, which usually have bright green, relatively soft foliage and large flower-spikes in shades of mauve, pink and white; the low alpine and alpine broad-leafed species which vary in size but tend to have leathery blue-green leaves and white flowers; and the whipcords, some of which are alpines while others come from very exposed areas at lower altitudes. Although the tightly appressed foliage of a whipcord hebe creates the impression of a tough alpine plant, they occur in the same places as the tougher broad-leafed species of *Hebe*. The Tekapo area of Canterbury is a good and easily accessible place to see whipcord hebes.

Hebes are entirely ornamental and appear to have held little or no significance for pre-European Maori or early European settlers.

For many years the plants grown in gardens were largely species, with just a few hybrids and selected forms, usually the fancy *H. speciosa* cultivars. In recent years, however, hebes have been the subject of intensive hybridizing with the result that new forms—many of which, like the 'Wiri' cultivars, are based on *H. diosmifolia*—offer considerable advantages over the species as garden plants in terms of growth-habit and flower display.

have been around for at least 100 million years.

The hardwood trees bear not cones but flowers, and they enclose their seeds in fruits, which may or may not be edible. The flowers may be large and showy or they may pass unnoticed. The leaves are the usual flat shape, leading to the term the broad-leafed trees. The flowering plants include not only trees but shrubs and non-woody plants (herbs) among their quarter of a million species. The fossil record suggests they arrived a bit later than the conifers, but even so there have been flowers on earth for around 80 million years.

THE FOREST EDGE

Let us leave the forest for the time being. The forest edge is not always a very clear-cut one, though there is usually an obvious reason why the domain of the trees has come to an end. As you climb a mountain, it eventually becomes too cold for trees to grow, leaving only shrubs and low-growing herbs. A few scattered trees may grow in sheltered pockets here and there, but the end of the forest is often quite abrupt. Or the trees may thin out as the soil changes and becomes too rocky or infertile for them. Again we are likely to find shrubs, whose smaller size puts less demand on the soil and which can flourish away from the shade of the trees. Or we may be crossing an otherwise invisible boundary between sufficient rainfall for trees and insufficient. We may now be in the rain shadow of a hill or mountain, or have moved that little, critical bit further from the sea or a lake.

There are shrubs in the forest, though they often grow in natural or artificial clearings or along the banks of streams where the trees cannot grow without being knocked over in floods. The shrubs' flexible branches offer less resistance, and their thicketing stems catch and hold soil that washes into them. When the forest canopy is an open one, either because the trees are spaced apart or they are not

Above: *In the grassland of a forest edge in Ireland,* Rhododendron ponticum *has gone wild, to adorn the land with purple blossoms in spring.*

very dense and shady in leaf, you may find an understorey of shrubbery, though often these are not so much shrubs as small, very low-branching trees. The camellia, a shrub of the open woodlands of China and Japan, is a typical

Left: *Cultivated land wrested from the forest in Nepal. In the foreground, the forest is reclaiming its own.*

example. We gardeners think of it as a shrub, but it is in fact a slow-growing small tree, with a quite noticeable habit of growing from one main stem. Some species, notably *Camellia reticulata*, can make forests in their own right, though not very lofty ones. A similar effect is seen in the New Zealand bush where *Pseudopanax* and *Pittosporum* species usually regarded as shrubs often form areas of low forest. Also, many of the species that in forests reach tree stature grow to barely knee high at the tree line.

The multi-stemmed plants that botanists recognize as shrubs, like the forsythia, lilac, oleander and the rose, are typically inhabitants of open ground, and they grow among grasses and other herbs.

THE IMPORTANCE OF CLIMATE

Trees and shrubs are usually grown outdoors, and some knowledge of the kind of climate and conditions under which they grow is very desirable to the gardener.

Taking a broad picture of climate, there are four main zones, namely cold, cool, warm and hot. However, such factors as altitude or the closeness of the sea can make a great difference to the climate. Bathed by the Gulf stream, the British Isles have a milder climate than parts of the USA which lie much closer to the Equator. And Taupo, at 1,200 ft (369 m) above sea level and as inland as it is possible to get in New Zealand, is considerably cooler than Greymouth, a couple of hundred miles to the south but coastal.

Cold climates (Zones 1 to 4)

Cold climates are those where the winters are long and frosty, with the ground frequently being covered with snow, and where summer is apt to both arrive and leave quite suddenly. While it is there, it can be surprisingly hot. Such places as Canada, Scandinavia, Central Europe, Russia, the northern parts of China and the New England and Rocky Mountain states, as well as much of the Midwest of the USA have cold climates.

In earth's coldest places—atop the highest mountains, about the poles—there are no trees, only more or less permanent snow and ice. The only plants to be seen are some lichens on rocks that face the sun or are too steep for the snow to cling to. These remarkable plants, half fungus, half seaweed-like alga, are of little interest to gardeners, but they grow in temperate climates as well as cold ones, and their presence or absence on walls, rocks and the trunks of trees are one index of how polluted the local environment is. They grow extremely slowly but live for a very long time.

If we retreat a little to lower latitudes where the snow melts in summer, we still find no trees: for we are now in the vast tundra that rings the North Pole, extending across the northernmost parts of Europe, Asia and North America. (In the southern hemisphere, the corresponding latitudes are occupied by the wild ocean that rings Antarctica.) Here the snow melts indeed, but the summers are still short enough that only the top layer of the soil thaws out. Below it stays frozen in the grip of permafrost, and trees cannot grow here. Any that tried would not be able to get their roots deep enough to support them and would be blown away in the cold winter wind.

The tundras are surprisingly rich in flowers but they are mostly low-growing perennials that burst into bloom in the long days of summer and then die down to spend the winter dormant beneath the snow. Among them are low shrubs

Hoheria populnea

HOUHERE (LACEBARK)
Hoheria populnea
Malvaceae

Apart from the kowhai and *Metrosideros* species, the lacebark is probably New Zealand's most striking tree when in flower. The flowers are white, so they don't have colour to make an impact, but they are borne in such large numbers that at flowering time, from late summer into autumn, the tree is largely hidden by bloom.

The name lacebark comes from the fibrous layer of inner bark which was used by early Maori as a cloth, for plaiting and weaving. It was also steeped in water and jellied for medicinal use. The wood pulp makes an excellent paper.

Hoheria populnea is the most common species of a genus that includes five species and which is confined to New Zealand. It is an evergreen, though some of the species, such as *H. lyallii,* are deciduous. Unlike *H. sexstylosa* which has a divaricating juvenile form, *H. populnea* looks much the same throughout its life, simply filling out from an upright sapling to a round-headed tree. Despite occurring naturally only from Waikato northwards, it is a hardy and adaptable tree that thrives throughout the country. It is fast growing when young and, apart from occasional damage by puriri moth larvae, is largely trouble free.

There are several selected foliage forms. The leaves of 'Variegata' have a large central yellow blotch; 'Alba Variegata' has a broad white margin; 'Osbornei' has a purple underside to the leaf and flowers with purple stamens; and 'Purpurea' has leaves with deep purple undersides. While the variegated forms provide added foliage colour throughout the year, they are not as striking when in bloom.

Hardiness Zone Map

This map has been prepared to agree with a system of plant hardiness zones which have been accepted as an international standard and range from 1 to 12. It shows the lowest minimum winter temperatures which can be expected on the average in different regions of New Zealand. Note that ZONES 1 to 6, which involve much lower temperatures, and ZONE 12, which involves very high temperatures, don't occur in New Zealand.

In the A–Z section of this book a zone number (for example, ZONE 8) is given at the end of each species entry. That number, which corresponds to a zone shown here, indicates the coldest areas in which the particular plant is likely to survive through an average winter. Note that these are not necessarily the areas in which it will grow best. Because the zone number refers to *minimum* temperatures, a plant given ZONE 7, for example, will obviously grow perfectly well in ZONE 8 but not in ZONE 6. Plants grown in a zone considerably higher than the zone with the minimum winter temperature in which they will survive might well grow but they are likely to behave differently—like the cherry tree taken from England (ZONE 7) to Singapore (ZONE 12) which became a non-flowering evergreen in its new home. Note also that some readers may find the numbers a little conservative; we felt it best to err on the side of caution. The map does not attempt to indicate a plant's water requirements or drought hardiness; where significant, this information is given in the text and reference table.

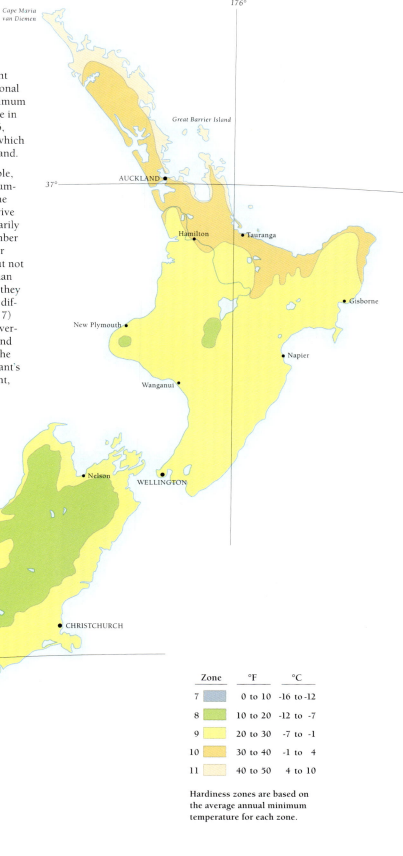

Zone	°F	°C
7	0 to 10	-16 to -12
8	10 to 20	-12 to -7
9	20 to 30	-7 to -1
10	30 to 40	-1 to 4
11	40 to 50	4 to 10

Hardiness zones are based on the average annual minimum temperature for each zone.

whose roots don't need to go deep and whose branches hug the ground; the dwarf birches and willows. The Arctic willow, *Salix arctica*, which comes from Greenland and the shores of Hudsons Bay, has the distinction of growing further north, on Melville Island, than any other woody plant in the world; and the even smaller *S. herbacea* rates as the smallest of all shrubs.

As we move further south we find the summer sun mounting higher and gaining sufficient strength to melt the permafrost. Now we encounter trees—larches and firs, then pines, spruces and hemlocks; and before we have gone too far we find ourselves in one of the world's great forests, the belt of coniferous trees that encircles the globe. Here we find nearly a third of the world's trees, but these are not forests rich in the number of their species; in any area you may find only three or four, often only one or two species. These are lands remote from civilization, though the forests are rich in things that civilization desires. Fur and resin were once coveted products of the coniferous forest; and timber has been exported from here to milder climates for centuries. However, conifers are not exclusively plants of the cold. There are some splendid species to be found in warm climates, such as the kauri of New Zealand and the araucarias of Australia and South America; but compared with the cold-climate ones, there are not very many of them, whether we consider number of species or number of trees.

The conifers are important to cold-climate gardeners, as they are just about the only evergreen trees and shrubs they have. The contrast they present with the broad-leafed deciduous trees and shrubs can be very beautiful, but they need careful placement if they are not to look silly in the winter. Most are conical in habit, and if they are just dotted about the garden they can look like so many leftover Christmas trees. They need to be grouped in broad masses and maybe linked with deciduous shrubs, so the garden retains the same continuity of form that it shows in summer. And they need to be carefully considered for colour. As they don't offer anything in the way of flowers (though the young cones of some species can be red, purple or even blue), gardeners have for the past 200 years been assiduously selecting forms with leaves of tints other than green, such as yellow and the steel-grey hue usually described as 'blue'. These need very careful placement if they are not to look artificial.

Cool climates (Zones 5 to 7)

Cool climates are those usually described as 'cool-temperate', where there will still be frost and maybe snow in winter, but not such intense cold. Spring and autumn are clearly marked, and summers are rather longer, though not necessarily hotter, than in the cold zones. Such climates are those of the British Isles, most of France; the north of Japan and much of China, the Pacific Northwest and the Mideastern states of USA, inland and southern parts of the South Island of New Zealand, Tasmania and the higher parts of south-eastern Australia and the cooler parts of southern Africa and South America. Such mountainous regions as the Himalaya and the Highlands of New Guinea might be included also.

The boundaries between the earth's climate zones are not sharply defined; altitude, the nearness or distance to the sea, and the local topography all conspire to make them so. This is reflected in the distribution of plants; we must not be surprised to find that the conifers of the cold regions are represented in the adjacent cool areas also. They do not, however, dominate the forests: the cool zones are the domain of the broad-leafed deciduous trees. These have evolved a different method from the conifers for coping with the change of seasons. Their wide leaves can soak up as much sunshine as they need in summer; as the winter approaches, they withdraw such nourishment as they can reuse, leaving the leaves to die.

That chlorophyll makes leaves green is incidental to its role in the process of photosynthesis; but as it is withdrawn we see the carotenoid pigments that were there all along—the leaves turn yellow (reduced mineral uptake in the cooler months also affects autumn colour). The precise shade of yellow varies with the species, from the burnished gold of the English elm (*Ulmus procera*) to the pale, clear tone of the aspens of Colorado (*Populus tremuloides*) and the silver birch (*Betula pendula*). These are very beautiful; but what gardeners most adore are those species in whose leaves anthocyanin pigments appear, to overlay the yellow with red so that the whole tree becomes gorgeous indeed. The variety of colours is extraordinary: the same tree can display leaves in any shade from yellow through coral pink to orange and scarlet, the red tones

Above left: *Picea engelmannii*. *Cold-climate forests often comprise a single species of tree.*
Left: *The planting of trees in formal avenues has a long history. This avenue is at Versailles.*

Dacrycarpus dacrydioides

KAHIKATEA (WHITE PINE)
Dacrycarpus dacrydioides
Podocarpaceae

The story of our tallest native tree, the kahikatea or white pine, like that of so many of New Zealand's large trees, is one of exploitation and decimation. Where once large forests stood, all that is seen now is the occasional survivor in the middle of a paddock. Having a useful and valuable timber was the downfall of the kahikatea. Many West Coast farmers made far more money from the timber of their kahikatea trees than from the animals raised on their farms.

One of the main uses of the timber was prosaic—butter boxes, those pale wooden boxes stamped with a green fern frond symbol. Each held a 56 lb (25 kg) slab of butter and a small portion of a national treasure. Butter is now packed in cardboard boxes but kahikatea timber is straight-grained and durable, which makes it ideal for furniture-making and shipbuilding. In pre-European times, Maori used kahikatea wood for bird spears and the fleshy orange drupes (found only on female trees) were eaten or used as bait in bird snares. When burnt, the soot of the heartwood provided a pigment for tattooing.

Originally present over most of New Zealand and often the dominant tree in damp or swampy areas, the kahikatea is now found in large numbers only in Westland. Remnants occur in many areas, Christchurch's Riccarton bush has some very old specimens, but the pure stands are largely gone. The kahikatea responds well to cultivation and, while ultimately too large for gardens, it can be very attractive in its juvenile stage and makes an excellent tree for parks. Its ability to grow in poorly drained soils is an asset.

being most intense in those leaves that get the most sun. The capital, so to speak, of the scarlet leaves is the New England states of the USA. There the autumn colours achieve a splendour unequalled anywhere else on earth. Vivid autumn colours are also found in New Zealand. The golden poplars of Otago and the stunning red maples and liquidambers of Nelson and Motueka are nearly as bright as those of New England, though not seen in the same quantity. We find brilliant colour in China and Japan also.

The deciduous hardwood forests are more complex than the coniferous forests, both in the fact that they usually contain a mixture of species and in their structure. The trees themselves tend to grow in two layers, so to speak; we have the tallest trees of the forest canopy proper, and below them an understorey of smaller, shade-tolerant ones, in greater or lesser numbers according to how thick and shady the main canopy is. Lower again we find shade-loving shrubs, and carpeting the ground there will be low-growing herbs and creeping shrubs. The balance depends on just where in the forest you are. At the edge of a clearing or along a path, where the sun can penetrate through gaps in the main canopy, the lower levels are apt to be more well developed than deeper in the forest.

The plants of the lower layers have of necessity attuned their life cycle to those of the dominant canopy trees. They almost always flower and make their annual growth in early spring, before the big trees have fully leafed out to block the sunshine, and many of the most desirable flowering trees of the temperate zones are forest understorey species. Among them we might note the American dogwood (*Cornus florida*); the dove or handkerchief tree (*Davidia involucrata*); many of the hawthorns (*Crataegus*), both European and American; the deciduous magnolias of Asia; and many of the *Prunus* species. The big canopy trees tend to be less showy in flower. Many, like the poplars, oaks and beeches, are indeed wind-pollinated and thus have no need for showy petals to attract pollinating insects.

The distinction between the understorey trees and the forest shrubs is not always very clear cut. Many of the trees are rather shrubby in habit, especially when they are grown in the open in gardens—*Magnolia quinquepeta* and its hybrid M. × *soulangeana* are good examples; many of the shrubs are capable of growing into small, multi-trunked trees if conditions suit them or where they need to struggle for the light. Here the classic example is the holly (*Ilex aquifolium*), which gardeners always think of as a shrub but which botanists prefer to regard as an understorey tree. The camellia is another. Both of these are evergreen; and it is in the shrub layers of the cool-climate forests that we meet our first examples of the

Right: *The fruit of the Chinese dogwood is as decorative as its cream spring blossoms.*

broad-leafed evergreens that dominate the flora of the warm and hot climates. These are invaluable to the garden designer, but their number—and their 'flower power'—is less in the coldest parts of the cool zone, where gardeners need to check very carefully the hardiness of species they propose to plant.

The cool zones, especially the uplands of Asia, are very rich indeed in flowering shrubs, most of them deciduous. Thickets of shrubs can often grow on land where the soil is too shallow, or the rainfall inadequate to support a forest; and they often grow on land where the forests have been cleared for agriculture. Deciduous shrubs play a leading role in temperate-climate garden design—where would the gardens of Europe and America, or those of the cooler parts of Australia or New Zealand, be without such things as lilac, forsythia, weigelas, deciduous azaleas, or roses?

Bottom: *The renewable resource: plantation-grown timber. Fast growers, pines are favourites for timber plantations.*
Below: *Desert plants set against a backdrop of native pines in a warm-climate garden.*

Warm climates
(Zones 8 to 10)

Warm climates, otherwise known as the warm-temperate and sub-tropical zones, include those of the Mediterranean countries (including the south of France), California, the Deep South and Gulf states of the USA, those of the Middle East and Kashmir; the southern parts of China and Japan; most of Australia, most of southern Africa and coastal and northern parts of New Zealand. Here winters are mild; though there may be occasional frosts, they are very rarely severe or prolonged. Summers can be quite hot and long, and spring and autumn often rather short.

In a sense, what we have chosen to describe as warm climates are a kind of transition zone between those where winter is cold enough to bring the growth of trees to a stop and the hot climates with their year-round summers. Here, winter may be sharp enough for us humans to reach for some woolly clothes, but it isn't cold enough to create a crisis for plants. Thus, they can keep their leaves all year, and we find that our forests are now dominated by evergreen hardwood trees and shrubs. Yet there are some deciduous species too: they may not be forced into a winter rest but they take it anyway.

More surprisingly, the conifers reappear in many places too; think of the famous pines of Rome or the cypresses of Italy, California and the rimu and totara of New Zealand. Cold is not their problem: drought is, and they are as adapted to resist warm dry seasons as they are the frigid dry ones where we first met them.

For the warm climates of the world tend to be dry. Not all are deserts, though it is in these latitudes that the great deserts are found: and there is a gradation between them and places where the rainfall is sufficient for the growth of forests not unlike the deciduous forests in their abundance of different species but basically evergreen. In between these extremes, we find the great grasslands—the steppes and pampas—and vast areas of country that indeed support forests, but forests where the trees stand apart—'like those of an English gentleman's park', as one of the early Australian explorers described them—and there is grass between to feed grazing animals.

That explorer spoke more truly than he realized, for these great parklands are not exactly in a state of nature. They are the natural habitat of mankind, and wherever man has gone, he has modified the landscape to suit himself. Even the New Zealand landscape has been heavily modified since the arrival of man. We may think of our country in its natural state as being dominated by evergreen forest in the wetter western areas with grasslands in the drier east. It was not always so. Those dry grasslands are in large part the result of fires started by early Maori to drive flightless birds into areas where they could be captured. The effects of this are most clearly seen in Canterbury, which has been grassland since well before European settlement, though remnants of bush occur in scattered pockets. Once the cover was cleared, erosion, drying north west winds and altered rainfall patterns made conditions unsuitable for regrowth, despite long periods without fire. Other parts of New Zealand, cleared for farmland since European settlement, would probably regain their former bush cover if left uncultivated.

Australian forests exhibit similar changes caused by fire and grazing, but there species have evolved that can cope with such treatment. The most characteristic are the eucalypts that thrive in myriad species over almost all of Australia.

That trees of such magnificence should flourish in the driest of continents, and on some of the oldest and least fertile soils in the world, is remarkable. And the eucalypts have been eagerly seized upon by foresters in other warm dry climates—in the Mediterranean countries, in the Middle East, in California, in North Africa.

The tallest trees live in the redwood groves of California. They are something of an anomaly, being a sort of southern outpost of the great coniferous forests of Washington, Oregon and British Columbia, and they grow only in favoured, well-watered places, especially where the summer air is cooled by fog. Like the eucalypts, they have travelled overseas, especially to Britain, where the tallest tree in every British county is now a specimen of either *Sequoia sempervirens* or *Sequoiadendron giganteum*.

American botanists failed in their bid to call the sequoia *Washingtonia* after their great former president. Washington—a keen gardener—had to content himself with having his name attached to a palm that grows in southern California, not all that far away from the sequoias. Here *Washingtonia filifera* grows around desert waterholes. An odd place for a palm perhaps—they are essentially creatures of the tropical rainforest—but they are surprisingly common in the arid zones. California is a major producer of dates: and the date palm itself (*Phoenix dactylifera*) is also a desert plant, from the Middle East where dates are a staple food. 'The just shall flourish as the palm tree' sang the psalmist; and the tree is invested with symbolic importance in Islam and Christianity.

The warm-climate forests are rich in garden shrubs both evergreen and deciduous, many of which have also acquired religious and cultural significance. There is the pomegranate, *Punica granatum*, an emblem of fertility and immortality since the days of the Babylonians; the fragrant bay tree (*Laurus nobilis*), sacred to Apollo, as was the oleander, *Nerium oleander*, a plant of watercourses and often the only shrubby plant to survive in places overgrazed by goats who realize how poisonous it is and avoid it; the yellow rose, *Rosa foetida*, which pious legend tells us sprang from the tears of the Prophet. Add to these the productions of California, the south of China, Australia, New Zealand and southern Africa.

Palms, pines, evergreen flowering trees, aromatic shrubs, fruit trees and many of the best cool-climate trees and some at least of those from hot climates—the gardener fortunate enough to live in a warm climate, with water on tap, can grow almost anything. No wonder legend placed Eden in the mild climate of what is now Iraq.

Hot climates
(Zones 11 to 12)

In hot climates, frost is unknown—or if it does occur, it makes the front pages of the newspapers—and there is sufficient warmth, rainfall permitting, for plants to grow throughout the year. Except for the highest uplands, every country that lies within the tropics is included, though some places outside those boundaries can be considered 'hot' also. Such include the southern parts of Florida, North Africa, much of Saudi Arabia, central Australia, and the warmest parts of southern Africa.

One of the things about the gardens of the tropics that strikes the visitor from a cool climate is the magnificence of the flowering trees. No temperate tree can approach the sheer splendour of the royal poinciana, *Delonix regia*, or the Indian laburnum (*Cassia fistula*) or the jacaranda: one scarlet, one gold, one blue, each arrayed with myriad flowers in its season.

They come from some of the most prodigious forests in the world. Richest of all are the great equatorial rainforests, where year-round warmth and moisture allows growth to be more or less continuous. There is no shutting down for the winter here; there is no winter. The tiered structure of understorey trees with a higher canopy above that we met in the cool-climate forests exists here in theory, but in practice the evergreen canopy is usually so dense that an understorey cannot develop, and the forest floor is often almost bare except for a mulch of fallen leaves. All around are slender trunks as the trees force each other ever higher to the light; it is not at all uncommon for the canopy itself to be 160 ft (50 m) above the floor, though each forest has its own height.

One of the most remarkable responses to the struggle for light is that displayed by the palms, such as the native nikau (*Rhopalostylis sapida*). They have dispensed with branches entirely, relying on the enormous size of their leaves to supply them with their crowns. They have no need to shed unwanted branches as they grow; they simply drop their old leaves. Their distinctive appearance and tolerance of deep shade has made some species familiar house plants in cool climates; but they are also favourite garden plants in hot climates. Few plants say 'tropics' more than palms do—you only have to look at a travel agent's window to see that. Not all are rainforest plants; the palms have adapted to many environments. But it seems the rainforest is their original home.

Rainforest trees have two distinguishing marks, no matter what family they belong to. One is the development of wide-spreading 'buttress' roots which give them a kind of pedestal for support. The other is indeed red leaves, but here the leaves are red when they first grow—spring rather than autumn colour. They are often limp, as though they were wilting too, and it is thought that this is to help them stand up to the pressure of the rain while they are still tender. Why they are red is uncertain.

It isn't quite true to say that every tree in the equatorial forest is of a different species, but it is almost so. In one less than one square mile patch of forest in Ecuador American scientists have counted over 1,300 species of plants. (Not all trees; there are vines, epiphytes like bromeliads and orchids, and other things too.)

This very diversity of species has until recently protected the equatorial forests from the worst effects of man's desire for forest products: the economically interesting species like rubber, mahogany or Brazil nuts were scattered through the woods, and were harvested one by one, often by indigenous people employed by agents of the dealers in these products. Even if we ignore the effects on exploited indigenous people—the appalling brutality with which the rubber-gatherers of the Congo were treated by their Belgian overlords during World War I for instance—the result has been to impoverish the forests. Mahogany (*Swietenia mahagoni*), first exported to Europe from Spanish colonies in Central America in the late seventeenth century, was already becoming rare by the end of the nineteenth, and other, closely

Right: *Forest meets sea: coconut palms, one of the most characteristic trees of the tropics.*

Clianthus puniceus

KAKA BEAK (KOWHAI NGUTU KAKA)
Clianthus puniceus
Fabaceae

The kaka beak has one of the most widely recognized flowers among the New Zealand native shrubs. Despite being one of the earliest New Zealand shrubs to be described (on Cook's first visit in 1769), it has probably never been very common and is now extremely rare in the wild. Because few specimens have been found far from habitation, it has been suggested that it was only through cultivation in Maori gardens that it survived to the present day.

The kaka beak is an evergreen shrub with sprays of mid-green ferny foliage on arching branches. While it is perfectly suitable as a free-standing shrub, the spreading, arching shape makes it ideal for espaliering, which lessens the possibility of wind damage and shows off the flowers to their best advantage. From spring to early summer it provides a lavish display of large, long-keeled, sweet pea-like flowers. The species has bright red flowers, and pink- and white-flowered forms are common. 'Kaka King' is a recently introduced heavy-flowering cultivar which has luxuriant foliage and a vigorous growth-habit.

Although it is an undemanding plant, the kaka beak tends to be short lived and is prone to a couple of problems. The first is a leaf miner that disfigures the foliage by mining around each of the leaflets. The second is a tendency to develop witches' brooms. These growths, which are caused by the action of minute mites, can fatally reduce the ability of the foliage to photosynthesise light. Kaka beak is best regarded as a temporary plant. If you tolerate the problems rather than try to beat them, you'll find it has a lot to offer.

Corynocarpus laevigata

KARAKA
Corynocarpus laevigata
Corynocarpaceae

The most immediately striking features of the karaka are its leathery, glossy green leaves and the conspicuous orange-brown fruit that ripens in autumn from panicles of tiny greenish cream, spring flowers.

The fruit is eaten by wood pigeons and was one of the most important sources of food for early Maori, so much so that it was one of the few plants they actively cultivated. Karaka drupes, which are up to 2 in (4 cm) long, contain a kernel that in its raw state is highly poisonous. The presence of the alkaloids cibarian, caronarian and karakin causes muscle spasms, permanent paralysis and can prove fatal. However, when these poisons are removed, usually by heating, leaching in running water for several days and removing the flesh, the kernels are safe to eat and very palatable. Considering the consequences of improperly treating the kernels, however, it is inadvisable to try them.

The leaves of the karaka had some medicinal use for Maori and the wood was occasionally used in construction. Nowadays the karaka is almost entirely grown as an ornamental.

The karaka is rather frost-tender, especially when young, and is usually restricted to coastal and lowland areas. It occurs naturally in the North Island and in the South Island down to Banks Peninsula in the east and Greymouth in the west. It is very tolerant of strong winds and salt air and is often one of the dominant coastal plants. In exposed positions it tends to be shrubby but when sheltered can grow to 5 ft (1.5 m) tall.

Above: *The garden as a place to collect favourite plants: here, dwarf conifers, coloured-leafed heathers, and perennials.*

related species from Africa and the Philippines have long been substituted for it. The same is true of such other highly desirable species as teak (*Tectona grandis*), which comes from Southeast Asia.

But the forest trees are all hardwoods, and the demand from the developed world for hardwood timbers has made it worthwhile cutting trees that formerly were ignored, and modern transport has made it worth doing so. Timber has become an international commodity. Since World War II, for instance, a significant percentage of the rainforests of Malaysia have been cut to supply Japan's need for timber, the forests of Japan itself having ceased to meet the demand long since; and the same story can be told in just about every country where the tropical hardwoods grow. Countries like New Zealand can take vigorous conservation measures, but when a developing country is offered large amounts of money in exchange for its trees, conservationists have a hard time convincing their governments that it is in their long-term interests to refuse them. But it is not only the need for timber: much of the present destruction of the Amazon forests, the oldest and richest on earth, is being done to provide land for agriculture, to grow oranges and beef for export. (In Malaysia, the desired crops are palm-oil and rubber.) The damage to the environment is not merely local. These huge forests provide a significant proportion of the world's oxygen—and when the soil is exhausted by cultivation, the forests will not return and the land will be reduced to semi-desert, with repercussions on the world's climate that we cannot foresee. For the soil that lies beneath these forests is not nearly as fertile as it looks. The very warmth and moisture that promotes the growth of the trees also speeds up the recycling process and most of the goodness of the soil is locked up in living vegetation. Remove that, and there is little surplus. The fate of the tropical forests concerns us all.

As you move away from the equator—but still within the tropics—the climate changes. Instead of the year-long summer, we find a sharp division of the year into two seasons, the wet and the dry. This is known as a 'monsoon' climate, from the Indian word for the winds that bring the yearly rains. Here we can find deciduous trees again, but this time they are not preparing for winter but for the dry season; they shed their leaves—not always all of them but most—to conserve moisture. That doesn't stop them from putting on a dazzling show of flowers in their season; indeed they can be showier than the rainforest trees, as they usually flower with the new growth and the flowers are less hidden among the foliage. Sometimes they flower on bare or almost bare branches, the leaves following as the flowers fade. The jacaranda is a typical example. It comes from the dry-winter forests of Brazil—and it is a disappointment in such places as Singapore or Bangkok with their rainforest climate; it grows all year and doesn't flower.

Planning the Garden

The creation of a garden is a very personal thing. Some people see their garden as primarily a source of food for the table; others as a place to grow flowers. Still others are not very interested in gardening and simply want a pleasant place for the children to play and the adults to sit, drink in hand, to enjoy the evening breeze after a long day's work. However you conceive your garden, trees are indispensable. Longest lived of plants, they will be there to give shape to the garden and shelter to the house long after more ephemeral plants and features have been replaced.

A garden is more than an artistic arrangement of plants, even trees: it needs to be planned as carefully for living as one does a house. You will need to consider privacy and shelter; and that is just in the backyard. The front garden is simpler to plan: the important thing is that it offers a comfortable route from the street to the front door, at the same time as it sets off the house itself. Trees and shrubs create the shade and moderate winds (cold in winter, drying in summer); they shape the spaces, the outdoor rooms of the garden; they block out undesirable views like the neighbours' washing and garage and frame desirable ones, including the view of your house from the street and from the garden itself.

In your planning, consider whether you will need to build or garden around existing trees. If so, take great care. Mature trees hate changes to their environment. Especially do they hate having the level of the soil around their roots altered. Lower it, and you expose the roots to air and dryness; raise it, and they will suffocate. If the tree is standing higher than the rest of the garden will be, you need to contain the area of its roots (roughly that beneath the spread of its branches) with a retaining wall of some kind, which may well become an attractive feature. If you want to *raise* the level, you have two options. You can either build a timber deck, so the natural ground level beneath is left unaltered; or you can fill with earth, after placing a conical 'breathing layer' of stones over the roots. This only needs to be a stone or two deep at the edge of the root system, but at the trunk it must reach to the full depth of the fill and be exposed—the effect is of the tree standing in a collar of stones—so the air can get in. Just how far this will allow you to raise the soil depends on the tree, and you should seek the advice of an expert arboriculturalist before you do anything. Your responsibilities don't end there. You must, must, make sure your builder neither drives his heavy equipment over the tree's roots nor stockpiles heavy materials there. If he does either, the soil will compact like a mud pie and the roots will suffocate. Then, you have to watch what sort of gardening you do beneath your tree. In dry climates like Central Otago's and East Cape's, you need to be sure you don't suddenly give your tree an artificial rainfall greater than it has been used to. Many an old tree has succumbed in a few years to root rot from having a heavily watered lawn created at its feet. (Either pave, or plant groundcovers or shrubs which don't need watering.)

Choosing the Trees & Shrubs

As you work out your ideas, try not to think of particular species but of the characteristics you need your trees and shrubs to have for the roles they are going to play. Here, perhaps, a biggish, deciduous, not-too-dense tree to shade the patio; there, a row of small evergreens to screen the neighbours' picture window. This makes it easier, once you have arrived at a design you think will be right for you, to short-list the species that might be suitable.

Chances are you'll have many more candidates than you have room for, so you need to think further. Is this species one that suits my soil and climate? Most trees are not really fussy about soil—few will quarrel if it is fertile and well drained—and shrubs are fairly easily pleased too. Poor drainage can be ameliorated by laying ground drains; or you can accept it and choose species that *like* wet feet. There are plenty. Of greater importance is the amount of lime in the soil, that is, whether it is classed as acid or alkaline. Again, most trees and shrubs have no preferences one way or the other, but there are some that dislike lime intensely. Rhododendrons, both the warm-climate and the cool-climate species, are the outstanding case, and so are azaleas, camellias, and the Chilean fire tree (*Embothrium coccineum*). If in doubt about your soil, you can have it tested by your university or technical college's soil sciences department or its equivalent for a small fee.

Climate is much more important. It is best to choose species which are native to your climate zone (refer to the text on climate earlier in this part) or most often planted there. You may be able to try growing species from the climate zones either side of your own. However, you should be very careful about falling in love with a species from further afield. If you expect frost each winter, the hot-climate species are not for you. They have evolved no resistance to it, and it will kill them. It is less obvious that a too-warm climate can be equally troublesome. The story is often told of the cherry tree taken to the Singapore Botanic Gardens by an expatriate Englishman hungry for cherries. It grew, but he never saw a cherry. Cherries must have their period of leafless winter rest in order to flower, and this one never got it. It became a non-flowering evergreen. Equally important is your rainfall. You can water a young tree, but eventually its roots go too deep for the hose, and should it come from a wetter climate than yours, it will suffer from drought too often for its own good.

Shrubs are a little more flexible. You can create a warmer microclimate by planting a tender species against a sunny wall, and you can give it extra assistance with the hose should the rain fail it. Still, it is not wise to make species that need extra care the backbone of your plantings, even if they always seem to be the most beautiful you have ever seen!

The very best way of all to see which species do well in your area is to take a tour of the neighbourhood, looking at other people's gardens. Your local nursery will be

Right: *Every child's fantasy: a tree house, securely supported in the branches of a healthy Monterey pine.*

able to give you good advice. Don't be afraid to ask if the species suggested has any problems like susceptibility to mildew or greedy roots. You are entitled to know: and it is a poor nursery that won't be able to offer you a choice of, say, small deciduous trees.

The only trouble with nurseries is that they only rarely have mature specimens of their selections to show you. The local botanic garden is the place to go for that; though here you may well encounter the opposite problem. Their specimen may well turn out to have been planted a hundred years ago—and you don't have that much time to wait. Refer to the tables at the end of this book for an estimate of how big you can expect each species to be at different ages, given the sort of growing conditions it likes. In these tables we haven't given recommended spacings, and that for a good reason. The usual recommendation is that you should space your trees so that they only just touch when they reach maturity, which means that if the species grows, say, 30 ft (10 m) wide, that is how far apart you plant it. When you are planting two species of different sizes next to one another, you average their spreads; so that a 30 ft (10 m) and a 15 ft (5 m) tree will go in about 23 ft (7.5 m) apart. This is fine when you are planting a shrubbery, as you don't want the plants to crowd each other; but it is not always the way you want to see your trees. You don't always want a group of perfect specimens lined up like ornaments on a mantelpiece; often you want a grove with its branches interlacing the way they do in a natural forest. Then, you will be planting them closer, how much closer depending on your artistic judgment. Some trees, like birches and many eucalypts, naturally grow in tight clumps and look best that way; others can look splendid in isolation.

Don't forget that if your willow gets its roots into your neighbour's drains, you may be liable for the cost of undoing the damage; and the same will be true if your tree encroaches on another's property. Gardeners are usually not bothered by the law, as their activities are harmless on the whole: but when you plant a tree you take on a legally enforceable duty of care for public safety, and your trees should not encroach on neighbouring properties. If they do, your neighbours may have the right to cut the branches off to a point above the boundary, and it is not going to make for good neighbours if they are tree-haters and always taking the saw to your favourite tree. They may be tree-lovers, of course, then you may co-ordinate your plantings, to the benefit of both properties and the beautification of the neighbourhood.

The Uses of Trees & Shrubs

SHADE, SHELTER & PRIVACY

If you think of garden and house as a unit, you can make the house much more comfortable and save energy costs, a consideration that is already important for most people

Left: Magnolia × soulangeana *raises its flowers over a carpet of azaleas, in an early-spring composition in pink.* Below: *Recycling in progress: leaves returning nutrients and humus to the soil.*

and will become more so in the future. You orient the house so that the sun streams in in winter and is blocked out in summer. You arrange for your most important rooms to face the sun, providing them with much glass to allow the sunlight to enter and warm them. This is fine in winter; but in summer the sun is the last thing you want. This is where the trees come in. By planting deciduous trees across that side of the house, you admit the winter sun when the trees are bare; in summer their leaves shade you. And they do more than that: the fact that they transpire water and thus use energy makes them natural air-conditioners. It is no illusion that the shade cast by a tree is cooler than that from a building. You can also place deciduous trees east and west, although in warm climates you may prefer to use evergreens to the west; even the winter afternoon sun can be unwelcome. As the sun sinks slowly in the west, its rays penetrate beneath a tree's canopy. You need foliage to the ground, and so you augment your trees with shrubs.

As our suburban gardens become smaller and houses are built ever closer to one another, maintaining privacy becomes an important issue. High hedges and screens are the first thought, yet they require regular trimming and can make a small area very dark and shady, and lawns may struggle to survive. Instead, check the potential lines of view. More than likely a few strategically placed large shrubs or small trees will be sufficient to shield you from prying eyes.

Some people don't like too many trees. They think they make the place gloomy. They might, if you chose only species with dense foliage; but there are many that only cast dappled, lacy shade, and the balance between these and the denser species can lend life and variety to your planting, before you even consider such ornaments as flowers. This is especially worth considering in hot climates, where year round shade is desirable and there are few deciduous trees anyway. The other thing to think about is scale. You need to choose trees that won't be too big for the space you have available. In a big country garden you can allow the forest giants full scope, but suburban gardens everywhere are getting smaller all the time, and smaller trees are usually more appropriate. But it is a fallacy that small gardens always need small, even miniature, plants. You simply can't have as many plants. You may prefer to allow just one or two dominating trees to set the theme for the entire garden, or you may prefer to use several smaller ones.

Agathis australis

KAURI
Agathis australis
Araucariaceae

Foremost among New Zealand trees and closely related to the Norfolk Island pine and the monkey puzzle tree, the majestic kauri is the only species of its genus found here.

Although every New Zealand child learns about the kauri and its associations with Maori legend, gumdiggers and timber milling, and is familiar with the stories of how the kauri forests of the north were laid waste in the 19th century, few would immediately recognize this giant tree. It has no fancy flowers, edible fruit or bold foliage, so it takes a little study to pick out the tree in a forest. It is perhaps for this reason that it was not described by Banks or Solander, the botanists who travelled with Captain Cook.

When young, the kauri is a slender, conical tree, but with age it becomes a round-headed tree most characterized by its massive trunk which gives a mature specimen enormous presence and grandeur. Very old specimens can reach 200 ft (60 m) tall, which puts them mid-range in terms of height among the world's trees, yet the trunk is so substantial that in terms of timber volume it is only outranked by the redwood (*Sequoiadendron giganteum*) and a few others.

The kauri is now relatively rare in the wild. The carnage wreaked on the species by early bushmen has left only one large stand: the Waipoua Forest Sanctuary. Those few remaining ancient specimens that pre-date European settlement give us just a hint of how the early forests may have looked. The species can still be seen quite readily, however, as it is widely planted in parks and large gardens. Naturally restricted to the northern North Island, the kauri will grow as far south as Dunedin, although it is very slow growing in southern areas.

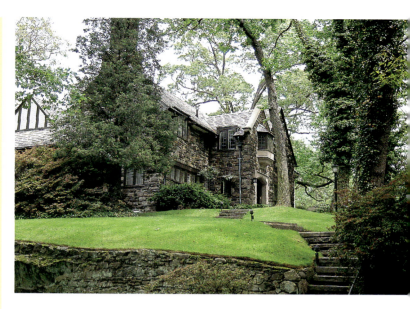

Above: *Forest trees setting the theme of a woodland garden in the suburbs of New York.*

WINDBREAKS

If you have a large garden, you could plant a row of trees as a windbreak. For smaller gardens, a hedge may be more appropriate. Hedges are usually formal, although they need not be—you can simply plant a row of shrubs of suitable height rather closer than normal, so their branches interlace in a billowing mass of foliage and flowers. You may need to prune occasionally to keep everything bushy.

A formal hedge, on the other hand, needs regular clipping, the aim being to shape it so it presents a vertical wall of foliage and an even flat top. If you part the foliage, you should see a whole lot of small twigs offering their greenery just where you want it. This is not the kind of growth that bears the best flowers, and clipped hedges are usually chosen for their fine textured greenery.

Conifers such as yew and cypresses are favourites, and so are small-leafed shrubs such as privet and box or tough coastal natives such as *Oleara* and *Griselinia*. The choice of species depends on just how high you want your hedge and where it is to be grown. If your fancy is the miniature edgings that enclose flower beds in Renaissance French and Italian gardens, you will opt for the dwarf box, *Buxus sempervirens* 'Suffruticosa', lavender or rosemary. Head-high hedges can be made from such tall shrubs as privet, photinia holly, *Camellia sasanqua* or *Tecomaria capensis*. Among the New Zealand natives you could use ake ake (*Dodonaea viscosa*), kohuhu (*Pittosporum tenuifolium*), Chatham Island ake ake (*Olearia traversii*) or broadleaf (*Griselinia littoralis*) according to your climate and your taste. Tall hedges can be clipped from trees also; yew, copper beech, hornbeam, *Ficus hillii*, the leyland cypress (× *Cupressocyparis leylandii*), and hawthorns all have their admirers. The competition that comes from close spacing—as close as 3 ft (1 m)—and the constant clipping keeps them from any thoughts of growing to full size: but should you stop, they'll lose no time in trying to do so.

Growing Trees & Shrubs

PLANTING

You have your design made and have selected and bought your trees and shrubs. Now comes one of the most satisfying tasks in all gardening, planting them. Any plant deserves the best start in life its owner can give it: a tree or shrub will be there for a long time. Give it a good start, and it will grow much faster too.

The first stage in planting is to carefully prepare the bed. Dig the soil as deep as the spade will go, meticulously getting rid of any weeds. Add lots of old manure and compost, then dust with a fertilizer such as blood and bone. Make the bed at least 3 ft (1 m) in diameter, more if the plant is being planted from a large container.

Planting from a container is easy enough. First water the plant thoroughly. It will make it heavier, sure: but if the root ball is dry it may not absorb the water after planting. Take the plant out with care. If it is too big to use the traditional method of holding the pot upside down, tapping the rim and then lifting the pot off, lay it on its side and slide it out. Don't ever try to pull it up by its stem; you'll only succeed in leaving half the roots behind. Check the roots; if the

Planting a rose bush. The bush itself, showing the mark where the soil level was in the nursery.

Digging the planting hole, deep and wide enough to hold the roots without crowding.

With the bush in place, soil is being filled around its roots. The next stage is to water it.

After watering, the bush is being given a mulch of compost. This is a warm-climate planting.

plant is pot bound and they are going round and round, they may never break out into their new home. Even if they do, a circular root can strangle a tree when its trunk tries to thicken over it, years later. Either tease them out gently or, better, make two or three vertical slashes about 1 in (2 cm) deep from the top of the root ball to the bottom with a sharp knife.

Then, make a hole deep enough so that the plant will finish up at the same depth as it was in the pot: no more, no less. Often this isn't critical; you can bury the roots a little without worry; but shallow-rooted plants like camellias resent having their roots buried too deep, and others, like citrus, can suffer the often-fatal condition known as collar rot. It isn't difficult. If you plan to stake, put the stake in first. That way you can be certain you aren't going to drive it through a delicate root. Place the stake on the sunny side to give a little shade to the tender bark. But don't tie the tree to the stake too rigidly; ensure that the topmost branches wave in the breeze.

The hole can be as wide as you please; if much wider than the root ball, so much the better. Not only do you have more room to manoeuvre, the roots will have plenty of soft soil to expand into. Ideally, you should dig the hole with a fork. Especially in clay soil, a spade can compress the sides of the hole, making a barrier that fine roots find difficult to cross. (Using a post-hole digger is even worse.) Then, you place the plant, fill the soil back around it, and water heavily to settle it all in. If you have prepared the bed properly, there should be no need to push it back with your boots.

Planting an 'advanced' tree from a large container is done in just the same way, the problem here being that the root ball is heavy and will almost certainly need two people to shift it. (Always lift by cradling the root ball: if you simply grab the

Sophora microphylla

KOWHAI
Sophora spp.
Leguminosae

Sophora is a widespread genus of evergreen and deciduous trees and shrubs. In New Zealand we have three native species (*S. microphylla*, *S. tetraptera* and the shrubby *S. prostrata*) from which several distinctive cultivars have been raised.
S. tetraptera is widely recognized as our national flower. The massed golden yellow blooms of the two tree-sized species are among the most distinctive and beautiful features of our spring gardens. They are also very attractive to nectar-feeding birds such as tuis and bellbirds.

One of the first New Zealand plants to be grown in European gardens, the kowhai is recorded in London nursery catalogues from as early as 1783. Being far from home is not unusual for the kowhai, which has always been something of a wanderer. *S. microphylla* is also found on several Pacific islands, in Chile and on Gough Island in the South Atlantic.

Now grown almost exclusively as an ornamental, the kowhai has had other uses. Its tough yet flexible wood is suitable for tool handles and is able to be bent quite sharply without breaking, a feature which led to its use in bow-saw frames and hay rakes. Yellow and gold dyes can be made from the flower petals and are still used by some enthusiasts. Also, the kowhai leaves were used medicinally by Maori, though these uses are now discouraged due to the poisonous alkaloids found in all parts of the plant.

Kowhais are easily cultivated plants that require no special care. They are subject to attack by the larvae of the kowhai moth but this rarely causes significant damage. While not deciduous in the manner of say an oak or a maple, the kowhais do shed their leaves. This is usually in late winter, just before the flowers appear, which makes the flowers even more striking as they are not hidden by foliage.

trunk the weight will certainly tear roots.) Big trees like this are usually grown in plastic bags, and you can plant bag and all, cutting it away and easing the bottom piece out from under before you fill the soil back in. It is a good idea to add extra compost to the filling soil, to create a transition zone between the fine-grained potting mix and the natural soil. This is especially worth doing in heavy soils. It's best to support a big tree by guying it, flagpole fashion, to three stakes rather than tying it to just one.

If the tree has been field-grown and came with its roots bundled up in burlap, don't bother trying to remove it. When the tree is in place, just cut any string and fill in. The burlap will rot quite quickly, and while it does the new roots can push through it.

If the tree has been supplied bare-root, that is with no soil around its roots—rose bushes and deciduous fruit trees are often sold thus—then you place it in its hole, using the dirt-mark on the stem to judge the depth, and gently fill the soil around the roots. (Roses should not be planted below the level at which they are budded, so double-check the dirt-mark.) A pointed stick can be a help to ease it in between them and make sure there will be no air pockets. Don't leave bare roots exposed to dry out, even for a minute; carry the plant to its new home in a bucket of water.

After you have finished planting, spread mulch all over the bed to conserve water and keep the weeds down. Weeds are great robbers of water and nutrients, and Australian research has shown that a young tree growing in a patch of bare soil about 3 ft (1 m) wide needs only about a quarter of the water that it would if the weeds were allowed to grow. Grass counts as weeds here, and if you are planting a tree on a lawn or in a paddock, you should keep that 3 ft (1 m) wide clear bed for at least two years, preferably three. Then you can allow the grass to grow back, though you should always take great care not to bang the tree with the lawn-mower. Many a young tree has been crippled by the mower cutting away its bark.

Don't leave your stakes in place for more than a year: by that time the tree or shrub will be self-supporting, and the ties can easily strangle the stem as it thickens. Furthermore, a steel stake protruding from the trunk where the tree has grown over it is not only an ugly sight, it is a perpetually open wound inviting rot and fungi to attack the tree.

If you promise to keep them watered in hot weather, you can plant container-grown trees and shrubs at any time except when the soil is in the grip of heavy frost; burlapped and bare-root specimens can only be planted in winter or early spring. If you garden in a dry climate, the beginning of the rainy season is the best time of all. Both sun and wind can dry a young plant out before you notice the problem, especially if the young tree or shrub is a long way from the house, in a paddock perhaps. If the plant is very small, you can put three sticks around it and drop a plastic shopping bag with the bottom cut out over them. For a bigger tree, do the same with burlap stretched between three stakes. It need only be kept in place for six months or so. Sure, it isn't pretty, but neither is a dying plant.

WATERING & FEEDING

Once we have chosen our trees and shrubs, arranged them to our liking and planted them with care, they demand very little attention from us. That is not to say that they need no care at all; but compared with flowers and vegetables their needs are modest. The first year or two after planting is the most important time, when they are still getting their roots established and building up their branches. Give them attention now, and you will be rewarded by much faster growth and more vigorous plants in the years to come. Allow them to struggle, and they may never establish properly and grow to their full beauty.

Keep their beds well weeded; weeds compete very strongly for water and nutrients, and if they grow luxuriantly they can shade small, young plants unduly. Pull them out: and spread a mulch to smother any that try to return. A mulch conserves moisture too, and reduces the amount of watering you have to do. You will have to water when the weather is dry, at least for the first year or two while the young plants are developing their root systems. Don't just sprinkle; wetting only the surface soil does more harm than good by encouraging the development of a lot of roots close to the surface, where they suffer when the soil dries out again. The aim is to encourage the roots to go deep where the soil dries out more slowly. Not often but thoroughly is the rule.

How often and how thoroughly depends on many factors: sandy soils absorb water fast, but don't hold it tight and so dry out fast; clay soils absorb it slowly but hold it for longer; water evaporates from the soil faster on hot summer days—and on windy ones—than it does when the weather is cooler. Do remember, though, that frost dries the soil: you may need to water young plants during a frosty spell to compensate. You need to learn the warning signs of drought. A plant that is actually wilting will need water at once: but long before that happens it will show signs of thirst. The leaves and flowers will go, not exactly limp, but flabby, dull and lustreless. The old notion that if you water during the heat of the day the water will boil and harm the plants is nonsense: but it is wasteful, as a lot of your water will evaporate at once. Watering in the cool of the early morning or evening is better.

As long as water restrictions are not in place, there is no reason why you can't water with sprinklers, either the kind you attach to the end of the hose or those you build in, attaching them every so often to a network of pipes. Hoses are certainly cheaper—though do-it-yourself systems have brought the price of fixed sprinklers down dramatically in recent years—but a fixed system is less trouble to operate; you can even buy gadgets that turn them on and off according to a pre-set program.

Even in places normally blessed with abundant rainfall, drought can sometimes strike to the extent that even long-established, deep-rooted trees suffer. They don't usually wilt the way lesser plants do, but reduce their rate of transpiration by shedding leaves out of season. This is serious as there is a real risk that when the rain returns they will make more growth and foliage than their drought-damaged roots can properly support. They may then suddenly die just when you thought the danger was over. What you must do is get water down deep into the roots, and to do that (especially if the soil is caked hard) you must apply it very slowly but for a long time. Simply leaving a hose to trickle at the base of the tree probably won't give you the feeling of doing good that turning on the sprinklers will, but it is the best thing to do. Leave it trickling there for at least 24 hours; 48 will be better. The same treatment is prescribed for large, drought-stricken shrubs also.

If you mulch with compost or old manure, you'll be giving your plants fertilizer as well as stemming moisture loss; and if you like you can boost that with a light dressing of something more concentrated as the regular growing season begins. Artificial fertilizer is fine, but it doesn't maintain the essential humus on which the continued health of the soil depends. For that, organic material is needed. Happily, trees and shrubs supply their own, simply by dropping their leaves. Leaving these to rot where they fall is one of the few times in life when laziness is rewarded!

Bark chips, ground bark and wood shavings and sawdust are widely used as mulches. They are

Right: A baby tree, mulched with bits of bark and leaves as though it were in its natural forest.

very effective at retaining soil moisture and will eventually break down and add humus to the soil. However, unless they are well rotted or composted before use their decomposition can take much of the nitrogen from the topsoil. This results in stunted plants and yellowing leaves. It is always best to use rotted products but if you must use fresh material remember to add a nitrogen-rich fertilizer like urea and water it in well. Apply further doses at three-monthly intervals until the mulch breaks down.

An established tree that doesn't seem to be growing as well as you might like will respond dramatically to being fertilized, but this is a bit more complicated than just sprinkling your chosen fertilizer on the ground. You need to get it down deep where the roots are. You can buy fertilizers specially formulated for trees but you can use any general-purpose fertilizer; blood-and-bone is good too. Allow about double the usual rate. Then, you make a number of holes about 3 ft (1 m) apart across the entire spread of the roots, that is in the area covered by the outermost branches. These should be about 2 in (4 cm) wide and at least 20 in (50 cm) deep. You can bore them with an augur or merely drive a stake to the required depth, which is easier to do if the soil is moist. Then you divide the allowance of fertilizer by the number of holes and pour in the calculated amount, watering it in with the hose. If you have bored the holes, you can fill the soil back in; if you used stakes, push it back to close the holes so visitors in high heels won't trip.

PRUNING

Pruning is the surgical removal of part of a tree or shrub in order to encourage it to grow the way its owner wants. Like a surgeon, the skilled pruner cuts cleanly, precisely, and with an overriding concern for the health of the organism.

The expert's fondness for the imperative voice suggests that pruning is a compulsory task. It is not. Trees and shrubs growing in the wild are not pruned, and there are very many that can spend all their lives in cultivation without ever needing to feel the saw or secateurs.

But a garden, park or city street is an artificial environment, and the gardener's aims may not be quite the same as nature's. In the extreme case, he or she may want to supplant the tree's natural form by an artificial shape, in the manner practised in Renaissance Italian or French gardens, when cypresses, yews or box were clipped into cones, spheres or even into representations of people or animals, an art invented by the Greeks and Romans and known as topiary. The aim may be to encourage more flowers and/or fruit; or to enhance the plant's natural form.

Now it is time to consider the tools you cut with. The general rule of good gardening applies: for your own comfort, you use the smallest tool adequate to the job. Adequate: don't try to force the tool to do more than it can. Hedge shears are not meant to cut woody branches; if you can't make the cut with secateurs, invest in a long-handled pair of lopping shears, which are just secateurs with extra-long handles that allow you to apply more force. They should handle branches as thick as a man's thumb, but bigger than that you need a saw. The best is the traditional curved-bladed, one-sided pruning saw, or rather two, one with coarse blades, one with fine.

Double-sided saws, coarse on one side, fine on the other, look like a bargain until you find yourself in a tight corner, cutting both the branch you want to keep as well as the one you are removing. We don't recommend that you buy a chainsaw; if you have to remove branches that big, you had best call in a tree surgeon who is experienced in the handling of these dangerous instruments. Whatever tools you choose, keep them *sharp*. Blunt instruments don't make clean cuts, they tear; and ragged wounds heal slowly if at all.

Although the principles are the same, the details of the actual operation are different for trees and shrubs, and we shall look at them separately.

Pruning trees

Pruning is only an occasional episode in the life of most cultivated trees: it is only if you want to create an artificial form like a cone or peacock that you would be considering pruning on an annual or semi-annual basis. If you find that you are constantly cutting the tree about trying to make it smaller, then you or your predecessor should have chosen a species more in scale with its location, and you might well be advised to consider replacing it with such. (Fruit trees, pruned to maximize the crop, are a special case.)

Before starting work make sure you are not prevented from pruning by conservation laws. Some trees, particularly well-established natives such as Auckland's pohutukawas, cannot even be pruned without written authority. If you wish to trim a large tree, even if it isn't marked for protection, check first!

From the point of view of pruning, a tree's life can be divided into three stages: infancy, maturity and senility.

INFANCY

A young tree growing in the forest grows upwards towards the light, concentrating its energy on gaining height, and only spreading its branches when they can receive their share of sunshine. Now a tree in a garden is usually planted in the sun—inevitably so if there are no trees there already to shade it—and it will start to develop its branches at once, and will grow with its branches much lower, even sweeping the ground, than it would do in the wild.

A tree can look quite magnificent thus; but if you eventually want to walk beneath it, you will not find having to push its branches out of your face very satisfactory. To get the tree to grow on a suitably long trunk you will need to discourage the side shoots. (You are doing with the secateurs what nature does by depriving these shoots of light.) This doesn't mean that you cut off the developing branches altogether. That would deprive the baby tree of leaves which it needs to sustain its growth. Rather, you shorten them—merely cutting back their tips once or twice during the growing season will often suffice—but leave the leading shoot untouched. These branches may well respond by shooting leafy twigs, which is fine; the more leaves the better at this stage. But the young tree will take the hint and divert its chief energy into the leader, with the result that it will gain height faster than it would otherwise.

When it has grown sufficiently that the lowest, previously shortened branches can be removed entirely, then go ahead. Resist the temptation to remove them before this time. How soon this will be depends both on the species and on your climate; where the growing season is long, a young tree will grow faster than it will in a short-summer climate. But generally, you can expect that it will be at least four or five years before your tree reaches this stage.

When the time comes to remove those lowest branches, you have your first test of technique. Most books say cut them off flush with the trunk, so that there will be no stub left to die back and rot. We say don't, or at least not quite. If you look carefully, you will see that where a branch springs from the trunk (or a larger branch) there is a sort of necklace of swollen bark called the 'branch collar'. It is sometimes perfectly obvious, sometimes less so; but it is always there. Now if you cut right to the trunk, you remove the collar, and that is inviting trouble. For the collar is the tree's natural defence against the loss of its branch. It is the cells of the collar that have the ability to proliferate over the wound and eventually cover it with bark: and if a branch dies, this is where it dies back to, no further. So you cut back to the collar, taking care to preserve it. (A nick or two won't matter.) This usually means that the cut is made at a slight angle to the trunk. It may not look quite so neat, but when the scar heals and the trunk thickens it will grow to a smooth line again. Be patient! If the collar remains intact, healing will be quick, and there will be no need to paint the wound with pruning compound to seal it against weather and rot-causing fungi. Sure, this is a traditional practice, but recent American research suggests it can do more harm than good by interfering with the healing process. Fresh cuts always draw the eye, being almost white against the darker tone of the trunk, but they soon darken. If they really do annoy you, paint them black with Indian ink.

The old-fashioned curved pruning saw allows you to get in close in tight corners like this one.

Here you can clearly see the uninjured branch collar. It's the raised ridge of bark surrounding the base of the branch.

Should the branch be too heavy to hold with one hand while you wield the saw with the other, then you must do the job in two stages, to avoid the disaster of the half-cut branch tearing away and taking a long strip of bark with it. Cut it back to say 6 in (15 cm) long, and then cut the stub to the collar. To be doubly sure, make that first saw cut on the underside of the branch. It only needs to be enough to cut the bark.

There are some trees, usually natives of the open-structured forests of dry warm climates, which virtually shape themselves and therefore need no pruning in infancy. The eucalypts and the jacaranda are prime examples, and they show a habit which is quite common among warm-climate trees and by no means unknown among cool-climate ones too; the ginkgo, some oaks and conifers for instance. They spend their first year or two growing almost like shrubs, concentrating their energy on making roots. Then they bolt straight up, in what is aptly known as their 'telephone pole' stage. They might spread their branches wide at maturity, but now they are as narrow as Christmas trees. Leave them untouched until this adolescent growth spurt is over; once they are mature enough to flower, their branches will begin to develop of their own accord. If you cut them back now to force the branches, you may well stunt them forever. This is especially true of some conifers like the Monterey cypress (*Cupressus macrocarpa*), the spruces and cedars—deprive them of their leaders now and they may never make new ones. If some disaster like a storm or caterpillar should do this, you can often save the situation by tying the topmost branch upright to a stake to form a new leader. Sometimes, you find a double leader on the Christmas-tree style conifers. Remove the weaker as soon as you see it. It may grow just as well as the other, but even if it does the tree will look most inelegant. More often, it slowly dies, leaving a great hole in the tree's outline that will take years to fill out again.

Once the young tree is up on its nice clean trunk and developing its crown, you can put your pruning tools away, perhaps forever. But keep an eye on how those branches are developing. You may need to remove a few which are crowding each other or threatening to unbalance the crown—the ideal is to have your main branches evenly spaced so the tree will grow shapely from its youth. Don't get obsessive about this; you are guiding the tree's development, not practising plastic surgery on it. But you should watch out for weak crotches. The wider the angle at which a branch grows from the trunk, the stronger it will be. While not all trees grow their branches straight out at right-angles like those of a Christmas spruce, you should prevent narrower-than-normal, V-shaped crotches from developing. They can easily tear asunder under the burden of rain-laden and storm-whipped foliage, often many years later. It is merely a matter of cutting out the offending branch when you see it.

Removing a branch altogether is invasive surgery, and this should never be done while the sap is actively running, that is when the tree is making new growth. The poor tree may not actually bleed to death, but it will suffer. The *best* time is when it is dormant, which usually means in winter; but you *can* prune in late summer after growth has stopped. Some cold-climate trees, the maples being the chief example, are exceptions. Cut them about in winter, and they bleed copiously, as any Canadian or New England reader who has made maple syrup will know. They must be pruned in late summer, the best time being just as the leaves are about to fall.

MATURITY

While young trees can be treated more or less alike, every mature tree is different, and how you treat it depends as much on where it is growing as on its species. It may be growing out in a paddock and seen mainly from a distance when you may decide that it can be left to its own devices. A mature tree in a garden or city street is a different matter; as its owner you need to be sure it is as safe as you can make it, that a dead branch won't drop on someone and injure them. And you may find it is casting more shade than you like.

This is actually very likely. A forest tree growing out in the sun often develops an unnatural (if handsome) luxuriance and relieving it of its excess leafage will allow more sunshine to the garden beneath.

The first thing you look at is whether there are any dead branches. It is not necessarily a cause for alarm if there are: as a forest tree grows, branches deprived of light die and eventually drop off, and a few dead bits inside the crown can be expected even in a healthy tree. Some species such as *Fraxinus oxycarpa*, *Paulownia tomentosa*, *Delonix regia* and many eucalypts and *Nothofagus* species tend to have many, and most of the American cypresses fill themselves full of dead twigs and leaves. Start by removing them. It is astonishing

Leptospermum scoparium 'Red Damask'

MANUKA (TEA-TREE)
Leptospermum scoparium
Myrtaceae

The manuka is one of the most abundant of native shrubs and is often the first woody plant to recolonize cleared ground. The wild species has simple, single white flowers but over the years plant breeders have introduced many fancy-flowered hybrids with single or double flowers in all shades of pink and red as well as white. It used to be thought that all the pink and red forms were descended from a plant found at Kaiapoi, but it now appears that such colour breaks occur quite commonly in the wild.

Another of the enduring legends about the tea-tree, that Cook used it to brew an anti-scurvy tea for his crew, now seems to be more legend than fact, although there is no doubt that manuka does contain some vitamin C as well as an important germicidal and insecticidal compound called leptospermone. Manuka twigs have been used for making brooms, the larger twigs for paddles and spears, and the sawdust for smoking food.

Farmers frequently despise the manuka for its colonizing ability and therefore countless hectares of the plant are cleared every year. Yet the manuka is a vitally important plant in the native ecosystem. It serves as a nursery and shelter plant for other more permanent shrubs and trees and helps in the control of erosion. Also, it is the favoured habitat of many birds which also feed on the nectar of the flowers, as do geckoes.

As might be imagined, the manuka is not difficult to cultivate. However, it is prone to attack by scale insects that suck the sap and secrete a honeydew on which a debilitating black fungus, sooty mould, grows. It covers the branches and foliage and affects photosynthesis. The first step in control is to remove the scale insects: use oil sprays to smother the scale and fungicides to clean up the mould.

the difference this simple job can make to the appearance of the tree. Often, removing dead wood is all you need to do.

Then, you can remove any small branches that are obviously being shaded by others immediately above them, cutting them right back to the main branches or the trunk whence they spring. It is important to remove unwanted branches entirely: cut them back only part way and you'll have a bunch of small branches springing from where you cut and the last state will be worse than the first. If you don't want to cut them all the way to their origin, simply cut to a junction with a side branch.

If that has not opened the crown out sufficiently, you can start on larger branches, but think very hard indeed before you cut away any of the main, largest branches which support the structure of the tree. (Of course, if a main branch is doing something anti-social like bashing the house, you must remove it.) Thinning calls for a certain amount of artistry. You want to lighten the tree and reveal its lines, not cut great holes in it. Ideally, when you have finished, your activities should not be obvious. That doesn't mean you should be timid; you can remove as much as a third of the foliage without leaving the tree looking like a plucked chicken. (Some people prefer to err on the side of too much, relying on a season or two's growth to fill the tree out again. It is a matter of aesthetic judgement.) The best season is, as always, while the tree is dormant, but there are advantages in doing a deciduous tree in late summer. You can judge the effect better when the leaves are on.

If the tree is branching too low to walk under comfortably, you can remove the lowest branches, an operation called 'raising the crown'. Go easy: it is often better to do this job progressively over two or three seasons so the tree isn't having to heal too many large wounds at once.

You won't recognize the garden; shafts of sunshine will have replaced the gloom, and your lowlier plants will show the benefit almost at once. And you will have made your tree much safer. Not only will there be no more dead branches, opening out the crown greatly reduces its resistance to the wind—in exactly the same way as the holes cut in banners—and you can sleep more soundly on stormy nights.

Go slowly: it has taken the tree many years to grow, and you don't want to ruin its beauty in an afternoon. It is a good idea to have a helper down on the ground to stand back and judge the effect to save you getting up and down all the time, and wise in the interests of safety too. Should an accident happen, you won't be lying there with a broken leg yelling to the neighbours for help.

Safety must always be paramount. A fellow cutting off the branch he is sitting on is only funny in comic strips. *You* won't be so silly: but you should ask yourself seriously whether you are sufficiently fit and agile to be clambering high among the branches with saw in hand. If you have any doubts at all, call in a qualified and experienced tree surgeon. His services won't come cheap, but they will be cheaper than a stay in hospital or perhaps worse. Choose with care: the profession seems to attract people whose only qualifications are muscles, a head for heights, and a chainsaw.

This certainly makes the tree smaller, but it scarcely improves it. And after a year or two it will have grown back denser and shadier than before. There is also a risk, particularly with eucalypts, that the new branches will not be as securely attached as the original ones were, and the tree will become dangerous. Sure, you can sometimes, by careful pruning and selection of that new growth, restore the tree to something like its original beauty, but this takes years. Other times, the operation may kill the tree. This is very likely to happen to conifers, few of which will sprout when cut into leafless wood. (The yew is perhaps the best known exception.)

After that, it may seem contradictory to say that cutting the branches back each year is in fact an ancient technique called pollarding. Apparently first developed by the Romans, it is much seen in the town squares of the South of France where the tree chosen for the treatment is usually the London plane, *Platanus × acerifolia*. The trees are trained in youth just as we have described, but when the crown is judged sufficiently developed, the branches are cut back to about 3 ft (1 m) and the resulting bunches of long, thin branches are themselves cut right back every winter. In leaf the tree looks like a lollipop and, though much smaller than it would be if it had been left to grow naturally, gives much denser shade. With age, the branches develop great knobs on their ends where the new shoots grow each year. Some people find the whole effect hideous, others enjoy the formality of a row or hollow square of such trees. They certainly need a formal setting of buildings and paving to look appropriate.

Planes are not the only possibility: the European lime (*Tilia cordata*) is often used in city streets in Britain and any tree that responds vigorously to hard pruning could be tried. The mulberries which feed the silkworms of China and Italy are pollarded to ensure lots of fresh, easy-to-pick leaves, and pollarded willows are still to be seen in the British countryside, especially in Somerset but also in East Anglia, Kent and in Scotland. In their case, the purpose is the production of the long, whippy shoots from which baskets are traditionally made. The advent of plastic has greatly reduced the numbers of both basket weavers and pollarded willows, however.

The evergreen trees of hot-climate areas are rarely pollarded. Partly this is because year-round

Below: *Thinning the branches of a juniper to show the structure of the tree. This is in a temple garden in Korea.*

Nothofagus solandri

NEW ZEALAND BEECHES
Nothofagus spp.
Fagaceae

The New Zealand beeches belong to a genus of over twenty-five species of trees with representatives also found in South America (primarily Chile) and Australia. Most of the plants seen locally are New Zealand natives. The three main species (all evergreens) are the red beech or tawhai raunui (*N. fusca*), the silver beech or tawhai (*N. menziesii*) and the black beech or tawhai rauriki (*N. solandri*). The fourth native species, the hard beech (*N. truncata*), is very similar to *N. fusca* and shares the same Maori name. All develop into large trees with rounded foliage canopies, although they may be rather columnar when young. Most have small rounded leaves with serrated edges but *N. solandri* has tiny smooth-edged leaves. *N. fusca* is probably the best choice as a garden specimen because of its attractive bronze foliage.

Beeches, primarily the red beech, black beech and its variety the mountain beech (*N. solandri* var. *cliffortioides*) are the dominant trees throughout much of the lower North Island and most of the South Island. Although once widely used for all manner of construction from railway sleepers to wall panels, beech timber was found to lack durability outdoors and the tool-blunting silica content of species other than *N. menziesii* led to beech being overlooked in favour of easier to work timber. For this reason large stands of beech remain, particularly in Nelson, Canterbury and Fiordland. How long they will last is hard to tell, now that huge quantities of beech timber are being chipped for export.

All of the native beeches are hardy and easily grown if you have the room for them. However, they are subject to attacks by honeydew-producing scale insects. The honeydew is an important resource for beekeepers but it leads to sooty mould, which has to be tolerated as such large trees are impossible to spray.

Above: *This tree has been eaten alive by termites. It will never return to glory, and there is no course but to remove it.*

shade is desirable in hot places and there will be very little in the months immediately following the operation, and partly because hot climates are blessed with a wide choice of trees that cast dense shade naturally. You do often see lollipop-shaped trees in warm and hot climates, but they are not usually the result of pollarding. Rather, the crown is simply clipped to shape with hedge shears.

SENILITY

Although senility is the term arboriculturalists and foresters use, it scarcely conveys the right impression to the gardener, who may consider a tree is at its most beautiful in the last years of its life when growth has passed its peak and the death of a few branches has brought it from the symmetry of youth to the character of an age greater than that ever attained by humans. The great landscape painters of China and Japan certainly thought so, and so do the gardeners of those countries. The meticulous care with which they prune and shape their trees is designed to give them the venerable aspect of extreme age.

But, however beautiful, an over-mature tree (also a forester's term) needs watchful care. It may be losing branches; its trunk may even be hollow; and as the roots lose vigour its hold on the soil may be less secure than formerly. Furthermore, it is likely to be less able to shake off the attacks of pests and diseases than it used to. All of which means that you need to be very concerned about its security. A tree is not immortal and sooner or later it *will* fall; but there is much that can be done to put off the evil day. Dead limbs can be removed; hollow trunks reinforced with concrete; limbs in danger of tearing braced with steel wire or propped from the ground with poles; the roots fertilized. But these are techniques needing the judgment of long experience, and we do advise that if you are the fortunate owner of a tree of great antiquity you have it inspected annually by a tree surgeon. And consider planting a replacement tree or trees, so posterity can have the pleasure bequeathed to you by your predecessors.

A tree need not be all that ancient to be senile. The trees that prepare the way for the climax forest—the acacias, willows, birches and their kind—are naturally short lived. Their role in the garden, as in the wild, is to clothe the land while the slower, permanent trees grow up. You can prolong their lives by the means we have outlined above, but scarcely for long enough to justify the effort. Removal and replacement is better in the long run.

Pruning fruit trees

Some books on growing fruit would have you believe that unless fruit trees were given elaborate pruning every winter they would never bear fruit. A moment's reflection will show that cannot be so. After all, fruit trees grow wild just as any others do, and if they didn't fruit they would die out.

We can state categorically that if you have a fruit tree, pruning is not a compulsory task. Assuming (as always) that it is suited to your climate, it will grow and fruit without feeling the shears. In fact, the evergreen fruit trees of hot and warm climates—the mangoes, jack fruits, lychees, avocados, citrus, olives and so on—are rarely pruned even by orchardists in those climates. They are given the usual guidance in infancy and then left. Should dead wood accumulate in their crowns, it is removed, that is all. Avocados, especially, should never have their crowns thinned out, much less be cut back. To do so is to invite the tender bark being sunburned. Citrus trees can sunburn easily too, which is why you often see orange and lemon trees in Italy and Spain with their trunks and main branches whitewashed.

Most of the deciduous fruit or nut trees of the cool zone—such as walnuts, persimmons, pecans, hazels—can be left to grow as they please too, after their initial shaping. It is the pome and stone fruits that have the elaborate literature.

The stone fruits—the cherries, plums, damsons, greengages,

Pittosporum cultivars

PITTOSPORUM
Pittosporum spp.
Pittosporaceae

Pittosporum includes some 150 species from Australia, New Zealand and Asia and, next to *Hebe,* is the genus for which New Zealand flora is best known internationally. The New Zealand species are primarily grown for their foliage because their flowers, while very fragrant, are inconspicuous. The most widely grown native species are *P. tenuifolium, P. eugenioides* and *P. crassifolium.*

The kohuhu (*P. tenuifolium*) is a very popular plant in Britain and British hybridizers have produced several forms with coloured foliage. It has recently become popular at home as a hedging plant and foliage filler with the result that local breeders have raised still more cultivars. All parts of the plant are aromatic or fragrant and were used by Maori for scenting sleeping areas and hair oils. A gum made from the sap was used medicinally and as a form of chewing gum.

The tarata or lemonwood (*P. eugenioides*) has been far less extensively cultivated. However, there is a variegated form which is very attractive and can become a small tree. Tarata timber is strong and flexible, and has been used in tool handles and for wood-turning.

The karo (*P. crassifolium*) and the similar *P. ralphii* have deep green, rounded, leathery leaves. In late spring they produce deep burgundy-coloured flowers that are fragrant and really very attractive but which seldom get noticed. Both species are natural coastal plants that make excellent foreshore hedging. 'Variegata' is a cream-edged form of *P. ralphii,* the foliage of which is among the best to be found in any variegated plant.

In all species the flowers are followed by rounded seed pods filled with the sticky seeds that give the genus its botanical name: *pitta* (pitch, from the sticky coating) and *spora* (seed).

peaches, nectarines, apricots and so on—are all members of the large northern-hemisphere genus *Prunus.* The early botanists included all the pome fruits as species of *Pyrus,* which now only includes the pears, European and Asian. The apples and quinces have been given genera of their own (*Malus* and *Cydonia* respectively). So have a small group grown mainly for ornament: the cotoneasters, the hawthorns and rowans (*Sorbus*), the ornamental quinces (*Chaenomeles*) and the pyracanthas.

The pome fruits bear their flowers (and then fruit, of course) on side shoots from the previous years' growth, in the manner which is typical of spring-flowering, cool-climate trees and shrubs. They do, however have the peculiarity that these side shoots ('spurs') continue to flower for years, unlike those of, say, a climbing rose. Once the tree is shaped, pruning consists of cutting the non-flowering shoots back to two or three leaves in late summer. This provokes the production of spurs and keeps the tree compact. Some stone fruits, certain plums for instance, bear and are pruned in the same way. Most of the rest don't, and the aim of pruning is simply to keep the tree compact. Cherries are spur-bearers, but they must not, repeat not, be pruned except in their earliest youth. A mature cherry heals its wounds slowly and ineffectually, and if you cut it you are inviting rot and premature death.

The recommended pruning varies too, even within a genus, with the chosen cultivar and with the understock to which it is grafted. Some 'need' harder treatment than others, others fruit more heavily if the tree is trained to a particular shape: and we do suggest that if the idea of backyard orcharding appeals, you arm yourself with a good textbook written by an expert familiar with your own area.

Pruning shrubs

As with trees, pruning is not compulsory with shrubs; and if you select with care you can spend your gardening life only using your secateurs to cut the occasional bunch of flowers for the house. Some shrubs are plants of the forest understorey, and often are almost tree-like in their habit of growing their many main branches not in a thicket but

Pinching out the tip of a young branch, to force side shoots and make the shrub bushier.

Here we are shortening the branch further, to the same end; forcing side branches to grow.

The result: two new branches where before there was only one.

from a single (very short) trunk. They include such plants as camellias, azaleas, hibiscus and the shrubby pittosporums, and require little or no pruning. On the other hand, those that come from the forest edge or grow in open country do often look much better for being pruned occasionally. They are more often browsed by animals, and have evolved the defence of making thickets of branches. They can always spare a few, and they replace them rapidly and easily. When you prune, you are taking the place of the browsing animal.

Happily, pruning shrubs is not nearly as big, nor as careful, a job as pruning trees. It's not very often you have to get up on a ladder to do it, and shrubs' in-built ability to quickly renew themselves means that removing the wrong branch is not a serious mistake.

The general principle is the same as for trees: by removing a branch, you encourage new growth elsewhere. To encourage a branch to elongate, you trim its side shoots; to encourage the side shoots, you shorten it; and if it's dead, you remove it altogether.

Just how you put the principles into practice depends on the shrub and its role in your garden design. Often, you want to make it bushier and more compact, when you will shorten the branches to encourage the side shoots. Other times, you might decide that it is altogether too bushy for your taste, in which case you will thin out the branches, almost as you did with the too-shady tree, either cutting them right to the ground or to where another strong branch is springing. Most often you will do both, thinning out old twiggy branches and shortening the others. When you shorten a branch, always cut it to a point where a new branch is already growing or where there is a dormant bud. This can sometimes be difficult to see; but if you cut back to just above a leaf, or where a scar on the bark shows there has been one, you will be cutting to the right place. If you're not sure what you're looking for, buy a rose from the florist. You'll see the little growth buds tucked neatly into the axils of the leaves where they join the stem.

Let your eye guide you. By the time a shrub is old enough to call for pruning, you should be sufficiently familiar with how it grows that the right course of action will suggest itself. You will have noticed how some shrubs flower on their current growth, the way a hybrid tea rose, a hibiscus, an oleander or a crape myrtle does. These almost always flower in summer; spring bloomers don't have time to make that much growth after their winter rest and so bloom on the branches they grew last year. Such include the azaleas, weigelas, forsythias, lilac, philadelphus, and the old-fashioned roses. If you prune these in winter, you will be cutting away your flowering wood. The time, therefore, is immediately after flowering but before the new growth begins. This is a fairly brief space, and you may prefer to prune while the shrubs are in bloom, combining pruning with cutting flowers for the house.

If in doubt, this can be taken as a general rule: prune after flowering but before new growth begins. Summer-bloomers can thus wait until winter, as they don't grow again before the spring. Dead branches, and dead flowers, can be removed at any time, as soon as you see them; and if a display of flowers are an issue, then you can prune either in winter or in late summer, the same as you do with trees.

There is a great exception to the prune-after-flowering rule, however. You may be faced with a great, overgrown shrub full of decrepit branches—an elderly lilac, for instance—and decide that the only way to restore it to youth and vigour is to cut it almost to the ground to force it to renew itself entirely. This must only be done while the plant is dormant, even if (as will be the case with the lilac) you thereby sacrifice flowers for a year or two. If that bothers you, take the job in stages over three years, cutting out a third of the bush each year so that

Above: *By regular shortening of the growing branches, the naturally lanky* Lantana 'Radiatron' *has been made bushy and shapely.*
Right: *When these roses fade, the stems carrying them will be shortened, both to encourage more and keep the bush compact.*

by the end of the third year you have replaced it entirely. This is a wise course if you are not sure that the species will in fact respond to drastic cutting back. Some evergreen shrubs are badly shocked by the sudden removal of all their foliage, and many from warm, dry climates, such as the Californian ceanothus and many Australian, Mediterranean and southern African shrubs will not sprout if you cut into leafless wood. Cut them back hard and you will kill them. (These are naturally rather short lived, but they are fast growing and it is almost always better to simply remove and replace rather than trying to renew them.) If in doubt, try cutting down one or two branches and see if they sprout.

Pollarding shrubs

There are some summer-flowering shrubs such as the poinsettia, crape myrtle, *Hydrangea paniculata* and *Buddleja davidii* where drastic cutting back every winter or early spring is the practice. In effect, you are pollarding them (refer to the text on pollarding trees earlier in

this section), and the shrub's natural habit will be as radically altered as that of a pollarded tree. The reward is much bigger flower clusters, but you don't *have* to do it. Try allowing them to grow naturally for a few years and see if the natural habit and smaller clusters appeal. You might also wish to pollard such shrubs as *Pittosporum tenuifolium*, *Cotinus coggygria* or those eucalypts that offer blue juvenile leaves, the aim here being to gain a constant supply of long sprays of foliage for cutting. Pollarded shrubs generally don't live as long as they would if allowed to grow naturally.

Left: *Weeping willows* (Salix babylonica) *at Giverny. The species is one of the easiest of all to transplant.*

Turning a shrub into a tree

Usually, you prune a shrub to make it bushier; but sometimes, you might want to do the opposite and make it more open. Then it is a matter of thinning. Simply cut the excess branches right out. This can be a good way to deal with a tall shrub that has grown bigger than you anticipated. Thin its main branches a little and remove the lowest side branches, and you have transformed it into a small, multi-stemmed tree under which you can now plant shade-loving flowers. This is usually the best way to treat those kinds that are on the borderline between tree and shrub, such as the larger-growing cotoneasters and calliandras, pittosporums, *Bauhinia galpinii*, even camellias and bamboo.

TRANSPLANTING OR REMOVING TREES

Modern machinery means that transplanting a mature tree no longer calls for the small army of strong backs that it used to, but it is still not a job to be undertaken lightly. Not all adult trees can in fact be transplanted; some never get over the inevitable damage to their roots. Magnolias, eucalypts and birches, for example have open, rather sparse root systems and rarely survive transplanting. The best candidates are species which either have densely fibrous root systems—rhododendrons are the outstanding example—or which grow new roots vigorously if the old ones are cut. Such include the willows, poplars, planes, and palms. Palms are perhaps the easiest of all trees to transplant, as they grow new roots very quickly.

Preparation for the move should begin at least a year before the big day, preferably two. Before you start you should of course check that no preservation or removal restrictions apply. Begin by pruning the roots. This has two functions: it reduces the root ball to more-or-less manageable size and it provokes the growth of a mass of fine new roots to nourish the tree in its new home and, incidentally, to bind the root ball together when it is lifted from the ground. Nurseries that grow advanced trees in the field—the ones you buy 'balled and burlapped'—prune their roots at least twice while they are growing, using huge mechanical spades. A long-established tree is best dealt with by cutting a circular trench about a third of the way out from the trunk to the outer branches and as deep as possible, using sharp spades and pruners if big roots are encountered. This is then filled in with fine soil enriched with organic matter and maybe watered a few times with the same root-provoking hormones you buy for striking cuttings. It's a good idea to mark the line of the trench in some way.

By doing this, when the time comes, you know where to dig so as not to damage your precious new roots. You'll have to dig beneath the root ball, of course: and then it is necessary to sever roots that you couldn't get the first time. happily, the majority of a tree's feeder roots are in the upper part of the root system, so the shock to the tree may not be as great as it will be to you. Specialist tree movers use a tractor-mounted gadget rather like an enormous ice-cream scoop which digs the tree and carries it to its new home and then deposits it in the planting hole. The rest of us will need to use spades and much sweat, and bundle the root ball up in burlap and string to keep it from falling apart under its own weight. When you remove it from the ground and transport it, always cradle it from below: if you try to pick up the tree by its trunk the roots will tear off, and the tender bark will be crushed.

Transporting the tree to its new home, and the actual planting, are done in just the same way as you did for a smaller one. Onto a truck with it: off again, and into a nice, freshly dug hole where it will end up at precisely the same depth as before. You should also orientate it as before, so the same side will be in the sun. The difference is that you are now dealing with an immensely heavy, fragile object—at all costs, you must not loosen the soil from the roots. If the tree is a really big one, the weight of the root ball may be enough to keep it steady once in place; but to be sure, give it three or four guy ropes.

Transplanting is best done in winter, though if you must you can do it in late summer, when you should spray the entire crown—every single leaf!—with a plastic anti-desiccant spray designed to reduce moisture loss from the foliage. Never, never try to shift a tree (or a shrub) that is actively making new growth.

No matter how careful you are, you cannot avoid some damage to the roots, and it is most desirable to reduce the top growth to keep everything in balance. Otherwise there is a real risk, even from a

Metrosideros excelsa

POHUTUKAWA AND RATA
Metrosideros spp.
Myrtaceae

The genus *Metrosideros* contains some of our most spectacular flowering plants, of which the most common are the pohutukawa (*M. excelsa*) and the northern and southern ratas (*M. robusta* and *M. umbellata* respectively). While shrubby and densely foliaged when young, they develop into heavy-limbed trees with gnarled, spreading branches. From late spring to early autumn they are ablaze with brilliant red filamentous flowers that often obscure the foliage.

As the northernmost and showiest species, the pohutukawa figures most in the Maori appreciation of these species. It was used medicinally, to treat dysentery and diarrhoea, and the nectar of its flowers was a sweet treat. It also features in legends and folklore, the most familiar of which is the idea that the nature of the flowering of the pohutukawas could be used as a guide to what the weather would be like in the coming summer.

The flowers of the northern rata, which occurs as far south as Westport, tend towards dusky orange rather than red and at a distance the plant is sometimes mistaken for a flowering gum (*Eucalyptus* spp.). It too was used medicinally by pre-European Maori and in more recent times its very hard, strong timber has seen to be ideal wherever strength and durability is required, such as in shipbuilding, for tool handles and mallet heads as well as for fine furniture.

The southern rata, which despite its name occurs as far north as Kaitaia, is seen at its spectacular best in the Southern Alps, particularly in the Otira Gorge, where the vivid red of its flowers contrasts beautifully with an intensely blue sky and white snow-capped mountains. As its other common name, ironwood, suggests, the southern rata's timber is just as tough as that of the northern rata. However, it is a smaller, more gnarled tree that yields little useable wood.

winter planting, of the damaged roots being unable to supply sufficient water to the leaves and the tree dying of thirst. Thinning the crown (see 'Pruning', earlier in this section) is a better option than just cutting it back.

The tree may look as though it has been growing in its new home forever, but this is an illusion. It will be at least two or three years before you can remove the guys and allow it to look after itself. In the meantime, you must water regularly, especially in hot weather, and give some fertilizer in spring. Adding a root-promoting hormone to the water is well worthwhile.

Transplanting an established shrub is done in the same way and with the same care. Happily, it isn't such a huge job, simply because the root ball will be smaller.

If you have to remove a tree altogether, there are certain legal obligations you must comply with. Check with your local authorities to see if you need permission to remove the tree. Some trees will have a preservation order on them. More rarely, you may also be legally obliged to remove a tree you'd rather keep, perhaps because it is posing a danger to drains or to public safety.

PESTS & DISEASES

It is customary in gardening books to give long lists of every kind of bug that might possibly be lying in wait to attack your plants, the reading of which would be enough to turn you off gardening forever. Happily, ornamental trees and shrubs are usually trouble free, and if they are flourishing in the sort of soil and climate they like, they can usually shake their troubles off for themselves. A few insect-eaten leaves are normally not much to worry about, though if they do bother you, a trip to the nursery with a specimen of the damage will usually bring forth the appropriate remedy. Often, this takes the form of a chemical that you spray on, which is fine if it is a shrub that is affected, but not so much if the victim is a large tree. Then you may have to rely on the fact that most bugs have natural enemies—birds and other bugs—and if they haven't been driven away by insecticides and other vile pollutants, they will

Right: *A group of plants from Japan, flourishing in a cool-temperate climate:* Cryptomeria japonica, Viburnum plicatum *and* Berberis thunbergii *'Atropurpurea'.*

Pseudopanax crassifolius

PSEUDOPANAX (LANCEWOOD, FIVE FINGER)
Pseudopanax spp.
Araliacae

The flora of New Zealand and Australia is notable for the many trees that have distinctly different juvenile and adult foliage forms. Few plants exhibit more profound changes than the lancewood (*P. crassifolius*) and toothed lancewood (*P. ferox*), both of which have drooping, very long and narrow, spined juvenile leaves that transform into upward-facing, relatively short, rounded, lobed leaves. The midribs of the young leaves are very tough and flexible and were occasionally used as thread substitutes. The shape of the plants also changes, from strongly upright, single-stemmed, narrow saplings to many-branched, round-headed trees. Not all species exhibit such marked changes: the five finger (*P. arboreum*) and *P. laetus* have broad, palmate leaves at all stages of growth and do not change shape as they mature.

All species share similar clusters of inconspicuous greenish flowers that develop into small, purplish berries. Although inedible, the berries are suitable for making a range of dyes.

Another feature of *Pseudopanax* is the sticky resin that covers the buds and developing new growth to the extent of sometimes forming lumps of jellied gum. The gum often traps insects but appears to serve little purpose other than preventing desiccation of the tender new growth.

Lancewoods have fairly narrow trunks that are unsuitable for board-making. Early settlers occasionally used the trunks for posts or piles but these days lancewoods are almost exclusively grown as ornamentals.

The larger species develop into small trees up to 30 ft (10 m) high. The shrubby forms grow to around 15 ft (5 m) and are suitable for massed shrubberies, informal hedging and container cultivation. Several selected foliage cultivars, such as the yellow-variegated 'Gold Splash' and the assorted bronze-leafed *P. lessonii* hybrids are available. The large-leafed *P. laetus* adds a tropical touch.

deal with the problem. Bugs, too, have bad and less bad years. A tree may be practically defoliated by an invasion of caterpillars one year but flourishing mightily again the next, the caterpillars having gone away (or been devoured by birds).

Every so often, however, a devastating disease strikes, the most famous being the Dutch elm disease which has almost destroyed the elms of America and Great Britain, though stringent quarantine has kept it out of most other countries so far. It is ironic that the finest specimens of the English elm are now to be met with in Australia and New Zealand (although Australia is free of the disease which is present in New Zealand but currently contained)—and that there are people in those countries who would like to see them removed to make way for indigenous species. Dutch elm disease is a fungus which destroys the inner bark, killing the tree, but it needs a certain bark-eating beetle to spread it from tree to tree. Control the beetle, and you have a chance of controlling the fungus: but it is a big task and, where the disease is present, it would be most unwise to plant any of the deciduous elms. (The evergreens, *Ulmus chinensis* and *U. parvifolia*, are immune, and so, it appears, are the related genera *Zelkova* and *Celtis*.) But they are not quite the same; and until resistant strains of elm can be developed, the glorious avenues of American elms that gave such beauty to the colonial towns of New England will remain a memory.

Equally alarming are two underground fungi, the honey fungus and the cinnamon fungus, *Armillaria mellea* and *Phytophthora cinnamomi* respectively, both of which do to the roots of many species of trees what Dutch elm disease does to the trunk and branches of elms. Honey fungus, a major worry in Britain, starts life on the roots of dead trees—it is one of the fungi that clear away the dead trees from the forest—but can then spread to attack live ones, which it usually kills. Some people say magnolias are immune, but the general view is that it will attack anything. It is to guard against it that it is standard practice in Britain to grub out every bit of stump and root when a tree has to be removed. It can be controlled by drenching the soil with rather dangerously toxic fungicides, a job for a specialist.

The cinnamon fungus is primarily a pest of warm climates. It is a major problem in the jarrah forests of Western Australia, and is a worry to foresters elsewhere in Australia too; it seems all eucalypts, and a great many other Australian trees and shrubs, are susceptible. It needs damp soil to establish itself, but it can be easily spread on the wheels of vehicles or even on the shoes of hikers. Stringent hygiene is called for, and should it strike in a garden—the symptoms are the sudden collapse and death of the plant, with mould on its roots—there is nothing for it but to replace with a resistant species. Be warned that even though the cinnamon fungus is not common in gardens, it is something to look out for when buying plants at a nursery.

Most gardeners won't encounter these problems; when they think of controlling pests on trees and shrubs they usually think of fruit trees. These are commonly attacked by such bugs as codling moths and fruit-flies, the species varying from place to place, and they may be attacked by various fungi also. If you are planning to grow your own fruit, you should take the advice of your government department of agriculture or equivalent as to the best types of trees for your area and whether you will be required by law to spray them against their enemies.

TREES & SHRUBS IN CONTAINERS

In principle, there is nothing particularly difficult about growing trees or shrubs in containers; nurseries do it all the time. You merely select a suitable container, making sure it has adequate holes for drainage, fill it with a good commercial potting mix, and plant. Then you water regularly—you must never let the plant dry out to the point of wilting—and fertilize regularly, as the constant watering will leach nutrients from the soil very rapidly. A slow release fertilizer is best.

The difference between your situation and the nursery is that the nursery pot is a temporary home but in the garden you will be expecting the plant to live for years in its container. As this needs to be big enough for the root system, you are

Left: *Rhapis excelsa*, perhaps the easiest and most elegant palm for indoors.

looking at quite large containers for an ordinary-sized shrub and an even bigger one for a tree; but even so the plant will eventually outgrow its root space. There are two ways to deal with this—plant into a bigger container, or remove it and prune the roots before putting it back with some fresh potting mix.

There is a limit to how big a container can be; even the very large concrete ones you see in some shopping centre malls are scarcely big enough to hold the roots of a fully grown tree. You and I can hardly cope with these; a half barrel is about as big as two people can man-handle into position when it is filled with soil. So some arrangement which allows us to trim the roots is almost always called for. You can, just, tip a half barrel on its side to ease the plant out, but then you have to stand it up to trim the roots and get it back in again. This is a task that will lead you to discover a vocabulary of obscenities you never realized you knew, though the job of root pruning is simple enough—shave away 2 in (5 cm) or so from the side of the root ball with a sharp knife. In early spring, just when new root growth is due to begin, is the best time.

The solution was devised by the gardeners whom Louis XIV charged with the care of his collection of orange trees at Versailles. (Oranges in those days were very much an expensive luxury.) They designed a square wooden tub with removable sides that allowed access to the roots and which is still called a *caisse de Versailles* or Versailles tub. A refinement was built-in handles so that two or four people could carry the trees into the greenhouse for the winter and then out onto the terrace for the summer. The orange trees flourished; it is said that a couple even survived into the present century, having lived in their tubs for over 250 years.

You can still buy these tubs, and they are not beyond a handyperson's skill to make. Though they are not cheap, if they are made of good, durable timber they should last a lifetime. They are available in a variety of sizes. Timber is just about the best material for a large container too. It is relatively light; unlike pottery or stone it doesn't break; and it is an excellent insulator, protecting the roots from over-heating in summer and to an extent from the cold in winter.

The story suggests some other important points. First, an orange tree is about as big a tree as you can comfortably accommodate in a container; second, that the best trees and shrubs for container growing are ones with a compact root system and which don't mind having their roots disturbed come pruning time. Oranges and lemons of course; camellias, hibiscus; apples; oleanders, mulberries and *Albizia julibrissin* are some which have been grown with success. There is another less obvious moral too: by pruning the roots and replacing at least some of the soil each year, you get over the problem that bedevils the growers of shopping mall trees in their concrete planters. That is the long-term deterioration of the soil. A container grown plant is deprived of that contact with the natural soil and all the various micro-organisms (and such bigger ones as worms) that constantly renew its quotient of organic matter. After a few years, the potting soil, deprived of humus, loses its structure and begins to compact like concrete or a mud pie. The fine feeding roots have trouble growing in this stuff—even if there is still room for them to grow—and so the poor plant starves to death. The addition of such bulk-enhancing substances as perlite to the mix can slow the deterioration down, but not stop it; and so the life span of most of these trees is rarely more than ten years or so.

The question arises; if it is so much trouble, why bother growing trees or shrubs in containers? If you live in an apartment, they allow you to turn your balcony or roof into a garden, a proper garden that is, not

Above: Caisses de Versailles *with their classic inhabitants, sour oranges, in front of the orangerie of the Jardin de Bagatelle in Paris.*
Right: *A blue spruce* (Picea pungens 'Glauca'), *enjoying the fresh air after its duty indoors as a Christmas tree.*

just a collection of small pot plants. Take care: a tree in a tub or even a shrub is heavy and you don't want to risk bringing the roof or balcony down. If you wish to go in for roof gardening, seek the advice of a structural engineer first. Don't forget that roofs and balconies are apt to be windy places and that wind dries plants out very efficiently. You need a tap, or you'll soon get tired of carrying watering cans out from the bathroom.

Even in a regular ground-based garden you might want to place a tubbed shrub or tree on a paved terrace simply to create a focal point. Certainly there are few things so effective for the purpose, though you need to place with care and artistry. A pot of tulips can be casually placed, almost like a bunch of flowers in a living room, but a big plant can't be. It is simply too big for the eye to accept it is only there for the moment. Then, you might be cursed with a limy soil and want to grow lime-hating plants. A container allows you to give your plant the soil it needs. Or you might be renting the place and want to take your choice plants with you when you move. Or you might want, like Louis XIV did, to grow a favourite that is too tender for your climate. If the plant is in a tub, you can bring it indoors for the winter to a greenhouse or even a sunny living room.

Left: *With unlimited funds you can grow forest trees under glass, as here at Longwood Gardens in Pennsylvania.*

TREES & SHRUBS INDOORS

Every gardener knows that if you want to grow plants from warmer climates than your own, all you have to do is build a greenhouse and grow them in that. Whether you need to heat it will depend on how much difference there is between your climate and that from which your chosen plants come. There is no reason why you can't include trees and shrubs, so long as you have unlimited wealth at your disposal—a greenhouse big enough to accommodate a fully grown tree is apt to be a costly item.

But if you can keep a winter minimum temperature of about 45°F (7°C) there is a great range of hot-climate shrubs that can be fitted into a modest greenhouse, either grown in pots (which allows you to take them outdoors for the summer) or planted directly into the greenhouse border. You might like to consider the Hawaiian hibiscus cultivars, oleanders, gardenias, *Tibouchina urvilleana*, and the South African ericas; or almost any of the shrubs indigenous to hot climates, if you have the room. They don't present special problems in cultivation: fertilize them in spring, water them regularly in summer, and don't let their feet get too wet in winter when the darker days slow down their growth. If the shrubs need pruning to keep them in bounds, wait until warm spring days are on the way. You don't want to force young growth too early.

The range of shrubs that can be grown in a merely frost-proof greenhouse is just as large, although perhaps not quite so exotic. Vireya rhododendrons and tea-scented roses are good examples of shrubs that do well under these conditions.

If you don't have a greenhouse, you can grow trees indoors. Not that most houses will have room for a forest giant: the height of the ceiling precludes that. But the choice of trees that will grow well indoors is surprisingly wide. Occasionally, New Zealand natives such as the puka (*Meryta sinclairii*) or the para (*Pisonia brunonianum*) are grown indoors. Most, however, are indigenous to tropical rainforests, used to constant warmth and able to put up with low light levels. Palms have been fashionable since Victorian times, and have been joined by such trees as the Norfolk Island pine (*Araucaria heterophylla*), the Moreton Bay chestnut (*Castanospermum australe*), the silky oak (*Grevillea robusta*), and the jacaranda. These will eventually outgrow their containers, but they will do quite well for a few years at least. They don't always branch out and develop a crown: in the same manner as the ubiquitous India-rubber tree (*Ficus elastica*), they have a tendency to grow up on one or two ceiling-high stems. The species that really does make an elegant branching tree from its earliest youth is the small-leafed weeping fig, *Ficus benjamina*, which has become so popular in recent years that interior decorators are apt to shun it as a cliché.

Others to try are citrus, though they can be temperamental (they don't really enjoy the level of warmth we do in winter); the coffee tree (*Coffea arabica*), though you are unlikely to get coffee beans from it; and the African hemp (*Sparrmania africana*). The easiest and most spectacular palms are probably the kentia (*Howea belmoreana*) and the lady palm (*Rhapis excelsa*), though these are slow growers and consequently expensive.

The important things for success with these trees, and with all indoor plants, are three: good light, humidity and just the right amount of water.

They must have good light: not direct sunlight necessarily, but light strong enough to cast a shadow. This means keeping the curtains open during the day; it is surprising how many people don't realize how much light drawn curtains exclude. (If privacy while you are out of the house all day is an issue, a light, transparent curtain will block prying eyes but still let in a reasonable amount of light.) You should turn the tree around every so often, so that all sides will have their turn in the light. Alas, the lightest place in the room is usually where we want to sit, so there may have to be a compromise between the tree's needs and the arrangement of the furniture: but you can't tuck *any* plant into a dark corner and expect it to grow.

Then, they must have humidity: dry air will cause them to drop their leaves in a hurry. Central heating and air-conditioning both dry the air out to desert-like levels. (This is not good for you either, and it will cause the piano to be always going out of tune.) A humidifier can help, though these can sometimes work all too well and you end up with a living room that resembles a Turkish bath. That isn't very good for the pictures or the carpets! You can try standing the tree on (not in) a tray of pebbles which you damp down every two or three days; or, simplest of all, place a bowl of water nearby. Even a vase of flowers will do the trick.

Third, they must never be overwatered, especially in winter when the shorter days will slow down growth, despite central heating keeping the temperature reasonably high. More house plants drown than die of thirst. The ideal is to have the soil in the pot just evenly moist but never wet. The pot itself should never stand in a saucer of water, or the roots will suffocate. It is easy enough to lift an African violet off its saucer to empty it, but not so easy to shift a tree. The best thing to do is to stand the pot on some blocks or stones. You can then leave the water in the saucer to evaporate and to raise the humidity.

Any standard commercial potting mix designed for indoor plants will grow these trees, and they won't mind tight shoes if you give them some fertilizer in spring and again in early summer. Re-potting should only be needed every two or three years. However, the pot needs to be big enough so the whole thing isn't top heavy and at risk of being easily knocked over.

Some of the shrubs we noted as good for the greenhouse will grow indoors too; hibiscus in particular have been popular in recent years. But don't expect much in the way of flowers unless you can give them a really sunny window. Some, such as poinsettias, hydrangeas and the Belgian hybrid azaleas, are a familiar sight in flower shops; but they are happiest in the greenhouse or in a mild-climate garden. If you have such, by all means transfer them there when the flowers fade; if you don't, resign yourself to treating them like bunches of flowers and discarding them when their beauty is over. If you keep them in a light place and give them a fine spray of water every day or so, they should outlast two or three bunches of cut flowers, so their cost isn't as high as it first seems.

Propagating Trees & Shrubs

Unless you are planting on a fairly large scale, you probably won't find the need to propagate your own trees and shrubs. Your local nurseries can most likely supply your needs, and you save time by buying plants rather than propagating them yourself. But propagation is a most interesting aspect of gardening, and it enhances your pleasure in a fine plant to know that you raised it from infancy. And should you come across an unnamed but desirable plant in a friend's garden, it can be easier to ask for some seeds or cuttings than to chase through books and nursery catalogues looking for its name and where to buy it.

Woody plants can be propagated in one of four basic ways. They can be grown from seed, struck from layers, struck from cuttings, or grafted.

SEED

Seed is the most common way of raising trees, especially when large numbers are desired for forest or park plantings. Not only are many trees difficult to raise from cuttings, seed is easier to handle in large numbers. (There is no worry about seeds drying out and dying before they can be planted.) By and large, trees and shrubs are not difficult to raise from seed. The seeds themselves are usually larger and easier to handle than those of flowers and vegetables. (Eucalypts are an exception, and it is wonderful to think that these tallest of all hardwood trees grow from some of the smallest of seeds.) The difficulty, from the gardener's point of view, can be obtaining the seed in the first place. Nurseries that specialize in growing tree seeds tend to cater primarily for foresters and other nurseries, so prefer to offer their seeds by the pound or the kilogram rather than in the small packets gardeners are used to. If you gather the seeds yourself from your own plants or a friend's, you can just take as many as you require. If you have any choice in the matter, try to select your seeds from the best specimen, the one with the strongest growth, best flowers, most attractive leaves or whatever is most important. A poor specimen may prove the parent of equally poor offspring.

However you obtain your seeds, make sure they are fresh. Many woody-plant seeds lose viability quite quickly, the most notorious being those of the magnolias and oaks. If in doubt, sow them as soon as you receive them. That will most likely be about the end of summer or shortly thereafter. They may well germinate almost at once; but if they are not planning to come up until the following spring, they will come to no harm provided you ensure that mice or such pests don't get a chance to eat them. Many cool- and cold-climate species won't germinate until they have been subjected to a period of cold anyway. It is a defence against their coming up too soon and being killed off by a late frost. Such include most members of the rose family, including the rose itself. Should you see a note in the catalogue that the seed needs 'stratification' or 'vernalization', that is what it means. You can give such seeds an artificial winter by bundling them up in just-moist peat or sphagnum moss and putting them in the refrigerator for a few weeks, then sowing at once. Alternatively, you can sow them in the autumn (in a tray or pot) and leave them to overwinter outdoors. They should germinate in spring just like nature intended provided the soil is kept just moist and free of weeds.

It is best to sow in small pots, maybe planting two or three seeds per pot and thinning the seedlings to keep only the strongest. The usual rule applies: cover your seeds with their own depth of soil. Any commercially mixed seed-raising compost will suit, or you can mix your own from half-and-half

Right: *The forests and gardens of the future: conifers (mainly thujas) in a nursery. Each is growing in its own pot.*

Vitex lucens

PURIRI
Vitex lucens
Verbenaceae

The puriri belongs to a largely tropical genus of trees. It has large lustrous leaves and unusual flowers for a New Zealand tree. These are a soft dusky pinkish red, and tubular with reflexed petals, rather like a small Cape primrose (*Streptocarpus*) bloom. The flowers are carried in large panicles and are most often seen in late winter, though they may occur at any time. The nectar-filled flowers and the bright red drupes that follow are very attractive to birds.

Found naturally in the northern half of the North Island, the puriri can be grown in any near frost-free or sheltered position: there is a very good specimen beside the main stairway of the Otago Museum in Dunedin. Once established, it is an undemanding tree, though gardeners should be aware of its eventual size.

That such a distinctive tree should have been among the first species collected by European botanists (on Cook's first visit in 1769) is not surprising, but it is unusual that Maori appear to have made little use of the puriri's extremely strong timber. They used the leaves medicinally—they contain a strong germicide—and the bark as a source of dye. It may have been the very toughness of the timber that limited its pre-European use: millers have been known to resort to small explosive charges to split puriri logs when conventional methods failed. Because it is difficult to work, the timber was mainly used for load-bearing tasks, such as railway sleepers, bridges and fence posts.

Puriri is a very impressive tree in all respects and, fittingly, is host to one of our most impressive insects: the puriri moth, which has a wingspan of up to 6 in (15 cm). The caterpillars of this large moth bore into the wood but seldom cause much damage.

Dacrydium cupressinum

RIMU
Dacrydium cupressinum
Podocarpaceae

This graceful tree has an unmistakable silhouette, especially when young. Until it reaches about 30 ft (10 m) high, the rimu has an open weeping habit; as it matures it develops into a columnar tree. The branches are clothed in very short, stiff needles which are green in spring and summer, turning reddish brown in autumn and winter.

While not extensively used for construction by Maori, who favoured it more for medicinal uses and for its resin, the rimu has since European settlement been the most extensively used of the native timbers. Not only is it seen in all manner of construction and furniture-making, it produces a dye and its tannins have been used in leather tanning. Rimu heartwood has a beautifully figured grain that makes it ideal for fine furniture, yet for such a valuable resource it is staggering to realize how much we still squander it: most wooden garden stakes are rimu.

Once common in higher rainfall areas over most of New Zealand, large stands of rimu are now restricted to the South Island's West Coast. While it is quicker to regenerate than most of the large native trees, the continued use of rimu timber puts even these few remaining fragments in jeopardy.

The rimu has always had a reputation for being difficult to cultivate, especially in dry areas like Canterbury and Hawke's Bay. However, provided it is planted out when very young and can be kept moist until well established, the rimu is surprisingly drought tolerant. In its juvenile state it is a very beautiful garden tree that deserves to be more widely planted.

peat-based potting mix and sharp sand. Keep your pots in a lightly shaded place, convenient enough that you won't forget about them: they will need regular watering, protection from pests like snails, and maybe a spray with fungicide as soon as they begin to germinate. If you are growing seeds which come from a climate warmer than your own, you may prefer to place your pots in a greenhouse.

When the young plants have developed a few leaves, they can be potted on to progressively bigger pots until they are big enough to go into their permanent homes in the garden. Don't be surprised if this takes two or three years; most trees and shrubs grow slowly at first.

CUTTINGS

A problem with seed from a gardener's point of view is that it doesn't always 'breed true'. The parent may be a selected variety (a cultivar) whose good qualities will be diluted in the seedlings—fruit trees are a case in point—or it may be a species that cross-breeds easily in gardens. To ensure that you are getting a new plant exactly like the parent, you must bypass the sexual processes that create the seeds and propagate, as some prudish English-speaking gardeners say, vegetatively; or as the French say, asexually. That is, you take cuttings, layers, or grafts. A group of plants propagated thus is called a clone. Most named cultivars of trees and shrubs, the camellias 'Adolphe Audusson' and 'Donation' for instance, or the 'Granny Smith' apple, are clones. You can recognize them by their names being given in quotation marks rather than the italics which botanists reserve for wild, true-breeding species. (Only bother growing such plants from seed if you want to create new cultivars.) Naturally, you'll only take your propagating material from plants with superior characteristics of growth, foliage, flower or fruit. It isn't worth the trouble perpetuating inferior ones.

A cutting is simply a piece of branch placed in the soil in the hope that before it dies it will make roots of its own. Many shrubs do this quite readily, others less do it readily; but many trees are reluctant strikers. You can take your cutting at any time it is offered, though the best times are usually said to be spring and summer. You can take the cutting from a soft, actively growing shoot, from one which has slowed down but not yet matured—a semi-mature cutting—or from mature wood, which may indeed have already lost its leaves for the winter. Each can give excellent results, depending on the species. Fuchsias and other fast-growing, warm-climate shrubs are usually grown from soft cuttings, camellias from semi-mature ones, roses from mature ones. Take your cuttings, if you can, from young, strongly growing plants. Those taken from older, less vigorous plants often don't strike so easily or grow less well when they do.

Having taken your cuttings, you need to trim them. Re-cut the base with a very sharp knife: if the cut is at all ragged, it won't heal, and it is from the healing callus that the new roots spring. Trim off excess leafage, but don't remove it all: usually you leave a few leaves. Dip it in rooting hormone, which does make a great difference so long as it is fresh, and insert it in a pot of sharp sand or the same half-sand-half potting mix you used for sowing seeds. Usually, you'll put several cuttings to the pot, and it saves confusion if you put only one variety to each pot and label it accordingly. Resist the temptation to tip the pot out to see if the cuttings have struck—you don't want to disturb the incipient roots, which are very delicate. When they have struck, you will see signs of new growth or of roots peeking out though the drainage holes, and then is the time to take your new plants out and pot them into individual pots.

Striking a cutting is a race with time, and you need to do everything you can to help. The ideal is to put your pots of cuttings in a greenhouse equipped with a heating system that will keep the soil in the pots just a little warmer than the air ('bottom heat') and a watering system that surrounds their tops in a constant, gentle fog. These 'mist systems' are widely used commercially and have made it possible to grow such formerly intractable things as rhododendrons from cuttings. You can buy small mist-propagating units; although the intial outlay for these is quite high, in terms of what they can produce they are extremely cost-effective. (If you want only a few plants it may well be more economical just to buy them ready-grown.) You can, however, create a poor-man's version by enclosing your cuttings, pot and all, in a clear plastic bag or bottle which will keep them moist. Keep it in a warm but shaded place.

LAYERING

The other way to assist a cutting is not to remove it from its parent at all until it has made its roots. This is called layering, and the usual way to do it is to take a low branch and bend it down to the ground (or to a strategically placed pot) and bury it about 2 in (4 cm) where it touches.

The Cultivation of Trees & Shrubs   41

Taking cuttings of a fuchsia. Stage one: trimming off any leaves that will be buried.

Stage two: inserting the cuttings in a pot of sharp sand with just a little compost.

Stage three: the cuttings are covered with a mini-greenhouse—a plastic jar.

Layering a magnolia. The branch chosen is one growing from the base of the tree.

Bending the branch to the ground, so that a short section can be buried.

The layer needs to be held immobile; here bent wires are pinning it to the ground.

If you have ever seen a blackberry take root wherever its branches touch the ground you have seen the process. Bending the branch sharply, or cutting a nick at the buried point, is often a help in giving it the idea that it should be making roots. A dab of rooting hormone won't be wasted either. You should tie your layer to a stake to keep it from blowing free, and then all you need is patience; it can take such slow-rooters as rhododendrons a year or three to make sufficient roots to allow you to cut your new plant away from its parent and transplant it.

Naturally, you can only layer a plant whose branches are low and flexible enough to be bent to the ground. If it can't be done, you can try a variation called air-layering or marcottage. Here you bring the soil (or rather, moist sphagnum moss) up to the branch. In the spring or early summer, select a branch one or two years old, make a nick in it (don't cut right through) and dab with rooting hormone. You might want give your branch a splint by tying it to a short piece of cane, just in case it breaks. Then pack the cut with a couple of handfuls of wet sphagnum moss and hold this in place by bandaging it in a sheet of clear plastic tied above and below the cut. An old shopping bag will do: if it is translucent, so much the better: you'll be able to see when roots are developed enough to detach your new plant. Don't forget to check the moss regularly to make sure it isn't drying out. If you want to try the technique, the best subject to practise on is that overgrown rubber tree (*Ficus elastica*) in the office. Air-layer a nice new plant with, say, eight or nine leaves, and throw the old plant away. Then you can transfer the new plant to the old plant's pot.

A further advantage of layering and air-layering is that you get a bigger plant than from a cutting; but this disappears in a few years. The cutting will catch up.

GRAFTING

Another way to deal with a cutting is to graft it on to a plant which already has roots. You sometimes see old trees or shrubs where two branches have rubbed together and joined up, and that is perhaps what gave gardeners the idea. If so, it was a very long time ago, for grafting has been practised in the West at least since the time of the Romans and in China since long before that.

There are many different methods of effecting the union between the cutting (the scion) and the already-rooted plant, the stock or understock. They all depend on a perfect meeting of the cambium layers, the bright green layer of actively growing tissue just inside the bark, and all call for exquisite care, a steady hand, and a razor-sharp knife. Let the cuts on either stock or scion be ragged, and the cambiums won't heal together. The best known methods are cleft grafting, when the stock is cut off and then split vertically to receive the end of the scion, trimmed to a wedge shape; and budding, where the scion is just a shield-shaped piece of bark bearing a growth bud and slipped beneath two flaps made by cutting a T-shaped cut in the bark of the stock. Budding is the easiest method, the one universally used for roses and fruit trees, though it is not always successful with other plants. Camellia or rhododendron growers, for instance, usually resort to cleft grafting. The other methods—veneer grafting, shield grafting, approach grafting and so on—are less often seen. In all cases, the stock can be either grown from seed or from a cutting; it doesn't matter.

With approach grafting, which is a kind of formalization of the two rubbing branches, it is quite common for both the stock and scion to have roots—you grow each in a pot and bring them together. That being so, why bother grafting at all? And why graft such things as roses, which grow easily from cuttings?

Grafting has many other advantages than just allowing asexual propagation from plants that don't grow from cuttings. By selecting the roots with care, you can to a great extent modify the characters of the resulting, composite plant. Hybrid roses, for instance, often have rather weak roots. By uniting them to the strong roots of a wild rose such as *Rosa canina*, *R. multiflora* or *R. rugosa*, you create a much stronger growing rose bush. Conversely, you might want to *reduce* the vigour of the scion. This is often the case with apples and pears, which tend to grow larger than the orchardist or gardener might wish when grown on their own roots (that is from cuttings). Here, the understocks are selected for *lack* of vigour, so the tree will be smaller. By careful selection of stock, you can have the same apple tailored to grow anything from the size of a large rose-bush to as tall as a two-storeyed house. Or you might want to give your plant roots with special disease resistance or ability to grow in otherwise unsuitable soils. Citrus are often grafted (budded, usually) on their close relative, *Poncirus trifoliata*, a much tougher, more cold-resistant species though its fruit is scarcely worth eating. Grape vines are grafted on to wild American grapes whose roots are not damaged significantly by the vine-louse, *Phylloxera vastatrix*, which cripples the classic European cultivars from which all the best wines are made. Other times, the stock is intended to be a 'nurse graft', designed to support the scion until it can make roots of its own. Tree peonies are grafted to a root of a herbaceous peony, and lilac to privet.

You might have an established plant, a camellia for instance, but

Cleft-grafting a camellia: understock, a sasanqua seedling; scion, a cultivar of C. japonica.

The stock is being cut down to receive the graft. Early spring is the time for grafting camellias.

Now the cleft is being cut in the stock. Notice the special grafting knife being used.

The base of the scion is being trimmed to a point, to exactly match the cleft.

Using the back of the knife to hold the cleft open, the scion is being inserted with care.

The completed graft; notice how the green cambiums line up precisely.

would prefer a different cultivar. You could place a number of grafts into its branches, removing all shoots of the original when the scions have taken and are growing strongly. You thus have a nice big bush of your new cultivar without having to wait for it to grow up from infancy. Grape growers did this on a large scale in the 1970s and early 1980s, when public taste suddenly switched from red to white wine. By grafting their existing red grape vines over to white varieties, they were able to meet the new demand in two or three years rather than the ten it would have taken otherwise.

The wine writers who were afraid the result would be pink grapes (and thus rosé wine) were displaying their ignorance of plants. The stock and scion do not hybridize. A white grape variety will bear white grapes, no matter what its understock would bear given the chance; an orange grafted on to a lemon will still bear oranges.

Grafting is one of the most skilled operations in all of horticulture, and it is not easy to learn from books. If you fancy trying it, we suggest you seek an opportunity to watch an experienced hand at work.

You should, however, be aware if a tree or shrub you buy has been grafted. The graft union does not become really firm for some time, and you need to handle grafted young plants gently. Yank a rose bush out from its packaging, and you may well find yourself with the scion in one hand and the stock in the other. It's a good idea to stake a grafted plant for a few years, just in case a storm rips the scion off.

Standard roses and such things as weeping cherries are grafted atop a long understock that forms the trunk, but normally the graft is made as low down as possible to obviate the worry of unwanted branches or suckers arising from the stock. Watch out for these and remove them as soon as you see them lest they take over and smother the scion. They will almost always have slightly different foliage but if in doubt you can usually recognize the swelling where the graft was made—the graft-union—and assume anything coming from below it is understock.

The general rule is to plant a grafted plant with the union above the soil. The union is not as resistant to cankers and rots as the rest of the plant—at least for the first few years—and you don't want to run the risk of constant contact with wet soil encouraging these. (This is especially true of citrus.) Nurse grafts are the exception. Here you must bury the union as deep as possible, so it will have the chance to throw out its own roots and eventually smother the stock. Lilac on privet is the classic example: the privet is really too strong for the lilac, and if you set the union above ground it will shake the lilac off its back in a few years. Most people like to set roses deep too, to encourage 'scion rooting'. This is well worth doing in a cold climate where there is danger of the top growth being killed by frost. You don't want to find the stock is all that has survived a hard winter!

Special Treatments of Trees & Shrubs

BONSAI

The art of bonsai originated in the Orient more than a thousand years ago. There a splendid bonsai is not a mere testament to a gardener's skill but a work of art which conveys profound spiritual meaning. It embodies the divine life that pulses throughout nature, and nowhere more than in an ancient and venerable tree.

Though the art of miniaturizing trees was first developed in China, it is the slightly different Japanese tradition that is most widely known in the West. The Chinese prefer to allow the creator freedom of expression in shaping his bonsai, often in emulation of some famous Song or Yuan dynasty painter: the Japanese reserve their highest appreciation for a tree that perfectly displays one of the dozen or so traditional styles. These are usually described by names that give no hint of the emotion they can evoke: the formal upright style, the informal upright, the slanting, the cascading, and so on. The tree will, of course, be in perfect proportion to the pot in which it lives, and the pot itself may be ancient and very precious: but there must be no hint of artifice. You must feel that what you are seeing is a tree living in its primeval forest, its branches shaped by decades of winter snow and summer wind.

Alectryon excelsus

TITOKI
Alectryon excelsus
Sapindaceae

This beautiful evergreen tree grows to about 30 ft (10 m) tall, making it ideal for most gardens. It is densely foliaged and, though the flowers are not very showy, the black seeds and bright red arils that are revealed when the seed capsules burst open are very striking. The fruit takes nearly a year to ripen and trees often bear ripe fruit and flowers at the same time. The titoki is self-fertile so a good crop of fruit is assured once the tree is mature. The fine pubescence that coats the young twigs and new leaves is also a feature of the titoki.

The titoki has had many uses, both to pre-European Maori and in modern times. Maori extracted an oil from the pulpy arils that was used medicinally and as a hair oil. It has also been used in lamps and in watch mechanisms. The fruit, which is very attractive to wood pigeons, is sometimes fermented to make a liqueur. Titoki timber, like that of the kowhai, is elastic and well suited to use in tool handles and bentwood furniture. In earlier times it was used in coach building.

Found over most of the North Island and in coastal parts of the South island to Westport in the west and Banks Peninsula in the east, the titoki is easily damaged by frost and strong winds when young. Because of this, titoki saplings are best planted in the shelter of other trees and shrubs that can be thinned and removed as the tree becomes established. Occasional light feeding with organic manures will boost the growth rate of young trees quite considerably.

If that suggests that bonsai is not for the casual gardener, you are right. This is not only an art requiring skill and sensitivity, the little trees need constant, devoted care. For all their beauty, they are growing on the edge of extinction, in just sufficient soil—and with only just sufficient nourishment—to support life, their growth slowed almost to a stop. They can do this indefinitely: there are bonsai trees

The Japanese black pine, (Pinus thunbergii), is the classic species for bonsai. This one is about 10 years old, its training still incomplete.

prune and it will grow out of the shape you have decreed, and cutting it back will leave scars that will ruin its beauty for years. If all you want is something cute, forget trying to grow bonsai trees and invest in a miniature rose bush from the florist.

If, however, the little trees touch your heart, the best course is to join your local bonsai society and learn the technique from experts. Bonsai isn't beyond the skills of the ordinary gardener: but it is very difficult to learn from a book. We can, however, make a few general suggestions. The traditional trees are the pines, zelkovas, willows, plums and maples of Japan, to which the Japanese add such shrubs as azaleas and wisteria, though these are not always taken very seriously: mere flowers are of less interest to the connoisseur than line and form. But there is no need to confine yourself to these, and if they do not flourish in your climate it would be wise to seek species that do, relying on the guidance of your local enthusiasts. There is scarcely a local market or street fair without a bonsai nursery offering ready-trained specimens, and you can assume they will be suitable.

Bonsai are not indoor plants, however enchanting they may look on the coffee table or mantelpiece. They must be grown outside, in a spot sheltered from drying winds and too much sun.

HEDGES

Hedges make ideal windbreaks and can also provide privacy. Refer to the text under 'Windbreaks' earlier in this part for the best species to use for hedge making.

To grow a formal hedge, you plant your chosen plants in a richly prepared bed, at about half the normal spacing, and you cut them back hard at once to force them to branch. This seems perverse, as you naturally want them to grow to their full height as fast as possible: but if you don't, they will never grow sufficiently solid. And you need to cut back the sides every winter until the hedge has grown up. Hedge making takes time and patience! Once the hedge has achieved its designed size, you clip with shears as often during the growing season as needed to keep it there. Don't attempt to make the walls exactly vertical: you'll inevitably misjudge it and the hedge will be wider at the top than at the bottom—which is how the plants will try to grow anyway. If that happens, the lowest branches will die off for lack of sun, and the effect will be spoiled. Slope the sides inwards a little.

If you miss out on a season or two of clipping, the hedge will get overgrown, and you'll need to cut harder to bring it back to shape. Beware: if you've chosen a species such as a cypress that won't sprout from bare wood, you may simply ruin it. If you can't accept making the hedge a little bigger than before, you may have to pull it out and start again. Yew is exceptional among conifers in growing back from stubs, which is one reason (apart from its velvet texture) why it is a classic species for hedge-making. It is, however, not a plant for hot, dry climates.

TOPIARY

Topiary, the cutting of trees or shrubs into fancy shapes, is handled in the same way as a hedge, and the same species are used (refer to the text under 'Windbreaks' earlier in this part). The difference is that you are clipping single plants rather than rows. Yew (*Taxus*) and the taller varieties of box (*Buxus*) are the classic species, although the Japanese clip Kurume azaleas to shapes reminiscent of clouds. (Clipped azaleas surrounding a tall rock are meant to evoke the clouds swirling around a mountain peak.)

Topiary can look wonderful in the right setting, which is almost always a formal one. If you fancy the idea, start with simple shapes like cones or spheres before you embark on such fantasies as peacocks, dinosaurs or a pack of hounds (in box) chasing a fox (in privet) across the lawn. Don't try to make your shape either too small or too detailed; you can't clip living greenery as finely as a sculptor can carve stone. Be patient; it takes many years to develop a topiary specimen.

ESPALIER

The word is French, but it appears that the technique was originally created by the ancient Romans as a means of encouraging fruit trees to ripen earlier in their season. Espalier is simple in principle. You plant your tree against a sunny wall, whose warmth will shelter it from the cold and assist the fruit to ripen earlier than it would out in the open. To make the most of this, you bend the branches back flat against the wall, tying them to wires or a trellis and removing any that insist on growing forward, so that the foliage and flowers are kept as close to the warmth of the wall as possible. By selecting some branches and rejecting others, you

Above: Naturally a tall tree, Pinus strobus *has here been disciplined—though not formally—into a splendid tall hedge.*
*Top: A beautiful contrast between the formally clipped box hedges (*Buxus japonica*) and the free-growing* Robinia *'Frisia' beyond.*

in Japan which are known to be centuries old. But they cannot live more than a couple of days without you. Forget to water one summer morning and you may return in the evening to find your tree dead. Forget to re-pot when it is needed and it will starve to death. Forget to

Opposite page: Tropical topiary: a zoo of animals shaped from a small-leafed species of Ficus *at Hua Hin in Thailand.*

The Cultivation of Trees & Shrubs

Podocarpus totara

TOTARA
Podocarpus totara
Podocarpaceae

When first seen, the most striking aspect of the totara is its very solid trunk and beautiful peeling bark. Large strips of the bark were used by pre-European Maori as a roofing material. The very straight, warp-free trunk of the totara led to it being the favoured tree for canoe-building as well as for general construction. Surprisingly, for a relatively common tree that was so widely used by Maori, it was not botanically described until 1826.

Large stands of the tree have now been decimated to provide timber for all manner of purposes: shipbuilding, wharves, telephone poles, fence posts, door and window frames, shingles and bridges. Small wonder that these days naturally occurring totara is most often seen as a single forlorn specimen in a paddock.

The totara does not bear true cones but produces bright red, fleshy fruit known as drupes. These are very attractive to birds. Totara drupes were also a favoured food of pre-European Maori. Make sure you actually have a totara drupe before trying one: when young, the totara can be mistaken for the yew (*Taxus baccata*) and yew drupes are poisonous.

Although the totara is one of the few native conifers to be widely grown in domestic gardens, such plantings can only be considered temporary because at over 65 ft (20 m) high, the mature totara is far too large for anything but parks and reserves. The golden-foliaged cultivar 'Aureus' is smaller and very slow growing, making it more suitable for general cultivation. Totara can be used for hedging and with regular trimming will remain shrubby with foliage to ground level.

can create any one of several patterns which can look wonderfully decorative. The tree might look like a fan, the most usual method for peaches; or it might be more like a menorah, the most favoured treatment for apples and pears. Figs cannot be trained quite so formally, and they don't really like the constant pruning. But in countries such as Britain they are tender and you either grow them espalier or not at all.

There is no reason why you can't train any smallish tree or shrub that can will put up with regular pruning as an espalier, and in fact if you have ever trained a 'climbing' rose flat against a wall that is what you have done. There is no need to force the branches into geometrical patterns; an informally trained espalier can look just as elegant. Some to experiment with are: *Camellia sasanqua*; the flowering quinces; hibiscus, both evergreen and deciduous; *Philadelphus mexicanus*; *Laburnum vossii*, and *Magnolia grandiflora*, always grown espalier in Britain for the same reason as the fig. In this case, you need a three storey house to train it on! A wall or fence clothed with espaliered shrubs can look wonderful, and they have the advantage over 'real' climbing plants that they grow much more slowly and you don't have the constant battle to keep them in bounds that ivy, wisteria, grapes or bougainvillea can lead you into.

STANDARDS

A standard is a shrub that would normally form a multi-stemmed bush that has been trained to form a single stem carrying a rounded head of branches—somewhat like a floral lollipop or a miniature tree. The effect can be deliciously formal, and for that very reason standard shrubs are favourites for growing in containers.

Below: *Here a standard lantana is displayed with a carpet of salvias and zinnias around its base.*

Carmichaelia odorata

LESSER KNOWN TREES & SHRUBS

The New Zealand flora includes many genera that are only occasionally seen in gardens or which are not always immediately recognized. Some, like the shrubby *Brachyglottis* (syn. *Senecio*) species, have their moment of glory when they burst into flower, while others such as the olearias perform year-round service as hedges and windbreaks.

The native brooms are among our most easily overlooked yet most distinctive plants. Species such as *Carmichaelia odorata* and *Notospartium carmichaeliae* could scarcely be called attractive when not in bloom, however as soon as the flowers open those dead-looking twigs come to life. The Marlborough rock daisy (*Pachystegia insignis*) is also among our best flowering shrubs and is increasingly seen in gardens. In all respects it is a superb plant, with magnificent deep green leaves that are heavily felted on the undersides, bright flowers and interesting seed heads. Equally attractive, though more tender, is the kumarahou (*Pomaderris kumeraho*), which produces masses of tiny golden yellow flowers in spring. Now grown as an ornamental, in earlier times it was used medicinally and the ability of its leaves to produce a lather when rubbed in water gave it the name gumdiggers' soap.

Some native plants seem to have all the attributes for extensive garden use but never seem to be taken up in large numbers by the public. *Corokia* is a genus that includes three species of evergreen shrubs. They have bright if small flowers, colourful foliage and showy berries yet are generally only used for windbreaks and amenity plantings. *Griselinia* and *Lophomyrtus* (syn. *Myrtus*) too deserve to be appreciated as much for their beauty as their utilitarian features.

Many of our native trees are just too large for small city gardens or are overlooked by mainstream nurseries and garden centres. This is a pity because trees like the rewarewa (*Knightia excelsa*), hinau (*Elaeocarpus dentatus*) and taraire (*Beilschmedia tarairi*), with its lustrous leaves and black, olive-like fruit that were a favourite food of pre-European Maori, are ideal candidates for cultivation.

Creating one is not unlike training a young tree; and indeed to train a standard, you need to start in the plant's youth. You select the strongest branch and ruthlessly remove all others. Tie your selected branch to a stake, trim away its side shoots, and when it has reached the desired height, pinch out the growing tip to force the branches that will make up the head. After that, prune as you would normally to keep the head bushy and compact.

Standard roses (also known as tree roses) are the best known example of this sort of thing, though perversely they are normally produced by budding the selected rose on to a long understock (refer to the text under 'Grafting' earlier in this part). Standard fuchsias, gardenias, azaleas, bay trees and even oleanders are familiar too, and they are produced in the manner described. You can in fact train almost any shrub as a standard if the fancy takes you; but you need to be very patient. It may take a couple of years of training before the stem is tall and the head well filled out. You will probably need to keep the plant staked all its life, as the stem is being expected to carry much more growth than it would naturally. Watch for unwanted shoots from the stem and rub them off as soon as they appear.

STREET TREES

There is a school of thought among architects that considers trees belong in the country and have no place in the city. Fine architecture, they say, needs no embellishment. They like to site such memorable places as St Mark's Square in Venice, St Peter's Square in Rome, the back streets of Paris. They have a point: but they forget that few cities are graced with magnificent historic buildings such as these—and that from the city centres of old the countryside was not far away. Modern cities are vastly bigger, their hearts are remote from the country, and their streets are apt to be composed of a jumble of inharmonious buildings, often ugly to boot. A row of trees can greatly improve such a street simply by providing a green frame that ties the composition together and by giving it a human scale; it is very pleasant to walk beneath a canopy of leaves, no matter how overwhelming the scale of the buildings that front the street. At least they give the citizens something beautiful to look at, both from the street and looking out the window.

Trees do more than just look attractive. They add their quota of oxygen to the often polluted air; they shade buildings and pavements which would otherwise simply reflect the summer heat; and they absorb at least some of the ever-present noise in our cities. Planting trees on the footpaths is one of the simplest, and the cheapest, ways of improving the quality of urban life.

The streets are not the only places where trees can lend beauty to the city; there are for instance the often bare and windy forecourts of office buildings, parks large and small—it is surprising how much a tiny park, just big enough for two or three seats and a tree or two to shelter them can contribute to a neighbourhood—and, of course, the private gardens of people like ourselves, both in the city and the suburbs. If every garden had a tree or two, how beautiful the city would be!

Above: *City parks attract a surprising amount of wildlife, like this squirrel resident in the heart of London.*
Above left: Paulownia tomentosa *is a favourite tree for city gardens and parks in cool climates. This splendid avenue is in Philadelphia.*
Top: *A sight rarely seen nowadays: an avenue of* Ulmus procera. *It is in Australia, one of the few countries so far spared Dutch elm disease.*

PART TWO

A–Z of Trees & Shrubs

AN EXPLANATION OF PLANT NAMES

The trees and shrubs featured in this book are arranged alphabetically by their scientific names. Because these names are in Latin they may not be familiar to every gardener, but there are many difficulties associated with using plants' common names.

One of the greatest problems would be that many plants share the same common name—for example, 'cedar' refers to quite unrelated trees in Asia, North America, South Africa and Australia. Another problem is that many plants have more than one common name even in the one language, not to mention common names that the same plant may have in different languages of the world. And to these difficulties should be added the fact that a large proportion of the world's plants have never received a common name, on account of being too rare, hard to distinguish, or found only in wilderness areas.

The reason that scientific names are in Latin is that, when the systematic description of plants began to receive attention in the Renaissance period, the common language of European scholarship was Latin. But for the next two or three centuries the names of plants were clumsy Latin phrases, which might be translated as, for example, 'Oak with lobed leaves and long-stalked nuts, its bark used for tanning'.

It was the famous Swedish naturalist Carolus Linnaeus (1707–78) who first hit on the idea of identifying each plant by two names. At first, in his book *Species Plantarum* of 1753, he showed the differentiating names merely as marginal annotations beside the longer phrase-names of the text, but it was not long before the convenience of this system was appreciated and these names were coupled with the genus names to give the Latin two-word names (binomials) we now use. These follow a similar principle to people's names, though with the surname and given name reversed, and so *Quercus alba* and *Quercus rubra* are both members of the 'family' *Quercus*, in the same way that Elizabeth Mann and Manfred Mann are both members of the family Mann. The parallel can be extended, in that the second part of the name, for example, *rubra*, can be the 'given' name in unrelated 'families'—thus there is an *Ulmus rubra* and a *Morus rubra* as well as a *Quercus rubra*.

The first part of the botanical name is the *genus* name, which is unique and can stand on its own: thus *Quercus* is the genus of oaks and no other plant genus can share the name. Each genus (plural: genera) may consist of several or many (or sometimes only one) *species*, each designated by a two-part name as just described—thus the name of the white oak species is *Quercus alba*, not just *alba*, the latter word being referred to by botanists as the 'specific epithet'.

There are standard ways of using botanical names: when appearing in other text they are distinguished by a different typeface, usually italic; and the genus name is usually abbreviated to its initial letter when additional species are itemized.

But in a way the use of binomials was not Linnaeus' most important contribution to the study of plants. He also put forward a comprehensive system of classification of plants and animals, with a full hierarchy of names from kingdom at the top to species at the bottom. Every plant known at the time could be allotted a place in his system, including the wealth of new species recently discovered in the Americas and tropical Asia. His classification of plants was based on the flower and in particular its organs of fertilization, the stamens and pistils. This revolutionary 'sexual system' used the respective numbers of stamens and pistils to place plants in a series of classes and subclasses—for example, a plant whose flowers have 5 stamens and 3 pistils would be placed in Linnaeus's *Pentandria Trigyna*. The advantage of this system was that all plants could be reliably pigeon-holed, but the disadvantage was that many plants that were obviously closely allied were placed in different classes simply on the basis of an extra stamen!

Linnaeus' successors soon realized this shortcoming and began to place species and genera in 'natural orders', now known as plant *families*, defined on the basis of a wider range of characters of flowers, fruits and foliage. By the late nineteenth century family names had stabilized into the form we now use, that is, using the name of the genus that typifies the family but with the ending -*aceae*. Thus *Rosa* gives its name to the family Rosaceae, of which it is a typical member.

Just as it is possible for a genus to consist of only one species or many species (over 1,000 in some cases), so a family may consist of only one genus or many genera. Family, genus and species are only the best known levels in the whole hierarchy of botanical names, which runs in descending order from kingdom, subkingdom, phylum or division, class, order, family, subfamily, tribe, genus, section, species, subspecies and cultivar.

There are other levels that can be squeezed in between some of these levels, for example, subsection between section and species. We should also emphasize that there are many different classifications of plants possible, depending on judgments of different botanists about the closeness of relationship between different genera, families and so on.

Often disagreement hinges on whether a botanist favours more broadly or more narrowly defined families, genera, etc. For example, the genus *Casuarina* has generally been regarded as the only genus in family Casuarinaceae, but recent study has shown that there is an argument for splitting this into 4 genera, of which 3, *Allocasuarina*, *Gymnostoma* and *Ceuthostoma* are newly named, while *Casuarina* itself is narrowed in scope to only 17 species out of the original 90. However, some botanists have rejected the arguments for this reclassification and choose to still treat *Casuarina* in the broad sense. Under the *International Code for Botanical Nomenclature* they are quite free to choose either classification—what this code governs is the correct use of names once a classification has been chosen, determined on rather legalistic grounds according to rules based on priority of publication. Thus the correct botanical name of the common larch is *Larix decidua*, not *L. europaea*, because the former name was published earlier and there is no dispute that both names refer to the same species.

Another subject that may need explanation is levels of classification below the rank of species. Linnaeus listed varieties (*varietas*) after some of the species in his *Species Plantarum*, indicating them with the Greek letters α, β, etc. Botanists in the nineteenth century continued to recognize mainly varieties, treating them as variants of the 'typical' species, thus *Acer saccharum* var. *leucoderme* was treated as distinct from *A. saccharum*. In the mid-twentieth century there was a move towards classifications that reflected evolving biological entities and many botanists moved to using *subspecies* in the same way as zoologists used it. In such a classification a species is divided into two or more subspecies, often regarded as species still in the process of evolving, with each subspecies usually having its own geographical range. The species *includes* all subspecies rather than being distinct from them, and one of them always repeats the species name. For example, the European *Pinus nigra* is now treated as consisting of three (sometimes more) subspecies: subsp. *nigra* is the Austrian pine, ranging from the Austrian Alps to Greece; subsp. *laricio* is the Corsican pine, restricted to Corsica, Sicily and Calabria; and subsp. *pallasiana* is the Crimean pine, occurring in the Balkans, Crimea and the Caucasus.

Variant forms of species that have been created or perpetuated by gardeners are now named as *cultivars* rather than varieties and must now be given names in modern languages, not Latin. We are all familiar with cultivar names such as those of roses ('Papa Meilland') and camellias ('Great Western'), names in this style having been in use for over 150 years. Note that a cultivar name is always in a different typeface from the botanical name, and has an initial capital letter; they are also usually in single quotes, though an alternative is to prefix them with the abbreviation cv.

You may notice that some cultivar names are attached to a species name while for others only the genus is mentioned. The latter is the practice for many plants of hybrid origin, particularly where more than two species are involved in the parentage, or for those cases where the species cannot readily be identified. Again, roses would be a major group where species name is seldom mentioned.

Cultivars, at least of trees and shrubs, are normally assumed to be single clones: that is, all individual plants of, for example, *Rosa* 'Peace' are derived from the original hybrid seedling by vegetative propagation, in this case by grafting or budding. A particular hybrid crossing may produce many seedlings with differing combinations of the parental characters; breeders select the best seedlings and perpetuate them as clones, naming the commercially promising ones as cultivars. An example of a hybrid is the cross between *Camellia japonica* and *C. saluenensis*, which has been repeated several times producing numerous seedlings. All seedling plants must take the hybrid name *C.* × *williamsii*, but some have been named as cultivars including the favourites 'Donation' and 'Caerhays'.

Because botanists the world over use the same system of plant nomenclature and follow its conventions, plants from all parts of the world can be identified and described without confusion. There are at least 100,000 species of trees and shrubs in the world, and the development of a simple system by which they can all be named and enumerated has been a triumph of human ability and cooperation. And having named and classified them, we have taken the first step towards understanding their part in the complex web of life on earth. For the gardener, knowing the names of plants and how they relate to each other can help in understanding the conditions in which they flourish.

ABELIA
Caprifoliaceae

A genus of both deciduous and evergreen shrubs, the abelias are valued for their elegant growth and abundant production of small tubular or trumpet-shaped flowers over a prolonged summer–early autumn season. They have dark green foliage on arching canes and can withstand heavy pruning, for example when used for low hedges, though poor flowering results if the long canes are constantly cut back. Species vary from moderately cold-hardy to somewhat tender. The hardy species are trouble-free plants, capable of surviving harsh conditions: even if cut back by frosts, they sprout again from the base. They prefer sun or light shade, and need regular water in summer. Abelias are easily propagated from cuttings.

Abelia chinensis

Like most of the hardier abelias, this one is from China. Deciduous or semi-deciduous, it makes a spreading bushy shrub about 6 ft (2 m) in height. It has reddish stems and small shiny leaves which turn bronze-purple in autumn. It blooms throughout summer and early autumn, with a succession of small white flowers, each with a conspicuous dull pink calyx which persists long after the flower falls. Little grown now, it has been supplanted in gardens by its hybrid *A. × grandiflora*. ZONE 8.

Abelia floribunda

With the largest and most brightly hued flowers among the abelias, this half-hardy species from the high mountains of central Mexico grows to around 6 ft (2 m) tall and wide. Its clusters of bright rose-carmine, 2 in (5 cm) long flowers are strung along arching branches in early summer. In cold areas it is best grown in a warm sheltered spot such as against a wall or fence. ZONE 9.

Abelia × grandiflora

This hybrid between *Abelia chinensis* and *Abelia uniflora* grows to 6–8 ft (2–3 m) tall and wide. It has arching reddish brown canes and small, glossy, dark green leaves. The gently fragrant pale mauve and white flowers appear in profusion in early summer, usually with a second flush at summer's end. After the flowers fall, their dull pink calyces persist into winter, in attractive contrast with the leaves which turn purplish bronze. The cultivar 'Frances Mason' has yellow or yellow-edged leaves on vigorous shoots; however it does have a tendency to revert to plain green. ZONE 7.

Abelia schumannii

Less vigorous than *A. × grandiflora*, this deciduous shrub appreciates a sheltered situation and grows to about 6 ft (2 m). It has arching red canes and small pointed leaves; the upper part of each cane produces a succession of showy bell-shaped flowers from late spring to early autumn. The flower is rose-pink with an orange blotch in the throat; the pale reddish calyx persists after the flower falls. ZONE 7.

ABIES
Pinaceae
FIR

The true firs, sometimes known as silver firs to distinguish them from *Picea* (from which they differ in their upright, not pendent, cones), comprise 40-odd species. They are among the most beautiful of all conifers with their regular spire-like shapes and richly textured, aromatic foliage. Most *Abies* come from cool- to cold-climate mountain areas, mainly in western China and western USA; a few species extend into the tropics on high mountains of Central America and Southeast Asia, and several occur in Alaska and Siberia. Because of their narrow shape and often slow growth, many species fit comfortably into a larger suburban garden, but they don't tolerate urban pollution and prefer a moist climate without extremes of heat or dryness. Soils are less of a problem, as long as depth, drainage and moisture retention are adequate. Propagation is from seed, though this is not always available in small packets. Grafting is used for selected clones (including named cultivars) but takes time, and a compatible seedling fir as rootstock. The only pruning or shaping needed is the removal of twin leading shoots as soon as they appear, and perhaps trimming of the lowest branches for mowing or walking space—though a column of foliage right down to the ground has its own attraction.

Abies alba
EUROPEAN SILVER FIR

This conifer comes from the mountains of central and southern Europe and has been planted as a timber tree for over 300 years, most successfully in Scotland where it has reached heights of 180 ft (60 m) and trunk diameters over 6 ft (2 m). It has dark greyish bark and glossy dark green needles with whitish undersides, arranged in two rows on the lateral branches; the cones are up to 6 in (15 cm) long and change from green to reddish brown as they ripen. It is capable of fast growth but may be damaged by unseasonal frost and is liable to attack by aphids. ZONE 6.

Abies amabilis
PACIFIC FIR

Amabilis means 'lovely', which was the impression this majestic tree made on David Douglas, the intrepid Scottish botanist who discovered it in 1832. It is native to the coastal mountains of north-western USA, western Canada and the south of Alaska and can grow to 260 ft (80 m) in the wild; in cultivation it has proved short lived and seldom reaches 100 ft (30 m). Its glossy green leaves, deeply grooved above and banded bluish white beneath, are notable for their smell when crushed which is similar to that of orange peel. The cones, 4–6 in (10–15 cm) long, ripen from red to deep purple. ZONE 5.

Abelia × grandiflora

Abelia schumannii

Abies alba

A plantation of *Abies alba*

Abies cephalonica

Abies balsamea
BALSAM FIR

The 'balsam' in this fir's name is a clear, thin resin in its bark which once had many uses in varnishes and pharmaceuticals; the resin has the same refractive index as glass and is used to glue compact lenses for telescopes, etc. The balsam fir is the most widespread North American species, especially in Canada where it is an important source of paper pulp; it extends south through mountains of eastern USA as far as West Virginia. A short-lived, spindly tree, it has little ornamental value and is seen in gardens mainly as dwarf cultivars, the most popular being 'Hudsonia', a compact miniature shrub up to 24 in (60 cm) high. ZONE 3.

Abies bracteata
SANTA LUCIA FIR

Among the rarest *Abies* species in the wild, this fir, formerly known as *A. venusta*, comes from higher parts of the Santa Lucia Mountains near the southern Californian coast. There it grows to 150 ft (46 m) tall. In cultivation it requires a mild climate, and may be short lived. It has a long-pointed crown, unusually long sharp needles, and the egg-shaped cones are covered in long appendages resembling the needles but narrower; these are what botanists call the 'bracts' of the scales that make up the cones, hence the specific name *bracteata*. ZONE 7.

Abies cephalonica
GREEK FIR

One of a distinctive group of firs from around the Mediterranean, with rather short, stiff, outward-pointing, prickly needles, this fir occurs naturally in the mountains of Greece and the Balkans, and is

Abies balsamea 'Hudsonia'

widely grown, hardy and vigorous. It was introduced to Britain as long ago as 1824, and trees there have reached heights equal to those in the wild, about 120 ft (38 m). The brown cones are roughly cylindrical and about 4 in (10 cm) long. ZONE 6.

Abies concolor
COLORADO WHITE FIR, PACIFIC FIR

Growing to 150 ft (46 m), *A. concolor* grows wild in the Rocky Mountains of western USA, with a taller race, var. *lowiana* (Pacific fir), found closer to the coast in Oregon and northern California. The needles are bluish green on both sides and blunt-tipped, and have a lemon scent when bruised. The cones are sometimes deep dull purple but may be paler brown. A fine ornamental fir, it is also hardy and vigorous. Seedlings vary in the blueness of their foliage and some of the best blue forms, propagated by grafting, are sold under the name 'Glauca'. Of an even more striking pale blue is 'Candicans', a rare and choice cultivar that is slower-growing. ZONE 5.

Abies delavayi
DELAVAY'S SILVER FIR

This extremely beautiful fir originated in the mountains of western China where it was collected by a

Abies amabilis

Abies concolor var. *lowiana*

French missionary, Jean Marie Delavay. Later studies have found a series of geographic varieties from this region of China and the border of Burma, including vars. *delavayi*, *fabri*, *faxoniana*, *forrestii* and *georgei*. Most commonly cultivated is var. *forrestii*, of medium height with crowded, short, broad needles and striking, barrel-shaped purplish blue cones. In its younger stages it is vigorous and decorative, with needles curving to display their white undersides. ZONE 7.

Abies bracteata

Abies koreana

Abies grandis

Abies lasiocarpa

Abies firma

Abies homolepis 'Prostrata'

Abies firma
MOMI FIR

With foliage of a deep shiny green, the momi fir reaches 150 ft (46 m) in the mountains of southern Japan. Its needles are stiff and leathery, up to 1½ in (3 cm) long, in two rows forming a wide V on twigs of the lower branches. The brown cones are egg-shaped and up to 5 in (12 cm) long. Densely branched, *A. firma* makes a fine ornamental tree, though it is less symmetrical than many other firs. ZONE 6.

Abies grandis
GIANT FIR

Among the world's tallest conifers, this fir reaches 300 ft (100 m) in forests on Vancouver Island, from where its natural range extends south to Sonoma County in California, a region noted for its high rainfall and mild but cool climate. The giant fir grows fast in cultivation, up to 3 ft (1 m) per year in suitable climates, and is widely planted for its timber. It does best in deep, moist soils. The foliage resembles that of *A. concolor* but has more contrasting white bands on the undersides, and when crushed smells like orange peel. The smallish cones ripen dark brown. ZONE 6.

Abies homolepis
NIKKO FIR

This species from central Japan has proved hardy and vigorous in Europe and North America, more tolerant of urban pollution than most firs. It can exceed 100 ft (30 m) in height, and is broadly conical when young. The crowded needles, up to 1½ in (3 cm) long, are dark green with broad blue-white bands on the undersides and blunt tips. The purplish grey immature cones can make a striking display. The bark, grey with purple tinges on young trees, becomes tessellated with age. The shrub-sized cultivar 'Prostrata' lacks erect leading shoots and is propagated from cuttings. ZONE 5.

Abies koreana
KOREAN FIR

A rare tree in the wild, this fir is known only from mountains in the far south of Korea. Since its introduction to the West in 1908 it has been popular for its compact size, seldom exceeding 20–30 ft (7–10 m), and its early coning—it may produce its attractive small bluish cones when as little as 3 ft (1 m) high! The crowded needles are short and broad with notched tips and wide blue bands on the undersides. Because of its size and relatively slow growth it is ideal for smaller gardens, or for a large rock garden. ZONE 5.

Abies lasiocarpa
SUBALPINE FIR

In the Rocky Mountains of western North America this species grows up to the tree line, from Arizona through Canada and into southern Alaska, and varies from a 100 ft (30 m) tall tree to a horizontal spreading shrub on mountain slopes. The needles are crowded and overlapping, with bluish stripes on both surfaces; cones are fat and dark purple. To the south-east of its range the typical species is replaced by var. *arizonica*, the corkbark fir, which has thick, corky, pale bark and beautiful blue-grey foliage. Selections from this variety are valued as garden plants, especially 'Compacta', which is a very strong silver-blue and a slow grower. However, as it is propagated by grafting, it is not easy to obtain. Another is 'Aurea', which has yellowish foliage. ZONE 4.

Abies magnifica
CALIFORNIAN RED FIR

This beautiful fir from the higher mountains of California and Oregon occurs chiefly in cool, moist valleys on the slopes of the Sierra Nevada. It makes a narrowly conical or columnar tree to 200 ft

(60 m) in the wild and has reddish bark and deep bluish green foliage. The individual needles are very narrow, blunt-tipped and curve upwards; the cones are very fat and barrel-like, bluish purple when young but ripening pale brown. In cultivation in a suitably wet climate this fir makes good growth to 65–100 ft (20–30 m), but is not as long lived as some other firs. ZONE 5.

Abies nordmanniana
CAUCASIAN FIR

Endemic to mountains of the Caucasus and Asia Minor, this handsome fir can reach 200 ft (60 m). The densely crowded needles are dark glossy green, with rounded and slightly notched tips and 2 whitish bands on the undersides; when crushed they smell like orange peel. The long fat cones are reddish brown when ripe, and conspicuous backward-pointing bract scales emerge from between the seed scales. Widely grown for ornament, it is vigorous and adaptable, attractive in shape, with a narrow outline and long straight leading shoot. ZONE 4.

Abies numidica
ALGERIAN FIR

One of the more adaptable firs for garden use, even in more urban environments, the Algerian fir is also a very handsome tree. In the wild it is known only from a small area in the Kabyle Ranges near Algiers, where it makes a broadly conical tree to 80 ft (25 m). The densely crowded needles, very flattened with broad blunt tips, are strongly banded with blue-white. The cones are long and narrowly cylindrical, ripening from deep green to dull brown. In cultivation this fir makes a symmetrical cone of dense foliage with lower branches touching the ground, and needs adequate space to develop properly. ZONE 6.

Abies pinsapo
SPANISH FIR

A handsome column-shaped tree reaching 100 ft (30 m), often with multiple leaders and densely crowded branches, this fir adapts to a wide range of soils and climates. The very short, rigid needles which appear on all sides of the thick, stiff twigs are less flattened than in most firs, and have fine bluish white stripes on both surfaces. Small purple pollen cones on the lower branch tips make a pretty display in spring. The seed cones, also purplish, are produced near the top of the tree as in most firs. Seedlings are selected for bluish foliage, collectively referred to under the cultivar name 'Glauca'. ZONE 5.

Abies procera
NOBLE FIR

Also known by its synonym *Abies nobilis*, this is a very tall conifer from the high-rainfall coastal region of north-western USA—trees over 250 ft (80 m) have been felled. Smooth-barked and broadly conical when young, with age it develops a mast-like trunk and a high, pointed crown with foliage in horizontal tiers. The narrow, bluntly pointed needles vary from bluish green to strong silvery blue. Cones are large, fat and purplish brown. The noble fir adapts well to cultivation in a cool, moist climate and good, deep soil, but can suffer disfiguring attacks from aphids in warmer climates. The blue-foliaged 'Glauca' cultivars are usually grown. ZONE 4.

Abies nordmanniana   *Abies pinsapo*

Abies numidica   *Abies procera* 'Glauca' (right)

Abies spectabilis
HIMALAYAN FIR

This tall fir occurs along much of the Himalaya, extending as high as 13,000 ft (4,000 m) in altitude, but despite this it is not reliably frost-hardy in the British Isles, being prone to damage by late frosts. It is one of the species which has long needles in 2 ranks forming a V between them; the needles are rather curved and tangled, with the white-banded undersides contrasting vividly with the dark green uppersides. The large, barrel-shaped cones are violet-purple at first but ripen brown. In cultivation it forms a conical tree of 60–80 ft (20–25 m). ZONE 7.

ABUTILON
Malvaceae
CHINESE LANTERN, FLOWERING MAPLE

This genus of mainly evergreen shrubs or subshrubs come from mostly warmer climates of South America, although additional species are found in Australia. They are grown for their flowers which are pendent and lantern-shaped in most cultivated species. Some have attractive variegated foliage. They need full sun or part-shade and well-drained soil. In cooler climates they can be grown in containers in sheltered, sunny spots or in greenhouses. They need good watering, especially if in containers (in which they bloom best if rootbound). Propagate from softwood cuttings in late summer. Flea-beetles, aphids and caterpillars can be problems in the garden. The species *A. vitifolium* and its hybrid belong to a small but very ornamental group of deciduous species from cool-temperate South America, sometimes split off by botanists as a distinct genus, *Corynabutilon*. Although the name 'Chinese lantern' is applied to other garden abutilons, it can hardly apply to these in view of their more saucer-shaped flowers.

Abutilon × hybridum
CHINESE LANTERN

Abutilon × hybridum is a collective name for the many cultivars derived from hybridizing some South American species, principally *Abutilon striatum* and *A. darwinii*. The lantern-like flowers, borne from spring to autumn, come in yellow, white, orange, pink, mauve and scarlet. Named cultivars include 'Golden Fleece', with rich golden yellow flowers; 'Orange King'; 'Ruby Glow'; and 'Souvenir de Bonn', with variegated foliage and red-veined orange flowers. In warm climates they will grow up to 8 ft (2.5 m), some with a similar spread, with a lax, open habit; some would call it untidy. Pruning hard in early spring will help keep growth in check and tip pruning will promote bushiness and flowering. These cultivars can be grown indoors in a cool but sunny room. ZONE 9.

Abutilon megapotamicum
BRAZILIAN BELL-FLOWER

This species from southern Brazil and Uruguay comes in two growth forms. One is an almost prostrate shrub with branches that may self-layer, making it a good ground-cover or rock-garden plant. The other form is a vigorous shrub of up to 8 ft (2.5 m) tall with arching cane-like branches. Flowers in both forms are smallish pendent bells with the deep red calyx larger than the pale yellow petals, and appear through much of the year. In cooler climates it is usually grown as a pot plant but it can be grown outdoors in Zone 8 if trained against a sheltered wall. 'Variegatum' is a cultivar with leaves heavily blotched yellow, in growth-habit conforming to the prostrate form. ZONE 9.

Abutilon megapotamicum 'Variegatum'

Abutilon megapotamicum

Abutilon × hybridum

Abies spectabilis

Abutilon × suntense

This cool-climate hybrid has the advantage of tolerating lower temperatures than *A. vitifolium*; its other parent is *A. ochsenii* from the colder south of Chile. It reaches 12 ft (4 m) tall and about 8 ft (2.5 m) wide, and has dark green leaves. Profuse flowers from spring to early summer are purple or mauve. The most popular clone is 'Jermyns', with deep mauve flowers becoming paler as they age. Moderately frost-hardy, it requires shelter from strong winds. ZONE 8.

Abutilon vitifolium

A soft-wooded deciduous shrub from Chile, *A. vitifolium* (syn. *Corynabutilon vitifolium*) grows to 9–12 ft (3–4 m), and is inclined to be short lived. In summer it bears profuse clusters of mauve-purple to white flowers up to 3 in (8 cm) wide. While needing a cool moist climate, it is one of the hardiest abutilons, but a position against a sheltered house wall or in a courtyard suits it best. Several forms have been named, including the white 'Album' and a fine, very pale lavender, 'Veronica Tennant'. Prune hard in early spring to prevent the shrub becoming straggly. ZONE 8.

ACACIA
Mimosaceae
WATTLE

This large genus contains over 1,200 species of trees and shrubs from warm climates. Over 700 are indigenous to Australia where they are a feature of both bushland and gardens, and many of these have been introduced to other countries for economic and ornamental purposes. Acacias are also common in tropical and subtropical Africa and are a feature of dry plains. Most African species are characterized by vicious spines and referred to as 'thorn trees'. Australian species range from low-growing shrubs to tall trees. Those described here are evergreen and include the most widely cultivated. Plants have either bipinnate leaves or their leaves are replaced by flattened leaf-stalks, known as phyllodes, which look like leaves and perform the function of photosynthesis. The tiny flowers range from deep golden yellow to cream or white, and are crowded into globular heads or cylindrical spikes, often fragrant and producing abundant, bird- and bee-attracting pollen. Fruits are either round or flattened pods, a distinction which is important for species identification. The hard-coated seeds remain viable for up to 30 years; they should be treated by heating and soaking for germination in spring. Some need fire to germinate. Seeds of some species

Acacia cultriformis

Acacia cultriformis

are edible and were ground into flour by Australian Aborigines. In cultivation many species are fast growing but short lived (10-15 years) and in their native regions often disfigured by insect or fungus attack. They are often grown as nurse plants to help establish other trees. They do best in full sun and well-drained soil. Some will take part-shade.

Acacia acinacea
GOLD-DUST WATTLE

This profusely branched shrub with very small, rounded phyllodes comes from the drier hill country of south-eastern Australia. It achieves a height and spread of around 6 ft (2 m), and bears bright yellow flower balls singly or in clusters from mid-winter to spring. This is one of the most ornamental species where a compact shrub wattle is desired, but needs full sun for best flowering. Fairly cold-hardy, it will also tolerate periods of dryness. ZONE 8.

Acacia baileyana
COOTAMUNDRA WATTLE

A fast-growing, small, spreading tree to 20 ft (7 m), the Cootamundra wattle has a short trunk and arching branches, silver, finely divided, feathery leaves and fragrant, golden yellow flower clusters in late winter. Widely used in warm-temperate gardens as a feature or shade tree, a specimen in full bloom can be a spectacular sight. Like most acacias, it tends to be short lived and prone to borer attack when declining. The cultivar 'Purpurea' has purplish foliage, especially on the growing tips. ZONE 8.

Abutilon vitifolium 'Album'

Abutilon × suntense 'Jermyns'

Acacia cultriformis
KNIFE-LEAF WATTLE, KNIFE ACACIA

This 6–12 ft (2–4 m) tall shrub differs in its foliage from most wattles. The blue-grey phyllodes, up to 1 in (2.5 cm) long, are shaped like small paring-knife blades and are attached directly to the branches, without intervening leaf-stalks. The showy spring flowers are in profuse short sprays of round, fluffy yellow balls. Endemic to the cooler tablelands of New South Wales, Australia, this undemanding species will tolerate light frost and is happy in any sunny, well-drained position. ZONE 8.

Acacia acinacea

Acacia decurrens

Acacia elata

Acacia karroo

Acacia longifolia

Acacia harpophylla

Acacia dealbata
SILVER WATTLE, MIMOSA

In gardens this tree reaches a height of 20–30 ft (10 m), though in nature in the eucalypt forests of south-eastern Australia it is much taller. Fast growing but rather short lived, it has a single trunk with smooth grey bark which has a mealy white bloom on the smaller branches. Each bipinnate leaf is made up of hundreds of tiny leaflets which are coated in white hairs that give the foliage a slight silvery cast. In late winter or spring the domed crown is decked in sprays of small, globular, golden yellow flower heads. This is the best known Australian acacia in the northern hemisphere, especially in Mediterranean countries where it is known as mimosa. In southern England it survives winter well enough, but flowers better in climates with a longer, drier summer. ZONE 8.

Acacia decurrens
GREEN WATTLE

This upright tree grows to 50 ft (15 m) tall, and has a domed crown atop a straight trunk and smooth brownish green bark. One of the fastest-growing and most attractive of the tall wattles, it has fine, feathery, rich green bipinnate leaves and in late winter bears very decorative, fragrant, golden yellow flowers that contrast especially well with the foliage. It prefers a warm-temperate climate and deep moist soil. ZONE 9.

Acacia elata
CEDAR WATTLE

One of the largest acacias, making a tree to 80 ft (25 m), the cedar wattle has a strong trunk and narrow conical crown. The leaves are larger than those of other bipinnate wattles, producing a graceful fern-like foliage texture. Long sprays of fragrant creamy yellow flowers appear in summer. The tree can live for 25 years or more, making it one of the longer lived wattles. It is less drought tolerant than many other acacias. ZONE 9.

Acacia harpophylla
BRIGALOW

One of the longest-lived acacias of Australia's semi-arid interior, the brigalow is also a very handsome tree, with a dense, spreading crown of blue-grey foliage and low-branched trunk with almost black, deeply furrowed bark. It once occurred as the dominant tree over large areas of east-central Queensland and parts of New South Wales, Australia, on deep fertile soils. Much of this former 'brigalow scrub' has been cleared for farming. Its height is mostly 30–50 ft (10–15 m), sometimes taller. Flowers are in clustered yellow balls, usually appearing in late winter or early spring. Seed production is erratic and the seeds have soft coats and must be planted and watered straight away to achieve germination. An alternative means of propagation is to detach lengths of root with sucker growths arising from them and treat them like large cuttings. ZONE 9.

Acacia karroo
KARROO THORN

This species from South Africa has been grown for ornament and hedging in southern Europe, where it has sometimes become naturalized. If left unpruned it will grow fairly fast into a small or medium-sized tree to 25 ft (8 m), although it can be taller in the wild. It has a stiff, irregular growth-habit, the branches armed with vicious long spines in V-shaped pairs, small bipinnate leaves and profuse deep yellow sweetly scented ball-shaped flower heads in summer. ZONE 9.

Acacia koa
KOA, HAWAIIAN MAHOGANY

The kings of Hawaii prized the hard, dark red wood of the koa above all others for the building of their war canoes, and today it is much used for furniture, carving and the making of musical instruments; before the introduction of polystyrene it was the wood of choice for the making of surfboards. In rich soil and a sheltered position, the tree can grow fast to a majestic 100 ft (30 m), with a broad, spreading crown; where the sea winds buffet it, it is apt to be much shorter and crooked in growth-habit. The evergreen phyllodes are long, narrow and dull green; the pallid flowers are of little account. In its native Hawaii it is regarded as one of the very best of all trees for reafforestation, though it is not often planted elsewhere. ZONE 10.

Acacia longifolia
SYDNEY GOLDEN WATTLE

Occurring naturally on dunes, heaths and sandstone ridges on Australia's east coast, this shrub has a height and spread of up to 15 ft (5 m). It has a short trunk and an irregularly shaped head, and in exposed conditions can be reduced to a semi-prostrate form. It bears long, golden fingers of fragrant, butter-yellow flowers from late winter to early spring and has narrow, oblong, dark green phyllodes. Excellent for a quick seaside hedge or low windbreak, it has been used for street planting in California and New Zealand. ZONE 9.

Acacia mangium

From the tropical rainforests of far north Queensland, Australia, this acacia has been planted as a fast-growing timber tree elsewhere in the wet tropics. It is also a fine ornamental tree, notable for the size of its phyllodes, up to 12 in (30 cm) long and 5 in (12 cm) wide on vigorous young plants, with several conspicuous parallel veins. Planted in a sunny position, it makes a medium-sized tree with a straight trunk topped by a dense pyramidal crown. However, with closer planting it grows tall and straight, reaching 80–100 ft (25–30 m). The cream flowers are not very showy but the pods are curious, long and twisted and tangled together. ZONE 12.

Acacia mearnsii
LATE BLACK WATTLE

Endemic to drier coastal woodlands of eastern and southern Australia, this fast-growing acacia makes a large shrub or a small erect tree with a spreading crown to about 30 ft (10 m) in height. The blackish bark is deeply ridged on the trunk. The fernlike, bipinnate leaves are dark green above, paler and downy beneath. Racemes of pale yellow, ball-shaped flowers borne in late spring and early summer are followed by dark brown, hairy pods. A useful screening plant, it is hardy and fairly frost tolerant. Late black wattle is much grown in warm climates for the production of tanning bark, a purpose for which some regard it as superior to the English oak. ZONE 8.

Acacia melanoxylon
BLACKWOOD

Unlike most acacias, this tree is long lived and moderately frost-hardy, occurring in the richer soils and humid forests of mainland eastern Australia and Tasmania, most commonly at higher altitudes. A large tree to 90 ft (28 m), it yields a valuable dark brown timber with blackish streaks which is prized for cabinet making. Planted in the open, it has a spreading bushy crown and short thick trunk. The phyllodes are a dark, dull green, and the profuse balls of pale yellow flowers appear in spring. Fertile, moist soil and humid climates suit it best, though it will survive on poorer soils; it is not drought resistant. ZONE 8.

Acacia neriifolia

Occurring in rather dry eucalypt woodlands on the tablelands of northern New South Wales and southern Queensland, this is one of the most abundantly flowering Australian wattles. A tall shrub or small tree to about 25 ft (8 m) of erect, open habit, it has narrow, straight, greyish phyllodes and numerous sprays of bright golden yellow flower heads all along the branches in late spring and early summer. ZONE 9.

Acacia pendula
WEEPING MYALL, BOREE

A small densely crowned tree to 20 ft (7 m) with vertically drooping branchlets like a small weeping willow, the boree makes a good shade or ornamental tree for gardens, streets and parks in semi-arid areas. Its narrow lance-shaped phyllodes are silvery grey-green; flowers are pale yellow and appear in spring. In its native plains country of inland eastern Australia it occurs on heavy clay soils that remain boggy after rain. It can survive harsh climates with low rainfall. ZONE 9.

Acacia melanoxylon

Acacia neriifolia

Acacia mangium

Acacia pendula

Acacia pendula

Acacia podalyriifolia
QUEENSLAND WATTLE, PEARL ACACIA, SILVER WATTLE

This handsome tall shrub or small tree from wooded hills of south-eastern Queensland, Australia, grows to about 20 ft (7 m), spreading to about half that, and is fast growing but short lived. The silvery phyllodes are rounded and have a felty texture. Large sprays of fragrant golden flowers appear in winter and early spring. Valued for its attractive foliage and abundance of bloom, it prefers well-drained soil, full sun and a mild to warm climate. Young trees can grow rapidly and become top heavy, so staking is advisable for the first year or two. ZONE 9.

Acacia pravissima
OVENS WATTLE

An evergreen, bushy shrub occasionally reaching a height of 18 ft (6 m) and spread of 15 ft (5 m) but commonly much smaller, this graceful wattle has drooping branches that form an arching mound. The short, triangular phyllodes are a dull olive green and small heads of bright golden yellow flowers appear in late winter or early spring. The bronze buds and gold-tipped foliage are attractive through winter. The common name comes from the Ovens Valley in Victoria, Australia, where the species is very common. There is a completely prostrate form. ZONE 8.

Acacia pycnantha
GOLDEN WATTLE

A small tree or medium shrub to 12–30 ft (4–10 m), this well-known wattle has a rounded crown of foliage with somewhat pendulous branches. The prolific panicles of large, fragrant, golden, ball-shaped flower heads appear in spring. From Victoria and adjacent parts of New South Wales and South Australia, this species is Australia's national floral emblem. It makes a fine garden specimen, although it is not long lived. Most soils and situations are suitable, though sandy soils are preferred, and it should be sheltered from heavy frost. Established trees are drought resistant. ZONE 9.

Acacia sieberiana var. *woodii*

This fast-growing, flat-topped tree, naturally occurring on the velds of south-eastern Africa, reaches a height of about 30 ft (9 m) with a spread of 50 ft (15 m), and casts a dappled shade. The 4 in (10 cm) long leaves have many small leaflets and are covered with velvety golden hairs. The corky bark, which is a yellowish brown, peels off in papery strips. The tree bears a profusion of creamy white flowers in spring, and the seed pods which follow are very attractive to birds. It is a hot-climate species, able to withstand severe drought and poor soil; it will also tolerate some frost. ZONE 9.

Acacia spectabilis
MUDGEE WATTLE

Occurring in the wild as a small tree to 15 ft (5 m) high with short trunk, this species comes from the western slopes of the Great Dividing Range in eastern Australia. In gardens it is normally a tall shrub of 8–10 ft (2.5–3 m) of open habit with drooping branchlets and small bipinnate blue-green leaves. Masses of rich golden yellow, fragrant, ball-shaped flower heads appear in winter and spring. Fine textured foliage and prolific flowers make this an excellent garden species, valued for screening or specimen planting. Light annual pruning will help to maintain shape. ZONE 9.

Acacia podalyriifolia

Acacia pravissima

Acacia pycnantha

Acacia spectabilis

Acacia verticillata
PRICKLY MOSES

Indigenous to Tasmania and mainland southern Australia, this shrub of upright but bushy habit grows to about 10 ft (3 m) tall. Its needle-sharp phyllodes are arranged in distinct whorls like spokes of a cartwheel. Creamy yellow flowers in dense cylindrical spikes are scattered all along the branches in spring and summer. It is moderately cold-hardy and can be grown in southern England, being especially suited to seaside gardens. Var. *latifolia* is a name used for semi-prostrate forms with broader, blunter phyllodes which grow on exposed coastal cliffs. ZONE 8.

Acacia xanthophloea

This tree has a straight main trunk and upright growth; only mature specimens will spread. It grows rapidly to a height of 30–40 ft (10–13 m) with sparse foliage that casts little shade. The bark is a pale, ghostly yellow. Yellow flowers, not especially showy, are borne in spring. *A. xanthophloea* needs warm summers, and winters with no severe frost to thrive. It can survive long periods of flooding. ZONE 9.

ACALYPHA
Euphorbiaceae

This genus of hot-climate, evergreen shrubs includes many species in tropical Asia and the Pacific, but only two or three are grown as ornamentals. Some are valued for their decorative spikes of tiny but massed female flowers (males are on different plants), and one species for its showy variegated foliage. They require a sunny to semi-shaded position, well-drained, light soil with plenty of water during summer and protection from wind. Plants are killed or damaged by frosts. Prune lightly to shape in late winter, followed by additional feeding and watering. Propagate from cuttings in summer. Watch for mealybug, red spider mite and whitefly.

Acalypha hispida
CHENILLE PLANT, RED-HOT CAT-TAIL

Thought to originate in the region around Malaysia, this plant is grown for its striking, tiny, bright red flowers that hang in pendulous, tassel-like spikes on the female plants in summer. The leaves are large, oval and bright green to reddish bronze. An evergreen, this upright, soft-stemmed shrub reaches a height and spread of 6 ft (2 m). Regular pruning will maintain its bushy shape, but it will become tree-like in habit if grown in poor light beneath taller plants. It does best in warm, sheltered sites in full sun. Outside the tropics it requires a warm spot in a courtyard, or a heated conservatory in cool climates. ZONE 11.

Acalypha wilkesiana
FIJIAN FIRE PLANT

Originating in Fiji and other Pacific Islands, this species grows to a height and spread of 10 ft (3 m), forming an irregularly rounded bush with erect stems branching from the base. It is grown for its attractive foliage—the large, serrated, oval leaves appear in a very wide colour range, depending on cultivar, from mid-green to reddish bronze, some with contrasting margins. Inconspicuous tassel-like catkins of reddish bronze flowers appear in summer and autumn. It prefers a warm, sheltered position and the foliage colours best in full sun. Cultivars include: 'Macrophylla' with very large leaves, each leaf differently variegated with bronze, copper, red, cream and yellow blotches; 'Godseffiana' with very narrow, drooping leaves, green edged with cream; 'Macafeeana' with leaves deep bronze splashed with coppery red; 'Marginata' with leaves bronze-red edged with cream or pale pink. ZONE 10.

Acacia verticillata

Acalypha hispida

Acacia xanthophloea

A group of *Acalypha* cultivars

Acalypha wilkesiana cultivar

Acer buergerianum, as a bonsai

Acer capillipes

Acer buergerianum

Acer cappadocicum 'Rubrum'

ACER
Aceraceae
MAPLE

Surely there is no group of trees to rival the maples for autumn colouring and variety of leaf shape and texture! And many are compact enough for the average garden. Maples are grown for their foliage, or for shade or timber. The distinctive 2-winged fruits (samaras) are more noticeable than the flowers, which in most species are inconspicuous. The bark is another beautiful feature of some maples—most commonly smooth and grey or greenish; in the group known as the 'snakebark maples' it has longitudinal grey or brown stripes and in others, including the striking *A. griseum*, it is flaky or papery.

There are a handful of well-known European species but the greatest richness is in East Asia, particularly China (over 80 species), Japan (over 20) and the eastern Himalaya. The other important area is North America: there, there are only 9 native maples, but they include the sugar maple (*A. saccharum*) famous for maple syrup as well as its valuable lumber, and the box-elder maple (*A. negundo*). And the large tree species *A. saccharum*, *A. saccharinum* and *A. rubrum* provide most of the superb autumn tones in the hills of eastern Canada and northern USA.

Virtually all the maples known to gardeners suit cool to cold climates and are deciduous but there are evergreen and semi-evergreen species from southern China and Southeast Asia, including the tall rainforest tree *A. laurinum*. The semi-evergreen *A. oblongum* is too tender for most of Britain and Europe but has been used as a street tree in Hong Kong and southern California.

Propagation is generally from seed for the species, by grafting for cultivars. Cuttings are very difficult to root, but layering of low branches is successful for some species. Seed is produced in abundance and is easily germinated; this can be aided by overwintering in damp litter, or refrigeration. Some species produce very few fertile seeds, so it may be necessary to sow a large quantity to obtain enough seedlings.

Acer buergerianum
TRIDENT MAPLE

This species from eastern China, though tall in its native forests, usually makes a bushy-topped small tree with a thick, strong trunk in cultivation. The bark is pale brown and attractively dappled. Its common name refers to the shape of the smallish leaves, usually with 3 short lobes close together at the upper end, but this is variable. Autumn colouring is often two-toned, with scarlet patches on a green or yellowish background. This species tolerates exposed positions and poor soils. Long cultivated in Japan, it is a traditional subject for bonsai. ZONE 6.

Acer campestre
FIELD MAPLE

A small to medium bushy-crowned tree, this European maple also occurs in western Asia and north Africa. In Britain it is also known as hedge maple, signifying its abundance in the traditional hedges that divide fields. It withstands heavy pruning and can be trimmed into dense, regular shapes. The corky bark is thick and furrowed. Autumn brings clear golden yellow or slightly bronzy tints. This vigorous species is easily grown from freshly collected seed. ZONE 4.

Acer capillipes
RED SNAKEBARK MAPLE

A Japanese member of the snakebark group of maples, the red snakebark grows quickly but may be short lived (20–30 years). It makes a broadly spreading small tree about 15–20 ft (5–7 m) high, with branches from just above the ground. The bark is indistinctly striped pale grey and dull green and the broad, 3-pointed leaves turn yellow, orange and crimson in autumn. It likes a sheltered but sunny position and is one of the few maples easily propagated from cuttings. ZONE 5.

Acer cappadocicum

Named for an ancient province of central Turkey known as Cappadocia, this maple has a vast range from southern Europe across temperate Asia to central China, with a number of geographic subspecies. Its smooth green leaves have very regular, radiating triangular lobes, each lobe drawn out into a slender point. A medium to large tree of rapid growth, reaching 100 ft (30 m) in the wild, it suits parks and street planting rather than suburban gardens. Autumn colour is a brilliant golden yellow. The cultivar 'Rubrum' has dark red new shoots, the young leaves expanding bright red before turning green. ZONE 5.

Acer carpinifolium
HORNBEAM MAPLE

A very beautiful maple from the mountain forests of Japan. The leaves are finely toothed rather than lobed, with closely spaced veins and a corrugated surface. Both scientific and common names refer to the resemblance of its foliage to that of the hornbeams (*Carpinus*).

In spring the new, half-expanded leaves have a silky coating and in autumn they turn a beautiful old-gold, hanging on the tree into early winter. A rather upright, narrow-crowned tree to 20 ft (7 m) or so, its growth is moderately slow. Seeds have a low rate of germination, so the species is often difficult to obtain. It is exceptionally cold-hardy. ZONE 3.

Acer circinatum
VINE MAPLE

Native to the west of North America, from British Columbia to northern California, the vine maple belongs to the same group as the Japanese maple, *A. palmatum*, and has leaves that are roughly circular in outline with 7–9 short lobes, like small grape leaves. It is usually a small, broadly spreading tree to 12 ft (4 m) high, branching at the base. Its gorgeous autumn tones are brilliant orange-scarlet to deeper red, particularly effective when underplanted in taller woodland or around edges of glades; it appreciates shelter from strong winds. Older specimens are often self-layering, providing a ready-made means of propagation. ZONE 5.

Acer cissifolium
VINE-LEAF MAPLE

A small tree or sometimes a large shrub, rarely reaching 30 ft (10 m), with a broadly spreading crown, the vine-leaf maple is native to Japan. Unlike most maples, it has compound leaves consisting of a number of separate leaflets; the name *cissifolium* refers to a resemblance between its leaves and those of some grape relatives with 3 leaflets. Autumn colour is yellow and orange or red. Although easily grown, it can be hard to obtain: male plants are rare so fertile seed is unavailable, and nurseries must propagate by the slower method of layering. ZONE 5.

Acer davidii
FATHER DAVID'S MAPLE

This beautiful Chinese maple was discovered in 1869 in the mountains of Sichuan by the French missionary-naturalist Armand David. One of the snakebark maples, it has a rather open habit and a flat-topped outline. The attractive bark has silvery grey stripes on an olive green background; the Dutch selection 'Serpentine' has more strongly contrasting stripes on a deep purplish brown background. Autumn brings shades of yellow, orange and dull scarlet. In a cool, humid climate *A. davidii* makes rapid growth to 20–25 ft (7–8 m). It is easily grown from fresh seed, but chance hybrids with other snakebark species are likely if these are growing nearby. ZONE 6.

Acer davidii

Acer cissifolium

Acer davidii

Acer carpinifolium

Acer cissifolium

Acer griseum

Acer ginnala
AMUR MAPLE

A large shrub or small tree of 20–30 ft (7–10 m), *A. ginnala* is native to northern Japan, Korea and Manchuria. It was from Manchuria's Amur River that it was first collected and named. Some botanists now classify it as a subspecies of *A. tataricum*. Frequently it branches near the ground into several long cane-like stems; the leaves are long-pointed and irregularly lobed, turning red in autumn and falling rapidly. In summer its pink fruits are quite decorative. A quick grower, it is very hardy. ZONE 4.

Acer glabrum
ROCK MAPLE, ROCKY MOUNTAIN MAPLE

This maple ranges from Alaska through western Canada to California and down the Rocky Mountains as far as New Mexico. Over this vast area it varies considerably, and has been divided into as many as 5 subspecies. It is nearly always low growing, usually with multiple stems from the base. In denser forests it occurs as a shade-loving understorey tree or shrub, or it may form lower scrubs on exposed hillsides. Not widely cultivated, its cold-tolerance and small size may be useful characteristics in some situations. ZONE 4.

Acer grandidentatum
BIGTOOTH MAPLE

Another North American species, the bigtooth maple's range extends from Alaska south to the mountains of northern Mexico and east as far as Oklahoma. The leaves are somewhat leathery, shiny deep green above and pale bluish beneath, with the typical 'maple leaf' outline of 5 bluntly toothed lobes. It makes an attractive small, bushy-topped tree to 35 ft (12 m) or so, with pale bark. The foliage turns brilliantly in shades of scarlet, orange and yellow. Its sugary sap was harvested by American Indians and the bark pounded to make a 'bread'. ZONE 4.

Acer griseum
PAPERBARK MAPLE

This species is a treasure among the maples, prized by collectors. Its chief glory is the bark, rich chestnut brown peppered with paler corky dots, which it sheds each year in wide curling strips. The foliage is also attractive, dark green and small-leafed, and autumn colour is deep scarlet. It makes a narrow-crowned tree to 30 ft (10 m) with a fairly straight trunk. Under moist, sheltered conditions in good soil, growth can be rapid. The paperbark maple grew widely in the interior of China but is no longer common in the wild. In cultivation it produces plenty of seed but most of these are infertile, so it is not easy to find in a nursery, and the price may be high. ZONE 5.

Acer griseum

Acer griseum

Acer grosseri

Acer ginnala

Acer ginnala

Acer macrophyllum

Acer grosseri

This is another of the snakebark maples, native to central China; the names *A. hersii*, *A. grosseri* var. *hersii*, and *A. davidii* subsp. *grosseri* have all been applied to it. It has short, broad leaves with 2 short lateral lobes, and the autumn tones are scarlet and red mixed with yellow. In summer the whole tree, trunk, twigs and leaves, appears very green, though the bark is beautifully striped with paler green. *A. grosseri* has proved vigorous and hardy as a tree for gardens and streets. ZONE 5.

Acer hookeri

Although grown as *A. hookeri* for several decades, some botanists now regard this tree as indistinguishable from *A. sikkimense*. Coming from the rainy eastern end of the Himalaya, it is quite frost-tender, thriving in cooler countries only in coastal areas warmed and humidified by ocean currents, or in humid highlands of subtropical regions. It grows rapidly at first, with long shoots and large oval leaves, often reaching 20 ft (7 m) within 10 years; thereafter it puts on little more height and may prove short lived. Leaves are an attractive bronze-green in early spring and rich orange in autumn; they sometimes hang on well into winter. ZONE 8.

Acer japonicum
FULL-MOON MAPLE

This maple's new growth is distinctive, very pale green with a coating of silky white hairs that disappear as the leaves mature. Its autumn colouring is subtly beautiful too, with leaves on some twigs changing early to orange or red, while others retain their summer olive-green tones into late autumn. Slow growing and intolerant of drying winds, it likes a moist, sheltered position,

Acer japonicum, showing pale green new growth, among the tall trunks of *Cryptomeria japonica*

and is of rather narrow, shrubby habit. *A. japonicum* has been grown for centuries in Japan and there are many cultivars: 'Aconitifolium' is among the most attractive, with ferny leaves. ZONE 5.

Acer macrophyllum
OREGON MAPLE, BIGLEAF MAPLE

Noteworthy for its large leaves, up to 12 in (30 cm) wide, the Oregon maple is not widely cultivated. It occurs wild from southern Alaska to southern California, usually as an understorey tree in tall conifer forests, but it can make a fine 100 ft (30 m) forest tree with a broadly domed crown and thick trunk. The flowers and fruits are larger than those of other maples: the yellowish flowers hang in dense sprays, and the 2- or 3-winged fruits are 3 in (7 cm) across. Autumn tones are gold and brown. It likes a moderately sheltered situation and deep, moist soil. ZONE 6.

Acer hookeri

Acer japonicum

Acer palmatum

Acer palmatum dwarf cultivars

Acer negundo

Acer palmatum

Acer nikoense
NIKKO MAPLE

Nikko is a mountain in Japan, site of an ancient shrine; it was from forests in this area that the maple first became known to Western botanists. *A. nikoense* (syn. *A. maximowiczianum*) has compound leaves consisting of 3 leaflets, which are closely veined with whitish undersides. Slow growing and of neat appearance, it reaches 50 ft (15 m) in the wild but is commonly under 20 ft (7 m) in gardens. Like the related *A. griseum*, it produces mainly infertile seed in cultivation and has similar problems of propagation. The autumn foliage is in shades of yellow and deep red.
ZONE 6.

Acer palmatum
JAPANESE MAPLE

The most widely grown maple in the world, the Japanese maple is valued for its compact size, delicate ferny foliage, and brilliant autumn colouring, from rich gold to deepest blood-red. Cultivated for centuries in Japan, and since 1830 in the West, there are now over 300 cultivars, from rock-garden miniatures to vigorous small trees, with great variety of leaf shape, size and coloration. Nearly all need to be grafted to preserve their characteristics, so are expensive to buy. But the ordinary seedling trees are beautiful too, if less predictable. The usual mature height in a garden is 12–15 ft (4–5 m); the tree branches low, with strong sinuous branches and a dense, rounded crown. Though easily grown and more tolerant of warmer climates than most maples, without some shade and shelter the leaves may begin to shrivel by late summer. The most popular cultivar of tree size is 'Atropurpureum', dense and spreading, with dark purple spring foliage giving way to paler olive-purple in summer and then suffused with deep scarlet tones in autumn; it largely comes true from seed. 'Sangokaku' ('Senkaki') has striking coral-red branches and twigs, displayed bare in winter, and brilliant gold autumn tones. 'Atrolineare' has foliage colour like 'Atropurpureum' but leaves divided almost to the base into narrow lobes. In the Dissectum group, the primary leaf lobes are deeply cut into a filigree pattern; their fine, drooping twigs grow down rather than upward, so they are grafted onto a standard, the height of which determines the height of the dome-shaped shrub. Despite the huge number of variants, it is hard to go past the original 'Dissectum' (green) and 'Dissectum Atropurpureum' for landscaping effect.
ZONE 5.

Acer negundo
BOX-ELDER MAPLE, BOX ELDER

Ranging from Canada to the mountains of Guatemala, and from the Atlantic to the Pacific, *A. negundo* is one of the easiest maples to grow. Occasionally reaching 50 ft (15 m) with a thick trunk and upright branching habit, it is more often seen as a smaller tree with very cane-like, bright green branches. American farmers often regard it as a 'weed tree' and its free-seeding habits have made it a minor nuisance in other countries. It is very fast growing and tolerates poor conditions, but its branches break easily in high winds. The cultivars 'Variegatum' and 'Aureomarginatum', with leaves attractively edged white or gold respectively, are often sold; the newer 'Flamingo' is like 'Variegatum' but with leaves strongly flushed pink on new growth. 'Violaceum' is a male clone with purplish new shoots and twigs, the male flower tassels also being pale purple. None of these reach more than half the size of the wild, green-leafed type. ZONE 4.

Acer pensylvanicum
STRIPED MAPLE

This species occurs wild from south-eastern Canada to the Appalachians and west to Wisconsin. Erect and vigorous, it has a single main trunk, the bark striping on younger limbs is the most richly coloured of any of the snakebark maples, suffused with red as well as olive and white. Autumn colour is a bright golden yellow. ZONE 5.

Acer platanoides
NORWAY MAPLE

This fine European tree occurs well north of the Arctic Circle in Scandinavia (reduced almost to a shrub) and ranges across Europe from France to the Urals but not to the Mediterranean coasts or the British Isles, though cultivated there for centuries both for beauty and for timber. It makes a large, round-headed tree and thrives in a wide range of soils and situations, but not in warm climates. Yellow flowers appear before the leaves; autumn colour is gold to reddish orange. 'Drummondii' has variegated leaves. Named cultivars with deep purplish foliage include 'Schwedleri', 'Faasen's Black' and 'Crimson King', between which there is much confusion. 'Columnare', with plain green leaves, has a narrow column shape. All are quite slow growing, so suit smaller gardens. ZONE 4.

Acer pseudoplatanus
SYCAMORE MAPLE

Occurring naturally across southern Europe and Asia Minor from Portugal to the Caspian Sea, this species was introduced to England 1,000 years ago and is so well established that many consider it a native; similarly in North America it seeds so profusely as to be regarded a weed. It can grow to 100 ft (30 m), with a trunk 6 ft (2 m) across. The bark is pale grey, thick and scaly. Useful for park and street planting, it grows rapidly to form a broad, dense crown of dark green. Autumn colour is not a feature: the leaves become brown and shrivelled. It prefers a sheltered situation with deep moist soil, but tolerates more exposed sites. The cultivar 'Purpureum' has leaf undersides of a deep plum, uppersides also slightly purplish. 'Erythrocarpum' has red fruits in conspicuous clusters. The spring foliage of 'Brilliantissimum' is pale creamy yellow flushed pink, changing in summer to whitish with green veining; it is slow growing and suits smaller gardens. 'Variegatum' has cream markings. ZONE 4.

Acer platanoides

Acer platanoides

Acer pensylvanicum

Acer pseudoplatanus 'Variegatum'

Acer pseudoplatanus

Acer rubrum
RED MAPLE

This large maple from eastern North America displays brilliant autumn tones of deep red with striking blue-white undersides. Native over much of eastern Canada, it extends south as far as Texas and Florida, making a tree of up to 100 ft (30 m) in the richest forests on deep alluvial soil. As a planted tree it makes rapid growth, with a straight trunk and narrow crown at first, but spreading broadly with age. The timber is prized for furniture. ZONE 4.

Acer saccharinum
SILVER MAPLE

Ranging over eastern USA and Canada (except the arctic north), the silver maple grows large, branching low into several trunks with a broad crown of foliage. As an ornamental it is popular for its hardiness, rapid growth and rich golden autumn colour. The cane-like branches are easily damaged by storms and heavy snow, but quickly grow back. American and European nurseries have developed many cultivars, featuring columnar habit, pendulous branches, more deeply divided leaves, or golden or variegated foliage. ZONE 4.

Acer saccharum
SUGAR MAPLE

In American culture and folklore this is the most famous of all maples. Its leaf adorns the Canadian flag, and maple syrup, tapped from its bark, is a traditional sweetener. The durable, close-grained wood is commercially important. It ranges across eastern North America from Newfoundland and Manitoba in the north to Florida in the south, and west to Utah. In the south and west, regional subspecies occur, including subsp. *floridanum*, subsp. *grandidentatum* and subsp. *leucoderme*. In the open garden a mature sugar maple is a low-branching, broad-crowned tree of 40–50 ft (12–15 m), though it will grow much taller in forests. Growth is often slow in the first 10 years or so. Autumn colour, one of its chief glories, varies from tree to tree, with yellow, orange, scarlet and crimson all common. The sugary sap is tapped in late winter, but it only runs where winters are severe. Even in Virginia maple sugar making is not possible. ZONE 3.

Acer truncatum
SHANTUNG MAPLE

Occurring in eastern Siberia as well as Japan, Korea and northern China, the Shantung maple is a small tree with very rough-barked trunk and a densely branched crown; the branches are rather tangled. In gardens its growth is often slow and it remains shrubby in habit for many years. Autumn colour is yellow. ZONE 5.

ACMENA
Myrtaceae
LILLYPILLY

This small genus of handsome evergreen trees has species in the rainforests of northern and eastern Australia, as well as New Guinea and the Malay archipelago. Like the related *Syzygium*, it was formerly included within the genus *Eugenia*. The trees have smooth-edged leaves arranged in opposite pairs on the twigs, at the tips of which appear sprays of small white flowers followed by pink, purple or white berries with edible though spongy flesh which can be used for making jam. Charming street and garden trees, they are grown successfully in other warm-climate countries. Seeds are readily germinated but must be fresh.

Acmena smithii
LILLYPILLY

The common lillypilly of eastern Australia occurs naturally in a wide range of rainforest types, from Queensland's Cape York Peninsula to southern Victoria. It is variable in growth-habit, from a 65 ft (20 m) tree to a low, salt-shorn shrub. Widely cultivated in Australia, it is a shapely and reliable garden subject which is adaptable to most locations. Leaves are somewhat similar in size, shape and texture to those of *Camellia sasanqua*. Sprays of tiny white flowers with prominent stamens appear in early summer followed by decorative white, pink or mauve fruits in late summer. In gardens it is usually seen as a compact 20–30 ft (7–9 m) tree or as a tall screening shrub or hedge. It prefers a frost-free climate and fertile, moist soil. It grows in sun or shade and, although pruning isn't necessary, it responds to clipping and extra water and fertilizer with flushes of coppery new growth. In more humid areas its foliage is sometimes marred by sooty mould fungus. ZONE 9.

ACOKANTHERA
Apocynaceae
WINTERSWEET

This is a small genus of warm-climate evergreen shrubs and trees from southern Africa with poisonous milky sap. The flowers are narrowly tubular, clustered in axils of the leathery leaves which are

Acer saccharum

Acer saccharum

Acer saccharinum

Acer rubrum

Acer truncatum

arranged in opposite pairs on the twigs. The fruits are medium-sized drupes with a spongy, milky flesh that is probably poisonous. Acokantheras prefer full sun and well-drained soil; established plants need little watering and will tolerate salt-laden winds near the sea. Propagate from seed in spring, or cuttings in summer.

Acokanthera oblongifolia
WINTERSWEET, BUSHMAN'S POISON

This dense, spreading shrub to 21 ft (7 m) tall and somewhat less in width, has large, oblong, leathery, glossy, dark green leaves which become purplish in winter. Fragrant white flowers, dull pink on the outside, appear in dense clusters through spring and summer followed by purplish black olive-sized fruits. It prefers a warm position. All parts of the plant are reputedly poisonous. The fruit are at their most toxic when unripe, and so it is wise to prune the shrub after flowering to prevent fruit from forming. The cultivar 'Variegata' is slightly smaller with grey-green and creamy white variegation; the young leaves have a pinkish tinge and a reddish maroon stain on the darker green parts. Propagate this species by grafting. ZONE 9.

ACROCARPUS
Caesalpiniaceae

A genus of only 2 species of large leguminous deciduous trees from tropical Asia, one of which is sometimes cultivated in warmer countries. They have very large bipinnate leaves and massed spikes of densely packed scarlet flowers all along the branches and twigs. Seeds are borne in flattened pods. Successful cultivation depends on an appropriate climate: although tropical they do not like lowland areas with a very hot dry season, preferring cooler hill country and deep moist soils. They also do well in warm-temperate coastal areas. Propagation is from seed, which may need soaking for good germination.

Acrocarpus fraxinifolius
PINK CEDAR

This is one of those tropical leguminous trees that can amaze by their speed of growth. As a young sapling it will shoot up to a height of 12–15 ft (4–5 m) in two years or less. At this stage it is normally single-stemmed with a palm-like appearance due to its huge bipinnate or tripinnate leaves. New leaves are attractively bronze-tinted. Originating in India, Burma and Sumatra, it is said to reach as much as 200 ft (60 m) in the wild with a massive trunk, but its size in cultivation is uncertain. Trees are deciduous in

Adansonia digitata

Acmena smithii

Adansonia gregorii

Acokanthera oblongifolia

the dry or cold season and towards the end of it produce a magnificent display of scarlet blossom, but they may not bloom until they reach a good size. In the highlands of East Africa the pink cedar has been extensively planted for timber, growing at rates of up to 10 ft (3 m) per year. ZONE 10.

ADANSONIA
Bombacaceae
BAOBAB, BOAB

These large trees, with trunks that become swollen with age into a bottle or flask shape, amazed European explorers in Africa, Madagascar and northern Australia. They are usually deciduous in the tropical dry season. Their leaves are divided into a number of leaflets radiating from the end of a common stalk. The cream flowers, which open only at night, are very large and attractive and hang singly on pendulous stalks, adapted to pollination by nectar-feeding bats. The large oval fruits contain seeds embedded in a sour, edible pulp. Cultivation of baobabs is not too difficult in the tropics or warmer subtropics. Although they come from monsoonal climates with a long dry season, they adapt to wetter regions quite well. Propagate from seed or semi-hardwood cuttings. Growth is somewhat slow until a good root system is established, but vigorous young trees with trunks beginning to swell make fine subjects for parks and streets.

Adansonia gregorii

Adansonia digitata
BAOBAB

The common name is thought to come from central Africa but this, the original baobab, ranges over much of the length and breadth of Africa, from dry sub-Saharan scrubland to the veld of northern Transvaal. Old trees can reach monstrous proportions, often branching near the ground into several hugely swollen trunks each of which may be 80 ft (25 m) or more high. ZONE 11.

Adansonia gregorii
AUSTRALIAN BAOBAB, BOTTLE TREE, DEAD RAT TREE

Confined in the wild to a relatively small area in the far north of Western Australia and a neighbouring region of the Northern Territory, this species is very closely related to the African baobab and young trees are hardly distinguishable. It does not generally grow quite as tall, but old trees reach an enormous girth. The unflattering name dead rat tree comes from the appearance of the grey seed pods. ZONE 12.

Adenium obesum

Adenandra uniflora

Aeonium arboreum

ADENANDRA
Rutaceae

This genus of small, shrubby evergreens from the Cape regions of South Africa is related to the boronias. Valued for their aromatic foliage as well as their flowers (fragrant in some species), they are half-hardy and grow best in full sun, in light, well-drained soil. Propagate from seed or semi-ripe cuttings.

Adenandra uniflora
CHINA FLOWER

This twiggy shrub grows only to about to 24 in (60 cm) high and 3 ft (1 m) wide, with small, aromatic, deep green leaves on fine reddish stems. Unlike some other species, its flowers are not fragrant, but make up for that by their great beauty. They are 5-petalled, white, about 1 in (2.5 cm) across and have an appearance like porcelain that gives the shrub its common name. Making a first-class rock garden plant, the China flower prefers light, well-drained soil and a sunny position and requires adequate water in winter. ZONE 8.

ADENIUM
Apocynaceae

The name of this small genus of curious succulent shrubs is taken from their Arabic name *aden*, and these plants may also have given their name to the port city of Aden on the Arabian Peninsula, from where they first became known to the West. They are shrubs, occasionally small trees, deciduous in dry seasons, and some develop very fleshy, swollen trunks. They range through tropical and subtropical Africa and Arabia. Popular in tropical gardens, they prefer a position in full sun or part-shade and thrive best in climates with a well-marked dry season. Vivid, funnel-shaped flowers are borne from mid-winter through to spring (or in the tropical dry season). As they are very prone to rotting, they require a gritty, well-drained soil. Propagate from seed or cuttings.

Adenium obesum
DESERT ROSE

This deciduous shrub may reach a height of 5 ft (1.5 m) and a spread of about 3 ft (1 m). Fleshy stemmed, it has a crooked, tapering trunk, sparsely branched, with fleshy twigs ending in tufts of shiny, oval leaves. Funnel-shaped pinkish red and white flowers are borne in mid-winter and spring. A number of cultivars with white, pale pink or red flowers have appeared in recent years in tropical countries, where these beautiful plants are becoming quite popular. ZONE 11.

AEONIUM
Crassulaceae

Most *Aeonium* species are found in the Canary Islands and the nearby north-west coast of Africa. Although classed as succulents they are also small shrubs, with semi-woody branches terminated by neat rosettes of very crowded, overlapping, fleshy leaves. Sooner or later each branch produces at its apex a panicle of many small, star-like flowers, yellow in most species. Aeoniums are sun-loving plants for subtropical regions, thriving in a dry atmosphere and requiring very good soil drainage. Some species are half-hardy, tolerating a degree or two of frost. Aeoniums can be grown as conservatory plants in frosty climates.

Aeonium arboreum

From the Atlantic coast of Morocco, this is one of the most popular aeoniums in Mediterranean gardens. Reaching a height of around 24 in (60 cm), it develops a number of branches with rosettes of bright green leaves. In spring some branches produce dense conical clusters of golden yellow flowers, the whole branch dying back when they are spent. ZONE 9.

AESCULUS
Hippocastanaceae
HORSE-CHESTNUT, BUCKEYE

These deciduous trees and shrubs have a finger-like arrangement of leaflets in their compound leaves, and eye-catching spikes of cream to reddish flowers at branch ends in spring or summer. The large, nut-like seeds, released from round capsules, resemble chestnuts but are bitter and inedible. At least half of the 20 or so species occur in North America, the remainder scattered across temperate Asia and Europe. They are primarily trees of valley floors, growing in sheltered positions in deep soil with good moisture. Although most are frost-hardy, they perform best in those cool climates where seasons are sharply demarcated and summers are warm. Renowned as majestic park and avenue trees in European cities, they are propagated from seed or, in the case of selected clones and hybrids, by bud-grafting.

Aesculus californica
CALIFORNIA BUCKEYE

This hardy Californian comes from the slopes of the Sierra Nevada and coastal ranges. In gardens this is a large spreading shrub or small tree of 10–15 ft (3–5 m) but in the wild it can reach 40 ft (13 m). The leaves are smaller than on most Aesculus species, the 5 to 7 narrow leaflets only 2–4 in (5–10 cm) long and greyish green. In summer it produces long, dense spikes of small, creamy white, often rose-flushed, fragrant flowers. *A. californica* often begins to lose its leaves at the end of summer. It is more drought tolerant than other species, able to survive hot dry summers. ZONE 8.

Aesculus × carnea
RED HORSE-CHESTNUT

This hybrid tree, thought to have originated by chance in Germany early last century, grows to about 30 ft (10 m) and often comes true from seed. It gets the reddish pink of its flowers from one parent, *Aesculus pavia*; the other parent is *A. hippocastanum*. A hardy and free-flowering tree (flowers in late spring), it adapts to slightly warmer and drier climates than *A. hippocastanum*. The cultivar 'Briotii' has larger spikes of brighter pink flowers. Both are very popular in the UK and suitable parts of the USA. ZONE 6.

Aesculus flava
YELLOW BUCKEYE, SWEET BUCKEYE

A handsome ornamental tree native to the central-eastern states of the USA, the yellow buckeye (syn. *Aesculus octandra*) occurs along fertile valleys, growing to 90 ft (28 m) in the wild. The smallish creamy yellow or occasionally pinkish flowers appear in 6 in (15 cm) panicles from late spring to early summer, followed by fruits each with 2 to 4 seeds. The dark green leaves turn yellow before falling. The bark is dark brown, becoming furrowed with age. There was once a popular belief in America that carrying buckeye seeds would ward off rheumatism. ZONE 4.

Aesculus glabra
OHIO BUCKEYE

This species is similar to *A. flava*, though usually a smaller tree, with rougher bark; the greenish yellow flowers with protruding stamens appear in spring, followed by prickly fruits. Its leaves have a disagreeable smell when bruised or crushed. In the wild it has a similar range to that of the yellow buckeye but extends further west, to Nebraska. Although a handsome tree with attractive foliage, the Ohio buckeye is found mainly in botanical gardens and other larger collections. ZONE 4.

Aesculus glabra

Aesculus californica

Aesculus californica

Aesculus glabra

Aesculus flava

Aesculus flava

Aesculus hippocastanum
HORSE-CHESTNUT

The common horse-chestnut of Europe, this tree originated in mountain valleys between Greece and Albania; it came to western Europe via Istanbul around 1615, causing quite a sensation, and is widely planted in parks, avenues and large gardens. It can reach 100 ft (30 m), though half that is its usual mature size. In full blossom in late spring or early summer it is one of the most beautiful of all flowering trees for cool climates, with white 'candles' of bloom held above the dense crown of dark green foliage. The individual flowers have crumpled white petals with a yellow basal patch which ages to dull red. Fruits, ripening through summer, have a leathery case covered with short prickles and in autumn release large seeds, known as 'conkers' to British children. Autumn colour is yellow-brown. ZONE 6.

Aesculus pavia 'Atrosanguinea'

Aesculus indica
INDIAN HORSE-CHESTNUT

From the north-west Himalaya, this species is similar in stature to *A. hippocastanum* and also valued as an ornamental. Trees planted in the open tend to branch very low and produce thick trunks and broad, spreading crowns with age. Blooming in early to mid-summer, it produces 12–16 in (30–40 cm) spikes of white flowers with petals tinged yellow or red. The shiny leaves turn yellow in autumn. The large fruits, brownish and slightly rough, lack prickles. The Indian horse-chestnut requires a sheltered but sunny position and reliable soil moisture. ZONE 6.

Aesculus parviflora

This attractive species is a many-stemmed shrub about 6–9 ft (2–3 m) high, spreading into a broad clump by new growths from the roots. The 5 large, strongly veined leaflets are downy on the undersides. In late summer it produces long spikes of spidery flowers with small white petals and masses of showy, long, pinkish stamens. *A. parviflora* occurs wild in moist woodland of south-eastern USA, in Georgia, Alabama and Florida. Although vigorous and adaptable, it is most at home in regions with a hot humid summer, in a sheltered position with deep moist soil. ZONE 7.

Aesculus pavia
RED BUCKEYE

A small tree to 20 ft (7 m) or frequently a shrub of about 10 ft (3 m) with dense, rather cane-like branches, the red buckeye is valued for its deep crimson flowers in upright spikes in early summer, and the reddish autumn tones of its rather small leaves, each of 5 leaflets. It originates on the coastal plain of eastern USA south of Virginia and extending to the Mexican Gulf, growing in moist woodland. Although attractive and easily grown, the red buckeye is rarely available from nurseries. The cultivar 'Atrosanguinea' has darker crimson flowers. ZONE 7.

Aesculus turbinata
JAPANESE HORSE-CHESTNUT

This large tree closely resembles the common horse-chestnut (*A. hippocastanum*) in shape but has larger leaves and slightly smaller panicles of cream flowers that open a few weeks later, in early summer. The fruits also differ, lacking any spines or prickles. It is rather slow growing and, with its less conspicuous flowers, would hardly be preferred to *A. hippocastanum* except for its very handsome foliage which turns a fine orange in autumn. ZONE 6.

AFROCARPUS
Podocarpaceae

Some 6 species make up this group of conifers from the more humid mountain regions of southern and eastern Africa; they were previously included in the genus *Podocarpus* and for a short period in *Nageia*. As in those genera, male and female organs are borne on different trees. The female trees bear large naked seeds with a resinous, fleshy outer layer, on slender stalks quite different from the swollen, juicy stalks that characterize *Podocarpus*. These handsome, large trees appreciate a sheltered position when young, and are ideal for areas of high humidity and rainfall with deep fertile soil. Propagation is from seed or cuttings.

Aesculus hippocastanum

Aesculus parviflora

Aesculus indica

Afrocarpus falcatus
OUTENIQUA YELLOWWOOD

This tall erect tree, formerly known as *Podocarpus falcatus,* can reach 100 ft (30 m) or more at maturity with a trunk diameter of 6 ft (2 m) in its native forests of eastern Cape Province, Natal and Transvaal. It is suitable for parks and large gardens, developing in the open a dense, bushy crown atop a straight thick trunk. The brown bark exfoliates in fine plates, giving the trunk an interesting texture. The pointed, deep green leaves are 1½–2 in (3–5 cm) long, and the ¾ in (2 cm) diameter seeds look like rounded berries; these ripen from dark green with a bloom of white wax, to yellow. ZONE 9.

Afrocarpus gracilior
AFRICAN FERN PINE, MUSENGERA

This species comes from high mountain forests of tropical East Africa, where it makes a tree of 65 ft (20 m) or more in height, with a straight trunk and smooth purplish bark. The foliage is dense and ferny with narrow, fine-pointed leaves 2 in (5 cm) or less long. The seeds are similar to those of *A. falcatus* but ripen to purplish brown, with a waxy bloom. ZONE 10.

AGAPETES
Ericaceae

These evergreen shrubs from the moist forests of Southeast Asia, mostly in the higher mountains, have leathery leaves and tubular flowers of a rather waxy texture. Most of the species grow as epiphytes in the forks of large trees, or frequently on cliffs or boulders. In some species the stems arise from a curious woody tuber which gets quite large with age. In cultivation they adapt to growing in the ground, but demand a well-drained soil of open texture and need to be planted high, with the tuber or root-bases exposed or covered only by coarse humus. As might be expected of such rainforest plants, they enjoy shelter and humidity, but adapt readily enough to garden conditions.

Agapetes serpens

A delightful shrub with low-arching branches from a large woody tuber, *A. serpens* (syn. *Pentapterygium serpens*) grows at altitudes of up to 10,000 ft (3,000 m) in the eastern Himalaya. It rarely exceeds 3 ft (1 m) in height but may be twice that in width. The bristly brown stems bear rows of small glossy leaves, beneath which hang single rows of tubular pale red flowers, each having 5 distinct angles and an interesting pattern of V-shaped bars of darker red. It is best planted on a shaded bank where its beauty is

Agapetes serpens

Afrocarpus gracilior

Afrocarpus gracilior

displayed near eye-level. 'Ludgvan Cross' is a hybrid between this species and *A. rugosa*, with slightly larger, paler flowers and larger leaves. ZONE 9.

AGATHIS
Araucariaceae
KAURI

This remarkable genus of large conifers consists of 20 or so species scattered through the south-west Pacific region from New Zealand to the Malay Peninsula. Nearly all are tall trees with massive straight trunks and broad leathery leaves quite unlike the needle-leaves of more familiar conifers. Their cones are curious, nearly spherical with a criss-cross pattern of scales—*Agathis* is Greek for 'ball of twine', which the cones were thought to resemble. Kauri (or kaori) is their

Aesculus turbinata

Polynesian name. They give very fine timber and also exude resin from the trunks which was used for varnishes and paints. The trees are marginally frost-hardy and prefer full sun, deep moist soil and high humidity. They can be pruned to limit size or to maintain shape. Propagation is from seed.

Aesculus turbinata

Agathis australis

Agave attenuata

Agathis australis

Agathis robusta

Agave americana

Agathis australis
NEW ZEALAND KAURI

The largest of New Zealand's native trees, the kauri occurs in lowland forests of the North Island. It reaches 150 ft (46 m) in height with trunk diameters exceeding 20 ft (7 m) and has great spreading limbs. In cultivation growth is slow and even 50-year-old trees are of modest size, with a dense, narrowly pyramidal crown. The short, blunt, stiff leaves are mid green, turning coppery brown in colder weather. Kauris prefer moderate temperatures. ZONE 9.

Agathis robusta
QUEENSLAND KAURI

The Queensland kauri occurs as a native in two limited areas of east-coastal Queensland, Australia, and in New Guinea. A tall tree of up to 160 ft (50 m), it was exploited in former years for its valuable timber. The thick, deep green leaves are about twice as large as those of the New Zealand kauri, and its growth is more vigorous. Young trees have very straight trunks with very short side branches. Its globular cones are the size of tennis balls. It prefers warm-temperate to tropical locations. ZONE 9.

AGAVE
Agavaceae

Occurring naturally in the Caribbean region including southern USA, Mexico and the West Indies, these perennial succulents are grown for their dramatic, sword-shaped, often sharply toothed leaves and tall flowering stems. The small species flower only after 5 to 10 years and the taller species may take up to 40 years to flower. All agaves flower only once in their lifetime and then the flowering shoot dies, in most species leaving offsets which continue the plant's growth. They are tough, drought-resistant plants from warm, dry climates; their frost-hardiness varies depending on species. Plant in a well-drained, gritty soil in full sun. Propagate from offsets or from seed in spring or summer. Water regularly in summer. With their arresting leaf shapes, these plants are popular for use in Mediterranean styles of landscape design.

Agave americana
CENTURY PLANT, AMERICAN ALOE

From Mexico, this species is suitable for dry banks where space is available. It consists of large, stemless rosettes of stiff, dull grey leaves with needle-like tips and fierce marginal teeth. Each rosette grows to a height and spread of 6 ft (2 m) but an old clump may be 30 ft (9 m) or more across. The rosette flowers when about 10 years old, the branched flower stem rising to about 20 ft (7 m) and bearing masses of yellow flowers. After fruiting the rosette dies, to be replaced by a ring of suckers. 'Marginata' is a popular cultivar with yellow-edged leaves. In Mexico the sap of the flowering stems of the century plant is tapped and fermented into pulque, a highly alcoholic drink. Tequila is the export version. ZONE 9.

Agave attenuata

Excellent for large rockeries and dry embankments, this spineless species has a thick stem to about 5 ft (1.5 m) high, crowned by a compact rosette of broad, soft-textured pale green leaves. Its eye-catching, arched flower-spike grows to about 10 ft (3 m) in length and bears densely packed greenish white flowers which open in succession over several months through spring and summer. Lateral rosettes branch off the main stem making, in time, a large mound of rosettes, which are very attractive in themselves. ZONE 9.

AGONIS
Myrtaceae

This is a small genus of warm-climate evergreen trees and shrubs indigenous to Western Australia, with narrow, thick-textured leaves and attractive small white flowers resembling those of tea-trees (*Leptospermum*). They do best in full sun and sandy soil that is well drained but preferably enriched with organic matter for moisture retention. They are frost-tender, but tolerate droughts when established. Propagation is from seed in spring or cuttings in summer. Plants sometimes self-propagate from seed contained in their small woody fruit capsules.

Agonis flexuosa
WILLOW-MYRTLE, PEPPERMINT TREE

The willow-myrtle is a tree to about 30 ft (10 m), broad-crowned with a spread eventually equalling its height, and rapidly developing a brown-barked trunk of quite surprising thickness, sometimes as much as 3 ft (1 m). It has attractive pendulous branches, rather like a small weeping willow. The long narrow leaves are aromatic when crushed and in late spring small white flowers are strung along the branches. The willow-myrtle is widely grown in parks and gardens in temperate areas of Australia, including seaside locations. The cultivar 'Variegata' is an attractive shrub with leaves striped cream and pinkish. ZONE 9.

AILANTHUS
Simaroubaceae
TREE OF HEAVEN, SIRIS

This tree genus from eastern Asia and the Pacific region includes both winter-deciduous and dry-season-deciduous species, though only the former are generally known in cultivation. They are vigorous growers of medium size with long pinnate leaves and branches terminating in large flower clusters—male and female flowers are on separate trees and neither is very conspicuous, but those on female trees develop in summer into masses of winged, papery fruits that are very decorative. The winter-deciduous species are hardy trees that adapt especially well to urban areas, even coming up from self-sown seed in the cracks of paving. They tolerate hard pruning, responding with vigorous new growths. Propagation is by means of the sucker shoots that are freely produced from the roots.

Ailanthus altissima
TREE OF HEAVEN

Valued in some cities for its ability to withstand urban pollution, in others the Chinese tree of heaven (syn. *A. glandulosa*) is scorned as a weed, spreading fast by suckers from its long-running roots. But planted on a large lawn it shows little inclination to sucker, growing into a handsome large tree of 50 ft (15 m), its tall dome-shaped crown scattered with bunches of pale reddish brown fruits in summer. The pinnate leaves, up to 3 ft (1 m) long on young trees, smell unpleasant if bruised. There is some debate as to whether *Ailanthus giraldii* deserves to be treated as a distinct species or is just a form of *A. altissima*. It has rather larger leaves and fruits. ZONE 6.

ALBERTA
Rubiaceae

Three species make up this genus of subtropical evergreen trees, one from South Africa and two from Madagascar, noted for their handsome gardenia-like foliage and showy tubular flowers. A curious feature is the way 2 of the 5 sepals enlarge after flowering to form coloured wing-like flaps on the woody fruit. The name honours the famous mediaeval scholar Albertus Magnus. Frost-tender, they do best in a warm coastal climate with ample rainfall and protection from salty winds. They prefer a fertile, well-drained but moist soil and plenty of water in summer. Propagate from autumn seed or root cuttings.

Ailanthus altissima

Ailanthus altissima

Ailanthus altissima

Ailanthus giraldii

Agonis flexuosa (below)

Alberta magna
NATAL FLAME BUSH

This species from South Africa makes a tree of around 30 ft (10 m) in the wild but in gardens is generally only a shrub of 6–10 ft (2–3 m), of erect habit. The leathery leaves are shiny deep green, and from late autumn through to summer it sporadically bears clusters of showy, upcurving scarlet flowers, followed by small fruits enclosed in pale red calyces. It is not frost-hardy and requires a subtropical climate to perform well, although it may survive in a warm sheltered site in cooler areas. ZONE 10.

Albizia julibrissin

Albizia julibrissin

ALBIZIA
Mimosaceae

Albizia species for the most part are quick-growing tropical trees and shrubs with globular clusters of long-stamened flowers, rather like those of many *Mimosa* and *Acacia* species but larger. They have feathery leaves and densely clustered small flowers in which the stamens are far longer and more conspicuous than the petals. In nature they are often rather weedy small trees, springing up quickly from seed and frequently short lived, but they can be quite ornamental. Cultivation is easy: their main requirements are summer warmth and moisture and a reasonably sheltered site.

Alberta magna

Albizia julibrissin
SILK TREE

Occurring from Iran east across temperate and subtropical Asia to China, this deciduous tree is named for the long, silky stamens, creamy white to deep pink, which are the visible part of the flower heads and stand above the leaves. Often staying under 6 ft (2 m) tall, though flowering freely, in ideal conditions it becomes a flat-crowned tree of 20–25 ft (7–8 m) with luxuriant feathery foliage. Its life span seldom exceeds 30 years. In colder climates it is sometimes used as a summer bedding or terrace plant, raised from seeds germinated under glass in early spring. ZONE 8.

Albizia lebbek
WHITE SIRIS, WOMAN'S TONGUE TREE, FRYWOOD TREE

This tree from tropical Africa, Asia and Australia, although fast growing, reaches only about 20–40 ft (7–13 m), developing quite early a broad, flat-topped crown. The bipinnate leaves, deciduous in the dry season, are composed of oblong leaflets up to 2 in (5 cm) long. Toward the end of the dry season new leaves appear, together with cream 'powder-puff' flower heads which darken to dull yellow as they age and droop. Long whitish papery pods follow, hanging on the tree for months; their seeds rattle with the breeze, hence the rather sexist common name. Easily grown in tropical and subtropical regions, it is useful for quick shade although with age it often becomes dangerously unstable. ZONE 11.

ALECTRYON
Sapindaceae

Grown for their attractive dense foliage, these evergreen trees occur naturally through islands of the Pacific, Australia and the Malay region. Their name comes from the Greek for 'cock', referring to a crest on the fruit like a cockscomb. All species have pinnate leaves, divided into several somewhat leathery leaflets; flowers are small, in sprays at the branch tips, and are followed by berry-like capsules that split to reveal large seeds with succulent, showy appendages which attract birds. Occurring in rainforest and coastal scrubs, they are tough trees surviving in exposed positions but will not tolerate severe frosts. Propagate from seed in autumn.

Alectryon excelsus
TITOKI

Indigenous to New Zealand, this interesting bushy tree has distinctive black bark, a short, thick trunk and hairy, reddish brown branches. It grows to a height of 30 ft (9 m) with a spread of 15 ft (5 m). The pinnate leaves are 12 in (30 cm) long and tiny reddish flowers appear in many-branched clusters in summer, followed by brown fruits that open to reveal shiny black seeds protruding from scarlet, fleshy envelopes. It makes a fine specimen or shade tree. ZONE 9.

ALEURITES
Euphorbiaceae

This small genus of evergreen or semi-evergreen trees ranges from

Albizia julibrissin

Alectryon excelsus

Allamanda neriifolia

Allamanda neriifolia

Southeast Asia through Indonesia to Australia and the Pacific Islands. Formerly included in the genus but now separated as *Vernicia* (listed later in this book) are some Chinese deciduous species including the tung-oil tree. Vigorous growers, *Aleurites* species have large, often lobed leaves and panicles of small cream bell-shaped flowers. The fruits are fairly large, consisting of a ball-like outer husk, like a walnut, enclosing a hard stone which contains oily kernels. The oil can be extracted and was traditionally used in Asia for lamps or, after treatment to remove toxins, as a cooking oil. Cultivation is easy in a warm or hot climate and the fast-growing trees are quite attractive, suitable for use in streets and parks. Young trees can be trained into a single trunk if necessary. Propagation is from seed, which germinates readily. The seeds of all species are poisonous.

Aleurites moluccana
CANDLENUT TREE

This evergreen grows rapidly to a height of 60 ft (20 m) or so, initially with a narrow, conical crown but with age spreading to a broader dome. It has a straight, thick trunk with smoothish brown bark and wide-spreading branches. The handsome, oval green leaves are lobed on young trees and are slightly aromatic when crushed. Abundant panicles of creamy white flowers are borne in summer, followed by the large round fruits. It is sometimes planted as a fast-growing timber tree in the tropics, and the waxy nuts are used to make candles. ZONE 10.

ALLAMANDA
Apocynaceae

Indigenous to South America, these evergreen climbers and shrubs are grown for their trumpet-shaped flowers, yellow in most species. Frost-tender, they require a warm or hot climate and well-drained humus-rich soil. Elsewhere they can be grown in large tubs in greenhouses. Water lightly in cooler weather, more heavily during the warmer months. Prune heavily in spring to retain shape. Propagate by soft-wood cuttings and watch for mites which damage the leaves. In cooler areas they may show some leaf fall.

Allamanda neriifolia
SHRUBBY ALLAMANDA

The only true shrub in the genus, this upright evergreen makes a fine display in a sheltered sunny position in the garden. It grows to a height and spread of around 6 ft (2 m) and has glossy green leaves. Its exotic, trumpet-shaped golden yellow flowers, occasionally streaked with orange, are borne in summer and into autumn, sometimes followed by large, shiny seed pods. Tending towards untidy growth, it needs to be pruned annually in spring to control shape and often benefits from the stems being tied to supports. ZONE 11.

ALLOCASUARINA
Casuarinaceae
SHE-OAK

The 60 species of this entirely Australian genus were until recently included in the genus *Casuarina* (listed later in this book). The latter in its present, narrower sense is left with only 17 species, some non-Australian, and generally larger trees of more fertile sites than most *Allocasuarina* species. The reclassification is based mainly on small differences in fruits but reflects differences in biology and habitat. Both genera are evergreen, with

Aleurites moluccana

needle-like branchlets which serve the function of leaves, while the true leaves are rings of tiny triangular scales at joints of the branchlets, needing a hand lens to be seen readily. Small male and female flower-spikes, adapted for pollination by wind, are usually carried on separate plants. Only the males are conspicuous, changing the branch tips to a rich brown when appearing in their countless thousands. With their attractive usually drooping foliage, she-oaks are grown as shade or windbreak trees, and for timber or firewood. The taller species are very fast growing and may be quite long lived; some will survive very dry conditions. Propagate from seed sown in spring.

Allocasuarina decaisneana

Allocasuarina decaisneana

Allocasuarina littoralis

Allocasuarina littoralis

Allocasuarina luehmannii

and dense crown of beautifully weeping grey-green branchlets. The seed 'cones' are the largest in the genus. In arid areas this tree makes a fine ornamental, thriving in conditions of extreme heat. ZONE 9.

Allocasuarina littoralis
BLACK SHE-OAK

Occurring along the whole east coast of Australia, often close to the sea, this erect, evergreen tree grows to a height of around 30 ft (9 m) with an irregularly conical, pointed crown, though often smaller in exposed coastal situations. It has closely fissured grey-brown bark on a short trunk and very fine, dark green foliage which in winter may be stained with brown from the innumerable fine male flower-spikes (only on male trees). The cylindrical 'cones' on female trees are rather narrow and often densely clustered. Fast growing and ornamental when young, it becomes sparse and unattractive after 15 to 20 years. It thrives in very poor soils and tolerates salt spray near the sea. ZONE 9.

Allocasuarina luehmannii
BULL OAK

One of the larger *Allocasuarina* species, the bull oak makes a fine, upright tree, occurring naturally on flats and low rises in semi-arid areas of south-eastern Australia. It reaches heights of up to 50 ft (15 m) with a stout, rough-barked trunk and thick ascending branches. The dense rather stiff branchlets are olive green and the seed 'cones' are smallish, usually wider than they are long. This species makes a useful shade tree for drier areas; it adapts to poor soils and tolerates poor drainage. ZONE 9.

Allocasuarina tessellata

One of many smaller species from the southern part of Western Australia, *A. tessellata* makes a stiff erect shrub 10–15 ft (3–5 m) tall with rather coarse dull green branchlets. The persistent seed 'cones' are longer than in most species, up to 2 in (5 cm), with the close-packed bracts fitting neatly together to make a smooth surface. It grows on rocky hillsides in a semi-arid region. ZONE 9.

Allocasuarina torulosa
FOREST OAK, FOREST SHE-OAK

Fast growing to 40–50 ft (13–15 m) or more on better soils, this graceful tree has corky, deeply furrowed bark. The drooping branches and branchlets are very fine-textured, green when young, turning a deep purple-bronze in cooler months. It occurs naturally in coastal ranges of eastern Australia and is useful for coastal planting on heavier soils for

Allocasuarina decaisneana
DESERT OAK

One of the most beautiful of all the she-oaks, this species also grows in the most extreme environment, among the red sand dunes of central Australia where annual rainfall is only about 3 in (8 cm). But these sands often conceal a large reservoir of deep subsoil moisture, tapped by the deep roots of these trees. The desert oak can grow to a 50 ft (15 m) tree with a thick straight trunk, deeply furrowed corky bark

Alloxylon flammeum

Allocasuarina tessellata

Allocasuarina tessellata

ornament or on farms for shade, shelter or fuel. The wood was once considered the best fuel for bakers' ovens; also it is easily hand-split for use as roofing shingles. Young trees can be lightly pruned to thicken growth. ZONE 8.

Allocasuarina verticillata
DROOPING SHE-OAK

This spreading tree from southeastern Australia grows to 30 ft (10 m) in protected inland sites, less on exposed seashores. It forms a neat mop-headed tree with densely weeping branchlets. Male flowers appear from winter to early spring, covering the tree in golden brown anthers. It tolerates most soils and aspects, is fairly frost, wind and drought resistant, and is frequently found as a much smaller specimen on exposed sea-cliffs, especially on shales. It responds well to lopping and can provide useful subsistence fodder for livestock. ZONE 8.

ALLOXYLON
Proteaceae

The few species in this genus of evergreen rainforest trees are native to the warm east coast of Australia and to New Guinea. Until recently they were included in the genus *Oreocallis*, now restricted to South American species, and earlier still in *Embothrium* (listed later in this book). Not widely available in nurseries, they are worth seeking out for their magnificent heads of scarlet or crimson flowers. While they can withstand very light frosts, they are really plants for tropical or subtropical gardens with regular summer rainfall. They do best on loamy or sandy soil with a high organic content and dislike root disturbance, so should be planted while still small. Sudden and unexplainable death of sapling trees is a common problem, the more so in areas that experience dry spells. Trees should be trained to a single trunk for the first 6 ft (2 m) or so. Propagate in spring from fresh seed.

Allocasuarina verticillata

Alloxylon flammeum
TREE WARATAH, SCARLET SILKY OAK

Alloxylon flammeum is still better known under the name *Oreocallis wickhamii*. The tree waratah reaches an eventual height of 30–50 ft (10–15 m). At first it has a bushy, erect growth-habit but with age it develops a wide, irregular head of branches. The variably lobed leaves are dark green in colour and leathery. Terminal clusters of spectacular orange-red flowers which look like waratahs (hence one of its common names) or spider chrysanthemums are borne in profusion in late spring or early summer. They are much loved by nectar-feeding birds. ZONE 9.

Allocasuarina torulosa

Alloxylon pinnatum

Alnus glutinosa

Alnus firma

Alnus acuminata

Alloxylon pinnatum
DORRIGO WARATAH

Less well known than *A. flammeum* and more difficult to grow to maturity, this species makes a tree to 30–60 ft (10–18 m) in its natural rainforest habitat but in gardens is usually an erect shrub of 12–20 ft (4–7 m). Its shiny, dark green leaves are divided right to the midrib into narrow lobes, appearing to be pinnate. The striking heads of crimson-pink flowers are borne at the branch tips in midsummer. ZONE 9.

ALNUS
Betulaceae
ALDER

Upright trees related to the birches (*Betula*), alders come mainly from cool to cold climates of the northern hemisphere, though in the Americas they range south along the Andes into Argentina. In far northern regions of Asia, Europe and America they are often important pioneers of vegetation, forming thickets on glacial moraines, landslides and floodplains of rivers. Though less attractive than the birches, they are very fast growing and their roots contain mico-organisms that can fix nitrogen from the air, adding to soil fertility. Light-loving trees themselves, alders act as nurse trees for slower-growing conifers but die soon after they are overtopped by them and shaded out. The female catkins are egg-shaped, hanging in groups at branch tips, and in the seeding stage they become hard and woody. The bark is brown or blackish and sometimes furrowed. All alders from cool-temperate regions are deciduous but produce little in the way of autumn colour. A few species from subtropical mountain areas are evergreen or semi-evergreen. Alders have many traditional uses: the bark was used in tanning and dying and the close-grained wood is tough and durable; its charcoal was used in making gunpowder.

Alnus acuminata
MEXICAN ALDER, EVERGREEN ALDER

This is one of a small group of alders from the mountains of Central and South America which have generally been lumped under the name *A. jorullensis*. This species ranges all the way from northern Mexico through the Andean mountain chain to north-west Argentina. It has become popular in cultivation in Australia and New Zealand in recent years, valued for its fast growth and broad crown of attractively weeping, birch-like foliage. It is promoted as being of compact size, and usually does not exceed about 30 ft (9 m); however, in a good site it can grow quite rapidly to 50 ft (15 m) or even more. Nonetheless it can be kept trimmed to a neat umbrella-like shape if necessary. ZONE 9.

Alnus cordata
ITALIAN ALDER

From the mountains of Corsica, Sardinia and southern Italy, this large alder has dense, deep green foliage and vigorous, upright growth to 30–40 ft (10–13 m), with relatively short side branches. The broad, rounded leaves are a shiny dark green, and the bark is grey and smooth. It flowers in late winter or very early spring, producing yellowish male catkins 3–4 in (8–10 cm) long at branch tips, followed by the maturing seed cones which are about 1 in (2 cm) long. The Italian alder adapts well to most situations and soils but makes best growth near water. ZONE 7.

Alnus firma
JAPANESE ALDER

This beautiful alder from the mountains of Japan has narrow, sharply toothed and prettily textured leaves on gracefully arching branches. It may remain a large shrub to about 10 ft (3 m) for many years, though ultimately it can reach about 30 ft (10 m). When a trunk finally develops it has attractive bark, with squares of older grey bark flaking off to reveal reddish new bark. The leaves often remain green late into autumn. Despite its beauty and ease of cultivation this species is not widely planted outside Japan. ZONE 5.

Alnus glutinosa
BLACK ALDER, COMMON ALDER

From Britain to the Urals and north almost to the Arctic Circle in Scandinavia, the common alder is valued more for its timber and its use to wildlife than as an ornamental tree. However in cold, bleak climates and on poor, boggy soils it is sometimes the only tree apart from certain willows that will thrive. It reaches heights of 60 ft (18 m) in the wild but planted trees are seldom more than half that. The dark brown bark becomes very deeply furrowed and checkered as the trunk increases in girth, and the high crown of the tree is often irregular and rather open. ZONE 4.

Alnus nepalensis
NEPAL ALDER

Though it comes from the eastern Himalaya and south-western China at medium altitude, this alder is not very frost-hardy, nor does it thrive in warm lowland climates. An erect tree of open, sparse branching habit with smooth, pale grey bark, it grows extremely fast. The broad oval leaves are up to 8 in (20 cm) long, bright green above, pale and satiny below. Unusually, the flowers appear in autumn as the leaves are falling. The striking male catkins are long and very thin, borne in large tangled masses at the branch tips. The Nepal alder thrives on a variety of soils but needs shelter and humidity or its large leaves become torn and scorched. ZONE 9.

Alnus orientalis
SYRIAN ALDER

The name *orientalis* goes back to the time when, to western Europeans, 'the Orient' meant anywhere east of about Italy, including Greece, Turkey, Syria and Palestine. This handsome alder occurs wild along river banks in Syria, southern Turkey and Cyprus, where it can grow to 50 ft (15 m). Its glossy green leaves are irregularly toothed. The male catkins, appearing in early spring, are covered in a sticky exudation before they expand to release their yellow pollen. ZONE 7.

Alnus rubra
RED ALDER

Ranging from Alaska to central California, this tree grows to about 40–50 ft (13–15 m), usually branching near the base into several trunks and with pendulous lower branches. The bark is thin and pale grey; the large leaves have coarse marginal teeth and are dark green above with paler grey-green undersides often covered with an orange down. It flowers in early spring before the leaves appear, producing at the branch tips profuse yellow male catkins that are quite showy. Valued for its graceful habit and attractive foliage, the red alder is reasonably frost-hardy but will soon outgrow a small garden. ZONE 6.

ALOE
Liliaceae

Occurring naturally in Africa and the Arabian Peninsula, this genus of succulent-leafed plants consists of over 200 species, including trees, shrubs, perennials and climbers. The 'aloes' of traditional medicine is a bitter drug obtained from some shrubby African species including *A. barbadensis* (*A. vera*). All aloes are evergreen, mostly with distinct rosettes of sword-shaped leaves terminating the stem or branches. Leaves vary greatly between species in size, colour, degree of succulence, and presence and distribution of prickles on the margins or faces. The flowers are tubular to bell-shaped, in long-stemmed racemes. Through much of southern and eastern Africa the many-branched tree aloes, up to 50 ft (15 m) in height, are a distinctive feature of dry, rocky hillsides and 'kopjes' (rocky hilltops). Nearly all aloes prefer a warm dry climate and very well-drained soil, but many will tolerate a few degrees of frost once established. Grow the larger species in full sun, the smaller types in part-shade. Propagate from offsets or stem cuttings. Infestation by mealybugs can be a problem.

Aloe candelabrum
CANDELABRA ALOE

This single-stemmed shrub, 6–12 ft (2–4 m) in height, is covered with old, dry leaves. Leaf edges are reddish and have small teeth. The flower heads are branched with up to 12 upright flower-spikes in winter. Flowers are scarlet, rose-pink or orange; the inner petals are tipped with white. This succulent shrub prefers protected areas in a subtropical area. ZONE 9.

Alnus rubra

Alnus nepalensis

Alnus nepalensis

Aloe candelabrum

Alnus orientalis

Aloe plicatilis

Aloe plicatilis
FAN ALOE

Distinctive for its fan-like clusters of pale, blue-green succulent leaves, this evergreen shrub grows to a height and spread of around 5 ft (1.5 m) with a stiff, many-branched habit. Tubular scarlet flowers are borne in spring. Frost-tender, it requires a sunny position with protection from hot afternoon sun and regular watering in winter and spring. ZONE 9.

ALOYSIA
Verbenaceae

A genus of few species of evergreen shrubs from subtropical and temperate South America, grown for their aromatic foliage. The branches are soft and cane-like with leaves arranged in opposite pairs or in whorls of three. Tiny flowers are borne in panicles terminating the branches. They prefer a well-drained, loamy or light-textured soil and plenty of summer watering. Tolerant of only mild frosts, they do best in sunny positions in warm, coastal environments. In cold areas they should be planted out new each year. Remove dead wood in early summer and prune well in late winter to maintain a bushy shape and encourage the flowers which are borne on current season's growth. Propagate by semi-hardwood cuttings in summer or soft-tip cuttings in spring.

Aloysia triphylla
LEMON-SCENTED VERBENA

Grown for its heavily lemon-scented, crinkly pale to mid-green leaves, this shrub has an open, rather straggling habit and reaches a height and spread of 10 ft (3 m). Racemes of dainty lavender-purple flowers appear in summer and autumn. It needs regular pruning to improve shape. Oil of verbena is produced from the leaves. ZONE 8.

ALPINIA
Zingiberaceae
ORNAMENTAL GINGER

Of Asian and Pacific origin, these plants are widely cultivated for their showy blooms in tropical and subtropical gardens and as commercial cut flowers. They grow from fleshy rhizomes to form large clumps, and are strictly speaking perennials, but do not die back and can be used in the garden like a shrub. The best known tropical species *A. purpurata*, known as red ginger, bears tall spikes of showy deep red flower bracts. Alpinias appreciate part-shade, a warm, humid atmosphere and rich soil. Propagate by division in late spring.

Alpinia zerumbet
SHELL GINGER

This evergreen, clump-forming perennial grows to around 10 ft (3 m) with a spread of 5–10 ft (1.5–3 m). It has long, densely massed leaves, and the drooping sprays of flowers appear in spring and intermittently in other seasons. They start as waxy white or ivory buds and open one at a time to reveal yellow lips with pink- or red-marked throats. A warm sheltered spot in part-shade and plenty of water will encourage strong growth. The cultivar 'Variegata' has leaves irregularly striped yellow; it tends to be lower-growing. ZONE 10.

ALYOGYNE
Malvaceae

These hibiscus-like shrubs come from the drier regions of southern and western Australia. The better known of the 2 species, *A. huegelii* (sometimes still listed as *Hibiscus huegelii*), has large flowers in the lilac-blue range and deeply lobed leaves. Alyogynes are fast growing, erect, leggy plants about 6–10 ft (2–3 m) tall. In the garden they can be improved by regular tip pruning after they have finished flowering. They will suit any frost-free warm climate and need full sun, shelter from strong winds and moderately fertile, well-drained soil. Propagate from seed or cuttings in summer.

Alyogyne hakeifolia
RED-CENTRED HIBISCUS

This Western Australian species grows to 10 ft (3 m) tall with upright habit and simple linear leaves. The funnel-shaped flowers may be

Aloysia triphylla

Aloysia triphylla

Alpinia zerumbet

Alyogyne hakeifolia

pale mauve, yellow or cream with dark red centres, and appear in spring and summer. ZONE 10.

Alyogyne huegelii

The most commonly grown species, this is instantly distinguishable from *A. hakeifolia* by its deeply lobed leaves and usually larger flowers that open wider. It has a wide natural range across southern Western Australia and into South Australia and runs into a number of regional races and forms. A spreading shrub of open habit and 4–8 ft (1.2–2.5 m) high, it can be pruned into a more compact, bush shape if desired. The lilac (or sometimes more pinkish) flowers are up to 6 in (15 cm) across and open in succession from early spring through to late summer. ZONE 10.

AMELANCHIER
Rosaceae
SERVICEBERRY, SNOWY MESPILUS

These shrubs and small trees, mostly native to cool climates of North America, belong to the pome-fruit group of trees and shrubs in the rose family, which includes apples, pears and quinces as well as many 'berry' shrubs. Most *Amelanchier* species are deciduous, with simple oval leaves, clusters of white flowers often with long narrow petals, and small rounded fruit ripening to purple or black and often sweet and edible. Some species make very attractive, graceful trees and are valued for the display of snowy white flowers in spring and for their autumn colouring. They do best in a grassy glade in the shelter of other trees but receiving ample sun. Propagation is normally from seed or by layering.

Amelanchier alnifolia
SASKATOON SERVICEBERRY

Commonly a shrub of 6 ft (2 m) or less, branching from the base, *A. alnifolia* may grow taller in sheltered situations. It produces clusters of white flowers in late spring, among the oval, coarsely toothed, rather small leaves, followed by small, sweet, blue-black fruit. As an ornamental this species is not of particularly high value, but it is extremely cold-hardy. It is native to a wide area from central Alaska down the Rocky Mountain chain as far as Colorado, growing in thickets on hillsides and along stream banks. ZONE 4.

Amelanchier arborea
DOWNY SERVICEBERRY

Occurring naturally in woodland on hills and along the banks of rivers through the eastern states of the USA, this tree reaches about 20 ft (7 m) in gardens, usually with a narrow crown and drooping lower branches. The finely toothed, pointed leaves are covered with white down as they emerge in spring. The profuse flowers, in short upright sprays, are followed in early summer by small fleshy fruit that ripen through red to purple-black. In autumn the foliage turns red, orange or yellow, making a fine display. Easily grown, this species (syn. *Amelanchier canadensis*) deserves wider cultivation. ZONE 4.

Amelanchier arborea

Amelanchier alnifolia

Alyogyne huegelii

Alyogyne huegelii (below)

Amherstia nobilis

Amelanchier lamarckii

Amelanchier lamarckii

Anacardium occidentale

Amelanchier laevis
ALLEGHANY SERVICEBERRY

Valued as an ornamental, this shrubby species from the Alleghany and Appalachian Mountain chains of the eastern USA grows on sheltered slopes and in ravines. The new leaves, as they expand in early spring, are bronze-purple, and the fragrant white flowers appear amongst them later in spring, in loose clusters. The sweet blackish fruits are traditionally used by American hill people for pies and preserves. Autumn foliage is usually red. ZONE 4.

Amelanchier lamarckii
SNOWY MESPILUS

For long confused in gardens with *A. canadensis*, this species is native to the mountains of central and southern Europe, making a spreading shrub or occasionally a small tree to 20 ft (7 m). The leaves are smallish and pointed, downy when first expanding and with a coating of white wool on the undersides. The white flowers, only a few per cluster but larger than in other species, about 1½ in (3 cm) across, make a fine show in late spring. The small edible fruits ripen through red to black, and in autumn the foliage colours attractively. ZONE 6.

AMHERSTIA
Caesalpiniaceae
PRIDE OF BURMA

Its one species considered among the most beautiful of all flowering trees, this genus was named in honour of Lady Sarah Amherst, early 19th-century botanist and collector whose husband became Viceroy of India. It has large bipinnate leaves. Briefly deciduous in the dry season, the drooping leaflets have whitish undersides. From beneath the canopy hang long pendulous sprays of orchid-like flowers, produced through much of the year in the wet tropics. In its native Burma handfuls of its flowers are offered at Buddhist shrines. It is strictly a tropical tree, succeeding only in equatorial regions with year-round rainfall, but even in these regions it is not common due to difficulties in propagation. Seed is almost impossible to obtain and cuttings very difficult to strike, so layering of branches using pots raised on stands is usually the only resort. *Amherstia* likes a very sheltered position, even part-shaded by larger trees.

Amherstia nobilis

A. nobilis is the only species in this genus. It is a spreading tree reaching a height of about 40 ft (13 m), with bipinnate leaves up to 3 ft (1 m) long. Each pendent spike bears 5 to 10 flowers about 4 in (10 cm) across with spreading crimson petals, the upper ones gold-tipped. New leaves are coppery pink and drooping. ZONE 12.

AMPHITECNA
Bignoniaceae
CALABASH

Often grown for their pulpy fruit or as ornamentals, these small trees from Central and South America and the West Indies should not be confused with the true calabash (*Crescentia cujete*), the gourd-like fruit of which is hollowed out to make carrying receptacles. In *Amphitecna* species the fruit develops from tubular white flowers. Tropical plants with elliptical leaves up to 8 in (20 cm) long, they demand steady, warm temperatures and regular water. They prefer a fairly light soil and most are at home in coastal conditions. Seed is the usual method of propagation.

Amphitecna latifolia
BLACK CALABASH, SAVANA CALABASH

Formerly known as *Enallagma latifolia*, this species occurs naturally in coastal areas from Costa Rica to Ecuador. It grows to around 30 ft (10 m) high and has dark green leaves 3–8 in (7–20 cm) long. The white tubular flowers are carried singly or in groups of 2 or 3 and develop into 3½ in (9 cm) long, oval, purplish green fruit. ZONE 11.

ANACARDIUM
Anacardiaceae
CASHEW

The cashew comes from a small tropical American tree related to the mango and the pistachio, semi-deciduous in the dry season with leathery pinnate leaves. Both branches and foliage have a very awkward, untidy aspect so it is not a tree you would grow purely for ornament. Stiff sprays of small pinkish flowers are followed by the curious fruits, consisting of two parts: the 'cashew apple', actually a swollen, fleshy stalk which is coloured and edible; and sitting in its hollowed apex the true fruit, curved like the nut, with an outer fleshy husk containing an extremely acrid, resinous sap which can badly burn the skin; this must be removed before the edible kernel can be used, requiring gloves to protect the skin. Most of the world's cashew crop comes from India, where the long, hot dry season suits its cultivation. The young leaves are also used as a salad vegetable in some countries but are only sweet and edible on selected trees. Propagation is easy from fresh seed, planted directly into the ground.

Anacardium occidentale

The cashew tree may grow as tall as 25 ft (8 m) but is usually about half that height with a spreading, irregular crown. In the dry season it sheds a proportion of its leaves. The pinkish flowers, produced early in the wet season, are fragrant at night. Fruits ripen later in the wet, the 'apple' yellow or orange and up to 4 in (10 cm) long and 2 in (5 cm) in diameter. Fast growing when young, cashews can be grown in the warmer subtropics as well as the tropics. ZONE 11.

ANDROMEDA
Ericaceae
BOG ROSEMARY

Only 2 species of low evergreen shrubs make up this genus from the colder parts of the northern hemisphere. They have tough short branches that root along the ground and small oblong leathery leaves. The small flowers, in short terminal sprays, are urn-shaped with a narrow aperture. Best grown in a shaded rockery, they prefer moist yet well-drained conditions. They will tolerate any frosts and prefer a cold climate. Propagate from seed or small tip cuttings.

Andromeda polifolia

This tough little evergreen shrub comes from the cool-temperate and near-arctic regions of northern Europe, Asia and North America. It grows to about 24 in (60 cm) high and wide, and has narrow, deep green 1 in (2 cm) long leaves with pale undersides. The tiny white to pink flowers appear in sprays in spring. ZONE 2.

ANGOPHORA
Myrtaceae
APPLE GUM

Consisting of 13 species of evergreen trees from eastern Australia, often on sandstone-derived soils of low fertility, this genus is closely related to *Eucalyptus*. While there are complex differences between the 2 genera, one rule-of-thumb to distinguish them is that *Angophora* has sharply ribbed fruit capsules and leaves in opposite pairs, while *Eucalyptus* has mostly smooth capsules and the adult leaves are arranged alternately. *Angophora* species vary considerably in size and habit, ranging from the almost shrubby dwarf apple, *A. hispida*, to 100 ft (30 m) which trees such as *A. costata* or *A. subvelutina* make under ideal conditions. The bark of most species is rough and scaly. Where space is available they make interesting subjects with their tortuous branches. Flowers are creamy white, usually profuse. Propagate from seed.

Angophora costata
SYDNEY RED GUM, SMOOTH-BARKED APPLE

From Australia's east coast sandstone regions, this tree may occasionally reach 100 ft (30 m) in height with a sturdy trunk up to 4 ft (1.2 m) in diameter and a high, spreading crown of twisting branches. These and the brownish pink bark, shed in spring to reveal salmon-pink new bark, are the chief attractions of this beautiful tree. The rather narrow leaves are orange-red on the summer growth-flushes, changing to dark green as they harden. In spring and summer it produces massed cream flowers. Suited to warm-temperate climates and sandy, well-drained soils, it is inclined to be rather unpredictable in both speed and form of growth. Propagate from seed in winter. ZONE 9.

ANISODONTEA
Malvaceae

This genus of shrubby mallows from southern Africa have tough, wiry stems and small flowers like miniature hibiscus, carried on slender stalks from short lateral shoots near the tips of the branches. The leaves are small and irregularly lobed. In recent years they have been rediscovered and popularized as free-blooming indoor plants, or in warm-temperate climates as garden shrubs also. However, if grown indoors they must receive some sun or very strong reflected light. They need frequent watering in the warmer half of the year, little in the cooler. Light pruning after flowers finish produces a more compact plant and encourages subsequent flowering. Propagation is normally from cuttings, which strike readily.

Anisodontea capensis

If left unchecked, this species will quickly grow to a shrub about 3 ft (1 m) high with long straggling branches and rather sparse foliage. Flowers, appearing in successive flushes from spring through summer or almost the whole year in warmer climates, open flesh-pink with darker veining and age to very pale pink. There is some confusion between this and the hybrid *A.* ×

Anisodontea capensis

Annona squamosa

Angophora costata

Angophora costata with *Xanthorrhoea* in foreground

hypomadarum (*capensis* × *scabrosa*), to which the cultivar 'African Queen' may belong: this differs in its larger, 1 in (2.5 cm) diameter, and more profuse flowers. ZONE 9.

ANNONA
Annonaceae

The genus *Annona* consists of 100-odd species of evergreen tree from the American tropics and subtropics. One species (*A. glabra*, the pond apple) extends to the USA, in southern Florida. They include some of the most delectably sweet tropical fruits, notably the cherimoya (*A. cherimolia*), custard apple (*A. atemoya*) and sweetsop (*A. squamosa*). The trees have broad, oblong, strongly veined leaves, and curiously shaped flowers, often with a pungent fruity aroma, which emerge from the old wood on short stalks. The fruits consist of many fused segments, with tough green or brownish skin which may be covered in soft prickles or other

Andromeda polifolia

protrusions, and a pulpy white flesh containing many brown seeds. *Annona* species are easily grown in most tropical and warmer subtropical areas, preferring sheltered sunny positions and fertile well-drained soils. They may flower and fruit through much of the year. Propagation is easy from freshly extracted seed, or by grafting for selected varieties.

Annona muricata
SOURSOP

From northern South America, this grows to 15–20 ft (5–7 m), branching low with strongly ascending lateral growths. New growths have brownish silky hairs; older leaves are glossy bright green. The large green fruits are asymmetrically oval, covered in soft spines, and may be borne throughout the year. Despite the name, the fluffy white aromatic flesh is not very sour. ZONE 10.

ANOPTERUS
Escalloniaceae

This genus consists of only 2 species of small evergreen tree or shrub; one confined to Tasmania, the other to east-coastal mainland Australia in subtropical hill forests. Both are very ornamental, with spathulate leaves and heavy-textured white flowers, but it is only the Tasmanian one that has been brought into cultivation to any significant extent.

Anopterus glandulosus
TASMANIAN LAUREL

This shrub of about 6–8 ft (2–2.5 m) is capable of growing to a tree of 20 ft (7 m) or more in moist Tasmanian forests. The glossy dark green leaves are very leathery, with blunt teeth, and the pure white cup-shaped flowers appear in spring in short sprays at branch tips. Plants grown from cuttings often flower when only a foot or so high. It requires a very sheltered position, moist humus-rich soil and a cool humid climate, but is not very frost-hardy. ZONE 9.

ARALIA
Araliaceae

This small group of cool-climate deciduous shrubs and small trees from North America and East Asia belongs to the ivy family. They have prickly stems, very handsome large compound leaves consisting of numerous leaflets, and large terminal panicles of densely packed small cream flowers. Younger plants often make a single unbranched trunk with the leaves confined to the top, but as they grow, lateral branches may develop and multiply to give a broad-headed small tree. Aralias can be eye-catching specimens when in full flower; they must have shelter from strong, drying winds and will tolerate full sun or part-shade beneath taller trees. While a moist, fertile soil suits them well, poorer soils are said to produce hardier, longer-lived specimens.

Aralia chinensis
CHINESE ARALIA

This species is widely distributed in China, occurring in subtropical as well as quite cool regions. As a young tree to 10 ft (3 m) or so it is single-stemmed with an irregular umbrella-like crown of dark green leaves each about 4 ft (1.2 m) long, consisting of large oval leaflets with closely toothed margins. Flowering in early autumn, it produces large panicles of creamy yellow flower-sprays which droop over the foliage. With age it branches into smaller crowns, with correspondingly smaller leaves and flower-sprays. In autumn the leaves turn yellowish. ZONE 7.

Aralia elata
JAPANESE ANGELICA TREE

Native to Japan and mainland north-east Asia, this ornamental frost-hardy species can grow to a spreading tree of up to 30 ft (10 m) but is most commonly seen as a shrub with few branches. The very decorative sprays of tiny flowers are carried into early autumn, by which time the leaves start to take on yellow and reddish tones. This species is easily propagated by detaching its basal suckers or even from sections of root taken late in winter. ZONE 5.

Aralia spinosa
DEVIL'S WALKING-STICK, HERCULES' CLUB

From forest understorey in eastern USA south from New York State, this species may remain a single-stemmed shrub for many years but with adequate light and nutrition it can ultimately make a tree of up to

Anopterus glandulosus

Aralia elata

Aralia elata

Aralia chinensis (left)

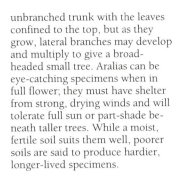
Annona muricata (above)

30 ft (10 m). It is notable for the stout thorns on its trunk. The large bipinnate leaves on younger trees are 3–4 ft (1–1.2 m) long, each consisting of many oval leaflets about 3 in (7 cm) long. The sprays of small white flowers can be up to 4 ft (1.2 m) long when they open in late spring. ZONE 6.

ARAUCARIA
Araucariaceae
ARAUCARIA, MONKEY PUZZLE PINE

This remarkable, geologically ancient genus of evergreen conifers is confined in the wild to the southern hemisphere, more specifically to South America, Australia, Norfolk Island, New Guinea and New Caledonia. The last-mentioned island accounts for 13 of the 19 species that make up the genus, no other landmass having more than 2 native species. Most araucarias are large trees with massive straight trunks that continue to the apex of the tree, sharply distinct from the crowded shorter lateral branches. The leathery leaves are incurved and densely overlapping in some species, flatter and spreading in others; male and female cones are on the same tree, the round bristly seed cones developing right at the top of adult trees. *A. araucana* is suited to cool climates; the others are warm-climate trees. Most are too large for home gardens but are used as park and street trees in warm climates. They will grow in a range of soil types but prefer a deep, moist, well-drained soil and a position in full sun. Growth may be quite fast when conditions suit them. Several make attractive indoor plants as seedlings, their growth slowing when roots are restricted. Propagate from seed in spring.

Araucaria angustifolia
PARANA PINE

One of the 2 South American *Araucaria* species, the parana pine is native to the plateaus of southwest Brazil, where extensive forests of it are managed for timber production. It makes a large tree with a very straight trunk and widely spreading branches which in old trees produce an umbrella-shaped crown. The leaves are flat, very like those of *A. bidwillii* but more prickly and rigid. A handsome tree, it adapts to climates from wet-tropical to moderately cool and will tolerate a few degrees of frost. Plants are not easily obtained in most countries. ZONE 9.

Araucaria araucana
MONKEY PUZZLE PINE

From the Andes slopes in Chile and Argentina, this bizarre tree enjoyed fad status in Britain in the 1840s.

Araucaria bidwillii

Araucaria bidwillii

The remark that 'it would puzzle a monkey to climb it' gave rise to its common name. Britain's climate suited it well and specimens 80 ft (25 m) tall and 4 ft (1.2 m) in trunk diameter are known. While vigorous young trees have a domelike shape with interwoven branches, with age the crown retreats to high above the ground, becoming progressively shallower, so that old trees resemble long-stemmed parasols. The glossy dark green leaves, rigid and fiercely prickly, remain on the branch for many years. Globular cones 4–7 in (10–17 cm) long are carried high on the crowns of mature trees. To grow a good specimen you need a climate where the summers are cool and misty, and soil that is deep, friable and well drained. ZONE 8.

Araucaria bidwillii
BUNYA PINE, BUNYA BUNYA

This tree from warm-temperate rainforests of south-east Queens-

Araucaria araucana

Araucaria araucana

land grows slowly to about 120 ft (38 m) high, developing a distinctive very symmetrical domed crown as it matures. The numerous long branches which jut out from the thick trunk have quite large, flat, dark green, prickly leaves. Mature trees bear huge, pineapple-like cones which weigh up to 18 lb (8 kg) and contain large edible seeds. Ideal for large gardens in subtropical to warm-temperate climates with good rainfall, it can adapt to somewhat cooler, drier conditions (but not seashores). Propagate from seed sown as soon as it is ripe, in late summer. ZONE 8.

Araucaria angustifolia

Araucaria cunninghamii

Araucaria heterophylla

Arbutus × *andrachnoides*

Araucaria cunninghamii

Araucaria cunninghamii
HOOP PINE

This tall, erect conifer is widely grown for timber in the Australian subtropical rainforest regions where it is native. It occurs also in New Guinea. Moderately fast growing, it will reach 100–130 ft (30–40 m), less in gardens, especially in cooler climates. Not very frost-hardy, it is fairly drought resistant once established, though preferring good summer rainfall. The tiny, pointed scale-leaves curve inwards on the branchlets, though on juvenile growths they are longer and very prickly. New bark is attractively copper-hued, but with age rougher transverse ridges or 'hoops' develop. ZONE 9.

Araucaria heterophylla
NORFOLK ISLAND PINE

Fast growing to 100 ft (30 m) or even more, this Norfolk Island endemic conifer is widely planted along Australian coasts. However, in recent years some close to cities have suffered as a result of polluting detergents breaking down the waxy cuticle that makes them salt-tolerant. They are also wind-tolerant and able to thrive in deep coastal sands. Though needing reliable water when young, they can tolerate dry spells once established. The upright and regular branching pattern of this species and its conical form make it very distinctive. It is widely grown as a shade-tolerant pot plant, indoors and outdoors, and can be long lasting in pots. In tropical countries it often does duty as a Christmas tree. ZONE 10.

ARBUTUS
Ericaceae
STRAWBERRY TREE, MADRONE

These smallish, spreading evergreen trees have thick trunks and sinuous limbs; the bark often peels attractively. The thick-textured leaves are finely toothed and the flowers are small white or pinkish bells in compact clusters at branch ends. A small proportion of flowers develop into fleshy but hard globular fruit often with wrinkled surfaces, which take almost a year to ripen. All *Arbutus* species prefer cool, humid climates, but tolerate summer droughts; continental climates with extreme heat and cold do not suit them. They adapt equally to peaty acid soils and limestone soils. All species are handsome, especially those with smooth, exfoliating bark. Propagation is normally from seed, easily extracted from the fleshy fruit. The 'strawberry' in the name refers to the hard, reddish yellow fruit which are edible but taste bland. Plant young: they hate root disturbance.

Arbutus andrachne
GRECIAN STRAWBERRY TREE

From the eastern Mediterranean, this tree has smooth reddish brown bark which peels attractively to reveal the new cream or greenish bark beneath. The glossy green leaves are smooth-margined on adult trees and the white flowers appear in early spring. The orange-red fruit, about ½ in (1 cm) across, are quite smooth. It adapts less well to cultivation than *A. unedo* and so is rarely seen. ZONE 6.

Arbutus × *andrachnoides*
HYBRID STRAWBERRY TREE

This hybrid of *A. andrachne* and *A. unedo* is similar in size and ease of cultivation to the latter but usually has the smooth, peeling bark of the former. Clusters of white flowers appear in late autumn. First found wild in Greece where the parent species grow together, it was introduced to England as early as 1800. Selected clones are grafted onto stock of *A. unedo*. ZONE 6.

Arbutus canariensis
CANARY ISLAND STRAWBERRY TREE

This species from the Canary Islands is similar to the common *A. unedo* but is different enough to attract attention. It is a neat, round-headed, evergreen small tree that grows to about 15 ft (5 m) high. In late summer and early autumn it produces pendulous clusters of small, light pink, lily-of-the-valley-like flowers that are followed by soft green fruit which ripen to red, though these are rare in cultivation. The flaking, reddish brown bark is attractive throughout the year. Plant in moist, well-drained soil in dappled shade. ZONE 8.

Arbutus menziesii
MADRONE

Considered by some to be California's most beautiful native tree, the madrone is the giant of the genus, reaching 100 ft (30 m) in height and 6 ft (2 m) in trunk diameter. It ranges in the wild from southern California to British Columbia in western Canada, mostly in humid areas amongst tall conifers such as redwoods. The madrone has completely smooth orange-brown bark and smooth-edged glossy green leaves with whitish undersides, and produces large clusters of pure white flowers, and profuse small, orange-red fruits. It is not common outside its native regions, but there are some fine specimens in Britain. ZONE 7.

Arbutus unedo
ARBUTUS, STRAWBERRY TREE

This bushy-crowned small tree is native to the western Mediterranean, with an outpost in the mildest south-western corner of Ireland. It can attain 30 ft (10 m), though 10–15 ft (3–5 m) is more usual in gardens. The bark is dark grey-brown, rather fibrous and scaly, but the smaller branches and twigs have an attractive reddish hue. In autumn the white or pinkish flower clusters, along with the 1 in (2 cm) orange fruits from the previous year, contrast prettily with the dark evergreen foliage. A hardy tree, it will tolerate neglect though responding to better conditions. It dislikes shade and damp ground. 'Compacta' is a smaller cultivar. ZONE 7.

ARCHONTOPHOENIX
Arecaceae

Majestic subtropical palms from the rainforests of eastern Australia make up this genus of 6 species. All have tall, solitary trunks topped by a green 'crownshaft' from which the long, gracefully arching fronds radiate. Old fronds fall cleanly from the trunk, leaving ringed scars. Large panicles of tiny but fragrant flowers burst one at a time from massive green buds that emerge at the base of the crownshaft which becomes laden with cherry-sized red fruits that follow the flowers. These palms are not at all frost-hardy but will grow in most fertile soils where organic matter and moisture are sufficient, even tolerating boggy conditions. They prefer part-shade when young, full sun as the crown gains height. They can also be grown as potted plants, indoors or outdoors in shade, though they are not as satisfactory for this purpose as many other palms. Propagate from seed which germinates readily in summer.

Arbutus unedo   *Arbutus unedo* 'Compacta'

Arbutus menziesii

Arbutus canariensis

Archontophoenix alexandrae
ALEXANDRA PALM

A tall, elegant palm, this species has a straight trunk up to 50 ft (15 m) tall and arching fronds 9–12 ft (3–4 m) long. Distinguishing features of the species are the silver-grey undersurface of the fronds which catches the light, especially when the sun is low, and the cream flowers on a spreading panicle which appear mostly in autumn. Endemic to coastal Queensland north of the Tropic of Capricorn, this species thrives in wet tropical climates but adapts well to warm-temperate climates. Because of its rapid seedling growth, it is sold as an indoor plant but often fails to thrive. ZONE 10.

Archontophoenix cunninghamiana
BANGALOW PALM, PICCABEEN PALM

This tall, slender palm is similar in appearance and requirements to the Alexandra palm, differing in the green undersides of the fronds, the rusty scurf coating the crownshaft, and the longer, vertically pendulous panicles of pale lilac flowers. It grows rapidly when young, and is usually taller than the Alexandra palm at first flowering. Occurring on the subtropical Australian east coast mainly south of the Tropic of Capricorn, it prefers slightly cooler climates and can tolerate extremely light frosts. It is also more shade-tolerant. ZONE 9.

ARCTOSTAPHYLOS
Ericaceae

This genus of evergreen shrubs or, rarely, small trees includes one species widely distributed through cool climates of the northern hemisphere but all others are native to western North America or Mexico. They are tough plants with very woody stems, smallish leathery leaves and small clusters of white or pink bell-shaped flowers. Some of the Californian species from the famous 'chaparral' evergreen scrub of the coastal ranges can survive the fires that periodically ravage it. They mostly have very ornamental bark; purple, red or orange and peeling in thin shreds or flakes. The seed, enclosed in a small fleshy fruit, is difficult to germinate, which may explain why these attractive plants are seldom cultivated; treatment with fire or acid may assist germination.

Arctostaphylos hookeri

Known in the wild only from a small stretch of the Californian coast near Monterey, this is a low-growing, almost prostrate shrub with smooth dark reddish brown bark, a coating of downy hairs on the young branches and small shiny light green leaves. The clusters of waxy flowers are dull pink and the small pale red fruits are sometimes borne in profusion. It suits a situation where it can spill over rocks or a retaining wall. ZONE 8.

Arctostaphylos manzanita
MANZANITA

The manzanita (Spanish for 'little apple') grows to 8 ft (2.5 m) in height and spread, more in its native California, but its growth is slow. A stiff, woody shrub, it has very thick oval leaves which are coated in a whitish scurf when young, giving the foliage a grey cast. Its bark is a striking reddish brown but tends to be concealed by peeling strips of duller, older bark. In early spring tight clusters of small urn-shaped deep pink flowers appear and may persist for many weeks, followed by ½ in (1 cm) red-brown berries. A sun-loving plant requiring well-drained soil, it tolerates long summer droughts. ZONE 8.

Archontophoenix cunninghamiana

Archontophoenix alexandrae (below)

Arctostaphylos manzanita

Arctostaphylos hookeri

Arctostaphylos manzanita

Arctostaphylos uva-ursi
BEARBERRY

This hardy low shrub ranges in the wild through most colder regions of the northern hemisphere in Eurasia and North America. Rather variable in habit, it is best known as a completely prostrate form which can cascade over walls, embankments or large rocks forming curtains of neat, dark green foliage that develops the most intense red tones in autumn and winter, and springy branches that become very woody at the base. In late spring it bears small clusters of dull pink, almost globular flowers, followed by green berries that ripen to red. By far the most easily grown species, it is readily propagated from cuttings. 'Point Reyes' is a drought tolerant cultivar. ZONE 4.

ARGYROCYTISUS
Fabaceae
MT ATLAS BROOM

This genus of only one species was previously included with many other brooms in the genus *Cytisus*. A large evergreen shrub or small tree from the Atlas and Rif Mountains of Morocco, it is distinctive for its dense foliage with leaves of 3 leaflets that are exceptionally large for a broom and coated in silky hairs giving them a beautiful silvery sheen. Spikes of yellow pea-flowers terminate the branches, followed by flattened hairy pods. As might be expected of a North African plant, it prefers a sunny position and rather dry atmosphere. It is more frost-tender than most European brooms but nonetheless prefers a mild climate. The soil should have excellent drainage, though this shrub is tolerant of a wide range of garden conditions. Propagate from seed or semi-ripe cuttings.

Argyrocytisus battandieri

This shrub or small tree grows to about 12 ft (4 m) high and as much in width. Although the closely packed spikes of early summer golden yellow flowers are attractive, it is mainly grown for its beautiful silvery trifoliate leaves. The 2½ in (5 cm) leaflets are covered in fine hairs that give them a metallic sheen. ZONE 8.

ARONIA
Rosaceae
CHOKEBERRY

A member of the pome-fruit group of the rose family, *Aronia* consists of only 3 deciduous shrub species from North America, but these make fine garden shrubs of compact size with abundant displays of glossy red or black berries in late summer and autumn. Frost-hardy and not demanding as to soil, they will grow well in part-shade but respond to full sun with more profuse fruit and brighter autumn foliage. They are easily propagated from seed or cuttings. The foliage is prone to disfigurement by the 'pear and cherry slug', the larva of a sawfly.

Aronia arbutifolia
RED CHOKEBERRY

Occurring over a wide area of eastern USA, this shrub reaches 8 ft (2.5 m) in height and spread in gardens, more in the wild. Its habit is rather open, with multiple stems closely grouped at the base and glossy leaves that are downy on the undersides. Late spring sees its spreading branches dotted with clusters of attractive white flowers with pink stamens, while at summer's end the berries ripen brilliant red, persisting as the leaves turn from dull scarlet to deep red. ZONE 5.

Arctostaphylos uva-ursi

Arctostaphylos manzanita

Aronia arbutifolia

Argyrocytisus battandieri

Artocarpus heterophyllus

Artocarpus altilis

Aronia melanocarpa

Atherosperma moschatum

Aronia melanocarpa
BLACK CHOKEBERRY

Very similar in foliage and flowers to the red chokeberry and originating in the same region of USA, the black chokeberry is a lower, more spreading shrub with more densely crowded stems. The leaves are less glossy and the berries, ripening a brilliantly glossy black, do not last long into autumn but fall soon after they ripen. ZONE 5.

ARTOCARPUS
Moraceae

Best known in the form of one of its many species, the breadfruit of Captain Bligh of the *Bounty* fame, *Artocarpus* is actually a very large tropical Asian genus of evergreen trees. It is closely related to *Ficus*, the fig genus, and in fact many of its species are hard to tell apart from figs when not in flower or fruit. Leaves, bark and twigs exude milky sap when damaged, and the minute greenish female flowers are crowded onto short fleshy spikes which after fertilization enlarge into aggregations of fleshy fruits, very large in the case of the species mentioned below. These edible-fruited species are cultivated in the wet tropics, thriving best in deep fertile well-drained soils in sheltered positions. Propagation is from seed, or more commonly from root-cuttings or aerial layers (marcotts) which perpetuate desirable clones.

Artocarpus altilis
BREADFRUIT

Despite its famous association with Tahiti, breadfruit is believed to be native to the Malay region, having been carried into the Pacific as much as 2,000 years ago by the colonizing Polynesians. It is very handsome for its foliage alone, with ascending branches bearing deeply incised leaves up to 30 in (75 cm) long, of a fresh green shade. Growth is rapid in younger stages, 10-year-old trees reaching about 25 ft (8 m) under good conditions; old trees are not much taller but develop a rounded, bushy crown. Flower-spikes are inconspicuous, the female ones developing into yellowish green, tough-skinned, globular fruit with very starchy flesh which is eaten after baking or boiling. ZONE 12.

Artocarpus heterophyllus
JACKFRUIT, JACA

This Southeast Asian species is easily confused with its close relative the chempedak (*Artocarpus integer*); both have similar gigantic compound fruits and leathery unlobed leaves, but the chempedak's fruit is slightly sweeter. The jackfruit tree grows to 30 ft (10 m) tall with a single main trunk and dense rounded crown of dark green leathery leaves. Hanging directly from the trunk and large branches, the fruits are irregular in shape and size but may be up to 24 in (60 cm) long and weigh up to 40 lb (18 kg)! Their outer surface is creamy brown with crowded small conical protuberances, and the sticky yellow or pink flesh contains many large brown seeds which are edible, as is the deliciously sweet though malodorous flesh. They are increasingly available at markets where Southeast Asian foods are sold. ZONE 11.

ASIMINA
Annonaceae

This small North American tree and shrub genus includes the most northerly—and cold-hardy—members of the custard-apple family. In the tropics this relatively primitive family shows enormous diversity with over 2,000 species, nearly all rainforest trees. *Asimina* comes from the American Indian name for the tree, adopted as the botanical name in 1763 by the French botanist Adanson. 'Pawpaw' is another of its Indian names. It should not be confused with the unrelated papaya (*Carica papaya*), a major tropical fruit sometimes also called papaw or pawpaw, though *Asimina* species also have edible fruit.

Asimina triloba
PAWPAW

A small deciduous tree to 35 ft (11 m), or a large shrub, the pawpaw is found in eastern USA from New Jersey to Florida and inland to Michigan and Texas. It has a slender habit but a rather bushy crown. The large leaves are broadest above the middle. The striking 2 in (5 cm) flowers have 6 deeply veined dull purple petals. Each flower may develop several yellowish fruits up to 5 in (12 cm) long, with sweet yellow or cream flesh. It occurs naturally as an understorey tree in deep, rich, moist soils in river valleys. Propagation is easy from the large seeds or by layering. ZONE 6.

ATHEROSPERMA
Atherospermataceae
BLACK SASSAFRAS, SOUTHERN SASSAFRAS

This genus of a single species occurs in the cool-temperate rainforests of Tasmania and south-eastern mainland Australia, commonly in association with the better known *Nothofagus* (southern beeches). Aromatic oily substances produced in the wood, bark and foliage include the compound safrole which is also found in the original North American sassafras (*Sassafras albidum*). It is these oils with their distinctive smell that earned it the name 'sassafras'. Sassafras oil, although used in traditional folk-medicine, is now regarded as dangerously poisonous.

Atherosperma moschatum

This evergreen, reaching almost 100 ft (30 m) in mountain gullies, appears conifer-like from a distance because of its fine greyish foliage and long-pointed crown. The narrow leaves in opposite pairs are dark green above and have a paler, furry coating beneath; they have a musk scent when crushed. Although rarely seen in cultivation, this species is worth growing in a large collection for its symmetrical shape and scattered small white flowers. It has been grown successfully in milder parts of Britain. ZONE 8.

ATHROTAXIS
Taxodiaceae

The island of Tasmania, with its cool-temperate rainforests, is unusually rich in conifers, including the extremely handsome *Athrotaxis*; this shows some resemblance in foliage and cones to the Japanese

Cryptomeria and American *Sequoiadendron* but its 3 species are much slower-growing and more compact in habit, though capable eventually of forming moderately large trees. Cultivation is not difficult in a cool, moist climate. Do not expect them to reach tree size for at least two or three decades, but as dense, bushy saplings they are highly ornamental.

Athrotaxis cupressoides
TASMANIAN PENCIL PINE

Occurring wild in the mountains of western Tasmania at the upper limits of tree growth, this species reaches a height of 50 ft (15 m) but is usually smaller with dense, symmetrical growth and a paler green foliage than most conifers, even slightly yellowish. The branchlets, covered in appressed scale-leaves, are much thicker and fleshier than in any of the true cypresses. Where conditions allow it to thrive it makes a handsome garden tree, but patience is required—even to reach shrub size may take 10 years or more. ZONE 7.

Athrotaxis selaginoides
KING BILLY PINE

Late last century this was one of Tasmania's most important timber trees, yielding a soft, dark reddish timber which resembles redwood (*Sequoia*), but the best stands have long since been exhausted. Its slow growth is often apparent in its wood: some samples have more than 30 annual growth rings per inch (2.5 cm) of diameter! The King Billy pine can grow to 100 ft (30 m) with a trunk diameter of 8 ft (2.5 m), though half that height is more usual. Leaves are long, incurved and sharp-pointed, bright green on top with contrasting white-banded undersides. Small orange-brown cones appear in spring. The soft reddish brown bark is very thick. ZONE 8.

AUCUBA
Cornaceae
AUCUBA, SPOTTED LAUREL

This is a small East Asian genus of shrubs, valued for their tolerance of heavy shade and large, often colourful, evergreen leaves. Clusters of large red berries appear in autumn but, with flowers of different sexes on different plants, it is only the females that fruit. The one species generally grown has given rise to many cultivars with variegated leaves in a range of patterns. It is a tough, resilient plant, tolerant of neglect, pollution and heavy shading but responding to better treatment and stronger light with more luxuriant growth. The long-lived but tender leaves should be protected from wind damage.

Aucuba japonica

Usually seen as a shrub of 4–6 ft (1.5–2 m), the Japanese aucuba will continue to spread by basal sprouting and self-layering of its weak, soft-wooded stems and, as it thickens up, the mass of stems will support one another, allowing an ultimate height of around 10 ft (3 m). The thick, soft, glossy leaves are up to 10 in (25 cm) long and very variably toothed. Sprays of small reddish flowers in spring may be followed by drooping clusters of ½ in (1 cm) long red berries in early autumn. One of the oldest cultivars is 'Variegata' (female), which has leaves densely spotted with yellow. 'Crotonifolia' (male) is among the best of many other cultivars with leaves more heavily splashed with yellow. ZONE 7.

AUSTROCEDRUS
Cupressaceae
CHILEAN CEDAR

This tree, the only member of its genus, is a conifer of the *Thuja* type, with flattened sprays of branchlets which are themselves strongly flattened, and small, narrow cones consisting of weak, hardly woody scales. In *Austrocedrus* the branchlets are quite fine and fern-like, attractively marked with bluish bands on the undersides.

Austrocedrus chilensis

Known as a timber tree in Chile, where it occurs on the Andean slopes at altitudes of 3,000–6,000 ft (900–1,800 m), the sole species of *Austrocedrus* can reach 80 ft (25 m). Young trees have a densely columnar habit but with age the crown lifts higher above a bare trunk and narrow cone of branches. The grey bark has fine scales, while the reddish wood is fragrant, durable and easily worked, in demand for fine cabinet work. Some trees have more bluish foliage than others and seedlings can be selected for this. In a reasonably moist climate it makes moderately fast growth. ZONE 7.

AVERRHOA
Oxalidaceae

It is hard to believe that these tropical fruit trees are close relatives of the humble *Oxalis* or wood-sorrels, some species of which are detested weeds. Until, that is, we look at the flower structure, with 5 overlapping pink or red petals, and the 5-angled fruit, which in miniature in *Oxalis* split open to scatter tiny seeds rather than remaining fleshy as in *Averrhoa*. The genus consists of only 2 species from Southeast Asia; *A. carambola* and *A. bilimbi*, the bilimbi or picklefruit which is of lesser importance as a commercial fruit. These are small trees with densely twiggy crowns and short pinnate leaves, some of which yellow and drop in the dry season. The slightly fragrant flowers appear in short lateral clusters from the old wood and the fruits, which enlarge and ripen quite slowly, hang in clusters from the branches. The trees are easily grown in full sun in tropical and warmer subtropical climates, making fine small shade trees. Propagation is from seed or more commonly by air-layers (marcotts) which preserve desirable clonal characteristics.

Averrhoa carambola
CARAMBOLA, STAR FRUIT, FIVE-CORNER

In cultivation this species normally makes a round-headed small tree about 12 ft (4 m) high. The leaflets of the compound leaves have the curious habit of folding together after being touched or at night. It flowers and fruits through much of the year, but with major flushes of flower in the middle of the wet and the middle of the dry season. The large, ornamental fruits ripen through pale yellow, when their flavour is pleasantly acid, to deep golden orange, when they become sweet and deliciously tangy, reminiscent of passionfruit. ZONE 11.

AVICENNIA
Avicenniaceae

This mangrove genus, of 6 species, occurs on seashores and in estuaries throughout the tropics and elsewhere in the southern hemisphere, ranging as far south as New Zealand's North Island and the eastern shores of South Africa. They are small to medium-sized, spreading trees with smallish, glossy, thick-

Averrhoa carambola

Austrocedrus chilensis

Aucuba japonica 'Crotonifolia'

Austrocedrus chilensis

Azara serrata

Avicennia marina

textured leaves in opposite pairs. Flowers are small with fleshy petals in stalked clusters near the branch tips and are followed by thin-walled fruits, each containing a single large seed which actually germinates on the tree, producing a thick taproot. After falling, the seeds may be carried away on receding tides; if stranded again on an exposed mudbank they can rapidly take root and colonize the new habitat. Another feature of *Avicennia* is the upward-growing aerial roots, stiff prongs which emerge from the mud to take in oxygen. Mangroves such as these are rarely if ever cultivated, but they cannot be overlooked as the trees that dominate such an extensive and difficult habitat as the intertidal zone.

Avicennia marina
GREY MANGROVE

This is the common *Avicennia* in tropical Asia, Africa and Australasia, occurring over a vast area, with at least 3 regional subspecies. All are small trees, 30 ft (10 m) or less in height. In temperate regions it forms pure stands in estuaries but in the tropics it is mixed with other, unrelated mangroves. The pointed leaves, longer and thinner in the tropical races, are whitish on the undersides and the small yellow-orange flowers appear in late summer (late dry to early wet season in the tropics). The hard, heavy wood is used for a variety of purposes. It is so dense that it sinks in water. ZONE 10.

AZADIRACHTA
Meliaceae
NIM, NEEM

Only one species belongs to this genus which is closely related to *Melia*; despite a similarity in growth-habit, *Azadirachta* is easily distinguished by its leaves being pinnate, not bipinnate as in *Melia*, with more regular ranks of leaflets which are curved in a sickle-like fashion. The leaves are deciduous in severe dry seasons but in better-watered situations are evergreen. Sprays of small white flowers at the branch tips are followed by profuse ovoid yellow fruits, which are eaten by birds. In its native India and Sri Lanka the nim has long been renowned for its medicinal and insecticidal uses, and its potential value is being increasingly recognized in other warm countries. It is also popular as a shade tree and for streets and parks, but it is susceptible to stem borers and termites, and sometimes suckers from the roots. Propagation can be effected from seed, tip cuttings or suckers, but it can be difficult to establish young plants in the ground in drier regions due to the shallowness of their roots, necessitating mulching or frequent watering.

Azadirachta indica

In its native southern Asia the nim grows in dry coastal forests on deep sandy soils. Planted specimens are mostly under 30 ft (10 m) tall with a dense rounded crown. Flowering occurs in the late dry season; fruits appear shortly after. ZONE 11.

Azara microphylla

Avicennia marina (below)

AZALEA
see RHODODENDRON

AZARA
Flacourtiaceae

Neat, glossy evergreen foliage and massed small yellow flowers characterize this temperate South American genus of shrubs and small trees. While they are quite attractive plants, azaras develop a certain 'legginess' with age. The 15 or so species cover a range of frost-hardiness and moisture requirements, including as they do trees from the Chilean subantarctic rainforests of the south as well as some from drier evergreen scrubs of the lower Andean slopes further north. Propagate from cuttings in summer.

Azara lanceolata

This southern Chilean azara is perhaps the most graceful species in growth-habit and foliage, making a slender shrub or small tree to 20 ft (7 m) with weak, drooping branches. The narrow, toothed, glossy dark green leaves are each accompanied by a much smaller 'leaf' (actually a stipule) attached at the same point on the stem, producing a distinctive pattern. In spring it produces from the leaf axils short clusters of small golden yellow flowers consisting mainly of stamens, which can make a fine show. It needs a mild humid climate and a very sheltered position for best results. ZONE 8.

Azara microphylla

This fairly erect small tree may reach 20 ft (7 m) in the garden, more in the wild in its native Chile and western Argentina. A vigorous grower, it has fine foliage, rather like a box (*Buxus*) though much more open in habit. In late winter it produces numerous small flower clusters, dull gold and delightfully fragrant, half hidden under the leaf sprays. This is the hardiest and most adaptable member of the genus, but it has been known to be damaged by frost in southern England. The cultivar 'Variegata' has leaves attractively variegated with cream. ZONE 7.

Azara serrata

This small tree grows to around 30 ft (10 m) in the wild in Chile, but in cultivation is usually seen as a shrub of 10–15 ft (3–5 m), often with a twiggy habit and rather sparse foliage. The glossy green leaves are thick-textured, with a broad blunt apex and coarse teeth. Stalked clusters of fragrant deep golden flowers are strung along all the branches in late spring or early summer. This species is perhaps the showiest in flower and in cool climates is easily grown in milder coastal areas. ZONE 8.

Backhousia citriodora

Backhousia citriodora

Banksia coccinea

Baeckea virgata dwarf cultivar

BACKHOUSIA
Myrtaceae

This is a small genus of evergreen trees and shrubs from coastal forests in warm-temperate latitudes of eastern Australia. The white flowers have small petals and prominent stamens and develop into small dry fruits with a persistent calyx attached. Cultivated for their attractive, often aromatic foliage, they prefer part-shade and moist humus-rich soil with good drainage; they do not tolerate salty winds or low temperatures. Some early shaping may be necessary to establish a single trunk. Propagation is from fresh seed in autumn, or from cuttings.

Backhousia citriodora
LEMON-SCENTED MYRTLE

A rainforest tree that is now extremely rare in its native southeastern Queensland, this species is widely planted in Australia as well as in some other countries with a warm-temperate climate. Growing to 10–30 ft (3–10 m) in cultivation, it has an erect, bushy growth-habit with a dense crown of dark green, lance-shaped leaves which have a clean, fragrant lemon scent when crushed; they yield a commercial oil when distilled and can be used for potpourri. Rounded clusters of greenish white flowers cover the tree in summer. It tolerates annual trimming to shape and limit height. ZONE 10.

BAECKEA
Myrtaceae

These evergreen shrubs, mostly heathlike in habit, are found all over Australia, growing in many habitats from subalpine marshes to exposed coastal heaths. A few species occur outside Australia, extending as far as southern China. They vary in size from wiry prostrate shrubs to tall, erect shrubs, almost small trees. They are grown for their neat foliage and attractive flowers which resemble tea-tree (*Leptospermum*) flowers but are mostly smaller. Several species make good rock-garden plants. They prefer full sun or part-shade, and moist but well-drained soil. Propagation is most readily achieved from cuttings. Plants benefit from a light pruning of flowering shoots after the petals have fallen.

Baeckea virgata
TWIGGY HEATH-MYRTLE, TALL BAECKEA

A bushy, erect shrub growing to a height and spread of 10 ft (3 m) or occasionally taller, this plant grows in a wide range of climatic and soil conditions but does best on well-drained, elevated sites away from the coast. It is valued for its dainty white flowers which are borne in abundance from late spring to late summer and is useful for screening purposes. Some remarkable miniature cultivars with extraordinarily fine, dense foliage have appeared recently. ZONE 8.

BANKSIA
Proteaceae

Named after the botanist Sir Joseph Banks, who discovered this genus in 1770, banksias are found all over Australia, but with the greatest number of species in the southwest. Habit and foliage vary, but all species are characterized by the strikingly dense fuzzy heads of small flowers, mostly cylindrical in shape, and odd woody fruits that protrude from among the dead flowers. Leaves are mostly long and narrow, often with toothed edges, and contain much woody tissue so that they remain stiff and springy even when dead. This 'sclerophyll' habit is believed to be an adaptation to soils very deficient in plant nutrients. As well as being attractive garden plants banksias have attracted much commercial interest as cut flowers, their rigid structure making them long-lasting; the more striking species are now grown in plantations (especially in Hawaii) for this purpose. All species prefer well-drained, sandy soil, free of added nitrates and phosphates. They do best in full sun, and some but not all species are frost-hardy. Plants in containers need moderate water during growth periods but little at other times. Regular light tip pruning maintains shape and foliage density. Propagate from seed, taking care to plant seedlings out before they become potbound. Some dwarf and prostrate groundcover forms of otherwise upright species are proving to be successful.

Banksia coccinea
SCARLET BANKSIA

One of the most beautiful species, from the far south of Western Australia and prized by the cut flower industry, the scarlet banksia has short, wide, erect brushes from winter through summer. The broad serrated leaves are medium green, paler underneath. The shrub grows to a height of about 10 ft (3 m), usually with a rather stiff, narrow habit. It can make rapid growth but does not always flower readily, and frequently succumbs to root rot fungi in climates with wet summers. ZONE 9.

Banksia 'Giant Candles'

A hybrid of 2 widespread east coast Australian species, *B. ericifolia* and *B. spinulosa*, 'Giant Candles' grows to about 12 ft (4 m), and is a dense shrub with abundant bronze-yellow flower-spikes which may be as much as 16 in (40 cm) long, tipped red through the cooler months. Tough and vigorous like its parents, it is a bushier shrub than either, though ultimately it becomes rather large and straggly. *B. spinulosa* 'Birthday Candles' is a dwarf cultivar with smaller golden bronze flower-spikes. ZONE 8.

Banksia integrifolia
COAST BANKSIA

This salt-tolerant species grows naturally along the east coast of Australia and has distinctive silver-backed leaves. At maturity it forms a gnarled tree of up to 50 ft (15 m) with a trunk 18 in (45 cm) in diameter, smaller on exposed sites. Lime green flowers fading to yellow form cylindrical spikes about 4 in (10 cm) long in the cooler months. The leaves are dull green above, silvery below. In cultivation *B. integrifolia* makes remarkably rapid growth, especially on deep sandy soils; it is a little more frost tolerant than most banksias. ZONE 9.

Banksia lemanniana

This is one of an unusual small group of Western Australian *Banksia* species in which the flower-spike points down toward the ground. Occurring close to the far southern coast in scrubland on stony ground, it makes a rather sparse shrub up to 15 ft (5 m) tall. The smallish, stiff leaves are jaggedly toothed, the new growths coated with rusty hairs, and the 4 in (10 cm) long flower-spikes are lemon-yellow. It blooms in late spring and early summer. ZONE 10.

Banksia lemanniana

Banksia integrifolia

Banksia integrifolia

Banksia 'Giant Candles'

Banksia 'Giant Candles' (right)

Banksia marginata
SILVER BANKSIA

The most cold-hardy of the banksias, this variable species occurs over a wide area of southeastern Australia including Tasmania, extending to altitudes of almost 5,000 ft (1,500 m) in the Snowy Mountains. Some forms from poor heath vegetation are dense, spreading shrubs of about 6 ft (2 m) in height, while the forms from mountain forests are slender and very upright small trees to as much as 40 ft (12 m), becoming broader and gauntly branched with age. The smallish, oblong, dark green leaves are toothed only at the apex and are silvery white beneath. Small dull yellow flower-spikes appear throughout the year, mainly in the cooler months. The compact forms make attractive garden shrubs, while taller forms are useful for screens and windbreaks. It is also a useful coastal plant, resistant to salt damage. Plants can be pruned to maintain shape. ZONE 8.

Banksia menziesii
FIREWOOD BANKSIA

Slow growing, the Western Australian *B. menziesii* can vary from a 10 ft (3 m) shrub to a small tree of 30 ft (10 m). Flower-spikes, from late summer through winter, are usually pinkish or reddish with a coating of silver hairs, but may also be pure yellow or occasionally dark or rusty brown. The hundreds of flowers on a spike start to open from the base and progress upward, producing the 'acorn' effect common to a number of western species. In the garden the firewood banksia needs full sun and free-draining, sandy soil. An organic mulch will help suppress weeds and reduce moisture loss. ZONE 10.

Banksia ornata
DESERT BANKSIA

The 'desert' in this common name should not be taken too seriously, being a local term for scrubby wilderness in western Victoria where this species is common on deep sandy soils. Growing to a height of 10 ft (3 m) with a spread of 5 ft (1.5 m), it is a handsome shrub with erect stems branching from the base and greyish, saw-toothed, wedge-shaped leaves. Stout silvery grey or pale yellow flower cones appear through summer and autumn. *Banksia ornata* is easily grown on well-drained sandy soil in an open sunny position. ZONE 9.

Banksia prionotes
ACORN BANKSIA

This fast-growing, open, small tree from Western Australia has grey bark and hairy branchlets with dull green, narrow, toothed leaves. Spectacular, orange-yellow flower cones opening from woolly white buds are borne in autumn and winter. It grows to a height of 18 ft (6 m) eventually forming a domed crown, though it is of shrubby habit in its early years. It can be grown in sandy, alkaline soils in areas with dry summer climates but does not thrive where summers are wet. This species produces outstanding cut flowers. ZONE 10.

Banksia serrata
OLD MAN BANKSIA, SAW BANKSIA

This east coast Australian species from sandstone soils is distinguished by its tough, gnarled appearance, leathery, saw-toothed leaves and thick, wrinkled, fire-resistant bark on a short crooked trunk. Even its bristly grey fruiting spikes with protruding fruits like small noses or chins make its common name, old man banksia, an appropriate one. Large greenish cream flower-spikes appear from summer through autumn. In the wild it makes a tree of up to 30 ft (10 m), ranging from coastal dunes to barren, cold, sandstone plateaus. It is easily cultivated, long lived and moderately frost-hardy. ZONE 9.

BARKLYA
Caesalpiniaceae

An Australian genus closely related to *Bauhinia* and consisting of one evergreen tree species only, *Barklya* is confined to a small area of rainforest in central-coastal Queensland and is now rare in the wild. Producing a summer display of brilliant gold blossom, it makes a handsome addition to warm climate parks, gardens or streetscapes. *Barklya* is subtropical and best grown in a frost-free climate; it requires full sun, fertile well-drained soil and plentiful summer water. Growth can be slow; the tree may take many years to reach flowering size if conditions are less than ideal. Propagation is normally from seeds, sown as soon as they ripen in autumn.

Barklya syringifolia
GOLD BLOSSOM TREE

A handsome tree to around 50 ft (15 m) in its natural habitat, this species is usually much smaller in gardens with a densely bushy, rounded crown. It has glossy dark green heart-shaped leaves, similar in shape to those of lilacs, and the crown is decked with stiff, erect spikes of crowded golden pea-flowers in early summer. They are followed by small seed pods. ZONE 10.

BARLERIA
Acanthaceae

This is a large genus of shrubs and subshrubs from the tropics of Asia, America and Africa. They have

Banksia ornata

Barklya syringifolia

Banksia serrata (left)

Banksia marginata (below)

simple leaves in opposite pairs. Flowers are generally tubular and 2-lipped, emerging from between overlapping bracts on short spikes terminating stems or in upper leaf axils. These are soft-stemmed, quick-growing plants, used in tropical gardens for quick effects and as bedding plants. In cooler climates they may be grown as indoor plants but require strong light. They are easily propagated from cuttings.

Barleria cristata
PHILIPPINES VIOLET

A shrub of around 3 ft (1 m) high, the Philippines violet is densely branched from ground level. For much of the year it produces small clusters of 2-lipped flowers from among bristly edged bracts in the upper leaf axils. Flowers vary from violet-blue to mauve, pink or white. It prefers a sheltered humid position in sun or part-shade. ZONE 10.

BARRINGTONIA
Lecythidaceae

This is a large genus of evergreen or dry-season-deciduous trees with species scattered throughout the tropics, from Africa eastward to southern China, and south to northern Australia and the Pacific Islands. They occur mostly in lowland areas, some near beaches or brackish-water estuaries, or in freshwater swamp forests. They have a somewhat distinctive habit of growth, with branches repeatedly forking in a candelabra-like fashion and terminating in rosettes of paddle-shaped leaves. Flowers are very striking, on usually pendulous spikes from the branch tips, with short petals and numerous long stamens. In many countries where they occur barringtonias are used as fish poisons: bark, leaves and fruit all contain the poison and are pounded or grated then thrown in the water to stupefy the fish. Some of the species have proved easy to cultivate in the tropics, making fine ornamental trees for parks and streets. They do best on sites with permanent subsoil moisture. Propagation is from the large seeds, which may take several months to germinate.

Barringtonia asiatica
FISH-KILLER TREE

Washed up on beaches all around the Pacific and Indian Oceans you will find large brown seeds that are egg-shaped in outline but square in cross section, with sharp angles. They are the fruit of this evergreen tree which grows in coastal areas of tropical Asia, the Malay archipelago and northern Australia. The buoyant seeds enable its dispersal across short ocean gaps. It normally grows to a height of about 20 ft (7 m) with multiple trunks and a vase-shaped crown. Leaves are dark green and glossy and the large flowers, appearing at the end of the dry season, are red and white. ZONE 12.

BAUERA
Baueraceae

Occurring naturally in eastern Australia, this small genus of evergreen shrubs is grown mainly for its star-shaped pink or white flowers. Branches are thin and wiry, often scrambling among other shrubs, and the small leaves are in whorls of 6 at each node, from which arise also the flowers on very fine stalks. Coming from a mild moist climate, they are moderately frost-hardy and grow best in moist, sandy or peaty soil in a sunny or part-shaded position. They appreciate soil kept cool by the shade of taller plants. Propagation is from cuttings. Light pruning after flowering produces a bushier plant and encourages abundant flowers.

Bauera rubioides
DOG ROSE, RIVER ROSE

Occurring naturally in higher-rainfall areas of south-eastern Australia including Tasmania, this attractive species grows in moist, shady places mostly on banks of small streams. It has a broad, straggling habit with a height up to 3 ft (1 m) and often greater spread. The glossy dark green leaves become reddish in winter, and bowl-shaped, deep carmine-pink to white flowers appear from winter to mid-summer. ZONE 8.

BAUHINIA
Caesalpiniaceae

This is a variable genus of evergreen and dry-season-deciduous trees, shrubs and climbers from the warmer latitudes of Asia, the Americas, Africa and Australia. All have characteristic 2-lobed leaves but are grown for their beautiful flowers whose likeness to orchids or butterflies has given rise to the common names of several species. The flattened brown seed pods which follow often persist on the branches for months. Bauhinias do best in tropical and subtropical areas and need protection from frost and cold winds. Full sun and light, fertile, well-drained soil suit them best. Propagate from seed.

Bauhinia × *blakeana*

B. blakeana resembles *B. variegata* in its compact growth and lavish display of orchid-like, scented flowers in spring, though they are usually a deeper, richer shade of magenta or even crimson. It has the advantage over *B. variegata* as an ornamental tree of not setting nearly so many brown seed pods, so its appearance after flowering is tidier and more attractive. Consequently many people prefer it. It is native to southern China and is the floral emblem of Hong Kong. ZONE 10.

Bauhinia galpinii
PRIDE-OF-DE-KAAP

An evergreen shrub with a sprawling, horizontal habit, this is the most spectacular shrub in its genus. It is a useful plant for large gardens because of its spreading growth-habit; it can reach a height of 10 ft (3 m) with a spread of 12 ft (4 m), though it can be kept smaller by pruning after flowering. The leaves have rounded lobes resembling a pair of wings, and showy clusters of apricot to brick red fragrant flowers are borne in summer and autumn. Fast growing, it will endure mild frosts and long periods without water. ZONE 9.

Bauhinia × *blakeana*

Bauera rubioides

Barringtonia asiatica

Barleria cristata

Beaucarnea recurvata

Berberis × *ottawensis* 'Superba'

Berberis × *ottawensis* 'Superba'

Bauhinia variegata

Bauhinia monandra

Bauhinia monandra

A rank-growing tropical species from the West Indies and northern South America, this species makes a spreading, multi-stemmed shrub or small tree to 20 ft (7 m) high with spreading branches and coarse foliage, the pale green leaves with only a small notch at the apex. At the end of the dry season and well into the wet it produces a succession of orchid-like flowers at the branch ends, the large petals opening cream but aging to flesh-pink with a dramatic red splash on the upper petal. They are unusual in having only a single stamen. This species is easily grown from seed. ZONE 11.

Bauhinia variegata
ORCHID TREE, MOUNTAIN EBONY

This lovely small tree bears abundant, fragrant, large orchid-like flowers in spring and intermittently in summer. These vary from tree to tree, from near-white to rose-pink, but always with a deeper shade on the upper petal. It grows to 15–25 ft (5–8 m), larger in the tropics, with a short trunk and spreading branches, and is half-hardy. In tropical climates it is semi-evergreen, in cooler locations almost deciduous. It's an attractive small street tree if given adequate water. 'Candida' has fragrant white flowers. Prune for early shaping and to ensure a single trunk. ZONE 9.

BEAUCARNEA
Agavaceae

Most commonly seen as potted plants, these evergreen trees and shrubs from desert regions of Mexico and far southern USA, related to yuccas, are grown for their remarkable thickened stems and long, thin, grass-like leaves. They can be grown outdoors in mild to warm climates, in full sun and well-drained, fertile soil. Water well while growing, but sparingly at other times for they are drought tolerant. As indoor potted plants they can reach ceiling height, flourishing in the warm, dry atmosphere of centrally heated rooms. Propagate from seed in spring or from suckers.

Beaucarnea recurvata
PONYTAIL PALM

This slow-growing evergreen tree, indigenous to the dry regions of Texas and Mexico, has adapted to arid conditions by storing water in its swollen base, which tapers to a palm-like trunk bearing a few branches with long, straplike, downward-curving leaves. Large feathery panicles of cream flowers are produced at the stem apex. Old specimens can achieve massive dimensions; the swollen base can be up to 13 ft (4 m) wide, from which emerge multiple stems up to 15–20 ft (5–7 m) tall. It resembles a yucca rather than a palm and can provide an interesting sculptural form in a dry spot in a warm garden. It can also be grown in a pot, indoors or outdoors, as long as it receives good light and moderate water. ZONE 9.

BEILSCHMIEDIA
Lauraceae

These evergreen trees and shrubs are grown for their foliage. Half-hardy, they are warm-climate plants and require a fertile, well-drained soil and an open sunny position. They are propagated from seed.

Beilschmiedia tarairi
TARAIRE

Growing to a height and spread of 15–65 ft (5–20 m), but usually no more than 30 ft (10 m) in garden situations, this New Zealand native is an ideal specimen tree for large gardens. Moderately fast growing, it has a slender, straight trunk and attractive reddish brown young growth, the leaves turning dark green at maturity. Insignificant small sprays of greenish flowers are borne in summer, followed by large, oval, purple fruits. ZONE 9.

BERBERIS
Berberidaceae
BARBERRY

The barberries are a large group of mostly very hardy shrubs, both evergreen and deciduous, with densely massed canes and weak spines where the small leaves join the stems. Small yellow, cream, orange or reddish flowers are followed by elongated, fleshy fruits. Most species come from temperate East Asia, a few from Europe and several from Andean South America. Barberries are easy to grow and thrive in most soil types; they are useful for hedges, withstanding hard pruning. Full sun suits them best. Propagate from seeds or cuttings. In some countries there are restrictions on growing barberries because some species can harbour the overwintering phase of the wheat rust fungus.

Berberis darwinii
DARWIN BARBERRY

The showiest of several evergreen species from Chile and Argentina, all with small leaves and neat clusters of deep yellow to orange flowers, *B. darwinii* has small dark green, glossy leaves with holly-like toothing and short, dense clusters of small bright yellow flowers in late winter and spring. It makes a shrub 6 ft (2 m) high and about as wide with irregular, open branching habit; the branches are less spiny than in most other species. It has been crossed with *B. empetrifolia* to produce the hybrid *B.* × *stenophylla*, with several named clones including the dwarf 'Corallina Compacta' and the tall and very floriferous 'Crawley Gem'. ZONE 7.

Berberis × ottawensis

This hybrid between *B. thunbergii* and *B. vulgaris*, bred in Ottawa early this century, is best known in the form of the clone 'Superba' which is similar to and often confused with *B. thunbergii* 'Atropurpurea' but is taller, around 6 ft (2 m), and more vigorous, with the new growths bronze-red rather than dark purplish. It is a popular and very hardy deciduous shrub with densely massed stems, useful for hedging or to provide contrast among green-leafed shrubs. ZONE 3.

Berberis thunbergii
THUNBERG BARBERRY, JAPANESE BARBERRY

This is the most widely planted of the barberries, though usually as one of its cultivars rather than the wild form. Native to Japan, it is a low-growing deciduous shrub (almost evergreen in warmer climates), only 5 ft (1.5 m) in height, with densely massed stems and small, neatly rounded leaves. Its spines are not particularly fierce. The small, not very decorative, bell-shaped flowers which appear in mid-spring, are greenish yellow with dull red stripes. The cultivar 'Atropurpurea' has deep purplish brown foliage turning a metallic bronze-black in late autumn. 'Atropurpurea Nana' (also known as 'Little Favourite') is a dwarf, very neat bun-shaped plant only 12–18 in (30–45 cm) high with similar toning plus green tints. 'Keller's Surprise' is compact and rather narrow with green or bronze leaves splashed with pink. ZONE 4.

Berberis vulgaris
COMMON BARBERRY

Ranging in the wild across Europe, northern Africa and western and central Asia, this is doubtfully native to Britain, though it is a common hedgerow plant there. A deciduous shrub 6–10 ft (2–3 m) tall with crowded spiny canes and round-tipped leaves with bristly teeth, it makes a fine show of yellow blossom in late spring but is at its most spectacular in autumn when laden with bright coral-red, cylindrical fruit. These are edible but have a strong acid taste, and have medicinal properties. The common barberry is easily grown and extremely hardy and drought resistant. It is naturalized in North America and is the main species harbouring wheat rust fungus there. ZONE 3.

Berberis wilsoniae
WILSON BARBERRY

Deciduous, or almost evergreen in warmer climates, this Chinese species has small, narrow, toothless leaves with rounded tips and a densely bushy habit. It reaches a height of about 5 ft (1.5 m) but

Berberis darwinii

spreads into a broad mass of foliage, touching the ground. Rather inconspicuous yellow flowers from late spring to early summer are followed in autumn by abundant pink fruit which persist into winter, turning deeper red at the same time as the foliage takes on tints of yellow, orange and red. This highly ornamental species requires ample space. ZONE 5.

BETULA
Betulaceae
BIRCH

Trees of the far northern regions of the globe, birches are deeply woven into the folklore and mythology of Germany, Russia, the Scandinavian countries, and the indigenous North American nations, and have a myriad of uses in traditional societies there. But *Betula* has its greatest riches of species in China and the Himalaya. As landscape subjects birches are among the most admired of all trees, despite having inconspicuous flowers and fruit; their appeal lies in the sparkling white to pinkish brown trunks, combined with vivid green spring foliage and delicate tracery of winter twigs. The broad serrated leaves turn gold in autumn. Their fast early growth yet fairly modest final height are added advantages for use in gardens or streets. In nature birches grow in dense stands rather than scattered among other trees. To grow them successfully you need a climate cool enough for at least the occasional winter snowfall. Propagation is normally from the small winged seed, produced in millions from the cylindrical female catkins. Birches grow best in deep, well-drained soils but some adapt to poorer, shallower soils.

Betula albosinensis

The most beautiful feature of this western Chinese birch is its pale coppery orange-red bark; the new bark is coated with a thin bloom of white powder which is revealed as large loose plates of the previous shiny bark layer peel off. *B. albosinensis* makes a medium-sized

Berberis wilsoniae

Berberis thunbergii 'Atropurpurea Nana'

tree of 30–40 ft (10–13 m), often branching low; its jaggedly toothed leaves are up to 3 in (8 cm) long. A sheltered but sunny spot with reliable soil moisture suits it best, if you can find a nursery that stocks it. ZONE 6.

Betula alleghaniensis
YELLOW BIRCH

Largest of the North American birches, the yellow birch, formerly known as *Betula lutea*, can reach 100 ft (30 m) in height in its native mountains and valleys of eastern USA and south-eastern Canada. The straight, high-branched trunk has smooth cream to golden bronze bark which peels off in thin papery sheets. The leaves are more elongated than in most birches, strongly veined and with sharply toothed margins. The bark of the twigs is aromatic, containing an oil like oil of wintergreen which is distilled commercially. The timber is also valuable and the species is extensively cut for lumber. It makes a fine ornamental for large gardens or parks with its attractive bark and clear yellow autumn foliage. ZONE 4.

Betula lenta
BLACK BIRCH, CHERRY BIRCH

Another American species, closely related to the yellow birch and

Betula lenta

rather similar in foliage but not growing as large, this species has a more restricted range in eastern USA, mostly in the Appalachian mountain chain. The trunk is smooth and straight with shiny dark reddish brown to almost black bark, which doesn't peel but on older trees breaks up into scaly plates. It shares with yellow birch the aromatic twigs. It does not always thrive in cultivation but is worth growing with other birches for its contrasting bark colour. ZONE 5.

Betula nana
DWARF BIRCH

Apart from dwarf willows, this birch is the woody plant that grows closest to the North Pole. It is abundant over large areas above the Arctic Circle in Europe, Asia and North America. A low shrub only 2–4 ft (60–120 cm) high, it forms extensive thickets on the tundra, in bogs or on low hills. Further south it is restricted to high, bleak regions such as the Scottish Highlands and parts of the Rocky Mountains. The leaves are much smaller than in other birches, and rather thick textured. As a garden plant it can make an interesting shrub, especially for damp, boggy areas, but will not thrive in mild climates. ZONE 1.

Betula nigra
RIVER BIRCH

Widespread in warmer parts of eastern USA, *B. nigra*'s natural habitat is along river banks, forming thickets with trees such as elms, poplars and willows. With maturity it becomes broader-crowned, forking 10–20 ft (3–7 m) above ground into several arching trunks. Older trunks have dark, furrowed bark at the base, but in young trees it is smooth and whitish. Foliage is luxuriant; the leaves are triangular with irregularly toothed edges. Though most at home beside water, the river birch thrives in well-drained soil, reaching 30 ft (10 m). The cultivar 'Heritage' has striking smooth bark, cream, salmon-pink or pale brown, which peels off in large curling plates. ZONE 4.

Betula papyrifera
PAPER BIRCH, CANOE BIRCH

Famed for its tough papery bark, used by Native North Americans for their light but strong canoes, the paper birch is one of the most wide-ranging North American species, extending across Canada and Alaska, much of northern USA, and south to the mountains of North Carolina. As might be expected, it is extremely cold-hardy. It reaches 65 ft (20 m) in cultivation with a rather sparse crown. The largish leaves are broadly heart shaped or egg shaped. The white or cream bark peels off in thin, curling layers exposing new bark of a pale orange-brown. Its chief ornamental value is in the bark, at times a dazzling white. ZONE 2.

Betula pendula
SILVER BIRCH, WHITE BIRCH

The common birch of northern Europe, extending eastward to Siberia, the silver birch is also one of the most elegant birch species, with smooth grey-white bark and fine arching branchlets bearing small shimmering leaves. It is more widely cultivated than any other birch and one of the most trouble-free in terms of pests and diseases. Its height is average for a birch, around 30–50 ft (10–15 m) in temperate climates. However, in Scandinavia it can reach 65–80 ft (20–25 m) and is an important timber tree there. Many cultivars have been named including 'Dalecarlica', with deeply incised leaves and strongly weeping branches, and 'Youngii', with growth like a weeping willow and no leading shoot, requiring it to be grafted on a standard. ZONE 2.

Betula platyphylla
JAPANESE WHITE BIRCH

Occurring naturally in western and northern China, Japan, Korea, Mongolia and eastern Siberia, this species has several geographical varieties, of which the one common in the West is var. *japonica*, from Japan and the Okhotsk Peninsula of Siberia. In leaves and fruit this birch is similar to the silver birch, but is distinguished from the latter by its striking pure white bark. It is a vigorous grower, making a shapely large tree of 30 ft (10 m) or more. ZONE 4.

Betula populifolia
GREY BIRCH

Native to eastern USA and Canada, this is the American equivalent of the European silver birch, growing in the most inhospitable climates and behaving as a pioneer tree on denuded lands such as eroded river floodplains. It is a 20–40 ft (7–13 m) tall tree with smooth pale grey bark, a narrowly conical crown and slightly pendulous branch tips. The leaves are sometimes over 3 in (7 cm) long and drawn out at the tips into fine points. Although an important species in its native forests, it has less ornamental value than many other birches. This is one of the species that the Native Americans used to make their birch bark canoes. ZONE 2.

Betula pubescens
DOWNY BIRCH

This is one of the two common birches of Europe and very similar to the silver birch in geographic range, habitat and stature, but somewhat less ornamental, usually

Betula papyrifera

Betula nigra

Betula papyrifera

Betula nigra

Betula pendula

Bixa orellana

with a more brownish cream bark (sometimes lighter) and less pendulous branchlets. Its main botanical distinction is the fine down on young twigs, though to detect this requires close examination. It tolerates more poorly drained soil than the silver birch. ZONE 2.

Betula utilis
HIMALAYAN BIRCH

From middle altitudes in the Himalaya region, these medium to large trees have pale, smooth, peeling bark and broadly domed crowns. The leaves, dark green with paler undersides and irregularly toothed, are up to 3 in (8 cm) long. Most widely grown is var. *jacquemontii*, which has dazzling white or cream bark that peels off in horizontal bands. Several clones of this variety have been selected for outstanding bark qualities and named as cultivars. Forms with darker orange-brown barks have also been introduced to Western gardens. ZONE 7.

BIXA
Bixaceae

Only 2 species belong to this tropical American genus, of which one is cultivated in warmer regions around the world, both for its ornamental value in gardens and for the fat-soluble orange dye that coats its abundant seeds which is used to colour foodstuffs such as butter. Although this dye (annatto) was largely displaced by synthetic dyes, it is coming back into favour as the demand for fully organic foods increases. South American Indians

Bixa orellana

used it as body paint and it has also been used to colour lipstick. The annatto plant is very distinctive, with its large heart-shaped, bronze-tinged leaves, erect clusters of attractive pink flowers like small single roses, and fruit capsules shaped like large almonds but covered in dense red bristles. It does well in all warm, frost-free climates and may be trained into a small tree or kept as a bushy shrub.

Bixa orellana
ANNATTO, LIPSTICK TREE

From the Amazon region of South America comes this colourful tree that can sometimes reach a height of 30 ft (10 m) but is more commonly seen as a spreading shrub of about 10 ft (3 m) or slightly less. The pink and white flowers are borne throughout summer, overlapping with the clusters of bristly red fruit that persist on the branches long after they have released their seed. ZONE 10.

Betula platyphylla var. *japonica*

Betula pubescens

BOLUSANTHUS
Fabaceae

This genus consists of one species: a slender tree grown for its flowers and as a specimen plant. Occurring naturally in open woodlands and grasslands of southern and eastern Africa, it does best in full sun, light to medium well-drained soil and an open position; it prefers hot summers with low rainfall. Propagate from seed in summer.

Betula utilis

Borassodendron machadonis

Boronia heterophylla

Boronia pinnata

Bolusanthus speciosus

Boronia megastigma 'Harlequin'

Bolusanthus speciosus
TREE WISTERIA

This small deciduous tree with a grey trunk reaches a height of 15–20 ft (5–7 m) or more. It is erect and slender with a narrow crown; the branches sometimes have a weeping habit. The small purple pea-shaped flowers, in pendent 6 in (15 cm) racemes resembling wisteria, appear in spring on leafless branches, followed by glossy green pinnate leaves. Large bunches of dry pods remain on the tree throughout summer. Mature specimens have neatly fissured bark. ZONE 9.

BOMBAX
Bombacaceae
SILK-COTTON TREE

This genus of soft-wooded, deciduous trees occurs in tropical forests of Asia, South America, Africa and Australia. Excellent specimen trees, they are grown in hot climate gardens for their foliage and flowers. Frost-tender, they require sun and a rich, moist, loamy soil. Young trees may need a little pruning and staking. Propagate from soft-tip cuttings in autumn or from seed when ripe.

Bombax ceiba
RED SILK-COTTON TREE

From Southeast Asia and northern Australia, this tall tree, formerly known as *Bombax malabaricum*, reaches a height of 100 ft (30 m) with a spread of about 40 ft (13 m). It has a buttressed, spiny trunk and, as the leaves fall in winter, clusters of large, waxy, bright red flowers appear at the ends of branches, followed by big seed pods. These pods are filled with a soft silky substance which is used as a substitute for kapok. ZONE 11.

BORASSODENDRON
Arecaceae

This genus consists of only 2 species of large tropical fan-leafed palms from the Malay Peninsula and Borneo. The name reflects the close relationship between this genus and the more common Asian *Borassus*, large palms which yield sugar and palm wine. The most striking feature of *Borassodendron* plants is the apparent disproportion between the slenderness of the tall straight trunk and the massive size of the long-stalked fronds, the segments of which are tangled and drooping. Male and female flowers appear on different trees, the male on very long, pendulous branched spikes which hang from among the frond bases, the female in shorter club-like spikes. Fruits are large nuts, packed in tight bunches. These dramatic palms will only grow well in the wet equatorial tropics, preferring very sheltered sites and deep moist alluvial soil or gravel.

Borassodendron machadonis

Named after an early 20th-century amateur botanist Machado, this species occurs sparsely in the Malay Peninsula, including far southern Thailand, in lowland rainforest. Its trunk is about 25 ft (8 m) tall with prominent rings, while the massive fronds are about 10 ft (3 m) long. Male flowers hang against the trunk in 5 ft (1.5 m) long branched spikes. Fruits are 4 in (10 cm) diameter. ZONE 12.

BORONIA
Rutaceae

Indigenous to Australia, this genus of small to medium-sized evergreen shrubs is noted for its attractive pink flowers (white, cream, brown or red in a minority of species) and aromatic foliage. Many of the species flower prolifically in the wild but do not adapt well to garden cultivation and are often short lived. They do best in sheltered positions in sun or part-shade, in well-drained acid soil which is kept moist. Tip pruning after flowering will maintain shape. Seeds are very difficult to germinate, so propagation is best achieved using semi-hardened tip cuttings.

Boronia heterophylla
RED BORONIA, KALGAN BORONIA

This erect, compact shrub to 5 ft (1.5 m) tall comes from the far south of Western Australia and has finely divided bright green leaves. Masses of rose-red, bell-shaped flowers are borne in late winter to early spring. A popular commercial cut flower in Australia, it prefers a cooler climate than some other boronias, and soil with added organic matter to ensure adequate moisture and provide a cool root run. ZONE 9.

Boronia megastigma
BROWN BORONIA

It is the sweet, heady perfume of this species, also from the far south of Western Australia, that is its main attraction. The hanging cup-shaped flowers that appear in late winter and spring are brownish purple to yellow-green outside and yellow-green inside. This shrub grows to 3 ft (1 m) and tolerates light frost, but is difficult to grow and short lived. A number of varieties have been selected with different flower coloration, but they often lack the fragrance of the typical species. 'Lutea' has yellow flowers and yellow-green leaves. 'Harlequin' is a brownish pink and white candy-striped variety. ZONE 9.

Boronia pinnata
FEATHER-LEAFED BORONIA

This open, sometimes semi-prostrate shrub grows to a height of 5 ft (1.5 m) with a spread of 4 ft (1.2 m). It has feathery, fern-like, strongly scented, dark green leaves with very narrow, somewhat irregular leaflets. Fragrant, star-shaped light pink or white flowers are borne in loose sprays in spring. 'Spring White' has clear white flowers. ZONE 9.

BOUVARDIA
Rubiaceae

A small genus of soft-wooded shrubs from Mexico and Central America, these frost-tender plants are grown for their attractive tubular flowers, which are popular with florists. They require a warm sunny position, preferably sheltered from wind. The soil needs to be fertile and well drained. Water well and feed regularly during the growing period. Cut back stems by half after flowering to maintain shape. Propagate from softwood or root cuttings. They are susceptible to attack by sap-sucking insects such as whitefly and mealybug. In cool climates they need a greenhouse.

Bouvardia longiflora
SCENTED BOUVARDIA

Previously known as *Bouvardia* 'Humboldtii', this tender, weak-stemmed evergreen grows to a height and spread of 3 ft (1 m) or more. Very brittle, it is easily damaged by strong winds. The strongly perfumed, snow-white flowers are about 1 in (2.5 cm) wide and are borne in terminal clusters in autumn and winter. The dark green leaves are small and lance-shaped. ZONE 10.

BRABEJUM
Proteaceae
WILD ALMOND

Although the South African flora is famous for its concentration of beautiful members of the family Proteaceae, including species of *Protea*, *Leucadendron*, *Leucospermum* and *Serruria*, these belong to a distinctly African tribe of the family, not closely related to its Australian and South American members. An exception to this is the single species of *Brabejum*, the wild almond, a member of the *Macadamia* tribe which has representatives in all landmasses where the family occurs. Like *Macadamia*, *Brabejum* has an edible nut, though the fruit is flattened and not so hard-shelled. It grows into a small tree 15 ft (5 m) high with long cane-like branches on which the leaves are arranged in whorls of up to 7 at regular intervals. In the axils of these appear short spikes of sweetly scented small white flowers, only a few of which develop into fruits. *Brabejum* has seldom been cultivated outside its native South Africa but is easily enough grown in a sunny position in a mild climate. It will endure long periods without water and makes a dense hedge or windbreak. Propagation is normally from seed.

Brabejum stellatifolium

The first indigenous tree cultivated by South Africa's early colonists, this small, round-headed tree grows to about 15 ft (5 m), often with many stems branching from ground level. In summer, the white, sweetly scented flowers appear in spikes about 4 in (10 cm) long, and in autumn it bears fruits similar in shape to a cultivated almond. ZONE 9.

BRACHYCHITON
Sterculiaceae

This variable genus consists of warm-climate, evergreen or dry-season-deciduous trees from Australia, some noted for their spectacular flowers. Some occur naturally in tropical and subtropical rainforests and others in semi-arid areas where their edible leaves and bark are used as fodder in dry seasons. Some of the arid-climate species have massive, swollen, water-storing trunks. Several species are widely planted in parks and streets. They need light, well-drained soils, preferably acidic. Propagate from fresh seed in spring or by grafting.

Brachychiton acerifolius
ILLAWARRA FLAME-TREE, FLAME KURRAJONG

The flame-tree, at its best one of the world's most spectacular flowering trees, is indigenous to warm, wet coastal slopes of eastern Australia. It can reach 35–50 ft (11–15 m) in cultivation, taller in its native rainforests. Profuse foamy sprays of bright scarlet flowers are borne in spring or early summer on the leafless crown, or on individual branches that shed their leaves just prior to flowering. Flowering is erratic from year to year and seems best following a dry, mild winter. Seedling trees may take many years to first flower, whereas grafted plants are more reliable and should flower in 5 to 8 years. The flame-tree needs a sheltered position with protection from cold or salty winds and from frost. ZONE 9.

Brachychiton discolor
LACEBARK KURRAJONG

A massive tree to 80 ft (25 m) or more in its native rainforest, the lacebark kurrajong is smaller when seen in parks and gardens, though retaining its distinctive form. Its thick trunk has greenish bark and it has a dense canopy of large maple-like leaves, dark green above and silvery beneath. Clusters of deep pink, velvety, bell-shaped flowers appear in early summer while the tree is briefly leafless. It requires similar growing conditions to *B. acerifolius*. ZONE 10.

Brachychiton populneus
KURRAJONG

Widely distributed on rocky hillsides of eastern Australia, this bushy-headed tree is grown chiefly for shade, or on farms for its fodder value in times of scarcity. The leaves are variably lobed, most strongly in the inland race. During summer it produces among the foliage masses of greenish cream bell-shaped flowers, spotted inside with purple or yellow to attract bees. It will tolerate limestone soil but not wet, heavy, clay soils. Saplings are best established in a sheltered area before transplanting to dry unattended sites; once established it is very drought resistant. ZONE 8.

Brachychiton populneus

Brabejum stellatifolium

Brachychiton discolor

Brachychiton acerifolius (below)

Bouvardia longiflora

BRACHYGLOTTIS
Asteraceae

This New Zealand genus of evergreen low shrubs and small trees of the daisy family now includes many additional shrubby species transferred from *Senecio*. *Brachyglottis* species are valued for their attractive foliage, stems and leaf undersides which all have a dense coating of white wool. Flowers (really flower heads) are in small to rather large sprays at the branch tips and may be golden-yellow with conspicuous petals, or small and greenish white with no evident petals. These are rewarding garden plants if climatic conditions are suitable: they do best in cool but mild and rainy climates, such as on the Atlantic coasts of the British Isles. Propagate from cuttings.

Brachyglottis repanda
RANGIORA

Worth growing for its foliage alone, the rangiora is a striking small tree of rapid growth, reaching about 20 ft (7 m). Saplings have straight, soft stems with opposite pairs of large, deep green glossy leaves with wavy edges and felted silvery white undersides. In late winter to early spring each branch produces at its tip a large frothy panicle of thousands of small greenish silver flowers. The large leaf size can be maintained by cutting branches back to the base after flowering, or the plant can be allowed to grow to a tree. It needs a sheltered position so leaves are not damaged by strong wind. 'Purpurea' has the upsides of the leaves deep purple. ZONE 9.

BRACHYLAENA
Asteraceae

This small genus of evergreen shrubs and small trees from Africa belongs to the huge daisy family, most members of which are subshrubs and herbaceous annuals and perennials. Its tree-like members are more evident in moist regions of the southern hemisphere. *Brachylaena* species are multi-stemmed but can develop quite strong, woody trunks with age. The leathery leaves are toothed and felted on the undersides and have whitish hairs. The small flower heads are carried in dense panicles terminating the branchlets. Fast growing and very wind resistant, they are useful for hedges and windbreaks especially near the sea and can be kept trimmed to a dense hedge. Propagation is from seeds or cuttings.

Brachylaena discolor
COAST SILVER-LEAF, SILVER OAK

A small tree from the Natal coast and escarpment of South Africa, the coast silver-leaf is common in low dune-forest, growing to about 20 ft (7 m) and forming a dense, impenetrable tangle of stems from an underground bole; in more sheltered forests it can be taller and straighter. Thicker trunks develop a scaly grey bark. The leaves are deep green above, in striking contrast with the silvery white undersides. Dense white flower clusters appear in spring. ZONE 9.

BRAHEA
Arecaceae

This genus of handsome fan-leafed palms is related to *Washingtonia* and the palms come from the same dry regions of western Mexico, including the peninsula of Baja California. They range from low-growing plants with no trunk developing, to quite tall, solitary-trunked palms with rather compact crowns. Tiny flowers are borne on panicles that may exceed the fronds in length and, as the date-like fruits develop, hang below the crown. Most of the species come from very hot dry areas, growing in dry gullies, on open grassy hills, limestone slopes and other inhospitable places. They adapt readily to cultivation but have never been widely planted. Some species will tolerate moderately severe frosts when established. Plants in containers should be watered frequently in summer; they are prone to attack by scale insects. Propagation is from seed only, with rapid germination as palms go, but seedling growth is slow.

Brahea armata
HESPER PALM

The outstanding feature of this species from Baja California is the striking pale blue-grey colour of its stiff fronds. It grows slowly to a height of 20 ft (7 m) with a crown 10 ft (3 m) wide. In flower and fruit it is an even more dramatic sight, with arching stems, up to 15 ft (5 m) long extending well beyond the foliage canopy. It takes decades to reach flowering size, but even young plants are beautiful for their foliage alone. ZONE 9.

BREYNIA
Euphorbiaceae

A small genus of shrubs and trees from Southeast Asia, Australia and the Pacific region, *Breynia* has one species which is grown for its decorative foliage. All species have tough stems and twigs, often suckering from the base, and small oval leaves that tend to alternate in 2 regular rows on either side of short lateral branches. Flowers and fruits are both inconspicuous, on short stalks in the leaf axils. They are

Brahea armata

Brahea armata

Brachyglottis repanda 'Purpurea'

Brachylaena discolor

Brugmansia species

Breynia disticha

Broussonetia papyrifera

easily grown in full light or part-shade and a coarse, well-drained soil with added organic matter. They are useful plants for warm, seaside environments, but need protection from frost and salt-laden winds. Tip pruning encourages thicker growth. Propagation is from cuttings.

Breynia disticha
SNOW BUSH

A small evergreen from the Pacific Islands, this shrub, formerly known as *Breynia nivosa*, grows to a height and spread of about 4 ft (1.2 m) with a rounded, well-branched habit. The new growths are pink with leaves becoming mid-green, variegated and mottled with white. Inconspicuous greenish flowers are borne in spring and summer. The cultivar 'Roseo-picta' has foliage more heavily splashed rose-pink. It is a popular plant in the tropics and can also be grown in warm positions in frost-free temperate areas. ZONE 10.

BROUSSONETIA
Moraceae
PAPER MULBERRY

This genus consists of 3 species of deciduous trees and shrubs from eastern Asia, closely allied to the true mulberries (*Morus*) but with thicker, pith-filled twigs and flowers of different sexes on different plants. The fruits are dry and hardly edible. The largest-growing species, *B. papyrifera*, is the famous paper mulberry which yields a fine silky fibre from its inner bark which was traditionally used in Japan to make paper. The tree was taken to the Pacific Islands by the Polynesians, who make from its bark fibre the renowned 'tapa cloth'. Broussonetias are fast growing, rather untidy plants with broad, thin-textured, toothed leaves, easily grown in a wide range of climates but preferring a sheltered humid position. They are easily propagated from cuttings taken in summer.

Broussonetia papyrifera
PAPER MULBERRY

Originating in China and Japan, the paper mulberry has spread to many other parts of the world, notably the islands of the south and central Pacific where it thrives despite the much warmer climate. Under suitable conditions it rapidly grows to a large tree of 40–50 ft (13–15 m) with a rather sparse rounded crown and dark trunk with an irregular surface. Leaves on saplings are up to 12 in (30 cm) long, often with 2 or 3 lobes; on adult trees they are smaller and seldom lobed. Male flowers are in long twisted catkins, females in much shorter, less conspicuous heads. ZONE 7.

BROWNEA
Caesalpiniaceae

This is a genus of about 8 species of evergreen trees from tropical America, closely allied to the Burmese *Amherstia nobilis* which they resemble in growth and foliage, though the flowers are different. The bell-shaped flowers are borne in summer, in dense round clusters, each flower attended by a velvety bract so the cluster—which from a little distance looks like a single enormous flower—resembles that of a rhododendron, a genus to which these trees are, of course, quite unrelated. Not that temperate-climate gardeners will often be able to make the comparison: these are strictly tropical trees. They flourish best in a climate blessed with regular rainfall and in rich, deep and perfectly drained soil. In cool climates they are occasionally grown in greenhouses for the sake of their magnificent flowers, though they need plenty of room and abundant heat. Propagation is from cuttings in summer.

Brownea grandiceps
ROSE OF VENEZUELA

The best known species of its genus and a splendid tree to about 65 ft (20 m) tall and wide for parks or large gardens in tropical climates, the rose of Venezuela bears scarlet to orange flowers in pendent clusters, each with as many as 70 flowers. The young leaves are red-tinted and drooping. Its hybrid *B.* × *crawfordii* makes a tree about half the size with flowers in brilliant deep pink. It is the *Brownea* most often seen in European greenhouses. ZONE 11.

BRUGMANSIA
Solanaceae
ANGEL'S TRUMPET

This small genus consists of exotic-looking evergreen or semi-evergreen trees and shrubs from the Andes of South America, still often found under the name *Datura* though botanists now restrict that genus to weedy annuals and biennials (thornapples). Brugmansias are grown for their very large, fragrant,

Brugmansia sanguinea

Brugmansia × candida

Brugmansia suaveolens

Brunfelsia australis

Whitefly and red spider mite can cause problems, as can snails. Propagate from soft-tip cuttings in spring or summer.

Brugmansia × candida

A small tree 10–15 ft (3–5 m) high of rather untidy habit, which can be kept to a lower shrub form by pruning, angel's trumpet branches from a short trunk and has long, oval, velvety leaves confined to the branch tips. The pendulous white flowers, strongly scented at night, are about 12 in (30 cm) long and have a widely flared mouth. They are borne mostly in summer and autumn but also at other times. Cultivars include 'Plena' with an extra frill of petals inside the main trumpet, and 'Apricot' (sometimes known as *Brugmansia versicolor*) with pale apricot-pink flowers. ZONE 10.

Brugmansia sanguinea
RED ANGEL'S TRUMPET

Reported to grow at altitudes up to 12,000 ft (3,600 m) in its native Andes and to become a small tree as much as 35 ft (11 m) high, this species is more cold-hardy than other brugmansias. It is normally seen in gardens as a many-stemmed shrub to about 8 ft (2.5 m) high. The flowers, narrower than those of other brugmansias, are usually orange-red with yellow veins, grading to yellowish green at the base, but there are variations with paler orange or yellow flowers. ZONE 9.

Brugmansia suaveolens

This many-branched spreading evergreen shrub or small tree to 15 ft (5 m) has downy oval leaves up to 12 in (30 cm) long. The pendulous flowers are slightly narrow pendent trumpet flowers. The leaves are large and soft, rather like tobacco leaves but smaller, and all parts of the plant are narcotic and poisonous. Frost-tender to half-hardy, they prefer a warm to hot climate, a sunny, sheltered site, and a light, fertile, well-drained soil. Best grown as small trees, they can be pruned when young to obtain a single trunk. Keep well watered during the growing season. Prune in spring to maintain shape.

and their tubes are heavily striped with green and may appear in great profusion, in flushes through summer and autumn or at other times of the year. Widely grown in tropical gardens, it is sometimes seen pruned to a round-headed shrub. Elsewhere it does well in a moderately heated greenhouse. The cultivar 'Plena' has semi-double blooms. ZONE 10.

BRUNFELSIA
Solanaceae

These evergreen shrubs from South and Central America bear delightfully fragrant, tubular flowers with 5 flat petals; these change colour from their first day of opening through successive days, with flowers of different ages sprinkling the bush. The tropical *B. americana* has white flowers which turn cream and pale golden as they age, while most others progress through purples, blues and white. Most species grow slowly to chest-height or taller bushy shrubs, with simple rather leathery leaves. They need a frost-free site, in full sun or with afternoon shade, and fertile, well-drained soil with adequate water in summer or during dry spells. They do well in pots and are widely grown in greenhouses in Europe. Prune after flowering if necessary to promote bushiness. Propagate from soft-tip cuttings. These plants may all contain poisonous alkaloids, particularly in their berry-like fruits which have been known to poison dogs.

Brunfelsia australis
YESTERDAY, TODAY AND TOMORROW

From southern Brazil, this is an attractive shrub growing to about 6 ft (2 m) tall and almost as wide, with a densely twiggy habit and slightly shiny leaves that are often purplish when young and in cool weather. At peak flowering, usually in mid-spring but sometimes in late winter or early summer, it bears massed blossoms which open violet and fade to pale blue then white, all three on the bush at the same time, hence the common name. A fairly tough plant, it does well in coastal gardens as long as salt spray is not too heavy. In older references it appears under the names *Brunfelsia latifolia* or *B. bonodora* and in fact the botanical identity of plants in this blue-flowered group is still not properly resolved. ZONE 9.

Brunfelsia pauciflora

This small deciduous or semi-evergreen Brazilian shrub (syn. *B. calycina*, *B. eximia*) is slower growing and less vigorous than *B. australis*, with longer, dark green, leathery leaves, growing to about 5 ft (1.5 m) tall and wide, but very open-branched. In bloom it is even more dramatic: large, abundant flowers opening a rich purple, fading to mauve and white over successive days, all through spring and early summer. Several varieties have been recognized. ZONE 10.

BRYA
Fabaceae

This is a small genus of pea-flowered trees from the West Indies and Central America. They have small, simple, stalkless leaves and small but abundant flowers (like those of some brooms) arising from the leaf axils. They appear to have potential as ornamentals for the tropics and warmer subtropics, growing in sheltered coastal areas. Propagation is from seed.

Brya ebenus
JAMAICA EBONY, WEST INDIAN EBONY, COCUS WOOD

A tree of 20–25 ft (7–8 m) high when grown in the open, this species has a short trunk and an open crown of broadly spreading branches with stiffly diverging twigs. The round-tipped leaves are shiny dark green and about 1 in (2.5 cm) long. Golden yellow flowers line the branches in autumn or late in the tropical dry season. *B. ebenus* yields a valuable timber with heartwood that becomes black with age. ZONE 11.

BUCKINGHAMIA
Proteaceae
IVORY CURL TREE

This genus consists of just 2 species of which one is widely cultivated: *B. celsissima*, a handsome, fast-growing evergreen rainforest tree from tropical Queensland, Australia. It is rather like some of the larger grevilleas in foliage and flower. It needs fertile, moist soil, a warm frost-free coastal climate, and full sun or part-shade. Pruning while young helps establish a single trunk, then prune only if required to maintain shape. Propagate from ripe seed. Minimize root disturbance when transplanting.

Buckinghamia celsissima

A tall, sparsely branched tree in its natural habitat, in cultivation *B. celsissima* makes an attractive densely crowned small tree of 20–30 ft (7–10 m) or a tall bushy shrub, the latter especially in cooler climates. Once valued as a timber tree, it is now popular as an ornamental park and street tree. Deeply lobed juvenile leaves become long and glossy on mature trees. In summer and early autumn even quite young trees bear creamy white, sweetly scented flowers in abundant spikes up to 8 in (20 cm) long. ZONE 10.

BUDDLEJA
Loganiaceae

The spelling was formerly *Buddleia* (named after 17th-century English botanist Adam Buddle) but *Buddleja* is now ruled the correct form. This genus consists of shrubs and small, mostly short-lived trees, both evergreen and deciduous. Most of the cultivated species originate in China, but the genus also occurs in Africa, Madagascar, southern Asia and South America and includes many tropical and subtropical species. Leaves are large, pointed and often crepe-textured, usually in opposite pairs. The spicily fragrant flowers are small and tubular, in dense spikes at branch tips or sometimes in smaller clusters along the branches. They range through pinks, mauves, reddish purples, oranges and yellows. Buddlejas prefer full sun. Some tough species and cultivars can survive neglect, dry shallow soils and harsh exposed positions, but they respond dramatically to kinder treatment. Propagate from semi-ripe cuttings in summer.

Buckinghamia celsissima

Brunfelsia pauciflora

Brya ebenus (below)

Buddleja alternifolia

Buddleja alternifolia

Buddleja davidii (below)

Buddleja davidii 'Royal Red'

Buddleja alternifolia

In full bloom in late spring and early summer this tall deciduous shrub from north-western China is transformed into a fountain of fragrant, mauve-pink blossom, the small individual flowers strung in clusters along its arching branches. It looks best trained to a single trunk so the branches can weep effectively from above, and should not be pruned back hard as it flowers on the previous summer's wood. A sunny but sheltered position suits it best. ZONE 6.

Buddleja davidii
BUTTERFLY BUSH

The butterfly bush is a deciduous shrub of about 12 ft (4 m). In late summer and early autumn its arching canes bear at their tips long narrow cones of densely packed flowers which are mauve with an orange eye. These are very attractive to butterflies, which feed on the nectar. Prune hard in late winter to encourage strong canes with larger flower-spikes. Cultivars with flowers in larger spikes and richer tones include 'White Bouquet' (cream with an orange eye), 'Royal Red' (magenta) and 'Black Knight' (dark purple). ZONE 7.

Buddleja globosa

Deep golden orange balls of tiny flowers, hanging like baubles from the branch tips in late spring and summer, make this South American species strikingly different from the other two. The strongly veined leaves are soft and covered in white 'fir', as are the twigs and flower-stalks. It is a tall shrub of 10–15 ft (3–5 m) or so, making fast growth under suitably sheltered conditions but inclined to be short lived. In cool but mild, moist climates it will do well close to the sea. ZONE 7.

BURCHELLIA
Rubiaceae
SOUTH AFRICAN POMEGRANATE

This genus contains only one species; the South African wild pomegranate, a slow-growing evergreen shrub which deserves to be more widely cultivated for its neat dark green leaves and showy summer flowers. It is somewhat frost-tender and prefers a sheltered, sunny position and well-drained soil with added organic matter. Prune lightly after flowering to prevent fruit production. Propagation is possible from half-hardened cuttings in summer.

Burchellia bubalina

A rounded to rather straggling, densely leafed shrub to 10 ft (3 m) and almost as wide, *B. bubalina* has faintly fragrant, vivid orange-red cylindrical flowers that appear in profusion on the branch tips for a long period over late spring and summer. ZONE 9.

BURSARIA
Pittosporaceae

Six species of evergreen shrubs and small trees make up this Australian genus; most of them have thorny twigs and small leaves arranged in rosette-like short shoots along the branches. In summer they bear panicles of numerous sweet-smelling small white flowers at the branch tips, often making a fine display and attracting many insects including butterflies. The flowers are followed by massed small, flattened brown seed capsules. These plants are seldom cultivated but have the potential to make useful screen or hedge plants, their thorns a deterrent to intruders. Propagate from seed or cuttings.

Bursaria spinosa
AUSTRALIAN BOXTHORN

A shrub of erect but often crooked, irregular habit, occasionally becoming a small tree to 20 ft (7 m), the Australian boxthorn occurs widely in south-eastern Australia as an understorey to open eucalypt forests, especially on drier clay soils of the coastal plains. Owners of grazing land regard it as nuisance because of its rapid regrowth. In summer it produces large, frothy sprays of fragrant white blossom. The masses of fruits which follow can also be quite striking when immature and pinkish red. ZONE 8.

BUTEA
Fabaceae

Not to be confused with the palm genus *Butia*, this tropical Asian genus of a few species of semi-deciduous small trees and woody climbers is noted for spectacular clusters of flowers, in shades of red, orange or yellow. These trees belong to the same tribe of legumes as the beans and *Erythrina* which are characterized by leaves with 3 leaflets and flowers with a prominent upper petal or 'standard', as in pea and bean flowers. Even in the tropics these trees are slow growing, but at the same time they will grow in poorly drained and even slightly saline soils in which few other ornamental trees survive. Propagation is from seed. A sunny position, regular watering and moist soil will ensure best growth.

Butea monosperma
FLAME OF THE FOREST, PALAS TREE

Grown for its brilliant orange-red pea-flowers that cover the tree in huge clusters on almost bare branches before the wet-season flush of new foliage, this small tree reaches a height of up to 30 ft (10 m) with a twisted, gnarled trunk and open crown of angular branches. Leaves are bluish green, bronze-tinged when newly expanded, with a silvery undersurface. This species is native to India, Bangladesh and Burma. The exudation from the bark, known as Bengal kino, has been used as an astringent medicine, and the flowers yield an orange dye. ZONE 11.

BUTIA
Arecaceae

This genus of moderately frost-hardy palms comes from central South America and is related to the coconut palm. They have short thick trunks and thick-textured, recurved fronds. These tough palms are adaptable to a range of climates and soils, thriving in full sun or part-shade. They periodically produce among the fronds large panicles of fruit-scented small cream flowers (reddish in bud), enclosed in bud in a very long, woody bract; these are followed by abundant fruits with juicy but fibrous flesh enclosing a very hard stone with 3 'eyes' like a miniature coconut. Propagate from seed in spring.

Buddleja globosa

Burchellia bubalina

Bursaria spinosa

Butia capitata
BUTIA PALM, JELLY PALM

Occurring naturally in Argentina, Brazil and Uruguay, this palm is somewhat variable in shape, but expect it to become a small, graceful palm of around 10 ft (3 m) after 15 years. It has a rough grey trunk and long, grey-green feather-shaped fronds which are arching and recurved. The orange-yellow fruits have edible pulp which is used for jellies or fermented to make wine. A hardy and easily grown palm, it makes vigorous growth when young and is a useful and reliable landscaping subject. Spent fronds should be cut off close to the trunk. ZONE 8.

Butia eriospatha

This species closely resembles *B. capitata* in size and foliage, differing chiefly in the remarkable dense, pale brownish 'fleece' that coats the very large bud-bract, and also in its deep reddish pink flower buds and petals which contrast attractively with the cream panicle branches. It appears to be a vigorous grower, reaching first flowering just as the short, thick trunk begins to develop beneath the fronds. The fruits are smaller and less juicy than those of *B. capitata*. ZONE 9.

BUXUS
Buxaceae
BOX

Traditional evergreens of cool climates, the boxes are grown for their small, neat, leathery leaves and dense growth-habit. Though regarded as shrubs, they are capable (except for some dwarf cultivars) of growing with age into small trees with strong, twisted trunks and branches. Creamy yellow box wood, with its high density and close, even grain, was once used for fine woodcut blocks for printing. Boxes withstand regular close clipping, making them ideal for topiary, formal hedges and mazes. Only a few species are normally grown in cool-climate gardens, but the genus also includes many tropical and subtropical species, which are mostly larger-leafed. Flowers are greenish yellow and appear in small clusters in the leaf axils in spring; although small, they may be very profuse and attract bees. Such tough plants have very simple requirements, thriving in most soils and in sun or shade, and adapting well to warmer climates. Pruning of hedges can be continued throughout the year. Propagate from cuttings.

Buxus microphylla
JAPANESE BOX

This East Asian box first came to Western gardens as a dwarf cultivar with distorted leaves, long grown in Japan but unknown in the wild. Later, wild forms were discovered in Japan, Korea and China and named as varieties, vars. *japonica*, *koreana* and *sinica* respectively. In North America var. *koreana* is popular for its compact, low-growing habit and great cold-hardiness. In milder climates var. *japonica*, with larger, shinier, more rounded leaves does well, sometimes reaching 10 ft (3 m) in height. ZONE 5.

Buxus sempervirens
EUROPEAN BOX, COMMON BOX

The common box has grown as tall as 30 ft (10 m) with a trunk 12 in (30 cm) thick, but as a garden shrub it is commonly only 3–6 ft (1–2 m) high, and is represented by a bewildering range of forms and cultivars. The edging box, cultivar 'Suffruticosa', has a very dense, bushy habit and can be maintained as very dwarf hedges of 12 in (30 cm) or less. There are also many variegated clones, the best known being 'Argentea', which has broad white margins to the leaves. ZONE 6.

Buxus sempervirens

Buxus microphylla

Butia eriospatha

Butia capitata

Caesalpinia gilliesii

Caesalpinia pulcherrima

Calamus australis

Caesalpinia ferrea

CAESALPINIA
Caesalpiniaceae

This genus gives its name to one of the three legume families (the others are Fabaceae and Mimosaceae), treated by some botanists as subfamilies of a single family. *Caesalpinia* is a diverse genus found in warmer regions around the world and includes trees, shrubs and scrambling climbers, often very thorny. Some shrub species from the Americas have been distinguished in the past as the genus *Poinciana*, as has the famous flamboyant from Madagascar, now separated as *Delonix* (listed later in this book). The leaves of all caesalpinias are bipinnate; the flowers are in spikes from upper leaf axils and may be quite showy, mostly in shades of red, yellow or cream, with separate petals and often conspicuous stamens. Seeds are in typical leguminous pods. Most species appreciate a sheltered sunny spot and deep sandy soil. Propagation is from seed, which may need treatment such as abrading and hot-water soaking to aid germination.

Caesalpinia ferrea
LEOPARD TREE, BRAZILIAN IRONWOOD

A long-lived tree of usually no more than 40 ft (13 m) in height, this species is grown in the tropics for its sinuous limbs and smooth cream bark which is beautifully dappled with darker grey-green. The crown is flat topped or slightly domed, with deep green foliage; in summer and autumn it is dotted with short erect spikes of yellow flowers, not particularly showy. Fast growing when conditions suit it, the leopard tree is often untidily branched when young and should be trained to a single trunk. ZONE 10.

Caesalpinia gilliesii
DWARF POINCIANA, BIRD OF PARADISE BUSH

Previously known as *Poinciana gilliesii*; in warm climates this can grow to a small tree, but in cultivation it seldom exceeds 10 ft (3 m). Native to subtropical Argentina and Uruguay, it is an attractive plant with fern-like foliage. Heads of yellow on cream flowers with prominent scarlet stamens are produced in summer. It grows best in light, well-drained soil in full sun. Shelter from strong wind and frosts is essential. Although evergreen in warm wet climates, it is elsewhere semi-deciduous or deciduous. ZONE 9.

Caesalpinia pulcherrima
PEACOCK FLOWER, BARBADOS PRIDE

Mostly seen as a shrub of about 8 ft (2.5 m), this species, once known as *Poinciana pulcherrima*, can in time grow to 15–20 ft (5–7 m). It is believed to originate in South America, though it has long been cultivated throughout the tropics. Short lived and fast growing, it has an open, moderately spreading habit with coarse, prickly leaves and branches with a whitish waxy bloom which terminate from spring to autumn in tall, upright sprays of vivid blossom, the flowers opening progressively from the base. Scarlet and gold in the most common form, they have very long, whisker-like stamens; there is also a yellow-flowered form and a darker red one. Profuse flat pods often follow the flowers. ZONE 11.

CALAMUS
Arecaceae
RATTAN, ROTANG

Imagine a palm with extremely long, thin stems that flop against other vegetation and hook onto its foliage with sharp grappling-hooks, and you will have a fair idea of what many of the 350-odd *Calamus* species look like. The stems of this genus are the source of the world's cane, or rattan, from which cane furniture is constructed. Most species are from the rainforests of tropical Asia and the Malay archipelago, with a smaller number found in Africa, eastern Australia and the Pacific Islands. They are graceful feather-leaved palms, usually multi-stemmed from the base. The frond mid-stalk may be extended into a whip-like grappling appendage, or this may arise from the rim of the sheathing base of the frond. Similar whip-like panicles bear the tiny flowers which are followed by distinctive small fruits with overlapping scales. Many *Calamus* species adapt to cultivation in warm, wet climates and in their juvenile state can make attractive container plants, best grown in semi-shade. Propagation is only possible from fresh seed, which requires much warmth and moisture to germinate and even so may take many months.

Calamus australis

One of the 8 *Calamus* species occurring in Australia, *C. australis* grows in dense rainforest in north Queensland. It is multi-stemmed with high-scrambling canes and graceful feather-like fronds about 6 ft (2 m) long. The grappling appendages are up to 10 ft (3 m) long and armed with vicious recurved hooks. The stalks and sheathing bases of the fronds are also armed with needle-like spines. The juvenile, clumping phase is less ferocious and can be maintained for years in a container. ZONE 10.

CALCEOLARIA
Scrophulariaceae

Most members of this quite large South American genus are herbaceous perennials or annuals, but a few are shrubs. Their chief attraction is the curiously shaped flower, the petals fused together and inflated into a pouch-like structure, mostly in bright shades of yellow, orange or red. The shrubby species are moderately cold-hardy outdoors but appreciate a sheltered sunny position and ample soil moisture. They are easily propagated from cuttings.

Calceolaria integrifolia

Native to Chile, this is a spreading shrub of rather loose and untidy habit, though easily kept in shape by pruning, reaching a height of 4 ft (1.2 m). It has closely veined leaves with an attractive fine 'seersucker' texture but is prone to insect damage. From late spring to early autumn a succession of bright yellow or bronze-yellow flowers appear in long-stalked clusters from the branch tips. ZONE 8.

CALLIANDRA
Mimosaceae

A few species of this large genus of evergreen shrubs and small trees from the American tropics and subtropics are cultivated as ornamentals, valued for their showy flower heads with numerous long stamens. The flowers are like those of acacias and mimosas but mostly on a larger scale. Leaves are always bipinnate but vary greatly in both number and size of leaflets; in most species the leaves 'sleep' at night or in dull, stormy weather, the leaflets folding together. Despite their often delicate appearance many calliandras are tough, long-lived plants, thriving in most soils and positions. Cold-hardiness varies between species, some being able to withstand a few degrees of frost as long as this is compensated for by hot summers. They are readily propagated from seed, but some species produce few or no pods in cultivation and these can be grown from cuttings.

Calliandra haematocephala
POWDERPUFF TREE, BLOOD-RED TASSEL-FLOWER

Indigenous to Bolivia, this species produces some of the largest flower heads, around 3 in (7 cm) diameter with densely massed stamens, but the heads are rather sporadically dotted through the luxuriant foliage. Flowers can be seen at most times of year but are most numerous in autumn and winter. It makes a large, broadly spreading shrub to a height of about 12 ft (4 m) and an even greater spread with age, with many tough, woody branches from ground level. Leaves consist of few oblong leaflets about 1½ in (4 cm) long, pink-flushed when first unfolding. Although a tropical species, this will grow and flower well in warm-temperate climates if sheltered from frost. The flowers attract nectar-feeding birds. ZONE 10.

Calliandra portoricensis
WHITE TASSEL-FLOWER

Delicate heads of pure white stamens, so thin and weak that they droop gracefully and appear like cottonwool balls dotting the foliage canopy, characterize this species. It makes a tall shrub of about 15 ft (5 m) with several erect straight stems from the base but is often kept cut back to a lower height. Leaves consist of numerous crowded, tiny leaflets on a rather untidy tangle of spreading branches. Flower heads in long racemes at branch ends open progressively from spring to autumn. From the West Indies, it performs surprisingly well in mild climates if sheltered from frost. ZONE 10.

Calliandra surinamensis
PINK TASSEL-FLOWER

More tropical in its preferences than the other species listed here, C. surinamensis comes from the Guianas region of northern South America. It is an elegant shrub of erect, open habit up to about 10 ft (3 m) tall with arching branches and ferny foliage. The flower heads are very distinctive, forming narrow erect cones that are scattered along the upper sides of the branches, white at the base but tipped rose-pink. They appear through much of the year and attract butterflies. ZONE 11.

Calliandra tweedii
RED TASSEL-FLOWER

Native to subtropical South America, this evergreen, graceful shrub has a height and spread of around 6 ft (2 m). Its fern-like bipinnate leaves consist of numerous tiny leaflets and striking crimson pompon flowers appear among the foliage through spring and summer. It prefers full sun, a light, well-drained soil and copious summer water. Prune after flowering to promote bushiness. ZONE 9.

Calliandra tweedii

Calliandra surinamensis

Calliandra haematocephala

Calliandra haematocephala

Calceolaria integrifolia

CALLICARPA
Verbenaceae
BEAUTY-BERRY

Deciduous and evergreen shrubs, *Callicarpa* species can be untidy in their growth but very appealing in flower and especially in fruit. The branches are long and cane-like, and the leaves, in opposite pairs, are usually downy on their undersides. Sprays of small pink to purple summer flowers are followed in autumn by dense clusters of small shiny berries, white or mauve to purple, which may persist into winter on the bare branches. Only 3 or 4 species are commonly grown in cool climates but others from subtropical and tropical regions make good garden subjects. *Callicarpa* species do best in full sun and fertile soil. Cut back older branches in late winter to encourage strong flowering canes. Propagate from tip cuttings. Fruiting branches are often cut for indoor decoration.

Callicarpa americana
Not as commonly grown as it deserves, this deciduous species from south-eastern USA makes a low, spreading shrub of 3–6 ft (1–2 m). It has broad, strongly veined leaves with downy undersides. The flowers are very small and violet-purple, but the fruits are very showy, brilliant mauve-magenta, in tight clusters like miniature bunches of grapes and persisting well into winter. ZONE 9.

Callicarpa bodinieri
Cold-hardy and very ornamental, this upright, bushy shrub from central China grows to about 6–10 ft (2–3 m) tall and wide. It has dark green leaves with paler, downy undersides, small dense sprays of lilac flowers in midsummer, and dense clusters of bluish mauve to purple fruit in late autumn. Var. *giraldii* differs in its less downy leaves and flower stalks and is the form most commonly grown; it fruits more abundantly in gardens than the type does. ZONE 6.

Callicarpa macrophylla
This evergreen species from the Himalaya is the giant of the genus, both in stature, up to 20 ft (7 m) high and 30 ft (10 m) spread, and in its large pale green leaves with white downy undersides. In a warm climate it makes rapid growth, with outward-leaning stems that develop into trunks up to 6 in (15 cm) thick. The small mauve flower clusters appear in autumn and are followed in winter and spring by whitish, pea-sized fruits in very large clusters. ZONE 10.

CALLICOMA
Cunoniaceae
BLACKWATTLE

This is a genus of one evergreen tree from temperate eastern Australia, where it grows in moist, shady gullies in coastal areas. It was the original 'wattle' of the first white settlers in Sydney, who used its flexible stems for the wattle-and-daub method of constructing dwellings. But the similarity of the flower heads of many species of *Acacia*, also common in the area, to the globular creamy white flower heads of *Callicoma* led to the use of 'wattle' for these as well, though *Acacia* and *Callicoma* are quite unrelated. Blackwattle is easily grown, preferring a sheltered site with its roots shaded and a moist soil rich in humus. It may be pruned when young to shape into a dense shrub or alternatively trained as a single-trunked tree. It is usually propagated from seed, collected in autumn.

Callicoma serratifolia
Although growing to a tree of 40 ft (13 m) or more in its native forests and ravines, in cultivation the blackwattle is usually a multi-stemmed large shrub or small tree, growing to 10–15 ft (3–5 m). Its distinctive oval serrated leaves are dark green above with downy undersides and it bears its cream puffball flowers in spring and early summer. ZONE 9.

CALLISTEMON
Myrtaceae
BOTTLEBRUSH

These evergreen Australian shrubs or small trees bear magnificent spikes of long-stamened flowers that look remarkably like a bottle brush, hence their common name. Many species are weeping in habit and a few have striking papery bark; most are excellent for attracting birds. Most species are easily grown and adaptable to a variety of conditions and climates, though in general they are only marginally frost tolerant and prefer full sun and moist soil; some, however, will tolerate poor drainage. Bottlebrushes have found their way into many gardens in the USA, Ireland, Mediterranean countries and South Africa, and greenhouses elsewhere, even putting on good displays in sheltered spots in cooler climates (Zone 8 or so). New leaves grow from the tips of the flower-spikes, leaving long-lasting woody seed capsules behind; a light pruning after flowering, especially of shrubby forms, will remove these and help promote bushiness and flowering. Prune to establish a single trunk on tree-like species. There are hybrids and cultivars with flowers in a variety of hues in the white/pink/red range. Propagate species from seed sown in spring, cultivars and clonal material from tip cuttings in late summer and autumn.

Callicarpa americana

Callicoma serratifolia

Callicarpa macrophylla

Callicoma serratifolia

Callistemon citrinus
SCARLET BOTTLEBRUSH

Widely distributed through the coast and ranges of south-eastern Australia, this rather stiff-leaved bushy shrub was among the first bottlebrushes to be taken into cultivation. *Citrinus* refers to the supposed lemon odour of the crushed foliage, but this is extremely faint and masked by a stronger eucalyptus-oil smell. A tough and vigorous plant, it usually grows quite rapidly to 6–8 ft (2–2.5 m) but may remain at much the same size for decades after, with a short basal trunk and many low branches. The fine scarlet to crimson bottlebrush flowers are about 5 in (12 cm) long and held rather erect, appearing in late spring and summer often with an autumn flush as well. A variable species, it has many wild races as well as many cultivars. Some of the latter have obscure origins and may involve hybrid influence from other species. They include 'Alba', with white flowers; 'Burgundy', with clustered wine-coloured brushes and leaves an attractive pinkish red when young; 'Mauve Mist', also with coloured new leaves and abundant brushes that start mauve and age to a deeper magenta; 'Reeves Pink', a denser shrub with clear phlox-pink flowers; and 'Splendens' ('Endeavour'), an early cultivar making a compact bush bearing bright scarlet brushes over a long period. ZONE 8.

Callistemon citrinus 'Reeves Pink'

Callistemon linearis

Growing to a height of 6–8 ft (2–2.5 m), with a similar spread, this shrub has very narrow, stiff leaves and very densely packed red flower-spikes with just a tinge of green. They appear from mid-spring and are from 3–5 in (7–12 cm) long. 'Pumila' is a 24 in (60 cm) dwarf form. ZONE 9.

Callistemon phoeniceus

One of only 2 species from south-western Australia, *C. phoeniceus* has thick, slightly glossy leaves and can grow to 10 ft (3 m) high. Its flower-spikes are deep scarlet tipped with golden pollen and are about 4 in (10 cm) long. It is one of the most intensely coloured bottlebrushes. ZONE 9.

Callistemon salignus
WHITE BOTTLEBRUSH, PINK-TIPS

Also known as the willow bottlebrush, this is a dense, erect tree with a wide natural distribution in coastal eastern Australia. It grows to 15–30 ft (5–10 m), the smaller size encouraged by pruning. Its bark is thick and papery and the narrow, pointed, dark green leaves are thinner than in most other species; the new growth flushes are a striking pinkish

Callistemon salignus

Callistemon phoeniceus

Callistemon salignus

Callistemon linearis (below)

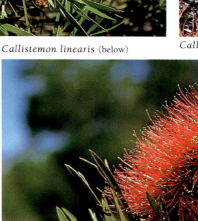

colour. The long spikes of flowers that appear in spring and sparsely through summer are normally pale greenish yellow, though red-flowered plants are also in cultivation. One of the hardiest of the bottlebrushes, it tolerates very wet or very dry conditions, salt and wind. ZONE 9.

Callistemon subulatus

Callistemon viminalis

a street tree or used for screening, this species is less cold-hardy but more damp loving than others. 'Captain Cook' is a dwarf seedling variation which forms a tree-like shrub to about 8 ft (2.5 m); leaves are smaller than the species and pinkish while young, becoming dark green. 'Harkness' grows as a tall shrub to 15 ft (5 m) on a short trunk with a dense crown and abundant scarlet flowers in spring and early summer. ZONE 9.

CALLITRIS
Cupressaceae
CYPRESS-PINE

The true cypresses (*Cupressus*) of warmer parts of the northern hemisphere have their counterpart in Australia in the genus *Callitris*, strikingly similar in foliage and cones and showing a similar range of growth-forms. A close examination shows that *Callitris* has its tiny scale-leaves arranged in whorls of 3, as opposed to pairs in *Cupressus*. The globular, woody cones likewise have 3 large seed-bearing scales alternating with 3 smaller ones. There is a total of 19 species in the genus of which 2 are endemic to New Caledonia and the remainder to Australia. These range widely through the continent mostly in the south-east and south-west but with one species occurring right across the inland and another in the far north. Only a few have been much cultivated, having similar requirements to *Cupressus*. They need full sun and well-drained soil, responding to summer watering. Propagation is from seed or cuttings.

Callitris columellaris
SAND CYPRESS-PINE, BRIBIE ISLAND PINE

This species occurs wild mainly on old, wooded sand dunes of coastal south-east Queensland, where it makes a broad-headed tree of 65 ft (20 m) or more with dark, furrowed bark and very fine, dark green foliage. However, in cultivation it is often strikingly different, making a dense column of slightly billowed form, retaining this shape even with age. Once popular in Australian gardens and still commonly seen as mature trees, its popularity has declined possibly due to nomenclatural confusion with the species now known as *C. glaucophylla*. ZONE 9.

Callitris glaucophylla
WHITE CYPRESS-PINE

This is the most widely distributed species, occurring in abundance over the plains and low hills of inland eastern Australia but with sparser occurrences on rocky ranges all the way to the far north-west of the continent. Growing to around 80 ft (25 m) tall with a straight trunk and short, spreading branches, it is an important timber tree in some regions, yielding a knotty, honey-coloured wood that is remarkably resistant to termite attack. The foliage varies in shade from deep green to a pale grey-green or even somewhat bluish, and the abundant silver-grey cones release their seed as soon as they mature, making it difficult to collect fully ripe seed. Growth is quite fast in deep sandy soils when water is adequate. This species has been lumped under *C. columellaris* by some botanists, though in horticulture and forestry these 2 species behave quite differently. ZONE 9.

Callitris rhomboidea
PORT JACKSON PINE, OYSTER BAY PINE

Occurring widely in rugged hills and ranges of south-eastern Australia, including also Tasmania, this species makes a columnar small tree of up to about 30 ft (10 m), easily recognized by the gracefully drooping shoots at the apex of the crown. The fine foliage is olive-green, changing in cold winters to a deep purplish brown. The woody cones form clusters on branches within the foliage and persist for years without releasing their seed. It thrives in shallow sandstone soils but more fertile soils produce faster growth. It will tolerate light shade, and can be trimmed as a hedge. ZONE 8.

CALLUNA
Ericaceae
HEATHER, LING

The sole species of this genus, heather is the dominant moorland plant of the colder parts of the British Isles and northern Europe; it is closely related to the heath genus *Erica*. In winter the plants turn brownish or dull purple. The numerous cultivars, selected for dwarf and compact growth, flower colour or foliage colour, are mostly grown. They are extremely hardy plants, thriving in very exposed situations though often performing poorly under kinder conditions. Soils should be acidic and gritty, and of low fertility. In climates with warm humid summers they are prone to

Callitris columellaris

Callitris columellaris

Callitris columellaris

Callistemon subulatus

An attractive spreading shrub from coastal valleys of New South Wales and eastern Victoria, this species produces its smallish dark red brushes among fine, almost needle-like foliage through spring and summer. It usually only reaches a height of 5 ft (1.5 m) and, if desired, can be kept trimmed to a neat rounded shape. It deserves wider cultivation. ZONE 9.

Callistemon viminalis
WEEPING BOTTLEBRUSH

This tree from the coastal lowlands of Queensland and northern New South Wales reaches up to 25 ft (8 m) in cultivation with a domed crown of gracefully weeping branches. Foliage is aromatic when crushed and the flowers, borne in profusion in spring and intermittently at other times, have scarlet or crimson stamens. Often planted as root and stem rot. Propagation is usually from tip cuttings, or rooted branches can be detached.

Calluna vulgaris

Common heather (called 'ling' in Yorkshire) makes a spreading subshrub 12–24 in (30–60 cm) high, rooting from the branches. Flowers of wild plants are pale pink to a strong purplish pink, occasionally white. Flowering time is variable: some races and cultivars flower through summer, others from mid-summer to early autumn, yet others entirely in autumn, such as the pink double-flowered 'H. E. Beale'. 'Mair's Variety' has pure white flowers and is a tall grower. 'Orange Queen' is a very compact plant grown for its foliage, golden yellow in summer changing to deep burnt-orange in winter. Over 400 other cultivars are available in Britain alone. ZONE 3.

CALOCEDRUS
Cupressaceae

Included in the cypress family (Cupressaceae) are several widely scattered small genera in both hemispheres that have their branchlets arranged in strongly flattened sprays, each branchlet with small scale-leaves that alternate between large (lateral) and small (facial) pairs. Best known of these genera are *Thuja*, *Thujopsis*, *Chamaecyparis*, *Calocedrus* and *Libocedrus*. These genera can be difficult to tell apart, though each has a characteristic cone structure; in *Calocedrus* the cones have only 4 seed-bearing scales, lying parallel in 2 opposite pairs, each scale with only 2 winged seeds. *Calocedrus* means 'beautiful cedar' and its 3 species, from western USA, Taiwan, and western China and adjacent Burma, are indeed beautiful trees, though only the American one is well known in gardens. They do best in cool, moist mountain areas and in deep, moderately fertile soils, but may survive under poorer conditions as small, bushy but still attractive trees.

Calocedrus decurrens
INCENSE CEDAR

Native to forests of the Californian Sierras and adjacent Oregon, this species is a large, conical tree in the wild, often broad at the base but tapering to a spire-like crown, with dense, aromatic foliage of a deep, rich green. The reddish brown bark has thick, spongy ridges separated by deep fissures on the lower trunk. The cones, about 1 in (2.5 cm) long, ripen to pale golden brown. The soft but durable timber is aromatic, and is valued for cabinet-making and interior fittings. Though not very drought-hardy, the incense cedar is normally trouble free; it transplants readily. ZONE 7.

Calluna vulgaris

Callitris glaucophylla

Calocedrus decurrens

Calluna vulgaris   *Calocedrus decurrens* (right)

Calodendrum capense

Calothamnus quadrifidus (below)

Calothamnus quadrifidus

Calophyllum inophyllum (below)

CALODENDRUM
Rutaceae
CAPE CHESTNUT

This genus contains one beautiful evergreen tree from southern Africa which is noted for its profuse pinkish flower panicles in late spring and early summer. It is widely cultivated as a street and park tree in southern hemisphere countries. It needs some protection from frost when young but once established will tolerate very light frosts. In colder regions it may be deciduous.

It prefers full sun, light, moist, fertile soil with good drainage, and adequate water in dry periods. Young trees can be pruned to shape. Propagate from seed sown in autumn; however seedling trees may take up to 12 years to flower while grafted trees will flower sooner.

Calodendrum capense
CAPE CHESTNUT

This shapely tree grows to 50 ft (15 m) tall, developing a wide domed crown. The glossy oval leaves, dark green above and paler on the undersides, are dotted with translucent oil glands. The pale pink to lilac flowers with prominent stamens appear in large terminal panicles, and are followed by woody, pustular seed pods which split into a star-like shape to release their large, nut-like but intensely bitter seeds. ZONE 9.

CALOPHYLLUM
Guttiferae

This is a large genus of evergreen shrubs and trees found primarily in the Indo-Malaysian and Pacific region with a few species in tropical South America. They are grown for their attractive oval leaves and sprays of fragrant, orange-blossom-like flowers. As with most tropical plants, they will not tolerate frost and require consistent warmth and moisture. Plant in humus-rich, well-drained soil in sun. Propagate from seed or from cuttings.

Calophyllum inophyllum
ALEXANDRIAN LAUREL, INDIAN LAUREL

Occurring naturally from coastal southern India and Malaysia to northern Australia, this tree grows up to 80 ft (25 m) high and has deep green leaves and smooth stems with grey bark. In summer it produces sprays of highly scented 5-petalled white flowers which are 1 in (2.5 cm) in diameter, followed by 1½ in (3 cm) yellow-brown fruit. Often growing on beaches, it is suitable for coastal tropical gardens or container cultivation elsewhere. ZONE 11.

CALOTHAMNUS
Myrtaceae
NET BUSH

Some 25 species of evergreen shrubs make up this genus which is endemic to Western Australia. They have narrow, almost needle-like, deep green leaves, 1–3 in (3–7 cm) long, with rolled edges. The flowers resemble those of their close relatives the bottlebrushes (*Callistemon*), except that the bunched clusters of filaments that make up the flower head are all on one side of the stem, usually the lower side. Most species have red flowers that open in late winter and spring. Although some may become rather woody, avoid pruning too heavily as the old wood is often reluctant to reshoot. Plant in light, well-drained soil in full sun and protect from frost when young. All species tolerate poor soil and drought. They are propagated from seed or small semi-ripe cuttings.

Calothamnus quadrifidus

This is by far the most widely grown species. It is a heavily wooded shrub that grows 6–8 ft (2–2.5 m) high and nearly as wide, with leaves up to 3 in (7 cm) long. The flowers are bright red tipped with yellow pollen. ZONE 9.

CALYCANTHUS
Calycanthaceae
ALLSPICE

The leaves, bark and wood of these deciduous cool-climate shrubs from

North America all have a spicy aroma when they are cut or bruised. Undemanding shrubs, they flower best in a sunny but sheltered position. They are grown for their curiously coloured flowers, which appear singly among the leaves in late spring or summer and resemble small *Magnolia* flowers with narrow petals that are deep red-brown or dull reddish purple; the flowers make interesting indoor decorations. Propagation is usually by layering branches, or from the seeds which are contained in soft, fig-like fruits.

Calycanthus floridus
CAROLINA ALLSPICE

A shrub from south-eastern USA, the Carolina allspice grows to about 6–8 ft (2–2.5 m) and has broad, glossy pale green leaves with downy undersides. Its 2 in (5 cm) wide flowers consist of many petals that are dull brownish red, often with paler tips. It flowers in early summer. ZONE 6.

Calycanthus occidentalis
CALIFORNIAN ALLSPICE

This species, from the ranges of northern California, makes a shrub of rather irregular growth, up to 13 ft (4 m) tall. The leaves are larger than *C. floridus*, and they don't have downy undersides. The flowers are also larger, sometimes 3 in (7 cm) across, but with similar colouring to those of *C. floridus*. ZONE 7.

CALYTRIX
Myrtaceae
FRINGE-MYRTLE

Calytrix consists of about 70 species of wiry-branched evergreen shrubs which are scattered across the Australian continent, though most are confined to the south-west. The small leaves, often very narrow, contain aromatic oils which give the crushed leaves a slightly pungent smell. The flowers are very distinctive, with an extremely fine tube flaring into 5 pointed petals; alternating with these are 5 threadlike stamens which persist on the small dry fruit as longer and stiffer bristles. Flowers are often massed and very showy, in shades of pink, red, purple and yellow. *Calytrix* requires very well-drained, light-textured soils of low nutrient content. Full sun and a rather dry atmosphere suits most species. Propagate from seed or cuttings.

Calytrix tetragona

This is the most wide-ranging *Calytrix* species, occurring in most parts of Australia except the central deserts and the monsoonal north. It

Calycanthus occidentalis

Calycanthus floridus

Calycanthus occidentalis (below)

Calytrix tetragona

is also very variable: it grows 2–6 ft (60 cm–2 m) high and has many stems from the base and narrow heath-like leaves of variable length. The starry white to pink flowers are densely massed in heads at all the branch tips. The bristly fruits, deep purple-brown, can also make a fine display. ZONE 9.

CAMELLIA
Theaceae

Indigenous to Japan and China, the first camellias reached England in the early 18th century. Today there are tens of thousands of cultivars, most of which have descended from *C. japonica*. A renewed interest in camellias and continuing interspecific hybridization is providing more and more cultivars. Unlike roses, it is the newer varieties that are often the most beautiful and reliable. Forming evergreen woody shrubs or small trees, camellias have glossy, deep green leaves and abundant blooms over a long period. Flowers are classified as single, semi-double, anemone-form, peony-form (sometimes called informal-double), double and formal-double, and range in size from miniature to over 5 in

(13 cm). There are so many that the best way to choose camellias for your garden is to visit a nursery to see them in flower. Camellias prefer warm-temperate climates and well-drained, slightly acid soil enriched with organic matter; they generally grow best in semi-shade. Good drainage is important to prevent phytophthora root rot, but they like to be kept moist. There are many varieties suited to pot culture and camellias make handsome tub specimens. Pruning is largely unnecessary, but plants can be trimmed after flowering or cut back harder if rejuvenation is required. Propagate from seed sown in spring or cuttings in late summer or winter, or by grafting.

Camellia 'Cornish Snow'
This is a hybrid between the species *C. saluenensis* and *C. cuspidata*, valuable for its vigorous growth, frost-hardiness and profusion of delicate, medium-small single white flowers, flushed with pink on the back, which are borne along arching branches in late winter and early spring. It grows to 8–10 ft (2.5–3 m) tall, with an open habit.
ZONE 7.

Camellia granthamiana
This half-hardy species from Hong Kong forms a large open shrub to about 9 ft (3 m) with a spread of 6 ft (2 m). It has distinctive crinkly, leathery leaves and in late autumn bears large saucer-shaped parchment-white flowers with a central mass of yellow stamens.
ZONE 9.

Camellia japonica
While the original species formed a small scraggy tree 20–30 ft (7–10 m) tall in its natural habitats in Japan, Korea and China, there is now so much variation in shape and size of cultivars and in flower form and coloration that no single description will suffice. Some will grow to a small tree, others can be kept as compact shrubs. Flowering time varies between winter and spring. They are moderately frost-hardy, and need semi-shade, with their blooms protected from the morning winter sun, plus adequate water when in bud. Among older cultivars are 'Betty Sheffield' and its various sports; 'C. M. Hovey', with medium-sized, formal-double, carmine flowers; 'Debutante', with large, full, informal-double, soft

Camellia japonica cultivar

Camellia japonica 'Debutante'

Camellia japonica cultivar

An attractive grouping of camellias (below)

Camellia reticulata 'Pavlova'

Camellia sasanqua cultivar

Camellia reticulata 'Dr Clifford Parks'

Camellia sasanqua cultivar

Camellia japonica 'Bernice Perfection'

pink flowers; and 'Hana Fuki' with large, semi-double, cup-shaped, soft pink flowers sometimes splashed white. 'Nuccio's Gem' has large formal-double white blooms with up to 10 tiers of rounded petals; it needs heavy disbudding for best results. ZONE 8.

Camellia reticulata hybrids

Taller than *C. japonica*, with a more upright form and open framework of sparser foliage, *C. reticulata* and its hybrids have large, leathery leaves and produce magnificent single and double saucer-shaped flowers often as large as 8 in (20 cm) across with ruffled and fluted petals. Less hardy than *C. japonica*, the plants appreciate more sun and light. 'Captain Rawes', the original type plant introduced in 1820, is still available and lovely, but many cultivars and hybrids are now superior garden subjects, bushier and easier to grow. Flower colours range from red ('Dr Clifford Parks') through pink ('Pavlova'); some are variegated with white but none is entirely white. ZONE 8.

Camellia sasanqua

Most versatile of all camellias, the sasanquas have greatly increased in popularity in recent years. They are densely leafed plants that can be grown as specimen trees or as hedges, and some can be espaliered against a wall or fence. They have small, shiny, dark green leaves and small, delicately fragrant, mostly single flowers in a variety of colours, profusely produced but individually short lived. Different cultivars extend the flowering season from early autumn to early winter. Sasanquas are faster growing and hardier than most other camellias and more sun tolerant, performing better in temperate than in cold climates. Among superior cultivars are 'Hiryu', a bushy and upright plant, excellent as a hedge or specimen tree, with bright to deep rosy red flowers; 'Jennifer Susan' has clear pink semi-double flowers; and the Australian-bred 'Plantation Pink' has large saucer-shaped single soft pink flowers and is excellent for hedging or espalier. ZONE 8.

Camptotheca acuminata

Camptotheca acuminata

Camellia × *williamsii* 'Donation' (below)

Picking tea (*Camellia sinensis*) in Sri Lanka (below left)

Camellia sinensis

Camellia sinensis
TEA

The world's most widely cultivated camellia, this is the plant that produces tea. It is believed to have originated in the mountains of south-western China, though var. *assamica* (Assam tea) comes from neighbouring parts of Burma and Assam. It does produce small nodding cream flowers in spring if allowed, although this does not happen when the plant is grown commercially as the tip growth is picked constantly for tea production. ZONE 8.

Camellia × *williamsii*

This hybrid camellia (*japonica* × *saluenensis*) and its hundreds of cultivars are tall, relatively fast-growing shrubs that flower prolifically over a long period in winter and spring. Raised initially in Britain, plants are more tolerant of alkaline soil and low summer humidity than *C. japonica*, and remain very popular in Britain. They tend to have the dense foliage of the *japonica* parent and the flowers of the *saluenensis*, mainly semi-doubles and in the pink range. They require the usual camellia conditions (see above) and need regular watering in summer. Typical flower forms include 'Caerhays' with medium-sized lilac-rose flowers on plants that have a somewhat pendulous habit; and the beautiful 'Donation' with large orchid pink semi-double flowers, regarded as one of the finest of all camellias. ZONE 7.

CAMPTOTHECA
Nyssaceae

A Chinese genus of a single deciduous tree species; it comes from low-altitude valleys of Yunnan and Sichuan and is not regarded as hardy in cool-temperate countries. A fast-growing tree in its first 10 years, its main attraction is in the foliage, the leaves being large, glossy and strongly ribbed; on new growth flushes they are pale pinkish bronze. In summer it bears stalked spherical heads of tiny white flowers close to the branch tips, followed in autumn by enlarged heads of curious yellow-green sharply angled fruits, which finally turn brown before falling. In a moist, warm-temperate climate and deep moist soil it makes a handsome tree but is too weak to tolerate strong winds, which break branches and disfigure the foliage. Propagation is from seed.

Camptotheca acuminata

This tree grows rapidly to a height of about 40 ft (12 m), with a straight, grey-barked trunk and spreading lateral branches. Growth subsequently slows and some trees go into early decline. Its expected life span is still uncertain. It is reported to be widely cultivated in parts of China. ZONE 10.

CANANGA
Annonaceae

This genus consists of fast-growing evergreen trees from tropical Southeast Asia and the north of Australia, which are prized for their wonderfully fragrant flowers. Like their relatives the custard apple and soursop (see *Annona*), they are easily cultivated in a sheltered position in tropical and warmer subtropical areas. Propagation is from seed or cuttings.

Cananga odorata
YLANG YLANG

This handsome tropical tree reaching 80 ft (25 m) in the wild has weeping, rather brittle branches and large, glossy green compound leaves. The flowers, with their long, twisted, drooping, greenish yellow petals and extraordinarily heavy perfume, appear mostly in summer, in thick clusters at leaf axils, and are followed by small greenish fruit. The ylang ylang (its Malay name) is widely cultivated in Hawaii for the perfume industry. ZONE 11.

CANTUA
Polemoniaceae
SACRED FLOWER OF THE INCAS

This small genus is made up of semi-evergreen shrubs from the Andes of South America, characterized by pendulous trumpet-shaped flowers on weak stalks. This characteristic is a feature of many unrelated flowers in the Americas that are pollinated by hummingbirds—with their amazing ability to hover they can obtain nectar from such flowers, inaccessible to other birds and insects. Only one species is widely cultivated, valued for the elegance of its profuse flowers, often in stark contrast with the bare, untidy stems and branches. Cantuas require a mild climate without extremes of hot or cold, and a sunny open position; in colder areas they prefer a sheltered position against a warm wall. Shape can be improved by tying back stems and pruning back longer growths; but keep in mind that flowers are borne on the previous season's twigs. Propagation is from cuttings, which strike fairly readily.

Cantua buxifolia

The only species usually grown, this makes a shrub of about 6 ft (2 m) high with erect stems and weak arching branches. Leaves are small, greyish green and rather fleshy. The flowers, borne in late spring, vary on different plants, most evident among plants raised from seed. In gardens a rose-purple shade is popular but pink, white and pink-and-white striped flowers are also seen. Sometimes the normal pink-flowering form also bears branches with yellow and white flowers and different foliage. ZONE 8.

CARAGANA
Fabaceae

Pea-flowered deciduous shrubs from central and eastern Asia, of which several are known in cultivation in Europe and North America, these are curious plants of a rather subdued nature, with lemon-yellow, orange, or reddish flowers and small pinnate leaves. Although at their best in climates with dry summers, they are adaptable in this respect, with root systems not prone to rot diseases. They tolerate very low temperatures. Most set plenty of seed in small dry pods which ripen in midsummer, providing an easy means of propagation.

Caragana arborescens
PEA TREE

This is the tallest species, attaining a height of 12–20 ft (4–7 m). A native of central Asia, Siberia and Mongolia, it has been cultivated in western Europe for almost 250 years, and is valued for its hardiness and tolerance of poor conditions. The leaves are soft and spineless, consisting of 8 to 12 fresh green leaflets. Loose clusters of slender-stalked pale yellow flowers hang among the leaves from late spring to early summer. Several cultivars have been named including 'Pendula' with weeping branches; it is usually grafted onto a standard. ZONE 4.

CARICA
Caricaceae
PAPAYA, PAW-PAW

Large succulent edible fruit distinguish this genus of 22 species from Central and South America. Although ultimately tree sized, they remain soft wooded and are short lived. The very large leaves are mostly deeply lobed in a snowflake-like pattern. Male and female flowers are normally borne on separate trees, but hermaphrodite trees have been developed in cultivation. The small cream male flowers are in long-stalked panicles while the larger, fleshy females are stalkless and solitary. Female flowers are followed by the pointed cylindrical fruit that yellows as it ripens. The lowland tropical species are not really suitable for temperate climate gardens but may ripen against a hot wall or can be container grown in greenhouses. Plant in rich, moist, well-drained soil in sun or part-shade. Propagate from seed, cuttings or by grafting.

Caragana arborescens

Cananga odorata

Cantua buxifolia (below)

Carmichaelia odorata

Carissa macrocarpa

Carica papaya

Carmichaelia odorata

Carica papaya

This is the true papaya. It is very much a tropical plant and will not tolerate freezing or even prolonged cold temperatures above freezing. It grows up to 20 ft (7 m) high with a single trunk and a palm-like head of foliage. Leaves are up to 24 in (60 cm) across and carried on 24 in (60 cm) stems. Young plants fruit most heavily and it is wise to keep a succession of plants coming on as replacements. Grow several together as both male and female plants are needed for pollination. Hermaphrodite flowering forms are available and preferred for commercial cultivation. ZONE 10.

CARISSA
Apocynaceae

This genus is made up of attractive evergreen, spiny shrubs which occur in eastern Africa, Asia and Australia. They are widely grown as hedges and container plants in warm-climate areas, valued for their masses of sweet-scented flowers, mostly snow-white, and for their neat appearance. All species bear edible fruit enjoyed by both humans and birds. The glossy, green leaves are thick and tough; leaves and stems exude abundant milky sap when cut or broken. These shrubs prefer warm summers and moderate rainfall, and require a well-drained soil. Plants in pots need moderate water in the growing season, less in winter. Propagate from seed when ripe in autumn, or from semi-ripe cuttings in summer.

Carica papaya (below)

Carissa macrocarpa
NATAL PLUM

Occurring naturally on margins of evergreen forest on the east coast of southern Africa, this dense shrub grows quickly to a height of 10 ft (3 m) and a spread of 15 ft (5 m). The small, rounded leaves are bright green and glossy, and among them are long, prickly spines. The fragrant white flowers appear from spring to summer. The fruits which follow are red, fleshy and oval; they can be made into a delicious jelly. Often planted for hedges, *C. macrocarpa* is particularly useful in sandy coastal gardens as it tolerates salt-laden winds. ZONE 9.

CARMICHAELIA
Fabaceae

Apart from one species endemic to nearby Lord Howe Island, all 40 species of this genus of interesting pea-flowered shrubs and small trees are from New Zealand, where they occur in a wide range of habitats. Their small leaves, consisting of 3 leaflets, are scarce or absent on adult plants of most species, the flattened green branchlets taking over their photosynthetic function. Flowers are mostly quite small, from white to pinkish or purplish, in small clusters freely produced along the branchlets; often scented, in mass they can make quite a display and attract bees and other insects. Seeds are borne singly or a few together in small pods of unusual structure, the softer 'shell' shedding to expose the red or orange seed encircled by the persistent pod rim. Carmichaelias are not often cultivated outside their native areas, but many species have ornamental qualities. They tolerate exposure and dry soils, but the taller species respond to shelter and better soil with denser foliage and more abundant flowers. Propagation is normally from seed, cuttings being difficult to strike.

Carmichaelia arborea

One of the largest-growing species, *C. arborea* can make a small tree of about 15 ft (5 m) with a woody, low-branching trunk and broad bushy crown. More commonly it is seen as a broadly spreading shrub half that height. The massed branchlets are flattened but very narrow, and dull olive-green. The very small, purple and white flowers are borne in great profusion in summer. ZONE 8.

Carmichaelia odorata

This species makes a shrub of 4–6 ft (1.2–2 m) tall with spreading branches and densely massed drooping branchlets that are flattened and very narrow. In late spring and summer it bears an abundance of sweetly scented white flowers with a purple blotch, in short, erect spikes. ZONE 9.

Carmichaelia williamsii

Endemic to the north-east of New Zealand, this species has very flattened stems. It bears pink-veined, creamy yellow flowers from late spring to early summer with occasional flowers at other times. The flowers have only a slight honey scent and are followed by conspicuous seed pods. ZONE 8.

CARNEGIEA
Cactaceae
GIANT SAGUARO

The sole species in this genus is familiar to most gardeners whether they know it or not. It is the tall, branching cactus seen in just about every movie about the American West. Found naturally in Mexico, Arizona and southern California, it is a very upright plant with a candelabra form that towers majestically over the low-growing shrubs common in its desert homeland. Due to their slow growth these dramatic plants are seldom propagated and sold in ordinary nurseries but mature plants are frequently poached from the wild by commercial landscapers, a cause of great concern to conservation authorities. They can be cultivated in gritty, very well-drained soil in full sun. Propagate from seed or offsets.

Carnegiea gigantea

This large, branching cactus can grow to 50 ft (15 m) high and has heavily fluted, spine-encrusted stems. In a low-humidity, low-rainfall climate it is suitable for garden or container cultivation, though it is not very easy to grow away from its native climate and growth is extremely slow—50-year-old plants may be hardly head high! The 4–5 in (10–12 cm) white flowers open at night in early summer and are followed by pulpy fruits that split when ripe. Driest and warmest parts of ZONE 9.

CARPENTERIA
Hydrangeaceae
TREE ANEMONE

Only one species from California belongs to this genus, an evergreen shrub with pure white flowers like those of the related *Philadelphus* but with 5 to 7 petals rather than 4 and a more conspicuous cluster of golden stamens. The leaves are narrow and rather soft, deep green above but paler and felty beneath, arranged in opposite pairs on the soft-wooded branches. Although requiring a fairly cool climate, it only flowers well in regions with warm dry summers, and needs ample sunshine and a well-drained,

Carnegiea gigantea

Carpenteria californica

gritty soil which must not dry out too much. At its best it is a shrub of great beauty when in full flower in late spring and early summer. Propagation is usually from cuttings, which do not root easily. Named for the American Professor Carpenter, it should not be confused with the Australian palm named *Carpentaria*.

Carpenteria californica

In the wild this very attractive shrub is known only from a small area of central California near Fresno, on dry mountain slopes. It can grow to 20 ft (7 m) tall but in gardens is usually 6–8 ft (2–2.5 m) tall and of bushy habit. The flowers, solitary or in small groups, are normally 2–2½ in (5–6 cm) wide but in the best forms may be up to 4 in (10 cm) wide with broadly overlapping petals. ZONE 7.

CARPINUS
Carpinaceae
HORNBEAM

The subtle beauty of hornbeams lies in their usually smoothly fluted trunks and limbs, their neatly veined, small, simple leaves that colour attractively in autumn, and their bunches of dry, winged fruits hanging from the twigs. *Carpinus* is a small genus of catkin-bearing deciduous trees, scattered across cool-climate areas of the northern hemisphere. In foliage and fruit there is not a huge variation between the species, though overall size and growth-habit are distinct for each. Most, and in particular the European *C. betulus*, yield a timber that is exceptionally strong, hard and close grained; it is much used in the mechanism of pianos. Hornbeams are useful small to medium-sized trees for parks, streets and lawns, they are long lived and often slow growing and colour pleasantly in autumn. Propagation is normally from seed except for certain named clones, which must be grafted.

Carpinus betulus
COMMON HORNBEAM

This handsome tree, which ranges from Asia Minor across Europe to eastern England, can grow to 80 ft

Carpinus betulus

Carpinus betulus

(25 m) but 30 ft (10 m) is an average garden height. It has a broad rounded crown and pale grey bark, fairly smooth and often attractively fluted. The ovate leaves are ribbed and serrated, downy when young, and change from dark green in summer to yellow in autumn. Inconspicuous flowers in early spring are followed by clusters of pale yellow fruit. *C. betulus* likes cool, moist conditions. Planted for ornament in parks and large gardens, it is also traditionally used for farm hedgerows as the tough branches will interlock closely; and it can be clipped as a formal hedge. ZONE 6.

Carya cordiformis

Carpinus japonica

Carpinus caroliniana
AMERICAN HORNBEAM, BLUE BEECH

Often shrubby in habit and rarely reaching 40 ft (13 m), this tree is capable of rapid growth—in fact farmers and foresters consider it rather a weed. It is widely distributed in eastern North America, from Canada to northern Mexico, but rarely cultivated. The bark is pale grey, the leaves large and pointed, turning deep orange or red in autumn. The small catkins appear in mid-spring, lengthening in fruit to 6 in (15 cm). This is an attractive and hardy tree combining compact size with vigorous growth.
ZONE 4.

Carpinus japonica
JAPANESE HORNBEAM

This Japanese species makes a medium-sized tree 30–40 ft (9–13 m) tall, forking rather low with broadly ascending branches. The smooth dark grey bark often has lighter streaks and becomes scaly and furrowed with age. Leaves are larger than those of the European

Carpinus caroliniana

Carpinus japonica

hornbeam, up to 4 in (10 cm) long and more closely veined, with edges more finely but sharply toothed and bases heart shaped. The fruiting catkins are very compact with broad, overlapping, jaggedly toothed bracts. As a young tree it is shapely and slow growing.
ZONE 5.

CARYA
Juglandaceae
HICKORY, PECAN

These deciduous trees are valued for the toughness and strength of their wood as well as for their edible nuts. Some 20 species occur in eastern or central USA, one in Mexico, and several in Asia. Closely related to the walnuts (*Juglans*), the hickories and pecans are medium to large trees with large pinnate leaves which turn yellow, orange or rich gold in autumn. The bark of most species is rough textured, giving the trunks a shaggy appearance. The male flowers appear in slender catkins at the base of the new year's growth, the female flowers in smaller clusters at its tip. The fruit is an oval nut enclosed in a leathery husk which divides neatly into 4 segments to open, the feature that distinguishes *Carya* from *Juglans*. *Carya* species are little cultivated with the exception of *C. illinoinensis*, the pecan. The seedlings have long fleshy taproots and are difficult to transplant; they should be grown from seed *in situ*, or planted out as very young seedlings before the taproot reaches the bottom of the container. Cold-hardy and quite fast growing, they prefer sheltered, fertile sites with deep, moist soil, in regions with cold winters and long, hot, humid summers.

Carya cordiformis
BITTERNUT HICKORY

Widespread through much of eastern USA, this fast-growing tree is of medium size, with spreading limbs and a rounded crown. The grey or pale brownish bark is smooth except on quite old trees, when it becomes shallowly furrowed. In winter its twigs are distinguished by striking yellow dormant buds. The rounded nut is smallish and thin shelled, its kernel too bitter to eat. The timber, of lower quality than some other species, is used in smoking hams and bacon. A fine ornamental for large gardens and parks, this tree has adapted well to the climatic conditions in Britain.
ZONE 4.

Carya glabra
PIGNUT HICKORY

Occurring from Maine in the north to Alabama in the south, this medium-sized tree has a tall straight trunk and rather narrow crown. Its grey bark is deeply furrowed with scaly ridges. Leaves consist of 5 to 7 pointed leaflets each 7 in (17 cm) long, turning yellow or orange in autumn. The nut, enclosed in a thin husk, is smallish and nearly spherical, and contains a small but sweet kernel. In the wild pignut hickory grows mainly on wooded slopes of higher hills. It adapts readily to cultivation, making vigorous growth. ZONE 4.

Carya illinoinensis
PECAN

One the world's most popular edible nuts comes from the pecan tree. From Indiana to Texas and Alabama, it occurs along broad river valleys in deep rich alluvial soils, growing to 100 ft (30 m) tall with scaly grey bark. In cultivation it makes fast growth, becoming an open-crowned tree of about 30 ft (10 m) within 10 to 15 years. Although quite frost-hardy, it needs long hot summers to make growth and set fruit. The leaves are long, with many narrow, glossy grey-green leaflets. The elongated nuts, in clusters, are enclosed in ridged, leathery husks; they are usually gathered after falling. Many selections have been named and are propagated by grafting. ZONE 6.

Carya illinoinensis (below)

Carya laciniosa
BIG SHELLBARK HICKORY

Found over much of eastern USA, this hickory is notable for its large handsome leaves and the remarkable bark, hanging from the straight trunk in long recurving plates. A vigorous grower, it reaches over 100 ft (30 m) in deep rich soils and yields an important hickory timber. A fast-growing sapling can be quite striking, with leaves up to 24 in (60 cm) long, downy on their undersides. These turn a magnificent clear yellow in autumn. The nuts, up to 2 in (5 cm) long and almost as wide, have a ridged shell and sweet edible kernel. ZONE 4.

Carya ovata
SHAGBARK HICKORY

Also known as little shellbark hickory, this species has a similar striking bark to that of *C. laciniosa*. In its native valley forests in central-eastern USA it grows as a tall slender tree to 80 ft (25 m) with a long straight trunk and high narrow crown, but in the open it makes a much lower, broader column with foliage reaching almost to the ground. The leaves, of medium size with only 5 broad leaflets, turn a fine golden-yellow in autumn. The smallish nuts are bluntly 4-angled and edible. ZONE 4.

Carya laciniosa

Carya illinoinensis

Carya ovata

Carya laciniosa

Caryota mitis

Carya tomentosa

Caryota urens

Carya tomentosa
MOCKERNUT HICKORY

This fine large tree has a broad, rounded crown and very large winter buds with brown scales which are covered in silky hairs. Native to most of the eastern USA, it favours drier hill slopes. The leaves, dark green with downy undersides and up to 8 in (20 cm) long, have a distinct fragrance when handled. The dark grey bark is close textured, shallowly furrowed and very hard. A very thick husk encloses the smallish oval nut; it contains a sweet, edible kernel. ZONE 4.

CARYOTA
Arecaceae
FISHTAIL PALM

Very unusual palms with bipinnate fronds rather than the more usual pinnate (feather) or palmate (fan) fronds of most palms, make up this genus from tropical Asia and Australasia. 'Fishtail' refers to the shape of the leaflets which are usually wedge shaped with the corners drawn out into points and veins radiating from the stalk end. They include both solitary-trunked palms, mostly large, and multi-stemmed palms which sucker from the base, these being medium-sized to quite small and slender. The mode of flowering and fruiting is remarkable, with the first tassel-like panicles produced among frond bases near tops of mature trunks, and later ones emerging over a number of years successively further down the trunk; the last to appear, sometimes almost at ground level, marks the beginning of the end for that trunk, or of the whole palm in the case of the single-trunked species. Marble-sized fruits, usually ripening dark red, are formed on some of the panicles but others are male only. The fruits contain 1 to 3 black seeds in a fibrous flesh which is quite irritating to the skin. Fishtail palms originate in very moist tropical rainforests and require sheltered, humid environments, but most will tolerate a surprising degree of cold, as well as poorly drained soils. They are easily propagated from seed, making fast growth once past the stemless seedling stage; some of the solitary ones gain height at an amazing rate in hot climates.

Caryota mitis
CLUSTER FISHTAIL PALM

This rainforest understorey palm, widely distributed in the wetter parts of Southeast Asia and the Malay archipelago, consists of a number of closely crowded stems up to about 30 ft (10 m) tall and 3–4 in (7–10 cm) in diameter, nearly always with a thicket of sucker growths at the base. The bipinnate fronds are rather erect, up to about 8 ft (2.5 m) long, with widely separated leaflets. Flowers and fruits appear in succession throughout the year. It is the most widely grown species for ornament, especially suited to sheltered courtyards, but its demand for humidity makes it less suited to permanent indoor use. ZONE 10.

Caryota no
GIANT FISHTAIL PALM

Its unique botanical name alone makes this palm a conversation piece. The epithet *no* was part of the name used by the Dayak people of Sarawak (north Borneo) for this palm. This is the largest of the fishtail palms, with a massive solitary grey trunk to about 80 ft (25 m) tall and over 24 in (60 cm) in diameter. The vast fronds have stiffly spreading stalks but pendulous leaflets. The flowering and fruiting panicles may hang down almost 10 ft (3 m). It makes very fast growth in the wet tropical lowlands and is therefore magnificent as an avenue palm. It can be grown successfully outside the tropics in locations protected from frost. ZONE 10.

Caryota urens
TODDY PALM

This handsome, single-stemmed species is not the only palm from which toddy or palm wine is derived, but it is very commonly grown for the purpose in its native countries (it comes from India, Burma and Malaysia). Toddy is made by cutting off the young flower clusters and collecting the sugary, vitamin-rich sap that flows from the wound; a tree can give as much as 180 gallons (800 litres) a year. It can be drunk fresh or fermented—or distilled into arrack, a highly alcoholic spirit often credited with aphrodisiac properties. The tree grows to about 30 ft (10 m) and is widely planted as an ornamental in tropical countries; though it is not very long lived, its life span of about 40 years is long enough for most people. The name *urens* means stinging, from the way the juice of the fruit irritates the skin. ZONE 10.

CASSIA
Caesalpiniaceae

This genus now consists of over 100 species of shrubs and trees from tropical and subtropical regions around the world. (Previously, *Cassia* was interpreted in a much broader sense, including a very large number of shrubs, small trees and herbaceous plants now separated as the genus *Senna*, listed later in this book.) Some are evergreen, some deciduous. Most have ferny pinnate leaves and clusters of simple, bright golden yellow flowers with prominent stamens, often borne for a long period; these are followed by bean-like seed pods which are often very large. They grow under a wide range of conditions, but most prefer well-drained soil and a sunny position. Propagation is from seed.

Cassia fistula
INDIAN LABURNUM, GOLDEN SHOWER TREE, PUDDING-PIPE OR MONKEY-POD TREE

Native to tropical Asia, this widely cultivated species is a deciduous to semi-evergreen tree that can grow to around 65 ft (20 m) high though often only half that height (or less) in cultivation. It has pinnate leaves from 12–24 in (30–60 cm) long made up of 3 to 8 pairs of large leaflets. In summer it produces large drooping panicles of fragrant pale yellow flowers. It prefers a moist, fertile soil in full sun. Though essentially a tropical plant, it can be grown in a sheltered position in frost-free temperate areas. ZONE 10.

Cassia javanica
PINK SHOWER

This deciduous tree is native to Southeast Asia where it may reach a height of 80 ft (25 m). Cultivated specimens are usually half that height, with a broad, flat-topped crown. It has long pinnate leaves made up of very long, narrow leaflets covered in fine down when young. The showy flowers are carried in large clusters and range from pale pink to red. This tropical species needs a warm climate and moist, fertile, well-drained soil. ZONE 11.

CASTANEA
Fagaceae

CHESTNUT, CHINQUAPIN

These cool-climate deciduous trees all bear edible nuts enclosed in a prickly burr-like husk. The leaves are elliptical with regularly toothed margins and a very regular feather-like arrangement of veins. In spring or early summer they produce showy clusters of stiff catkins of male flowers at the branch tips; the less conspicuous small groups of female flowers among the foliage on the same tree develop into the nuts. Most species are from North America; some are very small trees or even shrubs. Japan has two species and China at least two, while one (*C. sativa*) comes from the Mediterranean region. In a cool climate chestnuts are easily grown in deep, fertile soil. Hot dry summers suit them well as long as ample soil moisture is available in winter and spring. The larger species are important for the fine timber they produce. In the USA the chestnut blight disease all but wiped out many of the finest stands of native species following its accidental introduction in 1904. Some more resistant Eurasian species have been used as graft stocks for the American species. All species are readily propagated from fresh seed, and seedlings should be planted out early to avoid disturbing the taproot.

Castanea dentata
AMERICAN CHESTNUT

This tall North American chestnut was decimated by the chestnut blight early this century, never to recover in anything like its previous numbers and sizes. It grew up to 120 ft (38 m) tall with a straight trunk 3–4 ft (1–1.2 m) thick and was one of the most important timber trees in the eastern states. In foliage and fruit it closely resembles sweet chestnut and the nut is similarly edible. ZONE 4.

Castanea sativa
SWEET CHESTNUT, SPANISH CHESTNUT

The sweet or Spanish chestnut comes from countries around the Mediterranean, as well as the Black and Caspian Seas, but has been planted elsewhere in Europe for its edible nuts since time immemorial. In Britain it is believed to have been introduced in Roman times and some trees are 500 years old; specimens 120 ft (38 m) tall, with trunks 8 ft (2.5 m) in diameter are known. Vigorous young trees have a pyramidal crown with erect leading shoot, but with age lower limbs become massive and broadly spreading. It makes a magnificent, dense shade tree, spoiled only by the prickly burrs that strew the ground beneath at the end of summer. These contain the plump starch-filled nuts, normally with 3 squashed into a prickly husk, but in selected varieties this is often reduced to one larger nut. In autumn, the leaves turn from yellowish green to gold and russet. When planting for nuts it is usual to buy grafted named varieties from a source certified free of disease. ZONE 5.

CASTANOSPERMUM
Fabaceae

QUEENSLAND BLACK BEAN, MORETON BAY CHESTNUT

This genus consists of one species from the rainforests of north-eastern Australia which has long been valued for its beautifully figured, chocolate-brown timber, used for choice cabinet work and veneers. It is a slow-growing tree with a stout trunk and a dense, domed crown. The leaves are pinnate with glossy dark green oblong leaflets, sometimes semi-deciduous in late winter. In early summer it produces large orange and yellow pea-flowers in stiff panicles within the foliage canopy. These are followed in autumn by huge hanging pods, deep green ripening to brown, each containing 2 to 5, 1½ in (3 cm) wide brown seeds. In cultivation it needs a frost-free climate, well-drained fertile soil enriched with organic matter and regular watering. Pruning is rarely necessary. Propagate from seed in spring.

Castanea sativa

Castanea sativa

Cassia fistula

Cassia javanica   *Castanea sativa* (right)

Castanospermum australe

Castanospermum australe

Casuarina cunninghamiana

Casuarina cunninghamiana

Castanospora alphandii

Castanospermum australe

With its glossy leaves and showy orange and yellow flowers, this tree is widely planted in streets and for shade in parks and gardens on the east coast of Australia. It commonly reaches a height of around 40 ft (13 m). The chestnut-like seeds are poisonous but have been the source of international medical research, one of its alkaloids, castanospermine, being regarded as a potential cure for AIDS. Seeds are exported to Europe and Japan where the black bean has become a popular potplant marketed under a variety of names including 'Beany' and 'Bean Ball'. ZONE 10.

CASTANOSPORA
Sapindaceae

Consisting of a single medium-sized evergreen tree species, this is one of many genera of the family Sapindaceae found in rainforests of eastern Australia. Its chief attraction is its elegant foliage; the pinnate leaves curve downward and have 3 to 6 pairs of long, narrow, glossy leaflets, and new growth flushes are a very attractive paler green. Panicles of small white perfumed flowers appear at the branch tips, followed by clusters of reddish brown flattened seed capsules. With its dense crown of foliage, this species makes a fine ornamental and shade tree, but requires a sheltered position and deep, moist soil for good growth. It is propagated from seed.

Castanospora alphandii

Sometimes known as brown tamarind in its native Queensland and northern New South Wales, this tree grows rather slowly to 30–40 ft (10–13 m) tall, with a dense, dome-shaped crown of dark green foliage. The leaves consist of narrow, pointed leaflets about 8 in (20 cm) long. White flowers appear in spring followed by reddish brown fruits in summer and autumn. ZONE 10.

CASUARINA
Casuarinaceae
SHE-OAK

Members of this genus of evergreen trees are sometimes known as 'Australian pines' on account of their conifer-like appearance. It consists of 6 species widely distributed in Australia and about as many again in islands to the north. Many other species previously placed here are now classified under *Allocasuarina* or *Gymnostoma* (both listed elsewhere in this book). The branchlet structures are very similar in these 3 genera, the main difference being in the female 'cones'. Casuarinas are very much part of the Australian landscape (as well as being planted in many other countries) for despite bearing only inconspicuous (male and female) flowers they are graceful trees, fast growing, hardy and adaptable, often to very dry conditions, some to coastal headlands (*C. equisetifolia*), freshwater river banks (*C. cunninghamiana*), saltwater swamps (*C. glauca*), and heavy black inland soils (*C. cristata*). Casuarina wood makes excellent firewood. They are grown as shade or amenity trees and are valued by some farmers for the shade and shelter they provide for stock, while others maintain they poison the ground. They do have nitrogen fixing organisms in their roots and there is some evidence that compounds released from the fallen branchlets inhibit other plant growth. Different species have particular requirements. They are propagated from seed sown in spring. Pruning is rarely necessary.

Casuarina cunninghamiana
RIVER OAK, RIVER SHE-OAK

The largest of the casuarinas, growing to 65–100 ft (20–30 m), this species is much valued for its ability to stabilize river banks, its spreading roots helping to prevent erosion. A handsome tree for ornamental plantings, it is also grown for shade and shelter and, because of its rapid early growth with foliage persistent to ground level, it is useful for windbreaks. The tree requires adequate summer water; it will tolerate quite heavy frosts but growth will be slower and stunted in colder districts. ZONE 8.

Casuarina equisetifolia
BEACH SHE-OAK, AUSTRALIAN PINE

This graceful small tree to 15–30 ft (5–10 m) depending on soil and exposure, has a short trunk and long, weeping, silvery grey branchlets. It is the only species to have spread by natural means far beyond

Australia, being found on tropical seashores throughout the Pacific and Indian Oceans. It grows naturally on beaches and exposed coastal headlands, being very resistant to salt-laden winds and tolerant of poor sandy soil. It is not at all frost-hardy. Reputedly one of the best fuelwood species in the world, *C. equisetifolia* is extensively planted over some 2,000 miles (3,000 km) of China's coastline and is also used for boatbuilding, house construction and furniture making. ZONE 10.

Casuarina glauca
SWAMP OAK, SWAMP SHE-OAK

This upright tree with thick greyish green weeping branchlets grows to 50–65 ft (15–20 m) and occurs near saltwater tidal streams and estuaries of eastern Australia. Male flowers appear as reddish brown terminal spikes among the upper twigs, mostly in autumn. ZONE 9.

CATALPA
Bignoniaceae
CATALPA, INDIAN BEAN TREE

Fast-growing deciduous trees, catalpas have large ovate leaves in opposite pairs, panicles of showy bell-shaped flowers terminating the branches, and extraordinarily long, thin fruits which open to release quantities of very light winged seeds that float away on the breeze. At their best they are beautiful trees with a dense canopy of luxuriant foliage dotted with flower sprays, and are capable of very fast growth, but may look very scrappy if exposed to cold or dry winds or if soil is too poor. Some species yield valuable timber.

Catalpa bignonioides
INDIAN BEAN TREE, SOUTHERN CATALPA

This species comes from the warmer south-east of the USA, from Florida west to Mississippi, where it grows along river banks and around edges of swamps. It makes a reasonably compact tree of 25–50 ft (8–15 m) with a rounded, irregularly shaped crown and is cultivated as an ornamental tree for streets, large gardens and parks. The heart-shaped leaves taper to a fine point and have downy undersides; they have a slightly unpleasant smell when bruised, and turn black before falling in autumn. Sprays of 2 in (5 cm) bell-shaped white flowers with frilled edges appear in summer, with orange blotches and purple spots on their lower lips. The pendulous seed pods are up to 18 in (45 cm) long. The cultivar 'Aurea' has lime-yellow leaves. ZONE 8.

Catalpa bungei
BEIJING CATALPA

This very hardy species from north-eastern China makes a smallish tree with a dense bushy crown, and has ovate leaves with coarse teeth in the lower half, up to about 7 in (17 cm) long. The flowers are white and purple, of medium size and very few to a spray. Some trees grown in the West under this name have proved to be *C. ovata* or small forms of *C. bignonioides*. ZONE 5.

Catalpa speciosa
NORTHERN CATALPA

This handsome tree reaches over 100 ft (30 m) in its home region, the central Mississippi basin between Arkansas and Indiana, where it grows in forests on rich moist soil in valley bottoms and on lower slopes. It is sometimes planted for its timber, which is extraordinarily durable in the ground. The leaves, larger than those of *C. bignonioides*, have no unpleasant smell. The flowers, borne in mid-summer, are similar to those of *C. bignonioides* but individually slightly larger, though the species is usually regarded as less decorative overall. As a planted tree it is tall, upright and fast growing. ZONE 6.

Casuarina equisetifolia

Catalpa speciosa (below)

Catalpa speciosa

Catalpa bignonioides

Casuarina glauca

Casuarina glauca (below)

Ceanothus impressus

Cavendishia bracteata

Ceanothus griseus var. *horizontalis*

Ceanothus papillosus

CAVENDISHIA
Ericaceae

The Andes of South America are the home of the many species which make up this genus, consisting of evergreen shrubs with flowers a bit like some *Erica* species but with broad, leathery leaves. Many are epiphytes, growing on trees in mossy cloud-forests, or sometimes on rocks. Their origin should give a clue to their cultivation requirements: a peaty, humus-rich soil, a humid atmosphere, and a climate without extremes of either heat or cold. Only one species has found its way into gardens in other parts of the world, and this has proved reasonably hardy and vigorous. Propagation is normally from cuttings.

Cavendishia bracteata

This shrub to 3–6 ft (1–2 m) high (syn. *Cavendishia acuminata*) has somewhat scrambling reddish brown branches, becoming pendulous at the tips. New leaves are bronze-pink at the growing tips, hardening to glossy deep green. Clusters of tubular waxy flowers burst from bud bracts from spring to late autumn. These flowers are a shiny red with paler yellowish tips. ZONE 9.

CEANOTHUS
Rhamnaceae
CALIFORNIAN LILAC

Brilliant displays of blue or violet flowers are the feature of many species of these evergreen and deciduous shrubs, some reaching small tree size, all of them North American but the vast majority confined to the coast ranges of California where they form part of the scrubby evergreen 'chaparral' vegetation. Some which grow on coastal cliffs develop dense, prostrate forms highly resistant to salt spray. The leaves are small to medium sized, blunt tipped and usually toothed. The flowers, individually tiny with threadlike stalks, are massed in dense clusters at branch ends; they appear in spring in most species. As garden plants they can be outstandingly ornamental but often short lived, especially prone to sudden death in climates with warm wet summers. They require full sun and prefer exposed positions, in well-drained soil. Propagate from seed, often freely produced in small round capsules, or from cuttings.

Ceanothus arboreus

One of the largest-growing species, occurring wild only on Santa Catalina and nearby offshore islands of California, *C. arboreus* makes an evergreen tree of up to 30 ft (10 m) but in gardens it is normally only half that height, developing a thick, low-branching trunk. Leaves have downy undersides and are larger than in most other species, and the flowers, ranging from very pale blue to deep blue, are in loose clusters carried just above the leaves in spring and early summer. It makes fast early growth in suitable conditions. ZONE 8.

Ceanothus griseus

A spreading bushy shrub from the central Californian hills, this evergreen species grows to 10 ft (3 m) with rounded, hardly toothed leaves that are downy on the undersides. Starting in early spring, it produces abundant dense flower-clusters of a rather pale violet-blue. Var. *horizontalis* is a low-growing, densely spreading form from coastal cliffs, which makes a fine rock garden or groundcover plant for exposed sites: specific clones are grown under the names 'Yankee Point' or 'Hurricane Point', referring to collection sites. ZONE 8.

Ceanothus impressus

A free-flowering, small-leafed evergreen species of dense, spreading habit, this is a first-class garden shrub under suitable conditions. The leaves are ½ in (12 mm) long or less, very thick and with the veins deeply impressed into the upper surface. In spring it produces a profuse display of small clusters of deep blue flowers that appear purple in photographs. From 3–6 ft (1–2 m), this tall Californian species prefers tough, exposed conditions. ZONE 8.

Ceanothus papillosus

This vigorous evergreen shrub or small tree is endemic to California. It grows to around 12 ft (4 m) high and wide and has bright green, leathery leaves to about 1½ in (3 cm) long that densely clothe its strong branches. In spring the plant is covered in heads of deep blue flowers. It is tough and adaptable and will tolerate most soils provided they are well drained. It prefers full sun, does well in coastal conditions and withstands regular trimming. ZONE 8.

Ceanothus thyrsiflorus

A shrub or small tree to 30 ft (10 m), this is another tall evergreen Californian species, but the forms grown in gardens include some that are more compact shrubs of only 5–10 ft (1.5–3 m), with vigorous spreading branches. The shiny oval medium-sized leaves have 3 prominent longitudinal veins. In late spring and early summer it produces dense cylindrical clusters of pale blue to almost white flowers. ZONE 7.

Ceanothus × veitchianus

This hybrid is of unknown origin; *C. thyrsiflorus* may be one parent, the other an unknown smaller-leafed species. The small leaves are rounded and sharply toothed, with veins strongly impressed into the upper surface. The cylindrical flower-clusters are a rather pale lilac-blue, borne profusely in spring. Growing to about 10 ft (3 m) in height, it is a popular shrub. ZONE 7.

CECROPIA
Moraceae
CECROPIA

These fast-growing trees with large umbrella-like leaves are a striking feature of the Amazonian rainforest. They are soft-wooded, with large, open crowns that often project above the surrounding trees. The thick branches have a waxy surface and are often hollow, containing a series of chambers that are inhabited by fierce ants which attack intruders on the tree, including both humans and leafcutter ants that feed on the foliage. Some Amazonian Indians made trumpet-like instruments from the hollow stems. The genus is widespread in tropical America, including species of smaller size and less striking form. They are easily enough cultivated in sheltered sunny positions and deep moist soil, but the rank-growing saplings are weak and easily damaged. Propagation is from seed.

Cecropia palmata
SNAKEWOOD TREE

This species from the West Indies and north-eastern South America is particularly fast growing, making a tall lanky tree of up to 50 ft (15 m), with few branches. The umbrella-like leaves are about 24 in (60 cm) across, deeply segmented into 8 to 10 oblong lobes with rounded tips. The whole leaf is white on the underside. ZONE 11.

CEDRELA
Meliaceae
CIGAR-BOX CEDAR

The tropical tree genus *Cedrela* as formerly defined included many species from Asia, Australasia and the Americas, but is now treated as a purely American genus, the others constituting a separate genus, *Toona*. Both genera have long pinnate leaves and panicles of inconspicuous greenish flowers, and the soft, aromatic reddish timber of both is very valuable and has been exploited in the past to the point of scarcity. It is used to make traditional West Indian cigar-boxes.

Ceanothus thyrsiflorus

These trees are easily grown in any sheltered spot in a warm, humid climate, preferring deep moist soils. They make fast growth in the first decade or two, slowing down thereafter and making fine shade trees. Propagation is normally from fresh seed.

Cedrela mexicana

An evergreen forest tree of 100 ft (30 m) or more in its native Central and South America, this species when grown in the open takes on a broader form, with a stout, straight central trunk and widely spreading limbs. The crown is rather open and coarsely branched, the pinnate leaves being up to 24 in (60 cm) long with leaflets of a fresh green. ZONE 10.

CEDRUS
Pinaceae
CEDAR

A renowned genus of conifers belonging to the pine family; the 4 very similar species, from north-west Africa, Cyprus, Asia Minor and the Himalaya, are so similar that some botanists prefer to treat them as subspecies or varieties of a single species. The pollen cones, shaped like small bananas and up to 3 in (8 cm) long, release large clouds of pollen in early spring. The seed cones are broadly egg shaped or barrel shaped, pale bluish or brownish; they shatter to release seeds with papery wings. As cultivated trees the cedars are valued for the fine architectural effects of their branching, the texture and colour of their foliage, and

Ceanothus thyrsiflorus

Cecropia palmata

Cedrela mexicana (below)

their vigorous growth. In appropriate climatic conditions they are long lived and trouble free, growing massive with age. Propagation is normally from seed, though cuttings, layering and grafting are used for certain cultivars.

Cedrus atlantica
ATLAS CEDAR

The epithet *atlantica* refers not to the ocean but to the Atlas Mountains of Morocco and Algeria where this tree is endemic; some fine stands of trees 130 ft (40 m) tall can still be seen in the Atlas, mostly at altitudes above 3,000 ft (1,000 m). In cultivation it makes a pyramidal tree with stiffly ascending branches in its younger stage, which may last 30 years, but with age it spreads into a broadly flat-topped tree with massive limbs. The bark is dark and scaly, the cones barrel shaped. The densely clustered needles vary from dark green to bluish, though mainly the bluish forms are seen in gardens. This species is popular for ornamental effect in cool climates such as England and north-western Europe. The cultivar name 'Glauca' is used for selected seedling plants with bluish foliage. 'Glauca Pendula' has long, completely pendulous branches and no leading shoot; for long-term effect it should be grafted on a stock at least 10 ft (3 m) tall or allowed to spill over a vertical embankment. ZONE 6.

Cedrus brevifolia
CYPRUS CEDAR

The rarest species in cultivation, this is known in the wild only from a small area of the mountains of Cyprus at an altitude of around 4,500 ft (1,350 m). Botanists have frequently treated it as no more than a variety of *C. libani* but it differs consistently in its shorter needles, only ¼–½ in (6–12 mm) long and smaller overall size. In the wild it grows to a maximum size of 60 ft (18 m) with a trunk of 4 ft (1.2 m) diameter and the oldest trees in cultivation are considerably smaller. ZONE 6.

Cedrus deodara
DEODAR, DEODAR CEDAR

The deodar (its Indian name) occurs in the western Himalaya, reaching 250 ft (80 m) in the wild, but is now almost extinct over much of its former range. In cultivation it makes fast early growth. The long leading shoots nod over slightly, and smaller branches are quite pendulous. Foliage is a dark, slightly greyish green and the cones are about 4 in (10 cm) long. The deodar is at its best in milder, humid climates, in deep soil, making luxuriant growth and reaching 30 ft (10 m) in about 10 years. The most popular cultivar is 'Aurea', with golden branch tips. ZONE 7.

Cedrus libani
CEDAR OF LEBANON

This magnificent tree, the cedar of the Bible and Lebanon's national emblem, has been all but wiped out in that country, with only a few small groves surviving on Mount Lebanon; but larger populations survive in Turkey. It was introduced to western Europe centuries ago, and trees in England are up to 130 ft (40 m) in height and 8 ft (2.5 m) in trunk diameter. As a young tree it has a narrow, erect habit but with age adopts a flat-topped shape with massive spreading limbs. It prefers a moist, cool climate. It is slightly less ornamental than *C. atlantica* or *C. deodara* except for large, mature specimens, when the majestic architecture of the cedar of Lebanon can show to advantage. ZONE 6.

Cedrus brevifolia

Cedrus atlantica

Cedrus atlantica 'Glauca Pendula' (below)

Cedrus atlantica (below)

Cedrus deodara (below)

CEIBA
Bombacaceae
SILK COTTON

This genus consists of 4 deciduous trees with heavily buttressed, spiny trunks and large palmate (hand-shaped) leaves. They occur naturally in tropical parts of the Americas and Africa and their fibres still have some commercial use, though they have been largely replaced by synthetics. These trees are widely used by local people as sources of fibre, fuel and timber. These distinctly tropical trees are not suited to temperate zones. They need regular rainfall, moist, well-drained soil and steady warm temperatures. Propagate from seed or semi-ripe cuttings.

Ceiba pentandra
KAPOK

At up to 220 ft (70 m) high, this African species is the tallest tree found in that continent. Its trunk is very spiny and the branches are held horizontally giving the tree a distinctive pyramidal outline. It produces showy white, yellow or pale pink flowers, 6 in (15 cm) in diameter, followed by 6 in (15 cm) long, pointed, cylindrical fruit filled with seeds surrounded by white fibre. The fibre is kapok and was once extensively used in pillows, quilts, saddles and upholstery. ZONE 12.

CELTIS
Ulmaceae
NETTLE TREE, HACKBERRY

This large genus includes many evergreens, occurring mainly in the tropics, but the cool-climate deciduous species from North America, Europe and Asia are the ones mostly cultivated. They are medium to fairly large trees with smooth or slightly rough bark. Leaves are smallish, oval and pointed at the tip, with few or many marginal teeth. Insignificant flowers, of different sexes and lacking petals, appear with the new leaves, and fruits are small, hard, orange or blackish drupes carried singly in the leaf axils. Birds eat the fruits and disperse the seeds, and some species self-seed and can become a nuisance. *Celtis* species are planted mainly as shade trees in streets and parks, where they make shapely, long-lived and trouble-free specimens. Hackberry is their American name, while nettle tree is used in the UK.

Celtis africana
CAPE CHESTNUT

A warm-climate deciduous species that originates from coastal forests and grassland areas of South Africa, this is a large, well-shaped tree with smooth, silvery white bark. It grows rapidly to a height and spread of 30–40 ft (10–13 m) in cultivation, much taller in the wild. Insignificant, small, pale yellow flowers appear briefly in spring at the same time as the new foliage. The masses of orange or yellow berries which ripen during summer are enjoyed by birds. A useful shade tree, it is frost-hardy and reasonably drought tolerant. It does best in fertile, moist, well-drained soil. ZONE 9.

Celtis australis
NETTLE TREE

This deciduous small to medium-sized tree to 50 ft (15 m) originates from southern Europe, North Africa and Asia Minor. It has broadly lance-shaped serrated-edged leaves that are dark green and rough to touch on the upper surface, grey-green and downy on the underside. The small fruits which turn purple-black in autumn are edible. This species is a useful shade tree for streets or parks. ZONE 8.

Celtis laevigata
SUGARBERRY

The common name promises sweet fruit, but the small scarlet berries which turn black as they age are too small (and too lacking in pulp) to be worth eating, though birds adore them. Perhaps the handsomest species of its genus, the sugarberry (syn. *Celtis mississippiensis*) is a valued street tree in its native mid-west and southeastern USA and also in Australia as it is resistant to drought and urban pollution. This is surprising because in the wild it grows on river banks and moist ground. Officially deciduous, it is apt to be evergreen or almost so in mild-winter climates. The thin leaves taper to a very fine point and usually lack marginal teeth. It grows fast when young, eventually making a shapely, round-headed tree of about 50 ft (15 m) tall, with rich, deep green leaves. ZONE 5.

Celtis occidentalis
AMERICAN HACKBERRY

This species comes from the east of the USA, the Mississippi Basin, and eastern Canada. In its preferred habitat of forests on deep, rich alluvial soils, it can reach a very large size, but when planted in the open the American hackberry makes a shapely, spreading tree of 30–40 ft (10–13 m). The bark, smooth on saplings, develops irregular ridges of corky warts which combine into a darkish rough cover as the tree matures. The pea-sized fruit ripen through red to dull purple. It makes a fine shade tree with the foliage turning pale yellow in autumn, but it can become a pest along river banks and channels in some countries. ZONE 3.

Celtis occidentalis

Cedrus libani

Celtis sinensis
CHINESE HACKBERRY, CHINESE NETTLE TREE

Originating from China, Japan and Korea, this deciduous or semi-deciduous tree grows to 50–65 ft (15–20 m) with a rounded broad crown. It is notable for its dark green, glossy leaves. Small globe-shaped fruits start green and ripen to first dull orange then dull purple in mid-summer and autumn. In warmer temperate climates this species has proved very tough and adaptable, tolerating infertile and poorly drained soils and urban pollution. Unfortunately its seeds germinate easily and in large numbers and in humid coastal areas it rapidly becomes a weed. ZONE 8.

Ceiba pentandra

Celtis occidentalis

Celtis sinensis

Ceratopetalum apetalum

Cephalotaxus fortunei

Ceratopetalum apetalum

Ceratopetalum apetalum

Cephalotaxus harringtonia 'Fastigiata'

Ceratonia siliqua

CEPHALOTAXUS
Cephalotaxaceae
PLUM-YEW

This is an interesting genus of conifers, shrubs or very small trees, mostly with many stems sprouting from the base and attractive deep green leathery foliage. All originate in eastern Asia and they have similar foliage to the true yews (*Taxus*). The fleshy fruits, which are more like olives than plums, ripen reddish brown. Male pollen sacs are found in small globular clusters on separate trees. They are tough, resilient plants, but do best in cool, fairly humid climates and in sheltered positions. The occasional free-seeding specimen can cause minor problems by the quantity of 'fruits' dropping to rot on the ground beneath.

Cephalotaxus fortunei
CHINESE PLUM-YEW

The Chinese plum yew is a spreading shrub or small tree to 20 ft (7 m). It has brown bark peeling off in flakes. It originates from northeastern China, and was introduced to England in 1849 by Robert Fortune, the man who first brought the tea plant from China to India. The needle-like leaves, up to 3½ in (9 cm) long, have fine sharp points. The oval fruit, ripening to shiny brown, are about 1 in (2.5 cm) long. ZONE 7.

Cephalotaxus harringtonia
JAPANESE PLUM-YEW

First known from Japan, this species, with a range of forms, also occurs in Korea and parts of China. The typical form is a spreading bushy shrub 6–10 ft (2–3 m) tall. More commonly grown is var. *drupacea*, a domelike shrub to about 10 ft (3 m). The most remarkable and attractive form is 'Fastigiata': very erect, it sends up a dense mass of long straight branches from the base, each with radiating whorls of leathery, recurving dark brownish green leaves. It forms a tight column about 6 ft (2 m) high and 24 in (60 cm) across. It has been cultivated for centuries in Japan where it is called 'Chosen-maki'. ZONE 6.

CERATONIA
Caesalpiniaceae
CAROB, ST JOHN'S BREAD

The single species in this genus comes from the eastern Mediterranean where it forms a picturesque round-headed tree to 40 ft (13 m). It is more commonly seen as a smaller tree or large shrub in cultivation and can be pruned hard to keep it in check. While it requires hot summers to perform well, it will survive in warm sheltered positions in cooler climates. Marginally frost-hardy, carobs do best in full sun although they will tolerate light shade and are also drought tolerant; a moderately fertile, well-drained soil suits them. The bean-like pods, about 6 in (15 cm) long, commonly roasted and powdered as a chocolate substitute, can be picked in autumn when they are dark brown. They can also be eaten fresh and are used as stock fodder. Propagate from seed in autumn. The seeds are very uniform in size and used to be used by jewellers as standard weights—hence the term 'carat', derived from the Greek word for carob bean.

Ceratonia siliqua

A long-lived evergreen tree, the carob is used as a shade tree for streets, parks and large gardens, and as a farm shelter and fodder tree. It has glossy pinnate leaves and clustered spikes of small greenish flowers in spring and autumn. As some plants bear only male or female flowers, interplanting of clonal material may be needed for production of the pods. ZONE 9.

CERATOPETALUM
Cunoniaceae

Members of this small Australian genus come from forests of the east coast; the two most important species are found in New South Wales where they are valued for their timber and flowers respectively. They are evergreen and bear flowers with very small white petals, but with sepals that appear flower-like, enlarging and turning red as the small nut-like fruits mature. They prefer a warm, almost frost-free climate and free draining soil, with protection from salty winds, and plenty of water in spring and summer. Propagation is from fresh seed or from cuttings.

Ceratopetalum apetalum
COACHWOOD

This tree with its tall straight trunk and aromatic, greyish bark blotched with darker patches can reach a height of 80 ft (25 m) or more in deep shaded rainforest gullies. The long tapering leaves are dark green and heavily veined. Clusters of tiny white flowers appear in spring, the sepals enlarging and becoming red in early summer. A valuable timber tree, the coachwood is occasionally seen in parks and gardens. ZONE 9.

Ceratopetalum gummiferum
NEW SOUTH WALES CHRISTMAS BUSH

Occurring naturally in coastal gullies and sheltered slopes on mostly sandstone soils, this species grows naturally as an upright tree to about 25 ft (8 m). In gardens it is often kept pruned as a shrub or small tree to 12 ft (4 m), grown for its bright 'flowers' (calyces) which start white and become pink or bright red in early summer. The flowers are sold commercially in Australia as Christmas decoration and have found their way onto the cut flower export market. With their shiny soft green leaves, each divided into 3 serrated leaflets, the plants are also attractive when not in flower. As coloration is very variable from seedling stock, it is wise to buy plants when in flower or choose a clone such as 'Albery's Red'. Full sun suits it best. Cutting for flowers or trimming after flowering will promote shape and improve flowering next year. ZONE 9.

CERATOSTIGMA
Plumbaginaceae

This genus of 8 species of woody herbs and small shrubs is primarily of Himalayan and east Asian origin, with one species endemic to the Horn of Africa. The species grown in gardens are small deciduous shrubs and from spring to autumn they produce loose heads of blue phlox-like flowers that indicate the genus's relationship with *Plumbago*. The small leaves are deep green, turning to bronze or crimson in autumn before falling. *Ceratostigma* species will grow in any moist, well-drained soil in sun or part-shade. Propagate from seed or semi-ripe cuttings, or by division. In cold climates they will reshoot from the roots even though the top growth may freeze to ground level.

Ceratostigma willmottianum
CHINESE PLUMBAGO

This 24–36 in (60–90 cm) deciduous shrub from western Sichuan, China, is prized for its small heads of bright blue phlox-like flowers that open from late summer to autumn. The leaves are deep green, roughly diamond shaped and around 2 in (5 cm) long. In the autumn the foliage develops bronze or crimson tones before falling. It grows in any moist, well-drained soil in sun or part-shade, and survives heavy frosts with some stem dieback. Propagate from cuttings or by division. ZONE 6.

CERCIDIPHYLLUM
Cercidiphyllaceae
KATSURA TREE

Consisting of a single species of deciduous tree native to Japan and China, this genus is related to the magnolias. The flowers are rather insignificant, dull red and about $\frac{1}{4}$ in (6 mm) long, with different sexes on different trees. On female trees, clusters of small greenish pod-like fruit follow the flowers.

Ceratostigma willmottianum

Ceratostigma willmottianum

Ceratopetalum gummiferum

Cercidium floridum

Cercidium floridum

The katsura is valued chiefly for its foliage which is red when first expanding in spring, then dark green, changing in autumn to various mixtures of yellow, pink, orange and red. It is frost-hardy but the spring foliage is easily damaged by late frost, drought, or drying winds. Katsura is its Japanese name.

Cercidiphyllum japonicum

In cultivation in the West this is known as a small, rather slender tree about 30 ft (10 m) high but in Japan and China it is the largest native deciduous tree; ancient specimens up to 130 ft (40 m) tall, with trunks over 15 ft (5 m) thick are known! The trunk often forks at a narrow angle and the short branches spread horizontally in tiers. The heart-shaped leaves are mostly under 3 in (7 cm) wide, but larger in var. *magnificum*; var. *sinense* has slightly different leaves and flowers. The cultivar 'Pendulum' has a dome-shaped crown and pendulous branches. ZONE 6.

CERCIDIUM
Caesalpiniaceae

From the warmer and drier parts of the Americas, *Cercidium* consists of small wiry-branched trees that are commonly deciduous throughout dry periods, coming into leaf only after rain. Leaves are small and bipinnate but for much of the time it is the wiry green branches that perform the function of photosynthesis. The fine-stalked flowers are yellow and cup shaped, somewhat like *Cassia* flowers, and appear in profuse clusters all along the branches for a few weeks in spring. These trees have the potential to make fine ornamental and shade trees for very hot dry areas, though they do require a supply of deep subsoil moisture. Propagation is from seed, produced in small pods. If planted in other continents they should be watched carefully for excessive self-seeding—leguminous trees such as *Prosopis* and *Parkinsonia* from similar environments have already become problem weeds in some countries.

Cercidium floridum
PALO VERDE

The common name is Spanish for 'green stick' and describes the smooth bluish green bark and branches, leafless for much of the time in the desert stream-beds in which this species grows in the Colorado River region of southwestern USA and adjacent Mexico. It makes at maturity a broad-crowned small tree of 20–25 ft (7–8 m) tall with a short thick trunk and densely massed branches. In full flower it is briefly transformed into a mass of golden-yellow blossom. ZONE 8.

CERCIS
Caesalpiniaceae
JUDAS TREE, REDBUD

This genus is made up of small deciduous trees or shrubs from North America, Asia and southern Europe. Their profuse clusters of pea-like flowers, bright rose-pink to crimson, line the bare branches in spring; even the neat, pointed buds, slightly deeper in colour, make an elegant display, hence the American name redbud. The handsome heart-shaped to almost circular leaves follow, along with flat seed pods up to 4 in (10 cm) long. All of the 7 or 8 species are worth cultivating, though not all of them are easily obtained. They resent disturbance to their roots, especially transplanting. A sunny position suits them best and they thrive in hot dry summer weather, as long as the soil moisture is adequate in winter and spring. They are easily propagated from seed, though growth is usually slow and it may take many years for them to become larger than shrub size.

Cercidiphyllum japonicum (left)

Cercidiphyllum japonicum (above)

Cercis canadensis

Cercis occidentalis

Cercis siliquastrum

Cercis siliquastrum 'Rubra'

Cercis canadensis
EASTERN REDBUD

Endemic to eastern USA, from New Jersey and Minnesota south to Florida, this tree can reach 40 ft (13 m) in the wild and is strikingly beautiful in flower. In gardens it rarely exceeds 12 ft (4 m), branching close to the ground. The buds are deep rose, and the paler rose flowers, less than $\frac{1}{2}$ in (1 cm) long, are profuse and showy; flowering may continue into early summer. In the south-western part of its range the typical form is replaced by subsp. *texensis*, whose leaf undersides have a waxy bluish coating. ZONE 5.

Cercis occidentalis
WESTERN REDBUD

Geographically this species, found in the south-west of the USA, takes over more or less where *C. canadensis* leaves off. It is similar in growth-habit and flowers but usually remains shrubby. The leaves, sometimes kidney shaped, are bright green. The western redbud likes much the same conditions as the eastern redbud. ZONE 5.

Cercis siliquastrum
JUDAS TREE

Indigenous to the Mediterranean and Black Sea coasts, this tree can grow to 40 ft (13 m) but seldom exceeds 25 ft (8 m) even after several decades. The leaves are slightly bluish green with rounded tips, and the late spring flowers, larger and deeper pink than other species, arise in clusters on previous years' growths. It is the most reliable ornamental species in regions where winters are mild. Forms with distinct flower coloration include the white 'Alba' and the deeper reddish 'Rubra'. ZONE 7.

CERCOCARPUS
Rosaceae
MOUNTAIN MAHOGANY

These evergreen shrubs and small trees from western North America get their common name from their hard, strong, reddish wood and their occurrence high in the Rockies and Sierras. The small thick-textured leaves with blunt teeth and crowded parallel veins are carried on condensed knotty side shoots that also produce tight clusters of tiny petal-less flowers in spring and summer. The nut-like fruits may persist into winter; each has a long feathery plume, much more conspicuous than the small greenish flowers. Successfully cultivated in Europe, they remain rare there, but they are grown to a limited extent in their native regions. Tough and drought-hardy, propagation is from seed or small semi-ripe tip cuttings. Shoots near the ground can be layered and sometimes self-layer.

Cestrum fasciculatum 'Newellii'

Cercocarpus betuloides

Cestrum fasciculatum

Cercocarpus betuloides

Cercocarpus betuloides
BIRCHLEAF MOUNTAIN MAHOGANY

This species occurs wild in the mountains of California, north to Oregon and south through Arizona into northern Mexico, growing at altitudes up to 7,000 ft (2,500 m). There are several geographic varieties. Commonly shrub-like, it rarely reaches 20 ft (7 m) in height and has very hard, woody branches with smooth grey bark. The small leaves are dark green above with paler downy undersides. The decorative silvery plumes of the small dry fruits can be over 4 in (10 cm) long. ZONE 7.

CESTRUM
Solanaceae
JESSAMINE

This genus is made up of over 200 shrubs, mostly from the Americas, best suited to tropical and subtropical gardens and grown for their decorative tubular flowers, night-scented in some species. The flowers are followed by small round berries and all parts of the plants are poisonous. They make straggly bushes but can be pruned hard to shape. Some (especially *C. parqui*) are free-seeding and invasive, especially in warmer climates. They will grow fast in full sun and moderately fertile, well-drained soil with plentiful water in summer and regular fertilizing. Cestrums can be grown against a wall for frost protection in cooler climates and in areas with light frosts may be cut back and mulched heavily in early winter. A number of species are grown in conservatories and greenhouses. Plants in containers need plentiful water in the growing season, less at other times. Many will self-seed and also grow readily from soft tip cuttings in summer.

Cestrum fasciculatum
This slender evergreen shrub, fast-growing to 10 ft (3 m), has arching branches, long pointed leaves and terminal clusters of tubular rose-red flowers in summer and occasionally throughout the year. One-third of its wood can be removed after flowering to maintain shape. ZONE 9.

Cestrum fasciculatum 'Newellii'
Tougher than most other cestrums, this is a 6 ft (2 m) high, soft-stemmed evergreen shrub with deep green leaves, 4 in (10 cm) long, and clusters of tubular, crimson, unscented flowers through much of the year, followed by matching berries. It grows best in sunny, sheltered positions with rich, moist, well-drained soil and is regarded as something of a weed in some mild areas, particularly the north of New Zealand. Propagate from semi-ripe cuttings. ZONE 9.

Cestrum nocturnum
NIGHT-SCENTED JESSAMINE, LADY OF THE NIGHT

A rather untidy, easily grown evergreen shrub 10 ft (3 m) tall and almost as wide, this species has long, slender, arching branches growing from the base. Clusters of pale green flowers appear in late summer and are strongly and sweetly perfumed at night but scentless during the day. Berries are green at first but whitish when ripe in early winter. It is not fussy about soil and will grow in sun or part-shade. Older canes can be cut out annually. ZONE 10.

CHAENOMELES
Rosaceae
FLOWERING QUINCE

Related to the edible quince (*Cydonia*), with similar large, hard fruit, these many-stemmed shrubs are valued for the display of red, pink or white flowers on a tangle of bare branches in early spring or even late winter. Originating in China, Japan and Korea, they are extremely cold-hardy and adapt to a wide range of garden conditions. The tough, springy branches are often spiny on vigorous shoots; leaves are simple and finely toothed. Flowers appear in stalkless clusters on the previous year's wood, followed in summer by yellow-green fruits with waxy, strongly perfumed skin, which make fine jams and jellies. The flowering quinces perform best in a sunny spot in well-drained but not too rich soil, and a dry atmosphere. Some older branches may be cut back hard each year to encourage vigorous bushy growth, or it can be trained against a wall. Propagation is from hardwood cuttings. The wild forms have been replaced by a large selection of cultivars, only a few of which are generally available.

Chaenomeles speciosa
CHINESE FLOWERING QUINCE, JAPONICA

This species and its hybrids are the only flowering quinces usually grown. Shrubs of 5–10 ft (1.5–3 m) high, they spread by basal suckers to form dense thickets of stems. Flowering can start in mid-winter, the flowers scarlet to deep red in the original species. The many modern cultivars vary in availability, while several of the older ones are widely grown, including 'Nivalis' (white), 'Moerloosii' (white flushed and blotched pink and carmine) and 'Rubra Grandiflora' (crimson). Most hybrid cultivars belong to C. × superba (speciosa × japonica) and are somewhat lower growing, the flowers predominantly in rich oranges, scarlets and deep reds. ZONE 6.

CHAMAEBATIARIA
Rosaceae
FERNBUSH

The mountains of western USA are home to several unusual genera of shrubs and small trees in the rose family, of which this is one of the most distinctive. It consists of only one species, a low shrub with several erect stems that are covered with sticky, aromatic hairs when young, giving off a balsamic smell. The leaves are finely dissected in a bipinnate pattern and covered in a sticky whitish down. In summer the lateral branches terminate in short crowded panicles of white flowers like small apple blossoms, opening among a mass of woolly buds. Fernbush adapts well enough to cultivation, preferring a dry sunny spot and well-drained soil. It is best propagated from cuttings.

Chamaebatiaria millefolium

The sole species of the genus, this shrub ranges widely through the Rocky Mountains plateaus and Californian Sierras, growing in rocky places. It reaches between 24 in (60 cm) and 5 ft (1.5 m) depending on conditions. The reddish bark is loose and shredded. From mid to late summer it produces a profusion of white blossom. ZONE 5.

CHAMAECYPARIS
Cupressaceae
FALSE CYPRESS

Not long ago botanists classified these conifers as Cupressus (true cypresses) and indeed the differences between Cupressus and Chamaecyparis are slight. Nearly all Chamaecyparis species occur in cooler, moister, more northerly regions in North America and East Asia, while the true cypresses mostly occur further south and in drier regions, in western North America, Himalayan Asia, and the Mediterranean. Several species have given rise to a vast number of cultivars, which feature coloured foliage (usually gold, bluish or bronze); narrow, fastigiate, columnar or dwarf habit; bizarre foliage traits; or needle-like juvenile foliage. They are easily propagated from cuttings. Chamaecyparis species grow well in a cool, moist climate; they respond with fast growth to deep, rich, well-drained soils and a sheltered position. Under such good conditions, even some dwarf cultivars can reach many times their anticipated height; the best way to maintain dwarf forms in rock gardens is to use poor gritty soil; or in pots, tubs, or terrace gardens to allow only a limited root space.

Chamaecyparis funebris
CHINESE WEEPING CYPRESS

This attractive species, once known as Cupressus funebris, is widespread at lower altitudes in central China, where it is also widely planted. It commonly reaches a height of 30–50 ft (10–15 m) and is of broadly columnar habit, with a straight central trunk and ascending branches drooping at the tips, the small branchlets arranged in very elongated, pendulous, loosely flattened sprays. The foliage is a dull greyish green. Globular green cones about ⅓ in (1 cm) in diameter appear in profusion in summer on these branchlet-sprays. A very elegant tree, it does best in mild climates with good rainfall and low humidity. ZONE 9.

Chamaecyparis funebris

Chamaebatiaria millefolium

Cestrum nocturnum

Chaenomeles speciosa (right)

Chamaecyparis lawsoniana
LAWSON CYPRESS

From the humid coastal forests of north-western USA, this is one of the most majestic conifers, widely planted where space allows; trees in England are 120 ft (38 m) tall with trunks up to 4 ft (1.2 m) in diameter, narrowly conical with pendulous side branches producing rippling curtains of bluish green to deep green foliage. Adaptable and remarkably cold-hardy, it grows best in moist, sheltered sites on deep, fertile soils. Over 180 cultivars of this species are currently available and many more have been named. 'Allumii', of erect conical habit with very bluish dense foliage, grows to 10–15 ft (3–5 m) or more. 'Erecta', similar in shape, is plain green with very erect, narrow sprays of foliage tightly crowded together; slow growing at first, it can reach 30 ft (10 m) with age. 'Fletcheri' has grey-blue foliage in smaller, less regular sprays and is semi-juvenile, the leaves somewhat needle-like. 'Lane' makes a narrower column with lemony yellow foliage in late spring and summer changing to bronze-gold in winter; slow growing, it may still get larger than expected if conditions suit it. 'Stewartii', a golden cultivar, rapidly reaches 15–25 ft (5–8 m), with a broad base and crowded nodding sprays of rich buttery foliage; it is often used in landscaping for a gold effect on a large scale. 'Winston Churchill' is a popular recent cultivar; it has a very pronounced conical growth-habit and golden yellow foliage. ZONE 6.

Chamaecyparis obtusa

Chamaecyparis lawsoniana 'Winston Churchill'

Chamaecyparis nootkatensis
NOOTKA CYPRESS, ALASKA CEDAR, PORT ORFORD CEDAR

From western North America, this cypress ranges much further north than *C. lawsoniana*, through west-coastal Canada into Alaska. A large forest tree, it is conical in shape, growing to about 100 ft (30 m); the small blue-green cones have a recurved, pointed flap at the centre of each scale. The crushed foliage has a slightly unpleasant smell. Not quite as ornamental as *C. lawsoniana*, it is still an attractive tree, and thrives under more adverse conditions of soil and climate. ZONE 4.

Chamaecyparis obtusa
HINOKI CYPRESS

The normal, tall form of this fine tree from Japan, with richly textured deep green foliage, is seldom seen in gardens; it is usually represented by its dwarf or coloured cultivars. One of Japan's most valued timber trees, it reaches 120 ft (38 m) in the wild, with a trunk to 4 ft (1.2 m) in diameter and thick red-brown bark. In cultivation it grows to 60 ft (18 m), broadly columnar with dense, spreading branches that touch the ground. This species adapts to a wide range of climates and soil conditions. Cultivar 'Crippsii' makes a broad golden pyramid with a vigorous leading shoot; usually about 10–15 ft (3–5 m) tall. 'Tetragona' and 'Tetragona Aurea' are of similar height but narrower and more irregularly branched, their scale-leaves in 4 equal ranks and branchlets tightly crowded; the first is a deep slightly bluish green, the second green and gold. Of the dwarf cultivars, the smallest under 12 in (30 cm) in height, best known are 'Nana Gracilis' and its numerous variants, little bun-shaped plants normally 12–24 in (30–60 cm) high with crowded fans of tiny branchlets producing a richly textured effect; 'Nana Aurea' is much the same but with golden tips to the fans, the whole tree has more of a bronze tone in winter. ZONE 5.

Chamaecyparis nootkatensis

Chamaecyparis pisifera
SAWARA CYPRESS

Growing to 150 ft (46 m) in the wild, this vigorous Japanese species makes a broad conical tree; the lower sides of the branchlets are strongly marked bluish white and the tiny scale-leaves on juvenile growth are quite prickly. The cultivars fall into 3 groups, the Squarrosa group, the Plumosa group and the Filifera group. 'Squarrosa' itself is a broadly pyramidal small tree about 10 ft (3 m) tall, with pale bluish grey juvenile foliage that turns dull purple in winter. 'Squarrosa Intermedia' is a dwarf cultivar: 'Boulevard' is narrowly conical, about 6 ft (2 m) tall, with foliage of a bright steel-blue mixed with green. Plumosa is the largest group of cultivars, many of them dwarf. Of the Filifera group, best known is 'Filifera Aurea', a broadly pyramidal shrub 6–8 ft

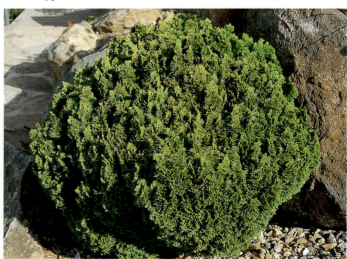
Chamaecyparis obtusa 'Nana Gracilis'

(2–3 m) tall; its bright gold and green foliage has flattened fans of branchlets mixed with elongated 'rat's-tail' branchlets that arch gracefully. ZONE 5.

Chamaecyparis thyoides
ATLANTIC WHITE CEDAR

From eastern North America and the Gulf Coast, this hardy tree reaches about 60 ft (18 m) in the wild, less in cultivation. It is narrowly columnar when young. The dull grey-green branchlets grouped into very small fans are crowded irregularly on the branches and do not produce the rippled foliage effect of most other species. In early American towns the wood was favoured for roofing shingles. The cultivar 'Ericoides' makes a broad pyramid 6–8 ft (2–3 m) high; its soft juvenile foliage is bronze-green in spring and summer, changing to deep plum tones in winter. ZONE 4.

CHAMAEROPS
Arecaceae
MEDITERRANEAN FAN PALM

Noteworthy as the only palm indigenous to Europe (except for a rare date palm on Crete), the single species of this genus occurs along all the warmer Mediterranean coasts, growing in seashore scrubs often on limestone, and in northwest Africa on rocky slopes of the Atlas and Rif Mountains to 5,000 ft (1,500 m) altitude. Wild plants, subjected to scrub fires and grazing, usually remain as a clump of stemless shoots less than 4 ft (1.2 m) high, with stiff greyish leaf-blades and very prickly stalks forming a dense mound. Cultivated plants develop taller multiple trunks clothed in shaggy fibre and stubs of leaf stalks. Flowers are of different sexes on different plants, the male yellow in dense short panicles, the female green in even shorter but sparser clusters, followed by shiny orange-brown fruits like short dates. These palms are easily cultivated, tolerating sun or shade and a wide range of soil types, but do best in warm sunny positions. They take many years to reach a respectable size and big specimens are prized for transplanting. Trimming of dead fronds should be done with sympathy for the natural appearance of the trunk; cut stalks neatly at a consistent length and take care not to rip off the fibre sheaths. Propagation is from seed which germinates readily, or by careful division of a clump. Take great care when handling as the thorns are very sharp.

Chamaerops humilis

Old plants of this palm have trunks up to about 12 ft (4 m) tall and 8–10 in (20–25 cm) in diameter including the coating of fibres and

Chamaecyparis pisifera, Plumosa group

Chamelaucium uncinatum

Chamelaucium uncinatum

old stalks. The leaves (fronds) are small for a fan palm, with stiff segments only 12–20 in (30–50 cm) long radiating from a stalk of about the same length, its edges fiercely armed. Fronds vary from plain olive-green to a strong blue-grey shade in different races. The perfumed yellow male flowers appear in late spring. ZONE 8.

CHAMELAUCIUM
Myrtaceae

A genus of dainty evergreen shrubs endemic to Western Australia, Geraldton wax flowers are perhaps the best known of Australian commercial cut flowers and are grown in many countries. Named hybrids and cultivars have flowers ranging from white through pale and dark pink to mauve, rose-purple and carmine. They are beautiful flowers, long-lasting in the vase, but the shrubs with their large, airy sprays of flowers have a reputation for being difficult to grow, since they do not tolerate cold winters, wet summers or high humidity. Try them in full sun and slightly alkaline, gravelly soil and prune fairly hard after flowering, but don't be surprised if they are short lived despite all your best efforts. Propagate from cuttings in summer.

Chamelaucium uncinatum
GERALDTON WAX

This is the most common species and the chief parent of most re-

Chamaerops humilis

cently bred cultivars; it grows to 10 ft (3 m) tall and almost as wide. In its natural habitat it is a brittle, spreading shrub with fine needle-like foliage and, most commonly, white, mauve or pink waxy flowers in late winter and through spring. New cultivars appear regularly but all seem prone to root-rot in wet soil. Avoid any root disturbance. ZONE 10.

Chionanthus retusus

Chionanthus retusus

Chilopsis linearis

Chimonanthus praecox

shaped, with a translucent waxy texture, and are followed by leathery-skinned fruits of a strange shape, like little bags stuffed with balls, which turn out to be the large seeds. These germinate readily, providing the easiest means of propagation, or the multiple stems can be layered by mounding with soil; cuttings are very difficult to strike. The plant itself is quite frost-hardy and will grow in most positions but does best against a warm wall in cold climates to protect the flowers. Pruning consists mainly of thinning out weaker stems and, if desired, shortening the larger stems, which should be done immediately after flowering.

Chimonanthus praecox

The wintersweet makes a thicket of stiff, angular stems 6–8 ft (2–2.5 m) high and about the same in width, with harsh-textured dark green leaves. Flowers appear in abundance on bare winter branches or, in milder climates, among the last leaves of autumn; the petals are pale yellow to off-white with a dull pink or red basal zone showing on the inside. The fruits are about 1½ in (4 cm) long, yellowish brown when ripe. ZONE 6.

CHIONANTHUS
Oleaceae
FRINGE TREE

The genus *Chionanthus* used to be regarded as consisting of only 2 species of deciduous tree, one from temperate North America and one from China, but botanists have now transferred to it a large number of tropical evergreens from the genus *Linociera*. The 2 deciduous species, however, are of most interest to gardeners. In late spring the crowns of these small trees are sprinkled with clusters of delicate white flowers above the green foliage; each slender-stalked flower has 4 narrow, diverging white petals. The smooth-margined leaves are in opposite pairs and the summer fruits are like small olives (not surprising as they belong to the olive family). These cool-climate trees are easily grown but may be slow to increase in size and can take 10 years to flower. A sunny but sheltered position with good soil and drainage suits them best.

Chionanthus retusus
CHINESE FRINGE TREE

This tree can reach 30 ft (10 m), developing a broad, umbrella-like crown with age, but in gardens it is often a large shrub. The shiny leaves are variable in shape and size on the one tree. The flowers, with petals about ¾ in (2 cm) long, form profuse small upright clusters which stand above the foliage in

CHILOPSIS
Bignoniaceae
DESERT WILLOW

Despite its common name this deciduous shrub, the only species in the genus, is quite unrelated to willows, being a member of the Bignonia family and producing the showy trumpet-shaped flowers typical of that family. From the arid valleys of inland south-western USA and northern Mexico, it grows in dry stream beds. The leaves do resemble those of many willows, narrow and drawn out into a long point. Flowers are borne in short spikes at branch ends, opening in succession. *Chilopsis* is a lank, untidy shrub, worth growing only for its beautiful flowers. It does best in a hot dry climate with cool, crisp nights. Soil should be open and well drained but with deep subsoil moisture available. Propagation is from seed or cuttings.

Chilopsis linearis

The desert willow is a shrub of 8–12 ft (2.5–4 m) with a slender, open habit of growth, the slender branches arching and twisted at odd angles. The sparse leaves are pale green and the 2 in (5 cm) flowers are borne through late spring and summer, and can be white, pale pink or a deep cerise-pink, paler in the throat. ZONE 9.

CHIMONANTHUS
Calycanthaceae
WINTERSWEET

This is a small genus of deciduous shrubs from China; one species is popular in gardens for its deliciously scented flowers produced from early to mid-winter. The leaves are simple and thin-textured, clustered at ends of the stiff branches. Smallish flowers are clustered just below the branch tips; they are multi-petalled and cup late spring or early summer. A good specimen in full flower is outstandingly beautiful. This seems to be the more climatically adaptable of the 2 species, flowering equally well in cool and warm, even subtropical regions. ZONE 7.

Chionanthus virginicus
AMERICAN FRINGE TREE

The individual flowers are similar to those of *C. retusus*, but the leaves are larger and less shiny, and the longer, drooping flower-sprays appear among the foliage rather than standing above it. Nonetheless a specimen in full flower in late spring is breathtakingly beautiful. In its native forests from Pennsylvania to Florida and inland to Oklahoma it grows on rich moist soil close to streams, occasionally 30 ft (10 m) tall but often only a shrub. Away from its native regions it can be a shy bloomer, performing better in continental climates of central Europe than in the British Isles and sulking in climates warmer than that. ZONE 5.

CHOISYA
Rutaceae

This genus consists of several evergreen shrubs from Mexico and the far south of USA, one species of which is widely grown in warm to temperate climates. It makes an excellent hedging plant as well as being an attractive addition to a shrubby border. It grows best in full sun, and preferably a slightly acid, humus-rich, well-drained soil, for it can be affected by root-rot. It will tolerate dry soil and also light frosts. Protect from strong winds, fertilize in spring and trim lightly after flowering to keep the plant dense and foliage close to the ground. Propagation is from tip cuttings in autumn.

Choisya ternata
MEXICAN ORANGE BLOSSOM

Related to citrus, with spring flowers that have the perfume of orange blossom, this species makes a compact rounded bush to 6 ft (2 m). Its attractive deep green glossy leaves have the oil glands of the Rutaceae family and are aromatic when crushed. The clusters of small white perfumed starry flowers appear in spring, sometimes again in late summer. ZONE 9.

CHORISIA
Bombacaceae
FLOSS-SILK TREE

This genus is made up of 3 deciduous South American trees with distinctively spiny trunks and branches that put on a wonderful display of flowers. These are followed by capsular fruit containing a soft, silk-like substance that has sometimes been harvested as kapok and which gives the trees their common name. They prefer a tropical or subtropical climate but will grow in a frost-free warm-temperate climate. They do best in full sun, in fertile, light, well-drained soil, with regular water in summer. Propagation is from seed sown as soon as it is ripe or by grafting of clonal forms for superior flowering quality.

Chorisia insignis
SOUTH AMERICAN BOTTLE TREE

This species, known as *palo botella* (bottle stem) in some of the tropical South American countries where it occurs, is worth growing for its thick green trunk alone. In young trees the trunk has scattered conical spines but these tend to disappear with age. It grows fairly rapidly to a height of 30–40 ft (10–12 m) but growth then slows and the crown widens. Leaves are deep green with broad, overlapping leaflets. In autumn pale creamy yellow flowers, sometimes brown-blotched in the centre, are borne in small groups at the branch ends. ZONE 10.

Chorisia speciosa
FLOSS-SILK TREE

Growing rapidly to 50 ft (15 m) or more with a spreading crown, this subtropical species is the one most commonly seen, grown for its striking large flowers that appear on bare branches throughout autumn. The saucer-sized, 5-petalled flowers range from rose-pink through salmon shades to burgundy, with gold or white throats. It is not grown as widely as the beauty of its flowers would lead one to expect, perhaps because of the vicious spines on its trunk and lower branches. Poorer or drier soils and harsher environments restrict its size. ZONE 10.

Chionanthus virginicus (below)

Chorisia speciosa (below)

Chorisia speciosa

Choisya ternata

Chorisia insignis

Chorisia speciosa

CHRYSALIDOCARPUS
Palmae

These feather palms from Madagascar and the nearby Comoros and Pemba Islands are very graceful plants that are really most at home in subtropical areas. Although there are 22 species, only one, *C. lutescens*, is widely grown, though the others are equally attractive plants. The flowers and fruit are unremarkable—simple yellow flowers in sprays followed by small green fruit—but the foliage is very luxuriant. Plant in moist, well-drained soil in sun or light shade. Propagate from seed.

Chrysalidocarpus lutescens
BUTTERFLY PALM, GOLDEN CANE PALM

This species from Madagascar is possibly the most widely cultivated ornamental palm. It is a clump-forming feather palm with fairly short fronds on cane-like stems up to 30 ft (10 m) high. The fronds tend to be yellowish in sun but when grown in the shade they are a beautiful light green. Although frost-tender and best in a tropical climate, it responds well to container cultivation and can be grown as a house plant. ZONE 10.

Chrysalidocarpus lutescens

CHRYSANTHEMOIDES
Asteraceae

This southern African genus of evergreen shrubs contains only 2 species, of which one is widely cultivated and naturalized in other parts of the world. They are somewhat short lived and soft wooded, with leathery, toothed leaves. The yellow flower heads are like small daisies and the fruitlets that follow are unusual in this family in being fleshy and juicy—these are attractive to birds which effectively disperse the seed. The species described here has been grown as an ornamental in Europe and other parts of the world; but following its introduction to Australia, where it was used for stabilizing coastal dunes, it rapidly became a weed. With low soil nutrient requirement it competes more than effectively with native vegetation, forming dense, impenetrable stands. In its native South Africa insect pests keep its growth in check, and it is valued as a hedge or windbreak plant, especially for exposed seashores. It should only be grown in countries and regions where it is sure not to become a problem. Easily grown from seed or cuttings, it may be useful as a summer bedding or tub plant in cool climates, but demands full sun.

Chrysanthemoides monilifera
BUSH-TICK BERRY, BITOU BUSH, BONESEED

This fast-growing shrub has 2 subspecies, rather different in growth-habit and ecology. Subsp. *monilifera* is an erect, bushy shrub of 4–6 ft (1.2–2 m) with dull green, thin-textured, coarsely toothed leaves and grows mainly away from the seashore. Subsp. *rotundata*, the coastal race, is usually 5–10 ft (1.5–3 m) tall and as much as 20 ft (7 m) across, forming a broad, dense mound of bright green foliage. The glossy leaves are rounded and barely toothed, with cobweb-like hairs on the undersides and young shoots. It can grow very quickly on dunes and seed itself freely. It is less frost-hardy than the inland race. Both subspecies can flower for most of the year. ZONE 9.

Chrysanthemoides monilifera

CHRYSOBALANUS
Chrysobalanaceae
COCO-PLUM, ICACO

A large group of tropical trees now form the family Chrysobalanaceae, though all were once included in the Rosaceae family. The family name comes from one of its smaller genera, *Chrysobalanus*, which consists of a few American and African species. They are evergreens with simple, rounded leaves and insignificant flowers in small axillary clusters. The fruits, though, are large drupes with juicy flesh clinging to an angular stone. Other parts of the trees such as bark and twigs have been used medicinally; they contain an astringent drug. The species listed below is sometimes planted as a fruit tree or an ornamental in the tropics or warmer subtropics, including southern Florida. Propagation is from seed.

Chrysobalanus icaco

From the Caribbean region, including the far south of Florida and the South American mainland, this species grows on stream banks, in 'hammocks' (evergreen thickets) and on seashores. It can become a small tree of about 20 ft (7 m) but is often only a shrub, with a reclining main stem and erect branches. The small cream flowers appear in spring and summer, followed by 2 in (5 cm) diameter sweet juicy fruits that can be yellow, white or pink; they taste rather insipid but are used for preserves in the West Indies. Icaco is a name believed to be of Spanish origin. ZONE 11.

CHRYSOLEPIS
Fagaceae
GOLDEN CHESTNUT

The single species of this tree genus from northern California and Oregon was formerly classified in the chestnut genus *Castanea*. The name *Chrysolepis* means golden-scaled, a reference to the thick coating of minute golden scales on the new shoots and the leaf undersides. The tree has a stout trunk and leathery leaves. Male flowers are in clusters of very short cream catkins at the branch tips, while the female flower-clusters at the base of the current year's growth develop into a tight group of spine-covered husks, the spines themselves branched into more spines, each husk enclosing 2 to 3 edible nuts that are triangular in cross-section. Though quite handsome, this is a tree for those who like growing novelties, and it could be difficult to obtain outside its native area.

Chrysolepis chrysophylla

Although some botanists recognize a second species (*C. sempervirens*) occurring further inland on the Sierra Nevada, *C. chrysophylla* is normally considered the only species in its genus. It can reach 100 ft (30 m) in the wild, but usually forms a small bushy tree of about 30 ft (10 m) in cultivation. The oval leathery leaves are 2–3 in (5–7 cm) long, dark green above and golden brown beneath. Flowering in mid-summer, the tree takes another 15 months or so to ripen its small pale brown nuts. ZONE 7.

CINCHONA
Rubiaceae
QUININE TREE

This genus is made up of some 40 species of deciduous tropical shrubs and trees from South America. Best known as the source of quinine, a bitter-tasting drug which is extracted from their bark and used to control malaria, they have simple large leaves in opposite pairs on the branchlets. The trumpet-shaped flowers, which come in white and shades of yellow, green, pink and red, are fragrant and carried in loose panicles. These tropical plants demand a consistently warm climate and are best with moist, humus-rich soil in sun or dappled shade. Propagate from seed or semi-ripe cuttings.

Chrysanthemoides monilifera (below)

Cinchona officinalis
CROWN BARK

Native to Peru, this species ultimately reaches 10–24 ft (3–8 m) high and may be shrubby or tree-like. Its small flowers, ¾ in (1.5 cm) long, range from yellowish green to light red and are pleasantly fragrant. The relatively small size and bushy habit of this species make it suitable for container cultivation. ZONE 11.

CINNAMOMUM
Lauraceae

This small genus consists of evergreen trees from tropical and subtropical Asia and Australasia with smooth, strongly veined leaves; highly aromatic compounds are present in leaves, twigs and bark of all species. Flowers are small and white or cream in delicate sprays and are followed by small fleshy berries containing a single seed. The genus includes *C. zeylanicum*, the bark of which yields the spice cinnamon, and which is nowadays cultivated in the form of a shrub; *C. cassia*, which is cultivated in China and Burma provides the spice cassia which is used in drinks and sweets. While *C. camphora*, described below, is a source of commercial camphor and its aromatic wood is traditionally used in China to make storage chests, it is more widely grown as an ornamental.

Cinnamomum camphora
CAMPHOR LAUREL

Originating in China, Japan and Taiwan, this fast-growing tree is known to reach 110 ft (35 m) in height with a rounded crown spreading to 50 ft (15 m) wide. The short, solid trunk has scaly grey bark. The leaves, pinkish when young, turn pale green and become darker as they age, and are strongly aromatic when crushed. Widely grown as a shade tree in parks and gardens and as a street tree, it self-seeds freely and grows so readily, especially in warm climates, that it can become an invasive weed. The roots reputedly release a compound which inhibits growth of other plants beneath the tree's canopy. Half-hardy, it is adaptable to a variety of climates and is best in full sun or dappled shade on light loamy or sandy free-draining soil with plentiful water in summer. It is easy to propagate from seed sown in autumn. ZONE 10.

Cinnamomum zeylanicum
CEYLON CINNAMON

A 30–40 ft (10–13 m) high evergreen tree from southern India and Sri Lanka, this species has light brown, papery bark. Its oval leaves are bright red when young, maturing to deep green with conspicuous white veins. Loose panicles of inconspicuous yellow flowers are followed by purplish fruit supported on structures very like acorn cups. This tree demands a tropical climate with regular rainfall; even, warm temperatures; and moist, humus-rich soil in sun or light shade. Propagate from seed or semi-ripe cuttings. When grown for cinnamon production, it is always pollarded to keep it small and to keep fresh branches coming for harvest. The bark is stripped and dried to yield the spice. ZONE 11.

CISTUS
Cistaceae
ROCK ROSE

These evergreen shrubs from around the Mediterranean are valued for their attractive flowers which have crinkled petals in shades of pink, purple or white and a central boss of golden stamens, like a single rose. In the wild they occur mainly in coastal scrubs (the *maquis* and *garigue* of France) often on shallow rocky soil, in areas with a hot dry summer and cool wet winter. They are very drought resistant and adapted to withstand scrub fires, sprouting again from the base, and their felty, resinous leaves are avoided by grazing animals. Most bloom over a long season, some for almost the whole year. They are easily cultivated provided they are given a warm sunny position and very well-drained, even rather dry soil; they prefer being among large rocks or other masonry, where their roots can seek out deep moisture. If necessary they can be tip pruned to promote bushiness, or main branches shortened by about a third after flowering. Most species are marginally hardy even in climates such as that of southern England, let alone the northern USA. They all thrive in the temperate southern hemisphere countries, but not in subtropical regions with hot, humid summers. Propagation is normally from cuttings, though seeds are readily germinated.

Cistus albidus

This attractive species, with felty grey-green foliage and large lilac-pink flowers with a small yellow blotch at the base of each petal, is very sensitive to excess moisture. From the far south-west of Europe and north-west Africa, it is a compact shrub rarely exceeding 4 ft (1.2 m) in height with foliage right down to the ground, concealing thick, twisted branches. Flowers appear mainly in spring. It is one parent of the hybrid *C.* × *pulverulentus*, which includes the cultivars 'Sunset' and 'Silver Pink'. ZONE 7.

Cinnamomum camphora

Cinnamomum camphora

Cistus albidus *Cistus* 'Silver Pink'

Cistus × *lusitanicus*

Cistus × *purpureus*

Cistus salviifolius

Citharexylum spinosum

Citharexylum spinosum

Cistus ladanifer

The most upright and slender *Cistus*, this species is easily recognized. The whole plant, apart from flower-petals, is coated with a shiny resin which in the heat of the day becomes semi-liquid and very aromatic. The Romans knew this as *ladanum* and valued it as an incense and perfume base, as well as for many medicinal purposes. Growing to 5–6 ft (1.5–2 m), *C. ladanifer* becomes sparse and leggy in only a few years from planting but does not take well to pruning. Its leaves are narrow and dark green and the flowers, among the largest in the genus at 3–4 in (7–10 cm) across, have pure white petals with a reddish chocolate blotch at the base of each petal; they appear from mid-spring to early summer. 'Albiflorus' has pure white petals. ZONE 8.

Cistus × lusitanicus

This hybrid between *C. ladanifer* and *C. hirsutus* develops into a densely foliaged shrub 24 in (60 cm) high and wide. It has narrow, dark green leaves and white flowers 2½ in (6 cm) across with a prominent crimson blotch at the base of each petal. 'Decumbens' is a low, spreading form with flowers that have darker crimson blotches. ZONE 8.

Cistus × purpureus

This hybrid between *C. ladanifer* and the eastern Mediterranean species *C. creticus* has deep pink flowers like *C. albidus*. The flower-coloration and growth-habit come mainly from *C. creticus* but the petals have prominent dark reddish chocolate blotches as in *C. ladanifer*. It is hardy and free flowering. Several clones have been named including 'Brilliancy' with clear pink petals, and 'Betty Taudevin', a deeper reddish pink. ZONE 8.

Cistus salviifolius

This species has dark green, less felty leaves and smaller, slender-stalked flowers that are predominantly white. It makes a rounded shrub of vigorous growth, about 24–36 in (60–90 cm) high and rather more wide, consisting of thin, densely massed twigs. The neat disc-like flowers, pure white except for a small orange-yellow basal blotch on each petal and gold stamens, are scattered profusely over the plant from late winter to early summer. It can be cut back harder than other species. ZONE 8.

CITHAREXYLUM
Verbenaceae

The tropical and subtropical trees and shrubs of this genus originate mainly in Central America and the West Indies. Evergreen or semi-evergreen, they are grown for their handsome, glossy leaves and fragrant flowers as well as the fine quality wood which is used for cabinet work. The species described below received its common name from the use of its wood in the manufacture of stringed instruments by the indigenous people of the Caribbean. It is not used in the manufacture of violins.

Citharexylum spinosum
FIDDLEWOOD

This fast-growing, evergreen, multi-stemmed small tree with a rounded crown grows to 40 ft (13 m) and comes from the Caribbean. The glossy, broadly oval leaves are about 8 in (20 cm) long and turn from bright green in summer to copper and orange in winter and spring, giving colour contrasts to the warm-climate garden. Some leaves fall in spring, particularly in colder climates. Long racemes of tiny, yellow-white, highly fragrant flowers appear in late summer to winter. Fiddlewood does best in subtropical to warm-temperate climates, but will tolerate light frosts. It prefers full sun and fertile, well-drained soil. Prune if necessary to maintain shape or to make a tall hedge. Propagate from semi-hardwood cuttings. ZONE 10.

CITRUS
Rutaceae

While largely cultivated for their fruit, most citrus trees have the bonus of looking attractive in the garden, with glossy evergreen leaves and fragrant flowers. The lemon is the most cold resistant, especially when grafted onto the related *Poncirus trifoliata* rootstock, and the lime is the least cold resistant, doing best in subtropical locations. All citrus can also be grown in pots, as long as the containers are large; cumquats are the most decorative for tubs. Citrus require excellent drainage as they are prone to root-rot. A friable, slightly acid loam soil is best. They need full sun, protection from wind and, as citrus are not deep rooted, they require regular watering, especially during the summer months. They also need regular fertilizing, including large amounts of nitrogen. Prune only to remove dead, diseased and crossing wood. Overlarge trees can be pruned severely. Citrus trees are subject to a range of virus diseases and can be invaded by a variety of pests, including scale, leaf miner, bronze orange bug and spined citrus bug. Fruit-fly can also be a problem in some areas. Citrus are rarely propagated by home gardeners as this is done by budding, a specialist task. Gardeners should seek advice on the selection of the best understock for their conditions and always buy citrus from a reputable nursery to ensure that plants are virus free.

Citrus aurantifolia
LIME

Originating from Southeast Asia, the lime is best suited to tropical and subtropical climates. The flesh and juice have a stronger acidity and flavour than the lemon. It is an erect tree growing to around 12 ft (4 m), more irregular and less ornamental than the lemon, with spiny branches. The Tahitian lime, the variety most commonly grown, bears fruit all year round. The Mexican lime has smaller fruits with high acidity and stronger flavour and is a thornier tree. Lime fruits should be picked as soon as they start to change colour from deep green. ZONE 10.

Citrus limon
LEMON

One of the most popular of all backyard fruit trees, lemons do best in warm, humid climates with mild winters. Trees grow to around 12 ft (4 m) and should be planted in well-drained, nitrogen-rich soil. Lemons are prone to collar rot, so plant them with their graft union well above the soil and keep mulch away from the stem. 'Eureka' is probably the most commonly grown cultivar, producing fruit and flowers all year round. It is an attractive, almost thornless tree, the best variety for temperate locations and coastal gardens. The smaller, hardier 'Meyer' produces smaller fruit and is the better variety for growing in pots. 'Lisbon' is popular with commercial growers and is reliable and heavy fruiting, good for hot areas, but thorny. ZONE 9.

Citrus limon

Citrus limon

Citrus aurantifolia

Citrus aurantifolia

Citrus paradisi
GRAPEFRUIT

Easily grown in mild areas, the grapefruit can make a tree to 20 ft (7 m). Its large, golden-skinned fruits are well known and widely appreciated. It requires shelter from strong wind to avoid damage to the heavy fruit. Plant it in moist, well-drained soil in full sun and feed regularly with citrus fertilizer. Popular hardy cultivars include 'Wheeny', 'Morrison's Seedless' and 'Golden Special'. The seedless and 'Ruby' cultivars are more tender, preferring a frost-free climate. All are usually grown from cuttings or grafts. *Citrus paradisi* × *Citrus reticulata* is a cross that has resulted in the tangelo, an excellent fruit. ZONE 10.

Citrus sinensis
ORANGE

Attractive trees to 12 ft (4 m) with a rounded head, glossy foliage and sweetly scented white flowers, oranges can be grown in most non-tropical climates. While they don't like heavy frosts, they will tolerate light frosts. 'Washington Navel', which fruits through winter, has very large, dark orange seedless fruit and is best suited to cooler areas. 'Valencia' is perhaps the hardiest of all oranges, producing fruit in spring and summer which is most commonly juiced but can also be eaten fresh. 'Joppa' is a good variety for tropical gardens. 'Ruby Blood' has somewhat oblong fruit with reddish rind, flesh and juice. It is the best known and best tasting of the 'blood oranges'. New varieties are available to commercial growers and gardeners could inquire at specialist nurseries about others that might suit their garden. ZONE 10.

CLADRASTIS
Fabaceae
YELLOW-WOOD

This genus of leguminous small trees come from cool climates of eastern USA, Japan and China. The pinnate leaves have rather few leaflets and the pendulous sprays of small to medium-sized, fragrant white or pinkish pea-flowers which appear in summer are slightly reminiscent of *Wisteria* flowers. The flowers are followed by flattened pods, each containing a row of small hard seeds. They are elegant trees, valued for their late flowering and, in the case of the American species, for autumn foliage. They adapt to a variety of situations in full sun, as long as soil drainage is good.

Cladrastis lutea
AMERICAN YELLOW-WOOD

The natural range of this species is from North Carolina to Alabama and Missouri, in rich soils on hill slopes or along ravines near streams. There it grows to 60 ft (20 m) with a trunk diameter to 3 ft (1 m), forking not far above the ground with steeply angled limbs. In cultivation it rarely exceeds 30 ft (10 m). The leaves consist of 5 to 9 broad, veined leaflets which are a fresh, rich green in summer turning clear yellow in autumn. The white flowers, in gracefully drooping panicles up to 12 in (30 cm) long, appear in early summer. Some trees flower only every second year. ZONE 6.

CLAUSENA
Rutaceae

A genus of tropical Asian trees related to *Citrus*, *Clausena* is usually known in the form of only one of its species, the Chinese wampee, cultivated for its edible fruit. It is a small evergreen tree with pinnate leaves of few leaflets which release an aromatic oil when crushed. Small white flowers like miniature orange blossom are borne in panicles terminating the smaller branches, followed by smallish, leathery-skinned, slightly downy fruit with a sweet, slightly acid and aromatic white pulp in which are embedded green seeds. In southern China it is one of the most prized fruits, thought to aid digestion and have other medicinal uses as well as a delicious flavour. It is propagated mainly from seed. A sheltered sunny position and deep, fertile soil will ensure good fruit production.

Clausena lansium
WAMPEE

A small tree of about 15 ft (5 m) in height, the wampee has a spreading bushy crown and glossy foliage, the leaves consisting of 5 to 9 leaflets about 2 in (5 cm) long. The flowers appear in spring, followed in summer by yellow oval fruits about 2 in (5 cm) long which can be eaten fresh or made into jam. ZONE 10.

CLERODENDRUM
Verbenaceae

This large genus of the tropics and warmer climates around the world contains trees, shrubs, climbers and herbaceous plants, both deciduous and evergreen, some with very showy flowers. The features that unite them are leaves in opposite pairs; tubular flowers, usually flared or bowl shaped at the mouth and with 4 long stamens and a style protruding well beyond the tube; and fruit, a shiny berry sitting at the centre of the calyx, which usually becomes larger and thicker after flowering. They vary greatly in their cold-hardiness, though only a few species from China and Japan are suited to cool climates. The shrub species are soft wooded, often rather rank growing, and the bruised leaves have a slightly unpleasant smell. They all appreciate a sunny position sheltered from the wind and deep, moist, fertile soil. Propagation is normally from cuttings which strike readily under heat, but many clerodendrums sucker from the roots and a large root cutting can produce much quicker results.

Citrus paradisi × *Citrus reticulata* (below)

Citrus sinensis

Cladrastis lutea

Citrus sinensis (below)

Cladrastis lutea (below)

Clerodendrum buchananii

This tropical species from Indonesia makes a tall, weak shrub of about 10 ft (3 m) with an open habit and large heart-shaped leaves with downy undersides. Flowers appear through much of the year in terminal panicles, the stalks and flowers all of a uniform scarlet colour; on any one panicle only a few flowers are open at a time. It is a rank-growing shrub, fast growing but short-lived. There may be confusion between this species and *C. speciosissimum*. ZONE 11.

Clerodendrum paniculatum
PAGODA FLOWER

Another fast-growing but short-lived species from tropical Asia, the pagoda flower is popular in the wet tropics for its huge conical panicles of small scarlet flowers that terminate the erect shoots, appearing through much of the year. Growing to about 6–8 ft (2–2.5 m) it branches from the roots into coarse, vigorous shoots with very large, deeply veined, glossy deep green leaves on long stalks. One of the most tender species, it is rarely seen outside humid tropical regions. ZONE 11.

Clerodendrum trichotomum

Native to Japan and China, this is one of the most frost-hardy species. It is an elegant small deciduous tree to 15–20 ft (5–6 m) in height, of erect growth and sparse branching habit; the lower branches droop with thin, downy leaves about 6 in (15 cm) long. In late summer it produces at the branch tips gracefully drooping panicles of slightly upturned, sweet-scented flowers, white aging pale mauve with large dull pinkish calyces that are sharply ribbed. The small blue fruits, cupped in enlarged red calcyces, can make quite a display. ZONE 7.

Clerodendrum ugandense
BLUE BUTTERFLY BUSH

While requiring a frost-free climate, this clerodendum from East Africa will take rather cooler conditions than most of the genus. It is a rangy and open evergreen bush to 10 ft (3 m) with a spread of 6 ft (2 m). Its long, slightly arching branches bear terminal sprays of delightful butterfly-shaped flowers in 2 shades of clear blue. The long flowering period over summer and autumn makes it a good shrub for the back of a border. Easily grown, it does best in full sun or light shade. It can be pruned back continually to keep the long branches in check. ZONE 10.

Clerodendrum zambeziacum

One of the low-growing shrubs among clerodendrums, this tropical African species puts up rather weak stems about 3–6 ft (1–2 m) tall from various points on the root system. Leaves are large, soft and heart shaped. Throughout the warmer part of the year it produces a succession of pure white flowers with tubes about 5 in (12 cm) long and sometimes curled stamens. ZONE 10.

CLETHRA
Clethraceae

A scattering of deciduous tree and shrub species across North America and eastern Asia, plus a larger number of evergreens in warmer climates, principally Southeast Asia, and one outlying species on the island of Madeira, make up this genus. The cold-hardy deciduous species mostly behave as spreading shrubs in cultivation, producing a thicket of stems concealed by dense foliage. Leaves are thin-textured with closely toothed margins. In summer and autumn small white flowers are borne in delicate loose sprays among the leaves, followed by numerous tiny seed capsules. Clethras prefer sheltered, moist spots half-shaded by taller trees, and peaty, acid soils. They can be propagated from seed, cuttings or layers.

Clerodendrum trichotomum

Clerodendrum ugandense

Clerodendrum zambeziacum

Clerodendrum paniculatum

Clerodendrum buchananii

Clianthus puniceus

Clianthus puniceus

Clethra arborea

Clethra barbinervis

Clethra alnifolia
SWEET PEPPERBUSH

One of the very few temperate North American species, *C. alnifolia* occurs wild along the eastern seaboard of the USA from Maine to Florida, in moist woods. It makes a broad dense thicket up to 8–10 ft (2.5–3 m) high with thin green leaves. Profuse sprays of fragrant white flowers with rounded petals are borne in late summer and early autumn. ZONE 4.

Clethra arborea
LILY-OF-THE-VALLEY TREE

While others of the genus are frost tolerant, this species from the Atlantic island of Madeira, an attractive shrub or small tree 20–25 ft (7–8 m) tall, requires milder conditions. It is a densely leafed plant with glossy leaves and long panicles of lily-of-the-valley-like flowers from summer to autumn. It is easily grown, needing moist, acid soil enriched with organic matter. Pruning is only necessary for occasional shaping. ZONE 9.

Clethra barbinervis

Widespread in mountain woodlands of Japan, *C. barbinervis* can make a 30 ft (10 m) tree in the wild with peeling orange-brown bark, but in gardens it usually makes a shrub of less than 10 ft (3 m) with crowded stems that tend to lean outward, and strongly veined leaves with a fuzz of very short hairs on the veins. The attractive white flowers appear in short panicles at the branch tips in late summer and early autumn. ZONE 6.

CLIANTHUS
Fabaceae

Until recently this genus was regarded as including 2 species, one from Australia and one from New Zealand. The Australian species is the famous Sturt's desert pea, a prostrate, hairy annual with spectacular red and black flowers; but recent botanical study shows that its correct classification is with the large Darling-pea genus *Swainsona*, to which it has been removed, leaving only the rather different New Zealand species in *Clianthus*. This is an evergreen shrub or scrambling climber with erect or arching cane-like stems springing from the base. The leaves are pinnate with many small, oval leaflets. Elongated pea-flowers are borne at ends of short lateral growths in stalked clusters. Easily grown in mild climates, *Clianthus* is moderately frost tolerant. Often rather short lived, it is inclined to become woody, and occasional cutting back helps to rejuvenate it. It is prone to attack by leaf-miners. Propagation is from seed, freely produced in bladdery pods, or from semi-ripe cuttings.

Clianthus puniceus
KAKA BEAK

The kaka is a New Zealand parrot and the long-pointed flowers of this shrub are reminiscent of its sharp beak. It is now rare in the wild but is widely cultivated. In gardens it normally makes a shrub of about 5 ft (1.5 m) but is capable of climbing to 20 ft (7 m) if supported by other vegetation or a wall. The flowers, borne in spring and early summer, are normally red, but pink and white forms are also available. ZONE 8.

CLUSIA
Clusiaceae

This is a very large genus of tropical American evergreen trees and shrubs, little known outside the Americas except as curiosities in botanical garden greenhouses but very diverse in their native rainforests. Many start life as epiphytes on other trees, but soon put down a curtain of aerial roots to the ground, which may ultimately fuse together into a self-supporting trunk—exactly like many (unrelated) tropical figs. Leaves of *Clusia* species may be quite large and are generally smooth and fleshy or leathery. The flowers, borne singly or in short sprays at branch tips, are often large and showy, with male flowers more conspicuous than female ones though both appear on the same tree. They are cup shaped or bowl shaped, often with 6 or more overlapping petals, and a dense, doughnut-shaped ring of stamens in the centre; in females this is replaced by a broad, domed ovary with shiny stigmas fused to its surface. Some species are hardy trees tolerant of exposed coastal conditions and these adapt well to street or park planting in tropical cities. Propagation is from cuttings under heat, or by air-layering.

Clusia rosea
COPEY

From the Caribbean region, this is one of the most widely planted species; it is popular in southern Florida. It makes a tree to about 50 ft (15 m) tall with a broadly spreading crown of irregular shape and rather dense foliage, often forked into several trunks from ground level. Descending from the lower branches are numerous aerial roots which take root when they contact soil or even cracks in pavement. The thick, grey-green leaves are paddle shaped with broad rounded tips. Pale pinkish flowers 2–3 in (5–7 cm) in diameter dot the crown in summer and early autumn. ZONE 11.

COCCOLOBA
Polygonaceae

About 150 species of mainly evergreen shrubs, trees and vines occurring in tropical areas of the Americas make up this genus. They have leathery leaves of variable shape and produce large fleshy spikes of very small separate male and female flowers. The flowers develop into segmented purple fruit carried in grape-like bunches. The fruit of the edible species often has some local economic importance. These tropical plants will not tolerate prolonged cool temperatures and do best with moist, well-drained soil in full sun. They have a preference for coastal conditions. Propagate from seed or semi-ripe cuttings.

Coccoloba uvifera
SEA GRAPE, JAMAICAN KINO

This tree from coastal tropical America can grow to 30 ft (10 m) high. It usually has a single trunk and a broad crown. The leathery, glossy leaves are almost circular, about 8 in (20 cm) long, with prominent white or pinkish veins. New leaves are an attractive translucent bronze. In spring and summer it produces erect, 8 in (20 cm) racemes of small white flowers that develop into green-spotted, edible purple fruit. Although very much a tropical plant, it is suitable for container cultivation in heated greenhouses. ZONE 11.

COCHLOSPERMUM
Cochlospermaceae

The 30-odd species of this genus of shrubs and small trees are scattered throughout the tropics, growing mainly in regions of strongly seasonal rainfall, and are mostly deciduous in the dry season. Although placed in a family of its own, it shows some relationship to *Bixa* (listed earlier in this book). The leaves are lobed, generally in the manner of grape or maple leaves, and beautiful large cream to golden yellow flowers are borne in clusters terminating the branches. The large seed pods are globular to sausage shaped and split open in a most unusual pattern to reveal masses of seeds embedded in a kapok-like down. The roots of *Cochlospermum* are swollen and fleshy and sometimes used as a food source, and other parts of the plants yield fibres and medicinal gums. Although not difficult to cultivate under tropical conditions, these are shrubs of very open, ungainly habit, but respond with denser growth to cutting back. Propagation is from seed or root-tuber cuttings.

Cochlospermum fraseri
YELLOW KAPOK

Native to far northern Australia, where it is one of 3 indigenous species, *C. fraseri* makes a crooked shrub or small tree of up to 30 ft (10 m) high. The leaves are slightly hairy, up to 6 in (15 cm) wide, with 3 to 7 shallow lobes. Flowers are bright golden yellow, up to 3 in (7 cm) across, borne on leafless branches late in the dry season (spring). If kept watered in a garden, the leaves may persist and be present with the flowers. ZONE 11.

COCOS
Arecaeae
COCONUT

As now recognized, the only species in this genus of tropical feather palms is the coconut (*C. nucifera*). So well known as to scarcely need description, it is the epitome of the tropical palm tree. Not only is it something of a cultural icon, it is also a vitally important plant with many commercial and local uses. A tall palm with a slender, usually curving trunk up to 100 ft (30 m) high, this species is very much a plant of the tropics, though it is occasionally grown in heated greenhouses in cooler climates. It does best in deep, porous soils with ample moisture and full sun, but will of course tolerate coastal conditions. It is raised from seed.

Cocos nucifera

A symbol of the tropics, this tall stately feather palm is everyone's idea of a palm tree. It is characterized by its slender trunk topped with a head of long, soft fronds. It is strictly a tropical plant and will not grow well where the temperature regularly falls below 60°F (15°C). In a suitable climate its panicles of small yellow flowers will develop into the familiar green fruit that dries and browns as it ripens. Coconut palms can be used as container plants for heated greenhouses in temperate areas. ZONE 12.

CODIAEUM
Euphorbiaceae

This genus includes a few species of evergreen shrubs and trees native to the Malay region and the tropical Pacific Islands. One species has given rise to a large number of cultivars with highly coloured and sometimes bizarrely shaped leaves. These are popular garden plants in tropical regions and house or greenhouse plants in temperate and cooler climates. Where they can be grown outdoors, the larger growing cultivars make good hedging plants. The small yellow flowers and the tiny seed pods are quite insignificant—this genus is grown strictly for its magnificent foliage. They will not withstand prolonged cold or drought and prefer moist, humus-rich, well-drained soil in sun or dappled shade. Propagate from seed or semi-ripe cuttings.

Cochlospermum fraseri

Cochlospermum fraseri

Codiaeum variegatum

Cocos nucifera (right)

Coleonema pulchellum 'Sunset Gold'

Coleonema pulchellum

Codiaeum variegatum
CROTON

Widely cultivated as a garden specimen in the tropics and as a potted plant elsewhere, this spectacular foliage plant is undemanding provided it has the warmth and humidity it needs. It shows enormous variation of leaf colour and pattern with shades of green, red, yellow, orange and purple all possible on one leaf. Some cultivars can grow to 8 ft (2.5 m) high, with leaves up to 12 in (30 cm) long. There are many cultivars and these must be propagated vegetatively, usually by cuttings, to maintain their foliage colour. ZONE 11.

Coffea arabica

COFFEA
Rubiaceae
COFFEE

This genus includes some 40 species of shrubs and small trees originating in tropical areas of Africa and Asia, the best known of which is *C. arabica*. Most species have tiered branches and deep green, oval leaves. Attractive white flowers are followed by small fleshy fruits that turn red as they ripen. The preferred growing environment is humus-rich soil with light shade and steady mild temperatures. Propagation is from by seed or semi-ripe cuttings. As would be expected of tropical plants, most are very frost-tender.

Coffea arabica
ARABIAN COFFEE

Originating in mountain rainforests of Ethiopia, this is the coffee of commerce and, while one or two are unlikely to supply your coffee needs, it is a very attractive evergreen shrub for frost-free gardens or for containers. It has tiered branches with deep green, 6 in (15 cm) oval leaves and can grow to 15 ft (5 m) high. Small, fragrant, white flowers are clustered along the branches behind the leaves and are followed by ½ in (1 cm) green fruit that redden as they ripen; each contains 2 'beans' which when extracted, dried and roasted are our familiar coffee beans. It can be grown as a house plant. ZONE 10.

COLEONEMA
Rutaceae
DIOSMA, BREATH OF HEAVEN

These small evergreen shrubs from South Africa are often confused with *Diosma* species. They have short needle-like leaves on very fine, wiry twigs and tiny starry flowers in spring or spring through summer. The foliage is spicily aromatic. They withstand regular trimming to shape, usually done immediately after flowering. Plant in light but moist well-drained soil in full sun. Propagate from semi-ripe cuttings.

Coleonema album
WHITE DIOSMA

Often misnamed *Diosma ericoides*, this species has white flowers. It grows to about 4 ft (1.2 m) high and wide. The foliage is deep green, but in poor soils or if neglected it can become a rather sickly yellowish green. Occasional applications of very dilute iron sulphate solution will keep the foliage looking healthy. ZONE 9.

Coleonema pulchellum

Formerly known as *Coleonema pulchrum*, this is the most widely grown species. It is a 5 ft (1.5 m) high shrub with soft foliage and pink flowers in spring and summer. Several forms are cultivated with white or deeper pink flowers. 'Sunset Gold' is a very popular form with bright yellow foliage and light pink flowers in spring. It is more compact than the species and usually grows as a low, flat-topped bush or groundcover. ZONE 9.

COLLETIA
Rhamnaceae
ANCHOR PLANT

A handful of species from temperate and subtropical South America make up this unusual genus. They are stiff, woody, evergreen shrubs with leaves and branchlets arranged in opposite pairs. Leaves are very small and in most species are present only on new growths; their photosynthetic function is taken over by the green branchlets, each tipped by a fierce spine. Small white bell-shaped flowers appear in clusters at the branchlet junctions and have a sweet honey-like smell. Colletias are curious plants which some people find attractive, others repellently fierce. They can be grown in any average garden soil and prefer full sun. Few shrubs are so well suited to forming an intruder-proof barrier. Propagation is from cuttings or seed, produced in small globular capsules. Plants can be pruned back to encourage denser growth.

Colletia cruciata

Indigenous to Uruguay and Argentina, this fiercely armed shrub is also known as *C. paradoxa*. It grows to about 10 ft (3 m) tall with an erect, very irregular growth-habit. Its leafless branchlets are deep grey-green with a white waxy bloom and mostly flattened in the vertical plane, but sometimes it produces branches with shorter, more slender branchlets as well. The texture of the plant is remarkable—tapping it with a fingernail is like tapping a sheet of hard plywood! White flowers appear in great abundance in autumn and are fairly long-lasting. ZONE 7.

COLVILLEA
Caesalpiniaceae
COLVILLE'S GLORY

This genus has only one species endemic to Madagascar but now widely planted in the tropics, a near-evergreen tree of medium size. It forms a large crown of fern-like bipinnate leaves and often has a good height of clear trunk below the branches, making it an ideal shade tree. Its bright scarlet flowers make a brilliant display in autumn. This tree does best in moist, well-drained soil in full sun. It needs a mild climate to grow well but will withstand very occasional light frosts. Propagation is from seed.

Colvillea racemosa

This 50 ft (15 m) high tree has finely divided feathery leaves up to 30 in (75 cm) long. It has a large spreading crown and the trunk is usually clear of branches for a considerable height, so it is suitable for park and street planting in warm climates. In autumn, long cylinders of yellow-tipped, bright scarlet flowers open from pendulous silky buds. ZONE 11.

COMBRETUM
Combretaceae

Members of this large genus occur across tropical and subtropical regions of Africa, Asia and the Americas and include small to medium-sized trees and shrubs as well as some climbers. While many are evergreen, some of the South African species are deciduous, the foliage colouring well in autumn. The flowers appear in spikes, and in many species have inconspicuous petals and prominent, colourful stamens not unlike the Australian bottlebrush (*Callistemon*) flowers. The attractive, 4-winged fruits which follow persist on the branches until dispersed by the wind. Combretums are adaptable to most soils provided drainage is good, and full sun suits them best. They are easy to propagate from fresh seed or from cuttings.

Combretum erythrophyllum
PAINTBRUSH, RIVER BUSHWILLOW

This deciduous South African species is a small, spreading tree to about 20–25 ft (7–8 m) high; it is also seen in gardens as a bushy shrub to about 9 ft (3 m). The new growth is pale, almost white, maturing mid-green, and foliage turns yellow, then deep red, in autumn. The bottlebrush-like flower-spikes are red, and these are followed by masses of pinkish or orange hop-like, 4-winged fruits which persist well after the leaves have fallen; they are often cut for use in dried arrangements. ZONE 9.

CONVOLVULUS
Convolvulaceae

Found in many temperate regions of the world, this genus consists mainly of slender twining creepers (the bindweeds) and small herbaceous plants. Only a few species are shrubby, and even these are soft stemmed and renewed by shooting from the base. They have simple, thin-textured, usually narrow leaves and the flowers are like morning glories, with a strongly flared tube that opens by unfurling 'pleats'. However, *Convolvulus* species differs from many true morning glories (*Ipomoea*) in having flowers that stay open all day, rather than shrivelling by mid-morning or early afternoon; they usually open in succession over a long season. These easily grown plants adapt to most soils, and exposed as well as sheltered positions, but always prefer full sun. Plants can be cut back hard after flowering if desired, to promote thicker growth. Propagation is from cuttings.

Convolvulus cneorum

This attractive subshrub from Mediterranean Europe has crowded, weak, upcurving stems sprouting from the base to a height of 12–24 in (30–60 cm). The leaves, in tufts along the stems, are soft and narrow with a coating of silky hairs which gives them a silvery sheen. The stems terminate in dense clusters of silky buds, each producing a long succession of flowers through spring and summer, flesh-pink in bud but opening pure dazzling white with a small yellow 'eye', and about 1½ in (3 cm) in diameter. This is a fine plant for a warm dry spot in the rock garden. ZONE 8.

COPROSMA
Rubiaceae

Most of the evergreen shrubs and some trees which make up this genus are native to New Zealand. Grown largely for their great tolerance of salt-laden winds, they are commonly seen as coastal hedging and shelter planting. They have tough, decorative foliage and small fruits, separate male and female plants being needed to obtain fruits. They do best in full sun on light, well-drained soil and are fast growing and easily maintained. Pruning will maintain leafiness. Propagate from seed in spring and semi-ripe cuttings in late summer.

Coprosma brunnea

Native to New Zealand, this species is a wiry-stemmed evergreen groundcover that can spread to 10 ft (3 m) wide. Narrow, olive-green leaves are rather inconspicuous against the light brown stems. Minute cream flowers in spring are followed by beautiful, translucent, ¼ in (6 mm), blue berries from late summer. ZONE 7.

Coprosma repens
TAUPATA, MIRROR BUSH, LOOKING GLASS PLANT

This is the species most commonly planted to withstand coastal winds, growing where little else will survive. Usually shaped to a mounded bush 3–6 ft (1–2 m), it will grow taller if left unpruned. It has brilliantly glossy, leathery, deep green leaves. Insignificant flowers are followed on female plants by small orange-red fruits in late summer and autumn. 'Marble Queen' is a variegated form with paler green and cream leaves often producing pure cream growths; 'Picturata' has a central yellow blotch surrounded by dark glossy green. ZONE 9.

CORDIA
Ehretiaceae

This genus is made up of around 300 species of evergreen and deciduous shrubs and trees from most tropical regions of the world. Some are used as timber trees, others hollowed out for canoes, and the leaves of a few species are used to make dyes. Most have large, smooth, oval leaves and small to moderately large, trumpet-shaped flowers that stand out against the dark foliage. This genus demands steady, warm temperatures and moist, well-drained soil. They are propagated from seed or semi-ripe cuttings. *Cordia wallichii* is an attractive but lesser known species from India. The fruit is typical of the genus.

Coprosma repens

Cordia wallichii

Convolvulus cneorum

Cordia wallichii

Coprosma brunnea (below)

Cordia dichotoma
BIRD LIME TREE

This handsome evergreen tree from tropical Asia and Australasia grows to 30 ft (10 m) high with a broadly spreading habit and broad, shiny leaves to 8 in (20 cm) long. It produces both male and hermaphrodite orange flowers. These flowers develop into ¾ in (2 cm) long soft, dull pinkish edible fruits with sticky flesh. ZONE 11.

Cordia sebestena
GEIGER TREE

This evergreen shrub or small tree is native to the West Indies, Florida and Venezuela and is widely cultivated for ornament in the tropics. It grows to around 25 ft (8 m) high and has 8 in (20 cm) long, oval leaves. It produces tight clusters of bright orange-red flowers through much of the year, followed by 1 in (2 cm) oval, white edible fruit. ZONE 10.

CORDYLINE
Asteliaceae
CABBAGE TREE, TI

Centred in the south-west Pacific region, most species of this genus of palm-like shrubs and small trees are tropical or subtropical, but a few of the New Zealand species are moderately frost-hardy. Most cordylines are easily grown from seed or cuttings and can be kept in pots or tubs for many years. A peculiarity is their underground rhizome-like stem that grows downward, sometimes emerging through the drainage apertures of a pot; its main function appears to be food storage. Cordylines somewhat resemble yuccas in habit and foliage but the flowers are small and starry in branched spikes. Propagate from stem cuttings or seed.

Cordyline australis
NEW ZEALAND CABBAGE TREE, TI KOUKA

This striking evergreen tree looks tropical but in fact it is half-hardy, occurring even in New Zealand's coldest regions. Seedlings with very narrow, elegantly arching leaves are sold as indoor plants and last for many years in this juvenile state. Planted outdoors in a sheltered position they begin to form a trunk and the leaves grow to almost 3 ft (1 m) long and 2 in (5 cm) wide. At 6–8 ft (2–3 m) tall, the first large panicle of small white sweet-scented flowers terminates the stem; the stem then branches into several leaf rosettes, each in time producing an inflorescence. Old plants may be 20 ft (7 m) tall with a thick trunk and numerous erect branches; in the wild trees 60 ft (18 m) high with trunk diameters to 5 ft (1.5 m) have been recorded! The foliage is brownish green. The cultivar 'Purpurea' with bronze-purplish leaves is popular and just as hardy. 'Albertii', a variegated cultivar with leaves striped cream, more pinkish on new growths, is less vigorous. ZONE 7.

Cordyline banksii
TI NGAHERE

From New Zealand, this small, compact tree or large shrub grows to 9 ft (3 m) with a similar spread. It looks somewhat like flax (*Phormium* spp.) with a clump of short trunks and cabbage tree flowers. Its dark green, drooping leaves reach 3 ft (1 m) in length and the small, fragrant white flowers in long panicles appear in late spring and summer. It does best in a protected, shaded position with regular water in the warm months. ZONE 8.

Cordyline fruticosa
TI

Formerly known as *Cordyline terminalis*, this evergreen, clump-form-

Cordyline australis

Cordyline fruticosa (below)

Cordyline indivisa

Cordyline banksii

Cordia sebestena (below)

ing shrub probably originated somewhere in eastern Indonesia, though it is widely regarded as a Polynesian plant. In tropical areas it grows to at least 10 ft (3 m) high, but is more often seen as a 4–6 ft (1.2–2 m) potted house plant. Heads of long, sword-shaped leaves cluster at the top of narrow stems. There are many coloured and variegated foliage forms. The 12 in (30 cm) panicles of small, scented white flowers are followed by small red berries. A frost-free climate is essential. ZONE 10.

Cordyline indivisa
MOUNTAIN CABBAGE TREE, TOII

Native to New Zealand, *C. indivisa* grows to 18 ft (6 m) and has a stout trunk topped with clumps of long, heavily ribbed, bluish green, sword-shaped leaves. The small white flowers, massed on panicles 24–36 in (60–90 cm) long, appear in spring or early summer. It demands a humus-rich soil and a cool, moist climate and does well in coastal fog belts. Light shade is best for young plants. It is propagated from seed or basal suckers. ZONE 9.

Cordyline stricta
SLENDER PALM LILY

In the garden this east Australian shrub forms a clump of cane-like stems to 6 ft (2 m) high with dark green strappy leaves at the tops of the weak stems. It can reach about the same height when grown in a pot but tends to grow more slender. Long, drooping panicles of pale purplish flowers appear in late spring and early summer, followed in late summer by small black berries. This species does best in moist, sheltered positions and is quite shade tolerant. ZONE 10.

CORNUS
Cornaceae
DOGWOOD, CORNEL

Most of these cool-climate shrubs and small trees from temperate regions of the northern hemisphere are deciduous. Flowers are always small, mostly white, cream, greenish or yellowish, arranged in clusters on short twigs. One small group of North American and East Asian species appears to have large 'flowers', but in fact these are bracts which surround tight heads of tiny flowers. To this group belong the most admired ornamentals, including *C. florida*, *C. nuttallii*, *C. kousa* and *C. capitata*. The fruits are small drupes, sometimes fused into a larger compound fruit. Some dogwoods have fine autumn colouring, others have bright red or yellow twigs that are showy in winter. Most species are easily grown in a cool climate. The multi-stemmed shrub species such as *C. alba* are the toughest and most adaptable, while the tree species are at their best in a sheltered but sunny position. Dogwoods are propagated from seed, or semi-ripe cuttings or layers in late spring.

Cornus alba
RED-BARKED DOGWOOD

Shiny red branches and twigs, brightest in winter or among the last yellow leaves of autumn, are the feature of this east Asian shrub. It makes a dense thicket of slender stems 6 ft (2 m) high and often twice that in spread, with lower branches suckering or taking root on the ground. In late spring and summer it bears 1½ in (3 cm) wide clusters of dowdy creamy yellow flowers, followed in autumn by pea-sized white or blue-tinted fruits. The red-barked dogwood thrives in damp ground and is effective in lakeside or streamside plantings. Prune in early spring to encourage new shoots which have the best bark colour. Cultivars include 'Spaethii' with brilliantly gold-variegated leaves. ZONE 4.

Cornus capitata
HIMALAYAN STRAWBERRY TREE

This is one of the few evergreen dogwoods, making a rounded, low-branched tree of 30 ft (10 m) after many years, with dense greyish green foliage. In late spring and early summer its canopy is decked with massed flower heads, each with 4 large bracts of a beautiful soft lemon-yellow. In autumn the large juicy (but tasteless) scarlet fruits can make almost as striking a display. The Himalayan dogwood thrives in cool to mild climates. Some botanists prefer to call it *Dendrobenthamia fragifera*. ZONE 9.

Cornus controversa

Cornus alba

Cornus controversa
TABLE DOGWOOD

Native to China, Korea and Japan, this handsome species makes a medium-sized tree to about 40 ft (13 m) with age, with a straight trunk and horizontal tiers of foliage. The glossy, strongly veined leaves are exceptional among the dogwoods in being arranged alternately on the reddish twigs, not in opposite pairs. It is perhaps the showiest in bloom of any of the *Cornus* species lacking large bracts, with white flowers in flat sprays about 4 in (10 cm) across, borne in early summer. The fruits are shiny black, and autumn foliage is red to purplish. ZONE 6.

Cornus florida
FLOWERING DOGWOOD

Early explorers in eastern North America declared this the most beautiful of the native trees, and it has remained popular for its beauty and reliability. Usually 10–20 ft (3–4 m) tall with a single crooked trunk, in mid-spring it bears profuse flower heads, each with 4 large white or rose-pink bracts. In late

Cornus florida

Cordyline stricta

summer the scattered red fruits make a fine showing and in autumn the foliage is a mixture of scarlet and deep purple, with a whitish bloom on the leaf undersides. *C. florida* prefers a warm summer and doesn't often flower well in cool-summer climates like that in the UK. Nurseries mostly stock 'Rubra', with dark rose bracts that are paler at the base next to the cluster of small greenish flowers. ZONE 5.

Cornus kousa

Cornus kousa

Cornus kousa

Cornus mas

Cornus mas

Cornus kousa
JAPANESE FLOWERING DOGWOOD

Occurring in the wild in Japan, China and Korea, *C. kousa* can reach 20 ft (7 m) or more at maturity, with dense, deep green foliage and tiered lower branches. At the beginning of summer when the leaves have fully expanded, the flower heads with large, pure white bracts appear, each bract tapering to an acute point. The dull red compound fruits are about ¾ in (2 cm) across. At least as popular in gardens as the typical Japanese race is var. *chinensis*, with slightly larger 'flowers' and of more vigorous growth. ZONE 6.

Cornus mas
CORNELIAN CHERRY

When it flowers in late winter or early spring on the leafless branches, this tree species looks unlike any other dogwood. The individual flowers are tiny and golden-yellow, grouped in small clusters without decorative bracts, but the flower-clusters are so profuse, and on thick old branches as well as the new twigs, that they make a fine display. Stiff and rather narrow at first, with maturity it becomes a spreading tree of 25 ft (8 m) or so. The edible fruits ripen bright red in late summer. Native to central and south-eastern Europe, *C. mas* provides much-needed winter colour for streets, parks and gardens. ZONE 6.

Cornus nuttallii
PACIFIC DOGWOOD

In the wild, in the Pacific Northwest of North America, this is a slender tree to 50 ft (15 m), but in gardens it is often only a tall shrub. The large flower heads have 4 to 7 pure white bracts, aging slightly pinkish, and the small flower-cluster at their centre is dull purple. Flowering occurs from mid-spring to early summer, and may start at a fairly early age, a partial compensation for its short-lived habit. Autumn foliage is a mixture of yellow and red. This beautiful tree is rather frost-tender, but thrives in a cool, rainy climate, in a part-shaded position. ZONE 8.

Cornus pumila
DWARF DOGWOOD

This unusual miniature species appeared in European gardens last century, but its origin is unknown. It has cane-like stems and inconspicuous flowers, and forms a dense mound of crowded suckers about 24 in (60 cm) high and twice as wide, spreading year by year. The small oval leaves are slightly bronze-tinted, turning bronze-yellow in autumn. In most seasons it provides an interesting landscape effect, not least in winter when the mass of fine reddish twigs is revealed. ZONE 5.

COROKIA
Cornaceae

This small genus consists of evergreen shrubs from New Zealand grown largely for their unusual, angular and interlacing branch pattern. Reasonably frost-hardy, they suit mild coastal climates and can tolerate wind. They should be planted in full sun and need moderately fertile, well-drained soil. A trim after flowering will maintain their shape and dense leaf growth. They are propagated from softwood cuttings in summer.

Corokia buddleioides

This densely foliaged evergreen shrub grows to about 10 ft (3 m) high and wide. It has long, narrow, bronze-green leaves that are quite glossy when young. In spring, very simple, 4-petalled, small yellow flowers open, followed by small red to black berries. A tough, adaptable bush that withstands regular trimming and is ideal for hedging, it also tolerates salt spray and is a very effective coastal plant. For best results, plant in moist well-drained soil in full sun or light shade. Propagate from seed or semi-ripe cuttings. ZONE 8.

Corokia cotoneaster
WIRE-NETTING BUSH

With small round dark green leaves that resemble those of some small-leafed cotoneasters, and a tangle of wiry, zig-zagging branches that give rise to its common name, this species grows to 9 ft (3 m). It bears lightly fragrant yellow flowers in summer followed by fleshy orange and red fruits in autumn. ZONE 8.

CORREA
Rutaceae

This small Australian genus is made up of irregularly shaped, downy, densely leafed evergreen shrubs, some semi-prostrate. They bear mostly bell-shaped or tubular flowers with protruding stamens, over a long period through winter and spring. The most common species, *C. reflexa*, is variable with a number of distinct forms. Correas grow naturally in cool, shaded spots often near streams and under trees. They are attractive to birds. In cultivation they are not fussy, adapting to most non-tropical climates and are grown in many countries, with new cultivars such as 'Dusky Bells' proving popular. They do best in part-shade in moderately fertile, free-draining but moist soil. Tip prune to promote a densely leafed bush. Propagate from semi-ripe cuttings taken between spring and autumn.

Correa alba
WHITE CORREA

A coastal shrub often found on the very edge of rocky coastal cliffs, *C. alba* will tolerate sandy soils and salt winds. It is a compact shrub to 5 ft (1.5 m) with thick, rounded, grey-green leaves, white underneath from densely matted hairs. The white flowers do not develop into a long tube as in most correas, but the 4 petals roll back into a star shape as the flower expands. This species is useful for mass planting in coastal gardens to bind the sand.
ZONE 9.

Correa lawrenciana

A less common and taller shrub, to 15 ft (5 m), this species is found usually in moist sheltered forests in the high country of New South Wales, Victoria and Tasmania. The dark green, oval leaves are white and downy beneath and the narrow yellow-green tubular flowers are covered in dense velvety hairs and have very long protruding stamens.
ZONE 9.

Correa pulchella

This species occurs naturally on better soils in sheltered places along creek margins in southern Australia. It is a compact shrub growing to less than 3 ft (1 m) and bears masses of attractive tubular flowers in shades of salmon, orange, pink and red through winter and spring.
ZONE 9.

CORYLOPSIS
Hamamelidaceae
WINTER HAZEL

These deciduous shrubs from China and Japan produce short, pendulous spikes of fragrant, 5-petalled, pale yellow or greenish flowers on the bare branches before the blunt-toothed leaves appear in spring. The fruits, ripening in summer among the leaves, are small woody capsules each containing 2 black seeds. Although they often bear flowers, the subtle appeal of these shrubs lies mostly in the repetitive pattern of flower-spikes on the bare branches. They are best suited to a woodland setting in a reasonably moist, cool climate, providing a foil for bolder shrubs such as rhododendrons. Propagation is normally from seed.

Correa alba

Correa pulchella

Correa lawrenciana

Corokia buddleioides

Cornus pumila

Corylopsis sinensis

Corylus avellana

Corylopsis glabrescens

Corylopsis glabrescens

Originating in Japan where it grows in the mountains, this species makes a broadly spreading shrub of 16 ft (5 m) tall or sometimes even taller. The fragrant small flowers are lemon-yellow with rather narrow petals and appear in mid-spring. ZONE 7.

Corylopsis sinensis

From western China, this is a variable species with several forms distinguished by name. It makes a spreading shrub 10–16 ft (3–5 m) high with pointed leaves. Flowers, borne in mid-spring on crowded spikes, have broad-tipped pale yellowish green petals with orange anthers. It is one of the most ornamental species. Forma *veitchiana* is lower growing; the flowers have darker reddish anthers and there are fewer of them on the flower-spikes. ZONE 7.

Corylopsis spicata

This species from Japan was the first one known in the West. It is low growing, seldom exceeding 6 ft (2 m) and often less, and broadly spreading. The narrow, pale greenish yellow flowers have red anthers, the short spikes bursting from particularly large pale green bracts which persist on the spikes. The arrangement of flowers is more informal than that of some other species. ZONE 6.

CORYLUS
Corylaceae
HAZEL, FILBERT

These deciduous large shrubs and small to medium-sized trees are best known for their edible nuts. Most species have massed stems springing from ground level; the branches are tough and supple and the leaves broad, somewhat heart shaped and strongly veined, with broad shallow teeth which themselves are toothed. Male and female flowers are on the same plant but in different positions, the male in slender pendulous catkins which shed their pollen before the leaves expand, the female in inconspicuous small greenish clusters at the branch tips. The latter develop into the distinctive nuts, each enclosed in a fringed green husk and ripening in summer. The stems of *Corylus* species have many traditional uses and the branches were often woven together or pleached to make living fences. Cultivation is simple, provided soil moisture is adequate and ample space is allowed. Propagation is often possible by detaching suckers, or by fresh nuts. For fruit set there is a cold requirement during winter of around 1,000 hours below 45°F (about 7°C), and cool moist summers also assist nut production.

Corylus avellana
HAZEL

The common hazel occurs through most of Europe (including Britain) as well as in western Asia and northern Africa. It typically makes a broad mass of stems about 12–15 ft (4–5 m) high. In winter the bare twigs are draped with the developing male catkins, which start to show their yellow pollen at winter's end, making quite a display. The ripening nut is enclosed in a green fringed tube that leaves the end of the nut showing. In autumn the leaves turn a pleasant pale yellow. Commonly grown for ornament is

Corylopsis spicata (below)

Corypha umbraculifera

Cotinus coggygria 'Purpureus'

Cotinus coggygria 'Purpureus'

Cotinus coggygria

Corylus maxima

the remarkable cultivar 'Contorta', with branches that wander and wriggle in all directions; when leafless they are cut for sale by florists. ZONE 4.

Corylus maxima
FILBERT

Similar in most respects to the hazel, the filbert is more inclined to become tree-like and has sticky hairs on the young twigs. The most obvious difference, though, is the much longer tubular husk completely enclosing each nut, which is also more elongated. As an ornamental it is best known by the cultivar 'Purpurea', which has deep, dark purple, spring foliage, softening to a dull greenish purple in summer. ZONE 4.

CORYPHA
Arecaceae

From tropical Asia, this genus includes some of the most massive of all palms, with huge fan-shaped fronds. Most remarkable is their manner of flowering; the growth of a mature palm, perhaps 30 to 40 years old, is terminated by a giant panicle of millions of small flowers, towering above the crown of fronds. The flowers are followed by an equally impressive crop of marble-sized fruits and after these ripen the whole palm dies, leaving the seeds to perpetuate the species. These are strictly tropical palms, growing normally in alluvial soils near rivers and swamps. They are usually seen in cultivation only in large parks and botanical gardens. Seed is easily germinated but even under the best growing conditions it will take 10 years at least before a trunk starts to elongate.

Corypha umbraculifera
TALIPOT PALM

Native to southern India and Sri Lanka, where it has many traditional uses, this massive species has a stout trunk up to 80 ft (25 m) tall supporting a crown of fronds with thick stalks about 12 ft (4 m) long from which radiate fan-like blades 15 ft (5 m) or more long. The terminal panicle of flowers rises about 20 ft (7 m) above the leaves, with crowded masses of white flowers on drooping lateral branches. By the time fruits have reached full size all the fronds have fallen, leaving the bare trunk which soon dies. ZONE 12.

COTINUS
Anacardiaceae
SMOKE BUSH, SMOKE TREE

Two species comprise this genus of cool-climate deciduous shrubs or small trees; one species is from temperate Eurasia, the other from eastern North America. Both have simple, oval, untoothed leaves. The remarkable inflorescences are very delicate and have many branches; few of these fine threadlike stems carry flowers, but they produce a curiously ornamental effect like fine puffs of smoke scattered over the foliage. Both flowers and fruit are very small and inconspicuous. Smoke bushes are easily grown, adapting to a range of temperate climates but most at home where summers are moderately warm and dry. Soils that are too moist or fertile tend to discourage free flowering. Propagate from softwood cuttings in summer or from seed in autumn.

Cotinus coggygria
SMOKE BUSH, VENETIAN SUMAC

A bushy shrub about 10–12 ft (3–4 m) in height and spread, this has oval, long-stalked leaves. The fuzzy, tiny, plume-like inflorescences appear in early summer, pale pinkish bronze, aging to a duller purple-grey. Some of the flowers produce small, dry, flattened fruits in late summer. Autumn foliage has strong orange and bronze tones. The cultivar 'Purpureus' is most widely grown; it has rich purplish spring foliage becoming greener in summer and glowing orange mixed with purple in autumn, though it doesn't flower very freely. ZONE 6.

Cotoneaster apiculatus

Cotoneaster franchetii

Cotoneaster conspicuus

Cotoneaster dammeri

COTONEASTER
Rosaceae

This temperate Eurasian genus of shrubs (rarely small trees) includes deciduous and evergreen species and is a member of the small-fruited pome-fruit group that includes *Pyracantha*, *Crataegus* and *Amelanchier*. The name *Cotoneaster* dates from Roman times, and means something like 'useless quince'. The lower-growing shrub species are popular in temperate gardens for their dense, spreading habit and display of red fruit, as well as their hardiness. Excellent for rock gardens, embankments and foundation plantings, some species are also used for hedges and espaliers. They are easily propagated from seed or cuttings. The evergreen species especially provide fine displays of berries even in subtropical areas. All do best in full sun. They are prone to fireblight.

Cotoneaster apiculatus

Growing to about 6 ft (2 m) high, this attractive shrub blooms in early summer, the petals commonly pinkish. Flowers and fruit are carried singly along the arching branches. It is deciduous, most of the leaves turning red before falling, though in warm climates it may not be fully so. ZONE 6.

Cotoneaster conspicuus

A stiffly twiggy evergreen shrub 4–6 ft (2–3 m) high (or in some forms almost prostrate) with small, thick leaves, *C. conspicuus* comes from the mountains of western China. A tough, space-filling shrub, its brilliant scarlet fruits are scattered profusely all along the branches through late summer and autumn. The small, solitary white flowers are borne in late spring. The lower-growing form is sometimes known as *C. conspicuus* 'Decorus', though that name has also been applied to the taller form. ZONE 6.

Cotoneaster dammeri

Most distinctive of the fully prostrate cotoneasters, the relatively large, round-tipped leaves on this species have veins deeply impressed into their dark green upper surfaces; the scattered starry white flowers through summer are followed by solitary ½ in (1 cm) scarlet fruits which last well into winter, when the leaves turn bronze. Planted on top of a retaining wall or above a large rock, it will spill over in a charming manner. The varietal name 'Radicans' is often added, but there is confusion as to which form of the species it belongs; all cultivated forms have very similar qualities. ZONE 5.

Cotoneaster franchetii

This attractive evergreen from western China has rather long cane-like branches to 10 ft (3 m). The smallish pointed leaves have curved veins strongly impressed into the glossy upper surface and downy undersides. In early summer it bears small clusters of pink-tinged white flowers, followed by tight groups of salmon-pink to pale orange berries which last into winter. This reliable shrub adapts well to most garden conditions, in warm and cool climates. ZONE 6.

Cotoneaster frigidus
HIMALAYAN TREE COTONEASTER

Deciduous or semi-evergreen, *C. frigidus* can reach 20 ft (7 m) in gardens, and old trees have grown to twice that. Normally branching near the ground into multiple, broadly diverging trunks, it can be trained into a single-trunked tree with an umbrella-like crown. The pointed leaves, 3–5 in (8–12 cm) long, may turn yellow or reddish in autumn. From late summer onwards profuse sprays of scarlet fruit deck the branches and persist well into winter. They are preceded in early summer by the less conspicuous cream flowers. This very beautiful tree, from cooler parts of the Himalaya, has proved quite easy and adaptable. ZONE 6.

Cotoneaster glaucophyllus

This large shrub species is variable in the wild in its native west and central China, but the most popular form is an evergreen (or semi-evergreen) known as var. *serotinus* or *Cotoneaster serotinus*. Branching low, it forms an irregularly shaped 10–12 ft (3–4 m) shrub. The leaves are broad and rounded, at first coated in white downy hairs on the underside, but these soon wear off and a thin bluish waxy bloom appears. Profuse but undistinguished white flowers appear in early summer, followed by an abundance of small, very glossy scarlet fruit, which may persist through winter. Self-sown seedlings are often plentiful. ZONE 6.

Cotoneaster horizontalis

Popular in cooler areas where its fine foliage takes on bronze-purple, orange and reddish autumn hues, this semi-prostrate shrub has horizontal, flattened sprays of branches building up in stiff tiers with age to 3 ft (1 m) high and up to 8 ft (2.5 m) wide. The small flesh-pink flowers are dotted along the twigs in early summer, followed by much showier deep red fruit. Native to mountain areas of western China, it is semi-deciduous except in severe climates when it drops all its leaves for the winter. The named forms include 'Variegatus' with leaves edged with white; var. *perpusillus* is a more compact, dwarf plant with tiny leaves. ZONE 5.

Cotoneaster glaucophyllus

Cotoneaster lacteus

Cotoneaster 'Hybridus Pendulus'

Cotoneaster 'Hybridus Pendulus'

This semi-deciduous hybrid is a shrub of high ornamental value, with weak pendulous branches and rather narrow leaves, enlivened from late summer onward by loose bunches of bright red berries. Planted on its own roots it mounds up eventually to about 3 ft (1 m) tall, and the branches can trail effectively over walls or rocks. Alternatively, grafted onto a standard of one of the taller species, it can make an attractive weeping specimen with curtains of foliage. ZONE 6.

Cotoneaster lacteus

This tall evergreen shrub grows to about 12 ft (4 m) high and wide. The white flowers appear early in summer, followed by a fine display of fruit in large bunches, ripening at the end of summer and persisting through winter. It is a species that adapts well to warmer climates. ZONE 7.

Cotoneaster horizontalis

Cotoneaster lacteus (below)

Couroupita guianensis

Cotoneaster salicifolius

Couroupita guianensis

Cotoneaster microphyllus

This compact twiggy species has small, thick, glossy evergreen leaves and plump crimson to purplish red fruit from late summer to winter. Growth-habit can vary from completely prostrate to upright or mound-like, sometimes 3–4 ft (1 m) in height; mature plants have a framework of tough woody branches. Vigorous and hardy, it needs a fairly exposed location in full sun. For a formal look, and to display its fruit more effectively, it can be clipped into dense mounds. Var. *cochleatus* is almost prostrate, with profuse fruit. Var. *thymifolius* is a stiffly upright shrub to 24 in (60 cm), with a finely twiggy habit and narrow, wedge-shaped leaves. ZONE 5.

Cotoneaster multiflorus

Rather different from most cotoneasters, this is a deciduous shrub of about 12 ft (4 m) with thin-textured, hairless leaves and arching branches with drooping tips. It produces a fine show of white blossom in late spring and small clusters of quite large, slightly pear-shaped bright red fruit which ripens in mid-summer. It has a wide distribution, from the Caucasus across central Asia to western China, and is very cold-hardy. ZONE 5.

Cotoneaster pannosus

This evergreen shrub to 12 ft (4 m) makes a tangle of tough, wiry branches with widely spaced, small, leathery, dull green leaves with white downy undersides. Clusters of small white flowers appear in late spring, followed by tight clusters of small pale red fruit that later deepen in colour. Hardy and vigorous, it readily withstands trimming and is useful for hedges; it adapts to warm climates as well as cool, and has become naturalized in some places in the southern hemisphere. ZONE 7.

Cotoneaster salicifolius

An attractive evergreen species, it features narrow leaves with a network of veins deeply impressed

Cotoneaster microphyllus (left)

Crataegus arnoldiana

into their convex, glossy upper surfaces. The very profuse large bunches of bright red berries last long into winter, when the leaves may also take on bronze and yellow tones. It is variable in habit; some forms are low and spreading, others reach 10 ft (3 m) with long arching growths. It takes well to trimming and makes a fine hedge plant. ZONE 6.

COUROUPITA
Lecythidaceae

Three species of trees from northern South America make up this genus. They have large, elliptical leaves, usually clustered at the branch tips. The flowers are large and complex in structure, usually 6-petalled, and sometimes smell like garlic. They are followed by spectacularly large, spherical fruits. These are plants for tropical or warm subtropical areas and will not tolerate frost or prolonged cold. They prefer to grow in deep moist, humus-rich soil in full sun but in a sheltered position. Propagation is normally from seed.

Couroupita guianensis
CANNONBALL TREE

This species is an upright evergreen tree that is capable of growing to 100 ft (30 m) high, though 30–40 ft (10–13 m) is a more usual size. Pendulous flowering branches emerge directly from the trunk, right down to the ground, and all year produce brilliant red and orange fragrant flowers with hundreds of stamens arranged in 2 groups, one in the flower's centre and the other on a lower petal. However, showy as the flowers are, the fruit is the main feature. It is a brown sphere up to 10 in (25 cm) across filled with a smelly, soft red pulp, and one tree bears hundreds of them! They look like small cannonballs and burst explosively on falling from the tree. ZONE 12.

CRATAEGUS
Rosaceae
THORN, HAWTHORN, MAY

Native to cool-climate areas of Europe, Asia and eastern North America, *Crataegus* belongs to the pome-fruit group of the rose family and the resemblance of the fruits to miniature apples can easily be seen (and tasted). Most species have long sharp thorns amongst the summer growth, leaves that are either toothed or lobed, and the white or rarely pink flowers cluster into circular umbels in late spring. They are followed in autumn by a display of fruit in shades of red or yellow, often also with attractive foliage colours. Hawthorns are very hardy deciduous trees, compact enough even for quite small gardens. They

Crataegus laevigata 'Paul's Scarlet'

are sun-lovers and not very fussy about soil type or drainage. Some species sucker from the base, but suckers can be removed to produce a tree form. The thorns can be an advantage if an intruder-proof hedge is wanted, but make pruned branches uncomfortable to dispose of. Some hawthorns are prone to the bacterial disease fireblight, controlled only by prompt removal and burning of affected branches. Foliage may also be disfigured by the 'pear and cherry slug' (larva of a sawfly); spray severe attacks with an insecticide. Hawthorns are propagated from seed with cold stratification, or by grafting for named clones. In winter they are easily transplanted bare-rooted.

Crataegus arnoldiana
ARNOLD HAWTHORN

This small, spreading tree from north-eastern USA grows to about 20 ft (7 m) and has grey scaly bark. The dark shiny leaves with pale undersides turn reddish in autumn. Clusters of scented large white flowers with conspicuous deep pink stamens are strung along the branches in mid-spring, followed by small bunches of crimson fruit each about ¾ in (2 cm) in diameter. Although quite ornamental, this species is not planted widely in North America or Europe but, surprisingly, has found a place in some southern hemisphere parks and gardens. ZONE 5.

Crataegus laciniata
ORIENTAL THORN

From Turkey and the Balkan and Caucasus regions, this species (syn. *Crataegus orientalis*) has been cultivated for ornament in western Europe for almost two centuries. It may reach 15–20 ft (5–7 m) but in gardens is frequently a spreading shrub, often virtually thornless. The broadly wedge-shaped leaves, green but frosted with whitish hairs, are deeply divided into narrow lobes. The individually large white flowers appear in early summer in rather small clusters, followed in autumn by ¾ in (2 cm) scarlet or yellowish fruit. An attractive species, it is not as widely planted as it deserves. ZONE 6.

Crataegus laevigata 'Paul's Scarlet'

Crataegus laciniata

Crataegus laevigata
MIDLAND HAWTHORN

This small, shrubby tree reaches 15–20 ft (5–7 m) in height and spread. Native to Europe, North Africa and the British Isles, it has dark green, glossy leaves and produces few thorns. The cultivar 'Paul's Scarlet' has bright red double flowers opening in late spring. ZONE 4.

Crataegus × *lavallei*
LAVALLE HAWTHORN

This hybrid of *C. crus-galli* and *C. pubescens* originated in the Segrez Arboretum in France in about 1880. Popularly grown for ornament, its beautiful autumn foliage tones, which intensify after the first hard frost, are a feature. It forms a densely branched, almost thornless tree of 15–20 ft (5–7 m). The leaves are ovate and irregularly toothed, and darker glossy green than most hawthorns. The white flowers with red stamens open in loose clusters in early summer, and are larger than those of most other hawthorns; they are followed by orange-red fruit. ZONE 6.

Crataegus monogyna
HAWTHORN, MAY

Originating in Europe and the British Isles, this small tree is most commonly cultivated as a hedgerow, but when growing wild and alone it can reach 35 ft (11 m). The leaves have 5 to 7 deep lobes, and turn yellow-brown in autumn. The fragrant single white flowers open in late spring (despite the may's historical association with May Day, it is very rarely in bloom by 1 May in England). The small dark red fruits which follow hang onto the twigs into winter. *C. laevigata* is very similar and the 2 species are often confused. ZONE 4.

Crataegus phaenopyrum
WASHINGTON THORN

From south-eastern USA, this elegant though very thorny tree reaches 20–30 ft (7–10 m), forming a round-headed, densely branched

Crataegus monogyna

Crataegus phaenopyrum

tree with sharp thorns. The leaves have 3 to 5 sharply toothed lobes, and are dark glossy green. Dense clusters of fragrant white flowers in mid-summer are followed in autumn by the shiny orange-red berries. It is often sold under an old name, *Crataegus cordata*. ZONE 4.

Crotalaria agatiflora

Crotalaria capensis

Crateva religiosa

Crinodendron hookerianum

Crataegus pubescens

Crataegus pubescens
MEXICAN HAWTHORN

This semi-evergreen species from the mountains of Mexico reaches 15–30 ft (5–10 m) and is often entirely thornless. The oblong, pointed leaves are coarsely toothed and dark shiny green, with downy undersides. Clusters of white flowers with pink stamens are produced in mid-spring, followed in autumn by large edible fruit that ripen to butter-yellow and are still a popular item in markets in some Mexican towns. ZONE 7.

CRATEVA
Capparaceae

These tropical evergreen shrubs and small trees come from Southeast Asia, the Pacific region and northern Australia. The most closely related genus is the herbaceous *Cleome*, as revealed by the flower structure. They usually have compound leaves, consisting of 3 leaflets, sometimes lightly felted on the undersides. The foliage of some species can cause a form of contact dermatitis in humans. Their flowers have large stalked petals notable for the long protruding stamens. These tropical plants demand warm, even temperatures year round and prefer rich, moist, well-drained soil with plenty of water in hot weather. Propagate from seed or semi-ripe cuttings.

Crateva religiosa
SPIDER TREE, TEMPLE PLANT

Growing to 20 ft (7 m) high, this tree has smooth grey bark with white spots and distinctive pale green young branches. Its handsome leaves are composed of 3 oval leaflets up to 6 in (15 cm) long. In winter it bears large creamy white flowers with distinctive, long, dark red to violet filaments. The flowers are followed by smooth green berries. Although tropical, it is suitable for container cultivation in a heated greenhouse. ZONE 10.

CRINODENDRON
Elaeocarpaceae

This genus consists of about 5 species of shrubs and trees from South America, 2 of which are prized ornamentals where climatic conditions allow their cultivation. They are evergreens with leathery, toothed leaves and stalked, bell-shaped flowers pendent from the leaf axils. Regions where they thrive best have cool but mild coastal climates with high rainfall or frequent mist, and include southwest England and Ireland, southern New Zealand, Tasmania, and the Pacific Northwest of the USA and Canada. In drier climates they are likely to be short lived, though a shaded, sheltered site with a humid microclimate and permanent soil moisture may increase their chance of survival. Propagation is normally from cuttings as the seeds, produced in a smallish capsular fruit, are rarely available.

Crinodendron hookerianum

This, the most admired species (syn. *Tricuspidaria lanceolata*), is from the rainforests of southern coastal Chile on and about the island of Chiloe, where rainfall exceeds 100 in (2,500 mm) a year and is heaviest in the winter months. In the wild it reaches heights of 30 ft (10 m) but in cultivation it is normally a bushy, upright shrub of 10 ft (3 m) or less, with narrow, strongly veined, deep green leaves. Conspicuous crimson buds appear in autumn but the flowers do not reach their full size of up to $1\frac{1}{4}$ in (3 cm) long until the next spring; they never open wide, retaining only a small aperture. Even so, this species produces great quantities of pollen; just the slightest tap and the flowers rain yellow pollen. ZONE 8.

Crinodendron patagua

Also from Chile, *C. patagua* (syn. *Tricuspidaria dependens*) comes from a region further north, in the hills around Valparaiso. It is a tree of similar size to *C. hookerianum*, but more vigorous and tolerant of drier conditions. The leaves are broader and flatter, dark green with downy undersides, and its $\frac{3}{4}$ in (2 cm) white, bell-shaped flowers are produced in late summer. ZONE 8.

CROTALARIA
Fabaceae
RATTLEBOX

The evergreen shrubs, perennials and annuals in this large genus are grown for their bright flowers and noted for the hard, inflated seed pods with loose rattling seeds at maturity which give them their common name—when the seeds have dried out they rattle inside the pods. They occur naturally in warm regions of Africa, Asia and Australia. It is the shrubby species with bright yellow or greenish yellow flowers that are most often seen in cultivation. These need a sheltered, almost frost-free location in full sun, and moderately rich, well-drained soil. Pruning after flowering will keep them compact and encourage a second blooming. Propagate from ripe seed in spring (soaked in water for 12 hours prior to sowing) or from soft-tip cuttings in spring.

Crotalaria agatiflora
BIRD FLOWER

This species is named the bird flower because just before they open the yellow-green flowers resemble small birds attached to the stem. A loose, open shrub reaching about 6 ft (2 m) in height, it occurs naturally from northern Australia to eastern India. It flowers for a long period from summer to early winter. Regular pruning will keep it compact. ZONE 10.

Crotalaria capensis

This fast-growing evergreen shrub can grow to about 9 ft (3 m) tall with a 6 ft (2 m) spread. The foliage is sparse, although with attractive trifoliate leaves. Masses of bright yellow pea-flowers are produced in summer. The fruits are contained in tubular pods that persist on the tree and rattle when the seeds have dried out. It prefers light to medium soils and moderate rainfall; it does not tolerate drought but can withstand light frosts. ZONE 9.

CROWEA
Rutaceae

Four species of attractive and easily grown small shrubs make up this Australian genus. They are compact evergreens with narrow, mid-green leaves and masses of smallish, 5-petalled, pink flowers. These are borne most heavily in late spring, but plants are seldom without bloom. They are easily grown in light but moist, well-drained soil in full sun or very light shade; a light trim after flowering helps to keep them neat. The dwarf cultivars make excellent rockery plants. Croweas are usually propagated from small semi-ripe cuttings.

Crowea saligna
RED WAX FLOWER

This species has the largest and most showy flowers; they are very bright pink, starry, and up to 1 in (2.5 cm) in diameter. Growing up to 3 ft (1 m) in sun or light shade, it demands perfect drainage. *C. exalata* × *C. saligna* has similar, bright pink flowers. ZONE 9.

CRYPTOMERIA
Taxodiaceae
JAPANESE CEDAR, SUGI

Only one species is generally accepted in this conifer genus from China and Japan, though many variations have been named. A fast-growing evergreen, its branches and branchlets are clothed in short leathery needle-leaves that are densely overlapping and curve inward slightly. Male (pollen) and female (seed) cones are on the same tree, the former in profuse clusters and releasing clouds of pollen in spring, the latter in sparser groups behind the branch tips. Its handsome shape and uniformity of growth make it highly suitable for windbreaks, hedges and avenues. In Japan it is grown for its timber, but is also venerated in historic groves and avenues. Cultivation presents few problems, though rainfall must be adequate, and dry or shallow soils are unsuitable. Propagation is from seed, or from cuttings for the cultivars.

Cryptomeria japonica

This species can make rapid growth, to 20–25 ft (7–8 m) in 10 years; old trees in Japan are up to 150 ft (46 m) high, with massive trunks. The bark is thick and brown and has straight vertical furrows. Trees are conical in shape with a long, pointed leader. The Japanese race has thicker branchlets and stiffer habit than the Chinese (var. *sinensis*) one. There are least 50 cultivars, most dwarf but a few approaching the wild types in size. Best known of the taller ones is 'Elegans', which makes a solid column of foliage of up to 30 ft (10 m) high and 8 ft (2.5 m) across; the needles remain long and soft, and in winter the whole tree turns a striking dull bronze or plum colour. 'Araucarioides', with a bizarre tangle of long rat's-tail branches, reaches 10 ft (3 m) and makes an interesting foliage contrast in a mixed conifers planting. 'Globosa Nana', the most popular lower-growing cultivar, makes a dense ball with intricate branching which is soft to the touch; it is plain green, with paler green new growth in spring and summer. While listed as a dwarf, in good soil it may grow to 10 ft (3 m) across in only 15 years! The very tiny 'Vilmoriniana' grows to about 12 in (30 cm) high and is suitable for rockeries. ZONE 7.

CUNNINGHAMIA
Taxodiaceae
CHINESE CEDAR, CHINA FIR

This unusual genus is made up of conifers from China, Taiwan and Indochina. Although quite handsome and not difficult to grow, *Cunninghamia* species are found mostly in botanical gardens and larger private collections. The stiff, springy, curved leaves taper to prickly points and have glossy upper surfaces. Dead leaves remain attached to the branches, making the interior of the trees untidy and prickly, but a well-grown specimen is among the more attractive conifers. Fully hardy, they require adequate rainfall and deep, fertile soil. Propagation is normally from seed, though seed set may be poor.

Cunninghamia lanceolata
COFFIN PINE, COFFIN FIR

In China, where it once had an extensive natural distribution, this tree provided a valued timber for coffins (it was thought the aromatic timber prevented bodies from corrupting), resulting in its over-exploitation. Trees of 150 ft (46 m) in height were recorded there, but in parks and gardens elsewhere it is mainly seen as a tree of 20–40 ft (7–13 m), sometimes multi-trunked and widest at the top, sometimes narrower with a single straight trunk and scattered clumps of lateral branches. Growth rates are likewise unpredictable, and it may remain shrubby for many years. ZONE 6.

CUNONIA
Cunoniaceae

One species in this small genus of evergreen trees and shrubs comes from South Africa, most of the rest come from New Caledonia. Fairly frost-tender, they do best in full sun on well-drained fertile soil, but will grow on sandy or gravelly soil if given sufficient moisture. Prune to establish a single leader if a tree form is desired. Propagate from seed or semi-ripe cuttings.

Cunonia capensis
SPOON BUSH

Also known as red alder, this species occurs wild in mild southern coastal districts of South Africa. It is quite fast growing and will become a rounded tree to 50 ft (15 m) on a single trunk where conditions suit it, or a bushy shrub in lesser conditions. It has attractive shiny leaves that are divided into pairs of lance-shaped, serrated leaflets, dark green with a reddish tinge. Tiny creamy white flowers with long stamens appear in autumn, densely crowded on long spikes. ZONE 9.

Cunninghamia lanceolata (below)

Cryptomeria japonica (below)

Cryptomeria japonica

Cunonia capensis (below & below left)

Crowea exalata × *saligna* (below)

CUPANIOPSIS
Sapindaceae

These tropical and subtropical evergreen trees with pinnate leaves from Australia, New Guinea, and islands of the south-west Pacific occur in rainforests and vine-thickets, or in stunted coastal scrubs. Small flowers in shades of green or yellow are borne in panicles at the branch tips, followed by leathery capsular fruits that split open to reveal 3 seeds, each cupped by a red or yellow fleshy appendage that is eaten by birds, thus dispersing the seeds. Some species are tough evergreens, coping with exposed situations including salt spray and urban pavements, often making surprisingly fast growth. Their branches are very strong and resilient. Propagation is always from seed, which germinates readily if freshly collected.

Cupaniopsis anacardioides
TUCKEROO

A small to medium tree to about 50 ft (15 m) high with an irregularly spreading crown, the tuckeroo occurs right along the eastern and northern coastlines of Australia. The leaves consist of 5 to 9 oblong, leathery, shiny leaflets about 6 in (15 cm) long with convex upper surfaces. The greenish yellow flowers appear in autumn and winter in panicles up to 12 in (30 cm) long, with yellow fruits ripening in summer, sometimes densely massed. It makes an attractive small tree, planted in streets and plazas, popular in California as well as Australia. The trunk is crooked and low branching, with limbs spreading widely at an early stage; for street planting it can be trained as a single trunk to above head height. ZONE 10.

CUPHEA
Lythraceae

From Central and South America, these small evergreen shrubs seldom exceed 30 in (75 cm) high and wide; they have weak stems and tubular red, pink or yellow flowers. Most are very frost-tender but as they are fast growing they are often treated as annuals. The large number of species differ quite considerably in appearance, especially with regard to the flowers. They bloom throughout the year and prefer moist, well-drained soil in sun or very light shade. Propagation is usually from small tip cuttings, though they are also easily raised from seed, which often self-sows.

Cuphea ignea
CIGAR FLOWER, CIGARETTE PLANT

This species gets its common names from its flowers, which are small, orange and tubular. Each has a white tip with a touch of black, suggesting the ash at the tip of a cigar or cigarette. The leaves are small, elliptical and bright green. The wiry-stemmed bush grows up to about 24 in (60 cm) high and benefits from occasional trimming to keep it compact. ZONE 10.

Cuphea micropetala

At first glance this Mexican species resembles one of the perennial lobelias or even a penstemon. However, closer examination shows it is really very like a larger version of C. ignea. The leaves are up to $2\frac{1}{2}$ in (6 cm) long, bright green and elliptical with a prominent midrib. The $1\frac{1}{2}$–2 in (3–5 cm) tubular flowers occur in rows at the branch tips and are orange-red with golden-yellow tones, tipped with greenish yellow. Tougher than most, this species will withstand occasional light frosts. Although in the wild it occurs on streamsides, it grows well in normal garden soils. ZONE 10.

× CUPRESSOCYPARIS
Cupressaceae
LEYLAND CYPRESS

The '×' in front of the name indicates that this is a bi-generic hybrid, that is, a hybrid between 2 different genera, in this case Cupressus and Chamaecyparis. First raised in England in 1888 as a chance hybrid between the frost-hardy Chamaecyparis nootkatensis and the less hardy Cupressus macrocarpa, it combines rapid growth with reasonable frost-hardiness, and adapts as well to poorly drained soil and very windy sites (but not arid climate). It is widely planted for fast-growing hedges as it responds well to frequent trimming, which it must have if it is not to rapidly grow to tree size. Propagation is from cuttings, which strike readily under nursery conditions. Although the seed is fertile, the resulting seedlings might vary.

× Cupressocyparis leylandii

This name encompasses a number of seedling clones, some of which have been named as cultivars. When used without specifying a cultivar name it usually refers to the clones 'Haggerston Grey' or 'Leighton Green', which both make very vigorous, upright trees with a long, open leading shoot and slightly irregular outline; foliage is deep green or slightly greyish. In good soil it will reach 30 ft (10 m) in 10 years and double that in 30 years, ultimately growing to 100 ft (30 m) or more. 'Naylor's Blue' has more strongly bluish grey foliage and is more columnar in habit. ZONE 5.

CUPRESSUS
Cupressaceae
CYPRESS

This important genus consists of conifers, well known since Classical times but seldom planted where winters are severe due to their limited cold tolerance. Most species originate in western USA, Mexico and Guatemala, with others in the

× Cupressocyparis leylandii (below)

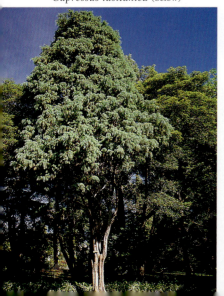

Cupressus lusitanica (below)

Cupressus macrocarpa (below)

× Cupressocyparis leylandii (below)

Cupaniopsis anacardioides (below)

Himalaya and western China; *C. sempervirens* is from the Mediterranean region and western Asia, and there is an allied but now almost extinct species in the Tassili-n-Ajjer mountains of the Algerian Sahara. The cypresses are handsome ornamentals which come in many foliage hues; they range from tall to dwarf, from columnar or high-crowned and spreading to weeping. Their dense foliage and rapid growth makes them especially useful for screens and windbreaks. Some species are very drought tolerant, others need moist conditions. They are easy to propagate from seed, always plentiful on adult trees, and cultivars are almost as easily raised from cuttings. However, some cypress species suffer from the disease cypress canker which disfigures the trees and finally kills them.

Cupressus cashmeriana
KASHMIR CYPRESS

One of the most beautiful of all cypresses, this species has long, weeping sprays of pale blue-green, aromatic foliage, but is difficult to grow. In a suitable warm, moist climate it makes fast growth at first, attaining 20–30 ft (7–10 m) in 15 years, but is easily damaged by wind and may die in spells of hot or dry weather. In cooler mountain areas of the wet tropics, for example in the Cibodas Botanical Garden in Java, are found some fine specimens, and it also does well in wetter hill areas of the Mediterranean, western USA, eastern Australia and New Zealand. In the UK it needs a greenhouse. ZONE 9.

Cupressus duclouxiana

This very attractive cypress from the hills of western China is narrowly columnar, with dense, very fine-textured foliage. Although not yet widely grown, it appears to be a useful landscaping subject for warm climates, tolerant of dry or exposed conditions. It can achieve a height of 20 ft (7 m) in 10 years on deep, rich soil. ZONE 9.

Cupressus glabra
SMOOTH ARIZONA CYPRESS

Cupressus glabra (syn. *C. arizonica* var. *glabra*) comes from the mountains of western Arizona, an area of low rainfall and quite low winter temperatures. With compact blue-grey foliage, waxy whitish twigs and reddish, flaking bark, it is highly ornamental; it is especially popular in warm regions with hot dry summers. Under such conditions it makes vigorous growth, is long lived, resistant to pests and diseases, and not fussy as to soil. There are different forms in cultivation, some fairly narrowly conical and others with much broader,

Cuphea ignea

Cuphea micropetala

looser crowns. It varies also in blueness of foliage, and seedlings can be selected for this character. Mature specimens are usually 30–40 ft (10–13 m) in height. ZONE 7.

Cupressus lusitanica
MEXICAN CYPRESS, CEDAR OF GOA

This cypress originated in the mountains of western Mexico. A common tree in parts of Portugal, it was introduced there by early voyagers to the New World. In warm climates it is a vigorous grower, but also tolerates cold and drought. It makes a bushy, broad-crowned tree with dense, somewhat greyish green foliage that has an attractive loose, foamy texture. Var. *benthamii*, from Mexico and Guatemala, has greener, more drooping foliage with branchlets in small flat sprays. Both this and the typical form are excellent windbreak and shelter trees, growing to 30 ft (10 m) or more in about 15 years. ZONE 8.

Cupressus macrocarpa
MONTEREY CYPRESS

Endemic to a limited area of central-coastal California near Monterey, this is the largest of all cypresses, reaching 120 ft (38 m) tall with a trunk diameter of 8 ft (2.5 m). When planted in a grove the trees form a tall straight trunk, but in the open in good soil they branch low with massive, spreading limbs, producing a broad, dense crown of deep green with a rather spiky outline. Close up, the foliage of the Monterey cypress is rather coarse, and it has a slightly sour smell when bruised. The cones are large and wrinkled. It thrives best

Cupressus duclouxiana

Cupressus glabra

in cool but mild climates with winter rainfall, such as southern England and Ireland, coastal South Africa, southern Australia and New Zealand. Often planted for windbreaks, it takes only 10 years or so to form dense 30–40 ft (10–13 m) trees. Golden cultivars include 'Brunniana', somewhat columnar, the foliage aging almost green; the very vigorous 'Aurea', with long golden spikes of foliage spreading almost horizontally; and 'Aurea Saligna' with remarkable weeping gold-tipped branchlets and elongated scale-leaves. A lower-growing cultivar to 4 ft (1.2 m) is 'Greenstead Magnificent', which spreads to form a flat-topped, remarkably dense mat of pale grey-green foliage, drooping around the edges; as the plant ages the whole becomes raised above the ground on a short trunk. ZONE 7.

Cupressus sempervirens
MEDITERRANEAN CYPRESS, FUNEREAL CYPRESS

This species, a familiar tree in Italy, France and Spain, was introduced to these countries from the eastern Mediterranean, from whence it

Cupressus cashmeriana

Cupressus sempervirens 'Swane's Golden'

ranges to the Caucasus and Iran. It has fine, dark greyish green foliage with very tiny scale-leaves in slightly flattened sprays, and large, slightly elongated, pale brown cones. In its growth-habit the Mediterranean cypress exhibits a curious phenomenon: the form usually cultivated, known as 'Stricta', is narrowly columnar, but a proportion of its seedlings grow into trees with side branches at a wide angle to the trunk, the form often known as 'Horizontalis'. Drought tolerant and slower growing than most other cypresses, it makes quite vigorous growth under good conditions in a warm climate. The 'Stricta' form can reach 15–20 ft (5–7 m) in 10 years, often as a slim column at this stage, but old trees of 30–40 ft (10–13 m) are usually much broader. It takes well to topiary and in some countries two trees planted either side of a gateway are trained to join in an arch above it. 'Swane's Golden', a cultivar with foliage flecked golden-yellow with deeper gold tips, is slower growing than 'Stricta' but can still reach 20 ft (7 m). It is rather tender. ZONE 8.

Cupressus torulosa (below)   *Cycas armstrongii* (above)

Cussonia spicata

Cussonia paniculata

Cupressus torulosa (below)

Cupressus torulosa
BHUTAN CYPRESS

This tall conifer reaches 150 ft (46 m) in its native Himalaya, though in cultivation 50–80 ft (15–25 m) is more usual. An elegant tree with long-pointed crown broader at the base, it is valued for its fast growth and fragrant timber. The deep green scale-leaves are blunt tipped; the cones, purple when young but ripening brown are about ½ in (1 cm) in diameter. The bark peels into strips. ZONE 8.

CUSSONIA
Araliaceae
SOUTH AFRICAN CABBAGE TREE

The small evergreen trees of this South African genus have unbranched trunks in their younger stages, topped by a thick mass of large compound leaves; the leaflets radiate from a central point. Densely clustered spikes of small, greenish flowers stand well above the canopy, and they are followed by the succulent fruits which are dull red to black. Though frost-tender, they will grow in cooler areas in a sheltered, sunny location. They can be grown in containers provided they have adequate water in the growing season. Propagation is from fresh seed or from cuttings in summer.

Cussonia paniculata
CABBAGE TREE

This upright evergreen tree from cool, mountainous areas of South Africa reaches a height of 12 ft (4 m); the trunk is thin, usually unbranched until the tree is mature, and is topped by a narrow, dense crown of foliage. The large, handsome leaves are rich bluish green with a silvery bloom, held on long stalks. Dense spikes of small yellowish flowers appear like candelabras in summer above the foliage. ZONE 9.

Cussonia spicata
SPIKED CABBAGE TREE, KIEPERSOL

This is the only species to be widely cultivated. Usually single trunked, it can grow to 20 ft (7 m) high and has 8 in (20 cm) diameter leaves that are divided into 5 to 9 leaflets and carried on long thick stalks. Long spikes of small, greenish flowers are borne above the canopy in spring and summer. Although often defoliated by heavy frosts, it can reshoot provided it is not repeatedly frozen. It is the best known species as a house plant. ZONE 9.

CYATHEA
Cyatheaceae

Evergreen tree ferns from tropical and subtropical forests, these species can reach 50 ft (15 m) in their natural habitat but are usually smaller in cultivation, their textured foliage making them useful additions to a shady garden or large shadehouse. Most species have an arching rosette of long bipinnate or tripinnate fronds emerging from the top of a slender trunk. Tree ferns prefer a warm climate, a humid atmosphere, part-shade, moist, humus-rich soil and plentiful water in warm weather. Established plants must be transplanted with care. Many species, when young, make attractive indoor plants; they require ample water in summer, less in cooler months. Propagation is by spores in spring.

Cyathea cooperi
STRAW TREE FERN, SCALY TREE FERN

Fast growing to 25 ft (8 m) with a spread of 15 ft (5 m), this tree fern from rainforests of eastern Australia has thick frond-bases densely covered in straw-coloured to brown chaffy scales. The much-divided, arching fronds are up to 12 ft (4 m) long. ZONE 10.

Cyathea dealbata
SILVER TREE FERN, PONGA

This attractive species has distinctive silver-white undersides to its fronds. It is slow growing to about 15 ft (5 m) in cultivation, although taller in the wild. The slender, erect stem has long fronds radiating from the top. It is half-hardy and needs a moist, humid atmosphere with shelter from wind. ZONE 9.

CYCAS
Cycadaceae
SAGO CYCADS

This ancient group of seed-bearing plants resemble palms, but they are not remotely related. Fossils show that cycads have been on earth for about 300 million years, twice as long as the flowering plants. *Cycas* itself is the only one of the 11 genera of cycads that occurs on more than one major landmass—it has species in Australia, mainland Asia, Madagascar and east Africa, as well as many of the islands in between, and out into the Pacific. Other cycad genera are confined to the Americas, or to Africa, or Australia. *Cycas* species are rather strange plants with long pinnate fronds like those of date palms arising from the top of a thick trunk packed with starchy tissue; male and female organs are on different plants, the male in long narrow cones terminating the stem, the female on the margins of furry, leaf-like organs that ring the trunk apex, enlarging after fertilization to make hard oval seeds that hang in a 'skirt' below the trunk apex. With the exception of *C. revoluta*, most *Cycas* species do not thrive outdoors except in tropical and warmer subtropical areas. They like sunny positions but with some shade in the younger stages, and deep, well-drained soil. Propagation is from seed, detached offsets, or by cutting off a whole trunk and plunging the base in a trench filled with gravel and organic matter. Trunk growth is normally very slow, so large specimens are prized and fetch high prices.

Cycas armstrongii

This species from the Top End of Australia's Northern Territory occurs in flat sandy country in open eucalypt woodland. It is usually unbranched, with a straight slender trunk 6–15 ft (2–5 m) tall, from the top of which emerges a circle of delicate new pale green fronds at the beginning of each wet season; during the long dry season they gradually shrivel and droop, hanging in a brown 'skirt'. Plants in moister positions may retain fronds for longer. Female trees mostly sport another 'skirt', of long-stalked seed-bearing organs, each with 2 to 4 orange-brown seeds the size of small hen's eggs. ZONE 12.

Cycas circinalis

Widely distributed in southern India, mainland Southeast Asia, the Malay archipelago and islands of the South Pacific, this is a robust plant commonly with multiple trunks, suckering from the base, up to 15 ft (5 m) high and over 12 in (30 cm) thick, with dense crowns of bright green glossy fronds 6–10 ft (2–3 m) long. On females the narrow seed-bearing organs hang among the frond bases. The large egg-like seeds ripen to shiny reddish yellow and are able to float in water (this has aided their wide dispersal). ZONE 10.

Cycas revoluta
JAPANESE SAGO CYCAD

Endemic to the islands of southern Japan, this palm-like species is a popular ornamental plant in Japan. It grows slowly on short single or multiple trunks to 10 ft (3 m) with a wide, flat rosette of stiff, pinnate leaves which have crowded spine-tipped leaflets. It is the most widely cultivated cycad in the world and is valued as a landscape subject, especially suited to courtyards and plazas. Slow growing, plants live for 50 to 100 years or even more and are readily transplanted. ZONE 9.

CYDONIA
Rosaceae
QUINCE

Quinces are familiar fruit, but most of us do not appreciate how attractive and unusual are the small deciduous trees from which they come. They belong to the pome-fruit group, with apples and pears and smaller-fruited genera such as *Cotoneaster* and *Crataegus*. From temperate Asia, they are small, crooked, very woody trees with smooth bark and simple, oval leaves, downy at least on the underside and clustered on short spur-shoots (as in apples) except on the long summer growths. The flowers are solitary at the ends of the spur-shoots, and have a downy calyx and pink petals. The large fruit has waxy or almost greasy skin which is pleasantly aromatic. Quinces only thrive in temperate climates, though the Chinese species tolerates warmer, more frost-free areas than the common quince does. They require moist, deep soil and a sunny position. Propagation is from seed, easily obtained from over-ripe fruit, or by grafting for named varieties. Both species of quince are well worth growing purely as ornamentals.

Cydonia oblonga
COMMON QUINCE

The origin of the quince is uncertain but it probably came from central or western temperate Asia. It has been cultivated in Europe for so long it is regarded as virtually a native. A spreading, bushy tree of 12–15 ft (4–5 m), it forks low into crooked limbs. The leaves are moderately large and oval, deep green above but downy on the underside and on the young twigs. Quince flowers are very attractive, about 2 in (5 cm) in diameter and usually a clear pale pink; they appear in late spring. The fruits, which ripen to pale or deep yellow, are up to about 5 in (13 cm) long, with hard flesh. They are always eaten cooked. The common quince is intolerant of summer humidity. ZONE 6.

Cydonia oblonga

Cydonia oblonga

Cydonia oblonga

Cycas revoluta

Cyathea dealbata (below)

Cyrilla racemiflora

Cytisus scoparius

Cydonia sinensis

Cydonia sinensis
CHINESE QUINCE

This interesting species has been placed at times in *Cydonia*, in *Chaenomeles,* or even in a genus of its own, as *Pseudocydonia sinensis*. However its appearance is most like that of a true quince, so we will keep it in *Cydonia*. Introduced from China to the West before 1800, it died out in England during the next few decades as the summer climate was too cool, but flourished in southern Europe where it is still widely grown. Old trees can be 30–40 ft (10–13 m) tall with a thick trunk and bark attractively dappled tan and dark grey, the lateral branches stiff and angular. Leaves, which colour deep scarlet in autumn, are smaller and less downy than those of the common quince and the flowers, borne on the old wood in late spring, are smaller but also an attractive flesh-pink. The pale yellow fruits, usually cylindrical in shape and up to 6 in (15 cm) long, have highly fragrant skin. ZONE 9.

CYRILLA
Cyrillaceae
AMERICAN LEATHERWOOD, SWAMP CYRILLA

This genus consists of only one species of small tree, often growing as a shrub, that includes both deciduous and evergreen races. This is partly explained by its very wide climatic range, from Virginia in eastern USA south through Florida and the West Indies and into South America as far as Brazil. However the plants usually grown in gardens are the northern, deciduous forms. They are tall shrubs with spatula-shaped leaves, producing many long tapering racemes of tiny white fragrant flowers from just below the new leaves. In the wild cyrillas form dense thickets along margins of swamps, while in gardens it is an undemanding shrub, worth growing for the elegance of its flowers. It does best in a sunny but sheltered spot. Propagation is normally from seed.

Cyrilla racemiflora

This shrub often only grows to about 5 ft (1.5 m) high, but under good conditions can reach 20 ft (7 m) or more, with a central woody stem and open branching habit, the lateral branches wiry and tending to curve upward. The rather sparse leaves are glossy green and turn dull red one by one before falling in late autumn. The white flower-spikes start opening in early summer and may continue almost to autumn. The flowers are followed by tiny dry fruits. ZONE 6.

CYTISUS
Fabaceae
BROOM

A diverse group of usually yellow-flowered leguminous shrubs from Europe and the Mediterranean countries, known in English as brooms, includes several genera. The most important of these are *Cytisus* and *Genista*; smaller genera are *Spartium*, *Retama* and *Argyrocytisus*. *Cytisus* is a large and variable genus, in habit ranging from erect to prostrate, some species having well-developed leaves, of 3 leaflets or simple and narrow, while others are almost leafless with all photosynthesis performed by the green angular branchlets. All have pea-like flowers, mostly in shades of yellow, in profuse small clusters along the current season's growths in mid to late spring. Generally easy garden subjects, they can be relied upon for a display of colour under most conditions except deep shade, tolerating both dry and boggy soils, fertile or highly infertile. Some of the smaller rock-garden species demand warm, dry positions in pockets of well-drained soil, but these are cultivated mainly by enthusiasts. Easily propagated from seeds, cuttings or, rarely, grafts are used for some named cultivars.

Cytisus 'Burkwoodii'

Although very similar to *Cytisus scoparius*, this reddish flowered cultivar is believed to be a hybrid with *C. multiflorus*. It makes a vigorous, bushy shrub of around 5 ft (1.5 m), starting to flower when quite small and developing arching branches as it ages. The upper petals (standards) are cerise, the inner (wings) crimson edged yellow. It blooms in late spring and early summer. ZONE 5.

Cytisus × *praecox*
WARMINSTER BROOM

This hybrid between the very tall species *C. multiflorus* and the lower *C. purgans* includes several popular cultivars which make free-flowering shrubs of 3–4 ft (1–1.2 m) with massed slender branchlets arising at ground level and spreading gracefully. The original hybrid has cream and yellow flowers with a heavy, perhaps overpowering, fragrance borne in mid to late spring. Later clones include 'Allgold', with cascading sprays of soft golden-yellow blossom, and 'Goldspear', a lower and broader shrub with deeper gold flowers. ZONE 5.

Cytisus scoparius
COMMON BROOM, SCOTCH BROOM

Widely distributed in central and western Europe including the UK, this is one of the tallest and most vigorous species of *Cytisus*, reaching 6–8 ft (2–2.5 m) in height and making a great show of golden-yellow blossom in late spring and early summer. The black seed pods may be abundant, ripening in mid-summer and scattering their seed with a sharp cracking sound in hot dry weather. In cool areas of some southern hemisphere countries this has become a troublesome weed, due to its prolific seeding habit and freedom from its normal insect pests; some of the latter are now being introduced in an attempt to check the broom's growth. ZONE 5.

D

Dacrydium cupressinum

Dacrydium cupressinum

Daboecia cantabrica

Dais cotinifolia

DABOECIA
Ericaceae
ST DABEOC'S HEATH

Only 2 species make up this genus of small-leafed, evergreen shrubs from north-western Atlantic coasts and islands. Commonly grouped with the heaths and heathers (*Erica* and *Calluna*) as fitting subjects for a heather garden, the genus has conspicuous white to purple urn-shaped flowers, which contract to a small mouth, on nodding stalks spaced along bare, ascending flowering branches that stand above the foliage. The petal tube falls after flowering, unlike that of many heaths and heathers, which makes for a neater effect in the garden. They are tough, easily grown plants suited to exposed situations in a rock garden or on retaining walls and make a fine show over a long flowering season. Naturally low and spreading, they can be trimmed after flowering to make even denser shrubs. Although wind tolerant, they require a moist climate and soil that is permanently moist and rather acid. Named varieties normally require propagation from cuttings, but they still produce fertile seed which may breed true to type.

Daboecia azorica
Endemic to the northern Atlantic Azores Islands, this is the less widely grown species and also the less frost-hardy. It is most at home in the milder parts of cool-temperate zones. More prostrate in habit than *D. cantabrica*, it has smaller leaves and deep red flowers. ZONE 8.

Daboecia cantabrica
Found along limited stretches of the Atlantic coasts of France and Ireland, this species becomes a somewhat straggling shrub of up to 24 in (60 cm) high if not pruned to a lower height. The flowers, borne throughout summer and autumn, are almost ½ in (1 cm) long and vary from white through pink to deep crimson-purple; clones representing these extremes are named 'Alba' and 'Atropurpurea' respectively. It has also been crossed with *D. azorica* to give the hybrid *D.* × *scotica*, of which the best known clone is 'William Buchanan' with deep rosy-red flowers. ZONE 7.

DACRYDIUM
Podocarpaceae

There are about 15 species of true *Dacrydium*, some species having been reclassified as *Lagarostrobos* and *Halocarpus*. All are from the South Pacific, mostly from New Caledonia and New Guinea, but one or two range as far as mainland Southeast Asia. They are all very beautiful trees with graceful branchlets clothed in overlapping fine needle leaves. They are true conifers but, like all other members of the podocarp family, their seed-bearing organs do not form a 'cone' but are solitary, large seeds each surrounded by fleshy scales. The small pollen cones are borne on different trees. *Dacrydium* species do not adapt well to cultivation; they require climates that are moderately cool but without severe frosts or high summer temperatures, as well as adequate rainfall and humidity. Even then growth is rather slow, but the young trees can be objects of great beauty.

Dacrydium cupressinum
RIMU, NEW ZEALAND RED PINE

In New Zealand this and the kauri (*Agathis australis*) are the tallest native trees, reaching 200 ft (60 m) in the wild, but in cultivation a rimu tree as much as 30 ft (10 m) tall would be quite rare. In its juvenile state, which persists until the sapling is at least 8 ft (2.5 m) tall, it is strikingly beautiful, with long weeping branchlets clothed densely in fine, spreading needles. In winter the whole turns a deep reddish brown. The saplings are delicate, requiring very sheltered conditions, and even then are liable to die suddenly. The adult foliage has shorter, fleshier needles and is more closely branched. Female trees bear small bluish seeds, each half-buried in a bright red fleshy cup. ZONE 8.

DAIS
Thymelaeaceae

This small genus consists of evergreen or semi-deciduous trees and shrubs from southern and eastern Africa and Madagascar, one species of which is grown in warm climates for its showy pompon heads of flowers. The branches have a thin, very rough bark; the leaves are simple and oval; and the silky-haired tubular flowers are not differentiated into petals and sepals. It does best in full sun and a moderately sheltered position, light, fertile soil with free drainage and adequate summer water. They can be pruned after flowering but normally maintain their shape well without pruning. Propagation is from seed or cuttings.

Dais cotinifolia
POMPON TREE

This partly deciduous shrub or small tree to about 12 ft (4 m) has small, oval, grey-green leaves, the branchlets terminating in starry heads of pink flowers through late spring and early summer. It tends to grow as a multi-stemmed shrub, but can be trained into a tree shape if required. ZONE 9.

DALBERGIA
Fabaceae

This large genus is made up of over 300 species including trees, shrubs, lianas and climbers, mostly from tropical rainforest areas. All have pinnate leaves with alternating leaflets, typical of the pea family. The small pea-shaped flowers, sometimes very numerous, are borne in hanging panicles; the seed pods are thin and do not split open easily. Some tree species are a valuable source of rosewood but are rarely cultivated for timber production, although they are sometimes planted around tea plantations as shelter and shade plants. They require a frost-free climate and high rainfall. Propagation is from seed, and treatment of the seed by abrading or placing them in boiling water overnight before planting may increase germination.

Dalbergia sissoo
SISSOO, SHISHAM

This deciduous tree grows to 80 ft (25 m) in its natural habitat in tropical areas of India and Southeast Asia, though it is usually much smaller and more spreading when grown out in the open. The leaves have 3 to 5 ovate leaflets; the white or cream pea-flowers are borne in short panicles, followed by the 4 in (10 cm) long fruits. The sissoo is an important timber tree in India, its hard and durable wood being used for timber floors or for making furniture. An excellent subject for permaculture, it grows best in well-drained soils. ZONE 10.

DAPHNE
Thymelaeaceae
DAPHNE

Few groups of shrubs are treasured by discerning gardeners as much as the daphnes. This quite large genus includes both deciduous and evergreen species, all from Europe or Asia, with simple, leathery leaves and small, mostly fragrant flowers clustered at the shoot tips or in the leaf axils. The flower parts are not differentiated into true petals and sepals, but for the sake of simplicity are referred to here as 'petals', of which there are always 4, characteristically pointed and recurving and rather fleshy in texture. In the wild, daphnes grow mostly in mountains in rocky or stony ground, often on limestone. As garden plants they prefer cool, well-aerated, gritty soil with high humus content; they are intolerant of disturbance to the roots and are best planted out while small. The taller species are best adapted to sheltered woodland situations, the smaller ones to rock garden conditions. Propagation is normally from cuttings or layers; seeds germinate readily enough but many of the species fail to fruit.

Daphne × burkwoodii

This hybrid between *D. cneorum* and *D. caucasica* was raised early in the 20th century by the Burkwood brothers, well-known English nurserymen, and ever since has been one of the most popular daphnes. Semi-evergreen, it is a low, rounded shrub up to about 3 ft (1 m) tall with profusely clustered, pale pink flowers, darker in bud. The main flowering is mid- to late spring but flowers may continue to appear through summer. The most easily grown of the deciduous daphnes, it flowers best in full sun but will also thrive in semi-shade. ZONE 6.

Daphne cneorum
GARLAND FLOWER

This evergreen shrub from southern Europe has a loose, semi-prostrate habit with the main shoots trailing but producing dense clusters of lateral branches with small, dark green leaves and profuse clusters of sweet-scented rose-pink flowers in mid-spring. It is a sun-loving plant but requires its soil to remain moist though perfectly drained. ZONE 6.

Daphne genkwa

Indigenous in China but long cultivated in Japan, this small deciduous shrub can grow to about 3 ft (1 m) or more tall, although in cultivation it tends to be short lived and may only reach half this height. It is sparsely branched, making long wiry growths in summer which the following spring bear clusters of delicate, long-tubed, lilac flowers at every leaf axil while still leafless. It seems to do best in a sheltered, sunny spot in very open-textured but moisture-retentive soil; however its performance is very unpredictable. It is sometimes damaged by late frosts. ZONE 6.

Daphne mezereum
MEZEREON

This is the only daphne native over the greater part of northern Europe and Asia, including the British Isles, growing in woodland and scrub. *Mezereum* is its classical name, thought to come from old Persian, and the common name 'mezereon' came into English from the French. It is an erect, bushy, deciduous shrub of up to 5 ft (1.5 m) tall with long narrow leaves. The fragrant flowers are a rich rose-pink, appearing in late winter and early spring clustered along the bare twigs of the previous year's growth. Conspicuous red juicy fruits

Daphne × burkwoodii (below)

Daphne genkwa (below)

(poisonous!) sit on the branches below the leaves, ripening in late summer. Preferring a very moist, sheltered situation, the mezereon makes a fine ornamental shrub although its performance is unpredictable. ZONE 5.

Daphne odora

A Chinese evergreen species long cultivated in Japan, *D. odora* is too frost-tender for many cooler regions of the northern hemisphere but its lovely sweet perfume has made it the most popular daphne in temperate southern hemisphere countries. Although capable of reaching almost 6 ft (2 m) in height, it is normally seen as a spreading, twiggy shrub of about 24 in (60 cm) with leathery, dark green leaves. From late autumn through to mid-spring it produces a succession of clusters of waxy flowers, typically rose-purple on the outside of the buds opening to almost pure white. 'Alba' has wholly white flowers, while 'Aureo-marginata', slightly more frost-hardy, has leaves edged with yellow and flowers with reddish purple outsides. ZONE 8.

DARLINGIA
Proteaceae

This genus contains 2 evergreen tree species endemic to tropical rainforests of north-eastern Australia, grown for their handsome foliage and erect spikes of creamy white grevillea-like flowers. The leaves are long and pointed, usually

Darlingia darlingiana (below)

lobed on young trees; the waxy flowers, often scented, are borne in dense, erect spikes at the ends of the growth and are generally hairy. The fruit is a follicle containing seeds that are thin, flat and winged. Attractive specimen trees for large gardens or parks, they need a sheltered position, ample moisture and moderately rich soil. Propagation is from fresh seed or cuttings.

Darlingia darlingiana
BROWN SILKY OAK

This handsome, tall, erect tree, growing to 80 ft (25 m) in the wild has been exploited for its timber but is not yet widely cultivated. Its shiny, dark green, variously lobed leaves can be up to 16 in (40 cm) long, with prominent veins. The dense white flower spikes, about 10 in (25 cm) long, appear in spring. ZONE 10.

Daphne odora (below)

Darlingia darlingiana (below)

Daphne cneorum (below)

DARWINIA
Myrtaceae

This medium-sized genus comprises evergreen shrubs that are endemic to Australia; most species occur in the far south-west but there is a smaller group in the south-east. They grow in heath vegetation in sandy or boggy soil. Darwinias have small, narrow leaves with translucent oil-dots containing aromatic oils. The flowers are hardly recognizable as belonging to the myrtle family, being narrow and tubular with long protruding styles, usually quite small but crowded into clusters terminating the lateral branches. However, in one group of south-western species the flower-clusters are surrounded by large, colourful bracts, appearing like a single flower and of striking appearance. Unfortunately, members of this group are among the most difficult to cultivate. Other darwinias grow quite readily in any light, well-drained soil in a sunny or partly shaded position; some will tolerate salty air near the sea. They vary from near-prostrate to tall, erect shrubs of about 10 ft (3 m), but most are low and spreading. Propagation is normally from tip cuttings.

Darwinia oxylepis
GILLIAM'S BELL

Despite its diminutive size, this shrub offers perhaps the best display of flowers in the genus. The flower heads hang from the ends of pendulous branches, with brilliant scarlet 'bells' of enclosing bracts. The leaves are small and prickly, and are crowded on the branchlets. Gilliam's bell grows to about 24 in (60 cm) high. ZONE 10.

DAVIDIA
Davidiaceae
DOVE TREE, HANDKERCHIEF TREE

'Like huge butterflies hovering' is how the plant explorer E. H. Wilson described the long-stalked flower heads of this tree in western China, each nestled between 2 large, drooping white or cream bracts. In full flower it is one of the most striking of all deciduous trees outside the tropics. The genus contains just one species, though sometimes a variety is distinguished within it. The large, toothed leaves have a soft texture with the surface deeply creased by veins. The tree is always raised from the large seeds, enclosed in a plum-like fruit about 1½ in (3 cm) long. Cold treatment assists germination.

Davidia involucrata

In its native China this graceful tree reaches heights of over 60 ft (18 m) with a rounded crown and thick trunk, often suckering from the base. In cultivation it can grow quite rapidly to 15–20 ft (5–7 m) in suitably deep, moist, friable soil and a sheltered situation, and in a few decades it may double that height. However, flowering rarely begins before the tree is 10 years old and does not peak for a further 5 years or so. The more common form in cultivation is var. *vilmoriniana*, with paler and less downy leaf undersides. ZONE 8.

DELONIX
Caesalpiniaceae

Only 2 species make up this genus of tropical deciduous trees from Africa, Madagascar, Arabia and south-west Asia. However, only one is widely grown for its striking flowers and feathery bipinnate leaves. The orchid-like flowers, produced in clusters all over the tree, are in shades of orange-red or yellow-white. The fruit, typical of the legume group, is a large, flattened, woody, bean-like pod. The poinciana needs rich, well-drained soil with plenty of moisture, and a position in full sun with plenty of room to spread. The vigorous root system can damage paths and even building foundations. Prune when young to establish a single trunk, but avoid heavy pruning thereafter. The trees are tolerant of a large range of soils but heavy, poorly drained clay soils do not suit them. They are easily propagated from seed or cuttings; however seedlings vary considerably in flower shape, colour and size, and may take 10 or more years to flower.

Delonix regia
POINCIANA, FLAMBOYANT TREE, FLEUR-DE-PARADIS, GUL MOHR

This magnificent deciduous tropical tree from Madagascar with its spectacular flowers grows only to about 40 ft (13 m) tall, but its umbrella-like canopy may be 3 times as wide. The long, feathery leaves are light green. Clusters of brilliant red or orange flowers, with one white petal marked with yellow and red, are produced in late spring or early summer over a period of about 6 weeks. They are followed by dark brown pods, up to 12 in (30 cm) long, which persist on the tree. ZONE 11.

DESFONTAINEA
Loganiaceae

This genus consists of evergreen shrubs from the Andean chain in western South America, one of which has long been cultivated for its interesting holly-like foliage and showy orange flowers. It is a stiff-branched shrub, spreading by basal branching, with leaves arranged in

Davidia involucrata (below)

Davidia involucrata

Darwinia oxylepis

Davidia involucrata (below)

Delonix regia

Delonix regia

opposite pairs. The flowers, borne singly in the upper leaf axils, are roughly trumpet shaped, with a gradually broadening tube and cupped, overlapping petals; they point downward and are presumably adapted to pollination by hummingbirds. In cool-temperate climates it is moderately frost-hardy but requires mild, rainy conditions for best results. Propagation is normally from cuttings.

Desfontainea spinosa

The only species in cultivation, this is usually seen as a rather slow-growing, erect shrub of up to 5 ft (1.5 m) tall, but when conditions suit it can reach twice this height and may spread with age to cover a large area. The shiny dark green leaves are remarkably similar to those of English holly (*Ilex aquifolium*) and the flowers, scattered among the branchlets in late summer, vary from pale yellowish orange to a bright orange-scarlet but generally paler at the petal tips. ZONE 8.

DEUTZIA
Hydrangeaceae
WEDDING BELLS

Summer-flowering deciduous shrubs from East Asia and the Himalaya, deutzias are closely related to *Philadelphus* but are easily distinguished by their smaller white or pink flowers in more crowded sprays, with 5 pointed petals rather than 4. Like *Philadelphus* they have long, straight, cane-like stems springing from ground level, developing a rather pale flaky bark if allowed to thicken. Leaves are always in opposite pairs, mostly finely toothed. The flower sprays terminate short lateral shoots from the previous year's growths, so hard pruning will delay flowering for a year; best results are obtained by selectively thinning out canes and shortening some of the thickest old stems. Propagation is straightforward using cuttings. There are many hardy species of deutzias which make excellent garden shrubs and also some fine hybrids,

Delonix regia

Desfontainea spinosa

especially those made in the famous Lémoine nursery at Nancy, France, between about 1890 and 1940, with wonderful soft pink shades added to the predominant whites. Deutzias are essentially shrubs for sheltered positions in moist, fertile soil, though appreciating plenty of sun.

Deutzia × *elegantissima*

Including some of the finest and largest-flowered pinks among its clones, this hybrid between the west Chinese *D. purpurascens* and the Japanese *D. sieboldiana* makes a shrub of 4–6 ft (1.2–2 m) with purplish red twigs and flower-stalks. The Lémoine nursery released the 2 original cultivars, 'Elegantissima' with flowers near-white inside and rose-pink outside, and 'Fasciculata' with a slightly

Deutzia × *kalmiiflora*

deeper rose flush. These were followed by the Irish hybrid 'Rosealind' with still deeper flesh-pink flowers. ZONE 7.

Deutzia gracilis

From Japan, where it occurs widely, this is still one of the most popular species for its graceful, spreading habit and pure white flowers produced in slender, arching sprays in late spring and early summer. It is one of the chief parent species of hybrid deutzias. Normally about 3 ft (1 m) tall, it is also known in gardens in the guise of a dwarf variant about half this height, widely sold as *Deutzia* 'Nikko'. ZONE 6.

Deutzia × *kalmiiflora*

Only one clone of this early Lémoine hybrid between *D.*

Deutzia gracilis

parviflora and *D. purpurascens* is normally available, so a cultivar name is not used. It makes an erect shrub of about 6 ft (2 m) with small neat leaves and rather tight clusters of flowers of which the deep pink outsides contrast with the pale rose insides. It flowers from early to mid-summer. ZONE 7.

Deutzia scabra

Deutzia × rosea

Dicksonia squarrosa

Deutzia × rosea

Deutzia × rosea

This was one of the earliest Lémoine crosses, involving the species *D. gracilis* and *D. purpurascens*. It has the low, spreading habit of the former species and the pink coloration of the second. The original clone has flowers of the palest pink, in shorter, broader sprays than in *D. gracilis*. 'Carminea' has larger panicles of pink flowers with a stronger carmine-pink on the back. ZONE 7.

Deutzia scabra

This longest established of the *Deutzia* species in Western gardens is also the most robust in growth, with tall, thick canes to about 10 ft (3 m) high, and one of the most cold-hardy. The name *scabra* means 'rough' or 'harsh' and refers to the rasp-like feel of the long, dull green leaves. The bell-shaped flowers are a dazzling white, produced in large panicles terminating all the upper branches from mid-spring to early summer. The pale brown bark peels attractively on the thicker growths. 'Flore Pleno' is a form with double flowers, striped dull pink on the outside; 'Candidissima' is a pure white double, while 'Pride of Rochester' is yet another double but with larger flowers faintly tinted mauve outside, very vigorous and floriferous. ZONE 6.

DICKSONIA
Dicksoniaceae
TREE FERN

Tree ferns are a common feature of forests in the wet tropics, among mountains where mist and drizzle are frequent. They are true ferns, distinguished from other ferns by their single bud terminating a vertical stem, at the core of which is a convoluted system of conducting and strengthening tissues, often clothed in a thick outer layer of matted aerial roots. The fronds are usually very large, divided into hundreds or thousands of small leaflets and with thick stalks covered in dense scales towards the bases. Outside the tropics the number of tree fern species drops off rapidly, and towards the limit of their range in the southern hemisphere is found the genus *Dicksonia*, which includes the most cold-hardy tree ferns. One New Zealand species (*D. squarrosa*) occurs throughout both islands, up to latitudes equivalent to central Europe. All tree ferns require very sheltered positions and will not tolerate a dry atmosphere.

Dicksonia antarctica
SOFT TREE FERN

This medium-sized tree fern comes from Tasmania and southern mainland Australia where it grows in tall, moist forests, often in great abundance. Old plants can be 20 ft (7 m) tall and often have thick mats of aerial roots on the trunk. The large, bright green fronds droop as they age and the dead ones form a 'skirt' concealing the upper trunk. In Australian nurseries it is sold as 'stumps' 24–36 in (60–90 cm) high, cut off above the ground but with the terminal bud intact; these take root readily when planted in moist soil. Elsewhere it may be necessary to raise it from spores. In cultivation in southern England and Ireland it has seldom reached more than 8 ft (2.5 m) in height. ZONE 8.

Dicksonia fibrosa
WHEKI-PONGA

This attractive tree fern from New Zealand grows slowly to a height of 20 ft (7 m) and produces dark green, arching fronds, each 5–8 ft (1.5–2.5 m) long. As the plant grows the stout stem becomes covered in thick, densely matted, fibrous, brownish red aerial roots. An easily grown species, it prefers cool, moist conditions. ZONE 8.

DILLENIA
Dilleniaceae

Some 60 species of evergreen trees and shrubs, most from tropical Asia, Africa, Madagascar and Australia, make up this genus. The large, leathery leaves have prominent veins and the showy yellow or white 5-petalled flowers are produced singly or in loose panicles. They are followed by fleshy fruit enclosed by enlarged fleshy sepals. These plants are moderately fast growing, transplant easily when young and are grown from seed. They need sun, a tropical or subtropical climate, ample water and some shelter when young. One species is widely planted as an ornamental in tropical regions.

Dillenia alata

Indigenous to the wet tropical regions of northern Australia, this evergreen tree grows to a maximum of 25 ft (8 m) on a crooked, low-branching trunk with attractive, bright red, flaking bark. Its glossy green leaves are long and thick, creating a dense canopy. The yellow flowers are 3 in (8 cm) across and open flat to reveal a cluster of golden yellow stamens. Its bright red seed pods, as attractive as the flowers, are popular with florists. *D. alata* tolerates salty winds but not frost or drought. ZONE 12.

Dillenia indica
ELEPHANT APPLE

This spectacular tree found in India and Southeast Asia grows to 20 ft (7 m) tall, with a domed canopy almost as wide, and is grown for shade as well as its attractive flowers and fruit. The large, thickened, dark green leaves have prominent parallel veins. The 6 in (15 cm) wide creamy yellow flowers are fragrant. The developing fruits, enclosed in fleshy sepals, look like smooth green apples and can be up to 7 in (17 cm) across when they mature in mid-summer. They are edible and are mostly used for jam; the mature fruit bracts are used for curries and preserves or are eaten as a vegetable. ZONE 12.

DIOON
Zamiaceae

Cycads are among the most ancient groups of plants; dinosaurs no doubt grazed on the tough foliage of their ancestral forms. Species of *Dioon* are grown primarily for their extraordinary primeval appearance. Their evergreen, pinnate fronds, greyish green with leaflet edges often fiercely serrated, either spring from a rosette at ground level or are borne on a rough trunk which in some species can eventually reach as much as 30 ft (10 m) tall. There are male and female plants. Like all

Dillenia indica

Dicksonia antarctica

Dicksonia antarctica (below)

Dillenia alata

Dicksonia fibrosa

cycads they have no flowers, but mature specimens may produce a cone which contains seeds. Mostly frost-tender, they grow in any well-drained soil, in sun or light shade, and live happily in containers. Pruning should be avoided as it ruins their perfect symmetry, except for removing old, untidy leaves. Endemic to Mexico and Honduras, most of the 10 species of *Dioon* are now rare in the wild. The genus name, Greek for 'two eggs' referring to the paired seeds on each cone-scale, should be pronounced with 3 syllables, Di-o-on. They are propagated from seed or offsets.

Dioon edule

Originating from Mexico, this rigid, symmetrical plant is the most widely grown member of the genus. It has handsome grey-green leaves; the tip of each stiff leaflet is armed with a spine, and the stalks are slightly downy when young. It produces edible seeds from a 12 in (30 cm) diameter cone. While slow to become established, *D. edule* is quite easy to grow; the thick trunk may reach 10–12 ft (3–4 m) in height. It can be grown almost indefinitely in containers but is difficult to transplant. ZONE 10.

DIOSPYROS
Ebenaceae
PERSIMMON, EBONY

This genus is made up of several hundred species of mostly evergreen trees from the tropics but with a number of important deciduous species in temperate Asia and America. *Diospyros ebenum* from Sri Lanka provides the hard, almost-black timber known as ebony, prized since the days of ancient Egypt though it is scarce now and most ebony comes from other African and Asian species. Not all species are black; some are very much paler. The genus also includes several species prized for their edible fruit, notably the black sapote (*D. dignya*) and the Japanese and American persimmons. All *Diospyros* species are trees with strong branches, smooth-edged leaves that unroll from the bud, and peculiar flowers with rolled-back petals and a leaf-like calyx that enlarges as the pulpy-fleshed fruit develops. The fruits of nearly all species are edible, if not to humans then to birds or mammals such as monkeys. Propagation is normally from seed.

Diospyros digyna
BLACK SAPOTE

This evergreen tropical tree can grow to 60 ft (20 m) tall in the wild in Mexico and Central America; it has also naturalized in tropical Asia. The shiny green leaves are up to 8 in (20 cm) long; the flowers are small, white and fragrant. The smooth, olive-green fruit is about 4 in (10 cm) across; as it ripens the skin may become almost black, and it ripens quickly after being picked from the tree, sometimes overnight. The flesh has a taste and consistency like chocolate mousse, and the fruit is high in vitamin C. There are many seedling variations, and some cultivars produce fruit without seeds. Budding (in autumn or midsummer) and grafting (spring or summer) are used for cultivars. Trees do best in well-drained, moist soil, with ample water in the growing season and shelter from strong wind because of their brittle branches. ZONE 11.

Diospyros kaki
PERSIMMON

Originally native to China, this well-known deciduous fruit tree was cultivated in Japan for many centuries before being introduced to the West in the 18th century. Growing to about 20 ft (7 m) with spreading branches and rather pendulous smaller branches, it has large glossy leaves that turn a fine yellow to deep orange colour in autumn. The small cream flowers appear among the leaves in early summer, followed by orange or pinkish fruit up to about 3 in (8 cm) in diameter from late summer to late autumn, persisting on leafless branches in some varieties. Some cultivars are astringent until very ripe and soft but others are sweet while still firm. ZONE 8.

Diospyros virginiana
PERSIMMON, AMERICAN PERSIMMON

This spreading tree can reach heights of over 100 ft (30 m) in its native eastern USA, in forests on deep alluvial soils in the river valleys, but in cultivation it commonly grows to only 20–30 ft (7–10 m). The leaves, glossy green with paler undersides, often turn an attractive pale yellow in autumn. The cream flowers open in mid-summer, and the globular, 1½ in (3 cm) diameter fruit ripens to orange or purple-red in early autumn; it is edible and tasty but must be fully ripe. The timber (known in the trade as white ebony) is very valuable, considered the finest in the world for the heads of golf 'woods' and other applications requiring high resistance to impact. ZONE 5.

DIPELTA
Caprifoliaceae

Only a few species from China make up this genus of deciduous shrubs, and only one is well established in Western gardens—but even that is uncommon. They are related to and resemble *Weigela* and *Kolkwitzia*, with richly marked, bell-shaped flowers in large clusters. The fruit is distinctive, with 2 rounded bracts enlarging at its base after the flowers are shed, partly concealing it. Though they are quite easily grown, these beautiful shrubs are not widely planted. They prefer a sunny position but with moist soil and some shelter

Dipelta floribunda (below)

Diospyros virginiana (below)

Diospyros kaki (below)

Diospyros virginiana (below)

Dioon edule

from strong winds. Dipeltas are easily propagated from cuttings.

Dipelta floribunda

From the lower mountains of east-central China, this species makes an erect, multi-stemmed shrub about 10 ft (3 m) in height, the stems becoming very woody with peeling layers of pale bark. In late spring and early summer it bears among broad, soft leaves large drooping clusters of fragrant flowers, 1½ in (3 cm) long, of the palest pink, deeper flesh-pink on the outside of the tube and with orange-yellow markings in the throat. ZONE 6.

DISANTHUS
Hamamelidaceae

Just a single species of deciduous shrub belongs to this Japanese genus in the witch-hazel family. It is ornamental though not showy. Its leaves are almost circular with pronounced bluish undersides; the flowers, appearing in autumn as the leaves colour, are small, strap-like and purplish red, borne in pairs along the old wood. Even in summer the strongly veined leaves are bronze tinted but by early autumn they turn a deep metallic bronze-purple and finally pale to red or orange not long before falling. Although fairly frost-hardy, *Disanthus* requires sheltered conditions and deep, moist, friable soil. The seeds, produced in small capsules maturing through summer, can be used for propagation, but cuttings or ground layering are more effective.

Disanthus cercidifolius

The only species in the genus makes a spreading shrub of rather slow growth, eventually reaching 8 ft (2.5 m) or more in height with stiff, wiry branches, usually with a number of stems diverging from the base. ZONE 7.

DODONAEA
Sapindaceae
HOPBUSH

This is a widespread and almost entirely Australian genus of evergreen trees and woody shrubs. Its common name, hopbush, is a reference to the abundant, winged, capsular, hop-like fruits which were used for brewing beer in the early days of European settlement. In many species, male and female flowers appear on separate plants. While the flowers are small and insignificant, these fruits are large and decorative on some species. Hopbushes will grown in full sun or partial shade and prefer moderately fertile, light, free-draining soil. They tolerate a wide range of climates and coastal salty winds. Light pruning in early spring helps re-

Dodonaea boroniifolia

strict height and maintain shape. Propagate from seed in spring or from cuttings in summer.

Dodonaea boroniifolia
FERN-LEAF HOPBUSH, HAIRY HOPBUSH

A bushy shrub to 5 ft (1.5 m) with dark green, fern-like leaves with hairy leaflets. The insignificant flowers are followed in summer by attractive red fruit capsules. ZONE 9.

Dodonaea viscosa
HOPBUSH

This very variable species grows throughout Australia and also in New Zealand, with very glossy, slightly sticky, light green foliage and decorative fruits in summer that are green turning to light brown. Dense and fast growing, it will grow to a small tree but is best pruned to an upright shrub form around 10 ft (3 m) tall; it is useful for screening and hedging. 'Purpurea', a bronze-leafed cultivar from New Zealand, has purplish red fruit capsules. ZONE 9.

DOLICHANDRONE
Bignoniaceae

A small genus, its shrubs and trees are found naturally in tropical areas of Africa, Asia, Australia and some Pacific islands. Most species are quite heavily wooded with dull to dark brown, attractively patterned bark. The leaves are pinnate and made up of around 3 to 13 leaflets that are usually elliptical though quite variable in shape. Phlox-like flowers appear in clusters at the branch tips. They are usually white and night scented. As with most tropical plants from regular rainfall areas, they prefer moist, humus-enriched, well-drained soil in sun or dappled shade. Temperatures below 56°F (13°C) will not be tolerated for long. Propagation is from seed or semi-ripe cuttings.

Dolichandrone heterophylla

From dry monsoonal woodland areas of northern Australia, this species is an 18 ft (6 m) tree with

Dolichandrone heterophylla

Dodonaea viscosa 'Purpurea'

deeply furrowed, dark brown bark. Its 6 in (15 cm) pinnate leaves are composed of leaflets up to 4 in (10 cm) long. The white flowers, about 1½ in (3 cm) long, have shorter petals than most other species. ZONE 11.

DOMBEYA
Sterculiaceae
WEDDING FLOWER

This genus of evergreen, deciduous or semi-deciduous shrubs and small trees has some species in Africa but many more in Madagascar; only a few species from southern Africa are widely cultivated. They come from the eastern, summer-rainfall regions of southern Africa, growing in dry scrubs and woodland on the escarpment and the Transvaal lowveld. The leaves are mostly circular, heart shaped or maple-like in outline, and have a

Dolichandrone heterophylla (below)

Disanthus cercidifolius (below)

Dombeya burgessiae

Dombeya rotundifolia

Dombeya burgessiae

Dombeya tiliacea

scurf of downy hairs at least on the underside. Flowers are very pretty, cup shaped with overlapping white, pink or red petals, in small to large clusters all over the crown. The petals persist while the small capsular fruits are ripening, turning a rusty brown. This can look unattractive, but after-bloom pruning will tidy the plants up. Dombeyas thrive in most warm-temperate and subtropical climates with good summer moisture; some species are moderately frost-hardy. Propagation is normally from fresh seed.

Dombeya burgessiae
PINK DOMBEYA

From parts of Natal, Transvaal and Zimbabwe, this species is often only a shrub of 10–15 ft (3–5 m) with a dense mass of stems from ground level. The leaves are hairy and quite large, with shallow, maple-like lobing. From mid-summer to mid-autumn loose clusters of showy, bell-shaped flowers are produced in succession, varying from the palest pink to deep pinkish red. It is a popular species for hedges and shelter-belts on account of its fast, early growth. ZONE 9.

Dombeya × cayeuxii

This hybrid of uncertain origin, but possibly with *D. burgessiae* as one parent, has long been grown in European greenhouses. It makes a shrub of similar size and growth-habit but the leaves have more long-pointed lobes. The pale pink flowers appear in great profusion in large, hemispherical heads at all branch tips, over a long season in summer and autumn. ZONE 10.

Dombeya rotundifolia
SOUTH AFRICAN WILD PEAR

This deciduous or semi-deciduous small tree to about 20 ft (7 m) tall has a dense, rounded canopy of foliage and rough, fissured bark on the thick crooked trunk. The leaves are roughly circular, very stiff to the touch with a harsh, furry surface; in late autumn they turn yellow, then brown, before falling. White flowers appear in profusion in early spring on the almost leafless branches, making this one of the most spectacularly flowering species. It makes fast early growth in a suitably warm climate. Trees cultivated in Australia with pale pink flowers are also assigned to this species—hardly surprising as it is widely distributed through eastern Africa from Natal northward, showing considerable variation. ZONE 10.

Dombeya tiliacea
NATAL WEDDING FLOWER

Also known as *D. natalensis*, this evergreen tree species with slim, blackish multiple trunks comes from areas of Natal and eastern Cape Province in South Africa. It has a leafier aspect than other species. Fast growing and slender in its younger stages, it widens into a bushy-crowned tree of up to 20–25 ft (7–8 m) with maturity. From autumn through winter to early spring it bears small pendulous clusters of pure white flowers. Some leaves may turn red in autumn. Water freely while in flower. Prune lightly after flowering to remove spent blooms and maintain shape. ZONE 9.

DORYANTHES
Agavaceae

The 2 species of *Doryanthes* are both indigenous to the east coast of Australia. Their winter to spring flowers are filled with nectar very attractive to birds. *Doryanthes* species are not commonly cultivated in private gardens, requiring up to 10 years to bloom, but are popular in warm-climate public gardens and are highly valued for dramatic floral vase displays. They do best in semi-shade in warm, frost-free conditions in light, humus-rich, well-drained soil. Propagation is from seed or suckers.

Doryanthes excelsa
GYMEA LILY

The larger and more common of the 2 species, *D. excelsa* is one of the largest lilies in the world, its cluster of deep red, torch-shaped flowers held on a stem that can be 18 ft (6 m) tall, arising from a rosette of giant, sword-shaped leaves that can spread to about 6 ft (2 m). ZONE 9.

DOVYALIS
Flacourtiaceae

This genus of evergreen trees and shrubs is largely restricted to Africa, with a few species also in Madagascar and Sri Lanka. Most are spiny, with lateral branchlets on the summer shoots modified as strong thorns. Leaves are simple and alternately arranged and the flowers small and inconspicuous, greenish or yellowish in clusters along the branches, with different sexes on different trees. The globular fruits are edible, mostly pale yellow when ripe. *Dovyalis* species are occasionally grown for fruit; heavily pruned, they make a formidable hedge barrier with their spines. They are propagated from seed or cuttings; if growing for fruit it is usual to bud females onto seedling stocks, with one or two male trees present for purposes of pollination.

Dovyalis caffra
KEI APPLE

From southern Africa, this evergreen shrub grows to about 10 ft (3 m) tall and spreads to about 6 ft (2 m). Of upright habit, it has thorny stems and small, shiny, oval leaves. The inconspicuous yellowish flowers are followed by rounded fruits which are edible but sharp-tasting. ZONE 9.

Dovyalis hebecarpa
CEYLON GOOSEBERRY

This bushy small tree which grows vigorously reaches to about 20 ft (7 m). The leaves have a velvety texture and attractively undulated surfaces with red stalks and veins. The green flowers appear in summer and autumn in leaf axils followed by velvety-skinned fruit about 1 in (2.5 cm) in diameter which ripen from yellowish green to dull purple. Fruits are not highly palatable, but this species has been crossed with *D. abyssinica* to give a hybrid fruit of greater commercial promise. ZONE 10.

DRACAENA
Agavaceae

This genus consists of evergreen trees and shrubs, many originating from equatorial regions of Africa and Asia, which are grown for their foliage, many as greenhouse or indoor potted plants. Those grown indoors are sometimes confused with species of *Cordyline* and are often termed 'false palms' because of their cane-like stems and crown of strappy leaves. In the garden dracaenas need warm-temperate to subtropical conditions, full sun or partial shade and well-drained soil.

Dracaena draco
DRAGON'S-BLOOD TREE, DRAGON TREE

This slow-growing, curious tree, endemic to the Canary Islands, is said to live to a very great age. A mature specimen may reach 30 ft (10 m) high with a rounded, umbrella-like crown consisting of clustered, stiff, lance-shaped, blue-green leaves about 24 in (60 cm) long and nearly 2 in (5 cm) wide. It bears insignificant flowers followed by berries in summer. Full-grown trees are usually only seen in arboretums and botanic gardens; it is also grown as a house plant. ZONE 10.

Dracaena marginata

A slow-growing tree or shrub from Madagascar, this species will reach 15 ft (5 m) in the garden in hot climates. It has narrow, strappy leaves with red margins. The cultivar 'Tricolor' with a cream stripe and red edge is most commonly seen as a house plant. They are easy to grow in pots, withstanding some shade, quite low winter temperatures (but not frost) and some neglect. ZONE 10.

DRIMYS
Winteraceae
WINTER'S BARK

This is an interesting genus of attractive evergreen shrubs or small trees from South and Central America; it belongs to the small family Winteraceae, related to the magnolias and believed to be one of the most primitive flowering plant families. These are cool-climate plants, requiring sheltered situations in the garden and reliable moisture. Propagation is normally from cuttings, or established plants can be layered. Species from Australia and New Guinea formerly placed under *Drimys* are now placed in the genus *Tasmannia*.

Drimys winteri

Of the 4 to 5 species only *D. winteri* is known in cultivation, grown mainly by gardeners with a passion for the rare and unusual. Native to Chile and Argentina, it can reach over 50 ft (15 m) in height but is variable, some forms remaining as shrubs of under 6 ft (2 m). Even as a tree it usually branches at ground level. Its fleshy foliage is dense and glossy, the leaf undersides pale and bluish beneath, and in spring is covered in small clusters of multi-petalled cream flowers. ZONE 8.

Doryanthes excelsa

Dovyalis caffra (below)

Drimys winteri

Dracaena draco

Dracaena draco

Duranta erecta

Durio zibethinus (below)

Durio zibethinus

DURANTA
Verbenaceae
GOLDEN DEWDROP, PIGEON BERRY

A genus of evergreen trees and shrubs from the American tropics and subtropics, *Duranta* is represented in gardens by just one of its many species, grown for its pretty blue flowers and chains of orange berries. The more vigorous growths are armed with spines, leaves are smallish and often toothed and the 5-petalled flowers, narrowed at the centre into a short tube, appear in delicate sprays from the upper leaf axils. They are followed by firm, fleshy fruits with hard stones, said to be poisonous. *Duranta* is a vigorous grower equally at home in the tropics and frost-free temperate regions. It can be trained to a small tree or kept cut back as a shrub; it is a useful subject for a hedge. Propagation is normally from cuttings, easily rooted with sufficient warmth.

Duranta erecta

Botanists took a long time to choose which of the names *D. plumieri*, *D. repens* and *D. erecta* was the correct one for this species, but the latter now seems to be the accepted one. Under good conditions it can reach 15–20 ft (5–7 m) if trained to a single-trunked tree, with dense, slightly pendulous foliage. Flowers are a pale mauve-blue with darker streaks on the 2 lower petals and a cream 'eye', borne from late spring to autumn but continuing into winter in the tropics. The very decorative fruits, ½ in (1 cm) long, can appear in profusion, overlapping with the flowers in late summer and autumn and often persisting into winter. The cultivar 'Variegata' has leaves that are edged with cream. The white-flowered 'Alba' has almost toothless leaves; this and other botanical differences set it rather apart from the species itself. ZONE 10.

DURIO
Bombacaceae

These evergreen trees are native to Burma, Indonesia and Malaysia. They are tall and have elliptical, dull green, scaly leaves. They produce their usually creamy white, heavily scented flowers on the old wood and often bloom twice a year. The flowers develop into large prickly fruit that fall and split open when ripe to reveal a strong-smelling, edible pulp. These are tropical plants that are not happy in areas where the temperature falls much below 65°F (18°C). They prefer a moist, humus-rich soil with full sun or dappled shade. The species may be propagated from seed but the best fruiting cultivars are grafted or budded.

Durio zibethinus
DURIAN

The durian is renowned among tropical fruits, as much for its smell as its taste, for while its many aficionados find the raw fruit delectable its aroma is indescribably putrid. A large tree, it grows to 130 ft (40 m) high in the wild. The leaves are 7½ in (18 cm) long, dark green above and paler on the undersides. The flowers, in clusters of 3 to 30 blooms, are borne directly on the trunk and branches. They are followed by the large, spiny, green to yellow fruit which are up to 15 in (38 cm) long. Greenish white flowers are the norm, though trees with pale pink flowers reputedly produce better fruit. ZONE 12.

DUVERNOIA
Acanthaceae

These small, evergreen shrubs are indigenous to tropical and southern Africa. They have large leaves with wavy margins, slightly ovate and smooth. The 2-lipped flowers are bisexual and grow in closely packed spikes, massed together in the axils of upper leaves. They are minutely hairy, as are the club-shaped fruit capsules.

Duvernoia adhatodoides
PISTOL BUSH

This sturdy, evergreen, flowering shrub or small tree reaches 10 ft (3 m) tall and 3 ft (1 m) wide. The ovate leaves are about 9 in (22 cm) long. During summer and autumn the pistol bush bears an abundance of showy, slightly aromatic, white to mauve flowers with beautiful purple stripes, particularly on the throat, in densely packed racemes. It grows easily and fairly quickly in frost-free areas in any compost-rich soil, in part-shade or even full sun; it needs plenty of water, especially in summer. Wind resistant and suitable for hedges, it can be pruned after flowering. The common name 'pistol bush' comes from the way in which the seed pods burst open with a loud crack to propel the seeds away from the parent plant. Propagation is from cuttings in summer.
ZONE 10.

Echium fastuosum

Edgeworthia chrysantha

Ekebergia capensis

ECHIUM
Boraginaceae

Most members of this genus from the Mediterranean and the nearby Atlantic Islands are annuals or short-lived perennials, some being troublesome weeds in warm countries despite their often showy blue, purple or pink flowers. The most spectacular are such species as *Echium candicans* and *E. wildprettii* from the Canary Islands, which bear 9 ft (3 m) tall spires of flowers, blue and red respectively; but they die after flowering and can scarcely be described as shrubs. The only shrubby species encountered in gardens is the pride of Madeira or tower of jewels, *E. fastuosum*.

Echium fastuosum
PRIDE OF MADEIRA, TOWER OF JEWELS

Sometimes confused with *Echium candicans*, this soft-wooded shrub from Madeira is a great favourite in mild-winter climates, as much for the handsome fuzzy grey-green leaves, broadly sword shaped and clustered in whorls along the branches, as for the spectacular summer display of 3 ft (1 m) spires of flowers, each only about ½ in (1 cm) wide but borne by the hundreds together. In the best forms they are pure sapphire blue, with crimson stamens, though violet-blue forms are often seen. The shrub is sprawling in habit, normally growing about 3 ft (1 m) tall when not in bloom but spreading wider. It needs full sun, sharp drainage and gentle pruning after bloom to keep it compact and is not very long lived. ZONE 9.

EDGEWORTHIA
Thymelaeaceae

This genus comprises 2 deciduous shrub species related to *Daphne*, one from China, the other from the Himalaya. Only the Chinese species is widely cultivated, famous for its traditional use in Japan as a source of high-quality paper prepared from the strong, fine, inner bark fibres. It is also an ornamental shrub of some distinction. Tight heads of small tubular flowers terminate the bare branches in spring; the outside of each flower is concealed by a layer of silky white hairs, the yellow, orange or red colour only appearing on the inner faces at the tip. As in *Daphne* the flower is not differentiated into petals and sepals. *Edgeworthia* is moderately hardy but easily damaged by late frosts. It prefers a sheltered sunny spot in well-drained soil. Pruning is not normally necessary as the plants are naturally rounded and bushy. Propagation is usually from cuttings.

Edgeworthia chrysantha
PAPER BUSH

Indigenous to central China, this species (syn. *E. papyrifera*) makes a shrub to about 6 ft (2 m) and similar spread, branching low from a single stem, but is more commonly seen at 3–4 ft (1–1.2 m). The red-brown twigs are extraordinarily tough and flexible and the soft, pale green leaves are inclined to wilt and shed in hot summer weather. The tips of the flowers, borne in mid-spring, are normally golden-yellow, contrasting prettily with the pure white silky tubes. Red-flowered forms are also grown, including the cultivars 'Red Robin' and 'Red Dragon'. ZONE 7.

EKEBERGIA
Meliaceae

This small genus of 3 or 4 members from tropical and southern Africa and Madagascar includes trees and small to large shrubs with smooth, compound leaves composed of 1 to 7 pairs of leaflets and a terminal leaflet; the midrib is sometimes winged. Flowers are borne in branching heads in the leaf axils, male and female flowers on different trees. The 4- to 5-lobed calyces are saucer shaped and flowers have 4 to 5 petals. These are followed by succulent fruits which contain one or more woody seeds.

Ekebergia capensis
CAPE ASH

This magnificent tree, the most widely cultivated species, is a useful shade tree growing to 30–65 ft (10–20 m) with a spreading crown. Generally evergreen, it may be semi-deciduous in cooler regions depending on rainfall, but new foliage quickly develops. The small white flowers which appear in spring are sweetly scented but insignificant; they are followed by fruits that ripen glossy red. Fast growing, wind resistant and able to tolerate some frost, it makes a useful tree for parks and open spaces. It is easily grown from seed. ZONE 9.

ELAEAGNUS
Elaeagnaceae

This genus consists of deciduous and evergreen shrubs, small trees and scrambling climbers mostly from Asia, where they range from lowland rainforests of Indonesia to the Central Asian steppes and mountains, and the cool woodlands of Japan. All have simple, toothless leaves which, together with the twigs, flower-buds and fruits, glisten with tiny circular scales, either silvery or rusty brown. Flowers, clustered in the leaf axils, have 4 small, fleshy 'petals' (actually sepals) opening narrowly, with a bulge at the stalk end indicating the ovary. The fruits are pale fleshy drupes, edible in some species. Generally vigorous and trouble free in cultivation, they thrive in most soils and positions. The evergreen species will tolerate shade, even if not looking their best there. Most species can be cut back heavily if a bushy shape is desired. Propagation is normally from seed for deciduous species (which fruit freely) and cuttings for the evergreens. The whole genus is often called oleaster, though the name is particularly given to the Russian olive.

Elaeagnus angustifolia
OLEASTER, RUSSIAN OLIVE

A deciduous species from Central Asia, this makes a large shrub or small tree to 30 ft (10 m) high, the new branches and the undersides of the narrow leaves coated in silvery scales. In late spring and early summer clusters of small, perfumed, pale yellow flowers appear in the leaf axils, followed in late summer by yellowish fruits ½ in (12 mm) long, also coated in silvery scales and with sweet edible flesh; they are sold in markets in some Middle Eastern countries. The oleaster makes a striking ornamental but needs a climate with warm dry summers to bring out its silvery foliage effect. ZONE 7.

Elaeagnus pungens

This vigorous, spreading, evergreen shrub of Japanese origin is widely cultivated. Growing to 12 ft (4 m) tall and even wider, with long, horizontal branches, it is often used for screening and shelter. The leaves are green and shiny above and dull white beneath with scattered brown glandular spots. It has rather insignificant but very fragrant bell-shaped white flowers in autumn. Among a number of cultivars with variegated foliage are 'Aurea', with leaves having a wide irregular margin of golden yellow; and 'Maculata', the leaves of which have a central splash of gold. It does best in full sun, but tolerates a wide range of climate and soils. ZONE 8.

Elaeagnus umbellata

From the Himalaya, China and Japan, this deciduous or semi-deciduous species is a large, spreading shrub 12–15 ft (4–5 m) high with broad green leaves that have wavy margins and silvery, reflective undersides. In late spring and early summer it bears numerous clusters of scented cream flowers in the upper leaf axils, followed in autumn by crowded, small, berry-like fruits that are initially silvery green but ripen eventually to pale red, blending attractively with the pale yellow autumn foliage. ZONE 7.

ELAEIS
Palmae

This tropical genus consists of feather palms with narrow, straight trunks topped with long drooping fronds. The individual leaflets also droop, which creates a soft, graceful effect. Small yellow flowers in large inflorescences are followed by the oil-bearing fruit. A warm, humid, tropical climate is necessary to grow these plants outdoors, though they may be container grown indoors in temperate zones. They are propagated from seed.

Elaeis guineensis
AFRICAN OIL PALM

A quick look around the supermarket shelves will yield countless products that contain palm oil, and this is the plant that is responsible for that vital oil. Originally from West Africa but planted in the millions in tropical countries to satisfy commercial demand, it is sometimes seen as a threat by conservationists because it is replacing rainforests. This palm grows to 70 ft (22 m) high with fronds up to 8 ft (2.5 m) long. The all-important fruit occurs in large, tightly packed bunches and changes from red to black when ripe. ZONE 11.

ELAEOCARPUS
Elaeocarpaceae

This small genus of evergreen trees and tall shrubs come from Southeast Asia, Australia and New Zealand. Most are slow growing, slender and graceful with sprays of lily-of-the-valley-type flowers, useful for warm temperate gardens. They prefer part-shade and fertile, well-drained but moist soil. Prune only to establish a single trunk. Propagate from seed sown in spring and soaked in warm water for 24 hours, or from semi-ripe cuttings in summer.

Elaeocarpus reticulatus
BLUEBERRY ASH

The most commonly grown Australian species is a lovely slender tree to 30 ft (10 m) tall, with shiny, leathery leaves. Racemes of fringed, bell-shaped, white flowers are borne from spring to summer, followed by globular, deep blue fruits in autumn. It is frost-tender. Pink-flowered cultivars such as 'Prima Donna' are even lovelier than the species. The tree grows well in a large container and can be pruned to form a 10 ft (3 m) shrub. It will tolerate damp shade and needs a plentiful supply of water in summer. ZONE 9.

EMBOTHRIUM
Proteaceae
CHILEAN FIRE BUSH

This evergreen South American genus, now regarded as having only one variable species, is one of the few tree members of the spectacular Protea family hardy enough to grow in climates such as that of Britain. A fine ornamental, it has vivid scarlet flowers, rare among temperate trees, and is fast growing for the first decade or two, given deep, well-drained soil and a sunny but sheltered site in a suitably moist climate. It needs 10 years to develop a good floral display but a free-flowering specimen is an eye-catching sight. Trees grown in too crowded a situation become very lanky and their weak lateral branches tend to flop outward or break off. Propagation is from seed, cuttings or basal suckers.

Elaeagnus pungens 'Aurea'

Elaeagnus umbellata (below)

Elaeis guineensis (below)

Embothrium coccineum

Coccineum is Latin for 'scarlet' and this aptly describes the brilliant hue of this tree's flowers, borne freely in late spring and early summer. Cultivated specimens seldom exceed more than 25 ft (8 m) and are generally of narrow habit to begin with, broadening out with age. They are not usually long lived. The slightly more than usually cold-hardy form commonly grown in Britain is known as 'Norquinco Valley',
after its collection locality on the Andean slopes of Argentina. ZONE 8.

ENCEPHALARTOS
Zamiaceae

These slow-growing cycads come from the subtropical regions of southern Africa and are commonly found on rocky outcrops among coastal dunes or on mountainsides. They appear as a great ball of spiky fronds for many years before eventually developing a stout trunk, up to 10–12 ft (3–4 m) high; the trunk contains an edible starchy pith which is sometimes used locally in a manner similar to sago. The stiff, palm-like leaves are deep bluish green; each leaflet is spine tipped and often toothed. As with all cycads, there are both male and female plants; the latter, in maturity, produce spectacular cones from the centre of the crown, either singly or in groups of up to 5. The plants tolerate an occasional frost, but they will do best in subtropical areas with full sun and plenty of moisture; they can withstand strong winds.

Encephalartos altensteinii
PRICKLY CYCAD, BREAD TREE

Indigenous to southern Africa, this cycad is extremely slow growing.

Embothrium coccineum

Embothrium coccineum (below)

The densely foliaged crown appears to grow directly out of the ground, and it takes many years to develop its thick, scaly trunk. The rigid, palm-like leaves grow to about 6 ft (2 m) long, and have an abundance of stiff, saw-toothed leaflets tipped with spines. There are male and female trees. A female mature specimen may produce large cones, which are held in the centre of the crown and resemble a giant, elongated pineapple 18 in (45 cm) tall. ZONE 9.

Encephalartos frederici-guilielmi
WHITE-HAIRED CYCAD

Of all the cycads, this species bears the greatest number of cones: male plants can have up to 12 cones, female plants 5 or 6. They are densely felty. The trunk is about 24 in (60 cm) thick, eventually reaching 12 ft (4 m) tall. The pinnate leaves are up to 3 ft (1 m) long, their undersurfaces covered with thick white hair. A new set of leaves is not necessarily formed every year, but old, dead leaves can be cut off to improve the appearance. They are easy to cultivate and tolerate mild frost; full sun and good drainage are essential. Propagation is from seed, which germinates easily, but seedlings take many years to develop into half-grown trees. Old specimens of *E. friderici-guilielmi* often form young plants around their base, which can be removed and planted elsewhere. ZONE 9.

Encephalartos altensteinii

ENKIANTHUS
Ericaceae

About 10 species of deciduous shrubs from East Asia make up this genus, valued for their small, bell-shaped flowers, densely clustered and prettily marked in most species, and their fine autumn foliage colours. Growth is rather open and the smallish leaves are clustered at the end of each season's growth, producing a layered effect. The stalked, pendulous flowers are produced in numerous short sprays from just below the leaves. *Enkianthus* species like similar moist woodland conditions to many rhododendrons and azaleas, with acid soil humus-rich but not too fertile. They will not thrive in heavy shade. Pruning into a rounded shape should be avoided, or the flowers will not be so well displayed. Propagation is usually from seed, produced in abundance in small capsules, though cuttings can also be used.

Enkianthus campanulatus

From Japan and southern China, this is the most popular species, making a shrub 9–12 ft (3–4 m) high of narrow, open habit and rather slow growth. The flowers, cream but heavily striped and tipped dull crimson, are produced in abundance in spring. In autumn the leaves turn to shades of gold, scarlet and dull purple. *E.* var. *palibinii* has more strongly reddish flowers. ZONE 6.

Enkianthus perulatus

Also from Japan, this is rather distinctive among *Enkianthus* species in its lower, bushier habit and more sparsely scattered waxy flowers that are pure white or greenish white, without markings and contracted at the mouth. They are borne on nodding stalks in early spring. It likes a very cool, sheltered position. This species has by far the best autumn foliage colour. ZONE 6.

EPACRIS
Epacridaceae

This genus of about 40 Australian and New Zealand natives occupies

Encephalartos frederici-guilielmi (below)

Ephedra distachya

a niche filled in the northern hemisphere by the heathers, *Erica* and *Calluna*, to which they are related. They are wiry-stemmed, evergreen shrubs with small, sometimes needle-like leaves and tubular or starry flowers. Those with tubular flowers are reminiscent of the showy southern African ericas. The cultivated species may grow to around 5 ft (1.5 m) high but are usually clipped back to keep them tidy. They thrive in moist, slightly acidic, well-drained soil in sun or part-shade, and a warm-temperate climate suits them best. Propagate the species from seed, cultivars from semi-ripe cuttings.

Epacris impressa

Endemic to southern and eastern mainland Australia and Tasmania, this species has small, pointed, deep green leaves directly attached to long, wiry stems that arch up from the base of the plant. From late winter, 1 in (2.5 cm) tubular flowers in 4–8 in (10–20 cm) terminal spikes develop. They range from white through light pink to reddish purple, with deep pink being the most common shade. There were a number of named cultivars developed in Britain last century, though they were displaced from greenhouses by the much showier Cape heaths (*Erica* species). ZONE 9.

Epacris longiflora

This species from eastern Australia blooms in spring and summer and has 1–1½ in (2–3 cm) red tubular flowers with white tips. The pendulous blooms hang from the undersides of the stems and occur in such profusion that the branches bend under their weight. The ½ in (1 cm) leaves are roughly diamond shaped with sharp tips. ZONE 9.

EPHEDRA
Ephedraceae

Ephedra is an ancient genus of around 40 species of gymnosperms from southern Europe, North Africa, Asia and the Americas. These near-leafless, drought-tolerant shrubs form a mass of slim, dull green, jointed stems. Tiny scale-like leaves are present for a brief period after rain. These shrubs do not produce true flowers, rather they have separate male and female, yellow, flower-like cones (strobili). These are usually followed by berry-like fruits. Plants of near-desert regions, they demand a light, stony or sandy soil with perfect drainage and full sun. Propagate from seed. This genus is best known for its association with ephedrine, an extract also known as Ma Huang or Mormon tea that is used as an allergy and asthma treatment, a stimulant and a metabolism accelerator. Pseudoephedrine is a synthetic form.

Enkianthus perulatus

Enkianthus campanulatus

Epacris longiflora

Epacris impressa

Ephedra distachya

Found from southern Europe to Siberia, this species often sprawls and is usually less than 3 ft (1 m) high. The ⅛ in (3 mm) diameter stems are bluish green and sprout from rhizome-like roots. The tiny yellowish cones develop into very small, globose, red fruit. ZONE 4.

Erica arborea 'Alpina'

Erica bauera

Eremophila polyclada (below)

Eremophila maculata

Ephedra viridis
MORMON TEA

Endemic to western North America from California to Colorado and Arizona, this 3 ft (1 m) high, stiffly erect bush is made up of a mass of very fine, deep green stems. The tiny yellowish male cones are short lived but the female cones last longer and develop into an ivory-toned fruit. ZONE 5.

EREMOPHILA
Myoporaceae
EMU-BUSH

This is a large and diverse genus of evergreen shrubs and small trees from arid and semi-arid interior regions of mainland Australia. The flowers are conspicuous: arising from the leaf axils on thin stalks, they are tubular at the base and are commonly 2-lipped, the lips and throat mostly spotted. The fruit is like a small berry but ripening hard and dry, often flattened and sitting in an enlarged calyx. Some species only grow in desert conditions while others (such as *E. maculata*) adapt well to moister climates. While they do best in full sun in hot, dry climates, in poor, sandy, slightly alkaline soil, they are frost-hardy and will tolerate cooler climates as long as there is low summer humidity, and other soil as long as drainage is excellent. Water sparingly or not at all. Light pruning after flowering will maintain bushiness. Several beautiful but difficult species are now grafted on to stock of the related *Myoporum*, which is much easier to grow. Seed is difficult to germinate, but cuttings are being successfully rooted using modern misting techniques.

Eremophila maculata
SPOTTED EMU-BUSH

The most commonly grown species, the spotted emu-bush makes a rounded shrub 6 ft (2 m) high and wide with grey-green leaves. The orange, red, pink or white tubular flowers with recurved petals and spotted throats appear most of the year, especially in winter and spring. There is a smaller-growing, golden yellow flowering form and new varieties are becoming available. ZONE 9.

Eremophila mitchellii
FALSE SANDALWOOD, BUDDA

Occurring over inland eastern and central Australia on deep sandy loam soils, this species makes a tree of up to 30 ft (10 m), often forming extensive stands of slender saplings spreading by root suckers. The glossy leaves are narrow and willow-like, coated with a sticky resin that is aromatic in the heat of the day. Smallish, trumpet-shaped flowers appear in profusion among the leaves, mainly in spring but with flushes at other times of the year; they are white or faintly mauve, with a large greenish white calyx. It yields a durable aromatic wood which at one time was substituted for true sandalwood (*Santalum*). ZONE 9.

Eremophila polyclada

This unusual species makes a tangled mound of green branches 3–6 ft (1–2 m) high and at least as much in spread, with very reduced, narrow leaves. It grows in clay soils on mostly treeless flood plains over a large area of eastern and central inland Australia. The showy flowers, large white trumpets with pinkish brown spots on the lower lip, appear for most of the year but mainly in spring and autumn. A fine ornamental shrub for arid areas, it has been successfully grown in moister climates grafted onto *Myoporum insulare*. ZONE 9.

ERICA
Ericaceae
HEATH

This remarkable genus is made up of small-leafed, free-flowering, evergreen shrubs. In Europe several *Erica* species plus the closely related *Calluna* (heather) dominate moorland vegetation. However, Europe and the Mediterranean region account for only a fraction of the 800 or more species. Unfortunately not frost-hardy, the Cape heaths enjoyed a vogue in Europe in the early 19th century as greenhouse plants and a number of attractive hybrids were developed then, though many desirable species have still not been introduced to cultivation. They are not very easy greenhouse plants and are rarely seen now, though they are very fine garden plants in mild-winter climates (Zones 8–9) where summer humidity is low. They like full sun and perfect drainage. The European species bear smaller flowers in a more limited white-to-deep-pink colour range but are much more hardy and are very fashionable garden plants in Britain, especially the many cultivars derived from *E. cinerea*, *E.* × *darleyensis* and *E. herbacea*. They are best grown in rather poor soil or they are apt to be all luxuriant growth and few flowers. They sulk in the sort of mild climates where the Cape heaths flourish. A great fault of almost all species is their reluctance to shed their dead flowers, though this can be alleviated by trimming the bushes immediately flowering is over.

Erica arborea
TREE HEATH, BRUYERE

The largest of the heaths, the tree heath also has the widest distribution, from the Canaries and Portugal right across to Iran and south through the high mountains of Arabia, Ethiopia and equatorial Africa, where it forms mist-shrouded forests of trees 20 ft (7 m) high with stout trunks. An interesting but not highly ornamental garden shrub, usually 6–8 ft (2–2.5 m) in height with contorted woody stems and finely fibrous bark, it bears masses of small white flowers in spring. Its stems and roots are the traditional source of 'briar' pipes. The cultivar 'Alpina' has bright green foliage. ZONE 8.

Erica bauera
BRIDAL HEATH

More cold-hardy than some other South African species, the bridal heath also has some of the most delicately beautiful flowers of all. The waxy tubes are china-white to soft rose-pink, about 1¼ in (3 cm) long and narrowed toward the mouth, opening progressively along the erect branches over a long season, from spring to autumn. It makes a small slender shrub only about 3 ft (1 m) high and appreciates a sheltered position. ZONE 9.

Erica canaliculata
PURPLE HEATH

This is the tallest and most floriferous of the South African ericas grown in gardens, usually reaching about 6 ft (2 m) but much taller in the wild. It has an open growth-habit, with densely foliaged shoots diverging from near the base. The massed bell-shaped small flowers vary, on different clones of the species, from pale pink to rose-purple, with darker anthers protruding from the mouth. Flowering season also seems to vary according to where it is grown: autumn through winter, and winter to early spring are the most common. One of the more adaptable species, it thrives in moderately cool as well as warm climates. ZONE 9.

Erica cerinthoides
SCARLET HEATH

This South African species has gaudy orange-scarlet flowers about 1½ in (3 cm) long, clustered at the ends of long, straight or slightly arching branches through winter and spring. There are also forms with white, pink and crimson flowers. It is low growing, not more than 3 ft (1 m) high and often only half that, branching from the base. Often sold in pots in full flower, it does not always transplant well into soil, but once established in a sheltered sunny spot in perfectly drained soil and without root disturbance it will grow and flower profusely for years. ZONE 9.

Erica cinerea
BELL HEATHER

Native throughout western Europe including the British Isles, bell heather is one of the prettiest of all the hardy heaths, producing its small, crowded, rose-pink bells over a long season from early summer to early autumn. This is a plant which is low and spreading with twisted branches. The stiff ends of the branches ascend to 12–20 in (30–50 cm) high. There are many clones which have been named as cultivars, and they vary chiefly in flower colour which can range from white to the richest rose-purple; some also have golden or coppery foliage. 'Kerry Cherry' and 'Crimson King' are attractive cultivars. Bell heather dislikes hot summer weather, which scorches its foliage and may kill the plant. ZONE 5.

Erica cinerea 'Kerry Cherry'

Erica cinerea 'Crimson King'

Erica arborea 'Alpina'

Erica cerinthoides (below)

Erica herbacea 'Springwood White' *Erica grandiflora* (above) *Erica erigena* 'W. T. Racklift' (below)

Erica × *darleyensis* (below)

Erica × darleyensis

This hybrid between the 2 hardy species *E. erigena* and *E. herbacea* has proved a valuable garden plant, forming a dense, spreading mass of stems up to 24 in (60 cm) high with dark green foliage, covered from late autumn through spring in crowded short spikes of cylindrical pale rose flowers with protruding darker stamens. The original clone is now known as 'Darley Dale' but others, with flowers ranging from white to deep pink, are listed including 'Darley Dale', with mauve flowers; 'George Rendall', a compact grower with purplish pink flowers; and 'Jack H. Brummage', with golden to red-tinted winter foliage. ZONE 6.

Erica erigena

This western European species has deep green foliage and massed, small, bright pink flowers in winter and spring. It grows to 6 ft (2 m) high and 3 ft (1 m) wide. This species has given rise to variously coloured cultivars including 'W. T. Racklift' and 'Silver Bells'. ZONE 7.

Erica grandiflora
LARGE ORANGE HEATH

Occurring naturally on mountain slopes of western Cape Province in South Africa, this sturdy, upright shrub grows to 3 ft (1 m) tall and wide. The attractive, orange, tubular flowers are up to 1½ in (3 cm) long and are slightly sticky. Wind resistant and half-hardy, it flowers abundantly, needing full sun, well-drained, acid soil and plentiful water. ZONE 9.

Erica herbacea
WINTER HEATH, SNOW HEATH

From the mountains of central and southern Europe, and formerly known as *E. carnea*, this species with its numerous cultivars is widely planted. It makes a low, spreading subshrub usually less than 1 ft (30 cm) high, with densely crowded branches. Through most of winter and into early spring it produces a fine display of small, tubular, pink flowers with protruding darker stamens. A tough shrub, responding to heavy trimming (after flowers finish) by thickening up its growth, it is ideal groundcover between taller shrubs or beneath deciduous trees, or in rock gardens. Well-known cultivars include 'Ruby Glow', 'Springwood Pink' and 'Springwood White'. ZONE 5.

Erica lusitanica
PORTUGAL HEATH

Of the European heaths, this is one of the least frost-hardy but also one of the most beautiful. From Portugal and Spain, it is a very slender, erect shrub seldom more than 6 ft

Erica regia

Erica lusitanica

Erica mammosa

Erica melanthera

(2 m) high with extremely fine, delicate foliage but a wiry main stem. Through winter it bears densely massed, small, tubular flowers, dull pink in bud but opening white flushed pale pink, the pink soon disappearing. Unfortunately this species is extraordinarily free-seeding: one plant produces millions of minute, wind-carried seeds which germinate on any moist ground, forming dense forests of seedlings. In Australia and New Zealand especially it has become something of a weed. ZONE 9.

Erica mammosa
RED SIGNAL HEATH

This South African species has bright green foliage and massed terminal clusters of red to deep pink tubular flowers, 1 in (2.5 cm) long, in spring. It grows to about 3 ft (1 m) high and 20 in (50 cm) wide. 'Coccinea' is a particularly heavy-flowering cultivar. ZONE 9.

Erica melanthera

This species from South Africa has small bell-shaped flowers reminiscent of the European ericas. It is a bushy shrub 3 ft (1 m) high and wide, with bright green foliage that from late autumn disappears beneath the pinkish purple flowers. This species is widely grown as a cut flower. ZONE 9.

Erica regia
ELIM HEATH

This attractive shrub from southern parts of South Africa's Cape Province is widely cultivated. It grows to about 30 in (75 cm) high and 20 in (50 cm) wide, is wind resistant and tolerates some frost. The flowers, which appear mainly in spring, are shiny and white with red or red and purple tips; about ¾ in (1.5 cm) long, they hang down in whorls from the stem tips. Propagation is from seed or cuttings. ZONE 9.

Erica tetralix
CROSS-LEAFED HEATH

This species from western and northern Europe usually has greyish green foliage, but the best forms are quite silvery. Its flowers, light pink or white and large for a European erica, appear in summer and autumn. A small shrub, around 12 in (30 cm) high and wide, it does very well in rockeries. ZONE 3.

Erica vagans
CORNISH HEATH

This European species, 12–24 in (30–60 cm) high and 24 in (60 cm) wide, has deep green foliage and pale pink flowers in clusters in summer and autumn. White forms are also available. ZONE 5.

Erica × wilmorei
WILMORE HEATH

This is representative of a group of hybrids between various South African species, the parent species usually unrecorded, characterized by showy, long, tubular flowers carried on erect branches. In the case of E. × wilmorei the flowers are a soft rose-pink with white tips, softly hairy on the outside. Some of these hybrids arose early last century in England and others were developed later in Australia, where they became popular as cut flowers. Among the finest are 'Aurora', 'Linton's Red' and 'Ruby Glow'. ZONE 9.

ERIOBOTRYA
Rosaceae

This genus belonging to the rose family includes 10 species of evergreen shrubs or trees of which *Eriobotrya japonica* is the most widely grown. Widely distributed through eastern Asia from the eastern Himalaya to Japan, the genus includes trees growing to 30 ft (10 m), all with somewhat leathery, deeply veined leaves with silvery or felty undersides. The insignificant, creamy white, scented flowers are held in loose sprays at the tips of the branches during autumn and are followed by edible, decorative fruit. Easily grown, they are frost-hardy and will tolerate dry as well as coastal conditions.

Eriobotrya japonica
LOQUAT

The loquat can grow to 20 ft (7 m), forming a dense, conical, shapely tree, but in gardens it is often kept considerably more compact by pruning, after harvesting the golden yellow fruit. The large, leathery, deep green leaves are pale and felty beneath. This species blooms in late autumn and fruit, setting in winter, ripens in spring. It is very susceptible to fruit-fly and birds can also damage the crop. Happy in fertile, well-drained soil in full sun or part-shade, this is a plant for temperate areas where ample moisture is available as fruit matures. ZONE 9.

ERIOSTEMON
Rutaceae
WAX FLOWERS

A wide-ranging genus of evergreen Australian shrubs, eriostemons mostly occur in the wild as understorey plants in forests, in dappled shade. They were popular pot plants with English gardeners as early as the 1820s and have proved extremely adaptable as long as good drainage is assured. Growing to around 3 ft (1 m) they dislike root disturbance, so a well-mulched, low-maintenance garden suits them best. The small, often aromatic leaves can almost disappear amongst the 5-petalled waxy pink or white blooms during the long flowering period. They are propagated from semi-ripe tip cuttings or scarified seed in late summer.

Eriostemon australasius
WAX PLANT

Though occurring naturally in eastern Australia in well-drained, sandstone soil in open forests, this species adapts to heavier soils in gardens provided drainage is adequate. It is an upright, evergreen shrub growing to around 4 ft (1.2 m) with small, rather sparse, grey-green leaves and star-like pink flowers heaped along the upright stems during spring. It looks well when mass planted. Pruning after flowering will promote bushiness. ZONE 9.

Eriostemon myoporoides
LONG-LEAF WAXFLOWER

This variably shaped, evergreen, woody shrub is the most popular of the genus. In spring, deep pink

Eriobotrya japonica

Eriobotrya japonica (below)

Erica tetralix

Erica vagans

Eriostemon australasius

Eriostemon australasius

Erythrina acanthocarpa

Eriostemon myoporoides 'Profusion' (below)

buds open to waxy, white, star-shaped flowers. The dark green, oval leaves are fragrant. Half-hardy, it prefers partial shade and well-drained soil. It grows to a height and spread of about 6 ft (2 m) and can be pruned regularly to promote compact growth. Although hardy to both frost and drought, mulching will provide the extra benefit of not disturbing the roots through weeding. Cultivars include 'Clearview Apple-blossom' with semi-double flowers, and 'Profusion' with masses of white blooms over a long flowering period. These are among the best available. ZONE 8.

ERYTHRINA
Fabaceae
CORAL TREE

The 108 species of deciduous and semi-evergreen trees and shrubs in this genus originate in tropical and warm-temperate areas of Africa, Asia, Central America, the Caribbean and Hawaii. They are usually grown as ornamentals, for their vividly hued flowers. Ranging in height from 6–65 ft (2–20 m), trunk and branches are protected with short, sharp spines; many species have weak branches which tend to fall in storms. Leaves are compound with 3 broad, often heart-shaped leaflets. Sweet-pea-like flowers in scarlet, crimson or orange are borne in racemes towards the ends of branches at varying times of the year (some species in mid-winter), followed by narrow seed pods that dry and brown as they ripen. Most species are not frost-hardy, but some are happy in exposed coastal locations. They enjoy full sun and well-drained soil. Propagation is from seed in spring or cuttings in summer, and also from suckers.

Erythrina acanthocarpa
TAMBOOKIE THORN

This deciduous shrub from southern Africa forms a thicket of stiff, thorny branches to 6 ft (2 m) tall and often wider. The elongated pea-flowers, scarlet tipped with green, make a spectacular show in late spring and early summer. *E. acanthocarpa* prefers full sun and will tolerate some frost if planted in a sheltered area. Not fussy about soil provided it is well drained, it responds to watering in the growing season. It can be propagated from the seeds held within the bean-like fruits; these plants should flower in their 3rd or 4th year. ZONE 9.

Erythrina × *bidwillii*

Erythrina caffra (below)

Erythrina caffra

Erythrina × *bidwillii*
HYBRID CORAL TREE

This hybrid between *E. crista-galli* and *E. herbacea* is an upright, deciduous shrub growing to around 10 ft (3 m) tall and 6 ft (2 m) wide. The vivid dark red flowers appear from late spring to mid-autumn on long racemes at the ends of the current season's growth, so it is important to prune well in early spring to ensure a good floral display. In cooler climates it is best treated as a herbaceous plant. It does best in full sun and moderately fertile well-drained soil and can be propagated from seed or by division. ZONE 9.

Erythrina caffra
SOUTH AFRICAN CORAL TREE

This semi-evergreen tree with a broad, open crown quickly reaches about 35–60 ft (12–18 m) and is often grown as a shade tree in South Africa. The compound leaves, 7 in (17 cm) wide, have 3 sharp oval leaflets on long stalks. Most often grown is the species, which from late spring to early summer bears clusters of brilliant orange-red flowers on almost bare branches (sometimes quite thorny). The cultivar 'Flavescens' has pale cream flowers and is equally attractive in a more subtle way. Propagation is from seed although in warm areas large branches strike readily to provide sturdy plants quickly. ZONE 9.

Erythrina crista-galli
COCKSPUR CORAL TREE

This species from Brazil is the best known coral tree in temperate climates, where it is treated almost as a herbaceous plant, being cut back almost to the ground in autumn after the flowers are over, transferred to a large pot and over-wintered under glass, or else grown permanently in the greenhouse and again pruned severely in late autumn. It grows about 6 ft (2 m) tall under these conditions. It is hardy only in the mildest parts of Zone 8, and even there the roots need the protection of a thick mulch in winter. In subtropical climates, it grows into a gnarled tree 15–30 ft (5–10 m) tall and bears its scarlet or coral-red flowers in spring and summer. Even there, the flowering branches tend to die back in winter and it is usual to prune quite heavily then to keep the tree presentable. ZONE 9.

Erythrina fusca
SWAMP IMMORTELLE

Found in many tropical areas, this deciduous tree grows to 80 ft (25 m) tall, with a crooked trunk and spine-covered branches. Its pinnate leaves are 8 in (20 cm) long. The flowers are orange-red with cream-green wings and keel. They are followed by slim pods up to 13 in (33 cm) long. ZONE 10.

Erythrina heardii

This small, deciduous tree grows to 15 ft (5 m) with a wide, dense canopy of glossy green leaves. The large, spiky clusters of elongated pea-flowers, borne on bare branches in spring, are brilliant crimson and produce a nectar which is especially irresistible to birds. They are followed by bumpy seed pods. ZONE 9.

Erythrina fusca

Erythrina heardii

Erythrina crista-galli (below)

Erythrina heardii

Erythrina heardii (below)

Erythrina lysistemon

Erythrina humeana
DWARF ERYTHRINA, NATAL CORAL TREE

This deciduous species from South Africa is a sturdy, erect shrub reaching 12 ft (4 m). In summer to early autumn it bears long, upright sprays of nodding tubular flowers of rich scarlet splashed with yellow and green. Distinctive pods develop and the seeds within can be used for propagation. This species will tolerate light frosts and prefers full sun and well-drained, reasonably fertile soil. ZONE 9.

Erythrina livingstoniana

A spreading 80 ft (25 m) tree from Mozambique, Malawi and Zimbabwe, *E. livingstoniana* has prickles on its bark and 8 in (20 cm) leaves made up of large oval leaflets. The bright scarlet flowers, borne in arching racemes, are followed by 14 in (35 cm) seed pods. ZONE 10.

Erythrina lysistemon
COMMON CORAL TREE

Growing to about 18 ft (6 m) tall, this deciduous tree from southern Africa has a fairly sparse crown; trunk and branches are usually pale and smooth. The large compound leaves have 3 oval leaflets. Clusters of magnificent scarlet flowers appear in spring before the leaves, and even the sepals are red. The long slender pods are segmented and the seeds, called 'lucky beans', are orange-red with a black spot. Drought resistant, it prefers a warm climate and full sun. It is easily grown from seed or cuttings, but large branches, planted towards the end of winter, will grow and flower within 1 to 2 years. ZONE 9.

Erythrina × sykesii
CORAL TREE

Formerly misidentified as *E. variegata* and *E. indica*, this large deciduous tree can reach 50 ft (15 m) tall and almost as wide, with a very short main trunk supporting

Erythrina humeana

Erythrina livingstoniana

Erythrina × sykesii

Escallonia × exoniensis

ascending branches, often spiny. Although with maturity it can form a very large crown, the canopy is not overly dense. In late winter and early spring it is covered with clusters of rich red flowers. The handsome, heart-shaped leaves follow. This tree prefers mild, frost-free climates and moist coastal areas. It is propagated from cuttings. The origin of *E. × sykesii* is a mystery but it is a commonly planted tree in warm temperate areas of Australia and New Zealand. ZONE 9.

Erythrina variegata
This strongly branched 90 ft (28 m) deciduous tree occurs naturally from eastern Africa and the Indian Ocean islands eastwards to Polynesia. The compound leaves are about 8 in (20 cm) long with large oval to rhomboidal leaflets. Although its floral racemes are only 8 in (20 cm) long, they are densely packed with bright scarlet to orange (rarely white) flowers, followed by 16 in (40 cm) pods. The cultivar 'Purcellii' has leaves strongly variegated with yellow. ZONE 11.

Erythrina vespertilio
BATS-WING CORAL TREE

From subtropical open forest areas of inland Australia, this deciduous tree grows to 50 ft (15 m), developing a sparse, open canopy. The stout trunk and branches are corky textured and thorny, and the leaves consist of 3 triangular leaflets each 5 in (12 cm) wide which look like the open wings of a bat. The leaves are shed briefly in summer before the appearance of the open, pea-shaped flowers. These are salmon-pink or red with prominent stamens, and are borne in long, pendent racemes. ZONE 10.

ESCALLONIA
Escalloniaceae

These evergreen shrubs and small trees come from temperate South America, mostly from Chile where they may grow in hillside scrubs or on exposed coasts. The smallish toothed leaves are usually shiny and

Escallonia × exoniensis

Escallonia 'Donard Star'

succulent and the flowers, crowded into dense panicles, have separate white or pink petals that in many species are pressed together to form a tube but with the tips recurving. The fruit is a small globular capsule, shedding fine seed. Escallonias are popular in the UK, though they are on the borderline of hardiness there; however they are capable of sprouting profusely from the base after being cut back by frost. They may be untidy in their growth, but as hedges the shrubby kinds will thicken up in response to trimming. Valuable seaside plants, they suffer salt damage only in the most exposed positions. They are easily propagated from softwood cuttings. A number of attractive cultivars have been raised by the Slieve Donard nursery in Ireland including 'Donard Beauty', 'Donard Star' and 'Pride of Donard'.

Erythrina variegata

Escallonia bifida

Escallonia bifida
Formerly known as *E. montevidensis*, this large-growing species can make a tree of up 20–25 ft (7–8 m) with a thick, low-branching trunk and spreading, irregular crown, but is usually lower than this, sometimes only a shrub. The shiny dark green leaves are up to 3 in (7 cm) long and the flowers are pure white, in dense clusters scattered over the crown from late spring to early winter. An interesting rather than spectacular tree, it is long lived in a suitably mild climate. It occurs naturally in Uruguay, extending into southern Brazil, and adapts to quite subtropical climates. ZONE 8.

Escallonia × exoniensis
This hybrid between the 2 Chilean species *E. rosea* and *E. rubra* originated last century in England. A vigorous shrub, it grows to heights of 20 ft (7 m) in suitable climatic conditions. It has a rather open, branching habit, becoming very woody at the base, and bears loose sprays of very pale pink flowers at the branch ends from late spring right through to autumn. Lopping back the branches will produce denser growth if desired. ZONE 8.

Eucalyptus brevifolia

Eucalyptus calycogona

Escallonia rubra

Eucalyptus calophylla

Escallonia rubra

This Chilean species has flowers of deeper colour and firmer texture than any other species, and is the dominant parent of most hybrid escallonias. Always shrubby and multi-stemmed, it varies greatly in the wild in stature as well as in leaves and flowers, and several forms have been introduced to gardens. Some shrubs are delicate and small, with small leaves and arching sprays of flowers with narrow red tubes and pale pink recurved ends of petals. In contrast is var. *macrantha*, a vigorous large shrub up to 10 ft (3 m) tall with succulent, glossy leaves and tight clusters of white to pink and sometimes crimson flowers. This and hybrid derivatives such as 'Apple Blossom' are the typical hedging and shelter-belt escallonias used in coastal plantings. ZONE 8.

EUCALYPTUS
Myrtaceae

This diverse genus contains over 600 species of evergreen trees and large shrubs prized for their beauty, shade, oils, timber and honey. Almost all originate in Australia, with only a few species from New Guinea and nearby islands, but these versatile plants are now grown in many countries. The name eucalyptus is taken from the Greek *eu*, meaning well, and *kalyptos*, to cover with a cap or lid. The flowers differ from most in having no separate sepals or petals as these have been fused together to form a cap which is pushed off by the densely packed emerging stamens which can be in shades of white, yellow, pink or red. Foliage varies from linear to heart shaped, and juvenile and adult leaves differ markedly, often making identification difficult. Trees vary in hardiness, with wide variation in shape, size and habitat; some species are able to withstand prolonged droughts, others are salt resistant and survive in swamps; others still, straight and tall, prefer cool mountain areas. Many eucalypts are grown for their striking trunk, bark and foliage, while a number of the Western Australian species are noted for their attractive blossoms. The latter are widely grown in California and around the Mediterranean. The smaller-growing, shrubby species known as 'mallees' have multiple stems arising from a lignotuber or swollen woody base, often below ground level.

Eucalyptus brevifolia
SNAPPY GUM

Occurring on the gravel plains, ridges and woodland margins of north-western Australia, the snappy gum grows to 37 ft (12 m) and has blue-green adult leaves up to 6 in (15 cm) long. The main attraction is the bark, which is white with darker patches that are shed in flakes. The small, creamy white flowers are rather insignificant. ZONE 11.

Eucalyptus caesia subsp. *magna*
GUNGURRU, SILVER PRINCESS GUM

The name *caesia* refers to the whitish bloom on the stems, buds and fruit of this garden gem which is quite hard to locate, even in its natural Western Australian habitat. The subspecies *magna* reaches about 15 ft (3 m) with an open growth-habit, silver grey foliage and striking red flowers. The weeping branches become more pendulous with the weight of the maturing fruit and these may need to be removed to ensure young branches don't split with the added weight. This species needs a well-drained soil and protection from prevailing winds. ZONE 9.

Eucalyptus calophylla
MARRI

Endemic to the south of Western Australia, this species can grow to

200 ft (60 m) tall, though 40–80 ft (12–25 m) is more common. It has a heavy, straight trunk with non-peeling greyish brown bark often stained with red sap. Its ovate juvenile and adult leaves are similar except that the adult leaves are smaller, around 5 in (12 cm) long. Large cream or rarely pink flowers are borne in summer and autumn, followed by 1 in (2.5 cm), goblet-shaped seed capsules. It hybridizes readily with the scarlet-flowering gum, *E. ficifolia*, the hybrids usually being pink. ZONE 9.

Eucalyptus calycogona
SQUARE-FRUITED MALLEE

A shrubby small tree found over much of southern Australia, this species grows to around 24 ft (8 m) tall. It has smooth grey bark overall that often sheds in strips or flakes. The narrow, lance-shaped adult leaves are up to 4 in (10 cm) long. With a preference for poor gravelly soils, it makes an excellent feature tree for frost-free, arid-area gardens. Small flowers, opening in spring and summer from angular buds, are followed by small seed capsules. ZONE 9.

Eucalyptus camaldulensis
RIVER RED GUM

A tree for large gardens, the river red gum can grow up to 160 ft (50 m) tall with a generous spread and trunk to 12 ft (4 m) in diameter. It is grown for its impressive overall stately appearance rather than for its flowers and has been a popular artists' subject.

Occurring over much of inland Australia, it is an invaluable shade and shelter tree able to withstand extended dry periods or water-logging. It does best on deep soils where subsurface water supply is available. Propagated from easily germinated seed, it will grow rapidly for the first 5 years. It is widely cultivated in warm-climate areas in Africa and Asia. ZONE 9.

Eucalyptus cinerea
ARGYLE APPLE

From tablelands and inland slopes of south-eastern Australia, this is one of the eucalypts familiar to flower arrangers for its distinctive silver-blue circular leaves. On some trees these juvenile-type leaves are replaced by sickle-shaped adult leaves, also silver-blue. Rather insignificant flowers, appearing in early summer, are creamy yellow. It has an interesting, somewhat gnarled growth-habit, reaching 50 ft (15 m) with a single short trunk and tall crown, often quite dense. Suited to most well-drained soils, it can be kept pruned. Propagation is from seed. ZONE 8

Eucalyptus citriodora
LEMON-SCENTED GUM

This adaptable tree from the open forests and dry slopes of tropical north-eastern Australia is widely grown in many more temperate areas. Tall and straight trunked, to 100 ft (30 m), it has smooth, sometimes dimpled bark in subtle shades of white, grey or pale pink which is shed during the summer months. The foliage is held aloft on an open crown and, when crushed, the long narrow leaves have a lemony scent. Winter flowers are creamy white. Young plants may be damaged by frost, but once established it is fast growing and hardy. Propagate from seed. ZONE 10.

Eucalyptus citriodora

Eucalyptus citriodora

Eucalyptus camaldulensis (below)

Eucalyptus cladocalyx

Eucalyptus curtisii

Eucalyptus desmondensis

Eucalyptus dumosa

Eucalyptus cladocalyx
SUGAR GUM

Often branching quite low, this fast-growing eucalypt from South Australia reaches 50–100 ft (15–30 m) and usually forms a wide, dense crown. The rough, reddish brown outer bark is shed in patches to reveal the smooth, chalky white new bark. Leaves are dark green and glossy, and the new growth is bronze-pink. The individual white flowers, smaller than many in the group, are borne in large clusters to make a pleasing display in summer. The small brown fruits are goblet shaped. The sugar gum is fairly drought resistant; it is not fussy about soil and tolerates salty coastal conditions. Its branches are apt to break in high winds. The tree should never be lopped as the new branches are notoriously unstable. ZONE 8.

Eucalyptus curtisii
PLUNKETT MALLEE

This tough little mallee shrub from south-east Queensland grows to 20 ft (6 m) high and 6 ft (2 m) wide, forming a thicket of smooth stems which are mottled greyish green and white. The leathery leaves are dark glossy green and the yellow buds open in spring in a profusion of pretty white blossoms held on long stalks. It makes an excellent low screen or shelter for windy or exposed gardens. ZONE 9.

Eucalyptus desmondensis
DESMOND MALLEE

Endemic to the Ravensthorpe Range in the south of Western Australia, this is a slender, willowy, large shrub or small tree that grows to around 15 ft (5 m) high. It has powdery white bark and twigs, and 4 in (10 cm) lance-shaped adult leaves. The pale yellow flowers occur in large clusters in late summer and are quite showy. Tiny seed capsules follow. ZONE 9.

Eucalyptus diversicolor
KARRI

An important timber tree from the south-west of Western Australia, the karri can grow to a height of 220 ft (70 m) with a massive trunk. It requires large space planting in warmer zones where well-drained soils are assured of moisture. The smooth, brown-tinted yellow bark is shed in irregular patches, and the crown is relatively open atop the straight trunk. It is propagated from seed, which germinates easily. ZONE 9.

Eucalyptus dumosa
CONGOO MALLEE

This hardy small tree from drier, inland areas of eastern Australia grows to 25 ft (8 m) and thrives in harsh conditions, tolerating wind, heat, drought and some frost provided the soil is well drained. A slender tree with smooth white bark above the rough blackish base of the trunk, it has curved, tapering, grey-green leaves up to 4 in (10 cm) in length. The creamy flowers appear in small clusters through spring and summer. ZONE 9.

Eucalyptus elata
RIVER PEPPERMINT

Usually growing to about 5 ft (15 m), this is a fast-growing shade tree for large gardens or farms in temperate regions where the soil is well drained. It forms a single trunk, the lower section of which is covered with rough greyish bark that falls away in long strips in summer. The upper trunk and branches are smooth and almost greenish white, blending well with the pendulous dark grey-green leaves. The creamy white late spring flowers are an attractive feature. Propagate from seed. ZONE 8.

Eucalyptus eremophila
TALL SAND MALLEE

Like other mallees, this species from semi-arid areas of Western Australia forms a thick clump about 10 ft (3 m) wide, and its numerous stems, to 30 ft (10 m) tall, are covered with smooth grey bark. The narrow adult leaves are blue-green. The horn-shaped yellow or reddish buds open to reveal bright yellow flowers, 1½ in (3 cm) across, which hang from the branches in fluffy clusters through winter and spring. It prefers sandy, well-drained soil in full sun, and tolerates drought and some frost. It dislikes humid summers. ZONE 9.

Eucalyptus erythrocorys
ILLYARIE

This Western Australian eucalypt is of the mallee type, a spreading shrub or small tree with thin stems rising from a lignotuber or swollen woody base that is often below ground level. The name *erythrocorys* refers to the red flower cap, which provides an interesting contrast to the early summer yellow flowers. Growing usually to about 27 ft (9 m), it is suited to warm, frost-free climates without summer humidity, preferring full sun and good drainage. If grown quickly it can become top heavy, but pruning will prevent this and at the same time keep the plant compact. Propagate from seed which germinates easily; guard against the disease damping-off in young seedlings. ZONE 9.

Eucalyptus globulus (below)

Eucalyptus ficifolia
SCARLET-FLOWERING GUM, RED-FLOWERING GUM

The most spectacular of all the flowering eucalypts, *E. ficifolia* bears enormous terminal clusters of scarlet to orange flowers in late spring to summer, followed by large, urn-shaped fruits. (Forms with crimson or pink flowers are suspected of being hybrids of *E. calophylla*.) It grows to about 30 ft (10 m) with rough bark and a spreading crown of lance-shaped foliage. This species is easily grown from seed. ZONE 9.

Eucalyptus forrestiana
FUCHSIA GUM

An extremely ornamental large shrub or small tree 9–15 ft (3–5 m) tall and nearly as wide, this species bears large, pendulous, 4-angled pink or red buds reminiscent of a fuchsia, hence its common name. These open to yellow blossom in summer. In common with many eucalypts, it has oval juvenile leaves of a soft grey-green; as the tree matures they are replaced by the long, deeper green, pointed adult leaves. While it has proved itself in cultivation over a wide range of soil types, it seems to prefer warm and fairly dry conditions. Seed germinates readily. ZONE 9.

Eucalyptus globulus
TASMANIAN BLUE GUM

This large tree can grow to 220 ft (70 m), with a trunk to 6 ft (2 m) in diameter. The thick trunk sheds its bluish bark in long strips. Juvenile foliage is silvery blue and rectangular, while the adult form is deep green and sickle shaped, to 18 in (45 cm) long. Occurring naturally in coastal areas of Tasmania and south-eastern mainland Australia, it is drought resistant. It is used for the building industry, for paper pulp and as a source of eucalyptus oil, and is widely planted in California and the Mediterranean countries. ZONE 8.

Eucalyptus gracilis
YORRELL

Widespread in semi-arid, sandy regions across southern Australia, this tree is commonly 15–25 ft (5–8 m) tall. It has rough, flaky bark on the lower 6 ft (2 m) of the trunk, with smooth grey to reddish brown bark above. The narrow adult leaves are lance shaped, glossy and around 3½ in (8 cm) long. Tiny cream flowers are followed by equally small seed capsules. It needs well-drained soil, but is tolerant of dry conditions, frost and salt winds, and is known to recover well after fire. ZONE 9.

Eucalyptus erythrocorys

Eucalyptus gracilis

Eucalyptus ficifolia (below)

Eucalyptus leucoxylon 'Rosea'

Eucalyptus maculata

Eucalyptus grandis (below)

Eucalyptus grandis
FLOODED GUM

One of the noblest of the large eucalypts, E. grandis originates in high-rainfall regions of the Australian east coast and can achieve a height of 200 ft (60 m) and a trunk up to 10 ft (3 m) in diameter in suitably deep, rich, moist soils. The base of its massive trunk is blackish and rough, with smooth, whitish bark above. The thin leaves are dark green and shiny on top, paler beneath. Clusters of white blossoms are borne in winter. It is much cultivated for timber in South Africa. ZONE 10.

Eucalyptus gunnii
ALPINE CIDER GUM

From the highlands of Tasmania, this 80 ft (25 m) tall tree is sometimes multi-trunked. It has light reddish brown bark that peels irregularly revealing white underbark. Young trees have the 'silver dollar' style foliage: opposite pairs of rounded grey-green leaves. Mature trees have 3 in (7 cm) long, lanceolate leaves. Small cream flowers in spring and summer are followed by tiny, goblet-shaped seed capsules. It is perhaps the most frost-hardy eucalypt and is regarded as the most reliable species in the UK. The common name comes from the sweet sap which was tapped and drunk by the Tasmanian Aborigines. ZONE 7.

Eucalyptus haemastoma
BROAD-LEAFED SCRIBBLY GUM

This species often has multiple twisted trunks arising from an underground lignotuber, its white bark distinctively scribble-marked by insect larvae (which seem not to affect the health of the tree). It grows to about 30 ft (10 m) with an uneven crown of thick, sickle-shaped leaves about 6 in (15 cm) long, and bears nectar-rich white blossoms for much of the year. Best suited to well-drained sandy soils of the ridges or seaside gardens where it can withstand salt-laden winds. ZONE 9.

Eucalyptus leucoxylon
YELLOW GUM, SOUTH AUSTRALIAN BLUE GUM

A tree from high rainfall regions of southern Australia, this shapely, slender eucalypt grows to 100 ft (30 m) with an open canopy. Its distinctive trunk is fissured at the base but becomes smooth and dappled with yellowish white and blue-grey spots as it extends upwards. Long, greyish green, sickle-shaped leaves taper to a point. The large 1½ in (3 cm) flowers, which may be cream or dark pink, are borne in small clusters from autumn through to spring. An attractive tree for parks and larger gardens, it does best in heavier, clay soils with adequate rainfall. ZONE 9.

Eucalyptus macrocarpa
MOTTLECAH

This species has the largest flowers and the most decorative nuts of the genus. Of spreading, mallee-type growth with multiple stems arising from an underground lignotuber, it reaches 12 ft (4 m) tall and wide. Both the juvenile and mature leaves are silvery, held close to the branch and offset by the large, bright red or sometimes pink blossoms also held along the length of the branches. It must have well-drained, slightly acid soil and a frost-free climate with low summer humidity; it has a well-deserved reputation for being difficult elsewhere. Propagate from seed. ZONE 9.

Eucalyptus maculata
SPOTTED GUM

This 100 ft (30 m), straight-trunked, open-headed tree occurs over much of the south-eastern coastal area of Australia. It has thick mottled grey-green bark that is shed in patches to create a patchwork of grey, green, pink and ochre. Pointed oval juvenile leaves give way to narrow adult leaves that are up to 8 in (20 cm) long. The large white flowers appear in winter, followed by small urn-shaped seed capsules. ZONE 9.

Eucalyptus mannifera
BRITTLE GUM

Erect, with an open, spreading crown, this frost-hardy tree grows quickly to about 30–50 ft (10–15 m). Its powdery whitish bark takes on orange-red tones in summer before being shed in strips. The sickle-shaped blue-green leaves are 3–6 in (8–15 cm) long. Small, creamy white flowers appear in clusters of 3 to 7 blossoms, usually in late spring to summer. The tree is fairly hardy and tolerates poor soil and dry conditions once established. Subsp. *maculosa* is the form most commonly grown and perhaps has the most attractively coloured bark. ZONE 8.

Eucalyptus microtheca
COOLIBAH

Sometimes known as E. coolabah, the coolibah comes from the semi-arid and arid inland areas of Australia. It is usually found near waterholes and on river banks. A small to medium-sized tree to about 50 ft (15 m) high, it branches fairly low with a twisted trunk. The narrow blue-green leaves are up to 8 in (20 cm) long, and the small white flowers are quite insignificant. The seed capsules are among the smallest of all eucalypts. The bark varies from fibrous to hard and furrowed,

Eucalyptus mannifera

Eucalyptus pauciflora subsp. *niphophila*; regrowth after fire

peeling to reveal a powdery white undersurface. This tree is extremely tolerant of drought and heat. ZONE 9.

Eucalyptus nicholii
NARROW-LEAFED BLACK PEPPERMINT

In maturity the strongly upright trunk with its furrowed bark is a feature of this tree growing to 50 ft (15 m), with its fine, sickle-shaped blue-grey leaves held aloft on a high crown. It makes an excellent large shade or street tree. This species bears white flowers that can only be appreciated when the tree is small. Adaptable to a wide climate and soil range, *E. nicholii* withstands mild frosts and strong winds. ZONE 8.

Eucalyptus nicholii

Eucalyptus pauciflora
SNOW GUM

This 30–65 ft (10–20 m) tree is found in south-eastern Australia and Tasmania. It tends to have a rather twisted trunk that is often distorted by the exposed conditions in which it grows. The reddish brown or grey bark peels in irregular strips, revealing white and beige under-bark. Small cream flowers in spring and summer are followed by small seed capsules. This species is noted for its erratic flowering— pauciflora means few flowers. Subspecies *niphophila*, which occurs at relatively cold high altitudes, is smaller and more low-branching. Both are grown successfully in England and Ireland. ZONE 7.

Eucalyptus papuana
GHOST GUM

Found along watercourses over much of northern inland Australia and around Port Moresby in Papua New Guinea, the ghost gum is a broad-crowned, single-trunked tree to 50 ft (15 m) high with an open, domed canopy of light green lanceolate leaves. Its common name comes from the pale, smooth, chalky bark. Small clusters of white flowers are produced in summer, followed by urn-shaped fruits. Well-drained soil and a warm, frost-free climate suit it best; it is extremely drought tolerant. ZONE 10.

Eucalyptus papuana (below)

Eucalyptus pauciflora (below)

Eucalyptus pauciflora (below)

Eucalyptus regnans

Eucalyptus ptychocarpa

Eucalyptus perriniana

Eucalyptus rubida

Eucalyptus perriniana
SPINNING GUM, ROUND-LEAFED SNOW GUM

This small, rather straggly tree grows to around 30 ft (10 m) high, often with multiple trunks. It has silver-grey, rounded, opposite juvenile leaves and 6 in (15 cm) long lanceolate mature leaves. Small white flowers in clusters of 3 appear in summer, followed by tiny seed capsules. This species often looks best grown as a shrub and can be cut back hard each year. ZONE 8.

Eucalyptus polyanthemos
RED BOX

A single-trunked tree growing to about 80 ft (25 m), the red box has distinctive grey, scaly bark on the lower trunk and subtly mottled above with grey, pink and cream. The creamy white flowers are nectar bearing and will encourage birds. Not fussy as to soil, it often grows naturally on well-drained, very shallow, stony sites where it produces a short crooked trunk, but given better soil conditions the trunk is usually upright. If space permits, a grove of these trees could be planted for future harvesting or thinning as firewood. Propagate from seed. It is popular in California. ZONE 9.

Eucalyptus ptychocarpa
SPRING BLOODWOOD

Found in the extreme north of Western Australia and the Northern Territory, this species grows to 50 ft (15 m) and has some of the largest leaves among the eucalypts; they are dark green and up to 16 in (40 cm) long. The fissured, grey-brown bark does not peel readily and remains attached to even the quite small twigs at the tips. The showy flowers range in colour from white or pink to apricot or red. Clusters of large, ribbed seed capsules follow. ZONE 11.

Eucalyptus regnans
MOUNTAIN ASH

This magnificent species which reigns over the mountain forests of far south-eastern Australia and Tasmania is the tallest hardwood tree in the world, specimens of over 300 ft (100 m) tall being found in Victoria. If 19th-century reports of 400 ft (135 m) trees are to be believed, it is the tallest of all trees, even outgrowing the redwoods (*Sequoia sempervirens*) of California: but no such trees are to be found now. The species has been much cut for timber, and has suffered more than most from the disastrous bushfires that have followed the

European settlers' impact on the Australian ecology. It has a long, straight trunk and relatively small, open crown, the bark being almost white and shed annually in long ribbons. The white flowers are small and rarely noticed. Despite the great beauty of mountain ash forests and the value of its timber, it is not a very commonly cultivated species. ZONES 9.

Eucalyptus rubida
CANDLEBARK

Found in New South Wales, Victoria, Tasmania and a small area of South Australia, this is an open-crowned tree that is usually 40–80 ft (12–25 m) tall. It has narrow, lanceolate leaves to 6 in (15 cm) long and light brown outer bark that peels away almost entirely to reveal white under-bark. Small cream flowers in clusters of 3 open from late summer, followed by cup-shaped seed capsules. ZONE 8.

Eucalyptus salmonophloia
SALMON GUM

From Western Australia, this handsome eucalypt is mostly 30–40 ft (10–12 m) tall with a long, sinuous, smooth trunk topped by a dense, umbrella-shaped crown. The new bark is an attractive salmon pink, turning grey as it ages before being shed. The mature leaves are shiny green and tapering, and the small white flowers appear in spring and summer. It does well in dry conditions and can withstand some frost. ZONE 9.

Eucalyptus sideroxylon
RED IRONBARK, MUGGA

This species from eastern and southern Australia is notable for its very variable leaves. The juvenile leaves can be bluish white, lanceo-

Eucalyptus tereticornis (below)

late or diamond-shaped. The adult leaves are around 4 in (10 cm) long and lanceolate to slightly sickle shaped. The bark is black and deeply furrowed and never shed. Showy pale pink to near crimson flowers open from autumn to spring, followed by small, goblet-shaped seed capsules. ZONE 9.

Eucalyptus tereticornis
FOREST RED GUM

Found over much of the eastern coastal area of Australia, this tree grows up to 150 ft (45 m) tall. It is open headed and single trunked, though it often branches quite low. Its outer bark is shed in irregular patches, showing a greyish white under-bark. The bright green adult leaves are narrow and up to 8 in (20 cm) long. Small cream flowers open from pointed oval buds from mid-winter. Small oval seed capsules follow. ZONE 9.

Eucalyptus tessellaris
CARBEEN, MORETON BAY ASH

Found in sandy soils along water-courses in eastern Australia, this 50 ft (15 m) tree is distinguished by its bark which is divided into squarish scales (which persist on the lower trunk) but is smooth and greyish white at the top of the trunk. The greyish green adult leaves are very narrow and up to 10 in (25 cm) long, and the summer-borne cream flowers are not particularly showy. ZONE 10.

Eucalyptus torquata
CORAL GUM

This small tree from Western Australia grows to about 20 ft (7 m) high with a fairly narrow, upright habit, though it may droop under the weight of its flowers and seed capsules. Its blue-green, sickle-shaped leaves are 4 in (10 cm) long, and the rough brown bark flakes rather than peels. Orange-red lantern-shaped flower buds, 1 in (2.5 cm) long, develop during spring, opening to a mass of creamy orange and yellow or pink and yellow stamens. The flowers are followed by quite large seed capsules. Light, well-drained soil and a sunny position suit it best; it is drought tolerant but does better with regular moisture. Propagate from seed. ZONE 9.

Eucalyptus salmonophloia (below)

Eucalyptus torquata (below)

Eucalyptus sideroxylon

Eucalyptus woodwardii
LEMON-FLOWERED GUM

The outstanding feature of this eucalypt is its showy, bright yellow flowers, up to 2 in (5 cm) across, which are borne on reddish twigs through winter and spring. The long, leathery leaves are dull green, often covered with a silvery bloom. It grows to about 50 ft (15 m), with an attractive weeping habit and smooth, greyish trunk. From arid areas of Western Australia, the lemon-flowered gum is successful

Eucommia ulmoides (below)

Eucalyptus woodwardii (below)

in dry, frost-prone areas, and prefers low summer rainfall. ZONE 9.

EUCOMMIA
Eucommiaceae

This Chinese deciduous tree genus consisting of a single species is placed in a family of its own, rather distantly related to the elm and witch-hazel families. While widely grown in north and east China it is not known in the wild state, but fossil leaves belonging to the genus have been found. A remarkable feature is the presence of latex in the leaves and bark, and earlier this century it was considered a potentially commercial rubber-yielding species. In China it is grown almost entirely for its medicinal properties, the dried bark being used in herbal medicine. It can be propagated from cuttings.

Eucommia ulmoides

Eucommia ulmoides

Usually a slender tree to 50 ft (15 m) high, of open habit with furrowed grey bark; the crown becomes broader and more rounded with age. The shiny green leaves are narrow and pointed. Male and female flowers, both inconspicuous, are carried on different trees and the winged fruits, rather like the 'keys' on an ash, are seldom seen on planted trees. This is a hardy and vigorous tree, though not an especially ornamental one. ZONE 5.

EUCRYPHIA
Eucryphiaceae

This small genus is made up of evergreen or semi-deciduous trees from the southern hemisphere. All species have pure white flowers of singular beauty, like small single roses with 4 petals and a 'boss' of red-tipped stamens. Two species are native to Chile and 2 to Tasmania, and another to mainland south-eastern Australia—and only in the last decade, 2 more have been discovered in the rainforests of Queensland. Eucryphias have been grown in the British Isles for more than a century, especially in mild, moist Atlantic coast districts where the climate suits them well. Several garden hybrids are more vigorous and floriferous than the species. Propagation is from seed, released from small ovoid capsules,

Eucryphia cordifolia

or more commonly from cuttings or sometimes layers. Like some other tree groups from temperate rainforests, eucryphias show a tendency to sudden death when climatic conditions are less than ideal, so they require careful siting, a humid microclimate and constant soil moisture combined with good drainage. Good flowering demands that the tree crown be in the sun but the roots shaded.

Eucryphia cordifolia
ULMO

Growing to a medium-large tree in the wettest coastal rainforests of southern Chile, this tree was called 'ulmo' (elm) by the Spanish settlers, no doubt on account of its strongly veined and toothed leaves. White flowers 2 in (5 cm) across are borne singly in late summer. In cultivation this species has proved tender, and while its foliage is interesting, with reddish new growths, it is not as free flowering as others. In very mild, wet climates it grows tall and slender, up to 20–25 ft (7–8 m) in under 10 years. ZONE 8.

Eucryphia glutinosa

Also endemic to Chile but from slightly drier mountain regions than *E. cordifolia*, this is the only deciduous species, though in mild climates it may be semi-evergreen. It is the hardiest and most ornamental species, forming a small, shrub-like tree with erect branches, slow growing to 20 ft (7 m) or more. Young shoots are coated in a sticky resin, hence the name *glutinosa*, and the leaves are compound with 3 to 5 glossy green leaflets that may turn orange and red before falling in autumn. The flowers, borne in profusion along the branches in late mid-summer, are very beautiful. A double-flowered form is sometimes seen. ZONE 7.

Eucryphia × intermedia

This hybrid between the Chilean *E. glutinosa* and the Tasmanian *E. lucida* first appeared as a chance seedling at Rostrevor in Ireland; several clones are available but 'Rostrevor' is the most widely planted. It makes an upright tree of

Eucryphia × intermedia 'Rostrevor'

Eucryphia moorei

slender habit, reaching 30 ft (10 m) in time, and under good conditions makes a profuse show of flowers in late summer. ZONE 8.

Eucryphia lucida
TASMANIAN LEATHERWOOD

From Tasmanian rainforests, this slender, evergreen tree can reach 100 ft (30 m) in the wild and has been felled for its close-grained pinkish timber, but it is best known for the aromatic honey that the introduced honey-bee makes from its abundant, fragrant early summer flowers. It has sticky buds and the small shiny leaves are simple, not compound. In cultivation it is rather slow growing and tender, seldom exceeding 20 ft (7 m). 'Pink Cloud' is a pink-flowered cultivar recently introduced, while 'Leatherwood Cream' has leaves irregularly margined with cream. ZONE 8.

Eucryphia moorei
PINKWOOD

From the far south-east of mainland Australia, this species grows in sheltered gullies in the coastal ranges. It reaches a similar size to *E. lucida* but differs in its pinnate leaves, each leaf consisting of about 5 to 7 neat, oblong leaflets with white undersides. Shoots and leaves are less sticky and shiny than on other eucryphias. Flowers are about 1¼ in (3 cm) wide, borne among the ferny foliage from mid-summer to early autumn. Pinkwood is very ornamental and sometimes makes vigorous growth in cultivation but is quite demanding in its moisture and humidity requirements. ZONE 8.

Eucryphia × nymansensis

This name covers all hybrids between the 2 Chilean species *E. glutinosa* and *E. cordifolia* and arose first at Nymans, Sussex, in 1914. A small, compact tree of narrow habit, in time it may exceed 30 ft (10 m). The leaves vary in shape and size and can be simple or composed of 3 leaflets. It flowers in late summer, and in a sunny spot the tree may be covered in white blossoms. Several clones have been raised but the most popular in Britain is still one of the original seedling clones now known as 'Nymansay' (from its initial tag 'Nymans A'). ZONE 7.

EUGENIA
Myrtaceae

This genus, though extensively revised and shorn of many of its species, still counts around 1,000 evergreen trees and shrubs from tropical to warm-temperate areas of the Americas with a few species in Asia and the Pacific. The best known is perhaps the least often seen in gardens: *Eugenia caryophyllus*, whose dried flower buds are cloves, familiar in every kitchen now but once the most prized and costly of all spices. The tree is native to the Molucca Islands in Indonesia, but 95 per cent of the world supply of cloves now comes from Zanzibar. If the buds are left to develop, they turn into small white or pale pink flowers with prominent stamens and then into fleshy berries. In this, and in its glossy, pointed-oval leaves, it is typical of the genus. The fruits of many species are decorative and often edible: being rich in pectin, they make excellent jams and jellies. The trees generally prefer rich soil, moisture and shelter. Propagation is from seed or semi-ripe cuttings—but not in Zanzibar, where unauthorized propagation of *E. caryophyllus* carries the death penalty.

Eugenia uniflora
SURINAM CHERRY, PITANGA, FLORIDA CHERRY

Indigenous to South America, this evergreen tree is popular in subtropical and tropical zones for the bright red new foliage that contrasts with the dark green older leaves. It grows very slowly to 21 ft (7 m) high but may be kept trimmed to 8 ft (2.5 m). Small, fragrant, white flowers with a mass of central stamens open in summer. They are followed by sweet, edible, red fruit the size of small tomatoes. The

Euonymus alatus

Eucryphia × nymansensis

darker the fruit, the better the taste. Drought- and frost-tender, it prefers rich, moist, humus-rich soil and part-shade. In cooler areas it is grown as a container plant. ZONE 10.

EUONYMUS
Celastraceae
SPINDLE-TREE

This genus consists of both deciduous and evergreen trees, shrubs and creepers of the northern hemisphere, centred mainly in East Asia including the Himalaya. All have simple leaves in opposite pairs, usually with toothed margins. Flowers are inconspicuous, greenish or yellowish, in small groups along the lower parts of the current year's growth. It is the capsular fruits that provide the main interest, splitting open in autumn to reveal bright yellow, orange or red seeds against a contrasting capsule; in the deciduous species their ripening coincides with rich autumn foliage. Birds, attracted by their nutritious oily outer layer, distribute the seeds. Cultivation presents few problems in a sheltered position with ample sun and fertile, well-drained soil. The deciduous species are usually propagated from seed, the evergreen ones from cuttings. Most species are fully frost-hardy.

Eucryphia × nymansensis

Euonymus alatus

From Japan, China and Korea, this decorative, spreading, much-branched shrub grows to about 6 ft (2 m) tall, the small branches distinctive for the broad 'wings' of corky tissue attached to either side of the green twig (*alatus* means 'winged'). In late spring it bears small green flowers in inconspicuous sprays and by autumn the small, purplish, 4-lobed capsules start splitting to reveal orange-red seeds. At the same time the leaves turn the most vivid deep red, sometimes showing paler scarlet tones as they are about to fall. An attractive shrub of compact growth and fairly shade tolerant, it is propagated from seed. ZONE 5.

Euphorbia grandicornis

Euphorbia grandicornis

Euonymus europaeus

Euonymus europaeus

Euonymus europaeus
EUROPEAN SPINDLE-TREE

'Tree' is a slight exaggeration, though this species is usually single stemmed at the base and occasionally reaches 20 ft (7 m). It is native in Europe, including the British Isles, growing in woodlands and often on limestone or chalk soils. The wood of this and the few other European species was once used to make spindles, used in spinning wool. It is a rather nondescript shrub until laden with pink or red fruit in late summer, and then as these split open to reveal the large orange seeds and the leaves turn to shades of yellow and scarlet, it becomes an object of beauty. ZONE 6.

Euonymus japonicus

Generally represented by its variegated cultivars, this spreading, evergreen shrub from Japan has dark green shiny leaves in its typical state, reaching heights of 10–13 ft (3–4 m). Pale greenish flowers appear in early summer, and autumn foliage may be enlivened by scattered pinkish capsules opening to reveal orange seeds. Sometimes used as a hedge, it is also useful for seaside planting. The variegated cultivars, all lower and denser, seldom produce flowers or fruit. 'Ovatus Aureus' has broad, irregular margins of bright yellow; 'Albomarginatus' has irregular white-margined leaves; and 'Microphyllus Variegatus' is

Euonymus japonicus cultivar

similar but has smaller, more crowded leaves. ZONE 8.

EUPHORBIA
Euphorbiaceae

The genus is a very large one with several hundred species, among them annuals, herbaceous perennials, shrubs and some succulent species that at first sight look remarkably like cacti. This variety of forms has suggested to many botanists that the genus should be divided; the trouble is that the flowers of all the species are almost indistinguishable from each other. They are very much reduced, consisting of only a stigma and a stamen, always green, and usually carried in small clusters. They are in fact a unique type of flower, called a cyathium. Many species, however, draw the eye by accompanying the flowers with showy bracts, and these are the most widely cultivated. Mainly tropical, the genus also includes some warm-temperate species, though as none of these are shrubs they are not included here.

Euphorbia abyssinica

Considered a succulent tree, *E. abyssinica* grows in an upright fashion to 30 ft (10 m). The leafless trunk and branches are made up of multi-angled, somewhat flattened, jointed, spiny segments that have evolved to take over the photosynthetic functions of true leaves. An architectural addition to the warm-climate garden where its form contrasts well with more conventional plants. ZONE 10.

Euphorbia grandicornis
COW'S HORN EUPHORBIA

This bright mid-green South African succulent has flattened triangular stems edged with spines up to 2 in (5 cm) long. Mature plants are around 4 ft (1.2 m) high with stems up to 6 in (15 cm) in diameter. Occasionally small, oval leaves will develop after warm, moist weather. It has yellowish green flower bracts followed by $\frac{3}{4}$ in (1.5 cm) diameter red fruit. This is one of the most frost-hardy succulents but demands bone-dry conditions in winter. ZONE 9.

Euphorbia pulcherrima
POINSETTIA, CHRISTMAS PLANT

Potted poinsettias are a familiar Christmas decoration all over the northern hemisphere—and even in the southern, where the plants are forced into bloom 6 months away from their natural winter season—but this native of Mexico is only a garden plant in frost-free climates. There it makes a rather gangling shrub up to 12 ft (4 m) tall, usually dropping its leaves as flowering commences. The attraction is the broad bracts, which give each flower-cluster the appearance of a single huge flower, the display lasting many weeks. There are many named cultivars, which extend the colour range from the original blood-red to pink and cream. The shrub is happiest in the tropics, and likes fertile soil and sunshine; it is usually pruned severely immediately after flowering to keep it reasonably compact. The leaves are large but not especially attractive. ZONE 10.

Euphorbia tirucalli
CAUSTIC BUSH, PENCIL EUPHORBIA

This sometimes shrubby succulent is from eastern and southern Africa as well as the Arabian peninsula.

Once used as a source of latex, it grows to a height and spread of about 10 ft (3 m), its twiggy stems covered with tiny deciduous leaves. The insignificant flower, called a cyathium, is unique to this genus. It can provide interesting sculptural form for a warm-climate garden, where it is easily cultivated in well-drained soil in full sun, and it makes an interesting house plant elsewhere. Propagation is from stem cuttings or from seed, which will only be fertile if plants of both sexes are available. ZONE 10.

EURYOPS
Asteraceae

Part of the large daisy family, this genus contains around 100 species of evergreen shrubs most of which come from southern Africa and are grown for their large yellow flower heads, held above the fern-like foliage. Well-drained soil and a position in full sun are the main requirements of this attractive genus, otherwise the shrubs tend to grow leggy and flowers are not as plentiful. They respond to light pruning after the flowers have faded.

Euryops chrysanthemoides
PARIS DAISY

Growing to around 3 ft (1 m) high, this shrub has soft, fern-like foliage and in winter is covered with bright yellow daisies; these continue sporadically through most of the year provided it is grown in well-drained soil in a sunny position. It does well in warm, dry climates; in cool areas it makes an attractive pot plant. Propagate from leafy cuttings taken towards the end of summer when the current year's growth has hardened slightly. ZONE 9.

Euryops pectinatus
GREY-LEAVED EURYOPS

This widely cultivated shrubby evergreen from south-western Cape, South Africa, grows well in most temperate conditions. Excellent for rock gardens and borders, it likes sun, partial shade in hot areas and moist, well-drained, gravelly soil. From winter to spring it bears bright yellow daisy flowers up to 2 in (5 cm) across, for which the finely cut grey-green leaves are an attractive foil. It is a single, short-stemmed, bushy shrub growing to around 3 ft (1 m), and can be lightly pruned to maintain a rounded bun shape. It likes a free-draining soil, kept moist during dry weather, and prefers a warm climate. ZONE 9.

Euryops virgineus
RIVER RESIN BUSH

A South African species easily distinguished by its small, bright green leaves and upright habit, this 4 ft (1.5 m) high evergreen shrub has stiff branches densely clothed in foliage. Flowering throughout the year, it blooms most heavily in late winter and spring, when it produces masses of small, bright yellow daisies at the branch tips. It is easily grown in any light, well-drained soil in full sun and very much at home in seaside gardens. A light trim after flowering keeps the growth compact. Propagate from seed or cuttings. ZONE 9.

Euryops pectinatus

Euryops chrysanthemoides

Euryops virgineus

Euphorbia pulcherrima

Euphorbia pulcherrima (below)

Euscaphis japonica

Euscaphis japonica

Exochorda × *macrantha*

EUSCAPHIS
Staphyleaceae

This genus includes just one species. It is a medium-sized deciduous tree with short, stout branches and attractive foliage, flowers and fruit. While none of these features is outstanding on its own, they combine to make an appealing, undemanding tree. Any well-drained soil in sun or dappled shade will do. Propagation is from seed, which may require 2 periods of stratification, or from softwood cuttings taken in early summer.

Euscaphis japonica
Endemic to China and Japan, this species grows to 30 ft (10 m) high. It has 10 in (25 cm) long pinnate leaves made up of 7 to 11 leaflets, each 2–4 in (5–10 cm) long. In spring it produces small yellow flowers in long panicles that develop into attractive red fruit. When the leaves fall, the white-striped, purple bark is an interesting feature. ZONE 6.

EXOCHORDA
Rosaceae
PEARL BUSH

These deciduous shrubs from central Asia and northern China have weak, pithy branches and thin-textured, paddle-shaped, rather untidy leaves, but in spring the branch ends are clustered with 5-petalled white flowers of delicate, informal beauty. The fruits are capsules with wing-like segments, splitting apart when ripe to release flattened seeds. As might be expected from their origin, they are quite cold-hardy but prefer climates with sharply defined seasons and dry summers for the best display of flowers. A sheltered position in full sun and well-drained soil are desirable. Prune older stems back to their bases after flowering to encourage vigorous new growth and lavish bloom. Propagation is usually from cuttings.

Exochorda × macrantha
This hybrid was raised in France around 1900 by crossing *E. racemosa* with the central Asian *E. korolkowii*. Sometimes reaching 10 ft (3 m) tall, in mid- to late spring it produces elongated clusters of pure white flowers, each about 1¼ in (3 cm) across, from every branch tip. ZONE 6.

Exochorda racemosa
From northern China this species, long established in Western gardens, makes a lovely display when well grown, though old, neglected plants may give a poor indication of its potential. It grows to about 10 ft (3 m) high and has narrower, thinner, paler green leaves than other species. Flowers appear in late spring in loose, slender sprays from the branch tips, each flower 1½ in (3 cm) wide with narrow petals. ZONE 6.

Fagus sylvatica (above)

Fagus sylvatica 'Pendula' (below)

Fagus sylvatica 'Purpurea' (below)

Fagus sylvatica 'Purpurea' (below)

Fagus grandifolia

Fagus grandifolia

FAGUS
Fagaceae
BEECH

In the British Isles and in Europe generally, few trees attract such admiration as the beech. *Fagus* has species scattered across Europe, Asia and North America, though the majority are confined to China and Japan. They occur in a rather narrow climatic zone, being absent from far northern forests as well as the lowland Mediterranean-type forests. North America has only one species, confined to the east but an important forest tree there. All beeches are deciduous trees with distinctive pointed winter buds with brown scales. The leaves are slender stalked and prominently veined while the flowers, in inconspicuous clusters of different sexes but on the same tree, appear briefly in spring with the new leaves. The fruits are small shaggy capsules which in early autumn split open to release several strongly angled seeds, or 'beech nuts'. Beeches are large, long-lived trees with smooth, grey trunks and a thin canopy of delicate foliage that moves with the slightest breeze. Autumn foliage is golden tending to golden brown. Their timber is valuable, close grained and readily worked, long used for flooring, furniture and small items such as kitchen utensils. The oil-rich nuts are a major food source for wildlife. Beeches have a very shallow, dense root system that robs moisture and nutrients from plants beneath their canopy. As ornamentals they are best suited to large gardens and parks, though some of the weeping and cut-leafed forms are more compact. They require an open, well-drained soil of reasonable fertility and make best growth with shelter from strong winds. Propagation is usually from seed, which should be sown as soon as it falls, while cultivars must be grafted.

Fagus grandifolia
AMERICAN BEECH

From the eastern USA and Canada with a variety in the highlands of Mexico, this beech grows to around 80 ft (25 m) in its native forests, with a long straight trunk, but when planted in the open it branches low down, developing a very broad, spreading crown with age. Root suckers are often present beneath mature trees. Foliage and nuts are not very different from the European *F. sylvatica*, though leaves are slightly larger. This beautiful tree is not commonly cultivated outside North America; in the cooler summers of the British Isles it makes poor growth. ZONE 4.

Fagus orientalis
ORIENTAL BEECH

'Oriental' here is used in its earlier sense of south-eastern Europe and Asia Minor. This species once formed extensive forests in Greece, Turkey, northern Iran and the Caucasus, replacing *F. sylvatica* at low altitudes. It resembles that species in most respects but the leaves are noticeably longer and the nuts are larger. In a suitably warm climate it is a vigorous tree capable of fast growth, but has not yet been tried in some countries and regions where it might be expected to thrive. ZONE 6.

F. sylvatica
COMMON BEECH, EUROPEAN BEECH

Although regarded as among the most 'English' of Britain's native trees, this species has a much wider natural distribution across Europe and into western Asia where in many areas it forms the most characteristic climax forests. It makes a large tree to 130 ft (40 m) high, with a long, smooth bole when close planted, but in the open it is low branching, the crown spreading with age. An average beech, though, is around 60 ft (20 m) tall. In spring appear drooping balls of yellowish male flowers and less conspicuous greenish clusters of female flowers at the branch tips, while the nuts are shed in abundance in early autumn. Many of the cultivars have darker bronze or purple foliage, including 'Purpurea' with unevenly edged purple leaves and 'Cuprea' (the copper beech, a favourite with British gardeners and foresters) with paler brownish purple foliage. 'Aspleniifolia' and 'Rohanii' both have deeply cut leaves, but in the latter they are brownish purple as well. 'Pendula' has branches drooping from a mushroom-shaped crown and is usually grafted on to a tall stock. *F. sylvatica* takes readily to pruning and is very often used in the UK for tall clipped hedges. ZONE 5.

FATSIA
Araliaceae

This genus has a single evergreen species from Japan closely related to ivy (*Hedera*), a relationship evident in the flowers and fruit as well as in leaf texture. However *Fatsia* is a shrub, with thick, erect, little-branched stems, and the deeply lobed leaves are far larger than those of ivies. The creamy white flowers are in spherical heads grouped in a large panicle that terminates the shoot, and are followed by small black berries. It is valued in gardens for its handsome foliage, shade tolerance and greater cold tolerance than almost any other evergreen with leaves of this size. It also adapts well to warmer-temperate and even subtropical climates, given shade and moisture. In colder regions it is frequently grown as an indoor plant. Propagate from seed or cuttings. The affinity of *Fatsia* and *Hedera* is further evidenced by the well-known hybrid × *Fatshedera lizei*, which is almost exactly intermediate in its characteristics.

Fatsia japonica

Sometimes known by its earlier name *Aralia japonica*, this handsome shrub reaches an average height of 8–9 ft (2.5–3 m), but the leaves are 12 in (30 cm) or more across. In moist forest undergrowth in its native Japan it is said to reach small tree size and in New Zealand 12 ft (4 m) tall specimens are not uncommon. The flowers appear in late autumn, with fruits ripening in late winter. It is a tough plant, ideal for a shaded situation beneath trees or in a courtyard, but should be protected from fierce summer sun or the leaves may be bleached or scorched. ZONE 8.

FEIJOA
Myrtaceae

This evergreen genus consisting of 2 species from South America is named after a Brazilian botanist, de Silva Feijo. They form compact shrubs to around 15 ft (5 m) tall and are grown in warmer climates for their edible fruit. In cooler climates, however, although fruit cannot be expected to set, they are often grown for their attractive flowers and foliage and are used in hedging where they respond to light pruning. It is the species *F. sellowiana* that is most widely grown, both as an ornamental and as a fruiting plant.

Feijoa sellowiana
PINEAPPLE GUAVA, FEIJOA

Growing to about 12 ft (4 m), the pineapple guava is an evergreen shrub but with pruning it can be formed into a single-trunked small tree or clipped as a hedge. It has deep green oval leaves with an attractive lustrous sheen above and a silvery white bloom on the undersides. The flowers, carried on the new season's growth, have red petals that are white underneath and prominent, dark red stamens. The elongated fruit, with a tangy pineapple-like flavour, is eaten raw or made into jam. Best suited to a sunny position in well-drained soil with added humus, it needs ample water while the fruit matures. Easily propagated from seed but cultivars are preferred for quality fruit. Fruit-fly can be a problem in areas prone to this pest. ZONE 9.

FICUS
Moraceae
FIG

Sweet and nutritious, figs have been eagerly sought after since the days of the ancient Egyptians, though the tree that bears them, *Ficus carica*, is something of an exception in this large genus in being deciduous and in preferring warm-temperate climates; most are tropical and evergreen. They range from climbers and shrubs to large trees, much planted in frost-free climates where there is room for their branches and invasive roots. Some, such as the India-rubber tree, *F. elastica*, are familiar house plants elsewhere. The flowers are unusual; they are completely enclosed in what will mature to be the fruit and they need certain species of wasps to penetrate their protection and fertilize them. Once the fruit ripens, it is eaten by birds and bats which spread the seeds, often into the branches of other trees where the young fig trees germinate, to send down roots to the ground. These soon become woody trunks, and the host tree is eventually strangled; strangler figs are one of the more dramatic features of the tropical rainforests. They will grow equally happily on masonry, and when you see a picture of a Maya or Khmer ruined temple in the clutches of roots and branches, they are usually those of a fig. Propagate from seed, semi-ripe cuttings or aerial layers.

Feijoa sellowiana

Fatsia japonica

Fatsia japonica

Ficus sp. (below)

Ficus aspera 'Parcellii'
MOSAIC FIG

This evergreen shrub or small tree has large, roughly oval leaves with white mottling, flecking and speckling against a dark green background; they are somewhat hairy on the undersides. The cultivar differs from the species in that its foliage markings are very pronounced; its fruit also differs from that of the species—it is pink to purple rather than orange red.

Ficus aspera 'Parcellii'

Ficus dammaropsis

It is sometimes grown as a house plant in cool climates. ZONE 11.

Ficus benghalensis
BANYAN, INDIAN BANYAN

Indigenous to India, the banyan displays the most outstanding aerial roots of any tree. Indeed these roots, descending from the branches to the ground, in time form secondary trunks; an old tree, though rarely more than about 65 ft (20 m) tall, can develop into a forest of 1 acre (0.5 ha) or more; there are examples of entire villages sheltering in the dense shade of a single banyan tree. The bark is pale grey; the leaves are large and dark green, tinted red in their youth; and the 1 in (2 cm) wide round figs are red. They are much eaten by bats, which distribute the seeds. These often germinate in the branches of other trees which the banyan eventually

Ficus benghalensis

strangles, a problem for Indian foresters and one made more difficult by the species being sacred to Hindus who refuse to destroy it. (The tree's ability to continue growing, supported and nourished by its extra trunks even when the original one has died, represents eternal life.) Young aerial roots are fibrous and used in India to make rope. ZONE 11.

Ficus benjamina
WEEPING FIG

A tropical evergreen tree that occurs through India and Southeast Asia, the weeping fig can reach 50 ft (15 m) tall and mature specimens can have a much greater spread, sometimes supported by aerial roots. The shiny, pointed-oval leaves form a dense canopy, its ascending branches having a graceful weeping habit towards the outer edges. Fruit is insignificant but as the tree matures it can be troublesome underfoot. The invasive root system needs to be kept well away from underground pipes. Frost-tender, it requires a warm to hot climate, full sun and plenty of water. The species and its cultivars are used extensively as potted indoor plants; these need adequate water in summer, less in cooler months. The cultivar 'Exotica' has twisted leaf tips; 'Variegata' has rich green leaves splashed with white. ZONE 10.

Ficus carica
FIG

The edible fig with its distinctive 3-lobed leaves is indigenous to countries surrounding the Mediterranean and has been cultivated for millenia. A deciduous small tree to 20 ft (7 m), it produces edible fruit in autumn—provided birds can be kept at bay. It needs a sunny position in a warm climate where dry summers are the norm, as rain can split the ripening fruit. Deep, fairly heavy soils hold the moisture necessary throughout the growing season, otherwise mulching will ensure the shallow roots are kept moist. In temperate climates such as the UK, the tree appreciates the shelter of a sunny wall. There are many named cultivars. ZONE 8.

Ficus dammaropsis
DINNER-PLATE FIG

From New Guinea, this small tree to 30 ft (10 m) has a somewhat open habit. It is single trunked, forming neither buttresses nor aerial roots as many *Ficus* do as

Ficus carica (below)

they mature. The large leaves, often rough to the touch, have dramatically corrugated margins; deep green above, they are paler beneath, sometimes with red veins. The fruits, held close to the branches and ripening to a deep purple, are hidden in a scaled covering. It can be grown in a pot in a well-lit room or a sheltered courtyard in warm climates. ZONE 10.

Ficus elastica
INDIA-RUBBER TREE

From tropical Asia this tree can grow to 100 ft (30 m), providing welcome deep shade in tropical areas and forming massive aerial roots and high buttresses with age. In gardens, the species and its variegated forms make attractive trees and can be pruned to restrict size; however, their aggressive root systems can damage foundations and drains. Outside the tropics it is usually seen as a potted plant, its attractive rosy sheath of new leaves contrasting with the deep green, shiny mature leaves. Cultivars include 'Decora' with bronze coloured new leaves; and 'Doescheri', with variegated grey-green and creamy white leaves with light pink midribs. They do best in deep soil where ample moisture is available. ZONE 10.

Ficus lyrata
FIDDLELEAF FIG

This 30 ft (10 m), spreading, evergreen tree from tropical Africa is often seen as a potted house plant. The violin-shaped leaves are the main attraction: they are bright glossy green, heavily veined, up to 15 in (38 cm) long and very broad. Insignificant cream flowers are followed by 1 in (2.5 cm) green fruits. Plant it in moist, humus-rich, well-drained soil in light shade. ZONE 10.

Ficus macrophylla
MORETON BAY FIG

This large, spreading evergreen tree occurs naturally in coastal rainforests of eastern Australia. It grows to about 130 ft (40 m) with a spread nearly as great and a handsomely buttressed trunk. The large, leathery, dark green leaves have distinctive rust-toned undersides. The abundant fruit, reddish brown when ripe, can be quite messy underfoot. It needs a subtropical or warm-temperate climate and its size restricts it to very large gardens or public plantings. Well-drained sandy soils and moderate to high rainfall areas suit it best. ZONE 10.

Ficus microcarpa
CHINESE BANYAN, WEEPING FIG

This large, evergreen tree with a spreading crown grows to 100 ft (30 m); the mature tree has masses of aerial roots forming 'curtains'. The pointed oval leaves are quite small and glossy, held on ascending branches, the tips of which have a decided weeping habit. The bark of the young shoots is green but this soon matures to a smooth grey. It is half-hardy and not very particular as to soil. The variety *hillii* (a native of Australia) is often used for muliple plaited plantings or as a single standard, either in a container or in a garden setting. ZONE 9.

Ficus religiosa
BO TREE, PEEPUL

Indigenous to India and much of Southeast Asia, the bo tree grows in much the same way as the banyan, though it is not so tall; its open crown and fluttering, poplar-like leaves make it a more elegant and attractive tree, and it is capable of very long life. The Buddha was meditating in the shade of a bo tree when he received Enlightenment, so it is commonly planted in the grounds of temples and elsewhere in those Buddhist countries whose climate is hot enough for it. (It is sacred to Hindus also.) Most of these trees are claimed to have originated as cuttings from the Buddha's tree or its descendants, and this may often be true; many have been propagated from the ancient tree at Anaradhapura in Sri Lanka, which is known to be authentic. It is recorded as having been planted in 288 BC, 200 years after the Buddha's death. ZONE 11.

Ficus elastica 'Decora'

Ficus macrophylla

Ficus lyrata (below)

Ficus microcarpa (below)

Ficus virens

Firmiana simplex

Flindersia australis

Fokienia hodginsii

Fokienia hodginsii

Ficus sur

considerable space and can damage paving and drains and even building foundations. It prefers a warm climate and grows well and fairly rapidly in any deep soil with regular water. ZONE 10.

Ficus virens
GREY FIG, SPOTTED FIG, JAVA WILLOW

Found from India to the Solomon Islands and northern Australia, this briefly deciduous species often starts life as an epiphyte and is one of the strangler figs, so-called because they smother and kill their host plants. Eventually the parasitic roots fuse together and the host tree rots away leaving a hollow-trunked fig. Cultivated plants, however, are usually more conventional single-trunked trees growing to about 50 ft (15 m) tall with a broad crown and heavy limbs. *F. virens* has pointed-tipped, poplar-like leaves up to 7 in (17 cm) long and produces pairs of small, red-spotted, white figs at the branch tips. ZONE 10.

FIRMIANA
Sterculiaceae

This genus was named after the 18th century patron of the Padua botanic garden, Karl Josef von Firmian. It comprises a few species of trees, mostly deciduous, one of which, the beautiful parasol tree, is widely grown. It is a great favourite in China and was commonly planted in the gardens of scholars and poets, whose emblem it was.

Firmiana simplex
PARASOL TREE, WU TREE

From China and Japan, this deciduous tree grows to about 65 ft (20 m), with smooth green bark. It is valued for its large, maple-like leaves and attractive sprays of small, greenish yellow spring flowers; the papery, pinkish gold, 5-bracted fruits with their seed developing on the exterior are also of interest. Warm, frost-free conditions suit it well, and it prefers a sheltered position with ample water in summer. It is easily propagated from freshly ripened seed. ZONE 8.

Ficus sur
BROOM CLUSTER FIG

This large, semi-deciduous to evergreen tree bears its large fruits in branched clusters. It is a superb shade tree, reaching a height of 65 ft (20 m) with a wide crown and large leaves that are reddish brown when young. Fruits are around ½ in (3 cm) in diameter and are edible—they are often used to make a delicious jam. This tree should only be planted in a large garden or park because surface roots take up

FLINDERSIA
Rutaceae

Named after the explorer Matthew Flinders, this genus comprises 17 species of evergreen trees of which all but 2 are indigenous to the Australian mainland. Several are valued for their timber. The attractive foliage is similar to that of the northern hemisphere ash trees (*Fraxinus*), hence the common names crow's ash (*F. australis*) and silver ash (*F. schottiana*). Flowers are small and white, and the woody fruits that follow are often covered with small sharp prickles. While most are from the tropical and subtropical rainforests, one popular species, the leopard tree, occurs in drier inland areas but has adapted extremely well to gardens where more moisture is available.

Flindersia australis
CROW'S ASH, AUSTRALIAN TEAK

This semi-evergreen tree from subtropical rainforests of eastern Australia is valued for its dense, durable timber. It grows to 120 ft (38 m) in the wild, less in cultivation, forming a sturdy trunk covered with scaly brown bark and a dense multi-branched crown. The large pinnate leaves are made up of shiny green leaflets. Small white flowers appear in profuse clusters in spring. The large fruits have 5 prickly, boat-shaped segments, and are often dried and used in floral arrangements. ZONE 10.

Flindersia maculosa
LEOPARD TREE

A graceful small tree from inland eastern Australia to 50 ft (15 m) with a fairly open crown of delicate foliage and very distinctive mottled bark in shades of cream, grey and white. Gardeners can be forgiven for thinking they are purchasing a shrub, for in its juvenile state this plant is quite a bushy, prickly plant but as it matures it forms a straight, slender trunk topped with a symmetrical crown. In early summer it is covered with profuse panicles of small, creamy white flowers. Relatively slow growing, it requires a frost-free climate, full sun and good drainage. It is easily propagated from seed. ZONE 10.

FOKIENIA
Cupressaceae

This coniferous genus contains one species. Discovered in 1908 in Fokien, China, this densely foliaged pyramidal tree resembles a *Chamaecyparis*. The foliage is made up of flattened sprays of tightly adpressed scales. The cones are also like those of *Chamaecyparis* but larger. Plant in moist, well-drained soil in sun or dappled shade. Propagate from seed or small cuttings.

Fokienia hodginsii

Usually seen as a 10–20 ft (3–7 m) pyramidal tree, this species can grow to 100 ft (30 m) in the wild. It has light olive green foliage and a solid trunk, reddish brown bark that peels off in small strips, and near-spherical cones up to 1 in (2 cm) in diameter. ZONE 7.

FORSYTHIA
Oleaceae

Since their introduction to Western gardens from China and Japan in the 19th century, forsythias have been popular shrubs, valued for their display of brilliant yellow or gold blossom in mid-spring; they make excellent cut flowers. Deciduous shrubs of medium stature, they have soft-wooded stems branching from near the ground. The rather narrow, bluntly toothed leaves appear after the 4-petaled yellow flowers, which are paired or clustered at the twig nodes. Cultivation is simple: they are not fussy about soil type but may require added fertilizer and compost for good growth. A sunny position aids flowering, however, climate is crucial: they virtually refuse to flower in warm climates, requiring minimum winter temperatures well below freezing point. The only pruning necessary is the occasional removal of some older branches. Propagation is from hardwood cuttings in early summer.

Forsythia × intermedia

This hybrid between *F. suspensa* and *F. viridissima* was first recorded in Germany around 1885 and some fine cultivars were named in the following 50 years, including the well-known 'Lynwood' and 'Spectabilis'. In 1939 Karl Sax at the Arnold Arboretum in Massachusetts created the first artificial tetraploid 'Arnold Giant', and subsequent breeding work resulted in 'Beatrix Farrand' and 'Karl Sax'. These are all fairly similar, carrying in mid-spring profuse large flowers of a brilliant gold on vigorous plants up to about 10 ft (3 m) tall. ZONE 5.

Forsythia suspensa

Indigenous to China, this species has been cultivated for centuries in Japan, whence it was first taken to Europe. It makes a shrub of 8–10 ft (2.5–3 m), or taller if supported, with dense, slender, arching branches. From early to mid-spring the branches are lined with profuse golden yellow flowers with rather narrow petals. ZONE 4.

Forsythia viridissima

This species, also from China, makes a lower growing shrub than *F. suspensa*, about 5–6 ft (1.5–2 m) high, with thicker and more stiffly ascending branches. The yellow flowers, held close to the branches, appear from mid- to late spring. Not as graceful a plant as *F. suspensa*, it has largely been replaced by the hybrid cultivars. ZONE 5.

FORTUNELLA
Rutaceae

The renowned Scottish plant collector Robert Fortune (1812–80) introduced the cumquat to the conservatories of Britain, where it has flourished ever since. The genus comprises 4 evergreen shrubs or small trees often with a small spine at the junction of the leaf and branch. Originally they were included in the *Citrus* genus, to which they are closely related. A little more frost-hardy than oranges, they make a compact small shrub, suited to garden or container, and covered with either fragrant white flowers or attractive small orange fruit.

Fortunella japonica
CUMQUAT

A small tree to 10 ft (3 m), although smaller when grown in a container, the cumquat is grown primarily for its decorative, edible, small golden-orange fruit which remain on the plant for a considerable time. The tart-tasting fruits are used for marmalade and are best picked as they ripen to maintain the tree's vigorous growth. The cumquat produces sweetly perfumed white blossoms. Given an open, full sun position and reasonably fertile, well-drained soil, cumquats are reliable, long-lived plants which respond to regular fertilizer. ZONE 9.

Forsythia suspensa

Forsythia × intermedia

Fortunella japonica, variegated

Forsythia × intermedia (below)

FOTHERGILLA
Hamamelidaceae

This mainly North American genus of deciduous shrubs is grown for spring flowers and autumn foliage colour. The flowers are upright, conical, brush-like spikes with conspicuous creamy white stamens. They appear before the foliage, which is roughly diamond shaped, heavily ribbed and hazel-like. The leaves start out bright green, mature to deep green and develop intense yellow, orange and red autumn tones. It does best in moist, acidic soil in sun or light shade and can be trimmed to shape after flowering if necessary. Propagate from seed or by layering in autumn.

Fothergilla gardenii
DWARF FOTHERGILLA

A small, deciduous, bushy shrub 24–36 in (60–90 cm) high from mountain areas of eastern USA, this species thrives in a cool climate with moist, well-drained soil. It produces its fragrant white flowers, 1½ in (3 cm) long, in early spring and the 2–3 in (5–7 cm) long leaves that follow develop brilliant autumn colours. ZONE 5.

FOUQUIERIA
Fouquieriaceae
OCOTILLO

This genus consists of some 11 species of woody, resinous, often succulent shrubs endemic to the south-western USA and Mexico. They have very upright, narrow, spiny stems that in some species can reach 50 ft (15 m) high and occasionally may produce small, bright green, oval leaves. The mass of thorny stems makes an impenetrable, if difficult to manage, hedge. Terminal clusters of showy tubular flowers usually appear after spring rains and may be red, pale purple, cream or yellow depending on the species. These desert or near-desert plants need a very dry winter and excellent drainage. They also need full sun. Propagation is from seed or cuttings taken from the short side branches.

Fouquieria splendens

This species (known as ocotillo, slimwood, candlewood, coach whip and flaming sword) briefly bursts into leaf and flower in spring and occasionally blooms later too if rainfall allows. It has very upright, grey-green, grooved, narrow, thorn-encrusted stems that can grow to 24 ft (8 m) high. The tubular, 1 in (2 cm) long, red flowers, which have prominent pollen-tipped stamens, are massed in terminal clusters. ZONE 9.

FRANKLINIA
Theaceae
FRANKLIN TREE

Named for Benjamin Franklin and consisting of a single species of a small deciduous tree, this genus became extinct in the wild shortly after its discovery in about 1765 in Georgia, USA, due to the rapid spread of white settlement and clearing of the forests. It has large white flowers with crinkled, overlapping petals and a central bunch of golden stamens—similar to those of the closely related *Gordonia*, and also *Camellia* and *Stewartia*, all members of the same family. The fruit of *Franklinia* is a large woody capsule, with 5 compartments each splitting to release 2 flattened seeds. Cultivation is not difficult, though growth is slow. It prefers deep, moist soil and a sheltered but warm position. Climates with a long, hot, humid summer produce the best flowering. Propagation is normally from seed.

Franklinia alatamaha

The name is taken from the Altamaha River in Georgia, beside which this species was first discovered. It makes a small, spreading tree of about 15–20 ft (5–6 m), often several trunked. The glossy, bright green leaves colour scarlet in autumn, while the 3 in (8 cm) wide fragrant white flowers open in late summer and early autumn. ZONE 7.

FRAXINUS
Oleaceae
ASH

This genus consists of mainly deciduous trees, ranging throughout the northern hemisphere except for the coldest northern regions and the lowland tropics. It differs from

Fraxinus americana var. *juglandifolia*

F. americana var. *juglandifolia* (below)

Franklinia alatamaha (below)

Fothergilla gardenii (below)

Franklinia alatamaha (below)

the northern hemisphere except for the coldest northern regions and the lowland tropics. It differs from other woody members of the olive family (Oleaceae) in having pinnate leaves consisting of a number of leaflets, and small flowers that in most species lack petals and appear with or before the new leaves in spring. The dry winged fruits or 'keys' are a characteristic feature, ripening among the leaves in summer. One group of species known as the 'flowering ashes', typified by *F. ornus*, has showier flowers with petals (albeit small ones) produced in large terminal panicles at the tips of the branches in late spring or early summer. Several of the larger species are famous for their very tough, pale timber, suited for such demanding uses as oars, tool handles and bentwood chair backs, and said to be the very best of all timbers for firewood. Ashes flourish in cultivation, making fast growth and surviving in exposed or arid conditions, though most respond to shelter and fertile, moist soils with more luxuriant growth. They are widely planted as street and park trees and are usually little affected by pests and diseases. Propagation is normally from seed or, for cultivars, by grafting on to stock of the same species.

Fraxinus americana
AMERICAN WHITE ASH

The most important ash in North America, this species occurs naturally through eastern USA as far west as Minnesota and just into the south-east corner of Canada. Growing normally to about 80 ft (25 m) in its native valley forests, with a long straight bole and furrowed grey-brown bark, it is valued for its high-quality timber, straight, symmetrical habit and fast growth rate. Leaves each consist of 7 to 9 large, dark green leaflets with paler undersides; the inconspicuous flowers appear before the leaves and are followed by small clusters of 2 in (5 cm) long winged fruits. Autumn colour is most commonly a fine yellow. As a park and street tree the white ash is popular in many countries, adapting even to subtropical climates. ZONE 4.

Fraxinus angustifolia

This name is now used in a broad sense to include a range of forms from the Mediterranean region and western Asia, formerly regarded as species but more appropriately ranked as subspecies of *F. angustifolia*. It is related to the more northerly *F. excelsior* and is rather similar in foliage, flowers and fruit, but differs in the darker bark and leaves arranged in whorls of 3 to 4 on the main shoots, rather than in pairs. This species is suitable for planting

Fraxinus americana

in semi-arid climates with hot dry summers, making a medium-sized tree with a broadly columnar to rounded crown of deep green foliage. With good soil it makes fast growth in the early stages. The best known subspecies is *oxycarpa* (the desert ash) which occurs in the eastern Mediterranean, Turkey and the Caucasus. It is upright with smooth bark; its leaves have up to 7 leaflets, hairy on the midribs beneath. The well-known cultivar 'Raywood', which originated in a South Australian nursery, appears to be a clone of this subspecies. It is known as the claret ash on account of the deep wine-purple colour of the autumn foliage. ZONE 7.

Fraxinus excelsior
EUROPEAN ASH

This tree is highly valued for its timber in its native Europe, from Britain to Turkey and the Caucasus, and is also popular as an ornamental and shade tree. It is one of the largest European deciduous trees, reaching as much as 150 ft (46 m), though when planted in the open 50–60 ft (15–18 m) is usual, with a broad but rather high, umbrella-shaped crown. Leaves consist of 9 to 11 narrow, toothed leaflets; both leaves and the small flower-clusters burst from velvety, blackish buds in spring, with the thin, pointed fruits following in summer in dense bunches. In autumn the leaves turn pale yellow. The golden ash, cultivar 'Aurea' (perhaps more correctly 'Jaspidea') has pale yellowish green summer foliage and a deeper yellow in autumn; the thick twigs are also a fine yellow, displayed in winter. 'Pendula' is a good weeping form, normally grafted on to a standard. ZONE 4.

Fraxinus griffithii

An evergreen or semi-evergreen tree from Southeast Asia growing to 20 ft (7 m), this ash has grey bark on its stately trunk. The leaves, shiny pale green above and silvery beneath, look most attractive when blowing in the breeze; the young, brown, square shoots are covered

Fraxinus excelsior 'Aurea'

with down. The white flowers appear in spring, in rare clusters at the end of the branches, just before the new leaves appear. A tree for warmer, drier regions where deep soil is present. ZONE 9.

Fraxinus latifolia
OREGON ASH

As the common name suggests, this species comes from the forests of the west coast of North America, in moister sites from British Columbia to southern California. Valued for timber, it can grow to 80 ft (25 m) tall with a 3 ft (1 m) trunk diameter but cultivated trees are seldom more than half that size. Its closest relative is the eastern red ash (*F. pennsylvanica*), which it resembles except that the leaflets are not narrowed into stalks at the base. ZONE 5.

Fraxinus ornus
FLOWERING ASH, MANNA ASH

From southern Europe and Asia Minor, the flowering ash makes a round-topped tree of 30–50 ft (10–15 m) with short, fluted trunk and smooth grey bark. At one time its sugary sap or 'manna', obtained by making cuts in the bark, was used medicinally. The leaves consist of 5 to 9 oval leaflets, dull green with downy undersides. In late spring foamy panicles of white blossoms are produced from branch tips all over the crown, followed shortly after by small,

Fraxinus ornus

Fraxinus angustifolia subsp. *oxycarpa*

Fraxinus latifolia

Fraxinus quadrangulata

Fraxinus quadrangulata

Fraxinus uhdei

Fraxinus pennsylvanica

Fraxinus pennsylvanica
AMERICAN RED ASH

With a wide natural distribution, from the prairie states of central USA and southern Canada to the east coast and Gulf of Mexico, this ash is smaller than *F. americana*, normally about 40–60 ft (12–18 m) at maturity, and is less valued for timber. It makes a fine ornamental and shade tree, growing vigorously in both cold and quite mild climates. The reddish brown bark is finely fissured and the crown is spreading but a little irregular in shape. Leaves consist of 7 to 9 narrow, dull green leaflets, very downy on the undersides and up to 6 in (15 cm) long; they turn rich yellow in autumn. Flowers are not conspicuous but the broad-winged fruits are quite prominent. ZONE 3.

Fraxinus quadrangulata
BLUE ASH

This medium to large ash comes from south-eastern and central USA, where it is valued for its exceptionally strong and durable wood. A blue dye was once obtained from the inner bark. Usually 50–70 ft (15–22 m) in height with a slender but open, rounded crown, it has thin grey bark breaking up into large flattened scales. A distinctive feature is the strongly 4-angled twigs, the angles often drawn out into 'wings'. The leaves consist of 7 to 9 largish leaflets. Purplish stamened flowers appear in spring before the leaves. Though seldom grown outside the USA, it is potentially as useful and attractive as other ashes. ZONE 4.

Fraxinus uhdei

Originating in Mexico and Central America, this evergreen tree grows to 50 ft (15 m) or more; it makes a good garden specimen or street tree in dry, warm areas. The dark green leaves have 5 to 9 leaflets and the dense flower heads are followed by winged fruits. Cultivars include 'Majestic Beauty', a vigorous, larger tree with rounded crown and deep green leaves, and 'Tomlinson', which is a more compact, upright tree that can grow to 12 ft (4 m). ZONE 9.

Fraxinus velutina
VELVET ASH, ARIZONA ASH

From the south-western USA and adjacent regions of Mexico, this species tolerates very hot, dry conditions as well as being quite cold-hardy. In the wild it grows along the bottoms of canyons, surviving oven-like heat, though with roots in moist alluvial deposits. 'Velvet' refers to the thick downy coating on the twigs and leaf undersides. It grows to 25–40 ft (8–12 m) tall with a spreading, bushy crown. The bark is silvery grey and the smallish leaves, of 3 or 5 thick, greyish green leaflets, turn deep yellow in autumn. Flowers are inconspicuous and the wedge-shaped fruits are notched at the tips. A useful shade tree for regions with hot, dry summers. ZONE 6.

FREMONTODENDRON
Sterculiaceae
FREMONTIA

This unusual small genus is made up of evergreen shrubs or small trees from the far south-western

USA and adjacent areas of Mexico, usually of ungainly habit but bearing cup-shaped, bright golden flowers in great profusion. The stems are often weak and when young have a coating of felty or scurfy hairs, as do the strongly lobed leaves at least on their pale undersides. The inner bark contains strong fibres and has a slippery layer of mucilage beneath it. The flowers lack petals but the large golden sepals are petal-like and also densely hairy on the outside. Fremontias are not difficult to grow in a sheltered, sunny position with well-drained soil, but they can be rather short lived. They do not perform well in climates with hot, wet summers.

Fremontodendron californicum

This is the best known and most cold-hardy species, ranging in the wild the length of California in the Sierra Nevada foothills and coast ranges. It may eventually become a small tree of 30 ft (10 m), but is usually seen as a shrub of sparse, crooked form 10–13 ft (3–4 m) tall, with dark brown bark. From mid- to late spring it produces a succession of 2 in (5 cm) wide flowers that clothe the branches with gold. It has been crossed with the larger-flowered but less hardy *F. mexicanum* to produce the hybrid 'California Glory'. ZONE 8.

FUCHSIA
Onagraceae

Every gardener would be familiar with this genus, mostly in the guise of its numerous hybrids with showy pendulous flowers in shades of red, white, pink and purple. These are all technically shrubs but when raised for sale in pots or hanging baskets they are treated almost as herbaceous plants. We deal here only with some of the larger and more obviously woody species. The genus has an odd distribution, being confined to South and Central America except for 4 species in New Zealand and one in Tahiti. Most of the larger-flowered American species inhabit areas of very high rainfall, sometimes growing as epiphytes or on boulders in moss forests, and their pendulous flowers are pollinated by hummingbirds, which do not require a strong stalk to hold on to as do nectar-feeding birds from other continents. An attractive feature of the larger fuchsias is the pale, spongy bark which peels off in thin flakes or strips. Hardier fuchsias are not difficult to cultivate; their basic needs are adequate shelter and humidity, freedom from extremes of heat and cold, and a moist but well-drained, acid soil of open texture.

Fuchsia arborescens
TREE FUCHSIA

This large, evergreen shrub from Mexico grows to about 12 ft (4 m) tall and can be pruned to tree-like proportions if desired. The fleshy, deep green leaves are offset by clusters of rose-purple tubular flowers held at the ends of the branches from autumn through to spring. It will tolerate a warmer climate than most other species, but a moist atmosphere in a protected position is necessary to ensure the foliage is not scorched by drying winds. ZONE 9.

Fremontodendron californicum *Fraxinus velutina*

Fremontodendron californicum *Fuchsia arborescens* (right)

Fuchsia hybrid

Fuchsia magellanica

Fuchsia denticulata

Fuchsia paniculata

Fuchsia denticulata

From Peru and Bolivia, this species has medium- to long-tubed, pinkish red flowers with sepals of the same colour as the base of the tube, fading to cream and green at the tips. The corolla (petals) is bright red. The leaves are very large, up to 6 in (15 cm) long. It can grow to 8 ft (2.5 m) high and 5 ft (1.5 m) wide. ZONE 9.

Fuchsia excorticata
NEW ZEALAND TREE FUCHSIA, KOTUKUTUKU

From New Zealand, this is the giant of the genus, a tree of up to 40 ft (12 m) tall in the wild with a trunk diameter of over 24 in (60 cm). However, it is quite slow growing and when cultivated usually makes only a shrub. In cool climates it is virtually deciduous. The bark on its thick trunk and branches peels off attractively. The small flowers are greenish purple or dull red and hang off quite thick branches. ZONE 8.

Fuchsia magellanica
HARDY FUCHSIA, LADIES' EARDROPS

'Hardy' is relative; though this species from Chile and Argentina is the very hardiest of the genus, it does best in a sheltered position even in Zone 8. It is very variable in the wild and many subspecies and varieties have been named, often with little justification; but it is usually seen as a large evergreen shrub, 15 ft (5 m) in the wild but only half that in cultivation, with pendulous red-sepalled, purple-petalled flowers. Often used for hedging in the milder parts of Ireland, it remains well worth growing despite the innumerable large-flowered hybrids. These can be white, red, pink, blue, purple or lavender—or any combination of these—many being double, with extra petals. Ranging in habit from almost prostrate sprawlers to upright shrubs nearly 6 ft (2 m) tall, they are apt to be more tender than the species itself. Favourite conservatory plants or even house plants in cool to cold climates, they like rich soil and dappled shade, and benefit from fairly hard pruning in early spring to keep them compact. ZONE 8.

Fuchsia paniculata

Indigenous to southern Mexico and Panama, this species is rather unusual. Its foliage resembles that of *F. magellanica*, but its pink flowers are very small and are massed in large heads (panicles). They are followed by near-spherical, deep purplish red berries that are often more conspicuous than the flowers. In the wild it grows to around 15 ft (5 m) high, though it is usually far smaller in gardens. ZONE 9.

Gardenia augusta 'Magnifica' (below) *Gardenia thunbergia* (above)

Gardenia thunbergia (below)

Gardenia thunbergia (below)

Garcinia xanthochymus

Garcinia xanthochymus

GARCINIA
Clusiaceae

By far the most important member of this genus of some 400 species of evergreen trees from tropical Asia and Africa is the mangosteen, *Garcinia mangostana*, whose fruit is often said to be the most delicious in the world. It is a small evergreen tree, 30 ft (10 m) or so tall, with glossy leaves and attractive pink flowers which are succeeded by the orange-sized purple fruit, whose rind when broken open reveals the fragrant white pulp. The species bears male and female flowers on separate trees, but male trees are extremely rare and most fruit are formed without fertilization. They thus contain no seeds; and as propagation from cuttings or by layering is difficult and the tree only consents to bear in equatorial climates, it (and its fruit) are rarely seen away from its homelands in Southeast Asia. Some other species are cultivated for the yellow latex in their stems, which is said to have medicinal properties.

Garcinia xanthochymus
GAMBOGE

A straight-trunked tree from northern India and the western Himalaya growing to about 40 ft (13 m) tall; its dense canopy is rounded and low to the ground. The glossy green leaves are narrow and up to 18 in (45 cm) long. In summer small white flowers precede the dark yellow fruit, which are not generally considered of table quality. The sap is dried to yield the yellow pigment gamboge, once much used by artists but superseded since the mid-19th century by the more durable chrome and cadmium yellows. Trees can be propagated from seed, and selected clones are budded on to seedling understock. ZONE 11.

GARDENIA
Rubiaceae

Gardenias provide some of the most delightfully fragrant of all the flowers and are popular in warm-climate gardens worldwide. The genus includes some 250 species, mostly from Southeast Asia or southern Africa. Evergreen shrubs or small trees with glossy deep green leaves and fragrant white or cream flowers, they require a fertile, well-drained, slightly acid soil and are suited to lightly shaded gardens. Generous water in warmer months and a regular dressing of compost and fertilizer will ensure good flowering and foliage that remains a deep glossy green. Frost-tender and lovers of humidity, they are grown in heated greenhouses in cooler climates. Propagation is easily done from semi-ripe cuttings in summer.

Gardenia augusta
GARDENIA, CAPE JASMINE

Formerly known as *G. jasminoides*, this is the best known species of the genus, an evergreen, glossy-leafed shrub from southern China, though long supposed native to the Cape of Good Hope, hence the name Cape jasmine. It is almost always seen in gardens and flower shops in one of its double-flowered cultivars, all with white, strongly perfumed flowers which change to pale yellow as they age. The best known is 'Florida', a 3 ft (1 m) tall shrub with flowers about 3 in (8 cm) wide; 'Magnifica' is larger in all its parts though less generous with its flowers; 'Radicans' is almost prostrate, with small flowers and leaves. All need a subtropical climate and in temperate climates are pampered by florists in greenhouses. Flowers appear over a long season from late spring. ZONE 10.

Gardenia thunbergia
WHITE GARDENIA

From humid forests of southern Africa, this erect shrub grows to 8 ft (2.5 m) high and wide. The large, fragrant, white flowers with reflexed petals are held singly towards the tips of the branches in early summer. This plant, being surface rooted, appreciates regular fertilizing and ample water plus a yearly mulch of compost. It can be propagated from cuttings taken once the new wood has hardened in early autumn. The grey woody fruit persist on the tree for some time. ZONE 10.

GARRYA
Garryaceae

The only genus in its family, *Garrya* comprises some 15 evergreen shrubs and small trees from North America, of which the most important in gardens is the silk-tassel bush, *Garrya elliptica*. This comes from California and Oregon, and is grown for the late-winter display of long catkin-like chains of flowers borne by the male plants. Those of the female plants are much shorter and less decorative, though they are succeeded by pleasant-looking berries in autumn. The species calls for a mild-temperate climate free of heavy frost, but there it is very easy to grow in almost any well-drained soil or position. It grows slowly and needs little pruning.

Garrya elliptica
SILK-TASSEL BUSH

This evergreen shrub has a bushy, dense habit and grows to 12 ft (4 m) in height with a spread of 10 ft (3 m). It can be trained in espalier form to display the attractive catkins. Leaves are broadly oval, dark green and leathery with a wavy edge. Distinctive tassel-like pale green catkins are borne from mid-winter to early spring. Those of male plants are much longer and more decorative than those of females. The male cultivar 'James Roof' is particularly attractive, bearing long silvery catkins with golden anthers. ZONE 8.

GAULTHERIA
Ericaceae

These 100 or so species of evergreen shrubs are from Asia, the Americas, Australia and New Zealand, where they are found as understorey plants in forests. They are valued for their attractive glossy leaves, their fragrance and their clumping growth-habit. The flowers are pink or white and are usually bell shaped. The fruit, though a capsule, is berry like and aromatic; that of the North American *Gaultheria procumbens* yields oil of wintergreen, used medicinally and to perfume tobacco. The plants prefer well-drained, humus-rich, acid soils, and a sheltered position in part-shade. They can be propagated from seed, semi-ripe cuttings or by division of suckers.

Gaultheria fragrantissima

Originating from the mountains of southern Asia, this dense plant is seen as a large shrub or a small tree to 10 ft (3 m). The new stems are shiny and the leathery, elliptical leaves, to 4 in (10 cm) long, smell strongly of oil of wintergreen when crushed. In maturity the green adult leaves develop a brown underside. The very fragrant bell-shaped flowers, white or pale pink, appear in spring, carried on the previous season's growth. The rounded fruit ripens mid- or pale blue. ZONE 8.

Gaultheria mucronata
PRICKLY HEATH

Formerly *Pernettya mucronata*, and often still sold under this name, this is a thicket-forming, suckering, evergreen shrub originating from Chile and Argentina. It grows to about 5 ft (1.5 m) high and wide, and has deep green, glossy leaves ½ in (1 cm) long with needle-sharp tips. In spring, clusters of small, white, pendulous flowers open, followed by small, fleshy, pinkish purple fruit. There are separate male and female plants; 1 male to 10 females will yield a good crop of berries. It may be trimmed to shape and prefers a humus-rich, acidic soil with a position in light shade. Cultivars include: 'Bell's Seedling', with deep carmine-pink berries; 'Mother of Pearl', pale pink berries; 'Mulberry Wine', purple berries; 'White Pearl', white berries. ZONE 7.

Gaultheria shallon
SHALLON

A suckering, evergreen shrub from western North America, this species has deep green, oval leaves to 4 in (10 cm) long and grows to about 4 ft (1.2 m) high and wide. In spring it produces terminal panicles of small, white, lily-of-the-valley flowers. These are followed by ½ in (1 cm) fleshy, purple fruit. It prefers humus-rich, acid soil and a position in light shade. ZONE 5.

Gaultheria fragrantissima

Gaultheria shallon

Garrya elliptica (right)

Gaultheria × wisleyensis

Gaultheria × wisleyensis

These vigorous hybrids were bred in England from *G. shallon* and *G. mucronata*. The plants are variable but are usually dense and less than 6 ft (2 m) high. The leaves are leathery and green, and the attractive white flowers are produced in spring. They are followed by large bunches of dark red berries that remain on the plant until late winter. This hybrid does well in containers and is used for bank stabilization in shaded areas. Some clones make effective groundcovers. Many named cultivars are available. ZONE 7.

GENISTA
Fabaceae
BROOM

Originating in the Mediterranean region, these ornamental shrubs are grown for their profusion of small, fragrant, pea-like flowers. They prefer a temperate climate and some are good seaside plants. Full sun and a not-too-rich, well-drained soil suit them best. They resent being transplanted. Propagate from seed in spring or semi-ripe cuttings in summer. Many of the species have very reduced leaves, sometimes bearing their flowers on leafless green branches. Prune to encourage a compact, bushy shape. In ancient times their flowers were used to make dyes.

Genista hispanica
SPANISH GORSE

From south-western Europe, this is an ideal dwarf shrub for rockeries and dry, sunny banks. Deciduous, it has few leaves but many spines. It grows to a height of 24 in (60 cm) and spread of about 4½ ft (1.5 m), forming a neat, prickly dome covered in spring and early summer with dense clusters of tiny, golden yellow flowers. ZONE 4.

Genista lydia

This deciduous shrub grows to a height of up to 24 in (60 cm), often spreading wider, in a domed shape with arching branches and bluish green leaves. A profusion of bright yellow flowers are borne through spring and early summer. This is an excellent subject for rockeries and for trailing over walls. ZONE 5.

Genista × spachiana

This evergreen broom is a hybrid between 2 species from the Canary Islands. Its fast growth and hardiness to wind, drought and infertile soils make it useful in difficult sites. Of dense habit, it may grow to 18 ft (6 m) tall but can be tip pruned to remain smaller. Leaves are dark green and shiny above, pale and silky beneath. A profusion of fragrant yellow pea-flowers are borne in winter and spring. This hardy plant is undemanding but needs ample sun. ZONE 6.

Genista tinctoria
DYER'S BROOM, DYER'S GREENWEED

Used as a medicinal herb and as a source of yellow dye, this deciduous, green-stemmed 3 ft (1 m) shrub occurs naturally in Europe westward to Siberia. It has 1 in (2.5 cm) elliptical leaves with a covering of fine hairs on the undersides. Golden yellow, pea-shaped flowers appear in summer after other brooms have finished flowering. 'Plena' is a dwarf cultivar 12 in (30 cm) high with double flowers. A tough, adaptable shrub, it prefers lime-free, well-drained soils and full sun. ZONE 3.

GINKGO
Ginkgoaceae
GINKGO, MAIDENHAIR TREE

This single species, *Ginkgo biloba*, represents an ancient class of plants, more 'primitive' than the conifers and even more ancient than they. The Ginkgoales first appeared in the Permian period (about 300 million years ago) and flourished all through the Jurassic, the age of dinosaurs. About 100 million years ago they began to die

Genista × spachiana

Genista hispanica (below)

Genista lydia

Ginkgo biloba

out, leaving the maidenhair tree as the sole survivor—and then only in China. It is now unknown in a wild state, and it appears it would no longer exist if ancient trees had not been preserved in the grounds of temples and young ones planted there. It is a tree of temperate climates, much grown as a city tree as it is resistant to pollution and seems to have outlived any pests it may have once had. It does, however, need shelter from strong winds and does best in deep, fertile soil. City authorities prefer to grow male trees, as females drop smelly fruit; in China female are preferred, as the seeds are edible and nutritious. They do not appear before the tree is at least 35 years old, however. Propagation is from seed or autumn cuttings.

Ginkgo biloba

Grown for its beauty of form and foliage, the ginkgo reaches a height of 80 ft (25 m) or more, upright when young and spreading to about 30 ft (10 m) with age. Deciduous, the 5 in (12 cm) long, matt green, fan-shaped leaves turn bright golden yellow in autumn. A fleshy, plum-like, orange-brown fruit with an edible kernel appears in late summer and autumn if male and female trees are grown together. The ginkgo has been cultivated for many centuries in both China and Japan, especially in temple grounds. The cultivar 'Fastigiata' has slender, erect growth to about 30 ft (10 m). ZONE 3.

GLEDITSIA
Caesalpiniaceae
HONEY LOCUST

Indigenous to North America and Asia, these deciduous, broadly spreading, usually thorny trees are grown for their attractive foliage, ease of cultivation and use as shade trees. They have inconspicuous

Ginkgo biloba

flowers and large, often twisted, brown, hanging seed pods that are filled with a sweetish, edible pulp. Gleditsias grow best in full sun in good alluvial soils but will tolerate higher land if watered well in summer. Cool-climate plants, they are fully hardy although young plants may need protection from frost. Young trees can be pruned to promote a single, straight trunk and thorns on the lower trunk can be removed. Propagate selected forms by budding in spring or summer and species from seed in autumn.

Gleditsia aquatica
WATER LOCUST

As the specific name suggests, this species likes wet ground; it is used for swamp plantings in Texas. Also much grown in Florida and North Carolina, this tree grows to 60 ft (18 m) and is not as thorny as the similar *G. triacanthos*. ZONE 4.

Genista tinctoria (below)

Gleditsia triacanthos var. *inermis* (below) *Gleditsia triacanthos* (above)

Glyptostrobus pensilis (below)   *Gleditsia triacanthos* var. *inermis*

Gleditsia triacanthos
HONEY LOCUST

Growing to 100 ft (30 m) high and 50 ft (15 m) wide, this species has an open, vase-shaped canopy and a very thorny trunk. Fern-like, shiny, dark green leaves turn deep yellow in autumn. The variety *inermis* is thornless. There are several cultivars including 'Ruby Lace', with reddish young growth turning dull bronze in autumn, and 'Sunburst', with bright yellow young leaves that turn to pale green in summer and deep yellow in autumn. ZONE 3.

GLIRICIDIA
Fabaceae

This genus contains about 6 species of trees and shrubs from tropical Central and South America; some are found on hillsides at altitudes of up to 6,500 ft (2,000 m). They are widely planted as shade trees in coffee and cocoa plantations and in tropical gardens. The pinnate leaves consist of 5 to 19 narrow leaflets and the showy flowers are borne in copious sprays in spring. The fruit are flat pods, and these and the leaves enrich the soil when they fall to the ground. The plants are not tolerant of frost and require a sunny position. Hard pruning after flowering is tolerated but is not essential. They are propagated from seed. The leaves, bark and seeds are all quite poisonous.

Gliricidia sepium
MADRE DE CACAO

This tree is grown for its attractive pea-flowers, lilac pink with a yellow eye, that hang in small racemes from the branches, trunk and twigs in early spring. It has a short, gnarled trunk and grows to 24 ft (8 m), with compact, fern-like leaves. It is valuable as a shade tree and for enriching the soil by nitrogen fixation. The seeds are used for rat poison in Central America and the Philippines. The common name comes from its widespread planting in cocoa plantations, where it shades the cocoa trees which will not grow well in full sun. ZONE 11.

GLYPTOSTROBUS
Taxodiaceae
CHINESE SWAMP CYPRESS

A genus comprising a single species, this is a deciduous conifer, allied to *Taxodium*, that in its natural habitat can grow to 80 ft (25 m) tall. It is adapted to waterlogged areas where a humid summer temperature can be expected for at least 3 months. Its name, derived from the Greek, means carved cone and while it is extinct in the wild it has been widely planted to stabilize river banks and walls of rice paddies in eastern Asia. It can be propagated from seed or by grafting; in the latter case plant the graft below the soil/water level to encourage roots to form above the graft.

Glyptostrobus pensilis

A tall, upright tree for warm, wet areas, its distinctive conical outline suggests the conifers of colder regions. It is deciduous, providing a wonderful display of new spring growth, summer foliage, unexpected rich red-brown autumn tones, then the distinctive twiggy outline of winter. It is a single-trunked tree but can become multi-stemmed if damaged by frost. Usually seen growing on its own rootstock, it sometimes produces stem-like roots that appear above the mud to help it breathe, and these are an indication that it has been grafted on to the closely related *Taxodium distichum* rootstock. ZONE 8.

GORDONIA
Theaceae

The evergreen and deciduous trees and shrubs of this small genus are, except for one North American species, all indigenous to East Asia. They have handsome flowers with showy, golden stamens. Warm-temperate plants, they do best in sun or dappled shade on a good-quality, friable, slightly acid soil—they enjoy similar conditions to camellias, to which they are related. Growth is improved if the plants are mulched, fed and watered regularly. Propagate from seed in autumn or spring or from semi-ripe cuttings in late summer. Tip pruning for the first few years of growth will improve their slightly open habit.

Gordonia axillaris

Though in time it becomes a tree about 25 ft (8 m) tall and wide, this beautiful evergreen from China grows slowly and is usually seen in gardens as a tall shrub. The leaves are bright green, turning scarlet before they fall a few at a time throughout the year, and as the tree matures its smooth variegated bark becomes an attractive feature. Clusters of buds in the leaf axils open in succession from autumn to spring. The camellia-like flowers are about 5 in (12 cm) wide and are white with golden stamens. A warm-temperate climate with only the mildest of frost and fertile, lime-free soil are called for. The tree is happiest in light shade, but will endure sun if it is adequately watered in summer. ZONE 9.

Gordonia lasianthus
LOBLOLLY BAY

From south-eastern USA, this evergreen species reaches a height of about 80 ft (25 m). It has a dense, narrow crown and finely toothed, glossy leaves. Pungently fragrant white flowers, about 2½ in (6 cm) in diameter, are borne on short stalks in summer. ZONE 6.

GRAPTOPHYLLUM
Acanthaceae

Generally seen as house plants, these shrubs from tropical Australia and the Pacific islands are admired chiefly for their decorative foliage, the summer flowers being of less account. They need a tropical climate to succeed as garden plants, doing best in dappled shade and fertile, well-drained soil. They respond well to gentle pruning to control their tendency to legginess. Propagation is from semi-ripe cuttings at any time in the tropics, in spring or summer elsewhere. As house plants they need regular watering except in winter when they should be kept on the dry side.

Graptophyllum pictum
CARICATURE PLANT

This evergreen shrub has an erect, open habit and reaches a height of 4½ ft (1.5 m) with a spread of about 30 in (75 cm). It is grown mainly for its attractive variegated foliage: the mid-green, oval leaves have creamy central blotches. The tubular purplish red flowers are borne in terminal spikes in spring and summer. In cooler areas it is often grown indoors or in greenhouses. 'Tricolor' has cream and green leaves, heavily flushed pink especially when young; 'Purpureum Variegata' is similar but replaces the pink with purple-red. ZONE 11.

GREVILLEA
Proteaceae

This Australian genus is the largest in the protea family, with around 350 species, ranging from prostrate shrubs to forest trees but all evergreen. The best known species is also the largest: Grevillea robusta, the silky oak. Strictly a tree for subtropical climates, it is a favourite with tea planters in Sri Lanka, as it grows fast and gives the dappled shade the tea bushes need without competing unduly with their roots. Young trees with their attractive foliage are popular house plants in cool climates. With their often handsome foliage and long season of bloom, the shrubby species are among the most important indigenous garden shrubs in Australia, and they are also well-liked in California and similar mild-winter, dry-summer climates, though South African gardeners are often inclined to regard them with suspicion. This is often a case of

Gordonia axillaris (below)

guilt by association, some species of the closely allied genus *Hakea* having become unpopular weeds in that country. Generally, grevilleas need full sunshine and perfect drainage and, being allergic to excess phosphorus in the soil, they should never be given fertilizers rich in that element. (Compost and manure are perfectly acceptable.) While the tree species are fairly long lived, most of the shrubby ones are not, often dying out after 10 years or so; they compensate for that by being very fast growing. Their lives can be prolonged a little by gentle pruning after bloom. The flowers are pollinated by nectar-eating birds, and where these exist a planting of grevilleas is a good way to attract them to the garden. Propagation is best from cuttings in summer; the species hybridize very freely in cultivation and seed often does not breed true. Many hybrid cultivars have been developed in Australia, some very meritorious, others much less so.

Grevillea banksii
BANKS'S GREVILLEA

Named after Sir Joseph Banks, this subtropical east coast species is a variable shrub or small open tree ranging in height from 3–30 ft (1–10 m). The finely cut, grey-green leaves offset cylindrical flower heads in cream, red or rich pink shades. Blooms can be increased with light pruning. This species is ideally suited to frost-free areas and well-mulched, open, sandy soils with good drainage. ZONE 9.

Grevillea dimorpha
FLAME GREVILLEA

This well-known shrub from western Victoria grows to 9 ft (3 m). It has stiff, long, narrow, undivided, deep green leaves and masses of bright red spider-type flowers held at the ends of branches from late autumn to spring. These plants respond to light pruning and can look very effective when planted as a single species hedge or screen. They need well-drained, acidic soil and prefer full sun but will flower in dappled shade. ZONE 9.

Grevillea banksii

Grevillea robusta

Grevillea 'Honey Gem'

Grevillea hilliana

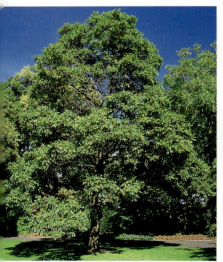
Grevillea hilliana

Grevillea juniperina

Grevillea fasciculata

This south-western species is a low shrub less than 3 ft (1m) high, spreading up to 8 ft (2.5 m) wide. It has small, deep green, roughly elliptical leaves with faint pale brown felting underneath. In late winter and spring it bears bright red, spidery flowers with yellow tips. It is useful for covering dry banks and can also be grown in large containers. It requires light, very well-drained soil in full sun. ZONE 9.

Grevillea hilliana
WHITE YIEL-YIEL

This tree from rainforests of the east coast of Australia has distinctive glossy green, deeply lobed juvenile leaves that give way to unlobed leaves as the tree matures. It grows to 25–65 ft (8–20 m) in subtropical areas, but is generally smaller in cooler climates. Tightly packed, curled, cylindrical rods hold hundreds of tiny greenish white individual flowers from late winter through to summer. Adaptable to most soil types, it grows best in deep loamy soil. Established plants will tolerate a light frost. ZONE 9.

Grevillea 'Honey Gem'

This cultivar is a dense evergreen shrub growing to 12 ft (about 4 m) tall with a spread of 6 ft (2 m). It carries large yellow-orange flowers for most of the year. The finely divided, dark green leaves have a silvery underside. Frost tender, it needs a sheltered position. ZONE 9.

Grevillea juniperina
SPIDER FLOWER

This species from eastern Australia is one of several given the common name spider flower, which comes from the shape of the flower-clusters. It is typically a tall shrub with conifer-like bright green, prickly leaves and scarlet to orange, sometimes yellow, flowers in summer. It is variable in the wild and several cultivars have been selected, varying in habit from prostrate types suitable for groundcover to head high or taller with an equal spread. Examples are 'Molonglo', a good groundcover with apricot-yellow flowers, not always borne very freely; and 'Sulphurea', about 6 ft (2 m) tall and wide with pale yellow flowers. Others offer shades of orange or coral-pink, and the species has given rise to a large number of hybrids such as 'Poorinda Queen', orange; or 'Pink Pearl', bright pink. Most of the taller types can be used for clipped hedges, though clipping greatly reduces the quantity of flowers. ZONE 8.

Grevillea lanigera
WOOLLY GREVILLEA

A bushy shrub from New South Wales and Victoria, this species takes its name from the greyish, furry leaves with which the red and cream flower-clusters make a very pleasing contrast in late winter and spring. It varies in size, some forms being quite prostrate, others growing to about 3 ft (1 m) tall and wide. This is one of the more cold-tolerant species, though it is inclined to be rather short lived in cultivation. ZONE 8.

Grevillea robusta
SILKY OAK

A tall, upright, evergreen tree from subtropical rainforests of the Australian east coast, the silky oak has long been valued for its beautiful timber, used for furniture making. Growing to 100 ft (30 m), the fern-like leaves with silvery undersides can be almost hidden by masses of golden yellow blooms in late spring. It is drought resistant, although mature trees growing in drier areas may lose their shapely crown, and it adapts to most soil types. Widely grown in larger gardens and parks in temperate regions, it is also a popular indoor plant in cooler climates. ZONE 9.

Grevillea 'Robyn Gordon'

Of the many hybrid grevilleas developed in Australia in recent years, this offspring of *G. banksii* and the less well-known *G. bipinnatifida* is widely regarded as the best, though some people have been known to experience skin allergies after contact with it. It makes a dome-shaped bush a little more than 3 ft (1 m) tall and rather wider. The olive-green leaves, tinted russet when young and sometimes grey-toned at maturity, are much divided and fern-like in effect though in fact rather stiff and prickly. The red flowers appear in showy clusters almost all year, with peak displays in spring and autumn. A sister seedling, almost identical but with pink and cream flowers, is called 'Ned Kelly'. ZONE 9.

Grevillea rosmarinifolia
ROSEMARY GREVILLEA, SPIDER FLOWER

This red or deep pink flowered species from New South Wales and Victoria is one of the most cold-tolerant grevilleas. It is a big shrub, usually taller than head high and spreading nearly as wide, well clothed to the base with bright green leaves shaped like needles and nearly as sharp. The flower clusters are borne in abundance in spring. Although the spider-like flower clusters are red, it is not one of the more colourful species as the flowers tend to be hidden among the leaves. Australian gardeners regard it as perhaps the best of their indigenous plants for formal hedging as it takes kindly to being clipped to shape and its prickly leaves make it quite impenetrable. ZONE 8.

GREWIA
Tiliaceae

Although there are over 150 species of this genus of trees, shrubs and climbers from tropical regions of Africa, Southeast Asia and Australia, there is really only one species, *G. occidentalis*, from southern Africa, that is commonly found in gardens. It is grown in California and the south-eastern states of the USA, around the Mediterranean, and in eastern Australia. The genus is named after Nehemiah Grew who was famous for his botanical drawings.

Grewia occidentalis
FOUR CORNERS

Also known as cross-berry, this evergreen with deep green, oval, toothed, somewhat leathery leaves, is an upright shrub that can grow to 10 ft (3 m) high. The star-shaped, mauve-pink flowers, held in small clusters, are dotted over it during spring and summer. Brownish, 4-valved berries ripen in autumn. In a sheltered, sunny position with well-drained, humus-rich soil *G. occidentalis* will form a neat, rounded bush that needs occasional pruning to keep its shape. Propagation is from cuttings or from seed. ZONE 9.

GREYIA
Greyiaceae

This genus from southern Africa encompasses 3 species of deciduous shrubs or small trees that make attractive additions to the dry, warm-climate garden where frosts are infrequent. Only one species is generally used in gardens.

Greyia sutherlandii
NATAL BOTTLEBRUSH

This dome-shaped, thick-wooded shrub grows to 10 ft (3 m). Its serrated leaves turn red in autumn, but it is mainly grown for its brilliant orange-red flowers. Appearing in late winter and early spring, the dense spikes of many small flowers with protruding stamens are borne towards the ends of the bare branches. It prefers a sunny position in fertile, well-drained soil; a light pruning after flowering will keep the plant compact. It needs generous water during the growing season, but less while the shrub is winter dormant. ZONE 9.

GRISELINIA
Cornaceae

This genus is made up of 6 species of evergreen shrubs and trees from New Zealand and Chile, of which only the 2 species here are commonly met with in cultivation. They are grown for their foliage and bushy habit, the pale greenish flowers being tiny and inconspicuous. The flowers are followed by black berries, though only on female plants. *G. littoralis*, especially, is a first-rate seaside shrub withstanding salty winds very well. It is well liked in England and popular in California. A temperate climate, well-drained soil and sunshine are called for. With a little trimming, the shrubs make good hedges. Propagation is from summer cuttings or seed.

Griselinia littoralis
KAPUKA

Growing to a height and spread of 18–37 ft (6–12 m), this tree or shrub has densely packed, bright green foliage and insignificant yellow-green flowers followed by black berries. It prefers full sun to partial shade and fertile soil, is resistant to salt-laden winds and will withstand drought. It appreciates the protection of a wall if grown in colder areas. If used as a hedge, the plants are best trimmed in summer. Cultivars include 'Dixon's Cream', with leaves spashed creamy white; and 'Variegata', with blotched white variegations. ZONE 8.

Greyia sutherlandii

Grevillea 'Robyn Gordon' (above)

Grewia occidentalis (below)

Griselinia littoralis (below)

Grevillea rosmarinifolia (below)

Griselinia lucida
PUKA

This somewhat more erect, open branching shrub than *G. littoralis* grows to 12 ft (4 m) high with slightly larger leaves that are a darker green. The leathery green leaves of the cultivar 'Variegata' are marked creamy yellow. ZONE 8.

GYMNOCLADUS
Caesalpiniaceae

Grown for their large, handsome leaves and for shade, the 2 deciduous trees of this genus come from North America and East Asia. The seeds and pods of different species have been used for soap and as a coffee substitute. Cool-climate plants, they require full sun and well-drained, fertile soil. They are propagated from seed in autumn, though only female trees bear fruit.

Gymnocladus dioica
KENTUCKY COFFEE TREE

From moist woodland areas of eastern USA, this slow-growing, deciduous tree has an attractive spreading habit, growing to a height of 65 ft (20 m) and 50 ft (15 m) wide. The large compound leaves, made up of oval leaflets, are pinkish bronze when young, turning dark green in summer and yellow in autumn. Fragrant, small, whitish flowers are borne in late spring to early summer and the fruit is a large, leathery, reddish brown hanging pod that persists for some time. The seeds can be roasted and ground to make a coffee-like beverage. ZONE 3.

GYMNOSTOMA
Casuarinaceae

This genus of around 20 species of attractive cypress-like trees occurs in islands of the south-west Pacific and Malay archipelago, with a single species in northern Australia. They are not conifers but close relatives of *Casuarina*, in which genus they were formerly included. The genus is distinguished from *Casuarina* and *Allocasuarina* by having only 4 tiny, scale-leaves at each joint of the slender needles, and by the long 'beaks' radiating from the cone-like structures that hold the seeds. One or two species are planted for ornament and shade in wetter parts of the Asian tropics, and the Australian species is becoming known in cultivation in that country. They prefer sheltered, humid situations and deep, moist, humus-rich soil. Propagation is from seed or cuttings.

Gymnostoma australianum

Known in the wild only from one high granite mountain near the mouth of the Daintree River in north-eastern Queensland, this is Australia's only member of the genus. It can make a small, bushy-crowned tree of around 20 ft (7 m) with age, but in gardens has so far made a neat conical shrub of up to 10 ft (3 m) with very fine, dense foliage of a rich deep green. It will thrive in gardens outside the tropics and will even cope with very light frosts. ZONE 10.

Gymnocladus dioica

Gymnocladus dioica (below)

Griselinia lucida

Gymnostoma australianum (below)

Gymnostoma australianum (below)

H

Hakea laurina

Hakea victoria

Hakea purpurea

HAKEA
Proteaceae

This genus consists of 130 species of evergreen shrubs and small trees from Australia. They are closely allied to the grevilleas and, like them, are well-regarded garden plants in their home country, though the easiest and most popular species are not always the most spectacular. They are popular in California also, though are rather frowned on in South Africa where several species have become troublesome weeds. Fast growing but not always long lived, they are happiest in mild-winter climates, sunshine and well-drained soil and dislike phosphorus-rich fertilizers. Many are outstandingly drought resistant and indeed tend to do poorly in summer-rainfall climates, especially the West Australian species. The bushier species are useful for informal hedges, those with prickly leaves being perfectly impenetrable. There is great variety in the foliage, from needle like to broad, though the leaves are always stiff and leathery; the flowers are borne in small clusters, often half-hidden among the leaves. Propagation is usually from seed; outstanding forms can be perpetuated from summer cuttings.

Hakea microcarpa

Hakea bucculenta
RED POKERS

This medium shrub from Western Australia to 18 ft (6 m) tall and half as wide has long, somewhat prickly leaves and magnificent spikes of nectar-rich orange blooms borne in winter. A useful plant for semi-arid, warm areas, it withstands moderate frosts. Given full sun and free-draining soil, it is relatively long lived, and light pruning will keep it compact. ZONE 9.

Hakea laurina
PINCUSHION BUSH

This shrub or small tree from Western Australia grows to 18 ft (6 m) tall, spreading to 10 ft (3 m), with a rather erect habit. The long, narrow leaves are grey-green and leathery. Through winter and spring its delightfully fragrant, ball-shaped, crimson flower heads appear, with long creamy styles protruding like pins from a pincushion. Useful for hedges and screens, this hakea must have perfect drainage and, if grown too fast, may become top heavy and liable to being toppled by strong winds. ZONE 9.

Hakea microcarpa
NEEDLE BUSH

This open, rounded shrub from mountain regions of eastern Australia grows to 6 ft (2 m) in height and spread. The green leaves are variable, but are usually needle shaped with sharp points. The small, creamy white flowers appear from late winter to summer; they have a honey-like fragrance and attract nectar-eating birds. This hakea is quite fast growing but does not transplant well. It requires a sunny aspect and well-drained soil. ZONE 8.

Hakea purpurea

This is a small dense shrub from Queensland, growing about 5 ft (1.5 m) high. Leaves are needle shaped, up to 4 in (10 cm) long, and are offset by clusters of vivid red flowers during winter and spring. It is indigenous to drier regions west of the Great Dividing Range in Queensland, and will flower best in full sun and well-drained, sandy soil in areas of low humidity. Once established, it is hardy both to drought and moderate frosts. ZONE 9.

Hakea salicifolia
WILLOW HAKEA

With narrow leaves like a willow and a graceful habit, this shrub from New South Wales and Queensland grows to 20 ft (7 m). Its delicate, creamy white flowers appear in spring, in clusters hiding in the leaves, and are followed by the distinctive woody fruit. It grows naturally in moist gullies as well as in shallow, dry soils, so has adapted well to a wide range of warm-climate garden conditions; in fact it has become a weed in some countries, particularly northern areas of New Zealand. Happy in full sun or part-shade, it tolerates strong winds and makes a good hedge plant as it benefits from pruning—the new growth is attractively purple tinted. ZONES 8–9.

Hakea victoria
ROYAL HAKEA

This upright, 10 ft (3 m) tall shrub from Western Australia is the most spectacular of the genus; not by reason of the flowers, which are pale pink and inconspicuous, but by its splendid foliage. The leathery leaves are shaped almost like scallop shells and display striking variegations in shades of yellow or orange on a grey-green ground, those on the long-flowering branches being the brightest. It is notoriously difficult to propagate and grow, needing a dry climate with little frost, sandy (or at least perfectly drained soil) and abundant sunshine and being difficult to transplant. Propagation is from seed. ZONE 9.

HALESIA
Styracaceae

Members of this genus of deciduous trees and shrubs are found from southern USA to Central and South America and also in East Asia in rich, moist woodlands and beside streams. They are grown mainly for their attractive bell-shaped flowers, which open in clusters as the leaves unfold, and the unusual winged fruit capsules that follow. Cool-climate plants, they prefer sheltered positions in full sun and grow best in well-drained, moist, neutral to acid soil. Propagation is from seed in autumn or from softwood cuttings in summer.

Halesia carolina
CAROLINA SILVERBELL, SNOWDROP TREE

This ornamental, spreading tree grows to about 24 ft (8 m) high and 30 ft (10 m) wide. It flowers profusely, even when young, producing masses of drooping, bell-shaped white or white flushed pink flowers in mid- to late spring as the young leaves emerge. The flowers are followed by 4-winged green fruit that ripen to pale brown. The mid-green leaves are downy when they first appear and turn yellow in autumn. ZONE 3.

Halesia monticola
MOUNTAIN SILVERBELL

A taller and more conically shaped species from the mountains of south-eastern USA, this tree is fast growing to a height of about 40 ft (13 m) with a spread of 25 ft (8 m). The pendent, bell-shaped white flowers are borne in profusion in late spring before the leaves, and the characteristic 4-winged fruit ripen in autumn. The rare var. *vestita* 'Rosea' has pale pink flowers and a white pubescence on the new growth. ZONE 4.

HAMAMELIS
Hamamelidaceae
WITCH HAZEL

These deciduous shrubs from East Asia and North America are prized for their fragrant flowers, borne on bare stems through winter, and for their autumn foliage. They are good shrubs for cool-climate gardens, preferring an open, sunny position (although they will tolerate semi-shade) in fertile, moist but well-drained loamy, acid soils. Old branches should be thinned out in spring to make way for new shoots. Propagate selected forms by grafting in winter, from heeled cuttings in summer or by budding in late summer. Species can be raised from seed, but germination may take a full year.

Hamamelis × intermedia
WITCH HAZEL

The name covers a group of cultivars derived from *H. japonica* and *H. mollis*, deciduous shrubs with oval leaves 3–5 in (7–12 cm) long that colour well in autumn. 'Arnold Promise' is the best for foliage colour. Fragrant flowers appear on bare twigs in winter. Their colour varies from light yellow to deep orange depending on the cultivar: 'Jelena' is bright orange. All cultivars are tough shrubs with a preference for moist, well-drained, humus-rich soils in dappled shade. Propagate by grafting or from semi-ripe summer cuttings. ZONE 4.

Halesia carolina (below)

Hamamelis japonica
JAPANESE WITCH HAZEL

This open, upright shrub grows to a height of 10–12 ft (3–4 m) and about as wide. Its sweetly perfumed yellow flowers with twisted petals are carried in clusters on the bare branches from mid- to late winter. Flowering branches are often cut for indoor decoration. The oval, mid-green leaves appear in spring and turn yellow before falling in autumn. ZONE 4.

Hamamelis mollis
CHINESE WITCH HAZEL

From central and western China this upright, open shrub has extremely fragrant, golden yellow flowers, borne on bare branches from mid-winter to early spring. It grows to a height and spread of 12 ft (4 m) and the large, thick leaves are mid-green above, downy beneath; they turn deep golden-yellow in autumn. 'Coombe Wood' is a cultivar selected for its slightly larger flowers. ZONE 4.

Hamamelis × *intermedia* 'Jelena'

Halesia carolina (below)

Hamamelis mollis

Hamamelis japonica

Hamelia patens

Hamamelis vernalis
OZARK WITCH HAZEL

This upright, suckering shrub is a smaller species, growing to a height and spread of about 6 ft (2 m). It flowers in spring with a profusion of sweet-smelling cream or dull yellow flowers with dark red centres. The leaves that follow are green above and greyish below, turning yellow in autumn. ZONE 4.

Hamamelis virginiana

Hamamelis virginiana
VIRGINIAN WITCH HAZEL

This witch hazel has an open, upright habit and grows to a height and spread of 12 ft (4 m) but can be readily adapted to tree-like form by training in early years to a single trunk. Small, sweetly fragrant, curled and twisted yellow flowers appear in autumn among the falling leaves. The dark green, broadly oval leaves turn a bright buttercup yellow in autumn. ZONE 2.

HAMELIA
Rubiaceae
HAMELIA, RAT POISON PLANT

This is a genus of about 40 evergreen shrubs and small trees from tropical America, of which only a few of the shrubby species are met with in tropical and subtropical gardens. They are related to the much better known ixoras—and indeed look confusingly like them—and have the same uses in the garden. The attraction is the clusters of flowers, borne over a long summer season. They prefer rich soil, light shade and plenty of moisture, and are propagated from summer cuttings. The inelegant common name comes from the poisonous nature of the fruit.

Hamelia patens
SCARLET BUSH, FIREBUSH

This dense, soft-wooded shrub grows to about 5 ft (1.5 m). The leaves are pale green with downy undersides, and the bright scarlet tubular flowers are held in clusters towards the ends of the branches in summer. The flowers are followed by yellow-green berries that ripen to purple black. ZONE 10.

HARPEPHYLLUM
Anacardiaceae
WILD PLUM

There is only one species in the genus, *Harpephyllum caffrum*. A most handsome evergreen tree, it is widely grown in subtropical climates both as a shade tree and for its edible fruit, though both male

Hamelia patens

Hamamelis vernalis (below)

Hamamelis virginiana (below)

Harpephyllum caffrum

Hebe albicans

Hebe diosmifolia

Hebe armstrongii

and female trees are needed if the female are to bear. It is a fine street tree, males being preferred as they don't drop fruit on to parked cars; but less desirable in a small garden as its shade is so dense it is difficult to grow other plants beneath it. Formerly known as kaffir plum, this is in fact no plum but a relative of the cashew nut and mango. Propagation is from seed or by grafting.

Harpephyllum caffrum

This dense, broadly domed tree grows to 40 ft (13 m) tall and about as wide, with an erect, short trunk. Its deep green, compound leaves rather resemble those of an ash (*Fraxinus*), and the inconspicuous whitish green blossoms held towards the branch tips are followed, on fertilized female plants, by small, oval fruit the size of a small plum that ripen to orange-red; these are tart tasting but make excellent jam. ZONE 10.

HEBE
Scrophulariaceae
VERONICA

The large genus *Veronica* used to contain both herbaceous perennials and shrubs, but the shrubby species (native to New Zealand and nearby islands, with a couple in Chile also) have now been given their own genus, *Hebe*. The hebes are first-rate evergreen shrubs, being neat and attractive in leaf and often showy in flower, though most are best suited to warm-temperate climates; only a few can be rated hardy in cooler places and none in cold climates. The species fall into 2 main groups: the broad-leafed hebes, fast-growing, more or less conventional shrubs with pleasing foliage and abundant spikes of small flowers in shades from white through pink to violet and blue over a long summer-to-autumn season; and the whipcord hebes, which have small leaves that give them the appearance of dwarf conifers and white or pale mauve flowers. Many of the latter are mountain plants and tricky to grow at low altitudes. That they are shy blooming in cultivation is perhaps not important, as their distinctive foliage is their main attraction. There are many garden cultivars, especially in the broad-leafed group; their ancestry is often a matter of speculation, as the broad-leafed hebes hybridize readily in gardens. As a rule, hebes like moist but well-drained soil and the broad-leafed types benefit from a post-flowering trim. In warm climates they grow equally well in sun or shade; in cooler ones sun is preferred. Propagation is easy, from summer cuttings.

Hebe albicans

This distinctive species has ½ in (1 cm) blue-grey leaves that are coated with a fine greyish, grape-like bloom. The leaves are tightly packed on the stems. Growing to about 20 in (50 cm) high and wide, it is a very neat plant that rarely needs trimming. The flowers, which appear in early summer, are white with purple anthers and are carried in short spikes. 'Boulder Lake' is a low, spreading cultivar. ZONE 8.

Hebe armstrongii

From summer to early winter this rounded, bushy, evergreen shrub bears dense clusters of tiny, 4-petalled, white flowers. One of the whipcord group, its narrow oval leaves are bronze when young and the twigs are a distinctive greenish gold. It has a height and spread of less than 3 ft (1 m). ZONE 8.

Hebe diosmifolia

A densely foliaged twiggy shrub growing 2–4 ft (0.6–1.2 m) high and 3–5 ft (1–1.5 m) wide. The leaves are small, about ½ in (1 cm) long, and are bright green. The branches tend to lie flat, creating a tiered effect. The flowers, which occur from spring to autumn, are pale mauve and are carried in short spikes near the branch tips. This species is usually compact, requiring little trimming, but is short lived and best replaced after about 10 years. ZONE 8.

Hebe speciosa 'Alicia Amherst'

Hebe odora

Hebe salicifolia

Hebe ochracea 'James Stirling'

Hebe ochracea
A whipcord species with olive-green to golden brown stems, it is most commonly represented by 'James Stirling', a particularly bright golden cultivar. The shrub grows to about 18 in (45 cm) high and 3 ft (1 m) wide. The inflorescences of about 10 white flowers are rarely seen in cultivation. Do not prune this species unless absolutely

Hebe venustula

necessary as it may lead to dieback. ZONE 8.

Hebe odora
Growing to about 4½ ft (1.5 m), this evergreen species from the South Island of New Zealand has tightly packed, neat green leaves arranged in a symmetrical pattern and spikes of white flowers during summer. Along with many others of the smaller-leafed species, it is tolerant of light frost. It does best in a protected position in full sun, with well-drained soil. ZONE 8.

Hebe salicifolia
This spreading evergreen shrub, usually to about 10 ft (3 m) tall and wide comes from New Zealand's South Island and from Chile, and is tolerant of pollution and salt winds. Of dense habit, it makes an effective screen. The waxy leaves are narrow and glossy and may be up to 6 in (15 cm) long. The fragrant flowers are white, tinged with lilac, produced in showy spikes up to 8 in (20 cm) long. Plants benefit from light pruning after flowering and old woody specimens can be pruned hard. They are easily transplanted. ZONE 9.

Hebe speciosa
This evergreen, compact shrub grows to about 3 ft (1 m) high, spreading to 4½ ft (1.5 m) wide in a broad, bun shape. It has oval, glossy foliage and bears a profusion of reddish purple flowers in terminal clusters from early summer to late autumn. This species is more prone to wilt than other hebes. Many attractive cultivars exist including 'Variegata', with creamy white leaf margins, and 'Alicia Amherst', with purple flowers. ZONE 8.

Hebe venustula
This is a tough little whipcord hebe that develops into a 3–4 ft (1–1.2 m) ball of twigs and foliage. The leaves are a light yellowish green on whippy, upright stems. The flowers, which are white to pale mauve, appear in early summer and are carried in loose clusters at the branch tips. It is a very heavy-flowering shrub. Prune lightly to shape each year after flowering. ZONE 8.

HEDYCHIUM
Zingiberaceae
GINGER LILY

Taking its name from the Greek words *hedys*, sweet and *choin*, snow, since one species has beautifully perfumed white flowers, the ginger lilies number about 40 species, originating from subtropical Asia and Madagascar. They are lush-growing, rhizomatous perennials with spathe-like leaves clasping reedy stems. Generally they prefer moist soil in a semi-shaded position. They flower in summer, and the spent stems should be cut out each season to ensure vigorous growth—or the blooms can be cut for indoor use. *H. coccineum* forms a low clump with spreading stems and narrow leaves. Erect flower spikes carry only a few flowers.

Hedychium gardnerianum
KAHILI GINGER

This plant grows to 6 ft (2 m), with long, bright green leaves clasping the tall stems. The fragrant red and creamy yellow flowers appear towards the end of summer, held in dense spikes. Propagation is by division in early spring. This species is considered a weed in some regions such as the northern areas of New Zealand. ZONE 9.

HERNANDIA
Hernandiaceae

This small genus of broad-leafed evergreen trees scattered through the wet tropics is rarely cultivated but some species have the potential to make fine ornamental and shade trees. They have rather large, often heart-shaped leaves, panicles of numerous small flowers and hard, nut-like fruit each enclosed in a hollowed reddish or yellowish structure formed from fused bracts; the structure may be a conspicuous and decorative feature. Cultivation is not difficult in humid tropical or subtropical regions. A sheltered position and deep, moist but well-drained soil are preferred. Propagation is from fresh seed.

Hernandia bivalvis
GREASE NUT

This small tree, rare in the wild in a small area of south-east Queensland, is becoming recognized in Australia as a desirable ornamental, reaching 30 ft (10 m) or more with a compact, bushy crown. In late spring it bears many panicles of cream flowers slightly above the foliage, followed in late summer and autumn by a fine show of orange to red bladder-like fruit about 2 in (5 cm) long, each consisting of 2 'valves' enclosing a large nut with very oily flesh. ZONE 10.

HETEROMELES
Rosaceae
CALIFORNIA HOLLY, TOYON

This genus consists of one species, an evergreen tall shrub or small tree that was formerly grouped with *Photinia*. Indigenous to drier regions of California, it needs full sun or part-shade and moderately fertile, well-drained soil. It is frost-tender. It is often planted as an informal screen, and can be clipped to form a tall hedge. When young it can be pruned to maintain a single trunk if a tree form is desired. A member of the rose family, its name comes from the Greek words for 'different' and 'apple tree'.

Heteromeles arbutifolia
CALIFORNIA HOLLY

This species grows to 27 ft (9 m) with thick, leathery, glossy, dark green leaves with quite sharply toothed margins. The flattened heads of flowers appear in summer; they are followed by bright red berries that persist, as they are not eaten by birds, until Christmas in its native region, hence its alternative common name, Christmas berry. ZONE 9.

HEVEA
Euphorbiaceae

A group of 9 species make up this genus which includes the rubber tree, *H. brasiliensis*, the major source of natural rubber. All members of the genus, as with others of the Euphorbia family, have a milky sap. Tropical heat and humidity are essential to the commercial cultivation of these trees although they will survive in large heated greenhouses, where they should be pruned in late winter to restrict size and maintain a neat shape. They need moist, free-draining soil and partial shade in the heat of summer.

Hevea brasiliensis
PARA RUBBER TREE

This tree reaches 130 ft (40 m) in its natural habit along the Amazon and Orinoco Rivers but elsewhere it seldom exceeds 65 ft (20 m). The thick, leathery leaves are divided into 3 leaflets and the greenish white perfumed flowers are insignificant. These flowers appear before or with new growth, which is a distinctive bronze-purple. It is rarely grown other than in commercial plantations or in botanical gardens. ZONE 11.

HIBISCUS
Malvaceae

While the genus name conjures up the innumerable cultivars of *Hibiscus rosa-sinensis*, perhaps the most widely grown and admired of all flowering shrubs in tropical and subtropical gardens, the genus is large and diverse, including hot-climate evergreen shrubs and small trees and also a few deciduous, temperate-zone shrubs and some annuals and perennials. The most important of these is *H. esculentus*, a bushy warm-climate annual whose immature fruit are the okra or gumbo so popular in Creole cooking. Easy to grow, the shrubby species thrive in sun and slightly acid, well-drained soil. Propagation is from late-summer cuttings. The *H. rosa-sinensis* cultivars make greenhouse subjects in frosty climates, and the compact-growing cultivars are gaining popularity as house plants. Grown thus, they need bright light and high humidity.

Hibiscus arnottianus

These shrubs of variable size, up to 20 ft (6 m), have long, arching canes, covered with mid-green leaves and lightly scented single flowers with 5 petals surrounding a central red column. These are warm-climate shrubs suited to full sun; they can stand neglect, but respond well to regular water and fertilizer. 'Wilder's White' is a free-flowering cultivar now regarded as belonging to this species rather than to *H. rosa-sinensis*. ZONE 9.

Hevea brasiliensis

Heteromeles arbutifolia

Hibiscus arnottianus (below)

Hedychium coccineum (right)

Hibiscus heterophyllus

Hibiscus insularis

Hibiscus heterophyllus
AUSTRALIAN ROSELLA, SCRUB KURRAJONG

This tall, evergreen shrub to 18 ft (6 m) has long, narrow, heavily veined leaves with serrated margins. Flowers, usually white or pale pink but sometimes yellow, with a darker centre, appear in summer and autumn. The flower buds and young shoots are edible, cooked or raw; however the small prickles on the stems under the leaves can cause skin irritations. It is adaptable to sun or shade in frost-free conditions, dry or moist, and can be pruned to avoid leggy growth. ZONE 9.

Hibiscus insularis
PHILLIP ISLAND HIBISCUS

Endemic to tiny Phillip Island, which lies off Norfolk Island in the south-west Pacific, this species is now close to extinction in the wild. It is a spreading shrub up to 12 ft (4 m) tall, branching low into a tangle of very woody stems supporting a twiggy canopy of fine foliage. The leaves are coarsely toothed and the 2 in (5 cm) diameter flowers appear all through autumn and winter and sporadically at other times; they open lemon-yellow with a maroon centre and age to dull pink. It is easily grown in a frost-free climate, where it is a useful shrub for exposed positions. Although naturally quite shapely, it can be pruned to a more compact size if desired. ZONE 10.

Hibiscus mutabilis
COTTON ROSE, CONFEDERATE ROSE

A multi-branched shrub or small deciduous tree with a low-branching habit, the cotton rose comes from China and grows to about 12 ft (4 m) tall and almost as wide. The large flowers open white and age from pale pink to deep pink; they appear in autumn and are held among the felty, multi-lobed, mid-green leaves. While the leaves fall, spent blooms often remain on the bush and these are best removed when pruning, by at least one-third, towards the end of winter. The hybrid 'Plenus', with its double flowers, is the most commonly grown. ZONE 9.

Hibiscus rosa-sinensis
CHINA ROSE, SHOE FLOWER

The name shoe flower is Jamaican, from the unromantic use of crushed flowers to polish black shoes. The species itself is of ancient hybrid origin from the Indian Ocean region and is a glossy-leafed evergreen shrub, sometimes as much as 15 ft (5 m) high and wide, with blood-red flowers borne just about all year. It is less often seen than its numerous garden cultivars, some pure-bred and others, like the enormous-blooming Hawaiian hybrids, carrying the blood of other species. They vary in height from 3 ft (1 m) or so to 3 times that, and the flowers can be 5-petalled singles, semi-double or fully double, the colours ranging from white through pinks to red: the Hawaiian hybrids offer yellow, coral and orange, often with 2 or 3 shades in each flower. The flowers range upwards in size from about 5 in (13 cm): some of the Hawaiian hybrids are as large as dinner plates. Each flower only lasts a day, opening in the morning and withering by evening, but they appear in long succession as long as the weather is warm. Any nursery in the tropics or subtropics will be able to offer a wide selection, and new cultivars are being introduced all the time. All like a frost-free climate, fertile well-drained soil and sun; where summers are dry they appreciate regular watering. They can be pruned for bushiness, quite hard if need be, in spring. ZONE 10.

Hibiscus mutabilis

Hibiscus insularis (below)

Hibiscus syriacus

Hibiscus rosa-sinensis, Hawaiian hybrid

Hibiscus rosa-sinensis

Hibiscus schizopetalus

Hibiscus syriacus

Hibiscus schizopetalus

From tropical Africa, this evergreen shrub grows to 12 ft (4 m) with rounded, toothed, deep green leaves and long-stemmed, pendulous, scarlet flowers; their petals are recurved and much cut, and the staminal column hangs as though on a silken thread. Pruning is not necessary as its natural, somewhat slender, drooping habit is part of this plant's charm. ZONE 10.

Hibiscus syriacus
ROSE OF SHARON, BLUE HIBISCUS

The specific name is misleading; this beautiful deciduous species is native to China. Hardiest of all hibiscus, it is of erect habit and while usually seen as a head-high shrub it can, by removal of the lower branches, be trained into a graceful small tree about 12 ft (4 m) tall. It is a very useful shrub to the temperate-climate gardener, as it flowers in great abundance from late summer and on into autumn after most other shrubs have finished blooming. The flowers are the size of a small hybrid tea rose and are borne in the axils of the leaves. They can be single or double and white, pink, mauve or lilac-blue, according to the cultivar; they almost always have red or maroon blotches at the base of the petals. Like all hibiscus, each one only lasts a day. The rose of Sharon is not fussy about soil as long as the drainage is good, though it does prefer a sunny position sheltered from strong winds. If pruning is needed, it can be done in late winter. ZONE 6.

Hibiscus tiliaceus (variegated)

Hoheria lyallii

Hibiscus tiliaceus

Hibiscus tiliaceus

Hibiscus tiliaceus
COTTONWOOD TREE, MANGROVE HIBISCUS

This evergreen, spreading tree, which occurs naturally around the shores of the Pacific and Indian Oceans, grows to a height of 30 ft (10 m) or more with a spread almost as great. It has large, heart-shaped, soft green leaves and bears scattered clear yellow flowers, with large crimson centres, that turn orange as they fade. There are cultivars with purple or variegated leaves. It flowers for most of the year, more prolifically in summer. Salt tolerant, it is an excellent coastal tree for frost-free areas, growing well in full sun in sandy soils. ZONE 10.

HIPPOPHÄE
Elaeagnaceae

These thorny, evergreen shrubs and trees are valued for their toughness and their showy autumn berries. Both male and female plants must be grown together to obtain the fruit. Indigenous to cold-climate regions of Asia, Siberia and northern Europe, they are found along the coast or river banks and in sandy woodlands. They are wind resistant and make excellent hedges for coastal areas, growing best in full sun and tolerating dry or very sandy soil. Propagation is from seed in autumn or from softwood cuttings in summer.

Hippophäe rhamnoides
SEA BUCKTHORN

Growing to a height and spread of about 18 ft (6 m) with a bushy, arching habit, this deciduous shrub or small tree has very narrow, grey-green leaves with paler undersides. Insignificant, small, yellowish flowers appear in clusters in spring, before the leaf growth. The bright orange berries are borne in dense clusters on the shoots of female plants and usually persist through winter. ZONE 2.

HOHERIA
Malvaceae

This small genus of evergreen and deciduous trees and shrubs is indigenous to the forests of New Zealand. Of slender, upright habit, they are grown for their clusters of faintly perfumed white flowers which appear in summer and autumn. Happiest in warm-temperate climates, they grow in sun or semi-shade in fertile, well-drained soils in areas with high summer rainfall. Straggly plants can be pruned by about one-third in winter and all plants benefit from a light annual pruning of the outer branches to maintain a tidy shape and abundant foliage. They are propagated from seed in autumn or from semi-ripe cuttings in summer.

Hoheria lyallii
LACEBARK

This deciduous tree is from subalpine areas of New Zealand, where it grows in thickets beside streams. Trees may grow to 18 ft (6 m) tall, and their thick and fibrous bark gives them their common name. The adult leaves are heart shaped and grey-green with a felty white underside; they are up to 4 in (10 cm) long. Juvenile leaves are smaller. The fragrant, white flowers appear in late summer and are followed by leathery, capsular fruit. The lacebark prefers soils rich in humus and is tolerant of alkaline soils. It does best in a sunny position. ZONE 7.

Hoheria populnea
HOUHERE, NEW ZEALAND LACEBARK

A fast-growing evergreen, this tree forms a slender dome about 20 ft (7 m) high. The attractive, glossy, toothed leaves resemble those of a poplar. Glistening white, 5-petalled flowers with golden stamens are borne in profuse clusters on the younger shoots in late summer and early autumn, followed by winged fruit capsules. Mature trees have distinctive, often flaky, pale brown and white bark. ZONE 9.

Hoheria sexstylosa
RIBBONWOOD

Narrowly conical in habit, this evergreen tree grows to 20 ft (7 m) tall; it has an erect trunk and main branches with drooping branchlets. Leaves are bright green and oval with sharply toothed margins. Small clusters of sweetly fragrant, star-shaped white flowers are borne abundantly in late summer and autumn, and are followed by small, brown, winged fruit capsules. When young, the plant is bushy and has more deeply toothed leaves. ZONE 7.

HOLMSKIOLDIA
Verbenaceae

This genus of evergreen sprawling shrubs is indigenous to warm-climate coastal regions from southeastern Africa and Madagascar to India. They are fast growing and generally suit tropical or subtropical gardens, but their range can be extended slightly by planting near a sheltering wall. Full sun and well-drained, fertile soil suit them best, and ideally some type of support that allows their attractive and unusual flowers to be viewed from below. They are propagated from cuttings in summer or from seed.

Holmskioldia sanguinea
CHINESE HAT PLANT, PARASOL FLOWER

Its unique flowers are the main interest of this scrambling shrub: each is a narrow, orange-scarlet tube backed by a circular calyx, appearing in dense terminal clusters through summer and autumn. The mid-green leaves are oval and slightly serrated. Its long, trailing canes make it ideal for espaliering. Rampant growth can be contained by pruning after flowering and old canes can be removed. There are also yellow and bronze-flowered forms. ZONE 10.

HOVENIA
Rhamnaceae

This genus consists of 2 species of trees from Asia, only one of which is widely grown. Graceful, deciduous trees for temperate-climate gardens, they prefer full sun and well-drained, reasonably fertile soil. Propagation is from fresh seed in autumn or cuttings in summer.

Hovenia dulcis
JAPANESE RAISIN TREE

Indigenous to China and Japan, this deciduous tree grows to 50 ft (15 m). Its large, heart-shaped leaves produce brilliant autumn hues. The summer flowers are inconspicuous and lightly fragrant and are borne in clusters on thick stalks. As the small capsular fruit ripen, the stalks become fleshy and are also edible. The fruit is sweet-tasting like raisins. ZONE 8.

HOWEA
Arecaceae

Two very similar palms make up this small genus endemic to Lord Howe Island, halfway between Australia and New Zealand. They have a smooth, ringed, single trunk and arching, feathered leaves on long, smooth stalks. Flowers are light brown (male) or green (female), borne on the same plant; held on long stalks at the base of the leaves, they are followed by small fruit. The plants are frost-tender and if grown outdoors they need moist, humid conditions and shade. Both species, but in particular *H. forsteriana*, have been popular indoor plants for many years; they tolerate less light and heat than many other palms. They are propagated from seed in spring; constant warmth is required for germination. They fruit readily in frost-free climates, but most plants are grown from seed or young plants obtained from Lord Howe Island.

Howea forsteriana
KENTIA PALM, THATCH PALM

Growing singly but in natural groves, these palms are best known worldwide as indoor plants. Outdoors in warm climates they are slow growing to about 30 ft (10 m) with a slender trunk, and can withstand coastal conditions; in strong prevailing winds they often form an attractive leaning silhouette. Most effective when planted in groups, they need to be protected from the sun when they are young. They do best in well-drained, humus-rich soil with regular mulching and fertilizer and adequate water during dry periods. ZONE 10.

Holmskioldia sanguinea

Hovenia dulcis

Howea forsteriana (below)

Hoheria sexstylosa (below)   *Hoheria populnea* (right)

HYDRANGEA
Hydrangeaceae

These deciduous shrubs occur over a wide area of temperate Asia and North America. Most species have large oval leaves with serrated edges; some develop good autumn foliage colour. The flower-clusters contain tiny fertile flowers and showy sterile ones with 4 petal-like sepals. Although most species produce panicles of flowers with few sterile flowers, many cultivated forms have heads composed almost entirely of sterile flowers and are called by gardeners mobcaps, mopheads, or hortensias. Intermediate forms with sterile flowers surrounding a central cluster of fertile flowers are called lacecaps. Flower colour may vary with the acidity or alkalinity of the soil: in acid soils the flowers are blue, in alkaline ones pink or red; white cultivars do not change. In some but not all cultivars the old flowers gradually fade to shades of green and pink, this colour being independent of soil type. The plants need shade or both leaves and flowers will scorch; and though soil should be constantly moist and rich in humus it should be well drained. Pruning is best done immediately after bloom, cutting out all stems that have just flowered and leaving the others alone. Propagate from cuttings or seed.

Hydrangea aspera

Formerly known as *Hydrangea villosa*, this species occurs naturally over much of southern and eastern Asia. In cultivation it grows to around 10 ft (3 m) high and wide. Its serrated-edged leaves vary from narrow to oval, and are 3–10 in (8–25 cm) long. The large flower heads that occur in summer are lacecap style with pale sterile flowers and tiny, purplish blue, fertile flowers. Flower colour varies little with soil type. ZONE 7.

Hydrangea macrophylla
HORTENSIA

The species itself comes from Japan and is rather rare in cultivation. The name usually covers a large race of hybrids derived from it and one or two other Japanese species. These are the best known hydrangeas, few temperate-climate shrubs matching them for their summer display of flowers. Mobcaps are the most familiar in gardens, though there are some handsome lacecap cultivars such as 'Blue Sky'. There are very many named cultivars, ranging in growth from less than 3 ft (1 m) tall and wide to twice that; 5 ft (1.5 m) is the average. As a rule, the deeper the colour the smaller the growth. ZONE 6.

Hydrangea macrophylla hybrid

Hydrangea macrophylla hybrid

Hydrangea macrophylla 'Blue Sky' (below)

Hydrangea macrophylla hybrid

Hydrangea aspera (below)

Hydrangea quercifolia in afternoon sunlight

Hymenosporum flavum

Hydrangea paniculata
PEEGEE HYDRANGEA

These large, deciduous shrubs from China and Japan grow to 10 ft (3 m) or more, with a broad, dome-shaped crown of equal width. They have large, oval, dark green leaves and in mid-summer bears small fertile cream flowers and larger flat, sterile, creamy white flowers that turn rose-purple as they age. Prune back hard in late winter or spring if larger flower heads are preferred. 'Grandiflora' is the form most commonly grown. ZONE 5.

Hydrangea quercifolia
OAK-LEAFED HYDRANGEA

Indigenous to the USA, mostly to the south-east of the Mississippi River valley, this deciduous shrub grows to a height of 6 ft (2 m), spreading to 12 ft (4 m) when conditions suit it. The deeply lobed, dark green leaves change to orange-scarlet in a spectacular autumn display. Flowers, borne from mid-summer to mid-autumn, are a mixture of small, fertile and sterile flowers. The white, sterile flowers eventually fade to pink and violet. This species does best in dappled shade. ZONE 5.

HYMENOSPORUM
Pittosporaceae
AUSTRALIAN FRANGIPANI

This genus consists of a single species of evergreen tree originating in subtropical rainforests of east coast Australia and New Guinea. A relatively fast-growing tree, it adapts to most soil types but prefers moist, humus-rich soils where it is less likely to be checked by long dry spells. It flowers best in full sun, but will tolerate some shade. The name comes from the Greek words *hymen*, a membrane, and *sporos*, a seed, referring to the winged seeds. Propagation is easily done from seed or from cuttings.

Hymenosporum flavum

Growing to 30 ft (10 m), taller in its natural rainforest environment, this tree develops a straight, smooth trunk and open, columnar shape, with widely spaced horizontal branches and dark green, glossy leaves clustered towards the ends. In spring it bears profuse clusters of very fragrant, trumpet-shaped cream flowers that age over several days to deep golden yellow. They are followed by flattish seed pods with small, winged seeds. ZONE 9.

HYPERICUM
Clusiaceae
ST JOHN'S WORT

This is a large and varied genus of herbaceous plants, shrubs and a few small trees, some evergreen but mostly deciduous, grown for their showy flowers in shades of yellow with a central mass of prominent golden stamens. Mostly cool-climate plants, they prefer full sun but will tolerate some shade. They do best in fertile, well-drained soil, with plentiful water in late spring and summer. Remove seed capsules after flowering and prune in winter to maintain a rounded shape. Cultivars are propagated from cuttings in summer, and species from seed in autumn or from cuttings in summer. *Wort* is the Anglo-Saxon word for 'medicinal plant'.

Hydrangea paniculata

Hypericum beanii

A vigorous, evergreen shrub from western China, this variable species may grow to 6 ft (2 m) tall with dense, arching branches. The mid-green leaves are usually elliptical and paler beneath. Large, star-shaped, golden yellow flowers with showy stamens appear in summer. This species is often used for bank retention, and full sun or part-shade suit it. Plants are propagated from softwood cuttings in summer and autumn. ZONE 5.

Hypericum calycinum

One of the best of all groundcovers for temperate climates, this species from Turkey is a low-growing evergreen shrub only about 15 in (35 cm) tall but spreading rapidly by creeping, runner-like stems to cover quite a large area: plants are usually set about 32–36 in (0.8–1 m) apart. The flowers, which appear at mid-summer, are about the size of a rose and very elegant with their long stamens. Any sort of soil suits and, though the plant will grow happily in the dry shade beneath deciduous trees, it flowers more profusely if given sunshine. ZONE 4.

Hypericum kouytchense

This broad shrub grows to 5 ft (1.5 m) tall, spreading to 6 ft (2 m). The golden yellow, flattish flowers with showy long styles and stamens are carried in profusion on the drooping branchlets in summer. ZONE 5.

Hypericum 'Hidcote'

Hypericum 'Hidcote'

Hypericum revolutum

Hypericum monogynum (below)

Hypericum 'Rowallane'

Hypericum patulum

This is a variable species in its native China, some forms growing about 3 ft (1 m) tall, others to 5 ft (1.5 m). It is a thin-wooded shrub, evergreen in warm-temperate climates but deciduous or almost so in cooler ones. The 2 in (5 cm) flowers are bright yellow and appear for several weeks around mid-summer. The species itself is a handsome plant, but most gardeners prefer the selected cultivars 'Hidcote' or 'Rowallane', whose flowers can be nearly twice as large. They pay the price of greater tenderness; while *H. patulum* is rated as hardy to Zone 7, these two need a sheltered, sunny spot in climates cooler than Zone 8. ZONE 7.

Hypericum revolutum
CURRY BUSH

Growing to about 8 ft (2.5 m) high, this dense, bushy shrub from south-eastern Africa has drooping branches. The dark green pointed leaves smell like curry after rain or when crushed. The large, bright yellow flowers with their masses of long golden stamens are loosely grouped at the branch tips. This shrub is easy to grow but does best in rich, well-drained soil in full sun. ZONE 9.

Hypericum monogynum

This long-flowering, semi-evergreen shrub originates from China, Japan and Taiwan. Variable in habit, it usually grows to 4½ ft (1.5 m) tall and 20 in (50 cm) wide, but there is also a low-growing form that makes a useful groundcover. The thick, rounded, leathery leaves are mid-green on their upper surface, paler beneath. The lemon or golden yellow, star-shaped summer flowers, 2½ in (6 cm) across, are crowded towards the outer parts of the plant; when spent they give way to the capsular fruit. ZONE 7.

Iboza riparia

Idesia polycarpa

Ilex × altaclarensis

Idesia polycarpa

IBOZA
Lamiaceae

Members of the mint family, these deciduous and semi-deciduous shrubs from southern Africa are grown for their sweet-scented flowers and aromatic foliage. Soft, woody, square-stemmed plants, they can be hard-pruned each year after the flowers are spent. They prefer a light, well-drained loam, though they do not put up with prolonged drought.

Iboza riparia
NUTMEG BUSH, MOSCHOSMA, GINGER BUSH

This deciduous shrub from southern Africa grows to 8 ft (2.5 m) tall and almost as wide. In winter or early spring, long fragrant panicles of tiny pale pink flowers with red stamens are borne at the branch ends. The toothed, velvet-textured, soft green leaves are spicily aromatic when crushed. It needs a sunny position, plenty of water in summer and protection from strong winds. ZONE 10.

IDESIA
Flacourtiaceae
WONDER TREE

There is just one species of deciduous tree in this genus. Indigenous to China, Korea, Japan and neighbouring islands, it is grown for its handsome foliage and fruit. To obtain the fruit both male and female plants are needed. It will grow in either sun or semi-shade. Moderately fertile, well-drained, neutral to acid soil and a warm-temperate climate suit it best. It can be pruned when young to establish a single main trunk, which will promote a well-shaped crown. Propagation is from seed in autumn or softwood cuttings in summer.

Idesia polycarpa

This fast-growing, shapely tree grows to a height of 40 ft (13 m) with a broadly conical crown spreading to 21 ft (7 m). It has most attractive large, heart-shaped, brownish red-stalked leaves, and fragrant, greenish flowers are borne in spring and summer. The female plants produce large hanging clusters of pea-sized berries that turn deep red in autumn and are not eaten by birds. ZONE 8.

ILEX
Aquifoliaceae
HOLLY

The evergreen and deciduous trees and shrubs which make up this large genus come predominantly from cool climates of the northern hemisphere. They are grown for their foliage and clusters of small glossy berries. Male and female plants must be grown together to obtain the berries. Produced in summer, autumn or winter, the berries are either red, yellow or black, and clusters of small, insignificant, greenish white blossoms precede them. Hollies grow well in deep, friable, well-drained soils with high organic content. An open, sunny position is best in cool climates. Water well in hot, dry summers. They do not like transplanting, but benefit from careful pruning in spring to check vigorous growth. Propagate from seed in spring or semi-ripe cuttings in autumn. Watch for holly aphid and holly leaf miner.

Ilex × altaclarensis
HIGHCLERE HOLLY

This group of evergreen hybrid hollies, reaching a height of about 50 ft (15 m), differ from the English holly (*I. aquifolium*) in having larger, less prickly leaves and larger flowers and berries. They have given rise to many cultivars, including 'Camelliifolia', a female with purple-tinged shoots, leaf stems and petal bases, larger berries and long leaves with only a few spines, and 'Golden King', another female with smooth-edged leaves with yellow margins. ZONE 5.

Ilex aquifolium
ENGLISH HOLLY

A valued ornamental, this is the parent plant of many cultivars. Evergreen, it is a popular Christmas decoration in the northern hemisphere with its glossy, spiny-edged dark green leaves and bright red winter berries. It can reach a height of 50 ft (15 m) and spread of about 15 ft (5 m) with an erect, many-branching habit. The most commonly grown cultivars include 'Ferox', the hedgehog holly, with more compact growth to 18 ft (6 m) and 15 ft (5 m) spread, and leaves with spines over the entire surface; 'Ferox Argentea', similar to 'Ferox' but with cream-edged leaves; 'Golden Milkboy', with variegated golden leaves; 'J. C. van Tol', 15 ft (5 m) tall with dark green, mostly spineless leaves and crimson berries; and 'Silver Queen', a male, non-berrying variety with leaves dark green in the middle with creamy white margins and grey-green in between. ZONE 5.

Ilex cornuta
CHINESE HOLLY

This dense, rounded shrub from China is self-fertile. Better suited than other species to mild-winter climates, it grows to about 12 ft (4 m) tall with a spread of 15 ft (5 m). The thick glossy leaves are almost rectangular with spiny points, and the berries, while not as profuse as on the English holly, are larger and are borne through summer, making it popular for Christmas decorations in the southern hemisphere. Plant in deep, humus-rich soil and water liberally during dry summer months. ZONE 4.

Ilex aquifolium

Ilex aquifolium 'Ferox Argentea'

Ilex aquifolium

Ilex cornuta (below)

Ilex crenata

Ilex crenata, espaliered

Ilex glabra 'Compacta'

Ilex decidua (below)

Ilex crenata

Ilex crenata
JAPANESE HOLLY

From Japan, this compact, evergreen shrub has stiff branches, small scalloped leaves, dull white flowers and glossy black berries. It is often used for densely clipped hedges and topiary. It can grow to a height of 15 ft (5 m) with a spread of 10 ft (3 m) but is usually far smaller. Cultivars include 'Convexa', almost spineless with glossy black-green leaves and purplish stems; 'Golden Gem', compact but rarely flowering, with soft yellow foliage; and 'Schwoebel's Compact', a low-spreading dwarf form to 3 ft (1 m) tall. Variegated or pale-leafed forms do best in full sun; green-leafed forms do well in semi-shade. ZONE 4.

Ilex decidua
POSSUMHAW HOLLY

From south-eastern USA, this shrub or small tree usually grows to 10 ft (3 m) high but can become tree like and reach 30 ft (10 m). It is deciduous, with a short trunk, slender pyramidal head, toothed leaves, slender stems and bright orange or red berries that last well into winter. ZONE 5.

Ilex glabra
INKBERRY

An evergreen from eastern North America, this erect shrub grows to 10 ft (3 m) with narrow, deep green leaves and glossy black fruit following the inconspicuous white flowers. There are several cultivars including 'Compacta' and 'Nordic', both ideal for hedging, and 'Ivory Queen' which is a white berried form. Seed can be used for propagating but germinates very slowly; cuttings, taken in late summer, are faster and more reliable. The species is surface rooted and easily upset by digging around its feet. ZONE 3.

Ilex opaca
AMERICAN HOLLY

The best known American species, this evergreen tree grows to a height and spread of about 30 ft (10 m); it has an erect habit and produces red berries in winter. Leaves are dull green above and yellowish underneath with spiny or smooth edges. It prefers a sunny position and does not do well near the sea. Its attractively grained wood is valued for fine cabinet-making. There are many named cultivars. ZONE 4.

Ilex paraguariensis
MATÉ

This slow-growing, evergreen tree reaches 18 ft (6 m) tall, its indented leaves deep green, the offset flowers greenish white. Deep red berries are

Ilex verticillata

Ilex opaca

Ilex verticillata

borne singly in leaf axils. In its native South America the dried leaves are used to make maté, a drink rich in caffeine. ZONE 9.

Ilex pernyi
PERNY'S HOLLY

From central and western China, this is a densely branched evergreen tree reaching a height of 30 ft (10 m). It has distinctive, diamond-shaped, triangular-spined leaves and oval red berries. Flowers are yellowish. It was named after the French missionary Paul Perny. ZONE 4.

Ilex serrata

Originating in Japan, this deciduous shrub reaches a height of 15 ft (5 m), with spreading branches, egg-shaped leaves and an abundance of tiny red berries. ZONE 5.

Ilex verticillata
BLACK ALDER, WINTERBERRY

From eastern USA, this deciduous shrub reaches a height of 6–10 ft (2–3 m). The leaves are purple-tinged in spring and turn yellow in autumn. The bright red berries stay on the bare branches for a long period. ZONE 4.

Ilex vomitoria
CAROLINA TEA, YAUPON

An evergreen tree from southeastern USA, this holly reaches a height of 30 ft (10 m) and has red berries and shallowly round-toothed leaves. Its leaves contain an emetic substance and were infused

Ilex serrata

by the North American Indians to prepare a purgative drink. ZONE 6.

ILICIUM
Illiciaceae

From the temperate to subtropical regions of East Asia and the Americas, this interesting genus contains about 40 evergreen shrubs and small trees, grown for their handsome foliage and fragrant flowers which are not unlike magnolias. The largest species, *I. verum*, is the source of star anise, a spice much used in Chinese cooking. *Illicium* species grow best in semi-shade or shade in moist, sandy, acid soil with added leaf mould.

Propagate from semi-ripe cuttings in summer or by layering in autumn.

Illicium anisatum
CHINESE ANISE

This evergreen shrub is notable for its bark, which has traditionally been dried and used for incense in Japan and China. It grows slowly to a height and spread of 18 ft (6 m) and has a conical form. The daphne-like leaves are aromatic and glossy dark green, and the fragrant greenish flowers with many narrow petals, are borne in mid-spring. The star-shaped, woody fruit are poisonous if eaten in quantity; they should not be used in cooking. This shrub prefers a sheltered position. ZONE 8.

Illicium anisatum

Indigofera decora

Illicium floridanum

Iochroma cyaneum

Iochroma grandiflorum

Illicium floridanum
PURPLE ANISE

This evergreen, bushy shrub from the southern states of the USA has spectacular star-shaped, red or purplish red flowers with numerous narrow, twisted petals, borne in late spring and early summer. The very aromatic leaves (not always pleasantly so) are deep green, leathery and lance shaped. The purple anise reaches a height and spread of 6 ft (2 m). ZONE 8.

INDIGOFERA
Fabaceae

This genus is a large one with over 700 species, and they come in just about every form imaginable: annuals, perennials, shrubs and small trees. One species, *I. tinctoria*, is the source of the blue dye indigo. Most hail from tropical and subtropical regions, with species found in both hemispheres. The cultivated species are generally subshrubs or small, deciduous, woody plants with bright green pinnate leaves and panicles of sweet-pea-like flowers, usually in summer. They tend to prefer light yet moist, well-drained soil in sun or partial shade and are propagated from seed, cuttings or basal suckers.

Indigofera decora

This deciduous shrub from China and Japan grows to 24 in (60 cm) high and wider in mild climates. The stems may die back to ground level, but the plant usually shoots again from the rootstock. The light green pinnate leaves, up to 10 in (25 cm) long, are composed of 5 to 13 leaflets. Panicles of mauve-pink pea-shaped flowers appear throughout the warmer months. ZONE 8.

IOCHROMA
Solanaceae

Members of the nightshade family, these brittle-wooded shrubs from tropical and subtropical areas of Central and South America are best suited to warm, humid climates. Usually erect, with soft-wooded, arching branches, the evergreen shrubs carry clusters of long tubular flowers in shades of blue, purple, red or white. Young plants can be pruned lightly to make them bushy, and flowered stems should be cut back heavily in early spring. Propagation is from semi-ripe cuttings or seed.

Iochroma cyaneum

This fast-growing evergreen shrub grows to 8 ft (2.5 m) high. It brings an interesting deep-purple accent to the warm-climate garden; in cooler areas it can be grown as a potted plant in a greenhouse. The felty leaves are grey-green and the tubular flowers are borne in large pendent clusters through summer and autumn. Prune to shape in early spring. ZONE 10.

Iochroma grandiflorum

Indigenous to Ecuador, this evergreen shrub or small tree grows 10–18 ft (3–6 m) high and 6–12 ft (2–4 m) wide. *I. grandiflorum* has soft, deep green, pointed oval leaves up to 8 in (20 cm) long that are slightly downy when young. The clustered flowers, which open in late summer and autumn, are long, pendent, bright purple tubes with widely flared mouths. They are followed by pulpy, purplish green, berry-like fruit. This species prefers a rich, moist soil in sun or light shade. ZONE 10.

ISOPOGON
Proteaceae
DRUMSTICKS

These small evergreen shrubs from Australia are grown in gardens for their attractive light green foliage which, though ferny in appearance, is hard and prickly—like that of so many Australian shrubs—and their globular heads of white, cream or pink flowers in spring or summer. Somewhat overshadowed by their more spectacular relatives the grevilleas and banksias, they are not widely grown even in their native land but they are plants of quiet charm. The flowers are followed by woody fruit like small pine cones, which persist on the bare, straight stems long after both flowers and leaves have died, giving rise to the common name. They need a sunny spot in a dry-summer climate free of severe frost and are propagated from seed.

Isopogon anemonifolius
BROAD-LEAF DRUMSTICKS

This is usually an upright shrub growing to about 6 ft (2 m) high and 3 ft (1 m) wide, although low-growing, prostrate forms are also seen. The leaves are similar to those of an anemone but are of a much more leathery texture. Flowering through spring, the blooms are creamy yellow and are held at the tips of the upright stems. It withstands dry periods and light frosts. ZONE 9.

ITEA
Escalloniaceae

The deciduous or evergreen trees and shrubs of this genus originate in cool-climate regions of North America and East Asia. They require sun or semi-shade and a sheltered position in cool climates. A fertile, well-drained, moist soil suits them best, and they are propagated from softwood cuttings in summer.

Itea virginica
SWEETSPIRE

An American species, this deciduous shrub is the best known of the genus. It reaches a height of 6 ft (2 m). It has an upright, slender form and is suitable for mass planting, particularly in wet, low places. Its slender leaves turn brilliant red in autumn and the lightly fragrant, greenish white summer flowers are borne in narrow, erect spikes at the ends of the stems. ZONE 3.

IXORA
Rubiaceae

From tropical regions of Africa, Asia and islands of the Pacific, this is a large genus of evergreen shrubs with spectacular heads of scarlet, orange, yellow, pink or white flowers. They need a warm, frost-free climate to grow outdoors; in the tropics they appreciate a partly shaded position, and in cooler climates they are grown in greenhouses. Humus-rich, freely drained, friable soils and high humidity suit them best, and they need regular water during the warmer months. Light pruning after flowering in autumn or late winter will maintain shape; spent flower heads should also be removed. These shrubs are used for massed bedding, hedges and screens and can be grown in containers. Propagation is from semi-ripe cuttings in summer.

Ixora chinensis

This evergreen shrub grows to 4 ft (1.2 m) tall and about as wide, its densely packed, erect branches clothed with narrowly pointed, deep green leaves. The large terminal clusters of tubular flowers are borne from spring to autumn in bright orange-red or sometimes yellow. The cultivar 'Prince of Orange' has even brighter, orange-scarlet flower heads that almost cover the bush in summer; 'Lutea' has yellow flowers. ZONE 10.

Ixora coccinea

From tropical Southeast Asia, this neat evergreen shrub reaches a height of 3 ft (1 m) with a spread of 5 ft (1.5 m). Small, scarlet, tubular flowers are borne in dense, ball-like clusters among the 4 in (10 cm) long, dark green leaves all through summer. ZONE 11.

Ixora 'Sunkist'

The cultivar 'Sunkist' originated in Singapore. It is usually under 24 in (60 cm) tall with narrow, shiny green leaves and massed heads of apricot-pink flowers which later turn brick red. 'Sunkist' likes well-drained soil and a sunny or part-shaded position in the tropical garden; it is not tolerant of frost. Best growth is achieved by pruning away half its growth after the autumn flowers have finished or in late winter. It is propagated from softwood cuttings in spring. ZONE 11.

Itea virginica (below)

Ixora coccinea (below)

Isopogon anemonifolius

Ixora chinensis 'Prince of Orange' (below)

Isopogon anemonifolius

JACARANDA
Bignoniaceae

This is a genus of about 50 species of medium-sized to large trees from Brazil and other parts of tropical and subtropical South America, all with fern-like, bipinnate leaves and bell-shaped flowers, which may be white, purple or, as in the best known species, *J. mimosifolia*, mauve-blue. The latter is one of the most widely planted and admired of all warm-climate flowering trees, though it is not happy in equatorial climates where the even temperatures and year-long rainfall do not allow it the period of dormancy it needs to flower. It can be grown in frost-free warm-temperate climates, though it never reaches the imposing size there that it does in hotter climates. It yields a richly figured timber, though as the tree is so valued for ornament it is rarely cut; the timber known as Brazil rosewood is usually that of *J. filicifolia*, a larger but less decorative species with white flowers.

Jacaranda mimosifolia
JACARANDA

A broadly spreading tree to about 50 ft (15 m) tall, the jacaranda has fern-like leaves that turn golden and are shed in early spring (rather than in autumn as is the case with most deciduous plants). A couple of months later the tree is covered in a glorious mass of mauve-blue flowers that last for just a few weeks, though there are often a few flowers in autumn. The new foliage then appears, together with round, flat seed pods that persist until the next spring. Pruning is not desirable because if branches are removed they are replaced by vertical shoots which spoil the shape of the tree. The trees are surface rooted, and this can pose problems for underplanting. ZONE 10.

JASMINUM
Oleaceae
JASMINE

The name jasmine is synonymous with sweet fragrance, though among this large genus of some 200 shrubs and vines from Asia and Africa there are many that offer nothing to the nose. The leaves are usually compound, the flowers white or more rarely yellow. Most of the species cultivated for their fragrance are climbing plants and so will not be discussed here. Some are hardy in temperate climates, though most definitely prefer subtropical to tropical ones.

Jasminum mesnyi
YELLOW JASMINE, PRIMROSE JASMINE

Originating in western China, this self-supporting, evergreen shrub grows to 6–9 ft (2–3 m) tall with long arching canes, eventually forming a wide, fountain shape. The deep green leaves are made up of 3 leaflets and bright yellow blooms (semi-double in the most usually grown form), held in leaf axils all along the branches, appear during late winter and early spring. The hardiest of the jasmines, this plant grows well in cool-temperate to subtropical areas; it needs full sun and plenty of space to display the full beauty of its arching branches. Pruning is not necessary, except to thin overgrown plants, which is best done by removing old canes at the base. Some authorities regard it as merely a form of the winter jasmine, *J. nudiflorum*, also from China and also yellow. This is smaller in all its parts and flowers in winter. ZONE 6.

Jasminum officinale
COMMON JASMINE, POET'S JASMINE

Introduced to Europe from China in the 16th century, this deciduous or semi-evergreen shrubby climber can be maintained as a neat 3–5 ft (1–1.5 m) shrub or allowed to ramble on arches, trellises or pergolas. The dark green leaves have 7 to 9 leaflets and the small clusters of deep pink buds, followed by wonderfully fragrant, starry white flowers, occur through summer and autumn. It does best in full sun and well-drained, reasonably fertile soil with ample water in warmer months. It makes an excellent container plant for a sunny terrace. ZONE 6.

JATROPHA
Euphorbiaceae

This genus consists of evergreen and deciduous shrubs, small trees and herbs. Originating in warm-temperate and tropical regions of Asia and the Americas, they have a distinctive milky sap and are grown primarily for the unusual, large, deeply divided leaves which can have 5 lobes. Flowers may be yellow, purple or scarlet, and male and female flowers are generally borne on separate plants; they are not especially ornamental. Because of their strong sculptural form, some *Jatropha* species are often cultivated as part of a collection of succulents—though they are not related. They do best in full sun but will tolerate light shade. Propagation is from seed or half-ripe cuttings.

Jatropha integerrima
PEREGRINA, SPICY JATROPHA

Previously known as *J. pandurata* or *J. pandurifolia*, this narrow-domed, evergreen tree may grow to 18 ft (6 m) tall and 6 ft (2 m) wide. The peregrina is indigenous to the West Indies and Peru. The glossy green leaves are mostly unlobed. The bright red, funnel-shaped flowers are grouped in clusters towards the ends of the branches. ZONE 10.

Jatropha multifida
CORAL PLANT, GUATEMALA RHUBARB

This shrub from Central America grows to 6 ft (2 m) tall. The large leaves, which may be up to 12 in (30 cm) wide, are deeply incised, with as many as 12 narrow lobes.

Jasminum mesnyi

Jatropha multifida

Jacaranda mimosifolia (below)

Juglans ailantifolia

Clusters of red flowers are borne on long, thin stalks high above the foliage. This plant does best in fertile, well-drained soil and a sheltered position; it tends to shed leaves as a response to both dryness and cold. The coral plant has been used as a purgative and all parts of the plant are highly poisonous. ZONE 10.

JUBAEA
Arecaceae
CHILEAN WINE PALM, COQUITO PALM

Consisting of one species of palm, this genus is named after King Juba of the old African kingdom of Numidia, though the plant itself comes from coastal Chile. The palms are now very rare in their natural habitat as they have been consistently cut for their sugary sap, which is distilled as palm wine or boiled down to make palm honey. They are slow growing when young, but once a trunk is formed growth is considerably quicker. More frost tolerant than most palms, they are widely grown in temperate climates, needing full sun and well-drained soil. Both male and female flowers are held on the same plant, so fertile seed is easily obtained; it must be sown while fresh but can take 6 to 15 months to germinate.

Jubaea chilensis

With maturity this handsome palm reaches 80 ft (25 m), with a very distinctive thick, cylindrical grey trunk topped with a dense mass of long, straight, feathery, deep green fronds. The yellowish flowers are borne in spring and are followed by fruit that look like small coconuts. The splendid specimen in the Temperate House at Kew Gardens is said to be the largest plant in any greenhouse. ZONE 9.

JUGLANS
Juglandaceae
WALNUT

Distributed from the Mediterranean region and the Middle East to East Asia, North and Central America and the Andes of South America, the deciduous trees of this genus are grown for their handsome form and elegant, aromatic foliage. Some species also bear edible nuts, and several yield fine timber used for furniture-making. Greenish yellow male catkins and inconspicuous female flowers appear on the same tree in spring, before the large pinnate leaves. They are followed by the hard-shelled nuts. Cool-climate trees, they prefer a sunny position. Deep, rich, alluvial soils of a light, loamy texture suit them best, and they need regular water. Propagate from seed, when ripe, in autumn. They make excellent ornamental trees for parks and large gardens. It is said that the fallen leaves are toxic to other plants that attempt to grow beneath walnut trees. Don't put them on the compost heap! The name *Juglans* is derived from the Latin *Jovis glans* (Jupiter's acorn).

Juglans ailantifolia
JAPANESE WALNUT

This species occurs naturally beside streams in Japan. It reaches a height of 50 ft (15 m) with grey brown bark and large, hairy, toothed, dark

Jubaea chilensis

green leaves. Catkins are greenish and the fruit is a shallow, pitted brown nut, enclosed in a sticky green husk. The husk is poisonous and is traditionally used in Japan to catch fish. The nuts are edible and the wood is used for carving and other purposes. ZONE 5.

Juglans cinerea
BUTTERNUT, WHITE WALNUT

From eastern North America, this species grows naturally in rich woodlands and river valleys. It reaches a height of 60 ft (18 m) and has grey, furrowed bark. The dark green pinnate leaves are hairy on both sides. Male and female catkins, borne on the same tree in late spring to early summer, are followed by the strongly ridged, edible, sweet-tasting, oily nuts, each enclosed in a sticky green husk. ZONE 2.

Juglans nigra
BLACK WALNUT, AMERICAN WALNUT

From central and eastern USA, this large, handsome tree is fast growing to a height of 100 ft (30 m), with a

Juglans nigra

single erect trunk and a broad, rounded crown. Greenish brown catkins appear in spring with the early leaves, followed by dark brown edible nuts enclosed in a green husk. Both the nuts and the dark-brown to blackish wood of this species are valuable commodities. The large aromatic leaves are made up of glossy, dark green leaflets. ZONE 3.

Juglans regia

Juglans regia

Juglans regia

Juniperus chinensis, as a bonsai

Juniperus chinensis 'Kaizuka'

Juniperus communis

Juglans regia
COMMON WALNUT

Believed to have originated in south-eastern Europe and temperate Asia, this slow-growing tree reaches 50 ft (15 m) tall and 30 ft (10 m) wide, and has a sturdy trunk. The branches form a broad, leafy canopy. The bark is pale grey and smooth, and the aromatic leaves are purplish bronze when young, maturing to a mid-green. Yellow-green flowers are borne in catkins in late spring to early summer, followed by the nut, enclosed in a green husk that withers and is cast off. The timber is valued for furniture and the nut is sweetly edible. Several cultivars are selected for the quality of their nuts. 'Wilson's Wonder' fruits younger than the norm, at about 7 years old. ZONE 4.

JUNIPERUS
Cupressaceae
JUNIPER

There are about 50 species of evergreen shrubs and trees in this conifer genus, distributed throughout the northern hemisphere. Slow growing and long lived, they range from small shrubs to trees big enough to be valued for their timber. Juvenile foliage is needle like, but at maturity many species develop shorter scale-like leaves, closely pressed to the stem and giving a pungent smell when crushed. Both types of foliage are found on adult trees of some species. Male and female organs usually occur on separate plants. The bluish black or reddish cones have fleshy, fused scales; known as berries, they are used to flavour gin. The fragrant, pinkish, cedar-like timber is soft but durable and widely used as shingles, weatherboards and window frames as well as for making pencils. Junipers are easily cultivated in a cool climate. They prefer a sunny position and any well-drained soil. Prune to maintain shape or restrict size, being careful not to make visible pruning cuts as old, leafless wood rarely sprouts. Propagate from hardwood cuttings in winter or from seed; cultivars can be propagated by grafting.

Juniperus chinensis
CHINESE JUNIPER

From the Himalaya, China, Mongolia and Japan, this species usually matures to a somewhat conical tree up to 50 ft (15 m) with a spread of 6–10 ft (2–3 m); but sometimes it forms a low-spreading shrub. Both adult and juvenile foliage may be found on adult trees. Berries are fleshy and glaucous white. It is a variable species with many cultivars. 'Kaizuka' forms a small tree about 18 ft (6 m) high, with twisted spear-like branches; 'Pyramidalis' has dense, blue-green leaves and a columnar habit, growing to 15 ft (5 m) in height; 'Variegata' is glaucous with white markings, growing to 18 ft (6 m). ZONE 4.

Juniperus communis
COMMON JUNIPER

From northern Europe, North America and south-western Asia, this species is either a slim, upright tree growing to 18 ft (6 m) or a sprawling shrub with a height and spread of 10–15 ft (3–5 m). It has brownish red bark and mid- or yellow-green leaves. Fleshy, greenish berries take 2–3 years to ripen to black and are used for flavouring gin. Many garden varieties have been raised: 'Compressa' is a dwarf, erect form, growing to 30 in (75 cm) tall with a spread of 6 in (15 cm); 'Depressa Aurea', a dwarf form with bronze-gold foliage, grows to 20 in (50 cm) in height with a spread of 6 ft (2 m); 'Hibernica' forms a dense column of dull, blue-green foliage when young, taking on a broader, conical shape with age and reaching a height of 10–15 ft (3–5 m) with a spread of 2–4 ft (0.6–1.2 m). ZONE 2.

Juniperus conferta
JAPANESE SHORE JUNIPER

A prostrate, spreading species from Japan, this shrub reaches a height of 6–12 in (15–30 cm) and spread of 5–6 ft (1.5–2 m). The soft foliage is a mixture of fresh, clear green and pale blue, aromatic, needle-like leaves. Berries are pale green. It tolerates seaside conditions and grows rapidly, making it a first-rate groundcover. ZONE 5.

Juniperus deppeana var. pachyphlaea
ALLIGATOR JUNIPER, CHEQUERBOARD JUNIPER

Rarely growing higher than 21 ft (7 m) with a spread of 5 ft (1.5 m), this conical small tree has a sharply pointed crown, silvery blue-grey foliage and reddish brown bark, divided into small square scales, hence the common name. It prefers a cool, dry climate. ZONE 4.

Juniperus horizontalis

A prostrate shrub, this cold-climate shrubby species from the north of North America is fast spreading and tough, and its cultivars come in a variety of attractive shades. Its branches form a mat up to 20 in (50 cm) thick of blue-green or grey leaves. 'Bar Harbor' has greyish green foliage, turning mauve in winter; 'Douglasii' has glaucous grey-blue leaves, turning plum-purple in winter; 'Wiltonii' is one of the best blue cultivars with trailing branches; 'Blue Chip' is another recently released blue-green cultivar. ZONE 4.

Juniperus deppeana var. *pachyphlaea*

Juniperus deppeana var. *pachyphlaea*   *Juniperus conferta* (right)

Juniperus horizontalis 'Wiltonii'

Juniperus horizontalis 'Blue Chip'

Juniperus × media

The name covers a group of garden cultivars, valuable in cool to cold climates for their foliage and mainly derived from *J. chinensis*. All are spreading shrubs, one or two being semi-prostrate. They have mainly scale-like, dull green leaves that have an unpleasant smell when crushed. Berries are white or blue-black. Many of the cultivars are suitable as specimen plants or groundcovers in small gardens.

Juniperus recurva

'Blaauw', a spreading shrub, grows to a height and spread of 6 ft (2 m) with blue-green foliage; 'Hetzii' has grey-green foliage and reaches a height of 10–12 ft (3–4 m) with a similar spread; 'Pfitzeriana' is broadly pyramidal with wide-spreading branches with weeping tips and grey-green leaves, to 10 ft (3 m) tall with a spread of 10–15 ft (3–5 m); 'Plumosa Aurea' has green-gold foliage turning bronze in winter, spreading branches with arched, weeping tips and reaches a height of 3 ft (1 m) and spread of 6 ft (2 m). ZONE 4.

Juniperus monosperma
REDBERRY JUNIPER, ONE-SEED JUNIPER

From south-western USA, this tree reaches a height of 15–21 ft (5–7 m) Both adult and juvenile foliage appear on the adult tree, the prickly juvenile foliage eventually being replaced by scale-like leaves. Fruit ripens to grey-blue and contains only one seed. ZONE 6.

Juniperus procumbens

This prostrate, shrubby juniper builds up to a height of 30 in (75 cm) with a spread of 12 ft (4 m). It has tufts of prickly, needle-like, bluish green foliage and brown or black berries. Its long, thick branches are held parallel to and slightly above the ground. The cultivar 'Nana' is not as vigorous and has a mat-forming habit, reaching a height of 12 in (30 cm) and spread of 5 ft (1.5 m). Some botanists consider this to be a variety of *J. horizontalis* rather than *J. procumbens*. ZONE 4.

Juniperus monosperma

Juniperus procumbens

Juniperus recurva
COFFIN JUNIPER

From Burma, south-west China and the Himalaya, this handsome shrub or small tree reaches a height of 50 ft (15 m) and spread of 15 ft (5 m). It has spreading, pendulous branches with needle-like, aromatic, grey-green or blue-green, incurved leaves. The bark is red-brown, peeling in vertical strips, and the berry is a glossy, dark purple. 'Coxii' has smaller leaves. It is fairly slow growing. The aromatic wood from this species was used in China to make coffins. ZONE 7.

Juniperus rigida
NEEDLE JUNIPER

From Japan and Korea, this cool-climate tree grows to 21 ft (7 m), though it often forms a shrub when grown in gardens. It has pendulous branches and needle-like leaves with a band of white on the upper surface. The fruit ripens through brown to blue-black. ZONE 4.

Juniperus sabina
SAVIN JUNIPER

A cold-climate species from Europe and Asia, this spreading shrub reaches 12 ft (4 m) with a spread of 10–15 ft (3–5 m) in its native mountains. It has flaking, red-brown bark and deep green, mainly scale-like leaves that have an unpleasant smell when crushed. The berries are blue-black. This conifer does well in limestone soil and is useful for covering a sloping bank. The cultivar 'Tamariscifolia' makes a broad mound about 3 ft (1 m) tall with a spread of 6 ft (2 m) and has mainly needle-like, grey-green leaves. It is much used for groundcover. ZONE 3.

Juniperus scopulorum
ROCKY MOUNTAINS JUNIPER

Slow growing to a height of 30 ft (10 m) and spread of 12 ft (4 m), this cold-climate tree has a rounded crown and scale-like, aromatic, grey-green to dark green leaves. The bark is reddish brown and peels on the branches. The berries are blue and fleshy. 'Blue Heaven' has a conical shape, growing to a height of 6 ft (2 m) and spread of 3 ft (1 m) with blue-green foliage; 'Repens', a prostrate form, is less than 8 in (20 cm) high with a spread of 5 ft (1.5 m) and has blue-green foliage. ZONE 3.

Juniperus squamata
HOLLYWOOD JUNIPER

This variable species ranges in height from 1–18 ft (30 cm–6 m) with a spread of 3–15 ft (1–5 m) depending on the variety. Needle-like green or blue-green leaves clothe densely crowded branchlets and the bark is flaky and red-

Juniperus × media 'Pfitzeriana'

Juniperus virginiana

Justicia spicigera

Juniperus squamata 'Blue Star'

Juniperus rigida

Juniperus sabina 'Tamariscifolia'

brown. The berries are fleshy and black. 'Meyeri' is a particularly beautiful form with steely blue foliage with a rich silver sheen; it reaches a height and spread of 15 ft (5 m). 'Blue Star', a dense, rounded shrub with blue foliage, grows to a height of 20 in (50 cm) and spread of 24 in (60 cm). ZONE 4.

Juniperus virginiana
PENCIL CEDAR

This tree is from eastern and central North America. It is the tallest of the junipers commonly grown in gardens, reaching up to 50–60 ft (15–20 m). Slow growing, it has a conical or broadly columnar habit and both scale- and needle-like, grey-green leaves borne on the same shoot. Berries are fleshy, small, glaucous and brownish violet. The wood is used in making cigar boxes and lead pencils. 'Glauca', a columnar form with blue-green foliage, grows to a height of 15 ft (5 m) and spread of 8 ft (2.5 m); 'Skyrocket' has a very narrow, columnar habit, reaching 10 ft (3 m) in height, with silvery blue foliage. ZONE 2.

JUSTICIA
Acanthaceae

These shrubs and woody perennials are found in subtropical and tropical areas of the world, especially the Americas, and are widely grown in gardens in most warm areas as well as in greenhouses in cooler climates. Leaves are simple and in opposite pairs, and the tubular flowers, in shades of cream, yellow, pink, orange or red, are mostly held in upright terminal spikes or clusters. Most species are frost-tender. They prefer well-drained soils in full sun or bright filtered light, and shelter from wind as many species have somewhat brittle stems. Plants can be kept neat and bushy by pinching out the growing tips. They are easily propagated from cuttings of non-flowering shoots taken in spring.

Justicia spicigera
MOHINTLI, PLUME-FLOWER

From Mexico and Central America, this erect, bushy shrub grows to 6 ft (2 m). The leaves are oval, glossy and deeply veined, and the terminal flower clusters produce a succession of orange flowers all through the warmer months. ZONE 10.

Kalopanax septemlobus

Kalopanax septemlobus

Kalopanax septemlobus

Kalmia latifolia

Kalmia angustifolia

Kalmia angustifolia
SHEEP LAUREL

This is usually an open, rather twiggy shrub that grows to 3 ft (1 m) high and 4 ft (1.2 m) wide. However, if trimmed after flowering it can be kept in a neat, compact shape suitable for shrubberies, rockeries or containers. The leaves, which are 1–2 in (2.5–5 cm) long, are bright green to bluish green. The flower heads are often carried some way down the stem (at the base of the new growth) and are usually bright reddish pink. The common name is ironic: the plant is very poisonous, though sheep are often stupid enough to eat it. ZONE 2.

Kalmia latifolia
MOUNTAIN LAUREL, CALICO BUSH

This delightful shrub, while reasonably attractive throughout the year with its leathery, deep green leaves and red-brown bark, is definitely grown mainly for its flowers. The clusters of distinctive, bright pink buds open to heads of small, pale pink flowers with stamens arranged like umbrella ribs—hard to describe but once seen, never forgotten. Mountain laurel can grow to 12 ft (4 m) but is more commonly 5 ft (1.5 m) high and wide. ZONE 3.

KALOPANAX
Araliaceae
TREE ARALIA

A genus which now contains only one species, the deciduous tree aralia is indigenous to the cool deciduous forests of China, Korea, Japan and eastern Siberia. When grown in moist, fertile soil it will develop into a good shade tree. It enjoys full sun but will also grow well in semi-shade. Propagation is from seed collected fresh in autumn or from cuttings.

Kalopanax septemlobus

Mature tree aralias develop a single stout trunk and a low-branching habit with a dense, rounded crown, and may eventually be as tall as 40–50 ft (13–15 m) in gardens. Most retain prickles on the trunk, branches and new growth. The leaves show some variation but are in general large, dark green, coarsely lobed, and may be as much as 14 in (35 cm) across on young saplings. The white summer flowers are held in large sprays radiating from the ends of branches. The small blue-black fruit are slightly split at the apex. ZONE 5.

KALMIA
Ericaceae

The kalmias are evergreen North American shrubs. They are usually very hardy and prefer to grow in a cool, moist climate in lime-free, humus-rich, well-drained soil and a position in partial shade. The 2 common species are quite different in their general appearance, but both bloom in spring and produce heads of pink flowers that open from buds that look as if they were made by a cake decorator. The flowers of *K. angustifolia* are far smaller than those of *K. latifolia*. Propagate from seed or cuttings, or by layering.

KERRIA
Rosaceae

This genus from China and Japan contains only one species, a deciduous shrub with many upright 6 ft

(2 m), deep green stems emerging directly from the ground. The leaves are 1 in (2.5 cm) long, bright green and roughly diamond shaped with finely serrated edges. The true species has simple, bright golden yellow flowers up to 2 in (5 cm) across. This is a very tough, adaptable plant that does well in any moist, well-drained soil in dappled shade. It is a good idea to give it a light trim to thin out some of the older canes after flowering. Propagate by basal suckers or from cuttings.

Kerria japonica
JAPANESE ROSE

The bright golden blossoms of this shrub, which appear in spring on lateral shoots all along the arching branches, make delightful cut flowers. The small leaves that follow, bright green and double toothed, only sparsely clothe the arching branches. Although the species is single flowered, the double form 'Pleniflora' is more common in gardens, and was introduced to European gardens nearly 50 years before the wild species was discovered! ZONE 5.

KIGELIA
Bignoniaceae

This unusual African genus contains 18 species of tropical and subtropical trees, one of which extends into northern South Africa. The compound leaves are made up of oval leaflets. The large bell-shaped flowers are borne in long pendent racemes and are mostly orange or red. They are adapted for pollination by bats. The huge, gourd-like, sausage-shaped fruit have thick skin enclosing a woody, fibrous pulp which contains many large seeds. The trees require a hot climate, full sun, well-drained soil and plenty of water, and do best in areas of high humidity. Propagation is from seed or cuttings.

Kigelia africana
SAUSAGE TREE

Growing to about 40 ft (13 m), this tree has a wide crown of spreading branches and compound leaves about 12 in (30 cm) long. In early summer the large, showy flowers are borne in pendulous sprays up to 6 ft (2 m) long. The cup-shaped flowers open at night and are crinkled and rich dark red inside but duller outside; they produce a lot of nectar but have a rather unpleasant smell which attracts the bats that pollinate them. The light brown, sausage-shaped fruit are up to 20 in (50 cm) long and can weigh over 8 lb (4 kg). Unfortunately, they are inedible. This tree needs lots of space and a tropical or subtropical climate. It grows vigorously in fertile, well-drained soil with adequate water. ZONE 10.

KINGIA
Xanthorrhoeaceae
SKIRTED GRASS-TREE

This genus of a single species is from higher rainfall areas in the south-west of Western Australia. A member of the distinctive grass-tree family of plants, it is very slow growing: the tallest plants have been estimated to be up to 1,000 years old! It thrives in sandy loam with good drainage and is happiest in full sun or light shade. Young plants can be grown in pots but larger plants resent transplanting. Propagation is from seed, which may take up to 6 months to germinate.

Kingia australis

Extremely slow growing to about 18 ft (6 m), this plant eventually forms a cylindrical, distinctively textured trunk packed with remnant leaf bases. This is topped by a dome-shaped tuft of smooth, needle-like leaves up to 2 ft (60 cm) long. The dead leaves persist for some time, hanging down like a skirt around the trunk. Creamy white flowers are clustered in ball-shaped heads on short stalks which appear in a ring among the upper leaves. ZONE 9.

KOELREUTERIA
Sapindaceae

Grown for their foliage, flowers and decorative fruit, this small genus of deciduous trees is from East Asia. They are useful small trees, mainly preferring cool climates. They thrive in full sun in fertile, well-aerated soil with free drainage. They can withstand hot, dry summers, but seaside conditions do not suit them. Propagate from root cuttings in late winter or from seed in autumn. Prune in the early years to establish a single trunk.

Kingia australis (below)

Kerria japonica 'Pleniflora' (below)

Koelreuteria bipinnata
PRIDE OF CHINA

From central and western China, this shapely tree grows to a height of 30–50 ft (10–15 m), with a single trunk and broadly conical crown. The bipinnate leaves are a clear yellow-green, turning deep golden in autumn. Bright yellow flowers, blotched scarlet at the base, are borne over summer. The fruit are like miniature Chinese lanterns, green at first then turning bright pink in autumn and paper-brown in winter. ZONE 8.

Kigelia africana

Kigelia africana

Kigelia africana (below)

Koelreuteria paniculata (below)   *Kolkwitzia amabilis*

Kunzea parvifolia (below)

Koelreuteria paniculata

Koelreuteria elegans
FLAMEGOLD TREE

Indigenous to Taiwan and naturalized in Fiji, this species is suited to most tropical and subtropical climates. It grows to 40 ft (13 m), forming in maturity a spreading, flat-topped, deciduous tree with large, mid-green, ferny, compound leaves. In late summer to autumn, long panicles of rich yellow flowers open towards the branch ends, and these are followed by bladder-like pods that split into 3 rose-hued segments. It prefers deep, well-drained soil and needs adequate water during its early years. It needs no pruning. Seeds germinate easily but plants can be variable. ZONE 9.

Koelreuteria paniculata
GOLDEN RAIN TREE, VARNISH TREE

From China and Korea, this wide-spreading, medium-sized tree reaches a height of 30–50 ft (10–15 m), though it is often rather smaller in gardens. Slow growing, it has a broad, convex crown and a single or divided main trunk. The bark is furrowed and the branches droop at the ends. The mid-green leaves turn deep golden yellow in autumn and large, showy clusters of clear yellow flowers are borne in summer; these are followed by papery, bladder-like, pinkish brown pods. This species is sun loving and does well in alkaline soil. The flowers are used in Chinese medicine and necklaces are made from the black seeds. ZONE 4.

KOLKWITZIA
Caprifoliaceae
BEAUTY BUSH

This genus consists of a single species of deciduous shrub from China, much admired in temperate and cool-climate gardens for its lavish spring display, though its foliage is undistinguished for the rest of the summer and it should be placed where other plants can attract the eye. Very easy to grow in any well-drained soil, it does well in sun or light shade. It can get very untidy if not pruned every 3 years or so, immediately after bloom; winter pruning will simply cut away the flowering wood. Propagation is from root cuttings.

Kolkwitzia amabilis

This shrub develops into a mass of upright, whippy stems to 8 ft (2.5 m) high, with small side branches. The leaves are in opposite pairs, a feature common to the honeysuckle family. They are oval, 1½ in (3 cm) long and deep green. The pale pink, trumpet-shaped flowers, which open in spring as the new leaves are developing, form profuse clusters at the ends of the side branches. ZONE 4.

KUNZEA
Myrtaceae

This Australian genus is made up of 30 species of small evergreen shrubs. Their individual flowers are simply a small fluffy bunch of stamens, but in their spring season they cover the bushes and the small heather-like leaves are pleasantly aromatic. The flowers are usually some quiet shade of white, pink or lilac, though *K. baxteri* is bright crimson. The need to grow the plants en masse to make an impact has led to their not being grown as widely as they might be, even in Australia; and some gardeners there report the bushes tend to be short lived and straggly. The straggliness can be overcome by a post-flowering trim, and old bushes are easily replaced from late-summer cuttings. They do best in mild climates, moist but well-drained soils, and light shade.

Kunzea baxteri

Growing to 8 ft (2.5 m) or more tall, this open, wiry-stemmed shrub from Western Australia is notable for the fluffy, crimson flower heads (the most richly coloured of the genus) it bears in spring and early summer. The stiff, narrow leaves are dull green, and the small fruit are red. This species tolerates light frosts and sandy, coastal conditions. It responds to light clipping or tip pruning, which is best done as the flower heads are fading. ZONE 9.

Kunzea parvifolia
VIOLET KUNZEA

This spreading shrub from cooler, hill areas of south-eastern Australia grows to about 5 ft (1.5 m) high. Often fairly open, it can be kept compact by regular clipping, making it ideal for use as a hedge. The tiny, heath-like leaves are hairy when young, and in late spring and early summer the shrub bears masses of showy, violet balls of blossoms towards the ends of branches. ZONE 8.

Laburnum sp.

× *Laburnocytisus adamii*

Laburnum × *watereri* 'Vossii' (below)   *Laburnum anagyroides* (above)

× LABURNOCYTISUS
Fabaceae

This curious small tree is the classic example of a graft hybrid, something that happens very rarely indeed; normally stock and scion remain distinct and their genetic material does not blend. It arose in a Paris nursery in 1826. It was fashionable at the time to create standard brooms by grafting *Cytisus purpureus* on to stems of the closely related *Laburnum anagyroides;* and in one plant the 2 fused to create the hybrid which has been perpetuated more as a curiosity than for its only moderate beauty. The hybrid is unstable, odd branches reverting to one parent or the other, so the trees usually show the golden laburnum flowers and the purple ones of the broom as well as the parti-coloured blossoms of the hybrid. It is propagated by grafting on to laburnum stock, and can be grown fairly easily in a sunny position in any temperate climate.

× *Laburnocytisus adamii*

This cross-generic hybrid resembles one parent, the popular golden chain tree, in overall habit, being a shrub or small tree to 20 ft (7 m) high. It has 3 small leaflets making up each compound leaf. The drooping flower heads are somewhat smaller than those of its parents and the flowers are purple, pink or bronze. It will thrive in any fertile soil in a sunny position.
ZONE 4.

LABURNUM
Fabaceae
GOLDEN CHAIN TREE

These deciduous, fast-growing shrubs and small trees from temperate regions of the northern hemisphere are grown for their attractive foliage and profuse clusters of bright yellow, pea-shaped flowers followed by brown, legume-like pods. Cold-climate plants, they prefer full sun and some humidity and tolerate any moderately fertile soil with free drainage—they do not like being waterlogged. Prune to remove competing leaders in the early years to establish a tree-like form. Watch for leaf miner, and young trees need protection from snails. Species are propagated from seed in autumn and hybrids by budding in summer. The leaves and seeds are poisonous.

Laburnum alpinum
SCOTCH LABURNUM

Originally from the Alps, Czechoslovakia and Yugoslavia, this broadly spreading, small tree can reach a height of about 20 ft (7 m). Large, dense, pendulous racemes, about 15 in (38 cm) long, of delicate bright yellow flowers are borne in spring and summer. They are followed by hairless, brown, fruiting pods containing brown seeds. The deep green leaves are smooth and glossy on the undersides. The bark is smooth and dark grey, shallowly fissured with age.
ZONE 3.

Laburnum anagyroides
COMMON LABURNUM

From the mountain regions of central and southern Europe, this small, spreading tree grows to a height and spread of 18 ft (6 m). The grey-green leaves are rather downy on the undersides. The densely clustered, golden yellow flowers are borne on 10 in (25 cm) long pendulous racemes in late spring to early summer, and are followed by hairy brown pods containing black seeds. ZONE 3.

Laburnum × watereri 'Vossii'
VOSS LABURNUM

A hybrid between common and Scotch laburnum, this spreading tree reaches a height and spread of 30 ft (10 m). It has thicker foliage than its parents and produces longer sprays of richer buttercup-yellow flowers up to 20 in (50 cm) in length. The fruit is sparsely produced, with only a few in each cluster. It is the cultivar most commonly seen in nurseries. ZONE 3.

LAGAROSTROBOS
Podocarpaceae
HUON PINE

This genus contains a single species of evergreen conifer, endemic to the cool, moist forests of south-western Tasmania. The Huon pine requires a mild climate with high year-round rainfall, high humidity and warm summers, and does best in deep, rich, well-drained, moist soils. Tolerant of shade, it needs protection from drying winds. The fine, fragrant, pale yellow wood is highly prized, used for turning and considered an excellent timber for shipbuilding. It is propagated from seed (if available) or cuttings.

Lagarostrobos franklinii

This species was formerly known as *Dacrydium franklinii*. The tree lives for hundreds of years in cool-temperate rainforest but is unfortunately becoming scarce in the wild. Extremely slow growing, it reaches a height of 50–80 ft (15–25 m) and spread of 12–18 ft (4–6 m) and is conical in shape, with slim, pendent, grey branches covered in fine, scale-like, dark green leaves. The bark is smooth, silvery to grey-brown. On female trees, the small, erect seed cones appear near the ends of the branches by autumn. It makes an excellent, long-lasting container specimen. ZONE 8.

LAGERSTROEMIA
Lythraceae

From East and Southeast Asia and some islands in the western Pacific, these evergreen and deciduous shrubs and small trees are grown in warm and hot climates for their showy flowers. They are excellent garden plants and are easily grown. They thrive in freely drained, fertile soil, preferably with high organic content. They need shelter from strong summer winds, which will destroy the delicate flowers. Propagation is from semi-ripe cuttings in summer or from seed in spring. Watch for powdery mildew. The timber of some species is highly prized for shipbuilding.

Lagerstroemia indica
CRAPE MYRTLE, PRIDE OF INDIA

Of neat appearance, this deciduous small tree or large shrub grows up to 20 ft (7 m) tall with an open, spreading, rounded head. In mid- to late summer it bears large clusters of frilly flowers in tones of white, pink, lilac or dark purplish red. The flower heads appear at the tips of the current season's growth; this gave rise to the practice of severe pruning to promote large, elongated flower heads, but if left unpruned the tree develops an attractive, open shape with massed smaller heads. In cooler areas the small, oval leaves turn shades of gold in autumn. Older plants are prone to attack by powdery mildew in areas of high humidity, but newer cultivars seem to have overcome this problem. Crape myrtles prefer an open, sunny position and well-drained, fertile soil. 'Eavesii' has an open, broader habit and pale mauve flowers; 'Petite Snow', of dwarf habit, has white flowers; 'Ruby Lace' has extremely frilly, deep red blooms. ZONE 6.

Lagarostrobos franklinii

Lagerstroemia indica (below)

Lagerstroemia indica, as a bonsai

Lagarostrobos franklinii (below)

Lagerstroemia indica (below)

Larix decidua

Larix decidua

Lagerstroemia speciosa
QUEEN'S FLOWER

A deciduous tree from the humid jungles of India, Sri Lanka and Burma where its timber is highly prized, this species can reach a height of 80 ft (25 m) in the wild, with a single trunk and a spreading broad head. It has long, leathery leaves that turn copper-red in autumn before falling. Very showy panicles of large, rose-pink to lilac and lavender-purple flowers are borne from summer through to autumn. The bark is shed in irregular patches, giving the smooth grey trunk an attractive yellowish, mottled appearance. ZONE 11.

LAGUNARIA
Malvaceae
NORFOLK ISLAND HIBISCUS, WHITE OAK

This genus consists of a single species, indigenous to the warm east coast of Australia as well as Norfolk and Lord Howe islands off the coast. A densely foliaged tree of neat proportions, it is well suited to seaside situations as its leathery, grey-green foliage seems to be immune to salt spray; it is often planted as a street tree there. The seed pods of this plant contain spicules, or tiny needles, which can cause extreme skin irritation—hence another common name, cow-itch tree.

Lagunaria patersonia

Usually seen as a neat, pyramid-shaped tree reaching to 40 ft (13 m) high, this warm-climate evergreen has somewhat oval, leathery leaves with a whitish bloom on the undersides. The pale to bright pink flowers that appear in the leaf axils during summer look like small hibiscus (to which they are closely related), with 5 reflexed petals surrounding a central column of stamens. It needs full sun, well-drained soil and adequate water; it tolerates occasional light frosts once established. Pruning is not usually necessary. It is propagated from seed, but take care when handling the seed pods. ZONE 10.

LARIX
Pinaceae
LARCH

From cool mountainous regions of the northern hemisphere, these deciduous, fast-growing conifers are grown for their handsome, graceful form and fresh green spring foliage as well as for their valuable timber. Mainly conical in shape, they lose their leaves in autumn, bursting into leaf in early spring. At this time too they bear bright red or purple-red female 'flowers'. The cones are erect and persist on the tree after shedding their seeds. Cold- to cool-climate plants, they do best in well-drained, light or gravelly soils; most species resent waterlogged soils. Propagation is from seed. Larches are prone to several diseases, including larch canker or blister and infestation by larch chermes (a type of aphid). The strong, durable timber is used for many purposes; the bark has been used for tanning and dyeing.

Larix decidua
EUROPEAN LARCH

From the mountains of central and southern Europe, this tree reaches a height of 100 ft (30 m); it has a conical crown when young, spreading with maturity. Branches are widely spaced and the branchlets

Larix decidua

Lagerstroemia speciosa (below)   *Lagunaria patersonia*

Larix kaempferi

Larix kaempferi

have a graceful, weeping habit. The soft, bright green, needle-like leaves turn yellow in autumn before falling. In spring, with the new foliage, the tree bears both drooping, yellow male flowers and upright, red female flowers. The cones are egg shaped, brown and upright. The grey bark becomes red-brown, fissured and scaly with age. This cold-climate species is valued for its durable timber and is also a source of turpentine. ZONE 2.

Larix gmelinii
DAHURIAN LARCH

From north-eastern Asia, this cold-climate tree reaches 100 ft (30 m) in the wild. Red and green female flowers and yellow-green male flowers appear in spring, the female flowers ripening through summer to a purple cone that finally turns brown. It has needle-like foliage and dark, reddish brown bark, broken into long scales. The branchlets are usually covered in fine hairs. ZONE 2.

Larix kaempferi
JAPANESE LARCH

This cool-climate species from Japan is widely used in forestry in Britain. Broadly conical, it is fast growing to a height of 100 ft (30 m) and spread of 30 ft (10 m). Its soft, needle-like leaves are grey-green to blue-green and it bears drooping yellow male flowers and creamy or pinkish upright female flowers in spring. The cones are egg shaped and upright, and the bark is reddish brown and scaly; on older branches it is orange-red. This is probably the most widely grown larch for ornamental landscape use. ZONE 4.

Larix kaempferi, dwarfed

Larix laricina
TAMARACK

A smaller species with a narrowly conical shape, this cool-climate tree reaches a height of 60–80 ft (18–25 m). Widely distributed through Alaska and Canada and south to Pennsylvania, it is most abundant in swampy areas, tolerating wet, peaty soils. Its timber has been used for telegraph poles and railway sleepers. The blue-green, needle-like foliage turns yellow in autumn and the drooping yellow male flowers and upright red female flowers are smaller than those of the other larches. The small, brown, upright cones have smooth scales and the bark is scaly and pinkish to reddish brown. ZONE 2.

Larix potaninii
CHINESE LARCH

From cool climates of western China, where it is the most important timber tree, and Tibet, this smaller species reaches a height of 60–70 ft (20–22 m). It bears greenish yellow male flowers and pink and green female flowers. The cones have shiny brown scales and long bracts. The needle-like foliage appears on rather stout shoots and has a strong, distinctive smell when crushed. The bark is dark, pinkish grey with scaly cracks. It is a similar looking tree to the European larch. ZONE 4.

LAURUS
Lauraceae

Two evergreen trees from the Mediterranean region and Atlantic islands make up this genus, grown for their highly aromatic leaves which are used in cooking. Cool- to warm-climate plants, they are moderately frost-hardy and do best in sheltered positions in sun or semi-shade in fertile, well-drained soil. They are valued as dense, evergreen screen plants and patio tub specimens;

Larix potaninii

Larix gmelinii

often used for topiary, they are tolerant of coastal conditions. Propagation is from seed in autumn or from semi-ripe cuttings in summer.

Laurus azorica
AZORES BAY, CANARY ISLAND BAY

Similar to the bay laurel (*L. nobilis*), this species is a large evergreen tree

Lavandula dentata

Laurus nobilis

Laurus nobilis

aromatic when crushed. It produces small, star-shaped, fragrant yellow flowers in spring, followed by small, round green berries that ripen to dark purplish black in autumn. This tree is particularly suited to clipping and shaping. 'Aurea' is a yellow-leafed form. ZONE 7.

LAVANDULA
Lamiaceae

These fragrant, evergreen, aromatic shrubs occur naturally from the Mediterranean region through the Middle East to India. Cultivated in southern Europe and elsewhere for the perfume industry, they are also valued for their attractive, silvery, lacy, fragrant foliage. Most species grow to 2–3 ft (60–90 cm) high and about as wide. The small mauve-purple flowers, held in silvery bracts, are borne in erect spikes above the foliage, mostly in spring. *L. angustifolia* and *L. stoechas* have oil glands at the base of the flowers that produce the pleasantly pungent oil of lavender used in the perfume industry. They prefer full sun and fertile, well-drained, alkaline soil. Excellent as low hedges, a light trim after blooming keeps them neat. They are propagated in summer from cuttings.

Lavandula angustifolia
ENGLISH LAVENDER

This dense, bushy, evergreen shrub from the Mediterranean region of southern Europe grows to about 24 in (60 cm) tall with narrow, furry, grey leaves. It is grown mainly for the long-stemmed heads of purple, scented flowers that appear in spring and through the warm months; these are easily dried for lavender sachets, pot pourri and the like. It makes an attractive low hedge and can be trimmed after flowering. There are a number of selected cultivars, of which 'Munstead' and the dwarf 'Hidcote' are outstanding. ZONE 6.

Lavandula dentata
FRENCH LAVENDER

The densely packed, soft spikes of tubular, mauve-blue flowers remain on this shrub from autumn through to late spring. The aromatic leaves are bluntly toothed, fern like and grey-green. It grows to a height and spread of about 3 ft (1 m). *L. dentata* is drought resistant and adaptable to most soils; it prefers full sun. It is often used as an edging plant, to soften the harsh lines of paving. ZONE 8.

Lavandula latifolia
SPIKE LAVENDER

This dwarf species grows as a rounded clump 30 in (75 cm) high and wide, its grey stems and foliage

up to 65 ft (20 m) high. Its flowers are a mass of yellow filaments, ½ in (1 cm) long and carried in clusters of 5 to 9 blooms. The flowers are followed by small black berries. The leaves, which are evergreen, are elliptical and up to 6 in (15 cm) long. It grows best in moist, well-drained soil in sun or part-shade. It is propagated from seed or cuttings. ZONE 8.

Laurus nobilis
SWEET BAY, BAY TREE, BAY LAUREL, LAUREL

An evergreen, broadly conical tree, this species grows up to 37 ft (12 m) high and 30 ft (10 m) wide, but is generally smaller in cultivation. Its glossy, dark green leaves are smooth and leathery and highly downy and fragrant. The heavily scented, dark purple flowers appear in spikes throughout summer. Its compact form makes it an ideal specimen for containers and low hedges. ZONE 7.

Lavandula stoechas
SPANISH LAVENDER, BUSH LAVENDER

This species has pine-scented, narrow, silvery green leaves with edges that curl inwards. A small, neat shrub 2 ft (60 cm) high and spreading to 3 ft (1 m) wide, it is covered with spikes of deep purple flowers in late spring and summer. Several bracts at the apex of each spike are elongated into pinkish purple petal shapes. It is also known as Italian lavender, though it is indigenous to Spain and Portugal. Not particular as to soil, it does need regular water and protection from frost. ZONE 7.

LAWSONIA
Lythraceae
HENNA, MIGNONETTE TREE

This genus consists of one species: a variable, somewhat open, evergreen shrub or small tree. Widely distributed in hot, semi-arid regions of northern Africa and southwestern Asia, it is cultivated for the orange dye called henna which is obtained from its crushed leaves. Hindu women in India traditionally use it to stain the palms of their hands and the soles of their feet for religious purposes. The tree requires a tropical or subtropical climate, full sun and well-drained soil. Light pruning in late spring encourages dense, more compact foliage. Propagation is from seed or cuttings.

Lawsonia inermis
HENNA

This evergreen shrub grows 12–25 ft (4–8 m) tall and has a loosely branching habit. Its grey twigs are covered with fine silvery grey-green foliage and the small,

Lavandula stoechas (below)

fragrant flowers, white, pink or red, are borne in terminal panicles. The fruit are tiny capsules. ZONE 11.

LEPIDOZAMIA
Zamiaceae

Two of this genus of 4 cycad species exist only as fossils, while the remaining pair are indigenous to forests of Australia's north-east. One species, *L. hopei*, with dark green frond-like leaves radiating from the crown of a slow-to-develop trunk, is among the taller growing cycads and may eventually reach 37 ft (12 m). Attractive garden and container plants in warm climates, they tolerate an occasional light frost, transplant easily and are best planted in the shelter of taller trees as the leaves tend to become faded and yellowish in full sun.

Lepidozamia peroffskyana
PINEAPPLE ZAMIA

Named for a Russian patron of botany, the pineapple zamia will, with time, become an erect tree to 20 ft (7 m), but it is more commonly seen in gardens with no trunk or a very short one. The glossy, bright green fronds are about 5 ft (1.5 m) long. The huge female cones, up to 30 in (75 cm) long, are a distinctive feature of this highly ornamental plant. (Both male and female plants are needed to produce fertile seed.) Pruning is not necessary, but allow for the mature spread of the palm-like fronds when deciding where to plant it. ZONE 10.

LEPTOSPERMUM
Myrtaceae
TEA-TREE

This genus of about 30 species of evergreen shrubs, sometimes small trees, from Australia and New Zealand, has no relation to the tea (*Camellia sinensis*) whose leaves are brewed into the familar drink; the name tea-tree arose because early sailors and settlers used the aromatic leaves as a substitute. (Captain Cook, seeking a remedy for scurvy in the South Seas, was the first to use them.) They are mainly upright growers with small, sometimes prickly leaves and 5-petalled flowers, mostly white or pale pink, in late spring or summer. They are widely grown in their native countries for their rapid growth, pretty flowers and graceful habit and are popular in California as well, where some

Lavandula latifolia

Lavandula angustifolia 'Munstead'

Lepidozamia peroffskyana (below)

very attractive cultivars with double flowers in shades from white to red have been developed, mostly from the red-flowered New Zealand form of *Leptospermum scoparium*. They all like a mild-winter climate and sunshine; most are drought resistant and some are outstanding seaside plants. They rarely need pruning and are propagated from summer cuttings.

Leptospermum scoparium 'Red Damask'

Leptospermum scoparium 'Ruby Glow'

Leptospermum laevigatum (below)

Leptospermum laevigatum
COAST TEA-TREE

Growing naturally in the sand dunes along much of the east coast of Australia, this tall, bushy shrub or small tree bears attractive small white flowers in spring and early summer. The evergreen leaves are small, oval and grey-green. Preferring moist, well-drained soil, it grows to about 20 ft (7 m) tall, with a spread of about the same and a trunk that becomes gnarled with age, especially when buffeted by salt-laden winds. It is an excellent plant for seaside areas, but not in South Africa where it has become a much-hated weed. ZONE 9.

Leptospermum petersonii
LEMON-SCENTED TEA-TREE

This evergreen shrub or small tree, indigenous to the eastern states of Australia, bears drifts of snow-white, 5-petalled flowers in spring and early summer. The narrow, lance-shaped leaves have a characteristic lemony scent when crushed; new foliage is bronze-red. It prefers light to medium, well-drained soil and does best in an open, sunny position. Drought-resistant but frost-tender, *L. petersonii* grows to a height of about 15 ft (5 m) and a spread of 8 ft (2.5 m). ZONE 9.

Leptospermum scoparium
MANUKA, TEA-TREE

This species occurs throughout New Zealand and also in the far south-east of Australia (mainly Tasmania). Since it was introduced to the British Isles and America last century, many popular hybrids have been developed. The species is an adaptable plant to 10 ft (3 m) tall with mainly erect growth, broadly needle-like foliage and sweetly scented, white or pale pink flowers. Among the many cultivars are 'Red Damask', with double crimson blooms; 'Abundance', with salmon-pink double flowers in winter; and 'Ruby Glow', with dark foliage and double, dark red blooms over winter and spring. Among the smaller growing hybrids are 'Kiwi' with red flowers and 'Pink Pixie' with pink blooms. ZONE 8.

LESPEDEZA
Fabaceae

Named for an 18th-century Spanish governor of Florida, this genus incorporates 40 species of perennial shrubs or herbs from across the tropics, including one species from northern Australia. Leaves are made up of 3 leaflets while flowers are held in long bunches. They are suited to a wide range of soil types, as long as good drainage is assured, and do best in a sunny position in warmer areas where cold winters will not cut them back. Mulch well, especially at the limit of hardiness, and prune to rejuvenate in spring.

Lespedeza thunbergii
BUSH CLOVER

An erect, open subshrub growing to 3–6 ft (1–2 m), this species has bright green leaves consisting of 3 narrow leaflets. The pendulous, rose-purple flowers appear in late summer and are followed by flattish seed pods. The cultivar 'Alba' bears white flowers. ZONE 4.

Lespedeza thunbergii

Leptospermum petersonii (below)

Leucadendron eucalyptifolium

Leucadendron argenteum

LEUCADENDRON
Proteaceae

This genus, indigenous to southern Africa, contains about 80 species of evergreen shrubs grown for their colourful foliage and flower heads. Male and female flowers are borne on separate plants; the female flowers are woody cones and the male are a mass of stamens. The flowers are quite undistinguished, but the bracts (modified leaves) that surround them are often richly coloured mainly in winter and spring, as are the stiff, upward-pointing leaves. Long lasting, they are prized as cut flowers. Frost-tender, they do best in full light and perfectly drained, sandy, peaty soil, preferably with low phosphates and nitrogen. Potted specimens should be well watered in periods of growth, less at other times. They are propagated from cuttings or seed.

Leucadendron argenteum
SILVER TREE

Indigenous to South Africa and growing to around 18 ft (6 m), the silver tree is very upright, developing a stout trunk with age. Its many branches are clothed with long, quite hairy, silver leaves that complement the silvery bracts surrounding the insignificant flowers in autumn and winter. This is a plant for a dry summer climate with low humidity; it needs full sun and well-drained, sandy soil. Cutting long stems for indoor decoration is sufficient pruning. ZONE 9.

Leucadendron comosum
YELLOW-BUSH

Endemic to the mountains in South Africa's southern and eastern Cape Province, this shrub grows to 5 ft (1.5 m) high and wide. The leaves of the male plants are narrow, almost needle shaped, while the female leaves are much wider. Flower heads are red, the surrounding bracts light green or yellow. Like all species, it needs acid soil and very good drainage. It grows very easily from seed. ZONE 9.

Leucadendron eucalyptifolium

This vigorous species is common in the wild in the coastal ranges of Cape Province, growing in deep sandy soils. It makes an erect shrub up to 15 ft (5 m) tall with a single trunk at the base and a dense, bushy crown. Despite the name, the narrow leaves are no more eucalyptus like than those of many other members of the protea family. In winter and spring it carries a profusion of small flower heads with long narrow bracts of a bright butter-yellow surrounding the cream knob of flowers. It is one of the most easily grown species, valuable for cut-flower production. ZONE 9.

Leucadendron argenteum

Leucadendron argenteum

Leucospermum 'Scarlet Ribbons'

Leucadendron tinctum

Leucadendron 'Safari Sunset'

Leucadendron 'Safari Sunset'

Leucadendron 'Safari Sunset'

A hybrid between *L. salignum* and *L. laureolum*, 'Safari Sunset' was developed in New Zealand where it is much grown for cut flowers. A vigorous, erect shrub, it grows rapidly to about 5 ft (1.5 m) with a densely branched, bushy habit. The deep green oblong leaves are flushed with red, and the stems and bracts are a deep wine red at the height of the autumn to winter flowering season; these turn pale to golden yellow as the season progresses. Full sun is needed for maximum colour. ZONE 9.

Leucadendron salignum

This evergreen shrub growing to about 3 ft (1 m) has many erect, branching stems holding bright green leaves that can become quite yellow during spring. Tiny, insignificant flowers are surrounded by long-lasting yellow bracts over the cooler months. These plants like a warm climate but will not tolerate humidity; they need full sun and free-draining soil that is not too rich. ZONE 9.

Leucadendron tinctum
TOLBOS

This evergreen shrub grows to about 3 ft (1 m) tall and wide, and both male and female flower heads are beautiful. The female cones are dark red, the males yellow, and both are enclosed by bright pinkish to reddish bracts. *L. tinctum* grows wild in southern and eastern Cape Province and is a popular garden specimen in South Africa, thanks to its beauty and tolerance of wind and some frost. ZONE 9.

LEUCOSPERMUM
Proteaceae
PINCUSHION

There are about 50 species of these evergreen shrubs, all from South Africa. Their flowers are borne in globular clusters, the projecting styles giving the whole inflorescence the appearance suggested by the common name. Long lasting and often brilliantly coloured, they are favourite cut flowers, both in South Africa and elsewhere where a mild winter and rather dry but not too hot summer provides the conditions needed for their successful cultivation. They are much grown in Australia, in the highlands of Hawaii from where they are exported to the flower shops of the USA, and in Israel whose crop goes to the markets of Europe. However, the florists usually sell them as 'proteas' rather than accustom their buyers to the long Greek name which means a white seed, from the shining seed vessels. They are mostly compact, attractive bushes full of flowers, the only pruning needed to keep them so being the cutting of the flowers. They bloom mainly in late spring, need well-drained soil and sunshine and are propagated from cuttings or seed, or by grafting, the best way to perpetuate the attractive hybrids now being produced.

Leucospermum cordifolium

Growing to 3–6 ft (1–2 m) tall with a spread of about 3 ft (1 m), this species has a well-branched habit with sturdy flowering branches bearing grey-green, very broad leaves and terminal flower heads. These distinctive, dome-shaped blooms in yellow and red tones are held over a long period through summer. 'Red Sunset', a hybrid with *L. lineare*, bears red and gold flowers in spring. ZONE 9.

Leucospermum erubescens

A somewhat rare species in the wild, *L. erubescens* is restricted to the Langeberg mountains east of Cape Town where it grows on dry rocky hills. It is an erect, rather stiff shrub up to 6 ft (2 m) high with narrow, blunt leaves toothed at the apex. From late winter to early summer it produces clusters of flower heads at the branch tips, opening honey-yellow but aging dull pink. This is only one of many beautiful *Leucospermum* species that await more general cultivation. ZONE 9.

Leucospermum reflexum
ROCKET PINCUSHION

This species makes an erect shrub up to 10 ft (3 m) with a spread of about 6 ft (2 m). The small, silvery leaves are clasped to the stems in a compact manner while the terminal salmon-red, yellow-tipped, spiky, reflexed flowers are borne profusely through spring and summer. This is a plant for the larger garden, where full sun and well-drained soil can be assured. ZONE 9.

Leucosperum tottum
FIREWHEEL PINCUSHION

This dense shrub grows to about 5 ft (1.5 m) high and wide. Its long, narrow, grey-green, elliptical leaves are covered with fine, short hairs. The dome-shaped flower heads, which are 3–4 in (7–10 cm) wide, open in spring and summer. The flower head is scarlet with numerous cream styles radiating from the central boss. It grows best in gritty, well-drained soil in full sun. It is not easy to propagate—seed often germinates well only to be killed by fungal diseases. Early autumn cuttings are the most likely to strike. 'Scarlet RIbbons' is a cross between *L. tottum* and *L. glabrum*. 'Golden Star', a cross between *L. tottum* and *L. cordifolium*, has light yellow flowers on long slender stems. Its flowering time can be extended to mid-winter when no other species are in bloom—which enhances its value as a cut flower. ZONE 9.

LEUCOTHÖE
Ericaceae

This genus containing about 50 species of deciduous and evergreen shrubs is widely distributed in cool- to warm-climate regions from southern USA to South America, with a few in East Asia. They have simple, alternate leaves and produce white or pink flowers in short axillary or terminal spikes. The fruit is a small capsule containing many seeds. *Leucothöe* species prefer moist, acidic, well-drained soil and a sheltered position in sun or part-shade. Propagation is from seed, cuttings or from the suckering root sections of the plant, or by division.

Leucothöe fontanesiana
PEARL FLOWER, FETTERBUSH

Indigenous to south-eastern states of the USA, this evergreen shrub grows to about 3–5 ft (1–1.5 m). The arching stems bear dark green, leathery leaves and pendulous spikes of small, bell-shaped white or pinkish flowers through spring. A very popular cultivar is the variegated 'Rainbow' or 'Golden Rainbow'. ZONE 6.

Leucospermum reflexum

Leucothöe fontanesiana

Leucosperum tottum (below) *Leucospermum cordifolium* (above) *Leucospermum erubescens* (below)

LIBOCEDRUS
Cupressaceae

These evergreen trees and shrubs, belonging to the cypress family, are from high-rainfall areas of New Zealand and New Caledonia. They have short, needle-like juvenile leaves and scale-like adult ones. Male and female cones appear on small branchlets arranged in flattened sprays on the same tree. Hardy, cool-climate plants, they prefer a sheltered position and fertile, moist soil. Their pleasantly aromatic timber is valued in building and for making pencils. Watch for dry rot. Propagate from seed.

Libocedrus plumosa
KAWAKA

From New Zealand, this narrowly upright conifer grows very slowly to a height of 37 ft (12 m) with a spread of about 8 ft (2.5 m). It has tiny, bright green scale-leaves on flattened, fern-like branchlets. The bark is stringy and the timber is deep red and beautifully grained. An excellent lawn specimen, it does well in containers. ZONE 8.

LIGUSTRUM
Oleaceae
PRIVET

For many temperate-climate gardeners the words 'hedge' and 'privet' are synonymous, but this genus of some 50 or so species from temperate Europe and Asia offers more than simply the ability to grow in almost any soil or position and to take the shears without protest; some species are in fact rather decorative. They range from shrubs to small trees, some evergreen, others deciduous; all grow very rapidly and bear abundant sprays of small white flowers in spring, almost always scented though sometimes unpleasantly. They follow up with black berries which can look very striking against the gold-splashed leaves of the variegated cultivars. Birds dote on these and can easily overpopulate the whole district with privet seedlings. The roots are very greedy, usually making growing anything else within their reach a frustrating exercise. Privets grow all too easily from seed but selected varieties need to be propagated from cuttings.

Ligustrum japonicum
JAPANESE PRIVET

This bushy evergreen shrub, with a dense habit, reaches 10 ft (3 m) tall with a spread of 8 ft (2.5 m). It has oval, glossy dark green leaves and bears large panicles of small white flowers from mid-summer to early autumn, followed by blue-black berries. It can be used as a hedge plant. The form 'Rotundifolium' is dense and slow growing, with thick rounded leaves. ZONE 6.

Ligustrum lucidum
COMMON PRIVET

An evergreen, upright shrub or tree, widely used as a tall hedging plant and, its lower branches trimmed, as a street tree where nothing else grows, this species can reach 30 ft (10 m) in height with a spread of 25 ft (8 m). Large panicles of small white flowers are borne among the glossy, dark green leaves in late summer and early autumn. This species can become invasive, its seed spread by birds which eat the small black fruit, invading and displacing native vegetation in higher rainfall warm-temperate areas of Australia and New Zealand. Prune after flowering to avoid this problem. The leaves of 'Tricolor' are variegated with yellow, pink when young. ZONE 6.

Ligustrum ovalifolium
CALIFORNIA PRIVET

Although originating from Japan, this shrub has become so entrenched in some parts of America it is commonly known as California privet. Growing to about 12 ft (4 m), it is usually seen in its variegated form 'Aureum'. Partly deciduous, it can form a thick mass of upright branches and is often used to good effect as a hedge. The leaves need full sun to become variegated with yellow; if green-leafed stems appear these should be cut out or they will eventually take over. The cultivar is grown from cuttings. ZONE 5.

Ligustrum vulgare
EUROPEAN PRIVET

This bushy shrub is deciduous or semi-evergreen and reaches a height and spread of 10 ft (3 m). It has dark green, pointed, oval leaves and bears panicles of small, strongly

Libocedrus plumosa

Libocedrus plumosa

Ligustrum japonicum 'Rotundifolium'

Ligustrum lucidum (below)

Ligustrum japonicum 'Rotundifolium' (below)

perfumed white flowers from early to mid-summer, followed by black berries. There are several cultivars with variegated leaves. If using as a hedge, prune back hard for the first few years of growth then trim regularly. ZONE 3.

LINDERA
Lauraceae

This large genus of evergreen and deciduous trees and shrubs is indigenous to East Asia and North America. Only a handful of cool-climate deciduous species are grown in gardens, valued for their autumn foliage. The leaves are variable, often lobed; when crushed the foliage releases a pungent and distinctly spicy odour. Male and female flowers, both yellow, are borne on the bare branches of separate plants in early spring. The fruit are globular and berry like. *Lindera* species grow naturally in part-shade in acid soils that are rich in organic matter. Though tolerant of extreme cold, they do best if protected from late spring frosts. Plants can be propagated from seed, which should be cleaned of pulp and sown fresh. Half-ripe stem cuttings taken in late summer are also used.

Lindera benzoin
SPICE BUSH, BENJAMIN BUSH

This deciduous shrub originates from damp woodland areas along much of the east coast of North America. Rounded in shape, it can grow up to 10 ft (3 m) tall. Small clusters of yellow-green flowers appear in spring, followed by berries that ripen glossy bright red in late summer. The leaves, unlike those of other species, are thin and unlobed and up to 6 in (15 cm) long; they turn orange and gold in autumn. This species is particularly cold-tolerant. It is the source of gum benzoin, used as a fixative in perfumery. ZONE 2.

Lindera obtusiloba

This shrub or small tree is native to Korea, China and Japan, and may grow as high as 30 ft (10 m). The leaves, usually 3-lobed, turn pale gold in autumn. The small, yellow-green flowers appear in spring, followed by shiny black, globose fruit that are about ⅓ in (8 mm) in diameter. ZONE 4.

LIQUIDAMBAR
Hamamelidaceae

This is a genus of deciduous trees belonging to the witch-hazel family, grown for their shapely form, handsome foliage and superb autumn colours. The leaves are deeply lobed, resembling a typical maple leaf. They are temperate-climate plants, requiring sun or semi-shade and fertile, deep loamy soil with adequate water during spring and summer. They will not thrive in shallow, sandy soil. Some species produce a resinous gum known as liquid storax that is used to scent soap, as an expectorant in cough remedies and as a fumigant in the treatment of some skin diseases. The trees are best allowed to develop their lower branches to ground level. Propagate by budding in spring or from seed in autumn.

Liquidambar formosana

From central and south-eastern China and Taiwan, this broadly conical species grows to 100 ft (30 m) with a spread of 50 ft (15 m). Its single trunk is erect, and the horizontal branches bear large, 3-lobed, toothed leaves that are bronze when young, mature dark green, then turn red, gold and purple in autumn. The bark is greyish white, becoming darker and fissured with age. Small, yellow-green flowers appear in spring at the same time as the new leaves emerge, followed by spiky, globular fruit clusters. The wood is used for making tea chests and the leaves to feed silk worms. ZONE 7.

Liquidambar orientalis
TURKISH LIQUIDAMBAR

This broadly conical tree from south-west Turkey reaches a height of 50–60 ft (15–18 m) with a spread of 30 ft (10 m). Slow growing, it bears bluntly lobed, smooth, matt green leaves that turn orange with purplish tones in autumn. Very small, yellow-green flowers appear along with the new leaf growth, followed by clusters of small, brown, rounded fruit. Liquid storax is obtained from the bark of this species which is orange-brown and thick, cracking into small plates. ZONE 5.

Liquidambar orientalis (above)

Ligustrum lucidum 'Tricolor' (below)

Ligustrum vulgare

Liquidambar styraciflua

Liriodendron chinense

Liriodendron chinense

Liquidambar styraciflua 'Variegata'

Liquidambar styraciflua 'Variegata'

Liquidambar styraciflua
LIQUIDAMBAR, SWEET GUM

Deciduous, with a broadly conical to spreading habit, this widely grown tree is from eastern USA. It reaches a height of 130 ft (40 m) and spread of 70 ft (22 m). The young branches and twigs are often ridged with a distinctive, corky bark and the wood of this species, known commercially as satin walnut, is used for furniture-making. It bears palmately lobed, glossy dark green leaves that turn orange to red and purple in autumn. Very small, yellow-green flowers appear with the new spring growth, followed by spiky, ball-like fruit clusters. The deeply furrowed bark is dark grey-brown with narrow ridges and yields liquid storax. 'Variegata' has leaves with paler green and yellowish blotches and streaks; 'Worplesdon' has more finely lobed leaves that turn orange in autumn. ZONE 5.

LIRIODENDRON
Magnoliaceae
TULIP TREE

Some botanists dispute there being two species in this genus; they prefer to recognize only one, *Liriodendron tulipifera*, regarding *L. chinense* as merely a variety of this. The majority, however, accept the two. Their leaves distinguish them at once from all other trees: they have 4 lobes and look as though someone has cut their ends off with scissors. The flowers are distinctive too, in pale green with orange at the bases of their petals and numerous stamens. They don't in fact look very much like tulips, more like their cousins the magnolias. They are both very handsome trees, straight of bole and symmetrical of crown, though they are rather too large—and too fast growing—to be suitable for any but the largest of gardens. They prefer a temperate climate and deep, fertile soil and are propagated from seed or by grafting. They are difficult to transplant.

Liriodendron chinense
CHINESE TULIP TREE

From China, this tree is the smaller and more dense growing of the 2 species, reaching a height of 80 ft (25 m) and spread of 37 ft (12 m). Fast growing, with a broadly columnar habit, it bears dark green, lobed leaves that turn yellow in autumn. The undersides of the leaves are grey-blue and covered with minute hairs. Orange-based, pale green flowers are borne singly on the ends of shoots in mid-summer, followed by conical, pale brown clusters of fruit which fall apart when ripe. ZONE 4.

Liriodendron tulipifera
TULIP TREE

From eastern USA, this is an outstanding specimen tree for cool climates, reaching 95 ft (30 m) or more with a spread of about 50 ft (15 m). A vigorous grower with a broadly conical habit, it bears deep green, lobed leaves that turn rich golden yellow in autumn. Orange-based, pale green flowers are borne singly at the ends of new shoots in mid-summer, followed by conical brown fruit. The flowers of this species are slightly larger than those of *L. chinense*. This is an important timber tree in the USA. The pale timber, called 'yellow poplar' in the trade, is not very hard or durable but it is fairly light and strong and much used in furniture-making, often hidden under veneers of more decorative wood. The bark is said to have medicinal properties. 'Aureomarginatum' has green leaves heavily edged with yellow; and 'Fastigiatum' is about half the size with an erect, columnar form. ZONE 3.

LITCHI
Sapindaceae
LYCHEE

This genus consists of just one evergreen tree from southern China and Southeast Asia, which is grown throughout the subtropics for its foliage and delicious fruit. It requires full sun and shelter from wind and cold (although it can withstand an occasional light frost) and prefers deep, moist soil and regular water. Propagate from seed in summer or by budding in spring. Trees raised from seed start to bear fruit after about 5 years. Lychees are grown commercially by air-layering or grafting of superior named varieties.

Litchi chinensis

A large, graceful, slim-trunked specimen, this tree reaches a height of 30 ft (10 m) and spread of 10–15 ft (3–5 m). Bright green compound leaves, gold or pink when young, form a low-spreading crown. Clusters of small, petal-less, greenish yellow flowers are borne in abundance in spring, followed by the bright red edible fruit that enclose a brown seed. The fruit contain a sweet pulp similar in texture to that of grapes. ZONE 10.

LITHOCARPUS
Fagaceae

This large genus comprises evergreen trees and shrubs from Asia, plus a single species, *L. densiflorus*, from California and Oregon. Grown for their foliage, these cool-climate plants require sun or semi-shade and a well-drained, neutral to acid soil. Young trees should be sheltered from strong winds. In appearance they fall somewhere between the oak and the chestnut. Their flower clusters are similar to that of the chestnut and their fruit, like those of the oak, are acorns. Propagation is from seed in autumn; the trees are difficult to transplant.

Lithocarpus densiflorus
TANBARK OAK

This species from western USA reaches a height and spread of 30 ft (10 m) or more. It has a spreading habit. The leaves are covered with thick, pale orange felt when young, becoming smooth and glossy green with maturity. The tiny, pale yellow male flowers, densely packed in narrow catkins, are borne in spring and often again in autumn. The female flowers and acorns, which mature in their second year, come in stout, stiff spikes below the male catkins. Tannins used in the leather industry are obtained from the thick, scaly bark. ZONE 6.

LIVISTONA
Arecaceae

This is a genus of medium to tall fan palms found in the wetter parts of Southeast Asia and Australia. They feature very large, round, pleated fronds up to 5 ft (1.5 m) across and a dense crown from which dead leaves may remain hanging for a short time. The leaf stalks are usually long and are edged with sharp teeth. These palms are widely used for outdoor landscaping; their clusters of blue, purple-black or, rarely, reddish, fruit and tapering leaves are shown to great effect. Most species are hardy enough to survive warm-temperate and subtropical climates, although they do best in mild, frost-free areas. Slow growing, they prefer deep, sandy soil and, while they tolerate full sun, they produce better deep green foliage in dappled shade. They make excellent indoor or outdoor container plants. Propagation is from seed in summer.

Litchi chinensis

Liriodendron tulipifera

Lithocarpus densiflorus (below)

Lithocarpus densiflorus (below)

Liriodendron tulipifera (below)

Liriodendron tulipifera

Livistona australis
CABBAGE PALM, CABBAGE-TREE PALM

Widely distributed along the east coast of Australia, this is one of the tallest species, growing to 80 ft (25 m) in the wild. The slender trunk shows the scars left by the shed fronds. The large, rounded leaves are held at the apex of the trunk, allowing understorey plants such as ferns to grow under mature specimens. Long sprays of small yellow flowers are borne in spring. The common names refer to the highly nutritious apical bud, which was eaten by Aborigines and early European settlers. ZONE 9.

Livistona chinensis
CHINESE FAN PALM

This palm will reach a height of 20–40 ft (7–13 m); it is quite fast growing in the tropics, slow in temperate climates. Its single trunk is heavily textured and the large circular fronds held on relatively short stalks droop attractively from the crown to give good foliage cover. A useful container specimen, it is one of the most frost-hardy palms and has been grown outdoors in sheltered gardens in England. ZONE 8.

LOBELIA
Lobeliaceae

This is a large genus with species in most parts of the world except the arctic and subarctic regions, though to gardeners it is best known in the form of North American herbaceous perennials such as *L. fulgens* and the South African annual *L. erinus*. However, in some regions, including the mountains of Mexico, it develops a range of remarkable shrubby forms. But none of these is as striking as the East African mountain lobelias, which reach almost tree size with massive upright spikes of crowded flowers terminating the often unbranched stem. As in all lobelias, the individual flowers are tubular at the base with the 3 longest petals forming a lower lip which is often recurved. The fruit is a capsule releasing many small seeds when ripe. Most lobelias are fairly easy to cultivate in an open, sunny position and well-drained soil. The shrub species vary in frost-hardiness but all are less hardy than the herbaceous perennials. Some of the African mountain lobelias have proved adaptable to cultivation in cool but mild, moist climates, though valued more as curiosities than as satisfactory garden subjects. Propagation is from seed or cuttings.

Lobelia keniensis

Kilimanjaro, Kenya, Ruwenzori, Elgon—these and other volcanic massifs reaching heights of more than 10,000 ft (3,000 m) in tropical East Africa are the habitats of the giant lobelias, each massif having its own distinct group of species. As the name suggests, *L. keniensis* comes from Mt Kenya where it occurs in large numbers in the heath zone not far below the permanent snow. ZONE 9.

LOMATIA
Proteaceae

Originating in eastern Australia and Chile, these evergreen shrubs and trees are members of the protea family. They are grown for their attractive foliage and flowers which have distinctive, narrow, spidery, twisted petals. Cool- to warm-climate plants, they require sun or semi-shade and sandy, acid, well-drained soil, preferably rich in organic matter. Growing in a wide moisture and temperature range, some are moderately frost-hardy but will need shelter from strong, cold winds. Propagate from cuttings.

Lomatia ferruginea
RUST-BUSH

This cool-climate shrub or small tree, indigenous to southern Chile and Argentina, grows to 20 ft (7 m) tall, with many erect basal stems. The new stem growth is covered with a brown, felt-like down. The fern-like, divided leaves consist of many olive green leaflets. The flowers, which appear in late winter and spring, are held in clusters in leaf axils; each flower has a red base, graduating to yellow-green at the petal tips. The fruit is a pod-like, somewhat woody follicle. The plants do best in well-drained, acid soils, in full sun or partial shade. ZONE 8.

Lomatia tinctoria
GUITAR PLANT

This small, stiffly erect, evergreen shrub from Tasmania has a dense, suckering habit and grows to about 3 ft (1 m) tall. The dark green leaves are finely divided. In summer the creamy white flowers are borne on erect sprays above the foliage. This shrub is quite easy to grow; it tolerates moderate shade to full sun. ZONE 8.

LONICERA
Caprifoliaceae
HONEYSUCKLE

The best known species of this genus of 180 species, found all over the northern hemisphere, are climbers, but there are some attractive shrubs among them. The chief attraction is the often delicious scent of the flowers, though there are scentless ones that are decorative enough in flower to earn their place in gardens. The species we deal with here are all plants of temperate climates, easily grown in sun or light shade and not fussy about soil. They benefit from occasional

Livistona chinensis (below)

Lobelia keniensis (below)

Lonicera nitida 'Aurea', as a bonsai

Lonicera fragrantissima

Lonicera tatarica (below)

Livistona australis (below)

pruning to keep them shapely and are propagated from cuttings.

Lonicera fragrantissima
WINTER HONEYSUCKLE

From China, this bushy, deciduous (sometimes evergreen) shrub reaches a height of 10 ft (3 m) with a spread of 12 ft (4 m). The most fragrant of the shrubby species, it bears tubular, paired, creamy white flowers, in some forms stained with rose-carmine, in winter and early spring. The dark green oval leaves appear shortly after the flowers. Except in the coldest climates where it grows, many will hang on the plant through winter. Prune after flowering to encourage a dense, leafy habit. ZONE 4.

Lonicera ledebourii

This is a large deciduous shrub from California, its upright branches wreathed in early summer with scentless but brightly coloured yellow and orange flowers which grow in pairs in the axils of the leaves. It can grow well over head high; to control its size it can be pruned after bloom. ZONE 7.

Lonicera nitida
BOX HONEYSUCKLE

An evergreen shrub endemic to Yunnan and Sichuan, China, this species forms a dense bush composed of masses of fine twigs covered with tightly packed, ½ in (1 cm) long, leathery, bronze-green leaves. Gold and variegated foliage forms, such as 'Aurea', are available. The small, creamy white, spring-borne flowers are not showy and the purple fruit is rarely seen in cultivation, so it is best regarded as a foliage plant. It withstands heavy trimming and is often used for hedging. It is tolerant of most soils in sun or light shade and is usually propagated from cuttings. ZONE 6.

Lonicera tatarica
TATARIAN HONEYSUCKLE

This deciduous, bushy, medium-sized shrub grows to a height of 8 ft (2.5 m) and spread of 10 ft (3 m). In late spring and early summer the dark green leaves are covered with trumpet-shaped flowers, in shades from white to deep pink, followed by red berries. ZONE 2.

LOPHOMYRTUS
Myrtaceae

This genus comprising several evergreen shrubs or small trees from New Zealand has been separated from the genus *Myrtus*. The plants are grown for their decorative foliage, which can be colourful and attractively aromatic, as well as the small white flowers and dark red berries. Moderately frost-hardy, they prefer full sun, well-drained, fertile soil and ample water in the warmer months. Tip pruning in spring will keep them compact. Propagate from seed or cuttings for the species; from cuttings for the cultivars.

Lophomyrtus bullata
RAMARAMA

Also known as *Myrtus bullata*, this New Zealand shrub, to 8 ft (2.5 m) high, is characterized by its 1–2 in (2–5 cm) long, puckered (bullate), oval leaves. The foliage varies in colour depending on where the plant is grown; in shade it is deep green, in the sun it develops purple and red tones. Small cream flowers open in summer, followed by reddish purple berries. ZONE 9.

Lophomyrtus obcordata

This erect, bushy shrub grows to about 6 ft (2 m) high, its many twiggy branches holding small, notched leaves. Young foliage turns bronze-purple during the winter months; the small, white summer flowers are followed by red berries that turn black as they ripen. The seeds within these berries can be used for propagation. ZONE 8.

Lophomyrtus × ralphii

There are many naturally occurring hybrids between the 2 species listed above. The widely seen 'Purpurea' grows to about 6 ft (2 m) high, bearing puckered or crinkly leaves of a deep purple bronze throughout the year; 'Lilliput' is a dwarf, compact shrub with tiny red leaves; 'Pixie' has leaves that are pinkish red. These forms are propagated from cuttings, best taken in early autumn as the new season's growths harden. ZONE 8.

LOPHOSTEMON
Myrtaceae
BRUSH BOX

The only species of note is *Lophostemon confertus*, the brush box of the rainforests of eastern Australia, where it is still perhaps better known by its old name *Tristania conferta*. It is a magnificent tree in the wild, rivalling some of the larger eucalypts in size, though few gigantic trees remain now. The reddish brown timber is hard and durable and, though difficult to season, is regarded as one of Australia's best. Nowadays it is mainly used for flooring, for which it is the equal of teak; formerly it was much used for heavy construction, especially the building of railway bridges. The tree is never quite so large in cultivation, though it is still rather large for most gardens; it is widely planted as a street tree, though sometimes chosen for its ability to recover from savage pruning rather than the beauty of its symmetrical crown and the shade

Loropetalum chinense

Lophomyrtus obcordata

Loropetalum chinense

offered by its broad evergreen leaves. It needs a frost-free climate and though it can put up with drought is much happier where it receives summer rainfall. Good soils are preferred.

Lophostemon confertus
BRUSH BOX

Tall and massive in its natural habitat, the brush box in a more open position is usually a dome-headed tree with dense, mid-green foliage. Flowers, although profuse, are hidden among the leaves and are followed by woody capsules. It is a very adaptable tree, able to withstand a wide variety of soil types but preferring free-draining fertile soil in full sun or semi-shade; once established it will tolerate light frosts. The cultivar 'Variegata' has cream central markings on the leaves, while 'Perth Gold' has yellow coloration towards the leaf margins. Propagation of the species is from seed, but the cultivars need to be grafted on to seedlings. ZONE 10.

LOROPETALUM
Hamamelidaceae
FRINGE FLOWER

This genus of only one species derives its name from the Greek words *loron*, a thong and *petalon*, petal, referring to the masses of flowers with twisted, strap-like, creamy white petals that hang on the shrub during spring. The plant has a distinctly horizontal branching habit which means it can be easily trained as an espalier, or pruned after flowering to emphasize the habit and give it a sculptured effect. The fringe flower does best in a warm-temperate climate, in sun or dappled shade. Well-drained, slightly acid soil is preferred. It is propagated from cuttings in summer.

Loropetalum chinense

This is an evergreen shrub reaching 6 ft (2 m) high, with horizontally inclined branches often forming a very wide profile. The small, neat, oval leaves are deep green and form a pleasant background to the fragrant, creamy white pendent flowers that appear during spring. It enjoys a sunny sheltered position in well-drained soil and, while undemanding, it does respond to regular water and fertilizer. ZONE 8.

LUCULIA
Rubiaceae

This is a genus of 5 species of evergreen shrubs from the foothills of the Himalaya. They are very much admired by gardeners for their attractive pointed leaves and clusters of scented pink or white

Lyonothamnus floribundus subsp. *aspleniifolius* (below left)   *Luculia gratissima* (above)

Luma apiculata

Lyonothamnus floribundus subsp. *aspleniifolius* (below)

Luma apiculata

flowers, but they have a reputation for being difficult to please. They need a warm-temperate climate free of both frost and drought, acid soil, and perfect drainage or there will be trouble with root-rot. If the plants grow straggly—they often do—they can be pruned gently after flowering. In cooler climates they succeed in mildly warmed greenhouses, there altering their natural flowering season from earliest spring to summer. Propagation is from seed or summer cuttings.

Luculia gratissima
This is a 5 ft (1.5 m) high, evergreen shrub that is grown in mild climates for its viburnum-like heads of fragrant pink flowers which appear in mid-winter. The leaves are bronze green, soft and up to 10 in (25 cm) long. ZONE 9.

LUMA
Myrtaceae
This genus consists of 4 species of evergreen shrubs and trees from Argentina and Chile closely related to *Myrtus*, in which genus they were formerly included. They have small, leathery, pointed, oval, deep green leaves and a dense, bushy growth-habit. The small creamy white, starry flowers appear from mid-summer. The bark of most species is very attractive and is, of course, a year-round feature; it is a reddish brown and flakes off to reveal white to pink wood underneath. Although generally shrubby, old specimens can eventually grow to tree size, but with trimming they can be kept to shrubs. Some species are suitable for hedging. They prefer moist, well-drained soil in sun or light shade. Propagate from seed or cuttings.

Luma apiculata
A Chilean evergreen shrub or small tree formerly known as *Myrtus luma*, this species grows to around 50 ft (15 m) in the wild but can be kept to 10 ft (3 m) with regular trimming and may be used for hedging. The small, pointed, oval leaves are deep green and the flaking bark is cinnamon-brown with white wood underneath; the growth is dense and bushy. From mid-summer it is smothered in small, starry white flowers with conspicuous stamens. The fruit is a dark purple berry. Plant in moist, well-drained soil in sun or light shade. Propagate from seed or cuttings. ZONE 8.

LYONOTHAMNUS
Rosaceae
CATALINA IRONWOOD

An early resident of Los Angeles, W. S. Lyon, discovered the evergreen tree that makes up this genus on Santa Catalina Island off the coast of southern California. It was earlier thought that there were 2 species, but the second is now considered a subspecies. *L. floribundus* needs fertile, well-drained soil and protection from cold drying winds. It does well in coastal conditions where frost is not a problem. This is a tree for a sunny or semi-shaded position in a warm climate. Propagate from seed or cuttings but these may prove difficult.

Lyonothamnus floribundus
This slender tree with its narrow crown, grows to about 50 ft (15 m). It is valued for its ferny compound leaves with narrow, wavy-edged leaflets, dark green above and soft grey-green below, and for its light reddish brown bark which is shed in slender strips. The early summer flowers, of soft creamy white, are held in large clusters towards the ends of the branches. These are followed by brown seed capsules. The subspecies *aspleniifolius*, with fern-like foliage, is more widely grown. ZONE 9.

Macadamia tetraphylla

Mackaya bella

Macropiper excelsum

MACADAMIA
Proteaceae

Consisting of 11 species, this relatively small genus of evergreen trees is native to Australia, Sulawesi in Indonesia, and New Caledonia. They are small to medium-sized rainforest trees. The leathery, narrow leaves are mostly arranged in whorls of 3 or 4 on the twigs, with smooth or toothed edges. Small flowers are crowded on to cylindrical spikes and are followed by the frequently edible nuts which can take up to 9 months to mature. Frost-tender, they should be grown in sun in fertile and moist soil. Two of the species which produce edible nuts have been widely cultivated and many selected seedlings and hybrids are now used as decorative and commercial nut producing trees. It is possible to propagate from seeds but for the best crop, selected grafted trees are preferred.

Macadamia tetraphylla
MACADAMIA NUT, BOPPLE NUT, QUEENSLAND NUT

Growing to around 40 ft (13 m) with a bushy habit when given room, this handsome tree is easily identified by its long, coarsely toothed leathery leaves which can be prickly to the touch. The young branchlets are a pinkish red before turning darker as they age. The spring flowers can be pink or white on long pendulous spikes. They are followed by the hard-shelled nuts. These nuts eventually fall, making harvesting in the garden situation easy. This species grows readily in well-drained fertile soil and appreciates mulching and regular watering during dry spells. Pruning is unnecessary as it is of a naturally neat habit, but regular fertilizing will ensure good-sized nuts. ZONE 10.

MACKAYA
Acanthaceae

A member of the Acanthus family, this South African genus is represented by only one species. Its lustrous deep green leaves give the appearance of a delicate plant but, given a semi-shaded position in a warm-climate garden or where such a sheltered microclimate is available, it will repay with a profuse display of pale lilac tubular flowers flared at the ends to show deep purple veining. Propagate from cuttings in spring or summer.

Mackaya bella
FOREST BELL BUSH

An evergreen shrub, this initially forms an erect habit, but with maturity develops a more spreading nature and eventually grows to around 8 ft (2.5 m) tall. As the flowers form on the current season's growth the shrub will require regular pruning, after the flowers have faded, to ensure that its prolific flowering habit continues. A shaded, moist, and fertile root run is preferred and this is provided by adding a yearly layer of mulch to the shrub border. ZONE 10.

MACLURA
Moraceae

A genus of 12 species of deciduous and evergreeen thorny trees, shrubs and scrambling climbers, scattered widely through warmer parts of the world. Only one species, a deciduous small tree from the southern USA, is generally cultivated, used as a hedging plant between country properties. Its branches bear long sharp thorns in every leaf axil. Insignificant yellowish flowers are of different sexes on different trees; on female trees they are followed by unusual compound fruit, the size of a large orange, ripening to pale yellow. The fruit is hard and tough and quite inedible. It does best in full sun and hot summers and grows well in a wide range of soils, its spreading roots making it resistant to drought. Propagate from seed in autumn, softwood cuttings in summer or root cuttings in late winter.

Maclura pomifera
OSAGE ORANGE

This spreading, deciduous tree can reach a height of 50 ft (15 m) and spread of 40 ft (13 m). It has dark orange, fissured bark and spreading, thorny branches that form an open, irregular crown. The oval, dark green leaves turn yellow before they drop and tiny yellow flowers are borne in summer, followed by large, wrinkled fruits. Broken leaves and fruits yield a sticky milky latex that can be a mild skin irritant. It is native to the southern states of USA where the Osage tribe once roamed. The yellow timber is hard and flexible, and valued for archery bows. ZONE 7.

MACROPIPER
Piperaceae

This genus is made up of 9 species of evergreen shrubs or small trees from the South Pacific countries where they are found in low altitude, humid forests. The large, soft leaves are held alternately along the branches and have unbroken margins, and the rather minute yellow flowers are crowded into fleshy, cylindrical spikes that stand out from the foliage. These are followed by small, round soft fruits. The plants prefer freely drained, moderately fertile soil and a partially shaded position. During the growing season they appreciate water to keep the soil evenly moist. They also benefit from mulching. Propagate from seed or from cuttings in the cooler months.

Macropiper excelsum
KAWA KAWA, PEPPER TREE

A shrub or small tree to 21 ft (7 m) tall, this native of New Zealand and Lord Howe Island has dark green, heart-shaped leaves and tiny yellow flowers. The orange fruits that follow cluster together on spikes. ZONE 10.

MACROZAMIA
Zamiaceae

About 24 species make up this genus of cycads. They produce

growth typical of cycads with cylindrical to almost globose stems that can be above or below ground level, topped with palm-like fronds of evergreen foliage that can be up to 8 ft (2.5 m) long. The trunks have attached dried persistent leaf bases, or if burnt a smoother blackened trunk will show. These plants produce large, light green, female and male cones, reminiscent of pineapples in shape, the female cone eventually breaking open to reveal mature bright orange, red or yellow seeds. The starchy kernels were eaten by the Australian Aborigines after lengthy preparation which removed toxic substances. They cannot be eaten fresh. The plants grow best in temperate to subtropical areas in open, well-drained soils in part-shade. Propagate from fresh seed, which may take up to 18 months to germinate. Growth will progress very slowly in cooler areas. Some species make good ornamental garden plants.

Macrozamia communis
BURRAWANG

In the wild this, one of the most beautiful of the *Macrozamia* species, is usually found growing in extensive stands in coastal areas of New South Wales. Sometimes forming a trunk as much as 6 ft (2 m) high, the plant carries up to 100 bright green, palm-like leaves about 6 ft (2 m) long in its crown. It produces male and female cones to 18 in (45 cm) long with oblong, orange or red seeds emerging from the latter. It can tolerate light frosts and being transplanted, and can be grown in pots or containers. ZONE 9.

Macrozamia miquelii
ZAMIA

This cycad is found only in southeastern Queensland, growing under

Macrozamia miquelii (below)

trees in rainforest and sheltered forest areas where its short trunk can reach 24 in (60 cm) in height. The 5 ft (1.5 m) leaves are dark green and contain many crowded leaflets about 10–15 in (25–38 cm) long with white or reddish bases. Some of the lower leaves are spine-like. The female cones are barrel shaped and up to 15 in (38 cm) in length, producing oblong orange or red seeds. The male cones are like bananas, up to 15 in (38 cm) long. *M. miquelii* can be grown in pots or in the garden, given well-drained soil, and responds to mulching and watering during dry periods.
ZONE 10.

MAGNOLIA
Magnoliaceae

This large and varied genus of deciduous and evergreen trees and shrubs occurs in the wild in East Asia and the Americas. They are grown for their handsome foliage and showy, often fragrant flowers. The leaves are mainly oval and usually smooth edged; the flowers are generally large and solitary. Flower colours are shades of white, yellow, pink or purple, but the flower shapes have great variety—shaped like a funnel, bell, cup, goblet, saucer, bowl or star. Fruit is conelike or roughly cylindrical. Some of the most popular orna-

Macrozamia communis with *Eucalyptus maculata* trunks

mental trees and shrubs are in this genus. Magnolias require deep, fertile, well-drained, mildly acid soil, preferably well aerated by the presence of fibrous matter. Roots are extremely fragile so the plants do not transplant readily. They will thrive in either sun or part-shade but need protection from strong or salty winds. The flower buds may be damaged by severe frosts. Pruning is unnecessary. Propagate species from semi-ripe cuttings in summer or from seed in autumn, selected forms from semi-ripe cuttings in summer or by grafting in winter. The genus was named for Pierre Magnol, a French botanist.

Magnolia acuminata
CUCUMBER TREE

The most stately of American deciduous magnolias, this tree grows

Magnolia acuminata (below)

to 90 ft (28 m) tall in the wild. It is upright when young, wide spreading with maturity. Pyramid shaped, it has 10 in (25 cm) long, dark green leaves with downy undersides. The cup-shaped, slightly fragrant, greenish yellow flowers have erect petals and are borne singly in early to mid-summer, followed by green fruits, similar in shape to cucumbers, that ripen to red. ZONE 4.

Magnolia acuminata

Magnolia denudata

Magnolia grandiflora

Magnolia campbellii

This broadly conical deciduous tree from the Himalaya is widely cultivated for its wonderful flowers. It can grow to a height of 80 ft (25 m) and spread of 40 ft (13 m) with a forked trunk and a broad, irregular crown. Very large, slightly fragrant, pale to deep pink to purplish pink or white flowers are carried on leafless branches from late winter to mid-spring. On plants raised from seed, flowers are only produced after 20 or more years growth. The leaves are bronze when young, becoming dark green with maturity. This species prefers open space and dislikes a lime soil. 'Alba' has pure white flowers; 'Mollicomata' has similar flowers to the parent but flowers at an earlier age and is more resistant to cold; 'Charles Raffill' is similar to the parent but the flowers are white with rose-purple shading; 'Lanarth' has larger flowers with deeper rose-purple hues.
ZONE 7.

Magnolia denudata
YULAN MAGNOLIA

Sometimes known as *M. heptapeta*, this small, deciduous tree from central China grows to a height and spread of 30 ft (10 m). It has spreading branches and produces masses of scented, pure white flowers from mid-winter to early spring, before the oval, mid-green leaves with downy undersides appear. The flowers are followed by rectangular cones containing orange seeds. This species is greatly admired by the Chinese who have cultivated it for centuries. It is depicted in ancient paintings as a symbol of purity and candour.
ZONE 5.

Magnolia grandiflora
SOUTHERN MAGNOLIA, BULL BAY

One of the few cultivated evergreen magnolias, this southern USA species forms a dense broad dome up to 60 ft (20 m), if the climate is sufficiently warm. It has thick, deep green leathery leaves with rusty tones on the undersides. The cup-shaped white or cream blooms are up to 10 in (25 cm) across and appear during the later summer months before being followed by reddish brown cones. The typical species prefers warm, moist conditions, however there are many cultivars of this plant (including the Freeman hybrids with *M. virginiana*) which are hardier in more temperate conditions, while others, such as 'Exmouth', have a more conical growth habit and very fragrant flowers from an early age. ZONE 6.

Magnolia liliiflora

A deciduous, bushy shrub, this Chinese species which is also known as *M. quinquepeta*, reaches a height of 10 ft (3 m) with a spread of 12 ft (4 m). The oval, dark green leaves are downy on the undersides and taper to a point. Fragrant, narrow, purplish pink flowers, whitish inside, are borne amongst the leaves from mid-spring until mid-summer. 'Nigra' has large, dark wine-purple flowers that are pale purple inside. ZONE 5.

Magnolia × loebneri

A hybrid between *M. kobus* and a pink form of the shrubby *M. stellata*, this deciduous tree has a broadly spreading habit, growing to 30 ft (10 m) with a spread of about 24 ft (8 m). The blunt-tipped leaves are glossy dark green to paler green. Variable white to pink, star-like flowers open from early to mid-spring. 'Leonard Messel' bears a profusion of many-petalled, lilac-pink flowers in late winter and early spring, before and after the leaves emerge and is of more compact growth form. 'Merrill' is a vigorous cultivar with large white flowers, initially flushed with faint pink. ZONE 5.

Magnolia macrophylla
BIGLEAF MAGNOLIA

This deciduous American tree grows up to 50 ft (15 m) with a broadly columnar shape. Its very large, rather thin, oval green leaves reach a length of 24 in (60 cm), sometimes as much as 3 ft (1 m)! Large, fragrant, cup-shaped creamy white to yellowish flowers, with pink or purple shading at the petal bases, appear with the leaves in mid-summer. ZONE 4.

Magnolia liliiflora

Magnolia campbellii 'Lanarth' (below)

Magnolia sprengeri 'Diva'

Magnolia × soulangiana

Magnolia stellata

Magnolia × soulangiana

This deciduous hybrid is a cross between *M. denudata* and the shrubby *M. liliiflora*. It first appeared in Europe in the 1820s and is now represented by many cultivars. It is an erect tree growing up to 24 ft (8 m) tall and 15 ft (5 m) wide, usually on a single trunk with low branches. The dark green leaves are tapered at the base and rounded at the tip, with a short point. Goblet- to cup- or saucer-shaped, white to pink or deep purple-pink flowers are borne from late winter to mid-spring, before and after the leaves emerge. 'Alexandrina' has large flowers which are pure white on the inside, flushed with rose-purple outside; 'Brozzoni' is one of the best of the cultivars with very large white flowers, shaded purple at the base; 'Lennei' has goblet-shaped flowers, beetroot-purple outside, white to pale purple inside; 'Rustica Rubra' has goblet-shaped flowers, rose-red outside, pink and white on the inside. ZONE 4.

Magnolia sprengeri 'Diva'

From central China, this deciduous, spreading tree reaches a height of 50 ft (15 m) with a spread of 30 ft (10 m). Closely related to *M. denudata*, it bears large, bowl-shaped and fragrant, rose-pink flowers from early to mid-spring, before the oval, dark green leaves appear. ZONE 5.

Magnolia × soulangiana 'Lennei Alba'

Magnolia stellata
STAR MAGNOLIA

A smaller growing magnolia from Japan, this deciduous shrub reaches a height and spread of about 10 ft (3 m). Many branched, its bark is aromatic when young and it has narrow, dark green leaves. Fragrant, star-like, pure white flowers open from silky buds in late winter and early spring before the leaves. A bush of spreading, though compact growth, it will flower when quite young. Protect from wind and frosts which will damage the delicate blooms. It has several cultivars in shades of pink. 'Waterlily', the most prolific flowerer, has more petals and slightly larger flowers. ZONE 5.

Magnolia × soulangiana 'Brozzoni' (below)

Mahonia lomariifolia

Mahonia aquifolium

Magnolia virginiana

Magnolia virginiana

Magnolia wilsonii
WILSON'S MAGNOLIA

From China, this spreading, deciduous shrub or small tree grows to 18 ft (6 m) high and wide. In late spring and early summer, fragrant, cup-shaped, white flowers with red or magenta stamens hang from the underside of arching branches among the narrow dark green leaves that are velvety beneath. The flowers are followed by pink fruit that ripen to release shiny red seeds. This species will tolerate alkaline soil. ZONE 5.

MAHONIA
Berberidaceae

This genus of evergreen, low-growing to tall flowering shrubs is grown for its beautiful foliage, often fragrant yellow flowers, blue-black fruits which usually have a bloom of whitish or blue-grey wax, and the interesting bark on some taller species and cultivars. The berries resemble miniature grapes and make an excellent jelly. They are useful plants for specimens, hedges, windbreaks and groundcovers. Cool-climate shrubs, they require a sunny aspect and a well-drained, fertile soil with adequate water. In warmer climates they do better in shade or part-shade. They usually do not need pruning, but old canes can be cut out at ground level. Propagate species from semi-ripe cuttings, basal suckers or seed; selected forms from semi-ripe cuttings or basal suckers. Some botanists still include these plants in the genus *Berberis*.

Magnolia virginiana
SWEET BAY

From America, this evergreen to semi-evergreen tree reaches a height of 15 ft (5 m) in gardens. In cooler climates it may become deciduous. Fragrant, creamy white, goblet-shaped flowers are produced in summer followed by 2 in (5 cm) long red fruits with scarlet seeds. The leaves of this species are smaller than most other magnolias. ZONE 3.

Mahonia aquifolium
HOLLY GRAPE, OREGON GRAPE

An evergreen shrub from western North America with a dense, bushy habit, this species grows to 6 ft (2 m) high and wide with 8 in (20 cm) long pinnate leaves made up of 5 to 9 holly-like, glossy, deep green leaflets. In the cooler months the foliage develops purple tones. Clustered heads of small, bright yellow flowers appear in spring and are followed by the fruits. It grows well in any well-drained soil in sun or shade. This species is usually propagated from cuttings or basal suckers. ZONE 3.

Mahonia fremontii
DESERT MAHONIA

From south-western USA and Mexico, this shrub has an open, branching habit, reaching a height of up to 12 ft (4 m). Pruning will assist in encouraging a more compact, leafy shape. It has glaucous, yellow-green leaves with spiny leaflets and bears racemes of buttercup-yellow flowers in late winter and early spring. These are followed by the fruits. This attractive foliage plant is ideal for dry-climate gardens as a specimen or barrier hedge. ZONE 7.

Mahonia japonica

An upright, spreading shrub, growing to a height of 6 ft (2 m) and spread of 10 ft (3 m), this species has deep green leaves with numerous spiny leaflets. From autumn to spring it bears long, slender, drooping sprays of fragrant yellow flowers, followed by the fruits. This species prefers part-shade. ZONE 6.

Mahonia lomariifolia

This species from central and western China, one of the tallest and most elegant of the mahonias, grows 10–15 ft (3–5 m) tall with a spread of about 6–10 ft (2–3 m). Very upright in habit, it has many erect bamboo-like shoots. The long, dark green leaves are mainly confined to the ends of the shoots and have narrow, holly-like spiny leaflets. Dense, upright racemes of fragrant, bright yellow flowers are borne during late autumn and winter, followed by the purplish fruits. This is a striking garden plant due to its very handsome foliage and interesting growth habit. ZONE 7.

Mahonia repens
CALIFORNIAN HOLLY GRAPE

From western USA, this is a low shrub, reaching a height of 20 in (50 cm) or less. It has a creeping habit and is a useful groundcover, especially on uneven, rocky ground. The glaucous green leaves, with spiny leaflets, often turn a reddish shade in colder winters.

Bunches of small, fragrant yellow flowers are borne in spring, followed by the globular fruits. ZONE 3.

MALLOTUS
Euphorbiaceae

Grown for foliage and decorative fruits, this is a genus of evergreen small to medium-sized trees. Warm-climate plants, they are frost-tender. They require a sunny position and do best in a deep, moist soil with plentiful summer water. Propagate from seed in summer or from semi-ripe cuttings.

Mallotus philippensis
RED KAMALA

From Australia and Southeast Asia, the red kamala is fast growing, to a height of 50 ft (15 m) and spread of 21 ft (7 m). It is an upright, single-trunked tree with whitish bark and stiff, oval, dark green leaves, with rusty brown, scurfy hairs. Small spring flowers are followed by interesting, scarlet, pea-sized fruit capsules in summer. This species can be grown in poor soil and makes a good street tree in warm areas. ZONE 10.

MALPIGHIA
Malpighiaceae

Several species of this genus of hot-climate evergreen trees and shrubs are grown for their delicate flowers and attractive foliage. Originating in the West Indies and Central and South America, they have distinctive flowers, pink, rose or red, with 5 slender-stalked petals, which are followed by berries in shades of orange, red or purple. These frost-tender plants need regular feeding and watering and do best in an open, sunny position in a well-drained, moderately rich, moist soil. If desired, prune to maintain a dense habit. Propagate from cuttings of ripe shoots.

Malpighia coccigera
BARBADOS HOLLY, SINGAPORE HOLLY

This beautiful little shrub from the West Indies is slow growing to a height and spread of 30 in (75 cm). It has small, shiny, holly-like leaves and neat pink flowers with fringed petals and golden stamens crowded along the branches, followed by edible red berries. This is an excellent plant for a miniature clipped hedge in the tropics. ZONE 10.

Malpighia glabra
BARBADOS CHERRY, ACEROLA, WEST INDIAN CHERRY

This is an evergreen shrub from tropical America, growing from 5–10 ft (1.5–3 m) in height, with smooth-edged leaves and clusters of small, pink flowers. The attraction is the cherry-sized fruits, which ripen to red, and although tart in flavour are very rich in vitamin C and are much used in the plant's native lands for cooking and making jams and preserves. ZONE 9.

Mahonia lomariifolia

Malpighia glabra (below)

Malpighia coccigera (below)

Mahonia repens

MALUS
Rosaceae

This genus of deciduous flowering and fruiting trees from the northern temperate zone is grown mainly for its beautiful spring blossom. The fruit of most varieties is edible and can be used for making sauces, jams and preserves. The genus also contains many varieties of the long-cultivated edible apple, which are probably the result of crosses between several species and usually given the name *Malus × domestica* or *M. pumila*. Many species offer a fine display both in spring with their delicate flowers, and in autumn when the fruit is complemented by foliage colour. Leaves are simple and toothed or sometimes lobed and the flowers are borne in clusters, varying from white to deep rose-pink or deep reddish purple. Their shapely form and moderate size make them ideal shade trees and lawn specimens in small gardens. They grow best in a cold, moist climate, preferring full sun but tolerating part-shade. Plant in a fertile, well-drained loamy soil with protection from strong winds. They will grow on poorer soils with annual applications of fertilizer. Cut out dead wood in winter and prune to maintain a balanced shape. Propagate by budding in summer or grafting in winter. Watch for aphids and fireblight.

Malus 'Aldenhamensis'
ALDENHAM CRAB

Growing to a height of 15–21 ft (5–7 m) and spread of 15 ft (5 m), this small hardy tree has red-bronze new foliage, turning to dark green later in the season. Wine-red, semi-double flowers are borne in profusion in spring, followed by decorative, purple-red crab apples. Aldenham crab is good choice for an ornamental tree. ZONE 3.

Malus coronaria
AMERICAN SWEET CRAB

A strong-growing species, this small tree reaches a height of 30 ft (10 m). Clusters of fragrant white flowers are borne in early summer, followed by green, unpalatable, acid crab apples. The vigorous growing shoots bear slightly lobed, broad, short, bright green leaves. ZONE 3.

Malus × domestica
APPLE

This large hybrid group includes upright and spreading trees usually with dark, grey-brown scaly bark and grey to reddish brown twigs. They can grow 30 ft (10 m) tall with a spread of 15 ft (5 m). The green leaves are generally downy on the undersides and the clusters of white flowers are usually suffused with pink. The juicy, sweet fruit is green or yellow to red. These common orchard trees are distinguished from the wild crab (*M. sylvestris*) by their downy shoots, blunter leaves and juicy fruits that sweeten on ripening. There are hundreds of cultivars including the American-bred 'Delicious', perhaps the most widely grown. It is necessary to grow 2 or more cultivars to have a crop as apple clones are not usually fertile to their own pollen. ZONE 3.

Malus 'Aldenhamensis'

Malus × domestica 'Jonathon'

Malus cultivar in bloom (below)

Malus × domestica 'Delicious'

Malus × domestica 'Starkspur Supreme Red Delicious'

Malus hupehensis

Malus 'Golden Hornet'

Malus floribunda
JAPANESE CRAB

Regarded as one of the most beautiful of the crab apples, this tree grows to a height of 24 ft (8 m) with a spreading, broad-domed crown of about 30 ft (10 m). The branches arch and droop at the ends. Pale pink flowers, red in bud, almost cover the entire tree in early spring, followed by tiny, pea-shaped, yellowish, blushed red, crab apples in autumn. This tree, despite its common name, is thought to have been introduced to Japan from China, and is the parent of many hybrids. ZONE 3.

Malus 'Golden Hornet'
CRAB APPLE

Bred in England, this shapely tree grows to a height of 30 ft (10 m) and spread of 24 ft (8 m), with a single trunk and a vase-shaped crown. The outer branches droop when in fruit. Leaves are dark green and shiny and pink buds open into cup-shaped white flowers in spring,

Malus floribunda

followed by a profusion of bright yellow crab apples in autumn, lasting well into winter. The best of the yellow-fruited crab apples, the heavy crops are excellent for preserving and making jelly. ZONE 4.

Malus hupehensis
HUPEH CRAB

From the Himalaya and central and western China, where a tisane called red tea is made from the leaves, this vigorous, spreading species grows to a height and spread of about 30 ft (10 m). The leaves are dark green, purple tinged when young, and large, fragrant white flowers, pink in bud, are borne from mid- to late spring,

followed by small crab apples that ripen to red from yellow and orange. ZONE 4.

Malus ioensis
IOWA CRAB

Growing to about 18 ft (6 m) tall with a spread of 24 ft (8 m), this leafy tree has a shrubby growth-habit and gives good autumn colour. Clusters of large, fragrant, pale pink flowers are borne in late spring—it is one of the last of the crabs to flower. One of the finest crab apples, it has a very heavy crop of flowers, good colour and sweet perfume. 'Plena' (the Bechtel crab) has double flowers and is more widely grown than the species. ZONE 4.

Malus hupehensis

Malus hupehensis

Malus sargentii

Malus toringoides

Malus sylvestris 'Bittenfelder'

Malus sargentii

Malus sargentii
SARGENT'S CRAB APPLE

A spreading shrub, this crab apple reaches a height and spread of about 8 ft (2.5 m). It has oval, dark green leaves with serrated margins and bears masses of white flowers in spring, followed by tiny, deep red fruits that last well into winter. Some of the branches may carry thorns. ZONE 3.

Malus sylvestris
CRAB APPLE, WILD CRAB

From Europe, this parent of orchard apples can grow to a height of 30 ft (10 m) with a spread of 10 ft (3 m). It has a rounded crown and dark bark. In spring it bears white flowers, flushed with pink, followed by yellow, flushed orange-red fruit that, although rather sour and bitter, make delicious conserves. The leaves have a partly red stalk and some branches may bear thorns. ZONE 3.

Malus toringoides

From China, this very attractive small tree reaches 24 ft (8 m) in height and has wide-spreading branches. The distinctive small, narrow leaves are often 2 or 3 lobed. Creamy white flowers are borne in spring, followed by round or pear-shaped red and yellow crab apples. ZONE 4.

MALVAVISCUS
Malvaceae

This genus of soft-wooded, frost-tender evergreen shrubs and small trees from South America is named from the Latin *malva* (mallow) and *viscidus* (sticky). They prefer a warm, humid climate but are successful in subtropical areas where there is no danger of frost. Given a well-drained soil of a loamy nature, they must have ample summer moisture. If container grown, they must be kept well watered. Prune flowering wood in winter to maintain the shape of the shrubs. Semi-ripe cuttings taken towards the end of summer will strike easily.

Malvaviscus arboreus
CARDINAL'S HAT, SLEEPING HIBISCUS

This rounded shrub from Mexico grows to 10 ft (3m) tall and almost as wide. It has large, mid-green leaves, but it is the bright red flowers that make this a significant shrub in the warm-climate garden. It prefers well-drained moist soil either in sun or part-shade. In early spring, prune back by half the last season's growth to ensure a good flowering during the later summer months. The form with long, pendulous, mostly scarlet flowers is now treated as a distinct species, *M. penduliflorus*. ZONE 10.

MANGIFERA
Anacardiaceae
MANGO

This is a genus of evergreen trees from India and Southeast Asia of which by far the most important is the mango, *Mangifera indica*. Now grown in every tropical country, mangoes have been cultivated in India for well over 2,000 years, both for their delicious fruit and for the cool shade cast by their dense, glossy leaves. The young leaves are drooping and tinted strongly with red, a common feature among tropical trees and thought to protect them from the sun and heavy rain. The fruit, a drupe, is interesting; the big central stone often contains 3 embryos, the first 2 being the result of pollination, but the third arising entirely from the mother tree. Normally it is one of the first 2 that grows, but if they are removed as the seed germinates, the third will grow and reproduce the character of the parent fruit exactly. Nonetheless, it is customary to graft selected varieties. While mangoes can be cultivated in the subtropics, they are much more reliable in tropical, monsoonal climates. Rain at flowering time can rot the blossoms and ruin the crop.

Mangifera indica
MANGO

The mango can grow as much as 80 ft (25 m) tall and wide, though grafted trees are normally smaller. The spring flowers are tiny and greenish, though they are borne in large sprays which look quite decorative against the long, glossy leaves. The fruit rather resembles an enormous peach, though its skin is smooth, ripening to orange or red. It can be eaten ripe, or cooked unripe in such dishes as mango chutney. Seedling trees are apt to have furry seeds, making the extraction of the juicy, pale orange flesh awkward—and their sweet flavour is often marred by a bitter aftertaste. Selected cultivars have much superior fruit; sweet to the last, and with smooth pits for easier eating. There are many cultivars, every tropical country having its own favourites; but the Bombay 'Alphonso' is universally regarded as the finest of all. It is a very much smaller tree than usual, orchardists planting it at half the normal spacing of 65 ft (20 m) each way. ZONE 11.

MAYTENUS
Celastraceae

Though there are over 200 species of this genus of evergreen trees and shrubs, mainly from South America and the Caribbean, the only one ever seen in gardens is *M. boaria*, admired for its attractive weeping habit. It is a popular street tree in the deep south of the USA. Most members of the genus are only suitable for cultivation in frost-free climates; some of the shrubby species bear decorative red or yellow seeds in autumn.

Maytenus boaria
MAYTEN

Growing to 24 ft (8 m) and spreading almost as wide, this Chilean tree has a graceful, weeping habit; in fact it looks rather like an evergreen weeping willow. It has narrow, glossy green leaves that are finely serrated and hang down from slender shoots. Inconspicuous, star-shaped flowers, white tinged with green, are clustered in small groups and appear in spring. These are followed by red and yellow seed pods. *M. boaria* tolerates frost. ZONE 8.

Mangifera indica

Mangifera indica

Maytenus boaria

Maytenus boaria

MEGASKEPASMA
Acanthaceae
BRAZILIAN RED CLOAK, MEGAS

The single species in this genus is a hot-climate shrub grown for its display of red flowers. Originally from Venezuela, the plants can grow to 10 ft (3 m) high and have a spreading habit. Plant them where they can enjoy sun or part-shade and a light soil, rich in organic matter. They will benefit from regular watering and fertilizing. Protect them from snails. Propagate from cuttings.

Megaskepasma erythrochlamys
The mid-green, oval leaves of this evergreen shrub are up to 12 in (30 cm) long, with prominent veining. The plants form spreading clumps, and the erect stems bear spikes of deep red flowers in summer. These are up to 12 in (30 cm) long and are held above the foliage in summer. ZONE 10.

MELALEUCA
Myrtaceae

The evergreen trees and shrubs that form this large genus are indigenous to Australia, except for a handful of species found in New Guinea, Indonesia and coastal Southeast Asia. Some species have beautiful papery barks. They are chiefly valued for their brush-like flowers with showy stamens. The profuse blooms produce nectar, making them an excellent food source for many native birds and animals. Some species make excellent hedges and they are used extensively in urban landscaping because of their capacity to tolerate pollution, salt winds and saline soils. The smaller shrubs make very useful fill-in plants and low, informal hedges. *Melaleuca* species are adaptable plants as they can tolerate wet and even boggy conditions (but they much prefer well-drained soil) and, although they are warm-climate plants, most species will also withstand cold if they are given full sun. They can be grown from seed or cuttings which should be taken just as the current season's growth begins to form. The shrubby species benefit from a light annual pruning straight after the main flowering period. Melaleucas are remarkably free from pests and disease.

Melaleuca argentea
SILVER-LEAFED PAPERBARK

This pendulous, spreading tree reaches a height of 80 ft (25 m) and spread of 24 ft (8 m). It has an attractive papery bark and its silvery green leaves are narrow and up to 5 in (12 cm) long. Spikes of cream flowers are borne in winter and spring. To thrive, the silver-leafed paperbark requires ample moisture. ZONE 11.

Melaleuca argentea

Melaleuca argentea

Megaskepasma erythrochlamys (left)

Megaskepasma erythrochlamys

Melaleuca bracteata 'Revolution Green'

Melaleuca armillaris
BRACELET HONEY-MYRTLE

A small to medium-sized tree to 30 ft (10 m), this species has a spreading canopy of deep green needle-like leaves while the flowers are in cylindrical spikes up to 2 in (5 cm) long. The buds are usually in shades of pink or red, opening to white in spring and summer. The bark is grey and furrowed and peels off in strips. This is a fast-growing species, adaptable to a wide range of soil types, and is popular as hedging as it adapts well to regular pruning. Its fast, bushy growth has made it very popular with highway designers in Australia who use it to shield houses from the sight and sound of traffic. ZONE 9.

Melaleuca bracteata
BLACK TEA-TREE, RIVER TEA-TREE

This popular tree, growing to 30 ft (10 m), has dark grey, fissured bark and grey-green leaves scattered along the length of the branches. Flowers held towards the ends of the branches are creamy white, appearing in summer. This is a very adaptable plant as to soil and climatic conditions: it grows well in wet locations, particularly along the coast. It has produced 3 cultivars suitable for warm-climate gardens. These are 'Revolution Gold', with red stems and fine golden foliage that can scorch if the weather is too hot; 'Revolution Green', growing to 12 ft (4 m) with fine bright green foliage and useful as a screen plant; and 'Golden Gem', growing to 6 ft (2 m). ZONE 9.

Melaleuca incana

Melaleuca fulgens
HONEY-MYRTLE

A shrub growing up to 5 ft (1.5 m), the honey-myrtle has an erect, open habit and fine green leaves acting as a foil to the yellow-tipped, bright scarlet flower-spikes that open during spring and summer. The seed capsules remain on the bush for some time. This species does best in full sun and a well-drained position. Tip prune regularly to prevent the bush from becoming leggy. ZONE 9.

Melaleuca incana
GREY-LEAFED HONEY MYRTLE

A pendulous-branched shrub growing to 10 ft (3 m) tall, this species

Melaleuca armillaris

usually has a low-branched main trunk, forming a spreading bush about 6 ft (3 m) across. The slender, arching branches carry narrow and hairy leaves that are reddish green at first, becoming grey-green with a red edge and then turning greyish purple in winter. Creamy yellow flower-spikes are borne in spring. Its graceful, weeping habit, makes it good for specimens, hedging or screening as it tolerates most soils. ZONE 9.

Melaleuca linarifolia

Melaleuca linarifolia

Melaleuca linarifolia

Melaleuca leucadendra
WEEPING PAPERBARK, CAJEPUT

This tree is notable for its thick, whitish, spongy bark. It has a tall, open crown and weeping branches, reaching a height of 65 ft (20 m) or more with a spread of 45 ft (14 m). Spirally arranged, narrow, dull green leaves are up to 6 in (15 cm) long. The fuzzy, creamy white fragrant flowers are borne in bottlebrush-like spikes in summer and autumn. This species thrives in waterlogged soil and the timber is used for posts and shipbuilding. It makes a good street tree. Cajeput oil, used in medicine, is distilled from the foliage. ZONE 10.

Melaleuca linarifolia
FLAX-LEAFED PAPERBARK, SNOW-IN-SUMMER

A small tree up to 30 ft (10 m) with a spreading crown and white, papery bark, this species derives one of its common names from its grey-green, flax-like leaves. The short white flower-spikes, held at the ends of the branches, are very profuse and appear from late spring into summer. These fast-growing trees grow naturally around swamps but are adaptable to most garden soil types. Multiple plantings make a good screen or windbreak. An essential oil is extracted from the leaves of this species. ZONE 9.

Melaleuca quinquenervia
BROAD-LEAFED PAPERBARK, PUNK TREE

Forming a medium-sized tree, up to 60 ft (20 m) with a spreading canopy, these paperbarks look particularly impressive when group planted in a large garden. Occurring naturally in and near water, they seem equally at home in drier positions such as street plantings. Notable for their pale orange-brown papery bark that peels in patches, they bear stiff, dark green leaves. The creamy white or pink flowers appear in spring and then bloom spasmodically throughout the year. In their native Australia they are a good food source for bats and nectar-eating birds. It has escaped from cultivation in Florida, in the USA, to become a major pest in the Everglades. ZONE 10.

Melaleuca tamariscina
Growing to about 15 ft (5 m) high and 10 ft (3 m) wide, this attractive species from Queensland has slender, crowded branches covered with tiny scale-like leaves closely pressed against the stems. Its bark is papery and it bears white to pale mauve, bottlebrush-like flowers. It needs a full sun position and can be variable in its flowers. ZONE 10.

Melaleuca thymifolia
An upright or spreading shrub, this species grows to a height and spread of about 3 ft (1 m). This vase-shaped shrub has small, erect blue-green leaves that give off a spicy aroma when crushed. Pale purple flowers with incurving stamens are borne from late spring to autumn. This species is adaptable to most soils but thrives in a wet position in full sun. To maintain a compact shape, it should be pruned in late summer. ZONE 9.

Melaleuca viridiflora
BROAD-LEAFED PAPERBARK
Closely related to *M. leucadendra* and *M. quinquenervia*, this attractive species occurs wild across the tropical north of Australia. It makes a tree of up to about 30 ft (10 m) of rather stiff habit, the trunk and branches clothed with thick cream papery bark. The leaves are among the largest in melaleucas, up to 4 in (10 cm) long and 2 in (5 cm) wide, very thick and stiff. The bottlebrush-type flower-spikes are most commonly greenish cream, but pink and bright red forms also occur. One red-flowering clone has become established in cultivation. Easily grown in a sunny position, the broad-leafed paperbark tolerates poorly drained soil. ZONE 10.

Melaleuca quinquenervia

Melaleuca thymifolia

Melaleuca quinquenervia

Melaleuca quinquenervia

MELASTOMA
Melastomataceae

This genus consists of 70 species of evergreen small trees and shrubs, all native to tropical regions. They have large, soft leaves with prominent veins. White, pink or purple terminal flowers bloom throughout most of the year in tropical climates, and in summer in subtropical areas. These are followed by deep red or blue-black berries. Frost-tender, they require full light or part-shade in fertile, well-drained soil. If necessary, they can be pruned in late winter. Propagate from cuttings taken in spring or summer.

Melastoma malabathricum

This tropical Asian shrub has large, soft leaves, easily damaged by cold winds, and distinctive, almost flat, light purple, single flowers that are often mistaken for those of a *Tibouchina*. Generally grown in warm areas where frost is not likely to occur, this is a low-branched plant that needs ample space to display its large flowers which are held in profuse clusters in summer and autumn. It needs to be well watered during its extensive flowering season. The berries that follow the flowers are reddish and have been long used for medicinal purposes by peoples of India and Southeast Asia. ZONE 10.

MELIA
Meliaceae

Recent botanical studies have shown that this genus consists of only one very variable species of deciduous tree, ranging across Asia from Iraq to Japan, and south to Australia. This is *Melia azedarach*, a favourite small to medium-sized tree in warm but not tropical climates, admired for its great ability to put up with drought and poor soil as well as for its elegance and attractive summer flowers. It has many common names: Persian lilac, pride of India, Chinaberry, white cedar (from the timber), bead tree or rosary tree. The last two arise from the way the seeds conveniently have a hole through the middle, which makes them suitable for bead-making; until the advent of more colourful plastic beads they used to be grown in southern Italy for making rosaries. The name *Melia* is Greek for the ash (*Fraxinus*), though the only connection is that the pinnate or doubly pinnate leaves are vaguely similar. Propagation is usually from seed.

Melia azedarach
CHINABERRY, WHITE CEDAR, PERSIAN LILAC

A fast-growing, spreading tree to about 30 ft (10 m), the Chinaberry is a favourite street tree in arid climates, though it is not always very long lived. The young leaves are accompanied in late spring or early summer by large sprays of small, delicately scented lilac flowers which are followed by bunches of pale orange berries, each containing a single woody seed, which persist until the leaves fall. They are decorative also and, though poisonous to humans, are much eaten by birds. The species is widespread throughout subtropical Asia, and the form *australasica* occurs in northern and eastern Australia. As the species is thus one of the very few deciduous trees native to Australia, it is much grown by patriotic gardeners there, though most trees in Australia have been propagated from seed originating in Iraq. The cultivar 'Umbraculiformis', the Texas umbrella tree, has a curiously attractive habit, like a blown-out umbrella. ZONE 8.

MESPILUS
Rosaceae
MEDLAR

This single species genus originated in Europe and south-west Asia and has been in cultivation for hundreds of years. A deciduous tree (sometimes thorny), it is adaptable to a range of soils and is frost resistant but should never be allowed to dry out. Reaching a height of 20 ft (7 m), it is grown primarily for its brown fruit which is edible only after it has been 'bletted' (almost rotten) and which stays on the tree until well into autumn. Its large hairy leaves form a dense canopy of foliage which turns russet in autumn, particularly if the tree is grown in full sun. Large, single white flowers appear in early summer and are unperfumed. Slow growing, *Mespilus* species resent being transplanted but are easy to cultivate, requiring only a light pruning in early winter. Propagation is from seed or by grafting.

Mespilus germanica

Medlars have been eaten since the time of the Romans. They are less favoured today, partly because

Melia azedarach form *australasica*

Melia azedarach form *australasica*

Melia azedarach form *australasica*

Metasequoia glyptostroboides

refrigeration has made fresh fruit available even in mid-winter, when medlars are at their peak, and partly because modern taste rejects a fruit which has to be beginning to decompose before it can be eaten. The tree is a pretty sight in early summer with its white flowers, and its gnarled branches give it an interestingly ancient look even when quite young. It grows easily in any temperate climate, liking well-drained soil and shelter from strong wind. Pick the fruit when the leaves fall, preferably after frost, and store them until they are sufficiently 'bletted', when they will be as soft as butter. ZONE 4.

MESUA
Clusiaceae

The lovely deciduous trees from the genus *Mesua* originate in Asia and are prized for their foliage, flowers and timber. They need well-drained, fertile soil, plenty of moisture and a sheltered sunny position. Young trees are slow to establish and have a formal conical appearance which becomes rounded with age. Eventually the tree can reach 60 ft (20 m). The new foliage is brilliant red maturing to rich green. The white flowers are fragrant. Propagate from seed or cuttings.

Mesua nagassarium

In India *M. nagassarium* is considered to be one of the most important timber species of the genus. It is also a popular specimen tree, providing shade in parks and gardens where its sumptuous foliage can be seen to best effect. Although a slow grower, it makes an excellent, dense screen tree. Its leaves are dark green above, pale green beneath and look attractive when fluttering in the breeze. ZONE 11.

METASEQUOIA
Taxodiaceae
DAWN REDWOOD

Until shortly after World War II, *Metasequoia glyptostroboides* was known only as a fossil, and it was indeed the best known of fossil conifers. Then a stand of living

Metasequoia glyptostroboides

trees was discovered in western China and from these it has been propagated, to be widely planted in temperate-climate gardens. The only living species in its genus, it is notable for the attractive way the foliage turns russet before falling in autumn. It is thus one of the few deciduous conifers. It grows very rapidly and, as the timber is durable and of fine quality, it is a very promising tree for cool-climate forestry. It prefers a deep, fertile soil, good summer rainfall, and shelter from strong winds.

Metasequoia glyptostroboides

Its gracefully conical outline and delicate foliage, light green in spring and summer and russet and gold in autumn, have given the dawn redwood wide acceptance as a specimen for parks and large gardens, quite apart from its curiosity value as the 'living fossil'. It is unusually rapid in growth if the climate is moist and the soil fertile, and it is thought that old trees will achieve 200 ft (60 m). As the trees mature, the rough textured bark turns from reddish to dark brown to grey. It can take clipping, so has been tried as a tall hedge. It is propagated from seed or cuttings taken from side shoots in autumn. ZONE 5.

Metasequoia glyptostroboides

Mespilus germanica

Metrosideros kermadecensis 'Variegata'

Metrosideros excelsa 'Variegata'

Metrosideros robusta

Metrosideros excelsa

Metrosideros umbellata

METROSIDEROS
Myrtaceae

The 20 or so species in this South Pacific genus are not all trees; some are shrubs or even vines. They are especially important in New Zealand where several species yield rata, the hard dark-red timber prized by the Maoris for sculpture, and where they are found from the very edge of the sea to the high mountains. They typically have hard, leathery, evergreen leaves, often with an attractive grey tinge, and red (sometimes bright yellow) summer flowers whose chief beauty, like those of the related *Eucalyptus* of Australia, comes from their long coloured stamens. As a group, they do best in subtropical or warm-temperate climates, and are adaptable to most soils. The shrubby species do very well as container plants.

Metrosideros excelsa
POHUTUKAWA

Growing to around 37 ft (12 m), these trees begin as shrubs with masses of low-growing branches forming a dense outline. As they mature a stout main trunk forms and an umbrella-shaped canopy develops (often with a very sculptured outline if buffeted by salt-laden winds). The oblong leaves are a dull deep green above with a grey felty texture underneath. The crimson stamens stand out from the flowers making a showy display from November to January in the warm zones of the southern hemisphere, hence an alternate common name of New Zealand Christmas tree. It makes an exceptional screen or can be used for hedging, requiring little pruning to keep a good outline. ZONE 10.

Metrosideros kermadecensis
KERMADEC POHUTUKAWA

This tree is very similar to *M. excelsa* but the leaves, as well as being slightly smaller, are more oval and the flowering season is usually more prolonged. Growing to much the same height as *M. excelsa*, it is more often seen in its variegated-leaf forms. 'Variegata' forms a neat shrub for many years before eventually becoming tree-like to around 18 ft (6 m). The grey-green leaves are edged with an irregular creamy yellow margin. 'Sunninghill' has the creamy yellow marking towards the middle of the leaf. The species and the cultivars make good hedges and screens. ZONE 10.

Metrosideros robusta
NORTHERN RATA

This species from the North Island and northern area of the South Island of New Zealand is a tree up to 70 ft (22 m) high. It is heavily wooded and in the wild the branches are often covered with epiphytic plants. It often begins its own life as an epiphyte, eventually sending down roots to ground level. In gardens it behaves normally and can be treated like any other evergreen tree. It is very slow growing. Masses of brilliant orange-red flowers open in summer. ZONE 9.

Metrosideros umbellata
SOUTHERN RATA

Similar to the northern rata though not as large, this species is found throughout much of New Zealand and extends into higher alpine regions. It produces a mass of magnificent, intensely scarlet blooms from late spring to autumn and its flowering is a feature of the bushlands of the Southern Alps. It is not difficult to cultivate but its rate of growth can be frustratingly slow. ZONE 8.

MICHELIA
Magnoliaceae

Closely related to the magnolias, the 50 or so species of *Michelia* are to be found in tropical and subtropical Asia, with a few species in the cooler foothills of the Himalaya. They range from shrubs to quite substantial trees, mainly evergreen, the chief attraction to gardeners being the often intense fragrance of their flowers. Some species are widely cultivated in India for the extraction of fragrant oil from these blooms, for use in the perfume and cosmetic industry. They like frost-free climates and fertile soil; like the magnolias, they resent being transplanted. Propagation is from seed or summer cuttings.

Michelia champaca
CHAMPAK

Originating in the lower reaches of the Himalaya, this evergreen tree reaches 100 ft (30 m) in its native habitat but is usually seen in gardens growing to only a third of this height. It is an upright, conical tree with long, slender, bright green leaves held in a drooping effect from the somewhat horizontal branches. Cup-shaped creamy orange petals sitting on a bed of recurved sepals are held in an upright fashion towards the ends of the branches during late summer. The flowers are particularly fragrant. ZONE 10.

Michelia doltsopa

Growing to around 30 ft (10 m), this tree from the eastern Himalaya has a slender habit while young which tends to a broader crown with age. The large, scented, white flowers, reminiscent of those of *Magnolia denudata*, appear in the axils of the greyish green leaves in late winter and early spring. ZONE 9.

Michelia figo
PORT-WINE MAGNOLIA, BANANA SHRUB

A slow-growing, compact, evergreen shrub from western China, the port-wine magnolia is usually seen as a dense shrub of about 10 ft (3 m) but eventually grows to twice that. The small, shiny, deep green leaves virtually obscure the tiny spring-blooming cream flowers which are streaked with purple and heavily scented. It is a neat bushy shrub and only needs pruning to produce an abundance of new flowering growth. ZONE 9.

Michelia yunnanensis

This small, open-crowned tree will grow to 15 ft (5 m) and produces large, round, perfumed, cream flowers with prominent yellow stamens in spring. Clustered along the length of the branches, the flowers burst from furry brown buds. The tree is well suited to cool climates if it can be given protection from strong winds. Slow growing, *M. yunnanensis* is a good tree for small gardens. It will also make a good container specimen when it will require consistent watering during its growing season. ZONE 9.

MICROBIOTA
Cupressaceae

There is just the one species in this genus, a dwarf conifer that is excellent either on its own or grouped together with other low-growing conifers or heathers. It also acts well as a foil to other more brightly hued plants such as bulbs. Accepting of most positions and soils, it should be pruned only if absolutely necessary and then only into the new wood. Propagate from seed or from tip cuttings.

Microbiota decussa

This conifer from Siberia needs dry, free-draining, sandy soil and an open aspect. It can tolerate extremes of temperature and high altitude. It is excellent as an evergreen groundcover as it only grows to 20 in (50 cm) high with a spread of 10 ft (3 m). Its foliage nods at the tips and consists of flat sprays of scaly, yellowish green leaves that turn bronze in winter. Its small, round cones are pale brown and contain only one fertile seed each. ZONE 3.

Michelia yunnanensis (right)

Michelia figo (below)

Microbiota decussa

Michelia figo, young shrub (below)

Michelia doltsopa (below)

MILLETTIA
Fabaceae

Over 90 species of vines, shrubs and trees from a vast area of the tropics together with several species from humid coastal South Africa make up this genus which is a member of the pea family. All species, both evergreen and deciduous, thrive in warm humid areas where their large compound leaves and great trusses of pea-shaped flowers demand admiration. They prefer a moist, well-drained soil situated in full sun and the trees in the genus are ideal as specimen shade trees. Prune only if necessary to keep the plant shapely. Propagation is from seed.

Millettia grandis
SOUTH AFRICAN IRONWOOD, UMZIMBEET

The most popular tree species of *Milletia* for warm humid areas, the ironwood provides year round shade from its dense, evergreen crown made up of long leaves which hold as many as 15 pairs of smaller, glossy green leaflets. Growing to around 30 ft (10 m), it begins to branch at head height. In late spring the ironwood carries large rose-purple flower spikes above the foliage. Flat furry pods develop after the flowers have faded and the seeds within are readily germinated. ZONE 10.

Morus alba (below)

Morus alba 'Pendula' (below)

Montanoa bipinnatifida (below)

MONTANOA
Asteraceae

This striking group of evergreen plants includes some quite large shrubs that can reach a height of 20 ft (7 m) and which may alternatively be treated as herbaceous plants. Leaves of most species are deeply indented giving a pleasant texture to a shrub border, while the daisy-like flowers make an interesting conversation point when seen growing on such large bushes. As these plants are frost-tender, a full sun position will result in a good floral display provided the soil is well drained with ample humus and water added. After flowering, the plants should be cut back hard. Propagate from seed or from root cuttings.

Millettia grandis

Morus alba (below)

Montanoa bipinnatifida
MEXICAN DAISY TREE

Growing upwards to about 15 ft (5 m) with large, soft green leaves that are deeply indented, this species comes from Central America. In late autumn and winter large clusters of white, daisy-like single flowers appear on the long, branching canes. The display can be prolonged with regular deadheading. When the flowers are spent the shrub can be pruned hard to encourage new growth. As the canes can be rather brittle, plant in a sheltered position. Water well while in growth and liquid feed when the flowers begin to form. ZONE 10.

MORINGA
Moringaceae

Originating in the drier parts of western Asia and Africa, this genus consists of small deciduous trees that are ideal for gardens with a sunny, protected aspect. They prefer a moist soil and need protection from frost and wind. The trees are admired for their soft, corky bark and attractive foliage. Propagation is from seed.

Moringa oleifera
DRUMSTICK TREE, HORSERADISH TREE

Growing to a maximum height of 24 ft (8 m) with a spread of 10 ft (3 m), this very attractive, small tree is cultivated all over India for the sake of its airy, much-divided leaves and sprays of white and gold, honey-scented spring flowers, but even more for its fruit. The name 'drumstick' is appropriate; each fluted, bright green pod can be 20 in (50 cm) long. The seeds are sometimes extracted to be eaten separately but more usually the entire, asparagus-flavoured pod is either pickled or boiled fresh. Both seeds and pods are much used in curries, the drumstick curry of Madras being a great favourite of Indian gourmets. The name horseradish tree is a relic of the British Raj, when expatriate Englishmen used to scrape the roots as a substitute for horseradish to accompany their roast beef. ZONE 11.

MORUS
Moraceae
MULBERRY

There are a dozen or so species of deciduous tree in this northern hemisphere genus, most of them originating in eastern Asia. They are characterized by broad, more or less heart-shaped leaves with closely toothed margins and inconspicuous greenish flowers on short catkins, the male and female flowers on separate catkins. The female catkins bear tiny fruits that are so closely packed together that they appear as a single fruit, the mulberry. On seedlings the leaves may be deeply lobed. Some of the species have been cultivated for centuries, both for edible fruit and for silk production, the silkworm larvae feeding on the leaves. Cultivation is simple, as the trees thrive under a wide range of conditions, but they do best in fertile, well-drained soils and a sunny, sheltered position. Propagation is easily achieved from cuttings, which can be quite large branches.

Morus alba
WHITE MULBERRY

It is this species that has always sustained the silk industry of China and Japan. It is a tree of vigorous growth, up to 40 ft (13 m) tall with a low-branching habit and broadly spreading crown, the smaller branches rather pendulous. The leaves are almost hairless and a fresh green shade, strongly veined, with sharp marginal teeth. The fruit are cylindrical, sometimes quite long and narrow, with a somewhat rubbery texture. Although 'white mulberry' refers to the white fruit colour, in fact the colour can vary from white through pink or red to purple-black. In east-coastal Australia a strain with purple-black fruit is regarded as the common mulberry. It prefers a climate with long, warm summers. ZONE 7.

Morus nigra
BLACK MULBERRY

Grown primarily for its fruit, this is the common mulberry of Britain and northern Europe. Its origin is uncertain but it is believed to have come from somewhere in China or central Asia. It makes a smaller tree than M. alba with a thicker trunk, more compact crown and darker green foliage. The leaves have a velvety down on the undersides and blunt marginal teeth. Fruits are dark red and slightly acid, though quite sweet when fully ripe. The leaves can be used to feed silkworms, though it is not as good for this as white mulberry. ZONE 6.

Morus rubra
RED MULBERRY

This North American mulberry is adaptable to most soils. It is grown for its unusual shape rather than for its fruit, which, although an attractive ruby shade, are relatively tasteless. As with M. nigra, care must taken with siting the tree as the fruit will stain paved areas. As the tree reaches its mature height of 65 ft (20 m) it takes on a characteristic twist which gives it a grotesque appearance. The trunk bears a spreading crown with serrated, heart-shaped leaves with a rough upper surface. The red mulberry is a reliable ornamental specimen. ZONE 2.

MUNDULEA
Fabaceae

This genus contains 30 species of more or less evergreen shrubs and small trees ranging from tropical Africa, Madagascar, southern India and Sri Lanka. Species have compound leaves made up of many smaller leaflets and distinctive purple-blue pea-shaped flowers held in clusters at the end of branches. It is a genus which occurs naturally in the dappled shade of taller trees in warm temperatures and success is assured if planted in a similar garden situation. In addition they need a well-drained, humus-rich soil. Prune lightly to maintain shape. Propagate from seeds soaked in hot water or from cuttings of short side shoots taken with a heel.

Mundulea sericea
SOUTH AFRICAN CORKBUSH

This slow-growing species grows to 10 ft (3 m) tall. Its leaves are compound and the branches tough and bendable when young. It bears reams of pea-shaped, purple-blue flowers with 3 in (8 cm) long tapering seed pods covered with velvet-like hairs. The bark and seed pods are reported for use as fish poison; it kills rather than stupefies them. However, the leaves are eaten by wild animals and livestock without any negative results. The corkbush is the only species of this genus found in South Africa. ZONE 9.

MURRAYA
Rutaceae

This is a small genus, allied to *Citrus*, of evergreen trees and shrubs from India and Southeast Asia, admired by gardeners for their aromatic foliage and attractive creamy white flowers, which rather resemble those of their relative the orange and are often strongly scented. *Murraya koenigii*, the curry tree, provides edible leaves that find their way, dried or fresh, into curry powder along with several other herbs and spices, but the best known ornamental species is M. paniculata, one of the best and most easily cultivated shrubs in frost-free but non-tropical climates. It is an understorey tree in nature, and does equally well in sun or quite deep shade. Gardeners in cooler areas should substitute the similar (though not so tall growing) *Choisya ternata*, which comes from Mexico.

Murraya koenigii
CURRY TREE

The leaves of this species are used in the preparation of curries and other spicy dishes, hence the common name. From the Indian sub-continent, this small, aromatic tree grows to about 10 ft (3 m). Bunches of fragrant creamy white flowers stand out against the fresh green foliage in summer and are followed by small, black fruit. ZONE 10.

Murraya paniculata
ORANGE JESSAMINE, MOCK ORANGE

Widely distributed in tropical Asia, the cosmetic bark (another of its common names) forms a compact and dense rounded bush up to 10 ft (3 m) tall that is thickly clothed with shiny, dark green leaflets. The small, creamy white, perfumed flowers are held in clusters at the ends of the branches in spring and at intervals thereafter. Red berries may appear after each flowering. It will flourish anywhere in warm climates, but when grown in borderline temperate situations a more sheltered though sunny aspect is advised. Early pruning will ensure a thickly branched shrub from the ground up and a yearly clipping, after the late flowering season, will maintain this bushiness. ZONE 10.

Morus rubra

Morus rubra

Morus nigra

Murraya paniculata

Mussaenda philippica (below)   *Musa ornata* (above)

Musa × paradisiaca

Musa × paradisiaca

Mussaenda philippica

Mussaenda erythrophylla (below)

MUSA
Musaceae

Bananas, originally native to India and adjacent countries, are now cultivated throughout the tropics; and, thanks to their ability to ripen in transit after being harvested green, they are a familiar fruit in temperate countries also. But the genus *Musa* includes several other important species, including *M. textilis* which yields the strong and useful fibre known as Manila hemp, and others grown for the decorative value of their enormous leaves or coloured flowers, though several of these have been translated to other genera such as *Ensete*. The nomenclature of the genus is in fact in some disarray, due to its very long history of cultivation and hybridization and to the ease with which hybrids can be propagated clonally by division of the rootstock, to the confusion of botanists. For though they often grow to tree size, the plants are really giant herbaceous perennials; each 'trunk' is composed of the bases of the leaves and when the flowering shoot has arisen from among them and borne its fruit, it dies. Some of the smaller species can be cultivated as house plants or in greenhouses in temperate climates.

Musa ornata
FLOWERING BANANA

As the name suggests, this species from Bangladesh and Burma is very decorative. The flowers are erect and contained in yellow bracts which are tinged with pink. It grows to a height of 10 ft (3 m), two-thirds of which is made up of foliage. The mid-green leaves have a red tinge along their midrib. It has unusual false stems which are waxy and pale green mottled with black. It is one of the few *Musa* species to produce inedible fruit. ZONE 11.

Musa × paradisiaca
BANANA, PLANTAIN

The bananas we know today are the result of cultivation and selection over the last three thousand years. Just about all the edible varieties—and there are many, with red or green fruit as well as the yellow familiar to temperate-climate markets, some designed for eating fresh, others (usually called plantains) for cooking—have no seeds at all. The 'tree' grows as tall as 25 ft (8 m), its long, wide leaves usually ripped to tatters by the wind. It grows very fast, often flowering and bearing fruit within 18 months of the shoot appearing from the rootstock. The immature flowers are enclosed in thick purplish bracts which drop off as the flowers mature and, as the female flowers are borne at the base of the stem and the male ones further along, by the time the fruit is beginning to ripen the flowers are separated from them by a long, dangling naked stem. The crop requires very fertile, moist soil and heat. Just about every part of the plant is used in the tropics; the leaves are used as thatch for roofing houses, the male flowers are cooked and eaten; sections of the wide, flat leaves are used as plates. ZONE 10.

MUSSAENDA
Rubiaceae

This is a genus of about 40 evergreen shrubs from tropical Africa, Asia and the Pacific Islands, widely cultivated throughout the tropics and subtropics for their year-long display, though it is not so much the petals of the small flowers in shades of red or yellow that are the chief feature but the way a single sepal is greatly enlarged into a kind of bract, which can be white, red or pink. The shrubs themselves are attractive in their bright green leaves, but they tend to become straggly and need regular trimming to keep them compact and about 3–5 ft (1–1.5 m) tall. They prefer a sunny or lightly shaded position and fertile, well-drained soil and are propagated from cuttings.

Mussaenda erythrophylla
ASHANTI BLOOD

Occurring naturally in tropical west and central Africa, this scrambling shrub can climb to a height of 30 ft (10 m), although 6 ft (2 m) is more normal, and produces slender, woody, strong stems. Also known as the red flag bush, its large, rounded, bright green leaves are covered with silky hairs. Those who persevere with this tender plant will be rewarded with a stunning late summer display of clustered creamy yellow flowers with a red felted middle accompanied by blood-red bracts up to 3 in (7 cm) long. ZONE 11.

Mussaenda philippica
LADY FLOWERS

The name is a botanical convenience, applied to a group of very attractive hybrids developed in the Philippines after World War II which feature much tighter flower-clusters than usual so that the 'bracts' appear to form large, many-petalled flowers, usually in some shade of pink. They are mostly named after prominent ladies, hence the common name *dona flores* or lady flowers, and include the bright pink 'Dona Imelda', 'Dona Luz', pink with red edges; and the pale pink and crimson 'Queen Sirikit'. It is thought that they were originally derived from *M. erythrophylla* and the widely cultivated *M. frondosa* from India, which has white bracts. ZONE 11.

MYOPORUM
Myoporaceae

About 30 species of evergreen trees and shrubs from a wide area throughout the southern hemisphere make up this genus. These plants are named from the Greek *myo* (to close) and the Latin *porum* (a pore), because of the high number of glands or transparent spots on their leaves. They make quick-growing screens and are especially useful in warm climates. To ensure a dense windbreak the plants will need to be clipped, although this may interfere with the attractive display of the fruit which follow the white to pinkish white flowers. Propagate from seed or from cuttings taken from young firm growth.

Myoporum floribundum
WEEPING BOOBIALLA

This small to medium-sized shrub reaches a height and spread of around 10 ft (3 m) with slender, somewhat horizontal and pendent branches. These are lightly clothed in long narrow leaves which adds to the weeping effect. During spring and early summer the shrub is covered with tiny white blossoms giving the appearance of snow resting on the weeping branches; however, many people dislike their heavy scent. Short lived, it does equally well in sun or part-shade in a light, slightly acid soil, and a light pruning from an early age will ensure a bushy plant. ZONE 9.

Myoporum insulare
BOOBIALLA

This very adaptable species, growing 3–21 ft (1–7 m) high has spreading, upright branches holding fleshy dark green leaves with toothed margins. The small white flowers are spotted purple and are clustered towards the ends of the branches. They are followed by succulent purple-streaked white fruit. It is not fussy as to soil type, even withstanding wet periods in heavy soils. Easily grown, it does best in full sun and responds to regular pruning. ZONE 9.

Myoporum laetum
NGAIO

Varying in height from 15–30 ft (5–10 m), this wind-resistant small tree is grown extensively in its New Zealand homeland as a shelter or screen tree on exposed sites. The light green leaves, about 3–4 in (8–10 cm) long, are lightly toothed towards their ends. The plant is easily recognized by its sticky shoots at the ends of the branches. White flowers, liberally sprinkled with purple dots, are insignificant and are followed by maroon fruits. It responds well to regular trimming, though in exposed conditions ngaio is often shaped by the prevailing winds. ZONE 10.

MYRICA
Myricaceae

Myrica is a genus of about 50 species of evergreen or deciduous shrubs and trees ranging in height from 5 ft (1.5 m) to 100 ft (30 m) that grow happily in awkward marshy spots where nothing else survives. They must never be allowed to dry out. *Myrica* species thrive in part-shade, but will not grow in alkaline or chalky conditions. The main attraction are the fruits which consist of clusters of bluish black berries enclosed in a white waxy crust. Tiny flowers appear in late spring with both sexes on the one plant, the males in elongated catkins and the females in globular clusters. Propagation is from seed or cuttings, or by layering in summer.

Myrica cerifera
WAX MYRTLE, BAYBERRY

This shrub flourishes in the southeastern region of North America where it enjoys swampy conditions, peaty soil and the shade of taller trees. An evergreen with a mature height of 30 ft (10 m), wax myrtle bears narrow, dark glossy green leaves with unusual downy undersides. Its golden brown catkins are followed by the fruits. The wax on the fruits is harvested for use in the manufacture of candles. ZONE 4.

Myrica gale
SWEET GALE

Indigenous to northern Europe and northern regions of North America, this is a deciduous shrub which grows to 5 ft (1.5 m) tall and wide. It is erect and bushy with oval leaves which are dark green on top with an attractive paler green underside. Its tiny fruits, crowded in dense spikes, are greenish yellow. With its compact growth, this plant makes a useful screen or understorey specimen in damp, peaty areas; it is also called bog myrtle. ZONE 4.

MYRISTICA
Myristicaceae

Myristica consists of about 80 species of tropical evergreen trees that grow to 100 ft (30 m). They must be protected from frost and drought, and planted in rich, moist, well-drained soils if they are to

Myrica cerifera

Myoporum floribundum

Myoporum laetum

Myoporum floribundum (below)

Myoporum laetum (below)

Myrtus communis

Myroxylon balsamum

Myristica fragrans

Myroxylon balsamum

Myrtus communis

flourish outside their native regions of tropical Asia, northern Australia and the islands of the Pacific. They perform best if allowed to grow in a hot, humid position away from sun, strong winds and pollution. Only the flowers of the female trees produce fruit, but they do so several times a year. Propagation is from seed, cuttings or by grafting in spring and autumn. ZONE 11.

Myristica fragrans
NUTMEG

The fruit of this tree from Indonesia is nutmeg, the exotic spice which has been used for centuries in many different ways. It is now cultivated commercially mainly in Indonesia and in Grenada, sometimes called the Nutmeg Island. A slender, evergreen tree maturing to a height of 50 ft (15 m), it is distinctive for its whorls of spreading branches and smooth grey bark. The aromatic leaves, which are said to contain insect repelling agents, are much more decorative than the flowers, which are small and pale yellow. *M. fragrans*' crowning glory is the nutmegs which appear as fleshy, pear-shaped brilliant scarlet berries when ripe. Their red jackets are harvested and processed separately to become mace, which is a milder spice than nutmeg. ZONE 12.

MYROXYLON
Fabaceae

Indigenous to tropical America, *Myroxylon* species insist on moist rich, fertile soil and plenty of warmth if they are to reach their height of 30 ft (10 m). Slender, graceful evergreen trees, they are grown for their attractive foliage and showy white flowers. The pinnate leaves are glossy green, borne on branches stemming from an erect, stout trunk. The fruits consist of 2-winged pods which appear in profusion in late summer. Propagation is from scarified seed.

Myroxylon balsamum
TOLU BALSAM

This native of Venezuela will produce a mass of white, butterfly-like fragrant flowers if grown in a hot, steamy environment. The glossy leaves have up to 13 oblong, alternate leaflets. *M. balsamum* must have heat to produce its large seed pods which are about 3 in (8 cm) long. ZONE 11.

MYRTUS
Myrtaceae
TRUE MYRTLE

The ancient Greeks and Romans knew this Mediterranean shrub as *Myrtus*, from which the English 'myrtle' came down to us via Old French. As a scientific name it has been used by botanists in both narrow and broad senses. The narrow sense is adopted here, following most present-day botanists who separate the southern hemisphere myrtles off into a number of other genera including *Lophomyrtus*, *Luma* and *Ugni*, leaving *Myrtus* with only the single species *M. communis*, the original Mediterranean myrtle. Myrtles are usually densely foliaged evergreen shrubs with small, deep green, pointed leaves and starry white flowers in spring. The flowers may be followed by blackish purple berries. True myrtle prefers moist, well-drained soil and will grow in sun or light shade. This shrub benefits from a light trimming to keep it compact, and can be used for informal hedging. It also makes a good container plant, when it is often seen clipped into a ball or pyramid. If container grown in cooler areas, it will need to be given protection during the cold months. Some foliage cultivars are available but there is little variation in the flowers. Propagate from semi-ripe cuttings or from seed.

Myrtus communis

This is an erect shrub to around 10 ft (3 m) with dense, small, deep green leaves, wonderfully fragrant when crushed. The highly perfumed white flowers appear in spring, followed by edible berries ripening to blue-black with a delicate whitish waxy bloom. Cultivated for hundreds of years, this is the myrtle that was prized by the ancient Greeks. A number of cultivars exist, including 'Flore Pleno' with double white flowers, 'Microphylla' with tiny leaves and flowers, and 'Variegata' with leaves edged white. ZONE 8.

Nauclea orientalis

Nandina domestica 'Nana'

Nandina domestica

Nandina domestica

NANDINA
Berberidaceae
SACRED BAMBOO, HEAVENLY BAMBOO

Nandina is a genus of a single species from China and Japan, related not to the bamboos—though it is rather bamboo like in its habit and the elegance of its compoundly pinnate leaves—but to the barberries. It grows as a clump of thin, upright stems, and bears sprays of white flowers in summer and red berries in autumn and winter. The plants come in male and female and both are needed to enjoy the fruit, though hermaphrodite cultivars are available. The plants like a little shade and fertile soil and a warm-temperate or subtropical climate. The scientific name is a corruption of the Japanese name nanten, and the common one comes from the Oriental tradition of planting it in the gardens of temples, though it is popular in secular gardens also.

Nandina domestica

This is a shrub with strongly upright, cane-like stems growing to 6 ft (2 m) high. The evergreen foliage is usually bipinnate and composed of many 1 in (2 cm), elliptical leaflets. These are red when young, become green and then develop intense yellow, orange and red tones when the cold weather arrives. The small white flowers appear in terminal panicles in summer. Although separate clones are usually needed to see the red berries that follow, self-fertile cultivars such as 'Nana', 'Richmond' and 'Firepower' are available and are generally preferable to seedlings. ZONE 5.

NAUCLEA
Rubiaceae

This genus is named from the Greek words *naus* (ship) and *kleio* (to close) because the seeds resemble the hull of a ship. These evergreen shrubs and trees from tropical Africa across Asia, Australia and Polynesia have smooth, leathery leaves. They are cultivated in warmer areas for their fragrant flowers and edible red fruit. They require filtered light and moist soil enriched with organic matter. Propagate from seed or cuttings taken towards the end of summer.

Nauclea orientalis
LEICHHARDT TREE

Growing to around 50 ft (15 m), this widely distributed tree has a conical shape and spreading branches. Its bark is deeply furrowed and the heart-shaped, deep green leaves are up to 10 in (25 cm) long. If there is a shortage of water, the tree may drop its leaves. Attractive yellow flowers are borne in clusters during late spring and summer. ZONE 11.

NEODYPSIS
Arecaceae

These feather-leafed palms from Madagascar are closely related to the genus *Dypsis*, and in fact recent botanical studies show that in the future they may be re-classified as *Dypsis*. Only one species is commonly cultivated, valued for its elegant fronds which are strikingly arranged in 3 vertical ranks, the large sheathing frond bases making a triangle in cross-section. The trunk itself is short and stout, ringed with scars from the fallen fronds. Short panicles of small cream flowers protrude from among the frond bases, with small oval fruit following, though these are rare in cultivation. These palms require a tropical or subtropical climate free of frost, but have proved surprisingly hardy under dry or exposed conditions as long as the roots are well watered. Propagation is only possible from seed.

Neodypsis decaryi
THREE-CORNERED PALM

As usually seen, this palm has a very short, thick trunk, seldom more than 6 ft (2 m) high, but topped by a vase-shaped crown of large fronds, up to about 12 ft (4 m) long, with elegantly recurved tips and very narrow leaflets arranged in 2 regular rows. A distinctive feature is the way the lowest leaflets are extended into long threadlike appendages that hang down to the ground. The broad frond bases are clothed in thick blue-grey felt with rusty tinges, and the fronds are also a pale greyish green. The three-cornered palm makes a striking landscape subject but requires an open space such as a lawn or courtyard for effective display. ZONE 11.

NERIUM
Apocynaceae
ROSE-LAUREL, OLEANDER

This small genus consists of evergreen shrubs native to northern Africa and southwest Asia. The most important is *Nerium oleander*, cultivated (and often naturalized) all through the drier subtropics and much grown in warm-temperate climates also for the sake of its lavish display of perfumed flowers, borne from spring to autumn. The wild form is pink, but cultivars offer shades from white to red. The oleander is a big, straggling bush with dull green, pointed leaves and usually grows on the banks of streams, which has led some scholars to think it is the 'willow of the brook' mentioned in the Bible; in gardens it flourishes in any sort of soil, dry or moist, so long as it gets plenty of sunshine. If the shrubs get overgrown and leggy, they can be rejuvenated by severe pruning in spring. In frosty climates, oleanders can be grown in containers and overwintered under glass. *Nerium* species are very poisonous, but this has not harmed their popularity, as all parts of the plant are so very bitter even goats won't eat them and it is rare for people to try. Propagate from summer cuttings.

Nerium oleander
OLEANDER

Depending on the cultivar selected, the plants can grow from 6–12 ft (2–4 m) tall. As it is a species often used for hedging, it is wise to keep the varying growth-habits of the cultivars in mind if a uniform appearance is wanted. Cultivars have long, deep green leaves and the flowers, ranging from white to salmon to deep pink, appear in late summer onwards and are held in clusters. Depending on the cultivar the blooms can be single or double, while some cultivars have variegated foliage. Some popular cultivars include 'Album', with single white flowers with a cream centre; 'Luteum Plenum', with double flowers of creamy yellow; 'Mrs Fred Roeding', with double salmon-pink blooms with a smaller growth-habit; 'Punctatum', a vigorous plant with single, pale pink blooms; and 'Splendens Variegatum', with pink double flowers and variegated gold-green foliage borne at the expense of the profuse flowering habit of its parent 'Splendens'. ZONE 9.

NOTHOFAGUS
Fagaceae
SOUTHERN BEECH

Nothofagus is a genus of over 25 species of evergreen and deciduous trees, many of which make tall trees in their native forests. These fast-growing trees have dark green leaves with margins often toothed. The foliage of several of the deciduous species displays rich bronze hues before dropping. The small fruits each contain 3 triangular seeds known as beechnuts. Thought to have originated in Antarctica (in the days before that continent took up residence at the South Pole!) before spreading to Australia, New Zealand and South America, they can be cultivated in a variety of climates providing they have protection from strong winds. They prefer acid soil, deep enough to support their large root system. They should be planted out when small and never transplanted. Position in full sun and water well when young. Propagate from cuttings in summer or seed in autumn.

Nothofagus cunninghamii

Neodypsis decaryi

Nothofagus cunninghamii
TASMANIAN BEECH

This magnificent tree, also known as myrtle beech and Tasmanian myrtle, attains a height of 160 ft (50 m) when grown in the cool, mountainous regions in the south of its native Australia. An evergreen, it is one of the faster growing species in the genus, and is valued for its reddish timber. Its small, dark green, triangular-toothed leaves are held in fan-shaped sprays and the young foliage is a deep bronze shade in spring. Small catkin flowers are borne in early summer. ZONE 8.

Nerium oleander 'Punctatum'

Nothofagus cunninghamii

Nerium oleander 'Album'

Nerium oleander cultivars in a garden setting in India

Nothofagus moorei

Nothofagus menziesii
NEW ZEALAND SILVER BEECH

Famed for its beautiful silver bark, this evergreen tree from New Zealand bears a mass of small, dense leaves with coarsely serrated margins. Reaching a height of 65 ft (20 m), it must have wind protection and plenty of sun. The flowers appear as small catkins in summer. ZONE 8.

Nothofagus moorei
ANTARCTIC BEECH

Unlike its siblings, this Australian tree prefers a partially shaded, frost-free position where its roots can stay moist during dry spells. An evergreen tree, it is sometimes known as the Antarctic beech. Growing to a mature height of over 65 ft (20 m) with a broad head, this species bears distinctive triangular leaves up to 4 in (10 cm) long. Its massive trunk is covered with brown, scaly bark. The tiny, insignificant flowers appear in early summer. ZONE 9.

Nothofagus obliqua
ROBLE

Deriving its name from its characteristic oblique leaf base, the roble or Chilean beech is a deciduous tree from Chile and Argentina. Growing to 160 ft (50 m), it has a broad spread of 21 ft (7 m) and is suitable for cold regions. Its deeply toothed leaves and attractive drooping habit make it one of the most popular *Nothofagus* species in cultivation. Its leaves turn a deep reddish orange before dropping. The roble is now grown as a plantation crop for its fine timber and its exceedingly rapid growth. ZONE 8.

Nothofagus procera
RAULI

One of the best timber species of the family and also the fastest growing, the rauli thrives in mild wet climates anywhere from its native South America to western Europe and the USA where it is enjoyed for the reddish gold hues the leaves attain before they drop. Fast growing, *N. procera* is delicate when young and should be protected during severe winters. It is also susceptible to pollution. ZONE 8.

Nothofagus solandri
BLACK BEECH

A 60 ft (18 m) high evergreen tree endemic to New Zealand, the black beech has small leaves, around ½ in (1 cm) long, but they are densely packed in fan-like sprays. The young growth is soft and downy. The black bark is a very distinctive feature. Small reddish brown flowers, heavy with pollen, open in spring. Although individually

Nothofagus solandri (below)

Nothofagus moorei (below)

Nothofagus obliqua

Nothofagus solandri (below)

the flowers are not very significant, when in full bloom the tree develops a reddish cast. To achieve best results, the tree should be grown in moist, humus-enriched, well-drained soil with light shade when young. ZONE 8.

NOTOSPARTIUM
Fabaceae

The species of broom-like shrubs that comprise this small genus thrive in any well-drained soil but must have full sun to flower. Medium-sized bushes reaching a maximum of 9 ft (3 m), *Notospartium* species grow naturally in New Zealand but have become popular in mild-winter climates elsewhere because of the profusion of charming pea-shaped flowers that appear in mid-summer. The shrubs are leafless at maturity and attain their shape from graceful arching branches which can spread to 6 ft (2 m). Propagation is from seed in spring or from cuttings taken in late summer.

Notospartium carmichaeliae
NEW ZEALAND PINK BROOM

This deciduous shrub bears leaves only when the plant is young, and spends the rest of its life as a flat-stemmed, erect, slender bush. When in full spring flower, the shrub is smothered in lilac-pink blossoms which appear all along the branches. If protected from the wind, flowering will continue for many weeks during warm weather. Preferring sandy soil, the pink broom must be kept moist during dry spells and protected from frosts during winter. ZONE 8.

NUYTSIA
Loranthaceae
WESTERN AUSTRALIAN CHRISTMAS TREE

This genus, consisting of a single species from Western Australia, was named after the Dutch navigator, Peter Nuyts. *N. floribunda* is a semi-parasitic shrub in nature, dependent on a host plant, but it seems in cultivation it is not particular as to the host type—it germinates easily and as long as a tuft of grass is added to the potting mix of young seedlings they seem to thrive. Plant out when quite young, in combination with the initial host plant, in the vicinity of another likely companion. Strawberries have been trialled with success as companions to this beautiful but unusual plant, sometimes called the golden bough.

Nuytsia floribunda

An evergreen tree growing to 30 ft (10 m), *N. floribunda* has widely spreading branches and slender leaves about 3 in (8 cm) long. A magnificent display of honey-scented, orange-yellow flowers are borne in elongated clusters towards the end of the branches during the summer months. It needs full sun and, as the plants grow naturally in a moist position, cultivated specimens will need to be well watered, especially while young. ZONE 9.

NUXIA
Loganiaceae

There are about 40 species in this genus of evergreen trees and shrubs spread throughout Africa, Madagascar and the Mascarene Islands. The leaves are simple and generally arranged in 3s around a node, very occasionally alternate or sometimes opposite. Smooth or hairy and sticky, the leaves can be toothed or lobed, either wavy or with entire margins. Small sweet-smelling flowers are borne terminally. The fruit is a capsule with small and numerous seeds. Propagate from cuttings.

Nuxia floribunda
FOREST ELDER

This decorative tree occurs mainly in the coastal forests of south-eastern Cape Province, South Africa. It grows to about 24 ft (8 m) with a spread of 12 ft (4 m) and has a rounded crown when mature. The glossy, evergreen leaves are simple, oblong and large, 6 in (15 cm) long. From autumn to spring the tree bears large clusters of fragrant, creamy white flowers, up to 12 in (30 cm) long, that give it a hazy, almost lacy, beauty. As forest elder does not grow easily from seed, cuttings are the only method of propagation. Plant it in a large hole in good, enriched soil. A fast grower, it likes plenty of sun and a frost-free winter. This attractive specimen tree deserves to be planted in greater numbers and could be used along streets in towns and cities. ZONE 9.

Notospartium carmichaeliae

Nuxia floribunda

Nuytsia floribunda

Olea europaea growing in Morocco

Ochna serrulata

Nyssa sylvatica

Olea europaea

Nyssa sylvatica

NYSSA
Nyssaceae

Occurring naturally in southern Asia and North America, the genus is named after Nyssa, the water nymph, because the trees insist on adequate year-round water to survive. Fast growing and wind tolerant, they must be left undisturbed after planting and may reach a maximum height of 110 ft (35 m) with a broad-based conical shape. Small clusters of greenish white flowers appear during summer to be followed by vivid, dark purple berries, up to 1 in (2 cm) long, which provide an effective contrast to the stunning foliage. Few trees attract as much attention as these when they are clad in their spectacular red, crimson, yellow and orange autumn foliage, though they must have acid soil and a cool climate. Prune only to remove dead or crowded branches. Propagate from seed in spring.

Nyssa aquatica
WATER TUPELO

This tree can commonly be found in swamps or shallow water where it develops a sturdy buttressed trunk. Its leaves are diamond shaped, green and 10 in (25 cm) long. The honey made by bees drinking the nectar from tupelo flowers has a distinctive and delicious taste. An important timber tree, *N. aquatica*, sometimes called a tupelo gum or cotton gum, is a pyramid-shaped specimen that reaches 110 ft (35 m) in optimum conditions. ZONE 5.

Nyssa sylvatica
BLACK TUPELO

This elegant tree is one of the most decorative and useful of all deciduous plants, as it flourishes in swampy conditions. The 4 in (10 cm) long leaves are a glossy dark or yellowish green turning brilliant red, often with shades of orange and yellow as well, before dropping and are slightly wider towards the tip than the base. A small tree growing to 65 ft (20 m) with a broad columnar conical habit, the sour gum, as it is also called, has an unusual trunk covered with brownish grey bark which breaks up into large pieces on mature specimens. ZONE 3.

OCHNA
Ochnaceae

The name is derived from the Greek *ochne* (wild pear), referring to the similarity of the foliage to that of a pear tree. Grown for their distinctive fruit, these small trees and shrubs also have attractive evergreen leaves and flowers making them a useful and bright addition to a shrub border in many areas. Numbering about 90 species, some can be invasive in warm, humid areas near bushland and care needs to be taken in selecting the plants and in managing them. Grow in full sun in any fertile and well-drained soil. Prune during spring, and propagate from seed in spring or from cuttings in summer.

Ochna serrulata
CARNIVAL BUSH, MICKEY MOUSE PLANT

A native of southern Africa, this shrub is sometimes referred to as bird's eye bush. It can grow up to 8 ft (2.5 m) with a rather open habit and has narrow, glossy mid-green leaves. The flowers open yellow-green and become large and reflexed with a red calyx. The berries ripen to a glossy black and when these drop, they seed easily causing the plant to become a pest if it is not controlled. ZONE 9.

OLEA
Oleaceae

There are about 20 species in this genus, all long-lived evergreen trees or shrubs from Africa, Asia and Australasia growing up to around 65 ft (20 m). The important species is the common olive (*Olea europaea*) which, in its many cultivars, is the source of olive oil. They have leathery, grey-green leaves and tiny off-white flowers which are followed by the fruit, known botanically as a drupe. Generally these plants require a frost-free climate, but the winters need to be sufficiently cool to induce flowering while the summers must be long and hot to ensure development and growth of the fruit. Although olives can survive on poor soils, better cropping will result if the trees are given well-drained, fertile loam where ample moisture is available when the fruit is forming. Propagation is from seed in autumn, from heel cuttings in winter, or from suckers. The wood of the olive tree is prized for carving and turning.

Olea europaea
OLIVE

The olive probably originated in northern Africa, but since ancient times has been cultivated around the Mediterranean for its nourishing fruit. There are many named cultivars, the selection depending on whether the grower wants black fully ripe olives, green almost-ripe ones, or olive oil. This is the best of all cooking oils—it is not only fine in flavour but free of saturated fats—and has long been used in cosmetics and lamps. The fruit is, however, too bitter to be eaten fresh; it must be treated with lye (sodium hydroxide) before being pickled in brine or preserved in its own oil. The tree grows slowly to about 30 ft (10 m) and is very long lived, to compensate for its not coming into full bearing until it is at least 10 years old. Its picturesque habit, rough grey bark and dull-green leaves, touched with silver on their undersides, make it a beautiful sight. Its timber is hard and durable; but, the tree being so valued for its fruit, it is rarely cut. ZONE 8.

OLEARIA
Asteraceae
DAISY BUSH

Indigenous to Australia and New Zealand, this large genus of evergreen shrubs and small trees thrives on neglect. Plants are characterized by daisy-like flower heads which can be white, cream, blue, lavender, purple or pink and which appear from spring to autumn. *Olearia* can grow in alkaline soils and most species are tolerant of salt, wind and atmospheric pollution. The dense foliage of many species makes them excellent shrubs for hedging, particularly if pruned hard after flowering to encourage growth. Propagate from seed or semi-ripe cuttings in summer.

Olearia argophylla
MUSK TREE

Deriving its name from the strong musk-like scent of its stems, this species prefers heavy, well-drained soils containing generous quantities of organic matter. Also called silver shrub, it makes a low-branched tree of over 50 ft (15 m) in its native southern Australian forests, with a trunk up to 3 ft (1 m) in diameter. The large, conspicuously veined leaves have a silvery underside. The flowers are creamy white and held in long terminal clusters. It grows well in a shady position. ZONE 8.

Olearia avicenniifolia

This species prefers well-drained soil and constant moisture during dry spells. It grows to a height of 12 ft (4 m) and has arching branches spreading from an erect stem. The leaves are an intense green with a white downy underside and the fragrant flowers are white and profuse. Removal of spent flowers prolongs flowering throughout the summer. ZONE 8.

Olearia ilicifolia

Commonly known as mountain holly because its foliage resembles that of *Ilex aquifolium*, this 9 ft (3 m) daisy bush has a rounded crown made up of stiff, dull, greyish green leaves with undulating margins. This is one of the few species in this genus whose white flowers are fragrant. It prefers light soils and a protected position. ZONE 9.

Olearia macrodonta

This New Zealand shrub is distinguished by its 2–4 in (5–10 cm) long, holly-like leaves. They are deep green above with greyish white hairs below. The flower heads are white and yellow in the middle and the bush blooms heavily from early summer. It grows to about 6 ft (2 m) in cultivation and prefers moist, well-drained soil in sun or light shade. If necessary, trim to shape after flowering. ZONE 7.

Olearia paniculata

Originating in New Zealand, *O. paniculata* can grow to 12 ft (4 m) with a coarsely grooved bark.

Olearia ilicifolia

Olearia macrodonta (below)

Its light yellow-green leaves have wavy edges and are greyish white on the undersides. The leaves are up to 2½ in (6 cm) long. The creamy white flower heads appear in autumn and, while scarcely a feature, they are pleasantly scented. This species withstands heavy trimming and is also tolerant of most soils and positions. ZONE 9.

Olearia phlogopappa
DUSTY DAISY BUSH

This 6 ft (2 m) rounded bush bears numerous white, blue or purple flowers up to 1 in (2 cm) across in heads. The oblong leaves, held on a single, many-branched stem, are greyish green, under 2 in (4 cm) long with serrated margins. Its height makes *O. phlogopappa* an effective screen or windbreak for seaside gardens or parks. Prune hard to encourage flowering or it can become very straggly. ZONE 7.

Olearia × *scilloniensis*

This cultivar originated in Tresco in the Scilly Isles in the English Channel as a cross between *O. lirata* and *O. phlogopappa*. Small white flowers appear in spring. ZONE 8.

Olearia 'Talbot de Malahide'

A hybrid of *O. avicennifolia*, sometimes sold as *O. albida*, this dense bushy shrub grows to 10 ft (3 m) with a spread of 15 ft (5 m). It is cloaked in dark green, leathery oval leaves with silvery undersides. Its fragrant creamy white flowers appear in late summer and form large showy heads. It is one of the best of the genus for coastal plantings in cooler climates. ZONE 8.

Olearia traversii

Endemic to the Chatham Islands of New Zealand, this species has a pale, furrowed bark. Its 2½ in (6 cm) oval leaves are deep glossy green above with fine greyish white hairs below. It can grow to 18 ft (6 m) but is most often a 6 ft (2 m) high trimmed hedge, for which it is ideal, especially in coastal areas. Despite producing numerous cream flower heads in summer, it is primarily a foliage plant. ZONE 8.

Olearia × *scilloniensis*

Olearia phlogopappa (below)

Olearia traversii (below)

Opuntia ficus-indica

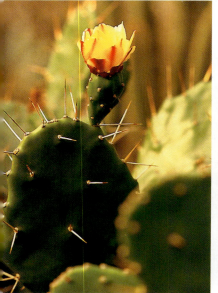
Opuntia vulgaris

Omalanthus populifolius

OMALANTHUS
Euphorbiaceae

These evergreen shrubs and small trees, from Australia and the Asian tropics, are grown for their large, heart-shaped leaves that turn a bright red one by one as they age. Their insignificant flowers are borne in tassel-like terminal clusters without petals. In the warm-temperate areas of the east coast of Australia they tend to appear as spontaneous seedlings in gardens near bushland and are ideal pioneer plants for a rainforest-type garden. They are not long lived, but usually after about 5 years will have self-seeded. They prefer a shaded site with moist, well-drained soil. Prune to shape if necessary, and propagate from seeds or cuttings if self-seeded plants are not available.

Omalanthus populifolius
BLEEDING HEART TREE, QUEENSLAND POPLAR

This large shrub or small tree grows to around 12 ft (4 m) with heart-shaped, dark green leaves which turn red individually throughout the year. Also referred to as native poplar, these plants require a rich, fertile soil to which plenty of humus has been added to help retain a moist atmosphere. Pruning is not usually required. When young, this species is a rewarding indoor plant. ZONE 10.

ONCOBA
Flacourtiaceae

Tropical Africa is the natural home of this genus of slow-growing, spiny, evergreen trees. In the wild some species may reach a height of 65 ft (20 m) but in a garden 20 ft (7 m) is more common. Although not widely cultivated domestically outside their native region, the trees are attractive and may be found as specimen trees in subtropical botanic gardens. The flowers can be white, yellow or light red and are followed by a leathery yellow fruit.

Oncoba spinosa

The trees need shelter from strong winds and a warm sunny position to flower. They prefer moist, well-drained soil with a generous application of mulch. Propagation is from seed or cuttings in summer and autumn.

Oncoba spinosa

O. spinosa has not only large, camellia-like and fragrant white flowers with showy yellow stamens, but also glossy serrated leaves. These, together with the roots of the tree, are used for medicinal purposes in Africa. Its golden yellow fruits are 2½ in (6 cm) in diameter and contain an edible pulp which is similar to that of a pomegranate. However, care should be taken when picking the fruit because of the prominent, 2 in (5 cm) long spines that grow on the trunk and branches. ZONE 11.

OPUNTIA
Cactaceae

Generally the succulent shrubs in this very large genus, numbering around 300 species, are easy to grow but vary greatly in their re-

Oncoba spinosa

Opuntia ficus-indica

quirements as they have evolved in widely differing geographic habitats. They range from prostrate to erect with cylindrical or flat, jointed stems or branches and tubular or 3-angled leaves. Most of the species have sharp spines as well as small bristles which are extremely hard to remove from the skin so care should be taken to position these plants away from areas where children or animals play. The flowers are generally yellow and are followed by edible fruit ('prickly pears') which range in shade from green to yellow to red. These plants need dry conditions in well-drained soil and a full sun position. Propagate from seeds or cuttings in spring or summer. The tree-like *O. vulgaris* was once widely planted to feed the cochineal insect, and develop the cochineal industry. Several species have become serious pests in some warmer countries, the worst being *O. stricta* in Australia and South Africa earlier this century.

Osmanthus × fortunei

Opuntia imbricata

Opuntia ficus-indica
PRICKLY PEAR

This species is native to somewhere in tropical America, but it has been so widely cultivated for its delicious fruit that just where is now not known. It grows to 10 ft (3 m) tall and wide, each branch made up of several flat, oval segments almost the size of a tennis racquet, and bears rather attractive yellow flowers in early summer. These develop into the pear-shaped red or orange fruit, whose skin is studded with bristles and which must be carefully stripped (wearing gloves) before the white pulp can be enjoyed. Spineless cultivars exist, but connoisseurs insist they are not as sweet as the prickly ones. ZONE 10.

Opuntia imbricata

From Mexico comes this tree-like cactus which can eventually grow to 10 ft (3 m). It has large, rounded stem segments with brownish white spines about 1 in (2 cm) long. Its flowers are in the pink and purple shades and are followed by rounded, spineless, yellow fruit. ZONE 8.

ORPHIUM
Gentianaceae
STICKY FLOWER

A small, evergreen shrub from South Africa makes up this genus. Sticky flower has become popular in subtropical gardens for its compact habit and long summer display of flowers.

Orphium frutescens

Growing to no more than 24 in (60 cm), *O. frutescens* is an erect, rather soft-wooded shrub. The 5-lobed, pink-purple flowers are

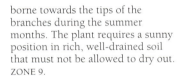
Osmanthus fragrans

borne towards the tips of the branches during the summer months. The plant requires a sunny position in rich, well-drained soil that must not be allowed to dry out. ZONE 9.

OSMANTHUS
Oleaceae

Originally from the Himalaya, China and Japan, these evergreen flowering shrubs are prized for their fragrance, which some admirers consider the sweetest and most attractive of all flowers. The white or cream flowers are almost inconspicuous but their fragrance is reminiscent of jasmine or gardenia. The Chinese use the flowers to enhance the scent of tea. Belonging to the olive family, the plants are slow growing with some species eventually reaching 45 ft (14 m). The dense foliage comprises thick, rigid leaves which may be edged with stout, often hooked, spiny teeth. Plants should be clipped after flowering to maintain this density. Plant in rich, well-drained soil in either the sun or in the shade. Propagate from semi-ripe cuttings in summer.

Osmanthus delavayi

This species is adaptable to most soils and conditions and grows to a height and width of 6 ft (2 m). It has serrated, oval, dark green leaves 1 in (2 cm) long which are held on

Osmanthus delavayi

Orphium frutescens

arching branches. Sweetly scented, creamy white flowers are tubular in shape, about ½ in (1 cm) long and are produced in the leaf axils and at the ends of the branches during summer. ZONE 7.

Osmanthus × fortunei

A cross between *O. fragrans* and *O. heterophylla*, this shrub boasts a showier display of flowers than its parents. Produced in spring, they are highly fragrant. *O. × fortunei* grows to a height and spread of 10 ft (3 m). ZONE 6.

Osmanthus fragrans
SWEET OSMANTHUS

Usually seen as a shrub with a height of around 9 ft (3 m), this species can be trained as a small tree and can also be grown in containers. Its glossy, deep green foliage acts as a foil to the highly fragrant creamy white or yellow flowers. These are small and 4-lobed and are held in tight clusters towards the ends of the branches. Also known as sweet olive, the plant flowers intermittently from spring to autumn. ZONE 7.

Oxydendrum arboreum

Ostrya virginiana

Ostrya virginiana

Osmanthus heterophyllus

Oxydendrum arboreum

Osmanthus heterophyllus
HOLLY OSMANTHUS

This shrub produces broad variable leaves, some of which are toothed like holly leaves and some that are oval and only bear spines at the tips. Its height and spread are similar, up to 10 ft (3 m), and it is slow to mature. Sometimes grown as a hedge, it flowers in early summer. ZONE 7.

OSTRYA
Carpinaceae

Deciduous and fast growing in rich, alkaline soils, these trees grow to 65 ft (20 m) tall. Originating in the northern hemisphere they are grown for the spectacular shades of red, yellow and orange that their leaves achieve before dropping. The toothed leaves are prominently veined and tapered to a point and are held on a short trunk with eye-catching bark. In spring, the yellow catkins look attractive against the bright green foliage. These are followed by brown winged nutlets that hang down in a chain. To flourish, the trees need a full sun or partially shaded site. Prune only to remove dead branches. Propagate from seed in spring.

Ostrya carpinifolia
HOP HORNBEAM

Preferring a partially shaded position, the hop hornbeam forms a compact conical crown reaching 60 ft (18 m). Its toothed, glossy dark green leaves turn a clear yellow before falling and look very attractive against the smooth, grey bark of its trunk. The nutlets are hoplike and hang in clusters 2 in (5 cm) long. ZONE 2.

Ostrya virginiana
EASTERN HOP HORNBEAM

Comparatively rare outside eastern North America, this tree is very similar to *O. carpinifolia* except for its dark brown bark which sometimes earns it the common name of ironwood. It normally grows to a height of 50 ft (15 m). The deeply saw-toothed, dark green leaves are 4 in (10 cm) long and turn a rich yellow before they drop. The wood is prized for carpentry. ZONE 3.

OXYDENDRUM
Ericaceae
SORREL TREE, SOURWOOD

The single deciduous species in this genus originates in eastern North America and is garden grown for its autumn foliage and flowers. The leaves are alternate and the fragrant, small flowers are held in drooping, terminal panicles. For the best autumnal hues, it should be planted in an open position in sun or part-shade in moist soil. Propagate from cuttings in summer or seeds in autumn. The genus takes its name from Greek words meaning 'sour tree', a reference to the sour-tasting foliage.

Oxydendrum arboreum

Making a small, 20–40 ft (7–13 m), tree this cool-climate species tolerates frost better than it does drought. It is best grown in a slightly acid soil, enriched with plenty of leaf mould and well-rotted organic matter. An occasional dressing of iron and/or ammonia after flowering may be required. The trunk is slender and the crown pyramid shaped. Streamers of white lily-of-the-valley flowers appear in late summer sometimes prior to, sometimes coinciding with, a display of scarlet foliage. ZONE 3.

Paeonia lutea

Paeonia suffruticosa cultivar

Pachira aquatica

Pachystegia insignis

Paeonia suffruticosa cultivar

PACHIRA
Bombacaceae

Originating in the tropical regions of America, this genus consists of a small number of evergreen or deciduous trees which can reach 90 ft (28 m). They are grown for their large, compound leaves and unusual flowers that are followed by big, woody pods. The flowers, which have a large number of protruding stamens, appear throughout the year, each bloom only lasting a short time. The trees need moist soil, full sun and, preferably, a tropical environment. They make excellent bonsai or container specimens. Propagate from seed or cuttings in late summer.

Pachira aquatica
SHAVING BRUSH TREE

An evergreen tree that can vary in height from 15 ft (5 m) to 60 ft (18 m), *P. aquatica* is grown for its fruit which can be roasted and eaten in a similar way to sweet chestnuts. Also known as the Guiana chestnut or provision tree, this species has compound leaves consisting of up to 9 leaflets up to 12 in (30 cm) long and slightly smaller, greenish or cream flowers. The long white stamens with red tips resemble a fine brush. Its large, brown fruit are 12 in (30 cm) long and about 5 in (12 cm) round. This is an unusual specimen tree for boggy areas. If *P. aquatica* is grown in a container, adequate water must be provided. ZONE 10.

PACHYSTEGIA
Asteraceae

These evergreen shrubs are closely related to the other bush daisies of New Zealand such as *Olearia* and *Brachyglottis*. They have a limited natural distribution in coastal regions of the north-east of the South Island. The large, thick, leathery leaves have glossy, wax-coated upper surfaces and felted undersides—superb protection against salt spray and coastal storms. In addition the plants produce showy white daisy-like flowers in summer followed by seed heads. Although a natural seaside plant, the rock daisy adapts well to garden cultivation and is generally undemanding. It grows in any well-drained soil in sun or light shade. Propagate from seed or cuttings.

Pachystegia insignis
MARLBOROUGH ROCK DAISY

The height of this attractive seaside plant is variable—1–5 ft (30 cm–1.5 m)—while it can spread to 3 ft (1 m). In early summer the white daisy-like flower heads open; they have golden yellow central florets. Fluffy, brown seed heads follow. Although the flowers are attractive, it is the foliage that is the main feature of the plant. The leaves are heavy and leathery, 3–7 in (8–18 cm) long, deep glossy green above with heavy white felting below. ZONE 8.

PAEONIA
Paeoniaceae

This genus is made up of about 30 herbaceous perennials and deciduous shrubs from Europe, northwestern USA, and China and Tibet. The shrubby species are known as 'tree peonies', the most beautiful being *P. suffruticosa* from China. They usually reach the size of a large rose bush. Peonies are grown for their large, lightly scented flowers, which come in every shade from white through pink to red, as well as orange; and they vary from poppy-like singles to extravagantly frilled doubles with 80 petals or more. Many garden cultivars are available. These long-lived plants prefer a cool climate and partial shade (in hot climates), and rich, moist but well-drained soil. Tree peonies should be pruned gently in early spring. Peonies are very difficult to propagate, which makes them rather expensive to buy. The name commemorates Paeon, a semi-mythical physician of ancient times.

Paeonia lutea
YELLOW TREE PEONY

This tree peony from western China was not introduced to the West until the end of the 19th century. A large shrub, it can reach a height and width of about 6 ft (2 m). In late spring to early summer it bears single, clear yellow flowers about

6 in (15 cm) across, which tend to hide among the leaves. The dark green leaves have saw-toothed margins. *P. lutea* is the parent of some beautiful hybrids with *P. suffruticosa*. ZONE 4.

Paeonia suffruticosa
TREE PEONY, MUDAN

A native of China, this handsome shrub has been so enthusiastically transplanted into gardens it is probably extinct in the wild. Reaching a height and width of 3–6 ft (1–2 m), it produces very large, single or double, cup-shaped flowers in spring. Depending on variety, these are white, pink or red or yellow, and are set among attractive, large, mid-green leaves. ZONE 4.

PALIURUS
Rhamnaceae

This genus is made up of 8 species of deciduous or evergreen spiny shrubs or trees from around the Mediterranean. The trees can reach up to 21 ft (7 m) in height. Because of their thorns, the shrubs have long been used as hedging plants. The oval leaves are a glossy green. Small, winged fruit appear after the summer flowers. The plants require a full sun position in well-drained, fertile soil. Propagate from cuttings taken in late summer or from seed in autumn.

Paliurus spina-christi
CHRIST THORN

The most common species grown, *P. spina-christi* is one of the plants thought to have been used for Christ's crown of thorns. Although it can be grown as a small tree, it is usually seen as a tall shrub and can be treated as a hedge, forming an excellent barrier plant as its branches are covered with pairs of long thorns. While these spiny branches are erect when young, they arch over as side branches appear. The tiny yellow blooms are followed by unusual, decorative fruit. Foliage turns a rich yellow before dropping in the cooler months. ZONE 6.

PANDANUS
Pandanaceae
SCREW PINE

This genus from East Africa, Malaysia, Australia and the Pacific contains about 200 species, a few of which make exceptionally decorative trees for seaside gardens and swampy areas in frost-free climates. Palm-like evergreens, some can reach a height of over 50 ft (15 m), although the plants may appear to be shorter as they often lean at an angle. The sword-shaped, spiny-edged green leaves, arranged spirally at the ends of branches, are long and narrow. While the white flowers are very small, the fruit are aggregations of reddish or yellow berries, up to 12 in (30 cm) in diameter, which look a little like a pineapple. Requiring a tropical or subtropical climate, full sun or partial shade, and moist, well-drained soil, *Pandanus* species can also be treated as house plants when young provided they are given ample water. Keep the plants tidy by removing dead and damaged leaves. Propagation is from seed, soaked for 24 hours before planting, or by detaching rooted suckers.

Pandanus tectorius
HALA SCREW PINE, PANDANG

The width of this species from Polynesia often exceeds its height of 25 ft (8 m), and the weight of its branches needs to be supported by stout, buttress-like aerial roots. The male flowers are strongly and sweetly scented, and produce an essential oil. The leaves have long spines on their edges and also on the undersides of the midrib. They are used for thatching and for weaving into grass skirts, mats, baskets and other essentials. ZONE 11.

PARASERIANTHES
Mimosaceae
CAPE LEEUWIN WATTLE, CRESTED WATTLE

Recently re-classified into a new genus (from the more familiar *Albizia*), the species below is a fast-growing, deciduous tree from Western Australia with the fern-like foliage so often seen among plants that thrive in subtropical areas. The bipinnate leaves are made up of numerous small leaflets. The yellowish green, brush-like flower spikes appear in winter and spring. Short lived, it is a tree to plant for instant effect while slower growing shrubs and trees are becoming established. The tree is not particular as to soil and can be positioned in shade or full sun. It may be used as a potted greenhouse plant in cold areas. Plants germinate more easily if the hard seeds, held within long flat pods, are gently nicked or filed before planting in autumn.

Paraserianthes lophantha

Growing very quickly to around 25 ft (8 m), this small tree has bright green feathery leaves which have the unusual habit of folding up as evening approaches. Given a warm climate, it can grow as much as 12 ft (4 m) during its first summer and often flowers within 12 months of germination. ZONE 9.

Paraserianthes lophantha

Pandanus tectorius (below)

Pandanus tectorius

Parrotia persica

PARKINSONIA
Caesalpiniaceae

The elegant weeping habit of these thorny deciduous trees from subtropical and tropical America, with one species in South Africa, is their chief attraction. *Parkinsonia* species dislike cold climates and acid soils but will grow happily in drought-prone areas where they will reach 30 ft (10 m) if they are in full sun. The bright green leaves are extremely short lived, so for most of the year the branches appear as slender bare stems. These set off to good effect the golden pea-shaped flowers that are produced in spring. The fruit is a brownish pea pod, the scarified seeds of which germinate rapidly when sown in spring.

Parkinsonia aculeata
JERUSALEM THORN, HORSE BEAN

This species prefers partial shade when grown in an inland desert area but can tolerate full sun near the coast. It is grown for its clusters of scented golden yellow flowers. It can reach 21 ft (7 m) high with a similar spread, and has greenish bark. The thorns that appear on the branches are up to 1 in (2 cm) long. Another common name, the Mexican palo verde (green hedge), comes from its widespread use as a hedge. ZONE 10.

PARROTIA
Hamamelidaceae
PERSIAN WITCH-HAZEL

From Iran and the Caucasus comes this genus of a single species cultivated for its rich autumnal hues and unusual flowers. The petal-less flowers consist of upright, wiry, dark red stamens enclosed in brown bracts and appear in early spring before the leaves. These are about 4 in (10 cm) long and have undulating edges. The branches on older trees dip down towards the ground. Propagate from softwood cuttings in summer or from seed in autumn. The genus was named after F. W. Parrot, a German botanist.

Parrotia persica

A spreading, short-trunked, deciduous tree with flaking bark, this species can reach about 40 ft (13 m) in the wild, but in a garden is unlikely to grow above 25 ft (8 m). The roughly diamond-shaped leaves with wavy margins are the tree's principal glory: they present a magnificent spectacle in autumn when they turn yellow, orange and crimson. A lime-tolerant tree, it is said to achieve these splendid hues best on a slightly acid soil. The tree grows well in full sun and in fertile soils in temperate climates. ZONE 5.

PAULOWNIA
Bignoniaceae

Originally from China and Japan, the genus is named for Anna Paulowna, a daughter of Paul I, Tsar of Russia. It includes some very fast-growing trees. In fact *Paulownia* species may grow to 8 ft (2.5 m) in their first year, reaching an eventual height of 50 ft (15 m). Their big, heart-shaped leaves and dense clusters of elegant flowers make them distinctive shade trees. The flower-spikes, similar to foxgloves, appear in spring with the new leaves, and are followed by capsules containing winged seeds. These deciduous trees do best in well-drained, fertile soil, with ample moisture in summer and shelter from strong winds. Propagate from seed or root cuttings taken either in late summer or in winter. Some of the species are grown for their timber in China and Japan.

Paulownia fortunei
POWTON

A spreading tree that may grow to 40 ft (13 m), this species grows best in a sheltered location. The broad

Parrotia persica

Parkinsonia aculeata (below)   *Parkinsonia aculeata*

Parkinsonia aculeata

Peltophorum pterocarpum

mid-green leaves are oval, 6–8 in (15–20 cm) long and 3–5 in (8–12 cm) across. The midrib and major veins are clearly visible on the underside which is hairy. In autumn the leaves turn a dull yellow before falling. The 3 in (8 cm) long, bell-shaped flowers are fragrant and arranged in clusters. They are cream to pale mauve with a creamy throat sporting purple spots, and bloom on the ends of the branches in early spring. ZONE 4.

Paulownia tomentosa
PRINCESS TREE

One of the more commonly grown of the *Paulownia* species, *P. tomentosa* (syn. *P. imperialis*) is chosen for its large, heart-shaped leaves and beautiful, pale-violet, fragrant flowers. The paired leaves can be as long as 12 in (30 cm) as can the erect flower spikes. Drought-tender, the tree reaches a height and width of 40 ft (13 m). Grown in both cool and warm-temperate climates, the tree can suffer damage to the flower buds if late frosts strike. If pruned almost to the ground each winter the tree will develop branches about 10 ft (3 m) long with enormous leaves, though it will not then flower. ZONE 4.

PELTOPHORUM
Caesalpiniaceae

At home in the tropical regions of the world, these are evergreen and deciduous trees that are grown primarily for the dense shade they cast. In the wild some species can reach 95 ft (30 m) but in cultivation they are more usually 60 ft (18 m) tall. The fern-like leaves are deep glossy green, with individual leaflets measuring up to 1 in (2 cm) long. Impressive spikes of perfumed yellow flowers, appearing in summer, develop into long, brown pods. The seeds from these pods need to be scarified before they will germinate. The trees prefer a sheltered, semi-shaded position although they can tolerate full sun provided their roots are kept moist in a light, sandy soil. Propagate from seed or cuttings taken during the wet season.

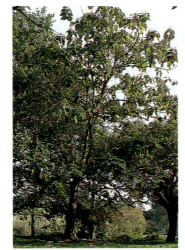
Paulownia fortunei

Peltophorum pterocarpum
RUSTY-SHIELD TREE, YELLOW FLAME TREE

The fern-like leaves of this handsome tree (also known as yellow poinciana and formerly *P. ferrugineum* and *P. inerme*) form a crown up to 24 ft (8 m) wide. This feature, allied to its mature height of up to 60 ft (18 m) in cultivation, makes it a good shade tree for tropical gardens. Clusters of heavily perfumed yellow flowers with unusual crinkled petals open in early summer from vivid rust-red buds. The abundance of rust-red, flattened seed pods that follow persist on the tree until the next flowering. ZONE 11.

PERSEA
Lauraceae

This genus is made up of about 150 evergreen trees and shrubs mostly from the tropical regions of Central and South America, although a few come from Asia and one, *P. indica*, is indigenous to the Canary Islands. The best known member of the genus is *P. americana* (syn. *P. gratissima*), the avocado. The trees can reach a height of 60 ft (18 m), though many do not grow that tall. They have glossy, dark green foliage and the small, greenish flowers, held in the axils, are insignificant. These are followed by the pear-shaped, green or black fruit. *Persea* species prefer moderately fertile, perfectly drained soil, and a position in full sun or very light partial shade. Propagation is from seed or cuttings.

Persea americana
AVOCADO

This species is usually grown for its fruit rather than its beauty or domestic habits—it sheds its leaves continuously throughout the year and is sometimes considered too messy for the garden. Drought- and frost-tender, the avocado can be nurtured in mild climates well south and north of the tropics. The stem is usually erect, and the leathery leaves a glossy dark green. The nutritious fruit can vary in shade from bright green to purple to black and in shape from pear like to round. Avocados are not self-pollinating and more than one tree will need to be planted to achieve the fruit. There are many named cultivars, each with different growth patterns and requirements and it is worth seeking the one best suited to individual climates and conditions. ZONE 10.

Paulownia tomentosa

Paulownia tomentosa

Phellodendron amurense

Phellodendron amurense

PHELLODENDRON
Rutaceae

These deciduous trees from East Asia are extremely hardy, tolerating both frost and harsh sun, although they prefer protection from wind. Growing to 50 ft (15 m) with a crown spreading to 12 ft (4 m), the trees are elegant and slender and require little maintenance. The shiny, light green pinnate leaves turn a rich shade of yellow in autumn. Small, yellowish green flowers appear in late spring or early summer, to be followed by black berry-like fruit. The trees grow best in full sun with fertile, well-drained soil. Seeds may be germinated in spring, or propagate from cuttings or by grafting or layering in summer.

Phellodendron amurense
AMUR CORK TREE

Earning its common name from its attractive, corky, older branches (though they are not a commercial source of cork), *P. amurense* is the commonest species in cultivation and forms a tree growing to 37 ft (12 m). Originally from China and Japan, it prefers humus-rich soil and moisture during periods of drought. Its tolerance of both heat and cold makes it a useful choice for extreme gardens. Its bright green leaves with between 5 and 11 leaflets have an unusual heart-shaped base and a pungent aroma. The 5-petalled, yellowish green flowers, male and female on separate trees, produce berries that are held above the foliage in dense bunches. ZONE 5.

Philadelphus coronarius

Philadelphus coronarius

PERSOONIA
Proteaceae

Persoonia species are evergreen shrubs native to Australia where about 60 different species occur. Some have a prostrate habit and are used as groundcovers, but most are tall—up to 15 ft (5 m)—open-growing shrubs or small trees. Several are gaining attention as garden plants for their attractive foliage. The 4-petalled flowers are yellow, and are followed by fleshy berries that are edible but rather astringent. The plants grow best in full sun and acid, sandy soil. They are notoriously difficult to propagate. Try freshly harvested seeds that have first been soaked in warm water for 24 hours to soften the hard seed coat. The genus takes its name from Christian Persoon, the German botanical author who first described *P. levis*.

Persoonia pinifolia
PINELEAF GEEBUNG

Soft, delicate, bright green and pine-like foliage is the main feature of this shrub from New South Wales and Queensland. The long arching stems further emphasize the dainty appeal of this, the most attractive of the genus. The pineleaf geebung reaches a height of 12 ft (4 m) and is nearly as wide. The small golden yellow flowers are borne in large clusters at the branch tips throughout summer and autumn. An additional highlight is provided by bunches of small, succulent green berries. By winter these berries have attractive red to purple tonings and they persist for several months. This species provides excellent cut foliage for flower arrangers. Propagate from seed or cuttings, but resist trying to transplant larger specimens. ZONE 10.

PHILADELPHUS
Hydrangeaceae
MOCK ORANGE, SYRINGA

This genus of deciduous shrubs comes from the temperate regions of the northern hemisphere, mainly from East Asia and North America. The cultivated species are all quite similar. They grow to about 10 ft (3 m) high and wide and have light green, roughly elliptical leaves to around 3 in (8 cm) long. They flower in late spring and early summer and bear 4-petalled flowers in

Persoonia pinifolia

loose clusters. The flowers are often strongly scented of orange blossom, hence the common name. Mock oranges are easily grown, preferring moist, well-drained soil and a position in sun or light shade. They may be pruned after flowering and can be used for informal hedging. Propagate from seed or from cuttings taken in summer.

Philadelphus coronarius

A native of southern Europe and Asia Minor, this species grows to around 6 ft (2 m) and has very fragrant 2 in (5 cm) wide white flowers. Its oval bright green leaves are slightly hairy on the undersides. 'Aureus' is a cultivar with bright yellow new growth and smaller flowers. ZONE 2.

Philadelphus 'Lemoinei'

This plant is a hybrid between *P. coronarius* and *P. microphyllus*. It was introduced in the late 1880s by the famous French hybridist Lémoine, who also raised many hydrangeas and lilacs. It grows to around 6 ft (2 m) and has arching branches. The 1 in (2 cm) flowers are white, very fragrant and usually carried in clusters of up to 7 blooms. ZONE 3.

Philadelphus lewisii

Indigenous to the USA, this shrub, the state flower of Idaho, is easily grown in both cold and temperate climates. The cream flowers are up to 2 in (5 cm) across and are held in clusters. They appear in mid-spring; the plant may also produce the occasional flower spasmodically through the warmer months. The stems, reaching heights of about 10 ft (3 m), can become woody and untidy if the plant is not cut back after flowering. It does best in a partly shaded spot and rich soil. This species must not suffer prolonged drought. ZONE 4.

PHILODENDRON
Araceae

This genus of over 200 species includes many well-known house plants. Native to tropical America and the West Indies, the plants are mainly epiphytic, evergreen vines and creepers with aerial roots, some dainty but others quite robust. The genus also includes small shrubs. All species need plenty of moisture and a tropical or subtropical climate to be cultivated outdoors. They need a sheltered, shady spot. Beautiful lush foliage is their trademark, often with a dramatic outline or deep lobes, mostly green but in some species attractively marked with white, pink or red. The flowers are inconspicuous. The soil should be well drained and enriched with organic matter. Water and fertilize house plants regularly, reducing watering during the cooler months. Most species are easily grown from cuttings taken in spring. All parts of the plant are poisonous.

Philodendron bipinnatifidum
TREE PHILODENDRON

Here the main feature is the large, shiny, oval, deep green leaves 16–24 in (40–60 cm) long, divided into up to 15 lobes; in some hybrids the leaves can be up to 3 times as large. Native to Brazil, this upright, robust plant can grow up to 9 ft (3 m). It grows best in a sheltered, sunny to partly shaded situation and needs a rich, moist but well-drained soil. The flowers are white or greenish. Propagation is from seed or cuttings. This species is variable in leaf outline; the common form with very irregular lobing is best known under the name *P. selloum*. Other cultivars and hybrids include some of the most spectacular of all foliage plants. ZONE 10.

PHOENIX
Arecaceae

These evergreen feather palms are native to subtropical and tropical parts of Asia, Africa and the Canary Islands. There are 17 very different species. Some are an important source of food (dates and also palm sugar which is derived from dates) while others are popular as house plants or avenue trees. *Phoenix* includes species with a single trunk as well as some that form clumps of stems. The long fronds have stiff, sharp spines at their bases and form a dense crown. The small yellow flowers grow in clusters and are followed by the fruit. Male and female plants will have to be planted to ensure pollination. The plants prefer full sun though they will tolerate partial shade, hot winds and poor soil, given good drainage. Hybrids between species are common. Propagation is usually from seed in spring. *Phoenix* is the ancient Greek name given to the date palm.

Phoenix canariensis
CANARY ISLAND PALM

This massive palm is endemic to the Canary Islands but a popular landscape feature in warm-temperate zones. It grows up to 50 ft (15 m) tall with a spread of 30 ft (10 m), the trunk being thick and sturdy—up to 3 ft (1 m) across—and marked by the scars of the older leaves. The deep green fronds are up to 12 ft (4 m) long, arching gracefully and making a dense crown. In summer small yellow flowers are arranged in large, drooping clusters. These are succeeded by orange-yellow acorn-like fruit that are inedible. Plant it in an open, sunny position with plenty of room for it to grow so that its dramatic symmetrical shape can be enjoyed. In areas prone to frosts, choose an advanced specimen and plant it out in spring when the danger of frosts is past. Trim off dead fronds to keep the plant neat. ZONE 9.

Philadelphus lewisii

Philodendron bipinnatifidum

Phoenix canariensis *Phoenix canariensis*

Phoenix canariensis and *P. dactylifera*, in the north African city of Melilla

Phoenix dactylifera
DATE

Date palms have been cultivated in their native lands of the Middle East and North Africa for over 5,000 years, though California is now also a major producer of dates. A large palm with a mature height of around 100 ft (30 m) and a spread of 20 ft (6 m), the trunk is more slender than that of the Canary Island palm. The fronds have a greyish tinge and spiny stalks. The fronds at the top of the plant point upwards, while the lower ones curve downward to make a spherical crown. The dates, 1–3 in (2–7 cm) long, are cylindrical and yellowish when fresh. The date palm adapts to a range of soil types but needs an open, sunny location. Suckers are preferred for the propagation of named, selected cultivars, of which there are several. ZONE 10.

Phoenix roebeleni
DWARF DATE PALM

This is an ornamental and versatile small palm from Laos, suitable for the hot-climate garden and also as a potted specimen indoors. It will grow to 10 ft (3 m) tall with a similar spread, given enough room. The dark green arching fronds give it an elegant, lacy effect. The short, slender stem is rough because the bases of the old leaves persist. The fruit are small, black, egg-shaped drupes. Plant outdoors in a sunny or partly shaded location but shelter it from frosts. Keep soil or potting mix moist. ZONE 9.

PHOTINIA
Rosaceae

These evergreen or deciduous shrubs and small trees of Asian origin are grown for their brilliant young foliage and, in the case of the deciduous species, for their autumn colour. The majority are fast growing. The leaves are alternate and the flowers mostly white and are fol-

Phoenix roebeleni (below)

Photinia × *fraseri*

Photinia sp., as a hedge (below)

Photinia × *fraseri*

lowed by either red or dark blue berries. Give the plants protection from strong winds, and plant in sun or partial shade in fertile, well-drained soil. The plants make excellent hedges and should be pruned to promote bushiness and new growth. The genus takes its name from a Greek word meaning 'shining'; a reference to the gleaming foliage. Propagate from seed or cuttings in summer, or by grafting on to hawthorn or quince stock.

Photinia × fraseri

These evergreen shrubs of garden origin grow well in temperate climates when given protection from strong cold winds. The young growths are attractive shades of bright red, bronze-red and purple-red and hold their colour over a long period. The mature leaves are glossy and green. 'Red Robin' has brilliant red new growth and 'Robusta' bears eye-catching coppery-red young leaves. The height of the shrub varies with the cultivar, but most are in the 9–12 ft (3–4 m) range. ZONE 8.

Photinia glabra

This evergreen shrub that grows to about 9 ft (3 m) is often used as a hedging plant as clipping promotes the reddish bronze new growth. As the leaves mature, they change to a glossy green. The spring-borne broad clusters of white flowers give an attractive, smoky effect and are succeeded by blue-black berries. Frost-hardy in short-winter climates, it can prove sensitive in prolonged cold conditions. 'Rubens' bears sealing-wax red new growth. ZONE 7.

Photinia serrulata

Indigenous to China, this small evergreen tree or shrub can grow to a height of 21 ft (7 m) with a bushy crown, but can also be kept to lower heights and clipped to form hedging. The glossy, oval leaves are large, serrated and bronze tinted in spring. The small, white spring flowers are followed by small, red berries. The plant is also listed as *P. serratifolia* and sometimes known as Chinese hawthorn. ZONE 7.

Photinia villosa

A deciduous upright shrub or small tree from Japan, Korea and China, this species grows to 15 ft (5 m) with a bushy crown. It is a great survivor in both cool and mild climates. The white flowers borne in late spring are followed by red berries which resemble those of a hawthorn. The leaves are oval with serrated edges and have a slightly downy surface. They are bronze tinted when young and turn scarlet, orange and gold in autumn. This species prefers acid soil. ZONE 3.

PHYLICA
Rhamnaceae

These evergreen shrubs from South Africa grow to around 10 ft (3 m) high. They have bright green, narrow, slight hairy leaves, and are grown for their decorative clusters of tiny flowers which appear in winter and are often used in flower arrangements. These shrubs thrive only in warm climates and need full sunshine and acid soil. They do well in areas of high humidity, including coastal situations. To propagate, take cuttings in autumn or use seed. Pruning is not generally necessary if the flowers are deadheaded regularly.

Phylica pubescens
FEATHERHEAD

This species is the most commonly grown. It grows into an upright, rounded shrub 6 ft (2 m) tall and wide and has slightly hairy, awl-shaped leaves. The striking creamy white, dense flower heads have interesting feathery bracts as long as the leaves and are covered with buff-toned hairs. They make excellent cut flowers. Plum-like fruit 2 in (5 cm) across follow the flowers. This species grows best in winter rainfall areas. Prune after flowering to keep the plants compact. ZONE 9.

PHYLLANTHUS
Euphorbiaceae

From tropical and subtropical regions of the world comes this large genus of evergreen or deciduous herbs, shrubs and trees. The stalkless leaves are arranged in 2 flattened ranks along the branches. Small red or greenish yellow petal-less flowers appear during spring and summer. Some tree species bear edible gooseberry-like fruit in late summer which are palatable only if cooked. The pea-sized fruit of the shrubs is inedible. Plant in

Phylica pubescens

Phylica pubescens

Photinia villosa

Photinia serrulata

Phyllostachys nigra

Phyllanthus acidus

Phylloclaus trichomanoides

Phyllostachys bambusoides

rich, sandy, well-drained soil with ample water. This is a good genus for seaside cultivation in hot climates. Propagation is from seed or cuttings.

Phyllanthus acidus
STAR GOOSEBERRY, OTAHEITE GOOSEBERRY

One of the arborescent members of the genus, the star gooseberry comes from India and Madagascar and is the only member of the genus to be widely cultivated. It reaches its mature height of 30 ft (10 m) quickly. With a spread of 10 ft (3 m), it has pale green, almost stalkless leaves and tiny red flowers arranged in dense clusters in spring. Tight bunches of ribbed bright yellow fruit 1 in (2 cm) long follow in late summer. These make excellent preserves, though they are rather tart to eat fresh. Birds adore them. ZONE 11.

PHYLLOCLADUS
Podocarpaceae

Seven species of evergreen conifers from the southern hemisphere make up this genus. The taller species grow to a height of 68 ft (21 m) but there are some lower growing shrubby members of the genus—reaching a maximum of 6 ft (2 m)—that can be made into very attractive bonsai specimens. The stems are erect, with horizontal branches bearing brownish green flattened phylloclades (a short stem that acts as a leaf) which sometimes darken in winter. Male cones are carried in terminal clusters, while the female cones appear on the base of the 'leaves'. Drought-tender, they perform best in well-composted, moist soils in sunny or semi-shaded positions away from strong winds. Propagation is from seed or cuttings.

Phyllocladus aspleniifolius
CELERY PINE

Indigenous to Tasmania, Australia, this is a slow-growing conifer to 50 ft (15 m) with an idiosyncratic foliage arrangement. It produces striking diamond-shaped thick cladodes (modified branchlets) up to 3 in (8 cm) long that are evergreen. But the true leaves, which appear as tiny scales, are deciduous. Its foliage bears a fancied resemblance to that of celery. Young trees do best if planted in partial shade such as they receive in their native forests. The hard, close-grained timber is valued. ZONE 8.

Phyllocladus trichomanoides
TANEKAHA, NEW ZEALAND CELERY PINE

In the wild this species can reach 50–70 ft (15–22 m), but in cultivation specimens rarely exceed 20 ft (7 m). A symmetrical conifer, it thrives in the cool, moist climate of its native New Zealand. Its stems, spreading to 12 ft (4 m), radiate in whorls from horizontal branches. The foliage (compressed stems) resembles the fronds of a maidenhair fern. Its slow rate of growth makes it suitable for small suburban gardens. This conifer is prized for its timber which is hard and close grained. ZONE 8.

PHYLLOSTACHYS
Gramineae

Made up of 80 species of medium- and large-growing bamboos from Asia, these evergreen plants have spreading rhizomes which are capable of sprouting some distance from the parent plant. They are ideally suited to grove planting and are mainly grown for their decorative foliage and graceful habit. They are also useful for preventing soil erosion. The woody stems have nodes at intervals, and the insignificant flowers take several years to appear; similar to most bamboos, the plants then die. If they need to be contained to a specific area, they can be grown in large tubs. Temperate-climate plants, they thrive in a sheltered position that is not too dry. Propagate from seed in either spring or autumn, or by division in spring.

Phyllostachys bambusoides
MADAKE, GIANT TIMBER BAMBOO

Originating in China and Japan, the madake grows to 70 ft (22 m). This easily grown species has large leaves and thick-walled culms (stems) which are dark green at first. The young shoots, which are edible, appear in late spring. This bamboo is widely used for all sorts of constructions in China and Japan. Like all bamboos, its wood is flexible. Many varieties have evolved including 'Holochrysa', smaller growing and with a more open habit with golden yellow culms, sometimes with green stripes; 'Castillonis', with green grooves to the culms; and 'Castillonis Inversa', with green culms and yellow grooves. ZONE 8.

Phyllostachys nigra
BLACK BAMBOO

The slender canes, growing to about 18 ft (6 m) with prominent joints, are green when young and only turn black in their second year. The long, thin leaves are green and pointed. Best in moist, fertile soil, in either semi-shade or sun, black bamboo needs protection from cold winds in cool climates. Grown for its statuesque stems, it can become seriously invasive in mild climates. Var. *henonis* bears a mass of lush dark leaves and yellow-brown canes. ZONE 5.

PHYSOCARPUS
Rosaceae
NINEBARK

The unusual inflated fruit of this genus of deciduous shrubs from Asia and North America are not edible—the dozen or so species are admired for their flowers and attractive foliage. Reaching a maximum height of 10 ft (3 m) in the wild, *Physocarpus* species require fertile, well-drained soil in a sunny position. They are easy to grow in temperate climates, but resent limy soil and dry roots. The leaves are prominently veined, lobed and serrated and change to a dull yellow in autumn. The 5-petalled white or pink flowers, appearing in spring or early summer, are small but are displayed in decorative clusters along the branches. Propagate from seed or cuttings of semi-ripened wood in summer. Thin out crowded plants by cutting back some of the arching canes after flowering.

Physocarpus opulifolius

Native to eastern USA and perhaps the most attractive species in the genus, this shrub has a height and spread of 5 ft (1.5 m) and has a graceful arching habit. The yellowish green, rounded heart-shaped leaves complement the dense pink-tipped white flowers which are at their best in early summer. Cheerful reddish pods with yellow seeds contrast well with the bright autumn foliage and the dark brown bark that peels off in many layers when it is mature. 'Aureus' has bright greenish yellow leaves and white flowers. ZONE 2.

PHYTOLACCA
Phytolaccaceae
POKEWEED, POKEBERRY

The 35 species in this genus are native to warm and tropical regions of the Americas; the taller plants can be 50 ft (15 m) tall. These perennial, evergreen trees and shrubs are valued for their general appearance and attractive though often poisonous rounded berries. The leaves can be quite large while the white flowers are small and arranged in clusters. They need adequate moisture to thrive and prefer rich soil in a sheltered position in full sun to part-shade. Propagation is from seed in spring or autumn.

Phytolacca americana

This soft-wooded shrub from North America is often treated as a herbaceous perennial. Summertime white flowers are followed by purple-blue berries in autumn. All parts of the plant are poisonous. ZONE 2.

Phytolacca dioica
OMBU, BELLA SOMBRA TREE

The ombu is a fast-growing evergreen tree that needs a sheltered sunny spot in a frost-free climate with moist soil. A mature specimen can grow to 50 ft (15 m) tall and 9 ft (3 m) wide. A native of Brazil, Paraguay, Argentina and Uruguay, it has a shallow root system and its sturdy trunk appears swollen. The dense crown of foliage consists of elliptical to oval-shaped leaves with a pointed tip. The white flowers are followed (on female plants) by yellow, fleshy berries, but the tree is chiefly grown to provide shade—as its name bella sombra (beautiful shade) tree suggests. ZONE 10.

Phytolacca dioica

Phytolacca americana

Physocarpus opulifolius

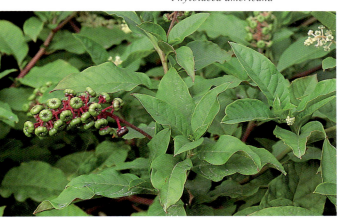
Phytolacca americana   *Physocarpus opulifolius* (below)

PICEA
Pinaceae
SPRUCE

A large, well-known genus of evergreen conifers, *Picea* contains about 45 species that originate in mountainous regions of the northern hemisphere where there are deep pockets of moist, rich, acidic, freely draining soil. Today these wonderfully fragrant plants are widely cultivated as they can tolerate poor soil, some lime and heat, although they are prone to fungal infections in warm, humid climates. These are among the faster growing spruces, sometimes reaching an impressive 220 ft (70 m). They develop a stiff, narrow, conical, sometimes columnar growth-habit, with short, upward-pointing branches. The foliage is unmistakable: the leaves are arranged spirally on short pegs and appear in a range of different shades from bright green to glaucous blue. Able to withstand strong winds, *Picea* species bear large cones which hang downwards, distinguishing the genus from the superficially similar firs (*Abies*). They will not survive transplantation when large, nor grow well in heavily polluted environments. The slow growth and contorted habit of some cultivars make them ideal bonsai specimens while others are prostrate and make excellent groundcovers. Propagate from seed or cuttings in autumn or by grafting. This genus produces valuable timber and pitch and turpentine.

Picea abies
NORWAY SPRUCE, COMMON SPRUCE

The traditional Christmas tree in Europe, *P. abies* is native to Scandinavia where it can grow to nearly 200 ft (60 m) tall. In cultivation it is often rather less though still a majestic tree. Its straight trunk is covered in orange-brown, maturing to reddish, bark which it sheds in scales. The leaves are dark green and rectangular and the reddish cigar-shaped cones, erect at first, become pendulous and grow to 7½ in (18 cm) long. Dwarf shrubby cultivars have usually been propagated from 'witches' brooms', tight clumps of congested foliage that sometimes appear on the plant. Shallow rooted, the Norway spruce can be upended by strong winds. The cultivar 'Maxwellii', the Maxwell spruce, originated in North America and is a low-growing, compact form ideal for rockeries and borders. 'Pumila Glauca' is a semi-erect dwarf form with lime green foliage. 'Pygmaea' is a slow-growing dwarf form. 'Reflexa' is a weeping cultivar distinguished by growing tips that point upwards when young. It makes a beautiful prostrate shrub. ZONE 2.

Picea breweriana
WEEPING SPRUCE, BREWER'S WEEPING SPRUCE

The branchlets of this North American conifer hang its foliage in 3 ft (1 m) curtain-like streamers from its horizontally held branches. The needles are blue-green and flattened and the light brown cones grow to 5 in (12 cm) long. The tree forms a strong trunk, reaching a height of 110 ft (35 m) with a broad conical shape that will become narrow if the tree is grown in crowded conditions. Seeds are slow to mature, so this spruce is mostly propagated by grafting. ZONE 2.

Picea abies with *Betula pendula* (below)

Picea abies 'Pygmaea'

Picea breweriana (below)

A mixed spruce (*Picea*) and birch forest in Sweden (below)

Picea abies (below)

Picea engelmannii, Yosemite National Park, USA

Picea engelmannii
ENGELMANN SPRUCE

Growing slowly to 160 ft (50 m), this is one of the most cold-tolerant evergreen trees. It also grows well in poor soil. The densely textured, pyramid-shaped crown spreads to 15 ft (5 m) and is made up of sharply pointed, 4-angled needles, up to 1 in (2 cm) long. The needles are soft grey to steel blue and the cones are cylindrical, green and tinged with purple. ZONE 1.

Picea glauca
WHITE SPRUCE

Grown commercially for the paper industry, this tree from Canada reaches a height of 80 ft (25 m) when mature, but is relatively slow growing. Characterized by the bright green shoots that appear in spring, it prefers sharply drained soil. The drooping branchlets carry the 4-angled needles that are strongly aromatic and grow to ½ in (1 cm) in length. The cones are small and narrow. The cultivar 'Conica', known as the dwarf Alberta spruce, is a compact, erect, cone-shaped shrub that reaches 32 in (80 cm) in 10 years but will grow taller if untrimmed. Grass-green foliage makes it an attractive rockery specimen. ZONE 1.

Picea engelmannii

Picea mariana
AMERICAN BLACK SPRUCE

This 60 ft (20 m) conifer from the USA prefers boggy soil and must have an open, sunny position to thrive. The pyramidal crown spreads to 15 ft (5 m) and is composed of whorled branches bearing blunt, bluish green needles. The 1½ in (3 cm) long cones are purplish brown and remain on the tree for up to 30 years. 'Nana' is a slow-growing dwarf cultivar. ZONE 1.

Picea mariana 'Nana'

Picea glauca 'Conica'

Picea omorika

Picea obovata

Picea orientalis

Picea obovata

Picea obovata
SIBERIAN SPRUCE

As its common name suggests, the Siberian spruce is extremely hardy and can grow to a height of 190 ft (60 m). Its erect, branching crown displays dark green foliage and long brown cones up to 8 in (20 cm) long. This spruce produces some of the most attractive 'flowers' of the genus, which appear as pinkish red catkins in spring. ZONE 1.

Picea omorika
SERBIAN SPRUCE

This spruce, from Serbia and Bosnia, reaches 110 ft (35 m) and has pendulous branches forming a narrow, spire-like crown. The bright green, flattened needles have a square tip and a greyish underside. The purplish cones mature to a deep brown shade. Growing happily in a range of soils from acid to limy, *P. omorika* is one of the best species of *Picea* for large, temperate-climate gardens. It is more tolerant of urban pollution than most species. ZONE 4.

Picea orientalis
CAUCASIAN SPRUCE

Reaching 95 ft (30 m) in its native Turkey and Caucasus, this slow-growing spruce produces abundant, pendent branches from ground level up. The brilliant, glossy green foliage is short and neat and provides a fine background for the spectacular brick red male 'flowers' that appear in spring, and the purple cones that grow to a length of 3 in (8 cm). This species prefers a sheltered site. The cultivar 'Atrovirens' displays attractive rich green foliage that flushes to golden yellow in early summer. ZONE 3.

Picea pungens
COLORADO BLUE SPRUCE

This beautiful spruce from the west coast of the USA is so popular that demand often exceeds supply because less than one third of the seed gathered for propagation is viable. It grows to 110 ft (35 m) in the wild, although it is usually much smaller in gardens. It has a pyramid of bluish green foliage composed of stiff and sharply pointed needles; the bark is grey. 'Glauca', a commonly grown cultivar, is slightly smaller than its parent and is slower growing. Its strong steel-blue new foliage makes it one of the most striking specimen trees in large gardens and parks. 'Hoopsii' is prized for its even bluer foliage; 'Iseli Fastigiate' has upward pointing branches and very sharp needles; 'Royal Blue' and 'Koster' are other striking blue cultivars; 'Moerheimii', originating in the Netherlands, has been bred to produce longer, silvery blue foliage than other forms. ZONE 2.

Picea sitchensis
SITKA SPRUCE

The trunk of this species bears pale bark and supports a pyramidal crown composed of whorled branches. The leaves are flattened, bluish grey and stiff. The 4 in (10 cm) long cones are covered with thin papery scales and release their winged seeds on warm spring days. Fast growing to 145 ft (45 m), this species is one of the few in the genus that can survive being transplanted when young. It also enjoys humid sites but it must have good summer rainfall. Its crown becomes broader at the top as the tree matures. The timber is not very durable or strong and is mainly used for packing cases and the like, though it is the timber of choice for sounding boards of musical instruments. ZONE 4.

Picea pungens

Picea pungens 'Hoopsii'

Picea pungens 'Royal Blue'

Picea sitchensis

Picea smithiana

Picea smithiana

Pieris formosa var. *forrestii* (above)

Pieris formosa var. *forrestii* (below)

Picea smithiana
WEST HIMALAYAN SPRUCE

This spruce from northern India develops graceful branches which hang in cascades. The foliage is dark green and composed of fine, 4-angled needles up to 1½ in (4 cm) long. The cones, which are green maturing to shiny brown and grow to 7 in (17 cm) long, often appear at the ends of the branches and accentuate their pendulous effect. ZONE 6.

PIERIS
Ericaceae

This genus consists of evergreen shrubs and, more rarely, small trees from North America and East Asia. The shrubby species are valued for their neat compact habit, attractive foliage and flowers. The height of the shrubs rarely exceeds 12 ft (4 m) and is often less. The flower buds are held throughout the winter, and in spring open into clusters of small, waxy, usually white flowers. The plants require a temperate climate, moist, peaty, acidic soil and a partially shaded site. They appreciate humidity. Propagation is from seed in spring or from cuttings in summer, or by layering.

Pieris formosa

This magnificent dense, bushy shrub from western China carries glossy, dark green leathery leaves and bears sprays of small, bell-shaped white flowers in mid-spring. Frost resistant, it grows well in both cool and mild climates but is drought-tender. It is one of the taller growing species, to 12 ft (4 m). *P. formosa* var. *forrestii* is usually smaller with scarlet-bronze young growth against which the flowers gleam in striking contrast. ZONE 6.

Pieris japonica
LILY-OF-THE-VALLEY SHRUB

This Japanese shrub can grow to 12 ft (4 m) high, but usually only reaches around 6 ft (2 m) in cultivation. It has pointed, elliptical, deep green leaves to 5 in (12 cm) long that are reddish copper when young. Panicles of small, white, bell-shaped flowers appear from early spring. The many cultivars include 'Bert Chandler', with pink and cream new growth; 'Christmas Cheer', with early, pale pink flowers; 'Flamingo', with bright pink flowers; 'Purity', with large, pure white flowers; and 'Variegata', with cream-edged foliage. ZONE 4.

PIMELEA
Thymelaeaceae
RICE FLOWER

These woody evergreen shrubs are native to Australasia and can grow to a height of 6 ft (2 m), though most species are smaller. Their great attraction is their terminal flower heads, in white, yellow, pink or purple often surrounded by prominent coloured bracts. Each flower is tubular and star shaped. They grow best in full sun in light, well-drained soil enriched with organic matter. Windy and seaside sites also suit them, but they dislike heavy frosts and lime. Lightly tip prune after flowering to keep them tidy. Propagate from tip cuttings. Attempts to transplant large specimens usually fail.

Pimelea ferruginea

This species, the most frequently seen in gardens, grows naturally in

Western Australia and forms a compact, well-branched rounded shrub with a height and spread of 3 ft (1 m). Tiny, recurved, oval leaves are crowded opposite each other along the stems. The leaves are smooth and light green on top and greyish green underneath. In spring compact rounded heads of small rose-pink flowers appear in large numbers. Each flower head may be up to 1½ in (4 cm) across. ZONE 9.

PINUS
Pinaceae
PINE

This genus of about 90 species of conifers, ranging from large shrubs to very large trees, includes some of the most commercially important of any tree species. Few parts go unused. Pines are most valued for their timber, which is used extensively in construction, manufacturing and as wood pulp for paper. The resin of some species yields turpentine, while other species have edible seeds. The cones are used as fuel, as is the bark, which is also composted to make potting mixes. Even the foliage—the familiar needles—has its uses: as a mulch or for surfacing woodland paths.

Pines originate from Europe, Asia, the Mediterranean region and North America; however, the European and American species are the most important today. When young they usually have a pyramidal shape but mature specimens are often much broader, even flat topped. While seldom suitable for small gardens, pines can be beautiful where they have room to develop and many are useful as shelter trees. Some pines are tolerant of drought and dry, sandy soil and some are able to withstand strong winds and coastal conditions. Although there is a species of pine for most situations, two factors are essential for satisfactory growth: good drainage and plenty of sun. Shallower rooted than other conifers, pines can often be transplanted if a large rootball is preserved.

The needle-like leaves range in length from 1 in (2 cm) to 18 in (45 cm) and are carried in bundles of 2, 3, 4 or 5, depending on the species. They fall to make a thick thatch under the tree, which can pose problems on lawns and walkways. The pollen released from late winter can also irritate hay-fever sufferers. Falling cones can also be a problem. Most cones release their seeds on ripening but some maintain intact cones for many years until stimulated to release their seed, often by fire. Propagate from seed.

Pinus aristata
BRISTLECONE PINE

This North American pine matures to 35 ft (11 m) high. It is very slow growing but lives to a great age. (The 5,000-year-old plants of California's White Mountains previously included in this species are now classified as *P. longaeva*.) As a garden plant it forms a dense shrubby tree, making an effective informal windbreak. Its 2 in (5 cm) long, deep green needles flecked with resin are pressed closely to the stem, and occur in groups of 5. Its cones are glossy and 4 in (10 cm) long. ZONE 5.

Pinus armandii
DAVID'S PINE

This pine from China and Taiwan does not like to dry out. It grows to 65 ft (20 m) with spreading branches and bears green leaves, up to 6 in (15 cm) long, in groups of 5. The thin cones, arranged in pairs or triplets, are as long as the leaves. ZONE 8.

Pinus ayacahuite
MEXICAN WHITE PINE

This pine, which occurs in Mexico and Guatemala, can tolerate pollution and so is a good choice for sheltered gardens. Growing to 110 ft (35 m), *P. ayacahuite* is characterized by the symmetry of its growth and by the bluish green, 7 in (17 cm) long needles in groups of 5, and 12 in (30 cm) cones which contain long-winged seeds. ZONE 8.

Pimelea ferruginea

Pinus armandii

Pinus aristata (below)

Pinus ayacahuite (below)

Pinus canariensis

Pinus canariensis

Pinus caribaea

Pinus bungeana

Pinus bungeana
LACEBARK PINE

This native of China can reach 100 ft (30 m) in the wild but is considerably smaller in cultivation. It is an attractive tree that branches down to near ground level and can be trained as a large, multi-trunked shrub. The common name comes from the patchwork of colours left by the smooth, flaking bark. It has dark green, 3 in (7 cm) long needles in groups of 3 and small, rounded, pale brown cones carried singly or in pairs. It tolerates extremes of winter cold and summer heat. ZONE 5.

Pinus canariensis
CANARY ISLAND PINE

This native of the Canary Islands is a moderately fast-growing tree. It has been successfully used as a timber tree in Portugal and has some potential for south-western USA. Though it is adaptable and drought tolerant, it prefers an open sunny spot where the soil is rich and moist yet well drained. *P. canariensis* matures to become an attractive spreading tree, reaching up to about 80 ft (25 m) in height. The upright trunk has attractive, reddish brown, fissured bark. The densely packed, shiny, grass green needles are 12 in (30 cm) long and carried in groups of 3. Outer branchlets assume a graceful habit. The brown cones are oval-shaped and are about 8 in (20 cm) long. ZONE 8.

Pinus caribaea
CARIBBEAN PINE, SLASH PINE

Native to Central America and reaching about 100 ft (30 m) in height, the Caribbean pine has an open, broad, rounded crown with grey to brown bark exfoliating in large flat plates. The needles are deep green, growing in bundles of 3, 4 or 5, up to 12 in (30 cm) long, and the cones are a glossy rust-brown in colour. *P. caribaea* is a commercially important tree that is used for timber and in the manufacture of turpentine. Varieties include *bahamensis,* the Bahamas pine, which grows to about 70 ft (22 m) tall; and the fast-growing *hondurensis,* the Honduran pine, which grows to 142 ft (44 m). ZONE 9.

Pinus cembra
AROLLA PINE, SWISS STONE PINE

This pine will grow to 80 ft (25 m) in its native Alps, central Europe, and in Siberia. It has been cultivated since 1746 and is appreciated for its neat, conical shape, dense foliage and long-lived needles. It needs to be kept moist but is otherwise very tough and disease resistant. The 5 in (12 cm) long, dark green, glossy needles occur in groups of 5. The 3½ in (9 cm) cones are a distinguishing feature, maturing from an attractive purplish shade to a deep bluish brown. Their seeds are edible but difficult to harvest unless the cone is rotted or forced apart. ZONE 4.

Pinus cembroides
MEXICAN PIÑON PINE, MEXICAN NUT PINE

Native to Mexico and southwestern USA, this compact, shrubby tree grows to 24 ft (8 m) or more and makes a neat screen. A short-needled pine, it produces many orange-brown branchlets and bears small, rounded cones that complement the shape of the pine's rounded crown. Its bark is silvery grey. The wingless seeds of this species are harvested and sold commercially. Slow growing, it tolerates both drought and wind. ZONE 6.

Pinus contorta var. latifolia
LODGEPOLE PINE

In its native Rocky Mountains this tapering tree usually grows to 75 ft (23 m), sometimes more, and forms a magnificent straight trunk valued by the North American building industry. However, it tends to be slow growing, low and rather bushy in cultivation. It has yellowish green, 2–3 in (4–7 cm) long needles in pairs, and small, oval cones that release fine seeds which can be carried great distances by wind. They germinate freely and self-seeded trees are proving a nuisance in parts of New Zealand. This pine is not drought tolerant. ZONE 5.

Pinus coulteri
BIG-CONE PINE, COULTER PINE

This tough pine from California withstands heat, wind and drought and tolerates most soils, including heavy clay. It gets one of its common names from its spiny brown cones that grow to a massive 15 in (38 cm) and weigh 5 lb (2.3 kg). Given enough space it will make an arresting specimen. *P. coulteri* is a bushy tree which can reach 95 ft (30 m) with attractive, stiff, bluish green needles, up to 12 in (30 cm) long, held in 3s. It is relatively fast growing. ZONE 8.

Pinus cembra

Pinus cembroides (below)

Pinus coulteri

Pinus coulteri (below)

Pinus contorta var. *latifolia* (below)

Pinus densiflora, growing at Kyoto in Japan

Pinus elliottii

Pinus densiflora

Pinus halepensis, growing at Fethiye, Turkey

Pinus densiflora
JAPANESE RED PINE

This lovely tree is grown for its red bark and naturally twisted shape. Although reaching 100 ft (30 m), and widely used as a timber tree in its native Japan, in cultivation it is slow growing, often multi-trunked, and can be pruned, which makes it very popular as a bonsai specimen. Ovoid, yellow-purplish cones stand out boldly from the bright green, 5 in (12 cm) long foliage. The dwarf cultivar 'Umbraculifera', commonly known as the Tanyosho pine, has an umbrella-like canopy. The bark on the multiple trunks is an appealing orange-red and flaky. An extremely slow grower, it eventually reaches a mature height of about 15 ft (5 m). 'Oculus-draconis', the dragon's eye pine, has yellow-banded needles. ZONE 4.

Pinus elliottii
SLASH PINE

This fast-growing species copes with most soils, even poorly drained ones. Its final height is around 80 ft (25 m) with a pyramidal shape. Native to south-eastern USA, its narrow, deep green leaves are in bundles of 2 or 3, at least 5 in (12 cm) long. The cones are 6 in (15 cm) long and each scale is armed with a sharp prickle. The slash pine is a valuable source of turpentine and rosin, as well as timber and wood pulp. Some botanists include this species in *P. caribaea*. ZONE 9.

Pinus halepensis
ALEPPO PINE

The most drought resistant of the pines, the Aleppo pine hails from the eastern Mediterranean area. It tolerates most conditions except severe frost when young. It quickly forms a tree 50 ft (15 m) tall with a spreading crown, and has a very distinctive rugged character. The young bark is ash grey, but ages to reddish brown. The soft, light green needles are 4 in (10 cm) long and usually carried in pairs, and the 3–4 in (7–10 cm) cones are reddish brown. Turpentine is also derived from this species and it is occasionally harvested for use as a Christmas tree. It is much valued for timber in Greece. ZONE 7.

Pinus jeffreyi
JEFFREY PINE

Native to western North America, from Oregon to Baja California, this slender, conical pine grows to a height of 180 ft (55 m), though trees grown under harsh conditions are often naturally dwarf. It is distinguished by 8 in (20 cm) long, thick, aromatic, bluish green needles and curved, often J-shaped cones up to 12 in (30 cm) long. Its fissured bark is deep reddish brown and flakes off to reveal bright new bark. It can be attacked by the disease *Elytroderma deformans,* which causes witches' brooms. ZONE 6.

Pinus koraiensis
KOREAN PINE

This lovely pine from Korea, Japan and the Amur region of China displays unusually rough, deep bluish green needles up to 4 in (10 cm) long which are carried in bundles of 5. Its bark is rough and greyish brown and the cones are from 3½–6 in (9–15 cm) long. In the wild it is a tall, narrow tree but in cultivation it grows to about 50 ft (15 m) with a rounded head. It is a tough, adaptable tree with a preference for well-drained soil. Though probably suitable for timber, it has not been much used for this purpose. ZONE 5.

Pinus monophylla
SINGLE-LEAF PIÑON

Native to western North America from Utah to Baja California, in cultivation this species grows very slowly to 25 ft (8 m) and is usually multi-stemmed. It matures from a slender sapling to an interesting, round-headed tree with a crooked trunk. Its single, stiff, prickly leaves are 2 in (5 cm) long. Its brown, woody cones are spheres with a diameter of 2 in (5 cm) and produce edible nuts. Ideal for exposed rocky positions, this species is tough and drought resistant. ZONE 7.

Pinus monticola
WESTERN WHITE PINE

Found from British Columbia to northern California, this large tree matures to 200 ft (65 m); the oldest recorded specimen is 500 years old. A timber tree used principally in the manufacture of matches, *P. monticola* keeps its shape without pruning. Its upward-growing branches are clad with dense clumps of 4 in (10 cm) long, bluish green needles, carried in bundles of 5, and display long, up to 8 in (20 cm), tapering, purplish cones from their tips. Though hardy, it is susceptible to white pine blister rust in north-western USA. ZONE 5.

Pinus mugo
MOUNTAIN PINE, SWISS MOUNTAIN PINE

Found in the mountains of Europe, this small tree grows slowly to 25 ft (8 m). Its windswept appearance reflects its alpine habitat and makes it an interesting plant for bonsai work. It can look very effective in rock gardens or arranged with other dwarf conifers in tubs. Its pairs of 2 in (5 cm) long, bright green needles develop from very resinous buds. The oval, dark brown cones are 1–2 in (2–5 cm) long. This species is very hardy but does not tolerate extreme heat or drought. 'Aurea' has golden foliage; 'Gnom', a particularly tight little bush, 20 in (50 cm) high and spreading to 30 in (75 cm), produces whitish new shoots that stand out dramatically against its rich, black-green mature growth; 'Mops' matures to 16 in (40 cm) over 10 years; var. *pumilio,* known as the dwarf Swiss mountain pine, grows into a compact, rounded bun achieving 32 in (80 cm) in 10 years. ZONE 2.

Pinus monophylla

Pinus koraiensis

Pinus jeffreyi

Pinus monticola

Pinus mugo 'Mops'

Pinus nigra
AUSTRIAN PINE

Originating from central and southern Europe, P. nigra has a dense crown of dark green foliage and grows to 130 ft (40 m), though cultivated specimens rarely exceed 50 ft (15 m). It has an open, conical habit with a whitish brown trunk and whorled branches. Its pairs of stiff, dark green needles are up to 6½ in (16 cm) long, while its cones are 3 in (7 cm) long. It grows happily in both chalk and clay and will tolerate coastal conditions. Var. *maritima*, commonly known as the Corsican pine, forms a denser crown and is slower growing than other forms. Its grey-green twisted needles are paired and grow to a length of 7 in (17 cm). It is distinguished by cracking bark and a very straight trunk that is harvested for timber. Interestingly, trees are harvested in Corsica at around 180 years old, while in New Zealand they mature in 50 years. ZONE 4.

Pinus palustris
LONGLEAF PINE

Found naturally from Virginia to Texas, this handsome pine lives up to its common name by producing needles up to 18 in (45 cm) long. Valued as a source of pitch timber and wood pulp, it grows to 100 ft (30 m). It will not tolerate strong winds or drought. A rather open crown is formed by sparse branches clad with blunt, bluish green needles arranged in groups of 3. Its 6–10 in (15–25 cm) long, reddish brown cones have spines on the tips of their scales and are held on the tree for up to 20 years. ZONE 4.

Pinus parviflora
JAPANESE WHITE PINE

This small pine usually matures to a height of 40 ft (13 m) in cultivation but in its native Japan it can reach 80 ft (25 m). It is usually a pyramidal tree that is nearly as wide as it is high. It produces some of the shortest needles in the genus—1½ in (3 cm) long—and forms a dense, bluish green foliage which, combined with its slow growth-habit, makes it a popular bonsai or tub subject. 'Brevifolia' is an upright, sparsely foliaged cultivar. 'Glauca' is a blue-foliaged cultivar that takes many years to reach 5 ft (1.5 m) high. The blue-green needles have distinctive blue-white bands on their inner sides. ZONE 3.

Pinus patula
MEXICAN YELLOW PINE, SPREADING-LEAFED PINE

Probably the most elegant of the pines, this species is always graceful with long, slender, drooping needles and a spreading canopy,

Pinus parviflora 'Brevifolia'

Pinus nigra

Pinus nigra

Pinus palustris

making it a good shade tree. It eventually reaches a height of 50 ft (15 m) with a 15 ft (5 m) spread, branching low to the ground. The 8 in (20 cm) long needles are soft, pale green to greyish green, and grouped in 3s. The clustered cones are 4 in (10 cm) long and oval in shape. This tree is becoming very important as a source of wood pulp and is being extensively planted in many parts of the world. ZONE 9.

Pinus pinaster
MARITIME PINE, CLUSTER PINE

Found in the Mediterranean region and growing quickly to 100 ft (30 m), the maritime pine demands a large garden. It is intolerant of drought and frost, but enjoys coastal locations and is a good windbreak. This tree has beautiful and very characteristic bark: bright reddish brown and deeply furrowed in a jigsaw-like pattern. The pairs of green needles are up to 10 in (25 cm) long, stiff and shiny. Its cones are rich brown, oval and 7 in (17 cm) long. Because the cones persist on the branches for many years without opening, they are useful as decorations. This species is an important resin-producing conifer and is widely planted in Portugal as a timber tree. ZONE 7.

Pinus pinea
ROMAN PINE, STONE PINE, UMBRELLA PINE

This species from southern Europe and Turkey, the seeds of which are edible and known as pine nuts (pinoli in southern Europe), has an interesting flattened crown atop a straight, though often leaning trunk. It copes with most conditions including extremes of drought and heat when established. It can reach a height of 80 ft (25 m) but in the wild is often stunted by harsh conditions. The trunk has furrowed, reddish grey bark, while the rigid paired needles are 4–8 in (10–20 cm) long and bright green. Globe-shaped cones are shiny and brown. ZONE 8.

Pinus ponderosa
PONDEROSA PINE, WESTERN YELLOW PINE

This pine originates in western North America where it is one of the most abundant trees. It has distinctive bark that is deeply fissured with a mosaic of broad, smooth, yellowish brown, reddish brown and pinkish grey plates. The USA's third most important timber tree, it is used in construction and furniture making as well as for more mundane items such as mouse traps. It can reach 200 ft (60 m), but in cultivation is usually smaller, and has dark brown cones on spire-like branches. Its dark green needles are carried in bundles of 3, and are up to 11 in (27 cm) long. ZONE 5.

Pinus radiata plantation

Pinus pinea

Pinus radiata
MONTEREY PINE, RADIATA PINE

This fast-growing pine from California is an important plantation species in other parts of the world and the number one timber tree in Australia and New Zealand. It adapts well to a range of conditions but does not tolerate extreme drought or heat. It grows best in well-drained soil. It is shallow rooted and inclined to be toppled by strong wind. The Monterey pine grows to a height of over 100 ft (30 m) and has a distinctive pyramidal shape when young, becoming more columnar with age. The deep green needles are 4–6 in (10–15 cm) long, and the bark greyish brown. The 4–6 in (10–15 cm) long cones are light brown. ZONE 8.

Pinus pinaster, growing on the island of Capri, Italy (below)

Pinus patula (below)

Pinus sylvestris

Pinus sylvestris (below)

Pinus roxburghii
CHIR PINE, HIMALAYAN LONGLEAF PINE

Native to the Himalayan foothills, this species grows very large in its native habitat—to 160 ft (50 m) tall with a 15 ft (5 m) spread—but is usually smaller in cultivation. The tree is slender when young but becomes round headed as it matures. It cannot withstand severe drought. The bark is mottled with light brown and greyish tones. The drooping needles are very long, to 12 in (30 cm), light green and carried in 3s. The cones are oval in shape with reflexed scales and are 8 in (20 cm) long. ZONE 6.

Pinus strobus
EASTERN WHITE PINE

Occurring naturally from Manitoba to Georgia, this eastern North American species is characterized by its deeply fissured, greyish brown bark and whorled branches. It grows to 200 ft (60 m) in the wild, but only 75 ft (23 m) in cultivation. The conical crown becomes flattish with age. Its fine, 4 in (10 cm) long, bluish green needles are soft and carried in groups of 5. Pointed cones, clustered at the ends of the branches, produce copious amounts of white resin. This species develops rapidly if grown away from a polluted environment, and is one of the most valuable timber trees of eastern USA. Though cold hardy, it is susceptible to drought and windburn. 'Fastigiata' has vivid green growth that is borne by upward-pointing branches. 'Nana' is a rounded dwarf cultivar with dense foliage that completely obscures the branches. ZONE 3.

Pinus sylvestris
SCOTS PINE

The Scots pine is the commonest pine in cultivation in Europe and, being fast growing and an excellent timber tree, is often used in forestry. Found throughout northern Europe and western Asia, it is the only pine indigenous to the United Kingdom. Growing to a height of 100 ft (30 m) with a characteristic rounded head of foliage, dwarf cultivars can make attractive tub specimens; young potted trees are

Pinus strobus 'Fastigiata'

Pinus strobus, as a hedge (below)

Pinus roxburghii (below)

Pinus roxburghii

often sold at Christmas. The twisted, bluish green needles grow in pairs and are 3 in (7 cm) long. The bark is orange-red and very much a feature of the tree. The Scots pine grows well in poor sandy soil but will not tolerate drought. ZONE 4.

Pinus thunbergii
JAPANESE BLACK PINE

This tree is commonly grown in Japan as an ornamental where its irregular, layered, horizontal branches have for centuries been an inspiration for artists and bonsai masters. It will stand any amount of pruning and trimming to shape and does very well in containers. Also known as *P. thunbergiana*, this species has a rugged trunk and intricate framework of branches and will grow to 130 ft (40 m) if left untrimmed. With purplish black bark, pairs of thick needles and conspicuous white buds, this pine makes an outstanding specimen. ZONE 5.

Pinus wallichiana
BHUTAN PINE

Sometimes known as the Himalayan white pine, this tree produces eye-catching 12 in (30 cm) long cones from graceful long branches. If grown in moist, deep soil, this handsome ornamental tree with its 6–8 in (15–20 cm) long, drooping, grey-green needles will attain a height of 145 ft (45 m). The growth form is conical and very broad at the base. This species is especially effective as the centrepiece for a large lawn. It is quite cold and disease resistant but suffers in hot, dry conditions. ZONE 5.

PISCIDIA
Fabaceae

This small genus consists of evergreen shrubs or small trees from the West Indies. They grow to 15 ft (5 m) and must be planted in rich, moist soil. The oblong, divided leaves contrast well with the yellowish brown bark. The red and white, pea flowers mature to pods with 4 broad wings. Seed must be scarified before sowing. Propagation is also from cuttings.

Piscidia piscipula
FLORIDA FISHPOISON TREE, JAMAICA DOGWOOD

This sun-loving species from the Caribbean grows to 30 ft (10 m) or so, making it a useful small shade tree. The 4 in (10 cm) long leaflets are held in 4 sets of pairs, and the red and white flowers look pink from a short distance. They appear in spring with the new leaves. This tree, apart from being grown as an ornamental, is also used as an aid to catching fish: leaves or pieces of bark are thrown into the water to stupefy the fish. In addition, the leaves of *P. piscipula* may irritate sensitive skin. This species is restricted to subtropical climates. ZONE 10.

PISONIA
Nyctaginaceae

These fast-growing, deciduous or evergreen small trees and shrubs are found growing naturally in tropical and subtropical areas, particularly in Australia and the Malay region. The trees are best known for producing extremely sticky fruits that trap small birds and insects. The reason for such an attribute remains a mystery. They require a sunny or partially shaded site with rich, well-drained soil. They will grow in containers provided ample water is available. Propagation is from seed or cuttings.

Pisonia grandis
BIRD LIME TREE

The pale green leaves of this species are 12 in (30 cm) or more long. The flowers are greenish and appear in late summer. The soft, spongy trunk branches shortly above the ground into a broad, open crown. The bird lime tree grows to 30 ft (10 m) and looks effective planted as an avenue. ZONE 10.

PISTACIA
Anacardiaceae

This is a small genus (9 species) of both deciduous and evergreen trees

Pistacia chinensis (below)

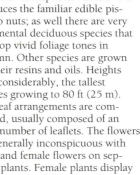

and shrubs. They originate in the warm-temperate regions of the northern hemisphere. *Pistacia vera* produces the familiar edible pistachio nuts; as well there are very ornamental deciduous species that develop vivid foliage tones in autumn. Other species are grown for their resins and oils. Heights vary considerably, the tallest species growing to 80 ft (25 m). The leaf arrangements are compound, usually composed of an even number of leaflets. The flowers are generally inconspicuous with male and female flowers on separate plants. Female plants display clusters of small berries or fleshy fruit in autumn and early winter. A site in full sun with a well-drained soil is preferred. Propagation is from seed sown in autumn and winter, or by budding or grafting.

Pistacia chinensis

Pistacia chinensis
CHINESE PISTACHIO

Growing to 25 ft (8 m) or so in gardens, this deciduous species has glossy green leaves which consist of up to 10 pairs of leaflets. In autumn the leaves turn spectacular shades of yellow, orange and scarlet. The inconspicuous flowers are borne in panicles, and are followed in summer by small red berries that turn blue in autumn and are particularly attractive to birds. They are too small to be worth eating as nuts. Its mild root system and modest maintenance requirements make it an excellent street tree, but it also performs well as a canopy for shade-loving shrubs. It often forms a double trunk. ZONE 5.

Pinus thunbergii

Pittosporum phylliraeoides

Pittosporum eugenioides

Pittosporum crassifolium

Pittosporum rhombifolium

Pistacia vera
PISTACHIO, PISTACHIO NUT

Native to western Asia and the Middle East, the pistachio is now grown in plantations in many warm-temperate parts of the world. It is a small deciduous tree that reaches a height and spread of about 30 ft (10 m). The leaves consist of 1 to 5 pairs of oval leaflets. The leaves turn red-gold in autumn and red male and white female flowers are borne on separate trees; at least one of each is needed for a crop of nuts. These are reddish, fleshy and oval with a central green or yellow edible kernel. The pistachio prefers a hot dry summer, but should be well watered, with a mild to cold winter to ensure good fruit set and yields. It does best in loamy, organic soil. ZONE 8.

PITTOSPORUM
Pittosporaceae

A large genus of attractive foliage trees and shrubs, these evergreens make good specimen plants, screens and windbreaks or dense hedges in mild-winter climates. There are some 150 species, mostly from tropical and subtropical regions of Australasia. The leaves are arranged alternately along the stems, or in whorls. Several species have striking foliage much sought after by flower arrangers. Fragrant flowers are followed by fruit consisting of a hard outer capsule surrounding round seeds with a sticky covering. Some species are frost tolerant and many are excellent for seaside gardens. Grow them in full sun or partial shade, choosing a sheltered position in colder areas. The soil must be well drained and kept moist over summer to maintain the foliage at its best. Propagate from seed in autumn or spring, or tip cuttings in summer.

Pittosporum crassifolium
KARO

This native of New Zealand forms a tall shrub or small tree, rarely over 25 ft (8 m) tall with a spread of 10 ft (3 m). The single trunk bears low-growing branches and has a dense, domed canopy. The oblong to oval leaves are dark green and leathery, 3 in (8 cm) long with the felted undersides a greyish white. Clusters of fragrant, star-shaped, reddish purple flowers are set among the branch tips in spring. Fleshy, greenish white, oval fruit up to 1 in (2 cm) long follow. The karo is drought tolerant and copes well with exposed seaside locations. It adapts to most soil types but needs an open, sunny aspect. 'Variegatum' has grey to bright green leaves with an irregular cream edge. ZONE 8.

Pittosporum eugenioides
TARATA, LEMONWOOD

The tarata is a beautiful, densely foliaged large shrub to small tree from New Zealand, pyramidal in shape when young. Mature specimens reach up to 40 ft (13 m) tall, with smooth, pale grey bark. The oval leaves have a wavy edge and are a shiny dark green. They have a citrus-like aroma when crushed. Terminal clusters of small, star-shaped yellow flowers with a honey-like perfume appear in spring. Large clusters of green oval fruit follow and persist through autumn and winter. Frost and drought tolerant, the tarata thrives in most soils when grown in an open, sunny spot. 'Variegatum' has beautiful mid-green leaves blotched along the edge with white. It grows to a height of 9–15 ft (3–5 m). The species and its cultivars are suitable for clipped hedges. ZONE 9.

Pittosporum phylliraeoides
BERRIGAN, WEEPING PITTOSPORUM, WILLOW PITTOSPORUM

This is a large, rounded shrub to small tree, 24 ft (8 m) tall with a graceful weeping habit. It forms an open canopy. The shiny, dark green leaves hang from pendulous branches. Narrowly lance shaped, and up to 4 in (10 cm) long, they end in pointed, curved tips. Creamy yellow flowers held singly or in small clusters at the branch tips are an added attraction in spring and summer. These are followed by decorative, fleshy, oval fruit about 1 in (2 cm) long. Ripening from yellow to reddish brown, they split in 2 to reveal red seeds against a yellow interior. Plant this species in well-drained soil and a sunny location. Berrigan tree seeds were used by Australian Aborigines to treat pain and cramps. ZONE 9.

Pittosporum rhombifolium
QUEENSLAND LAUREL, AUSTRALIAN LAUREL

Native to rainforests of eastern Australia, masses of round, bright orange fruit in autumn and winter are the main attraction of this species. About $\frac{1}{2}$ in (1 cm) across, they split when ripe to reveal sticky black seeds. This tree can be up to 80 ft (25 m) tall when grown in a sheltered position, usually smaller in an open spot. Upward-sweeping branches form a dense pyramidal crown. Toothed, leathery, shiny green leaves are, as the species name indicates, rhombus shaped, and are about $4\frac{1}{2}$ in (11 cm) long. In spring star-shaped, creamy white flowers are arranged in dense clusters at the branch tips, up to 5 in (12 cm) across. This species grows best in loamy to heavy soil. Drought tolerant, it needs adequate moisture during the warmer months to ensure a spectacular display of fruit. It makes a good street tree in frost-free climates. ZONE 9.

Pittosporum tenuifolium
KOHUHU

The kohuhu is a New Zealand native. A tall shrub to small tree, 30 ft (10 m) tall, the young plants are columnar, rounding in shape as they mature. The ornamental leaves have a wavy edge, and are pale green and oblong in shape and 3 in (8 cm) long. They contrast beautifully with the black twigs and bark. Small, dark chocolate flowers appear in late spring, either singly or in small clusters. Their sweet honey perfume is most intense at night. In late summer, round fruit that turn from green to almost black when ripe are produced. A species that will tolerate heavy pruning, it prefers an open, sunny site with light to medium soils enriched with organic matter. There are a number of cultivars with variegated or purple-toned foliage suited to floral arrangements. To obtain suitably long-stemmed sprays, the shrubs are pruned in spring. ZONE 9.

Pittosporum tobira
JAPANESE MOCK ORANGE

Native to Japan and China, this is a slow-growing shrubby species, about 8 ft (2.5 m) tall, that is mainly admired for its beautiful shiny green leaves. Oval to oblong in shape and 4 in (10 cm) long, these are arranged in whorls along the stems. Star-shaped, cream flowers with an orange blossom scent are clustered among the foliage in late spring and summer. The species will thrive only in mild climates, but it is tolerant of dry conditions. A popular hedge plant, particularly in coastal regions, it should be grown in an open, sunny position in a light to medium soil that is well drained. 'Wheeler's Dwarf' is a mound-like shrub under 24 in (60 cm). 'Variegatum' has an irregular silvery white edge to its leaves. ZONE 9.

PLAGIANTHUS
Malvaceae

There are 2 species in this genus including one of the few deciduous trees native to New Zealand. One (P. betulinus) is a 40 ft (13 m) high tree and the other (P. divaricatus) is a shrub that eventually reaches 8 ft (2.5 m) high and wide. They have light olive green leaves with serrated edges and greenish white flowers in summer. They are not spectacular plants, but are very tough and adaptable. Plant in moist, well-drained soil with light shade when young. Propagate from seed or grow selected male forms from cuttings.

Plagianthus betulinus
RIBBONWOOD

Ribbonwood has very coarsely toothed leaves up to 4 in (10 cm) long. When young the tree is a densely twiggy, spreading shrub and stays in this form for a number of years. There are separate male and female plants; both produce panicles of yellowish or greenish white flowers in summer, but those of the male are slightly larger and more decorative. The name ribbonwood comes from the lacy inner bark. ZONE 7.

PLANCHONIA
Lecythidaceae

This genus consists of semi-deciduous trees indigenous to the monsoonal regions of Australia and New Guinea. They have an upright habit reaching 20 ft (7 m) and a trunk covered with corky bark. The circular leaves are 4 in (10 cm) long. Large, pale green flowers appear on the branch tips in summer. The edible fruit look like green eggs. The trees thrive in poor, infertile soil providing they are given constant moisture and plenty of sun. Propagate from seed or cuttings.

Planchonia careya
COCKY APPLE

This species is grown for its attractive flowers and leaf hues. It forms an open tree to 20 ft (7 m) with circular leaves held on long stalks. The young foliage is pale green and becomes brilliant orange before dropping during the dry season. Its flowers, which appear in winter and spring, have long white stamens that are stained scarlet at the base. They open in the morning but normally fall by the afternoon. P. careya is a useful small specimen tree for gardens in tropical climates. ZONE 11.

Plagianthus betulinus

Pittosporum tenuifolium (below)

Planchonia careya (below)

Pittosporum tobira 'Variegatum'

Pittosporum tobira 'Wheeler's Dwarf'

PLATANUS
Platanaceae

A genus of large, vigorous, wide-crowned, deciduous trees from Eurasia and North America, it contains some of the world's largest deciduous shade trees for dry summer climates, many of which are widely used as street trees. The most conspicuous feature is the mottled bark that is shed in winter. The 5-lobed leaves are large and maple like, and the brown seed balls hang in clusters on the trees in winter. The flowers are of little visual significance. The majority tolerate severe pruning, air pollution and hard man-made substances, such as paving, partially covering the root run. They thrive in deep, rich, well-drained soil in a sunny site and can be transplanted. Propagation is from seed, cuttings or by layering. The trees are called planes or plane-trees in some countries, sycamores in others.

Platanus × acerifolia
LONDON PLANE

Used as a street tree for many years, this obliging tree is resistant to leaf blight and can withstand poor atmospheric conditions, deep shade, hot sunlight, severe pollarding and a concrete cover over its roots. However, the roots can lift paving and the large, bright green, leathery leaves can block small drains. This fast-growing tree can reach heights of 120 ft (38 m). The trunk, attractively blotched in grey, brown and white, is straight and erect. Decorative brown seed balls hang through the winter months. ZONE 3.

Platanus occidentalis
AMERICAN PLANE, BUTTONWOOD, SYCAMORE

A large tree with a broad open head, it can top 150 ft (46 m). The bark is generally a creamy white but, on older trees, usually takes on a dark brown hue close to the ground. The large, bright green leaves, up to 10 in (25 cm) wide, are toothed, and the seed heads hang singly. This species prefers a continental climate (cold winters and hot summers). It is prone to attack by leaf blight. Its timber is used in the USA for furniture and for firewood. ZONE 3.

Platanus orientalis
CHINAR, CHENNAR, ORIENTAL PLANE

Native to the Mediterranean and the Middle East, this is a large tree to about 100 ft (30 m) tall with spreading branches and a relatively short, stout trunk. The flaking bark is grey to greenish white. The leaves are deeply incised forming 5 narrow, pointed lobes. The round, brown seed heads hang like 3–5 beads on a thread. It gives good shade and is used as a street tree in Australia, southern Africa and southern Europe. The leaves of 'Digitata' have elongated, narrow lobes that are more deeply cut. ZONE 6.

Platanus racemosa
ALISO, WESTERN SYCAMORE

Indigenous to the mountains of California, the tree can fail in areas where the winters are long and harsh. It does best in a deep, fertile soil in an open sunny site. The trunk is stout, erect and pale when young. The tree, a rapid grower, can reach heights of 110 ft (35 m), while the canopy is usually about half the tree's height. The lobed leaves are green, and have a downy whitish underside. The greenish flowers hang in clusters and are followed by between 2 and 7 spiky seed heads hanging on a stalk. 'Wrightii' is very similar except that the seed heads are smooth. ZONE 7.

PLATYCLADUS
Cupressaceae

Platycladus is a genus that contains only the one species, an evergreen conifer featuring flat, fan-like sprays of aromatic foliage. However, you may also find it listed with the closely related *Thuja* or *Biota*. The type species is a tall, conical tree but the attraction for gardeners lies in the wide choice of selected small to dwarf varieties. These offer a diversity of neat, conical or rounded bushes with changing foliage tones through the seasons. As all the branches are retained right down to the ground, these conifers form excellent informal hedges and screens, rockery features or tub specimens. The leaves are tiny, scale-like needles that clasp the twigs. Female trees have small, erect, fleshy brown cones with overlapping scales hidden among the foliage. The species prefers warmer climates than many conifers. Choose a spot sheltered from strong winds, though preferably in full sun. A partly shaded position will also be suitable. Most moist, well-drained soils are suitable. Clip plants lightly in spring, if desired, to shape them. Propagation is from seed, or from cuttings taken in the cooler months.

Platanus orientalis

An avenue of *Platanus* × *acerifolia* in Medoc, France

A row of *Platanus* × *acerifolia* attractively pollarded

Platanus racemosa

Platycladus orientalis
ORIENTAL ARBOR-VITAE

This conifer grows into a densely branched large shrub or small tree, up to 40 ft (13 m) tall. Native to north and west China and Japan, it features sprays of bright green foliage held vertically when young, but almost horizontal on older branches. Young plants are dense and conical to columnar in shape. In older trees, a domed crown of upward sweeping branches tops the short trunk. Better known are the smaller-growing varieties, which have a multitude of uses in the garden. Some have very dense, crisp foliage and a symmetrical shape while others are softer looking with a more irregular form. They are good accent plants in a rockery or can be grown in tubs. Some dwarf types keep their fuzzy, juvenile foliage. The cultivars vary from round to columnar in shape, with leaves in shades of green, grey, gold or grey and white. ZONE 6.

PLUMBAGO
Plumbaginaceae

The leadworts are a small genus of perennials, evergreen shrubs and scrambling climbers and semi-climbers. Their main appeal for gardeners lies in the clusters of blue, white or red flowers. The flowers have 5 petals narrowing to a long slender tube and are massed together on short stems near the tips of the arching branches. The leaves are arranged alternately. Plumbagos grow best in warm climates. In frost-ridden places, they do well in a mildly warmed greenhouse. They require well-drained soil, perhaps enriched with a little organic matter. Although an established plant is drought tolerant, keeping the soil moist through the summer ensures a good flowering display. They will benefit from pruning in late winter to tidy their vigorous stems and remove old wood. This will also ensure a good flower display, as flowers are produced on the new growth. Propagate from tip cuttings taken in the warmer months or from semi-hardwood cuttings taken in autumn.

Plumbago auriculata
BLUE PLUMBAGO

Originating in South Africa, P. auriculata (formerly known as P. capensis) is the main species cultivated. Its beautiful flowers are a shade of sky-blue rarely seen elsewhere. Fast growing to a height of around 6 ft (2 m) with a similar spread, it flowers prolifically through the warmer months of the year. A partly shaded location will ensure the flowers retain their colour. The pale green leaves are oblong and 2 in (5 cm) long. It produces suckers readily, and will quickly increase its size and sprawling habit unless pruned once or twice a year. This species will grow higher if supported and will also climb up nearby shrubs. The plant makes a striking informal hedge or can be trimmed to make a more formal hedge. Often grown in a large pot or hanging basket, it is also a favourite conservatory or cool greenhouse plant. The cultivar 'Alba' has clear white blooms. 'Royal Cape' has flowers of a more intense blue that hold their colour and is considered slightly more tolerant of frost and drought. ZONE 9.

PLUMERIA
Apocynaceae
FRANGIPANI, TEMPLE TREE

The scent of frangipani on a tropical evening is simply unforgettable. The genus contains 8 species of mainly deciduous shrubs and trees, originally from Central America. The trees can reach a height of 30 ft (10 m), though they are generally much smaller. Their fleshy branches contain a poisonous, milky sap. In the tropics the terminally held flowers (generally white) appear before the leaves and continue to flower for most of the year. In sub-tropical climates, the flowers appear in spring after the leaves and continue growing until the next winter. In colder climates, you can grow frangipani in a greenhouse. The fruit consists of 2 leathery follicles, though the trees rarely fruit in cultivation. Most frangipanis in gardens are hybrids. Propagate from cuttings in early spring. Plumeria commemorates Charles Plumier, a 17th-century French botanist who described a number of tropical species.

Plumbago auriculata

Plumbago auriculata 'Royal Cape'

Platycladus orientalis 'Aurea Nana'

Platycladus orientalis

Plumeria rubra var. acutifolia

Podocarpus henkelii

Plumeria rubra

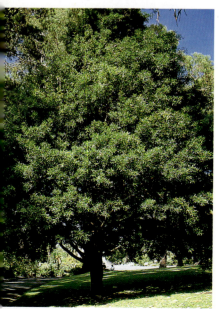

Podocarpus elatus

Plumeria obtusa
WHITE FRANGIPANI

This small tree grows up to 24 ft (8 m) high and is best suited to a tropical climate. It can be grown in frost-free subtropical climates but requires a sheltered position and a fairly constant supply of water. The broad leaves are 7 in (17 cm) long and blunt ended and, unlike most frangipanis, this plant is reliably evergreen in the tropics. The scented, creamy white flowers have a bright yellow centre and are held as long as the days and nights are warm. The stems are stout and fleshy. Propagation is from cuttings which have been allowed to dry out for a couple of weeks. ZONE 10.

Plumeria rubra

This deciduous large shrub or small tree with a broadly rounded canopy can grow to a height of 24 ft (8 m). It is distinguished by its pale pink to crimson flowers which are used extensively for decoration. This species is widely cultivated. *P. rubra* var. *acutifolia* is usually seen more commonly than the species. It features creamy white flowers, sometimes flushed pink, with a yellow centre. ZONE 10.

PODALYRIA
Fabaceae

This is a genus of about 25 species of evergreen shrubs and small trees that occur naturally in the winter rainfall areas of southern Africa. They have oval, 1–2 in (2–5 cm) long leaves covered with very fine hairs that create a silvery effect. The flowering season varies but usually starts in very early spring when fragrant clusters of mauve or white sweet pea flowers open. A light trimming after flowering keeps the bushes compact. Plant in light, well-drained soil in full sun; these plants are excellent in coastal conditions. Propagate from seed in spring or cuttings in summer or by layering.

Podalyria calyptrata
SWEETPEA BUSH

This species grows to be a rather open, small tree of about 12 ft (4 m) high and nearly as wide. Its foliage is distinctly silver-grey and is as much a feature as the masses of pink flowers that open in spring. Provided the climate is mild enough, this is an undemanding plant that performs reliably. Though perhaps not in the first rank of garden specimens, it is a good foliage specimen with the added bonus of a flower display. ZONE 9.

PODOCARPUS
Podocarpaceae
PLUM PINE

All the species in this coniferous genus are evergreen, varying in size from groundcovers of 3 ft (1 m) to large trees reaching 145 ft (45 m). There are about 100 different species, native to South America, southern Africa, southern and East Asia and Australasia. Grown for their dense foliage and attractive habit, they are, in some ways, the warm-climate equivalent of the yew (*Taxus*), with a similar appearance and ornamental uses. The flat, generally narrow leaves are spirally arranged. There are separate male and female plants. Male plants have catkin-like yellow cones. Female plants have naked seeds held on short stalks that later develop into the fleshy, berry-like 'fruit' that give them their common name of plum pines. The fruit ranges from plum purple to blue-black to red. The genus includes species harvested commercially for softwood. *Podocarpus* is moderately fast growing and reliable in a range of soils from rich to poor, either in full sun or part-shade, depending on the species, though warm-temperate climates, free of heavy frost, suit them best. In cooler areas, plum pines can be successfully grown indoors. Leave the plants unpruned unless grown as a hedge. Propagation is from seed or cuttings.

Podocarpus elatus
PLUM PINE, BROWN PINE

Originally from eastern Australia where it can grow into a large tree to 110 ft (35 m) with a spreading crown, it is generally considerably smaller in cultivation. Its dense canopy makes it a good choice as a shade tree. It has flaky dark brown bark and shiny dark green leaves that are oblong and end in a sharp point. They are up to 4½ in (11 cm) long. The edible fruit are rounded and purplish to black, and 1 in (2 cm) across. This species can tolerate mild frosts, but must be watered in dry periods. *P. elatus* copes with heavy pruning, best done during the growing season which extends throughout the warmer months. This makes it a good choice for a clipped hedge. ZONE 9.

Podocarpus henkelii
NATAL YELLOWWOOD, HENKEL'S YELLOWWOOD

A native of South Africa, this species has a weeping appearance, with drooping branches and foliage. Individual leaves, up to 7 in

(17 cm) long, are often curved. The fruit are rounded and waxy green, up to ½ in (1 cm) across. ZONE 9.

Podocarpus latifolius
REAL YELLOWWOOD

This is a big tree, up to 130 ft (40 m) in its natural habitat of southern African mountain and coastal forests. Under garden conditions it will probably grow to 50 ft (15 m). It is slightly tender to frost but is wind resistant. In fully grown trees the leaves are grouped close to the tips of the branches, while the bark is longitudinally grooved. Male trees produce pinkish, relatively large, 1½ in (3 cm) long cones. When mature, the fruit turn blue or purplish. In South Africa, the real yellowwood is considered an excellent choice for gardens, parks and streets. There the wood is also used in the timber industry. ZONE 9.

Podocarpus lawrencei
MOUNTAIN PLUM PINE

Originally from Australia, this tree, also known as *P. alpinus*, can withstand drought and some frost but it must be grown in a sunny position. Variable in height from 5 ft (1.5 m) in mountain areas to 24 ft (8 m) in woods, its trunk has a gnarled, picturesque appearance. The small leaves are narrow, greyish green and flat and contrast well with the attractive, red, fleshy berries. It is a good species for container planting as it grows fairly slowly. ZONE 8.

Podocarpus macrophyllus
KUSAMAKI

This large-leafed species from mountainous areas of Japan and China prefers moist, humus-rich soil and is relatively tolerant of cold. Its informal pyramidal crown with a height of 65 ft (20 m) and spread of 12 ft (4 m) in the wild is composed of 5 in (12 cm) long, thick, dark green leaves that are crowded onto the branchlets. It responds well to pruning and makes a good thick hedge. It also makes a good container plant. Also known as the Buddhist pine because it is often grown in the gardens around Japanese temples, this conifer bears little black berries. 'Maki' has a distinctly erect habit with almost vertical branches. It is rarely bigger than a shrub. ZONE 7.

Podocarpus neriifolius
BLACKLEAF PODOCARP

In the warm climate of its native Borneo and New Guinea, this species grows to 65 ft (20 m) and is characterized by relatively large leaves and small fruit. The unusually glossy dark green, thin leaves have prominent midribs and are up to 6 in (15 cm) long. Its flowers appear as catkins: the male brown, female green. Its fruit are oval, fleshy, green berries. ZONE 10.

Podocarpus salignus
WILLOWLEAF PODOCARP

This Chilean conifer differs from other members of the genus in its willow-like leaves (hence its common name). These glossy blue-green leaves are up to 6 in (15 cm) long. The bushy, columnar crown reaching 65 ft (20 m) is held on a trunk bearing shaggy, orange-brown bark. It does not like to dry out and should be mulched heavily in cultivation. ZONE 8.

Podocarpus latifolius

Podocarpus salignus

Podocarpus macrophyllus

Podocarpus lawrencei

Podocarpus totara
TOTARA

One of the tallest of the genus and reaching 100 ft (30 m), this tree from New Zealand is a slow grower. Its magnificent trunk grows to a diameter of 10 ft (3 m) and yields one of New Zealand's most valuable timbers. It can live for 200 years. Its dense leaves are stiff and bronze green with sharp points. Also known as the mahogany pine, it produces a very distinctive reddish brown bark when fresh which ages to a greyish brown and peels off in strips. Its crimson fruit, about $\frac{1}{2}$ in (1 cm) round, are carried on red stalks. 'Aureus' has a pyramidal form and rich golden yellow foliage. It is smaller than its parent, maturing to 15 ft (5 m), and has more graceful branches. It can be dwarfed by pruning to suit confined spaces. ZONE 9.

Polygala virgata

Polygala myrtifolia 'Grandiflora' (below)

POLYGALA
Polygalaceae
MILKWORT

Over 500 different species hail from warm areas all over the world. They include trees, annuals and perennials and some shrubs, only a few of which are successful and showy garden shrubs. Some species were used by the ancient Greeks to stimulate the secretion of milk in lactating mothers, hence the common name. The 2 biggest sepals of the pea-like flowers are rose-purple, petal like and known as wings. The keel terminates in a crown-like tuft which is characteristic of polygalas. The flowers are carried in racemes and are followed by a 2-chambered seed pod. Plant them in a sunny to partly shaded spot with light, well-drained soil. Pot culture is another option. To keep the growth dense, prune off any straggly stems after the main flowering has finished. Propagate from seed (sown in spring or early summer), or soft tip cuttings or semi-hardwood cuttings taken late in summer.

Podocarpus totara (below)

Polygala myrtifolia
SEPTEMBER BUSH

Probably the best known of the species in gardens, this is an evergreen shrub from South Africa. It has an upright habit, its many twiggy branches covered with soft, dull green leaves. These are rounded to oval in shape, and 1 in (2 cm) long. The shrub grows to a height of 8 ft (2.5 m). Greenish white flowers with purple hues smother this bush for many months, beginning in late winter. The flowers are concentrated in large clusters near the branch tips. Each flower is up to 1 in (2 cm) across. This shrub can cope with light frost but it does best in subtropical areas. It may become invasive. Propagate from cuttings. 'Grandiflora' is a cultivar which has especially rich purple flowers and is a little larger than the species. ZONE 9.

Polygala virgata
PURPLE BROOM

P. virgata is an open-growing shrub that will grow rapidly to 6 ft (2 m). It carries graceful clusters of deep purplish pink, winged flowers. The narrow, lance-like leaves are alternate and simple, up to 2 in (4 cm) long. Purple broom is self-seeding and small plants often appear around the parent plant after the first flowering season; these transplant easily. Wind resistant, this plant needs no special care. Once established it will tolerate drought and some frost and will give a beautiful display in a shrub garden or rockery. ZONE 9.

POLYSCIAS
Araliaceae

Originally from tropical Asia, Australia and the Pacific, these evergreen shrubs and trees are cultivated for their attractive, aromatic foliage. The leaves are pinnate, with 2 or more pairs of leaflets, while the flowers are insignificant. Slow growing, they require warm-temperate to tropical climates and plenty of water. They prefer well-drained, humus-rich soil and partial shade. In tropical climates they are appealing outdoor accent plants or can be grown as hedges. In cooler climates they make exotic house plants. Prune any leggy stems in spring. Propagate from seed in spring or cuttings in summer.

Polyscias filicifolia
FERN LEAF ARALIA

This shrub earns its common name from its graceful foliage. It grows to 15 ft (5 m) with a spread of 6 ft (2 m). Its bright green leaves are leathery, deeply dissected with prominent purple veining and can be up to 12 in (30 cm) long. This Pacific Islander prefers a protected, partially shaded position. ZONE 11.

Polyscias guilfoylei
GERANIUM-LEAF ARALIA, WILD COFFEE

Native to Polynesia, this sparsely branched shrub of up to 18 ft (6 m) is cultivated for its handsome foliage. The dark green leaves are large and fern-like, composed of serrated leaflets that spread to 18 in (45 cm) and develop white margins. Prune only to remove damaged foliage. ZONE 10.

Polyscias scutellaria

This many-branched shrub has glossy green, round leaves with prominent midribs. Growing to 5 m (15 ft), it spreads to 6 ft (2 m). It prefers fertile soils and must be kept moist in hot weather. Decorative in the garden, it is also excellent for growing in a container. ZONE 10.

POMADERRIS
Rhamnaceae

These woody evergreen shrubs and small trees are natives of Australia and New Zealand. Only a few of the 50 different species have become garden subjects. They are most spectacular in flower in late spring when large, feathery masses of small cream, yellow or pale green flowers cover the plants. The foliage consists of alternate hairy green leaves. Twigs and branches are hairy too. These plants cope with occasional light frosts, but will need to be grown in a sheltered spot or even in a greenhouse in colder areas. Select a well-drained, even

gravelly, soil where the plant gets shelter from strong winds. Trim to keep a compact shape. Propagate these plants from seeds or soft tip to semi-hardwood cuttings.

Pomaderris aspera
HAZEL POMADERRIS

This species grows into an open shrub 15 ft (5 m) tall and about half as wide. In spring, tiny greenish white flowers are massed together into large plumes. The branches are hairy and clothed with oval leaves. The leaves have conspicuous veins and are 5 in (12 cm) long. This species is native to shady gullies in eastern Australia and grows best in a shady spot in well-drained soil enriched with organic matter. Keep the plant moist as it will not tolerate drought. ZONE 8.

Pomaderris kumeraho
KUMARAHOU, GUMDIGGER'S SOAP

This shrub originates from New Zealand and was used by the Maoris to treat asthma and other chest problems. The kumarahou grows to a height of 9 ft (3 m) and up to 6 ft (2 m) wide. Its slender branches are clothed with bluish green, wrinkled leaves. The oval leaves are 4 in (10 cm) long, their undersides are densely covered with hairs. The large fluffy clusters of tiny yellow flowers may be up to 8 in (20 cm) across. Peak flowering is in early spring. Plant it in full sun and choose a well-drained soil, sandy or even stony in texture; this is not a plant for rich fertile soils. Established plants will tolerate mild frost. Keep the plant well watered during the growing season. ZONE 8.

PONCIRUS
Rutaceae
TRIFOLIATE ORANGE, BITTER ORANGE

Containing only one species, this genus is closely related to *Citrus*. It is a fast-growing, deciduous, small tree originally from China which looks most attractive in winter without its leaves. Though mainly used as a rootstock for oranges and some other *Citrus* species, it is an attractive plant in flower. It also makes an impenetrably thorny hedge. Propagate from seed or semi-ripe cuttings in summer.

Poncirus trifoliata

A deciduous small tree with flattened stems, long, stout spines and trifoliate leaves, this species has white, scented, 5-petalled flowers that open before or with the new growth in spring. These are followed by yellow fruit which becomes quite fragrant when ripe but is inedible. This plant can be grown in any garden soil in a temperate climate. Prune in early summer when used in hedging. ZONE 5.

Populus alba 'Pyramidalis'.

Poncirus trifoliata

POPULUS
Salicaceae

The poplars form a genus of 35 to 50 species of majestic, deciduous trees and are from the northern hemisphere. Fast growing, many blaze with spectacular colours in autumn. The leaves are set on long, flexible stalks and rustle pleasantly in the wind. Poplars are important specimen trees in parks and large gardens and also make good avenue trees. They serve as windbreaks and screens and are also valued for their soft white timber which is used for making matches, packing cases and other utilitarian articles. Male and female flowers, borne on separate trees, are hanging catkins and appear in late winter and early spring before the leaves. The fruit is a capsule containing seeds covered with fine hairs. Plant in deep, moist, well-drained and fertile soil in full sun. These trees dislike arid conditions, and many species have vigorous root systems notorious for blocking drains and lifting paving,

Poncirus trifoliata

so these trees are not suitable for small gardens. Many sucker freely from the roots, so unless you want a forest in your garden, choose carefully. Propagate from cuttings in winter. Most species are short lived—60 years or so.

Populus alba
WHITE POPLAR, SILVER POPLAR

This beautiful tree from Europe and the Middle East grows rapidly up to 80 ft (25 m). On account of its suckering roots, it is best used in

Pomaderris kumeraho

open country. The bark is greyish white. The tree carries reddish catkins in spring. The leaves have between 3 and 5 lobes, and their undersides are covered with white, downy hairs giving a silvery effect in the wind. The leaves turn a beautiful gold in autumn. This species can withstand low-level drought conditions, salt winds and poor alkaline soils. 'Pyramidalis' (sometimes known as *P. bolleana*) is conical in shape and 'Richardii' bears yellowish leaves. ZONE 2.

Populus tremula (below)   *Populus deltoides* (above)

Populus nigra

Populus lasiocarpa (below)

Populus fremontii
FREMONT COTTONWOOD, ALAMILLO

Growing, quite fast, to a height of about 110 ft (35 m), this tree from the west of USA carries a fairly narrow, rounded crown. The 2½ in (5 cm) long leaves are triangular and turn yellow late in the season. The catkins are also yellow. The tree adapts well to most soils and conditions and is tolerant of both frost and drought in cool or mild climates. ZONE 5.

Populus lasiocarpa
CHINESE NECKLACE POPLAR

Growing more slowly than some members of the genus, this poplar is less inclined to sucker. Usually seen in large gardens and parks, the tree reaches heights of about 30 ft (10 m), though larger specimens have been known. The tree carries very large, leathery, heart-shaped leaves that are veined in red and are held on red stems with a light green upper side and a silvery underside. The leaves can become disfigured when exposed to hot winds. Fat yellow catkins are displayed in spring. ZONE 7.

Populus nigra
BLACK POPLAR

This noble tree is too often included in small gardens where its stature of 100 ft (30 m) is out of place and its suckering habit a nuisance. The dark bark is deeply furrowed. The diamond-shaped leaves are bronze when young, becoming bright green and then yellow in autumn. These large leaves are held on thin stalks and give an impression of constant movement. The male trees produce black catkins in the mid-winter. There are many cultivars, the best known being 'Aurea', the golden poplar, and 'Italica', the Lombardy poplar, which is a male cultivar. Its narrow, columnar shape and fast growth make it a much planted tree. ZONE 6.

Populus deltoides
COTTONWOOD

An upright, broad-headed tree from eastern North America growing to 100 ft (30 m), this species is less likely to sucker than other poplars. It is, however, notably short lived and brittle in high winds. The triangular, glossy green leaves are large, up to 8 in (20 cm) long and coarsely toothed, while the bark is grey and deeply corrugated. The long yellow and red catkins are particularly decorative. The common name is derived from the very great quantities of fluff that surrounds the seeds; this can be a nuisance in summer. A tough tree for extreme inland conditions. Var. *monilifera*, the northern cottonwood, bears slightly smaller leaves with the toothed margins more sharply delineated. ZONE 3.

Populus tremula
ASPEN

A vigorous, spreading tree from Europe for cool climates, this species grows to about 50 ft (15 m). The rounded, toothed leaves are bronze-red when young, grey-green in maturity and turn a clear yellow in autumn. They are held on slim, flat stems and quiver and rustle at the hint of a breeze. In late winter the tree carries long grey catkins. This is a good choice for large gardens and parks where constant mowing will sever the ever-present suckers. ZONE 1.

Populus tremuloides
QUAKING ASPEN, AMERICAN ASPEN

Growing fast to heights of up to 50 ft (15 m) this spreading tree from the west of North America thrives in cool climates and looks best when given plenty of space and planted in groves. The bark is smooth and grey with silvery markings; the glossy, dark green leaves are finely toothed, small and fluttery—hence the common name. Before dropping in autumn, the leaves turn a lovely golden shade. ZONE 1.

Populus trichocarpa
BLACK COTTONWOOD, WESTERN BALSAM

A conical, dense tree from the west of USA, this species can reach heights of 100 ft (30 m) but is usually smaller. This is a balsam poplar with an especially fragrant, young wood. The leaves, which turn yellow in autumn, are oval, glossy and dark green and have white undersides. The tree will endure maritime winds. It is said to be prone to canker in some places and can prove short lived in mild climates. ZONE 7.

Populus yunnanensis
YUNNAN POPLAR

This species originates from Yunnan, in south-western China. It grows into a broad tree, 80 ft (25 m) tall. It copes with warmer and drier conditions than other poplars and does not have a freely suckering habit. It bears bright green, triangular leaves, 6 in (15 cm) long with reddish stalks and midribs and a whitish underside. The twigs are also reddish. This species resists poplar rust, a disease that causes premature leaf fall in some other species. It adapts to a wide range of soils. ZONE 7.

PORTULACARIA
Portulacaceae
JADE PLANT, ELEPHANT BUSH, ELEPHANT'S FOOD

This genus has only the one member, a succulent, evergreen shrub with many branches, often horizontal or twisted. It may reach a height of 12 ft (4 m) but looks like a twisted dwarf tree even when very young. In its native hot, dry habitat of southern Africa it bears tiny pink flowers arranged in clusters, followed by insignificant, pinkish, 3-cornered berries. Choose a position with well-drained soil and keep plants dryish, especially during winter. It grows in sun or shade and tolerates drought but only the lightest frost. In dry parts of South Africa the shrub is used to feed livestock and game, hence some of its common names. Propagate from cuttings in summer and from seed.

Portulacaria afra
The branches of this shrub are reddish to purplish and are dressed with opposite pairs of silky smooth leaves. Each fleshy leaf is lime green, round to oval and set directly into the stem or into short spur-like twigs. Leaves are ½ in (1 cm) across. The tiny pink flowers and berries are rarely seen on cultivated plants. Adapting well to a wide range of soils and climates, it thrives by the sea. It makes an interesting, low maintenance rockery and tub plant, and is also a good subject for bonsai. Cultivars include 'Tricolor' (green, cream and pink tones) and 'Variegata' (green leaves edged with cream). ZONE 9.

PROSTANTHERA
Lamiaceae
MINTBUSH

These 40 or so species of woody, evergreen shrubs grow naturally in Australia. Glands dotted over the leaves release a minty smell when crushed, hence the common name. Flowers appear during spring and summer. They are trumpet like with 2 lips. The upper lip is erect and hooded with 2 lobes while the broader, lower lip has 3 lobes. Flower colours include green, white, blue and purple, even red and yellow. The fruit is a small nut. A warm climate is essential to grow mintbushes, which prefer a sunny location sheltered from strong winds with very well-drained soil, which must be kept moist during the growing season. Even with the best of care, some species are notorious for their ability to die suddenly. Prune after flowering. Propagate new plants from seed or cuttings taken in summer. Some of the more difficult species can be grafted.

Prostanthera caerulea
BLUE MINTBUSH

Native to eastern Australia, the blue mintbush flowers in spring. The flowers are blue to violet and carried in showy sprays up to 4 in (10 cm) across. This is an upright, densely foliaged shrub, 8 ft (2.5 m) tall with a 3 ft (1 m) spread. The dark green, lance-shaped leaves are up to 2 in (5 cm) long, with toothed edges. This species prefers light shade and medium to heavy soil. ZONE 9.

Prostanthera cuneata
ALPINE MINTBUSH

This is a compact shrub from the mountains of south-eastern Australia that reaches 3 ft (1 m) in height but spreads over 5 ft (1.5 m). It blooms in summer, bearing white to mauve flowers with purple spots in the throat. The flowers appear in small, quite profuse clusters that provide an excellent contrast with the soft, dark green leaves. These are round in shape, ½ in (1 cm) across and very aromatic, forming a dense crown. The alpine mintbush will thrive in medium to heavy soils, provided it is kept moist over summer. ZONE 8.

Portulacaria afra

Populus trichocarpa

Prostanthera cuneata

Populus tremuloides, in autumn tones, outside Fairbanks, Alaska

Prostanthera lasianthos
VICTORIAN CHRISTMAS BUSH

This makes a fast-growing, large shrub to small tree growing from 15–30 ft (5–10 m) tall. The canopy is open, spreading out from a short trunk. From spring to mid-summer it bears sprays of white flowers tinged with either pink or light blue and marked with purple and orange spots in the throat. The flowers have a faint perfume. Lance-shaped leaves are up to 3½ in (9 cm) long. This species comes from eastern Australia. It copes with sun or shade and tolerates an occasional light frost. ZONE 8.

Prostanthera ovalifolia
PURPLE MINTBUSH

Perhaps one of the most spectacular of the mintbushes, this bears large sprays of rich purple flowers in spring. It is the most commonly grown species despite its short life. The purple mintbush forms a large shrub to small tree 8 ft (2.5 m) tall, either upright and dense or more spreading. The small, oval leaves are dark green above and greyish green on the underside, and up to ½ in (1 cm) long. Both the foliage and the stems are very aromatic. ZONE 9.

Prostanthera rotundifolia
ROUND-LEAFED MINTBUSH

This species features lilac or mauve, but sometimes whitish flowers, arranged in large, open or more compact clusters. It is a shrub with a bushy crown only 6 ft tall (2 m) and 5 ft (1.5 m) wide. The dense, dark green leaves are very aromatic, oval to round and small, ½ in (1 cm) across, with smooth edges. It prefers partial shade. ZONE 9.

PROTEA
Proteaceae

This outstanding genus of evergreen shrubs and small trees from South Africa is cultivated widely in areas with acid, sandy soil and hot, sunny climates. Most species grow 3–10 ft (1–3 m) tall. The plants are prized for their heads of flowers, which are becoming an important contribution to the cut flower industry. 'Pink Ice' is the hybrid cultivar most important commercially as cut flowers. The characteristic cone-shaped flowers are in fact a dense, central mass of hairy flowers surrounded by brightly coloured leaf-like bracts. These range from violet to red, crimson, pink, orange, silver and white, and flowering usually extends over several months. The leathery green leaves often have hairy or undulating margins. Often difficult to grow, proteas prefer an open, sunny position, with light, usually acid, well-drained soil. They can cope with occasional light frosts, but young plants need protection during their first 2 winters. Mulch to suppress competition from weeds. Prune after flowering to maintain shape and to promote new growth. Propagate from seed or from cuttings in summer, or by grafting or budding.

Protea aristata
KLEINDENSUIKERBOS

This slow-growing species forms a compact, round shrub 8 ft (2.5 m) tall and spreading over 10 ft (3 m). It features dainty, pine-like foliage. Each leaf is fresh green in colour, about 3 in (8 cm) long with a black pointed tip. Blooms are cup shaped with a central cone of dark pink, hairy flowers surrounded by deep pink to red bracts. Each bloom can be 4½–5½ in (11–14 cm) long and 4–5 in (10–12 cm) across. Plants bear flowers at the branch tips from early to mid-summer. ZONE 9.

Protea compacta
BOT RIVER PROTEA

In this species the cup-shaped flower heads are delicate and almost oblong, 3½–5 in (9–12 cm) long and 3–4 in (8–10 cm) across. Velvety bracts are a rich, clear pink and are fringed with silver, the flowers themselves being paler. This species flowers from late autumn to early spring. A stiff, upright shrub with relatively few but rangy branches arising from the

Protea 'Pink Ice'

Protea ovalifolia (below)

Protea compacta (below)

Protea aristata (below)

Prostanthera lasianthos (below)

Protea cynaroides

Protea cynaroides

single main stem, it grows to 10 ft (3 m). Light green leaves are stemless and vary from oblong to broadly lance shaped, and grow up to 5 in (13 cm) long. New leaves are downy, while the mature leaves are smooth. ZONE 9.

Protea cynaroides
KING PROTEA, GIANT PROTEA

The 'king' of flowers is South Africa's floral emblem. It grows about 5 ft (1.5 m) tall with several sprawling stems. Each flower head is a huge, shallow bowl up to 12 in (30 cm) across. Widely spaced, pointed, downy pink bracts enclose a central dome of pink flowers which are snowy with white hairs. Flowering usually lasts from mid-winter until spring. The oval, leathery leaves are shiny green with a long red stalk and about 5 in (12 cm) long. Although best for warm climates, it can be grown in a greenhouse in cooler climates. ZONE 9.

Protea eximia
RAY-FLOWERED PROTEA

The leaves on this protea are broadly oval to heart shaped and silvery to purplish green. The large blooms have long, spoon-shaped outer rose pink to crimson bracts around a cone of pink, hairy flowers tipped with purple. Blooms are held well above the foliage and are 4–5½ in (10–14 cm) long and 3–5 in (8–12 cm) across. Flowering peaks in the spring months. *P. eximia* grows into a dense, upright shrub up to 15 ft (5 m) tall with relatively few branches. This species has been the parent of some notable cultivars such as 'Sylvia' (*P. eximia* and *P. susannae*), which bears its deep pink to red flowers profusely through summer. ZONE 9.

Protea grandiceps
RED SUGARBUSH, PEACH PROTEA

This species is known as the peach protea because of the deep peach-pink to scarlet bracts that surround the flower. These bracts are fringed with reddish purple hairs which protect the showy white stamens within. Its large flower heads grow

Protea grandiceps

to 6 in (15 cm) across, and its dull greyish green leaves are oval and 5 in (12 cm) long. Slow to mature, it will reach a height and spread of 5 ft (1.5 m). ZONE 9.

Protea longifolia
SIR LOWRY'S PASS PROTEA

This species features exquisite, creamy white blooms with dramatic peaked centres. Each has pointed cream bracts tinged with green or yellow, surrounding a mass of fluffy white flowers and a central peak of hairy black flowers. Blooms may be 3–6½ in (8–16 cm) long and 2–3½ in (4–9 cm) across. Flowering lasts from autumn until late spring. Leaves are long and narrow, pointing upwards, and are 7 in (17 cm) long. *P. longifolia* forms a spreading small shrub up to 5 ft (1.5 m) tall. It is restricted to the winter rainfall areas of southern Africa. ZONE 9.

Protea grandiceps

Protea eximia

Protea repens

Protea neriifolia

Prumnopitys ferruginea, juvenile

Prunus cultivar

Protea neriifolia
BLUE SUGARBUSH, OLEANDER-LEAFED PROTEA

Probably the most widely grown protea, this species has narrow, grey-green leaves up to 6 in (15 cm) long, covered with fine felting when young. From autumn to spring upright, 5 in (12 cm) long, goblet-shaped flower heads open at the tips of the branches. They have a felty central cone surrounded by overlapping, upward-facing, petal-like, deep reddish pink bracts tipped with a fringe of black hairs. There are forms with deeper or paler flowers, as well as a very beautiful greenish white one. ZONE 9.

Protea repens
SUGARBUSH, HONEY PROTEA

One of the easiest of the species to grow, this protea features deep, V-shaped blooms with shiny, sticky bracts, creamish white to crimson or white with candy pink tips surrounding an open cone of downy white flowers. Each flower head is up to 3½ in (9 cm) across. Flowering is from early autumn through winter. The common name derives from the prolific nectar, formerly collected from the flowers to make a sweet syrup, 'bossiestroop'. This upright, multi-branched, rounded shrub grows up to 10 ft (3 m) tall and wide. The mid-green leaves are tipped with a bluish tinge and are narrowly oblong to lance shaped, 2–6 in (5–15 cm) long. ZONE 9.

Protea scolymocephala

This charming small shrub, 3 ft (1 m) high, grows on sandy coastal flats on the Cape Peninsula and further south-east. It produces dainty flowers during spring and summer. The flower heads measure 2 in (5 cm) across and are cream to greenish, composed of bracts arranged in the form of a bowl. The shrub is well branched, while the narrow leaves, massed along the stems, partly obscure the flowers. The flowers are ideal for long-lasting arrangements and corsages. Slightly tender to frost but wind resistant, it needs sandy soil. ZONE 9.

PRUMNOPITYS

This genus includes several species formerly listed under *Podocarpus*, though they more closely resemble the newly recognized genus *Afrocarpus* than they do *Podocarpus* in the narrow sense which is characterized by large, juicy seed stalks. *Prumnopitys* species mostly come from South America, New Zealand and eastern Australia, and differ in small botanical details but are very similar in general appearance.

Prumnopitys elegans
PLUM-FRUITED YEW

The graceful foliage on this elegant Chilean conifer is similar to that of the yew family and is composed of narrow, rich green leaves set opposite each other on thin green branches. It forms a compact, pyramidal shape reaching 12 ft (4 m) and yields valuable timber. Its attractive fruit are round, red and plum like. ZONE 8.

Prumnopitys ferruginea
MIRO

The bark on this handsome tree from New Zealand is almost black and bears distinct indentations. Preferring well-composted soil, it will grow to a height of 80 ft (25 m) and a spread of 15 ft (5 m). Its foliage is dark green and the leaves are set in 2 rows on narrow branchlets. Its bright red, succulent berries are very attractive to birds but are poisonous to humans. These fruit, which smell of turpentine, are covered with a waxy bloom when they first appear and grow to a width of 1 in (2 cm). ZONE 8.

PRUNUS
Rosaceae

Prunus is a large genus, mostly from the northern hemisphere, that includes the edible stone fruit—cherries, plums, apricots, nectarines and almonds—but is also represented in gardens by ornamental species and cultivars with their beautiful flowers. While the genus includes several shrubby species, most are trees growing on average to 15 ft (5 m). All but a few are deciduous and bloom in late winter to spring with scented, 5-petalled, rose-like, pink or white flowers. Their leaves are simple and often serrated and all produce a fleshy fruit (inedible in the ornamental species) containing a hard stone. Many give brilliant autumnal colours while others have interesting bark. *Prunus* species vary in hardiness, some being warm-temperate in origin, others from cold climates. Plant in moist, well-drained soil in sun with some protection for the blossoms from strong wind. Pests and diseases vary with locality. Many of the fruiting varieties respond well to espaliering. Propagation is normally by grafting or from seed. Ornamental plants are usually grafted or budded on to species seedlings. The timber is sometimes used commercially; *P. serotina,* for example, native to the USA, provides one of that country's most prized timbers.

Prunus armeniaca
APRICOT

From eastern Asia, the apricot displays white or pinkish blossoms in early spring before the leaves appear. Growing to a height of 24 ft (8 m), its trunk becomes characteristically gnarled with age. The branches are reddish, and the heart-shaped leaves 3 in (8 cm) long. The fruit is yellow-orange with a smooth, flattened stone that separates easily from the sweet-tasting flesh. After flowering the apricot should be pruned moderately to encourage a good fruit crop the following year. ZONE 8.

Prunus avium
GEAN, MAZZARD, WILD CHERRY, SWEET CHERRY

A broadly spreading deciduous tree with reddish bark, this species can reach 40 ft (13 m) high. The pointed, dark green leaves are up to 6 in (15 cm) long and turn red, crimson and yellow before dropping. The profuse white flowers are cup shaped and appear before the leaves. These are followed by black-red fruit. *P. avium* is the parent of many cultivated sweet cherries. Most of these are not self-fertile so 2 trees are needed to produce fruit. Cherry wood is prone to fungus so the tree should not be pruned in winter or in wet weather. There are dwarf hybrids which live and fruit happily in tubs. The ornamental cultivar 'Plena' carries a mass of drooping, double, white flowers. ZONE 3.

Prunus campanulata
TAIWAN CHERRY, CARMINE CHERRY

This slow-growing, narrow, deciduous tree from Taiwan can grow to 30 ft (10 m) but like most cherries, it resists pruning. One of the earliest flowering *Prunus* species, it looks spectacular in late winter when its bare branches are festooned with clusters of single, bell-shaped, carmine or pale pink flowers. The small fruit that follow are a deep red. Its bright green foliage turns bronze-red in autumn. ZONE 8.

Prunus cerasifera
PURPLE-LEAFED PLUM, CHERRY PLUM, MYRABOLAN

A deciduous, decorative tree for either cool or mild climates, this species can grow to about 30 ft (10 m). A profusion of small white flowers appears before the leaves, in spring in cool climates and in late winter in milder ones. These are followed by edible, yellow-red cherry plums. The leaves are somewhat sparse and glossy green. Some cultivars have pink flowers. 'Nigra' is grown for its blackish purple leaves and single, pink or white blossoms. 'Pissardii' carries foliage that opens in a shade of deep red and turns blackish purple with age, while its blossoms are pink in bud but open out white. Its fruit are red. 'Elvins' is a smaller tree to 12 ft (4 m), with prolific rose-tinged white spring flowers. *P.* × *blireiana* is a common hybrid. It displays single or double, fragrant, pink blossoms in spring that look extremely effective against the bare, purplish black branches. The oval leaves are bronze-purple and change to golden brown in autumn. ZONE 3.

Prunus cerasoides

A lovely tree from western China and the Himalya, this species reaches 24 ft (8 m) in its natural habitat. It has leathery, sharply toothed leaves and in late spring bears rose-pink flowers that are deeper pink in bud. It was introduced into cultivation in 1931. ZONE 7.

Prunus domestica
PLUM, EUROPEAN PLUM

This widely cultivated plum grows up to 30 ft (10 m) and is famous for its delicious, sweet fruit of which there are many types. Some European plums, however, are grown purely for their delightful white or creamy blossoms or their attractive leaves. The trunk is smooth, and the foliage is somewhat thorny on new growth; the leaves are usually dull green and serrated. It grows well in cool to temperate climates but must be protected from wind. The European plum comes in many named varieties which usually produce fruit which is best suited to cooking or drying for prunes. The flesh is yellow while the skin can be red, purple, yellow or green. 'Coe's Golden Drop' produces a sweet, juicy, amber-yellow plum with red spots. ZONE 2.

Prunus campanulata

Prunus cerasoides

Prunus cultivar, a weeping cherry

Prunus cerasifera cultivar (below)

Prunus lusitanica

Prunus persica

Prunus laurocerasus

Prunus persica

Prunus ilicifolia

Prunus mume 'Geisha'

Prunus ilicifolia
HOLLY-LEAFED CHERRY

This low-growing, evergreen species from California is often used as a hedge, its holly-like foliage forming a dense and effective screen. While the white flowers are small, they form large clusters that stand out against the glossy, dark green leaves. The flowers are followed by small, dark red berries. Growing to 24 ft (8 m) with a spread of 6 ft (2 m), *P. ilicifolia* needs little pruning except to shape. ZONE 7.

Prunus laurocerasus
LAUREL CHERRY, CHERRY-LAUREL

This handsome evergreen native of the eastern Mediterranean bears large, shiny, bright green leaves that are pointed and up to 7 in (17 cm) long. A vigorous grower, it is sometimes used as a hedge, but if unclipped it can grow to 50 ft (15 m). It can tolerate alkaline soils and withstand low temperatures and shade. It bears upright sprays of small, sweetly scented, single, white flowers in mid to late spring; these are followed by red berries that ripen to black. ZONE 5.

Prunus lusitanica
PORTUGAL LAUREL

This evergreen tree from the Iberian Peninsula makes a large shrub or small tree up to 50 ft (15 m) and can be used as a tall hedge or screen. It requires plenty of sun and well-drained soil but is tolerant of cold and drought. It produces a dense cover of glossy, dark green leaves that are yellow-green on the undersides, with long, pointed tips. Up to 5 in (12 cm) long, the leaves have finely serrated edges. Masses of drooping, small, white flowers appear in early summer, followed by spikes of red berries that later turn black. ZONE 6.

Prunus mume
JAPANESE APRICOT

This very early flowering species is native to China and Japan. It is a 15 ft (5 m) high, round-headed tree with sharply pointed leaves up to 4 in (10 cm) long. The 1 in (2 cm) flowers are white to deep pink and carried in small clusters along the stems. They are lightly scented and are followed by yellowish apricot-like fruit. This is one of many species of the blossom that features so prominently in Chinese and Japanese paintings; it is also a popular species for bonsai work. There are several cultivars including 'Albo-plena', with white double flowers; 'Beni-shidon', a later flowerer with fragrant, pink double flowers; 'Pendula', with a weeping habit; and 'Geisha' with semi-double deep rose flowers. ZONE 5.

Prunus persica
PEACH

The peach is one of the most popular and important species in the genus. Originally from China, it is noted for the profusion of its pinkish red blooms. The 6 in (15 cm) long, mid-green leaves appear after the blossoms. Its delicious fruit are also pinkish red and are covered with a velvety down. The stone is deeply pitted and grooved. Growing to 12 ft (4 m), peach trees look best when mass planted, but can also make attractive formal standards. 'Alba Plena' is one of the most commonly grown cultivars, with single white flowers. 'Klara Meyer' has double peach-pink flowers with frilled petals. 'Magnifica' is noted for its double deep crimson-red blooms that cover the branches, producing a magnificent looking tree in early spring. 'Versicolor' bears semi-double white and red-striped flowers on the same tree and grows to 10 ft (3 m) high and wide. ZONE 5.

Prunus serrulata 'Shirotae'

Prunus serrula

Prunus serrulata cultivar

Prunus sargentii
SARGENT CHERRY

This Japanese cherry is covered with single pink flowers with deeper pink stamens in spring. Its long, sharply pointed foliage, which opens at the same time as the blossoms, gives a brilliant display of young reddish bronze leaves. These are among the first leaves to turn in autumn, giving a splendid display of orange and reddish hues. One of the loveliest of all cherries, it has dark chestnut-coloured bark and can grow to 50 ft (15 m). It performs best if grown away from polluted environments. ZONE 4.

Prunus serotina
BLACK CHERRY, RUM CHERRY

Reaching a height of 100 ft (30 m), this fast-growing large cherry is indigenous to North America where it enjoys fertile soil. It is sometimes planted in avenues. It has dark brown bark and its timber is of very high quality, highly prized in the USA for furniture making. The leathery, pointed leaves, up to 6 in (15 cm) long, are green above with paler undersides and often have a downy midrib. They turn yellow before falling. The small, fragrant flowers are white and are followed by small, black fruit. ZONE 2.

Prunus serrula
TIBETAN CHERRY

A deciduous, neat, round-headed tree growing to about 50 ft (15 m), this species has spectacular gleaming, mahogany-red bark peeling like that of a birch. Clusters of small white flowers appear in spring at the same time as the new dark-green leaves. The leaves turn yellow in autumn while the tiny round fruit are red to black. This species does best in cool climates. ZONE 6.

Prunus serrulata
JAPANESE FLOWERING CHERRY

This ornamental cherry from Japan grows quickly up to 30 ft (9 m). The sharply serrated leaves turn from shiny green to yellow before dropping in autumn. The flowers are white and appear before or with the leaves. The scaly bark is a shiny reddish brown. *P. serrulata* is the parent of numerous cultivars. 'Amanogawa' has a narrow habit, growing to 30 ft (10 m) high and carries fragrant, semi-double white to shell-pink flowers. 'Kanzan' is a vigorous grower, to 10 ft (3 m), carrying double purple-pink flowers in mid-spring. 'Kikushidare' (Cheal's weeping cherry) flowers early, carrying double deep pink flowers on weeping branches that grow almost to the ground. 'Mount Fuji' ('Shirotae'), up to 18 ft (6 m), has slightly drooping spreading branches and, mid-spring, carries a wealth of fragrant, double white blossoms. 'Shiro-fugen', growing to 21 ft (7 m), blooms late in the season and the purplish pink buds intermingle attractively with the young, copper leaves. The flowers open white and turn purplish pink. 'Tai Haku' is known as the great white cherry and the name sums it up well. It can reach 20 ft (6 m). 'Ukon', an upright tree to 30 ft (9 m), bears interesting pink-tinged greenish cream flowers in mid-spring. ZONE 4.

Prunus subhirtella
HIGAN CHERRY, ROSEBUD CHERRY

This deciduous spreading tree from Japan produces a profusion of pale pink flowers early in spring. The leaves are dark green, pointed and fade to shades of yellow before dropping. Growing to a height of 30 ft (9 m), the higan cherry thrives in cool climates. 'Autumnalis', growing to 15 ft (5 m), bears pink-budded white flowers intermittently from late autumn through winter and into early spring. 'Pendula' carries pink flowers in spring on the weepiest of branches from late winter into spring. ZONE 4.

Prunus sargentii

Prunus subhirtella 'Pendula'

Prunus serotina

Prunus tenella
DWARF RUSSIAN ALMOND

This charming, vase-shaped shrub from south-eastern Europe makes an excellent tub specimen if repotted and root-pruned every second year. It grows to 5 ft (1.5 m). It bears bright pink flowers on long, slender branches before the glossy, narrow, 3 in (8 cm) long leaves. It is frost resistant but dislikes drying out. 'Fire Hill' has erect stems that are wreathed with brilliant, deep rose flowers. ZONE 4.

Pseudolarix amabilis (below)   *Pseuderanthemum reticulatum* (above)

Prunus × *yedoensis*

from green to purplish black with oval leaves growing to 6 in (15 cm); these have an intricate network of golden veins and undulating edges. Its large flower spikes occur at the ends of the branches and hold a number of tubular white blossoms with cerise markings in the centres. ZONE 11.

PSEUDOLARIX
Pinaceae
GOLDEN LARCH

This genus consists of only one species, the golden larch. A deciduous conifer, it originates in China. Slow growing to a maximum of 130 ft (40 m), in cultivation it seldom exceeds 65 ft (20 m). It grows almost as wide as it does high. It differs from the larch in that the cone scales taper to a point. The male cones are held in clusters rather than singly, while the scales on the female cones spread and drop off. Plant in moist, rich, deep, well-drained, acid soil. It requires shelter from strong winds and abundant light. Propagation is from seed.

Pseudolarix amabilis

The horizontal branches on this species, which is also known as *P. kaempferi,* form a broad conical crown, held on a trunk with reddish brown bark that is fissured and scaly. Its fine leaves are soft and pale green with bluish undersides and are arranged in rosettes along slender twigs. The foliage turns golden yellow in the cooler months before dropping, making this conifer a beautiful ornamental tree for cool-temperate gardens. Its flowers appear as catkins which are followed by green cones, maturing to yellow, which persist on the tree. It can make an excellent bonsai specimen. ZONE 3.

PSEUDOPANAX
Araliaceae

Members of this small genus of evergreen trees and shrubs are grown for their interesting fruit and foliage. Most of the 15 species are endemic to New Zealand with 1 each in Tasmania, New Caledonia

Pseudolarix amabilis

Prunus × *yedoensis*
YOSHINO CHERRY

A hybrid of uncertain origin, this tree grows rapidly to about 30 ft (10 m) high and wide. The massed display of fragrant, white or pale pink flowers usually opens before the new foliage develops; the deep green, 4 in (10 cm) leaves that follow colour well in autumn. It is an excellent lawn specimen or avenue tree. It comes from Japan where it is extensively cultivated, and it is the famous flowering cherry so prominently featured in Washington DC. 'Ivensii' has an arching and weeping growth-habit. ZONE 3.

PSEUDERANTHEMUM
Acanthaceae

This genus consists of small evergreen perennials and shrubs native to Asia, Australia and Polynesia. They are grown for their unusual foliage and spectacular spikes of white flowers that are spotted with red, pink and magenta. Varying in height from 12 in (30 cm) to 5 ft (1.5 m), these charming plants can either make effective groundcovers or small, ornamental bushes. Well-drained, moist and composted soil in partial shade ensures healthy growth and a good flowering display. Tip prune to encourage bushiness or, if the plants become too straggly, cut back hard in spring. Year-round propagation is from seed or by division.

Pseuderanthemum reticulatum
GOLDEN NETBUSH

This shrub from Vanuatu thrives in hot climates and enjoys rich, moist soil. Growing to a height and spread of 3 ft (1 m), it prefers partial shade and protection from winds. The showy foliage varies

Pseudolarix amabilis (below)

and Chile. The leaves are simple when young, becoming compound as they mature. The 5-petalled, greenish summer flowers are inconspicuous. They are followed by clusters of berries. These plants suit warm-climate gardens and make good tub specimens. They also make attractive house plants. Grow them in well-drained soil enriched with organic matter, either in sun or part-shade. Propagate from seed or semi-hardwood cuttings taken in summer.

Pseudopanax crassifolius
HOROEKA, LANCEWOOD

Horoeka is the Maori name of this small tree native to New Zealand. The plant changes dramatically with age. Young plants have a single stem up to 8 ft (2.5 m) tall and stiff, sword-like, narrow leaves. These are dark shiny green above, purplish beneath, with sharply serrated edges and a reddish midrib. The leaves point downwards and are up to 3 ft (1 m) long. Older plants are branched, 35 ft (11 m) tall with a rounded canopy 9 ft (3 m) wide. Then the leaves become compound, with the leathery leaflets 12 in (30 cm) long, and have more deeply toothed edges. Small, black, ornamental fruit are produced by female plants. ZONE 9.

Pseudopanax lessonii
HOUPARA

Rich green, leathery leaves feature on this shrub or small tree that reaches a height of 20 ft (7 m). Each leaf consists of 3 to 5 oval to lance-shaped leaflets up to 4 in (10 cm) long and has smooth or toothed edges. In warm-temperate areas, the leaves may be tinged bronze to purple in winter. The houpara grows into a well branched, slender plant that maintains its fresh, rich foliage even in exposed windy conditions. It is a good tub specimen. There are hundreds of different forms of *P. lessonii*, with variable leaf shapes and colouring. These are raised from seed and sold as *P. lessonii* hybrids. ZONE 9.

PSEUDOTSUGA
Pinaceae

Some of the largest of all conifers, *Pseudotsuga* species are seldom seen at their maximum height outside their native North America and China. They may reach heights of up to 300 ft (90 m) with a cylindrical trunk supporting an attractive, broad pyramidal shape. The leaves are soft, green, flattened and tapered towards the tip, with 2 bands of white on their undersides. The brown cones are 2 in (4 cm) long with pointed bracts and hang downwards; they take a year to mature. This magnificent genus prefers cold climates, cool, deep soil and sunny, open spaces. Propagation is from seed or by grafting.

Pseudotsuga menziesii
DOUGLAS FIR, OREGON PINE

This fast-growing conifer can reach a height of 300 ft (90 m) and live for 400 years. The stately Douglas fir has long been valued in North America for the quality of its timber. Its sturdy trunk is covered with dark, reddish brown, thick, corky bark. Its branches curve up towards the ends and are clad with soft, densely set needle-like foliage that is fragrant, bluish green and fragrant. At the end of each branch wine-red buds form in winter, opening as apple-green rosettes of new growth in spring. Pendulous cones appear after the plant is 20 years old. ZONE 4.

PSIDIUM
Myrtaceae
GUAVA

Named after the Greek word for pomegranate, this genus of evergreen shrubs, growing to 30 ft (10 m) high, originated in Central and South America. Grown for their fruit and foliage, their simple leaves are arranged opposite one another. The clusters of 5-petalled, white flowers are usually large and are followed by the decorative fruit. Each fruit is a globular to pear-shaped berry that has red or yellow skin. Guavas need a warm to hot climate, a protected position and rich, moist, free-draining soil. The fruit are mostly used to make jellies, jams and juice but are available fresh in subtropical areas. Tip prune for a compact shape. Propagate from seed or cuttings, or by layering or grafting.

Psidium cattleianum
STRAWBERRY GUAVA

This evergreen shrub or small tree derives its common name from its deep red to purplish fruit about 1 in (2 cm) across. The strawberry guava has an upright trunk with smooth, beautifully mottled bark, growing to a height of 20 ft (7 m). The strawberry guava's shiny green leaves are leathery in texture and rounded, 3 in (8 cm) long, and form a canopy to 12 ft (4 m) across. Single white flowers have 5 petals and are 1 in (2 cm) across. The fruit are acidic and are used in jellies and jams. Var. *littorale* has yellow fruit; 'Lucidum' has sweet purplish fruit. ZONE 9.

Pseudotsuga menziesii (below)

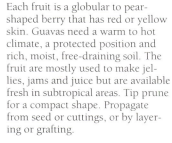

Pseudopanax crassifolius

Psidium cattleianum (below)

Pseudopanax lessonii hybrid

Psidium guajava
YELLOW GUAVA

Now grown in all tropical and sub-tropical regions for its nutritious abundant fruit, this tree will grow to 30 ft (10 m) with a dense bushy canopy. It has scaly, greenish bark. The 6 in (15 cm) long leaves are leathery with prominent veins and downy undersides. The white spring flowers are bunched in the leaf axils from where round fruit with pink flesh and yellow skins later appear. These grow to 3 in (7 cm) in diameter and are used mainly in jellies and juices. *P. guajava* is a useful shade tree for small gardens. ZONE 9.

Punica granatum (below)

Ptelea trifoliata (below)

PTELEA
Rutaceae

From the cooler parts of North America, *Ptelea* is a genus of small, deciduous trees or large shrubs that grow slowly to an eventual height of 24 ft (8 m). The branching stems carry bushy foliage with leaves composed of 3 oblong leaflets. In common with the citrus family, to which they are related, the leaves have oily glands that release a scent when crushed. They turn a beautiful shade of gold in autumn. The small, greenish white flowers are fragrant and appear from late spring to early summer. Plant in a shady site in free-draining soil and protect from drought. Propagate from seed in autumn or by layering and grafting in spring.

Ptelea trifoliata
HOP-TREE

Also known as the water ash, the fruit of this tree resemble a bunch of keys. It can grow to 24 ft (8 m), given the shade of taller trees and plenty of mulch in the warmer months to conserve soil moisture. The bark is a rich brown, and the oval, dark green leaflets up to 4 in (10 cm) long. *P. trifoliata* makes an attractive ornamental for cool-temperate gardens. ZONE 2.

PTEROCARYA
Juglandaceae

Ranging from the Caucasus to China, this genus consists of about 10 species of deciduous trees that are grown for their handsome leaves and pendent flowers. Reaching a height of 110 ft (35 m), they have spreading crowns with abundant, pinnate, bright green leaves, each leaflet up to 5 in (12 cm) long. *Pterocarya* species can be readily identified by the spring flowers that appear as yellowish green catkins and grow to 20 in (50 cm) long. Winged nutlets, forming a chain up to 18 in (45 cm) long, are an eye-catching feature of these trees that will grow in any fertile soil, given plenty of sun and water. Propagation is from cuttings in summer or from suckers or seed in autumn.

Pterocarya fraxinifolia
CAUCASIAN WINGNUT

This large tree, a relative of the walnut, originated in the Caucasus and Iran and quickly reaches 100 ft (30 m) if grown in loamy, moist soil. Its wide crown is adorned with numerous leaflets. Its greenish flowers form long, pendulous, greenish golden catkins in spring followed by the winged fruit that hang from the branches in ribbons. This species needs to be grown in a sheltered position. It is an excellent shade tree for a large garden or park, especially near water. ZONE 5.

PTEROSTYRAX
Styracaceae

From Asia comes this genus of 3 species of deciduous shrubs and trees reaching up to 50 ft (15 m) with a spread of 37 ft (12 m). The slender branches carry serrated leaves, up to 7 in (17 cm) long, that are bright green and oval. Creamy white, fluffy flowers are produced in pendulous sprays up to 10 in (25 cm) long. Fruits appear as bristly seed capsules from which the plant can be propagated in the cooler months. Plant in deep, moist, well-drained soil in sun or partial shade. Apart from seed, this genus can also be propagated from cuttings in summer or by layering. They are useful shade trees which should be pruned only to control shape and size.

Pterostyrax hispida (below)

Pterostyrax hispida

Pterostyrax hispida
EPAULETTE TREE

This lovely species from China and Japan attains a height of 50 ft (15 m). Rich green, oval leaves, with wedge-shaped bases and downy undersides, form a dense crown. During summer it displays fragrant white flowers in drooping sprays up to 10 in (25 cm) long. Grey, furry, 10-ribbed fruit appear in early autumn and stay on the bare branches during winter. ZONE 4.

PTYCHOSPERMA
Arecaceae

Indigenous to northern Australia, New Guinea and other Pacific islands, these clump-forming or solitary feather palms can grow to 30 ft (10 m) on erect, slender trunks. Their leaves are dark green and pinnate, forming a canopy up to 12 ft (4 m) wide. The flowers are cream or yellow and occur in large, branching sprays. Red, orange or black berries cluster in bunches along the length of the stems. These tropical plants need humidity, full sun and well-drained soil with plenty of moisture. Propagation from seed is slow, as it takes several months to germinate.

Ptychosperma macarthurii
MACARTHUR PALM

The Macarthur palm is a good specimen for a partially shaded position in the wet tropics. Growing to 30 ft (10 m), it forms a clump displaying large leaves up to 5 ft (1.5 m) long. It is characterized by its leaflets, having a 'chewed' appearance at the tip. Its yellowish flowers are held in long, pendulous sprays and the berries that follow are red. Prune only to remove badly wind-damaged leaves. *P. macarthurii* looks elegant as an understorey plant in a mixed palm grove. It also makes a good tub specimen. ZONE 11.

PUNICA
Punicaceae

There are 2 species belonging to the pomegranate genus but *P. granatum* is the only one cultivated. This deciduous shrub or small tree has 3 in (8 cm) long, blunt-tipped, glossy leaves and large, 8-petalled flowers. Pomegranates can be grown in a wide range of climates from tropical to warm-temperate, but the red or orange fruit will only ripen where summers are hot and dry. Pomegranates can be pruned as a hedge and also make good tub specimens. Plant in deep, well-drained soil, preferably in a sheltered, sunny position. Propagate from seed in spring or from cuttings in summer or by removing suckers.

Punica granatum
POMEGRANATE

Originating from Mediterranean countries and southern Asia, this rounded shrub for tropical and subtropical climates has been cultivated for centuries for its edible fruit. It grows to 15 ft (5 m) tall and 10 ft (3 m) wide. Slender stems bear shiny, light green oblong leaves that are coppery when young. The leaves are 3 in (8 cm) long and turn yellow in autumn before falling. From spring to summer there are red-orange flowers held at the branch tips. Each bloom is funnel shaped with crinkly petals. These are followed by the apple-like fruit known as pomegranates. Green at first before ripening to orange-red, each has a thick rind surrounding masses of seeds in reddish, sweet pulp. A range of cultivars is available, the fruit varying from very sweet to acidic and the flowers red, pink or white. 'Nana' is a dwarf cultivar growing up to 3 ft (1 m) high. It has single orange-red flowers and small fruit. The commercially cultivated 'Wonderful' has double, orange-red flowers and large fruit. ZONE 8.

PUYA
Bromeliaceae

This large genus from South America consists of spectacular plants which are in fact giant terrestrial herbs growing to about 20 ft (7 m). They are used in gardens in the same way as shrubs. The leaves stand out boldly from a basal rosette and they often have hollow stems. Giant blue, purple or yellow flowers are held on unbranched spikes or in dense panicles. The fruit are capsules that enclose winged seeds. The plants can grow in a wide range of soils provided these are well drained, and prefer a sunny position. As with all members of the bromeliad family, Puya species should be positioned away from footpaths because the leaves bear sharp spines along their margins. Prune to remove damaged foliage and propagate by division of offsets or from seed.

Puya berteroniana

Native to Chile, P. berteroniana (also known as P. alpestris) loves rocky outcrops where its blue-green foliage can stand out against a barren landscape. The stems are prostrate, and the 3 ft (1 m) long, narrow leaves are strap like and arching. During summer, metallic blue flowers with vivid orange stamens form dense panicles up to 6–10 ft (2–3 m) tall at the ends of long stems. The rosette of leaves dies after flowering, leaving offsets to carry on. Preferring some protection from hot sun, this bromeliad will benefit from mulch to prevent water evaporation from its roots. In cool climates it can be grown in a greenhouse. ZONE 9.

PYCNOSTACHYS
Lamiaceae

These woody stemmed perennials or soft-wooded shrubs come from southern Africa and have evergreen, narrow, hooked leaves up to 12 in (30 cm) long. They can grow to about 6 ft (2 m) high. Their cobalt blue flowers are displayed on dense, 5 in (12 cm) long spikes in late summer. They need a warm, sheltered position in moist, well-drained soil. In cool climates they can be grown in a greenhouse. Prune back after flowering. Propagate from seed or from cuttings in spring.

Pycnostachys urticifolia
HEDGEHOG SAGE

This much-branched shrubby plant grows to 5 ft (1.5 m) and has 4 in (10 cm) long, oval leaves that are deeply cut and toothed. The bugle-shaped heads of royal blue flowers are held in summer on spikes 4 in (10 cm) high; these can be damaged by frost. It thrives in a warm-temperate to tropical climate. ZONE 9.

PYRACANTHA
Rosaceae
FIRETHORN

Originally from Asia and the Mediterranean, these large shrubs are grown in temperate-climate gardens everywhere for their evergreen foliage and abundant, bright red, orange or yellow berries in autumn and winter. Although tasteless, the berries are edible and are much enjoyed by birds. Growing up to 20 ft (7 m), the branches are armed with spines, and the foliage is usually glossy green. Clusters of small, white flowers are borne on short spurs and crowd along the branches in spring. Firethorns can adapt to a wide range of soils from sandy to clay. They tend to naturalize and become invasive where conditions are to their liking. Choose a sunny position for the brightest berry display, and ensure adequate moisture in dry weather. The spiny shoots make these plants awkward to prune, but this is often necessary to control their size. It should be borne in mind when pruning that fruit are produced on second year wood. Often espaliered, they also make dense, informal hedges and screens. Propagate from seed or cuttings. The diseases fireblight and scab can be a problem.

Pyracantha angustifolia
ORANGE FIRETHORN

A native of western China, this species can reach a height and width of 10 ft (3 m) or more. A dense shrub with graceful, horizontal branches, this firethorn has narrow, oblong, dark green leaves, 2 in (5 cm) long, with grey downy undersides. The leaves are clustered in whorls on the flowering twigs but spirally on new shoots. It bears clusters of small, white flowers from late spring to early summer. The yellow-orange berries persist for most of the winter. These have a floury texture inside. ZONE 6.

Puya berteroniana

Pyracantha coccinea 'Lalandei'

Pycnostachys urticifolia

Pyracantha coccinea

Pyracantha coccinea

One of the most popular species of the genus, P. coccinea produces a spectacular display of fiery scarlet fruit that resemble tiny apples. This species is originally from southern Europe, and both its fruit and foliage will become darker if grown in cool climates. P. coccinea reaches a height of 15 ft (5 m) and its arching branches spread to about 6 ft (2 m). Its narrow leaves grow to $1\frac{1}{2}$ in (3 cm) long and are held on long stalks. 'Kasan' is one of the hardiest of the Pyracantha cultivars, and carries striking orange-red fruit. 'Lalandei', a cultivar developed in France in the 1870s, is a vigorous plant with erect branches that display abundant fruit which ripen to bright red. ZONE 5.

Pyrus ussuriensis

Pyrus salicifolia 'Pendula'

Pyrus communis 'Beurre Bosc'

Pyracantha crenatoserrata
YUNNAN FIRETHORN

Originating from China, the leaves on this species are deep green and plentiful. Its berries are orange, ripening to crimson-red. It grows to a height and spread of 12 ft (4 m) and looks particularly effective if trained against a brick wall. ZONE 6.

PYRUS
Rosaceae
PEAR

The 20 or so species in this genus from temperate Eurasia and North Africa are related to the apple (*Malus*). Slow-growing deciduous or semi-evergreen trees occasionally reaching 80 ft (25 m) but often smaller, *Pyrus* species are ideal for cool-temperate climates. They have been cultivated since antiquity for their grainy-textured, sweet, juicy, yellowish green stone fruit, not all of which are pear shaped. Many species are also valued for their attractive autumn foliage (for which they need plenty of sun) and their clusters of 5-petalled white flowers (sometimes tinged with pink) which waft a cloying sweet scent and appear at the same time as the new leaves, or just before them, in spring. The glossy leaves vary from almost round to quite narrow. Modest moisture requirements mean that pear trees are suitable for coastal conditions, thriving in heavy, sandy loams with good drainage in a sunny position. They need to be cross-pollinated to produce fruit. Prune to remove damaged branches and to improve the shape of the trees in late winter or early spring. Propagate from seed or by grafting.

Pyrus calleryana
CALLERY PEAR

This shapely semi-evergreen tree from China is grown as an ornamental. It is valued for its showy clusters of white flowers which appear in early spring. These are often followed by small, brown, inedible fruit. The greyish green, 3 in (8 cm) long leaves stay on the tree until late autumn when they turn attractive shades of rich purplish claret, red, orange or yellow. Reaching about 60 ft (18 m) with a broad canopy, and tolerating heat, drought, wind and poor soil, it makes an ideal street tree and is planted extensively as such in its native land. It is resistant to fire blight, however it is not very long lived. 'Bradford', the Bradford pear, is a common cultivar which flowers profusely and grows well in poor conditions. ZONE 5.

Pyrus communis
COMMON PEAR

This wild pear of uncertain origin is the parent of many garden cultivars and is grown for its beautiful single, pinkish white flowers with red stamens. Long lived, it reaches 50 ft (15 m) but its short branches can look unappealing when the tree is not covered in flowers. The bark is dark grey or brown and cracks into small plates. Its rather leathery leaves are dark green with serrated margins and long stalks. The greenish fruit are up to 2 in (5 cm) long and ripen to yellow and are usually gritty in texture and dull in flavour—the fruit of the cultivars are sweeter and are best when picked before they fully ripen. 'Beurre Bosc' is widely cultivated for commercial orchards for its heavy crops of large, soft, sweet, brown-skinned pears that are good for baking. 'Williams Bon Chrétien' has medium-sized, succulent fruit and has been in cultivation since medieval times. It is the parent of the famous English Williams pear. In North America it is known as the Bartlett pear and is grown for canning. ZONE 2.

Pyrus pyrifolia
NASHI PEAR, JAPANESE PEAR

This compact tree, growing to 50 ft (15 m), is grown both for its beauty and for its fruit. Its small flowers appear either just before or at the same time as the oblong, sharply toothed leaves. These leaves are glossy green when young, becoming an attractive rich orange-bronze in autumn. The small, round, brown fruit are hard and have a gritty, sand-like texture; they are an acquired taste. The nashi pear has been grown for hundreds of years in China and Japan where there are many cultivars; there are also some bred in North America. ZONE 4.

Pyrus salicifolia
WILLOW-LEAFED PEAR

One of the best known of the ornamental pears, this small tree comes from the Caucasus and Iran. Also known as the silver pear, its beautiful willow-like foliage is long, silver-grey and covered with silky down when young. It bears small, creamy white flowers but these are somewhat hidden by the foliage. The small, brown fruit are pear shaped and ripen in autumn. Growing to about 25 ft (8 m), its slender branches arch. 'Pendula' is of willowy habit and is more popular than the species itself. Its foliage is smaller than that of its parent. ZONE 4.

Pyrus ussuriensis
MANCHURIAN PEAR

Also known as the Ussuri pear, this splendid tree is the largest growing of the pears and can reach 65 ft (20 m) or more, with a broad pyramidal shape. The tree is covered with a profusion of small, scented white flowers in spring which are followed by small, yellow-brown fruit. Its dark shiny green leaves are almost heart shaped and up to 4 in (10 cm) across. They turn brilliant red and coral in autumn. *P. ussuriensis* makes a neat, attractive street tree. ZONE 3.

QR

Quercus acutissima

Quercus acutissima

Quercus alba

Quercus alba, young tree

QUERCUS
Fagaceae

The oaks are the northern hemisphere's most important group of broad-leaved trees. Most are from temperate regions but a surprisingly large number of the 450 or so species come from tropical and subtropical regions of Mexico, Southeast Asia, and even New Guinea. Including both evergreen and deciduous species, oaks range from shrubs 3 ft (1 m) high to trees of 50 ft (15 m), are very long lived and develop tremendous character. Most grow too large for the average garden, but are excellent shade trees for parks and large gardens. Their leaves, mostly lobed and leathery but in some species thin and lustrous, provide a dense canopy for a multitude of animals, birds and insects and make wonderful compost for acid-loving plants. The leaves of some deciduous oaks develop magnificent hues during the cooler months before they drop. Oaks can be divided into 'white oaks' and 'red oaks'. White oaks usually have rounded leaves and offer edible acorns which mature in 1 year. Red oaks (which include the evergreen species) usually have pointed leaves (often bristle tipped) and acorns which mature in 2 years and are too bitter to eat. Female flowers are small, insignificant and greenish, while the male flowers appear as yellow catkins in spring. The acorn, a greenish brown fruit, is enclosed or sits in a small, cup-like structure. These range in size from ½ in (1 cm) to 3 in (8 cm). Prune only to remove damaged limbs. *Quercus* species thrive in a range of soils providing they are deep, damp and well drained. Some like alkaline soils and full sun; other species prefer partial shade. They have extensive root systems and do not like to be transplanted. Grown as specimens in large gardens and parks, *Quercus* species are also exceptional when planted as an avenue. Otherwise easy to maintain, oaks are susceptible to oak-leaf miner in humid climates, as well as oak root fungus and aphids. Prized for their moisture- and salt-resistant timber, they were used to make ships, furniture and barrels. Propagation is from seed or by grafting in autumn. Acorns are sometimes ground to make a beverage similar to coffee and were often ground into flour during times of famine.

Quercus acutissima
JAPANESE OAK, SAWTOOTH OAK

The 7 in (17 cm) long, narrow, glossy green leaves on this deciduous oak from China, Japan and Korea are similar to those of the chestnut and turn yellow in autumn. This slow-growing, lime-hating tree eventually reaches a height of 50 ft (15 m). The narrow foliage remains on the tree until well into winter and attractive long catkins appear in spring. The name sawtooth oak comes from the regular serration of the leaves, as was emphasized by the old name *Q. serrata*. ZONE 5.

Quercus agrifolia
CALIFORNIA LIVE OAK

This Californian oak is identified by its stiff, evergreen, spiny-toothed leaves and its relatively large acorns maturing to 1 in (2 cm) long. The trunk has black bark and, growing up to 60 ft (18 m), supports a somewhat untidy canopy. This is an important species in California and old specimens are often protected by law. It is notably drought resistant and must be kept dry in summer or its roots will rot; it is difficult to transplant. ZONE 6.

Quercus alba
AMERICAN WHITE OAK

This deciduous oak grows up to 100 ft (30 m) high with a similar spread. It has scaly, fissured, pale ash-grey bark and oblong, lobed leaves that are up to 9 in (22 cm) long and turn purplish red in autumn. Its acorns are small. The timber of this species is important commercially, particularly in the eastern USA and Canada where it is also an important member of mixed hardwood forests. It is one of the stateliest of the American oaks. ZONE 3.

Quercus bicolor
SWAMP WHITE OAK

This oak is distinguished by its flaking bark, particularly on young trees. Its deciduous foliage forms a round crown and is composed of shallowly lobed, glossy green leaves that are sometimes white and downy beneath. Its acorns occur in pairs. From the eastern USA, it matures to a height of 70 ft (22 m). ZONE 4.

Quercus canariensis
CANARY OAK

Originating from North Africa, the Canary Islands and the Iberian Peninsula, this deciduous species keeps its 5 in (12 cm) long, coarsely toothed leaves until well into winter by which time they are a yellowish brown shade. Also known as *Q. mirbeckii*, the Mirbeck's oak, it grows quickly to 40 ft (13 m). To a gardener, this is effectively a larger-leafed, more drought-resistant version of the English oak, though it is not suitable for semi-arid zones. In the wild it grows naturally in river valleys. ZONE 5.

Quercus castaneifolia
CHESTNUT-LEAFED OAK

This deciduous tree from Iran and the Caucasus is related to the Turkey oak but has leaves remarkably similar to that of a chestnut. These sharply toothed leaves are up to 7 in (17 cm) long and are narrowly tapered with parallel veins. *Q. castaneifolia* grows to 100 ft (30 m) and forms a broad crown. ZONE 5.

Quercus cerris
TURKEY OAK

Originating in central and southern Europe and Turkey, this deciduous oak is one of the grandest in the genus, reaching 130 ft (40 m) on a stout trunk. Its black bark is deeply fissured and its narrow leaves are grey and coarsely toothed, up to 5 in (12 cm) long. It can tolerate alkaline soils and seaside situations, though it rarely reaches its full size there. Its acorns are enclosed within shaggy cups and mature during their second year. The Turkey oak is often planted in parks and is much used in European forestry as it grows faster than the English oak; its bark is just as rich in tannin, though its timber is not quite so strong. The common name comes from the species having been introduced to the UK from Turkey in the 18th century. ZONE 7.

Quercus chrysolepis
MAUL OAK, CANYON LIVE OAK

Originating from Oregon and California on the west coast of the USA, this evergreen oak grows up to a height of about 65 ft (20 m). *Q. chrysolepis* is characterized by a short trunk and spreading crown and dark green, glossy foliage up to 4 in (10 cm) long. This tree is also known as the goldcup oak because its acorn is contained within a cup which is covered in yellow hairs. ZONE 7.

Quercus cerris

Quercus canariensis

Quercus castaneifolia

Quercus bicolor (below)

Quercus ilex

Quercus dentata (below)

Quercus coccinea
SCARLET OAK

This deciduous eastern North American oak has deeply lobed, glossy, bright green leaves with bristle tips. The 6 in (15 cm) long leaves turn brilliant scarlet in a cool, dry autumn, and stay on the tree for a long time. It reaches 80 ft (25 m) on a strong central leader and is distinguished by its drooping branches. The bark is grey and darkens as it matures. The acorns are smaller than average and cone-shaped, ripening in their second year. This can be the most brilliant of all the genus for autumn colour but trees often disappoint by merely turning brown. *Q. coccinea* can tolerate pollution and makes a good specimen for urban environments. ZONE 2.

Quercus dentata
DAIMYO OAK

This deciduous oak from China and Japan grows to 50 ft (15 m). Its canopy extends to 40 ft (13 m) and bears dense foliage with very large, coarsely lobed leaves that can be as long as 12 in (30 cm) on young trees. It prefers acid soil. ZONE 7.

Quercus ilex
HOLM OAK, HOLLY OAK

This oak grows naturally in North Africa and southern parts of Europe. Up to 60 ft (18 m) tall, with grey rough bark that breaks into distinctive small squares, it casts dense shade. It is one of the largest, broad-leafed evergreen trees for cool-temperate climates and grows well in exposed seaside locations and limestone soils. Its dark greyish green leaves have downy, whitish green undersides. On young trees and lower branches of mature trees, the leaves are oval in shape and prickly to discourage grazing animals. As the leaves mature, they become more lance-like with a smooth edge, up to 3 in (8 cm) long. Acorns are small, in groups of 1 to 3, maturing from green to chocolate. The timber is used for furniture. *Q. ilex* can be clipped to formal shapes or grown as a tall hedge. ZONE 6.

Quercus kelloggii
CALIFORNIAN BLACK OAK

This adaptable deciduous tree grows to 90 ft (28 m). An erect trunk bears an open crown with bristly margined leaves that are 6 in (15 cm) long with narrow lobes. Native to California and Oregon, it is occasionally cultivated in temperate climates elsewhere. ZONE 6.

Quercus macrocarpa
BUR OAK

Native to the USA from the Midwest to the Appalachian Mountains, this species has scaly, deeply furrowed, light brown bark and matures to a height of 70–80 ft (22–25 m). It is identified by its oblong, deeply lobed leaves that are shiny and up to 10 in (25 cm) long. They turn yellowish brown in autumn. The cup which encloses the acorn has a moss-like fringe. ZONE 2.

Quercus mongolica
MONGOLIAN OAK

This striking deciduous tree grows to 100 ft (30 m). Originating from Japan and north-east Asia, it bears coarsely but regularly toothed leaves grouped at the ends of the branches. These characteristic leaves are 8 in (20 cm) long and have a fine pale down on the undersides. Its acorns are cone shaped. ZONE 4.

Quercus nigra
WATER OAK

The leaves of this mostly deciduous North American oak are bluish green on top and glossy green underneath. Broad toward the tip, they are 3 in (6 cm) long and are held on a slender stalk. Growing to a height of 50 ft (15 m) with a broad rounded crown, the water oak thrives in moist soil. ZONE 6.

Quercus palustris
PIN OAK

Coming from eastern and central USA, this species tolerates dry, sandy soil, although it favours moister, acidic soil. Moderately fast growing, it matures to a height of 80 ft (25 m). Its smooth, grey trunk supports horizontal branches towards the top of the tree, while the lower branches droop gracefully and so this species needs plenty of room. Its handsome, deeply lobed, lustrous green leaves are 5 in (12 cm) long and become crimson-red in autumn. They persist on the tree well into winter. *Q. palustris* has a shallow root system. ZONE 3.

Quercus kelloggii (below)

Quercus palustris

Quercus phellos
WILLOW OAK

Native to eastern USA south of New York state, this graceful, deciduous tree reaches about 60 ft (18 m) and makes a good shade tree. The narrow leaves of this oak are up to 4 in (10 cm) long and differ from those of most oaks in being willow-like and not lobed. The foliage turns from a shiny, light green to a brilliant orange in autumn. The willow oak prefers moist soil. ZONE 5.

Quercus prinus
SWAMP CHESTNUT OAK, BASKET OAK

Originating from eastern central USA, this deciduous oak can grow to 100 ft (30 m) with an open crown. Its shiny, dark green leaves have pale grey, downy undersides and turn rich yellow in autumn. They have shallow, coarse teeth, and are up to 7 in (17 cm) in length. The acorns are oval. This species prefers deep, moist soil. The swamp chestnut is a commercial source of tannin and its timber is also considered of value. ZONE 3.

Quercus robur
ENGLISH OAK, PEDUNCULATE OAK

Arguably the most famous of all the oaks and with a life span of 600–700 years, the common oak,

Quercus nigra

as it is also known, is native to most of northern and central Europe. It performs best on heavy clay soils where its roots can penetrate deeply. Its immense branches are heavily leafed, providing good shade. Its 5 in (12 cm) long leaves are deciduous, with 5 to 8 pairs of rounded lobes, and remain dark green through autumn. The English oak's elliptical acorns are held, often in pairs, on long stalks, and are partially enclosed in small cups. This majestic, slow-growing tree eventually reaches a height of 110 ft

Quercus robur

(35 m) and makes an exceptional canopy for rhododendrons and azaleas when grown in a woodland setting. The species prefers a cool-temperate climate, but performs surprisingly well in some warmer temperate climates. It is one of Europe's most valuable timber trees. The timber is of importance for building, and is the timber of preference for wine barrels; once it was used in shipbuilding. An important cultivar is 'Fastigiata', grown for its narrow, upright habit which makes it suitable for small

Quercus phellos

spaces. 'Concordia', known as the golden oak, is a rounded tree and is one of the smallest of the oaks, a weak grower to 30 ft (10 m). It was raised in 1843 to produce bright yellow, juvenile foliage that becomes a light greenish yellow in summer. ZONE 3.

Quercus rubra 'Aurea'

Quercus shumardii

Quercus rubra 'Aurea'

Quercus salicina

Quercus rubra
NORTHERN RED OAK

Originating in eastern USA and eastern Canada, this robust, deciduous tree reaches up to 90 ft (28 m) with a broad canopy formed by strong, straight branches. Its shiny, grey bark forms flat-topped grey ridges that become dark brown as it ages. The matt green leaves with pointed lobes are up to 9 in (22 cm) in length and display rich, red-brown autumnal hues. The large acorn is held in a shallow cup. The red oak grows relatively quickly and does well in sun or partial shade. The young leaves of 'Aurea' are bright yellow. ZONE 3.

Quercus salicina

An evergreen species of oak growing to 60 ft (18 m), this is a native of Japan. Its slender branches are a greyish brown, with narrow, smooth-edged, glossy, green foliage. White on the undersides, the lance-shaped leaves measure 4 in (10 cm) in length. The acorns ripen in their second year. This species is occasionally mistaken for *Q. bambusifolia*, because the foliage is similar, and for *Q. myrsinifolia*, because the acorns are similar. ZONE 8.

Quercus shumardii
SHUMARD RED OAK

The attractive, 6 in (15 cm) long leaves of this oak are deeply lobed and turn red or golden brown in autumn. Originating from southeastern USA, this species will grow to 80 ft (25 m). It is very similar to the northern red oak (*Q. rubra*) but prefers a warmer climate and can withstand a moister soil. ZONE 5.

Quercus suber
CORK OAK

The thick, furrowed, grey bark of *Q. suber* is the main source of commercial cork, the production of which is concentrated in its native lands of Portugal, Spain and northwest Africa. A short, sturdy, often gnarled and twisted trunk gives the tree character. It reaches a height of 60 ft (18 m) with a broad, spreading canopy of 50 ft (15 m). The oval, evergreen leaves with a slightly toothed edge are up to 3 in (8 cm) long. They are a dark, shiny green on top and silvery beneath. Single or paired acorns mature to chocolate brown and are held loosely in a cup covering just over one-third of the acorn. ZONE 6.

Quercus velutina
BLACK OAK, YELLOW OAK

This deciduous oak with velvety buds originates from eastern North America but is now cultivated in Europe. Growing to 100 ft (30 m), it has yellow bark that yields tannin. The inner bark is a source of a yellow dye. Its large, dark green, glossy leaves, downy beneath, are lobed and grow to 12 in (30 cm). The ovoid acorns are half-enclosed in a deep cup. ZONE 3.

Quercus virginiana
LIVE OAK

This evergreen species is native to south-eastern USA and Gulf states west to Mexico. It grows up to 60 ft

(18 m) tall, with a short trunk that supports horizontally spreading branches. The live oak grows best in warm-temperate climates, with plenty of moisture; it also copes with coastal conditions. The dark green leaves are white and downy underneath, oblong to rounded in shape and up to 4 in (10 cm) long. Acorns are small, arranged singly or in 2s or 3s, ripening to dark brown, almost black within a year, which is unusual for a red oak. This species resembles Q. ilex but is even more beautiful and its smooth-edged leaves are a slightly brighter green. ZONE 7.

Quercus wislizenii
INTERIOR LIVE OAK

An evergreen tree from California, this species matures to 80 ft (25 m) with a rounded crown. It has black to red fissured bark, while the young branches are quite rigid and downy. The glossy green leaves (like holly) can be either entire or toothed and are up to 4 in (10 cm) in length. The small acorns are half-enclosed in their cups. ZONE 8.

QUILLAJA
Rosaceae

About 3 species of evergreen trees make up this genus from southern South America, but only one is of economic importance and is sometimes cultivated. It is a narrowly branched tree to a height of 60 ft (18 m), with drooping branches, and thick, glossy green, leathery leaves held on short stalks. The unperfumed, 5-petalled flowers are greenish white, appearing in spring and are followed by capsular fruit that open into a star shape. It must have moist but well-drained soil and protection from strong winds. It can be clipped to form a hedge. Propagate from seed or cuttings.

Quillaja saponaria
SOAPBARK TREE, QUILLAI

The distinguishing characteristic of this tree from Chile and Peru is its bark. Thick, rough and dark, it contains a substance called saponin which acts like soap. Its leaves are round, bluntly toothed and leathery and its flowers are held in clusters of 3 or 5 at the ends of the branches. These are greenish white with purple centres. Q. saponaria is the best known species in this genus. ZONE 8.

Quillaja saponaria

Quercus suber

Quercus wislizenii

Quercus virginiana

Quercus velutina

Radermachera sinica

Rauvolfia caffra (below)

Radermachera sinica

Ravenala madagascariensis (below)

RADERMACHERA
Bignoniaceae

This genus is made up of evergreen trees from tropical Asia, though only one, *R. sinica*, is seen in gardens. Native to the tropical regions of China, this small tree has large bipinnate leaves up to 3 ft (1 m) long. The panicles of white trumpet-shaped flowers are held either terminally or in the axils of the branches and are followed by slender capsular fruit. Provide a sheltered spot and choose a light, sandy soil. Propagation is from seed, cuttings or by layering.

Radermachera sinica
CHINA DOLL, ASIAN BELL-FLOWER

This attractive tree is native to southern China where it grows to 35 ft (11 m) tall. The plant has an upright habit and features glossy, dark green bipinnate leaves with leaflets up to 2 in (4 cm) long. Mature trees have large clusters of trumpet-shaped white flowers at the branch tips during summer and autumn. The fruit is a capsule up to 16 in (40 cm) in length. This species can be grown indoors in cool climates. ZONE 10.

RAUVOLFIA
Apocynaceae

There are over 50 species in this genus, growing in the tropics of both hemispheres. The glabrous, often attractive, trees and shrubs have large, glossy leaves held in whorls of 3 or 5. The flowers are held terminally and are either white or greenish and are followed by a berry containing 1 or 2 seeds. Different parts of the plants, including the watery or milky white sap which is poisonous, have been used, variously, as a tranquillizer, poison, purgative, sexual stimulant, as well as for treating wounds, snakebite and malaria. Plant in rich, deep soil in a sunny position and water well. Propagation is from seeds and cuttings. The generic name commemorates a 16th-century German physician, Leonhart Rauwolf, who travelled widely to collect medicinal plants.

Rauvolfia caffra
QUININE TREE

The quinine tree occurs wild in tropical and southern Africa and is the only species of this genus that occurs naturally in South Africa. The beauty of the tree lies in its graceful form, wide, round crown and branches with slightly drooping foliage. Fast growing, it can reach a height of 40 ft (13 m). A single, straight trunk, up to 5 ft (1.5 m) in diameter, is covered with a cream to grey or sometimes dark brown bark that can be rough and cork-like or smooth. The bark contains reserpine which is used in tranquillizers. The slender branches contain a bitter, milky sap. The glossy, dark green leaves, up to 8 in (20 cm) long, are crowded onto the ends of the branches and the fragrant, terminally held white flowers make a showy display in summer. The small, glossy black fruit that follow are eaten by birds and monkeys but are poisonous to humans. Despite the common name, it is not the source of the quinine that is used for treating malaria. That comes from *Cinchona*. ZONE 9.

RAVENALA
Strelitziaceae
TRAVELLER'S PALM, TRAVELLER'S TREE

Originally from Madagascar but now commonly grown throughout the tropics, there is only the one species in this genus that forms part of a very striking family. The huge, paddle-like leaves attached to long stalks are similar to those of a banana, spreading like a fan from the base and looking exceptionally graceful when swaying in the breeze. The whole arrangement grows to a height of 27 ft (9 m) and spreads out to form a wide, flat fan of foliage. Clusters of white flowers emerge from between the leaf bases in summer. The plants need rich soil and a sunny spot in a hot climate. Propagate from seed in spring or by division of suckers at any time.

Ravenala madagascariensis

The bright green leaves of *R. madagascariensis*, up to 10 ft (3 m) long, form 2 opposite rows and are held on tightly overlapped long stalks. They have a tendency to become frayed with age. Its trunk terminates in the sheathing bases of the leaf stalks that lap together in an almost geometric pattern. The tree's unusual habit makes it an eye-catching specimen for a tropical garden. ZONE 11.

RETAMA
Fabaceae

This small genus of brooms is made up of about 3 species of graceful, semi-evergreen shrubs from the Mediterranean region. They are a joy in spring when covered with a mass of white flowers. The leaves are small and short lived, lasting only a couple of days. Reaching a height of 5 ft (1.5 m), the plants are easy to grow providing they have well-drained soil and plenty of sun. *Retama* species respond to a light pruning after flowering to keep them bushy. Tolerating a range of climates from cold to hot, they dislike humidity. The small fruit are pea-shaped pods that are sometimes downy. Propagation is from seed in spring. The species are commonly included in *Genista*.

Retama monosperma
WHITE BROOM

Like all brooms, this shrub is popular for its profusion of sweetly scented flowers that appear on bare branchlets in spring. These branchlets have a weeping habit from a short trunk and are silvery green. *R. monosperma* will bloom for a long period if grown away from strong winds. It thrives in cool climates but can withstand long, hot summers if adequate moisture is available. When not in flower it has a straggly appearance so it is best displayed in a mixed border of shrubs and perennials. ZONE 7.

RHAMNUS
Rhamnaceae
BUCKTHORN

This is a genus of over 100 species of deciduous and evergreen shrubs and small trees from temperate regions. They are also grown for their attractive, though somewhat sombre, foliage. Occurring in a range of climates from cold to warm and tolerant of drought and salt-laden atmospheres, the trees are versatile if slightly dull-looking plants. Their modest requirements extend only to well-drained soil and shade in the hottest areas. They are distinguished by smooth dark bark and simple green leaves often with serrated edges. The flowers appear in clusters and are fairly insignificant. The fruit is a fleshy, pea-sized berry that is very popular with birds. Pruning is unnecessary except if the plants are used as hedges. Some of the species are thorny. Propagate the deciduous species from seed and the evergreen species from cuttings in summer. Some of the species produce dyes that are used commercially, while the bark of other species is used medicinally, being the source of the purgative, cascara sagrada.

Rhamnus alaternus
ITALIAN BUCKTHORN, ALATERNUS

This large, evergreen multi-stemmed shrub comes from the Mediterranean region, as its common name indicates. It is valued in its native lands for its ability to tolerate polluted environments. It grows fast to 15 ft (5 m) and makes an excellent hedge or screening plant. The thorny branches are covered in a mass of small, dark green, glossy leaves. These hide the tiny greenish yellow flowers which attract all manner of insects. Its berries are purple-black. A drought-tolerant shrub, this is a good choice for a seaside planting, although it can become invasive in certain areas. *R. alaternus* 'Argenteo-variegata' is more attractive than its parent but less hardy. Its leaves are marbled with grey and edged with creamy white. ZONE 6.

Rhamnus californica
COFFEEBERRY, CALIFORNIA BUCKTHORN

This shrub from California and Oregon bears finely toothed, oval leaves up to 2 in (5 cm) long that carry 12 pairs of veins. It is semi-evergreen and forms a medium-sized shrub to 6 ft (2 m). Honey bees are attracted to the greenish flowers. Its fruit change from red to black as they ripen. ZONE 6.

Rhamnus purshiana
CASCARA SAGRADA, BEARBERRY

Unlike other species in this family, this deciduous tree prefers an open, sunny position and requires plenty of moisture during dry spells. Reaching 24 ft (8 m) with a spread of 10 ft (3 m) or more, it makes a tough nurse plant for other coastal species that need shelter when young. It has an erect, branching habit and a trunk clothed in reddish brown bark. Its leaves are large, up to 8 in (20 cm) long, oblong and finely toothed, with prominent veins and downy undersides. They appear after the clusters of greenish flowers. The drug cascara sagrada is produced from its bark. ZONE 5.

RHAPHIOLEPIS
Rosaceae
INDIAN HAWTHORN

These are slow-growing but tough evergreen shrubs, mostly wider than they are tall. Suitable for warm-temperate climates only, their leaves are leathery and up to 3 in (7 cm) long and half as wide, and have pale undersides. New shoots are often coppery red. The attractive, 5-petalled flowers are white or pink and are arranged in loose clusters that are often held rigidly away from the foliage at the branch tips. The fruit is a berry, usually blue-black. These shrubs do best in a sandy soil enriched with organic matter and thrive in seaside gardens. Grow them in full sun or heavy shade, massed as an informal, low screen, or clipped to make a formal hedge. Propagate new plants from seed, from semi-hardwood cuttings or by layering.

Rhamnus alaternus 'Argenteo-variegata'

Rhamnus alaternus 'Argenteo-variegata'   *Rhamnus californica* (below)

Retama monosperma

Rhaphiolepis × delacourii
HYBRID INDIAN HAWTHORN

This is a hybrid between *R. indica* and *R. umbellata* and bears the name of its French breeder, M. Delacour. It forms a rounded shrub up to 6 ft (2 m) tall. Attractive, upright, 4 in (10 cm) high clusters of pale pink or rose-pink flowers are borne at the branch tips from late winter through spring. Flowers are slightly larger than those of the parent species. The leaves are oval

Rhaphiolepis umbellata (below)

Rhaphiolepis indica (below)

Rhaphiolepis indica (below)

and slightly toothed at their tips. They are shiny green on top and paler underneath, while the new leaves are bronze-green. ZONE 7.

Rhaphiolepis indica
INDIAN HAWTHORN

Contrary to its common name, the Indian hawthorn originates in southern China. It is a compact shrub up to 8 ft (2.5 m) high and wide. During late winter and spring it bears perfumed, 3 in (8 cm) long flower clusters. Each flower is white with a pink blush, made more appealing by the central, long, pink stamens. The flowers are followed by black berries with a bluish tinge. The shiny, dark green leaves are narrow and pointed with a serrated edge. New foliage is reddish and downy. ZONE 8.

Rhaphiolepis umbellata
YEDDO HAWTHORN

A dense, rounded mound normally 6 ft (2 m) tall, this shrub has paddle-shaped, quite thick leaves with a smooth edge. Newly emerging leaves are covered with grey, downy hairs. Clusters of perfumed white flowers are a summer feature and in warm climates the flowers spot bloom for much of the year. The fruit ripen to bluish black berries arranged in clusters and persist into winter. Adapted to seashore

Rhapis subtilis (below)

conditions, this species is native to Japan and Korea; the Japanese produce a dye from its bark. ZONE 7.

RHAPIDOPHYLLUM
Arecaceae
BLUE PALMETTO, NEEDLE PALM

The single species in this genus grows naturally in the American states of South Carolina, Georgia and Florida. It forms a low, dense clump of deeply divided, fan-shaped leaves. The 3-petalled reddish flowers are tiny but densely clustered. The fruit is oval and downy, up to 1 in (2 cm) long. The needle palm prefers moist soil with plenty of organic matter. It adapts to a range of climates from cool to warm and can be grown in temperate regions where most palms will not thrive. Propagate from seed, which take up to 6 months to germinate, or from suckers.

Rhapidophyllum hystrix

Needle palm is the right name for this plant that features many long black spines hidden among the leaf stalks. The stems hug the ground and form clumps of foliage. Each leaf is bluish green on top and silvery below, up to 30 in (75 cm) wide and deeply divided into 12 or more segments. The flowers are dark red. ZONE 8.

RHAPIS
Arecaceae
LADY PALM

Rhapis is a small genus of low-growing, very decorative palms. They grow naturally from southern China to Thailand and form clumps of bamboo-like stems carrying deeply divided fan-shaped leaves. The stems are slender and recent growth is covered with interwoven fibres arising from the base of each leaf. The yellow, male and female flowers are found on separate plants. The fruit is a small berry containing a single seed. They are often grown in tubs, or used ornamentally as feature clumps, or grown as hedges in warm, humid climates where they can be grown outdoors. Elsewhere they are favourite house plants. They require some shade and an enriched, moist soil. These palms are most commonly propagated by dividing a clump but may also be reproduced from seed.

Rhapis excelsa
LADY PALM, RHAPIS PALM

The lady palm, originally from southern China, is a favourite choice as an indoor plant. Its many stems form a dense clump up to 6 ft (2 m) tall. The leaves are light to rich green and divided into 5 to 8 stiff, finger-like segments. The flowers, arranged in dense spikes, arise from within the clump. This palm will grow outside in warm climates but is slow growing there. Choose a spot in filtered sunlight as leaves may burn in full sun. Mulch and keep soil moist and enriched with organic matter. *R. subtilis* is a more recently cultivated species. Its stems are more slender and the foliage more delicate than *R. excelsa*. ZONE 10.

RHODODENDRON
Ericaceae

The rhododendrons form a spectacular and diverse genus of deciduous, semi-evergreen and evergreen trees and shrubs, numbering some 800 species with thousands of cultivars. Rhododendrons range from miniature shrubs to small trees and are grown for their massed display of flowers which come in white and every shade of pink and red to purple, and yellow and orange. Spotted petals often occur. Some are sweetly perfumed. The bell- to funnel-shaped flowers have 5 or more petals and are usually held in clusters at the branch tips, forming a blaze of colour in late winter, spring or summer. Warm-climate rhododendrons can flower sporadically all year. In some cultivars either the calyx or stamens of the flower develop into petal-like structures—this form is known as 'hose in hose'. The alternate, oval leaves, often held in whorls along the stems, are mid to dark green. Those of some deciduous species colour beautifully in autumn. The fruit is a small capsule containing minute seeds. Most species require semi-shade and prefer light, well-drained but moist soil with slightly acid pH, enriched with organic matter with a cool root run. They benefit from an autumn dressing of mulch. They do not tolerate lime. Protect most species from afternoon sun and strong winds. These shrubs require little maintenance apart from a light trim after flowering. They can be prone to infestation by thrips, two-spotted mite (red spider mite) and powdery mildew in humid areas. Taller varieties make good woodland specimens and hedges while the dwarf forms are perfect for mass planting and rock gardens. Their shallow roots make them ideal for tubs and easy to transplant. Propagate from cuttings, or by layering, or grafting.

This important genus can be grouped horticulturally into 3 divisions: azaleas, Vireyas and 'true' rhododendrons.

AZALEAS

Once given their own genus, azaleas can be divided into deciduous and evergreen species and their numerous hybrids. The deciduous azaleas include some of the most spectacular of all cool-temperate flowering shrubs; some are notable for their perfume. Flowering before the leaves appear, their colours of white, yellow through pink and orange to flame blaze undiluted with green. These are followed in autumn by a brilliant display of foliage colour. Most of those seen in gardens are hybrids, grouped under such names as Mollis hybrids, Ghent hybrids, Knap Hill hybrids, Exbury hybrids, and others. They make wide-spreading shrubs up to 10 ft (3 m) tall.

The evergreen azaleas are mostly plants for warm-temperate gardens. The most important group are the so-called Indica azaleas which may be from 18 in (45 cm) to up to 10 ft (3 m) high and smothered in single or double flowers in a range of colours—mostly shades of pink, rose, red or white. Most bloom from spring to early summer. Some of the Belgian Indicas—developed mainly as indoor plants for the European climate—have flowers up to 5 in (12 cm) wide. Other groups include the Gumpo, Satsuki and Kurume azaleas.

VIREYA RHODODENDRONS

Also known as Malesian rhododendrons, these are native to Malaysia, Indonesia, Borneo and the Highlands of New Guinea, with one species, *R. lochiae*, coming from far northern Australia. Vireyas are mostly evergreen shrubs growing as high and wide as 6 ft (2 m). They can flower at any time of the year with clusters of beautiful wide open trumpet- or funnel-shaped flowers, ranging in colour from yellow, orange, coral or pink to white. Some are sweetly scented. They thrive in humid, mild conditions, but few can survive even the lightest frost. They will not tolerate pollution. Many hybrids have been developed in recent years in addition to a fine group of hybrids raised in the Veitch Nursery in England over 100 years ago.

RHODODENDRONS

These evergreen shrubs to small trees are very important to temperate-climate gardeners. The clusters of flowers appear from spring to early summer and come in almost all shades. The individual blooms can be wide open to trumpet shaped. The plants are also interesting for their handsome foliage even when they are not in flower. The group known as the Hardy hybrids are the most widely grown of the rhododendrons. *R. catawbiense* was the main early parent of these hybrids. They are mostly large shrubs up to 10 ft (3 m) tall, flowering spectacularly in spring with clusters of wide open flowers generally in shades of white, pink, red or purple. There are many named cultivars.

Rhododendron arboreum, growing in shade in the Himalaya

Rhododendron arboreum

Rhododendron arboreum

This tree can grow to 40 ft (13 m) and forms a narrow, cylindrical crown. Evergreen leaves up to 8 in (20 cm) long are rough and leathery and have whitish or rust-coloured undersides with prominent veins. Red, white or deep pink bell-shaped flowers appear in dense globular heads in very early spring. This species needs a mild but cool climate to flourish. *R. arboreum* was one of the first species to be introduced from the Himalaya and is the parent of many cultivars. ZONE 6.

Rhododendron Kurume azalea hybrid, as a bonsai

Rhododendron decorum

Rhododendron calendulaceum

Rhododendron augustinii

Rhododendron catawbiense

Rhododendron augustinii

Discovered in China in 1886, this species has unusually small evergreen leaves that are dark green and tapered, with a prominent midvein. A medium-sized shrub reaching a height and width of 5 ft (1.5 m), *R. augustinii* is covered in late spring by a profusion of 1½ in (3 cm) wide, tubular blue or violet flowers, ranging from pale to deep hues—the deeper the colour, the more tender the plant. The flowers occur in clusters of 3 or 5. It performs best in dappled shade. It is the parent of many blue-flowered hybrids. ZONE 6.

Rhododendron calendulaceum
FLAME AZALEA

This azalea from south-eastern USA is one of the largest of the azaleas, reaching a height and width of 10 ft (3 m). It has hairy branches, while its deciduous leaves are oblong and turn bright orange and red in autumn. Funnel-shaped flowers, 2 in (5 cm) across and coloured rich flame red, yellow, orange or scarlet, often appear just before the leaves in late spring. Many of the orange to flame deciduous azaleas derive their bright colours from this species. ZONE 4.

Rhododendron catawbiense

Named after the Catawba River in south-eastern USA, this evergreen shrub is the parent of many Hardy hybrid rhododendrons. It grows to 10 ft (3 m), though occasionally becomes a small tree up to 21 ft (7 m) high, while its oval, glossy green leaves are up to 6 in (15 cm) long. The bell-shaped flowers are lilac, purple, pink or white and appear in early summer in large trusses. Old plants have the tendency to layer, forming a dense thicket over a period of years. ZONE 3.

Rhododendron cinnabarinum

This evergreen species was introduced into cultivation in 1849 and is one of the most beautiful of the Himalayan rhododendrons. An upright shrub to 6 ft (2 m), it has beautiful peeling bark and tubular flowers shaded an unmistakable cinnabar red, although they sometimes vary in colour from pink to crimson, even yellow. One of the last of the genus to flower, *R. cinnabarinum* provides a lively splash of early summer colour. ZONE 8.

Rhododendron decorum

Originally from China, this large 20 ft (7 m), extremely decorative rhododendron has evergreen leaves with pale undersides, forming a bushy crown. Trusses of fragrant white or shell-pink flowers festoon the shrub in groups of 8 to 10; they appear in late spring or early summer. These flowers are cup shaped and are 4 in (10 cm) in diameter with very pretty frilled petals. Sometimes spotted, they are among the most attractive in the genus. ZONE 7.

Rhododendron degronianum

This Japanese rhododendron grows into a neat small shrub, 4–6 ft (1.2–2 m) high, with a domed crown. It produces dark green leaves up to 6 in (15 cm) long with light brown, fuzzy undersides. Its bell-shaped flowers are a delicate, soft pink and appear in late spring. ZONE 6.

Rhododendron 'Fragrantissimum'

In summer this rhododendron bears trusses of fragrant white flowers flushed with pale pink. It can be susceptible to frost and makes an excellent house plant in cold-climate areas. ZONE 9.

Rhododendron Ghent azalea hybrids

These popular, deciduous azaleas originating in Belgium grow to a height of 6–8 ft (2–2.5 m) and prefer an open position. They generally have trumpet-shaped, double flowers with long tubes, similar to those of the honeysuckle, and come in a wealth of sparkling colours. They are sweetly perfumed and appear in late spring. Many have rich autumn leaf colour. While once very popular, not many Ghent azaleas are cultivated today. Some of the oldest established hybrids include 'Coccinea Speciosa', prized for its brilliant orange-red flowers; 'Daviesii', with fragrant white flowers that have an orange-yellow flare on the petals; and 'Narcissiflora', with fragrant, light yellow flowers. ZONE 6.

Rhododendron griffithianum

This evergreen rhododendron reaching 18 ft (6 m) has reddish brown peeling bark and unusually large, oblong leaves up to 12 in (30 cm) long. Because of their size, the leaves can be easily damaged by wind and therefore the plant should only be grown in a sheltered position. It holds its enormous, bell-shaped, white flowers tinged with pink in loose trusses of 6 blossoms, each 6 in (15 cm) in diameter. Flowers are faintly speckled with green and sweetly perfumed, peaking in late spring. It is regarded as one of the best white-flowered species but, as it is rather tender, is not often seen in gardens. ZONE 8.

Rhododendron Hardy hybrids

Hardy hybrids are described in the genus entry above. The following are just 5 of the thousands of popular Hardy hybrids. 'Bow Bells' grows to 3 ft (1 m) with coppery foliage when young. Its buds are deep cerise pink and open to shell pink. 'Crest' has large trusses of tubular, butter yellow flowers with darker throats, 4 in (10 cm) across. 'Cynthia', a vigorous grower to 18 ft (6 m), produces conical trusses of funnel-shaped, crimson-rose flowers with blackish markings on the insides. 'Mrs E. C. Stirling' has large heads of pale pink flowers. 'Cilpinense' is a dwarf cultivar with pale, bell-shaped flowers. ZONES 4–8.

Rhododendron 'Mrs E. C. Stirling', a Hardy hybrid

Rhododendron griffithianum

Rhododendron 'Cilpinense' (foreground), a Hardy hybrid, with other hybrids

Rhododendron Indica azalea hybrids

These are rounded, evergreen shrubs varying in height from 3–8 ft (1–2.5 m) high and wide with a dense, leafy canopy. The slightly hairy, oval to lance-shaped leaves are 2–4 in (5–10 cm) long. These azaleas are good for massed plantings, especially in warmer, temperate climates. They are less tolerant of cold than the Kurume azaleas. *R. simsii* from China and Taiwan is one of the main parents of the Indica azaleas. Varieties are many and the mainly spring flowers range from pure white, pink, purple and violet, to scarlet and dark red. The single-flowered hybrids tend to grow larger than the doubles. A sample includes 'Alba Magna', large white flowers marked with green in the throat; 'Splendens' or 'Salmonea', with salmon pink flowers with magenta spots; and and 'Bertina', with salmon pink flowers. ZONE 9.

Rhododendron litiense (below)

Rhododendron kiusianum

The foliage of this azalea from Kyushu, Japan, develops yellow, red and purple tones as it ages and then most of the ½ in (1 cm) long, oval, hairy leaves are actually dropped by the end of winter, despite this species being classed as an evergreen. A very dense, twiggy bush that forms a rounded hummock to around 3 ft (1 m) high and 5 ft (1.5 m) wide, from early spring it is hidden beneath masses of tiny pinkish purple flowers. White- and light pink-flowered forms are also available. Best grown in sun or very light shade to keep it compact, it can also be trimmed as a hedge. This is one of the parents of the Kurume azalea hybrids. ZONE 8.

Rhododendron Kurume azalea hybrids

Some of these evergreen azaleas have a dwarf habit to 20 in (50 cm) high, while others grow to 6 ft (2 m). Very slow growing, each bush has a width similar to its height. A twiggy growth habit produces a dense foliage effect of small, narrow, dark green leaves. The bushes become a mass of flowers in spring and the leaves are almost totally obscured. The small flowers are funnel shaped, sometimes hose-in-hose, white, pink, purple and mauve. Kurumes grow best in warm climates or sheltered spots in cool climates, as a massed display or in pots. Mainly derived from the Japanese *R. kiusianum* and *R. kaempferi*, many varieties were selected in Japan and bear Japanese names. Some of these hybrids are 'Azuma-Kagami' or 'Pink Pearl', rose-pink hose-in-hose blooms; 'Hatsugiri', crimson to purple flowers; 'Hinodegiri', deep crimson flowers; 'Kirin' or 'Daybreak', silvery rose hose-in-hose flowers;

Rhododendron 'Alba Magna', an Indica azalea hybrid

Rhododendron 'Hinodegiri', a Kurume azalea hybrid (below)

Rhododendron Indica azalea hybrid

Rhododendron 'Bertina', an Indica azalea hybrid

Rhododendron lochiae

Rhododendron nuttallii

'Osaraku' or 'Penelope', single white flowers with a lavender edge; 'Seikai' or 'Madonna', white hose-in-hose flowers; 'Suetsumu' or 'Flame', single crimson flowers. ZONE 8.

Rhododendron litiense

Sometimes known as *R. wardii*, this medium-sized, evergreen rhododendron from China has oblong leaves up to 4 in (10 cm) long. It has a compact habit to 10 ft (3 m). Its wide, bell-shaped, soft yellow flowers, appearing in early and mid-summer, contrast attractively with the dark foliage. ZONE 6.

Rhododendron lochiae
AUSTRALIAN RHODODENDRON

A Vireya, this is the only rhododendron that is native to Australia. It grows on rocks and trees in the higher mountains of north-east Queeensland. An evergreen shrub, it grows to 5 ft (1.5 m) high with a similar spread, and in spring and summer carries bright red, trumpet-shaped, pendent flowers. Flowers may be 2 in (5 cm) across. Its low-spreading branches have thick, dark green, oval leaves, 3 in (7 cm) long. Grow in a shady spot. ZONE 9.

Rhododendron macgregoriae

Widespread in the mountains of New Guinea, this Vireya rhododendron is most often found as an upward branching shrub to 15 ft (5 m) tall, although small trees are occasionally seen. The elongated leaves are up to 3 in (8 cm) long, and the small flowers, massed in large, rounded heads, appear in shades of yellow, dark orange and brick red. They bloom during winter in the wild but in cultivation may bloom in summer and autumn. The flowers will last for at least a week indoors if picked as soon as they open. This species is used by the local people in New Guinea's Western Highlands to make rat bait—human fatalities have also been recorded. ZONE 9.

Rhododendron maximum
ROSEBAY RHODODENDRON

Also known as the great laurel, this native of eastern North America is an evergreen shrub usually reaching 10 ft (3 m) but can grow to 20 ft (7 m). Its narrow leaves are oblong, 12 in (30 cm) long and dark green with paler undersides, and can hide the flowers. The trumpet-shaped, early summer flowers are rose-purple or pink. They are slightly fragrant and hang in large, loose clusters at the ends of the branches. *R. maximum* can be grown to form an impenetrable hardy hedge. ZONE 3.

Rhododendron Mollis azalea hybrid

Rhododendron Mollis azalea hybrids

Mollis hybrids are deciduous, rounded shrubs up to 6 ft (2 m) tall. Their trusses of vividly coloured flowers in shades of red, orange or yellow appear in early spring on the bare stems, sometimes later when the foliage is young. Their distinctive perfume does not appeal to everyone. 'Spek's Orange' bears deep orange flowers in late spring. ZONE 5.

Rhododendron nuttallii

This superb species from Bhutan can grow to 25 ft (8 m) but usually makes a shrub 6 ft (2 m) high in gardens. The flowers are among the largest of any rhododendron, up to 5 in (12 cm) wide. Fragrant and funnel shaped, they form loose trusses of 3 to 9 blooms. They are white, tinted with yellow and pink. This species bears leaves up to 12 in (30 cm) long. These are metallic purple when young, becoming dark green and wrinkled as they mature. In cool climates it makes a handsome tub specimen for greenhouses. ZONE 9.

Rhododendron Indica azalea hybrid

Rhododendron ponticum

Rhododendron occidentale 'Exquisita'

Rhododendron ponticum

Rhododendron occidentale
WESTERN AZALEA

This deciduous North American azalea from Oregon and California has oval, glossy green leaves that colour richly in autumn. Its fragrant, funnel-shaped flowers are creamy white to pale pink with yellow or orange throats and appear in early summer. This shrub grows to 8 ft (2.5 m). 'Exquisita' has fragrant, frilled flowers that are flesh pink inside and deep pink outside. ZONE 5.

Rhododendron aurigeranum × *macgregoriae,* a Vireya hybrid

Rhododendron ponticum
This evergreen species, originally from Pontus in Turkey, has naturalized in many parts of the British Isles. It bears large heads of mauve flowers in late spring or early summer; the heads are about 10 in (25 cm) wide and the individual flowers are 2½ in (6 cm) wide. A height of 12 ft (4 m) and its density make the plant an excellent choice for hedges or shelter belts. It is also useful for underplanting in densely wooded areas. This species provides the rootstock on to which many cultivars are grafted. ZONE 5.

Rhododendron Satsuki and Gumpo azalea hybrids
These evergreen hybrids are closely related to the Indica azaleas and have been cultivated in Japan for over 400 years. However, they have only been widely grown since the 1950s. Most Satzukis are small, spreading bushes generally about 20 in (50 cm) high and 3 ft (1 m) wide. Late flowering, these hybrids bear large, single flowers in a wide variety of colours. However, the plants tend to produce sports, that is, flowers of various colours on the one plant. Flowers need protection from summer sun. Hybrids include 'Chinzan', with deep, reddish pink flowers; 'Gunrei', with white-flushed flowers striped mid-pink; and 'Shugetsu' which has white flowers edged with purple. ZONE 8.

Rhododendron schlippenbachii
ROYAL AZALEA

Found naturally in Korea, this 12 ft (4 m) deciduous azalea has very thin, soft green leaves to 5 in (12 cm) long. This species does best in shade. The white, pale pink or deep pink flowers are fragrant and up to 3 in (8 cm) in diameter. Held in loose trusses, they open from mid-spring and are of extremely delicate appearance. When leafless, the new growth is frost-tender. This species needs a continental climate to grow well. ZONE 4.

Rhododendron simsii
CHINESE EVERGREEN AZALEA, 'AZALEA INDICA'

This evergreen to semi-evergreen shrub grows naturally in China and Taiwan. It reaches a height of 5 ft (1.5 m) and grows up to 6 ft (2 m) wide. The branchlets of this dense spreading species are hairy. Small, oval leaves, to 2 in (5 cm) long, with a pointed tip are borne in spring, changing in summer to a broader shape. Deep pink or red funnel-shaped flowers, arranged in clusters, appear in winter and spring. *R. simsii* is one of the parents of the Indica hybrids. ZONE 9.

Rhododendron sinogrande
This superb evergreen Tibetan rhododendron is distinctive for its huge, glossy green leaves that reach 32 in (80 cm) in length and 12 in (30 cm) in width and are silvery underneath. These are matched in spring by enormous trusses of bell-shaped creamy white to yellow flowers with crimson blotches. Growing to a height of 40 ft (13 m), it was introduced to the Western world in 1913. This species needs a sheltered spot and a cool but mild climate to grow successfully. ZONE 8.

Rhododendron Vireya hybrids
Vireya rhododendrons are described in the genus entry on page 375. Some popular Vireya hybrids include 'Christo Ray', with deep orange flowers; 'Gilded Sunrise', with bright golden yellow flowers; 'Pink Ray', with delicate pink flowers; and 'Simbu Sunset', with yellow flowers edged with orange. ZONE 9.

RHODOLEIA
Hamamelidaceae

These small evergreen trees, native to Asia, feature attractive flowers and foliage. Leaves are alternate and leathery, waxy underneath. Spring flowers appear in hanging clusters in the leaf axils. Each flower is surrounded by coloured bracts. The flower itself is rose-red. The fruit are capsules arranged in clusters. A genus for a warm climate, the plants should be grown in sun or partial shade, but they will need to be sheltered from wind. They require a light, slightly acid, well-drained soil that has been enriched with organic matter. Propagate from seed in spring or from cuttings in winter.

Rhodoleia championii
SILK ROSE, HONG KONG ROSE

Native to China and Hong Kong, this is a small bushy tree. While it can grow to 18 ft (6 m) or more tall, it is often trained as a large shrub. The thick, rounded to oval leaves are crowded together at the branch tips and are about 5 in (12 cm) long. Their upper surface is dark green with a contrasting cream midrib. The leaves are held on pink stalks. The drooping clusters of between 5 and 10 rose-red flower heads appear near the ends of younger shoots. Each bell-shaped flower head has a whorl of pink bracts which is 2 in (5 cm) across. ZONE 9.

RHODOSPHAERA
Anacardiaceae
YELLOWWOOD, TULIP SATINWOOD

A genus native to tropical and subtropical areas of north-eastern Australia, *Rhodosphaera* contains only one species; a small evergreen tree with the male and female flowers being produced on separate plants. The genus is closely allied to *Rhus* and sometimes placed in that genus. The leathery leaves are pinnate, made up of between 4 and 12 pairs of leaflets, each leaflet up to 3 in (7 cm) long. They are covered in minute, soft, erect hairs. The 5-petalled red flowers appear in spring on a dense branching inflorescence, followed by berry-like fruit, each with a single seed. The tree will grow in subtropical areas in sunny positions or partial shade and needs a well-drained soil and moisture during dry periods. Propagate from fresh seed or cuttings in autumn.

Rhodosphaera rhodanthema

The yellowwood is a bushy tree growing to about 40 ft (13 m) in its natural environment and has been logged to supply wood for furniture making and cabinet work. As its common name indicates, it polishes to a beautiful yellow. The rough, grey-brown trunk sheds its bark in thick, scale-like plates. If cut, the bark will produce a white gum-like liquid. The 16 in (40 cm) leaves have a wavy surface and are glossy dark green above and pale green beneath. New growth on the tree is an attractive contrasting pale green. The glossy brown fruit will hang for a long time on the tree, and can be used in dried flower arrangements. This wide-spreading tree is excellent for providing shade. ZONE 10.

RHOPALOSTYLIS
Arecaceae

The 3 species in this genus of palms grow naturally in New Zealand, Norfolk Island and the Kermadec Islands. The trunk is topped by a swollen shaft made up of the leaf bases, called the crownshaft. The pinnate leaves are obliquely erect and feathery, giving these palms a distinctive outline. The flowers are carried in a branched cluster below the leaves. Red berry-like fruit

Rhodoleia championii

Rhodosphaera rhodanthema (below)

Rhododendron sinogrande

Rhododendron 'Pink Ray', a Vireya hybrid

follow. These palms need a sheltered sunny spot in a frost-free climate. A moist but well-drained, light to medium soil enriched with organic matter is ideal. Propagate from fresh seed in spring.

Rhopalostylis sapida
NIKAU PALM, FEATHER DUSTER PALM

This species grows naturally in New Zealand and is the world's most southerly wild palm. Slow growing to a height of 30 ft (10 m), its stout trunk is closely ringed with the scars of old leaf bases. The distinctive crownshaft is shiny green and bulging at the base. A mass of fronds stiffly crowded together arises from it. Each frond is up to 10 ft (3 m) long with a short stalk and is divided into many narrow, lance-shaped leaflets up to 3 ft (1 m) long. The short clusters of flowers are cream to mauve, up to 12 in (30 cm) long and appear just below the crownshaft. The Maori ate the young flowers and the heart of the palm tree, and wove the leaves into baskets and thatch. ZONE 10.

Rhus chinensis 'September Beauty' (below)

RHUS
Anacardiaceae

Rhus is a large and diverse genus of shrubs and trees and occasionally scrambling vines found in many parts of the world, but less numerous in the southern hemisphere. It includes both deciduous and evergreen species. One group of species, often now separated into a new genus *Toxicodendron*, contains trees and shrubs notorious for their allergy-causing properties; they include the creeping American poison ivy shrubs as well as some east Asian species whose resinous sap is used to make lacquerware. Most species of *Rhus* in the narrower sense are relatively innocuous, but the sap may cause irritation to the skin. Some of the deciduous species are grown for their attractive foliage, often turning brilliant shades of red, purple, orange, yellow and bronze in autumn, and in the case of others, they are grown for the dense clusters of reddish or brownish velvety fruit. In many species, male and female flowers occur on different trees. As well as the deciduous species, there is a large group of evergreen species from regions such as southern Africa and California, some of which are moderately frost-tolerant. Many species are tolerant of pollution and make useful background plants in a mixed shrubbery or border in suburban gardens. They like a sunny position with adequate moisture and protection from wind. Propagate from seed or cuttings, or by division of root suckers.

Rhus aromatica
FRAGRANT SUMAC

This species from eastern USA reaches a height of 3 ft (1 m) and spread of 5 ft (1.5 m), making it a sprawling shrub that needs regular pruning to maintain its shape. The insignificant yellow flowers are borne in spikes on bare stems and are followed by downy, deep green, coarsely toothed and aromatic foliage that matures to spectacular shades of orange and purple in autumn. Small red berries appear in mid-summer. ZONE 2.

Rhus chinensis
CHINESE SUMAC

This small, broad-headed shrub or small tree reaches 18 ft (6 m) or more and is grown for its marvellous autumnal hues. Its compound leaves are coarsely toothed, and

Rhopalostylis sapida (below)

Rhus lancea (below)

arranged on winged stalks. Clusters of whitish flowers are produced in late summer which are followed by red, downy berries. 'September Beauty' is an outstanding cultivar, grown for its blaze of autumn colour. ZONE 6.

Rhus lancea
KARREE

A native of South Africa where it is one of the most widely grown trees, the karree grows quickly to a height of 18 ft (6 m). Its stems and branches are almost black and its rough bark is split and very dark. Its branches grow in a crooked fashion, producing a thin, spreading crown with hanging branch tips. The slender leaves are arranged in groups of 3, with the leaflets being up to 5 in (12 cm) long. The insignificant yellowish flowers appear in late summer and are grouped in clusters at the tips of the branches. The yellowish brown fruit is often eaten by birds. This species grows well in dry regions where it can endure drought once established. ZONE 9.

Rhus pendulina
WHITE KARREE

A native of South Africa, this fast-growing tree, to 15 ft (5 m), has a willow-like habit and attractive, compound, fresh green leaves. The leaflets, held in 3s, are lance shaped and evergreen. The trunk and branches are a tawny grey, and its abundant branches bear a beautiful crown. Tiny whitish green flowers appear on the female trees in summer, followed by fruit resembling

Rhus aromatica

Rhus pendulina

miniature mangoes that are quickly eaten by birds. Resistant to drought and wind, it thrives in mild coastal regions. This species can be easily propagated by simply planting a branch. An excellent shade tree, this is a useful species for the garden and as a street tree. ZONE 9.

Rhus typhina
STAG'S-HORN SUMAC

This deciduous shrub or small tree from temperate eastern North America has a slender erect trunk or frequently suckers from the roots to produce a thicket of stems. It is usually under 15 ft (5 m) high with a spreading crown up to about 12 ft (4 m) wide. The pinnate leaves have toothed, 5 in (12 cm) long leaflets. The clusters of terminal flowers are yellowish green and insignificant; the plant is grown for its brown stems, bunches of red fruit and intense scarlet, red, yellow and orange autumn foliage. The fruit that accompany the brilliantly coloured leaves are covered with velvety red hairs. The cultivar 'Laciniata' carries its dark fruit well into winter and has deeply dissected fern-like foliage. Tannin is produced from this species while its wood is used to make toys. ZONE 3.

RIBES
Grossulariaceae
CURRANT, GOOSEBERRY

From the temperate regions of the northern hemisphere comes this genus of evergreen and deciduous ornamental and fruiting currants and gooseberries. The fruit is a juicy berry varying in colour from white, scarlet, purple, green to black. In many species the fruit is edible, some delicious eaten in the hand, some juiced, many used in cooking. These extremely hardy and popular shrubs can grow to 10 ft (3 m) with long arching stems. Some species of *Ribes* have very attractive reddish brown branches that stand out in winter gardens. In some species either the stems or fruit, or both, have prickles. The

Ribes odoratum

lobed, mid-green leaves are pungent when crushed. The leaves can also have downy or felted undersides and toothed edges. In other species the foliage turns brilliant red and orange before dropping. Masses of sometimes fragrant blossoms in shades of yellow, red or pink cover the bushes in late winter or early spring. The stems must be thinned by one quarter after flowering to encourage vigorous growth, but it should be borne in mind that flowers and hence the fruit are produced on the previous year's growth. Some species are unisexual and will need to be planted in groups to ensure good displays of flowers and fruit. A good choice for the cool-temperate garden, *Ribes* species need moist, rich soil and full sun to semi-shade. In the USA some species host white pine blister rust and are not recommended for planting. Propagation is from seed or cuttings.

Ribes alpinum
MOUNTAIN CURRANT

This dense, twiggy European shrub makes an informal hedge, with a height and spread of up to 6 ft (2 m). Reddish purple, smooth, arching stems are clad in heart-shaped, serrated leaves. The flowers are pale greenish yellow clusters of about 7 to 15 blossoms. These are

Ribes sanguineum

Ribes alpinum, as a hedge

followed by large bunches of scarlet berries, provided both male and female plants are grown. *R. alpinum* is a neat and versatile shrub that is tolerant of heavy shade. ZONE 5.

Ribes fasciculatum

Korea and Japan are the natural homes of this deciduous shrub. The arching stems are slender and smooth, carrying dark green, deeply serrated leaves. In good soil and a sunny position the bush will rise to about 5 ft (1.5 m), achieving a spread of about 6 ft (2 m). The flowers are fragrant, clustered, creamy yellow and borne in early summer. As the flowers of this species are unisexual, the decorative scarlet berries will only appear if plants of both sexes are grown. ZONE 5.

Ribes odoratum
BUFFALO CURRANT, GOLDEN CURRANT

A spreading shrub with an attractive, downy young stem growth, this species can reach about 8 ft (2.5 m). The 3-lobed leaves are shiny and colour well in autumn. The clustered, down-turned flower heads are large and greenish yellow, turning a deeper shade as they age.

Rhus typhina

They exude a spicy, clove-like fragrance and are the main reason why the plant is cultivated. The berries are black. This species does not bear prickles. ZONE 6.

Ribes sanguineum
FLOWERING CURRANT

This is an attractive, ornamental shrub, deciduous and prickle free. The aromatic, lobed leaves are held on arching stems that can reach 12 ft (4 m). The deep pink or red flowers, appearing in late spring, are borne on erect to drooping spikes. Bluish black berries follow in summer. There are several named cultivars of this popular species including 'King Edward VII' which bears carmine flowers; 'Brocklebankii' which bears golden leaves and pink flowers; 'Tydeman's White', with white flowers; and 'Pulborough Scarlet' which carries a mass of deep red flowers. ZONE 6.

Robinia pseudoacacia 'Frisia'

Robinia pseudoacacia 'Tortuosa'

Ribes sativum

Robinia pseudoacacia 'Tortuosa'

ition. In its native Tasmania it has grown as high as 50 ft (15 m), though it is generally considerably smaller. It remains unbranched for many years. Its leaves are oval and 3 ft (1 m) long with waxy margins. The tiny, cup-shaped flowers of pink or white cluster along the branches in summer. ZONE 8.

ROBINIA
Fabaceae
BLACK LOCUST

These North American deciduous shrubs and trees are valued for their rapid growth and lovely, fresh green leaves. They can withstand the grime of heavily polluted cities and are often used as street trees. Some species can reach a height of 80 ft (25 m) but many are shrub like, maturing to 6 ft (2 m). Many species will spread easily by suckers and self-seeding. The leaves are divided pinnately into small, oval leaflets, sometimes turning buttery yellow in autumn. There is commonly a pair of spines on the branch at the base of each leaf. The fragrant pea flowers are clustered in pendulous sprays of pink, purple or white blossoms, appearing in spring. The fruit is a flat pod less than 4 in (10 cm) long. Cultivars that have been grafted to produce a mop-like head of foliage look very attractive when grown in planter boxes. Pruning is only necessary to contain growth, and can be difficult

Ribes uva-crispa

Ribes sativum
REDCURRANT

This deciduous, prickle-less species from western Europe can grow to about 6 ft (2 m) but is usually kept to a more manageable size with judicious pruning. The stems are slender and smooth. The mid-green leaves have a dull green topside and a silvery white underside. The spring-borne flowers are greenish yellow and undistinguished whereas the juicy berries which follow are a sparkling scarlet or an opaque shade of white. These are valued for their culinary uses. ZONE 6.

Ribes uva-crispa
GOOSEBERRY

A stiff spiny deciduous shrub growing to about 3 ft (1 m), this species, also known as *R. grossularia*, is native to central Europe and North America. It is grown for its greenish fruit that are made into jams, jellies and preserves. The canes are upright and the small green leaves are held at stiff angles from the stems. The flowers are pinkish green and are followed by the greenish fruit that are covered with soft prickles. An open position, fertile, well-drained soil and protection from birds during the fruiting season are all that is required for this species to do well in a cool climate. These shrubs (there are many different cultivars in a variety of sizes and shapes bearing green, russet-green or yellow-green fruit) rarely fruit well in frost-free climates. ZONE 6.

RICHEA
Epacridaceae

All but one of the beautiful but rarely cultivated species of this Australian genus is endemic to Tasmania. Evergreen, stiff, woody shrubs and trees, most species are bushy shrubs, but some can grow as tall as 50 ft (15 m). The strap-like leaves can vary from ½ in (1 cm) to over 3 ft (1 m) long. Flowers appear in summer and are pink, white, yellow or cream. These are thrust above the foliage on upright spikes of densely clustered blossoms. *Richea* species must have moist, preferably acid soil and shelter from full sun and wind to produce the best blooms. Plants benefit from an annual mulch of organic matter. Prune spent flower heads in early autumn. Propagate from seed in autumn or cuttings in summer. These plants do well in containers.

Richea pandanifolia
TREE HEATH

This species needs to be grown in plenty of compost in a shady posas some species are very spiny. Preferring poor, moist soil in a sunny position, *Robinia* species will do well just about anywhere except where exposed to strong winds. Propagation of the species is from scarified seed or cuttings, or by suckers or division. Cultivars need to be grafted.

Robinia hispida
ROSE ACACIA

This deciduous shrub comes from dry woods and scrub of southeastern USA. The pinnate leaves are fresh green, long and fern like while the erect stems and branches are clothed in brown bristles. In summer, the shrub carries lavish rose-pink, pea flowers that are followed by bristly seed pods up to 3 in (7 cm) long. Given favourable conditions, the plant will grow quickly to about 6 ft (2 m). This species is sometimes grafted on to stems of *R. pseudoacacia* to produce a small, mop-headed tree. ZONE 3.

Robinia pseudoacacia
BLACK LOCUST, FALSE ACACIA

This fast-growing tree comes from eastern and central USA. It has dark, deeply grooved bark. Growing up to 80 ft (25 m), the prickly branches have a graceful habit. The fern-like leaves are finely divided into about 23 leaflets and turn yellow in autumn. The scented pea flowers are white and are borne in late spring or summer. Bees are very attracted to the fragrant blooms. These are followed by the 2–4 in (5–10 cm) long reddish brown seed pods that persist into winter once they have released their black, kidney-shaped seeds during autumn. The tree suckers strongly so it must be sited with care. 'Frisia' carries an airy head of distinctive golden foliage that intensifies in autumn. It is thornless. 'Tortuosa' has an interesting growth habit with short branches that are twisted. 'Umbraculifera', the mophead acacia, rarely flowers but carries a neat rounded dense dome of foliage and is thornless. These named cultivars rarely exceed 30 ft (10 m). ZONE 3.

Robinia viscosa
CLAMMY LOCUST

This species reaches 40 ft (13 m) and is characterized by its sticky, glandular young shoots and twigs that are smooth and spineless. The dark trunk and mature stems of this species contrast beautifully with its rich foliage as it turns golden yellow in autumn. The 3 in (7 cm) long bunches of flowers are pale rose-pink, stained with yellow and are very attractive to bees. This seldom planted species is one of the more ornamental members of the genus. ZONE 5.

RONDELETIA
Rubiaceae

These exotic, evergreen trees and shrubs are native to tropical America and the West Indies. Only 3 of the 100 plus species are commonly cultivated; they grow to 10 ft (3 m) in warm climates. The tough foliage is distinctly veined and remains attractive all year. The red, yellow or white tubular flowers appear in terminal or axillary clusters in spring and summer; being rich in nectar, they attract birds. The seed pods are capsules containing many seeds. The plants can be pruned by cutting back the flowered stems each year in early spring. Grow in sun to semi-shade. Choose a well-drained, slightly acid soil enriched with organic matter. These plants can also be grown in pots when they should be kept well watered during growth. Propagate them from seed in spring or semi-hardwood cuttings.

Rondeletia amoena

Native to Mexico and Guatemala, this shrub attains a height and spread of 8 ft (2.5 m). The upright, multi-stemmed shrub forms a bushy crown. The leathery leaves are broadly oval, olive green above and slightly felted beneath, and up to 5 in (12 cm) long. In spring small tubular flowers appear in hues of salmon to rose-pink, with a golden-yellow throat. Arranged in large rounded clusters at the ends of the branches, they have a faint perfume. ZONE 10.

ROSA
Rosaceae

Everyone knows the rose, though most of the roses grown by the average gardener are hybrids many generations removed from their wild parent species. Many thousand hybrid cultivars have been raised over the last century and a half, of which only a few hundred have achieved lasting popularity. The most important parent species has been *R. chinensis*, responsible for

Rosa 'Pink Peace', a modern hybrid cultivar

Rondeletia amoena (below)

Rosa 'Intervilles', a modern hybrid cultivar (below)

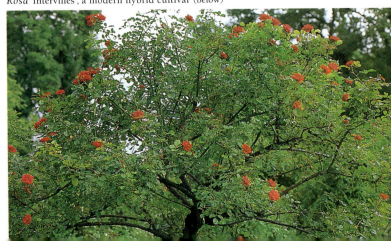

such characteristics as repeat flowering and the bronze-coloured new foliage. The subject of hybrid roses is too vast for this book to cover adequately and is amply dealt with in the many books on roses that are available. We describe here mainly some of the species that are shrubby rather than climbing. Roses are deciduous or near-evergreen shrubs or scrambling climbers that are distributed over most of the temperate parts of the northern hemisphere, ranging in height from only a few inches (or centimetres) high to giant climbers. The wild species usually produce simple, single flowers, often in large clusters, that are for the most part fragrant, blooming in spring or early summer and are followed by bright orange to red oval fruit known as hips or heps. The branches carry prickles and the leaves are mostly pinnate. Roses generally prefer cool to cool-temperate conditions and grow best in reasonably sunny positions, which reduces the incidence of fungal diseases such as mildew, black spot and rust. They prefer a fairly rich soil with regular spring watering and occasional mulching. However, do not make conditions too rich or the foliage will become soft—an invitation to fungal diseases. Cultivated roses are also prone to insect pests, especially aphids, mites and thrips. Wild roses, however, are more resistant to pests and diseases. Pruning consists of removing elderly or weak branches and shortening the rest. Most may be propagated from stratified seed or cuttings. Garden cultivars are usually budded onto seedlings or cutting-grown stocks of wild briar rose or dog rose.

Rosa 'Fragrant Cloud', a modern hybrid cultivar (below)

Rosa carolina

This species from eastern USA bears clusters of soft-pink 5-petalled flowers in a single burst occurring in early and mid-summer. These are followed by roundish, red ornamental hips. The slender branches are covered with prickles, and the leaves consist of 5 to 9 dull green leaflets with coarsely serrated margins. In the wild the plant is found on the cool uplands of northern America where it forms a dense, leafy bush about 3 ft (1 m) in height. When grown on its own roots the plant suckers freely. Two forms are commonly recognized: 'Alba', bearing single white flowers; and *R. carolina* 'Plena', bearing double pink flowers. ZONE 3.

Rosa chinensis

A near-evergreen shrub or scrambler from western China, this rose grows to around 15 ft (5 m) high and wide. It bears widely spaced prickles, and its leaves are divided into 3 or 5 leaflets. The 5-petalled, 2½ in (6 cm) flowers, which are usually borne in small groups, open pink and rapidly age to red. They are followed by orange hips. The repeat-flowering habit of this species was a vital ingredient in the development of modern garden

Rosa foetida (below)

Rosa chinensis (below)

Rosa carolina (below)

Rosa gallica

Rosa moyesii

roses. The introduction to the West of the 4 Chinese cultivars of this species in the late 18th and early 19th century was responsible for the breeding of modern roses. ZONE 6.

Rosa foetida
AUSTRIAN BRIAR

This deciduous species from southern and eastern Europe is possibly of ancient hybrid origin, the parent species being yellow-flowered shrubs from western Asia. It develops into a dense, twiggy shrub up to 10 ft (3 m) high and wide with numerous prickles. The branches carry pinnate leaves with between 5 and 9 leaflets that are 1 in (2 cm) long. The late spring flowers are 5-petalled and bright yellow, up to 2½ in (6 cm) in diameter. 'Persiana' is a double-flowered cultivar and 'Bicolor' has flowers that are yellow on the outside and coppery red inside. ZONE 4.

Rosa gallica
FRENCH ROSE, RED ROSE

A suckering species, this occurs naturally in southern Europe from France to the Caucasus. It is a dense, low-growing, 3 ft (1 m) tall shrub that bears few prickles. The leaves are divided into 3 or 5 leathery leaflets, and the flowers, which are slightly scented and up to 3½ in (9 cm) across, are pink. Because of its tendency to produce double flowers, it has been an important species in the development of modern roses. 'Officinalis' has semi-double deep pink flowers; its sport 'Versicolor' has semi-double pink and white striped flowers. The dried petals of a form of *R. gallica* 'Officinalis' were used medicinally in the 16th and 17th centuries. ZONE 3.

Rosa glauca

Rosa glauca

A cool-climate species from central and southern Europe, *R. glauca* (syn. *R. rubrifolia*) is valued for its stems that are glaucous purple-plum in colour, and for the foliage that persists for most of the year. The branches are much employed by flower arrangers. The single flowers, carried in clusters, are small but still showy and are composed of 5, well-separated, soft pink-mauve petals with soft lemon stamens. The red-brown hips that follow are decorative. Bush heights of 6 ft (2 m) are common. Two hybrids are in cultivation, 'Carmenetta' with slightly larger flowers and 'Sir Cedric Morris', a huge bush bearing a lavish display of single scented white flowers. ZONE 2.

Rosa moyesii

From western China comes this densely suckering rose that bears rich crimson flowers in a single summertime flush. The branches carry straight prickles and the dark green leaves are divided into between 7 and 13 leaflets. This is a vigorous, bushy plant that can reach heights of 10 ft (3 m). The pendent, deep scarlet flask-shaped hips are very attractive and may persist into winter. The best known of a number of forms and hybrids is 'Geranium' with paler leaves, carmine-red petals and an eye-catching display of scarlet hips. This does not grow as large as its parent, to about 6 ft (2 m) high and wide. ZONE 3.

Rosa xanthina

Rosa sericea var. *pteracantha*

Rosa rugosa

Rosa rugosa 'Alba' (below)

Rosa rugosa
JAPANESE ROSE, RAMANAS ROSE

This sprawling shrub species from north-eastern Asia is valued for its beautiful, clear flower colour and its extreme hardiness under exposed conditions. It has thick, glossy, deep green, heavily veined leaves that are divided into as many as 9 leaflets. One of the best of the flowering shrubs, its habit is dense and bushy to about 5 ft (1.5 m) high and wide. Its branches are thickly covered with prickles and bristles. It blooms in repeated flushes over a long season and the white to deep pink flowers are 5-petalled, clove scented and up to 3½ in (9 cm) across. They are followed by showy, large, pinkish orange-red hips. The leaves turn a clear yellow in autumn. It is a good choice for a coastal situation in a cool climate and is also excellent for hedging. This tough, disease-resistant species has given rise to a group of hybrids known collectively as Rugosas. 'Alba' is a white-flowered cultivar. ZONE 2.

Rosa sericea var. *pteracantha*
BROAD-SPINED ROSE

This large, cool-climate rose bush from China will reach about 10 ft (3 m). It is unusual in that it is often garden grown for the beauty of its huge, broad-based prickles, deep red on young shoots which when backlit by the morning or evening sun, take on a magnificent glowing tone. As the shoot matures, the prickles turn pale grey and opaque. Its leaves are divided into a large number of leaflets, as many as 17. The single burst of charming, white, 4-petalled flowers appears in late spring and is followed by small, oval, orange-red hips and attractive autumnal foliage. The plant is also listed as *R. omeiensis* var. *pteracantha*. ZONE 6.

Rosa xanthina

This angular, cool-climate shrub, reaching heights of 10 ft (3 m), rarely performs or displays well in frost-free climates. The scented, yellow flowers are small, semi-double and appear in a single flush in late spring. The wood and fern-like leaves are dark. Closely allied is the cultivar 'Canary Bird', which is much more widely grown and has a stronger yellow flower colour and is very free flowering. ZONE 3.

ROSMARINUS
Lamiaceae

Some botanists recognize a dozen species in this genus but most suggest there is only one, *R. officinalis*. An evergreen shrub grown for its foliage and flowers, it is native to the Mediterranean region and has long been used in medicine, the perfume industry and the kitchen. These small shrubs, rarely growing more than 4 ft (1.2 m), have narrow, needle-like leaves that are dark green and aromatic. The blue flowers are held in short clusters. They prefer a sunny site and will thrive in poor soil if it is well drained; they tolerate salt-laden air. Prune regularly to encourage new growth. They can be grown as a specimen shrub or as a hedge. Propagate from seed or cuttings in summer.

Rosmarinus officinalis
ROSEMARY

Widely grown as a culinary herb, this aromatic shrub is also a very attractive ornamental plant. The habit is upright with strong woody branches that are densely clothed with narrow, 1 in (2 cm) deep green leaves. Simple, lavender blue to deep blue flowers smother the bush in autumn, winter and spring. Regular trimming will keep the plant compact. It can also be grown as a low hedge. 'Prostratus' is a groundcover form that is ideal for spilling over walls or covering banks. ZONE 6.

ROTHMANNIA
Rubiaceae

These are evergreen shrubs to small trees native to tropical and southern Africa. They were once classified with *Gardenia* which they closely resemble. Growing to 15 ft (5 m), they can form several stems. They feature lance- to oval-shaped, opposite leaves, up to 6 in (15 cm) long, that are a glossy green. Stalkless, bell-shaped flowers with a strong fragrance appear in spring through summer and are followed by fleshy, rounded fruit. Grow these plants in a sheltered sunny to semi-shaded spot. A well-drained soil enriched with organic matter is ideal, preferably with a neutral to slightly acid pH. Propagate these warm-climate plants from seed in spring or from cuttings in summer.

Rothmannia capensis
CAPE GARDENIA

Growing widely in evergreen forests, ravines and on rocky slopes in warm coastal areas of its native South Africa, in cultivation this fast-growing species reaches 15 ft (5 m). The glossy green, leathery, lance- to oval-shaped leaves are up to 4 in (10 cm) long and have slightly wavy edges. The grey-brown bark cracks to reveal the pink underbark. Its beautiful cream to yellow, bell-shaped flowers, up to 3 in (7 cm) long, are sweetly scented even when dried. The blooms are patterned with reddish spots in the throat. The green, rounded fruit exude a sap that leaves blue stains and was once used in the healing of wounds and burns. This plant is only suitable for tropical and subtropical areas. ZONE 10.

Rothmannia globosa
TREE GARDENIA

This shrub to small tree bears masses of decorative, creamy white, spring flowers, sometimes with yellowish throats. Bell shaped and waxy, they have a strong gardenia-like perfume. The flowers are arranged in groups of 1 to 3 in leaf axils or at branch tips. The glossy green leaves are lance to oval shaped. Indigenous to South Africa, it reaches 12 ft (4 m) with a narrow domed canopy and a dark-coloured bark. Its fruit are hard and ball-like, 1 in (2.5 cm) in diameter, held in large clusters, and are brownish black when ripe. ZONE 10.

ROYSTONEA
Arecaceae
ROYAL PALM

This genus of striking, evergreen palms from tropical South America, the West Indies and southern Florida is only seen in tropical and subtropical climates. It needs moist, rich and well-drained soil. These are graceful palms reaching 130 ft (40 m) with a single, erect whitish brown trunk. Their enormous fronds can extend to 21 ft (7 m) with a width of 6 ft (2 m). The small white flowers are followed by deep purple berries. Propagation is from seed. These palms are often seen planted along avenues or in a mass planting.

Roystonea regia
CUBAN ROYAL PALM

This palm matures to a height of 100 ft (30 m) with a spread of 30 ft (10 m). It is spectacular when used

Rosmarinus officinalis

Rothmannia capensis (below)

Roystonea regia (below)

Rothmannia globosa

Rubus occidentalis

Rubus idaeus

Rubus idaeus

RUBUS
Roseaceae
BRAMBLE, BLACKBERRY, RASPBERRY

This large genus of deciduous and evergreen shrubs and scrambling climbers is represented in most parts of the world. A few species are cultivated widely for their delicious berries but there are also some ornamental species that are grown for their flowers. The plants can grow to a height and width of 8 ft (2.5 m) and have attractive though often prickly stems; canes bear flowers and fruit in their second year. The leaves are mostly compound with 3–7 leaflets arranged pinnately or palmately and are usually felted underneath. The flowers appear in summer and are white, pink or purple, resembling those of a small single rose. The sweet, juicy fruit are a mass of tiny drupes and are usually either red or black. After fruiting, the canes should be cut back to the ground. Easy to cultivate, the plants like moist, well-drained soil in a sunny position. Some forms of *Rubus* have naturalized and have become a persistent menace. Propagate by division of roots in winter or from seeds, cuttings or suckers.

Rubus idaeus
RASPBERRY

The European raspberry performs well in a cool climate. A deciduous perennial shrub growing to a height and spread of 5 ft (1.5 m), it is distinguished by attractive, smooth, reddish brown stems that can bear many or few prickles. The large, serrated leaflets are up to 5 in (12 cm) long and grey underneath. The small, 5-petalled flowers of *R. idaeus* appear after the second year, on the side shoots of the branches that grew the previous summer. Reaching their peak in late spring and early summer, they festoon the shrub in open white clusters. The succulent aromatic berries are usually red, occasionally white or yellowish. This species has given rise to many cultivars. ZONE 4.

Rubus occidentalis
BLACK RASPBERRY

A parent of the many cultivars of black raspberries, this erect shrub can reach 5 ft (1.5 m). Its prickly canes arch and root from their tips. The 3-lobed leaves are serrated and whitish on their undersides. Small white flowers, held in dense clusters, are followed by the black and occasionally golden berries. ZONE 2.

Rubus odoratus
THIMBLEBERRY, ORNAMENTAL RASPBERRY

A vigorous, thicket-forming, shrub, this deciduous species is prickleless with peeling stems. The vine-like leaves are dark green and velvety; while the fragrant flowers, produced all through the warmer months, are a warm rose-pink, or sometimes white, and carried in sprays. The red fruit that follow are tasteless and slightly shrivelled. The shrub's eventual height of around 6 ft (2 m) is achieved when planted in a rich soil in semi-shade. ZONE 2.

as a feature in tropical gardens or as an avenue tree. Its straight trunk is often thickened in the middle before narrowing at the top. Its fronds are up to 18 ft (6 m) long and are composed of numerous narrow, deep green leaflets. Its small white flowers are clustered in pendulous spikes up to 3 ft (1 m) long. The deep purple berries are spheres up to 1 in (2 cm) in diameter. ZONE 11.

Sabal minor

Salix alba

Sabal palmetto

Sabal palmetto

SABAL
Arecaceae
PALMETTO PALM

These fan palms are indigenous to southern USA and the Caribbean region. Some species have erect tall trunks while others feature very short stems. Hybrids are common. Leaves are fan shaped and deeply cut into segments of irregular size. The leaf stalks often persist for years on the trunk after the leaves have fallen. Clusters of creamy flowers appear among the leaves, their stalks enclosed by tubular bracts at the base. The fruit are rounded to pear-shaped berries. Leaves of palmetto palms are traditionally used for thatching roofs while the buds of some species are one source of hearts-of-palm, also known as millionaire's salad. These palms suit warm to hot climates and moist or dry conditions. They prefer a sheltered sunny spot in well-drained soil rich in organic matter. Propagate from fresh seed.

Sabal minor
DWARF PALMETTO

This shrub-sized palm is usually about 6 ft (2 m) tall and half as wide. The stem is usually mostly underground but occasionally upright and short, and leaves appear from the crown at ground level. Each leaf is green to bluish green, stiff and almost flat, and cut into regular ribbed segments. Flowers are small, white and scented, on slender erect panicles projecting high above the foliage. The small fruit are black and shiny. The dwarf palmetto grows naturally over a wide area of south-western and south-central USA. ZONE 8.

Sabal palmetto
PALMETTO, CABBAGE PALM

This evergreen tree species originates from south-eastern USA, Cuba and the Bahamas and thrives in swampy coastal areas. It is very popular in Miami for street and park planting. It can reach a height of 80 ft (25 m), with a sturdy trunk, scarred where the leaf bases have been. Leaves are dark green above and greyish underneath, up to 6 ft (2 m) long. Each leaf is divided into regular segments cut two-thirds of the way to the main axis and split at the tips. Leaves are characteristically twisted. The small, whitish flowers are held in long, branched clusters. The fruit is a small black berry. ZONE 8.

SALIX
Salicaceae
WILLOW

This genus includes about 300 species of deciduous trees, shrubs and groundcovers from cold and temperate regions in the northern hemisphere. The fast-growing but relatively short-lived trees are the most widely grown. These hardy plants are largely grown for their timber, their twigs which are used in basket-making, and their strong suckering habit which aids soil retention. Willow bark was the original source of aspirin. The leaves are usually bright green, lance shaped and narrow. The flowers, which are borne in fluffy catkins, are conspicuous in some species appearing before or with the new leaves; male and female catkins are usually borne on separate trees. Willows do best in areas with clearly defined seasons and prefer cool, moist soil with sun or partial shade. Propagate from hardwood or semi-ripe cuttings, layers or seed.

Salix alba
WHITE WILLOW

A very adaptable tree from Europe and western Asia, this species grows to about 40 ft (13 m) high. Its erect branches weep somewhat at the tips and are clothed with 3 in (8 cm) long, narrow leaves that are bright green above with flattened silky hairs on the undersides. The white willow makes a good windbreak tree, albeit with invasive roots. It is often pollarded to gain long, flexible shoots for basket-making. There are several varieties and cultivars including 'Britzensis', bright red new stems; 'Chrysostela', yellow shoots tipped with orange; var. *caerulea*, blue-green leaves, the willow from which cricket bats are made; and var. *sericea*, very silvery foliage. ZONE 2.

Salix apoda

This deciduous shrub from the Caucasus grows to about 3 ft (1 m) high and spreads to 8 ft (2.5 m) wide. The pointed oval leaves are 2½ in (6 cm) long, covered with hair when young, dark green when mature. In early spring reddish brown buds open to reveal striking 1 in (2 cm) silver-grey catkins with a felt-like texture. While larger than the stunted arctic willows, this species has a bonsai-like quality that makes it a marvellous plant for a large rockery. ZONE 3.

Salix babylonica
WEEPING WILLOW

Probably the most widely grown and recognized willow, this Chinese species grows to about 50 ft (15 m) high and wide. The narrow, bright green leaves, 3–6 in (8–15 cm) long, densely clothe flexible, arching branches that often droop right down to ground level. The catkins are insignificant. 'Crispa' (syn. 'Annularis') is a cultivar with twisted leaves and a narrower growth-habit. ZONE 4.

Salix × chrysocoma
WEEPING GOLDEN WILLOW

This French cultivar, a hybrid between *S. alba* and *S. babylonica*, grows rapidly to about 60 ft (18 m) with a similar spread. Its arching limbs produce long, thin, yellow branchlets that droop to the ground. Lance-shaped, yellow-green leaves turn a golden colour in autumn. Both male and female flowers are borne on the same tree. This tree needs full sun and moist soil to thrive. ZONE 2.

Salix fragilis
CRACK WILLOW

This fast-growing erect species from Europe and north-western Asia can reach 80 ft (25 m) tall, its many branches forming a broad crown. The toothed leaves, to 7 in (17 cm) long, turn yellow in autumn. Its wood has been used to produce high quality charcoal. This tree grows easily and can naturalize and become a problem, spreading along the banks of streams. Several cultivars are known. The common name comes from the trees' brittle twigs; old trees rot easily and break apart in storms. ZONE 2.

Salix humboldtiana
SOUTH AMERICAN WILLOW

Almost fully evergreen, this willow, formerly known as *S. chilensis*, occurs naturally in warmer areas of Chile and other parts of Central and South America. It grows to 50 ft (15 m) tall, often with several upright trunks and upward-sweeping branches, giving a columnar shape. The tough, flexible branches are used for making wicker furniture. The bright green, waxy leaves are 4–6 in (10–15 cm) long and narrow to lance shaped; similar to those of the familiar weeping willow. New growth can be damaged by frosts, making this willow best suited to warm climates. ZONE 9.

Salix integra

This upright deciduous shrub grows to 9 ft (3 m) and is similar to *S. purpurea*, having purplish branches and 4 in (10 cm) long leaves that are whitish below and mid-green above. The cultivar 'Alba Maculata' has white mottled leaves and is also called 'Hakuro-nishki'. ZONE 5.

Salix matsudana 'Tortuosa'
CORKSCREW WILLOW

This popular cultivar originated as a sport of *S. matsudana*, which is hardly distinguishable from *S. babylonica* but is smaller growing. The lance-shaped, serrated leaves turn from dark green to yellow in autumn. The catkins appear at the same time as the leaves. ZONE 4.

Salix matsudana 'Tortuosa' *Salix matsudana* 'Tortuosa'

Salix babylonica (below) *Salix apoda* *Salix integra* 'Alba Maculata' (below)

Salix purpurea
PURPLE OSIER, ALASKA BLUE WILLOW

The tree-sized willows will all grow to at least 25 ft (8 m) but there are some small species, of which *S. purpurea* from northern North America is the best known. It grows to about 15 ft (5 m) high. In its darkest forms the catkins are an intense reddish purple. The leaves are silver-grey, often with a hint of purple on the undersides, and the stems are tinted purple. ZONE 2.

SALVIA
Lamiaceae
SAGE

This large genus of annual and perennial herbs and soft-wooded shrubs (mainly evergreen) is widely distributed in warm climates; it includes species whose leaves are used as edible herbs as well as for a host of folk remedies. These include the familiar garden and kitchen sage, *S. officinalis*, a peren-

Salix purpurea (below)

Sambucus nigra (below)

Salvia africana-lutea (below)

nial not quite woody enough to be called a shrub but what botanists would call a subshrub. The leaves are aromatic and the small 2-lipped tubular flowers are arranged in spikes or panicles. In some species showy bracts or calyxes are the most conspicuous part of the flower spikes. Most of the shrubby species are frost-tender, and do best in full sun and well-drained, light to medium soil with ample water in warmer months. They are propagated from seed or cuttings.

Salvia africana-lutea
BEACH SALVIA, GOLDEN SALVIA

This very attractive evergreen shrub from southern Africa grows to about 6 ft (2 m) tall and wide, and has greyish green aromatic leaves. It blooms profusely during spring and early summer; the yellow flowers fade to brick-red then reddish brown, and after they fall the showy purple-and-yellow calyxes remain. Beach salvia tolerates light frost and is wind resistant. A fine rockery plant, it needs no special soil but prefers full sun and adequate water in winter. Occasional pruning will keep it neat. ZONE 9.

SAMANEA
Mimosaceae

This genus from tropical regions of Central and South America contains about 20 species of trees and shrubs. They have fern-like, bipinnate leaves, dense clusters of flowers and are without the spikes, thorns or other protective growths

Sambucus canadensis (below)

often seen in members of this family. The fruit is like a curved, sectioned, pea pod with the seeds embedded in the pulp. These plants need reasonably rich soil, ample water and good drainage. They are propagated from seed.

Samanea saman
RAIN TREE, MONKEY POD TREE

This fast-growing tree from South America can grow to 90 ft (28 m) with a short trunk and a great umbrella-shaped canopy spreading to as much as twice its height. The leaflets of the large, deep green leaves fold together in the evening or when the sky becomes overcast. The clusters of summer flowers consist of many prominent stamens, pink at the tips and white at the base, giving a fluffy effect. This tree is widely grown as a park and shade tree in large tropical gardens and parks. It is much planted as a street tree throughout the tropics; and it is perhaps the most magnificent street tree in the world. ZONE 11.

SAMBUCUS
Caprifoliaceae
ELDERBERRY

This genus includes about 25 species of perennial herbs, deciduous shrubs and soft-wooded trees, with representatives spread widely over the temperate regions of the world. Although most are rarely cultivated because of their tendency to be somewhat weedy and invasive, some species are useful and attractive. Most have pinnate leaves and, in late spring and early summer, large radiating sprays of tiny white flowers which are followed by clusters of purple-black, blue or red berries. The most commonly cultivated species, *S. nigra*, is grown for its edible flowers and berries and there are also several forms with coloured or variegated foliage. Other species such as *S. sieboldiana* have bright red berries that are very popular with birds. *Sambucus* species are usually undemanding plants that thrive in any reasonably well-drained soil in sun or shade. Propagate from seed or cuttings.

Sambucus caerulea
BLUEBERRY ELDER

This small deciduous tree species from northern and western areas of North America is often seen in California. It grows up to 10–45 ft (3–15 m); the leaves usually have 7 leaflets and the creamy yellow flowers are produced in early summer in flat-topped sprays. The edible fruit which follow are black but covered with a powdery bloom which makes them look blue. *S. caerulea* is grown commercially for the tasty berries that should be cooked before they are eaten. ZONE 4.

Sambucus canadensis
AMERICAN ELDER

An upright, deciduous shrub from cold-climate regions in the northeast of North America, this fast-growing species reaches about 10 ft (3 m) tall with a similar spread, and has soft pithy stems. The compound leaves have 5 to 11 leaflets and the tiny, white, starry flowers appear in spring, borne in large sprays about 8 in (20 cm) across; they are followed by purple-black berries. ZONE 2.

Sambucus nigra
EUROPEAN ELDER, ELDERBERRY

This species, sometimes regarded as a weed, is cultivated for its large, spring-borne sprays of tiny white flowers and the clusters of purple-black berries that follow. Originally from Europe, northern Africa and western Asia, this deciduous shrub or small tree to 18 ft (6 m) high has pinnate leaves made up of 5 to 9 deep green, serrated-edged leaflets. The berries are used in pies, the flowers and fruit to make wine or liqueurs. ZONE 4.

SANTALUM
Santalaceae
SANDALWOOD

From low-rainfall areas of Southeast Asia, Australia and the Pacific, these evergreen trees and shrubs are semi-parasitic, relying on the roots of other plants to supply their nutrients. Because of this they are

Sapindus drummondii

considered difficult to cultivate, but research continues as some bear edible fruit suitable for growing in warm, arid areas. The traditional sandalwood, from which small precious objects are made and fragrant oil is distilled, is *S. album*, from Asia, the Pacific and northern Australia. *S. lanceolatum* from Australia is also valued for its scented wood.

Santalum acuminatum
SWEET QUANDONG

This stately small tree from dry inland regions of Australia grows 10–20 ft (3–7 m) tall, with pendulous, leathery, grey-green leaves and small greenish white 4-petalled flowers in spring and summer. But it is the bright red succulent fruit, resembling a small plum, which are of most interest. These are borne after the tree is about 4 years old, and are used for making jam; the kernels within the nut are also edible, being oily and nutritious. Grasses have been used successfully to provide hosts for this semi-parasitic plant; though it is, like most such plants, not very easy to establish in gardens. The sweet quandong needs full sun or light shade and light, well-drained soil with water during the warmer months. ZONE 9.

SAPINDUS
Sapindaceae

This genus contains about 20 species of evergreen and deciduous trees and shrubs, very few of which feature in gardens. Originating in tropical and subtropical regions of the Americas and Asia, they thrive on sandy, dry, rocky soil. Some species are grown as ornamental and shade trees as well as for their inedible berry-like fruit, which are fleshy and leathery. The fruits contain a substance called saponin, which lathers in water and therefore allows the berries to be used as a soap substitute in their native lands. The leaves are pinnate and the small 5-petalled summer flowers are in shades of white, yellow or orange with prominent hairy stamens. *Sapindus* species are not fussy about soil as long as it is well-drained, and prefer full sun. Propagation is from seed or softwood cuttings.

Sapindus drummondii
WESTERN SOAPBERRY, WILD CHINA-TREE

Indigenous to arid regions of southern USA and Mexico, this deciduous tree matures to 50 ft (15 m). It forms a spreading canopy with pinnate leaves composed of up to 18 leaflets, each 3 in (8 cm) long. The yellowish white summer flowers are held in clusters at the ends of the branches. They are followed by small yellow fruit which ripen to black. *S. drummondii* makes an attractive small shade tree which is tolerant of cold and drought. ZONE 8.

SAPIUM
Euphorbiaceae

This is a genus of about 100 species of trees and shrubs, evergreen to semi-deciduous, found naturally in warm-climate areas from East Asia to tropical America. Like other members of the euphorbia family, they have a milky sap which is poisonous to humans and animals. This congeals on drying and some of the South American species, notably *S. verum*, have been tapped for rubber. The leaves are arranged alternately along the stems. Flowers are in spikes but are insignificant. The fruit are hard-shelled capsules. These plants thrive in well-drained soil enriched with organic matter and need full sun. Propagate them from freshly collected seed or semi-hardwood cuttings. Superior forms of *S. sebiferum* are sometimes grafted on to seedling rootstocks.

Sapium sebiferum
CHINESE TALLOW TREE

From warm-climate areas of China and Japan, and the only species commonly seen in cultivation, this fast-growing tree reaches 20–40 ft (7–13 m), with a spreading crown. It is semi-deciduous in hot climates, deciduous where winters are cooler. The bright green leaves, heart shaped to oval with a pointed tip, colour attractively to shades of yellow, orange, red and purple in autumn, even in a subtropical cli-

Santalum acuminatum

Saraca indica

Sapium sebiferum

mate. In late spring spikes of tiny greenish yellow flowers are borne at the branch tips. The autumn fruit are capsules ½ in (1 cm) across, containing 3 seeds which are covered with white wax. This waxy coating is used in China to make soap and candles. This is one of the most reliable trees for autumn colour in mild-winter climates. ZONE 8.

SARACA
Caesalpiniaceae

This leguminous genus contains small evergreen trees from tropical Southeast Asia; they occur naturally as understorey trees in forests. They are grown for their dense clusters of showy flowers and attractive foliage. The leaves are pinnate with paired leaflets; new foliage is often soft and bronze-red, maturing to mid-green. The flowers have no true petals, but very colourful tubular calyx opening into 4–5 flat sepals and long, prominent stamens, and are borne in clusters on older branches. They are followed by narrow oblong pods. Saracas need a hot, humid climate, moist, well-drained soil and some shade. In cooler climates they can be grown in greenhouses. They are grown from seed.

Saraca indica
ASOKA, SORROWLESS TREE

The best known species of the genus, this erect evergreen tree occurs naturally from India to the Malay Peninsula. It can grow to 30 ft (10 m) and has long, shiny, compound leaves with 3 to 6 pairs of leaflets which are soft and reddish when young. The flowers, held in dense clusters, appear mainly in summer, though a few can be seen almost all year. They are yellow-orange to scarlet with long, showy, dark red stamens, and the pods which follow are deep reddish purple. ZONE 11.

Scaevola sericea

Sassafras albidum

Sarcococca ruscifolia

Saxegothaea conspicua

Sarcococca hookeriana

SARCOCOCCA
Buxaceae
SWEET BOX, CHRISTMAS BOX

These wiry-stemmed evergreen shrubs from Asia have glossy, deep green, elliptical leaves and in late winter to spring produce small white to pink flowers that while not very showy are sweetly scented. The flowers are followed by conspicuous berries. While often grown in difficult, dry, shady areas, the sweet boxes look better with a little care and attention. They prefer a relatively cool, moist climate with well-drained soil to match. They are largely trouble free. Propagate from seed, cuttings or layers.

Sarcococca hookeriana
Indigenous to the Himalayan region, this species develops into a dense clump of upright, somewhat arching stems. Its scented cream flowers have reddish pink anthers, a feature emphasized in var. *hookeriana*. The berries are black. 'Purple Stem' is a cultivar with narrow leaves and red-purple stems. ZONE 5.

Sarcococca ruscifolia
From Yunnan, Hubei and Sichuan in China, this species bears scented white flowers which are followed by red berries. It grows to about 5 ft (1.5 m) high and forms a densely foliaged clump. ZONE 6.

SASSAFRAS
Lauraceae

This small genus of the laurel family contains 3 species of tall deciduous trees from China, North America and Taiwan. All parts of the trees have a spicy aroma which repels insects, and the wood has been used to make insect-proof cabinets and furniture. The alternate leaves of the trees can be entire or lobed and it is not unusual to see both on the same plant. The unisexual or bisexual flowers have no petals; usually greenish yellow, they are borne in clusters and appear with the leaves in spring. The fruit is an oval-shaped, blue-black drupe (not edible). Propagation is from seed, stem cuttings, suckers or root pieces.

Sassafras albidum
SASSAFRAS

This handsome tree occurs naturally in forests on the east coast of North America from Quebec to Florida; it grows to 70 ft (22 m). The leaves are up to 5 in (12 cm) long, sometimes lobed, glossy dark green above and paler beneath; the foliage turns spectacular orange and scarlet shades in autumn. The spring flowers are small, greenish yellow and insignificant, and the fruit are blue-black. The inner bark yields the aromatic oil of sassafras, which was once used as a food flavouring and in cosmetics, but is now suspected of being poisonous; it is also used as an insecticide. Sassafras thrives in temperate climates in rich, well-drained soil with constant moisture, and does best in full sun. It has a reputation for being difficult to transplant. ZONE 2.

SAXEGOTHAEA
Podocarpaceae
PRINCE ALBERT'S YEW

This genus comprises a single species of conifer with yew-like foliage, indigenous to cool, moist climates of southern Chile. Although it is hardy, Prince Albert's yew prefers full sun and a well-drained soil. The timber is used in its native country for general carpentry as it is easy to work. The tree is propagated from seed or cuttings. The species is of great botanical interest, forming as it does a link between the yews, the podocarps and the pine family. Some botanists have placed it in the yew family, Taxaceae.

Saxegothaea conspicua
This slow-growing, evergreen conifer can grow to over 45 ft (14 m). In warm-temperate areas it forms a neat conical shape, but it tends to be more columnar and bushy in cooler regions. The needle-like dark green leaves are about ½ in (1 cm) long, and spirally arranged; young foliage is somewhat pendulous. The cones differ from those of other conifers in being fleshy, spine tipped, and powdery blue. ZONE 7.

SCAEVOLA
Goodeniaceae
FAN FLOWER

This is a genus of about 60 species of subtropical evergreen shrubs, subshrubs, perennials and vines mainly from Australia. They are valued for their attractive flowers and adaptability to a wide range of conditions, including seaside gardens. The shrub species range from prostrate groundcovers 6 in (15 cm) high and up to 6 ft (2 m) wide to shrubs reaching 10 ft (3 m) tall. The larger species have fleshy leaves, while the groundcovers have soft foliage. The distinctive flowers have their 5 petals arranged on one side only, giving them a curious asymmetrical appearance. *Scaevola* species tolerate a wide range of soils but prefer them to be light and well-drained; they do best in sun or semi-shade. The fan-shaped flowers are blue, white or mauve, usually covering the plant in a profusion which lasts for many months. Propagate from seed or cuttings.

Scaevola sericea
SEA LETTUCE

One of the few species occurring beyond Australia, it grows on tropical beaches and atolls throughout the Pacific and Indian Oceans. This attractive evergreen shrub (syn. *S. taccada*) grows to 5 ft (1.5 m) high and about as wide. The bright green leaves are about 5 in (12 cm) long. The small white flowers are streaked with purple; they are borne at branch ends for most of the year. The fruit is a small, succulent, purplish blue berry. ZONE 10.

SCHEFFLERA
Araliaceae

A vast genus of small trees, shrubs and scrambling climbers, with over 700 species occurring through most wetter tropical and subtropical regions of the world; a few are grown for their luxurious green foliage. The leaves consist of a number of leaflets of similar size arranged like a cartwheel at the ends of long stalks. The small flowers are arranged in branching, usually radiating spikes. The fruit are small, fleshy berries. In their native rainforests, many schefflera grow as epiphytes, high on other trees, or in cliffs or rock outcrops. Several species are popular house plants in cool and cold climates. In warm to hot climates they can be planted in the garden, in a spot sheltered from wind, either in the sun or partly shaded. Young plants make excellent tub specimens. Grow them in a well-drained soil, preferably enriched with organic matter, keeping soil moist over summer. Propagate new plants from fresh seed or cuttings.

Schefflera actinophylla
QUEENSLAND UMBRELLA TREE

Each 16 in (40 cm) wide leaf of this species resembles an umbrella; they consist of 7 to 15 light green glossy leaflets. From rainforests of northern Australia, it reaches about 30 ft (10 m) in cultivation. Multiple erect trunks form a dense canopy 20 ft (7 m) wide. Numerous clusters of flowers are arranged in spectacular radiating spikes on red stems. These appear near the top of the plant from late summer to early spring. Each ruby red flower has contrasting cream stamens and is rich in nectar. Reddish fleshy berries follow. ZONE 10.

Schefflera arboricola
MINIATURE UMBRELLA TREE

Endemic to Taiwan, this smaller version of *S. actinophylla* makes a shrub 6–15 ft (2–5 m) tall with a similar spread. It produces many branches near the ground and can be pruned to a rounded shape, making it a popular pot plant for indoors and out. Leaves consist of 5 to 10 leaflets radiating from the leaf stalk; each is shiny green and up to 6 in (15 cm) long. Greenish yellow flowers in branching sprays appear near the branch tips in spring and summer, followed by massed orange fruit which ripen to purple. Cultivar 'Renate' has variegated leaves. ZONE 10.

SCHINUS
Anacardiaceae

These evergreen trees, indigenous to Central and South America, are grown for their graceful habit and great resistance to drought. Leaves usually consist of many leaflets but are sometimes simple. Flowers are tiny and arranged in clusters, male and female flowers on the same or separate trees. Female trees feature attractive round berries later in the season. They make excellent shade and street trees and tolerate hot, dry conditions. An open sunny location suits them, as well as well-drained, coarse soil, but they will adapt to poorer soils. Propagate from fresh seed or cuttings. *Schinus* species grow best in warm to hot climates. They are not good garden trees, having very strong surface roots.

Schinus areira
PEPPER TREE, PEPPERCORN

This fast-growing tree with graceful drooping leaves and branchlets occurs naturally in Argentina, Paraguay and Bolivia and is also known as *S. molle*. Older trees develop an attractive gnarled trunk topped by an irregular weeping crown to a height of 40 ft (13 m). The dark green, shiny leaves are about 6 in (15 cm) long, composed of 10 to 18 pairs of small pointed leaflets. In late spring to early summer, pendulous open clusters of tiny cream flowers are borne at the branch tips. Long hanging bunches of poisonous peppercorn-like berries appear later in summer on female trees. These ripen to coral red and persist for several months. ZONE 9.

Schinus terebinthifolia
BRAZILIAN PEPPER TREE

A round-headed tree, up to about 30 ft (10 m) high, this Brazilian species has bronze-green pinnate leaves, usually of 7 leaflets. The drooping panicles of tiny cream flowers that appear in summer are followed by small green berries that redden as they ripen in winter. It is easily grown and tolerates most soils but requires good drainage. When trimmed it makes an excellent shade tree. In some warm, wet climates, such as Hawaii, it has become a serious weed. ZONE 10.

SCHIZOLOBIUM
Caesalpiniaceae

Indigenous to tropical regions of South America, the 2 evergreen or deciduous trees of this small genus are valued for their huge, feathery leaves and wonderful display of golden yellow flowers in spring. They do best in deep, rich, moist soil, in full sun but with shelter from strong winds, and plenty of water. Propagate from seed.

Schizolobium parahybum
TREE-FERN TREE, BACURUBU

This tall, slender-trunked tree, indigenous to tropical Brazil, is fast-growing to about 90 ft (30 m), with a sparse, open growth-habit. The large, bipinnate, fern-like leaves are up to 3 ft (1 m) long, and are borne in crowded whorls at branch ends. Young trees remain unbranched up to 20 ft (7 m) or more, resembling a slender tree fern. The leaves are shed in late winter, and by late spring the tree is covered with golden flowers in large clusters. The fruit which follow are brown pods, each holding a single seed. ZONE 10.

SCHOTIA
Caesalpiniaceae

This genus includes some 20 species of evergreen or deciduous shrubs and small trees indigenous to tropical and subtropical Africa. They are grown for their showy clusters of flowers. Leaves are alternately arranged and composed of an even number of leaflets. The fruit is an oblong leathery pod. These plants are propagated from seed or semi-hardwood cuttings. They need a warm frost-free climate and shelter from wind, and grow best in full sun and light to medium well-drained soil.

Schinus terebinthifolia (below)

Schinus areira

Schefflera actinophylla (below)

Sciadopitys verticillata

Sciadopitys verticillata

Senecio grandifolius

Scolopia braunii

Schotia brachypetala

Schotia brachypetala

Schotia brachypetala
WEEPING BOER-BEAN, TREE FUCHSIA

This large shrub or wide-spreading deciduous tree from South Africa reaches a height of 30–40 ft (10–13 m). In spring it sheds most of its leaves before producing large clusters of deep red flowers with tiny, bristly petals and projecting red stamens. Copious nectar drips from the flowers, giving rise to the common name weeping boer-bean. Birds adore this nectar, but the nectar ferments in the sun so the birds get drunk. Leaves are shiny green and consist of 4 to 5 pairs of oval to oblong leaflets. The fruit are oblong pods, 4 in (10 cm) long. ZONE 9.

SCIADOPITYS
Sciadopityaceae
JAPANESE UMBRELLA PINE

This genus consists of just one species, a very distinctive and handsome conifer from Japan. It is an upright, single-trunked, conical tree that eventually grows to over 100 ft (30 m) tall, though it is very slow growing; it can be kept in a container for long periods and is often used as a bonsai subject. The Japanese umbrella pine prefers a cool maritime climate with cool, moist, humus-rich soil and light shade when young. It is propagated from seed.

Sciadopitys verticillata

What makes this species distinctive is its foliage. The deep green flattened needles, up to 6 in (15 cm) long, are carried in stiff whorls of 20 to 30 and face upwards, creating an effect like the ribs of an umbrella. Interestingly, the needles are not true leaves at all but they do photosynthesize. The true 'leaves' are the tiny scales that lie almost flat along the stems. The small oval cones take 2 years to mature. ZONE 5.

SCOLOPIA
Flacourtaceae

This genus contains 45 species of trees and shrubs indigenous to tropical and subtropical areas of southern Africa, Asia and Australia. All species have simple alternate leaves and small flowers in unbranched elongated clusters usually borne near the ends of branches. They produce a berry-like fruit. The plants do best in full sun, planted in well-drained soil with adequate water. Propagation is from fresh seed or cuttings.

Scolopia braunii
BROWN BIRCH

From forests of eastern Australia, this erect tree grows to 50 ft (15 m). It has a dense crown of smooth, glossy, sometimes toothed, green leaves that are up to 3–4 in (9–10 cm) long; the young foliage is diamond shaped with toothed edges. The clusters of small creamy white flowers are followed by ½ in (1 cm) globular, black, red or yellow fruit. The trees adapt to most soils, can be pruned hard and are adaptable to pot culture; they make attractive house plants. ZONE 10.

SENECIO
Asteraceae

This large genus of vigorous leafy plants includes some 2,000 to 3,000 species from all over the world, though many botanists now recognize many smaller genera split off from this large one. Plants range from annuals and perennials to evergreen tree-like shrubs and climbers. The daisy-like flowers, usually yellow but sometimes red, orange, blue or purple, are arranged in small to large clusters at the top of the plant. Reasonably fertile, well-drained soil suits these plants, as well as a sunny location. Regular tip pruning encourages a bushy plant. Propagation of shrub species is from seed or semi-hardwood cuttings. Some species contain alkaloids and are poisonous to humans and animals.

Senecio grandifolius
MEXICAN TREE GROUNDSEL

Indigenous to Mexico, this large, rounded, upright, evergreen leafy shrub grows up to 10 ft (3 m) tall. Leaves are large (as the species name indicates), oval to oblong in shape, and 10–16 in (25–40 cm) long, with toothed edges and prominent veins. They are soft dark green on top and paler green underneath, and are held on long thick stalks. From late summer to winter the yellow flowers appear, clustered in broad heads up to 18 in (45 cm) across, held well above the foliage. Some botanists place this species in the genus *Telanthophora*. ZONE 10.

Senecio greyii

This very adaptable and easily grown, 5 ft (1.5 m) high shrub withstands drought, coastal conditions and neglect. Although common in cultivation, it has a natural distribution restricted to coastal areas of the North Island of New Zealand. Its stems and the undersides of the deep green oval leaves, up to 4 in (10 cm) long, are covered in fine silver-grey hair. The bright yellow flowers occur in loose heads and open from late spring. Annual trimming after flowering will keep the bush compact. In recent botanical treatments this species has been placed in the genus *Brachyglottis*. ZONE 8.

Senecio laxifolia
NELSON MOUNTAIN GROUNDSEL

This species is very similar to *S. greyii* except for a slightly more open growth-habit. It has heavily felted foliage and is relatively small growing, to 3 ft (1 m) high. The oval leaves are 2–3 in (5–7 cm) long, deep green above and silver-grey below. The flowers, which are clustered in loose heads and open in mid-summer, are bright golden yellow daisies up to 1 in (2 cm) in diameter. In some botanical treatments this species has been placed in the genus *Brachyglottis*. ZONE 7.

Senecio petasitis
MEXICAN GIANT GROUNDSEL

Also called the velvet geranium, this shrub reaches 8 ft (2.5 m) tall and is up to 10 ft (3 m) wide. Many branches from the base form a dense mass of foliage. Both stems and leaves are covered with velvety hairs. Leaves are large and plate like, oval to round and 10 in (25 cm) long, on a stalk of equal length. They have deep wavy lobes, and are yellowish green on top. Golden flowers are arranged in large loose heads 8–12 in (20–30 cm) across, supported by a fleshy red stalk. This species flowers from late winter to spring. Some botanists place this species in the genus *Roldana*. ZONE 10.

Senecio viravira
DUSTY MILLER

This shrub from central Argentina (syn. *S. leucostachys*) gets its common name because of its soft, silver-grey foliage. It is a loosely branched shrub to 24 in (60 cm) tall, with branches from the base all densely covered with white hairs. The 2 in (5 cm) long leaves are dissected into linear segments and are slightly furry. White, daisy-like flower heads with golden centres are held above the foliage in summer.

SENNA
Caesalpiniaceae

This large genus consists of fast-growing, mostly evergreen shrubs as well as some herbaceous perennials and small trees. It includes several species grown for medicinal use (senna). Formerly classified under *Cassia*, they occur in most warmer parts of the world with most species in the Americas, Africa and Australia. They are grown for their clusters of buttercup-like flowers, mostly golden yellow but sometimes pink. The compound leaves consist of paired leaflets. Fruit are long pods, either flattened or rounded. *Senna* species are commonly propagated from seed (first soaked in warm water for 24 hours) but sometimes from semi-hardwood cuttings. Most thrive in light, well-drained soil, with full sun and shelter from wind. Prune plants lightly after flowering to maintain dense foliage.

Senna alata
CANDLE BUSH, RINGWORM SENNA

This fast-growing evergreen tropical shrub, previously named *Cassia alata*, grows to about 8 ft (2.5 m) tall and wide. Its large leaves have up to 14 leaflets and the bright yellow cup-shaped flowers are borne through summer in upright, candle-like spikes; the winged seed pods are up to 6 in (15 cm) long. The plants are a source of chrysophanic acid which is used in the treatment of some skin diseases, hence its common name, ringworm senna. *S. alata* thrives in full sun and rich, well-drained soil with plenty of water through summer. It is easily grown from seed. ZONE 10.

Senna artemisioides
SILVER CASSIA, PUNTY

This dense, rounded, evergreen shrub reaches 4 ft (1.2 m) tall and is endemic to dry parts of southern Australia. The foliage is silver-grey and silky due to a covering of minute hairs. Leaves are up to 2 in (5 cm) long, with 3 to 8 pairs of narrow leaflets. The flowers are a rich yellow with contrasting brown anthers, arranged in clusters of 10 to 12. Flowering extends from winter to early summer. The fruit is a flattened pod which matures dark brown. The silver cassia thrives best in dry climates. ZONE 8.

Senecio greyii

Senecio petasitis (below)

Senna artemisioides (below)

Senecio viravira (below)

Senna alata (below)

Senna didymobotrya

Senna didymobotrya

Senna pendula

Senna spectabilis

Senna multijuga

Senna didymobotrya
Indigenous to tropical Africa, this evergreen shrub grows to 10 ft (3 m) and has a rounded canopy on a short trunk. Fine downy hairs cover both leaves and shoots. The foliage has an unpleasant smell when crushed. Leaves may be 12–18 in (30–45 cm) long. From summer to winter, the yellow flowers are carried near the shoot tips in erect spikes up to 12 in (30 cm) long, bursting from bud scales. Fruit are flattened, long pods. ZONE 10.

Senna multijuga
This species from Central and South America is a fast-growing evergreen tree that grows to 25 ft (8 m) and forms a rounded crown with attractive, pinnate leaves with 10 to 15 pairs of leaflets. It bears golden yellow flowers on large, terminal panicles in late summer, followed by long seed pods. Full sun and fertile, well-drained soil suit it best. ZONE 10.

Senna pendula
This shrub or small tree, formerly known as *Cassia bicapsularis*, reaches a height of 6–10 ft (2–3 m) and forms a broadly spreading mass of evergreen foliage up to 8 ft (2.5 m) across. Bright yellow flowers are borne in large clusters in autumn. The fruit is a cylindrical pod. A decorative, fast-growing plant for the subtropics, it is short lived and apt to spread from self-sown seed and become a nuisance. In cool climates it makes a fine plant for a mildly heated greenhouse. ZONE 9.

Senna spectabilis
This evergreen species from Central and South America varies greatly in size, ranging from a 6 ft (2 m) shrub to a 65 ft (20 m) tree. It is mainly seen as a rangy, small tree with ferny leaves up to 18 in (45 cm) long, covered with fine down when young. In summer it produces clusters of bright yellow flowers, followed by seed pods up to 12 in (30 cm) long. It prefers moist, well-drained soil in full sun. ZONE 10.

SEQUOIA
Taxodiaceae
CALIFORNIA REDWOOD, COAST REDWOOD

The sole species in this genus is *S. sempervirens*, renowned for being the tallest living trees, some measured at over 360 ft (110 m). It is a very long-lived, evergreen conifer indigenous to the west coast of the USA from Monterey, California, north to Oregon. Valued for its timber, it has been necessary to provide statutory protection for the most notable groves in national parks and elsewhere to save it from exploitation. The California redwood grows quickly when young and needs plenty of water. It does best in sun or partial shade with deep, well-drained soil. Propagation is usually from seed or heeled cuttings; this genus is one of the few conifers that will sprout from the cut stump.

Sequoia sempervirens
This single-trunked conical tree has bright green, flattened, leaf-like needles up to 1 in (2 cm) long. The foliage is held horizontally on small side branches, with the main branches drooping slightly. The whole tree has a resinous aroma like pine wood, especially the red-brown, fibrous bark which is very thick and deeply fissured in parallel

lines running straight up the trunk. There are several cultivars: 'Adpressa', very dwarf, for many years around 3 ft (1 m) high and 6 ft (2 m) wide, maturing to 10 ft (3 m) high; 'Aptos Blue', blue green foliage and slightly pendulous branch tips; 'Los Altos', deep green, heavy textured foliage on arching branches; 'Santa Cruz', pale green, soft-textured, slightly drooping foliage. ZONE 7.

SEQUOIADENDRON
Taxodiaceae
GIANT SEQUOIA, BIG TREE

From the Sierra Nevada area of California, the only species in this genus is a true giant of a tree. While not quite as tall as the California redwood (*Sequoia sempervirens*), it is far more heavily built and contains the largest timber volume of any tree. Like the California redwood, it is very long lived, at least 3,500 years! Its massive trunk is covered in rough, deeply fissured, reddish brown bark. This is an impressive tree for large parks and gardens. Where space allows it is an ideal specimen to plant for your great-grandchildren to marvel over. A tree of this size needs a solid base, so plant it in deep, well-drained soil and water it well when young. Propagate from seed or cuttings.

Sequoiadendron giganteum
This conifer can grow to 275 ft (84 m) tall with a trunk up to 40 ft (13 m) in diameter at the base. It is an upright, single-trunked, conical tree with sprays of deep green, slightly prickly, cypress-like foliage. Known as the General Sherman tree, a specimen of this species in the Sequoia National Park in California is said to be 3,800 years old and the world's largest tree.

SERENOA
Arecaceae

This genus contains just one palm species which occurs naturally in south-eastern USA. It is an evergreen fan palm with creeping or, rarely, short upright stems. The plants form immense colonies in their natural habitat. This palm prefers full sun or semi-shade and dislikes frost. It grows best in well-drained soil and is very tolerant of exposed coastal locations; it also tolerates boggy conditions. It can be propagated from seed or suckers.

Serenoa repens
SAW PALMETTO

This palm has stems that are mostly prostrate or creeping, about 24–36 in (60–90 cm) high, with a spread about twice that, but occasionally there is an upright stem to 10 ft (3 m). Fan-shaped leaves are held stiffly upwards and vary from green to bluish green or even silver. Each leaf is 18–30 in (45–75 cm) across, and divided into about 20 strap-shaped segments. The leaf stalks are toothed along the edges. In summer creamy white perfumed flowers are hidden among the foliage. The fruit which follow are egg shaped and ripen blackish. ZONE 9.

Serenoa repens

Sequoiadendron giganteum

Sequoia sempervirens   *Sequoia sempervirens* (right)

SERRURIA
Proteaceae

Members of the protea family, *Serruria* includes over 40 species of shrubs that are endemic to the south-western Cape area of South Africa. Each flower head consists of a central tuft of flowers surrounded by leafy bracts which are often the dominant feature of the bloom. The compact flower heads may be solitary at the branch ends or in clusters. Some have a very feathery appearance from the mass of central stamens. Serrurias range from prostrate shrubs to plants 5 ft (1.5 m)

Simmondsia chinensis (below)

Simmondsia chinensis (below)

Sideroxylon inerme (below)

tall. The leaves are fern like, with each leaf divided into many fine segments. The fruit are small hard nuts covered with hairs. These proteas must have sandy perfectly drained soil and a warm climate to thrive. Choose an open sunny spot. Serrurias grow faster than most other proteas and are best propagated from seed.

Serruria florida
BLUSHING BRIDE

This species forms a slender shrub to 4 ft (1.2 m) tall. It is rare in the wild, but in recent years it has become popular with florists as the dainty white to pale pink flower heads are long lasting. These consist of very showy, broad, papery, creamy white bracts, flushed with pink or rarely green, surrounding a central tuft of feathery silvery white to pinkish flowers. Each flower head is up to 2 in (5 cm) across, and they appear in clusters of 3 to 5 from winter to spring. The leaves are delicate and fern like, divided into needle-like segments. Regular pruning will maintain a compact

Sideroxylon inerme (below)

Serruria florida (below)

shrub. Plants may be short lived in cultivation. 'Sugar'n'spice' is a hybrid between *S. florida* and *S. rosea*. It has white bracts flushed deep rose-pink surrounding the central mass of pale pink flowers.
ZONE 9.

SIDEROXYLON
Sapotaceae
COASTAL MILKWOOD

The evergreen trees of this genus from Africa are grown for their timber which is widely used in ornamental carving. They are elegant, tall trees with trunks flanged at the base and covered with wrinkled, corky, mottled brown bark. The young branchlets are covered with distinctive small, pimple-like swellings. The thick, firm leaves are oval. White bell-shaped flowers appear from spring to autumn; they are mildly fragrant, and clustered in groups of 2 or 6 on hairy stalks. The flesh of the succulent plum-like berries is edible when made into jam. These trees prefer light to medium, well-drained soil in a protected, sunny or part-shaded position. Propagate from seed, cuttings or layering.

Sideroxylon inerme

This smallish, dense, leafy tree up to 30 ft (10 m) tall grows along the east coast of South Africa from the South Western Cape to Zululand. The glossy green leaves are oval with rounded tips. A milky latex appears whenever leaves or branches are broken. This superb foliage tree is a good choice for the garden and does well in full sun. It tolerates considerable wind and sea air, but is sensitive to frost. ZONE 9.

SIMMONDSIA
Buxaceae
JOJOBA

There is only one species in this genus. An evergreen shrub, it occurs naturally in dry, frost-free areas of south-western USA and Mexico, despite the specific name *chinensis*. It needs a warm to hot climate, and thrives in full sun, in any well-drained soil. Propagation is from seed or cuttings.

Simmondsia chinensis

This is a stiffly branched, upright shrub to 8 ft (2.5 m) tall. The dull green, leathery leaves have almost no stalks; they are oblong to oval and arranged in opposite pairs. Flowers are carried on short stalks in summer. Male and female flowers are borne on separate plants, with male flowers arranged in clusters while female flowers are solitary. In spring nut-like leathery capsules appear. Jojoba has attracted attention because oil from the capsules is a substitute for whale oil and is used in a range of products including cosmetics.
ZONE 9.

SKIMMIA
Rutaceae

Spread over much of East Asia from the Himalayan region to eastern Siberia, Japan, Taiwan and the Philippines, this genus includes 4 species of evergreen shrubs. They have deep glossy green oval leaves about 4–6 in (10–15 cm) long and about half as wide. The small starry flowers, which open from late winter, are white or cream and densely packed in conical clusters. They are followed by red or black berries depending on the species. At least one species, *S. reevesiana*, is self-fertile, but others require male and female plants to be present for pollination. Skimmias are plants for shade or partial shade and grow very well with rhododendrons, azaleas and camellias. Like them they prefer moist, humus-rich, well-drained soil. They can be raised from seed but are most commonly grown from semi-ripe cuttings.

Skimmia japonica

This hardy shrub from Japan, eastern Siberia and Taiwan grows to about 5 ft (1.5 m) high and wide. It has 4 in (10 cm) long, glossy, deep green, leathery, oval leaves. In spring terminal clusters of slightly fragrant, creamy white flowers are borne, followed by ½ in (1 cm) long, bright red berries that last well into winter. Both male and female plants are required to obtain berries. ZONE 7.

SLOANEA
Elaeocarpaceae

These tall, handsome evergreen trees come from tropical and subtropical rainforests of eastern Australia. Once valued for their timber, they are erect and straight with a wide, domed crown and buttressed trunk. The dark green leaves, up to 12 in (30 cm) in length, have serrated edges, and the flowers, usually cream or white, have broad, fleshy petals. They are held in clusters and are followed by capsular berries whose fleshy coating is eaten by birds; the attractive woody, spiny, seed cases are sometimes used in dried flower arrangements. The trees need a frost-free climate, shelter when young, and plenty of water. They are propagated from cuttings or seed in summer.

Sloanea woollsii
YELLOW CARABEEN

This tall subtropical rainforest tree reaches 160 ft (55 m) in the wild, about half that in cultivation; its massive buttressed trunk can be up to 8 ft (2.5 m) in diameter and is covered with wrinkled grey-brown bark. The long, shiny, dark green leaves are ovate with toothed mar-

Sloanea woollsii

Skimmia japonica

gins and conspicuous veins. The velvety white flowers appear in spring, borne in clusters in leaf axils. They are followed by prickly, light brown, capsular fruit which hold 2 seeds. The wood from the trees was once used for building and joinery. This is a handsome tree for parks and large gardens in the subtropics. ZONE 10.

SOLANUM
Solanaceae

There are over 1,700 species in this genus including trees, shrubs, annuals, perennials and even climbers. Some are evergreen, others semi-evergreen or deciduous. The genus includes important food plants like the potato and eggplant (aubergine), though many species are dangerously poisonous. Ornamental species are grown for their flowers and fruit. Leaves are arranged alternately. Flowers are solitary or in clusters, showy and star shaped to bell shaped, ranging from white and yellow to blue and purple. The fruit are berries which contain many seeds. These warm-climate plants have a wide range of requirements; most prefer rich, well-drained soil. They are commonly grown from seed or soft-tip cuttings.

Solanum aviculare
KANGAROO APPLE, PORO PORO

Indigenous to Australia and New Zealand, this evergreen shrub is fast growing but short lived. Reaching 9–12 ft (3–4 m) tall, its single upright stem has spreading branches forming a wide crown. The large, dark green to bluish green leaves are oval to lance shaped, often with deeply lobed edges. In spring and summer the star-shaped purple flowers, 1½ in (3 cm) across, appear in large clusters at branch tips. The fruit, oval berries about 1 in

Solanum aviculare

(2 cm) long, hang from thin stalks and ripen from green to yellow to red. The plants grow well in full sun to semi-shade and need a position that is sheltered from the wind. ZONE 9.

Solanum mammosum
NIPPLE FRUIT, COW'S UDDER PLANT

A tropical plant indigenous to lowlands of Central America, this perennial herb or soft-wooded subshrub grows to about 4 ft (1.2 m) with angular, spiny stems and large hairy leaves. The smallish white flowers are undistinguished, but the yellow or orange fruit are striking—about 2 in (5 cm) long, sometimes waisted, bloated structures resembling a cow's udder with several nipples at the calyx end. Branches bearing the fruit are often cut for indoor use, with the leaves removed; they last for several weeks. The plants need full sun with shelter from the wind. ZONE 11.

Sophora tetraptera

Solanum rantonnei

Sophora japonica

Solanum rantonnei

Sophora japonica

Solanum rantonnei
PARAGUAY NIGHTSHADE

Indigenous to Paraguay and Argentina, this evergreen rounded shrub, once known as *Lycianthes rantonnei*, is grown for its clusters of very attractive violet-blue flowers, borne through spring and summer. These have a yellow eye and open out flat; each is 1 in (2 cm) across. The shrub is 6 ft (2 m) tall and wide, with a vigorous branching woody stem. The oval leaves are bright green and smooth, up to 4 in (10 cm) long, and the fruit are heart-shaped berries about 1 in (2 cm) long. It grows best in full sun to semi-shade. ZONE 9.

SOPHORA
Leguminosae

This genus of some 50 species of deciduous or semi-evergreen trees and shrubs is widespread in the temperate regions of the northern hemisphere, with a few species from South America and New Zealand. Most are open many-branched trees that grow to about 30 ft (10 m) high and wide. They generally flower in spring and produce pendulous racemes of pea flowers. Most species have cream or lavender blooms, the brightest being the yellow of the kowhai (*S. tetraptera*). These are followed in summer by bean-like pods with noticeable constrictions between each seed. Sophoras are generally adaptable plants that thrive under a wide range of conditions. They can be grown in small groves, used as shade trees or lawn specimens. Most prefer moist, well-drained soil in sun or partial shade. Propagate from seed, or semi-ripe or hardwood cuttings. In Australia and New Zealand caterpillars of the Kowhai moth can defoliate plants in summer.

Sophora japonica
PAGODA TREE

Despite its name, this deciduous tree originates in central China. It grows to around 40 ft (13 m) high. The light green pinnate leaves are 8 in (20 cm) long, and the cream, or occasionally pale pink, flowers are borne in long panicles. 'Pendula' is often grafted on to 8 ft (2.5 m) standards to produce a small weeping tree. ZONE 4.

Sophora microphylla
WEEPING KOWHAI

This species occurs naturally in New Zealand and Chile. It is a fully to partly deciduous tree, growing 12–18 ft (4–6 m) tall. Weeping, interlocking, wiry branches form a wide, rounded crown. The leaves, made up of many tiny dark green oval leaflets, have a fern-like appearance; many of them are shed in late winter before the flowers appear. The flowers, lemon to deep orange but usually deep yellow and up to 1½ in (3 cm) long, are borne in dense clusters from late winter to early summer. The fruit is a pod about 6 in (15 cm) long. Propagate *S. microphylla* from soft tip cuttings to obtain a plant with a good shape and preferred flower colour. Var. *longicarinata* has lemon flowers and smaller, more numerous leaflets. 'Golden Shower' forms a symmetrical tree with strongly weeping outer branches and golden yellow flowers. ZONE 7.

Sophora tetraptera
KOWHAI

This free-flowering usually evergreen small tree from the North Island is New Zealand's national flower. It may grow to 30 ft (10 m) tall but is usually smaller. Mature specimens develop a semi-pendulous habit with the branches somewhat interlocked. The leaves consist of 20 to 30 pairs of small, grey-green leaflets. The abundant spring pea-flowers are about 1½ in (3 cm) long; pale to golden yellow, they are borne in showy pendulous clusters. The fruit is a narrow pod which ripens to dark grey. ZONE 8.

SORBARIA
Rosaceae

The shrubs of this small genus originate in cool to cold mountain regions of Asia. All are deciduous and have bright green pinnate leaves with serrated leaflets. The small white flowers, usually in large terminal panicles, have a cup-shaped calyx, 5 reflexed petals and many prominent stamens. The fruit are berries. Most species sucker freely; they thrive in full sun, in rich, moist soils, and prefer cool climates. They can be pruned in winter to restrict size and some older canes removed if necessary. Propagation is from seed, root cuttings, softwood cuttings or suckers.

Sorbaria arborea
FALSE SPIRAEA

This large spreading shrub grows to 18 ft (6 m) tall, with cany stems and compound leaves consisting of up to 17 long, narrow leaflets. The flowers are held in upright fluffy panicles 12 in (30 cm) long. The young growth is often covered in masses of hair. ZONE 4.

SORBUS
Rosaceae
ROWAN, SERVICE TREE, WHITEBALM

This genus is made up of deciduous trees and shrubs from cool-climate regions of the northern hemisphere, grown for their foliage, timber and decorative fruit. Most species have pinnate leaves and terminal clusters of small creamy white flowers in spring. The flowers, which are often rather unpleasantly scented, are followed by showy berries. Some species have attractive autumn foliage but most show little autumn coloration. Rowans are easily grown in any well-drained soil and are most at home in areas with distinct winters. The species may be raised from stratified seed; selected forms are usually grafted.

Sorbus aria
WHITEBEAM

This European species is a 15 ft (5 m) high tree with very coarsely toothed, simple leaves, 4 in (10 cm) long, that have white felting on the undersides. They develop orange and yellow autumn tones. The ½ in (1 cm) berries are red. This species is very tough, tolerating chalky soils, salt winds and air pollution. There are several cultivars including 'Aurea', light yellowish green leaves; 'Chrysophylla', yellow leaves; 'Lutescens', young foliage is covered with fine silvery hairs; and 'Majestica', larger leaves and berries than the species. ZONE 2.

Sorbus aucuparia
MOUNTAIN ASH, ROWAN

The most commonly grown species, the mountain ash grows to about 18 ft (6 m) high in gardens, much taller in its native European forests. The pinnate leaves, made up of 11 to 15 small, toothed leaflets, turn rich gold in autumn. The white spring flowers are followed by bright orange berries. There are several cultivars including 'Asplenifolia', very finely cut leaves; 'Edulis', a large-berried form whose fruit is used for jams and preserves; 'Pendula', wide-spreading growth with a weeping habit; and 'Xanthocarpa', yellow berries. ZONE 2.

Sorbus chaemaemespilus

This shrub from central Europe grows to about 10 ft (3 m). Its finely toothed, simple, leathery leaves are 3 in (7 cm) long, deep green above and yellow-green beneath. The young growth tends to be hairy and the clusters of pink flowers are followed by tightly packed bunches of small, bright red fruit. ZONE 5.

Sorbus commixta
JAPANESE ROWAN, KOREAN ROWAN

This erect tree grows to 15–25 ft (5–8 m) or more. It is grown for its handsome pinnate leaves, dark green and shiny above, grey-green beneath (in autumn they turn brilliant shades of orange and red) and for the massed clusters of scarlet berries which are borne in summer. An unusual feature is that the winter buds are very sticky. The Japanese rowan does best in areas with cool to cold winters. It needs a sunny position, well-drained, fertile soil and plenty of water in warmer months. ZONE 4.

Sorbus domestica
SERVICE TREE

This 30 ft (10 m) high, spreading tree, indigenous to southern and eastern Europe and northern Africa, has deeply fissured bark. The leaves are made up of 13 to 21 toothed leaflets. The 1 in (2 cm) long fruit, brownish green with a rosy tint, is somewhat pear shaped and edible when fully ripe. ZONE 3.

Sorbus aucuparia (below)

Sorbus commixta (below)

Sorbus commixta (below)

Sorbus domestica (below)

Sorbus aucuparia (below)

Spartium junceum

Sorbus pohuashanensis 'Pagoda Red'

Sparrmania africana 'Flore Plena'

Sorbus megalocarpa

Sorbus hupehensis

Stems and leaves are covered with soft hairs. The large, soft leaves have a toothed edge and may be cut into lobes. Attractive flowers on long stalks are arranged in clusters near the shoot tips or arise from the leaf axils. The fruit is a spiny capsule. Plants need a sunny position, sheltered from wind and frost, and well-drained soil enriched with organic matter. Keep the soil moist while the plant is making active growth. These plants are for warm climates but are often grown in greenhouses in cooler areas. Propagation is from softwood cuttings.

Sparrmania africana
AFRICAN HEMP, WILD HOLLYHOCK

This fast-growing shrub or small tree reaches 20 ft (7 m). It bears clusters of striking white flowers with prominent purple and gold stamens. Flowering peaks in winter to early spring but the species flowers sporadically throughout most of the year. The large leaves may be oval to heart shaped with a pointed tip, or have several finger-like lobes. The stem is erect and woody with many spreading branches. The fruit is rounded. 'Flore Plena' has double flowers. ZONE 10.

SPARTIUM
Fabaceae
SPANISH BROOM

This genus includes just one species of evergreen shrub which is indigenous to the Mediterranean region but has naturalized in a few areas with a similar climate. A yellow dye is derived from the flowers. It is an adaptable plant but thrives in well-drained soils enriched with a little organic matter. Full sun is best. This shrub is for warm to coolish climates. Pruning after flowering will maintain a compact well-shaped bush. The Spanish broom is propagated from seed or soft-tip cuttings.

Spartium junceum

The shiny green leafless twigs give the Spanish broom a rush-like appearance and the name *junceum* is derived from the Latin word for 'rush'. The species bears masses of large, golden yellow, fragrant pea-flowers carried in loose spikes 10–12 in (25–30 cm) long at the shoot tips. It flowers profusely through spring into early summer. The leaves are bluish green, lance shaped to linear and up to 1 in (2 cm) long; they are only seen on the new growth, falling by mid-summer. The Spanish broom makes a bushy shrub 6–10 ft (2–3 m) tall and on older specimens the stems arch downwards. The fruit is a flat pod, silvery maturing to brown. ZONE 6.

Sorbus hupehensis
CHINESE ROWAN

Indigenous to Hubei province in central China, this tall, vigorous tree has blue-green pinnate leaves made up of 9 to 17 leaflets. The foliage develops orange, red and purple autumn tones. Long-lasting berries are white, tinted pink, and are carried on red stems. ZONE 5.

Sorbus 'Joseph Rock'

This vigorous upright tree of unknown east Asian origin grows to about 18 ft (6 m) high. Its leaves are made up of 15 to 21 sharply toothed leaflets that develop rich red, orange and purple tones in autumn. It produces large clusters of bright yellow berries that last well. ZONE 4.

Sorbus megalocarpa

Rare in cultivation but very striking, this tree grows to about 15 ft (5 m) in its natural environment in China, with large, bright green, obovate, double-toothed leaves and creamy white woolly flower heads borne at the ends of branches in late winter before the leaves appear. The flowers have a rather pungent smell. The brown egg-shaped fruit are about 1 in (2 cm) long, which is unusually large for the genus. ZONE 4.

Sorbus pohuashanensis

Indigenous to mountainous regions of northern China where it reaches 30 ft (10 m) tall, this deciduous tree is closely related to the European rowan (*S. aucuparia*). The pinnate leaves are up to 8 in (20 cm) long, green above but hairy and blue-green beneath; young shoots and flower buds are also covered in hair. The flat-topped clusters of flowers are held above the foliage, as are the shiny red fruit. 'Pagoda Red' has been selected for its fine display of fruit. ZONE 4.

SPARRMANIA
Tiliaceae

This small genus of evergreen trees and shrubs is indigenous to tropical and temperate southern Africa.

SPATHODEA
Bignoniaceae

This genus contains 2 or 3 species of evergreen trees which occur naturally in tropical and subtropical Africa. One species is widely planted as a street tree and ornamental all over the tropics. The large, bell-shaped, orange or scarlet flowers are produced in dense, terminal clusters. The large pinnate leaves are deep green. The fruit is an oblong capsule that splits open when ripe to release the seeds. These are trees for warm, frost-free areas. They prefer rich, well-drained soil, shelter from wind and a sunny position. Propagation is usually from seed which can be variable.

Spathodea campanulata
AFRICAN TULIP TREE, FOUNTAIN TREE

This spectacular, fast-growing evergreen tree from tropical east Africa grows to about 50 ft (15 m). The large, flat clusters of velvety, bronze-green buds and big, bell-shaped, orange-red flowers with yellow frilly edges are borne through spring and summer. The nectar-rich flowers attract bats which are thought to be their pollinating agent. The pinnate leaves are bronze when young, maturing to deep glossy green. The fruit are 8 in (20 cm) long. The common name fountain tree comes from the way the buds are full of moisture which squirts out when they are squeezed. ZONE 11.

SPIRAEA
Rosaceae

This genus consists of deciduous shrubs primarily from China, Japan and North America, which are valued for their spring and summer flower display and autumn foliage colour. Spiraeas form clumps of wiry stems that shoot up from the base. The plants are densely covered with narrow, toothed leaves. They are in the rose family, and under a magnifying glass the flowers do resemble tiny roses, but they are so small that the individual flower is lost among the mass of blooms carried on each flower cluster. Spiraeas are adaptable plants that thrive under most garden conditions in temperate climates, though they prefer a warm summer. They thrive in moist, well-drained soil and a position sheltered from the hottest sun, especially in warm summer areas where the foliage may burn. They are propagated from cuttings. Most should be pruned after flowering.

Spiraea cantoniensis
MAY, REEVES' SPIRAEA

This species is very showy when in flower in spring, with rounded 2 in (5 cm) clusters of small white 5-petalled flowers densely clothing the reddish, gracefully arching branches. The narrow leaves are dark green above and blue-green below. This 3–6 ft (1–2 m) shrub originated in China. It can be used for hedging and is the best spiraea for warmer temperate regions. The double-flowered form is the most popular in gardens. ZONE 5.

Spiraea douglasii
WESTERN SPIRAEA

Occurring naturally from northern California to Alaska, this upright shrub grows to about 6 ft (2 m) tall and almost as wide. The oblong leaves are dark green above, velvety white beneath. The rose-pink cylindrical flower clusters, about 8 in (20 cm) long, are borne at the ends of branches in summer. Prune (if necessary) in early spring, as this species flowers on new season's wood. ZONE 4.

Spiraea japonica

This species from Japan and China grows to 5 ft (1.5 m), with many upright stems forming a dense clump. It blooms in summer with clusters of tiny pink flowers. It has many varieties and cultivars, like var. *fortunei*, up to 6 ft (2 m) with large flower heads; 'Little Princess', to 3 ft (1 m); 'Anthony Waterer', pale and deep pink flowers, some branches with white or cream leaves; and 'Nana', a dwarf cultivar with pink flowers. ZONE 4.

Spiraea japonica 'Anthony Waterer'

Spiraea japonica 'Nana'

Spathodea campanulata (below)

Spathodea campanulata (below)

Spiraea cantoniensis (below)

Spiraea nipponica
From Japan, this species reaches 6 ft (2 m) high and wide. Its rounded leaves are finely serrated and its early summer flowers are pure white, in neat, round heads crowded along the branches. 'Snowmound' is a cultivar with white flowers. ZONE 5.

Spiraea prunifolia
BRIDAL WREATH SPIRAEA

This shrub from China, long grown in Japan, grows to 6 ft (2 m) tall. The 5-petalled, snowy white flowers with greenish centres are arranged in small clusters of 3 to 6 all along its pendulous branches in early spring before the oval leaves appear. These turn red in autumn. The double 'Plena' is the only form commonly grown. ZONE 4.

Spiraea prunifolia 'Plena'

Stachyurus praecox

Spiraea thunbergii
An early flowering species, this dense, arching shrub is indigenous to China but long cultivated in Japan. It grows to 5 ft (1.5 m) tall and about 3 ft (1 m) wide. The small white 5-petalled blossoms on threadlike stalks appear all along its slender, wiry branches in early spring. The lance-like, finely serrated leaves are light green; they may stay on the plant all year in mild climates, while in cooler areas they often turn shades of pink and orange before falling. ZONE 4.

STACHYURUS
Stachyuraceae

This genus includes some 10 species of deciduous shrubs and trees from the Himalaya and East Asia. Although reminiscent of the witch hazels and *Corylopsis*, they belong in a different family. They are generally not spectacular plants, though one species, *S. praecox*, is fairly widely grown. In common with others in the genus, it blooms in late winter or early spring before or just as the leaves are developing. It produces small cream to pale yellow flowers in drooping racemes at every leaf bud and has broadly lance-shaped leaves. The only other species likely to be encountered is *S. chinensis*, which is very similar to *S. praecox* but flowers about 2 weeks later. The plants prefer a humus-rich, well-drained, acidic soil in sun or light shade and are usually propagated from seed or semi-ripe cuttings.

Stachyurus praecox
A 7 ft (2 m) high and wide shrub indigenous to Japan, this species is noted for its early flowering habit. Its gracefully drooping, 3 in (8 cm) long racemes of buds appear on the bare branches in autumn, opening as small pale yellow flowers in late winter or early spring. The leaves that follow are up to 6 in (15 cm) long and are carried on somewhat tiered, reddish brown stems. ZONE 5.

STENOCARPUS
Proteaceae

These evergreen trees belonging to the protea family and indigenous to Australia and New Caledonia, bear striking flowers and foliage. *S. sinuatus* is the main species cultivated in warm to hot climates. It prefers full sun and deep, well-drained soil enriched with organic matter, and needs plenty of water over summer. It is propagated from seed or by grafting.

Stenocarpus sinuatus
FIREWHEEL TREE

A handsome but slow-growing tree endemic to rainforests of Australia's warm east coast, the firewheel tree can reach 30–65 ft (10–20 m); it has an upright thick trunk with dark brown bark topped by a dense crown of foliage. Leaves are shiny and dark green, lance shaped to oblong or deeply lobed, and up to 12 in (30 cm) long. The interesting skittle-shaped buds, opening to contorted flowers, are often partly concealed by the foliage; they are orange to red, and arranged in a cluster like spokes on a wheel. This 'firewheel' is about 3 in (7 cm) across. Trees do not begin to produce flowers until they are 10 to 12 years old, and they are generally more prolific after a hot dry summer. The woody, boat-shaped fruit are 2–4 in (5–10 cm) long. ZONE 10.

STEPHANANDRA
Rosaceae

This genus is made up of 4 species of deciduous shrubs related to *Spiraea*. From the East Asian region, they tolerate low temperatures. The toothed and lobed mid-green leaves, which turn orange-gold in autumn are very ornamental, as are the sepia-tinted bare stems in winter. Tiny star-shaped white or greenish flowers appear in summer, in soft panicles; each has many stamens. *Stephanandra* species grow in sun or semi-shade, preferring rich, moist, loamy soil, and can be pruned to shape in winter if necessary. Propagate from hardwood or softwood cuttings, or by division in autumn.

Stenocarpus sinuatus (below)

Stewartia pseudocamellia

Stephanandra tanakae

Stewartia pseudocamellia

Stephanandra incisa

Stephanandra incisa
LACE SHRUB

Occurring naturally in Japan and Korea, this shrub grows to about 6 ft (2 m) tall with a similar spread. The lace shrub has graceful arching branches and the diamond-shaped leaves are lobed and deeply incised. The leaves turn a vivid orange and gold colour in autumn. The tiny greenish white flowers appear in summer. This shrub tolerates neglect. 'Crispa' is a dwarf-growing cultivar with slightly curled leaves. ZONE 4.

Stephanandra tanakae

Valued for its decorative, arching habit and attractive leaves, this shrub from Japan grows to about 5 ft (1.5 m) tall and has a similar spread. The plant's leaves are mid-green and are 2–4 in (5–10 cm) long and have shallow, toothed lobes with long points. The new foliage is pinkish brown, and in autumn the leaves turn gold and orange. The tiny white starry flowers are borne through summer. ZONE 4.

STEWARTIA
Theaceae

This East Asian and North American genus—sometimes spelt *Stuartia*—of deciduous small trees is closely allied to the camellias. The flowers are usually white with prominent golden anthers, about 3 in (8 cm) across, and resemble single camellia blooms. The leaves are elliptical, 2–5 in (4–13 cm) long, and often develop bright orange and red autumn tones. Stewartias grow best in moist, humus-rich, well-drained, slightly acidic soil in sun or partial shade. They can be propagated from seed or from semi-ripe cuttings.

Stewartia malacodendron
MALLOW TREE

This species is indigenous to southeastern USA and is usually seen as a 10 ft (3 m) high and wide shrub, though it is capable of reaching 30 ft (10 m). It blooms from early summer and its flowers sometimes have purplish stamens. The autumn foliage is reddish purple. The mallow tree needs warm summers to flower well. ZONE 7.

Stewartia pseudocamellia
FALSE CAMELLIA

Indigenous to Japan (not Hokkaido) and Korea, this species can grow to 30 ft (10 m) high in the wild, but is more commonly about 18 ft (6 m) in cultivation. It blooms from late spring to early summer and the white flowers are followed by small, spherical, nut-like seed capsules that are a prominent feature from mid-summer. In addition to the flowers it has attractive peeling bark and yellow, orange and red autumn foliage. ZONE 6.

Stewartia sinensis

A 20 ft (7 m) tree indigenous to China, this species blooms in late spring and summer with small flowers about 2 in (5 cm) across. The colour of the flaking bark is a warm reddish brown to purple and the autumn foliage is crimson. ZONE 6.

Strelitzia reginae

Streptosolen jamesonii

Strelitzia nicolai

Styrax japonica

Styrax japonica

STRELITZIA
Strelitziaceae

Strelitzias have most exotic flowers that resemble the head of a bird. Each bloom consists of several spiky flowers arising from a boat-like bract. Leaves are large and dramatic. Strelitzias form large clumps of evergreen banana-like foliage. They occur naturally in southern Africa but are grown in warm climates around the world; in cool areas they are enjoyed as greenhouse specimens. The fruit is a capsule. They need full sun or part shade, and prefer well-drained soil enriched with organic matter and dryish conditions in cooler months. You can produce new plants by dividing a clump, but this is hard work as the clump and roots are very dense.

Strelitzia nicolai
WILD BANANA, BLUE STRELITZIA

Banana-like leaves characterize this tree-sized species. Erect woody palm-like stems reach a height of 20 ft (7 m) and the clump spreads over 12 ft (4 m). This species has large greyish leaves over 5 ft (1.5 m) long, on long stalks. Flowers appear in summer near the top of the plant from the leaf axils. These rather striking flowers are greenish blue and white, and open a few at a time from a reddish brown bract. ZONE 10.

Strelitzia reginae
BIRD-OF-PARADISE FLOWER, CRANE FLOWER, STRELITZIA

This shrub-sized species is the most common. Its blooms really do look like a crane's crested head, bright orange and sky blue sitting in a pointed green bract edged with red; the main flowering season is spring to summer. This species grows to 5 ft (1.5 m) high and spreads over 6–9 ft (2–3 m), forming an erect clump of leaves and smooth flower stalks arising from underground stems. Leaves are greyish green and spoon like with an oblong to lance-shaped blade on a long stalk. Var. *juncea*, sometimes called *S. juncea*, has similar flowers but the leaves have virtually no blade, giving the plants a rush-like appearance. ZONE 10.

STREPTOSOLEN
Solanaceae
MARMALADE BUSH

This genus consists of only one shrub species, occurring in parts of the northern Andes. The marmalade bush is grown outdoors in warm to hot climates, as a greenhouse plant in cooler areas; it will not tolerate frost. In the garden, it does best in full sun with shelter from strong winds. A light well-drained soil is ideal, preferably enriched with organic matter, and adequate moisture is needed during warmer months. Light pruning after flowering will keep it compact. It is propagated from soft-tip or semi-hardwood cuttings.

Streptosolen jamesonii

This fast-growing evergreen shrub reaches 6 ft (2 m) high, with long flexible stems that arch slightly under the weight of the flower heads. Flowers are typically bright orange, hence its common name marmalade bush, but there is a yellow-flowered form. Flowering peaks in spring to summer but continues for much of the year. Individual flowers are tubular on a thin stalk and are strangely twisted. They form large dense clusters at the branch tips. Leaves are neat, oval and shiny dark green above, paler on the undersides. Both foliage and flowers bear fine hairs. The fruit is a small capsule. ZONE 9.

STYRAX
Styracaceae
SNOWBELL

These small deciduous and evergreen trees occur naturally over a wide area of the Americas and eastern Asia, with one species native to Europe. Several cool-temperate deciduous species are cultivated for their neat growth-habit and attractive spring display of slightly drooping sprays of small, bell-shaped, white flowers. They prefer cool, moist, well-drained soil and cool, moist summer climates. Usually raised from stratified seed, they may also be grown from hardwood or semi-ripe cuttings.

Styrax japonica
JAPANESE SNOWBELL, JAPANESE SNOWDROP TREE

This species is a native of Japan, Korea and China. It grows to around 25 ft (8 m) high and flowers from mid-spring. Its branches, which are clothed with rather narrow, 3 in (8 cm) long, deep green, shiny leaves, tend to be held horizontally which creates a somewhat tiered effect. This species does best shaded from the hottest sun. ZONE 7.

Styrax obassia

Indigenous to Japan, Korea and north-eastern China, this species grows to 30 ft (10 m) high. Its flowers are not as pendulous as those of other species, but they are slightly fragrant. The large deep green, paddle-shaped leaves are up to 8 in (20 cm) long and covered in whitish down on the undersides. It is worth growing for the foliage alone. ZONE 6.

SUTHERLANDIA
Fabaceae

This small African genus is made up of about 6 species of small shrubs, most coming from southern Africa. The pinnate leaves are soft grey-green and slightly to very hairy. The pea flowers are borne in small clusters. With regular water, the plants grow quickly and flower in the same year. Frost-hardy and wind-resistant, they prefer full sun and are not fussy about soil—a rockery suits them well. They tend to get straggly with age and should be cut back each year after flowering. They are propagated from seed sown in spring.

Sutherlandia frutescens
CANCER BUSH

This soft-wooded shrub from drier parts of southern Africa grows to 5 ft (1.5 m) tall and spreads about as wide, with soft, grey-green foliage. The compound leaves are divided into small oval leaflets which give the plant a graceful appearance. Showy, drooping, coral-red pea flowers are borne from late winter to summer, and these are followed by inflated pale green seed pods which often appear simultaneously with the flowers thus creating a very decorative effect. Despite the common name, there is no proof this plant can cure cancer. ZONE 8.

SWIETENIA
Meliaceae
MAHOGANY

This small genus consists of evergreen or semi-deciduous trees from the tropical forests of Central America and the West Indies, prized as the source of one of the world's most precious timbers for fine furniture. The trees grow tall and straight, and the timber is dense and finely grained; it is a rich reddish brown when seasoned. The large pinnate leaves consist of smooth, shiny leaflets, and the small, insignificant flowers are greenish yellow. The fruit which follows is a large woody capsule containing winged seeds which are used for propagation. Mahoganies are widely grown for shade in frost-free areas. They need deep, fertile soil and high rainfall. In subtropical areas with distinct seasons the leaves often turn golden in autumn and most are shed. 'Mahogani' is their local name in the West Indies.

Swietenia macrophylla
HONDURAS MAHOGANY

First introduced to the furniture-makers of Europe in the 1600s, these handsome trees supply one of the world's most coveted timbers. In their native forests they grow, straight-trunked, to 165 ft (50 m) high, but in cultivation as shade or street trees they are usually smaller. The compound leaves are 14 in (35 cm) long, and the brown woody fruit are about 6 in (15 cm) long. ZONE 10.

Swietenia mahagoni
WEST INDIES MAHOGANY

While still a majestic tree, this species is overall smaller than *S. macrophylla*; it grows only to 75 ft (23 m), the pinnate leaves are 4–8 in (10–20 cm) long, and the fruit 5 in (12 cm) long. It is widely grown as a shade and street tree in the tropics. ZONE 11.

SYAGRUS
Arecaceae

The 30 or so palms in this genus are indigenous to drier parts of tropical and subtropical South America. They have single, smooth, horizontally ridged trunks crowned with a mass of feathery, pinnate leaves arising from a fibrous sheath. Leaf stalks are mostly smooth but sometimes edged with teeth. Separate male and female flowers are borne in a large panicle which bursts from a huge, spindle-shaped enclosing bract, emerging from among the leaves. The fruit are fleshy fibrous drupes. Several species are a commercial source of palm oil. They are usually propagated from seed.

Syagrus romanzoffiana
COCOS PALM, QUEEN PALM

This species was formerly called *Arecastrum romanzoffianum* and *Cocos plumosa*. It occurs naturally in coastal areas of Brazil and is an excellent specimen tree, especially when planted in groups. It is also a source of edible palm cabbage. The cocos palm adapts to a range of climates from hot to warm and enjoys coastal locations. In cooler climates it is grown as a house plant. Fast growing, it has a slender, upright, smooth grey trunk to 50 ft (15 m) tall, topped with a crown of arching plume-like leaves. Each leaf is green, up to 15 ft (5 m) long, with long leaflets radiating out from the central stalk on several planes. Dead leaves are usually retained and can make the tree look untidy. Flowers are small and inconspicuous. The fruit, fat orange-red fleshy berries up to 1 in (2 cm) long, are edible and may attract bats and insects. This palm transplants very easily and is a favourite subject for 'instant' landscaping. ZONE 10.

SYMPHORICARPOS
Caprifoliaceae

This genus is made up of 15 deciduous shrubs allied to *Lonicera* from North America, and one rare and obscure species from China. They have elliptical to nearly round

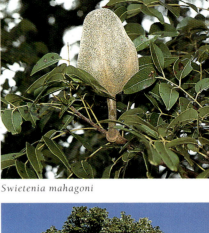
Swietenia mahagoni

Swietenia mahagoni

Sutherlandia frutescens

Styrax obassia

Sutherlandia frutescens

Syringa meyeri 'Palabin' as a standard

Symphoricarpos orbiculatus

Syncarpia glomulifera

Syringa meyeri 'Palabin'

Syncarpia glomulifera

leaves and very small, bell-shaped, pink or white flowers in spring. They are primarily grown for their large crops of distinctive berries that stand out clearly in winter when the branches are bare. They are easily grown in any moist, well-drained soil in sun or shade and are usually propagated from open-ground winter hardwood cuttings. Being resistant to shade, poor soil and pollution, they are very suitable for city gardens.

Symphoricarpos albus
SNOWBERRY

Found east of the Rocky Mountains from Colorado to Quebec, this wiry-stemmed, suckering shrub grows to 6 ft (2 m) high and wide. Its small spring flowers are followed by clusters of ½ in (1 cm), stark white berries that persist well after the leaves have fallen. An otherwise undistinguished shrub, its pure white berries are striking. Any pruning or thinning should be left until the berries have fallen. ZONE 4.

Symphoricarpos orbiculatus
INDIAN CURRANT

This tough, adaptable shrub from the USA and Mexico grows to about 6 ft (2 m) high and 10 ft (3 m) wide. It is very dense and twiggy, with oval leaves around 1½ in (3 cm) long. The fruit is small, under ¼ in (10 mm) in diameter, but abundant and a conspicuous bright pink. The berries last long after the leaves have fallen. A hot summer will yield a heavier crop of berries. ZONE 4.

SYNCARPIA
Myrtaceae
TURPENTINE

This genus consists of 2 species of tall evergreen trees indigenous to coastal forests of eastern Australia. Not dissimilar to the (related) eucalypts, they grow tall and straight, with a domed crown atop a trunk of thick, fibrous bark. The trees are exploited in Australia for their timber. The dense, straight hardwood has a high silica content which makes it exceptionally resistant to marine borers; *S. hillii*, endemic to Queensland's Fraser Island, was used last century for sidings in the construction of the Suez Canal and for wharves worldwide. Turpentines need a frost-free climate, moist, well-drained soil and reliable rainfall. Propagation is from seed.

Syncarpia glomulifera
RED TURPENTINE

Valued as a shade tree as well as for its durable reddish timber, this species is cultivated in subtropical USA and Africa as well as Australia. In the wild it grows to 200 ft (60 m) tall, its straight trunk clothed in red-brown, deeply fissured bark; the leaves, mid-green with paler, hairy undersides, are aromatic when crushed. Small cream flowers with long stamens are fused into fluffy globular flower heads which are borne through spring and summer, and the woody fruit are also fused into a spiky ball shape. ZONE 9.

SYRINGA
Oleaceae
LILAC

Lilacs are prized for their upright to arching panicles of small, highly fragrant spring flowers, which are massed in loose heads. They appear from mid-spring and range in colour from white and pale yellow to all shades of pink, mauve and purple. Most of the common garden hybrids were raised in France in the late 1800s to early 1900s, though new forms appear from time to time; not all cultivars are fragrant. The genus contains about 25 to 30 species, all deciduous shrubs, from Europe and north-eastern Asia. Most reach about 8 ft (2.5 m) high and 6 ft (2 m) wide, with opposite leaves. The foliage sometimes colours well in autumn. Lilacs prefer moist, humus-rich, well-drained soil in sun or light shade. They do best where the winters are cold because they require at least a few frosts in order to flower well. Species may be raised from seed or cuttings. Hybrids will sometimes strike from hardwood or semi-ripe cuttings, but most are grafted. Established plants produce suckers that can be used for propagation. Any other pruning is best done immediately after flowering.

Syringa × *hyacinthiflora*

This is a French hybrid between *S. oblata* and *S. vulgaris*. There are several cultivars and they closely resemble the common *S. vulgaris* cultivars in appearance but are generally not as fragrant. 'Blue Hyacinth' has rounded lavender-blue flower heads; 'Buffon', pale lavender-pink; 'Clarke's Giant', mauve to lavender-blue; and 'Esther Staley', bright deep pink. ZONE 6.

Syringa meyeri
LILAC

From China, this small spreading shrub grows to about 3 ft (1 m) tall and wide. The leaves are elliptical and the deep purplish mauve flowers appear in spring in dense panicles. 'Palabin' is a slow-growing dwarf cultivar. ZONE 4.

Syringa patula
KOREAN LILAC

This neat shrub grows to 10 ft (3 m), with a roundly spreading crown. Its branches are tinged purple, and the leaves are velvety green and slightly hairy with paler undersides. The flowers, mauve outside and white inside, appear in small terminal panicles in late spring. 'Miss Kim' has bright lavender-pink flowers which are profuse and fragrant, the same size as the species, and appear at about the same time. It grows to about 4–5 ft (1.2–1.5 m) high and wide. ZONE 4.

Syringa reflexa
A native of Hubei province in central China, this species grows to 12 ft (4 m) high and its 8 in (20 cm) pendulous panicles of deep pink flowers are borne in abundance from late spring. The pointed elliptical leaves are up to 8 in (20 cm) long. This beautiful species is just different enough from the common hybrids to attract attention. It is the parent of a number of hybrids raised in Canada and collectively known as S. × prestoniae. ZONE 3.

Syringa reticulata
This Japanese lilac has comparatively small flowers but they produce a wonderful spring display of creamy white clusters at the ends of the branches. Sweetly fragrant, they stand out boldly against the dark green foliage, and also make excellent cut flowers. S. reticulata grows to 27 ft (9 m) and forms a squat, wide-crowned tree. Remove spent flowers regularly to prolong the display. ZONE 3.

Syringa vulgaris
This is the species from which most of the garden cultivars were derived. It is indigenous to Turkey and south-eastern Europe and grows to around 12 ft (4 m) high, with pointed, oval or heart-shaped leaves up to 3½ in (9 cm) long and panicles of fragrant white to pale mauve flowers. The cultivar 'Aurea' has yellowish green leaves and darker flowers. Other cultivars include 'Charles Joly', with purplish pink, very fragrant flowers and strongly upright growth; 'Edith Cavell', white; 'Katherine Havemeyer', lavender-blue, very fragrant, semi-double; 'Maréchal Foch', purplish pink; 'Mme F. Morel', also purplish pink; 'President Lincoln', light blue; 'Primrose', pale yellow flowers and compact growth-habit; and 'Souvenir d'Alice Harding', small heads of white flowers in summer. ZONE 2.

SYZYGIUM
Myrtaceae
LILLYPILLY, BRUSH CHERRY

These evergreen trees and shrubs, at one time included in the genus *Eugenia*, originated in tropical and subtropical rainforests of Southeast Asia, Australia and Africa. They are grown for their attractive foliage, flowers and berries. The edible berries—white, pink, magenta or purple—ripen in late summer to autumn. Plants have a lush dense canopy of shiny green leaves; new growth in spring is often a contrasting red, pink or copper. The spring and summer flowers are mostly small with protruding white to mauve or crimson stamens giving a fluffy appearance. The plants prefer full sun to semi-shade, and deep, moist, well-drained soil enriched with organic matter, and do best in warm climates with only occasional light frosts. Prune to shape if necessary; propagate from fresh seed or semi-hardwood cuttings.

Syringa patula 'Miss Kim'

Syringa vulgaris

Syringa vulgaris 'Mme F. Morel'

Syringa reticulata

Syzygium luehmannii

Syzygium jambos

Syzygium luehmannii

Syzygium paniculatum

Syzygium jambos
ROSE APPLE

Indigenous to the Malay Archipelago, this tree reaches a height of 30–40 ft (10–12 m), with a rounded crown. The leaves are dark green and glossy, and the fluffy greenish white flowers are borne in large rounded clusters. The edible, creamy pink to yellow fragrant fruit have a decided taste of rosewater. ZONE 10.

Syzygium luehmannii
SMALL-LEAFED LILLYPILLY, RIBERRY

Formerly called *Eugenia luehmannii*, this is a large tree with a buttressed trunk in the wild in eastern Australian rainforests, but when cultivated it usually reaches only 20 ft (7 m) or so with spreading branches low to the ground and a domed crown. An attractive shade and specimen tree for warm to hot climates, it can also be grown as a formal hedge. Leaves are very shiny, oval to lance shaped with a prominent midrib, and 1½–2½ in (3–6 cm) long. New growth is pink to red. The creamy white summer flowers in small clusters are followed by coral red pear-shaped fruit, ½ in (1 cm) long. ZONE 10.

Syzygium paniculatum
MAGENTA BRUSH CHERRY

This small to medium tree (syn. *Eugenia paniculata*) can grow up to 50–60 ft (15–18 m) tall with an irregular rounded and densely foliaged crown. It is often confused with the similar but less ornamental *S. australe*. Leaves are shiny green, variable in shape from oval to rounded, coppery brown when young, and held on reddish stalks. Fragrant flowers are creamy white, each ½ in (1 cm) across; they are held in dense clusters, mainly in late spring. The large, decorative fruit is rose-purple, oval to rounded and up to 1 in (2 cm) long; it appears in late summer and autumn. This lilly-pilly suits coastal gardens. ZONE 10.

Syzygium wilsonii
POWDERPUFF LILLYPILLY

This oval-crowned shrub grows to about 6 ft (2 m) tall and wide; in moist, shady spots it scrambles to a greater height and width. Leaves vary from lance shaped to more rounded; each is 4–6 in (10–15 cm) long, often on a twisted stalk, smooth and dark green. New foliage is orange-red to red. Flowers have insignificant white petals and showy magenta stamens. They appear in spring and summer arranged in dense heads on the tips of arching stems. Fruit is a whitish round to oval berry, ½ in (1 cm) long. ZONE 10.

T

Tabebuia heterophylla

Tabebuia chrysotricha

Tabebuia chrysotricha

Tabebuia chrysantha

TABEBUIA
Bignoniaceae
TRUMPET TREE

The shrubs and trees of this genus occur naturally in tropical America and the West Indies where some are valued for their timber. They feature spectacular flowers and attractive foliage. Many are briefly deciduous during the tropical dry season, but some are almost evergreen. Flowers are tubular to bell-shaped and may be shades of white, yellow, pink, red or purple. They are usually clustered at the branch tips, commonly when the leaves have fallen in late winter to spring. The fruit are bean-like capsules. Leaves vary in shape, and include simple leaves and compound leaves with 3 to 7 leaflets; the edges are often toothed. Trumpet trees need a hot to warm frost-free climate and deep, humus-rich soil with good drainage. A sunny position is best, with some shelter from wind to protect the flowers. Propagate from seed; selected types are grafted.

Tabebuia avellanedae
PAU D'ARCO

This handsome tree from tropical Argentina matures to a height of 65 ft (20 m) and a spread of 5 ft (1.5 m). Its rounded crown is formed by a network of branching stems sparsely clad with slender palmate leaves with 5 leaflets; leaves are shed briefly in spring. Spectacular clusters of rose-pink or purple-pink flowers are borne on bare branches. ZONE 11.

Tabebuia chrysantha
GOLDEN TRUMPET TREE

This small deciduous tree from Venezuela grows to a height of 20 ft (7 m) and forms an open crown of slender branches. Its leaves are composed of 5 hairy, finger-like leaflets. It bears a profusion of rich mustard-yellow, trumpet-shaped flowers 3 in (7 cm) long and grouped in large heads at the ends of leafless branches in spring. Its fruit are slightly hairy. ZONE 11.

Tabebuia chrysotricha
GOLDEN TRUMPET TREE

This Central American tree develops an open canopy and reaches 30–50 ft (10–15 m) high. The species name is Greek for 'golden hair', referring to the brownish hairs on the branches, flower stalks, leaf stalks and lower leaf surfaces, fruit and parts of the flower. During the brief time the tree is bare of leaves, clusters of flowers almost smother the crown. Each is trumpet shaped, about 2 in (5 cm) across, with bright yellow ruffled petals. Brownish lines and golden brown hairs highlight the throat. Leaves are dark green, mostly with 3 to 5 oval to oblong leaflets, held on long stalks. Fruit are golden brown capsules. ZONE 10.

Tabebuia heterophylla
IPE ROXO

From Brazil, this is one of the most magnificent species, producing a mass of flowers on leafless branches. The blossoms hang in large, loose clusters and come in various shades of pink, from the palest eggshell to the deepest rose. ZONE 11.

TABERNAEMONTANA
Apocyanaceae

Widespread throughout tropical and subtropical regions, these evergreen shrubs and small trees resemble gardenias (to which they are related), in both leaf and flower. The leaves are deep green and roughly oval; the funnel-shaped flowers are usually white. The plants can tolerate very occasional light frosts. Where it is possible to grow them outdoors, they are often used as informal hedging. They grow best in humus-rich, moist, well-drained soil, and sun or dappled shade. Propagate the species from seed and the cultivars from semi-ripe cuttings.

Tabernaemontana divaricata
MOONBEAM, CREPE JASMINE

Formerly known as *Ervatamia divaricata* and occurring naturally from northern India to China's Yunnan province and northern Thailand, this twiggy, heavily foliaged shrub grows to about 6 ft (2 m) high and has leathery leaves up to 4 in (10 cm) long. Clusters of white tubular flowers in terminal clusters open throughout the warmer months; their scent is stronger in the evening. 'Flore Pleno' is a double-flowered cultivar and is much more widely grown than the species. These beautiful shrubs are excellent container plants and can be lightly trimmed to shape. ZONE 11.

TAIWANIA
Taxodiaceae

This genus of evergreen conifers occurs wild in Burma, China and Taiwan and consists of only 2 species, *T. cryptomerioides* and *T. flousiana*, which are not widely grown elsewhere. It is closely related to *Cryptomeria*. The juvenile leaves are narrow, greyish green, almost needle like, while mature leaves are small and scale like. The seed-bearing cones are cylindrical and woody. In China the wood from these trees has been used for centuries to make coffins and now they are almost extinct in the wild. They prefer well-drained soil and a sheltered position with plenty of moisture and sun. Propagation is from seed or cuttings.

Taiwania cryptomerioides

This conifer forms an impressive conical tree, reaching 200 ft (60 m) in the wild, with a massive trunk up to 20 ft (7 m) in diameter. Young trees are vigorous and columnar, with gracefully dropping branches. Juvenile leaves are rigid, sharply pointed and narrow, about ½ in (1 cm) long in flattened rows angled away from the stem. The adult leaves are less than half that length, softer, triangular and pressed against the stem. Small, cylindrical brown cones hang from the drooping ends of the branches. ZONE 8.

TAMARINDUS
Caesalpiniaceae
TAMARIND

There is one species in this genus, a tall evergreen tree which originated in eastern Africa but is naturalized in many areas of tropical Southeast Asia. Valued as a shade and street tree, it is also grown for its bean-like pods which contain large seeds encased in an edible, sweet, fibrous pulp. This pulp, with high tartaric acid content, is cooked and strained to produce a tart-sweet syrup which is used to make a refreshing drink in Middle Eastern countries, and is an important ingredient of many curries. The tree needs a tropical climate to thrive, but is not fussy about soil and once established will tolerate drought and exposed positions. The roots can be invasive. It is grown from seed or cuttings.

Tamarindus indica
This handsome tree grows to 65 ft (20 m), with a broad spreading crown and dense foliage. The short trunk is covered with shaggy brown bark. The fern-like, compound, vivid green leaves are held on slender, pale brown branchlets. The small flowers, pale orange-yellow or cream with red veins, are borne in small clusters among the leaves in summer. These are followed by the 8 in (20 cm) long pods which ripen from green to dark brown and have brittle shells. ZONE 12.

TAMARIX
Tamaricaceae

These tough shrubs and small trees occur naturally in southern Europe, North Africa and temperate Asia in dry riverbeds, often in saline soils. Most *Tamarix* species are deciduous but a few are evergreen. They develop a short trunk and a graceful dense canopy of drooping branchlets. Leaves are minute and scale like and have salt-secreting glands. Flowers are small and white or pink, in slender spikes. The fruit is a capsule. Grown for ornament and as a windbreak, these trees adapt to a wide range of soils and climates, and cope with salt spray and very dry conditions. They do best in deep sandy soil with good drainage and can be pruned after flowering. *Tamarix* species are propagated from seeds, or from semi-hardwood or hardwood cuttings.

Tamarix aphylla
ATHEL TREE

This is a vigorous evergreen small tree to 30 ft (10 m) with dense, weeping branches. A spreading crown tops the short, single, greyish trunk. It has greyish twigs and grey-green linear leaves. In summer and autumn tiny, white to pale pink flowers appear, arranged in slender spikes 2 in (5 cm) long. It is indigenous to North Africa and the eastern Mediterranean region. It helps stabilize sandy soil, but in Central Australia is causing alarm by its rapid spread along watercourses. It prefers an open, sunny spot in warm to hot, dry climates, with adequate water for the first 2 years until established. ZONE 8.

Taiwania cryptomerioides (below)

Taiwania cryptomerioides

Tamarix aphylla (below)

Tamarindus indica (below)

Tamarindus indica (below)

Tamarix parviflora

Taxodium distichum

Tamarix chinensis
CHINESE TAMARISK

This deciduous shrub does best in mild climates. Although it tolerates hot, dry conditions, it must have a supply of moisture to the roots. It makes an elegant shrub, growing to about 12 ft (4 m) with an upright stem and slightly weeping branchlets. The leaves are small, linear and slightly drooping. A haze of massed tiny pink flowers appears in summer and can last for several months. ZONE 7.

Tamarix parviflora
EARLY TAMARISK

Indigenous to south-eastern Europe, this species grows well in mild climates where it is frost-hardy but drought sensitive. An open position is preferable. Making a small deciduous open tree about 15 ft (5 m) in height, the plant is a pretty sight when smothered in spring with a haze of tiny rose-pink flowers which are carried in small spikes along the previous year's growth. At this stage it makes an eye-catching mist of soft colour. The leaves are small and narrow. The plant is often confused with *T. gallica*, the French tamarisk, which is similar but is rarely cultivated and blooms in summer and autumn. ZONE 4.

Tamarix ramosissima
LATE TAMARISK

This open deciduous elegant shrub, previously known as *T. pentandra*, grows to about 15 ft (5 m) and carries tiny blue-green leaves on dark red-brown stems. The trunk and branches too are a dark red-brown. Panicles up to 5 in (12 cm) long of profuse small pink flowers are borne in upright plumes during the late summer months. The plant grows well in cool climates. This is perhaps the most widely grown species. 'Pink Cascade' is a vigorous cultivar which bears rich rose-pink flowers. ZONE 3.

TAXODIUM
Taxodiaceae

This small genus of deciduous or evergreen conifers consists of only 3 species that occur naturally on the edges of rivers and lakes in eastern North America and parts of Mexico. The genus name comes from the supposed similarity of their foliage to that of the yews (*Taxus*). *Taxodium* species shed their leaves in autumn, still attached to the delicate small branchlets. These are feather-like and turn coppery brown. Male (pollen) cones are tiny; female ones are globular, up to 1 in (2 cm) in diameter. These trees thrive in damp boggy soils and will grow in shallow water but do not do well in very dry soils in their native countries. They are a source of strong, tough, termite-resistant wood. Propagate from seed or cuttings.

Taxodium ascendens
POND CYPRESS

Occurring mainly in the sandy 'pine barrens' of east-coastal USA, *T. ascendens* grows in shallow pools in the wild. This narrowly conical tree, reaching a height of 60 ft (18 m) in cultivation, has spirally arranged leaves on erect branchlets. The new spring growths are erect and fresh green, becoming rich brown in autumn. The small cones hang from the tips of the branches. As its common name suggests, it

Taxodium distichum   *Taxodium ascendens* (below)

Tamarix ramosissima 'Pink Cascade' (above & below)

makes an excellent feature beside rivers, ponds and lakes. 'Nutans' has shoots that are erect at first, becoming nodding as they mature. ZONE 4.

Taxodium distichum
BALD CYPRESS, SWAMP CYPRESS

From eastern USA where it enjoys swampy conditions and plenty of sun, this fast-growing tree reaches 120 ft (38 m) in the wild, nearer to 80 ft (25 m) in cultivation. It is distinguished by its deeply fissured, fibrous, reddish brown bark and knobbly 'knees'. These special structures are vertical woody growths sent up from the roots and are thought to allow the tree to breathe with its root system submerged. The pyramidal crown spreads to 20 ft (7 m) or more, and bears tiny, light green, slender, pointed leaves arranged in 2 rows. The feathery new foliage appears in early summer. As it matures it becomes rusty red in autumn then golden brown before falling. The wood is very brittle, and trees are easily damaged by storms and strong winds. Its resinous, round, purple cones, 1 in (2 cm) across, disintegrate when they fall to the ground. ZONE 4.

Taxodium mucronatum
MEXICAN BALD CYPRESS, MONTEZUMA CYPRESS

Indigenous to Mexico, this conifer is only deciduous in cooler climates. It reaches a height of 100 ft (30 m) with a massive trunk and widely spreading branches. The leaves are identical to those of *T. distichum* and cones are inconspicuous. Grow it in an open sunny position, where the soil is permanently moist and enriched with organic matter. This species suits warm to cool climates and tolerates only slight frosts. It is propagated from seed or cuttings. There are some huge specimens in the Mexican highlands, most notably the great tree of Tulé with a trunk over 30 ft (10 m) in diameter and possibly 1,000 years old. ZONE 9.

TAXUS
Taxaceae

The evergreen conifers of this small genus, from cool-climate regions of the northern hemisphere, are slow growing but very long lived. They are hardy and tolerate a wide range of conditions including heavy shade and chalky soil but do not enjoy warm winters or hot dry summers. Young trees are conical in shape, but as they age—over the centuries—they develop a domed crown and a massive, thick trunk clothed in reddish brown or greyish brown bark which peels off in thin scales. The flat green leaves are shortly needle like and sharply pointed,

Taxodium mucronatum

Taxus baccata 'Repandens'

and male and female flowers appear on separate trees in spring. The single, small brown seed is enclosed in a vivid red fleshy cup which is the only part of the plant that is not poisonous to humans and animals. Yews make excellent dense hedges, often used for topiary. Propagate from seed or cuttings or by grafting.

Taxus baccata
ENGLISH YEW, COMMON YEW

Indigenous to western Asia, North Africa and Europe, this dense, dark tree has had legendary and religious associations for centuries. This yew grows best in a moist alkaline soil in an open position. The dark-coloured trunk is erect and very thick in maturity; leaves are needle like and dark green. The male tree bears scaly cones and the female cup-shaped, scarlet berries which encase a poisonous seed. Old trees may reach 45 ft (14 m) but cultivars rarely achieve this height. 'Aurea' has golden green foliage; 'Fastigiata', the Irish yew, is columnar; and 'Repandens' has a spreading habit. ZONE 4.

Taxus cuspidata
JAPANESE YEW

Faster growing than the English yew, this conifer is popular in cold climates and can grow in dense shade. It forms a large shrub or small tree with an erect trunk which is covered in greyish brown bark. The dense foliage is composed of small, narrow leaves arranged in V-shaped rows on the stem. The leaves are dull green above and lighter below. Tolerant of pollution, *T. cuspidata* is one of the few conifers that performs well in difficult urban environments. The dwarf cultivar 'Densiformis' forms a dense, compact mound, about 3 ft (1 m) high. ZONE 3.

Taxus cuspidata

Taxus cuspidata

TECOMA
Bignoniaceae

These showy shrubs and small trees grow naturally in tropical areas of Central and South America and are close relatives of *Tecomaria* and *Tabebuia*. They bear clusters of showy yellow to orange tubular to trumpet-shaped flowers. Their leaves can be simple or compound with an odd number of leaflets. Fruit are smooth bean-like capsules. *Tecoma* species are suitable for warm to hot climates—they can withstand only minimal frosts. They thrive in full sun with shelter from strong winds, and need adequate soil moisture in summer. Use either seeds or cuttings to propagate them.

Taxus baccata 'Fastigiata' (below)

Tecomaria capensis

Telopea speciosissima

Telopea speciosissima 'Wirrimbirra White'

Tecoma stans

Telopea oreades

Tecoma stans
YELLOWBELLS, YELLOW TRUMPET TREE, YELLOW ELDER

This shrub or small tree features bright yellow trumpet-shaped flowers, 2 in (5 cm) long arranged in sprays at the branch tips. It has a long flowering season, from early summer to late autumn. The fruit is a capsule about 8 in (20 cm) long, ripening to chocolate brown. This species reaches a height of 15–20 ft (5–7 m) but can be pruned heavily after flowering to keep it compact. Leaves are mid-green, composed of 5 or 7 leaflets each 2$\frac{1}{2}$–3 in (6–8 cm) long with deeply serrated edges, resembling those of the European elder (*Sambucus*). Propagate new plants from cuttings. ZONE 10.

TECOMARIA
Bignoniaceae

These upright to clambering and semi-climbing evergreen shrubs, closely related to *Tecoma*, grow naturally in tropical and subtropical southern Africa. They feature trumpet-shaped flowers in shades of yellow, orange or scarlet, in clusters at the ends of shoots. Leaves are arranged opposite each other or in groups of 3, with an odd number of leaflets. The fruit is an oblong narrow capsule. *Tecomaria* species grow best in full sun in a position where they are protected from wind; soil should be well drained with added organic matter. The plants are propagated from seed or cuttings.

Tecomaria capensis
CAPE HONEYSUCKLE

The Cape honeysuckle is a scrambling shrub with orange-red to scarlet curved trumpet-shaped flowers, each 2 in (5 cm) long, borne in short spikes from late summer to late autumn. The branches are slender and sprawling, forming roots where they touch the ground and able to climb to a height of 15 ft (5 m). The glossy green leaves are 6 in (15 cm) long, divided into 5 to 9 rounded to oval leaflets with a serrated edge. 'Aurea' has yellow flowers. With regular clipping, the Cape honeysuckle can be grown as a hedge. It thrives in hot and warm climates, and is good near the seaside. ZONE 10.

TECTONA
Verbenaceae
TEAK

These fast-growing deciduous trees from tropical India and monsoonal forests of Southeast Asia form tall, majestic trees. There are 3 species in the genus but *T. grandis* is the only one of note and the one renowned for timber. The trees require high rainfall, heat, humidity and deep, rich soil to make good growth. In tropical Asia these trees have naturalized widely. They are often planted in parks and gardens where they are valued for their dense shade and handsome foliage. The fruit are round and dark purplish red. Propagation is from seed or cuttings.

Tectona grandis

The large-scale felling of stands of teak in Southeast Asia is still posing great problems as this is a tree of the hills and watersheds and the removal of the forests is causing devastating erosion. Harvested for use since the early 19th century by the British, particularly for shipbuilding and fine furniture, it is still regarded in Europe as a timber for quality furniture. However, in Southeast Asia it was used for general purposes, being hard, durable and immune to insect attack. Where space allows, *T. grandis* makes a fine specimen tree up to about 80 ft (25 m); its large, rounded leaves are up to 24 in (60 cm) long and have wavy edges and prominent veins. The bluish white summer flowers are borne in large, upright, misty clusters up to 16 in (40 cm) across. The fruit is a fleshy plum-like berry. ZONE 11.

TELOPEA
Proteaceae

Commonly known as waratahs, these evergreen sturdy shrubs and small trees are indigenous to open forests of south-eastern Australia including Tasmania; only 4 species exist, but there are some attractive hybrids as well. They bear spectacular flowers in spring, each distinctive bloom a dense head of tubular flowers surrounded by often showy, leafy bracts. Flowers develop at the shoot tips. Leathery green leaves are alternate along the woody stems and have long stalks. The fruit are leathery pods. They prefer full sun to partial shade, and need shelter from the wind. Waratahs can be difficult to grow successfully, needing well-drained sandy soil with low fertility and an acid pH and excellent drainage; they are prone to fungal root and stem rot. Regular pruning after flowering will keep them bushy. Waratahs are best propagated from seed or cuttings and can also be grafted.

Telopea oreades
GIPPSLAND WARATAH, VICTORIAN WARATAH

From the cool hill forests of south-eastern mainland Australia, this waratah has a slender, upright, well-branched habit and forms an open crown. Young plants are shrubby but become tree like with maturity. Mature trees have one to several dominant shoots and masses of shorter stems. They reach a height of 18–24 ft (6–8 m). Red flowers arranged in broad loose spidery heads, up to 3 in (7 cm) across, have pale reddish to green oval to oblong bracts at the base. There is also a white-flowered form. The oval to lance-shaped leaves have a smooth edge and are 6–10 in (15–25 cm) long. The fruit is a boat-shaped pod. This species enjoys a shady location. ZONE 9.

Telopea speciosissima
WARATAH

This waratah grows naturally in New South Wales, and is that state's floral emblem. It is the most spectacular species, with magnificent scarlet to crimson flowers in large domed heads 4–6 in (10–15 cm) across in spring. These are supported by red lance-shaped bracts of variable size and prominence; on some plants the bracts are insignificant but on others they dominate the bloom. This sturdy vigorous shrub with many branches and an open crown grows to 10 ft (3 m) tall and 6 ft (2 m) wide. Leaves vary from oblong to wedge shaped and are leathery, often with a serrated edge and sometimes slightly lobed. The fruit are brown pods. There is a white-flowered cultivar, 'Wirrimbirra White', which features creamy white flowers and cream to greenish bracts. In recent years several named cultivars have become available in Australia with flowers in shades of deep pink. ZONE 9.

TERMINALIA
Combretaceae
TROPICAL ALMOND

The trees of this large genus originating in tropical and subtropical regions of India, Southeast Asia, Australia and southern Africa are valued for their timber, attractive foliage and fruit. The bark is deeply fissured and the branches are blackish and horizontally whorled. The leaves are generally large and leathery. The 5-petalled, greenish white flowers are generally not showy; they appear on spikes or in clusters. The fruit are yellow, dark red or black oval berries, some of which are edible, though it is said that eating too many will make you drunk. Tropical almonds need well-drained soil and plenty of sun, and some species tolerate salty winds and long periods of drought. They are propagated from seed.

Terminalia catappa
INDIAN ALMOND

This attractive tree has horizontal, tiered branches and a broad, flattened canopy often twice as wide as its height of 60 ft (20 m). Indigenous to countries from India through Southeast Asia to northern Australia, it is often found growing along tropical beaches and coastal streams. The leaves are glossy green, and broadly oval with prominent veins; as they age, they turn bright orange, then red, and fall at any time of year, though the tree is never completely bare. The inconspicuous but lightly fragrant white flowers are held on spikes near the ends of branches from summer to autumn. The oval fruit, 2½ in (6 cm) long, are yellow tinged with red when ripe; they consist of fibrous flesh surrounding an almond-like seed of which the kernel is edible, either raw or roasted. The Indian almond is widely cultivated in India and Southeast Asia, and also in Florida, being especially favoured for avenue planting. ZONE 11.

TERNSTROEMIA
Theaceae

This genus of shrubs and small trees originates from the warm-climate areas of East and Southeast Asia. They are grown for their evergreen foliage, which resembles that of the camellia, to which they are closely related though they are less hardy. Well-drained, slightly acid soils suit them best, with plenty of moisture during dry spells. They benefit from an annual dressing of organic mulch spread thickly over the roots. Young plants can be transplanted in winter and trained to form a dense hedge. Propagation is from seed or from cuttings in autumn.

Ternstroemia gymnanthera

This attractive shrub or small tree is one of the few species that is cultivated. Originating from Japan, it reaches a height of 15 ft (5 m) with a rounded crown about 8 ft (2.5 m) wide. The oval, glossy green, pointed leaves are thick and leathery and arranged in spirals; young foliage is coppery red. The small white flowers hang in clusters of 3; they are delicately perfumed. Berries that ripen to scarlet follow. ZONE 7.

Ternstroemia gymnanthera (below)

TETRADIUM
Rutaceae

This genus consists of 9 species of deciduous small trees from East Asia. They do best in full sun to part-shade, and prefer deep, fertile soil that is moist but well drained. They are often planted as part of a shrub border. The leaves are pinnate and the leaflets have translucent oil dots and a slightly aromatic smell when crushed. Flowers appear in flat sprays at the ends of new growth. Both the flower and fruit parts of the trees usually occur in 4s. Propagate from seed or semi-hardwood cuttings. The genus is included by some botanists in *Euodia* or *Phellodendron*.

Ternstroemia gymnanthera

Terminalia catappa (below)

Tetradium daniellii

This tree from the mountain woodlands of northern China and Korea grows to 50 ft (15 m) and forms a canopy of broad, spreading, upwardly pointing branches. Its 12 in (30 cm) long leaves are composed of 5 to 11 ovate leaflets, each narrowing to a sharp point. They are smooth, glossy, dark green above, and blue-green and hairy below. Sprays of small white perfumed flowers appear in late summer. Small, beaked, reddish black capsular fruit are produced in generous clusters in autumn. ZONE 8.

TETRAPANAX
Araliaceae
RICE-PAPER PLANT

The genus consists of one species, an evergreen, suckering shrub or small tree from Taiwan. Both the common name and the species name come from the fact that a type of fine 'rice-paper' is made from the white pith of the stems. It is grown in even quite temperate gardens for its very large, fan-like leaves where an exotic, tropical effect is required and space is available for its often rampant growth. *Tetrapanax* does best in a mild climate, in a sheltered, preferably lightly shaded spot and well-drained soil. Tolerant of salt winds and sandy soil, it is an ideal specimen for seaside gardens. Prune to remove damaged foliage and spent flower heads, and remove canes at ground level to control the size of the plant. Propagate from seed or cuttings.

Tetrapanax papyrifera

This freely suckering shrub grows vigorously to 20 ft (7 m) tall and spreads about as wide. The huge, umbrella-like lobed leaves are shiny mid-green above, felty underneath. New growth has a distinctive whitish bloom. The individual flowers are creamy white fluffy balls, held in large, loose, showy clusters; they appear during the autumn months to be followed by black berries. 'Variegata' has leaves of cream to white tinged with bright to dark green. ZONE 6.

THEOBROMA
Sterculiaceae

This genus consists of about 30 species of evergreen trees from tropical America; one species, *T. cacao*, provides one of the world's most valuable and widely consumed foods—cacao which is the source of chocolate. The trees grow naturally as understorey plants in forests. They do best in well-drained soil containing a large percentage of organic matter, with regular water and shelter from sun and wind. They are propagated from seed or grafting.

Theobroma cacao
COCOA, CACAO

In its native tropical forests of Central America, this erect tree grows to 30 ft (10 m) or more, but in commercial cultivation it is generally kept smaller to facilitate harvesting. The pointed, oval leaves are large, up to 10 in (25 cm) long, and leathery. Throughout the year, small creamy yellow flowers are borne on the trunk and larger woody branches. These are followed by the fruit: large ribbed pods, about 12 in (30 cm) long and 8 in (20 cm) wide, which ripen to a rich, glossy reddish brown. The fruit contain many seeds which are used to make chocolate. ZONE 12.

THEVETIA
Apocynaceae

Members of this small genus of trees and shrubs have a poisonous milky sap. Relatives of the oleander (*Nerium*), they are indigenous to tropical America. They feature clusters of large, mostly yellow, funnel-shaped flowers at the shoot tips; flowering peaks in summer. The fruit are berry like. The leaves are arranged alternately on the stems. The plants grow best in a sandy soil enriched with organic matter and with good drainage. They need plenty of water while in flower. The ideal location provides shelter from wind and full sun to partial shade. Prune the plants after flowering to maintain dense growth. Propagate from seed or cuttings. All parts of these plants are very poisonous.

Thevetia peruviana
YELLOW OLEANDER, LUCKY NUT

This domed, evergreen shrub grows 9–12 ft (3–4 m) tall. The yellow to soft orange, slightly perfumed flowers, each 2 in (5 cm) across, are held on long stalks. They bloom on and off for most of the year in their native habitat; in cooler climates they bloom in summer. The fruit is an oddly shaped, fleshy drupe, rounded with a prominent ridge. It ripens from green to red to black and is regarded by some as a lucky charm, even though dangerously poisonous. The long, shiny, rich green leaves are hard and strap like to narrowly lance shaped, with barely any stalk. ZONE 10.

Thevetia thevetioides
LARGE-FLOWERED YELLOW OLEANDER, BE-STILL TREE

This species from Mexico grows as a shrub or small tree to 15 ft (5 m) tall. Its erect stems and spreading branches form a dense crown. The flowers, about 3 in (8 cm) across, are orange or pale to strong yellow and funnel shaped, though more open than those of *T. peruviana*. Leaves are narrowly lance shaped, 4 in (10 cm) long and ½ in (1 cm) wide, with a pointed tip and prominent veins. The fruit is a green drupe. ZONE 10.

THRYPTOMENE
Myrtaceae

This Australian genus is made up of about 40 species of wiry-stemmed, evergreen shrubs, only a few of which are cultivated. They grow up to 5 ft (1.5 m) high and wide and have tiny, heath-like, deep green leaves that are aromatic when

Tetradium daniellii (below)

Thevetia peruviana (below)

Tetradium daniellii

Theobroma cacao

Thevetia peruviana (below)

Tetrapanax papyrifera (below)

Thevetia thevetioides

Thryptomene saxicola

Thryptomene calycina

Thuja plicata, young tree

Thuja occidentalis

Thuja occidentalis 'Smaragd'

crushed. An abundance of small, starry flowers appear all along the branches. Thryptomenes make good cut flowers and, as they need regular trimming to keep them compact, using the flowers is a good way to prune. They prefer light, well-drained soil in full sun or semi-shade, and a mild climate, frost-free or almost so. They are usually propagated from semi-ripe cuttings.

Thryptomene calycina
GRAMPIANS THRYPTOMENE

This species from a limited area of western Victoria, in particular the rugged sandstone Grampians Mountains, has slightly pointed leaves and white flowers carried in great profusion through winter and spring. The species is widely cultivated for cut flowers. A distinctive characteristic of the Grampians thrytomene is that the 5 sepals are identical in shape, size and colour to the 5 petals. There are several cultivars. ZONE 9.

Thryptomene saxicola

This species has somewhat rounded leaves and light pink flowers which occur mainly in winter and spring. It is a neat, compact plant that seldom exceeds 4 ft (1.2 m) high and only requires light trimming after flowering. ZONE 9.

THUJA
Cupressaceae
ARBOR-VITAE

This small genus contains 5 evergreen conifers from high-rainfall, cool-temperate regions of East Asia and North America. All are valuable timber trees, and several are widely cultivated on a commercial basis. They feature erect, straight trunks covered in deeply fissured, fibrous bark, and are columnar to pyramidal. The aromatic foliage consists of sprays of scale-like leaves which are often flattened. The egg-shaped cones are covered with overlapping scales and are green, maturing to brown; they are notably small for such large trees, mostly under $\frac{1}{2}$ in (1 cm) long. Dwarf cultivars, some no more than 16 in (40 cm) high, make excellent rockery or container specimens; most are juvenile forms. The plants tolerate cold and are not fussy about soil as long as it is well drained; most species prefer full sun and dislike drought. Propagation is from seed or cuttings in winter.

Thuja occidentalis
AMERICAN ARBOR-VITAE

Ornamental and easy to grow, this is a popular specimen for conifer gardens and as a feature in large lawns. Growing to 50 ft (15 m) with a pyramidal crown, it has attractive reddish brown, peeling bark. Its dense foliage is composed of yellow-green glandular leaves with bluish undersides held on flat, spreading branchlets. The leaves are smooth and shiny, and turn bronze in autumn. Its tiny cones are less than $\frac{1}{4}$ in (6 mm) long. This species has given rise to over 140 cultivars ranging from dwarf shrubs to large trees, some of which are notable for their winter coloration. All need full sun. 'Ericoides', 20 in (50 cm) tall, has soft, loose, bronze juvenile foliage which becomes brownish green as it matures. 'Lutea' grows to 8 ft (2.5 m) in 10 years, forming a tight pyramid; it has creamy yellow young leaves which become rich golden bronze in winter, while the mature foliage remains coppery green. Slow-growing 'Rheingold' forms a spreading, semi-prostrate dome 30 in (75 cm) high and $4\frac{1}{2}$ ft (1.5 m) wide and is the best known cultivar; new leaves are pinkish gold, yellow and bronze in spring and summer, then turn rich golden brown in winter. 'Smaragd', of compact pyramidal growth-habit, has bright green foliage all year, and is sometimes used to form a dense hedge 6 ft (2 m) high; it makes an ideal rockery or tub specimen. ZONE 4.

Thuja plicata
WESTERN RED CEDAR

This fast-growing conifer reaches about 80 ft (25 m) in cultivation, much taller in its natural habitat of the cool, moist valleys of north-western North America. It has long been harvested for its durable and versatile softwood timber. Of conical habit, it becomes columnar in maturity, with branches sweeping the ground. When the rich coppery green foliage is crushed, it exudes a sweet, tangy aroma. *T. plicata* tolerates shade and heavy soils. It transplants well when young. The dwarf cultivar 'Rogersii' forms a round bun shape 20 in (50 cm) across, with fine golden yellow new growth which becomes bronze as the weather cools. Compact 'Zebrina', growing to 18 ft (6 m) high and 5 ft (1.5 m) wide, has glossy bright green foliage striped with yellow and, unlike many cultivars of this species, it keeps its colour all year round. ZONE 5.

Thujopsis dolabrata

Thujopsis dolabrata 'Nana'

Thuja plicata 'Zebrina'

Tibouchina granulosa

Tibouchina lepidota

THUJOPSIS
Cupressaceae
MOCK THUJA

This genus from Japan contains only a single species, *T. dolabrata*, which resembles *Thuja* but is distinguished by several important features, namely round, woody cones, winged seeds and larger leaves. Tolerant of cold, it thrives in moist, well-drained soil, acid or alkaline, and an open, sunny position. It is the parent of several cultivars, varying in habit and foliage colour. Propagation is from seed, or cuttings for selected forms.

Thujopsis dolabrata
This evergreen conifer is variable in growth-habit, from upright and pyramidal to spreading and bushy, 20–50 ft (7–15 m). Its foliage is composed of flattened, scale-like leaves which are dark green above with frosted white undersides. Both leaves and branchlets are thicker and less delicate than those of *Thuja* species. Small cones are bluish grey, round and scaly. The dwarf cultivar 'Nana' forms a spreading bun shape 24 in (60 cm) high by 5 ft (1.5 m) wide, with fresh green foliage, sometimes tinged bronze; it tolerates poor, shallow soils. Slow-growing 'Variegata' matures to a broad pyramid 10 ft (3 m) high and 5 ft (1.5) wide, its vivid green, shiny foliage splashed with white, giving it a frosted appearance. ZONE 4.

TIBOUCHINA
Melastomataceae
LASIANDRA, GLORY BUSH

There are over 300 species of these evergreen shrubs, small trees and climbers from South America. Flowers are large and vivid, commonly purple, pink or white, with 5 satiny petals. They are borne either singly or in clusters at the shoot tips, and sometimes the whole plant is smothered with blooms over several months, usually from late summer to early winter. Flower buds are rounded and fat. The leaves are simple and hairy, deeply marked with 3 to 7 veins. New growth is often contrasting reddish bronze, and stems are square; fruit is a capsule. They prefer full sun and do best in light soil with added organic matter and a slightly acid to neutral pH, kept moist during the growing season. Prune them after flowering. Plants have brittle stems and need shelter from wind. They do not like frost. Propagation is from tip cuttings.

Tibouchina granulosa
Sometimes tree-like to 30–40 ft (10–13 m), this Brazilian species is usually a large shrub 12–15 ft (4–5 m) high and wide. Flower clusters are 12 in (30 cm) long and may completely hide the foliage in autumn; each bloom is rose-purple to violet or pink, and 2 in (5 cm) across. The branching stems are thick and woody. Leaves are lance shaped to oblong, 5–8 in (12–20 cm) long; dark green and shiny on top and bright green and hairy underneath and hairy along the edge. It suits warm to hot climates. ZONE 9.

Tibouchina lepidota
From Ecuador and Colombia, this is a leafy shrub with a short trunk to 12 ft (4 m) high, but may become tree like with a neat round canopy, to 40 ft (13 m) tall. Its violet to purple flowers are borne in clusters; the flower buds are enclosed by pink silky bracts and stems have reddish hairs. Leaves are dark green and shiny, oblong to lance shaped, with 5 main veins and 2 outer minor ones; underneath they are paler and hairy. Full sun to part shade suits them. 'Alstonville' has particularly vibrant flowers. ZONE 9.

Tibouchina urvilleana
PRINCESS FLOWER

This species (syn. *T. semidecandra*) from southern Brazil, develops a short trunk topped by a bushy rounded crown and reaches 15 ft (5 m) high. Young stems are reddish and slightly hairy, turning brown later. The oval to slightly oblong leaves are 2–4 in (5–10 cm), shiny dark green above and slightly hairy below. The rich purple to violet flowers, 3 in (7 cm) wide, with purple stamens, are borne singly or in small groups. Flower buds are large, reddish and hairy. It is the longest established in gardens in warm-temperate climates. In the UK and most of the USA where it is cultivated as a greenhouse plant, it is often grown as an espalier because of its lax habit. ZONE 9.

TILIA
Tiliaceae
LIME TREE, LINDEN

From cool-temperate regions of Asia, Europe and North America, these tall, handsome deciduous trees are often planted in avenues and streets, because they are fast growing and withstand regular heavy pruning and atmospheric pollution. They are generally upright with thick, buttressed trunks and have a tendency to sucker. Rounded to heart-shaped leaves, held on thin stalks, turn briefly yellow in autumn. The small, fragrant, cup-shaped cream flowers are borne in clusters; each cluster has a whitish bract which persists and helps to disperse the fruit on the wind. Both the flowers and the bracts are dried to make linden tea. The flower clusters produce large quantites of nectar and attract bees. Unfortunately the nectar of some East Asian species is toxic to bees. The fruit are small, round, hard, green berries ¼ in (6 mm) across. Several species are valued for their pale, strong but lightweight wood, used for making musical instruments and for wood carving. Lime trees do best in cool climates, and prefer full sun, neutral, well-drained soil and plenty of water in dry periods. Even quite large trees can be readily transplanted during their winter dormancy. Propagation is from seed, cuttings or layering.

Tilia americana
BASSWOOD, AMERICAN LINDEN

This attractive, sturdy tree from east-central USA and Canada grows to 130 ft (40 m), its erect trunk with smooth grey bark which becomes fissured with age. Its young branches are green and form a compact narrow crown. The heart-shaped, dull green leaves, up to 6 in (15 cm) long, have toothed edges. Yellowish white, fragrant flowers in pendent clusters appear in summer, followed by small, hairy fruit. ZONE 3.

Tilia cordata
SMALL-LEAFED LINDEN

A denizen of European woodlands, this species grows to 100 ft (30 m) with a dome-shaped crown. Its leathery, round leaves, 2 in (5 cm) across, are bright green on top with pale undersides. Its small flowers are pale yellow and sweetly scented and its fruit are grey. This long-lived species can make a handsome specimen for parks and formal gardens where it has plenty of space. The small-leafed linden's soft whitish timber is often used for wood carving. ZONE 2.

Tilia × europaea 'Wratislaviensis'

Tibouchina urvilleana

Tilia × europaea
EUROPEAN LINDEN, COMMON LIME TREE

Widely grown in Europe, this handsome hybrid between 2 European species, *T. platyphyllos* and *T. cordata*, grows to 100 ft (30 m) and has been used as an avenue tree for centuries. It is characterized by a dense, shapely crown held on a stout trunk which has a strong tendency to sucker. The smooth, green shoots grow in a distinct zig-zag pattern and the bright green, rounded to heart-shaped leaves have toothed edges. Its pale yellow flowers appear among the leaves in early summer; they are sometimes infused and drunk as a tea. The small, rounded fruit are faintly ribbed. 'Wratislaviensis' has golden yellow young foliage which becomes green as it matures. ZONE 3.

Tilia americana

Tibouchina urvilleana

Tilia cordata

Tilia heterophylla
WHITE BASSWOOD

Rarely seen outside its native eastern North America, this species reaches 100 ft (30 m) with a rounded crown supported by a network of smooth branches. The dark green leaves are large, broad and oval, with coarsely toothed edges and pale hairy undersides. ZONE 4.

Tilia platyphyllos
BROAD-LEAFED LINDEN

Reaching a height of 80 ft (25 m), this vigorous European species has a straight, rough, grey trunk and rounded crown spreading to broadly. The young shoots are reddish brown and downy and the large, dark green leaves are heart shaped and bluish beneath. Pale yellow flowers in groups of 3 are followed by small, hard, pear-shaped, ribbed fruit. In 'Rubra' the bark of the young twigs is a vivid red. ZONE 3.

Tilia tomentosa
SILVER LINDEN

This graceful tree indigenous to south-eastern Europe and Turkey is distinguished by its young shoots which are pale grey and felted. Growing to 90 ft (28 m), its ascending branches are often pendulous at the tips. Large round leaves, with serrated edges and whitish undersides, seem to shimmer in the wind. The lime green summer flowers are followed by small, rough, oval fruit. Tolerant of dry conditions and smog-laden atmospheres, the only disadvantage of this species is that the nectar it produces is sometimes toxic to bees. 'Petiolaris' has a more pronounced weeping habit and leaves on long pendent stalks. In the past this was regarded as a distinct species but has not been found in the wild and is now regarded as a form of *T. tomentosa*. ZONE 4.

TIPUANA
Fabaceae

This genus is made up of just a few species of trees indigenous to South America. They are evergreen or semi-deciduous with clusters of bright pea flowers at the branch tips. The pinnate leaves consist of an odd number of leaflets. Tipuanas need full sun and a frost-free, humid, warm to hot climate. Fast growing, they thrive in deep, well-drained soil enriched with organic matter, and are propagated using freshly collected scarified seed.

Tipuana tipu
TIPU TREE, PRIDE OF BOLIVIA

This attractive shade tree with spreading branches and an irregular crown reaches a height of 50–65 ft (15–20 m) with a similar spread. Indigenous to parts of Brazil and Bolivia, it is evergreen in the tropics, but partly to completely deciduous in the subtropics. Spring highlights are the yellow to orange pea flowers arranged in large clusters which bloom for several weeks. They are replaced in autumn to winter by decorative, brown, winged, oblong pods 2–4 in (5–10 cm) long, in the upper part of the canopy. Dark green leaves are up to 10 in (25 cm) long, composed of 15 to 19 oblong leaflets. ZONE 9.

TITHONIA
Asteraceae

This genus of 10 species consists mainly of herbaceous annuals, biennials and perennials, *T. diversifolia* being the only one which becomes a true shrub. Originating from Central America and the West Indies, they are related to sunflowers and bear large, vivid yellow, orange or scarlet, daisy-like flower heads in summer and autumn. The leaves are often hairy on the undersides and are often sharply lobed. The plants thrive under hot, dry conditions but require a plentiful supply of water. They grow best in

Tilia heterophylla (below)

Tipuana tipu (below)

Tilia heterophylla

Tilia platyphyllos 'Rubra' espaliered (below)

Tithonia diversifolia

Toona ciliata

Toona sinensis 'Flamingo'

well-drained soil and need full sun to thrive, but even so may need staking. Deadhead regularly to promote a longer flowering season and prune hard after flowering to encourage new growth. Propagation is from seed.

Tithonia diversifolia
MEXICAN SUNFLOWER, TREE MARIGOLD

A very large perennial growing to 15 ft (5 m) tall, this species is best suited to the rear of a shrub border where it can supply visual impact during the late summer months with its large, single, yellow flower heads. Because of its height, removing dead flowers may be difficult, and in fact the seed heads themselves are of interest. ZONE 9.

TOONA
Meliaceae

Previously included in the closely related genus *Cedrela*, these deciduous and evergreen trees from China, the Himalaya, Southeast Asia and northern Australia are valued for their fine, often aromatic, timber. Attractive pinnate leaves have many oval to lance-shaped leaflets. *Toona* species grow best in deep rich soil in moist climates. Their cold tolerance depends on their country of origin. *T. ciliata* and *T. sinensis* thrive in warm rather than tropical climates, with shelter from wind. They are propagated from seed or suckers.

Toona ciliata
AUSTRALIAN RED CEDAR

Formerly known as *T. australis* and *Cedrela toona*, this species ranges widely from southern Asia to eastern Australia and shows much variation. It includes a number of forms native to eastern Australia and for long regarded by botanists as a distinct species, *T. australis*. The Australian red cedar was once abundant in coastal rainforests but nearly all the larger trees were felled for the valuable timber in the 19th century; it was used as a local substitute for mahogany. A deciduous tree 50–110 ft (15–35 m) tall, its stout upright trunk features scaly reddish bark. The spreading canopy is up to 50 ft (15 m) wide. Leaves are deep green, 10–20 in (25–50 cm) long, mostly with 10 to 18 oval leaflets. The new foliage has attractive bronze tones. Inconspicuous flowers are perfumed, whitish to pink, and held in dense clusters in mid- to late spring. The fruit is a capsule 1 in (2 cm) long. ZONE 9.

Toona sinensis
CHINESE TOON

Indigenous to China as its name suggests, this deciduous tree, 30–40 ft (10–13 m) tall, produces many suckers and is commonly grown as a clump of these, reaching 12 ft (4 m) wide. If trained as a single-trunked tree, it develops rough bark and a spreading canopy. Leaves are 12–24 in (30–60 cm) long, with 16 to 24 alternate to almost opposite leaflets along a red stalk. The leaves open pale green, turning orange yellow in autumn. The young leaves are edible, smelling of onions. Tiny, fragrant, pink flowers are arranged in long hanging clusters in spring. The pink-leafed 'Flamingo' is a cultivar of Australasian origin. ZONE 7.

TORREYA
Taxaceae

The yew-like evergreen coniferous trees and shrubs of this small genus of 6 or so species occur wild in eastern Asia and North America. They adapt to a wide variety of soils, from chalk to heavy clay and poor sand, and are reasonably cold tolerant provided they are planted in a sheltered position. All demand adequate water during dry spells. The spiny-pointed leaves are spirally arranged on twisted shoots

Toxicodendron succedaneum

Trichilia emetica

Torreya californica

Trachycarpus fortunei

and are often paler on the undersides. Fruit are oval berries which contain a single seed. Propagation is from seed or grafting.

Torreya californica
CALIFORNIA NUTMEG

This neat, erect, evergreen conifer grows to a height of 65 ft (20 m); conical in habit, in maturity its horizontal branches sweep the ground. The dark green, spine-tipped, needle-like leaves, about 1½ in (3–7 cm) long, are yellowish green beneath. Male and female flowers are borne on separate trees; small, woody, olive-like fruit follow on female trees. Indigenous to the hill forests of California and Oregon, it thrives in temperate climates with high rainfall and needs protection from frost and cold winds. ZONE 6.

Torreya nucifera
KAYA

From Japan, this attractive, symmetrical conifer reaches about 70 ft (22 m). Its stiff, spiky, yew-like foliage is dark grey-green and pleasantly pungent when crushed. The bark is a smooth reddish brown. The fruit are edible green berries which ripen to purple with a white bloom; they contain a rich oil. ZONE 4.

TOXICODENDRON
Anacardiaceae

This genus (formerly included in *Rhus*) is made up of trees, shrubs and climbers. The milky or resinous sap of all species is highly caustic and irritant to the skin and mere contact with the leaves causes severe allergic reaction, sometimes life threatening. For this reason cultivation of the species is prohibited in some places. The genus includes the notable *T. radicans* (the poison ivy of North America). The species occur naturally in temperate and subtropical regions of North America and East Asia. Several are grown for their brilliant autumn foliage. The leaves are ash like, with a few to many paired leaflets. The small flowers are arranged in clusters, with separate male and female flowers. The fruit are small, rounded, grey, slightly flattened drupes with dry flesh. These plants prefer full sun, and adapt to most soils but prefer well-drained soil. Propagation is from seed or cuttings.

Toxicodendron succedaneum
RHUS TREE, WAX TREE, POISON SUMAC

This deciduous shrub to small tree grows up to 18–24 ft (6–8 m) tall with a single trunk and spreading crown. It is also called *Rhus succedanea*. The large compound leaves have 9 to 15 oblong, slightly drooping leaflets. They are shiny green and in autumn turn vibrant scarlet and orange even in warm climates. Clusters of inconspicuous yellowish green flowers are followed by large clusters of black to brown drupes that persist for long time. The rhus tree grows naturally from East Asia to India. A wax is derived from the berries and a lacquer from the substance which exudes from the stem. ZONE 7.

TRACHYCARPUS
Arecaceae
WINDMILL PALM

This genus is made up of a few species of highly ornamental palms bearing large, fan-shaped leaves. They are valued for their ability to tolerate cooler climates than most palms. Indigenous to southern China and the Himalaya, they often occur at high altitudes. Provided adequate moisture is available they adapt to any free-draining soil, and partial shade or full sun is suitable. *Trachycarpus* species are small to medium trees and their trunks are usually covered with coarse, shaggy fibre. The fan-like, dark green leaves are divided into narrow, pointed blades and can be as much as 5 ft (1.5 m) across. Small yellowish flowers are followed by dark-coloured berries. These palms are shallow rooted and can be transplanted quite easily. Windmill palms make excellent tub specimens for patios and larger greenhouses. Propagation is from seed.

Trachycarpus fortunei
CHINESE FAN PALM, CHUSAN PALM

This remarkable palm has been cultivated in Europe for 160 years where it is prized for its exotic appearance and tolerance of cold—it grows outdoors in Britain—but it does not enjoy tropical conditions. It reaches 30 ft (10 m) tall, the slim trunk swathed in brownish fibre. The fan-shaped leaves, held on long stalks, are dark green above, blue-green below; dead leaves tend to persist as a 'skirt' on the tree. Dense, showy clusters of small yellow flowers precede the marble-sized, dark blue berries which have a coating of whitish wax. Slow growing until it is established, young plants make good tub specimens. ZONE 8.

TRICHILIA
Meliaceae

This genus includes about 300 species of tropical and subtropical trees and shrubs, mostly from the Americas, with a few species found in southern and eastern Africa. The large compound leaves are alternate, the leaflets untoothed. Male and female flowers are borne in sprays in leaf axils. The fruit are about 1½ in (3 cm) across and contain several black seeds almost covered by a scarlet, fleshy aril. Oil derived from the fruit has a number of uses in traditional medicine in the trees' native countries. Propagation is from seed or cuttings.

Trichilia emetica
RED ASH, NATAL MAHOGANY

This handsome evergreen shade tree is indigenous to southern Africa and is widely seen in warm, humid areas. It grows to 30 ft (10 m) with a rounded, spreading crown and brownish grey bark. The leaves have 7 to 11 leaflets and are dark green with shiny upper surfaces, paler undersides. In summer, small, creamy white, fragrant, bell-shaped flowers are borne in long sprays. Fruit are small, creamy brown and shaped like figs; when ripe they contain 3 to 6 black seeds, each with a scarlet covering. The red ash tolerates wind and does well close to the sea; it needs a frost-free climate and adequate water in summer months. ZONE 10.

TRISTANIOPSIS
Myrtaceae

This genus of evergreen trees is closely related to *Tristania* and used to be included in that larger genus. It contains several species indigenous to high-rainfall coastal forests of eastern Australia. These trees adapt to a range of situations but grow best in deep, well-drained, moist soil, in shade or partial shade. Propagate from seed.

Tristaniopsis laurina
WATER GUM, KANUKA BOX

An evergreen conical tree reaching a height of 30–50 ft (10–15 m), the water gum has a smooth, creamy brown trunk, attractively streaked with grey. Branches start low to the ground and form a dense canopy. It is a good shade or specimen tree for situations of both full sun and full shade. Leaves are oblong to lance shaped, 4 in (10 cm) long, the upper surface dark green and the undersides paler. New leaves are pinkish. Clusters of small, deep yellow flowers appear in summer, each blossom up to ½ in (1 cm) across and rich with nectar. Some people dislike their privet-like scent. The fruit is a round capsule. This species is much planted as a street tree in the warmer parts of Australia. ZONE 10.

TSUGA
Pinaceae
HEMLOCK

These 10 or so species of elegant evergreen conifers from cool-temperate areas of North America and East Asia are widely grown as ornamentals in cool climates. They range from tall trees to (in the case of dwarf cultivars) small shrubs suitable for hedging and rockeries. Conical to pyramidal in growth-habit, the spreading branches droop gracefully. Tsugas are tolerant of shade and thrive in slightly acid, deep, well-drained soil containing plenty of compost. These trees do not enjoy urban environments or very exposed positions and dislike being transplanted. Male cones are small, female cones are scaly and contain winged seeds. The common name hemlock has no connection to the poisonous herb—the trees are not poisonous. Propagation is from seed in spring or cuttings in autumn.

Tsuga canadensis
EASTERN HEMLOCK

From the cool north-east of North America, this conifer thrives near rivers and streams where it has constant moisture. A slow-growing tree, it reaches 80 ft (25 m) with a trunk which is often forked at the base. It forms a broad pyramidal crown with thin branches and pendulous tips. The short, oblong needles, ¼–½ in (6–12 mm) are arranged in 2 rows and are greyish brown and hairy when young, maturing to dark green with 2 greyish bands on the undersides. Oval cones, 1 in (2 cm) long, are borne at the ends of the branchlets and disperse their seeds in autumn. 'Pendula', a lovely weeping conifer, forms a semi-prostrate mound, to 6 ft (2 m) high and wide; it looks spectacular if planted where its graceful branches can cascade down a wall or bank. Juvenile foliage is lime green, becoming greyish green with age. ZONE 2.

Tristaniopsis laurina

Tristaniopsis laurina

Tsuga canadensis

Tsuga canadensis 'Pendula'   *Tristaniopsis laurina* (below)

Tsuga heterophylla

Tsuga chinensis (below)   Tsuga caroliniana (above)

Tsuga mertensiana

Tsuga caroliniana
CAROLINA HEMLOCK

Originating in south-eastern USA, this evergreen conifer grows to 70 ft (22 m). It has attractive bark, dark purple-brown and fissured. The shiny young shoots are grey, red or yellowish brown and needles are a soft greenish yellow. It is a better garden tree than *T. canadensis*. ZONE 4.

Tsuga chinensis
CHINESE HEMLOCK

This small conifer reaching 65 ft (20 m) has been in cultivation for thousands of years and is often a feature of formal Japanese gardens. It forms a narrow crown with a spread of 12 ft (4 m) and is one of the neatest members of the family. Its yellowish young shoots precede glossy green needles that are distinctly notched at the tip. ZONE 6.

Tsuga heterophylla
WESTERN HEMLOCK

From moist, cool, coastal regions of north-western North America, this large, fast-growing tree can reach nearly 200 ft (60 m) in the wild, generally less in cultivation, and is harvested commercially for its pale yellow timber and tannin-rich bark. As with *Sequoia*, the harvest comes almost entirely from natural forests, to the concern of environmentalists. As a specimen in parks and large gardens it is particularly elegant, with a spire-like habit, weeping branchlets and a rusty brown, fissured trunk. New young shoots are greyish, and the flat needles are deep green. ZONE 4.

Tsuga mertensiana
MOUNTAIN HEMLOCK

One of the smallest species, the mountain hemlock seldom exceeds 50 ft (15 m) high and performs best in areas similar to the mild coastal regions of its native western Canada and Alaska. Narrow and columnar, with a straight single trunk and pendent branches, it bears blue-green, distinctly rounded needles, banded top and bottom. These are arranged spirally on the branches and habitually point forward. Its comparatively large, cylindrical, purplish black cones mature to 3 in (8 cm) long. A slow grower, *T. mertensiana* is susceptible to pollution and drought. ZONE 4.

Ulmus americana

Ugni molinae

Ulmus americana

Ulmus glabra

UGNI
Myrtaceae

Members of this genus of evergreen shrubs from temperate regions of Central and South America are grown for their attractive, edible fruit and their glossy green leaves. They need well-drained, moist, acid soil and prefer full sun. Most species form a clump of slender branches clothed in deep green, glossy leaves. They can be pruned in winter to keep the plant compact and bushy. Propagation is from seed or cuttings. This genus is closely related to the myrtles (*Myrtus*) and was formerly included with them.

Ugni molinae
CHILEAN GUAVA, CHILEAN CRANBERRY

Indigenous to Chile and Bolivia, this species is cultivated for its interestingly shaped, fragrant, purplish red, berry-like fruit. These are edible, though tart, and are often made into jam. The small, bell-shaped flowers are pink or white, with prominent stamens, and are borne in leaf axils. Its dense growth, to about 15 ft (5 m), makes the Chilean guava suitable for hedges, and it tolerates light shade. ZONE 8.

ULMUS
Ulmaceae

There are 20-odd species in the elm genus, occuring naturally in temperate regions of the northern hemisphere, though absent from all but the northern fringe of Africa and from North America west of the Great Divide. It is only in the British Isles and north-western Europe that elms have generally been a dominant and much loved feature of the landscape, though sadly that is no longer the case since the advent of Dutch elm disease. With the exception of *U. parvifolia* and perhaps one or two other East Asian species, elms are deciduous, the foliage turning yellow in autumn. The genus is recognized by a combination of leaf and fruit features: the leaves are with few exceptions very one-sided at the base, usually have many prominent, parallel, lateral veins, and the margins are regularly toothed; the small fruit are disc like and dry with a membranous wing, and are carried in clusters near the branch tips usually in late spring or early summer. Most of the European and some North American elms make majestic large trees with furrowed grey bark and high, domed crowns supported by massive limbs. Elms will grow in a wide range of conditions but require cool to cold winters. They grow best in deep, moist soil and can tolerate waterlogging for short periods. They have a high demand for water and soil nutrients. Propagation is from semi-ripe cuttings, suckers or, for selected clones, by grafting or budding; seed can also be used but germination rate is often low.

During the 1920s and 1930s Europe and North America were swept by an epidemic of Dutch elm disease, followed by a second more virulent strain in the 60s and 70s. The disease, which causes wilting and eventual death of the trees, is caused by the fungus *Ophiostoma ulmi*. The fungus is transmitted from tree to tree by the elm bark beetle, which can fly quite long distances. Dutch elm disease has wiped out most of the elms in both Europe and North America. There is no cure for affected trees but not all elms are equally affected, the Asian species generally being immune. Australia is now just about the only country with large numbers of planted elms that is still free of the disease.

Ulmus americana
AMERICAN ELM, WHITE ELM

The largest of the North American elms, this species can make a majestic tree of up to 120 ft (35 m) in height in the wild, or about half that when planted in an open situation, with high-arching limbs and a vase-shaped crown, spreading broadly only with considerable age.

The trunk of old trees may become strongly buttressed at the base and the grey bark is divided by deep fissures into flat-topped ridges. The 4–6 in (10–15 cm) long leaves are distinguished from those of most European elms by having none of their lateral veins forked; they have smooth upper sides and slightly downy undersides. The American elm occurs over a vast area of eastern and central USA and southern Canada, mostly in moist valley bottoms and lower hill slopes, but is in danger of extinction in many areas from the ravages of Dutch elm disease. It was prized for street planting as well as for the valuable, tough timber it produced. ZONE 3.

Ulmus glabra
WYCH ELM, SCOTCH ELM

One of the major European elms, this species occurs over much of Europe including the British Isles. It can make a tree of over 100 ft (30 m) high with a rather open crown of large, spreading limbs, though on younger trees the crown may be dense and rounded. It is easily identifiable by its leaves which are up to 6 in (15 cm) long, broadest near the apex, and with an extremely rough upper surface. The wych elm does not sucker from the roots like other European elms and is also one of the most resistant species to urban pollution. The 'wych' in the name has nothing to do with witches but is an old Anglo-Saxon word for trees with flexible branches, as in 'witch-hazel' and 'wicker'. Popular cultivars are 'Camperdownii' which forms a dome-like mound of weeping branches when grafted on to a standard; and 'Lutescens', the common golden elm, with spring and summer foliage lime-green tipped pale yellow—in some countries it has often been misidentified as *U. procera* 'Louis van Houtte', another golden cultivar. ZONE 3.

Ulmus × hollandica
DUTCH ELM

This hybrid name covers a number of distinct clones, all believed to originate from crosses between the European species *U. glabra* and *U. minor*. Their leaves are mostly smaller and less raspy-textured than *U. glabra* but broader and shorter stalked than *U. minor*. They include some of the most widely planted elm clones, making large, handsome trees with high, spreading crowns. The original is now referred to as cultivar 'Hollandica' and has very broad, rounded leaves. 'Vegeta', the Huntingdon elm, is another very old clone (first noted in 1760), with pale yellowish green leaves in distinct flattened sprays. 'Purpurascens' is a vigorous, open tree with purplish green new growth. 'Jacqueline Hillier' is a modern cultivar of miniature size, usually 4–6 ft (1.2–2 m) high with dense, weeping branches; it is useful for hedging. ZONE 4.

Ulmus laevis
RUSSIAN ELM

From central and eastern Europe and east to the Caucasus region, the Russian elm makes a large tree of vigorous growth and rather coarse dark green foliage. The leaves resemble those of *U. americana*, to which it is closely related, but are shorter and relatively broader with a grey down on the undersides. The crown spreads very broadly, even on quite young trees, and the dark grey bark is strongly furrowed. ZONE 3.

Ulmus minor
FIELD ELM, SMOOTH-LEAFED ELM

Also known as *U. carpinifolia*, this species has a wide occurrence in Europe, western Asia and North Africa. It is a vigorous tree but usually smaller than the other European elms and the crown is pointed. Leaves also are smaller, tapering toward both ends, with smooth upper sides and a slender stalk. Unfortunately, it is one of the worst species for root suckers and a tree may spread into a small dense grove in time, especially if subjected to soil disturbance or lopping. More widely planted now is 'Variegata', with leaves variably flecked and streaked with white; just as vigorous, it seems less inclined to sucker. ZONE 4.

Ulmus × hollandica

Ulmus parvifolia
CHINESE ELM, LACEBARK ELM

Very different from the European and North American elms, the Chinese elm is prized for its elegant, open growth-habit with spreading, sinuous limbs and in particular for its beautiful bark which sheds in small flakes to produce a mottled effect with dark grey, red-brown and cream variously mixed, depending on age and season. In mild climates it is semi-evergreen. The dark green leaves are quite small and leathery, smooth and shiny on the upper sides, with small blunt teeth. They colour individually yellow or dull reddish before each drops. The small, thick fruit mature in autumn, much later than most other elms. Found wild in China and Japan, this species is the best elm for warmer temperate climates though lacking the character of the English elms. It is relatively resistant to Dutch elm disease. ZONE 5.

Ulmus parvifolia (below)

Ulmus parvifolia

Ulmus minor (below)

Ulmus pumila

Ulmus procera
ENGLISH ELM

In England, to which it is believed to be endemic, this elm is regarded as the noblest of native trees, reaching heights of up to 150 ft (45 m) with a high-branched crown of billowing foliage and a straight or slightly sinuous trunk so commonly seen in paintings of traditional landscapes. Sadly, most of these majestic trees have now succumbed to Dutch elm disease. In cultivation in the southern hemisphere, it makes a tree with a compact, rounded crown, up to about 80 ft (25 m) high with age. The species is recognized by its smallish, rounded leaves, almost as broad as they are long, with a slightly rough surface. The English elm has often been confused with other European elms, especially with some forms of the Dutch elm. It seldom sets fertile seed and is usually propagated by suckers. The quite rare cultivar 'Louis van Houtte' has golden leaves. ZONE 4.

Ulmus pumila
SIBERIAN ELM, DWARF ELM

Occurring from eastern Siberia right across northern China and central Asia, this small elm is valued for its rapid growth and hardiness under severe conditions. It is easily distinguished from other elms by its small leaves, which are almost completely symmetrical at the base, on slender stalks. It has become especially popular in the USA in the Midwestern states, withstanding drought and bitter cold and assisting in erosion control. Its branches have a reputation for brittleness, breaking in strong winds, but it appears resistant to Dutch elm disease and for this reason has been used as a breeding parent of new hybrid cultivars; one of the most promising is 'Sapporo Autumn Gold', with dense foliage which turns deep golden yellow in autumn. ZONE 3.

UMBELLULARIA
Lauraceae
CALIFORNIA LAUREL, HEADACHE TREE

This genus includes just one species, the California laurel, indigenous to California and Oregon. It is an evergreen tree with leathery leaves. When crushed under the nose, their pungent smell can cause an instant (though temporary) headaches. Frost-hardy once established, it likes full sun, shelter from strong winds and deep, moist, but well-drained soil. Propagate from seed.

Umbellularia californica

The California laurel reaches a height of 80 ft (25 m), its spreading branches forming a dense, shady crown. The trunk has scaly bark, and leaves are oval to lance shaped, 5 in (12 cm) long. They are dark green, leathery and shiny on top. Inconspicuous yellowish green flowers are carried in clusters near the branch tips in spring. The fruit is a purple, pear-shaped berry. The timber is valued for delicate woodworking. ZONE 7.

VACCINIUM
Ericaceae
BLUEBERRY, CRANBERRY

This large and varied genus includes small trees and vines but the species seen in gardens are deciduous shrubs valued for the edible berries of some species and notable autumn colour in others. These berries, known according to the species as bilberry, blueberry, cranberry, huckleberry or whortleberry,

Ulmus procera (below)

are red or blue-black and often covered with a bloom when ripe. They are grown commercially for fresh fruit, as well as for juicing and canning. Indigenous to Asia, Europe and North and South America, *Vaccinium* species are generally cold tolerant and shade loving; many form dense, thicket-like shrubs. The plants need acid, well-drained soil with plenty of humus and regular water; some, indeed, prefer boggy ground. Leaves are narrow, bright green, leathery and sometimes copper-red when young; their edges can be toothed or smooth. Small bell-shaped flowers, pale pink, white, purple or red, appear in late spring or early summer. Propagate by division or from cuttings in autumn.

Vaccinium arboreum
TREE SPARKLEBERRY

This medium to large deciduous or semi-evergreen shrub from south-eastern USA, also known as the farkleberry or tree huckleberry, can achieve tree-like proportions in the wild. Its glossy, dark green leaves, 2 in (5 cm) long, are leathery with downy undersides. The foliage colours well in autumn but the berries are food appealing only to birds. ZONE 7.

Vaccinium corymbosum
HIGHBUSH BLUEBERRY

Also known as the swamp blueberry because of its preference for boggy soils, this deciduous species from New England is mainly grown for its edible blue-black berries. It also displays exceptionally fine scarlet autumn foliage. Forming a dense thicket with upright stems with a height and spread of 6 ft (2 m), its new leaves are bright green and its clusters of pendulous flowers are pale pink. 'Blue Ray' has delicious, sweet, juicy fruit. ZONE 2.

Vaccinium ovatum
EVERGREEN HUCKLEBERRY

From Oregon through to southern California, this is a dense, compact shrub. Its dark green, glossy foliage is much in demand by florists as it lasts well in water; in fact, they have driven the wild plants very nearly to extinction. The plant forms a spreading clump 3 ft (1 m) high and 5 ft (1.5 m) wide. White or pink flowers appear in early summer. Its tangy edible berries are red when young, maturing to blue-black, and are rich in Vitamin C. ZONE 4.

VEITCHIA
Arecaceae

The elegant feather-leaved palms of this genus occur naturally in tropical forests of Fiji, Vanuatu and the Philippines. They need a tropical or warm subtropical climate, protec-

Vaccinium ovatum

Vaccinium corymbosum

tion from wind, moist, well-drained soil and do best in part-shade or full sun. Species range in height from 20–100 ft (7–30 m) and most have a slender, pale grey, smooth or lightly ringed trunk. The bright green, gently arching fronds form an umbrella-like crown. Bunches of insignificant flowers are followed by dense clusters of bright red or orange berries. Mature trees make attractive lawn and landscape specimens while young plants grow well in tubs, even indoors in well-lit conditions. Propagation from seed is slow.

Veitchia merrillii
MANILA PALM

From the Philippines, this is an attractive small palm widely grown in tropical gardens. Maturing to 20 ft (7 m), it has a slender trunk marked with rings. The feathery, bright green leaves form a compact crown, springing from a short green crownshaft. The bright red fruit, about 1½ in (3 cm) long, hang in clusters below the crown in autumn and winter. The Manila palm is often seen planted in the shelter of buildings where its delicate fronds are protected from wind damage. ZONE 11.

Vaccinium ovatum

Veitchia merrillii

Viburnum × bodnantense

Viburnum × bodnantense

Vestia lycioides

VERNICIA
Euphorbiaceae

Formerly included in *Aleurites*, this small genus consists of mainly deciduous trees from China and Indo-China. They are grown commercially for their seeds which contain chinawood oils, drying oils used extensively in paints and varnishes, and are also valued as shade trees. The large seeds are poisonous. They are enclosed in large rounded fruit that look a bit like walnuts. The leaves are oval to heart shaped, sometimes lobed, and the flowers appear in clusters at the branch tips. Profuse hairs cover the attractive flowers as well as the young stems and leaves. The trees grow best in full sun, in an open position and in light, well-drained soil. *Vernicia* species thrive in warm climates. Propagation is from seed (sown directly where the tree is to grow) or from hardwood cuttings.

Vernicia fordii
TUNG-OIL TREE

From southern China, the tung-oil tree grows to 18–30 ft (6–10 m) high; branches extend horizontally from the trunk, forming a round to flat-topped canopy. The leaves are oval, about 5 in (12 cm) long, with 3 lobes; each has 2 red glands at the base where it joins the long stalk. Mature leaves are held horizontally and are light, yellowish green. Spring flowers are trumpet shaped and cream, streaked with orange or red, each 1 in (2 cm) long, on a long thin stalk. Fruit are 2–3 in (5–8 cm) across, ripening from green to brown. Tung-oil, used in paints and varnishes, is derived from the seeds. ZONE 10.

VESTIA
Solanaceae

Like its relative the potato, this evergreen shrub, the only member of its genus, comes from temperate areas of South America. It appreciates shelter from strong winds and does best in rich, well-drained soil with plenty of water in warmer months. Full sun or light shade suit it. In warm-temperate or even subtropical climates it can be cut back hard in winter and will shoot from the base in spring. Propagation is from seed or cuttings.

Vestia lycioides

Indigenous to Chile, this fast-growing shrub reaches 6 ft (2 m) high, with many erect stems. Its shiny green leaves are thin and narrow, crowding down the stems; they have an extremely unpleasant smell when crushed. Dainty, lemon-yellow, tubular flowers with prominent stamens are produced through spring and summer. The fruit is a small, inedible, blue berry. ZONE 9.

VIBURNUM
Caprifoliaceae

This important genus is made up of some 150 species of evergreen and deciduous cool-climate shrubs, primarily of Asian origin with a few species from North America, Europe and northern Africa. Many of the cultivated species and forms are noted for their fragrant, showy flowers and may also produce colourful berries or bright autumn foliage. The evergreen species, especially *V. tinus,* are often used for hedging. Most viburnums are remarkably trouble-free plants. They grow in any well-drained soil in sun or light shade. They can be trimmed heavily after flowering, though this will prevent fruit forming. Viburnums are usually grown from cuttings. In several species, such as *V. plicatum, V. macrocephalum* and *V. opulus,* the flowers are arranged in a similar way to those of the lacecap hydrangeas; with small fertile flowers and large, sterile ones on the same plant. These species have all given rise to cultivars with all-sterile flower heads, known as 'snowball viburnums'.

Viburnum × bodnantense

A hybrid between *V. farreri* and *V. grandiflorum,* this 9 ft (3 m) high deciduous shrub has slightly glossy, deep green, oval leaves that are pale green on the undersides. Before they fall in autumn they develop intense orange, red and purple tones. The flowers, which open from autumn to early spring depending on the climate, are bright pink in the bud, open pale pink and fade to white. They are heavily scented. 'Dawn' has slightly darker flowers, especially those that open in spring; 'Deben' has light pink to white somewhat tubular flowers. ZONE 6.

Viburnum × burkwoodii

A hybrid between *V. carlesii* and *V. utile*, this 8 ft (2.5 m) high semi-evergreen plant has glossy, deep green, pointed, oval leaves to about 3½ in (9 cm) long. They are pale sage green on the undersides and those that are to fall in autumn develop bright yellow and red tones. From early to late spring ball-shaped clusters of small starry flowers open; they are pink in the bud, opening white, and are heavily fragrant. ZONE 4.

Viburnum carlesii
KOREAN VIBURNUM

Indigenous to Korea and Tsushima Island, this densely foliaged deciduous shrub grows to about 5 ft (1.5 m) high with a similar spread. The Korean viburnum has pointed oval leaves 2–3½ in (5–9 cm) long, with finely serrated edges. The starry flowers open from mid- to late spring; they are pale pink aging to white, around ½ in (1 cm) across and sweetly scented. The flowers are carried in rounded clusters up to 2½ in (7 cm) in diameter. The fruit ripens to black and is sporadic in cultivation. Several cultivars are available, including 'Aurora', with deep pink buds; 'Charis', with white flowers; and 'Diana', slightly larger growing, with deep pink buds. ZONE 3.

Viburnum davidii

This evergreen species from Sichuan, China, grows to around 3 ft (1 m) high and spreads slowly to form a densely foliaged clump up to 6 ft (2 m) across. It makes an excellent large-scale groundcover. The pointed, oval leaves are bright glossy green and up to 6 in (15 cm) long. The leaf petioles and new wood are reddish brown. The spring-borne clusters of white flowers are not spectacular but are followed by turquoise blue berries. 'Femina' is a reliable, heavy-fruiting cultivar. ZONE 6.

Viburnum dentatum
SOUTHERN ARROW-WOOD

The Native Americans used the stems of this shrub from eastern USA for the shafts of arrows. Today its uses are purely decorative, as it makes a pleasant deciduous shrub 12 ft (4 m) high and about 6 ft (2 m) wide, with rounded, prominently veined, toothed leaves which are occasionally tufted beneath. Glossy green when young, they turn rich red in autumn. Flowering in early summer, the southern arrow-wood's white blooms are borne in clusters on the ends of long stalks. The egg-shaped fruit are bluish black. This species makes an attractive informal hedge. ZONE 2.

Viburnum farreri

Discovered in mountain regions of western China at the beginning of the century by Reginald Farrer and formerly known as *V. fragrans*, this deciduous shrub grows to about 8 ft (2.5 m) tall. Its lightly arching branches are clad in oval, deeply toothed leaves with prominent veins; bronze when young, they mature to rich green and turn red before falling. The pink buds open to white, sweetly smelling flowers clustered at the tips of branches in early spring before the leaves appear. Glossy red fruit are produced only occasionally. In 'Candidissimum' the flowers and buds are pure white, leaves bright green. ZONE 5.

Viburnum dentatum

Viburnum davidii

Viburnum farreri   *Viburnum carlesii* (below)   *Viburnum carlesii*

Viburnum lantana
WAYFARER TREE

Often used as hedging, this deciduous species from Europe and northwestern Asia is tolerant of cold climates. It forms a tall branching shrub 15 ft (5 m) high and is distinguished by its new shoots which are unusually furry for a viburnum. The oval leaves have hairy undersides and turn burgundy red in autumn. In early summer small creamy white flowers are profusely borne in flat clusters. The oblong red fruit ripen to black. ZONE 3.

Viburnum opulus 'Compactum'

Viburnum opulus   *Viburnum odoratissimum* (below)

Viburnum macrocephalum
CHINESE SNOWBALL TREE

The distinctive characteristic of this species is the presence of small, fertile flowers and large, sterile ones, but the cultivated plants represent a form with all-sterile flowers. Huge rounded trusses of white flowers, up to 6 in (15 cm) across, give a spectacular display in early summer on this upright shrub from China. The dark green, leathery leaves are oval and 4 in (10 cm) long; normally deciduous, this species may be semi-evergreen in milder climates. It does best in a sunny, protected position in cold areas, growing to 6–10 ft (2–3 m). ZONE 5.

Viburnum odoratissimum
SWEET VIBURNUM

As the species name implies, *V. odoratissimum* has very fragrant flowers in late spring. They are white and star shaped, in dense clusters 4 in (10 cm) across. This fast-growing species forms a dense, rounded shrub or small tree 15–18 ft (5–6 m) high. Red berries mature to black. The sweet viburnum ranges from the Himalaya to the Philippines and Japan. Evergreen, its shiny green leaves are thick, leathery and rounded, 6 in (15 cm) long. It is one of the few viburnums to thrive in warm to hot climates (it dislikes frost). ZONE 8.

Viburnum opulus
GUELDER ROSE, SNOWBALL TREE

This lovely deciduous shrub from Europe and North Africa has several outstanding qualities. It produces splendid clusters of snowy white, lacy flowers in summer, it has attractive fruit and autumn colour, and it can be grown in wet or boggy situations. A large shrub growing to 12 ft (4 m), *V. opulus* has grey bark and a spreading habit with long, pale green shoots. Its paired leaves are lobed and turn deep crimson in autumn. Generous bunches of shiny, translucent, orange-red fruit remain on the bush until well into winter. The variety *americanum* (formerly known as *V. trilobum*) bears dense clusters of white flowers and deeply toothed leaves which turn claret red in autumn. 'Compactum' is a dense, compact shrub bearing large quantities of flowers and fruit. 'Sterile', the snowball bush, has snowball-like heads of pale green to white, sterile flowers so large they weigh the branches down; the slightly hairy foliage colours richly in autumn but it bears no fruit. 'Xanthocarpum' has clear yellow fruit, which are quite translucent when ripe. ZONE 2.

Viburnum plicatum

This deciduous shrub from Japan and China grows to about 15 ft (5 m) high and wide. It has hazel-like, 3 in (8 cm) long, mid-green, pointed, oval leaves with serrated edges and a somewhat tiered growth-habit, a feature emphasized in the cultivar 'Mariesii'. Large creamy white flower clusters with a mass of tiny fertile flowers in the

Viburnum opulus var. *americanum*

Viburnum lantana

Viburnum macrocephalum (below)

Viburnum setigerum

Virgilia divaricata

centre, surrounded by large sterile flowers, open in spring; they are followed by small berries that are red at first, ripening to black. *V. plicatum* var. *plicatum* is a sterile form. This shrub grows best in moist, well-drained, humus-rich soil with its roots shaded. The attractive cultivar 'Pink Beauty' has a pale pink tinge to the flowers. ZONE 5.

Viburnum prunifolium
BLACK-HAW

This species from eastern USA features deciduous leaves that turn orange and red in autumn; broadly oval to round with a finely toothed edge, each is 3 in (8 cm) long, on a reddish stalk. This shrub grows to about 15 ft (5 m) tall. Black-haw grows naturally in eastern parts of the USA. In spring the small white flowers are borne in flat-topped clusters 4 in (10 cm) across. Berries are bluish black in flattened clusters. Each berry measures just over ½ in (1 cm) long. The root of this plant is used for medicinal purposes. This species tolerates frost. ZONE 3.

Viburnum rhytidophyllum

This fast-growing evergreen shrub from China has distinctive, handsome foliage. The long leaves of *V. rhytidophyllum* are corrugated, deeply veined and dark glossy green, with grey felted undersides. Growing to 12 ft (4 m) high and spreading almost as wide, it can tolerate alkaline soil. The spring flowers, which are small and creamy white, appear in large, flat clusters at the ends of branches, and the fruit are oval berries, red at first, later turning black. To ensure fruiting, this shrub should be planted in groups. ZONE 4.

Viburnum prunifolium

Viburnum setigerum

This species from China grows to about 12 ft (4 m) high and can be trimmed to keep it compact. The rich orange-yellow autumn foliage is matched in beauty by oval, yellow fruit which mature to a brilliant red. By comparison, the flowers are unspectacular, appearing as white clusters in early summer. The leaves were said to be made into tea by Chinese monks, hence the (obsolete) name *V. theiferum*. ZONE 5.

Viburnum tinus
LAURUSTINUS

This very densely foliaged evergreen shrub from the Mediterranean region may eventually grow to 15 ft (5 m) high and 18 ft (6 m) wide, though it is usually kept smaller by trimming. It is an excellent hedging plant and is very tolerant of heavy shade. The dark green, pointed, elliptical leaves are up to 4 in (10 cm) long and develop purplish tones in cold weather. Cream and yellow variegated foli-

Viburnum tinus

age forms are available. Clusters of white flowers open from pink buds from late winter and are followed by blue-black berries. Some people find the scent of the flowers unpleasant. ZONE 6.

VIRGILIA
Fabaceae

Only 2 species belong in this genus, both evergreen trees and both indigenous to southern Africa. They

Viburnum rhytidophyllum

Viburnum plicatum 'Pink Beauty'

are notable for their fast growth. Over the warmer months they make a great display of showy pea-flowers. *V. divaricata* bears pink flowers in spring. The fruit is a flat pod. Leaves are fern like with an odd number of leaflets. Very adaptable, they grow best in an open sunny position and well-drained soil. They cope well with wind and suit warm climates, being tender to frost. Propagate from seed (soaked in warm water for 24 hours).

Virgilia oroboides

Vitex negundo

Vitex negundo

Vitex lucens

Vitex lucens

Virgilia oroboides
CAPE LILAC, TREE-IN-A-HURRY

This species is also known as *V. capensis*. It features masses of small, mauve-pink, fragrant flowers in clusters scattered through the crown from early summer to autumn. It is called tree-in-a-hurry because of its speedy growth-habit—up to 15 ft (5 m) in only 2 years. However, it is often short-lived and older trees become quite straggly, so it is mainly useful for new gardens or as a nurse plant. It makes a rounded shrub to small tree 18–30 ft (6–10 m) tall. Leaves are dark green, up to 8 in (20 cm) long, with 13 to 21 oblong, leathery leaflets. The pod is 2–3 in (5–7 cm) long. ZONE 9.

VITEX
Verbenaceae

This genus is made up of about 100 mainly tropical and subtropical trees and shrubs; some evergreen, some deciduous. The leaves are compound with 3 to 7 leaflets radiating from the stalk—less commonly, leaves are simple. Highlights are sprays of tubular flowers in shades of white, yellow, red, blue or purple, and fleshy drupes, usually not a feature. In some species both the leaves and the flowers are aromatic. These plants adapt to most soils but do best in fertile soil with good drainage, with plenty of summer moisture. A sheltered spot in full sun is ideal. Propagate from seed or cuttings.

Vitex agnus-castus
CHASTE TREE

This shrub, indigenous to southern Europe and western Asia is also called monk's pepper for its aromatic leaves; as well as being a cheap spice, the leaves were believed to induce chastity. These are 6–8 in (15–20 cm) long with 5 to 7 lance-shaped to rounded leaflets, deep green on top and felty grey underneath. The chaste tree is a deciduous, rounded shrub or small tree, 10–18 ft (3–6 m) tall, with an upright, branching, woody stem. From early summer to autumn it bears dense, erect sprays up to 12 in (30 cm) long of faintly perfumed, lavender flowers. Small purple fruit follow. White-flowered and variegated-leaf forms are also available. It is used medicinally and its flexible branches are popular for basket weaving. It thrives in warm to cool climates. ZONE 7.

Vitex lucens
PURIRI

This fine evergreen tree is from New Zealand. It reaches a height of 30–50 ft (10–15 m) and features a rounded crown and a smooth pale trunk. Sprays of bright red or pink flowers are a winter bonus. Each flower measures 1 in (2 cm) long. Large, bright red drupes mature in spring. The leaves consist of 3 to 5 large, oval to round leaflets, smooth and shiny rich green, with a wavy edge. This tree prefers to grow in moist soil enriched with organic matter; it suits mild climates. ZONE 9.

Vitex negundo

This useful shrub or small tree, indigenous to warm-climate areas from southern and eastern Asia, is grown for its pleasantly aromatic foliage and fragrant flowers. It grows to 24 ft (8 m) high and produces long leaves composed of deeply cut leaflets which are dark green above with pale, furry undersides. The fragrant flowers are mauve and appear in loose sprays in spring. ZONE 6.

Vitex trifolia

An evergreen, rounded shrub or bushy small tree to 10 ft (3 m) high, this species comes from coastal areas from eastern Australia to Southeast Asia. The leaves usually have 3 leaflets (the middle leaflet larger), and are oblong to lance shaped, mid-green above, white and downy on the undersides. Flowers are coloured blue to purple, in sprays to 9 in (22 cm) long, from late spring to autumn. The flower stalks are white and hairy. The fruit are black drupes. 'Purpurea' has leaves with deep purple undersides, while 'Variegata' has bright green leaves edged with creamy yellow. This is a shrub for warm climates. It copes with coastal exposure and poor sandy soil. ZONE 10.

W X Y Z

Washingtonia filifera (below) *Weigela florida* 'Variegata' (above)

Washingtonia robusta (below)

Washingtonia filifera

WASHINGTONIA
Arecaceae
WASHINGTONIA PALM

This genus is made up of 2 species of evergreen palms from arid parts of western Mexico, southern California and Arizona. Their stately appearance makes them an excellent choice as a specimen or avenue tree. They have an upright single trunk. They are also called petticoat palms because of the dense mass of dead fronds which hangs down and sheaths the trunk, almost to the ground. Leaves are large and fan shaped, with many strap-like segments. The leaf stalks are armed with spines. Small white flowers are clustered at intervals on long flowering branches that arch out well beyond the leaves, while the fruit are small brown drupes. These palms enjoy warm to hot climates, full sun, well-drained soil and an open position. Propagate from seed.

Washingtonia filifera
CALIFORNIA FAN PALM, COTTON PALM

From southern California and Arizona, this palm develops quite a fat trunk and reaches a height of 40–50 ft (13–15 m). The massive greyish green leaves consist of many segments pointed at the tips, and very spiny leaf stalks. They form a broad spherical crown to about 15 ft (5 m) across, the lower leaves hanging downwards or horizontally and the upper ones standing upright and well separated. The common name of cotton palm derives from the white cotton-like threads on and between the leaf segments. The white flowers are unobtrusive. Black berries ripen in winter. ZONE 9.

Washingtonia robusta
MEXICAN WASHINGTONIA PALM

This species, taller and more slender than *W. filifera* and with a more tapering trunk, occurs naturally in north-western Mexico. It grows to 80 ft (25 m) and has a crown about 10 ft (3 m) across. Its shiny, bright green leaves are almost circular, being less deeply cut into segments. Cotton-like threads are missing on mature specimens. The white flowers are borne in small clusters. Fruit are tiny, dark brown berries. This species is easier to grow than *W. filifera* and many find it a better garden tree, though it is a little more frost-tender. ZONE 10.

WEIGELA
Caprifoliaceae

This genus includes about 10 species of deciduous shrubs from Japan, Korea and north-eastern China. Most grow to 6–10 ft (2–3 m) high and wide, and have pointed, elliptical, deep green leaves, about 4 in (10 cm) long. The foliage often develops orange, red and purple tones in autumn before falling. In spring, weigelas bear masses of white, pink or crimson, sometimes yellowish, bell- or trumpet-shaped flowers, about 1½ in (3 cm) long. If necessary, the shrubs can be pruned after flowering. Most species do best in full sun or light shade in moist, well-drained soil. They are usually propagated from summer cuttings.

Weigela 'Bristol Ruby'

This erect hybrid, bred from *W. florida* and *W. coraeensis,* is grown for the profusion of crimson flowers which adorn the shrub through spring. It grows to 6 ft (2 m) tall, with slender, arching branches. ZONE 4.

Weigela florida

This arching deciduous shrub from Japan, Korea and north-eastern China grows up to 10 ft (3 m) or so. It is grown for the lavish spring display of flowers, white, pink or crimson according to cultivar (the wild plant is usually rose-pink). 'Variegata' has bright green leaves edged with cream and in spring bears masses of 1½ in (3 cm) wide, bright pink, trumpet-shaped flowers. ZONE 4.

Weigela middendorffiana

This attractive deciduous shrub grows to a height and width of about 6 ft (2 m), and is distinctive for its plump, bell-shaped, spring flowers which come in tones from pale creamy yellow to deep amber, with reddish markings in the throat. Although it can tolerate heat, it needs shelter from strong winds to perform at its best. ZONE 6.

WESTRINGIA
Lamiaceae

These evergreen shrubs are indigenous to Australia. The square woody stems are clothed in small stiff leaves arranged in whorls of 3 or 4. The tubular flowers consist of 2 lips, the upper one with 2 lobes, the lower with 3. They appear for many months in the leaf axils, flowering peaking in spring. The fruit are tiny and nut like. Westringias thrive in mild-winter climates. Many grow naturally near the sea and relish these conditions. They prefer an open sunny spot and adapt to most well-drained soils; some species benefit from the addition of organic matter. All species will thrive where there is adequate water over summer. Clip them annually to maintain a compact bush. They are propagated from soft-tip or semi-hardwood cuttings.

Westringia fruticosa
COAST ROSEMARY, AUSTRALIAN ROSEMARY

This species is also known as *W. rosmariniformis* due to its rosemary-like leaves. It makes a compact rounded shrub 6 ft (2 m) high and about as wide, but can be kept more compact. Slender spreading branches bear narrow leaves arranged in 4s; they are grey-green on top, white and felty underneath. The small flowers, white with purple blotches in the throat, are present much of the year. The coast rosemary can be grown as a clipped or informal hedge. ZONE 9.

WIDDRINGTONIA
Cupressaceae

This small genus of conifers belongs to the cypress family and occurs naturally in eastern and southern Africa. *Widdringtonia* species are evergreen trees and bear male and female flowers on the same tree. Their attractive greyish green foliage is linear on young trees, scale like on mature ones. Woody female cones are held upright and are rounded. These are cypresses for warm climates and tolerate only moderate frost. An open sunny location and well-drained soil suit them best. They are grown from seed.

Widdringtonia cupressoides
SAPREE-WOOD

The sapree-wood is a low, shrubby tree reaching 12 ft (4 m) high. The young leaves are linear, up to ½ in (1 cm) long, while the scale-like adult leaves overlap and are closely pressed together, arranged in 4 vertical rows. Female cones, held in groups of up to 3, are about ¾ in (2 cm) across. ZONE 8.

WODYETIA
Arecaceae
FOXTAIL PALM

This genus contains only one species, a striking, evergreen palm endemic to tropical open forests of Australia's Cape York Peninsula. *W. bifurcata* was identified only in the early 1980s, but is already widely grown in the tropics and subtropics in many countries. Unfortunately, the palm is now believed to be threatened in the wild due to poaching. Foxtail palms are easily grown in warm, frost-free areas. They need very well-drained soil but tolerate dry conditions, hot sun and even strong wind—though wind will damage the fronds. They are easily raised from seed. The genus is named for Wodyeti, the last male Aborigine of his clan, who died in the 1970s.

Wodyetia bifurcata

This attractive palm has distinctive, bright green, dense, bushy fronds which look very like foxtails and are up to 8 ft (2.5 m) long. It grows to 50 ft (15 m) tall. The sturdy trunk is slightly bottle shaped, smooth and banded, with a prominent pale green crownshaft. Flowers are borne in large branched clusters at the base of the crownshaft, male and female together. The large, oval fruit which follow the flowers measure about 2½ in (6 cm) long and ripen orange-red. ZONE 10.

WOLLEMIA
Araucariaceae
WOLLEMI PINE

This conifer genus, endemic to a very restricted area in the Blue Mountains of south-eastern Australia, was discovered in late 1994. The only known species is *W. nobilis*. Closely related to *Agathis* and *Araucaria*, *Wollemia* belongs to an ancient family of conifers. It is one of the world's rarest plants, with only about 20 trees surviving in a deep, moist sandstone canyon, and is considered to be a 'living fossil'. Although botanists have begun to propagate it, seeds or plants of the Wollemi pine are unlikely to be available to gardeners for a good few years yet. To date there is little information on how to grow it. In the wild it grows in moist soils derived from sandstone and high in organic matter.

Wollemia nobilis

This remarkable conifer grows to a height of 130 ft (40 m) tall and has a slender columnar growth-habit. The bark of mature trees features many soft spongy nodules while young stems have bark that peels away in thin reddish brown scales. The Wollemi pine has a unique branching habit that produces a double crown effect on older trees. The lateral main branches are in whorls up the trunk; these do not

Westringia fruticosa

Westringia fruticosa (below)

Wollemia nobilis

Wollemia nobilis (below)

branch again but those near the apex of the crown terminate in a male or female cone. After coning, each whole branch is subsequently shed from the trunk rather than the leaves being shed individually. Once these primary branches have fallen, buds on the trunk below the crown grow out to produce a second generation of branches which form a 'second crown'. Some new branches may also sprout from the base of the trunk to eventually produce a tree with multiple trunks of different ages. The leaves of the Wollemi pine vary according to their position on the tree: on the lower lateral branches they are long, narrow and flexible, in 2 comb-like rows forming a flattened spray; at the top of the crown they are short, broad and rigid, arranged in 4 rows but all directed upwards. The female (seed) cones are about 4 in (10 cm) long and globular with many bristle-pointed scales, while the cylindrical male (pollen) cones are up to 5 in (12 cm) long; they are borne on lower branches than the female cones. ZONE 9.

XANTHORRHOEA
Xanthorrhoeaceae
GRASS-TREE, BLACK-BOY TREE

This is a small genus of evergreen, grass-like plants indigenous to Australia; they are very slow growing but long lived. Mature plants are stemless or have a thick, palm-like trunk topped by a thick clump of long, arching, grass-like leaves up to 3 ft (1 m) in length. Young plants are clumps of erect or arching leaves, and they take 20 years or more to form a trunk. The long, spear-like flower spikes are produced spasmodically, usually in spring and in response to burning. The spike, up to about 5 ft (1.5 m) long, consists of many densely packed, small, white flowers, held on a long woody stalk up to about 6 ft (2 m) long. The fruit are leathery capsules, packed along the length of the spike and surrounded by the blackened dead flowers; as the flowers are fleeting, for most of the time the flower spike looks

Wollemia nobilis, bark (below)

Xanthorrhoea malacophylla (below)

Xanthorrhoea preissii

Xylomelum occidentale

black. Grass trees need an open sunny spot and well-drained soil as they are susceptible to root rot. They can also be grown in containers. The substance which exudes from the base of the old leaves was formerly used as a source of resins and varnish. Propagate from seed.

Xanthorrhoea glauca

Formerly known as *X. australis*, this species eventually develops a trunk up to 12 ft (4 m) high which sometimes divides into 2 or more stems some distance above the ground. Each very narrow grey-green leaf is up to 3 ft (1 m) long and squarish in cross-section. They are erect to arching, and old dead leaves persist, hanging down in a 'skirt' around the trunk. The crown of foliage is about 5 ft (1.5 m) across. The flower spike plus stalk stands 6–9 ft (2–3 m) above the foliage, accounting for about half the total length. From rocky hills of coastal eastern Australia, this is a plant for warm climates. ZONE 9.

Xanthorrhoea malacophylla

This grass-tree is one of the tallest species, with a trunk as much as 20 ft (7 m) high and often branched when older, each branch terminating in a luxuriant rosette of long, bright green leaves that are rather soft and drooping. Each rosette may send up a flower spike up to 5 ft (1.5 m) long on top of a stout stalk up to 6 ft (2 m) long. The numerous small white flowers open from late autumn to mid-spring. The species is confined to subtropical eastern Australia, occuring on wet coastal ranges in north-eastern New South Wales where it grows on steep rocky hillsides. ZONE 10.

Xanthorrhoea preissii

From mild-climate areas of Western Australia, this evergreen plant has an upright or slightly twisted trunk, often black and scorched-looking, which can reach 20 ft (7 m) with maturity. The crown of long arching grass-like leaves sits in a clump on top. The small creamy yellow flowers are densely packed at the top of a long spike which stands high above the crown. Brownish capsular fruit follow; they contain 1 or 2 black shiny seeds. This species can be grown as a tub specimen for patios and courtyards. It is drought tolerant, needs full sun and light, well-drained soil. ZONE 10.

XANTHOSTEMON
Myrtaceae

The evergreen trees of this small genus originated in tropical rainforests of north-eastern Australia. The leathery, oval leaves are glossy dark green, up to 6 in (15 cm) long, and held on short stalks; new growth is often bronze-pink. The 5-petalled flowers are white, gold or yellow and are held in clusters at the ends of the branches. The trunk and branches are smooth and pale, and the canopy is rather open. The trees need a warm, frost-free climate, full sun or light shade, humus-rich soil and plenty of moisture. Shelter from strong winds is beneficial. Propagate from seed or cuttings.

Xanthostemon chrysanthus
BLACK PENDA

Becoming popular in tropical and subtropical gardens in Australia, this tree reaches 25 ft (8 m) or so in cultivation, though it is taller in its native rainforests of tropical north-eastern Australia. The showy heads of bright acid-yellow flowers with masses of long stamens are borne mainly in winter, but rain may stimulate flowering at other times. The large leaves have a pale green mid-vein. ZONE 10.

Xanthostemon chrysanthus

XYLOMELUM
Proteaceae
WOODY PEAR

This small Australian genus contains about 4 evergreen small trees with leathery leaves and flowers resembling those of grevilleas and hakeas, which are members of the same family. Indigenous to dry, warm regions, these unusual plants are grown for the attractive flowers and for the unique felty seed capsules in the shape of a pear, hence their common name. They need well-drained, sandy soil in full sun, but young plants, which germinate readily from seed, need to be given ample water.

Xylomelum occidentale
WESTERN WOODY PEAR

This Western Australian tree reaches 25 ft (8 m) tall, with a spreading crown and dark brown,

Xanthostemon chrysanthus

Yucca aloifolia 'Variegata'

Yucca elephantipes

Yucca aloifolia

flaky bark. The large, deep green leaves resemble those of some oaks and have prickly edges. Sprays of creamy flowers appear in summer. These are followed by the showy pear-shaped fruit, up to 4 in (10 cm) long, which ripen reddish brown and persist on the plant after they have split open to release their seeds. The western woody pear can be used in arrangements of dried flowers. ZONE 9.

YUCCA
Agavaceae

These unusual evergreen plants, found in drier regions of North America, add strong dramatic shapes to a garden. Usually slow growing, they form rosettes of stiff, sword-like leaves usually tipped with a formidable spine; as the plant matures some species develop an upright woody trunk, often branched. Yuccas bear showy tall panicles of drooping, white or off-white, bell- to cup-shaped flowers. The fruit can be fleshy or a dry capsule, but in most species is rarely seen away from the plants' native lands as the flowers must be pollinated by the yucca moth. Yuccas do best in areas of low humidity; they prefer full sun and sandy soil with good drainage. Depending on the species, they suit frost-free to cool climates. They are propagated from seed (if available), cuttings or suckers.

Yucca aloifolia
SPANISH BAYONET

This species gets its common name from its very sharp, sword-like, greyish green leaves, each 24 in (60 cm) long and 1–2 in (3–5 cm) wide. It develops a branched trunk up to 24 ft (8 m) high, but in cultivation it is often much smaller. The flowers are carried in an upright spike up to 24 in (60 cm) long, mainly in summer. Each bell-shaped flower is white flushed with purple and about 2 in (5 cm) across. The fruit is fleshy. There are several cultivars with variegated leaves: 'Variegata' has leaves edged with creamy white; 'Tricolor' has white or yellow in the centre of the leaf; and 'Marginata' has yellow-edged leaves. ZONE 9.

Yucca brevifolia
JOSHUA TREE

This striking tree reaches 40 ft (13 m) tall in its natural habitat and has twisted branches. The long leaves are narrow and sharply pointed, with minute teeth along the edge. The Joshua tree has greenish white flowers about 2½ in (6 cm) long, arranged on a long erect spike; these are followed by a dry capsule. Extremely slow growing, the Joshua tree can be difficult to cultivate, even in its native regions. It is indigenous to the area from Utah through Arizona and Nevada to southern California). ZONE 9.

Yucca elephantipes

This yucca grows naturally in Mexico. There it develops a rough thick trunk that often branches and reaches a height of 30 ft (10 m), but under cultivation it grows very slowly and is usually smaller. The leaves are 4 ft (1.2 m) long and 3 in (7 cm) across, shiny dark green with rough serrated edges. They are held in rosettes at the tips of the branches and droop downwards. White to off-white bell-shaped flowers are clustered along spikes through summer. ZONE 9.

ZELKOVA
Ulmaceae

Occurring from Asia Minor across cool-climate areas of western Asia to China and Japan, these fine deciduous trees are cultivated for their attractive habit and handsome foliage, and are important timber trees in China and Japan. The leaves resemble but are smaller than the English or American elms, giving an effect of airy elegance. Though related to the elms, they are not plagued by the same diseases and are becoming popular as elm-substitutes. They need deep, well-drained soil and plenty of water in summer months. The small, greenish, spring flowers are sometimes perfumed but both these and the fruit are insignificant. The trees are propagated from seed or root cuttings, or by grafting.

Zelkova carpinifolia

From the Caucasus and Asia Minor, this slow-growing tree can live to a great age, reaching a height of 100 ft (30 m) and a spread of 50 ft (15 m) or so. It has a dense rounded head, slender upright branches and weeping branchlets. The mid-green, pointed leaves have serrated edges and their upper sides are rough to the touch. Fragrant but insignificant flowers appear in spring. ZONE 4.

Zelkova serrata
JAPANESE ELM

This ornamental tree grows to 80 ft (25 m) or more with a wide-spreading crown. It has smooth bark dappled grey and brown and the new shoots are tinged purple. The pointed, oblong, sharply serrated leaves are light green and slightly hairy above, with shiny undersides. Foliage turns golden yellow to rusty brown in autumn. It is valued in Japan for its timber. ZONE 3.

ZIERIA
Rutaceae

This genus is made up of about 20 species of evergreen shrubs which occur wild in eastern Australia. Ranging from 24 in (60 cm) to 8 ft (2.5 m) tall, they are erect and often spreading, and can be kept compact by light pruning after flowering. Leaves are small and compound with 3 leaflets; they contain aromatic oils in small translucent dots. Small, starry flowers are white or shades of pale to deep pink, with bright yellow stamens. Zierias need humus-rich, sandy soil with perfect drainage; like the related boronias, they prefer shade, though several species tolerate full sun. They are propagated from cuttings.

Zieria buxijugum

This is one of a number of rare and localized *Zieria* species discovered in recent years on rocky hilltops in south-eastern Australia, though in the case of this one, it has particular ornamental qualities combined with ease of cultivation that have attracted native plant enthusiasts. A shrub to 6 ft (2 m) tall, its fine lacy foliage consists of leaves with 3 very narrow leaflets that have finely warted surfaces and are also velvety to the touch. In spring it bears numerous small sprays of starry white flowers on fine stalks. ZONE 9.

ZIZYPHUS
Rhamnaceae

These trees and shrubs, either deciduous or evergreen, are commonly called jujubes for their sugary fruit. They occur naturally in warm- to hot-climate areas of the northern hemisphere, from the Mediterranean region across western Asia to China. Some have spiny stems. Their leaves are usually marked with 3 veins and there are spines at the base of each leaf stalk. The insignificant flowers are small, greenish, whitish or yellow, arranged in clusters in the leaf axils. *Z. jujuba* is cultivated in Asia for its sweet berries; these are eaten fresh, dried, pickled or stewed, or made into confectionery. The plants are propagated from seed or root cuttings, or by grafting.

Zizyphus jujuba
JUJUBE, CHINESE DATE

This deciduous tree, indigenous from western Asia to China, grows to 40 ft (13 m) high. The leaves, oval to lance shaped and 1–2 in (3–5 cm) long, are green with two spines at the base of the leaf stalk, one of which is usually bent backwards. The small greenish flowers are borne in spring. The reddish fruit are oblong to rounded and up to 1 in (2 cm) long; they ripen from autumn to winter on the bare branches. ZONE 9.

Zelkova serrata

Zelkova serrata

Zelkova carpinifolia (below)

Zieria buxijugum (below)

Zizyphus jujuba

Zizyphus jujuba, in Rajasthan, India (below)

Reference Table

The aim of this table is to help in selecting suitable trees or shrubs for a particular place or purpose. For example a tree that gives useful shade in summer but sheds its leaves to allow winter sun into a room can be chosen from the appropriate columns. If you would prefer a fast-growing species, or one with interesting bark, edible fruit or fragrant flowers, these qualities can be selected.

NAME

Botanical names are listed in alphabetical order, common synonyms are given in brackets. To find a plant by its common name refer to the index.

CLIMATE & ZONE

As a broad guide, plants are assigned to Cold, Cool, Warm or Hot climate.

- **Cold** refers to climates with very low winter temperatures, e.g. northern Europe, most of Canada, far northern USA.
- **Cool** refers to climates with milder winters (not falling below about 5° F (-15° C)), but cool enough to experience at least occasional snowfall.
- **Warm** refers to climates that are frost free or experience only light frosts, but have a distinct winter season.
- **Hot** refers to tropical climates, where temperatures rarely or never fall below 50° F (10° C).

Hardiness zones: As given in the main text of this book, these indicate the lowest winter temperature a plant can survive and resume growth, and the map on p.16–17 shows corresponding temperature ranges and regions. In this table a range of zones (e.g. 'Z 5–9') is given for each plant, the higher number indicating the warmest zone in which the plant can be expected to grow happily. Zone 1 corresponds to a subarctic climate such as central Canada or Siberia, while Zone 12 covers much of the equatorial tropics (but not tropical highlands). Zone 10 is the lowest zone in which frost and snow are not normally experienced.

GARDEN HEIGHT

As an aid to garden planning, anticipated average heights are given for 5, 10 and 20 years from planting. It is assumed that when planted the plant is a small seedling or recently rooted cutting, not an advanced plant. It should be emphasized that growth rates can vary greatly depending on climate, soil, shelter and other factors, as well as the variety or cultivar chosen. You will notice that patterns of height growth differ greatly between species: for example a tree with fast early growth but short life has listed the heights 15 ft (5 m), 20 ft (6 m), 20 ft (6 m), whereas a tall, long-lived tree may have listed heights of 8 ft (2.5 m), 15 ft (5 m), 30 ft (10 m), indicating progressive growth that continues well beyond 20 years. In the case of some shrubs and very short-lived trees no 20-year height is given, suggesting that the plant is generally unlikely to reach this age.

DECIDUOUS/EVERGREEN

These are generally self-evident, except that some species have 'Decid*' (with an asterisk): these are tropical or subtropical trees and shrubs that shed their leaves in the dry season, sometimes quite briefly, often not gaining new foliage until the start of the wet season. When planted in slightly cooler climates such plants often do not lose their leaves until spring, the new leaves appearing with or after the flowers in late spring or early summer (jacaranda is an example of this phenomenon).

ARID CLIMATES

A 'Yes' in this column indicates that the plant is suited to cultivation in very low-rainfall regions, with very hot, dry summers. It does not imply that all these species are able to survive long droughts without some added source of soil moisture, for example from irrigation.

CHIEF ATTRACTIONS

This column shows the main feature for which the plant is valued, or features in descending order of importance. In the case of flowers the colour (or range of colours) and flowering season are given in brackets, as an aid to garden planning.

USES

This column indicates some of the wide range of possible uses to which a tree or shrub may be put. Obviously many of these overlap, for example 'lawn specimen' and 'parks', though the former is meant mainly to indicate a tree or shrub suited to a lawn in a private garden. 'Courtyard' should be taken in a broad sense to indicate any paved or partially paved area sheltered by walls. 'Rock garden' likewise can refer to any area of garden where rocks or masonry are featured on a large or a small scale, usually with enhanced drainage. 'Plaza' refers to mainly paved areas, possibly with planting boxes, associated with streets, shops or large buildings. 'Coastal planting' indicates plants whose foliage can withstand some salt spray off the sea in stormy weather, though not all species so listed are equally tolerant. 'Timber' generally refers to trees that might usefully be planted for future timber harvesting, but includes also some that, while too slow-growing for plantations, are renowned for their timber.

DRAWBACKS

Points about a species that might be regarded as a disadvantage for garden use are listed here. Note though that a drawback for some purposes may be an advantage for others. Fierce thorns may be undesirable on a courtyard shrub, but quite useful if it is planted as an intruder-proof hedge!

Careful selection of trees and shrubs will result in a garden that looks good all year.

Reference Table

NAME	KIND	CLIMATE & ZONE	HEIGHT AT 5 yrs	HEIGHT AT 10 yrs	HEIGHT AT 20 yrs	DECIDUOUS EVERGREEN	ARID CLIMATES	CHIEF ATTRACTIONS	USES	DRAWBACKS	COMMENTS
Abelia chinensis	Shrub	Cool Z 8-10	4 ft 1.2 m	6 ft 2 m	6ft 2m	Everg	—	Flowers (white, summer-autumn)	Shrub border, informal hedge	—	The showiest *Abelia* but frost-tender
Abelia floribunda	Shrub	Warm Z 9-10	4 ft 1.2 m	6 ft 2 m	6ft 2m	Everg	—	Flowers (rosy-red, early summer)	Courtyard, shrub border	—	Showy but frost-tender
Abelia × grandiflora	Shrub	Cool Z 7-11	6 ft 2 m	8 ft 2.5 m	8 ft 2.5 m	Everg	—	Flowers (white & mauve, spring-autumn); graceful habit	Shrub border, informal hedge, courtyard	—	Climatically adaptable, vigorous, trouble-free
Abelia schumannii	Shrub	Cool Z 7-10	6 ft 2 m	6 ft 2 m	6ft 2m	Decid	—	Flowers (pink & white, late spring-early autumn)	Shrub border, courtyard	—	—
Abies alba	Tree	Cool Z 6-8	6 ft 2 m	15 ft 5 m	30 ft 9 m	Everg	—	Foliage; symmetrical form	Timber, windbreaks	Damaged by aphids, late frosts	Needs cool, moist conditions
Abies amabilis	Tree	Cool Z 5-9	4 ft 1.2 m	12 ft 4 m	25 ft 8 m	Everg	—	Foliage; symmetrical form	Parks, timber, windbreaks	Short-lived in cultivation, climatically sensitive	Needs cool, moist conditions
Abies balsamea	Tree	Cold Z 3-7	6 ft 2 m	12 ft 4 m	25 ft 8 m	Everg	—	Foliage	Windbreaks, rock-gardens ('Hudsonia'), Christmas trees	One of the shortest-lived firs (30 yrs)	Source of Canada balsam (resin from bark)
Abies bracteata	Tree	Cool Z 7-9	6 ft 2 m	15 ft 5 m	30 ft 9 m	Everg	—	Foliage; symmetrical form	Lawn specimen, parks	Damaged by late frosts, often short-lived	Remarkable spire-shaped crown
Abies cephalonica	Tree	Cool Z 6-9	6 ft 2 m	15 ft 5 m	30 ft 9 m	Everg	—	Foliage; symmetrical form	Lawn specimen, parks, Christmas trees	—	—
Abies concolor	Tree	Cool Z 5-9	6 ft 2 m	15 ft 5 m	25 ft 8 m	Everg	—	Aromatic foliage; symmetrical form	Lawn specimen, parks, streets	—	Blue-leaved selections most prized
Abies delavayi	Tree	Cool Z 7-9	6 ft 2 m	15 ft 5 m	30 ft 9 m	Everg	—	Foliage; purple cones	Lawn specimen, parks	—	Several varieties cultivated
Abies firma	Tree	Cool Z 6-9	6 ft 2 m	15 ft 5 m	25 ft 8 m	Everg	—	Foliage	Lawn specimen, parks, streets	—	Rich green foliage. Requires very moist climate
Abies grandis	Tree	Cool Z 6-9	8 ft 2.5 m	20 ft 6 m	40 ft 12 m	Everg	—	Foliage; symmetrical form; fast growth	Lawn specimen, parks	—	One of the tallest known conifers
Abies homolepis	Tree	Cool Z 5-9	8 ft 2.5 m	20 ft 6 m	30 ft 9 m	Everg	—	Foliage; purple young cones	Lawn specimen, parks	—	Suits urban conditions better than other firs
Abies koreana	Tree	Cool Z 5-9	4 ft 1.2 m	10 ft 3 m	20 ft 6 m	Everg	—	Foliage; decorative cones at early age	Rock gardens, shrub border, Christmas trees	—	—
Abies lasiocarpa	Tree	Cool Z 4-8	6 ft 2 m	15 ft 5 m	25 ft 8 m	Everg	—	Foliage; symmetrical form	Lawn specimen, parks	—	Requires very cool, wet climate
Abies magnifica	Tree	Cool Z 5-8	8 ft 2.5 m	15 ft 5 m	30 ft 9 m	Everg	—	Foliage; symmetrical form	Lawn specimen, parks, timber	—	—
Abies nordmanniana	Tree	Cool Z 4-9	6 ft 2 m	15 ft 5 m	25 ft 8 m	Everg	—	Foliage	Lawn specimen, parks, Christmas trees	—	—
Abies numidica	Tree	Cool Z 6-9	8 ft 2.5 m	20 ft 6 m	30 ft 9 m	Everg	—	Foliage; symmetrical form	Parks, lawn specimen, Christmas trees	—	Suits urban conditions better than other firs
Abies pinsapo	Tree	Cool Z 5-9	8 ft 2.5 m	15 ft 5 m	25 ft 8 m	Everg	—	Foliage; purple pollen cones	Parks, lawn specimen	Prickly needles	'Glauca' form is most commonly grown
Abies procera	Tree	Cool Z 4-9	4 ft 1.2 m	15 ft 5 m	25 ft 8 m	Everg	—	Foliage; symmetrical form	Parks, lawn specimen, timber	—	—
Abies spectabilis	Tree	Cool Z 7-9	8 ft 2.5 m	15 ft 5 m	25 ft 8 m	Everg	—	Foliage; purple cones	Parks, lawn specimen	Damaged by late frosts	—
Abutilon × hybridum	Shrub	Warm Z 9-11	6 ft 2 m	8 ft 2.5 m	8 ft 2.5 m	Everg	—	Flowers (yellow, red, pink, orange, summer-autumn)	Shrub border, tubs, indoors	—	Cultivars available in various colours
Abutilon megapotamicum	Shrub	Warm Z 9-11	6 ft 2 m	6 ft 2 m	6ft 2m	Everg	Yes	Flowers (yellow & red, most of year)	Shrub border, informal hedge, rock gardens, groundcover	—	Cultivar 'Variegatum' is semi-prostrate, has colourful foliage
Abutilon × suntense	Shrub	Cool Z 8-9	10 ft 3 m	12 ft 4 m	12 ft 4 m	Everg	—	Flowers (purple, mauve, spring-early summer)	Shrub border, courtyard, espalier	—	—
Abutilon vitifolium	Shrub	Cool Z 8-9	10 ft 3 m	12 ft 4 m	12 ft 4 m	Everg	—	Flowers (mauve, white, spring-early summer)	Shrub border, courtyard, espalier	Short-lived	Requires shelter
Acacia acinacea	Shrub	Warm Z 8-10	6 ft 2 m	6 ft 2 m	6ft 2m	Everg	Yes	Profuse flowers (yellow, midwinter-spring)	Shrub border, road banks	—	Fine, neat foliage
Acacia baileyana	Tree	Warm Z 8-11	12 ft 4 m	20 ft 6 m	20 ft 6 m	Everg	Yes	Profuse flowers (yellow, late winter)	Streets, parks, shrub border	Short-lived, prone to borers	—
Acacia cultriformis	Shrub	Warm Z 8-11	8 ft 2.5 m	10 ft 3 m	10 ft 3 m	Everg	Yes	Flowers (yellow, spring) foliage	Shrub border, informal hedge, road banks	Short-lived, prone to borers	—
Acacia dealbata	Tree	Cool Z 8-11	20 ft 8 m	30 ft 9 m	30 ft 9 m	Everg	—	Flowers (yellow, spring); foliage	Windbreak, firewood, cut foliage	Short-lived; may get galls in native area	The 'mimosa' of Europe (introduced)
Acacia decurrens	Tree	Warm Z 9-12	25 ft 8 m	40 ft 12 m	40 ft 12 m	Everg	Yes	Flowers (yellow, late winter-early spring); foliage	Streets, parks, tanning bark	Often short-lived	—
Acacia elata	Tree	Warm Z 9-12	25 ft 8 m	40 ft 12 m	50 ft 15 m	Everg	—	Flowers (cream, early summer); foliage	Streets, parks	Sometimes gets unsightly galls in native areas	One of the handsomest of the tall tree *Acacias* and longest-lived
Acacia harpophylla	Tree	Warm Z 9-12	12 ft 4 m	20 ft 6 m	30 ft 9 m	Everg	Yes	Foliage; flowers (yellow, summer)	Parks, farms, shelter, timber	Suckers from roots	Long-lived tree with dense crown of blue-grey foliage
Acacia karroo	Tree	Warm Z 9-12	10 ft 3 m	20 ft 6 m	30 ft 9 m	Everg	Yes	Flowers (yellow, spring)	Farm hedges, parks, large gardens	Can become a weed in warm dry climates	Large, fierce spines
Acacia koa	Tree	Warm Z 10-12	10 ft 3 m	20 ft 6 m	30 ft 9 m	Everg	Yes	Foliage	Timber, parks, streets	—	Native of Hawaii but resembles some Australian acacias

NAME	KIND	CLIMATE & ZONE	HEIGHT AT 5 yrs	HEIGHT AT 10 yrs	HEIGHT AT 20 yrs	DECIDUOUS EVERGREEN	ARID CLIMATES	CHIEF ATTRACTIONS	USES	DRAWBACKS	COMMENTS
Acacia longifolia	Shrub	Warm Z 9-11	10 ft 3 m	15 ft 5 m	15 ft 5 m	Everg	—	Flowers (yellow, late winter-early spring)	Seashore gardens, windbreaks, road banks	Short-lived, becomes galled in native regions	Can become a weed in countries beyond Australia
Acacia mangium	Tree	Hot Z 11-12	20 ft 6 m	40 ft 12 m	60 ft 18 m	Everg	—	Foliage, flowers (cream, summer)	Timber, parks, streets	—	One of the fastest-growing timber trees for the wet tropics
Acacia mearnsii	Tree	Warm Z 8-11	15 ft 5 m	30 ft 9 m	40 ft 12 m	Everg	—	Flowers (late spring); foliage	Tanbark, parks, streets, windbreaks	—	The most widely grown Acacia in tanbark plantations
Acacia melanoxylon	Tree	Warm Z 8-12	15 ft 5 m	25 ft 8 m	30 ft 9 m	Everg	—	Flowers (cream, spring); foliage	Parks, streets, shelter, timber	—	Long-lived; heartwood timber makes high-quality furniture
Acacia neriifolia	Tree	Warm Z 9-11	12 ft 4 m	15 ft 5 m	20 ft 6 m	Everg	—	Flowers (yellow, late winter-spring); graceful habit	Shrub border, lawn specimen, screen	—	—
Acacia pendula	Tree	Warm Z 9-11	10 ft 3 m	15 ft 5 m	20 ft 6 m	Everg	Yes	Foliage	Parks, streets, farms	—	Foliage browsed by livestock
Acacia podalyriifolia	Shrub	Warm Z 9-11	10 ft 3 m	15 ft 5 m	15 ft 5 m	Everg	—	Flowers (yellow, winter-early spring); foliage	Shrub border, parks, road banks	Short-lived	—
Acacia pravissima	Shrub	Warm Z 8-10	6 ft 2 m	8 ft 2.5 m	10 ft 3 m	Everg	—	Flowers (yellow, late winter-early spring)	Shrub border, road banks	—	One of the most frost-hardy acacias
Acacia pycnantha	Tree	Warm Z 9-11	12 ft 4 m	15 ft 5 m	20 ft 6 m	Everg	Yes	Flowers (yellow, spring)	Lawn specimen, parks, streets	May be short-lived	Australia's floral emblem
Acacia sieberiana var. woodii	Tree	Warm Z 9-11	12 ft 4 m	15 ft 5 m	20 ft 6 m	Everg	—	Flowers (yellow, spring)	Lawn specimen, parks, streets	May be short-lived	Australia's floral emblem.
Acacia spectabilis	Shrub	Warm Z 9-11	8 ft 2.5 m	10 ft 3 m	10 ft 3 m	Everg	Yes	Flowers (yellow, winter-spring)	Shrub border, road banks	—	—
Acacia verticillata	Shrub	Cool Z 8-10	6 ft 2 m	8 ft 2.5 m	10 ft 3 m	Everg	—	Flowers (yellow, spring-summer); foliage	Seaside gardens, shrub border, hedges	Prickly foliage	—
Acacia xanthophloea	Tree	Hot Z 9-12	10 ft 3 m	20 ft 6 m	30 ft 9 m	Everg	Yes	Smooth yellowish bark; flowers (yellow, spring)	Parks, streets, farms	Fierce spines	Possible risk of weediness in continents other than Africa
Acalypha hispida	Shrub	Hot Z 11-12	4 ft 1.2 m	6 ft 2 m	6 ft 2 m	Everg	—	Flowers (red, summer)	Shrub border, courtyards, indoors	—	—
Acalypha wilkesiana	Shrub	Warm Z 10-12	4 ft 1.2 m	6 ft 2 m	8 ft 2.5 m	Everg	—	Coloured foliage	Shrub border, courtyards, plazas, indoor	—	Cultivars vary in height
Acer buergerianum	Tree	Cool Z 6-10	8 ft 2.5 m	12 ft 4 m	20 ft 6 m	Decid	—	Autumn foliage; bark	Lawn specimen, parks, streets, bonsai	—	A good species for city gardens
Acer campestre	Tree	Cool Z 4-9	10 ft 3 m	15 ft 5 m	30 ft 9 m	Decid	—	Autumn foliage	Parks, streets, hedge, shade	—	Common in hedgerows in Britain and Europe
Acer capillipes	Tree	Cool Z 5-9	10 ft 3 m	15 ft 5 m	25 ft 8 m	Decid	—	Autumn foliage; bark	Lawn specimen, parks, streets	Stressed by summer droughts	One of the 'snakebark' maples
Acer cappadocicum	Tree	Cool Z 5-9	8 ft 2.5 m	15 ft 5 m	30 ft 9 m	Decid	—	Autumn foliage	Lawn specimen, parks, streets	—	Interesting leaf shape with 5-7 neatly pointed lobes
Acer carpinifolium	Tree	Cool Z 3-9	6 ft 2 m	12 ft 4 m	20 ft 6 m	Decid	—	Autumn foliage	Lawn specimen, parks, streets	—	Strongly veined leaves; one of the most frost-hardy maples
Acer circinatum	Tree	Cool Z 5-9	6 ft 2 m	12 ft 4 m	15 ft 5 m	Decid	—	Autumn foliage	Lawn specimen	—	Brilliant autumn colour; lieks sheltered position
Acer cissifolium	Tree	Cool Z 5-9	6 ft 2 m	12 ft 4 m	20 ft 6 m	Decid	—	Autumn foliage	Lawn specimen, parks	Sets little or no fertile seed	—
Acer davidii	Tree	Cool Z 6-9	10 ft 3 m	15 ft 5 m	25 ft 8 m	Decid	—	Autumn foliage; bark	Lawn specimen, parks, streets	—	One of the 'snakebark' maples with striped bark
Acer ginnala	Tree	Cool Z 4-10	8 ft 2.5 m	10 ft 3 m	10 ft 3 m	Decid	—	Autumn foliage	Lawn specimen	—	Often remains shrubby
Acer glabrum	Tree	Cool Z 4-8	8 ft 2.5 m	10 ft 3 m	12 ft 4 m	Decid	—	Shade-tolerant, very cold-hardy	Woodland garden	—	Often remains shrubby
Acer grandidentatum	Tree	Cool Z 4-9	6 ft 2 m	10 ft 3 m	20 ft 6 m	Decid	Yes	Autumn foliage, shade	Lawn specimen, parks, streets	—	—
Acer griseum	Tree	Cool Z 5-9	8 ft 2.5 m	12 ft 4 m	25 ft 8 m	Decid	—	Striking cinnamon bark, peeling in large flakes	Lawn specimen, parks	—	A showpiece species
Acer grosseri	Tree	Cool Z 5-9	8 ft 2.5 m	12 ft 4 m	20 ft 6 m	Decid	—	Striped bark, autumn foliage	Lawn specimen	—	The only American 'snakebark' maple
Acer hookeri	Tree	Warm Z 8-10	8 ft 2.5 m	15 ft 5 m	25 ft 8 m	Decid	—	Autumn foliage, bronzy spring growth	Lawn specimen	New growth damaged by late frosts	Large, unlobed leaves
Acer japonicum	Tree	Cool Z 5-9	4 ft 1.2 m	8 ft 2.5 m	10 ft 3 m	Decid	—	Foliage texture, autumn tones	Lawn specimen	Foliage easily damaged by wind or sun	Many cultivars exist
Acer macrophyllum	Tree	Cool Z 6-9	8 ft 2.5 m	12 ft 4 m	30 ft 9 m	Decid	—	Very large leaves, autumn colour	Lawn specimen, parks, streets	Foliage damaged by late frosts	The largest-leafed maple, rare in cultivation
Acer negundo	Tree	Cool Z 4-11	8 ft 2.5 m	20 ft 6 m	25 ft 8 m	Decid	Yes	Fast early growth, delicate flowers on leafless twigs	Lawn specimen, parks, streets	Free-seeding, can become a weed	Variegated cultivars are popular
Acer nikoense	Tree	Cool Z 6-9	6 ft 2 m	12 ft 4 m	20 ft 6 m	Decid	—	Autumn foliage	Lawn specimen, parks	—	—
Acer palmatum	Tree	Cool Z 5-10	6 ft 2 m	10 ft 3 m	12 ft 4 m	Decid	—	Foliage shapes and textures, compact size, autumn colour	Lawn specimen, parks	Foliage scorched by dry summer winds	Over 300 named varieties listed, from low shrubs to trees

Reference Table

NAME	KIND	CLIMATE & ZONE	HEIGHT AT 5 yrs	HEIGHT AT 10 yrs	HEIGHT AT 20 yrs	DECIDUOUS EVERGREEN	ARID CLIMATES	CHIEF ATTRACTIONS	USES	DRAWBACKS	COMMENTS
Acer pensylvanicum	Tree	Cool Z 5-9	8 ft / 2.5 m	12 ft / 4 m	20 ft / 6 m	Decid	—	Striped bark, autumn foliage	Lawn specimen, parks, streets	—	—
Acer platanoides	Tree	Cool Z 4-9	8 ft / 2.5 m	20 ft / 6 m	30 ft / 9 m	Decid	—	Shade, autumn foliage	Lawn specimen, parks, streets; shade tree	—	The hardiest European maple
Acer pseudoplatanus	Tree	Cool Z 4-10	10 ft / 3 m	20 ft / 6 m	40 ft / 12 m	Decid	—	Fast growth, shade	Lawn specimen, parks, streets; shade tree	Very free-seeding, a weed in some countries	The sycamore of Europe but not of North America
Acer rubrum	Tree	Cool Z 4-9	8 ft / 2.5 m	20 ft / 6 m	25 ft / 8 m	Decid	—	Autumn foliage, shade	Lawn specimen, parks, streets; shade tree	—	The most brilliant red-colouring maple
Acer saccharinum	Tree	Cool Z 4-9	8 ft / 2.5 m	15 ft / 5 m	25 ft / 8 m	Decid	—	Autumn foliage, fast early growth	Lawn specimen, parks, streets; shade tree	Branches brittle, prone to storm damage	—
Acer saccharum	Tree	Cool Z 3-9	6 ft / 2 m	15 ft / 5 m	25 ft / 8 m	Decid	—	Autumn foliage	Maple syrup; lawn specimen, parks, streets; shade tree	Slow-growing in early stages	Important for both timber and maple syrup in native regions
Acer truncatum	Tree	Cool Z 5-9	8 ft / 2.5 m	15 ft / 5 m	20 ft / 6 m	Decid	—	Leaf shape, autumn foliage	Lawn specimen, parks	—	—
Acmena smithii	Tree	Warm Z 9-11	10 ft / 3 m	20 ft / 6 m	30 ft / 9 m	Everg	—	Display of pale violet to mauve fruit (autumn to spring)	Lawn specimen, streets, parks; jelly from fruit	Drops fleshy fruit on lawns and paths	Rainforest tree but adaptable to quite exposed positions
Acokanthera oblongifolia	Shrub	Warm Z 9-11	4 ft / 1.2 m	8 ft / 2.5 m	8 ft / 2.5 m	Everg	Yes	Flowers (white, fragrant, spring-summer)	Shrub border	Fruit said to be poisonous	'Variegata' has leaves variegated pink and cream
Acrocarpus fraxinifolius	Tree	Warm Z 10-11	15 ft / 5 m	25 ft / 8 m	40 ft / 12 m	Decid*	—	Large compound leaves, flowers (scarlet, spring-summer)	Timber, parks	—	Exceptionally fast-growing tropical tree
Adansonia digitata	Tree	Hot Z 11-12	6 ft / 2 m	12 ft / 4 m	20 ft / 6 m	Decid*	Yes	Swollen trunk, flowers (cream, summer)	Parks	—	Long-lived; swollen trunk develops with maturity
Adansonia gregorii	Tree	Hot Z 12	6 ft / 2 m	12 ft / 4 m	20 ft / 6 m	Decid*	Yes	Swollen trunk, flowers (cream, summer)	Parks	—	Long-lived; swollen trunk develops with maturity
Adenandra uniflora	Shrub	Warm Z 8-10	1 ft / 0.3 m	2 ft / 0.6 m	2 ft / 0.6 m	Everg	—	Flowers (white, spring-autumn)	Rock garden, courtyard, container	—	Petals like white porcelain
Adenium obesum	Shrub	Hot Z 11-12	2 ft / 0.6 m	4 ft / 1.2 m	5 ft / 1.5 m	Decid	Yes	Flowers (red, pink or white, midwinter-spring)	Container, courtyard, rock gardens	Susceptible to root rot	Stems semi-succulent; must be kept dry in winter
Aeonium arboreum	Shrub	Warm Z 9-10	1 ft / 0.3 m	2 ft / 0.6 m	2 ft / 0.6 m	Everg	Yes	Succulent leaves, flowers (yellow, spring)	Container, rock garden	—	Each stem flowers once, then dies back
Aesculus californica	Tree	Cool Z 8-10	6 ft / 2 m	10 ft / 3 m	4m / 13ft	Decid	Yes	Fragrant flowers (cream, summer)	Shrub border, lawn specimen	May lose leaves at end of summer	—
Aesculus × carnea	Tree	Cool Z 6-9	6 ft / 2 m	15 ft / 5 m	25 ft / 8 m	Decid	—	Flowers (red, late spring)	Lawn specimen, parks, streets	—	More compact than A. hippocastanum
Aesculus flava	Tree	Cool Z 4-8	8 ft / 2.5 m	20 ft / 6 m	30 ft / 9 m	Decid	—	Flowers (yellowish, late spring-early summer)	Parks, streets	—	—
Aesculus glabra	Tree	Cool Z 4-8	6 ft / 2 m	15 ft / 5 m	30 ft / 9 m	Decid	—	Flowers (yellow-green, spring)	Parks, streets	Bruised leaves smell unpleasant	—
Aesculus hippocastanum	Tree	Cool Z 6-9	6 ft / 2 m	12 ft / 4 m	25 ft / 8 m	Decid	—	Flowers (white, late spring-early summer); autumn foliage	Parks, avenues	—	The stately horse-chestnut of European avenues
Aesculus indica	Tree	Cool Z 6-9	6 ft / 2 m	15 ft / 5 m	25 ft / 8 m	Decid	—	Flowers (white, early-mid summer)	Parks, streets	—	Similar to A. hippocastanum but smaller, more tender
Aesculus parviflora	Shrub	Cool Z 7-9	5 ft / 1.5 m	8 ft / 2.5 m	8 ft / 2.5 m	Decid	—	Flowers (white & pink, summer)	Shrub border, lawn specimen, edge of stream or pond	—	Multi-stemmed, spreads to broad clump
Aesculus pavia	Tree	Cool Z 7-9	6 ft / 2 m	10 ft / 3 m	15 ft / 5 m	Decid	—	Flowers (crimson, early summer), autumn foliage	Shrub border, lawn, parks	—	—
Aesculus turbinata	Tree	Cool Z 6-9	6 ft / 2 m	10 ft / 3 m	20 ft / 6 m	Decid	—	Flowers (cream, early summer), autumn foliage	Lawn specimen, parks	—	Similar to A. hippocastanum but slower-growing
Afrocarpus (Podocarpus) falcatus	Tree	Warm Z 9-11	8 ft / 2.5 m	15 ft / 5 m	30 ft / 9 m	Everg	—	Foliage, 'fruit' (actually seeds, yellow, autumn)	Parks, streets	Seeds litter pavement	Separate male and female trees
Afrocarpus (Podocarpus) gracilior	Tree	Warm Z 10-11	8 ft / 2.5 m	15 ft / 5 m	25 ft / 8 m	Everg	—	Foliage, 'fruit' (actually seeds, purplish, autumn)	Parks, streets	—	Separate male and female trees
Agapetes serpens	Shrub	Warm Z 9-10	2 ft / 0.6 m	3 ft / 1 m	3 ft / 1 m	Everg	—	Flowers (red, late winter-midsummer)	Woodland garden, rock garden, courtyard, containers	—	Prefers partly shaded position
Agathis australis	Tree	Warm Z 9-10	4 ft / 1.2 m	8 ft / 2.5 m	15 ft / 5 m	Everg	—	Foliage, compact shape	Lawn specimen, parks	Very slow growth	New Zealand's largest, most famous native tree
Agathis robusta	Tree	Warm Z 9-11	6 ft / 2 m	10 ft / 3 m	25 ft / 8 m	Everg	—	Foliage, straight narrow habit	Lawn specimen, parks, timber	—	Attains very large size with age
Agave americana	Shrub	Warm Z 9-11	4 ft / 1.2 m	6 ft / 2 m	6 ft / 2 m	Everg	Yes	Bold succulent foliage, tall flowering stems	Large rock gardens, embankments	Vicious spines on leaves	Source of tequila; individual rosettes take 10 years or more to flower, then die
Agave attenuata	Shrub	Warm Z 9-11	2 ft / 0.6 m	4 ft / 1.2 m	5 ft / 1.5 m	Everg	Yes	Foliage; flowers (greenish-white, spring-summer)	Large rock garden, embankment, container	—	One of the few completely spineless agaves
Agonis flexuosa	Tree	Warm Z 9-11	8 ft / 2.5 m	15 ft / 5 m	20 ft / 6 m	Everg	Yes	Weeping foliage, flowers (white, late spring)	Gardens, parks, streets, coastal planting	—	Remarkably thick trunk for a small tree

NAME	KIND	CLIMATE & ZONE	HEIGHT AT 5yrs	HEIGHT AT 10yrs	HEIGHT AT 20yrs	DECIDUOUS EVERGREEN	ARID CLIMATES	CHIEF ATTRACTIONS	USES	DRAWBACKS	COMMENTS
Ailanthus altissima (incl. A. giraldii)	Tree	Cool Z 6-10	10 ft 3 m	20 ft 6 m	40 ft 12 m	Decid	Yes	Dense foliage; decorative fruit	Lawn specimen, parks	Suckers from roots, can become a weed	Foliage smells unpleasant when bruised
Alberta magna	Shrub	Warm Z 10-11	5 ft 1.5 m	8 ft 2.5 m	10 ft 3 m	Everg	—	Flowers (red, summer-autumn); decorative fruit	Shrub border, large containers	Very slow growth	Spectacular in flower
Albizia julibrissin	Tree	Cool Z 8-10	6 ft 2 m	10 ft 3 m	15 ft 5 m	Decid	Yes	Flowers (pink & white, late spring-early summer)	Lawn specimen, shrub border, container	Sometimes stays shrublike	—
Albizia lebbek	Tree	Hot Z 11-12	10 ft 3 m	20 ft 6 m	30 ft 9 m	Everg*	Yes	Flowers (cream aging yellow, spring)	Shade, shelter for slower-growing plants	Short-lived, limbs decay with age	Pods rattle in the wind
Alectryon excelsus	Tree	Warm Z 9-10	8 ft 2.5 m	15 ft 5 m	20 ft 6 m	Everg	—	Dense foliage, decorative fruit & seeds (scarlet & black, autumn)	Shade, lawn specimen, parks	—	—
Aleurites moluccana	Tree	Hot Z 10-12	15 ft 5 m	30 ft 9 m	50 ft 15 m	Everg	—	Rapid growth, large handsome leaves	Shade, parks	Large seeds may litter ground	Seeds yield a useful oil but poisonous in raw state
Allamanda neriifolia	Shrub	Hot Z 11-12	4 ft 1.2 m	6 ft 2 m	6 ft 2 m	Everg	Yes	Flowers (yellow & orange, summer-autumn)	Shrub border, courtyards, plazas, espalier	—	Branches long and scrambling if left unchecked
Allocasuarina (Casuarina) decaisneana	Tree	Warm Z 9-11	5 ft 1.5 m	10 ft 3 m	20 ft 6 m	Everg	Yes	Dense needle-like drooping foliage	Park specimen in arid areas	—	The most striking tree of Australia's driest desert regions
Allocasuarina (Casuarina) littoralis	Tree	Warm Z 9-11	10 ft 3 m	20 ft 6 m	25 ft 8 m	Everg	—	Fine needle-like foliage, massed male flowers (red-brown, winter)	Woodland garden, shrub border, parks	Short-lived, dead wood appears with age	—
Allocasuarina (Casuarina) luehmannii	Tree	Warm Z 9-11	10 ft 3 m	20 ft 6 m	30 ft 9 m	Everg	Yes	Dark needle-like foliage	Shade, parks, farms, firewood	—	Tolerates poor drainage
Allocasuarina (Casuarina) tessellata	Shrub	Warm Z 9-11	8 ft 2.5 m	12 ft 4 m	15 ft 5 m	Everg	Yes	Needle-like foliage	Shrub border	—	—
Allocasuarina (Casuarina) torulosa	Tree	Warm Z 8-11	10 ft 3 m	20 ft 6 m	30 ft 9 m	Everg	—	Drooping, needle-like foliage, purplish in winter	Lawn specimen, parks, timber, firewood	—	Timber split for shingles, burnt in bakers' ovens
Allocasuarina verticillata (Casuarina stricta)	Tree	Warm Z 8-11	8 ft 2.5 m	15 ft 5 m	20 ft 6 m	Everg	Yes	Dense crown of drooping needle-like foliage	Coastal planting, lawn specimen, hedges, parks, streets, firewood	Drops quantities of dead 'needles'	—
Alloxylon flammeum (Oreocallis wickhamii)	Tree	Warm Z 9-11	6 ft 2 m	10 ft 3 m	20 ft 6 m	Everg	—	Flowers (orange-red, late spring-early summer)	Lawn specimen, parks	Liable to sudden death in early growth	Spectacular flowers attract nectar-feeding birds
Alloxylon pinnatum (Oreocallis pinnata)	Tree	Warm Z 9-11	6 ft 2 m	10 ft 3 m	15 ft 5 m	Everg	—	Flowers (crimson, mid-summer) bird-attracting	Lawn specimen	Liable to sudden death in early growth	Flowers attract nectar-feeding birds
Alnus acuminata (jorullensis)	Tree	Warm Z 9-11	10 ft 2.5 m	20 ft 5 m	30 ft 9 m	Everg	—	Dense pendulous foliage	Lawn specimen, shade, parks, streets	Greedy root system	The only Alnus native to South America
Alnus cordata	Tree	Cool Z 7-9	10 ft 3 m	20 ft 6 m	30 ft 9 m	Decid	—	Foliage	Lawn specimen, edge of stream, pond or lake, parks	Sometimes short-lived	Long yellow male catkins at branch tips
Alnus firma	Tree	Cool Z 5-9	6 ft 2 m	10 ft 3 m	15 ft 5 m	Decid	—	Foliage	Shrub border, woodland garden	—	Slow-growing for an alder
Alnus glutinosa	Tree	Cold Z 4-9	8 ft 2.5 m	20 ft 6 m	30 ft 9 m	Decid	—	Foliage	Edge of stream or pond, boggy lawn, woodland garden	—	Untidy growth; cone-like fruits used for dried decorations
Alnus nepalensis	Tree	Warm Z 9-10	10 ft 3 m	20 ft 6 m	30 ft 9 m	Decid	—	Large leaves, long tangled catkins, smooth greenish bark	Lawn specimen, windbreak and shelter	Foliage damaged by dry summer winds	One of the largest-leaved alders
Alnus orientalis	Tree	Cool Z 7-10	10 ft 3 m	20 ft 6 m	40 ft 12 m	Decid	Yes	Foliage	Shade, parks, streets	—	—
Alnus rubra	Tree	Cool Z 6-9	10 ft 3 m	20 ft 6 m	30 ft 9 m	Decid	—	Foliage, male catkins (yellow, early spring)	Shade, parks, streets	—	—
Aloe candelabrum	Shrub	Warm Z 9-11	2 ft 0.6 m	4 ft 1.2 m	8 ft 2.5 m	Everg	Yes	Flowers (red, pink or orange, winter), succulent leaf rosette	Rock gardens, courtyards, containers	—	Generally a single stem, terminated by leaf rosette
Aloe plicatilis	Shrub	Warm Z 9-11	2 ft 0.6 m	3 ft 1 m	5 ft 1.5 m	Everg	Yes	Fans of succulent foliage, flowers (scarlet, spring)	Rock gardens, courtyards, containers	Growth extremely slow	Exceptional among aloes in fanlike arrangement of leaves
Aloysia triphylla	Shrub	Warm Z 8-11	4 ft 1.2 m	5 ft 1.5 m	6 ft 2 m	Everg	—	Flowers (pale lavender, summer-autumn), aromatic foliage	Shrub border, herb garden, espalier	—	Leaves have strong lemon scent when crushed
Alpinia zerumbet	Shrub	Warm Z 10-11	6 ft 2 m	8 ft 2.5 m	10 ft 3 m	Everg	—	Flowers (white & orange, spring-summer), bold foliage	Shrub border, courtyards, cut flowers	—	Technically not a shrub but functions as one for garden use; likes shade
Alyogyne hakeifolia	Shrub	Warm Z 10-11	6 ft 2 m	8 ft 2.5 m	10 ft 3 m	Everg	Yes	Flowers (blue-mauve or cream, spring-summer)	Shrub border	Usually short-lived	—
Alyogyne (Hibiscus) huegelii	Shrub	Warm Z 10-11	6 ft 2 m	8 ft 2.5 m	8 ft 2.5 m	Everg	Yes	Flowers (lilac or mauve, spring-summer)	Shrub border	Usually short-lived	One of the best shrubs for warm dry climates
Amelanchier alnifolia	Shrub	Cool Z 4-9	4 ft 1.2 m	6 ft 2 m	6 ft 2 m	Decid	—	Flowers (white, late spring); decorative fruit	Shrub border	—	Ornamental value not high
Amelanchier arborea	Tree	Cool Z 4-9	6 ft 2 m	10 ft 3 m	20 ft 6 m	Decid	—	Flowers (white, spring); decorative fruit; autumn foliage	Lawn specimen	—	—
Amelanchier laevis	Tree	Cool Z 4-9	6 ft 2 m	10 ft 3 m	15 ft 5 m	Decid	—	Flowers (white, spring); decorative fruit; bronze new leaves	Lawn specimen, shrub border	—	—
Amelanchier lamarckii	Shrub	Cool Z 6-9	6 ft 2 m	8 ft 2.5 m	12 ft 4 m	Decid	—	Flowers (white, late spring), autumn foliage	Shrub border	—	—

NAME	KIND	CLIMATE & ZONE	HEIGHT AT 5yrs 10yrs 20yrs	DECIDUOUS EVERGREEN	ARID CLIMATES	CHIEF ATTRACTIONS	USES	DRAWBACKS	COMMENTS
Amherstia nobilis	Tree	Hot Z 12	6 ft 12 ft 20 ft / 2 m 4 m 6 m	Decid*	—	Orchid-like flowers (crimson & gold, most of year)	Lawn specimen	Difficult to propagate	One of the most beautiful flowering trees for hot climates
Amphitecna latifolia	Tree	Hot Z 11-12	8 ft 15 ft 25 ft / 2.5 m 5 m 8 m	Everg	—	Flowers (white & purple), decorative fruit	Streets, parks	—	—
Anacardium occidentale	Tree	Hot Z 11-12	8 ft 12 ft 15 ft / 2.5 m 4 m 5 m	Everg	Yes	Edible nut & fruit-stalk	Orchard	Sap irritant to the skin	The cashew nut; not very ornamental
Andromeda polifolia	Shrub	Cold Z 2-8	2 ft 2 ft 2 ft / 0.6 m 0.6 m 0.6 m	Everg	—	Flowers (pink or white, spring)	Shrub border, rock garden, woodland garden	—	Branches root along ground
Angophora costata	Tree	Warm Z 9-11	8 ft 15 ft 25 ft / 2.5 m 5 m 8 m	Everg	—	Smooth pinkish bark, contorted limbs, flowers (white, spring-summer)	Lawn specimen, woodland garden	Erratic growth rate, unreliable in cultivation	One of Australia's most beautiful native trees
Anisodontea capensis	Shrub	Warm Z 9-10	3 ft 3 ft 3 ft / 1 m 1 m 1 m	Everg	—	Flowers (pink, most of year)	Courtyards, containers, indoors	—	Needs regular pruning to keep neat
Annona muricata	Tree	Hot Z 10-12	8 ft 15 ft 20 ft / 2.5 m 5 m 6 m	Everg	—	Edible fruit (soursop)	Orchard	—	Named cultivars most reliable
Annona squamosa	Tree	Hot Z 10-12	8 ft 15 ft 20 ft / 2.5 m 5 m 6 m	Everg	—	Edible fruit (sweetsop)	Orchard	—	Named cultivars most reliable
Anopterus glandulosus	Shrub	Cool Z 9	3 ft 5 ft 8 ft / 1 m 1.5 m 2.5 m	Everg	—	Flowers (white, spring)	Shrub border, woodland garden	Growth very slow and erratic	—
Aralia chinensis	Tree	Cool Z 7-10	4 ft 8 ft 15 ft / 1.2 m 2.5 m 5 m	Decid	—	Flowers (cream, autumn)	Shrub border, lawn specimen	—	Very large compound leaves
Aralia elata	Tree	Cool Z 5-10	4 ft 8 ft 15 ft / 1.2 m 2.5 m 5 m	Decid	—	Flowers (white, late summer-early autumn), autumn foliage	Shrub border, lawn specimen, woodland garden	—	—
Aralia spinosa	Shrub	Cool Z 6-10	4 ft 8 ft 15 ft / 1.2 m 2.5 m 5 m	Decid	—	Flowers (white, late spring), autumn foliage	Shrub border, lawn specimen, woodland garden	Prickly stems	Very large compound leaves
Araucaria angustifolia	Tree	Warm Z 9-12	6 ft 12 ft 30 ft / 2 m 4 m 9 m	Everg	—	Symmetrical branching habit	Lawn specimen, parks, timber	Sheds prickly branches	—
Araucaria araucana	Tree	Cool Z 8-9	4 ft 8 ft 20 ft / 1.2 m 2.5 m 6 m	Everg	—	Symmetrical branching habit	Lawn specimen	Prone to sudden death if climate not ideal	The famous 'monkey puzzle pine'
Araucaria bidwillii	Tree	Warm Z 8-11	6 ft 12 ft 25 ft / 2 m 4 m 8 m	Everg	Yes	Symmetrical branching habit, perfect domed crown; edible seeds	Lawn specimen, parks	Huge cones may drop from high in crown	The most climatically adaptable araucaria
Araucaria cunninghamii	Tree	Warm 9-12	8 ft 20 ft 40 ft / 2.5 m 6 m 12 m	Everg	—	Distinctive branching habit, shiny brown bark	Coastal planting, lawn specimen, parks, timber	—	Vigorous grower
Araucaria heterophylla	Tree	Warm Z 10-11	5 ft 10 ft 25 ft / 1.5 m 3 m 8 m	Everg	—	Symmetrical form; foliage	Lawn specimen, parks, coastal planting, indoor	Sensitive to urban pollution	Seedlings popular as indoor plants in cooler climates
Arbutus andrachne	Tree	Cool Z 6-10	6 ft 10 ft 15 ft / 2 m 3 m 5 m	Everg	Yes	Attractive bark, flowers (white, early spring)	Shrub border, lawn specimen, parks	—	Difficult to transplant
Arbutus × andrachnoides	Tree	Cool Z 6-10	8 ft 12 ft 15 ft / 2.5 m 4 m 5 m	Everg	Yes	Attractive bark, flowers (white, late autumn)	Shrub border, lawn specimen, parks	—	Difficult to transplant
Arbutus canariensis	Tree	Cool Z 8-10	6 ft 12 ft 15 ft / 2 m 4 m 5 m	Everg	—	Attractive bark, flowers (pink, late summer-early autumn)	Shrub border, lawn specimen, parks	—	—
Arbutus menziesii	Tree	Cool Z 7-10	8 ft 12 ft 20 ft / 2.5 m 4 m 6 m	Everg	—	Bark; flowers (white); decorative fruit	Lawn specimen, parks, streets	—	Regarded as most beautiful native tree in California
Arbutus unedo	Tree	Cool Z 7-10	8 ft 12 ft 15 ft / 2.5 m 4 m 5 m	Everg	Yes	Flowers (white or pink, autumn); decorative fruit	Parks, streets, informal hedges	—	Fruit is edible but not palatable
Archontophoenix alexandrae	Palm	Warm Z 10-12	6 ft 12 ft 25 ft / 2 m 4 m 8 m	Everg	—	Elegant fronds; smooth straight trunk; flowers (cream, winter)	Lawn grouping, courtyard, swimming pools, plazas, container	—	—
Archontophoenix cunninghamiana	Palm	Warm Z 9-11	4 ft 8 ft 20 ft / 1.2 m 2.5 m 6 m	Everg	—	Elegant fronds; smooth straight trunk; flowers (puplish, winter-spring)	Lawn grouping, courtyard, swimming pools, plazas, container	—	—
Arctostaphylos hookeri	Shrub	Cool Z 8-10	1 ft 2 ft 2 ft / 0.3 m 0.6 m 0.6 m	Everg	—	Foliage; flowers (pink); decorative fruit	Rock garden, coastal planting, groundcover, banks	—	—
Arctostaphylos manzanita	Shrub	Cool Z 8-10	4 ft 6 ft 8 ft / 1.2 m 2 m 2.5 m	Everg	—	Attractive bark	Shrub border, lawn specimen, coastal planting	—	—
Arctostaphylos uva-ursi	Shrub	Cool Z 4-9	1 ft 2 ft 2 ft / 0.3 m 0.6 m 0.6 m	Everg	—	Foliage; flowers (white or pink, late spring); decorative/edible fruit	Groundcover on walls, banks, rock garden	—	Foliage has deep red tones in autumn and winter
Argyrocytisus battandieri	Shrub	Cool Z 8-10	8 ft 12 ft — / 2.5 m 4 m	Everg	Yes	Flowers (yellow, early summer); silvery foliage	Shrub border, informal hedge	Short-lived	—
Aronia arbutifolia	Shrub	Cool Z 5-9	4 ft 6 ft 8 ft / 1.2 m 2 m 2.5 m	Decid	—	Decorative fruit; autumn foliage	Shrub border, courtyard, woodland garden	—	—
Aronia melanocarpa	Shrub	Cool Z 5-9	4 ft 5 ft 6 ft / 1.2 m 1.5 m 2 m	Decid	—	Decorative fruit; autumn foliage	Shrub border, courtyard, woodland garden	—	—
Artocarpus altilis	Tree	Hot Z 12	10 ft 25 ft 30 ft / 3 m 8 m 9 m	Everg	—	Edible fruit; foliage	Lawn specimen, home orchard, coastal planting	—	Handsome tropical tree, has very large lobed leaves
Artocarpus heterophyllus	Tree	Hot Z 11-12	10 ft 20 ft 30 ft / 3 m 6 m 9 m	Everg	—	Edible fruit; foliage	Orchard, lawn specimen	—	One of the largest tropical fruits
Asimina triloba	Tree	Cool Z 6-9	8 ft 15 ft 20 ft / 2.5 m 5 m 6 m	Decid	—	Edible fruit; flowers (purple, early summer); autumn foliage	Lawn specimen, shrub border	Fruits rarely produced	The pawpaw of North America, not to be confused with papaya

NAME	KIND	CLIMATE & ZONE	HEIGHT AT 5yrs	10yrs	20yrs	DECIDUOUS EVERGREEN	ARID CLIMATES	CHIEF ATTRACTIONS	USES	DRAWBACKS	COMMENTS
Atherosperma moschatum	Tree	Cool Z 8-9	8 ft 2.5 m	15 ft 5 m	30 ft 9 m	Everg	—	Symmetrical habit, flowers (white, spring)	Informal hedge, woodland garden	—	Leaves and bark contain sassafras oil (safrole)
Athrotaxis cupressoides	Tree	Cool Z 7-9	3 ft 1 m	8 ft 2.5 m	15 ft 5 m	Everg	—	Foliage texture, symmetrical shape	Lawn specimen, rock garden	—	Very slow-growing conifer
Athrotaxis selaginoides	Tree	Cool Z 8-9	4 ft 1.2 m	10 ft 3 m	20 ft 6 m	Everg	—	Foliage texture, symmetrical shape	Lawn specimen, timber	—	Very slow-growing conifer
Aucuba japonica	Shrub	Cool Z 7-10	4 ft 1.2 m	6 ft 2 m	8 ft 2.5 m	Everg	—	Foliage; decorative fruit	Shrub border, woodland garden, container	—	Variegated cultivars popular; male, female plants needed for fruit
Austrocedrus chilensis	Tree	Cool Z 7-9	8 ft 2.5 m	15 ft 5 m	30 ft 9 m	Everg	—	Foliage texture	Formal hedge, screen, lawn grouping	—	—
Averrhoa carambola	Tree	Hot Z 11-12	8 ft 2.5 m	10 ft 3 m	12 ft 4 m	Everg	—	Edible fruit	Orchard, lawn specimen, shade	—	5-angled fruit are ornamental as well as delicious
Avicennia marina	Tree	Warm Z 10-12	8 ft 2.5 m	20 ft 6 m	30 ft 9 m	Everg	—	Foliage	Stabilizing tidal mud and sand banks	—	One of the most widespread mangrove trees
Azadirachta indica	Tree	Hot Z 11-12	10 ft 3 m	20 ft 6 m	25 ft 8 m	Decid*	Yes	Flowers (white, late spring); decorative fruit	Medicinal and insecticidal properties, shade	—	Popular shade tree in the tropics
Azara lanceolata	Tree	Cool Z 8-9	6 ft 2 m	12 ft 4 m	20 ft 6 m	Everg	—	Foliage; flowers (yellow, fragrant, spring)	Shrub border, screen, hedge, woodland garden	—	—
Azara microphylla	Tree	Cool Z 7-9	6 ft 2 m	12 ft 4 m	20 ft 6 m	Everg	—	Foliage; flowers (yellow, fragrant, late winter)	Shrub border, screen, hedge, woodland garden	—	Hardiest & most adaptable azara
Azara serrata	Tree	Cool Z 8-9	8 ft 2.5 m	10 ft 3 m	15 ft 5 m	Everg	—	Flowers (yellow, late spring-early summer)	Shrub border, hedge, woodland garden	—	—
Backhousia citriodora	Tree	Warm Z 10-11	6 ft 2 m	12 ft 4 m	20 ft 6 m	Everg	—	Flowers (greenish white, summer); aromatic foliage	Lawn specimen, informal hedge	—	Crushed leaves have strong lemon scent
Baeckea virgata	Shrub	Warm Z 8-11	6 ft 2 m	8 ft 2.5 m	10 ft 3 m	Everg	—	Flowers (white, late spring-summer); graceful habit	Shrub border, screen	—	—
Banksia coccinea	Shrub	Warm Z 9-10	6 ft 2 m	8 ft 2.5 m	10 ft 3 m	Everg	—	Flowers (scarlet, winter-summer)	Cut flowers	—	Only succeeds in semi-arid climate, alkaline soil
Banksia 'Giant Candles'	Shrub	Warm Z 8-11	6 ft 2 m	10 ft 3 m	12 ft 4 m	Everg	—	Flowers (bronze-yellow, autumn-winter)	Shrub border, informal hedge	—	Very long flower spikes
Banksia integrifolia	Tree	Warm Z 9-11	8 ft 2.5 m	20 ft 6 m	30 ft 9 m	Everg	—	Flowers (greenish-yellow, autumn-winter); foliage	Coastal planting; lawn specimen, container	—	—
Banksia lemanniana	Shrub	Warm Z 10-11	8 ft 2.5 m	12 ft 4 m	15 ft 5 m	Everg	—	Flowers (lemon-yellow, late spring-early summer)	Shrub border	—	Flower-spikes are pendulous
Banksia marginata	Tree	Warm Z 8-10	6 ft 2 m	10 ft 3 m	12 ft 4 m	Everg	—	Flowers (greenish-yellow, autumn-winter)	Coastal planting, informal hedge, screen, shrub border	—	Some forms may grow much taller
Banksia menziesii	Shrub	Warm Z 10-11	6 ft 2 m	12 ft 4 m	15 ft 5 m	Everg	Yes	Flowers (pinkish or yellowish, late summer-winter)	Cut flowers, shrub border, lawn specimen	—	—
Banksia ornata	Shrub	Warm Z 9-11	5 ft 1.5 m	8 ft 2.5 m	10 ft 3 m	Everg	Yes	Flowers (pale yellow, summer-autumn)	Shrub border	—	—
Banksia prionotes	Tree	Warm Z 10-11	6 ft 2 m	15 ft 5 m	18 ft 6 m	Everg	Yes	Flowers (orange-yellow, autumn-winter); foliage	Cut flowers, shrub border	—	—
Banksia serrata	Tree	Warm Z 9-11	6 ft 2 m	12 ft 4 m	25 ft 8 m	Everg	—	Flowers (greenish-white, summer-autumn); decorative fruit	Seaside planting, woodland garden	—	Curious gnarled fruiting cones persist on tree
Barklya syringifolia	Tree	Warm Z 10-11	6 ft 2 m	10 ft 3 m	15 ft 5 m	Everg	—	Flowers (orange-yellow, early summer)	Lawn specimen	—	—
Barleria cristata	Shrub	Warm Z 10-12	3 ft 1 m	3 ft 1 m	3 ft 1 m	Everg	—	Flowers (blue, mauve or white, most of year)	Shrub border, courtyard, conservatory	—	Needs humid climate
Barringtonia asiatica	Tree	Hot Z 12	8 ft 2.5 m	15 ft 5 m	20 ft 6 m	Everg	—	Flowers (red and white, late spring)	Fish poison, parks, streets	—	Some leaves turn orange & fall at any time of year
Bauera rubioides	Shrub	Warm Z 8-11	2 ft 0.6 m	3 ft 1 m	3 ft 1 m	Everg	—	Flowers (deep pink to white, winter-midsummer)	Woodland garden, rock garden, courtyard	—	Likes damp soil; prune to keep compact
Bauhinia × blakeana	Tree	Warm Z 10-12	8 ft 2.5 m	12 ft 4 m	20 ft 6 m	Everg	—	Flowers (crimson, spring)	Parks, streets	—	Sterile, so ugly seed pods not a problem (as in B. variegata)
Bauhinia galpinii	Shrub	Warm Z 9-12	6 ft 2 m	8 ft 2.5 m	10 ft 3 m	Everg	Yes	Flowers (brick red, summer-autumn)	Lawn specimen, embankment, courtyard, espalier, container	—	Unusual flower colour
Bauhinia monandra	Tree	Hot Z 11-12	12 ft 4 m	20 ft 6 m	20 ft 6 m	Everg	Yes	Flowers (cream to pink, late spring-summer)	Shrub border, parks	—	—
Bauhinia variegata	Tree	Warm Z 9-12	8 ft 2.5 m	12 ft 4 m	20 ft 6 m	Decid*	Yes	Flowers (pink to white, spring-summer)	Lawn specimen, shrub border, streets, parks	Massed seed pods may be unattractive	Popular flowering tree in tropics and subtropics
Beaucarnea recurvata	Tree	Warm Z 9-12	3 ft 1 m	6 ft 2 m	12 ft 4 m	Everg	Yes	Swollen trunk; drooping foliage	Courtyard, plaza, swimming pool, container	—	Young plants sold as 'ponytail palm'; old plants develop very thick base
Beilschmiedia taraire	Tree	Warm Z 9-11	8 ft 2.5 m	15 ft 5 m	25 ft 8 m	Everg	—	Foliage; dense canopy	Parks, streets	Prone to root rot in moist climate	—
Berberis darwinii	Shrub	Cool Z 7-9	4 ft 1.2 m	6 ft 2 m	6 ft 2 m	Everg	—	Flowers (orange, late winter-spring)	Shrub border, informal hedge, courtyard	Somewhat spiny	—

NAME	KIND	CLIMATE & ZONE	HEIGHT AT 5yrs	10yrs	20yrs	DECIDUOUS EVERGREEN	ARID CLIMATES	CHIEF ATTRACTIONS	USES	DRAWBACKS	COMMENTS
Berberis × ottawensis	Shrub	Cool Z 3-10	4 ft 1.2 m	6 ft 2 m	6 ft 2 m	Decid	—	Foliage	Shrub border, formal hedge	—	Purple-leaved cultivar 'Superba' is most commonly grown
Berberis thunbergii	Shrub	Cool Z 3-10	3 ft 1 m	5 ft 1.5 m	5 ft 1.5 m	Decid	—	Foliage	Formal hedge, shrub border, courtyard, rock garden	—	Semi-evergreen in mild climate, colour deepens in winter
Berberis vulgaris	Shrub	Cool Z 3-10	5 ft 1.5 m	8 ft 2.5 m	10 ft 3 m	Decid	—	Flowers (yellow, late spring); decorative fruit	Informal hedge, lawn specimen, shrub border	Very spiny; alternate host to wheat rust	—
Berberis wilsoniae	Shrub	Cool Z 5-9	3 ft 1 m	5 ft 1.5 m	5 ft 1.5 m	Decid	—	Foliage; decorative fruit	Informal hedge, shrub border, groundcover	—	—
Betula albosinensis	Tree	Cool Z 6-9	10 ft 3 m	20 ft 6 m	30 ft 9 m	Decid	—	Bark; winter twigs	Lawn specimen, parks, streets	—	—
Betula alleghaniensis	Tree	Cold Z 4-8	10 ft 3 m	25 ft 8 m	40 ft 12 m	Decid	—	Autumn foliage; winter twigs	Lawn specimen, parks, streets, timber	—	—
Betula lenta	Tree	Cold Z 5-8	10 ft 3 m	20 ft 6 m	30 ft 9 m	Decid	—	Bark; winter twigs	Lawn specimen, parks, streets	—	—
Betula nana	Shrub	Cold Z 1-8	2 ft 0.6 m	4 ft 1.2 m	4 ft 1.2 m	Decid	—	Foliage	Rock garden, hedge	—	One of the most cold-tolerant of all woody plants
Betula nigra	Tree	Cold Z 4-8	10 ft 3 m	20 ft 6 m	30 ft 9 m	Decid	—	Attractive bark; winter twigs	Lawn specimen, parks, streets, boggy areas	—	Copper-coloured bark turns almost black as tree matures
Betula papyrifera	Tree	Cold Z 2-8	10 ft 3 m	25 ft 8 m	40 ft 12 m	Decid	—	Attractive bark	Lawn specimen, parks, streets	—	—
Betula pendula	Tree	Cold Z 2-9	10 ft 3 m	20 ft 6 m	40 ft 12 m	Decid	—	Attractive bark; graceful habit	Lawn specimen, parks, streets	—	Silvery bark, graceful weeping branches (some cvs more weeping)
Betula platyphylla	Tree	Cool Z 4-9	10 ft 3 m	20 ft 6 m	40 ft 12 m	Decid	—	Attractive bark	Lawn specimen, parks, streets	—	—
Betula populifolia	Tree	Cold Z 2-8	10 ft 3 m	20 ft 6 m	40 ft 12 m	Decid	—	Attractive bark	Lawn specimen, parks, streets	—	—
Betula pubescens	Tree	Cold Z 2-9	10 ft 3 m	20 ft 6 m	40 ft 12 m	Decid	—	Bark	Lawn specimen, parks, streets	—	—
Betula utilis	Tree	Cool Z 7-9	12 ft 4 m	30 ft 9 m	50 ft 15 m	Decid	—	Attractive bark	Lawn specimen, parks, streets	—	—
Bixa orellana	Shrub	Warm Z 10-12	8 ft 2.5 m	10 ft 3 m	12 ft 4 m	Everg	—	Flowers (pink, summer); decorative fruit	Dye from seeds, lawn specimen, dried decoration	—	Size easily controlled by pruning
Bolusanthus speciosus	Tree	Warm Z 9-10	6 ft 2 m	12 ft 4 m	15 ft 5 m	Decid	Yes	Flowers (purple, spring)	Lawn specimen	—	—
Bombax ceiba (malabaricum)	Tree	Hot Z 11-12	15 ft 5 m	30 ft 9 m	50 ft 15 m	Everg*	Yes	Flowers (red, winter-spring)	Parks, lawn specimen	—	Flowers attract nectar-feeding birds
Borassodendron machadonis	Palm	Hot Z 12	5 ft 1.5 m	10 ft 3 m	20 ft 6 m	Everg	—	Foliage; symmetrical form	Lawn specimen, parks	—	—
Boronia heterophylla	Shrub	Warm Z 9-10	4 ft 1.2 m	5 ft 1.5 m	—	Everg	—	Flowers (red, late winter-early spring)	Rock garden, courtyard, cut flowers	Must have perfect drainage	Can be temperamental in gardens
Boronia megastigma	Shrub	Warm Z 9-10	3 ft 1 m	3 ft 1 m	—	Everg	—	Fragrant flowers (brown & yellow, late winter-spring)	Woodland garden, courtyard, cut flowers	Short-lived	Delicious fragrance, flowers used in perfumery
Boronia pinnata	Shrub	Warm Z 8-10	3 ft 1 m	5 ft 1.5 m	—	Everg	—	Flowers (pink, spring)	Woodland garden, cut flowers	Short-lived	—
Bouvardia longiflora	Shrub	Warm Z 10-11	3 ft 1 m	3 ft 1 m	—	Everg	—	Fragrant flowers (white, autumn-winter)	Courtyard, balcony, indoor, cut flowers	—	—
Brabejum stellatifolium	Tree	Warm Z 9-11	5 ft 1.5 m	10 ft 3 m	15 ft 5 m	Everg	—	Edible nuts, flowers (white, fragrant, summer)	Shrub border, orchard	—	—
Brachychiton acerifolius	Tree	Warm Z 9-12	6 ft 2 m	12 ft 4 m	25 ft 8 m	Decid*	—	Flowers (scarlet, spring-early summer)	Lawn specimen, parks	Dead leaves very untidy	May take many years to flower but spectacular when it does
Brachychiton discolor	Tree	Warm Z 10-12	8 ft 2.5 m	15 ft 5 m	30 ft 9 m	Decid*	—	Flowers (pink, early summer)	Lawn specimen, parks, streets	—	—
Brachychiton populneus	Tree	Warm Z 8-11	6 ft 2 m	12 ft 4 m	20 ft 6 m	Everg	Yes	Foliage; flowers (cream, summer)	Streets, parks, shade on farms, fodder for livestock	—	Extremely drought-resistant
Brachyglottis repanda	Tree	Warm Z 9-11	12 ft 4 m	15 ft 5 m	20 ft 6 m	Everg	—	Foliage; flowers (greenish silver, late winter-early spring)	Shrub border	—	—
Brachylaena discolor	Tree	Warm Z 9-11	10 ft 3 m	15 ft 5 m	20 ft 6 m	Everg	—	Foliage, flowers (cream, spring)	Informal hedge, coastal planting, windbreak	—	—
Brahea armata	Palm	Warm Z 9-11	3 ft 1 m	6 ft 2 m	10 ft 3 m	Everg	Yes	Foliage; symmetrical form	Lawn specimen, plaza	—	—
Breynia disticha	Shrub	Warm Z 10-12	4 ft 1.2 m	4 ft 1.2 m	4 ft 1.2 m	Everg	—	Foliage (variegated pink and white)	Courtyard, swimming pool	—	—
Broussonetia papyrifera	Tree	Warm Z 7-11	15 ft 5 m	30 ft 9 m	40 ft 12 m	Everg	—	Foliage	Bark fibre, lawn specimen	—	Bark can be made into paper and 'tapa cloth' of Polynesians
Brownea grandiceps	Tree	Hot Z 11-12	8 ft 2.5 m	12 ft 4 m	20 ft 6 m	Everg	—	Flowers (scarlet to orange, summer)	Lawn specimen, shade, streets	—	Spectacular in flower, requires very hot climate
Brugmansia (Datura) × candida	Tree	Warm Z 10-11	6 ft 2 m	12 ft 4 m	15 ft 5 m	Everg	Yes	Flowers (white, fragrant, summer-autumn)	Courtyard, shrub border, conservatory	Leaves and flowers highly poisonous	Can be pruned to more compact size
Brugmansia (Datura) sanguinea	Shrub	Warm Z 9-11	6 ft 2 m	8 ft 2.5 m	10 ft 3 m	Everg	Yes	Flowers (orange-red, late spring-summer)	Courtyard, shrub border	Leaves and flowers highly poisonous	Can be pruned to more compact size

NAME	KIND	CLIMATE & ZONE	HEIGHT AT 5yrs	HEIGHT AT 10yrs	HEIGHT AT 20yrs	DECIDUOUS EVERGREEN	ARID CLIMATES	CHIEF ATTRACTIONS	USES	DRAWBACKS	COMMENTS
Brugmansia (Datura) suaveolens	Shrub	Warm Z 10-12	6 ft 2 m	12 ft 4 m	15 ft 5 m	Everg	Yes	Flowers (white, summer-autumn)	Courtyard, shrub border, conservatory	Leaves and flowers highly poisonous	Can be pruned to more compact size
Brunfelsia australis (bonodora)	Shrub	Warm Z 9-11	3 ft 1 m	6 ft 2 m	6 ft 2 m	Everg	—	Flowers (violet-blue-white, spring)	Informal hedge, shrub border, courtyard, container	—	Flowers pass through three colours as they age
Brunfelsia pauciflora	Shrub	Warm Z 10-12	3 ft 1 m	4 ft 1.2 m	5 ft 1.5 m	Everg	—	Flowers (purple-mauve-white, spring-early summer)	Shrub border, courtyard, woodland garden	—	Flowers pass through three colours as they age
Brya ebenus	Tree	Hot Z 11-12	8 ft 2.5 m	15 ft 5 m	20 ft 6 m	Everg	—	Flowers (orange-yellow, autumn)	Lawn specimen, courtyard, plaza	—	—
Buckinghamia celsissima	Tree	Warm Z 10-12	6 ft 2 m	12 ft 4 m	20 ft 6 m	Everg	—	Flowers (white, fragrant, summer-early autumn)	Street, park, lawn specimen	—	Can be trained to single trunk with weeping branches
Buddleja alternifolia	Shrub	Cool Z 6-9	6 ft 2 m	10 ft 3 m	12 ft 4 m	Decid	—	Flowers (mauve-pink, fragrant, late spring-early summer)	Lawn specimen, shrub border	—	—
Buddleja davidii	Shrub	Cool Z 7-10	8 ft 2.5 m	10 ft 3 m	12 ft 4 m	Decid	—	Flowers (purple, red, pink, white, late summer-early autumn)	Shrub border	Dead flowers are unattractive	Fast-growing, tolerates poor soil; attracts butterflies
Buddleja globosa	Shrub	Cool Z 7-10	8 ft 2.5 m	12 ft 4 m	15 ft 5 m	Everg	—	Flowers (orange, late spring-summer)	Lawn specimen, shrub border	Often short-lived	Unusual globular flower heads for a buddleja
Burchellia bubalina	Shrub	Warm Z 9-11	4 ft 1.2 m	6 ft 2 m	10 ft 3 m	Everg	Yes	Flowers (orange-red, late spring-summer)	Informal hedge, shrub border, courtyard	—	—
Bursaria spinosa	Shrub	Warm Z 8-11	6 ft 2 m	12 ft 4 m	15 ft 5 m	Everg	Yes	Flowers (white, summer); decorative fruit	Informal hedge, woodland garden	Thorns on branches	—
Butea monosperma	Tree	Hot Z 11-12	6 ft 2 m	12 ft 4 m	20 ft 6 m	Decid*	—	Flowers (orange-red, late spring)	Park, lawn specimen	Growth can be ungainly	Popular in tropics for brilliant flowers, shade
Butia capitata	Palm	Warm Z 8-11	4 ft 1.2 m	8 ft 2.5 m	12 ft 4 m	Everg	Yes	Foliage, decorative/edible fruit	Park, lawn specimen, courtyard, plaza	Spiny frond bases	Fruit edible but stringy, has been used for wines & jellies
Butia eriospatha	Palm	Warm Z 9-11	4 ft 1.2 m	8 ft 2.5 m	12 ft 4 m	Everg	—	Foliage, decorative/edible fruit	Park, lawn specimen, courtyard, plaza	Spiny frond bases	—
Buxus microphylla	Shrub	Cool Z 5-10	3 ft 1 m	6 ft 2 m	8 ft 2.5 m	Everg	—	Foliage texture	Formal hedge, topiary	—	—
Buxus sempervirens	Shrub	Cool Z 6-10	3 ft 1 m	6 ft 2 m	10 ft 3 m	Everg	—	Foliage texture	Formal hedge, topiary, formal bed edging	—	Height depends on variety and pruning
Caesalpinia ferrea	Tree	Hot Z 10-12	8 ft 2.5 m	12 ft 4 m	20 ft 6 m	Everg	Yes	Attractive bark	Lawn specimen, shade, parks, streets	—	—
Caesalpinia gilliesii	Shrub	Warm Z 10-11	6 ft 2 m	8 ft 2.5 m	10 ft 3 m	Decid*	—	Flowers (yellow & scarlet, summer)	Shrub border, courtyard	—	Prune after flowering for more shapely plant
Caesalpinia (Poinciana) pulcherrima	Shrub	Hot Z 11-12	6 ft 2 m	12 ft 4 m	15 ft 5 m	Everg	Yes	Flowers (scarlet & gold, spring-autumn)	Shrub border, plaza	Can be short-lived	Fast-growing, one of the most popular tropical flowering shrubs
Calamus australis	Palm	Hot Z 10-12	4 ft 1.2 m	10 ft 3 m	20 ft 6 m	Everg	—	Foliage	Cane (rattan), rainforest garden	Fierce spines on stems & climbing appendages	Mainly a curiosity in gardens
Calceolaria integrifolia	Shrub	Cool Z 8-9	2 ft 0.6 m	4 ft 1.2 m	4 ft 1.2 m	Everg	—	Flowers (yellow, late spring-early autumn)	Shrub border, courtyard, container	Somewhat short-lived	Can be treated as a herbaceous perennial
Calliandra haematocephala	Shrub	Warm Z 10-12	5 ft 1.5 m	10 ft 3 m	12 ft 4 m	Everg	—	Flowers (red, most of year)	Shrub border, swimming pool, informal hedge	—	Flowers attract birds
Calliandra portoricensis	Shrub	Warm Z 10-12	8 ft 2.5 m	15 ft 5 m	15 ft 5 m	Everg	—	Flowers (white, spring-autumn)	Shrub border, courtyard, lawn specimen, plaza	—	—
Calliandra surinamensis	Shrub	Hot Z 11-12	6 ft 2 m	8 ft 2.5 m	10 ft 3 m	Everg	—	Flowers (pink & white, most of year)	Shrub border, lawn specimen	—	—
Calliandra tweedii	Shrub	Warm Z 9-11	4 ft 1.2 m	6 ft 2 m	6 ft 2 m	Everg	—	Flowers (crimson, spring & summer)	Shrub border, informal hedge	—	May grow straggly, can be kept compact by pruning after flowers
Callicarpa americana	Shrub	Warm Z 9-10	3 ft 1 m	6 ft 2 m	6 ft 2 m	Decid	—	Flowers (purple, summer), decorative fruit	Shrub border, cut fruiting stems	—	—
Callicarpa bodinieri	Shrub	Cool Z 6-9	6 ft 2 m	8 ft 2.5 m	10 ft 3 m	Decid	—	Flowers (lilac, summer); decorative fruit	Shrub border, cut fruiting stems	—	Fruit display best if several plants grown together
Callicarpa macrophylla	Shrub	Warm Z 10-11	10 ft 3 m	15 ft 5 m	20 ft 6 m	Everg	—	Flowers (mauve, autumn) decorative fruit	Informal hedge	—	—
Callicoma serratifolia	Tree	Warm Z 9-11	8 ft 2.5 m	12 ft 4 m	15 ft 5 m	Everg	—	Flowers (cream, spring-early summer)	Woodland garden, shrub border	—	Fast growing, tolerates shade, likes damp soil
Callistemon citrinus	Shrub	Warm Z 8-11	4 ft 1.2 m	6 ft 2 m	8 ft 2.5 m	Everg	—	Flowers (scarlet to crimson, late spring-summer)	Informal hedge, shrub border, courtyard	—	Can be pruned after flowering to keep compact
Callistemon linearis	Shrub	Warm Z 9-11	4 ft 1.2 m	6 ft 2 m	8 ft 2.5 m	Everg	—	Flowers (red, spring-early summer)	Shrub border	—	—
Callistemon phoeniceus	Shrub	Warm Z 9-11	5 ft 1.5 m	8 ft 2.5 m	10 ft 3 m	Everg	Yes	Flowers (red, spring-early summer)	Shrub border, informal hedge	Straggly habit	Can be pruned after flowering to keep compact
Callistemon salignus	Tree	Warm Z 9-11	8 ft 2.5 m	15 ft 5 m	25 ft 8 m	Everg	Yes	Flowers (greenish yellow or red, spring-summer); pink new growths	Lawn specimen, streets, parks, hedge, boggy areas	—	Can be kept as large shrub by pruning; red-flowered form becoming popular
Callistemon subulatus	Shrub	Warm Z 9-11	3 ft 1 m	5 ft 1.5 m	5 ft 1.5 m	Everg	—	Flowers (dark red, spring-summer)	Shrub border, informal hedge	—	—

NAME	KIND	CLIMATE & ZONE	HEIGHT AT 5 yrs	10 yrs	20 yrs	DECIDUOUS EVERGREEN	ARID CLIMATES	CHIEF ATTRACTIONS	USES	DRAWBACKS	COMMENTS
Callistemon viminalis	Tree	Warm Z 9-11	8 ft 2.5 m	12 ft 4 m	20 ft 6 m	Everg	Yes	Flowers (scarlet, spring)	Lawn specimen, street, park, shrub border	—	Weeping habit, old trees develop gnarled trunks
Callitris columellaris	Tree	Warm Z 10-11	6 ft 2 m	12 ft 4 m	25 ft 8 m	Everg	—	Foliage; symmetrical form	Informal hedge, lawn group, against wall	—	—
Callitris glaucophylla	Tree	Warm Z 9-11	6 ft 2 m	12 ft 4 m	25 ft 8 m	Everg	Yes	Foliage; symmetrical form	Farm planting, timber, lawn specimen	—	—
Callitris rhomboidea	Tree	Warm Z 9-11	6 ft 2 m	15 ft 5 m	20 ft 6 m	Everg	—	Foliage; symmetrical form	Shrub border, screen, formal or informal hedge	—	—
Calluna vulgaris	Shrub	Cold Z 3-9	1 ft 0.3 m	2 ft 0.6 m	2 ft 0.6 m	Everg	—	Flowers (pink to purplish, summer-autumn)	Rock garden, embankment, heather garden	—	Large number of cultivars exist
Calocedrus decurrens	Tree	Cool Z 7-9	5 ft 1.5 m	12 ft 4 m	25 ft 8 m	Everg	—	Foliage; symmetrical form	Lawn specimen, informal hedge, park	—	Like a sequoia in appearance but of more compact size
Calodendrum capense	Tree	Cool Z 9-11	6 ft 2 m	15 ft 5 m	30 ft 9 m	Everg	Yes	Flowers (pink, late spring-early summer)	Street, park, lawn specimen	—	—
Calophyllum inophyllum	Tree	Hot Z 11-12	10 ft 3 m	20 ft 6 m	30 ft 9 m	Everg	—	Flowers (white, fragrant, summer); foliage; dense canopy	Seaside planting	—	—
Calothamnus quadrifidus	Shrub	Warm Z 9-11	5 ft 1.5 m	8 ft 2.5 m	8 ft 2.5 m	Everg	Yes	Flowers (red, late spring-early summer); foliage	Shrub border, informal hedge	Can be short-lived	—
Calycanthus floridus	Shrub	Cool Z 6-9	5 ft 1.5 m	8 ft 2.5 m	8 ft 2.5 m	Decid	—	Flowers (brownish red, late spring-summer)	Shrub border	—	Crushed leaves have spicy aroma
Calycanthus occidentalis	Shrub	Cool Z 7-9	5 ft 1.5 m	8 ft 2.5 m	12 ft 4 m	Decid	—	Flowers (brownish red, late spring-summer)	Shrub border	—	Needs care in pruning, can be reluctant to sprout
Calytrix tetragona	Shrub	Warm Z 9-11	3 ft 1 m	5 ft 1.5 m	6 ft 2 m	Everg	Yes	Flowers (pink to white, late winter-early summer)	Woodland garden, rock garden, seaside	—	—
Camellia 'Cornish Snow'	Shrub	Cool Z 7-10	5 ft 1.5 m	8 ft 2.5 m	10 ft 3 m	Everg	—	Flowers (white flushed pink, late winter-early spring)	Shrub border; woodland garden	—	Hybrid cultivar, very popular in the UK, one of the most cold-tolerant camellias
Camellia granthamiana	Shrub	Warm Z 9-11	3 ft 1 m	6 ft 2 m	10 ft 3 m	Everg	—	Flowers (white, late autumn); foliage	Shrub border; woodland garden	—	—
Camellia japonica	Shrub	Warm Z 8-11	4 ft 1.2 m	8 ft 2.5 m	12 ft 4 m	Everg	—	Flowers (red, pink, white, winter-early spring)	Shrub border; woodland garden, cut flowers, container	—	Thousands of cultivars available
Camellia reticulata	Shrub	Cool Z 8-10	5 ft 1.5 m	10 ft 3 m	15 ft 5 m	Everg	—	Flowers (red, pink, white, midwinter-early spring)	Shrub border; woodland garden, cut flowers	—	Cultivars include the largest-flowered of all camellias
Camellia sasanqua	Shrub	Warm Z 8-11	8 ft 2.5 m	12 ft 4 m	20 ft 6 m	Everg	—	Flowers (pink, white, early autumn-early winter)	Informal or formal hedge, lawn specimen, street, espalier, container	—	Informal habit; flowers short-lived but abundant, fragrant
Camellia sinensis	Shrub	Warm Z 8-11	4 ft 1.2 m	6 ft 2 m	8 ft 2.5 m	Everg	—	Foliage; flowers (white, spring)	Tea plantation, hedge, espalier	—	Young leaves are fermented to make tea
Camellia × williamsii	Shrub	Cool Z 7-10	5 ft 1.5 m	12 ft 4 m	15 ft 5 m	Everg	—	Flowers (pink, winter-spring)	Shrub border; woodland garden, cut flowers, container	—	—
Camptotheca acuminata	Tree	Warm Z 10-11	10 ft 3 m	30 ft 9 m	40 ft 12 m	Decid	—	Foliage; flowers (white, summer); decorative fruit	Lawn specimen, parks	—	—
Cananga odorata	Tree	Hot Z 11-12	10 ft 3 m	20 ft 6 m	30 ft 9 m	Everg	—	Flowers (greenish-yellow, summer)	Perfumery, lawn specimen, parks	—	The heavily scented flowers are used to make perfume
Cantua buxifolia	Shrub	Cool Z 8-9	4 ft 1.2 m	6 ft 2 m	6 ft 2 m	Everg	—	Flowers (purple to pink, late spring)	Shrub border, courtyard	Straggly habit	Very fine in flower but can be temperamental
Caragana arborescens	Tree	Cool Z 4-9	6 ft 2 m	12 ft 4 m	20 ft 6 m	Decid	Yes	Flowers (yellow, late spring-early summer)	Shrub border, lawn specimen	—	—
Carica papaya	Tree	Hot Z 10-12	8 ft 2.5 m	12 ft 4 m	20 ft 6 m	Everg	—	Edible fruit, foliage	Orchard, kitchen garden, courtyard	—	Grown mainly for fruit but has striking foliage
Carissa macrocarpa	Shrub	Warm Z 9-11	4 ft 1.2 m	8 ft 2.5 m	10 ft 3 m	Everg	Yes	Edible fruit; flowers (white, spring-summer)	Shrub border, courtyard, thorny hedge, container	—	Curious forked spines, milky sap
Carmichaelia arborea	Tree	Cool Z 8-10	5 ft 1.5 m	10 ft 3 m	15 ft 5 m	Everg	—	Flowers (purple & white, summer)	Shrub border, lawn specimen	—	—
Carmichaelia odorata	Shrub	Warm Z 9-10	3 ft 1 m	5 ft 1.5 m	6 ft 2 m	Everg	—	Flowers (white & purple, fragrant, late spring-summer)	Shrub border, courtyard	—	—
Carmichaelia williamsii	Shrub	Cool Z 8-10	3 ft 1 m	8 ft 2.5 m	12 ft 4 m	Everg	—	Flowers (creamy-yellow, late spring-early summer)	Shrub border, lawn specimen	—	—
Carnegiea gigantea	Tree	Warm Z 9-10	1 ft 0.3 m	2 ft 0.6 m	3 ft 1 m	Everg	Yes	Succulent stems; flowers (white, early summer)	Desert garden	Extremely slow-growing, difficult to cultivate	Flowers open at night; the famous saguaro cactus of the American southwest
Carpenteria californica	Shrub	Cool Z 7-9	4 ft 1.2 m	6 ft 2 m	8 ft 2.5 m	Everg	—	Flowers (white, early summer)	Shrub border, courtyard	—	—
Carpinus betulus	Tree	Cool Z 6-9	8 ft 2.5 m	15 ft 5 m	30 ft 9 m	Decid	—	Autumn foliage; decorative fruit; bark	Lawn specimen, hedge, shade	—	Used for hedgerows in Europe
Carpinus caroliniana	Tree	Cool Z 4-9	8 ft 2.5 m	20 ft 6 m	30 ft 9 m	Decid	—	Autumn foliage; decorative fruit; bark	Lawn specimen, shade	—	—

NAME	KIND	CLIMATE & ZONE	HEIGHT AT 5yrs 10yrs 20yrs	DECIDUOUS EVERGREEN	ARID CLIMATES	CHIEF ATTRACTIONS	USES	DRAWBACKS	COMMENTS
Carpinus japonica	Tree	Cool Z 5-9	6 ft 12 ft 25 ft / 2 m 4 m 8 m	Decid	—	Autumn foliage; decorative fruit; bark	Lawn specimen, shade	—	Slow-growing but shapely
Carya cordiformis	Tree	Cool Z 4-9	8 ft 15 ft 30 ft / 2.5 m 5 m 9 m	Decid	—	Autumn foliage; winter twigs	Lawn specimen, shade	—	—
Carya glabra	Tree	Cool Z 4-9	8 ft 15 ft 30 ft / 2.5 m 5 m 9 m	Decid	—	Autumn foliage; edible nuts	Timber, lawn specimen, shade	—	—
Carya illinoinensis	Tree	Cool Z 6-10	10 ft 25 ft 40 ft / 3 m 8 m 12 m	Decid	Yes	Edible nuts (pecans)	Orchard, parks, avenues	—	Must have a hot summer for good nut crop
Carya laciniosa	Tree	Cool Z 4-9	8 ft 15 ft 30 ft / 2.5 m 5 m 9 m	Decid	—	Edible nuts, autumn foliage, striking bark	Lawn specimen, shade	—	—
Carya ovata	Tree	Cool Z 4-9	8 ft 12 ft 25 ft / 2.5 m 4 m 8 m	Decid	—	Edible nuts, autumn foliage, striking bark	Lawn specimen, shade	—	—
Carya tomentosa	Tree	Cool Z 4-9	8 ft 15 ft 30 ft / 2.5 m 5 m 9 m	Decid	—	Autumn foliage, edible nuts	Lawn specimen, shade	—	—
Caryota mitis	Palm	Hot Z 10-12	6 ft 12 ft 20 ft / 2 m 4 m 6 m	Everg	—	Foliage	Courtyard, lawn specimen, container	Fruit has irritant juice	Fishtail-shaped leaflets, stems in clumps
Caryota no	Palm	Hot Z 10-12	8 ft 20 ft 50 ft / 2.5 m 6 m 15 m	Everg	—	Foliage, symmetrical form, fast growth	Lawn specimen, avenue, park	Short-lived	—
Caryota urens	Palm	Hot Z 10-12	8 ft 15 ft 30 ft / 2.5 m 5 m 9 m	Everg	—	Foliage, fast growth	Sugar from sap	—	Sap from flower stalk used to make toddy and arrack
Cassia fistula	Tree	Hot Z 10-12	8 ft 20 ft 30 ft / 2.5 m 6 m 9 m	Decid*	Yes	Flowers (pale yellow, late spring-summer)	Lawn specimen, parks, streets	Large woody pods litter ground	—
Cassia javanica	Tree	Hot Z 11-12	10 ft 25 ft 40 ft / 3 m 8 m 12 m	Decid*	—	Flowers (pink, late spring-summer)	Lawn specimen, parks, streets	Somewhat short-lived	Spectacular in flower
Castanea dentata	Tree	Cool Z 4-9	8 ft 15 ft 30 ft / 2.5 m 5 m 9 m	Decid	—	Edible nuts; autumn foliage	Orchard, timber, shade	Susceptible to chestnut blight disease	Now rare in wild due to chestnut blight disease
Castanea sativa	Tree	Cool Z 5-9	8 ft 15 ft 30 ft / 2.5 m 5 m 9 m	Decid	—	Edible nuts; autumn foliage	Orchard, timber, lawn specimen	Prickly husks litter ground	Majestic shade tree; grafted disease-free plants best for nuts
Castanospermum australe	Tree	Warm Z 10-12	8 ft 15 ft 30 ft / 2.5 m 5 m 9 m	Everg	—	Flowers (orange & yellow, early summer); curious fruit	Lawn specimen, shade, parks, streets, timber, indoor	Seeds poisonous; pods & seeds litter ground	Chocolate-brown timber very valuable, used for cabinet work, veneers
Castanospora alphandii	Tree	Warm Z 10-11	6 ft 12 ft 20 ft / 2 m 4 m 6 m	Everg	—	Foliage; decorative fruit	Lawn specimen, rainforest garden	—	—
Casuarina cunninghamiana	Tree	Warm Z 8-12	15 ft 30 ft 50 ft / 5 m 9 m 15 m	Everg	Yes	Foliage; pine-like growth form; vigorous growth	Parks, streets, farms, shade, screens, windbreaks	Dead twigs and female 'cones' litter pavements	Very fast-growing; useful for river banks, resists flooding and prevents erosion
Casuarina equisetifolia	Tree	Warm Z 10-12	10 ft 20 ft 30 ft / 3 m 6 m 9 m	Everg	Yes	Foliage; pine-like growth form	Coastal planting, streets, parks, lawn specimen	Dead twigs litter ground	Grows on sand and coral beaches
Casuarina glauca	Tree	Warm Z 9-12	12 ft 25 ft 40 ft / 4 m 8 m 12 m	Everg	Yes	Foliage; pine-like growth form	Coastal planting, parks, streets, farms, poorly drained areas	Dead twigs and prickly 'cones' litter pavements	—
Catalpa bignonioides	Tree	Cool Z 8-10	8 ft 15 ft 25 ft / 2.5 m 5 m 8 m	Decid	Yes	Flowers (white, summer); foliage	Lawn specimen, parks, streets	Leaves have unpleasant smell when bruised	Fast-growing, spectacular in flower, needs shelter from wind
Catalpa bungei	Tree	Cool Z 8-10	8 ft 15 ft 20 ft / 2.5 m 5 m 6 m	Decid	—	Flowers (white); foliage	Lawn specimen, parks, streets	—	—
Catalpa speciosa	Tree	Cool Z 6-10	8 ft 15 ft 30 ft / 2.5 m 5 m 9 m	Decid	Yes	Flowers (white, summer); foliage	Parks, streets, timber, shade	—	Leaves lack the odour of C. bignonioides
Cavendishia bracteata	Shrub	Warm Z 9-10	4 ft 6 ft 6 ft / 1.2 m 2 m 2 m	Everg	—	Flowers (red, spring-late autumn); pink new growths	Shrub border, courtyard, woodland garden	—	Needs a humid climate
Ceanothus arboreus	Shrub	Cool Z 8-10	6 ft 10 ft 15 ft / 2 m 3 m 5 m	Everg	—	Flowers (pale to deep blue, spring-early summer)	Shrub border, lawn specimen	—	Prefers winter-rainfall climates (all ceanothus)
Ceanothus griseus	Shrub	Cool Z 8-10	5 ft 8 ft 10 ft / 1.5 m 2.5 m 3 m	Everg	—	Flowers (pale blue, spring)	Coastal planting, rock garden, swimming pool	May be short-lived	Some sea-coast clones are prostrate, make good groundcover
Ceanothus impressus	Shrub	Cool Z 8-10	3 ft 4 ft 6 ft / 1 m 1.2 m 2 m	Everg	Yes	Flowers (deep blue, spring)	Coastal planting, rock garden, embankment, swimming pool	May be short-lived	Many named cultivars & hybrids exist
Ceanothus papillosus	Shrub	Cool Z 8-10	4 ft 8 ft 12 ft / 1.2 m 2.5 m 4 m	Everg	—	Flowers (deep blue, spring)	Coastal planting, rock garden, hedges	May be short-lived	—
Ceanothus thyrsiflorus	Tree	Cool Z 7-9	6 ft 12 ft 20 ft / 2 m 4 m 6 m	Everg	—	Flowers (pale blue, late spring-early summer)	Shrub border, lawn specimen, courtyard	—	—
Ceanothus × veitchianus	Shrub	Cool Z 7-9	5 ft 8 ft 10 ft / 1.5 m 2.5 m 3 m	Everg	—	Flowers (pale blue, spring)	Shrub border, lawn specimen, courtyard	—	A number of cultivars exist
Cecropia palmata	Tree	Hot Z 12	15 ft 25 ft 40 ft / 5 m 8 m 12 m	Everg	—	Foliage	Lawn specimen, parks, plazas	Branches very weak	Very fast growing, dramatic foliage
Cedrela mexicana	Tree	Hot Z 10-12	8 ft 20 ft 40 ft / 2.5 m 6 m 12 m	Everg	—	Foliage	Parks, streets, timber	—	Yields the traditional cigar-box timber
Cedrus atlantica	Tree	Cool Z 6-9	6 ft 12 ft 25 ft / 2 m 4 m 8 m	Everg	—	Foliage; symmetrical form	Lawn specimen, parks, avenues	—	'Glauca' forms (blue foliage) preferrred for ornamental use
Cedrus brevifolia	Tree	Cool Z 6-9	5 ft 10 ft 20 ft / 1.5 m 3 m 6 m	Everg	—	Foliage; symmetrical shape	Lawn specimen	—	Rare in cultivation
Cedrus deodara	Tree	Cool Z 7-10	8 ft 25 ft 40 ft / 2.5 m 8 m 12 m	Everg	—	Foliage; symmetrical form	Lawn specimen, parks, streets, windbreak	—	The fastest-growing Cedrus species

Reference Table 459

NAME	KIND	CLIMATE & ZONE	HEIGHT AT 5yrs 10yrs 20yrs	DECIDUOUS EVERGREEN	ARID CLIMATES	CHIEF ATTRACTIONS	USES	DRAWBACKS	COMMENTS
Cedrus libani	Tree	Cool Z 6-9	6 ft / 12 ft / 25 ft; 2 m / 4 m / 8 m	Everg	—	Foliage; majestic form	Lawn specimen, parks, avenues	—	The cedar of the Bible, also shown on the Lebanese flag
Ceiba pentandra	Tree	Hot Z 12	20 ft / 40 ft / 80 ft; 6 m / 12 m / 25 m	Decid*	—	Foliage, flowers (white, yellow, pink, winter); massive trunk	Parks, avenues, kapok from seed pods	Spiny trunk when young	Main source of kapok, from floss surrounding seeds
Celtis africana	Tree	Warm Z 9-11	10 ft / 20 ft / 30 ft; 3 m / 6 m / 9 m	Decid	Yes	Foliage	Parks, streets, shade	—	—
Celtis australis	Tree	Warm Z 8-11	10 ft / 20 ft / 30 ft; 3 m / 6 m / 9 m	Decid	Yes	Foliage	Parks, streets, shade	—	Tolerates urban conditions
Celtis laevigata	Tree	Cool Z 5-10	10 ft / 20 ft / 30 ft; 3 m / 6 m / 9 m	Decid	Yes	Autumn foliage	Shade, parks, streets	—	—
Celtis occidentalis	Tree	Cool Z 3-10	10 ft / 20 ft / 30 ft; 3 m / 6 m / 9 m	Decid	Yes	Autumn foliage	Shade, parks, streets	Spreads by seed along river channels	The best *Celtis* for autumn colour
Celtis sinensis	Tree	Warm Z 8-11	10 ft / 25 ft / 40 ft; 3 m / 8 m / 12 m	Decid	—	Foliage	Shade, parks, streets	Becomes a weed in moist subtropical climates	Tolerates urban conditions
Cephalotaxus fortunei	Tree	Cool Z 7-10	4 ft / 8 ft / 15 ft; 1.2 m / 2.5 m / 5 m	Everg	—	Foliage, decorative fruit	Shrub border, courtyard	Fallen fruits can be a nuisance	—
Cephalotaxus harringtonia	Shrub	Cool Z 6-10	3 ft / 6 ft / 10 ft; 1 m / 2 m / 3 m	Everg	—	Foliage, compact form	Shrub border, lawn specimen, courtyard, container	—	Cultivar 'Fastigiata' is the most ornamental form
Ceratonia siliqua	Tree	Warm Z 9-10	6 ft / 12 ft / 25 ft; 2 m / 4 m / 8 m	Everg	Yes	Foliage; edible pulp around seeds	Lawn specimen, parks, streets, farms, fodder, chocolate substitute	—	Male and female plants required for pod production
Ceratopetalum apetalum	Tree	Warm Z 9-11	8 ft / 15 ft / 30 ft; 2.5 m / 5 m / 9 m	Everg	—	Bark; decorative fruit (red, early summer)	Parks, lawn specimen, timber	—	Valued for timber but too slow-growing for plantations
Ceratopetalum gummiferum	Tree	Warm Z 9-11	8 ft / 12 ft / 25 ft; 2.5 m / 4 m / 8 m	Everg	—	Flowers (white, late spring); decorative fruit (red, early summer)	Cut flowers, lawn specimen, woodland garden	—	Selected clones have richer 'flower' colour
Ceratostigma willmottianum	Shrub	Cool Z 6-10	2 ft / 3 ft / 3 ft; 0.6 m / 1 m / 1 m	Decid	—	Flowers (blue, late summer-autumn)	Rock garden, shrub border, herbaceous border, courtyard, swimming pool	—	One of the most brilliant deep blue flowers of any shrub
Cercidiphyllum japonicum	Tree	Cool Z 6-9	6 ft / 12 ft / 25 ft; 2 m / 4 m / 8 m	Decid	—	Autumn foliage	Lawn specimen, woodland garden, parks, streets	Spring foliage very tender	—
Cercidium floridum	Tree	Warm Z 8-11	6 ft / 12 ft / 20 ft; 2 m / 4 m / 6 m	Decid*	Yes	Flowers (yellow, spring)	Lawn specimen, streets, plazas, desert garden	—	—
Cercis canadensis	Tree	Cool Z 5-9	4 ft / 8 ft / 12 ft; 1.2 m / 2.5 m / 4 m	Decid	—	Flowers (pink, spring-early summer)	Lawn specimen, shrub border, courtyard	—	Very beautiful when flowering on leafless branches
Cercis occidentalis	Tree	Cool Z 5-9	4 ft / 8 ft / 10 ft; 1.2 m / 2.5 m / 3 m	Decid	—	Flowers (pink, spring)	Lawn specimen, shrub border, courtyard	—	—
Cercis siliquastrum	Tree	Cool Z 7-10	4 ft / 10 ft / 15 ft; 1.2 m / 3 m / 5 m	Decid	Yes	Flowers (deep pink, late spring)	Lawn specimen, parks, streets	—	Very pretty tree for small garden
Cercocarpus betuloides	Shrub	Cool Z 7-9	4 ft / 8 ft / 12 ft; 1.2 m / 2.5 m / 4 m	Everg	Yes	Decorative plumed fruit	Lawn specimen, courtyard, cut stems	—	—
Cestrum fasciculatum	Shrub	Warm Z 9-11	6 ft / 10 ft / 10 ft; 2 m / 3 m / 3 m	Everg	—	Flowers (red, summer)	Shrub border, courtyard, container, espalier	Poisonous; foliage unpleasant smelling	—
Cestrum 'Newellii'	Shrub	Warm Z 9-11	6 ft / 6 ft / 6 ft; 2 m / 2 m / 2 m	Everg	—	Flowers (crimson, most of year)	Shrub border, courtyard, espalier	Poisonous; foliage unpleasant smelling	—
Cestrum nocturnum	Shrub	Warm Z 10-11	6 ft / 8 ft / 10 ft; 2 m / 2.5 m / 3 m	Everg	Yes	Flowers (pale green, very fragrant, late summer); decorative fruit	Shrub border, courtyard	Poisonous	—
Chaenomeles speciosa	Shrub	Cool Z 6-10	5 ft / 8 ft / 10 ft; 1.5 m / 2.5 m / 3 m	Decid	—	Flowers (red, pink, white, midwinter-early spring); edible/decorative fruit	Shrub border, courtyard, cut flowers, espalier	Branches sometimes thorny	Many cultivars, some double; fruit used for preserves
Chamaebatiaria millefolium	Shrub	Cool Z 5-9	2 ft / 4 ft / 5 ft; 0.6 m / 1.2 m / 1.5 m	Decid	—	Flowers (white, summer); foliage	Shrub border	—	—
Chamaecyparis (Cupressus) funebris	Tree	Warm Z 9-10	8 ft / 20 ft / 30 ft; 2.5 m / 6 m / 9 m	Everg	—	Foliage; weeping habit	Lawn specimen, parks, streets	—	This species regarded as a link between *Cupressus* and *Chamaecyparis*
Chamaecyparis lawsoniana	Tree	Cool Z 6-9	8 ft / 20 ft / 40 ft; 2.5 m / 6 m / 12 m	Everg	—	Foliage; symmetrical form	Lawn specimen, parks, group plantings, windbreak	—	Cvs include dwarf/columnar habit, gold/blue foliage, juvenile forms
Chamaecyparis nootkatensis	Tree	Cool Z 4-9	8 ft / 15 ft / 30 ft; 2.5 m / 5 m / 9 m	Everg	—	Foliage; symmetrical shape	Lawn specimen, parks, group plantings	—	—
Chamaecyparis obtusa	Tree	Cool Z 5-10	8 ft / 12 ft / 25 ft; 2 m / 4 m / 8 m	Everg	—	Foliage; symmetrical form	Lawn specimen, parks, courtyard, rock garden (dwarf cultivars), timber	—	Cvs include dwarf habit, gold foliage, juvenile forms
Chamaecyparis pisifera	Tree	Cool Z 5-10	6 ft / 12 ft / 25 ft; 2 m / 4 m / 8 m	Everg	—	Foliage; symmetrical form	Lawn specimen, parks, courtyard, rock garden (dwarf cvs)	—	Juvenile cultivars are known as 'retinosporas'
Chamaecyparis thyoides	Tree	Cool Z 4-9	8 ft / 15 ft / 30 ft; 2.5 m / 5 m / 9 m	Everg	—	Foliage	Lawn specimen, parks, windbreaks, timber	—	—
Chamaerops humilis	Palm	Warm Z 8-10	2 ft / 5 ft / 10 ft; 0.6 m / 1.5 m / 3 m	Everg	Yes	Foliage; flowers (yellow, fragrant, late spring)	Lawn specimen, courtyard, plaza, container, coastal planting	Sharp spines on leaf stalks	One of the most cold-hardy palms; male and female flowers on different plants

NAME	KIND	CLIMATE & ZONE	HEIGHT AT 5yrs	10yrs	20yrs	DECIDUOUS EVERGREEN	ARID CLIMATES	CHIEF ATTRACTIONS	USES	DRAWBACKS	COMMENTS
Chamelaucium uncinatum	Shrub	Warm Z 10-11	8 ft 2.5 m	10 ft 3 m	10 ft 3 m	Everg	Yes	Flowers (mauve-pink-white, late winter-spring); aromatic foliage	Cut flowers, shrub border, courtyard	Can be short-lived	Many named cultivars now available, varying in flower colour
Chilopsis linearis	Shrub	Warm Z 9-10	6 ft 2 m	10 ft 3 m	12 ft 4 m	Decid	Yes	Flowers (pink, late spring-summer)	Shrub border, courtyard, desert garden	Untidy habit	—
Chimonanthus praecox	Shrub	Cool Z 6-10	4 ft 1.2 m	6 ft 2 m	8 ft 2.5 m	Decid	—	Flowers (pale yellow, fragrant, late autumn-winter)	Shrub border, courtyard	—	Valued for very sweet perfume in winter
Chionanthus retusus	Tree	Cool Z 7-10	5 ft 1.5 m	10 ft 3 m	20 ft 6 m	Decid	—	Flowers (white, late spring-early summer)	Lawn specimen, parks	—	Outstanding floral display
Chionanthus virginicus	Tree	Cool Z 5-10	5 ft 1.5 m	10 ft 3 m	15 ft 5 m	Decid	—	Flowers (white, late spring)	Lawn specimen, parks	Reluctant to flower well in some climates	—
Choisya ternata	Shrub	Warm Z 9-10	4 ft 1.2 m	6 ft 2 m	6 ft 2 m	Everg	—	Flowers (white, fragrant, spring)	Shrub border, courtyard, hedge	—	Leaves aromatic when crushed
Chorisia insignis	Tree	Warm Z 10-11	10 ft 3 m	20 ft 6 m	30 ft 9 m	Decid*	Yes	Flowers (cream, autumn), interesting trunk form	Lawn specimen, parks, streets	Trunk has large prickles when young	—
Chorisia speciosa	Tree	Warm Z 10-11	10 ft 3 m	30 ft 9 m	40 ft 12 m	Decid*	Yes	Flowers (pink, autumn), interesting trunk form	Lawn specimen, parks, streets	Trunk has large prickles when young	Every seedling tree has different colour pattern in flowers
Chrysalidocarpus lutescens	Palm	Hot Z 10-12	5 ft 1.5 m	10 ft 3 m	20 ft 6 m	Everg	—	Foliage; elegant stems	Lawn specimen, courtyards, plazas, indoor	Leaves scorched by cold or dry winds	One of the most popular palms in tropical landscaping
Chrysanthemoides monilifera	Shrub	Warm Z 9-11	5 ft 1.5 m	8 ft 2.5 m	10 ft 3 m	Everg	—	Flowers (yellow, most of year)	Coastal planting (Africa only); containers	A pernicious weed in Australia & New Zealand	—
Chrysobalanus icaco	Tree	Hot Z 11-12	6 ft 2 m	12 ft 4 m	15 ft 5 m	Everg	—	Foliage; edible fruit	Coastal planting, lawn specimen, hedge	—	Fruit used for jams & preserves
Chrysolepis chrysophylla	Tree	Cool Z 7-9	6 ft 2 m	12 ft 4 m	25 ft 8 m	Everg	—	Foliage; edible nuts	Lawn specimen, parks, streets	—	Rare in cultivation
Cinchona officinalis	Tree	Hot Z 11-12	8 ft 2.5 m	12 ft 4 m	20 ft 6 m	Everg	—	Foliage; medicinal bark; flowers (yellow, fragrant)	Source of quinine	—	Requires a wet tropical climate
Cinnamomum camphora	Tree	Warm Z 10-11	8 ft 2.5 m	15 ft 5 m	30 ft 9 m	Everg	—	Foliage; flowers (cream, spring); pink new growths	Parks, avenues, timber	Becomes a weed in warm wet climates; greedy roots	Timber is a traditional source of camphor, & used to make storage chests
Cinnamomum zeylanicum	Tree	Hot Z 11-12	8 ft 2.5 m	15 ft 5 m	20 ft 6 m	Everg	—	Foliage; spice from bark	Spice plantation	—	Bark stripped from coppice stems, dried for cinnamon
Cistus albidus	Shrub	Cool Z 7-9	2 ft 0.6 m	4 ft 1.2 m	4 ft 1.2 m	Everg	Yes	Flowers (lilac pink, spring); aromatic foliage	Courtyard, coastal planting, rock garden	—	—
Cistus ladanifer	Shrub	Cool Z 8-10	4 ft 1.2 m	6 ft 2 m	6 ft 2 m	Everg	Yes	Flowers (white & chocolate, mid spring-early summer)	Shrub border, courtyard, coastal planting	Becomes leggy, not readily pruned	Aromatic resin ('ladanum') coats stems, leaves & buds
Cistus × lusitanicus	Shrub	Cool Z 8-10	2 ft 0.6 m	2 ft 0.6 m	2 ft 0.6 m	Everg	Yes	Flowers (white, spring-early summer)	Shrub border, courtyard, coastal planting	—	—
Cistus × purpureus	Shrub	Cool Z 8-10	2 ft 0.6 m	3 ft 1 m	3 ft 1 m	Everg	Yes	Flowers (rose pink, summer)	Shrub border, courtyard, coastal planting, rock garden	—	Several cultivars available
Cistus salviifolius	Shrub	Cool Z 8-10	2 ft 0.6 m	3 ft 1 m	3 ft 1 m	Everg	Yes	Flowers (white, late winter-early summer)	Shrub border, courtyard, coastal planting, rock garden	—	Can be pruned harder than other Cistus species
Citharexylum spinosum	Tree	Warm Z 10-11	8 ft 2.5 m	15 ft 5 m	30 ft 9 m	Everg	Yes	Flowers (cream, fragrant, late summer-winter); foliage	Shrub border, parks, streets, hedges	—	Foliage colours orange & bronze in winter & spring
Citrus aurantifolia	Tree	Warm Z 10-12	4 ft 1.2 m	8 ft 2.5 m	12 ft 4 m	Everg	Yes	Edible fruit; flowers (white, fragrant, spring-early summer)	Home orchard (lime), courtyard, containers	Susceptible to drought, pests & diseases	Selected cultivars always grown, sold as grafted plants
Citrus limon	Tree	Warm Z 9-11	6 ft 2 m	10 ft 3 m	12 ft 4 m	Everg	Yes	Edible fruit; flowers (white, fragrant, most of year)	Home orchard (lemon), courtyard, containers	Susceptible to drought, pests & diseases	Selected cultivars always grown, sold as grafted plants
Citrus paradisi	Tree	Warm Z 10-12	6 ft 2 m	10 ft 3 m	15 ft 5 m	Everg	—	Edible fruit	Home orchard (grapefruit), courtyard	—	Selected cultivars always grown, sold as grafted plants
Citrus sinensis	Tree	Warm Z 10-11	6 ft 2 m	10 ft 3 m	12 ft 4 m	Everg	Yes	Edible fruit; flowers (white, fragrant, spring-summer)	Orchard (orange), lawn specimen, courtyard	Susceptible to drought, pests & diseases	Selected cultivars always grown, sold as grafted plants
Cladrastis lutea	Tree	Cool Z 6-9	8 ft 2.5 m	15 ft 5 m	25 ft 8 m	Decid	—	Flowers (white, early summer)	Lawn specimen, parks, streets	—	Some trees flower only every second year
Clausena lansium	Tree	Hot Z 10-12	8 ft 2.5 m	12 ft 4 m	15 ft 5 m	Everg	—	Edible fruit; flowers (white, spring)	Orchard, lawn specimen, courtyard	—	—
Clerodendrum buchananii	Shrub	Hot Z 11-12	8 ft 2.5 m	10 ft 3 m	—	Everg	—	Flowers (scarlet, most of year)	Shrub border, courtyard	Short-lived	—
Clerodendrum paniculatum	Shrub	Hot Z 11-12	6 ft 2 m	8 ft 2.5 m	8 ft 2.5 m	Everg	—	Flowers (scarlet, most of year)	Shrub border, courtyard	Short-lived	Requires a very humid tropical climate
Clerodendrum trichotomum	Shrub	Cool Z 7-10	6 ft 2 m	12 ft 4 m	20 ft 6 m	Decid	—	Flowers (white to mauve, fragrant, late summer); decorative fruit	Shrub border, lawn specimen, courtyard	—	One of the most cold-hardy clerodendrums
Clerodendrum ugandense	Shrub	Warm Z 10-11	6 ft 2 m	8 ft 2.5 m	10 ft 3 m	Everg	—	Flowers (blue, summer-autumn)	Shrub border, courtyard	—	Unusual colour for a clerodendrum
Clerodendrum zambesiacum	Shrub	Warm Z 10-12	5 ft 1.5 m	6 ft 2 m	6 ft 2 m	Everg	—	Flowers (white, spring-autumn)	Shrub border, courtyard	—	Flowers have very long tube

Reference Table

NAME	KIND	CLIMATE & ZONE	HEIGHT AT 5 yrs	HEIGHT AT 10 yrs	HEIGHT AT 20 yrs	DECIDUOUS/EVERGREEN	ARID CLIMATES	CHIEF ATTRACTIONS	USES	DRAWBACKS	COMMENTS
Clethra alnifolia	Shrub	Cool Z 4-9	5 ft 1.5 m	8 ft 2.5 m	8 ft 2.5 m	Decid	—	Flowers (white, late summer-early autumn)	Shrub border, woodland garden	—	—
Clethra arborea	Tree	Warm Z 9-10	6 ft 2 m	12 ft 4 m	20 ft 6 m	Everg	—	Flowers (white, summer)	Lawn specimen, shrub border, woodland garden	—	—
Clethra barbinervis	Shrub	Cool Z 6-9	6 ft 2 m	10 ft 3 m	12 ft 4 m	Decid	—	Flowers (white, late summer-early autumn); foliage	Shrub border, woodland garden	—	—
Clianthus puniceus	Shrub	Warm Z 8-10	5 ft 1.5 m	6 ft 2 m	6 ft 2 m	Everg	—	Flowers (red, pink, white, spring-early summer)	Shrub border, courtyard, container, espalier	Often short-lived	—
Clusia rosea	Tree	Hot Z 11-12	10 ft 3 m	20 ft 6 m	30 ft 9 m	Everg	—	Flowers (pale pink, summer-early autumn); foliage	Lawn specimen, parks, streets, shade	Difficult to propagate	—
Coccoloba uvifera	Tree	Hot Z 11-12	6 ft 2 m	12 ft 4 m	20 ft 6 m	Everg	—	Foliage; bronze new growths; decorative fruit	Coastal plantings, swimming pools, tubs, screening	—	Tolerates salt spray, brackish groundwater
Cochlospermum fraseri	Tree	Hot Z 11-12	8 ft 2.5 m	15 ft 5 m	20 ft 6 m	Decid*	Yes	Flowers (yellow, late spring); decorative fruit	Lawn specimen, courtyard	Ungainly habit	Can be evergreen if watered in dry season
Cocos nucifera	Palm	Hot Z 12	6 ft 2 m	15 ft 5 m	30 ft 9 m	Everg	—	Edible nuts; foliage; graceful trunk	Lawn grouping, coastal planting, plantations	Heavy coconuts can fall from a height	One of the world's most important palms
Codiaeum variegatum	Shrub	Hot Z 11-12	6 ft 2 m	8 ft 2.5 m	8 ft 2.5 m	Everg	—	Coloured foliage	Shrub border, hedges, courtyards, plazas	—	—
Coffea arabica	Shrub	Hot Z 10-12	6 ft 2 m	12 ft 4 m	15 ft 5 m	Everg	—	Fruit (coffee berries); flowers (white, fragrant, spring); foliage	Shrub border, courtyard, indoor, plantation	—	Likes shade; coffee comes from the dried & roasted seeds ('beans')
Coleonema album	Shrub	Warm Z 9-10	2 ft 0.6 m	3 ft 1 m	4 ft 1.2 m	Everg	—	Flowers (white, spring)	Shrub border, courtyard, rock garden, cut flowers	—	—
Coleonema pulchellum	Shrub	Warm Z 9-10	3 ft 1 m	5 ft 1.5 m	5 ft 1.5 m	Everg	—	Flowers (pink, spring-summer)	Shrub border, courtyard, rock garden, cut flowers	Foliage has pungent, ant-like smell	Cultivars with gold foliage and darker pink flowers available
Colletia cruciata	Shrub	Warm Z 7-10	4 ft 1.2 m	8 ft 2.5 m	10 ft 3 m	Everg	Yes	Bizarre stems; flowers (white, fragrant, autumn)	Protective hedge, shrub border, courtyard	Vicious spines	—
Colvillea racemosa	Tree	Hot Z 11-12	10 ft 3 m	25 ft 8 m	40 ft 12 m	Everg	—	Flowers (orange, late spring-autumn)	Parks, avenues	—	—
Combretum erythrophyllum	Tree	Hot Z 9-11	8 ft 2.5 m	12 ft 4 m	20 ft 6 m	Decid	Yes	Decorative fruit	Lawn specimen, windbreak, parks	—	—
Convolvulus cneorum	Shrub	Cool Z 8-10	1 ft 0.3 m	2 ft 0.6 m	2 ft 0.6 m	Everg	Yes	Flowers (white, spring-summer); silvery foliage	Rock garden, courtyard, herbaceous border, container	—	Must have full sun, good drainage
Coprosma brunnea	Shrub	Cool Z 7-10	1 ft 0.3 m	2 ft 0.6 m	2 ft 0.6 m	Everg	—	Foliage, decorative fruit	Coastal planting, hedge	Can be short-lived	—
Coprosma repens	Shrub	Cool Z 9-11	3 ft 1 m	6 ft 2 m	8 ft 2.5 m	Everg	—	Foliage	Coastal planting, hedge, courtyard, container	—	Several variegated cultivars available
Cordia dichotoma	Tree	Hot Z 11-12	10 ft 3 m	15 ft 5 m	25 ft 8 m	Everg	Yes	Flowers (white, spring); decorative fruit	Lawn specimen, courtyard, plaza	—	—
Cordia sebestena	Tree	Hot Z 11-12	8 ft 2.5 m	12 ft 4 m	20 ft 6 m	Everg	Yes	Flowers (orange-red, most of year)	Lawn specimen, courtyard, plaza	—	Popular small tree in the tropics
Cordyline australis	Tree	Cool Z 7-10	4 ft 1.2 m	8 ft 2.5 m	15 ft 5 m	Everg	—	Foliage; flowers (white, fragrant, late spring-early summer)	Shrub border, courtyard, swimming pool, container, indoor	—	Several cultivars available with purple or variegated leaves
Cordyline banksii	Shrub	Warm Z 8-10	4 ft 1.2 m	8 ft 2.5 m	10 ft 3 m	Everg	—	Foliage; flowers (white, late spring-summer)	Shrub border, courtyard	—	—
Cordyline fruticosa (terminalis)	Shrub	Hot Z 10-12	6 ft 2 m	10 ft 3 m	12 ft 4 m	Everg	—	Foliage	Shrub border, courtyard, plaza, swimming pool, container, indoor	Foliage tattered by strong winds	Numerous coloured-leaved cultivars available, some dwarf
Cordyline indivisa	Tree	Cool Z 9	3 ft 1 m	6 ft 2 m	10 ft 3 m	Everg	—	Foliage; flowers (white, spring-early summer)	Shrub border, woodland garden, courtyard	Climatically sensitive	Handsome foliage but requires high humidity
Cordyline stricta	Shrub	Warm Z 10-11	3 ft 1 m	6 ft 2 m	6 ft 2 m	Everg	—	Foliage; flowers (pale purplish, late spring-early summer); decorative fruit	Shrub border, courtyard, container, rainforest garden	—	—
Cornus alba	Shrub	Cool Z 4-9	4 ft 1.2 m	6 ft 2 m	6 ft 2 m	Decid	—	Winter twigs; flowers (cream, late spring-summer)	Shrub border, edge of pond or lake, hedge	—	—
Cornus capitata	Tree	Warm Z 9-10	6 ft 2 m	12 ft 4 m	25 ft 8 m	Everg	—	Flowers (lemon-yellow, late spring-early summer); decorative fruit	Lawn specimen, parks	Fruit attacked by birds & litters ground	Attractive both in flower and fruit
Cornus controversa	Shrub	Cool Z 6-9	6 ft 2 m	12 ft 4 m	20 ft 6 m	Decid	—	Autumn foliage; flowers (white, early summer)	Lawn specimen, parks	—	—
Cornus florida	Tree	Cool Z 5-9	6 ft 2 m	12 ft 4 m	15 ft 5 m	Decid	—	Flowers (pink or white, spring), autumn foliage, decorative fruit	Lawn specimen, woodland garden	—	Needs hot summer and cold winter to grow & flower well
Cornus kousa	Tree	Cool Z 6-9	6 ft 2 m	12 ft 4 m	20 ft 6 m	Decid	—	Flowers (white, early summer); autumn foliage; decorative fruit	Lawn specimen, woodland garden	—	—
Cornus mas	Tree	Cool Z 6-9	6 ft 2 m	12 ft 4 m	20 ft 6 m	Decid	—	Flowers (yellow, late winter-early spring)	Lawn specimen, parks, streets	—	Small yellow flowers quite different from most other *Cornus* spp.
Cornus nuttallii	Tree	Cool Z 8-9	5 ft 1.5 m	10 ft 3 m	15 ft 5 m	Decid	—	Flowers (white, mid spring-early summer)	Lawn specimen, woodland garden	—	Largest-flowered but most tender & difficult of *Cornus* spp.

NAME	KIND	CLIMATE & ZONE	HEIGHT AT 5yrs 10yrs 20yrs			DECIDUOUS EVERGREEN	ARID CLIMATES	CHIEF ATTRACTIONS	USES	DRAWBACKS	COMMENTS
Cornus pumila	Shrub	Cool Z 5-9	2 ft 0.6 m	2 ft 0.6 m	2 ft 0.6 m	Decid	—	Autumn foliage; coloured twigs	Shrub border, courtyard, edge of pond or lake	—	—
Corokia buddleioides	Shrub	Cool Z 8-9	4 ft 1.2 m	8 ft 2.5 m	10 ft 3 m	Everg	—	Foliage; flowers (yellow, spring)	Coastal planting, hedge, shrub border, container	—	Can be kept compact by pruning
Corokia cotoneaster	Shrub	Cool Z 8-9	4 ft 1.2 m	6 ft 2 m	10 ft 3 m	Everg	—	Foliage; flowers (yellow, fragrant, summer)	Shrub border, courtyard, container	—	Intricate mass of tangled wiry branches
Correa alba	Shrub	Warm Z 9-11	3 ft 1 m	4 ft 1.2 m	5 ft 1.5 m	Everg	—	Flowers (white, winter–mid spring)	Coastal planting, rock garden, erosion control	—	Withstands strong winds
Correa lawrenciana	Shrub	Warm Z 9-10	6 ft 2 m	8 ft 2.5 m	10 ft 3 m	Everg	—	Flowers (yellow-green, late autumn-winter)	Shrub border, woodland garden	—	Likes shelter and humidity
Correa pulchella	Shrub	Warm Z 9-11	2 ft 0.6 m	3 ft 1 m	3 ft 1 m	Everg	—	Flowers (orange-pink, winter-spring)	Shrub border, courtyard, container	—	—
Corylopsis glabrescens	Shrub	Cool Z 7-9	6 ft 2 m	10 ft 3 m	15 ft 5 m	Decid	—	Flowers (lemon-yellow, mid spring)	Shrub border, lawn specimen, woodland garden	—	—
Corylopsis sinensis	Shrub	Cool Z 7-9	6 ft 2 m	10 ft 3 m	15 ft 5 m	Decid	—	Flowers (pale yellow, mid spring)	Shrub border, lawn specimen, woodland garden	—	One of the most ornamental members of this genus
Corylopsis spicata	Shrub	Cool Z 6-9	3 ft 1 m	4 ft 1.2 m	6 ft 2 m	Decid	—	Flowers (greenish yellow, early spring)	Shrub border, woodland garden, courtyard, cut flowers	—	—
Corylus avellana	Shrub	Cool Z 4-9	6 ft 2 m	12 ft 4 m	15 ft 5 m	Decid	—	Edible nuts; male flowers (yellow, late winter-early spring)	Orchard, lawn specimen, hedge, cut stems ('Contorta')	—	Usually coppiced for hazelnut production; 'Contorta' has bizarre twisted twigs
Corylus maxima	Tree	Cool Z 4-9	6 ft 2 m	15 ft 5 m	20 ft 6 m	Decid	—	Edible nuts; foliage	Orchard, lawn specimen, hedge	—	'Purpurea' with purplish spring foliage is more ornamental
Corypha umbraculifera	Palm	Hot Z 12	6 ft 2 m	12 ft 4 m	30 ft 9 m	Everg	Yes	Foliage; majestic stature; flowers (once only, white)	Parks	Flowers only once, then dies	Spectacular palm with huge fronds and flowering panicle
Cotinus coggygria	Shrub	Cool Z 6-10	5 ft 1.5 m	8 ft 2.5 m	10 ft 3 m	Decid	Yes	Foliage; flower-stalks (pinkish, early summer)	Lawn specimen, shrub border, hedge	Sap can irritate skin	Purple-leaved forms most popular in cultivation
Cotoneaster apiculatus	Shrub	Cool Z 6-10	2 ft 0.6 m	4 ft 1.2 m	6 ft 2 m	Decid	—	Flowers (pinkish, early summer); decorative fruit; autumn foliage	Shrub border, courtyard, hedge, espalier	Prone to fireblight (most cotoneasters)	—
Cotoneaster conspicuus	Shrub	Cool Z 6-10	3 ft 1 m	4 ft 1.2 m	4 ft 1.2 m	Everg	—	Decorative fruit	Shrub border, courtyard, espalier, rock garden, hedge	—	—
Cotoneaster dammeri	Shrub	Cool Z 5-10	1 ft 0.3 m	1 ft 0.3 m	2 ft 0.6 m	Everg	—	Foliage; decorative fruit	Rock garden, retaining wall, courtyard, groundcover	—	Mounds up with age
Cotoneaster franchetii	Shrub	Cool Z 6-10	6 ft 2 m	8 ft 2.5 m	10 ft 3 m	Everg	—	Decorative fruit	Shrub border, hedge, espalier	—	Berries last into winter, good display even in warm climates
Cotoneaster frigidus	Tree	Cool Z 6-9	8 ft 2.5 m	15 ft 5 m	20 ft 6 m	Decid	—	Autumn foliage decorative fruit	Lawn specimen, shrub border	—	Can be semi-evergreen in warmer climates
Cotoneaster glaucophyllus	Shrub	Cool Z 6-10	8 ft 2.5 m	10 ft 3 m	12 ft 4 m	Everg	—	Decorative fruit	Shrub border, hedge	Self-sown seedlings a nuisance	Some forms may be deciduous in cool climates
Cotoneaster horizontalis	Shrub	Cool Z 5-9	2 ft 0.6 m	3 ft 1 m	3 ft 1 m	Decid	—	Autumn/winter foliage; decorative fruit	Groundcover, courtyard, rock garden, espalier	—	Semi-evergreen in warmer climates
Cotoneaster 'Hybridus Pendulus'	Shrub	Cool Z 6-9	1 ft 0.3 m	3 ft 1 m	3 ft 1 m	Everg	—	Pendulous habit; decorative fruit	Retaining walls, groundcover, rock garden, courtyard	—	Makes a weeping shrub grafted as a standard
Cotoneaster lacteus	Shrub	Cool Z 7-10	6 ft 2 m	10 ft 3 m	12 ft 4 m	Everg	—	Decorative fruit	Shrub border, hedge	—	Good display of berries even in warm climates
Cotoneaster microphyllus	Shrub	Cool Z 5-10	1 ft 0.3 m	2 ft 0.6 m	3 ft 1 m	Everg	—	Foliage; decorative fruit	Embankments, rock gardens, courtyards, espalier	—	Prostrate and taller mounding forms are grown
Cotoneaster multiflorus	Shrub	Cool Z 5-9	6 ft 2 m	10 ft 3 m	12 ft 4 m	Decid	—	Flowers (white, late spring); decorative fruit	Shrub border, lawn specimen	—	—
Cotoneaster pannosus	Shrub	Cool Z 7-10	6 ft 2 m	10 ft 3 m	12 ft 4 m	Everg	—	Decorative fruit	Shrub border, hedge	Free-seeding, can become a weed	Adapts to warm climates as well as cool
Cotoneaster salicifolius	Shrub	Cool Z 6-9	4 ft 1.2 m	6 ft 2 m	8 ft 2.5 m	Everg	—	Autumn/winter foliage; decorative fruit	Shrub border, hedge, groundcover, embankments	—	Includes almost prostrate & taller shrubby forms
Couroupita guianensis	Tree	Hot Z 12	8 ft 2.5 m	15 ft 5 m	30 ft 9 m	Everg	—	Flowers (red & orange, fragrant, most of year); curious fruit	Lawn specimen, parks	—	Flowers & large spherical fruit borne on trunk
Crataegus arnoldiana	Tree	Cool Z 5-9	6 ft 2 m	10 ft 3 m	15 ft 5 m	Decid	—	Flowers (white, fragrant mid spring); decorative fruit	Lawn specimen, shrub border	Prone to fireblight (most Crataegus spp.)	—
Crataegus laciniata	Shrub	Cool Z 6-9	4 ft 1.2 m	8 ft 2.5 m	10 ft 3 m	Decid	Yes	Flowers (white, early summer); decorative fruit	Shrub border, cut stems with berries	—	—
Crataegus laevigata	Tree	Cool Z 5-9	8 ft 2.5 m	12 ft 4 m	20 ft 6 m	Decid	—	Flowers (white to red, late spring); decorative fruit	Lawn specimen, parks, streets	—	Double red & pink cultivars more popular as ornamentals
Crataegus × lavallei	Tree	Cool Z 6-10	6 ft 2 m	12 ft 4 m	15 ft 5 m	Decid	—	Flowers (white, early summer); decorative fruit	Lawn specimen, parks, streets, cut foliage with berries	—	Has larger flowers than most other hawthorns; often almost thornless

NAME	KIND	CLIMATE & ZONE	HEIGHT AT 5 yrs	10 yrs	20 yrs	DECIDUOUS/EVERGREEN	ARID CLIMATES	CHIEF ATTRACTIONS	USES	DRAWBACKS	COMMENTS
Crataegus monogyna	Tree	Cool Z 4-9	8 ft 2.5 m	15 ft 5 m	20 ft 6 m	Decid	—	Flowers (white, late spring-early summer); decorative fruit	Hedges, shrub border	Spreads by seeds and suckers, may become a weed	Has long sharp thorns
Crataegus phaenopyrum (cordata)	Tree	Cool Z 4-9	8 ft 2.5 m	12 ft 4 m	15 ft 5 m	Decid	—	Flowers (white, midsummer), decorative fruit	Lawn specimen, hedge, cut foliage with berries	Numerous fierce thorns	—
Crataegus pubescens	Tree	Cool Z 7-10	6 ft 2 m	12 ft 4 m	15 ft 5 m	Everg	Yes	Edible/decorative fruit; flowers (white, mid spring)	Lawn specimen, shrub border, cut foliage with berries	—	Often entirely thornless
Crateva religiosa	Tree	Hot Z 11-12	8 ft 2.5 m	15 ft 5 m	20 ft 6 m	Everg	—	Flowers (cream, winter-spring)	Lawn specimen, courtyard, conservatory	—	—
Crinodendron hookerianum	Shrub	Cool Z 8-9	4 ft 1.2 m	8 ft 2.5 m	12 ft 4 m	Everg	—	Flowers (crimson, winter-spring)	Lawn specimen, woodland garden	Climatically sensitive	Requires humid climate, sheltered position
Crinodendron patagua	Tree	Cool Z 8-9	6 ft 2 m	10 ft 3 m	15 ft 5 m	Everg	—	Flowers (white, late summer)	Lawn specimen, woodland garden	—	Easier to grow than *C. hookerianum*
Crotalaria agatiflora	Shrub	Warm Z 10-11	6 ft 2 m	6 ft 2 m	—	Everg	Yes	Flowers (yellow-green, summer-early winter)	Shrub border	Short-lived	Easily renewed from seed
Crotalaria capensis	Shrub	Warm Z 9-11	8 ft 2.5 m	10 ft 3 m	—	Everg	Yes	Flowers (yellow, summer)	Shrub border, courtyard	Short-lived	—
Crowea saligna	Shrub	Warm Z 9-10	2 ft 0.6 m	3 ft 1 m	3 ft 1 m	Everg	—	Flowers (pink, late summer-early winter)	Shrub border, rock garden, container	Prone to root rot	Needs perfect drainage
Cryptomeria japonica	Tree	Cool Z 6-10	10 ft 3 m	20 ft 6 m	40 ft 12 m	Everg	—	Foliage; winter colouring (cultivar 'Elegans')	Lawn specimen, screen, windbreak, timber, parks	'Elegans' prone to wind damage	Many cultivars include dwarf & juvenile leaf forms
Cunninghamia lanceolata	Tree	Cool Z 6-10	6 ft 2 m	15 ft 5 m	25 ft 8 m	Everg	—	Foliage	Lawn specimen, timber, parks	Prickly dead branches persist on tree and litter ground	Growth unpredictable in cultivation
Cunonia capensis	Shrub	Warm Z 9-10	6 ft 2 m	10 ft 3 m	15 ft 5 m	Everg	—	Foliage; flowers (white, autumn)	Shrub border, courtyard, woodland garden	—	—
Cupaniopsis anacardioides	Tree	Warm Z 10-12	8 ft 2.5 m	15 ft 5 m	30 ft 9 m	Everg	Yes	Foliage; decorative fruit	Parks, streets, plazas, coastal planting, rainforest garden	—	Hardy tree for city streets and plazas
Cuphea ignea	Shrub	Warm Z 10-11	1 ft 0.3 m	2 ft 0.6 m	2 ft 0.6 m	Everg	Yes	Flowers (orange, summer-autumn)	Courtyard, container, rock garden	—	Often grown in pots as an annual
Cuphea micropetala	Shrub	Warm Z 10-11	2 ft 0.6 m	3 ft 1 m	3 ft 1 m	Everg	Yes	Flowers (orange-yellow, summer-early winter)	Courtyard, container, shrub border	—	—
× Cupressocyparis leylandii	Tree	Cool Z 5-10	12 ft 4 m	30 ft 9 m	50 ft 15 m	Everg	—	Foliage; vigorous growth	Windbreak, hedge	—	Very fast-growing; several clones available, varying in foliage hue
Cupressus cashmeriana	Tree	Warm Z 9-11	8 ft 2.5 m	15 ft 5 m	30 ft 9 m	Everg	—	Foliage; weeping habit	Lawn specimen, woodland garden	Easily wind-damaged	Needs warm moist climate to succeeed
Cupressus duclouxiana	Tree	Warm Z 9-10	10 ft 3 m	20 ft 6 m	30 ft 9 m	Everg	—	Foliage; columnar shape	Lawn specimen, screen, courtyard	—	—
Cupressus glabra	Tree	Warm Z 7-10	10 ft 3 m	20 ft 6 m	30 ft 9 m	Everg	Yes	Foliage; conical shape	Lawn specimen, screen, windbreak, parks	—	Foliage colour varies, some trees quite blue-grey
Cupressus lusitanica	Tree	Warm Z 8-10	10 ft 3 m	20 ft 6 m	40 ft 12 m	Everg	Yes	Foliage; vigorous growth	Lawn specimen, screen, windbreak	—	—
Cupressus macrocarpa	Tree	Warm Z 7-10	12 ft 4 m	30 ft 9 m	50 ft 15 m	Everg	—	Foliage vigorous growth	Parks, windbreak, shade, hedges, timber, coastal planting	Dead foliage held in tree (fire hazard)	Golden cultivars grown for ornament
Cupressus sempervirens	Tree	Warm Z 8-10	8 ft 2.5 m	15 ft 5 m	30 ft 9 m	Everg	Yes	Foliage; columnar shape	Courtyard, screens, parks, hedge, topiary, coastal planting	Dead foliage held in tree (fire hazard)	Columnar form ('Stricta') traditionally associated with cemeteries
Cupressus torulosa	Tree	Warm Z 8-10	10 ft 3 m	20 ft 6 m	40 ft 12 m	Everg	—	Foliage; conical shape	Lawn specimen, screen, hedges, timber, windbreak	Greedy roots	—
Cussonia paniculata	Tree	Warm Z 9-11	4 ft 1.2 m	8 ft 2.5 m	12 ft 4 m	Everg	—	Foliage; flowers (greenish-yellow, summer)	Lawn specimen, courtyard, container	—	Leaves have complex pattern of lobing
Cussonia spicata	Tree	Warm Z 9-11	5 ft 1.5 m	10 ft 3 m	20 ft 6 m	Everg	—	Foliage; flowers (greenish-white, spring-summer)	Lawn specimen, courtyard, container, indoor	—	Juvenile state used as an indoor foliage plant
Cyathea cooperi	Tree fern	Warm Z 10-11	5 ft 1.5 m	10 ft 3 m	20 ft 6 m	Everg	—	Foliage; symmetrical form	Shrub border, woodland garden, courtyard, conservatory	Large dead fronds to be disposed of	Needs humid, sheltered postion, tolerates shade
Cyathea dealbata	Tree fern	Warm Z 9-10	4 ft 1.2 m	6 ft 2 m	12 ft 4 m	Everg	—	Foliage; symmetrical form	Shrub border, woodland garden, courtyard	—	Needs humid, sheltered postion, tolerates shade
Cycas armstrongii	Cycad	Hot Z 12	3 ft 1 m	4 ft 1.2 m	6 ft 2 m	Decid*	—	Foliage; symmetrical shape; decorative seeds	Courtyard, lawn grouping, rock garden	—	Fronds die and hang from trunk in tropical dry season
Cycas circinalis	Cycad	Hot Z 10-12	3 ft 1 m	5 ft 1.5 m	8 ft 2.5 m	Everg	—	Foliage	Courtyard, lawn specimen	—	The most densely foliaged *Cycas* species
Cycas revoluta	Cycad	Warm Z 9-11	22 ft 0.6 m	3 ft 1 m	5 ft 1.5 m	Everg	—	Foliage; symmetrical shape	Courtyard, plaza, container, bonsai	Very slow-growing	The most widely grown cycad; easily transplanted
Cydonia oblonga	Tree	Cool Z 6-9	5 ft 1.5 m	8 ft 2.5 m	12 ft 4 m	Decid	Yes	Edible fruit; flowers (pale pink, late spring)	Home orchard, lawn specimen, jams & preserves	Prone to fireblight	Worth growing for beauty of flowers as well as for fruit
Cydonia (Pseudocydonia) sinensis	Tree	Warm Z 9-10	6 ft 2 m	12 ft 4 m	20 ft 6 m	Decid	—	Edible/decorative fruit; flowers (pink, late spring); bark; autumn foliage	Lawn specimen, home orchard	—	Tolerates warmer climate than *C. oblonga*

NAME	KIND	CLIMATE & ZONE	HEIGHT AT 5yrs 10yrs 20yrs	DECIDUOUS EVERGREEN	ARID CLIMATES	CHIEF ATTRACTIONS	USES	DRAWBACKS	COMMENTS
Cyrilla racemiflora	Shrub	Cool Z 6-9	4 ft 6 ft 8 ft / 1.2 m 2 m 2.5 m	Decid	—	Flowers (white, fragrant, summer)	Shrub border, woodland garden, edge of pond	—	Some forms of the species are evergreen
Cytisus 'Burkwoodii'	Shrub	Cool Z 5-9	3 ft 5 ft 5 ft / 1 m 1.5 m 1.5 m	Everg	—	Flowers (red & yellow, late spring-early summer)	Shrub border, courtyard	Usually short-lived	Grows best in full sun, with perfect drainage
Cytisus × praecox	Shrub	Cool Z 5-9	3 ft 3 ft 4 ft / 1 m 1 m 1.2 m	Everg	—	Flowers (yellow, white, fragrant, mid to late spring)	Shrub border, courtyard, rock garden	Usually short-lived	Several cultivars grown, varying in colour & height
Cytisus scoparius	Shrub	Cool Z 5-9	5 ft 8 ft 8 ft / 1.5 m 2.5 m 2.5 m	Everg	—	Flowers (yellow, late spring early summer)	Shrub border, courtyard, screen	A bad weed in some countries	—
Daboecia azorica	Shrub	Cool Z 8-9	1 ft 1 ft 1 ft / 0.3 m 0.3 m 0.3 m	Everg	—	Flowers (red, summer-autumn)	Rock garden, courtyard, groundcover, heather garden	—	Less common than sits hybrid D. × scotica
Daboecia cantabrica	Shrub	Cool Z 7-9	1 ft 2 ft 2 ft / 0.3 m 0.6 m 0.6 m	Everg	—	Flowers (pink, purple or white, summer-autumn)	Rock garden, shrub border, heather garden, coastal planting	—	Cultivars vary mainly in flower colour
Dacrydium cupressinum	Tree	Cool Z 8-9	5 ft 10 ft 20 ft / 1.5 m 3 m 6 m	Everg	—	Foliage; weeping habit	Shrub border, woodland garden, lawn specimen	Climatically sensitive	Requires sheltered, humid position
Dais cotinifolia	Shrub	Warm Z 9-10	8 ft 10 ft 12 ft / 2.5 m 3 m 4 m	Decid*	—	Flowers (pink, late spring-early summer)	Shrub border, courtyard, lawn specimen	—	Can be pruned after flowering for more compact shrub
Dalbergia sissoo	Tree	Warm Z 10-11	10 ft 20 ft 30 ft / 3 m 6 m 9 m	Decid*	Yes	Flowers (white)	Timber (rosewood), shelter, shade	—	Used as shade tree for tea plantations
Daphne × burkwoodii	Shrub	Cool Z 6-9	2 ft 3 ft 3 ft / 0.6 m 1 m 1 m	Everg	—	Flowers (pink, spring)	Rock garden, woodland garden, shrub border	—	—
Daphne cneorum	Shrub	Cool Z 6-9	1 ft 1 ft 1 ft / 0.3 m 0.3 m 0.3 m	Everg	—	Flowers (rose-pink, spring)	Rock garden, embankment	—	—
Daphne genkwa	Shrub	Cool Z 6-9	1 ft 2 ft 3 ft / 0.3 m 0.6 m 1 m	Decid	—	Flowers (lilac, spring)	Rock garden, shrub border, courtyard	—	—
Daphne mezereum	Shrub	Cool Z 5-9	2 ft 4 ft 5 ft / 0.6 m 1.2 m 1.5 m	Decid	—	Flowers (pink, fragrant, late winter-early spring); decorative fruit	Woodland garden, shrub border	Fruit poisonous	—
Daphne odora	Shrub	Cool Z 8-10	1 ft 2 ft 3 ft / 0.3 m 0.6 m 1 m	Everg	—	Flowers (purple & white, fragrant, late autumn-spring)	Rock garden, courtyard, cut flowers	Prone to virus disease and root rot	Resents root disturbance; variegated form hardier
Darlingia darlingiana	Tree	Warm Z 10-11	6 ft 12 ft 25 ft / 2 m 4 m 8 m	Everg	—	Flowers (white, spring)	Lawn specimen, parks	—	Leaves of saplings larger, more lobed
Darwinia oxylepis	Shrub	Warm Z 10	2 ft 2 ft 2 ft / 0.6 m 0.6 m 0.6 m	Everg	—	Flowers (scarlet, spring)	Rock garden, woodland garden	—	Difficult to cultivate successfully
Davidia involucrata	Tree	Cool Z 8-9	8 ft 15 ft 25 ft / 2.5 m 5 m 8 m	Decid	—	Flowers (white, late spring)	Lawn specimen, parks	—	Seldom flowers until 10-15 years old
Delonix regia	Tree	Hot Z 11-12	10 ft 20 ft 25 ft / 3 m 6 m 8 m	Decid*	Yes	Flowers (scarlet, late spring-early summer)	Parks, streets, lawn specimen	Greedy root system	Spectacular flowering tree, colour varies; large brown pods persist
Desfontainea spinosa	Shrub	Cool Z 8-9	2 ft 4 ft 6 ft / 0.6 m 1.2 m 2 m	Everg	—	Flowers (orange, late summer)	Shrub border, courtyard, hedge	—	Holly-like leaves, striking tubular flowers
Deutzia × elegantissima	Shrub	Cool Z 7-9	4 ft 5 ft 6 ft / 1.2 m 1.5 m 2 m	Decid	—	Flowers (pink, late spring-early summer)	Shrub border, woodland garden	—	Best pruned immediately after flowering (all deutzias)
Deutzia gracilis	Shrub	Cool Z 6-10	2 ft 3 ft 3 ft / 0.6 m 1 m 1 m	Decid	—	Flowers (white, late spring-early summer)	Shrub border, woodland garden, rock garden	—	A dwarf form is frequently grown
Deutzia × kalmiiflora	Shrub	Cool Z 7-9	4 ft 6 ft 6 ft / 1.2 m 2 m 2 m	Decid	—	Flowers (pink, early-midsummer)	Shrub border, woodland garden	—	—
Deutzia × rosea	Shrub	Cool Z 7-9	2 ft 3 ft 3 ft / 0.6 m 1 m 1 m	Decid	—	Flowers (pink, late spring-early summer)	Shrub border, woodland garden	—	Several clones available, varying in depth of colour
Deutzia scabra	Shrub	Cool Z 6-10	4 ft 8 ft 10 ft / 1.2 m 2.5 m 3 m	Decid	—	Flowers (white, mid spring-early summer)	Shrub border	—	The tallest, most vigorous deutzia
Dicksonia antarctica	Tree fern	Cool Z 8-10	2ft 4ft 6ft / 0.6m 1.2m 2m	Everg	—	Foliage; graceful form	Courtyard, conservatory, woodland garden	Very slow height growth	Needs sheltered position, high humidity
Dicksonia fibrosa	Tree fern	Cool Z 8-9	2ft 4ft 6ft / 0.6m 1.2m 2m	Everg	—	Foliage, thick black trunk	Courtyard, conservatory, woodland garden	Very slow height growth	Needs sheltered position, high humidity
Dillenia alata	Tree	Hot Z 12	5 ft 12 ft 20 ft / 1.5 m 4 m 6 m	Everg	—	Flowers (yellow, spring-summer); bark; decorative fruit	Lawn specimen, parks, coastal planting	—	Cut fruiting branches used indoors
Dillenia indica	Tree	Hot Z 12	8 ft 15 ft 25 ft / 2.5 m 5 m 8 m	Everg	—	Flowers (white & yellow, fragrant, spring); edible fruit; foliage	Lawn specimen, parks, jams, preserves & curries	—	Large, strongly veined leaves are a striking feature
Dioon edule	Cycad	Warm Z 10-11	2 ft 3 ft 6 ft / 0.6 m 1 m 2 m	Everg	—	Foliage; large cones	Courtyard, conservatory, swimming pool	Slow-growing, difficult to transplant	—
Diospyros digyna	Tree	Hot Z 11-12	8 ft 20 ft 30 ft / 2.5 m 6 m 9 m	Everg	—	Edible fruit	Orchard, shade	Brittle branches	Fruit high in vitamin C; selected clones preferred for fruit
Diospyros kaki	Tree	Warm Z 8-10	6 ft 10 ft 15 ft / 2 m 3 m 5 m	Decid	—	Edible fruit; autumn foliage	Orchard, lawn specimen	—	Good autumn colour even in warm climates, as well as fruit
Diospyros virginiana	Tree	Cool Z 5-9	6 ft 15 ft 25 ft / 2 m 5 m 8 m	Decid	—	Autumn foliage; edible fruit	Timber, lawn specimen	—	Timber highly valued for golf 'woods'
Dipelta floribunda	Shrub	Cool Z 6-9	4 ft 8 ft 10 ft / 1.2 m 2.5 m 3 m	Decid	—	Flowers (pink, fragrant, late spring-early summer)	Shrub border, lawn specimen	—	Winged fruit is distinctive
Disanthus cercidifolius	Shrub	Cool Z 7-9	3 ft 6 ft 8 ft / 1 m 2 m 2.5 m	Decid	—	Autumn foliage; flowers (purple-red, autumn)	Woodland garden, shrub border	—	Requires shelter, moist soil

NAME	KIND	CLIMATE & ZONE	HEIGHT AT 5 yrs	10 yrs	20 yrs	DECIDUOUS EVERGREEN	ARID CLIMATES	CHIEF ATTRACTIONS	USES	DRAWBACKS	COMMENTS
Dodonaea boroniifolia	Shrub	Warm Z 9-11	3 ft 1 m	5 ft 1.5 m	—	Everg	—	Foliage; decorative fruit	Shrub border	—	Male and female flowers on separate plants (all dodonaeas)
Dodonaea viscosa	Tree	Warm Z 8-11	8 ft 2.5 m	10 ft 3 m	12 ft 4 m	Everg	Yes	Foliage; decorative fruit	Shrub border, informal hedge, coastal planting	—	The bronze-foliaged 'Purpurea' is more widely planted
Dolichandrone heterophylla	Tree	Hot Z 11-12	6 ft 2 m	10 ft 3 m	15 ft 5 m	Everg	Yes	Flowers (white, night-scented, winter-spring)	Lawn specimen	—	Rarely cultivated
Dombeya burgessiae	Shrub	Warm Z 9-11	6 ft 2 m	10 ft 3 m	15 ft 5 m	Everg	Yes	Flowers (pink, midsummer-mid autumn)	Informal hedge, shrub border, dried flowers	—	Fast early growth
Dombeya × cayeuxii	Shrub	Warm Z 10-11	6 ft 2 m	10 ft 3 m	15 ft 5 m	Everg	—	Flowers (pink, summer-autumn)	Informal hedge, shrub border, conservatory	—	—
Dombeya rotundifolia	Tree	Warm Z 10-11	6 ft 2 m	15 ft 5 m	20 ft 6 m	Decid	Yes	Flowers (white or pink, spring)	Shrub border, lawn specimen, dried flowers	—	One of the most spectacularly flowering Dombeya species
Dombeya tiliacea	Tree	Warm Z 9-11	8 ft 2.5 m	15 ft 5 m	20 ft 6 m	Everg	—	Flowers (white, autumn-early spring)	Lawn specimen, parks, cut flowers (bridal posies)	—	—
Doryanthes excelsa	Shrub	Warm Z 9-11	2 ft 0.6 m	5 ft 1.5 m	6 ft 2 m	Everg	—	Flowers (red, late winter-spring)	Shrub border, courtyards, plazas, cut flowers	May take 10 years to bloom	Flowering stem can be over 15 ft (5 m) tall
Dovyalis caffra	Shrub	Warm Z 9-11	6 ft 2 m	12 ft 4 m	12 ft 4 m	Everg	Yes	Edible fruit	Protective hedge (spiny); preserves and pickles	Viciously spiny	Trees are of different sexes
Dovyalis hebecarpa	Tree	Warm	6 ft 2 m	12 ft 4 m	20 ft 6 m	Everg	Yes	Edible fruit	Protective hedge (spiny)	—	Trees are of different sexes
Dracaena draco	Tree	Warm Z 10-11	2 ft 0.6 m	5 ft 1.5 m	8 ft 2.5 m	Everg	Yes	Foliage; symmetrical form	Courtyard, plaza, swimming pool, conservatory, container	Height growth extremely slow	Trunk exudes a red resin ('dragon's blood') once used medicinally and in varnishes
Dracaena marginata	Tree	Warm Z 10-12	4 ft 1.2 m	8 ft 2.5 m	10 ft 3 m	Everg	Yes	Foliage	Courtyard, plaza, swimming pool, indoor, container	—	Variegated cultivars have become popular
Drimys winteri	Shrub	Cool Z 8-9	3 ft 1 m	6 ft 2 m	8 ft 2.5 m	Everg	—	Flowers (white, spring)	Shrub border, courtyard, woodland garden	—	Bark has peppery taste
Duranta erecta	Shrub	Warm Z 10-12	8 ft 2.5 m	12 ft 4 m	15 ft 5 m	Everg	Yes	Flowers (blue, late spring-autumn); decorative fruit	Shrub border, informal hedge, courtyard	Vigorous growths have long spines	Extremely tough plant; often displays flowers & berries together
Durio zibethinus	Tree	Hot Z 11-12	12 ft 4 m	20 ft 6 m	30 ft 9 m	Everg	—	Edible fruit	Orchard, shade	Large fruit may fall from high up	The famous durian of SE Asia, fruit flesh smells offensive but is prized by connoisseurs
Duvernoia adhatodoides	Shrub	Warm Z 10-11	6 ft 2 m	10 ft 3 m	10 ft 3 m	Everg	Yes	Flowers (white & purple, summer-autumn)	Shrub border, informal hedge, courtyard	May be short-lived	Fast growing shrub for warm climates
Echium fastuosum	Shrub	Warm Z 9-10	3 ft 1 m	4 ft 1.2 m	6 ft 2 m	Everg	Yes	Flowers (violet-blue, late spring-summer)	Rock garden, courtyard, herbaceous border	Usually short-lived	Flower spikes rise well above foliage
Edgeworthia chrysantha	Shrub	Cool Z 7-9	2 ft 0.6 m	4 ft 1.2 m	6 ft 2 m	Decid	—	Flowers (yellow & silver, spring)	Shrub border, courtyard	Leaves wilt in hot summer weather	A fine paper is made from the inner bark in Japan
Ekebergia capensis	Tree	Warm Z 9-11	8 ft 2.5 m	15 ft 5 m	30 ft 9 m	Everg	—	Decorative fruit; flowers (white, fragrant)	Parks, streets, shade, shelter	—	May be semi-deciduous in dry or cool climates
Elaeagnus angustifolia	Tree	Cool Z 7-9	8 ft 2.5 m	12 ft 4 m	20 ft 6 m	Decid	Yes	Flowers (yellow, fragrant, late spring-early summer); edible fruit	Shrub border, lawn specimen	—	Does best in winter-rainfall climates
Elaeagnus pungens	Shrub	Warm Z 7-10	3 ft 1 m	5 ft 1.5 m	8 ft 2.5 m	Everg	—	Foliage; flowers (white, fragrant, autumn)	Shrub border, informal hedge	Long scrambling canes	Grown primarily for its foliage, variegated cvs popular
Elaeagnus umbellata	Shrub	Cool Z 7-9	6 ft 2 m	10 ft 3 m	12 ft 4 m	Decid	—	Flowers (cream, fragrant, spring-summer); decorative fruit, autumn foliage	Shrub border, lawn specimen	—	—
Elaeis guineensis	Palm	Hot Z 11-12	6 ft 2 m	12 ft 4 m	20 ft 6 m	Everg	—	Foliage; decorative/useful fruit	Palm oil, parks, avenues	Fallen fruit may litter ground	The economically important oil palm
Elaeocarpus reticulatus	Tree	Warm Z 9-11	8 ft 2.5 m	15 ft 5 m	25 ft 8 m	Everg	—	Flowers (white or pink, spring-summer); decorative fruit	Lawn specimen, courtyard, container	—	Small berries (drupes) are a deep blue, eaten by birds
Embothrium coccineum	Tree	Cool Z 8-9	6 ft 2 m	12 ft 4 m	20 ft 6 m	Everg	—	Flowers (scarlet, late spring-early summer)	Lawn specimen, shrub border	Branches very weak if too sheltered	Flowers well only after 10 years; can be a temperamental subject
Encephalartos altensteinii	Shrub	Warm Z 9-11	3 ft 1 m	4 ft 1.2 m	6 ft 2 m	Everg	Yes	Foliage; large cones	Lawn specimen, courtyard, plaza	Very slow-growing	Rare, large plants very valuable
Encephalartos friderici-guilielmi	Shrub	Warm Z 9-11	2 ft 0.6 m	3 ft 1 m	5 ft 1.5 m	Everg	Yes	Foliage; large cones	Lawn specimen, courtyard, plaza	Very slow-growing	Rare, large plants very valuable
Enkianthus campanulatus	Shrub	Cool Z 6-9	4 ft 1.2 m	8 ft 2.5 m	10 ft 3 m	Decid	—	Flowers (cream & red, spring); autumn foliage	Shrub border, woodland garden	—	—
Enkianthus perulatus	Shrub	Cool Z 6-9	3 ft 1 m	4 ft 1.2 m	6 ft 2 m	Decid	—	Flowers (white, early spring), autumn foliage	Shrub border, woodland garden	—	—
Epacris impressa	Shrub	Warm Z 9-10	2 ft 0.6 m	2 ft 0.6 m	—	Everg	—	Flowers (white, pink or red, late winter-spring)	Rock garden, courtyard	Short-lived, prone to root rot	Needs damp, acid soil, good drainage
Epacris longiflora	Shrub	Warm Z 9-10	2 ft 0.6 m	3 ft 1 m	4 ft 1.2 m	Everg	—	Flowers (red & white, spring-summer)	Rock garden, courtyard, container	—	Needs damp, acid soil, good drainage

NAME	KIND	CLIMATE & ZONE	HEIGHT AT 5 yrs	HEIGHT AT 10 yrs	HEIGHT AT 20 yrs	DECIDUOUS/EVERGREEN	ARID CLIMATES	CHIEF ATTRACTIONS	USES	DRAWBACKS	COMMENTS
Ephedra distachya	Shrub	Cool Z 4-9	1 ft 0.3 m	2 ft 0.6 m	2 ft 0.6 m	Everg	Yes	Foliage	Rock garden, groundcover, embankment	—	Original source of the drug ephedrine; plants very tough
Ephedra viridis	Shrub	Cool Z 5-9	1 ft 0.3 m	2 ft 0.6 m	3 ft 1 m	Everg	Yes	Foliage	Rock garden, embankment	—	—
Eremophila maculata	Shrub	Warm Z 9-11	3 ft 1 m	5 ft 1.5 m	6 ft 2 m	Everg	Yes	Flowers (orange, red, pink, white)	Shrub border, courtyard, embankment	—	Flower colour varies with different wild sources
Eremophila mitchellii	Tree	Warm Z 9-11	6 ft 2 m	10 ft 3 m	20 ft 6 m	Everg	Yes	Flowers (white, spring)	Lawn specimen, timber, shade	—	Wood very aromatic, has been substituted for sandalwood
Eremophila polyclada	Shrub	Warm Z 9-11	3 ft 1 m	5 ft 1.5 m	6 ft 2 m	Everg	Yes	Flowers (white, most of year)	Shrub border, courtyard	—	Plants almost leafless, a tangle of green branches
Erica arborea	Shrub	Cool Z 8-10	3 ft 1 m	6 ft 2 m	8 ft 2.5 m	Everg	—	Flowers (white, spring)	Shrub border, screen, hedge	—	The largest erica, not highly ornamental; roots used for briar pipes
Erica bauera	Shrub	Cool Z 8-9	2 ft 0.6 m	3 ft 1 m	3 ft 1 m	Everg	—	Flowers (white or pink, spring-autumn)	Rock garden, courtyard, cut flowers	—	A South African erica; these are all less frost-hardy than the European spp. & hybrids
Erica canaliculata	Shrub	Cool Z 8-10	3 ft 1 m	6 ft 2 m	6 ft 2 m	Everg	—	Flowers (pink to purple, autumn-winter or winter-spring)	Shrub border, courtyard, cut flowers	—	South African sp.
Erica cerinthoides	Shrub	Cool Z 8-10	2 ft 0.6 m	2 ft 0.6 m	3 ft 1 m	Everg	—	Flowers (orange, scarlet, pink, winter-spring)	Rock garden, courtyard, container, cut flowers	Prone to root rot	South African sp.; has largest, most brilliantly coloured flowers of the ericas
Erica cinerea	Shrub	Cool Z 5-9	1 ft 0.3 m	1 ft 0.3 m	1 ft 0.3 m	Everg	—	Flowers (pink, summer-early autumn)	Rock garden, courtyard, groundcover	—	European sp.; dislikes strong sun; many cultivars available
Erica × darleyensis	Shrub	Cool Z 6-9	2 ft 0.6 m	2 ft 0.6 m	2 ft 0.6 m	Everg	—	Flowers (pink, late autumn-spring)	Rock garden, groundcover, embankment	—	European sp.
Erica erigena (mediterranea)	Shrub	Cool Z 7-9	2 ft 0.6 m	2 ft 0.6 m	2 ft 0.6 m	Everg	—	Flowers (pink, winter-spring)	Rock garden, groundcover, embankment	—	European sp.
Erica grandiflora	Shrub	Warm Z 9-10	2 ft 0.6 m	3 ft 1 m	3 ft 1 m	Everg	—	Flowers (orange, winter-spring)	Rock garden, courtyard, cut flowers	—	South African sp.
Erica herbacea (carnea)	Shrub	Cool Z 5-9	1 ft 0.3 m	1 ft 0.3 m	1 ft 0.3 m	Everg	—	Flowers (pink, winter-early spring)	Groundcover, rock garden, shrub border, embankment	—	European sp.
Erica lusitanica	Shrub	Warm Z 9-10	3 ft 1 m	5 ft 1.5 m	6 ft 2 m	Everg	—	Flowers (pink & white, winter-spring)	Shrub border, boggy areas, cut flowers	Naturalizes freely in mild, wet climates	European sp., but one of the least frost-hardy of these
Erica mammosa	Shrub	Warm Z 9-10	2 ft 0.6 m	3 ft 1 m	3 ft 1 m	Everg	—	Flowers (red, spring)	Rock garden, courtyard, cut flowers	—	South African sp.
Erica melanthera	Shrub	Warm Z 8-10	2 ft 0.6 m	3 ft 1 m	3 ft 1 m	Everg	—	Flowers (purple-pink, late autumn-winter)	Cut flowers, rock garden, courtyard, container	—	South African sp.
Erica regia	Shrub	Warm Z 9-10	2 ft 0.6 m	2 ft 0.6 m	2 ft 0.6 m	Everg	—	Flowers (white & red, spring)	Rock garden, courtyard, container, cut flowers	—	South African sp.
Erica tetralix	Shrub	Cool Z 3-9	1 ft 0.3 m	1 ft 0.3 m	1 ft 0.3 m	Everg	—	Flowers (pink or white, summer-autumn)	Rock garden, courtyard	—	European sp.; many cultivars available
Erica vagans	Shrub	Cool Z 5-9	1 ft 0.3 m	2 ft 0.6 m	2 ft 0.6 m	Everg	—	Flowers (pink or white, summer-autumn)	Rock garden, embankment, groundcover	—	European sp.; many cultivars available
Erica × wilmorei	Shrub	Warm Z 9-10	2 ft 0.6 m	3 ft 1 m	3 ft 1 m	Everg	—	Flowers (pink & white, winter-spring)	Shrub border, cut flowers	—	Hybrids of South African spp.
Eriobotrya japonica	Tree	Warm Z 9-10	6 ft 2 m	12 ft 4 m	20 ft 6 m	Everg	—	Edible fruit; flowers (white, late autumn)	Home orchard, lawn specimen	Susceptible to fruit fly	Selected clones have larger, juicier fruit
Eriostemon australasius	Shrub	Warm Z 8-10	2 ft 0.6 m	4 ft 1.2 m	4 ft 1.2 m	Everg	—	Flowers (pink, spring)	Shrub border, cut flowers	Prone to root rot, difficult to propagate	Needs perfect drainage, poor gritty soil
Eriostemon myoporoides	Shrub	Warm Z 8-10	2 ft 0.6 m	4 ft 1.2 m	6 ft 2 m	Everg	—	Flowers (pink & white, spring)	Shrub border, courtyard	—	The most easily grown eriostemon; several forms available
Erythrina acanthocarpa	Shrub	Warm Z 9-11	2 ft 0.6 m	4 ft 1.2 m	6 ft 2 m	Decid	Yes	Flowers (scarlet & green, late spring-early summer)	Shrub border, courtyard	Slow growing, very prickly	Strikingly beautiful flowers from a gaunt, unattractive shrub
Erythrina × bidwillii	Shrub	Warm Z 9-11	3 ft 1 m	5 ft 1.5 m	8 ft 2.5 m	Decid	—	Flowers (dark red, late spring-mid-autumn)	Shrub border, lawn specimen, courtyard	—	Grown as a herbaceous plant in cooler climates but can make thick trunk with age
Erythrina caffra	Tree	Warm Z 9-11	8 ft 2.5 m	15 ft 5 m	30 ft 9 m	Decid	Yes	Flowers (scarlet, late spring-early summer)	Lawn specimen, parks, shade	—	Attracts nectar-feeding birds; cv. 'Flavescens' has cream flowers
Erythrina crista-galli	Tree	Warm Z 9-11	6 ft 2 m	10 ft 3 m	15 ft 5 m	Decid	Yes	Flowers (red, spring-summer)	Lawn specimen, shrub border	—	Attracts nectar-feeding birds; grown as herbaceous plant in cool climates
Erythrina fusca	Tree	Hot Z 10-12	8 ft 2.5 m	12 ft 4 m	20 ft 6 m	Decid*	—	Flowers (orange-red)	Lawn specimen	—	—
Erythrina haerdii	Tree	Hot Z 9-12	6 ft 2 m	10 ft 3 m	15 ft 5 m	Decid*	Yes	Flowers (crimson, spring)	Lawn specimen	—	Attracts nectar-feeding birds
Erythrina humeana	Shrub	Warm Z 9-11	4 ft 1.2 m	8 ft 2.5 m	12 ft 4 m	Decid	Yes	Flowers (scarlet, summer-early autumn)	Shrub border, courtyard	—	—

NAME	KIND	CLIMATE & ZONE	HEIGHT AT 5 yrs	10 yrs	20 yrs	DECIDUOUS/EVERGREEN	ARID CLIMATES	CHIEF ATTRACTIONS	USES	DRAWBACKS	COMMENTS
Erythrina livingstoneana	Tree	Warm Z 10-12	8 ft 2.5 m	15 ft 5 m	30 ft 9 m	Decid*	Yes	Flowers (scarlet, spring)	Lawn specimen	—	—
Erythrina lysistemon	Tree	Warm Z 9-10	8 ft 2.5 m	15 ft 5 m	20 ft 6 m	Decid	Yes	Flowers (scarlet, spring); decorative seeds	Lawn specimen, parks, shade	—	—
Erythrina × sykesii (indica)	Tree	Warm Z 9-10	8 ft 2.5 m	15 ft 5 m	25 ft 8 m	Decid	—	Flowers (red, winter-spring)	Parks, windbreaks	Branches brittle, sharp prickles	Attracts nectar-feeding birds; can be grown from very large cuttings
Erythrina variegata	Tree	Hot Z 11-12	10 ft 3 m	20 ft 6 m	30 ft 9 m	Decid*	—	Flowers (orange or scarlet, winter-spring)	Parks, streets	—	—
Erythrina vespertilio	Tree	Hot Z 10-12	6 ft 2 m	12 ft 4 m	20 ft 6 m	Decid*	Yes	Flowers (salmon or red, winter)	Lawn specimen, parks	—	Attracts nectar-feeding birds
Escallonia bifida	Tree	Warm Z 8-10	5 ft 1.5 m	12 ft 4 m	20 ft 6 m	Everg	—	Flowers (white, late spring-early winter)	Lawn specimen, windbreak, coastal planting	—	—
Escallonia × exoniensis	Shrub	Cool Z 8-10	6 ft 2 m	12 ft 4 m	20 ft 6 m	Everg	—	Flowers (pale pink, late spring-autumn)	Shrub border, windbreak, coastal planting, hedge	Branches weak & brittle	Long flowering season
Escallonia rubra	Shrub	Cool Z 8-10	5 ft 1.5 m	8 ft 2.5 m	10 ft 3 m	Everg	—	Flowers (pink, spring-early autumn)	Shrub border, informal hedge, coastal planting, espalier	—	Parent of many hybrids; the robust var. macrantha is most widely grown
Eucalyptus brevifolia	Tree	Hot Z 11-12	6 ft 2 m	12 ft 4 m	20 ft 6 m	Everg	Yes	Bark; foliage	Lawn specimen	—	Tropical species, rare in cultivation
Eucalyptus caesia subsp. magna	Tree	Warm Z 9-10	8 ft 2.5 m	12 ft 4 m	15 ft 5 m	Everg	Yes	Flowers (crimson, autumn-spring)	Shrub border, courtyard, lawn grouping	Straggly habit, branches weak	White bloom on twigs and buds contrasts with brilliant large flowers
Eucalyptus calophylla	Tree	Warm Z 9-10	10 ft 3 m	20 ft 6 m	30 ft 9 m	Everg	Yes	Flowers (cream or pink, summer-autumn)	Lawn specimen, parks, timber	—	Hybridizes spontaneously with E. ficifolia, hybrids usually pink
Eucalyptus calycogona	Tree	Warm Z 9-10	8 ft 2.5 m	12 ft 4 m	20 ft 6 m	Everg	Yes	Flowers (cream, spring-summer)	Lawn specimen, shrub border, streets	—	—
Eucalyptus camaldulensis	Tree	Warm Z 9-10	15 ft 5 m	30 ft 9 m	50 ft 15 m	Everg	Yes	Foliage; bark; massive stature	Parks, river banks, timber, shelter, shade	—	Grown in Africa & Asia for timber, fuel, erosion control
Eucalyptus cinerea	Tree	Warm Z 8-10	10 ft 3 m	20 ft 6 m	30 ft 9 m	Everg	—	Foliage	Lawn specimen, parks, streets, cut foliage	—	Foliage blue-grey; most trees retain the rounded juvenile leaves
Eucalyptus citriodora	Tree	Warm Z 10-11	10 ft 3 m	25 ft 8 m	40 ft 12 m	Everg	Yes	Bark; elegant form	Lawn specimen, parks, streets, lemon-oil	—	Crushed leaves have strong lemon smell, oil extracted commercially
Eucalyptus cladocalyx	Tree	Warm Z 8-10	10 ft 3 m	25 ft 8 m	40 ft 12 m	Everg	Yes	Foliage; bark; vigorous growth	Windbreaks, parks, shade	Brittle branches; foliage can poison livestock	—
Eucalyptus curtisii	Tree	Warm Z 9-10	8 ft 2.5 m	12 ft 4 m	15 ft 5 m	Everg	—	Flowers (white, spring)	Shrub border, screen, shelter	—	Flowers in large panicles terminating shoots
Eucalyptus desmondensis	Tree	Warm Z 9-11	8 ft 2.5 m	10 ft 3 m	15 ft 5 m	Everg	—	Flowers (pale yellow, late summer); bark	Lawn specimen, parks, shrub border	—	Waxy white bloom on branches & twigs
Eucalyptus diversicolor	Tree	Warm Z 9-11	15 ft 5 m	30 ft 9 m	60 ft 18 m	Everg	—	Massive size; bark	Timber, parks	—	One of the tallest eucalypts and Western Australia's largest tree
Eucalyptus dumosa	Tree	Warm Z 8-10	8 ft 2.5 m	15 ft 5 m	20 ft 6 m	Everg	Yes	Flowers (white, spring-summer)	Shrub border, shelter	—	One of the 'mallee' eucalypts, normally multi-stemmed
Eucalyptus elata	Tree	Warm Z 8-10	10 ft 3 m	20 ft 6 m	40 ft 12 m	Everg	—	Weeping foliage; bark; flowers (white, late spring)	Lawn specimen, parks, streets, farms, shelter	—	Remains small under exposed conditions and poor soil
Eucalyptus eremophila	Tree	Warm Z 9-10	8 ft 2.5 m	12 ft 4 m	20 ft 6 m	Everg	Yes	Flowers (yelllow, winter-spring)	Lawn specimen, shrub border	—	Unsuited to summer-rainfall climates
Eucalyptus erythrocorys	Tree	Warm Z 9-10	6 ft 2 m	12 ft 4 m	20 ft 6 m	Everg	Yes	Flowers (yellow & red, early summer)	Lawn specimen, shrub border	Habit often ungainly	Can be kept shapely by judicious pruning
Eucalyptus ficifolia	Tree	Warm Z 9-10	8 ft 2.5 m	15 ft 5 m	20 ft 6 m	Everg	—	Flowers (orange or scarlet, late spring-summer); curious fruit	Lawn specimen, parks, streets	Can be short-lived	Spectacular in flower; does best in winter-rainfall climates
Eucalyptus forrestiana	Tree	Warm Z 9-10	6 ft 2 m	8 ft 2.5 m	10 ft 3 m	Everg	Yes	Flowers (red & yellow, summer)	Shrub border, lawn specimen, streets	—	Red buds and flower bases contrast with yellow stamens
Eucalyptus globulus	Tree	Warm Z 8-10	20 ft 6 m	40 ft 12 m	60 ft 18 m	Everg	—	Bark; vigorous growth; foliage	Timber, parks, avenues, windbreaks, eucalyptus oil	—	Widely grown in countries other than its native Australia
Eucalyptus gracilis	Tree	Warm Z 9-10	8 ft 2.5 m	12 ft 4 m	20 ft 6 m	Everg	Yes	Bark; foliage; flowers (cream, autumn-winter)	Lawn specimen, screen, coastal planting	—	One of the 'mallee' eucalypts, often multi-stemmed
Eucalyptus grandis	Tree	Warm Z 10-11	20 ft 6 m	40 ft 12 m	60 ft 18 m	Everg	—	Bark, stately form	Timber, parks, farms	Drops dead branches from high up	One of the fastest-growing eucalypts, used in plantations
Eucalyptus gunnii	Tree	Cool Z 7-9	10 ft 3 m	20 ft 6 m	30 ft 9 m	Everg	—	Foliage; bark	Lawn specimen, cut foliage, shelter	—	Among the most frost-hardy eucalypts, popular in the UK
Eucalyptus haemastoma	Tree	Warm Z 9-10	10 ft 3 m	20 ft 6 m	30 ft 9 m	Everg	—	Bark ('scribbly')	Lawn specimen & groups, parks, coastal planting	—	Scribble-like bark markings are caused by larvae of a small moth
Eucalyptus leucoxylon	Tree	Warm Z 9-10	12 ft 4 m	25 ft 8 m	40 ft 12 m	Everg	Yes	Flowers (cream, pink or crimson, autumn-spring)	Parks, streets, lawn specimen	—	Wild trees vary in flower colour, pink forms popular

NAME	KIND	CLIMATE & ZONE	HEIGHT AT 5 yrs	HEIGHT AT 10 yrs	HEIGHT AT 20 yrs	DECIDUOUS/EVERGREEN	ARID CLIMATES	CHIEF ATTRACTIONS	USES	DRAWBACKS	COMMENTS
Eucalyptus macrocarpa	Tree	Warm Z 9-10	5 ft 1.5 m	8 ft 2.5 m	12 ft 4 m	Everg	Yes	Flowers (red or pink, late winter-early summer)	Lawn specimen, courtyard, cut foliage/flowers	—	The largest flowers and fruits of any eucalypt
Eucalyptus maculata	Tree	Warm Z 9-10	15 ft 5 m	25 ft 8 m	40 ft 12 m	Everg	—	Bark; flowers (white, winter)	Timber, parks, streets, windbreaks	—	Bark is attractively mottled and dimpled, peeling in patches
Eucalyptus mannifera	Tree	Cool Z 8-9	10 ft 3 m	20 ft 6 m	30 ft 9 m	Everg	—	Bark; elegant form	Lawn specimen, parks, streets, windbreaks	Branches brittle, prone to wind damage	Subsp. *maculosa* is the form most commonly grown
Eucalyptus microtheca (coolabah)	Tree	Warm Z 9-11	10 ft 3 m	20 ft 6 m	30 ft 9 m	Everg	Yes	Foliage	Parks, farms, river banks, firewood	—	The famous 'coolibah' of Australian folklore
Eucalyptus nicholii	Tree	Warm Z 8-9	12 ft 4 m	25 ft 8 m	40 ft 12 m	Everg	—	Foliage; bark	Lawn specimen, parks, streets	—	Popular medium-small eucalypt; crushed leaves have peppermint smell
Eucalyptus papuana	Tree	Hot Z 10-12	15 ft 5 m	30 ft 9 m	40 ft 12 m	Everg	Yes	Bark; elegant form	Lawn specimen, parks	—	Grows in very hot dry areas; the 'ghost gum' of northern Australia
Eucalyptus pauciflora	Tree	Cool Z 7-9	12 ft 4 m	20 ft 6 m	30 ft 9 m	Everg	—	Bark; twisted trunk	Lawn specimen, parks, windbreaks	—	Subsp. *niphophila* grows at high altitudes in snow
Eucalyptus perriniana	Tree	Cool Z 8-9	12 ft 4 m	20 ft 6 m	30 ft 9 m	Everg	—	Foliage	Cut foliage, lawn specimen	—	Juvenile leaves very ornamental, encouraged by coppicing
Eucalyptus polyanthemos	Tree	Warm Z 8-10	12 ft 4 m	25 ft 8 m	40 ft 12 m	Everg	Yes	Foliage; bark; flowers (white, spring)	Cut foliage, honey, timber, lawn specimen, streets	—	Bluish rounded leaves ornamental, popular in California
Eucalyptus ptychocarpa	Tree	Hot Z 10-12	15 ft 5 m	25 ft 8 m	40 ft 12 m	Everg	Yes	Flowers (white to red, most of year); large fruit	Lawn specimen, parks, dried arrangements	—	Becoming popular in tropical Australia as an ornamental
Eucalyptus regnans	Tree	Cool Z 8-9	15 ft 5 m	30 ft 9 m	60 ft 18 m	Everg	—	Stately form	Timber, paper pulp	—	The tallest eucalypt and the world's tallest hardwood tree
Eucalyptus rubida	Tree	Cool Z 8-9	12 ft 4 m	25 ft 8 m	40 ft 12 m	Everg	—	Bark	Windbreaks, cut foliage (juvenile)	—	Old bark hangs from trunk & branches, very inflammable
Eucalyptus salmonophloia	Tree	Warm Z 9-10	12 ft 4 m	20 ft 6 m	30 ft 9 m	Everg	Yes	Bark	Lawn specimen, parks	—	Bark of striking orange-salmon colour, polished appearance
Eucalyptus sideroxylon	Tree	Warm Z 9-11	12 ft 4 m	25 ft 8 m	40 ft 12 m	Everg	Yes	Bark; foliage; flowers (white to crimson, autumn-spring)	Lawn specimen, parks, farms, firewood	—	One of the 'ironbark' eucalypts with blackish, furrowed bark
Eucalyptus tereticornis	Tree	Warm Z 9-11	12 ft 4 m	25 ft 8 m	40 ft 12 m	Everg	—	Bark; vigorous growth	Parks, windbreaks, farms, firewood	—	—
Eucalyptus tessellaris	Tree	Hot Z 10-12	15 ft 5 m	30 ft 9 m	50 ft 15 m	Everg	Yes	Bark	Lawn specimen	Difficult to propagate	Striking bark pattern, scaly on lower trunk, smooth above
Eucalyptus torquata	Tree	Warm Z 9-11	6 ft 2 m	12 ft 4 m	20 ft 6 m	Everg	Yes	Flowers (orange & yellow, spring-autumn); curious fruit	Lawn specimen, parks, streets	—	Very showy in flower; suits small gardens
Eucalyptus woodwardii	Tree	Warm Z 9-11	12 ft 4 m	20 ft 6 m	30 ft 9 m	Everg	Yes	Flowers (yellow, winter-spring); weeping habit	Lawn specimen, parks, streets	—	Prefers winter-rainfall climates
Eucommia ulmoides	Tree	Cool Z 5-10	10 ft 3 m	25 ft 8 m	40 ft 12 m	Decid	—	Foliage	Herbal medicine, lawn specimen	—	Widely grown in China for medicinal bark
Eucryphia cordifolia	Tree	Cool Z 8-9	10 ft 3 m	20 ft 6 m	30 ft 9 m	Everg	—	Flowers (white, late summer); foliage	Lawn specimen, woodland garden	—	The most tender and climatically sensitive eucryphia
Eucryphia glutinosa	Tree	Cool Z 7-9	6 ft 2 m	12 ft 4 m	20 ft 6 m	Decid	—	Flowers (white, midsummer)	Lawn specimen, woodland garden	—	A double-flowered cv is sometimes grown
Eucryphia × intermedia	Tree	Cool Z 8-9	6 ft 2 m	12 ft 4 m	20 ft 6 m	Decid	—	Flowers (white, late summer)	Lawn specimen, woodland garden	—	Hybrid between *E. glutinosa* & *E. lucida*
Eucryphia lucida	Tree	Cool Z 8-9	6 ft 2 m	12 ft 4 m	20 ft 6 m	Everg	—	Flowers (white, fragrant, early summer)	Lawn specimen, woodland garden, honey production	—	Famous for its honey in Tasmania; a pink-flowered cv is available
Eucryphia moorei	Tree	Cool Z 8-9	8 ft 2.5 m	15 ft 5 m	25 ft 8 m	Everg	—	Flowers (white, midsummer-early autumn)	Lawn specimen, woodland garden	—	Requires high humidity, moist soil
Eucryphia × nymansensis	Tree	Cool Z 7-9	8 ft 2.5 m	15 ft 5 m	20 ft 6 m	Decid	—	Flowers (white, late summer)	Lawn specimen, woodland garden	—	Hybrid between *E. cordifolia* & *E. glutinosa*
Eugenia uniflora	Tree	Hot Z 10-12	5 ft 1.5 m	8 ft 2.5 m	10 ft 3 m	Everg	—	Edible/decorative fruit; flowers (white, summer)	Home orchard, lawn specimen, courtyard, container	—	Fruit translucent red, usually acid
Euonymus alatus	Shrub	Cool Z 5-9	3 ft 1 m	6 ft 2 m	6 ft 2 m	Decid	—	Autumn foliage; decorative fruit	Shrub border; woodland garden, cut foliage/fruit	—	Twigs have interesting corky wings; autumn colour brilliant
Euonymus europaeus	Shrub	Cool Z 6-9	5 ft 1.5 m	10 ft 3 m	12 ft 4 m	Decid	—	Autumn foliage; decorative fruit	Shrub border, lawn specimen	—	Oily seeds attract birds; male & female plants needed for fruit
Euonymus japonicus	Shrub	Cool Z 8-10	3 ft 1 m	6 ft 2 m	8 ft 2.5 m	Everg	—	Foliage	Hedge, seaside planting, shrub border, rock garden, container, topiary	—	Variegated cultivars most commonly grown
Euphorbia abyssinica	Tree	Warm Z 10-11	3 ft 1 m	6 ft 2 m	12 ft 4 m	Everg	Yes	Succulent angled stems	Courtyard, plaza	—	Stems have numerous short spines
Euphorbia grandicornis	Shrub	Warm Z 9-11	2 ft 0.6 m	3 ft 1 m	4 ft 1.2 m	Everg	Yes	Succulent spiny stems	Courtyard, rock garden, container	—	Stems have long interlocking spines

Reference Table

NAME	KIND	CLIMATE & ZONE	HEIGHT AT 5yrs 10yrs 20yrs	DECIDUOUS EVERGREEN	ARID CLIMATES	CHIEF ATTRACTIONS	USES	DRAWBACKS	COMMENTS
Euphorbia pulcherrima	Shrub	Warm Z 10-11	4 ft 8 ft 12 ft / 1.2 m 2.5 m 4 m	Decid	Yes	Flowers (red bracts, late autumn-spring)	Shrub border, courtyard, container	Sap poisonous, can damage eyes	Many compact cultivars developed for indoor use
Euphorbia tirucalli	Shrub	Warm Z 10-11	3 ft 8 ft 10 ft / 1 m 2.5 m 3 m	Everg	Yes	Succulent branches	Courtyard, container, indoors, swimming pool	Sap poisonous, can damage eyes	Interesting sculptural form
Euryops (Gamolepis) chrysanthemoides	Shrub	Warm Z 9-11	2 ft 3 ft 3 ft / 0.6 m 1 m 1 m	Everg	—	Flowers (yellow, winter and most of year)	Courtyard, seaside planting, conservatory, cut flowers	—	—
Euryops pectinatus	Shrub	Warm Z 9-11	2 ft 3 ft 3 ft / 0.6 m 1 m 1 m	Everg	—	Flowers (yellow, winter-spring); foliage	Courtyard, conservatory, rock garden	Often short-lived	Grey foliage makes effective contrast with yellow flowers
Euryops virgineus	Shrub	Warm Z 9-11	3 ft 4 ft 4 ft / 1 m 1.2 m 1.2 m	Everg	—	Flowers (yellow, late winter-spring)	Seaside planting, hedge, courtyards, perennial border	—	Can be pruned hard after flowering to prevent legginess
Euscaphis japonica	Tree	Cool Z 6-9	6 ft 12 ft 20 ft / 2 m 4 m 6 m	Decid	—	Foliage; decorative fruit; bark	Lawn specimen, shrub border	—	—
Exochorda × macrantha	Shrub	Cool Z 6-9	4 ft 6 ft 8 ft / 1.2 m 2 m 2.5 m	Decid	Yes	Flowers (white, mid-late spring)	Shrub border	—	Prefer climates with warm, dry summer, cold winter
Exochorda racemosa	Shrub	Cool Z 6-10	5 ft 8 ft 8 ft / 1.5 m 2.5 m 2.5 m	Decid	Yes	Flowers (white, late spring)	Shrub border	—	—
Fagus grandifolia	Tree	Cool Z 4-9	8 ft 20 ft 30 ft / 2.5 m 6 m 9 m	Decid	—	Foliage, elegant form	Parks, streets, timber	—	Seeds are valuable food for wildlife
Fagus orientalis	Tree	Cool Z 6-9	8 ft 20 ft 30 ft / 2.5 m 6 m 9 m	Decid	—	Foliage, elegant form	Parks, streets	—	Sometimes regarded as a form of F. sylvatica, leaves larger
Fagus sylvatica	Tree	Cool Z 5-9	8 ft 20 ft 30 ft / 2.5 m 6 m 9 m	Decid	—	Foliage, elegant form	Parks, streets, woodland garden, timber	Surface roots inhibit other plantings beneath	Purple-foliaged cultivars most often planted in gardens
Fatsia japonica	Shrub	Warm Z 8-11	3 ft 4 ft 6 ft / 1 m 1.2 m 2 m	Decid	—	Foliage; flowers (white, autumn); decorative fruit	Courtyards, swimming pools, woodland garden	Leaves scorched by strong sun	Good for creating tropical effect in cool climate
Feijoa sellowiana	Shrub	Warm Z 9-11	4 ft 6 ft 12 ft / 1.2 m 2 m 4 m	Everg	Yes	Edible fruit; flowers (white & red, late spring-early summer)	Home orchard, informal hedge, shrub border	Attracts fruit fly	Named cultivars best for fruit; can be pruned to more compact size
Ficus aspera	Tree	Hot Z 11-12	6 ft 12 ft 15 ft / 2 m 4 m 5 m	Everg	—	Foliage	Shrub border, conservatory, courtyard, container	—	Variegated cv. 'Parcellii' is most often grown
Ficus benghalensis	Tree	Hot Z 11-12	10 ft 20 ft 30 ft / 3 m 6 m 9 m	Everg	Yes	Aerial roots forming multiple trunks; foliage	Parks	—	The original banyan, sacred in Hindu religion
Ficus benjamina	Tree	Hot Z 10-12	8 ft 20 ft 30 ft / 2.5 m 6 m 9 m	Everg	—	Foliage	Containers, indoors, swimming pools, streets, topiary & plaited trunks	Fallen fruit can be a nuisance	Cultivars varying in leaf shape and colour
Ficus carica	Tree	Warm Z 8-10	6 ft 8 ft 15 ft / 2 m 2.5 m 5 m	Decid	Yes	Edible fruit	Home orchard, courtyards	Damaged by birds and fruit fly	The common fig; some cultivars require a wasp for fruit set; fruits best in poor soil
Ficus dammaropsis	Tree	Warm Z 10-11	6 ft 12 ft 20 ft / 2 m 4 m 6 m	Everg	—	Foliage	Courtyard, swimming pools, indoors, shrub border	—	Huge leaves have striking corrugated surface
Ficus elastica	Tree	Hot Z 10-12	10 ft 20 ft 30 ft / 3 m 6 m 9 m	Everg	—	Foliage	Indoors, parks, plazas	Invasive roots, rapidly outgrows small spaces	The common rubber tree; several cultivars are grown
Ficus lyrata	Tree	Hot Z 10-12	6 ft 12 ft 20 ft / 2 m 4 m 6 m	Everg	—	Foliage	Indoors, courtyard, plaza, conservatory	—	Distinctive leaf shape, like body of violin
Ficus macrophylla	Tree	Warm Z 9-11	8 ft 15 ft 30 ft / 2.5 m 5 m 9 m	Everg	—	Foliage, massive trunk	Parks, avenues	Greedy roots; fruit & leaves litter pavement	Enormous crown spread, trunk has large buttresses
Ficus microcarpa	Tree	Warm Z 9-12	10 ft 20 ft 30 ft / 3 m 6 m 9 m	Everg	—	Foliage, smooth bark	Parks, avenues, topiary & plaited trunks, containers	Invasive roots often damage pavements	Var. hillii is widely planted in Australia
Ficus religiosa	Tree	Hot Z 11-12	6 ft 12 ft 20 ft / 2 m 4 m 6 m	Decid*	Yes	Foliage; graceful habit	Courtyards, parks, plazas	—	The sacred 'bo tree' of Buddhism
Ficus sur (capensis)	Tree	Hot Z 10-12	10 ft 20 ft 30 ft / 3 m 6 m 9 m	Decid*	Yes	Foliage, decorative/edible fruit	Parks, avenues, shade	Invasive roots	—
Ficus virens	Tree	Hot Z 10-12	10 ft 20 ft 30 ft / 3 m 6 m 9 m	Decid*	Yes	Foliage, massive trunk, aerial roots	Parks, rainforest garden	Invasive roots	One of the 'strangler figs', with curtain of aerial roots
Firmiana simplex	Tree	Warm Z 8-11	6 ft 10 ft 15 ft / 2 m 3 m 5 m	Decid	—	Autumn foliage, decorative fruit	Lawn specimen, courtyard, streets, shade	—	Large lobed leaves ornamental, featured in traditional Chinese paintings
Flindersia australis	Tree	Warm Z 9-11	8 ft 15 ft 30 ft / 2.5 m 5 m 9 m	Decid*	Yes	Foliage; flowers (white, winter-spring); decorative fruit	Streets, parks, lawn specimen, timber, dried arrangements	—	Often flowers on bare branches; star-shaped prickly fruit are ornamental
Flindersia maculosa	Tree	Warm Z 10-11	4 ft 8 ft 15 ft / 1.2 m 2.5 m 5 m	Everg	Yes	Attractive bark; foliage; flowers (white, late spring-summer)	Lawn specimen, parks	Slow-growing	Goes through long shrub-like juvenile stage
Fokienia hodginsii	Tree	Cool Z 7-10	6 ft 12 ft 20 ft / 2 m 4 m 6 m	Everg	—	Foliage	Lawn specimen, parks	—	Rare Chinese conifer, seldom grown
Forsythia × intermedia	Shrub	Cool Z 5-9	4 ft 6 ft 8 ft / 1.2 m 2 m 2.5 m	Decid	—	Flowers (yellow, mid-spring)	Shrub border, courtyard, lawn grouping	—	Includes the most popular forsythia cultivars

NAME	KIND	CLIMATE & ZONE	HEIGHT AT 5 yrs	HEIGHT AT 10 yrs	HEIGHT AT 20 yrs	DECIDUOUS EVERGREEN	ARID CLIMATES	CHIEF ATTRACTIONS	USES	DRAWBACKS	COMMENTS
Forsythia suspensa	Shrub	Cool Z 4-9	6 ft 2 m	8 ft 2.5 m	12 ft 4 m	Decid	—	Flowers (yellow, early-mid-spring)	Shrub border, courtyard, lawn grouping, espalier	—	Requires cold winter for good flowering (all forsythias)
Forsythia viridissima	Shrub	Cool Z 5-9	4 ft 1.2 m	6 ft 2 m	6 ft 2 m	Decid	—	Flowers (yellow, mid-late spring)	Shrub border, courtyard, espalier	—	—
Fortunella japonica	Shrub	Warm Z 9-11	4 ft 1.2 m	6 ft 2 m	8 ft 2.5 m	Everg	—	Edible/decorative fruit	Containers, courtyards, conservatories, home orchard	—	Fruit (cumquats) like miniature sour oranges, used for jams & preserves
Fothergilla gardenii	Shrub	Cool Z 5-9	2 ft 0.6 m	3 ft 1 m	3 ft 1 m	Decid	—	Flowers (white, fragrant, early spring), autumn foliage	Shrub border, rock garden, woodland garden	—	Prefers moist acidic soil
Fouquieria splendens	Shrub	Warm Z 9-11	4 ft 1.2 m	8 ft 2.5 m	15 ft 5 m	Everg	Yes	Flowers (red, spring); spiny stems	Courtyard, desert garden, hedge	—	Seldom grown outside SW USA
Franklinia alatamaha	Tree	Cool Z 7-9	6 ft 2 m	10 ft 3 m	15 ft 5 m	Decid	—	Flowers (white, late summer-autumn); autumn foliage	Lawn specimen, shrub border, woodland garden	—	Extinct in the wild, has been maintained in gardens for 200 years
Fraxinus americana	Tree	Cool Z 4-10	10 ft 3 m	20 ft 6 m	40 ft 12 m	Decid	—	Autumn foliage	Parks, streets, timber	Greedy surface roots (most *Fraxinus* spp.)	Strong, tough timber has many uses
Fraxinus angustifolia (incl. oxycarpa, syriaca)	Tree	Warm Z 7-10	10 ft 3 m	20 ft 6 m	30 ft 9 m	Decid	Yes	Autumn foliage	Parks, streets	—	Includes several geographic subspecies; cv. 'Raywood' is the popular claret ash
Fraxinus excelsior	Tree	Cool Z 4-9	10 ft 3 m	20 ft 6 m	30 ft 9 m	Decid	—	Autumn foliage (summer colour in 'Aurea')	Lawn specimen, parks, streets, timber	—	The golden cultivar 'Aurea' is most commonly grown
Fraxinus griffithii	Tree	Warm Z 9-11	10 ft 3 m	15 ft 5 m	20 ft 6 m	Everg	—	Flowers (white, spring-summer); decorative fruit	Lawn specimen, streets, plazas	—	Tiny flowers massed in large clusters above foliage
Fraxinus latifolia	Tree	Cool Z 5-9	10 ft 3 m	20 ft 6 m	40 ft 12 m	Decid	—	Autumn foliage	Parks, streets, timber	—	—
Fraxinus ornus	Tree	Cool Z 6-9	8 ft 2.5m	15 ft 5 m	25 ft 8 m	Decid	Yes	Flowers (white, late spring); autumn foliage	Lawn specimen, parks, streets	—	Flowers massed in large panicles above foliage
Fraxinus pennsylvanica	Tree	Cool Z 3-10	10 ft 3 m	20 ft 6 m	30 ft 9 m	Decid	—	Autumn foliage	Parks, streets	—	Handsome species in leaf, adapts to city conditions
Fraxinus quadrangulata	Tree	Cool Z 4-9	10 ft 3 m	20 ft 6 m	40 ft 12 m	Decid	Yes	Autumn foliage	Parks, streets, timber, dye from bark	—	4-angled twigs are a distinctive feature
Fraxinus uhdei	Tree	Warm Z 9-11	15 ft 5 m	30 ft 9 m	50 ft 15 m	Everg	—	Foliage	Parks, streets, timber	—	Extremely fast-growing species for warm climates
Fraxinus velutina	Tree	Cool Z 6-10	8 ft 2.5m	15 ft 5 m	25 ft 8 m	Decid	Yes	Autumn foliage	Parks, streets, shade	—	Good shade tree for dry climates
Fremontodendron californicum	Shrub	Cool Z 8-10	8 ft 2.5m	12 ft 4 m	15 ft 5 m	Everg	Yes	Flowers (yellow, mid-late spring)	Shrub border, courtyards, espalier	Branches brittle, hairs can irritate skin	—
Fuchsia arborescens	Shrub	Warm Z 9-10	4 ft 1.2 m	8 ft 2.5 m	10 ft 3 m	Everg	—	Flowers (purple, autumn-spring)	Shrub border, courtyards	—	Tolerates shade, prefers sheltered position
Fuchsia denticulata	Shrub	Warm Z 9-10	3 ft 1 m	6 ft 2 m	8 ft 2.5 m	Everg	—	Flowers (red & green, spring-summer)	Shrub border, courtyards, woodland garden	—	Prefers shade
Fuchsia excorticata	Tree	Cool Z 8-9	4 ft 1.2 m	8 ft 2.5 m	12 ft 4 m	Everg	—	Attractive bark; flowers (green & pink, late winter-early summer)	Shrub border, woodland garden	—	The largest fuchsia, can reach 40 ft (12 m) in wild with thick trunk
Fuchsia magellanica	Shrub	Cool Z 8-10	4 ft 1.2 m	6 ft 2 m	8 ft 2.5 m	Everg	—	Flowers (red & purple, summer-autumn)	Shrub border, courtyard, espalier, containers, informal hedge, conservatory	—	Several colour-forms grown; can be pruned to compact form
Fuchsia paniculata	Shrub	Warm Z 9-10	4 ft 1.2 m	8 ft 2.5 m	12 ft 4 m	Everg	—	Flowers (pink, spring); decorative fruit	Shrub border, courtyard, woodland garden	—	—
Garcinia mangostana	Tree	Hot Z 12	6 ft 2 m	12 ft 4 m	20 ft 6 m	Everg	—	Edible fruit	Orchard, courtyard, lawn specimen	Slow-growing	Delicious fruit, can only be grown in fully tropical climates
Garcinia xanthochymus	Tree	Hot Z 11-12	6 ft 2 m	12 ft 4 m	20 ft 6 m	Everg	—	Decorative/edible fruit; foliage	Shrub border, lawn specimen, pigment from sap	—	The traditional artist's pigment gamboge is obtained from sap
Gardenia augusta (jasminoides)	Shrub	Warm Z 9-11	4 ft 1.2 m	5 ft 1.5 m	6 ft 2 m	Everg	—	Fragrant flowers (white, late spring-autumn)	Courtyard, container, informal hedge, conservatory, cut flower	Flowers may brown in hot sun	Several cultivars grown, all double-flowered
Gardenia thunbergia	Shrub	Warm Z 10-11	4 ft 1.2 m	6 ft 2 m	8 ft 2.5 m	Everg	Yes	Fragrant flowers (white, early summer)	Shrub border, lawn specimen	—	Produces large woody fruit
Garrya elliptica	Shrub	Cool Z 8-9	6 ft 2 m	10 ft 3 m	12 ft 4 m	Everg	—	Flowers (pale green, midwinter-early spring)	Shrub border, courtyard, espalier	—	Only male plants grown for ornamental catkins
Gaultheria fragrantissima	Shrub	Cool Z 8-10	4 ft 1.2 m	6 ft 2 m	8 ft 2.5 m	Everg	—	Flowers (white or pink, fragrant, spring, decorative fruit	Shrub border, courtyard, woodland garden	—	—
Gaultheria (Pernettya) mucronata	Shrub	Cool Z 7-9	2 ft 0.6 m	3 ft 1 m	5 ft 1.5 m	Everg	—	Flowers (white, spring); decorative fruit	Shrub border, courtyard, rock garden, woodland garden	—	Male and female plants required for fruit display
Gaultheria shallon	Shrub	Cool Z 5-9	2 ft 0.6 m	3 ft 1 m	4 ft 1.2 m	Everg	—	Flowers (white, spring); decorative fruit	Shrub border, courtyard, rock garden, woodland garden	—	—
Gaultheria (Gaulthettya) × wisleyensis	Shrub	Cool Z 7-9	2 ft 0.6 m	3 ft 1 m	4 ft 1.2 m	Everg	—	Flowers (white, spring); decorative fruit	Shrub border, courtyard, rock garden, embankment	—	Many named cvs available, some useful as groundcovers

NAME	KIND	CLIMATE & ZONE	HEIGHT AT 5yrs 10yrs 20yrs			DECIDUOUS EVERGREEN	ARID CLIMATES	CHIEF ATTRACTIONS	USES	DRAWBACKS	COMMENTS
Genista hispanica	Shrub	Cool Z 4-9	1 ft 0.3 m	2 ft 0.6 m	2 ft 0.6 m	Decid	Yes	Flowers (yellow, spring-early summer)	Groundcover, rock garden, embankments	Prickly; often short-lived	—
Genista lydia	Shrub	Cool Z 5-9	1 ft 0.3 m	2 ft 0.6 m	2 ft 0.6 m	Decid	—	Flowers (yellow, spring-early summer)	Rock garden, retaining walls	—	Resents transplanting (all genistas)
Genista × spachiana (fragrans)	Shrub	Cool Z 6-9	3 ft 1 m	5 ft 1.5 m	8 ft 2.5 m	Everg	—	Flowers (yellow, winter-spring)	Containers, courtyards, rock garden, embankments	Often short-lived	Fast-growing, hardy plant
Genista tinctoria	Shrub	Cool Z 3-9	3 ft 1 m	3 ft 1 m	3 ft 1 m	Decid	—	Flowers (yellow, summer)	Shrub border, herb garden, rock garden	—	Once used as a source of yellow dye
Ginkgo biloba	Tree	Cool Z 3-10	6 ft 2 m	12 ft 4 m	25 ft 8 m	Decid	—	Autumn foliage	Lawn specimen, courtyards, parks, streets	Female trees drop smelly fruit	Grown in China for edible seeds; good for city conditions
Gleditsia aquatica	Tree	Cool Z 4-10	10 ft 3 m	20 ft 6 m	40 ft 12 m	Decid	—	Autumn foliage	Farms, boggy areas	—	Not as fiercely spiny as G. triacanthos
Gleditsia triacanthos	Tree	Cool Z 3-10	10 ft 3 m	20 ft 6 m	40 ft 12 m	Decid	—	Autumn foliage; large pods with edible pulp	Parks, lawn specimen, farms, boggy areas	Fierce spines on trunk; can become a weed	Spineless forms available, also cvs with yellow or bronze foliage
Gliricidia sepium	Tree	Hot Z 11-12	12 ft 4 m	20 ft 6 m	25 ft 8 m	Decid*	—	Flowers (pink & yellow, early spring)	Shade for coffee and cocoa plantations, lawn specimen	Short-lived, poisonous	Enriches soil by nitrogen fixation
Glyptostrobus pensilis	Tree	Warm Z 8-10	6 ft 2 m	12 ft 4 m	20 ft 6 m	Decid	—	Autumn foliage, symmetrical shape	Water-edge planting, lawn specimen	—	Planted in east Asia to stabilize banks of rice paddies
Gordonia axillaris	Tree	Warm Z 9-10	6 ft 2 m	10 ft 3 m	15 ft 5 m	Everg	—	Flowers (white, autumn-spring)	Lawn specimen, shrub border, streets	—	Related to camellias, similar flowers with yellow stamens
Gordonia lasianthus	Tree	Cool Z 6-9	6 ft 2 m	12 ft 4 m	20 ft 6 m	Everg	—	Flowers (white, fragrant, summer)	Lawn specimen, parks, streets, woodland garden	—	—
Graptophyllum pictum	Shrub	Hot Z 11-12	3 ft 1 m	5 ft 1.5 m	5 ft 1.5 m	Everg	—	Coloured foliage; flowers (red, spring-summer)	Indoors, containers, courtyards, swimming pools, conservatories	—	Cultivated forms mostly have coloured or variegated leaves
Grevillea banksii	Shrub	Warm Z 9-11	6 ft 2 m	10 ft 3 m	12 ft 4 m	Everg	Yes	Flowers (red or cream, most of year)	Shrub border, bush garden	Often short-lived	Flowers attract nectar-feeding birds
Grevillea dimorpha	Shrub	Warm Z 9-10	2 ft 0.6 m	4 ft 1.2 m	6 ft 2 m	Everg	—	Flowers (red, late autumn-spring)	Shrub border, courtyard, informal hedge	Often short-lived	—
Grevillea fasciculata	Shrub	Warm Z 9-10	2 ft 0.6 m	2 ft 0.6 m	2 ft 0.6 m	Everg	—	Flowers (red, late winter-spring)	Rock garden, embankment, container	Often short-lived	—
Grevillea hilliana	Tree	Warm Z 9-11	8 ft 2.5m	15 ft 5 m	25 ft 8 m	Everg	—	Flowers (white, late winter-summer)	Lawn specimen, streets	—	—
Grevillea juniperina	Shrub	Warm Z 9-10	4 ft 1.2 m	6 ft 2 m	6 ft 2 m	Everg	—	Flowers (scarlet, orange or yellow, summer)	Informal hedge, shrub border, embankments, groundcover	Often short-lived	Some forms are upright growers, others prostrate
Grevillea lanigera	Shrub	Warm Z 8-10	2 ft 0.6 m	3 ft 1 m	3 ft 1 m	Everg	—	Flowers (red & cream, late winter-spring); foliage contrast	Shrub border, rock garden	Often short-lived	—
Grevillea pteridifolia	Tree	Hot Z 11-12	10 ft 3 m	15 ft 5 m	20 ft 6 m	Everg	Yes	Flowers (orange, most of year)	Shrub border, screen, streets	Often short-lived	Flowers attract nectar-feeding birds
Grevillea robusta	Tree	Warm Z 9-11	10 ft 3 m	20 ft 6 m	40 ft 12 m	Everg	Yes	Flowers (orange-yellow, late spring)	Lawn specimen, parks, streets, timber	—	In cool climates often grown indoors as a foliage plant
Grevillea 'Robyn Gordon'	Tree	Warm Z 9-11	3 ft 1 m	3 ft 1 m	3 ft 1 m	Everg	Yes	Flowers (pink, most of year)	Informal hedge, shrub border, embankments, courtyard	Foliage causes skin allergy in some people	Flowers attract nectar-feeding birds
Grevillea rosmarinifolia	Tree	Warm Z 8-10	5 ft 1.5 m	6 ft 2 m	8 ft 2.5 m	Everg	—	Flowers (red, spring)	Formal hedge, shrub border, screen	Often short-lived; foliage prickly	Can be shaped by frequent trimming
Grewia occidentalis	Shrub	Warm Z 9-10	8 ft 2.5m	10 ft 3 m	10 ft 3 m	Everg	Yes	Flowers (pink, spring-summer)	Informal hedge, shrub border, espalier	—	Broadly spreading habit
Greyia sutherlandii	Shrub	Warm Z 9-11	3 ft 1 m	6 ft 2 m	10 ft 3 m	Decid	—	Flowers (scarlet, late winter-early spring)	Shrub border, rock garden, courtyard	Gaunt habit	Flowers attract nectar-feeding birds
Griselinia littoralis	Shrub	Warm Z 8-11	6 ft 2 m	12 ft 4 m	20 ft 6 m	Everg	—	Foliage, decorative fruit	Seashores, informal hedge, shrub border	—	—
Griselinia lucida	Shrub	Warm Z 8-11	5 ft 1.5 m	8 ft 2.5 m	12 ft 4 m	Everg	—	Foliage	Informal hedge, shrub border, rock garden, containers	—	Variegated cultivars available
Gymnocladus dioica	Tree	Cool Z 3-10	8 ft 2.5m	15 ft 5 m	25 ft 8 m	Decid	—	Foliage; flowers (white, fragrant, late spring-early summer)	Beverage from seeds, lawn specimen, parks	—	Only female trees bear pods
Gymnostoma australianum	Tree	Warm Z 10-11	4 ft 1.2 m	8 ft 2.5 m	15 ft 5 m	Everg	—	Foliage, symmetrical form	Shrub border, screen	—	—
Hakea bucculenta	Shrub	Warm Z 9-11	6 ft 2 m	12 ft 4 m	15 ft 5 m	Everg	Yes	Flowers (orange, lwinter-spring)	Shrub border, screen, informal hedge	—	Attracts nectar-feeding birds; prefers winter-rainfall climate
Hakea laurina	Shrub	Warm Z 9-11	5 ft 1.5 m	10 ft 3 m	12 ft 4 m	Everg	Yes	Flowers (crimson & cream, winter-spring)	Shrub border, screen, informal hedge	Easily wind-thrown	Needs good drainage; prefers winter-rainfall climate
Hakea microcarpa	Shrub	Cool Z 8-10	3 ft 1 m	4 ft 1.2 m	5 ft 1.5 m	Everg	—	Flowers (white, late winter-summer)	Shrub border, rock garden, waters-edge	—	Attracts nectar-feeding birds
Hakea purpurea	Shrub	Warm Z 9-11	2 ft 0.6 m	3 ft 1 m	4 ft 1.2 m	Everg	Yes	Flowers (red, winter-spring)	Shrub border, rock garden	—	—
Hakea salicifolia	Tree	Warm Z 9-11	8 ft 2.5m	15 ft 5 m	20 ft 6 m	Everg	—	Foliage; flowers (white, spring)	Informal hedge, screen, windbreak	Becomes a weed in some countries	Can be pruned to improve shape; new growths purplish

NAME	KIND	CLIMATE & ZONE	HEIGHT AT 5yrs	HEIGHT AT 10yrs	HEIGHT AT 20yrs	DECIDUOUS EVERGREEN	ARID CLIMATES	CHIEF ATTRACTIONS	USES	DRAWBACKS	COMMENTS
Hakea victoria	Shrub	Warm Z 9-10	5 ft 1.5 m	8 ft 2.5 m	10 ft 3 m	Everg	—	Coloured foliage	Shrub border, rock garden	Difficult to transplant	Needs perfect drainage, winter-rainfall climate
Halesia carolina	Tree	Cool Z 3-9	6 ft 2 m	12 ft 4 m	20 ft 6 m	Decid	—	Flowers (white, spring); curious fruit; autumn foliage	Lawn specimen	—	Profuse display of flowers, even when young
Halesia monticola	Tree	Cool Z 4-9	8 ft 2.5 m	20 ft 6 m	30 ft 9 m	Decid	—	Flowers (white, late spring); curious fruit; autumn foliage	Lawn specimen	—	A pink-flowered form is also known
Hamamelis × intermedia	Shrub	Cool Z 4-9	5 ft 1.5 m	10 ft 3 m	12 ft 4 m	Decid	—	Flowers (yellow to orange, fragrant, winter); autumn foliage	Shrub border, lawn specimen, cut flowers	—	Includes a number of cultivars
Hamamelis japonica	Shrub	Cool Z 4-9	5 ft 1.5 m	10 ft 3 m	12 ft 4 m	Decid	—	Flowers (yellow, fragrant, mid-late winter); autumn foliage	Shrub border, lawn specimen, cut flowers	—	Resents hard pruning (all *Hamamelis* spp.)
Hamamelis mollis	Shrub	Cool Z 4-9	5 ft 1.5 m	10 ft 3 m	12 ft 4 m	Decid	—	Flowers (golden, midwinter-early spring); autumn foliage	Shrub border, lawn specimen	—	—
Hamamelis vernalis	Shrub	Cool Z 4-9	4 ft 1.2 m	8 ft 2.5 m	12 ft 4 m	Decid	—	Flowers (cream to yellow, spring); autumn foliage	Shrub border, lawn specimen	Suckers from roots	—
Hamamelis virginiana	Shrub	Cool Z 2-9	6 ft 2 m	10 ft 3 m	12 ft 4 m	Decid	—	Flowers (yellow, fragrant, autumn); autumn foliage	Shrub border, lawn specimen	—	Flowers open as leaves colour and fall
Hamelia patens	Shrub	Warm Z 10-11	5 ft 1.5 m	5 ft 1.5 m	5 ft 1.5 m	Everg	—	Flowers (scarlet, summer); decorative fruit	Shrub border, swimming pool, courtyard	Fruits poisonous	—
Harpephyllum caffrum	Tree	Warm Z 10-11	8 ft 2.5 m	15 ft 5 m	25 ft 8 m	Everg	Yes	Foliage; decorative/edible fruit	Parks, streets, shade	—	Fruits used for jam
Hebe albicans	Shrub	Cool Z 8-9	1 ft 0.3 m	2 ft 0.6 m	2 ft 0.6 m	Everg	—	Flowers (white, early summer)	Rock garden, coastal planting	—	—
Hebe armstrongii	Shrub	Cool Z 8-9	1 ft 0.3 m	2 ft 0.6 m	3 ft 1 m	Everg	—	Flowers (white, summer-early winter)	Rock garden, courtyard, container	—	One of the 'whipcord' hebes, with cypress-like branchlets
Hebe diosmifolia	Shrub	Cool Z 8-10	2 ft 0.6 m	4 ft 1.2 m	—	Everg	—	Flowers (pale mauve, spring-autumn)	Shrub border, courtyard, coastal planting	Short-lived	—
Hebe ochracea	Shrub	Cool Z 8-9	1 ft 0.3 m	2 ft 0.6 m	3 ft 1 m	Everg	—	Foliage	Rock garden, container, coastal planting	—	One of the 'whipcord' hebes; does not like being pruned
Hebe odora	Shrub	Cool Z 8-9	2 ft 0.6 m	3 ft 1 m	4 ft 1.2 m	Everg	—	Flowers (white, summer)	Shrub border, courtyard, coastal planting	Short-lived	—
Hebe salicifolia	Shrub	Warm Z 9-10	5 ft 1.5 m	8 ft 2.5 m	10 ft 3 m	Everg	—	Flowers (white, fragrant, summer)	Coastal planting, informal hedge, screen	—	Tolerates urban pollution and hard pruning
Hebe speciosa	Shrub	Cool Z 8-10	2 ft 0.6 m	3 ft 1 m	3 ft 1 m	Everg	—	Red to purple (summer-autumn)	Seashore, shrub border, courtyard	Short-lived, prone to wilting	Many cultivars listed; tolerates some shade
Hebe venustula	Shrub	Cool Z 8-9	2 ft 0.6 m	3 ft 1 m	4 ft 1.2 m	Everg	—	Flowers (white to mauve, early summer)	Rock garden, container, courtyard	—	One of the 'whipcord' hebes; flowers profuse
Hedychium gardnerianum	Shrub	Warm Z 9-11	5 ft 1.5 m	6 ft 2 m	6 ft 2 m	Everg	—	Flowers (yellow & red, fragrant, late summer)	Woodland garden, courtyard, cut flowers & fruit	Can become a weed in mild wet climates	A herbacous plant but functions as a shrub in gardens
Hernandia bivalvis	Tree	Warm Z 10-11	6 ft 2 m	15 ft 5 m	25 ft 8 m	Everg	—	Flowers (cream, late spring); decorative fruit	Lawn specimen, rainforest garden, parks	—	—
Heteromeles arbutifolia	Tree	Warm Z 9-10	6 ft 2 m	10 ft 3 m	15 ft 5 m	Everg	Yes	Flowers (white, summer); decorative fruit	Shrub border, screen, hedge	—	—
Hevea brasiliensis	Tree	Hot Z 11-12	12 ft 4 m	25 ft 8 m	40 ft 12 m	Everg	—	Foliage	Commercial rubber production	—	Seldom grown except in commercial plantations & botanical gardens
Hibiscus arnottianus 'Wilder's White'	Tree	Warm Z 10-11	8 ft 2.5 m	12 ft 4 m	20 ft 6 m	Everg	—	Flowers (white, summer-autumn)	Informal hedge, screen, coastal planting	—	Has been listed as a *H. rosa-sinensis* cultivar
Hibiscus heterophyllus	Shrub	Warm Z 9-11	10 ft 3 m	15 ft 5 m	20 ft 6 m	Everg	—	Flowers (white or yellow & purple, summer-autumn)	Shrub border, rainforest garden	Irritant prickles on stems and leaves	—
Hibiscus insularis	Shrub	Warm Z 10-11	4 ft 1.2 m	8 ft 2.5 m	12 ft 4 m	Everg	—	Flowers (yellow & maroon, autumn-winter)	Coastal planting, informal hedge, lawn specimen	—	Useful for exposed positions; flowers turn pink as they age
Hibiscus mutabilis	Shrub	Warm Z 9-12	8 ft 2.5 m	10 ft 3 m	12 ft 4 m	Everg	Yes	Flowers (white aging pink, autumn)	Shrub border	—	Double-flowered cv is most widely grown
Hibiscus rosa-sinensis	Shrub	Warm Z 10-12	5 ft 1.5 m	8 ft 2.5 m	12 ft 4 m	Everg	Yes	Flowers (various colours, summer-early winter)	Shrub border, courtyard, swimming pool	—	Many newer cultivars are more compact, 4-6 ft (1.2-2 m)
Hibiscus schizopetalus	Shrub	Warm Z 10-12	4 ft 1.2 m	8 ft 2.5 m	10 ft 3 m	Everg	—	Flowers (scarlet, summer-autumn)	Shrub border, courtyard	—	Finely slashed petals & pendulous stalk give a delicate effect to flowers
Hibiscus syriacus	Shrub	Cool Z 6-10	6 ft 2 m	10 ft 3 m	12 ft 4 m	Everg	Yes	Flowers (white, pink or lilac & red, late summer-autumn)	Shrub border, screen, informal hedge	—	The most cold-hardy hibiscus; many cultivars; tolerates alkaline soil
Hibiscus tiliaceus	Tree	Hot Z 10-12	12 ft 4 m	20 ft 6 m	25 ft 8 m	Everg	—	Flowers (yellow & purple, most of year)	Coastal planting, lawn specimen, parks, streets	—	Tolerates soil salinity
Hippophae rhamnoides	Shrub	Cool Z 2-9	5 ft 1.5 m	8 ft 2.5 m	10 ft 3 m	Decid	Yes	Silvery foliage; decorative fruit	Seashore and streamside planting, shrub border	—	Male and female plants required for fruit set
Hoheria lyallii	Tree	Cool Z 8-9	5 ft 1.5 m	10 ft 3 m	15 ft 5 m	Everg	—	Flowers (white, fragrant, late summer)	Shrub border, lawn specimen	—	—

NAME	KIND	CLIMATE & ZONE	HEIGHT AT 5 yrs	10 yrs	20 yrs	DECIDUOUS EVERGREEN	ARID CLIMATES	CHIEF ATTRACTIONS	USES	DRAWBACKS	COMMENTS
Hoheria populnea	Tree	Warm Z 9-10	5 ft 1.5 m	12 ft 4 m	20 ft 6 m	Everg	—	Flowers (white, late summer-early autumn)	Shrub border, lawn specimen, screen, windbreak	—	Likes semi-shade; variegated cvs popular
Hoheria sexstylosa	Tree	Cool Z 8-10	5 ft 1.5 m	12 ft 4 m	20 ft 6 m	Everg	—	Flowers (white, fragrant, late summer)-autumn	Shrub border, lawn specimen	—	Likes semi-shade
Holmskioldia sanguinea	Shrub	Warm Z 10-12	8 ft 2.5m	10 ft 3 m	10 ft 3 m	Everg	—	Flowers (yellow to scarlet, summer-autumn)	Shrub border, courtyard, espalier	—	Unusual flower structure; several colour-forms available
Hovenia dulcis	Tree	Cool Z 8-10	8 ft 2.5m	15 ft 5 m	25 ft 8 m	Decid	—	Edible fruit stalks; autumn foliage	Lawn specimen	—	Fruit stalks become sweet as capsules ripen, taste like raisins
Howea forsteriana	Tree	Warm Z 10-11	3 ft 1 m	6 ft 2 m	10 ft 3 m	Everg	—	Foliage	Indoor, courtyard, container, swimming pool	Very slow-growing	The most widely grown potted palm
Hydrangea aspera	Shrub	Cool Z 7-9	4 ft 1.2 m	6 ft 2 m	8 ft 2.5 m	Decid	—	Flowers (mauve & blue, summer)	Shrub border, courtyard	—	Several subspecies grown; colour does not vary with soil
Hydrangea macrophylla	Shrub	Cool Z 6-10	4 ft 1.2 m	6 ft 2 m	6 ft 2 m	Decid	—	Flowers (pink or blue, summer)	Shrub border, courtyard, conservatory, cut flowers	—	The common hydrangeas (Hortensia group); flower colour varies with soil
Hydrangea paniculata	Shrub	Cool Z 4-9	4 ft 1.2 m	8 ft 2.5 m	8 ft 2.5 m	Decid	—	Flowers (cream, midsummer)	Shrub border, courtyard	—	Can be pruned hard in early spring for larger flower heads
Hydrangea quercifolia	Shrub	Cool Z 5-10	4 ft 1.2 m	5 ft 1.5 m	6 ft 2 m	Decid	—	Autumn foliage; flowers (cream, midsummer-mid-autumn)	Shrub border, courtyard	—	Likes semi-shade
Hymenosporum flavum	Tree	Warm Z 9-11	8 ft 2.5m	15 ft 5 m	25 ft 8 m	Everg	—	Flowers (cream aging gold, spring)	Shrub border, lawn specimen, streets	—	Excellent tree for small gardens
Hypericum beanii	Shrub	Cool Z 5-9	3 ft 1 m	5 ft 1.5 m	6 ft 2 m	Everg	—	Flowers (yellow, summer)	Shrub border, embankments, courtyards	—	Tolerates shade (most hypericums)
Hypericum calycinum	Shrub	Cool Z 4-9	1 ft 0.3 m	1 ft 0.3 m	1 ft 0.3 m	Everg	—	Flowers (yellow, summer)	Groundcover, shaded embankments, woodland garden	Prone to spider mite	Spreads by runners to cover large area
Hypericum kouytchense	Shrub	Cool Z 5-9	3 ft 1 m	4 ft 1.2 m	5 ft 1.5 m	Everg	—	Flowers (yellow, summer)	Shrub border, courtyard, embankment	—	Forms broad mound
Hypericum monogynum (chinense)	Shrub	Cool Z 7-10	2 ft 0.6 m	2 ft 0.6 m	3 ft 1 m	Everg	—	Flowers (yellow, summer)	Shrub border, courtyard, embankment, rock garden	—	A low-growing form is used as a groundcover
Hypericum patulum	Shrub	Cool Z 7-10	3 ft 1 m	5 ft 1.5 m	5 ft 1.5 m	Everg	—	Flowers (yellow, midsummer)	Shrub border, courtyard, woodland garden	—	Larger-flowered cvs 'Hidcote' & 'Rowallane' most popular
Hypericum revolutum	Shrub	Warm Z 9-11	6 ft 2 m	8 ft 2.5 m	8 ft 2.5 m	Everg	—	Flowers (yellow, spring-summer)	Shrub border, informal hedge	—	Smallish flowers; crushed or wet foliage smells like curry
Iboza riparia	Shrub	Warm Z 10-11	4 ft 1.2 m	6 ft 2 m	8 ft 2.5 m	Everg	—	Flowers (pale pink, aromatic, winter-early spring)	Shrub border, courtyard, swimming pool	Sometimes short-lived	Foliage sticky & aromatic
Idesia polycarpa	Tree	Cool Z 8-10	8 ft 2.5m	20 ft 6 m	30 ft 9 m	Decid	—	Foliage; decorative fruit	Lawn specimen, streets	—	Only female plants produce fruit; male plant needed also
Ilex × altaclarensis	Tree	Cool Z 5-10	8 ft 2.5m	15 ft 5 m	25 ft 8 m	Everg	—	Foliage; decorative fruit (summer)	Shrub border, lawn specimen, screens, cut foliage & berries	—	Many cvs, most with variegated leaves, some male, some female (fruiting)
Ilex aquifolium	Tree	Cool Z 5-10	6 ft 2 m	12 ft 4 m	20 ft 6 m	Everg	—	Foliage; decorative fruit (summer)	Shrub border, lawn specimen, screens, cut foliage & berries	—	Many cvs, especially with variegated leaves, some male, some female (fruiting)
Ilex cornuta	Shrub	Cool Z 4-10	3 ft 1 m	6 ft 2 m	12 ft 4 m	Everg	—	Foliage; decorative fruit (summer)	Shrub border, courtyard, hedge	—	Fruits well in warmer climates, fruiting through summer
Ilex crenata	Shrub	Cool Z 4-9	4 ft 1.2 m	6 ft 2 m	8 ft 2.5 m	Everg	—	Foliage, decorative fruit	Formal hedge, topiary, courtyard, rock garden, containers	—	Many cultivars, varying in colour, leaf size and stature
Ilex decidua	Shrub	Cool Z 5-9	5 ft 1.5 m	8 ft 2.5 m	10 ft 3 m	Decid	—	Decorative fruit	Shrub border	—	Berries persist on branches through winter
Ilex glabra	Tree	Warm Z 3-9	5 ft 1.5 m	8 ft 2.5 m	10 ft 3 m	Everg	—	Foliage, decorative fruit	Shrub border, informal hedge	—	A number of cultivars available
Ilex opaca	Tree	Cool Z 4-9	6 ft 2 m	12 ft 4 m	20 ft 6 m	Everg	—	Decorative fruit	Shrub border, lawn specimen, hedge	—	—
Ilex paraguariensis	Tree	Warm Z 9-11	6 ft 2 m	10 ft 3 m	15 ft 5 m	Everg	—	Foliage	Beverage from leaves	—	Maté, caffeine-rich beverage from dried leaves, is Argentina's national beverage
Ilex pernyi	Tree	Cool Z 4-9	6 ft 2 m	10 ft 3 m	15 ft 5 m	Everg	—	Foliage; decorative fruit	Shrub border, lawn specimen, cut foliage with berries	—	Small neat leaves have interesting shape
Ilex serrata	Shrub	Cool Z 5-9	5 ft 1.5 m	8 ft 2.5 m	10 ft 3 m	Decid	—	Decorative fruit; autumn foliage	Shrub border, lawn specimen, cut stems with berries	—	Tiny red berries in dense clusters, make good show
Ilex verticillata	Shrub	Cool Z 4-9	5 ft 1.5 m	8 ft 2.5 m	10 ft 3 m	Decid	—	Decorative fruit; spring & autumn foliage	Shrub border, cut stems with berries	—	Bright red berries persist on bare branches
Ilex vomitoria	Tree	Cool Z 6-9	6 ft 2 m	10 ft 3 m	15 ft 5 m	Everg	—	Decorative fruit; foliage	Shrub border, cut foliage with berries	—	Leaves contain an emetic drug

NAME	KIND	CLIMATE & ZONE	HEIGHT AT 5yrs 10yrs 20yrs	DECIDUOUS EVERGREEN	ARID CLIMATES	CHIEF ATTRACTIONS	USES	DRAWBACKS	COMMENTS
Illicium anisatum	Shrub	Cool Z 8-10	6 ft / 2 m, 10 ft / 3 m, 15 ft / 5 m	Everg	—	Flowers (white, fragrant, spring)	Shrub border, woodland garden, incense from bark	Woody fruit poisonous	Has been confused with the true star anise (*I. verum*)
Illicium floridanum	Shrub	Cool Z 8-10	2 ft / 0.6 m, 4 ft / 1.2 m, 6 ft / 2 m	Everg	—	Flowers (red, late spring-early summer)	Shrub border, woodland garden	—	—
Indigofera decora	Shrub	Cool Z 8-10	2 ft / 0.6 m, 2 ft / 0.6 m, 2 ft / 0.6 m	Decid	—	Flowers (mauve-pink, spring-autumn)	Shrub border, courtyard, rock garden	—	Spreads by root suckers into broad clump
Iochroma cyaneum	Shrub	Warm Z 10-11	5 ft / 1.5 m, 8 ft / 2.5 m, 8 ft / 2.5 m	Everg	—	Flowers (violet, summer-autumn)	Shrub border, courtyard, containers	—	Can be cut back in spring to keep compact
Iochroma grandiflorum	Shrub	Warm Z 9-11	6 ft / 2 m, 10 ft / 3 m, 12 ft / 4 m	Everg	—	Flowers (purple, late summer-autumn)	Shrub border, courtyard	—	Can be cut back in spring to keep compact
Isopogon anemonifolius	Shrub	Warm Z 9-11	4 ft / 1.2 m, 5 ft / 1.5 m, 6 ft / 2 m	Everg	—	Flowers (cream, spring)	Shrub border, courtyard, coastal planting, rock garden, cut flowers	—	Woody spherical fruiting heads
Itea virginica	Shrub	Cool Z 3-9	4 ft / 1.2 m, 5 ft / 1.5 m, 6 ft / 2 m	Decid	—	Flowers (white, fragrant, summer); autumn foliage	Shrub border, woodland garden, boggy areas	—	—
Ixora chinensis	Shrub	Warm Z 10-12	2 ft / 0.6 m, 3 ft / 1 m, 4 ft / 1.2 m	Everg	—	Flowers (orange-red, spring to autumn)	Containers, courtyards, hedge, plazas	—	Many cultivars; likes shade in hot climates
Ixora coccinea	Shrub	Warm Z 10-12	2 ft / 0.6 m, 3 ft / 1 m, 3 ft / 1 m	Everg	—	Flowers (scarlet, spring-summer)	Containers, courtyards, swimming pool, plazas	—	Many cultivars; likes shade in hot climates
Ixora 'Sunkist'	Shrub	Hot Z 11-12	2 ft / 0.6 m, 2 ft / 0.6 m, 2 ft / 0.6 m	Everg	—	Flowers (apricot aging red, most of year)	Containers, courtyard, plazas, swimming pools	—	—
Jacaranda mimosifolia	Tree	Warm Z 10-11	10 ft / 3 m, 20 ft / 6 m, 30 ft / 9 m	Decid*	Yes	Flowers (mauve-blue, late spring)	Lawn specimen, parks, streets	—	Leaves turn gold and are shed in early spring; flowers poorly in tropical lowlands
Jasminum mesnyi	Shrub	Warm Z 6-10	5 ft / 1.5 m, 8 ft / 2.5 m, 8 ft / 2.5 m	Everg	Yes	Flowers (yellow, late winter-early spring)	Shrub border, informal hedge, lawn specimen, cut flowers	—	Fountain-like habit; dead stems should be removed periodically
Jasminum officinale	Shrub	Warm Z 6-10	4 ft / 1.2 m, 5 ft / 1.5 m, 5 ft / 1.5 m	Decid	—	Flowers (white, fragrant, summer-autumn)	Courtyards, containers, swimming pools, espalier	—	—
Jatropha integerrima	Shrub	Hot Z 10-12	8 ft / 2.5 m, 10 ft / 3 m, 15 ft / 5 m	Everg	Yes	Flowers (red, most of year)	Shrub border, courtyard	—	Grown primarily for its red flowers, unlike other jatrophas
Jatropha multifida	Shrub	Hot Z 10-12	4 ft / 1.2 m, 5 ft / 1.5 m, 6 ft / 2 m	Everg	Yes	Foliage; flowers (red, most of year)	Shrub border, courtyard, rock garden	Highly poisonous	Lacy dissected leaves
Jubaea chilensis	Palm	Warm Z 9-11	5 ft / 1.5 m, 10 ft / 3 m, 20 ft / 6 m	Everg	—	Massive trunk	Lawn specimen, parks, avenues	Early growth very slow	Sap was extracted to make syrup or wine
Juglans ailantifolia	Tree	Cool Z 5-9	8 ft / 2.5 m, 12 ft / 4 m, 25 ft / 8 m	Decid	—	Edible nuts, foliage	Parks, timber	Fruit husk is poisonous	—
Juglans cinerea	Tree	Cool Z 2-9	8 ft / 2.5 m, 15 ft / 5 m, 30 ft / 9 m	Decid	—	Edible nuts, foliage	Parks, timber	Leaf litter toxic to other plants (most *Juglans* spp.)	—
Juglans nigra	Tree	Cool Z 3-9	10 ft / 3 m, 20 ft / 6 m, 40 ft / 12 m	Decid	—	Edible nuts, foliage	Orchard, parks, timber	—	—
Juglans regia	Tree	Cool Z 4-9	8 ft / 2.5 m, 15 ft / 5 m, 25 ft / 8 m	Decid	—	Edible nuts	Orchard, timber	—	Husks yield a black dye; named cultivars preferred for nuts
Juniperus chinensis	Tree	Cool Z 4-10	8 ft / 2.5 m, 15 ft / 5 m, 25 ft / 8 m	Everg	—	Foliage	Lawn specimen, parks, shrub border (cultivars)	—	Many lower-growing cultivars
Juniperus communis	Tree	Cool Z 2-9	4 ft / 1.2 m, 8 ft / 2.5 m, 15 ft / 5 m	Everg	—	Foliage	Shrub border, hedges, berries used for flavouring	Dead foliage builds up among branches	Columnar and dwarf cultivars mostly grown
Juniperus conferta	Shrub	Cool Z 5-10	1 ft / 0.3 m, 1 ft / 0.3 m, 1 ft / 0.3 m	Everg	—	Foliage	Groundcover, coastal planting, rock garden	—	Creeps over coastal dunes in its native NE Asia
Juniperus deppeana var. pachyphlaea	Tree	Cool Z 4-10	6 ft / 2 m, 10 ft / 3 m, 15 ft / 5 m	Everg	Yes	Foliage; bark	Shrub border, lawn specimen	—	Bark has interesting pattern of square scales
Juniperus horizontalis	Tree	Cool Z 4-9	1 ft / 0.3 m, 2 ft / 0.6 m, 2 ft / 0.6 m	Everg	—	Foliage	Groundcover, rock garden, embankments	—	Many cultivars, some fully prostrate
Juniperus × media	Tree	Cool Z 4-10	5 ft / 1.5 m, 8 ft / 2.5 m, 10 ft / 3 m	Everg	—	Foliage	Lawn specimen, shrub border	—	'Pfitzeriana' is the most popular of many cvs
Juniperus monosperma	Tree	Cool Z 6-9	5 ft / 1.5 m, 10 ft / 3 m, 15 ft / 5 m	Everg	Yes	Foliage; decorative fruit	Lawn specimen	Prickly juvenile foliage	—
Juniperus procumbens	Tree	Cool Z 4-10	1 ft / 0.3 m, 2 ft / 0.6 m, 3 ft / 1 m	Everg	—	Foliage	Groundcover, embankments	—	—
Juniperus recurva	Tree	Cool Z 7-9	5 ft / 1.5 m, 10 ft / 3 m, 20 ft / 6 m	Everg	—	Weeping foliage; decorative fruit	Lawn specimen	—	Cultivar 'Coxii' is the form commonly grown
Juniperus rigida	Tree	Cool Z 4-9	5 ft / 1.5 m, 10 ft / 3 m, 15 ft / 5 m	Everg	—	Weeping foliage; decorative fruit	Shrub border, lawn specimen, courtyard	Foliage very prickly	—
Juniperus sabina	Shrub	Cool Z 3-10	2 ft / 0.6 m, 4 ft / 1.2 m, 6 ft / 2 m	Everg	—	Foliage	Shrub border, groundcover, embankments, plazas	Bruised foliage smells unpleasant	Low-growing 'Tamariscifolia' is the form commonly planted
Juniperus scopulorum	Tree	Cool Z 3-9	6 ft / 2 m, 12 ft / 4 m, 20 ft / 6 m	Everg	—	Foliage; bark; decorative fruit	Shrub border, rock garden, courtyard	—	Dwarf and prostrate cultivars most commonly grown
Juniperus squamata	Shrub	Cool Z 4-9	5 ft / 1.5 m, 10 ft / 3 m, 15 ft / 5 m	Everg	—	Foliage	Shrub border, rock garden, courtyard	—	'Meyeri' is most widely grown, also dwarf cultivars
Juniperus virginiana	Tree	Cool Z 2-10	6 ft / 2 m, 12 ft / 4 m, 25 ft / 8 m	Everg	—	Foliage; symmetrical shape; decorative fruit	Shrub border, lawn specimen, timber	—	Wood used for pencils; many cvs available

NAME	KIND	CLIMATE & ZONE	HEIGHT AT 5 yrs	10 yrs	20 yrs	DECIDUOUS EVERGREEN	ARID CLIMATES	CHIEF ATTRACTIONS	USES	DRAWBACKS	COMMENTS
Justicia spicigera	Shrub	Warm Z 10-12	4 ft 1.2 m	6 ft 2 m	6 ft 2 m	Everg	—	Flowers (orange, spring-autumn)	Shrub border, courtyard, swimming pool	—	Soft-stemmed shrubs, easily damaged
Kalmia angustifolia	Shrub	Cool Z 2-9	2 ft 0.6 m	3 ft 1 m	3 ft 1 m	Everg	—	Flowers (pink, late spring-early summer)	Shrub border, courtyard, rock garden, woodland garden	Foliage poisonous to livestock	—
Kalmia latifolia	Shrub	Cool Z 3-9	3 ft 1 m	5 ft 1.5 m	6 ft 2 m	Everg	—	Flowers (pink, mid spring-early summer)	Shrub border, courtyard, woodland garden	Foliage poisonous to livestock	Many cultivars now available, mostly in deeper colours
Kalopanax septemlobus	Tree	Cool Z 5-9	8 ft 2.5m	20 ft 6 m	30 ft 9 m	Decid	—	Flowers (white, summer); decorative fruit; foliage	Lawn specimen, parks, shade	Trunk & branches may be prickly	Distinctive large lobed leaves & radiating flower heads
Kerria japonica	Shrub	Cool Z 5-10	4 ft 1.2 m	6 ft 2 m	6 ft 2 m	Decid	—	Flowers (yellow, spring)	Shrub border, courtyard	—	Double-flowered cultivar is most commonly grown
Kigelia africana	Tree	Warm Z 10-12	8 ft 2.5m	15 ft 5 m	25 ft 8 m	Decid*	Yes	Flowers (dark red, most of year); curious fruit	Parks, lawn specimen	Woody fruits litter ground	Grown mainly as a curiosity, for its striking long-stalked fruit
Kingia australis	Shrub	Warm Z 9-10	1 ft 0.3 m	2 ft 0.6 m	3 ft 1 m	Everg	—	Grassy foliage, symmetrical form	Courtyard, container, rock garden	—	Extremely slow-growing, may reach 1,000 years old
Koelreuteria bipinnata	Tree	Cool Z 8-10	10 ft 3 m	20 ft 6 m	30 ft 9 m	Decid	—	Foliage; flowers (yellow, summer); decorative fruit	Lawn specimen, parks, streets	—	Has tallest flower & fruit panicles among koelreuterias
Koelreuteria elegans	Tree	Warm Z 9-11	8 ft 2.5m	15 ft 5 m	25 ft 8 m	Decid	—	Foliage; flowers (yellow, late summer-autumn); decorative fruit	Lawn specimen, parks, streets	—	Suits humid tropical & subtropical climates
Koelreuteria paniculata	Tree	Cool Z 4-9	8 ft 2.5m	15 ft 5 m	25 ft 8 m	Decid	—	Flowers (yellow, summer); decorative fruit; autumn foliage	Lawn specimen, parks, streets	—	Requires full sun; tolerates alkaline soil, city conditions
Kolkwitzia amabilis	Shrub	Cool Z 4-9	6 ft 2 m	8 ft 2.5 m	8 ft 2.5 m	Decid	—	Flowers (pink, spring)	Shrub border; informal hedge	—	Dense mass of untidy canes but beautiful in full bloom
Kunzea baxteri	Shrub	Warm Z 9-10	5 ft 1.5 m	8 ft 2.5 m	8 ft 2.5 m	Everg	Yes	Flowers (crimson, spring-early summer)	Shrub border; seaside planting	Straggly, often short-lived	Attracts nectar-feeding birds
Kunzea parvifolia	Shrub	Cool Z 8-10	3 ft 1 m	5 ft 1.5 m	5 ft 1.5 m	Everg	—	Flowers (mauve, late spring-early summer)	Shrub border, rock garden, boggy areas	—	Flowers tiny but profuse
× Laburnocytisus adamii	Tree	Cool Z 4-9	8 ft 2.5m	12 ft 4 m	15 ft 5 m	Decid	—	Flowers (yellow & pink, late spring-early summer)	Shrub border, courtyard	—	One of the few known *graft hybrids*, a pretty curiosity
Laburnum alpinum	Tree	Cool Z 3-8	6 ft 2 m	12 ft 4 m	15 ft 5 m	Decid	—	Flowers (yellow, spring-summer)	Lawn specimen	Prone to insect & snail damage (all laburnums)	—
Laburnum anagyroides	Tree	Cool Z 3-8	6 ft 2 m	12 ft 4 m	15 ft 5 m	Decid	—	Flowers (yellow, late spring-early summer)	Lawn specimen	Leaves & seeds poisonous (all laburnums)	May be trained over trellis to make a 'laburnum arch'
Laburnum × watereri	Tree	Cool Z 3-9	8 ft 2.5m	15 ft 5 m	20 ft 6 m	Decid	—	Flowers (yellow, late spring-early summer)	Lawn specimen, espalier	—	May be trained over trellis to make a 'laburnum arch'
Lagarostrobos franklinii	Tree	Cool Z 8-9	3 ft 1 m	6 ft 2 m	10 ft 3 m	Everg	—	Foliage	Lawn specimen, woodland garden, waters-edge, container, bonsai	Very slow growing	Long-lived in the wild, some trees over 2,000 years old
Lagerstroemia indica	Tree	Warm Z 6-11	6 ft 2 m	12 ft 4 m	20 ft 6 m	Decid	Yes	Flowers (white to dark red, summer); bark	Lawn specimen, streets	Suffers from leaf mildew in summer	Many cultivars, some of hybrid origin
Lagerstroemia speciosa	Tree	Hot Z 11-12	8 ft 2.5m	15 ft 5 m	30 ft 9 m	Decid*	Yes	Flowers (pink to purple, summer-autumn)	Lawn specimen, parks, streets	—	—
Lagunaria patersonia	Tree	Warm Z 10-11	6 ft 2 m	12 ft 4 m	20 ft 6 m	Everg	—	Flowers (pink, summer)	Lawn specimen, parks, streets, coastal lanting	Irritant hairs in seed capsules	Hibiscus-like flowers age to paler pink
Larix decidua	Tree	Cold Z 2-8	10 ft 3 m	20 ft 6 m	40 ft 12 m	Decid	—	Weeping foliage; autumn colour	Timber, lawn specimen, parks, shelter	Prone to diseases & insect attack	Unsuited to mild or warm climates
Larix gmelinii	Tree	Cold Z 2-8	10 ft 3 m	20 ft 6 m	40 ft 12 m	Decid	—	Foliage	Timber, lawn specimen, parks	—	Requires a climate with very cold winter
Larix kaempferi	Tree	Cool Z 4-9	10 ft 3 m	20 ft 6 m	40 ft 12 m	Decid	—	Foliage, vigorous growth	Timber, lawn specimen, parks	—	One of the most ornamental larches, adapts to mild climate
Larix laricina	Tree	Cold Z 2-8	10 ft 3 m	20 ft 6 m	30 ft 9 m	Decid	—	Autumn foliage	Timber, boggy areas	—	—
Larix potaninii	Tree	Cool Z 4-9	10 ft 3 m	20 ft 6 m	30 ft 9 m	Decid	—	Autumn foliage	Timber, parks, lawn specimen	—	Similar to *L. decidua*; crushed leaves distinctively aromatic
Laurus azorica	Tree	Cool Z 8-10	8 ft 2.5m	15 ft 5 m	25 ft 8 m	Everg	Yes	Foliage; flowers (yellow-green, spring)	Lawn specimen, hedge, screen, container	—	Male & female flowers on different trees, male more conspicuous
Laurus nobilis	Tree	Cool Z 8-10	6 ft 2 m	12 ft 4 m	20 ft 6 m	Everg	Yes	Aromatic foliage; flowers (yellow, fragrant, spring)	Lawn specimen, hedge, screen, container, culinary herb	—	Dried leaves used as flavouring herb; good subject for topiary
Lavandula angustifolia	Shrub	Cool Z 6-10	2 ft 0.6 m	2 ft 0.6 m	2 ft 0.6 m	Everg	Yes	Flowers (purple, spring-autumn); aromatic foliage	Herbaceous border, rock garden, container	Can be short-lived	The lavender grown commercially for perfumery
Lavandula dentata	Shrub	Cool Z 7-10	2 ft 0.6 m	3 ft 1 m	3 ft 1 m	Everg	Yes	Flowers (mauve-blue, autumn-spring); aromatic foliage	Shrub border, low hedge, container, cut flowers, coastal planting	—	—
Lavandula latifolia	Shrub	Cool Z 7-10	2 ft 0.6 m	2 ft 0.6 m	2 ft 0.6 m	Everg	Yes	Flowers (purple, summer); aromatic foliage	Herbaceous border, rock garden, container, coastal planting, low hedge	—	—

NAME	KIND	CLIMATE & ZONE	HEIGHT AT 5yrs	10yrs	20yrs	DECIDUOUS EVERGREEN	ARID CLIMATES	CHIEF ATTRACTIONS	USES	DRAWBACKS	COMMENTS
Lavandula stoechas	Shrub	Warm Z 8-10	2 ft 0.6 m	2 ft 0.6 m	2 ft 0.6 m	Everg	Yes	Flowers (purple, spring-early summer)	Herbaceous border, rock garden, container, coastal planting	—	Distinctive for 'crown' of large bracts at top of flower spike
Lawsonia inermis	Shrub	Hot Z 11-12	5 ft 1.5 m	8 ft 2.5 m	12 ft 4 m	Everg	Yes	Flowers (pink or red, fragrant)	Shrub border, dye from leaves	—	Source of henna hair dye
Lepidozamia peroffskyana	Cycad	Warm Z 10-11	3 ft 1 m	5 ft 1.5 m	6 ft 2 m	Everg	—	Foliage, symmetrical form	Courtyard, plaza, rainforest garden, container	Very slow-growing	Giant cones; glossy leaves less prickly than other cycads
Leptospermum laevigatum	Shrub	Warm Z 9-11	8 ft 2.5m	12 ft 4 m	20 ft 6 m	Everg	—	Flowers (white, spring-early summer)	Coastal planting, informal hedge, screen, windbreak	Can become a weed in some countries	Trunk becomes gnarled & twisted with age
Leptospermum petersonii	Tree	Warm Z 9-11	6 ft 2 m	10 ft 3 m	15 ft 5 m	Everg	—	Aromatic foliage; flowers (white, spring-early summer)	Shrub border, lawn specimen, streets, screen	—	Crushed foliage strongly lemon-scented
Leptospermum scoparium	Shrub	Warm Z 8-11	6 ft 2 m	8 ft 2.5 m	10 ft 3 m	Everg	—	Flowers (white, pink or red, late winter-summer)	Shrub border, informal hedge, courtyard, container	Can be short-lived	Many cultivars, some double; dwarf cvs suit rock gardens
Lespedeza thunbergii	Shrub	Cool Z 4-9	3 ft 1 m	5 ft 1.5 m	6 ft 2 m	Decid	—	Flowers (purple, late summer)	Shrub border, courtyard	—	Semi-herbaceous, stems die back in winter
Leucadendron argenteum	Tree	Warm Z 9-10	5 ft 1.5 m	10 ft 3 m	20 ft 6 m	Everg	—	Foliage	Shrub border, lawn specimen, screen, cut foliage	Prone to sudden death from root rot	One of the most striking of all silver-foliaged plants
Leucadendron comosum	Shrub	Warm Z 9-10	4 ft 1.2 m	5 ft 1.5 m	5 ft 1.5 m	Everg	—	Flowers (red & yellow, spring)	Cut flowers, shrub border, courtyard	—	Prefers winter-rainfall climate, needs good drainage
Leucadendron eucalyptifolium	Shrub	Warm Z 9-10	6 ft 2 m	10 ft 3 m	12 ft 4 m	Everg	—	Flowers (yellow, winter-spring)	Cut flowers, shrub border, courtyard	—	One of the most easily grown leucadendrons
Leucadendron 'Safari Sunset'	Shrub	Warm Z 9-10	4 ft 1.2 m	5 ft 1.5 m	5 ft 1.5 m	Everg	—	Flowers (deep red, autumn-winter)	Cut flowers, shrub border, courtyard	—	Important cut flower variety, fairly frost-hardy
Leucadendron salignum	Shrub	Warm Z 9-10	2 ft 0.6 m	3 ft 1 m	3 ft 1 m	Everg	—	Flowers (yellow, autumn-spring)	Cut flowers, shrub border, courtyard	—	Prefers winter-rainfall climate, needs good drainage
Leucadendron tinctum	Shrub	Warm Z 9-10	2 ft 0.6 m	3 ft 1 m	3 ft 1 m	Everg	—	Flowers (pink-red, winter)	Cut flowers, shrub border, courtyard	—	Wind & frost tolerant
Leucospermum cordifolium	Shrub	Warm Z 9-10	4 ft 1.2 m	5 ft 1.5 m	6 ft 2 m	Everg	—	Flowers (yellow & red, late winter-early summer)	Cut flowers, shrub border	Can be short-lived, easily wind-damaged	—
Leucospermum erubescens	Shrub	Warm Z 9-10	4 ft 1.2 m	6 ft 2 m	6 ft 2 m	Everg	—	Flowers (yellow to pink, late winter-early summer)	Shrub border	—	Rare species
Leucospermum reflexum	Shrub	Warm Z 9-10	6 ft 2 m	10 ft 3 m	10 ft 3 m	Everg	—	Flowers (red & yellow, spring-summer)	Cut flowers, shrub border	Easily damaged by wind	Highly distinctive downward slanting flowers
Leucospermum tottum	Shrub	Warm Z 9-10	4 ft 1.2 m	5 ft 1.5 m	5 ft 1.5 m	Everg	—	Flowers (scarlet & cream, spring-summer)	Cut flowers, shrub border	—	Parent of some hybrid cultivars
Leucothoe fontanesiana	Shrub	Cool Z 6-10	3 ft 1 m	4 ft 1.2 m	5 ft 1.5 m	Everg	—	Flowers (white or pink, spring)	Shrub border, courtyard, woodland garden	—	Spreads by basal suckers; branches droop attractively
Libocedrus plumosa	Tree	Cool Z 8-9	5 ft 1.5 m	10 ft 3 m	20 ft 6 m	Everg	—	Foliage; columnar form	Lawn specimen, group, courtyard, container	—	Likes sheltered position, semi-shade; picturesque with age
Ligustrum japonicum	Shrub	Cool Z 6-10	5 ft 1.5 m	8 ft 2.5 m	10 ft 3 m	Everg	—	Foliage; flowers (white, midsummer-early autumn); decorative fruit	Shrub border, lawn specimen, hedge, container	—	One of the least invasive privet species
Ligustrum lucidum	Tree	Warm Z 6-11	12 ft 4 m	20 ft 6 m	30 ft 9 m	Everg	—	Flowers (white, late summer-early autumn); decorative fruit	Shrub border, lawn specimen, streets, hedge	Can become invasive in mild wet climates	Variegated cultivars less likely to be a problem
Ligustrum ovalifolium	Shrub	Cool Z 5-10	8 ft 2.5m	10 ft 3 m	12 ft 4 m	Everg	—	Foliage	Shrub border, hedge, cut foliage	Flowers suspected of causing hay-fever	Cultivar 'Aureum' is commonly grown (prune out green branches)
Ligustrum vulgare	Shrub	Cool Z 3-9	6 ft 2 m	8 ft 2.5 m	10 ft 3 m	Decid	—	Flowers (white, fragrant, summmer); decorative fruit	Shrub border, hedge	Can become invasive in cooler climates	—
Lindera benzoin	Shrub	Cool Z 2-9	5 ft 1.5 m	8 ft 2.5 m	10 ft 3 m	Decid	—	Autumn foliage; decorative fruit	Shrub border, woodland garden	—	Source of gum benzoin, used in perfumery
Lindera obtusiloba	Shrub	Cool Z 4-9	5 ft 1.5 m	10 ft 3 m	20 ft 6 m	Decid	—	Autumn foliage; decorative fruit	Shrub border, lawn specimen, woodland garden	—	Male & female flowers on separate trees
Liquidambar formosana	Tree	Cool Z 7-10	10 ft 3 m	20 ft 6 m	40 ft 12 m	Decid	—	Summer & autumn foliage	Lawn specimen, parks, timber	—	New growth attractively bronze-tinted
Liquidambar orientalis	Tree	Cool Z 5-10	8 ft 2.5m	15 ft 5 m	30 ft 9 m	Decid	—	Autumn foliage; dense spreading habit	Lawn specimen, parks, streets, shade	—	Source of storax, a once valued resin
Liquidambar styraciflua	Tree	Cool Z 5-10	10 ft 3 m	25 ft 8 m	50 ft 15 m	Decid	—	Autumn foliage	Lawn specimen, parks, streets, shade, timber	Roots invasive	Colours well in autumn even in quite warm climates
Liriodendron chinense	Tree	Cool Z 4-10	10 ft 3 m	20 ft 6 m	40 ft 12 m	Decid	—	Autumn foliage; flowers (green & orange, midsummer)	Lawn specimen, parks, streets	—	Larger leaves than the more commonly grown L. tulipifera
Liriodendron tulipifera	Tree	Cool Z 3-10	12 ft 4 m	25 ft 8 m	50 ft 15 m	Decid	—	Autumn foliage; flowers (green & orange, midsummer)	Lawn specimen, parks, streets, timber	Difficult to transplant	Fast-growing, long-lived deciduous tree

NAME	KIND	CLIMATE & ZONE	HEIGHT AT 5yrs 10yrs 20yrs	DECIDUOUS EVERGREEN	ARID CLIMATES	CHIEF ATTRACTIONS	USES	DRAWBACKS	COMMENTS
Litchi chinensis	Tree	Hot Z 10-11	6 ft 12 ft 20 ft / 2 m 4 m 6 m	Everg	—	Edible fruit	Orchard, lawn specimen, courtyard	Slow-growing	For early fruiting a grafted or air-layered plant is superior
Lithocarpus densiflorus	Tree	Cool Z 6-9	6 ft 12 ft 25 ft / 2 m 4 m 8 m	Everg	—	Foliage	Lawn specimen, parks, streets, shade, tanbark	Slow-growing	New foliage coated with felty orange-brown hairs
Livistona australis	Palm	Warm Z 9-11	5 ft 10 ft 20 ft / 1.5 m 3 m 6 m	Everg	—	Foliage; symmetrical form; flowers (yellow, early spring)	Lawn grouping, streets, plazas	Scorched by hot winds; frond stalks spiny	Edible apical bud was eaten by Australian Aborigines
Livistona chinensis	Palm	Warm Z 8-12	4 ft 8 ft 15 ft / 1.2 m 2.5 m 5 m	Everg	—	Foliage; symmetrical form; decorative fruit	Lawn grouping, courtyard, plazas, container	Very slow height growth	China-blue fruit unusual among palms
Lobelia keniensis	Shrub	Warm Z 9-10	4 ft 8 ft — / 1.2 m 2.5 m	Everg	—	Foliage; massive flower-spike	Shrub border, conservatory	Dies after flowering	Very rare in cultivation, a spectacular plant
Lomatia ferruginea	Tree	Cool Z 8-9	6 ft 12 ft 20 ft / 2 m 4 m 6 m	Everg	—	Foliage; flowers (red & yellow, late winter-spring)	Lawn specimen, shrub border	—	Likes a dry summer climate
Lomatia tinctoria	Shrub	Cool Z 8-10	3 ft 3 ft 3 ft / 1 m 1 m 1 m	Everg	—	Flowers (white, summer); foliage	Shrub border, courtyard, dried arrangements (fruit)	—	Spreads by basal suckers, free-flowering
Lonicera fragrantissima	Shrub	Cool Z 4-10	6 ft 8 ft 10 ft / 2 m 2.5 m 3 m	Decid	Yes	Flowers (cream, fragrant, winter-early spring)	Shrub border, courtyard	Untidy habit	Semi-evergreen in warmer climates; very fragrant
Lonicera ledebourii	Shrub	Cool Z 7-10	5 ft 6 ft 8 ft / 1.5 m 2 m 2.5 m	Everg	Yes	Flowers (yellow & orange, early summer); decorative fruit	Shrub border, cut flowers	—	Unusual flower structure for a lonicera, with coloured bracts
Lonicera nitida	Shrub	Cool Z 6-10	3 ft 4 ft 5 ft / 1 m 1.2 m 1.5 m	Everg	Yes	Foliage	Courtyard, hedge, topiary	Can be short-lived	Gold & variegated cultivars often grown
Lonicera tatarica	Shrub	Cool Z 2-9	4 ft 6 ft 8 ft / 1.2 m 2 m 2.5 m	Decid	—	Flowers (white to pink, late spring-early summer); decorative fruit	Shrub border, courtyard, hedge	—	—
Lophomyrtus (Myrtus) bullata	Tree	Warm Z 9-10	4 ft 6 ft 8 ft / 1.2 m 2 m 2.5 m	Everg	—	Foliage; flowers (cream, summer); decorative fruit	Shrub border, lawn specimen	—	Unusual crinkled leaves, reddish when grown in full sun
Lophomyrtus (Myrtus) obcordata	Shrub	Warm Z 8-10	3 ft 5 ft 6 ft / 1 m 1.5 m 2 m	Everg	—	Foliage; flowers (white, summer); decorative fruit	Shrub border, lawn specimen, hedge	—	Small leaves, turning purplish in winter
Lophomyrtus (Myrtus) × ralphii	Shrub	Warm Z 8-10	3 ft 5 ft 6 ft / 1 m 1.5 m 2 m	Everg	—	Foliage; bark	Shrub border, lawn specimen, hedge	—	Dwarf & variegated cultivars available
Lophostemon confertus	Tree	Warm Z 10-11	10 ft 20 ft 40 ft / 3 m 6 m 12 m	Everg	—	Foliage; flowers (white, late spring-early summer); bark	Parks, streets, timber	—	Widely used as street tree in Australia; variegated cvs exist
Loropetalum chinense	Shrub	Warm Z 8-10	3 ft 5 ft 6 ft / 1 m 1.5 m 2 m	Everg	—	Flowers (cream, fragrant, late winter-spring)	Shrub border, courtyard, espalier, embankment	—	Spreading dense, bushy habit
Luculia gratissima	Shrub	Warm Z 9-10	3 ft 5 ft 5 ft / 1 m 1.5 m 1.5 m	Everg	—	Flowers (pink, fragrant, autumn-midwinter)	Shrub border, courtyard	Prone to root root	Choice shrub; requires perfect drainage, reliable moisture
Luma apiculata (Myrtus luma)	Shrub	Cool Z 8-9	5 ft 10 ft 15 ft / 1.5 m 3 m 5 m	Everg	—	Flowers (white, summer); decorative fruit; bark	Shrub border, hedge, lawn specimen	—	—
Lyonothamnus floribundus	Tree	Warm Z 9-10	6 ft 12 ft 25 ft / 2 m 4 m 8 m	Everg	—	Flowers (white, early summer); foliage; bark	Lawn specimen, parks, coastal planting	—	Subsp. *aspleniifolius* is more widely grown: leaves fern-like
Macadamia tetraphylla	Tree	Warm Z 10-11	6 ft 12 ft 25 ft / 2 m 4 m 8 m	Everg	—	Edible nuts; flowers (white or pink, spring)	Orchard, lawn specimen, parks	Prickly leaves litter lawns	Australia's only commercial nut; named varieties preferred
Mackaya bella	Shrub	Warm Z 10-11	4 ft 8 ft 8 ft / 1.2 m 2.5 m 2.5 m	Everg	—	Flowers (pale lilac, spring-summer)	Shrub border, courtyard, swimming pool	—	Darker-veined flowers very attractive
Maclura pomifera	Tree	Cool Z 7-10	8 ft 15 ft 25 ft / 2.5 m 5 m 8 m	Decid	Yes	Foliage; curious fruit (inedible)	Farm hedges, timber	Milky sap can irritate skin	Male and female trees needed for fruit
Macropiper excelsum	Shrub	Warm Z 10-11	5 ft 8 ft 10 ft / 1.5 m 2.5 m 3 m	Everg	—	Foliage; decorative fruit	Courtyard, woodland garden	—	Striking large rounded leaves
Macrozamia communis	Cycad	Warm Z 9-11	2 ft 4 ft 6 ft / 0.6 m 1.2 m 2 m	Everg	—	Foliage; symmetrical form; striking cones and seeds	Courtyards, plazas, swimming pools, containers	Slow-growing; seeds poisonous	Male & female cones on different plants; seeds colourful
Macrozamia miquelii	Cycad	Warm Z 9-11	2 ft 4 ft 5 ft / 0.6 m 1.2 m 1.5 m	Everg	—	Foliage; symmetrical form; striking cones and seeds	Courtyards, plazas, swimming pools, containers	Slow-growing; seeds poisonous	Male & female cones on different plants; seeds colourful
Magnolia acuminata	Tree	Cool Z 4-9	6 ft 12 ft 25 ft / 2 m 4 m 8 m	Decid	—	Flowers (greenish-yellow, fragrant, early-midsummer)	Lawn specimen, parks, shade	—	Flowers less conspicuous than most magnolias
Magnolia campbellii	Tree	Cool Z 7-9	5 ft 10 ft 20 ft / 1.5 m 3 m 6 m	Decid	—	Flowers (pink, white or purple, late winter-mid-spring)	Lawn specimen, woodland garden	—	Seedlings may take 30 years to flower, grafted cultivars much sooner
Magnolia denudata (heptapeta)	Tree	Cool Z 5-10	6 ft 12 ft 20 ft / 2 m 4 m 6 m	Decid	—	Flowers (white, winter-early spring)	Lawn specimen, shrub border, courtyard	—	The finest white magnolia, long cultivated in China & Japan
Magnolia grandiflora	Tree	Warm Z 6-11	6 ft 12 ft 25 ft / 2 m 4 m 8 m	Everg	—	Flowers (white, summer); foliage	Lawn specimen, parks, streets	—	One of the largest-flowered magnolias; adapts to city conditions
Magnolia liliiflora (quinquepeta)	Shrub	Cool Z 5-10	5 ft 8 ft 10 ft / 1.5 m 2.5 m 3 m	Decid	—	Flowers (purple-pink, mid-spring-midsummer)	Shrub border	New leaves & flowers damaged by birds	Several cultivars available, often flowers out of season

NAME	KIND	CLIMATE & ZONE	HEIGHT AT 5 yrs	10 yrs	20 yrs	DECIDUOUS EVERGREEN	ARID CLIMATES	CHIEF ATTRACTIONS	USES	DRAWBACKS	COMMENTS
Magnolia × loebneri	Tree	Cool Z 5-9	6 ft 2 m	12 ft 4 m	20 ft 6 m	Decid	—	Flowers (white to pink, early-mid-spring)	Shrub border, lawn specimen	—	'Leonard Messel' is most commonly grown form
Magnolia macrophylla	Tree	Cool Z 4-9	6 ft 2 m	12 ft 4 m	25 ft 8 m	Decid	—	Huge leaves; flowers (white to yellow & purple, fragrant, midsummer)	Lawn specimen	—	Leaves can be up to 3 ft (1 m) long on saplings
Magnolia × soulangiana	Tree	Cool Z 4-9	6 ft 2 m	10 ft 3 m	20 ft 6 m	Decid	—	Flowers (white to pink or purple, late winter-mid-spring)	Shrub border, lawn specimen, courtyard	Flowers and new leaves damaged by birds	Many cultivars, varying in flower colouring
Magnolia sprengeri	Tree	Cool Z 5-9	6 ft 2 m	12 ft 4 m	25 ft 8 m	Decid	—	Flowers (pink, early-mid-spring)	Lawn specimen, woodland garden	Flowers and new leaves damaged by birds	'Diva' is the form most commonly grown
Magnolia stellata	Shrub	Cool Z 5-10	4 ft 1.2 m	6 ft 2 m	8 ft 2.5 m	Decid	—	Flowers (white, fragrant, late winter-early spring)	Shrub border, courtyard, container	Flowers easily scorched by sun	Distinctive starry flowers, borne from an early age
Magnolia virginiana	Tree	Cool Z 3-9	6 ft 2 m	10 ft 3 m	15 ft 5 m	Everg	—	Flowers (cream, fragrant, summer)	Shrub border, lawn specimen	—	Can be deciduous in cooler climates
Magnolia wilsonii	Tree	Cool Z 5-9	6 ft 2 m	10 ft 3 m	15 ft 5 m	Decid	—	Flowers (white, fragrant, late spring-early summer)	Shrub border, lawn specimen	—	Unusual downward facing, cup-shaped flowers
Mahonia aquifolium	Shrub	Cool Z 3-9	2 ft 0.6 m	3 ft 1 m	6 ft 2 m	Everg	Yes	Foliage; flowers (yellow, spring); decorative fruit	Shrub border, rock garden, courtyard, informal hedge	—	May spread by root suckers; leaves turn bronze in winter
Mahonia fremontii	Shrub	Cool Z 7-10	4 ft 1.2 m	6 ft 2 m	8 ft 2.5 m	Everg	Yes	Foliage; flowers (yellow, late winter-early spring); decorative fruit	Shrub border, informal hedge	—	Prickly foliage
Mahonia japonica	Shrub	Cool Z 6-10	3 ft 1 m	5 ft 1.5 m	6 ft 2 m	Everg	—	Foliage; flowers (yellow, autumn-spring); decorative fruit	Shrub border, courtyard	—	Prefers part-shade
Mahonia lomariifolia	Shrub	Cool Z 7-10	6 ft 2 m	10 ft 3 m	12 ft 4 m	Everg	—	Foliage; flowers (yellow, fragrant, late autumn-winter); decorative fruit	Shrub border, screen, courtyard	—	One of the tallest mahonias
Mahonia repens	Shrub	Cool Z 3-9	1 ft 0.3 m	1 ft 0.3 m	2 ft 0.6 m	Everg	—	Foliage; flowers (yellow, spring); decorative fruit	Groundcover, rock gardens, embankments	—	Leaves turn reddish or purplish in cold winters
Mallotus philippensis	Tree	Hot Z 10-12	12 ft 4 m	20 ft 6 m	30 ft 9 m	Everg	—	Foliage; decorative fruit	Parks, streets, source of a dye	—	Fruits have a red powdery resinous coating, used as a dye
Malpighia coccigera	Shrub	Hot Z 10-12	2 ft 0.6 m	3 ft 1 m	3 ft 1 m	Everg	—	Flowers (pink, summer); foliage; decorative/edible fruit	Shrub border, courtyard, hedge	—	Neat, attractive foliage, tolerates clipping
Malpighia glabra	Shrub	Hot Z 10-12	4 ft 1.2 m	6 ft 2 m	8 ft 2.5 m	Everg	—	Flowers (pink, summer); edible/decorative fruit	Shrub border, informal hedge	—	Fruit rich in vitamin C, acid flavour
Malus 'Aldenhamensis'	Tree	Cool Z 3-9	8 ft 2.5 m	12 ft 4 m	20 ft 6 m	Decid	—	Flowers (purple-red, spring); decorative fruit	Lawn specimen	Prone to fireblight (all *Malus*)	Purplish foliage
Malus coronaria	Tree	Cool Z 3-9	8 ft 2.5 m	15 ft 5 m	25 ft 8 m	Decid	—	Flowers (white, fragrant, early summer)	Lawn specimen	—	—
Malus × domestica	Tree	Cool Z 3-9	8 ft 2.5m	15 ft 5 m	20 ft 6 m	Decid	—	Edible fruit (apples); flowers (white & pink, spring)	Orchard	Prone to insect, fungal and bacterial attack	Hundreds of cultivars; several cultivars can be grafted on the one stock
Malus floribunda	Tree	Cool Z 3-9	8 ft 2.5m	15 ft 5 m	20 ft 6 m	Decid	—	Flowers (pink, early spring); decorative fruit	Lawn specimen	—	Very floriferous, one of the most beautiful crab apples
Malus 'Golden Hornet'	Tree	Cool Z 4-9	8 ft 2.5 m	15 ft 5 m	20 ft 6 m	Decid	—	Flowers (pink & white, spring); decorative/edible fruit	Lawn specimen, orchard	—	The finest yellow-fruited crab apple
Malus hupehensis	Tree	Cool Z 4-9	8 ft 2.5 m	15 ft 5 m	20 ft 6 m	Decid	—	Flowers (white & pink, spring); decorative fruit	Lawn specimen	—	Leaves used for a herbal tea in China
Malus ioensis	Tree	Cool Z 4-9	6 ft 2 m	10 ft 3 m	15 ft 5 m	Decid	—	Flowers (pink, fragrant, late spring); autumn foliage	Lawn specimen, shrub border	—	The double Bechtel crab, cv 'Plena', is most widely grown
Malus sargentii	Shrub	Cool Z 3-9	4 ft 1.2 m	6 ft 2 m	8 ft 2.5 m	Decid	—	Flowers (white, spring); decorative fruit	Shrub border, courtyard, lawn specimen	Branches may be thorny	—
Malus sylvestris	Tree	Cool Z 3-9	8 ft 2.5m	15 ft 5 m	25 ft 8 m	Decid	—	Flowers (white & pink, spring); decorative/edible fruit	Lawn specimen	—	One of the wild parent species of eating apples
Malus toringoides	Tree	Cool Z 4-9	6 ft 2 m	12 ft 4 m	20 ft 6 m	Decid	—	Flowers (white, spring); decorative fruit	Lawn specimen	—	Leaves with narrow lobes, unusual in apples
Malvaviscus arboreus	Shrub	Warm Z 10-11	6 ft 2 m	8 ft 2.5 m	10 ft 3 m	Everg	—	Flowers (red, summer-winter)	Shrub border, courtyards, swimming pools	—	Form with longer, pendent flowers now named *M. penduliflorus*
Mangifera indica	Tree	Hot Z 11-12	10 ft 3 m	20 ft 6 m	30 ft 9 m	Everg	Yes	Edible fruit (mango)	Orchard, shade	Wet spring can prevent fruit set	Large number of cultivars available
Maytenus boaria	Tree	Cool Z 8-9	8 ft 2.5m	15 ft 5 m	20 ft 6 m	Everg	—	Foliage; graceful form	Shrub border, lawn specimen, streets, screen	—	Willow-like habit, used as street tree in USA
Megaskepasma erythrochlamys	Shrub	Hot Z 10-12	6 ft 2 m	10 ft 3 m	10 ft 3 m	Everg	—	Flowers (red, summer)	Courtyard, swimming pools, shrub border, hedge	Leaves & flowers damaged by snails	Dramatic upright red-bracted flower spikes
Melaleuca argentea	Tree	Hot Z 11-12	12 ft 4 m	25 ft 8 m	40 ft 12 m	Everg	—	Foliage, bark, flowers (cream, winter-spring)	Parks, streets	—	Willow-like habit, silvery leaves
Melaleuca armillaris	Tree	Warm Z 9-11	8 ft 2.5m	15 ft 5 m	25 ft 8 m	Everg	—	Flowers (white, spring-summer); dense foliage	Coastal planting, lawn specimen, screen, streets	Dead twigs build up inside (fire risk)	Very dense, deep green foliage
Melaleuca bracteata	Tree	Warm Z 9-11	6 ft 2 m	12 ft 4 m	20 ft 6 m	Everg	Yes	Flowers (white, summer); foliage	Lawn specimen, screen, shrub border, informal hedge	—	Cultivars with yellow or lime-green foliage popular

Reference Table

NAME	KIND	CLIMATE & ZONE	HEIGHT AT 5yrs / 10 yrs / 20yrs	DECIDUOUS EVERGREEN	ARID CLIMATES	CHIEF ATTRACTIONS	USES	DRAWBACKS	COMMENTS
Melaleuca fulgens	Shrub	Warm Z 9-11	4 ft / 5 ft / 5 ft (1.2 m / 1.5 m / 1.5 m)	Everg	Yes	Flowers (scarlet, spring-summer)	Shrub border, courtyard	—	A pale orange form is also commonly grown
Melaleuca incana	Shrub	Warm Z 9-11	6 ft / 8 ft / 10 ft (2 m / 2.5 m / 3 m)	Everg	Yes	Weeping habit; flowers (cream, spring)	Informal hedge, shrub border, courtyard	—	Foliage greyish, hairy
Melaleuca leucadendra	Tree	Hot Z 10-12	15 ft / 25 ft / 40 ft (5 m / 8 m / 12 m)	Everg	Yes	Bark; weeping habit; flowers (white, summer-autumn)	Lawn specimen, parks, streets, medicinal oil	—	Cajeput oil distilled from leaves of this tropical species
Melaleuca linariifolia	Tree	Warm Z 9-11	10 ft / 20 ft / 25 ft (3 m / 6 m / 8 m)	Everg	—	Dense habit; flowers (white, late spring-summer)	Lawn specimen, windbreak, parks, boggy areas	—	Canopy covered by mass of blossom in summer
Melaleuca quinquenervia	Tree	Warm Z 10-11	15 ft / 30 ft / 40 ft (5 m / 9 m / 12 m)	Everg	—	Bark; flowers (white, mainly spring)	Lawn specimen, parks, streets, boggy areas	Becomes a weed in some countries	Flowers attract nectar-feeding birds and bats
Melaleuca tamariscina	Shrub	Warm Z 10-11	6 ft / 12 ft / 15 ft (2 m / 4 m / 5 m)	Everg	Yes	Fine foliage; flowers (white, spring, autumn)	Lawn specimen	—	As yet rare in cultivation but very ornamental
Melaleuca thymifolia	Shrub	Warm Z 9-11	2 ft / 3 ft / 3 ft (0.6 m / 1 m / 1 m)	Everg	—	Flowers (purple-pink, late spring-autumn)	Shrub border, rock garden, boggy areas	—	One of the most compact melaleucas, flowers pretty
Melaleuca viridiflora	Shrub	Hot Z 10-12	8 ft / 15 ft / 25 ft (2.5m / 5 m / 8 m)	Everg	—	Bark; flowers (greenish or red, autumn-winter)	Lawn specimen, parks, streets, boggy areas	—	Flowers mostly greenish in wild but red-flowered form widely grown
Melastoma malabathricum	Shrub	Warm Z 10-11	4 ft / 6 ft / 6 ft (1.2 m / 2 m / 2 m)	Everg	—	Flowers (pink, late summer-autumn)	Shrub border, courtyard, container	—	Similar to *Tibouchina*; fruit used in traditional medicine
Melia azedarach	Tree	Warm Z 8-12	10 ft / 20 ft / 30 ft (3 m / 6 m / 9 m)	Decid	Yes	Foliage; flowers (lilac, late spring-early summer; decorative fruit	Lawn specimen, shade, streets	Berries poisonous	Variable species, several forms in cultivation
Mespilus germanica	Tree	Cool Z 3-9	5 ft / 10 ft / 15 ft (1.5 m / 3 m / 5 m)	Decid	—	Edible fruit; flowers (white, early summer)	Shrub border, lawn specimen, home orchard	—	Fruits (medlars) need to be aged or 'bletted' before eating
Mesua nagassarium	Tree	Hot Z 11-12	6 ft / 12 ft / 25 ft (2 m / 4 m / 8 m)	Decid*	—	Foliage (red new growth); flowers (white, fragrant)	Lawn specimen, courtyard	Slow early growth	—
Metasequoia glyptostroboides	Tree	Cool Z 5-10	10 ft / 20 ft / 40 ft (3 m / 6 m / 12 m)	Decid	—	Autumn foliage	Lawn specimen, parks, screen	—	Conifer, first known as a fossil, later found live in China
Metrosideros excelsa	Tree	Warm Z 10-11	6 ft / 12 ft / 20 ft (2 m / 4 m / 6 m)	Everg	—	Flowers (crimson, late spring-summer); dense foliage	Coastal planting, screen, lawn specimen, hedge, streets	—	Renowned for floral display in its native New Zealand
Metrosideros kermadecensis	Tree	Warm Z 10-11	6 ft / 10 ft / 15 ft (2 m / 3 m / 5 m)	Everg	—	Flowers (crimson, spring-summer); foliage	Coastal planting, screen, lawn specimen, hedge, streets	—	Variegated cultivars are most popular
Metrosideros robusta	Tree	Warm Z 9-10	6 ft / 12 ft / 20 ft (2 m / 4 m / 6 m)	Everg	—	Flowers (orange-red, summer)	Lawn specimen, hedge	—	In the wild often begins life as an epiphyte
Metrosideros umbellata	Tree	Cool Z 8-10	3 ft / 6 ft / 10 ft (1 m / 2 m / 3 m)	Everg	—	Flowers (scarlet, late spring-autumn)	Shrub border, courtyard, container	Very slow-growing	The most cold-hardy *Metrosideros*
Michelia champaca	Tree	Warm Z 10-11	10 ft / 20 ft / 30 ft (3 m / 6 m / 9 m)	Everg	—	Flowers (pale orange, very fragrant, late summer)	Lawn specimen, courtyard, shade, perfumery	—	Strong, sweet fragrance, can carry some distance
Michelia doltsopa	Tree	Warm Z 9-10	6 ft / 12 ft / 20 ft (2 m / 4 m / 6 m)	Everg	—	Flowers (white, fragrant, late winter-early spring)	Lawn specimen, courtyard	Dead flowers persist	Can be semi-deciduous; narrow growth habit, spreads with age
Michelia figo	Shrub	Warm Z 9-11	3 ft / 6 ft / 10 ft (1 m / 2 m / 3 m)	Everg	—	Flowers (purple & cream, very fragrant, spring-summer)	Courtyard, shrub border, container, hedge	—	Intense, fruity fragrance, can carry some distance
Michelia yunnanensis	Tree	Warm Z 9-11	5 ft / 8 ft / 12 ft (1.5 m / 2.5 m / 4 m)	Everg	—	Flowers (cream, fragrant, spring)	Courtyard, shrub border, lawn specimen, container	—	Rust-brown buds contrast with pure white petals
Microbiota decussata	Shrub	Cool Z 3-9	1 ft / 1 ft / 2 ft (0.3 m / 0.3 m / 0.6 m)	Everg	—	Foliage	Groundcover, rock garden	—	Foliage bronze in winter
Millettia grandis	Tree	Warm Z 10-11	4 ft / 8 ft / 15 ft (1.2 m / 2.5 m / 5 m)	Everg	Yes	Flowers (purple, late spring-summer)	Lawn specimen	Slow-growing	Pea flowers in large, erect spikes
Montanoa bipinnatifida	Shrub	Warm Z 10-11	10 ft / 15 ft / 15 ft (3 m / 5 m / 5 m)	Everg	—	Flowers (white, late autumn-winter); foliage	Shrub border	—	Soft stems can be cut back to ground; white daisy flowers
Moringa oleifera	Tree	Hot Z 11-12	6 ft / 12 ft / 20 ft (2 m / 4 m / 6 m)	Decid*	Yes	Flowers (white & yellow, fragrant, spring); edible fruit; foliage	Courtyard, culinary herb	—	Large compound leaves, very long seed pods
Morus alba	Tree	Cool Z 7-10	8 ft / 15 ft / 25 ft (2.5m / 5 m / 8 m)	Decid	Yes	Edible fruit; foliage	Lawn specimen, home orchard, shade, silkworms	Fallen fruit stain paved areas	Fruit inferior in quality to black mulberry (*Morus nigra*)
Morus nigra	Tree	Cool Z 6-9	6 ft / 10 ft / 15 ft (2 m / 3 m / 5 m)	Decid	Yes	Edible fruit; foliage	Home orchard	Fallen fruit stain paved areas	—
Morus rubra	Tree	Cool Z 2-9	8 ft / 15 ft / 30 ft (2.5m / 5 m / 9 m)	Decid	—	Foliage; decorative fruit	Lawn specimen, shade, streets	Fallen fruit stain paved areas	Fruit inferior in quality to black mulberry (*Morus nigra*)
Mundulea sericea	Tree	Warm Z 9-11	6 ft / 8 ft / 10 ft (2 m / 2.5 m / 3 m)	Decid*	Yes	Flowers (purple, spring-summer); foliage; bark	Shrub border, lawn specimen	Bark poisonous	Wisteria-like flowers, silvery foliage
Murraya koenigii	Shrub	Hot Z 10-12	3 ft / 6 ft / 10 ft (1 m / 2 m / 3 m)	Everg	—	Aromatic foliage; flowers (white, fragrant, summer)	Herb garden, courtyard, shrub border	—	Fresh leaves used in curries and other Asian dishes
Murraya paniculata	Shrub	Warm Z 10-12	3 ft / 6 ft / 10 ft (1 m / 2 m / 3 m)	Everg	—	Flowers (white, fragrant, mainly summer-autumn); foliage	Courtyard, containers, hedges, shrub border	—	Red berries decorative but rarely produced; prune for compact shape

NAME	KIND	CLIMATE & ZONE	HEIGHT AT 5 yrs	HEIGHT AT 10 yrs	HEIGHT AT 20 yrs	DECIDUOUS EVERGREEN	ARID CLIMATES	CHIEF ATTRACTIONS	USES	DRAWBACKS	COMMENTS
Musa ornata	Shrub	Hot Z 11-12	8 ft 2.5m	10 ft 3 m	10 ft 3 m	Everg	—	Flowers (pink & yellow, summer); foliage	Courtyard, swimming pool	—	Fruit are inedible
Musa × paradisiaca	Tree	Hot Z 10-12	20 ft 6 m	20 ft 6 m	20 ft 6 m	Everg	—	Edible fruit	Home orchard; leaves have multiple uses	Prone to virus diseases	Includes most of the edible bananas and plantains
Mussaenda erythrophylla	Shrub	Hot Z 11-12	4 ft 1.2 m	6 ft 2 m	6 ft 2 m	Everg	—	Flowers (red, late spring-early autumn)	Shrub border, courtyard, swimming pool	—	Spectacular blood-red flowers; prune to maintain shrubby habit
Mussaenda philippica	Shrub	Hot Z 11-12	4 ft 1.2 m	6 ft 2 m	8 ft 2.5 m	Everg	—	Flowers (white to pink, spring-summer)	Shrub border, courtyard, swimming pool	—	Several cvs commonly grown in tropics
Myoporum floribundum	Shrub	Warm Z 9-10	6 ft 2 m	10 ft 3 m	—	Everg	Yes	Weeping habit; flowers (white, spring-early summer)	Shrub border	Can be short-lived, prone to root rot	—
Myoporum insulare	Shrub	Warm Z 9-10	6 ft 2 m	8 ft 2.5 m	10 ft 3 m	Everg	Yes	Dense foliage; flowers (white, spring-early summer)	Seaside planting, hedge, windbreak	—	Does best in winter-rainfall climates
Myoporum laetum	Tree	Warm Z 10-11	8 ft 2.5m	12 ft 4 m	20 ft 6 m	Everg	Yes	Dense foliage; flowers (white, spring-summer)	Seaside planting, hedge, windbreak	—	Responds well to trimming
Myrica cerifera	Shrub	Cool Z 4-9	5 ft 1.5 m	8 ft 2.5 m	10 ft 3 m	Everg	—	Foliage; decorative fruit	Shrub border, boggy areas	—	Thick wax coating on small fruit is used to make candles
Myrica gale	Shrub	Cool Z 4-9	2 ft 0.6 m	4 ft 1.2 m	5 ft 1.5 m	Decid	—	Foliage; decorative fruit	Shrub border, screen, boggy areas	—	—
Myristica fragrans	Tree	Hot Z 12	8 ft 2.5m	15 ft 5 m	30 ft 9 m	Everg	—	Foliage; decorative/ useful fruit	Spice (nutmeg and mace), shade	Difficult to transplant	Can only be grown in tropics
Myroxylon balsamum	Tree	Hot Z 11-12	10 ft 3 m	20 ft 6 m	30 ft 9 m	Everg	Yes	Flowers (white, fragrant, spring); curious fruit	Parks, shade, resin from bark	—	Source of tolu balsam, used in cough mixtures
Myrtus communis	Shrub	Warm Z 8-10	3 ft 1 m	5 ft 1.5 m	8 ft 2.5 m	Everg	Yes	Flowers (white, spring); decorative fruit	Courtyard, container, hedge, topiary	—	The true myrtle of the ancient Greeks & Romans
Nandina domestica	Shrub	Cool Z 5-10	4 ft 1.2 m	6 ft 2 m	6 ft 2 m	Everg	—	Foliage; decorative fruit; flowers (white, summer)	Courtyard, swimming pool, shrub border	—	Dwarf cultivars very popular, foliage red in autumn-winter
Nauclea orientalis	Tree	Hot Z 11-12	10 ft 3 m	20 ft 6 m	30 ft 9 m	Everg	—	Flowers (yellow, fragrant, late spring-summer); foliage	Lawn specimen, parks, streets	—	Grows along streams; leaves turn red before falling
Neodypsis decaryi	Palm	Hot Z 11-12	4 ft 1.2 m	8 ft 2.5 m	15 ft 5 m	Everg	—	Foliage; symmetrical form	Lawn specimen, courtyard, plaza, swimming pool	—	Fronds in 3 vertical ranks, very distinctive
Nerium oleander	Shrub	Warm Z 9-11	8 ft 2.5m	10 ft 3 m	10 ft 3 m	Everg	Yes	Flowers (white, pink, red, late spring-autumn)	Shrub border, screen, streets, container	Twigs & leaves poisonous but very bitter	Many cultivars, including double and variegated
Nothofagus cunninghamii	Tree	Cool Z 8-9	8 ft 2.5m	15 ft 5 m	30 ft 9 m	Everg	—	Foliage	Lawn specimen, screen, timber	—	Leaves small, neat, glossy
Nothofagus menziesii	Tree	Cool Z 8-9	8 ft 2.5m	12 ft 4 m	25 ft 8 m	Everg	—	Bark; foliage	Lawn specimen, screen, woodland garden	—	Bark of young trees silvery-grey, smooth
Nothofagus moorei	Tree	Cool Z 8-9	10 ft 3 m	20 ft 6 m	40 ft 12 m	Everg	—	Foliage	Lawn specimen, screen	—	New growths bronze, old leaves colour orange-brown before falling
Nothofagus obliqua	Tree	Cool Z 7-9	10 ft 3 m	25 ft 8 m	50 ft 15 m	Decid	—	Autumn foliage; drooping habit	Lawn specimen, parks, streets, timber	—	One of the faster-growing Nothofagus spp.
Nothofagus procera	Tree	Cool Z 8-9	12 ft 4 m	25 ft 8 m	50 ft 15 m	Decid	—	Autumn foliage, vigorous growth	Lawn specimen, parks, streets, timber	—	The fastest-growing Nothofagus spp.; dislikes urban pollution
Nothofagus solandri	Tree	Cool Z 8-9	8 ft 2.5m	15 ft 5 m	25 ft 8 m	Everg	—	Bark, foliage	Lawn specimen, screen, woodland garden	—	Smooth, blackish bark is distinctive
Notospartium carmichaeliae	Shrub	Cool Z 8-9	5 ft 1.5 m	8 ft 2.5 m	10 ft 3 m	Decid	—	Flowers (pink, late spring-midsummer)	Lawn specimen, courtyard, shrub border	Often short-lived	Broom-like habit
Nuxia floribunda	Tree	Warm Z 9-11	6 ft 2 m	12 ft 4 m	20 ft 6 m	Everg	—	Flowers (white, fragrant, autumn-spring)	Lawn specimen, streets	—	Tiny flowers in large frothy panicles
Nuytsia floribunda	Tree	Warm Z 9-10	3 ft 1 m	8 ft 2.5 m	15 ft 5 m	Everg	—	Flowers (orange, summer)	Lawn specimen	Difficult to propagate	Root-parasitic shrub, does not adapt easily to cultivation
Nyssa aquatica	Tree	Cool Z 5-9	10 ft 3 m	20 ft 6 m	40 ft 12 m	Decid	—	Foliage, decorative fruit	Lawn specimen, parks, streets, boggy areas, honey	—	Much less common in cultivation than N. sylvatica
Nyssa sylvatica	Tree	Cool Z 3-10	8 ft 2.5m	15 ft 5 m	30 ft 9 m	Decid	—	Autumn foliage	Lawn specimen, parks, streets	—	Among the most brilliantly colouring of all deciduous trees
Ochna serrulata	Shrub	Warm Z 9-11	5 ft 1.5 m	8 ft 2.5 m	8 ft 2.5 m	Everg	—	Flowers (yellow, late winter-spring); decorative fruit	Shrub border, hedge	Self seeding and invasive in some areas	—
Olea europaea	Tree	Warm Z 8-10	8 ft 2.5m	15 ft 5 m	25 ft 8 m	Everg	Yes	Edible fruit; gnarled trunk	Preserved fruit, edible oil, timber, lawn specimen, streets	Can become a weed in some countries	Many named cultivars, differing in size & qualities of fruit
Olearia argophylla	Tree	Cool Z 8-9	6 ft 2 m	12 ft 4 m	20 ft 6 m	Everg	—	Flowers (cream, spring-autumn); foliage	Lawn specimen, shrub border, woodland garden	—	Broad leaves, silvery on undersides
Olearia avicenniifolia	Shrub	Cool Z 8-9	6 ft 2 m	10 ft 3 m	12 ft 4 m	Everg	—	Flowers (white, fragrant, summer); foliage	Shrub border, informal hedge, coastal planting	—	Woolly white felt on underside of leaves
Olearia ilicifolia	Shrub	Warm Z 9-10	5 ft 1.5 m	8 ft 2.5 m	10 ft 3 m	Everg	—	Flowers (white, fragrant, summer)	Shrub border, courtyard	—	Sharply toothed leaves
Olearia macrodonta	Shrub	Cool Z 7-9	4 ft 1.2 m	6 ft 2 m	6 ft 2 m	Everg	—	Flowers (white, late spring-summer)	Shrub border	—	Sharply toothed leaves

NAME	KIND	CLIMATE & ZONE	HEIGHT AT 5yrs 10yrs 20yrs	DECIDUOUS/EVERGREEN	ARID CLIMATES	CHIEF ATTRACTIONS	USES	DRAWBACKS	COMMENTS
Olearia paniculata	Shrub	Warm Z 9-10	6 ft / 2 m — 10 ft / 3 m — 12 ft / 4 m	Everg	—	Foliage; flower (cream, fragrant, autumn)	Screen, hedge, seashore planting	—	Flowers rather inconspicuous
Olearia phlogopappa	Shrub	Cool Z 7-9	3 ft / 1 m — 4 ft / 1.2 m — 6 ft / 2 m	Everg	—	Flowers (white to purple, late spring-early autumn)	Shrub border, rock garden, coastal planting	—	—
Olearia × scilloniensis	Shrub	Cool Z 8-9	3 ft / 1 m — 4 ft / 1.2 m — 6 ft / 2 m	Everg	—	Flowers (white, spring)	Shrub border, seaside planting	—	Hybrid between O. lyrata & O. phlogopappa
Olearia 'Talbot de Malahide' (albida)	Shrub	Cool Z 8-9	6 ft / 2 m — 8 ft / 2.5 m — 10 ft / 3 m	Everg	—	Flowers (white, fragrant, summer-autumn)	Coastal planting, informal hedge	—	Hybrid of O. avicenniifolia
Olearia traversii	Shrub	Cool Z 8-9	8 ft / 2.5m — 10 ft / 3 m — 12 ft / 4 m	Everg	—	Foliage	Informal hedge, windbreak, coastal planting	—	Flowers inconspicuous
Omalanthus populifolius	Tree	Warm Z 10-12	5 ft / 1.5 m — 12 ft / 4 m — —	Everg	—	Foliage	Shrub border, rainforest garden	Short-lived	Self-seeds freely
Oncoba spinosa	Tree	Hot Z 11-12	4 ft / 1.2 m — 8 ft / 2.5 m — 12 ft / 4 m	Everg	—	Flowers (white & yellow, fragrant, spring-summer); decorative/edible fruit	Shrub border, lawn specimen, hedge	Long spines	Fruit pulp unpleasant tasting though edible
Opuntia ficus-indica	Shrub	Warm Z 10-11	3 ft / 1 m — 6 ft / 2 m — 10 ft / 3 m	Everg	Yes	Edible fruit; succulent stems; flowers (yellow, early summer)	Home orchard, courtyards	Fruit skin has barbed bristles	Of Mexican origin but popular fruit in Mediterranean region
Opuntia imbricata	Shrub	Warm Z 8-11	2 ft / 0.6 m — 5 ft / 1.5 m — 8 ft / 2.5 m	Everg	Yes	Succulent stems; flowers (pink to purple, summer)	Rock garden	Fierce spines; has become a weed in Australia	Differs from many other opuntias in its cylindrical stems
Orphium frutescens	Shrub	Warm Z 9-11	2 ft / 0.6 m — 2 ft / 0.6 m — —	Everg	Yes	Flowers (pink to purple, summer)	Shrub border, courtyards, rock garden, container	Short-lived, stems weak & floppy	Flowers have sticky, shiny petals
Osmanthus delavayi	Shrub	Cool Z 7-9	3 ft / 1 m — 5 ft / 1.5 m — 6 ft / 2 m	Everg	—	Flowers (white, fragrant, summer)	Shrub border, courtyard	Slow-growing	The showiest-flowered Osmanthus sp.; likes shade
Osmanthus fragrans	Shrub	Cool Z 7-10	3 ft / 1 m — 6 ft / 2 m — 10 ft / 3 m	Everg	—	Very fragrant flowers (white to pale orange, spring-autumn)	Shrub border, courtyard, container	Slow-growing	One of the sweetest-scented of all shrubs, fragrance carries some distance
Osmanthus × fortunei	Shrub	Cool Z 6-9	3 ft / 1 m — 5 ft / 1.5 m — 8 ft / 2.5 m	Everg	—	Flowers (white, fragrant, late summer-early winter); foliage	Shrub border, courtyard, lawn specimen	—	Holly-like leaves
Osmanthus heterophyllus	Shrub	Cool Z 7-10	3 ft / 1 m — 5 ft / 1.5 m — 8 ft / 2.5 m	Everg	—	Foliage; flowers (white, fragrant, early summer)	Shrub border, hedge, courtyard	—	Holly-like leaves
Ostrya carpinifolia	Tree	Cool Z 2-9	10 ft / 3 m — 20 ft / 6 m — 30 ft / 9 m	Decid	—	Autumn foliage; decorative fruit clusters; bark	Lawn specimen, parks, streets, shade	—	Very similar to the related Carpinus
Ostrya virginiana	Tree	Cool Z 3-9	10 ft / 3 m — 20 ft / 6 m — 30 ft / 9 m	Decid	—	Autumn foliage; decorative fruit clusters	Lawn specimen, parks, streets, shade, timber	—	—
Oxydendrum arboreum	Tree	Cool Z 3-9	8 ft / 2.5m — 15 ft / 5 m — 25 ft / 8 m	Decid	—	Autumn foliage; flowers (white, fragrant, late summer)	Shrub border, lawn specimen, woodland garden	—	Leaves have distinct acid taste, like sorrel; autumn colour very fine
Pachira aquatica	Tree	Hot Z 10-12	8 ft / 2.5m — 15 ft / 5 m — 25 ft / 8 m	Everg	—	Edible seeds; flowers (white to yellow, most of year)	Lawn specimen, shade, boggy area	—	Flowers have bunch of long stamens like a shaving brush
Pachystegia insignis	Shrub	Cool Z 8-10	1 ft / 0.3 m — 2 ft / 0.6 m — 3 ft / 1 m	Everg	—	Foliage; flowers (white, summer)	Rock garden, courtyard, seaside planting	—	Thick, round leaves with woolly undersides very striking
Paeonia lutea	Shrub	Cool Z 4-9	3 ft / 1 m — 6 ft / 2 m — 6 ft / 2 m	Decid	—	Flowers (yellow, late spring-early summer)	Shrub border, courtyard	—	The var. ludlowii has larger flowers and is more popular
Paeonia suffruticosa	Shrub	Cool Z 4-9	2 ft / 0.6 m — 3 ft / 1 m — 4 ft / 1.2 m	Decid	—	Flowers (white, pink or red)	Shrub border, perennial border, courtyard	Difficult to propagate, plants expensive	Many named cultivars; like shade, rich soil
Paliurus spina-christi	Shrub	Cool Z 6-10	6 ft / 2 m — 10 ft / 3 m — 10 ft / 3 m	Decid	Yes	Decorative fruit; flowers (yellow, summer); autumn foliage	Thorny hedge	Gaunt, spiny stems	Said to have made Christ's crown of thorns
Pandanus tectorius	Tree	Hot Z 11-12	5 ft / 1.5 m — 10 ft / 3 m — 15 ft / 5 m	Everg	—	Symmetrical habit; foliage; decorative fruit	Seaside planting, courtyards, swimming pools	Sheds large prickly leaves onto ground	Has striking stilt-roots
Paraserianthes (Albizia) lophantha	Tree	Warm Z 9-11	12 ft / 4 m — 25 ft / 8 m — —	Everg	Yes	Foliage; flowers (yellowish-green, winter-spring)	Lawn specimen, screen, shelter, coastal planting	Short-lived, freely self-seeding	Good quick shelter tree for shade-loving shrubs
Parkinsonia aculeata	Shrub	Hot Z 10-11	8 ft / 2.5m — 15 ft / 5 m — 20 ft / 6 m	Everg	Yes	Flowers (yellow, fragrant, spring-summer); foliage; bark	Lawn specimen, shrub border, informal hedge	Sharp thorns; can become a weed	Suited to very hot, dry climates
Parrotia persica	Tree	Cool Z 3-9	8 ft / 2.5m — 15 ft / 5 m — 20 ft / 6 m	Decid	—	Autumn foliage; flowers (reddish-yellow, spring); bark	Lawn specimen, parks	—	Picturesque growth habit
Paulownia fortunei	Tree	Warm Z 4-11	20 ft / 6 m — 30 ft / 9 m — 40 ft / 12 m	Decid	—	Fast growth; flowers (cream & mauve, fragrant, early spring)	Lawn specimen, parks, farms, timber	—	Leaves enormous on vigorous young saplings
Paulownia tomentosa	Tree	Cool Z 4-9	10 ft / 3 m — 20 ft / 6 m — 30 ft / 9 m	Decid	—	Flowers (violet, spring)	Lawn specimen	Flower buds damaged by late frosts	—
Peltophorum pterocarpum	Tree	Hot Z 11-12	12 ft / 4 m — 25 ft / 8 m — 40ft / 12 m	Everg	Yes	Flowers (yellow, fragrant, early summer)	Lawn specimen, parks, avenues	—	Useful shade tree, showy flowers
Persea americana	Tree	Warm Z 10-11	10 ft / 3 m — 20 ft / 6 m — 30 ft / 9 m	Everg	—	Edible fruit; foliage	Orchard, lawn specimen, courtyard	Heavy leaf fall; intolerant of pruning	Many avocado cvs with differing fruit characters

NAME	KIND	CLIMATE & ZONE	HEIGHT AT 5yrs 10yrs 20yrs			DECIDUOUS EVERGREEN	ARID CLIMATES	CHIEF ATTRACTIONS	USES	DRAWBACKS	COMMENTS
Persoonia pinifolia	Shrub	Warm Z 10-11	6 ft 2 m	10 ft 3 m	12 ft 4 m	Everg	—	Flowers (gold, summer-autumn); weeping habit; foliage	Shrub border, courtyard, cut foliage	Very difficult to propagate	Fruits edible when fully ripe, used by Australian Aborigines
Phellodendron amurense	Tree	Cool Z 5-9	8 ft 2.5m	15 ft 5 m	25 ft 8 m	Decid	—	Autumn foliage; decorative fruit; bark	Lawn specimen, parks	—	Bark smooth & red when young, thick & corky bark on old trees
Philadelphus coronarius	Shrub	Cool Z 2-10	4 ft 1.2 m	5 ft 1.5 m	6 ft 2 m	Decid	—	Flowers (white, fragrant, mid to late spring)	Shrub border, woodland garden, courtyard	—	Like sheltered position, damp soil, tolerates shade (most philadelphus)
Philadelphus Lemoine hybrids	Shrub	Cool Z 3-9	5 ft 1.5 m	6 ft 2 m	6 ft 2 m	Decid	—	Flowers (white, fragrant, mid to late spring)	Shrub border, woodland garden, courtyard	—	—
Philadelphus lewisii	Shrub	Cool Z 3-9	6 ft 2 m	8 ft 2.5 m	10 ft 3 m	Decid	—	Flowers (white, mid spring)	Shrub border, courtyard	—	—
Philodendron bipinnatifidum (incl. P. selloum)	Shrub	Warm Z 10-12	5 ft 1.5 m	8 ft 2.5 m	10 ft 3 m	Everg	—	Foliage	Courtyard, plaza, swimming pool, indoor	Aerial roots wander uncontrollably	Spectacular foliage
Phoenix canariensis	Palm	Warm Z 9-11	4 ft 1.2 m	8 ft 2.5 m	15 ft 5 m	Everg	Yes	Symmetrical form; decorative fruit	Parks, avenues, plazas	Ferocious spines on frond bases	Male and female plants required for fruit display
Phoenix dactylifera	Palm	Warm Z 10-11	4 ft 1.2 m	8 ft 2.5 m	15 ft 5 m	Everg	Yes	Edible fruit	Orchard, plazas, avenues	—	Hot, dry climate needed for fruit production; many named cvs, male tree needed to pollinate
Phoenix roebelenii	Palm	Warm Z 10-12	2 ft 0.6 m	5 ft 1.5 m	8 ft 2.5 m	Everg	—	Foliage; graceful form	Courtyard, swimming pool, indoor	—	Delicate, drooping bright green fronds
Photinia × fraseri	Shrub	Cool Z 8-10	6 ft 2 m	8 ft 2.5 m	10 ft 3 m	Everg	—	Foliage (new growths red)	Formal and informal hedge, windbreaks	—	Red new growths appear repeatedly following trimming
Photinia glabra	Shrub	Cool Z 7-10	6 ft 2 m	8 ft 2.5 m	10 ft 3 m	Everg	—	Foliage (new growths red)	Formal and informal hedge, windbreaks	—	'Rubens' is the form commonly grown
Photinia serrulata (serratifolia)	Tree	Cool Z 7-10	6 ft 2 m	10 ft 3 m	15 ft 5 m	Everg	—	Flowers (white, spring); decorative fruit	Lawn specimen, streets, windbreaks	Prone to mildew attack	Clipping encourages mildew, best allowed to grow as small tree
Photinia villosa	Tree	Cool Z 3-9	6 ft 2 m	10 ft 3 m	15 ft 5 m	Decid	—	Autumn foliage; flowers (white, spring); decorative fruit	Lawn specimen, shrub border, informal hedge	—	Very fine autumn colour, quite different from the evergreen photinias
Phylica pubescens	Shrub	Warm Z 9-10	4 ft 1.2 m	6 ft 2 m	6 ft 2 m	Everg	—	Flowers (cream bracts, winter-spring); foliage	Shrub border, cut flowers	—	Very striking feathery flower-heads (long hairs on bracts & leaves)
Phyllanthus acidus	Tree	Hot Z 11-12	10 ft 3 m	15 ft 5 m	20 ft 6 m	Everg	—	Edible/decorative fruit	Shrub border, home orchard	Ungainly growth habit; fruit attacked by birds	Fruit makes excellent preserves
Phyllocladus aspleniifolius	Tree	Cool Z 9	3 ft 1 m	6 ft 2 m	12 ft 4 m	Everg	—	Foliage	Lawn specimen, woodland garden, bonsai	Slow-growing	Remarkable foliage for a conifer
Phyllocladus trichomanoides	Tree	Warm Z 9-10	4 ft 1.2 m	8 ft 2.5 m	15 ft 5 m	Everg	—	Foliage	Lawn specimen, woodland garden, bonsai	Slow-growing	—
Phyllostachys bambusoides	Bamboo	Cool Z 7-10	10 ft 3 m	20 ft 6 m	20 ft 6 m	Everg	—	Smooth straight stems; foliage	Timber, screen	Long-running rhizomes can be invasive	Important structural bamboo in east Asia
Phyllostachys nigra	Bamboo	Cool Z 5-10	10 ft 3 m	20 ft 6 m	20 ft 6 m	Everg	—	Smooth blackish stems; foliage	Timber, screen, woodland garden, container	Long-running rhizomes can be invasive	Spreads to cover a large area; older stems darker in colour
Physocarpus opulifolius	Shrub	Cool Z 2-9	4 ft 1.2 m	5 ft 1.5 m	5 ft 1.5 m	Decid	—	Flowers (white, early summer); autumn foliage	Shrub border, hedge	—	Golden cultivars more ornamental
Phytolacca americana	Shrub	Cool Z 2-10	6 ft 2 m	6 ft 2 m	—	Everg	Yes	Decorative fruit; flowers (white, summer); foliage	Shrub border, perennial border	All parts of plant poisonous	Traditional folk medicine in USA but known to be dangerous
Phytolacca dioica	Tree	Warm Z 10-11	10 ft 3 m	20 ft 6 m	30 ft 9 m	Everg	Yes	Massive swollen trunk	Lawn specimen, parks, shade	—	Trunk expands rapidly to very large girth at base
Picea abies	Tree	Cold Z 2-9	8 ft 2.5m	15 ft 5 m	30 ft 9 m	Everg	—	Symmetrical form, foliage	Timber, lawn specimen, Christmast tree	—	Dwarf cultivars used for rock gardens and containers
Picea breweriana	Tree	Cold Z 2-9	6 ft 2 m	12 ft 4 m	25 ft 8 m	Everg	—	Symmetrical form; weeping branches	Lawn specimen	Slow-growing	Choicest ornamental species but often performs poorly
Picea engelmannii	Tree	Cold Z 1-8	6 ft 2 m	12 ft 4 m	25 ft 8 m	Everg	—	Symmetrical form	Lawn specimen, tall hedge, timber	—	One of the most cold-hardy conifers
Picea glauca	Tree	Cold Z 1-8	6 ft 2 m	12 ft 4 m	25 ft 8 m	Everg	—	Symmetrical form	Timber, paper pulp	—	Cultivar 'Conica' is most commonly grown for ornament
Picea mariana	Tree	Cold Z 1-8	6 ft 2 m	12 ft 4 m	20 ft 6 m	Everg	—	Symmetrical form	Lawn specimen	—	Not widely cultivated outside its native region
Picea obovata	Tree	Cold Z 1-8	6 ft 2 m	12 ft 4 m	25 ft 8 m	Everg	—	Symmetrical form; pinkish male cones	Lawn specimen	—	—
Picea omorika	Tree	Cool Z 4-9	6 ft 2 m	15 ft 5 m	30 ft 9 m	Everg	—	Symmetrical form; pendulous foliage	Lawn specimen; parks, Christmas tree	—	Unusual for its flattened needles; very narrow habit
Picea orientalis	Tree	Cold Z 3-9	6 ft 2 m	12 ft 4 m	20 ft 6 m	Everg	—	Symmetrical form; foliage, red male cones	Lawn specimen; Christmas trees	Slow-growing	Very short needles, a fine ornamenal
Picea pungens	Tree	Cool Z 2-10	6 ft 2 m	12 ft 4 m	25 ft 8 m	Everg	—	Symmetrical form; stiff blue foliage	Lawn specimen, parks	Prickly needles	Many cultivars, selected for bluer foliage or dwarf habit

NAME	KIND	CLIMATE & ZONE	HEIGHT AT 5yrs 10yrs 20yrs	DECIDUOUS EVERGREEN	ARID CLIMATES	CHIEF ATTRACTIONS	USES	DRAWBACKS	COMMENTS
Picea sitchensis	Tree	Cool Z 4-9	10 ft / 20 ft / 40 ft; 3 m / 6 m / 12 m	Everg	—	Symmetrical form; vigorous growth	Timber, lawn specimen, parks	Foliage prone to aphid attack	One of the fastest growing spruces, timber valuable
Picea smithiana	Tree	Cool Z 6-9	10 ft / 20 ft / 40 ft; 3 m / 6 m / 12 m	Everg	—	Symmetrical form; vigorous growth; weeping foliage	Lawn specimen, windbreak, parks	Short-lived in drier climates	The longest-needled spruce
Pieris formosa	Shrub	Cool Z 6-9	5 ft / 8 ft / 10 ft; 1.5 m / 2.5 m / 3 m	Everg	—	Flowers (white, mid-spring); red new growths	Shrub border, lawn specimen, courtyard	—	Var. *forrestii* is the form usually grown
Pieris japonica	Shrub	Cool Z 4-10	4 ft / 6 ft / 6 ft; 1.2 m / 2 m / 2 m	Everg	—	Flowers (white or pink, late winter-early spring); pink or red new growths	Shrub border, woodland garden, container, bonsai	—	Prefers semi-shade (all pieris)
Pimelea ferruginea	Shrub	Warm Z 9-10	2 ft / 3 ft / —; 0.6 m / 1 m	Everg	Yes	Flowers (rose-pink, spring)	Shrub border, rock garden, container	Short-lived	Requires full sun
Pinus aristata	Tree	Cool Z 5-9	4 ft / 8 ft / 15 ft; 1.2 m / 2.5 m / 5 m	Everg	—	Foliage	Lawn specimen, courtyard	Very slow-growing	Among the longest-lived of all conifers
Pinus armandii	Tree	Cool Z 8-10	8 ft / 15 ft / 30 ft; 2.5m / 5 m / 9 m	Everg	—	Foliage; symmetrical form	Lawn specimen, parks	—	—
Pinus ayacahuite	Tree	Cool Z 8-10	8 ft / 15 ft / 30 ft; 2.5m / 5 m / 9 m	Everg	—	Foliage; symmetrical form; large cones	Lawn specimen, parks	—	Tolerates urban pollution; prefers summer-rainfall climate
Pinus bungeana	Tree	Cool Z 5-9	5 ft / 10 ft / 20 ft; 1.5 m / 3 m / 6 m	Everg	—	Bark; foliage	Lawn specimen, courtyard, parks, bonsai	—	Bark mottled in different shades; famous specimens in Beijing
Pinus canariensis	Tree	Warm Z 8-10	10 ft / 20 ft / 40 ft; 3 m / 6 m / 12 m	Everg	—	Foliage; symmetrical form; bark	Timber, windbreak, parks, avenues	—	More fire tolerant than many pines
Pinus caribaea	Tree	Warm Z 9-11	12 ft / 20 ft / 40 ft; 4 m / 6 m / 12 m	Everg	—	Vigorous growth; straight trunk; foliage	Timber, windbreak, avenues	—	Important timber tree in summer-rainfall subtropical regions
Pinus cembra	Tree	Cool Z 3-9	6 ft / 12 ft / 20 ft; 2 m / 4 m / 6 m	Everg	—	Foliage; neat form	Edible seeds, lawn specimen	—	Seeds used as food item but difficult to extract
Pinus cembroides	Tree	Cool Z 6-9	5 ft / 10 ft / 15 ft; 1.5 m / 3 m / 5 m	Everg	Yes	Foliage; bushy form	Edible seeds, lawn specimen	—	Seeds sold in markets in Mexico
Pinus contorta var. latifolia	Tree	Cool Z 5-9	8 ft / 15 ft / 30 ft; 2.5m / 5 m / 9 m	Everg	—	Straight trunk; symmetrical form	Timber, windbreak	Self-seeds freely, can be a nuisance	Pole-like saplings
Pinus coulteri	Tree	Cool Z 8-10	6 ft / 12 ft / 25 ft; 2 m / 4 m / 8 m	Everg	—	Foliage; spreading crown; very large cones	Lawn specimen, parks, timber	—	The largest (but not longest) pine cones
Pinus densiflora	Tree	Cool Z 4-9	6 ft / 12 ft / 25 ft; 2 m / 4 m / 8 m	Everg	—	Foliage; bark; twisted limbs	Lawn specimen, courtyard, bonsai	—	One of the best known trees in formal Japanese gardens
Pinus elliottii	Tree	Warm Z 9-11	10 ft / 20 ft / 40 ft; 3 m / 6 m / 12 m	Everg	—	Foliage; straight trunk	Timber, paper pulp, turpentine, windbreaks	—	Very similar to *P. caribaea*, sometimes treated as synonym
Pinus halepensis	Tree	Warm Z 7-10	8 ft / 15 ft / 30 ft; 2.5m / 5 m / 9 m	Everg	Yes	Vigorous growth; dense foliage	Windbreak, lawn specimen, parks, Christmas trees	—	One of the best pines for low-rainfall areas
Pinus jeffreyi	Tree	Cool Z 6-9	8 ft / 15 ft / 30 ft; 2.5m / 5 m / 9 m	Everg	—	Symmetrical form; bark; foliage	Timber, lawn specimen, parks	—	Has large, prickly cones
Pinus koraiensis	Tree	Cool Z 5-9	8 ft / 15 ft / 30 ft; 2.5m / 5 m / 9 m	Everg	—	Foliage; dense habit	Lawn specimen, parks	—	Foliage very attractive, blue-banded and curling
Pinus monophylla	Tree	Cool Z 7-9	5 ft / 10 ft / 15 ft; 1.5 m / 3 m / 5 m	Everg	Yes	Foliage	Edible seeds, lawn specimen, courtyard	—	Unique among pines for needle held singly, not in bundles
Pinus monticola	Tree	Cool Z 5-9	10 ft / 20 ft / 40 ft; 3 m / 6 m / 12 m	Everg	—	Smooth straight trunk; foliage	Timber, lawn specimen	—	One of the smoothest-barked pines
Pinus mugo	Shrub	Cool Z 2-9	5 ft / 10 ft / 15 ft; 1.5 m / 3 m / 5 m	Everg	—	Dense foliage; bushy habit	Rock garden, bonsai, container, hedge	—	Some cultivars even smaller growing
Pinus nigra	Tree	Cool Z 4-9	10 ft / 20 ft / 30 ft; 3 m / 6 m / 9 m	Everg	—	Symmetrical form	Timber, lawn specimen, windbreak	—	Several subspecies, including Corsican, Austrian and Crimean pines
Pinus palustris	Tree	Cool Z 4-10	5 ft / 15 ft / 30 ft; 1.5 m / 5 m / 9 m	Everg	—	Foliage; straight trunk	Timber, lawn specimen, turpentine	—	Remarkable pole-like saplings remain unbranched for years
Pinus parviflora	Tree	Cool Z 3-9	5 ft / 10 ft / 20 ft; 1.5 m / 3 m / 6 m	Everg	—	Foliage; crooked habit	Lawn specimen, courtyard, bonsai	—	Needles very short; traditional bonsai subject in Japan
Pinus patula	Tree	Warm Z 9-11	10 ft / 20 ft / 40 ft; 3 m / 6 m / 12 m	Everg	—	Weeping needles; symmetrical form	Lawn specimen, shade, parks, timber, wood pulp	—	Most elegant foliage of all pines
Pinus pinaster	Tree	Warm Z 7-10	10 ft / 20 ft / 40 ft; 3 m / 6 m / 12 m	Everg	—	Foliage; bark	Timber, rosin, coastal planting, parks	—	Unsuited to summer-rainfall climates
Pinus pinea	Tree	Warm Z 8-10	8 ft / 15 ft / 25 ft; 2.5m / 5 m / 8 m	Everg	Yes	Umbrella-shaped crown; bark	Edible seeds, lawn specimen, avenues, coastal planting	—	Distinctive outline; unsuited to summer-rainfall climates
Pinus ponderosa	Tree	Cool Z 5-9	8 ft / 15 ft / 30 ft; 2.5m / 5 m / 9 m	Everg	—	Symmetrical form; foliage; bark	Timber, parks, avenues	—	Important North American timber tree
Pinus radiata	Tree	Warm Z 8-10	15 ft / 30 ft / 50 ft; 5 m / 9 m / 15 m	Everg	—	Vigorous growth	Timber, wood pulp, windbreaks	Seedlings invade native forests in some countries	The most important plantation tree in southern hemisphere countries
Pinus roxburghii	Tree	Warm Z 6-10	8 ft / 15 ft / 30 ft; 2.5m / 5 m / 9 m	Everg	—	Open, symmetrical form; bark; drooping needles	Lawn specimen, parks, avenues	—	Bark coarsely tessellated with rich orange-brown tones

NAME	KIND	CLIMATE & ZONE	HEIGHT AT 5yrs 10yrs 20yrs	DECIDUOUS EVERGREEN	ARID CLIMATES	CHIEF ATTRACTIONS	USES	DRAWBACKS	COMMENTS
Pinus strobus	Tree	Cool Z 3-9	10 ft 20 ft 40 ft / 3 m 6 m 12 m	Everg	—	Foliage; symmetrical form	Timber, lawn specimen, parks, avenues	Exudes messy resin	Attractive fine bluish foliage
Pinus sylvestris	Tree	Cool Z 4-9	8 ft 15 ft 30 ft / 2.5m 5 m 9 m	Everg	—	Slender form; bark	Timber, lawn specimen, parks, Christmas trees	—	Dwarf cultivars are grown in tubs and rock gardens
Pinus thunbergii	Tree	Cool Z 5-9	8 ft 15 ft 30 ft / 2.5m 5 m 9 m	Everg	—	Open form; bark	Courtyard, lawn specimen; container; bonsai	Prone to attack by scale insects	One of the preferred tree species for formal Japanese gardens
Pinus wallichiana	Tree	Cool Z 5-9	10 ft 20 ft 40 ft / 3 m 6 m 12 m	Everg	—	Broad symmetrical form; foliage; interesting cones	Lawn specimen, parks	—	Cones long & pendulous with papery scales
Piscidia piscipula	Tree	Hot Z 10-12	10 ft 15 ft 20 ft / 3 m 5 m 6 m	Everg	—	Flowers (pink, spring); foliage	Lawn specimen, courtyard	Leaves may irritate skin	Leaves used to stupefy fish
Pisonia grandis	Tree	Hot Z 10-12	8 ft 15 ft 20 ft / 2.5m 5 m 6 m	Everg	—	Foliage	Lawn specimen, avenue, coastal planting, container	—	Sticky fruits trap small birds
Pistacia chinensis	Tree	Warm Z 5-10	8 ft 15 ft 20 ft / 2.5m 5 m 6 m	Decid	Yes	Autumn foliage; decorative fruit	Lawn specimen, streets, parks	—	Good deciduous tree for small gardens, colours well in mild climates
Pistacia vera	Tree	Warm Z 8-10	8 ft 15 ft 25 ft / 2.5m 5 m 8 m	Decid	Yes	Edible nuts	Orchard	—	Male and female trees required for nut production (pistachios)
Pittosporum crassifolium	Tree	Warm Z 9-10	8 ft 15 ft 20 ft / 2.5m 5 m 6 m	Everg	—	Bushy habit; flowers (reddish-purple, spring); decorative fruit	Seaside planting, hedge, lawn specimen, screen	—	—
Pittosporum eugenioides	Tree	Warm Z 9-10	8 ft 15 ft 25 ft / 2.5m 5 m 8 m	Everg	—	Bushy habit; foliage; decorative fruit	Seaside planting, hedge, lawn specimen, screen	—	Cultivar 'Variegatum' more widely grown than wild form
Pittosporum phylliraeoides	Tree	Warm Z 9-11	6 ft 12 ft 20 ft / 2 m 4 m 6 m	Everg	Yes	Weeping habit; decorative fruit	Lawn specimen, parks	—	Best in a dry climate
Pittosporum rhombifolium	Tree	Warm Z 9-11	8 ft 15 ft 25 ft / 2.5m 5 m 8 m	Everg	Yes	Dense, symmetrical form; decorative fruit; flowers (cream, spring)	Lawn specimen, parks, streets	Sticky seeds litter paths	Upright narrow habit; display of massed orange fruit
Pittosporum tenuifolium	Tree	Warm Z 9-10	6 ft 12 ft 20 ft / 2 m 4 m 6 m	Everg	—	Dense foliage; flowers (chocolate, fragrant, late spring)	Shrub border, hedge, windbreak, cut foliage	—	Cultivars with purplish or variegated foliage
Pittosporum tobira	Shrub	Warm Z 9-10	3 ft 5 ft 8 ft / 1 m 1.5 m 2.5 m	Everg	Yes	Flowers (cream, fragrant, late spring-summer)	Hedge, shrub border, courtyard, container	—	Dwarf and variegated cultivars
Plagianthus betulinus	Tree	Warm Z 7-10	6 ft 15 ft 30 ft / 2 m 5 m 9 m	Decid	—	Foliage; flowers (cream, mid-spring-midsummer)	Lawn specimen, windbreak, screen	—	Early stage is shrubby with tangled twigs, later grows erect
Planchonia careya	Tree	Hot Z 11-12	8 ft 12 ft 15 ft / 2.5m 4 m 5 m	Everg	Yes	Flowers (white & red, winter-spring); edible fruit; foliage changes colour	Lawn specimen, courtyard, streets	—	Flowers short-lived, turn pink before falling
Platanus × acerifolia	Tree	Cool Z 3-10	8 ft 15 ft 30 ft / 2.5m 5 m 9 m	Decid	—	Stately habit; bark; autumn foliage	Parks, avenues, shade	Prone to anthracnose leaf disease	One of the world's hardiest trees for urban environments
Platanus occidentalis	Tree	Cool Z 3-9	8 ft 15 ft 30 ft / 2.5m 5 m 9 m	Decid	—	Stately habit; bark; autumn foliage	Parks, avenues, shade	—	Not so climatically adaptable as other *Platanus* spp.
Platanus orientalis	Tree	Cool Z 6-10	8 ft 15 ft 30 ft / 2.5m 5 m 9 m	Decid	Yes	Vigorous growth; foliage	Parks, avenues, shade	Leaves prone to mildew attack	Reaches great age and size
Platanus racemosa	Tree	Cool Z 7-10	8 ft 15 ft 30 ft / 2.5m 5 m 9 m	Decid	Yes	Bark; foliage	Parks, avenues, shade	Leaves prone to mildew attack	Best suited to dry climates
Platycladus orientalis	Tree	Cool Z 6-11	6 ft 12 ft 20 ft / 2 m 4 m 6 m	Everg	—	Foliage	Lawn specimen, courtyard, container	—	Many dwarf and coloured-leaved cultivars
Plumbago auriculata	Shrub	Warm Z 9-11	4 ft 6 ft 6 ft / 1.2 m 2 m 2 m	Everg	Yes	Flowers (pale blue, late spring-early winter)	Informal hedge, courtyard, shrub border, espalier	—	Grown as conservatory plant in cooler climates
Plumeria obtusa	Tree	Hot Z 10-12	6 ft 10 ft 15 ft / 2 m 3 m 5 m	Everg	—	Flowers (white & yellow, fragrant, spring-autumn)	Lawn specimen, courtyard, parks, plazas	Poisonous milky sap	Flowers all year in the wet tropics
Plumeria rubra	Tree	Hot Z 10-12	6 ft 10 ft 15 ft / 2 m 3 m 5 m	Decid*	—	Flowers (pink, crimson, yellow or white, fragrant, late spring-late autumn)	Lawn specimen, courtyard, parks, plazas	—	Flowers all year in the wet tropics; many cultivars
Podalyria calyptrata	Shrub	Warm Z 9-10	8 ft 12 ft 12 ft / 2.5m 4 m 4 m	Everg	Yes	Flowers (pink, spring); foliage	Shrub border, courtyard, lawn specimen	—	Foliage silver-grey
Podocarpus elatus	Tree	Warm Z 9-11	8 ft 15 ft 30 ft / 2.5m 5 m 9 m	Everg	—	Foliage; bark; edible/decorative fruit	Lawn specimen, parks, streets, hedge	Fallen fruit stain paved areas	Only female trees produce fruit (all *Podocarpus* spp.)
Podocarpus henkelii	Tree	Warm Z 9-11	5 ft 10 ft 20 ft / 1.5 m 3 m 6 m	Everg	—	Foliage; edible/decorative fruit	Lawn specimen, informal hedge	—	—
Podocarpus latifolius	Tree	Warm Z 9-11	8 ft 15 ft 30 ft / 2.5m 5 m 9 m	Everg	—	Foliage	Lawn specimen, parks, streets	—	—
Podocarpus lawrencei	Shrub	Cool Z 8-9	2 ft 4 ft 5 ft / 0.6 m 1.2 m 1.5 m	Everg	—	Foliage; decorative fruit	Rock garden, courtyard, container	—	—
Podocarpus macrophyllus	Tree	Cool Z 7-11	4 ft 8 ft 15 ft / 1.2 m 2.5 m 5 m	Everg	—	Foliage	Lawn specimen, courtyards, plazas, containers	—	The form commonly planted is very slow-growing
Podocarpus neriifolius	Tree	Hot Z 10-12	5 ft 10 ft 20 ft / 1.5 m 3 m 6 m	Everg	—	Foliage	Lawn specimen, courtyard, rainforest garden	—	—

NAME	KIND	CLIMATE & ZONE	HEIGHT AT 5 yrs	HEIGHT AT 10 yrs	HEIGHT AT 20 yrs	DECIDUOUS EVERGREEN	ARID CLIMATES	CHIEF ATTRACTIONS	USES	DRAWBACKS	COMMENTS
Podocarpus salignus	Tree	Cool Z 8-9	6 ft 2 m	12 ft 4 m	25 ft 8 m	Everg	—	Foliage; bark	Lawn specimen	—	—
Podocarpus totara	Tree	Cool Z 9-10	6 ft 2 m	15 ft 5 m	30 ft 9 m	Everg	—	Foliage; bark; decorative fruit	Lawn specimen, parks, streets	—	Grows to a very large tree in its native New Zealand
Polygala myrtifolia	Shrub	Warm Z 9-11	5 ft 1.5 m	8 ft 2.5 m	8 ft 2.5 m	Everg	—	Flowers (purple & green, most of year)	Shrub border, hedge, screen, courtyard	—	Cultivar 'Grandiflora' is the form usually grown
Polygala virgata	Shrub	Warm Z 9-11	6 ft 2 m	6 ft 2 m	—	Everg	—	Flowers (purple, late winter-early summer)	Shrub border, rock garden	Free-seeding, can become a weed	—
Polyscias filicifolia	Shrub	Hot Z 11-12	6 ft 2 m	10 ft 3 m	12 ft 4 m	Everg	—	Foliage	Courtyard, plaza, swimming pool, container	—	Semi-shaded position preferred; a golden cultivar is popular
Polyscias guilfoylei	Shrub	Hot Z 10-12	6 ft 2 m	10 ft 3 m	12 ft 4 m	Everg	—	Foliage	Courtyard, plaza, swimming pool, container	—	Several variegated cultivars are grown
Polyscias scutellaria	Shrub	Hot Z 10-12	6 ft 2 m	10 ft 3 m	12 ft 4 m	Everg	—	Foliage	Shrub border, courtyard, plaza, swimming pool, container	—	Several variegated cultivars are grown
Pomaderris aspera	Shrub	Warm Z 8-10	10 ft 3 m	12 ft 4 m	15 ft 5 m	Everg	—	Flowers (white, spring); foliage	Shrub border, woodland garden	—	Likes shade, moist soil
Pomaderris kumeraho	Shrub	Warm Z 8-10	5 ft 1.5 m	8 ft 2.5 m	10 ft 3 m	Everg	—	Flowers (yellow, spring); foliage	Shrub border, courtyard	—	Crushed leaves foam in water, used as soap substitute
Poncirus trifoliata	Shrub	Warm Z 5-10	5 ft 1.5 m	10 ft 3 m	12 ft 4 m	Decid	—	Decorative fruit; flowers (white, fragrant, spring)	Thorny hedge, lawn specimen, rootstock for citrus	Fierce thorns	Fruit skin is very aromatic
Populus alba	Tree	Cool Z 2-10	12 ft 4 m	25 ft 8 m	40 ft 12 m	Decid	Yes	Autumn foliage; bark; flowers (reddish, spring)	Parks, streets, farms	Suckers freely from roots	Cultivar 'Pyramidalis' is less inclined to sucker
Populus deltoides	Tree	Cool Z 3-11	15 ft 5 m	30 ft 9 m	60 ft 18 m	Decid	—	Stately habit; autumn foliage; flowers (reddish (male), spring)	Timber, windbreaks, parks, avenues	Branches brittle; seed fluff carried by wind	Some cultivated clones are female, others male
Populus fremontii	Tree	Cool Z 5-10	15 ft 5 m	25 ft 8 m	50 ft 15 m	Decid	Yes	Autumn foliage	Parks, avenues	—	—
Populus lasiocarpa	Tree	Cool Z 7-9	8 ft 2.5 m	12 ft 4 m	25 ft 8 m	Decid	—	Summer and autumn foliage; flowers (yellow, spring)	Lawn specimen, courtyard	Leaves scorched by hot winds	Grown for its handsome summer foliage
Populus nigra	Tree	Cool Z 6-10	15 ft 5 m	30 ft 9 m	50 ft 15 m	Decid	—	Stately habit; autumn foliage	Avenues, windbreaks, farms, parks	Suckers from roots	Cultivar 'Italica' (Lombardy poplar) is form usually grown
Populus tremula	Tree	Cold Z 1-9	12 ft 4 m	25 ft 8 m	40 ft 12 m	Decid	—	Autumn foliage; bark	Lawn specimen, parks	Suckers from roots	Famed for its leaves that quiver in slightest breeze
Populus tremuloides	Tree	Cold Z 1-8	12 ft 4 m	25 ft 8 m	40 ft 12 m	Decid	—	Autumn foliage; bark	Lawn specimen, parks, windbreaks	—	—
Populus trichocarpa	Tree	Cool Z 7-9	10 ft 3 m	20 ft 6 m	30 ft 9 m	Decid	—	Autumn foliage	Lawn specimen, timber, windbreak, parks, streets	Short-lived in mild climates	—
Populus yunnanensis	Tree	Warm Z 7-10	10 ft 3 m	20 ft 6 m	30 ft 9 m	Decid	—	Foliage	Parks, streets	—	Suckers less than most other poplars; adapts to warmer climates
Portulacaria afra	Shrub	Warm Z 9-11	2 ft 0.6 m	5 ft 1.5 m	8 ft 2.5 m	Everg	Yes	Foliage; flowers (pink, spring)	Courtyards, containers, bonsai, swimming pools, fodder	—	Flowers rarely seen in countries outside South Africa
Prostanthera caerulea	Shrub	Warm Z 9-10	6 ft 2 m	8 ft 2.5 m	—	Everg	—	Flowers (blue-violet, spring)	Rock garden, shrub border, courtyard	Short-lived	Massed display of blue flowers
Prostanthera cuneata	Shrub	Cool Z 8-9	2 ft 0.6 m	3 ft 1 m	3 ft 1 m	Everg	—	Flowers (white to pale mauve, summer)	Rock garden, courtyard	—	—
Prostanthera lasianthos	Tree	Warm Z 8-10	10 ft 3 m	15 ft 5 m	20 ft 6 m	Everg	—	Flowers (white, late spring-midsummer)	Shrub border, lawn specimen, woodland garden	—	The 'Christmas bush' of Victoria
Prostanthera ovalifolia	Shrub	Warm Z 9-11	6 ft 2 m	8 ft 2.5 m	—	Everg	—	Flowers (violet-purple, spring); aromatic foliage	Shrub border, courtyard	Short-lived, prone to root rot	Massed display of violet flowers
Prostanthera rotundifolia	Shrub	Warm Z 9-10	6 ft 2 m	6 ft 2 m	—	Everg	—	Flowers (mauve, spring)	Shrub border, courtyard, woodland garden	—	—
Protea aristata	Shrub	Warm Z 9-10	4 ft 1.2 m	6 ft 2 m	8 ft 2.5 m	Everg	—	Flowers (deep pink, summer); foliage	Rock garden, shrub border, courtyard, cut flowers	—	Narrow, needle-like leaves
Protea compacta	Shrub	Warm Z 9-10	6 ft 2 m	8 ft 2.5 m	10 ft 3 m	Everg	—	Flowers (pink, late autumn-early spring)	Shrub border, cut flowers	—	All proteas need perfect drainage, dry summers
Protea cynaroides	Shrub	Warm Z 9-10	3 ft 1 m	5 ft 1.5 m	5 ft 1.5 m	Everg	—	Flowers (pink, midwinter-spring)	Cut flowers, rock garden, container, conservatory	—	The largest flower-head in proteas, South Africa's floral emlem
Protea eximia	Shrub	Warm Z 9-10	5 ft 1.5 m	8 ft 2.5 m	12 ft 4 m	Everg	—	Flowers (pink to crimson, winter-spring)	Cut flowers, shrub border, lawn specimen	—	—
Protea grandiceps	Shrub	Warm Z 9-10	2 ft 0.6 m	4 ft 1.2 m	6 ft 2 m	Everg	—	Flowers (pink, late spring-summer)	Shrub border, rock garden, cut flowers	—	Becomes a small tree in the wild
Protea longifolia	Shrub	Warm Z 9-10	3 ft 1 m	5 ft 1.5 m	5 ft 1.5 m	Everg	—	Flowers (cream, green & black, autumn-spring)	Shrub border, rock garden, cut flowers	—	—
Protea neriifolia	Shrub	Warm Z 9-10	5 ft 1.5 m	8 ft 2.5 m	8 ft 2.5 m	Everg	—	Flowers (deep pink & black, autumn-spring)	Cut flowers, shrub border, lawn specimen	—	Unusual floral bracts tipped with black furry hairs
Protea repens	Shrub	Warm Z 9-10	5 ft 1.5 m	8 ft 2.5 m	10 ft 3 m	Everg	—	Flowers (white to crimson, autumn-winter)	Shrub border, cut flowers	—	Nectar from flowers was made into a syrup by settlers in Capetown area

NAME	KIND	CLIMATE & ZONE	HEIGHT AT 5yrs	10yrs	20yrs	DECIDUOUS EVERGREEN	ARID CLIMATES	CHIEF ATTRACTIONS	USES	DRAWBACKS	COMMENTS
Protea scolymocephala	Shrub	Warm Z 9-10	2 ft 0.6 m	3 ft 1 m	3 ft 1 m	Everg	—	Flowers (cream to greenish, sping-summer)	Rock garden, container, cut flowers	—	Interesting small nodding flower-heads, dwarf habit
Prumnopitys elegans (Podocarpus andinus)	Tree	Cool Z 8-9	6 ft 2 m	10 ft 3 m	12 ft 4 m	Everg	—	Foliage; decorative fruit	Lawn specimen, hedge, windbreak	—	—
Prumnopitys ferruginea (Podocarpus ferrugineus)	Tree	Cool Z 8-9	6 ft 2 m	10 ft 3 m	20 ft 6 m	Everg	—	Foliage; decorative fruit	Lawn specimen	Fruit poisonous	—
Prunus armeniaca	Tree	Cool Z 5-10	6 ft 2 m	12 ft 4 m	20 ft 6 m	Decid	Yes	Edible fruit (apricot); flowers (white or pink, early spring)	Home orchard, courtyard, lawn specimen	—	Prefers climates with warm dry summers
Prunus avium	Tree	Cool Z 3-9	10 ft 3 m	20 ft 6 m	30 ft 9 m	Decid	—	Edible fruit; flowers (white, spring), autumn colour	Orchard, lawn specimen, timber	—	Eating cherries derived from this species, but the wild form has very small fruit
Prunus campanulata	Tree	Cool Z 8-10	10 ft 3 m	20 ft 6 m	30 ft 9 m	Decid	—	Flowers (carmine pink, late winter-early spring)	Lawn specimen	—	Flowers better in warm climates than other cherries
Prunus cerasifera	Tree	Cool Z 3-10	8 ft 2.5 m	15 ft 5 m	25 ft 8 m	Decid	—	Flowers (white, late winter-spring); decorative/edible fruit; foliage	Lawn specimen, parks, streets	—	Purple-leaved cultivars most popular as ornamentals
Prunus cerasoides	Tree	Cool Z 7-9	8 ft 2.5m	15 ft 5 m	25 ft 8 m	Decid	—	Flowers (rose-pink, late spring)	Lawn specimen	—	—
Prunus domestica	Tree	Cool Z 2-10	8 ft 2.5 m	15 ft 5 m	20 ft 6 m	Decid	—	Edible fruit (plums); flowers (white, spring)	Orchard, lawn specimen	Branches often thorny	Many fruiting cultivars
Prunus ilicifolia	Tree	Cool Z 7-10	6 ft 2 m	12 ft 4 m	20 ft 6 m	Everg	—	Foliage; flowers (white, spring); decorative fruit	Lawn specimen, courtyard, hedge	—	Holly-like evergreen leaves
Prunus laurocerasus	Tree	Cool Z 5-9	8 ft 2.5 m	15 ft 5 m	25 ft 8 m	Everg	—	Foliage; flowers (white, spring); decorative fruit	Hedge, screen, windbreak, cut foliage (funeral wreaths)	Foliage poisonous to livestock	Fruit edible, sometimes used for jam or jelly
Prunus lusitanica	Tree	Cool Z 6-9	10 ft 3 m	20 ft 6 m	30 ft 9 m	Everg	—	Foliage; flowers (white, early summer); decorative fruit	Hedge, screen, windbreak, lawn specimen	—	Closely related to P. laurocerasus
Prunus mume	Tree	Cool Z 5-9	8 ft 2.5 m	12 ft 4 m	15 ft 5 m	Everg	—	Flowers (white to deep pink, winter-early spring); edible fruit	Lawn specimen, parks, cut flowers	—	Fruits eaten in Japan and China, grown elsewhere for ornament
Prunus persica	Tree	Cool Z 5-10	5 ft 1.5 m	8 ft 2.5 m	12 ft 4 m	Decid	Yes	Edible fruit; flowers (white, pink or red, late winter or early spring)	Orchard, lawns specimen, cut flowers	Susceptible to fruit fly	Different peach cvs grown for fruit and flowers
Prunus sargentii	Tree	Cool Z 4-9	8 ft 2.5m	15 ft 5 m	25 ft 8 m	Decid	Yes	Flowers (pink, spring); autumn foliage	Lawn specimen, parks, streets	—	—
Prunus serotina	Tree	Cool Z 2-9	10 ft 3 m	20 ft 6 m	30 ft 9 m	Decid	—	Autumn foliage; flowers (white, fragrant, spring); decorative fruit	Timber, parks, avenues	Seed spread by birds, can become a weed	—
Prunus serrula	Tree	Cool Z 6-9	8 ft 2.5m	15 ft 5 m	25 ft 8 m	Decid	—	Bark; flowers (white, spring); autumn foliage	Lawn specimen, parks	—	Striking shiny reddish bark, banded transversely
Prunus serrulata	Tree	Cool Z 4-9	10 ft 3 m	20 ft 6 m	30 ft 9 m	Decid	—	Flowers (white, pink, mid-spring); autumn foliage	Lawn specimen, courtyard, parks, streets	Prone to stem cankers, insect & fungal attack	Cultivars include double and semi-double flowers, weeping habit
Prunus subhirtella	Tree	Cool Z 4-9	8 ft 2.5 m	15 ft 5 m	20 ft 6 m	Decid	—	Flowers (pale pink, early spring); autumn foliage	Lawn specimen, courtyard, woodland garden	—	Cultivar 'Pendula' is most widely grown, usually grafted as a standard
Prunus tenella	Shrub	Cool Z 4-9	3 ft 1 m	5 ft 1.5 m	5 ft 1.5 m	Decid	—	Flowers (pink, mid to late spring)	Shrub border, courtyard	—	Prefers full sun, moist soil
Prunus × yedoensis	Tree	Cool Z 3-9	8 ft 2.5m	15 ft 5 m	25 ft 8 m	Decid	—	Flowers (white or pale pink, spring); autumn foliage	Lawn specimen, streets	—	—
Pseuderanthemum reticulatum	Shrub	Hot Z 11-12	3 ft 1 m	3 ft 1 m	3 ft 1 m	Everg	—	Foliage; flowers (white & pink, spring-summer)	Courtyard, shrub border, container, indoor, groundcover	—	Several cultivars, varying in leaf coloration
Pseudolarix amabilis	Tree	Cool Z 3-9	4 ft 1.2 m	8 ft 2.5 m	20 ft 6 m	Decid	—	Autumn foliage	Lawn specimen, parks, bonsai	Slow-growing	Larch-like foliage very attractive
Pseudopanax crassifolius	Tree	Warm Z 9-10	5 ft 1.5 m	10 ft 3 m	20 ft 6 m	Everg	—	Foliage	Courtyard, shrub border, woodland garden	—	Thick sword-like leaves on saplings change dramatically on adult plants
Pseudopanax lessonii	Tree	Warm Z 9-10	6 ft 2 m	12 ft 4 m	20 ft 6 m	Everg	—	Foliage	Courtyard, shrub border, container, swimming pool	—	Several cultivars available, varying in foliage
Pseudotsuga menziesii	Tree	Cool Z 4-9	8 ft 2.5m	15 ft 5 m	30 ft 9 m	Everg	—	Foliage; symmetrical form	Timber, lawn specimen, parks, farms, windbreak	—	Fast-growing conifer, one of the world's important timber trees
Psidium cattleianum	Shrub	Warm Z 9-12	5 ft 1.5 m	10 ft 3 m	15 ft 5 m	Everg	—	Edible fruit; bark; foliage	Home orchard, shrub border, courtyard	Becomes a weed in wet tropical climates	Fruits make a delicious tangy jelly
Psidium guajava	Shrub	Hot Z 10-12	6 ft 2 m	12 ft 4 m	20 ft 6 m	Everg	—	Edible fruit; bark	Orchard, courtyard	Prone to fruit fly attack	Fruit canned or juiced, makes a tasty jelly
Ptelea trifoliata	Tree	Cool Z 2-9	6 ft 2 m	12 ft 4 m	20 ft 6 m	Decid	—	Autumn foliage; decorative fruit	Shrub border, lawn specimen, woodland garden	—	Interesting disc-shaped fruit; prefers semi-shade
Pterocarya fraxinifolia	Tree	Cool Z 5-9	10 ft 3 m	20 ft 6 m	40 ft 12 m	Decid	—	Foliage; flowers (greenish-yellow, spring); curious fruit	Lawn specimen, parks, streets, shade	—	Relative of walnuts & hickories but nuts small, winged

NAME	KIND	CLIMATE & ZONE	HEIGHT AT 5 yrs	HEIGHT AT 10 yrs	HEIGHT AT 20 yrs	DECIDUOUS/EVERGREEN	ARID CLIMATES	CHIEF ATTRACTIONS	USES	DRAWBACKS	COMMENTS
Pterostyrax hispida	Tree	Cool Z 4-9	6 ft 2 m	12 ft 4 m	25 ft 8 m	Decid	—	Flowers (white, fragrant, summer); decorative fruit	Lawn specimen, parks, woodland garden	—	Bristly fruit clusters interesting & attractive
Ptychosperma macarthurii	Palm	Hot Z 11-12	6 ft 2 m	12 ft 4 m	25 ft 8 m	Everg	—	Foliage; decorative fruit	Lawn specimen, courtyard, parks, streets, plazas	Fleshy fruits litter pavements	Popular landscaping palm in humid tropical areas; multi-stemmed
Punica granatum	Shrub	Warm Z 8-11	5 ft 1.5 m	10 ft 3 m	15 ft 5 m	Everg	Yes	Edible/decorative fruit; flowers (red-orange, spring-summer)	Shub border, courtyard, home orchard, container	Untidy growth habit, wiry dead twigs	Different cultivars grown for fruit & ornament
Puya berteroniana	Shrub	Warm Z 9-11	2 ft 0.6 m	8 ft 2.5 m	8 ft 2.5 m	Everg	—	Foliage; flowers (blue & orange, summer)	Rock garden, courtyard, plaza, desert garden	Leaves very spiny	Most of height consists of flowering panicle and stalk
Pycnostachys urticifolia	Shrub	Hot Z 10-12	5 ft 1.5 m	5 ft 1.5 m	5 ft 1.5 m	Everg	—	Flowers (blue, summer)	Shrub border, courtyard, conservatory	Weak, untidy stems	Flowers are a very rich blue
Pyracantha angustifolia	Shrub	Cool Z 6-10	4 ft 1.2 m	8 ft 2.5 m	10 ft 3 m	Everg	—	Decorative fruit; flowers (white, late spring-early summer)	Hedge, shrub border	Very thorny; seeds spread by birds	Red, orange or yellow fruits characterize different plants
Pyracantha coccinea	Shrub	Cool Z 5-9	4 ft 1.2 m	8 ft 2.5 m	10 ft 3 m	Everg	—	Decorative fruit	Hedge, shrub border, courtyard	—	Several cultivars available, some lower-growing
Pyracantha crenatoserrata	Shrub	Cool Z 6-10	4 ft 1.2 m	8 ft 2.5 m	12 ft 4 m	Everg	—	Decorative fruit	Hedge, shrub border, courtyard	—	—
Pyrus calleryana	Tree	Cool Z 5-10	8 ft 2.5 m	15 ft 5 m	30 ft 9 m	Decid	—	Flowers (white, early spring); autumn foliage	Lawn specimen, parks, streets, graft stock	Can be short-lived	Cultivars include 'Bradford', useful for city streets
Pyrus communis	Tree	Cool Z 2-9	6 ft 2 m	15 ft 5 m	25 ft 8 m	Decid	—	Edible fruit; flowers (white, spring)	Orchard (pear), lawn specimen	—	Right mix of cultivars needed for effective pollination for fruit
Pyrus pyrifolia var. culta	Tree	Cool Z 4-10	6 ft 2 m	15 ft 5 m	25 ft 8 m	Decid	—	Edible fruit; flowers (white, spring); autumn foliage	Orchard (nashi pear), lawn specimen	—	Fruit had gritty texture, but improved forms now available
Pyrus salicifolia	Tree	Cool Z 4-9	6 ft 2 m	12 ft 4 m	20 ft 6 m	Decid	Yes	Silvery foliage; flowers (white, spring)	Lawn specimen	—	'Pendula' is form most commonly grown
Pyrus ussuriensis	Tree	Cool Z 4-9	8 ft 2.5 m	20 ft 6 m	40 ft 12 m	Decid	—	Autumn foliage; flowers (white, spring)	Lawn specimen, parks, streets	—	Popular as a street tree
Quercus acutissima	Tree	Cool Z 5-10	6 ft 2 m	15 ft 5 m	30 ft 9 m	Decid	—	Autumn foliage; bark	Lawn specimen, parks, avenues	—	Leaves have many small bristly teeth
Quercus agrifolia	Tree	Cool Z 6-10	6 ft 2 m	15 ft 5 m	30 ft 9 m	Everg	—	Foliage	Lawn specimen, parks	—	Prefers winter-rainfall climates
Quercus alba	Tree	Cool Z 3-9	8 ft 2.5m	20 ft 6 m	40 ft 12 m	Decid	—	Autumn foliage; bark	Timber, parks, avenues, wine casks	—	One of the USA's important timber trees
Quercus bicolor	Tree	Cool Z 4-10	6 ft 2 m	15 ft 5 m	30 ft 9 m	Decid	—	Foliage; bark	Lawn specimen, parks, streets	—	Leaves whitish on undersides
Quercus canariensis (mirbeckii)	Tree	Cool Z 5-10	8 ft 2.5m	15 ft 5 m	30 ft 9 m	Decid	Yes	Foliage; symmetrical form	Lawn specimen, parks, streets	—	Similar to English oak (Q. robur) but more drought tolerant
Quercus castaneifolia	Tree	Cool Z 5-9	8 ft 2.5 m	15 ft 5 m	30 ft 9 m	Decid	—	Autumn foliage	Lawn specimen, parks, streets	—	Leaves resemble those of chestnuts
Quercus cerris	Tree	Cool Z 7-10	8 ft 2.5 m	15 ft 5 m	30 ft 9 m	Decid	Yes	Autumn foliage	Timber, lawn specimen, parks	—	Magnificent large tree, attractive foliage
Quercus chrysolepis	Tree	Cool Z 7-9	6 ft 2 m	12 ft 4 m	25 ft 8 m	Everg	—	Foliage	Lawn specimen	—	Young leaves have coating of yellow down
Quercus coccinea	Tree	Cool Z 2-9	10 ft 3 m	20 ft 6 m	40 ft 12 m	Decid	—	Autumn foliage	Lawn specimen, parks, streets	—	Rich red autumn colouring, but some trees disappoint
Quercus dentata	Tree	Cool Z 7-9	6 ft 2 m	12 ft 4 m	25 ft 8 m	Decid	—	Autumn foliage	Lawn specimen	Slow-growing	Striking large leaves
Quercus ilex	Tree	Warm Z 6-10	8 ft 2.5m	15 ft 5 m	30 ft 9 m	Everg	Yes	Dense foliage; rounded shape	Parks, streets, hedge, coastal planting, topiary	—	Holly-like leaves on young trees; magnificent shade tree
Quercus kelloggii	Tree	Cool Z 6-10	6 ft 2 m	12 ft 4 m	25 ft 8 m	Decid	—	Foliage	Parks	—	—
Quercus macrocarpa	Tree	Cool Z 2-9	8 ft 2.5 m	15 ft 5 m	30 ft 9 m	Decid	—	Autumn foliage	Lawn specimen, parks, streets	—	Large acorns sit in cups with long shaggy scales
Quercus mongolica	Tree	Cool Z 4-9	8 ft 2.5 m	15 ft 5 m	30 ft 9 m	Decid	—	Autumn foliage	Lawn specimen, parks, streets	—	Thin leaves, pale on undersides
Quercus nigra	Tree	Cool Z 6-10	8 ft 2.5m	15 ft 5 m	30 ft 9 m	Decid	—	Foliage, bark	Lawn specimen, parks, boggy areas	—	Holds leaves well into winter
Quercus palustris	Tree	Cool Z 3-10	10 ft 3 m	20 ft 6 m	40 ft 12 m	Decid	—	Autumn foliage	Lawn specimen, parks, streets	—	Deeply lobed leaves make fine autumn display
Quercus phellos	Tree	Cool Z 5-9	6 ft 2 m	12 ft 4 m	25 ft 8 m	Decid	—	Autumn foliage	Lawn specimen, parks, streets	—	Unusual among oaks for its narrow, willow-like leaves
Quercus prinus	Tree	Cool Z 3-9	8 ft 2.5 m	15 ft 5 m	30 ft 9 m	Decid	—	Autumn foliage	Lawn specimen, parks, streets, timber	—	—
Quercus robur	Tree	Cool Z 3-10	8 ft 2.5 m	15 ft 5 m	30 ft 9 m	Decid	—	Foliage, broad canopy	Lawn specimen, parks, streets, timber, tanbark, wine casks	Foliage disfigured by leaf-miner insects	The best known oak, famed for timber; acorns long-stalked
Quercus rubra (borealis)	Tree	Cool Z 3-9	10 ft 3 m	20 ft 6 m	40 ft 12 m	Decid	—	Autumn foliage	Lawn specimen, parks, streets	—	Vigorous grower, fine autumn colour
Quercus salicina	Tree	Cool Z 8-10	8 ft 2.5m	15 ft 5 m	30 ft 9 m	Everg	—	Foliage	Lawn specimen, parks, streets	—	Narrow leathery leaves

NAME	KIND	CLIMATE & ZONE	HEIGHT AT 5yrs	10yrs	20yrs	DECIDUOUS EVERGREEN	ARID CLIMATES	CHIEF ATTRACTIONS	USES	DRAWBACKS	COMMENTS
Quercus shumardii	Tree	Cool Z 5-10	8 ft 2.5m	15 ft 5 m	30 ft 9 m	Decid	—	Autumn foliage	Lawn specimen, parks, streets	—	Similar to Q. rubra but adapted to warmer climate
Quercus suber	Tree	Warm Z 6-10	6 ft 2 m	12 ft 4 m	25 ft 8 m	Everg	Yes	Bark, gnarled trunk	Cork, lawn specimen, parks	—	Bark is the source of cork; prefers winter-rainfall climates
Quercus velutina	Tree	Cool Z 3-9	8 ft 2.5m	15 ft 5 m	30 ft 9 m	Decid	—	Autumn colour	Lawn specimen, parks, streets, tanbark, dye	—	Larged lobed leaves are downy on underside
Quercus virginiana	Tree	Warm Z 7-11	8 ft 2.5m	15 ft 5 m	30 ft 9 m	Everg	—	Foliage, dense canopy	Parks, streets, coastal plantings, woodland garden	—	Thrives in humid warm-temperate climates
Quercus wislizenii	Tree	Warm Z 8-10	8 ft 2.5m	15 ft 5 m	30 ft 9 m	Everg	—	Foliage	Lawn specimen, parks, streets	—	Similar to Q. agrifolia, narrower leaves
Quillaja saponaria	Tree	Warm Z 8-10	6 ft 2 m	15 ft 5 m	30 ft 9 m	Everg	—	Foliage; bark; flowers	Lawn specimen, hedge, screen	—	Bark foams in water, used as a soap substitute
Radermachera sinica	Tree	Warm Z 10-12	12 ft 4 m	20 ft 6 m	30 ft 9 m	Everg	—	Foliage; flowers (white, summer)	Indoor, courtyard, swimming pool, lawn specimen	Stems weak	Introduced as an indoor foliage plant, flowers only on larger trees
Rauvolfia caffra	Tree	Warm Z 9-11	10 ft 3 m	20 ft 6 m	30 ft 9 m	Everg	—	Flowers (white, fragrant, summer); decorative fruit	Lawn specimen, medicinal drugs	Fruit and sap are poisonous	One of the sources of the drug reserpine
Ravenala madagascariensis	Tree	Hot Z 11-12	8 ft 2.5m	12 ft 4 m	20 ft 6 m	Everg	Yes	Foliage; symmetrical form	Lawn specimen, courtyard, plaza, swimming pool	—	Eye-catching palm-like plant for tropical gardens
Retama monosperma	Shrub	Cool Z 7-10	4 ft 1.2 m	5 ft 1.5 m	5 ft 1.5 m	Everg	Yes	Flowers (white, fragrant, spring); weeping foliage	Shrub border, courtyard	Often short-lived	Prefers winter-rainfall climates
Rhamnus alaternus	Shrub	Cool Z 6-10	6 ft 2 m	10 ft 3 m	12 ft 4 m	Everg	Yes	Foliage; flowers (greenish-yellow, late winter-early spring)	Hedge, shrub border, courtyard, container	—	Variegated cultivars more commonly grown
Rhamnus californica	Shrub	Cool Z 6-10	4 ft 1.2 m	6 ft 2 m	6 ft 2 m	Everg	Yes	Decorative fruit; foliage	Shrub border, medicinal drug	—	One of the sources of the drug cascara sagrada
Rhamnus purshiana	Shrub	Cool Z 5-9	8 ft 2.5m	15 ft 5 m	20 ft 6 m	Decid	—	Foliage, decorative fruit	Shrub border, woodland garden, medicinal drug	—	Principal source of the drug cascara sagrada
Rhaphiolepis × delacourii	Shrub	Warm Z 7-10	3 ft 1 m	5 ft 1.5 m	6 ft 2 m	Everg	—	Flowers (pale to deep pink, late winter-spring); decorative fruit	Shrub border, courtyard, swimming pool, hedge	—	—
Rhaphiolepis indica	Shrub	Warm Z 8-11	4 ft 1.2 m	6 ft 2 m	8 ft 2.5 m	Everg	—	Flowers (white & pink, late winter-spring); decorative fruit	Shrub border, courtyard, hedge	Seeds spread by pigeons	—
Rhaphiolepis umbellata	Shrub	Warm Z 7-11	2 ft 0.6 m	4 ft 1.2 m	6 ft 2 m	Everg	—	Foliage; flowers (white, spring-early summer); decorative fruit	Coastal planting, hedge, rock garden, courtyard, swimming pool	Seeds spread by pigeons	Makes broad, rounded hummock, good for very exposed position
Rhapidophyllum hystrix	Palm	Cool Z 8-11	2 ft 0.6 m	4 ft 1.2 m	5 ft 1.5 m	Everg	—	Foliage	Courtyard, swimming pool, container	Sharp spines hidden among leaf bases	Densely massed deep green fronds, remains compact
Rhapis excelsa	Palm	Warm Z 10-11	4 ft 1.2 m	6 ft 2 m	6 ft 2 m	Everg	—	Foliage; bamboo-like stems	Courtyard, container, plaza, indoor, shrub border	Difficult to propagate	First-class indoor palm but needs adequate humidity
Rhapis subtilis	Palm	Warm Z 10-12	2 ft 0.6 m	4 ft 1.2 m	5 ft 1.5 m	Everg	—	Foliage; bamboo-like stems	Courtyard, container, plaza, indoor, shrub border	—	Smaller than R. excelsa, often raised from seed
Rhododendron arboreum	Tree	Cool Z 6-9	4 ft 1.2 m	8 ft 2.5 m	12 ft 4 m	Everg	—	Flowers (white, pink or red, early spring)	Shrub border, woodland garden	Leaves disfigured by spider-mites	An important parent of Hardy hybrid rhododendrons
Rhododendron augustinii	Shrub	Cool Z 6-9	2 ft 0.6 m	4 ft 1.2 m	5 ft 1.5 m	Everg	—	Flowers (blue, late spring)	Shrub border, woodland garden, rock garden	—	One of the bluest-flowered rhododendrons
Rhododendron calendulaceum	Shrub	Cool Z 4-9	4 ft 1.2 m	6 ft 2 m	8 ft 2.5 m	Decid	—	Flowers (scarlet, orange or yellow, spring); autumn foliage	Shrub border, woodland garden	—	A parent of deciduous azalea hybrids
Rhododendron catawbiense	Shrub	Cool Z 3-9	4 ft 1.2 m	6 ft 2 m	8 ft 2.5 m	Everg	—	Flowers (lilac, purple or white, early summer)	Shrub border, woodland garden	—	An important parent of Hardy hybrid rhododendrons
Rhododendron cinnabarinum	Shrub	Cool Z 8-9	3 ft 1 m	5 ft 1.5 m	6 ft 2 m	Everg	—	Flowers (orange-red, early summer)	Shrub border, woodland garden	—	Unusual drooping, trumpet shaped orange flowers
Rhododendron decorum	Shrub	Cool Z 7-9	3 ft 1 m	5 ft 1.5 m	8 ft 2.5 m	Everg	—	Flowers (white or pale pink, fragrant, late spring-early summer)	Shrub border, woodland garden	—	Large, open flowers have very delicate colouring
Rhododendron degronianum	Shrub	Cool Z 6-9	2 ft 0.6 m	4 ft 1.2 m	5 ft 1.5 m	Everg	—	Flowers (pale pink, late spring); foliage	Shrub border, woodland garden, rock garden	—	Distinctive narrow leaves, delicately coloured flowers
Rhododendron 'Fragrantissimum'	Shrub	Cool Z 9-10	2 ft 0.6 m	4 ft 1.2 m	6 ft 2 m	Everg	—	Flowers (white & pink, fragrant, spring-summer)	Shrub border, woodland garden, conservatory	—	Loosely clustered flowers have delicious fragrance
Rhododendron Ghent azalea hybrids	Shrub	Cool Z 6-9	4 ft 1.2 m	6 ft 2 m	8 ft 2.5 m	Decid	—	Flowers (white, yellow, orange, red, fragrant, late spring); autumn foliage	Shrub border	—	—
Rhododendron griffithianum	Tree	Cool Z 8-9	4 ft 1.2 m	8 ft 2.5 m	12 ft 4 m	Everg	—	Flowers (white, fragrant, late spring)	Shrub border, woodland garden	—	Important parent of some large-flowered hybrids
Rhododendron Hardy hybrids	Shrub	Cool Z 4-9	—	—	—	Everg	—	Flowers (many colours, midwinter-midsummer)	Shrub border, woodland garden, lawn specimen	—	Great variation in cold-hardiness and size among the many cultivars

Reference Table

NAME	KIND	CLIMATE & ZONE	HEIGHT AT 5yrs	10yrs	20yrs	DECIDUOUS EVERGREEN	ARID CLIMATES	CHIEF ATTRACTIONS	USES	DRAWBACKS	COMMENTS
Rhododendron *Indica azalea hybrids*	Shrub	Warm Z 9-10	2 ft 0.6 m	4 ft 1.2 m	5 ft 1.5 m	Everg	—	Flowers (white, pink, orange, red, winter-spring)	Shrub border, courtyard, container, woodland garden	Susceptible to spider mite and petal blight fungus	Many cultivars, mature size varies
Rhododendron kiusianum	Shrub	Cool Z 8-10	2 ft 0.6 m	3 ft 1 m	3 ft 1 m	Everg	—	Flowers (purple-pink, spring); autumn-winter foliage	Shrub border, rock garden, woodland garden, bonsai	Susceptible to petal blight fungus	One of the parents of the Kurume azalea hybrids
Rhododendron *Kurume azalea hybrids*	Shrub	Cool Z 8-10	1 ft 0.3 m	2 ft 0.6 m	3 ft 1 m	Everg	—	Flowers (white, pink, orange, purple, spring)	Shrub border, courtyard, container, woodland garden, bonsai	—	Similar to Indica azalea hybrids but smaller
Rhododendron litiense	Shrub	Cool Z 6-9	3 ft 1 m	6 ft 2 m	8 ft 2.5 m	Everg	—	Flowers (yellow, early-midsummer)	Shrub border, woodland garden	—	Sometimes regarded as a synonym of *R. wardii*
Rhododendron lochiae	Shrub	Warm Z 9-11	2 ft 0.6 m	3 ft 1 m	5 ft 1.5 m	Everg	—	Flowers (red, spring-summer)	Courtyard, woodland garden	—	Australia's only native rhododendron
Rhododendron macgregoriae	Shrub	Warm Z 9-11	2 ft 0.6 m	4 ft 1.2 m	6 ft 2 m	Everg	—	Flowers (yellow, orange, red, summer-autumn)	Courtyard, woodland garden	Reported to be poisonous	Tallest of the Vireya rhododendrons; large heads of small flowers
Rhododendron maximum	Shrub	Cool Z 3-9	4 ft 1.2 m	6 ft 2 m	10 ft 3 m	Everg	—	Flowers (purple to pink, early summer)	Lawn specimen, hedge, shrub border	—	Rarely cultivated outside USA but parent of early hybrids
Rhododendron *Mollis azalea hybrids*	Shrub	Cool Z 5-9	3 ft 1 m	5 ft 1.5 m	6 ft 2 m	Decid	—	Flowers (red, orange, yellow, early spring); autumn foliage	Shrub border, woodland garden	—	Mainly derived from the Japanese *R. japonicum*
Rhododendron nuttallii	Shrub	Cool Z 9	4 ft 1.2 m	6 ft 2 m	8 ft 2.5 m	Everg	—	Flowers (white, pale yellow & pink, fragrant, spring); bark; foliage	Woodland garden, conservatory	Sparse, leggy habit	One of the largest-flowered of all rhododendrons
Rhododendron occidentale	Shrub	Cool Z 5-9	4 ft 1.2 m	6 ft 2 m	8 ft 2.5 m	Decid	—	Flowers (white to pink & yellow, fragrant, early summer); autumn foliage	Shrub border, woodland garden	—	Parent of the Occidentale azalea hybrids
Rhododendron ponticum	Shrub	Cool Z 5-9	5 ft 1.5 m	8 ft 2.5 m	12 ft 4 m	Decid	—	Flowers (mauve, late spring-early summer)	Woodland garden, hedge, windbreak, rootstock for cultivars	Has become a weed in Britain	Important parent species of Hardy hybrids
Rhododendron *Satsuki & Gumpo azalea hybrids*	Shrub	Cool Z 8-10	1 ft 0.3 m	2 ft 0.6 m	2 ft 0.6 m	Everg	—	Flowers (white, pink, orange, red, late spring)	Containers, courtyards, conservatory, bonsai	—	Some cultivars feature striped and variably coloured flowers on the one plant
Rhododendron schlippenbachii	Shrub	Cool Z 4-9	4 ft 1.2 m	6 ft 2 m	10 ft 3 m	Decid	—	Flowers (white to pink, fragrant, spring)	Shrub border, woodland garden	—	—
Rhododendron simsii	Shrub	Warm Z 9-11	2 ft 0.6 m	4 ft 1.2 m	5 ft 1.5 m	Everg	—	Flowers (deep pink or red, winter-spring)	Shrub border, woodland garden	—	The major parent of Indica azalea hybrids
Rhododendron sinogrande	Tree	Cool Z 8-9	2 ft 0.6 m	5 ft 1.5 m	10 ft 3 m	Everg	—	Foliage; flowers (cream to yellow, spring)	Woodland garden	Slow-growing	Huge leathery leaves; takes 10 years or more to flower
Rhododendron *Vireya hybrids*	Shrub	Warm Z 9-11	2 ft 0.6 m	4 ft 1.2 m	6 ft 2 m	Everg	—	Flowers (white, yellow, pink, orange, red, most of year)	Courtyard, woodland garden, conservatory	Sparse, leggy habit	Cultivars vary in size and growth habit; most prefer shade
Rhodoleia championii	Tree	Warm Z 9-11	5 ft 1.5 m	10 ft 3 m	15 ft 5 m	Everg	—	Flowers (red, winter-early spring)	Shrub border, lawn specimen	—	Unusual bell-shaped flower heads with long red bracts
Rhodosphaera rhodanthema	Tree	Warm Z 10-11	8 ft 2.5 m	15 ft 5 m	30 ft 9 m	Everg	—	Foliage; decorative fruit; flowers (red, spring)	Lawn specimen, parks, rainforest garden	Fallen fruit litter ground	Clusters of shiny red-brown berries with dry flesh
Rhopalostylis sapida	Palm	Warm Z 10-11	3 ft 1 m	6 ft 2 m	12 ft 4 m	Everg	—	Foliage; symmetrical form	Shrub border, lawn group, courtyard	—	The world's most southerly wild palm
Rhus aromatica	Shrub	Cool Z 2-9	2 ft 0.6 m	3 ft 1 m	3 ft 1 m	Decid	—	Autumn foliage	Shrub border, courtyard, embankment, groundcover	—	—
Rhus chinensis	Shrub	Cool Z 6-9	6 ft 2 m	12 ft 4 m	15 ft 5 m	Decid	—	Autumn foliage; flowers (white, late summer)	Shrub border, lawn specimen	—	Autumn colour very fine, red & orange shades
Rhus lancea	Tree	Warm Z 9-11	8 ft 2.5 m	15 ft 5 m	20 ft 6 m	Everg	Yes	Foliage	Shrub border, hedge, screen, shelter	—	Fruit eaten by birds
Rhus pendulina	Tree	Warm Z 9-11	8 ft 2.5 m	12 ft 4 m	15 ft 5 m	Everg	Yes	Foliage	Shrub border, hedge, screen, shelter, shade	—	Willow-like habit, fruit eaten by birds; large cuttings can be rooted
Rhus typhina	Shrub	Cool Z 3-9	6 ft 2 m	10 ft 3 m	15 ft 5 m	Decid	—	Autumn foliage; decorative fruit	Shrub border, lawn specimen	—	Dense spikes of velvety reddish fruit terminate branches in autumn
Ribes alpinum	Shrub	Cool Z 5-9	3 ft 1 m	6 ft 2 m	6 ft 2 m	Decid	—	Decorative fruit; foliage	Shrub border, hedge, courtyard	—	Male & female plants required for fruit set
Ribes fasciculatum	Shrub	Cool Z 5-9	3 ft 1 m	4 ft 1.2 m	5 ft 1.5 m	Decid	—	Decorative fruit	Shrub border, courtyard	—	Male & female plants required for fruit set
Ribes odoratum	Shrub	Cool Z 6-9	3 ft 1 m	6 ft 2 m	8 ft 2.5 m	Decid	—	Flowers (yellow, fragrant, spring); decorative fruit	Shrub border, courtyard	—	Spicy fragrance of the small flowers is the chief attraction
Ribes sanguineum	Shrub	Cool Z 6-9	5 ft 1.5 m	8 ft 2.5 m	10 ft 3 m	Decid	—	Flowers (pink to red, late spring)	Shrub border, hedge, lawn specimen, courtyard	—	The finest-flowered *Ribes* species, a first class shrub
Ribes sativum	Shrub	Cool Z 6-9	3 ft 1 m	5 ft 1.5 m	6 ft 2 m	Decid	—	Edible/decorative fruit (redcurrant)	Kitchen garden, courtyard	—	Named cultivars usually grown for fruit
Ribes uva-crispa (grossularia)	Shrub	Cool Z 6-9	2 ft 0.6 m	3 ft 1 m	3 ft 1 m	Decid	—	Edible fruit (gooseberry)	Kitchen garden, hedge	Very prickly	Requires cool to cold climate for good fruiting
Richea pandanifolia	Tree	Cool Z 8-9	2 ft 0.6 m	6 ft 2 m	12 ft 4 m	Everg	—	Foliage; symmetrical form; flowers (white or pinkish, summer)	Shrub border, woodland garden, courtyard	Slow-growing	Striking sword-leaved plant, remains unbranched for many years

NAME	KIND	CLIMATE & ZONE	HEIGHT AT 5 yrs	HEIGHT AT 10 yrs	HEIGHT AT 20 yrs	DECIDUOUS EVERGREEN	ARID CLIMATES	CHIEF ATTRACTIONS	USES	DRAWBACKS	COMMENTS
Robinia hispida	Tree	Cool Z 3-9	6 ft 2 m	6 ft 2 m	6 ft 2 m	Decid	Yes	Flowers (pink, summer); decorative fruit	Shrub border, courtyard, lawn specimen	Suckers from roots	Sometimes grafted onto R. pseudoacacia to make a tree
Robinia pseudoacacia	Tree	Cool Z 3-10	10 ft 3 m	20 ft 6 m	30 ft 9 m	Decid	—	Autumn foliage; flowers (white, fragrant, late spring-summer)	Lawn specimen, streets, farms, timber, boggy areas	Suckers from roots, invasive	Golden cultivar 'Frisia' is now more widely planted
Robinia viscosa	Tree	Cool Z 5-10	8 ft 2.5 m	15 ft 5 m	20 ft 6 m	Decid	—	Flowers (pink, early summer); autumn foliage	Lawn specimen, courtyard, parks, streets	—	Young branches and pods have a sticky coating
Rondeletia amoena	Shrub	Warm Z 10-11	4 ft 1.2 m	6 ft 2 m	8 ft 2.5 m	Everg	—	Flowers (pink, spring)	Shrub border, lawn specimen, courtyard	—	Flowers attract nectar-feeding birds
Rosa carolina	Shrub	Cool Z 3-9	3 ft 1 m	3 ft 1 m	3 ft 1 m	Decid	—	Flowers (white or pink, late spring-summer); decorative fruit	Shrub border, embankment, rock garden	—	Spreads by basal suckers to form clump
Rosa chinensis	Shrub	Cool Z 6-10	5 ft 1.5 m	8 ft 2.5 m	12 ft 4 m	Decid	—	Flowers (pink-red, spring-autumn)	Shrub border, formal garden, courtyard	—	Repeat-flowering habit incorporated in most modern roses
Rosa foetida	Shrub	Cool Z 4-9	4 ft 1.2 m	8 ft 2.5 m	10 ft 3 m	Decid	—	Flowers (yellow, late spring)	Shrub border, courtyard	Very prickly	Source f the rich yellows in modern rose hybrids
Rosa gallica	Shrub	Cool Z 3-9	3 ft 1 m	3 ft 1 m	3 ft 1 m	Decid	—	Flowers (pink, fragrant, spring-early summer)	Shrub border, woodland garden	—	One of the earliest cultivated roses, early hybrid parent
Rosa glauca	Shrub	Cool Z 2-9	4 ft 1.2 m	6 ft 2 m	6 ft 2 m	Decid	—	Flowers (pink, summer); foliage; decorative fruit	Shrub border, cut foliage & hips	—	Summer foliage is bluish or purplish
Rosa moyesii	Shrub	Cool Z 3-9	4 ft 1.2 m	6 ft 2 m	6 ft 2 m	Decid	—	Flowers (crimson, summer); decorative fruit	Shrub border, woodland garden, cut fruiting stems	Very prickly	Hips very attractive; cv 'Geranium' selected for flower colour
Rosa rugosa	Shrub	Cool Z 2-10	3 ft 1 m	5 ft 1.5 m	5 ft 1.5 m	Decid	—	Flowers (white, pink, crimson, spring-autumn); foliage; decorative fruit	Coastal planting, embankments, hedges	Rampant spreader	Distinctive strongly veined leaves, fine display of hips
Rosa sericea var. pteracantha	Shrub	Cool Z 6-9	3 ft 1 m	4 ft 1.2 m	6 ft 2 m	Decid	—	Decorative prickles; flowers (white, late spring)	Shrub border, woodland garden	Very prickly	Striking broad-based prickles, translucent red when young
Rosa xanthina	Shrub	Cool Z 3-9	4 ft 1.2 m	6 ft 2 m	10 ft 3 m	Decid	—	Flowers (yellow, fragrant, late spring)	Shrub border, courtyard	—	Needs cold winter, dry summer to flower well; 'Canary Bird' is more adaptable
Rosmarinus officinalis	Shrub	Cool Z 6-10	2 ft 0.6 m	3 ft 1 m	4 ft 1.2 m	Everg	Yes	Flowers (blue, autumn-spring); aromatic foliage	Herb garden, rock garden, hedge, courtyard, container	—	Variable in growth habit, some cvs prostrate or have brighter blue flowers
Rothmannia capensis	Tree	Warm Z 10-11	6 ft 2 m	12 ft 4 m	15 ft 5 m	Everg	—	Flowers (cream to yellow, summer)	Shrub border, lawn specimen	—	—
Rothmannia globosa	Tree	Warm Z 10-11	5 ft 1.5 m	10 ft 3 m	12 ft 4 m	Everg	—	Flowers (cream, fragrant, spring-summer)	Shrub border, lawn specimen, courtyard	—	Hard globular fruit persist on branches, blacken with age
Roystonea regia	Palm	Hot Z 11-12	8 ft 2.5 m	12 ft 4 m	25 ft 8 m	Everg	—	Foliage; symmetrical form; smooth columnar trunk	Lawn grouping, parks, avenues	Fallen fruit litter pavements	Some famous avenues in tropical cities
Rubus idaeus	Shrub	Cool Z 4-9	5 ft 1.5 m	5 ft 1.5 m	5 ft 1.5 m	Decid	—	Edible fruit (raspberry)	Kitchen garden, orchard	—	Numerous cultivars available, differing in fruit qualities
Rubus occidentalis	Shrub	Cool Z 2-9	5 ft 1.5 m	5 ft 1.5 m	5 ft 1.5 m	Decid	—	Edible fruit (black raspberry)	Kitchen garden	—	—
Rubus odoratus	Shrub	Cool Z 2-9	4 ft 1.2 m	6 ft 2 m	6 ft 2 m	Decid	—	Flowers (pink, fragrant, summer-early autumn)	Shrub border, woodland garden	Suckers freely, untidy habit	Prefers semi-shade
Sabal minor	Palm	Warm Z 8-11	2 ft 0.6 m	4 ft 1.2 m	6 ft 2 m	Everg	—	Foliage; decorative fruit	Shrub border, courtyard, swimming pool	—	Dwarf palm, usually lacks a trunk; stiff greyish foliage
Sabal palmetto	Palm	Warm Z 8-11	2 ft 0.6 m	5 ft 1.5 m	10 ft 3 m	Everg	—	Foliage; symmetrical form	Lawn grouping, parks, streets	Fallen fruit litter pavements	Old frond bases form interesting pattern on trunk
Salix alba	Tree	Cool Z 2-9	12 ft 4 m	25 ft 8 m	40 ft 12 m	Decid	—	Foliage; vigorous growth	Stream & lake edges, boggy areas, timber	Carried by floods, can become a weed	Var. caerulea is the willow used for cricket bats
Salix apoda	Shrub	Cool Z 3-9	2 ft 0.6 m	3 ft 1 m	3 ft 1 m	Decid	—	Furry catkins (silvery, early spring); foliage	Rock garden, courtyard	—	Broadly spreading habit
Salix babylonica	Tree	Cool Z 4-10	12 ft 4 m	25 ft 8 m	40 ft 12 m	Decid	—	Weeping habit; autumn foliage	Lawn specimen, stream & lake edges, boggy areas	Invasive roots, spreads along rivers	The weeping willow; displaced in cooler climates by S. × chrysocoma
Salix × chrysocoma	Tree	Cool Z 2-9	12 ft 4 m	25 ft 8 m	40 ft 12 m	Decid	—	Weeping habit; yellow twigs; autumn foliage	Lawn specimen, waters-edge	—	—
Salix fragilis	Tree	Cool Z 2-9	12 ft 4 m	25 ft 8 m	40 ft 12 m	Decid	—	Vigorous growth; autumn foliage	Lawn specimen, stream & lake edges, boggy areas	Branches very brittle	Hybrids with S. alba are more commonly found
Salix humboldtiana	Tree	Warm Z 9-11	10 ft 3 m	20 ft 6 m	30 ft 9 m	Everg	—	Foliage; columnar form	Lawn grouping, screen, courtyard	Often short-lived	Best suited to moist subtropical climates
Salix integra	Shrub	Cool Z 5-9	5 ft 1.5 m	8 ft 2.5 m	10 ft 3 m	Decid	—	Purplish twigs; foliage	Shrub border, courtyard, pond edge	—	—
Salix matsudana 'Tortuosa'	Tree	Cool Z 4-10	12 ft 4 m	20 ft 6 m	30 ft 9 m	Decid	—	Bizarrely twisted branches	Lawn specimen, dried arrangements	—	Species hardly distinguishable from S. babylonica

NAME	KIND	CLIMATE & ZONE	HEIGHT AT 5yrs	10 yrs	20 yrs	DECIDUOUS EVERGREEN	ARID CLIMATES	CHIEF ATTRACTIONS	USES	DRAWBACKS	COMMENTS
Salix purpurea	Shrub	Cool Z 2-9	6 ft 2 m	10 ft 3 m	12 ft 4 m	Decid	—	Foliage; catkins (red-purple, spring)	Shrub border, pond edge	—	Fine purplish twigs good for winter effect
Salvia africana-lutea	Shrub	Warm Z 9-11	3 ft 1 m	5 ft 1.5 m	6 ft 2 m	Everg	Yes	Flowers (yellow to brown, spring-early summer)	Rock garden, shrub border, courtyard	—	Remarkable flower colour
Samanea saman	Tree	Hot Z 11-12	15 ft 5 m	30 ft 9 m	40 ft 12 m	Everg	—	Broad canopy; flowers (pink & white, late spring-summer)	Parks, avenues, wood carving, stock fodder	Surface roots interfere with lawns	Wood is the 'monkey pod' used for hand-carved items
Sambucus caerulea	Tree	Cool Z 4-9	6 ft 2 m	12 ft 4 m	20 ft 6 m	Decid	—	Flowers (yellow, early summer); decorative/edible fruit	Shrub border, lawn specimen, home orchard	—	One of tallest, longest-lived Sambucus spp.; berries blue
Sambucus canadensis	Shrub	Cool Z 2-10	8 ft 2.5m	10 ft 3 m	10 ft 3 m	Decid	—	Flowers (white, spring); decorative fruit; foliage	Shrub border, lawn specimen	—	A golden cultivar is popular
Sambucus nigra	Shrub	Cool Z 2-10	6 ft 2 m	12 ft 4 m	15 ft 5 m	Decid	—	Flowers (white, spring); decorative/edible fruit; foliage	Shrub border, lawn specimen, kitchen garden	—	Fruit used in pies, preserves; flowers used to flavour wine
Santalum acuminatum	Tree	Warm Z 9-11	3 ft 1 m	6 ft 2 m	10 ft 3 m	Everg	Yes	Edible fruit	Lawn specimen	Difficult to propagate (semi-parasitic)	Plum-sized red fruit have acid flesh, good flavour
Sapindus drummondii	Tree	Warm Z 8-11	10 ft 3 m	20 ft 6 m	30 ft 9 m	Decid	Yes	Foliage; decorative fruit	Lawn specimen, parks, streets, shade	—	Crushed fruit lather in water, used as soap substitute
Sapium sebiferum	Tree	Warm Z 8-11	10 ft 3 m	20 ft 6 m	30 ft 9 m	Decid	—	Autumn foliage; decorative seeds	Lawn specimen, parks, streets	Seeds may litter pavements	Good autumn colour even in subtropical climates
Saraca indica	Tree	Hot Z 11-12	6 ft 2 m	12 ft 4 m	20 ft 6 m	Everg	—	Flowers (yellow to scarlet, mainly summer)	Lawn specimen, parks	Slow growing, crooked habit	—
Sarcococca hookeriana	Shrub	Cool Z 5-9	3 ft 1 m	5 ft 1.5 m	5 ft 1.5 m	Everg	—	Foliage; flowers (cream, fragrant, late winter-spring); decorative fruit	Shrub border, courtyard, hedge, woodland garden	—	—
Sarcococca ruscifolia	Shrub	Cool Z 6-9	3 ft 1 m	5 ft 1.5 m	5 ft 1.5 m	Everg	—	Foliage; flowers (cream, fragrant, late winter-spring); decorative fruit	Shrub border, courtyard, hedge, woodland garden	—	Glossy evergreen foliage
Sassafras albidum	Shrub	Cool Z 2-9	8 ft 2.5m	15 ft 5 m	25 ft 8 m	Decid	—	Autumn foliage	Shrub border, lawn specimen, aromatic oil from leaves	—	—
Saxegothaea conspicua	Tree	Cool Z 7-9	5 ft 1.5 m	10 ft 3 m	20 ft 6 m	Everg	—	Foliage	Lawn specimen, woodland garden	—	Yew-like foliage but leaves sharper-pointed
Scaevola sericea	Shrub	Hot Z 10-12	4 ft 1.2 m	5 ft 1.5 m	6 ft 2 m	Everg	—	Foliage; flowers (white, most of year); decorative fruit	Coastal planting, courtyard, shrub border	—	Most other Scaevola spp. lower-growing Australian shrubs
Schefflera actinophylla	Tree	Hot Z 10-12	6 ft 2 m	15 ft 5 m	25 ft 8 m	Everg	—	Foliage; flowers (red, late summer-early spring); decorative fruit	Courtyard, plaza, swimming pool, container, indoor	Greedy root system	Popular indoor plan; in nature it is usually an epiphyte
Schefflera arboricola	Shrub	Warm Z 10-11	4 ft 1.2 m	8 ft 2.5 m	12 ft 4 m	Everg	—	Foliage; decorative fruit	Courtyard, plaza, swimming pool, container, indoor	—	Popular indoor plan; in nature it is usually an epiphyte
Schinus areira (molle)	Tree	Warm Z 9-11	10 ft 3 m	20 ft 6 m	30 ft 9 m	Everg	Yes	Foliage; weeping habit; gnarled trunk; decorative fruit	Lawn specimen, parks, streets, plazas	—	Tolerates hot dry climates, also urban pollution
Schinus terebinthifolia	Tree	Hot Z 10-12	8 ft 2.5m	15 ft 5 m	25 ft 8 m	Everg	Yes	Foliage; decorative fruit	Lawn specimen	Becomes a weed in warm wet climates	Requires warmer, wetter conditions than S. areira
Schizolobium parahybum	Tree	Hot Z 10-12	10 ft 3 m	25 ft 8 m	50 ft 15 m	Decid*	—	Foliage; symmetrical form; flowers (gold, spring)	Lawn specimen, parks, plazas, timber	—	Very fast-growing tropical tree, remains unbranched for considerable height
Schotia brachypetala	Tree	Warm Z 9-11	6 ft 2 m	12 ft 4 m	20 ft 6 m	Decid*	—	Flowers (red, spring)	Lawn specimen	—	Flowers attract nectar-feeding birds
Sciadopitys verticillata	Tree	Cool Z 5-9	2 ft 0.6 m	6 ft 2 m	12 ft 4 m	Everg	—	Foliage; symmetrical form	Lawn specimen, courtyard	Slow-growing	Unique leaf formation among conifers, very attractive
Scolopia braunii	Tree	Warm Z 10-11	8 ft 2.5m	15 ft 5 m	25 ft 8 m	Everg	—	Foliage; bronze new growths; decorative fruit	Lawn specimen, rainforest garden	—	—
Senecio grandifolius	Shrub	Warm Z 10-11	4 ft 1.2 m	8 ft 2.5 m	10 ft 3 m	Everg	—	Flowers (yellow, late summer-winter); foliage	Shrub border, lawn specimen	—	Striking large hairy leaves, flat heads of daisy flowers
Senecio greyii	Shrub	Warm Z 8-10	2 ft 0.6 m	4 ft 1.2 m	5 ft 1.5 m	Everg	—	Foliage; flowers (yellow, late spring-summer)	Coastal planting, shrub border, hedge	—	Foliage grey & green
Senecio laxifolia	Shrub	Warm Z 7-10	2 ft 0.6 m	3 ft 1 m	3 ft 1 m	Everg	—	Flowers (yellow, midsummer); foliage	Rock garden, coastal palnting, hedge	—	Similar to S. greyii, more open habit
Senecio petasitis	Shrub	Warm Z 10-11	4 ft 1.2 m	6 ft 2 m	8 ft 2.5 m	Everg	—	Flowers (yellow, late winter-spring); foliage	Shrub border, pond edge, boggy areas	—	Attractive large felty leaves, stems with reddish hairs
Senecio viravira	Shrub	Warm Z 9-10	2 ft 0.6 m	2 ft 0.6 m	—	Everg	—	Flowers (white, summer); foliage	Rock garden, courtyard, container	Often short-lived	Whitish foliage: one of the 'dusty miller' senecios
Senna (Cassia) alata	Shrub	Hot Z 10-12	6 ft 2 m	8 ft 2.5 m	—	Everg	—	Flowers (yellow, summer)	Shrub border, courtyard	Short-lived	Medicinal drug obtained from the plant
Senna (Cassia) artemisioides	Shrub	Warm Z 8-11	3 ft 1 m	—	—	Everg	Yes	Flowers (yellow, winter-early summer); foliage	Shrub border, courtyard	Short-lived	Highly variable, many wild forms now placed under this name
Senna (Cassia) didymobotrya	Shrub	Warm Z 10-11	5 ft 1.5 m	8 ft 2.5 m	—	Everg	Yes	Flowers (yellow, summer-winter)	Shrub border, courtyard	Short-lived	Distinctive blackish scales enclosing flower spikes in bud

NAME	KIND	CLIMATE & ZONE	HEIGHT AT 5yrs	HEIGHT AT 10yrs	HEIGHT AT 20yrs	DECIDUOUS EVERGREEN	ARID CLIMATES	CHIEF ATTRACTIONS	USES	DRAWBACKS	COMMENTS
Senna (Cassia) multijuga	Tree	Hot Z 10-12	6 ft 2 m	12 ft 4 m	20 ft 6 m	Everg	Yes	Flowers (yellow, late summer)	Lawn specimen, courtyard, plaza	—	Massed display of flowers above foliage
Senna pendula (Cassia bicapsularis)	Shrub	Warm Z 9-11	6 ft 2 m	8 ft 2.5 m	10 ft 3 m	Everg	—	Flowers (yellow, autumn)	Shrub border, courtyard, conservatory	Self-seeding in warm, wet climates	One of the easiest autumn-flowering shrubs for warm climates
Senna (Cassia) spectabilis	Tree	Hot Z 10-12	8 ft 2.5 m	15 ft 5 m	25 ft 8 m	Everg	—	Flowers (yellow, summer)	Lawn specimen, plaza	—	—
Sequoia sempervirens	Tree	Cool Z 7-10	8 ft 2.5 m	20 ft 6 m	40 ft 12 m	Everg	—	Foliage; stately habit; bark	Parks, avenues, timber, farms	—	The world's tallest living tree
Sequoiadendron giganteum	Tree	Cool Z 6-9	6 ft 2 m	15 ft 5 m	30 ft 9 m	Everg	—	Foliage; stately habit; bark	Parks, avenues	—	The largest living tree, in terms of bulk, but not the tallest
Serenoa repens	Palm	Warm Z 9-11	2 ft 0.6 m	3 ft 1 m	3 ft 1 m	Everg	—	Foliage; flowers (white, fragrant, summer); decorative fruit	Courtyard, woodland garden, container, swimming pool	Oily fruit develop unpleasant smell	Stem creeping, usually below ground; stiff grey-green foliage
Serruria florida	Shrub	Warm Z 9-10	3 ft 1 m	4 ft 1.2 m	4 ft 1.2 m	Everg	—	Flowers (white to pale pink, winter-spring); foliage	Shrub border, rock garden, Cut flowers	Prone to root rot	Important commercial cut flower, cultivation tricky
Sideroxylon inerme	Tree	Warm Z 9-11	6 ft 2 m	12 ft 4 m	20 ft 6 m	Everg	—	Foliage; edible/decorative fruit	Coastal planting, lawn specimen, parks	—	—
Simmondsia chinensis	Shrub	Warm Z 9-11	3 ft 1 m	5 ft 1.5 m	8 ft 2.5 m	Everg	Yes	Foliage	Oil from seeds	Slow-growing	The jojoba, promoted for plantations; requires hot dry climate
Skimmia japonica	Shrub	Cool Z 7-9	2 ft 0.6 m	4 ft 1.2 m	5 ft 1.5 m	Everg	—	Foliage; decorative fruit; flowers (white, spring)	Rock garden, shrub border, courtyard	—	Male and female plants required for fruit display
Sloanea woollsii	Tree	Warm Z 10-12	10 ft 3 m	20 ft 6 m	40 ft 12 m	Everg	—	Foliage; flowers (white, spring)	Lawn specimen, parks, rainforest garden	—	Mature trees develop large buttresses
Solanum aviculare	Shrub	Warm Z 9-11	6 ft 2 m	8 ft 2.5 m	—	Everg	—	Flowers (purple, spring-summer); decorative fruit; foliage	Shrub border, courtyard, rainforest garden	Short-lived	Large lobed juvenile leaves; used for manufacture of contraceptive drugs
Solanum (Lycianthes) rantonnei	Shrub	Warm Z 9-10	4 ft 1.2 m	6 ft 2 m	6 ft 2 m	Everg	—	Flowers (violet-blue, spring-summer); decorative fruit	Shrub border, courtyard	—	Very free-flowering, showy
Solanum mammosum	Shrub	Hot Z 11-12	3 ft 1 m	4 ft 1.2 m	—	Everg	—	Decorative fruit	Cut stems with fruit	Short-lived, straggly habit	Large fruit resembles a cow's udder
Sophora japonica	Tree	Cool Z 4-10	6 ft 2 m	12 ft 4 m	25 ft 8 m	Decid	—	Autumn foliage; flowers (cream, summer)	Lawn specimen	—	Leaves, bark and wood contain a purgative drug
Sophora microphylla	Tree	Warm Z 7-10	5 ft 1.5 m	10 ft 3 m	15 ft 5 m	Decid	—	Flowers (yellow, late winter-early summer); foliage	Shrub border, lawn specimen	Often defoliated by larvae of kowhai moth	Similar to S. tetraptera, leaflets slightly smaller
Sophora tetraptera	Tree	Warm Z 8-10	5 ft 1.5 m	10 ft 3 m	15 ft 5 m	Decid	—	Flowers (yellow, spring); foliage	Shrub border, lawn specimen	Often defoliated by larvae of kowhai moth	New Zealand's national flower
Sorbaria arborea	Shrub	Cool Z 4-9	6 ft 2 m	12 ft 4 m	15 ft 5 m	Decid	—	Flowers (white, midsummer); foliage	Shrub border	—	Feathery pinnate leaves, large sprays iof small white flowers
Sorbus aria	Tree	Cold Z 2-9	3 ft 1 m	8 ft 2.5 m	12 ft 4 m	Decid	—	Autumn foliage; flowers (white, late spring); decorative fruit	Lawn specimen	Leaves disfigured by 'pear & cherry slug' (most Sorbus)	One of the Sorbus spp. with simple rather than pinnate leaves
Sorbus aucuparia	Tree	Cold Z 2-9	6 ft 2 m	12 ft 4 m	20 ft 6 m	Decid	—	Decorative fruit; autumn foliage; flowers (white, spring)	Lawn specimen, parks, streets	—	Larger-fruited form is used for jams and preserves
Sorbus chamaemespilus	Shrub	Cool Z 5-9	2 ft 0.6 m	4 ft 1.2 m	8 ft 2.5 m	Decid	—	Decorative fruit; autumn foliage	Shrub border, courtyard, woodland garden	—	One of the smallest spp. with simple, hardly toothed leaves
Sorbus commixta	Tree	Cool Z 4-9	6 ft 2 m	12 ft 4 m	20 ft 6 m	Decid	—	Decorative fruit; autumn foliage	Lawn specimen, parks, streets	—	—
Sorbus domestica	Tree	Cool Z 3-8	6 ft 2 m	12 ft 4 m	25 ft 8 m	Decid	—	Edible/decorative fruit	Lawn specimen	—	One of the largest-fruited Sorbus spp., fruit used for preserves
Sorbus hupehensis	Tree	Cool Z 5-9	8 ft 2.5 m	15 ft 5 m	25 ft 8 m	Decid	—	Autumn foliage; decorative fruit	Lawn specimen, parks, streets	—	Vigorous growth, unusual whitish berries ageing dull pink
Sorbus 'Joseph Rock'	Tree	Cool Z 4-9	6 ft 2 m	12 ft 4 m	20 ft 6 m	Decid	—	Decorative fruit; autumn foliage	Lawn specimen, courtyard, parks, streets	—	Bright yellow berries
Sorbus megalocarpa	Tree	Cool Z 4-9	3 ft 1 m	8 ft 2.5 m	15 ft 5 m	Decid	—	Flowers (white, late winter); decorative fruit	Lawn specimen, courtyard	Flowers have pungent smell	Simple, toothed leaves, large brown fruit
Sorbus pohuashanensis ('Pagoda Red')	Tree	Cool Z 4-9	6 ft 2 m	12 ft 4 m	20 ft 6 m	Decid	—	Decorative fruit; flowers (late spring)	Lawn specimen, courtyard, parks, streets	—	Fine display of red fruit
Sparrmania africana	Tree	Warm Z 10-11	6 ft 2 m	12 ft 4 m	15 ft 5 m	Everg	—	Flowers (white, winter-spring); foliage	Lawn specimen, shrub border	Weak, straggly branches	A double-flowered form is often grown
Spartium junceum	Shrub	Warm Z 6-10	4 ft 1.2 m	8 ft 2.5 m	10 ft 3 m	Everg	Yes	Flowers (yellow, fragrant, spring-early summer)	Shrub border, screen, courtyard	Sometimes short-lived	One of the most colourful brooms in flower
Spathodea campanulata	Tree	Hot Z 11-12	10 ft 3 m	20 ft 6 m	30 ft 9 m	Everg	Yes	Flowers (spring-summer); foliage	Lawn specimen, parks, streets	Damaged by strong winds	May be deciduous in climates with a severe dry season
Spiraea cantoniensis	Shrub	Warm Z 5-10	3 ft 1 m	5 ft 1.5 m	6 ft 2 m	Decid	—	Flowers (white, spring)	Shrub border, courtyard, hedge, cut flowers	Builds up dead twigs in centre	Suits subtropical climates better than other spiraeas
Spiraea douglasii	Shrub	Cool Z 4-9	3 ft 1 m	5 ft 1.5 m	6 ft 2 m	Decid	—	Flowers (pink, summer)	Shrub border, woodland garden	—	—
Spiraea japonica	Shrub	Cool Z 4-9	3 ft 1 m	5 ft 1.5 m	5 ft 1.5 m	Decid	—	Flowers (pink, summer)	Shrub border, courtyard, rock garden, container	—	A number of cultivars available

NAME	KIND	CLIMATE & ZONE	HEIGHT AT 5yrs 10yrs 20yrs	DECIDUOUS EVERGREEN	ARID CLIMATES	CHIEF ATTRACTIONS	USES	DRAWBACKS	COMMENTS
Spiraea nipponica	Shrub	Cool Z 5-9	3 ft 5 ft 6 ft / 1 m 1.5 m 2 m	Decid	—	Flowers (white, early summer)	Shrub border, courtyard, rock garden	—	Lower-growing selections are available
Spiraea prunifolia	Shrub	Cool Z 4-9	3 ft 5 ft 6 ft / 1 m 1.5 m 2 m	Decid	—	Flowers (white, early spring); autumn foliage	Shrub border, courtyard, cut flowers	—	Only the double-flowered form is usually grown
Spiraea thunbergii	Shrub	Cool Z 4-10	3 ft 5 ft 5 ft / 1 m 1.5 m 1.5 m	Decid	—	Flowers (white, early spring); autumn foliage	Shrub border, courtyard	—	Semi-evergreen in milder climates
Stachyurus praecox	Shrub	Cool Z 5-10	4 ft 6 ft 8 ft / 1.2 m 2 m 2.5 m	Decid	—	Flowers (pale yellow, winter-early spring); autumn foliage	Shrub border, courtyard, woodland garden	—	Elegant drooping flower spikes on bare winter branches
Stenocarpus sinuatus	Tree	Warm Z 10-11	6 ft 12 ft 20 ft / 2 m 4 m 6 m	Everg	—	Flowers (scarlet, autumn); foliage	Lawn specimen, parks, rainforest garden	Slow-growing, flowers erratically	Unique wheel-like arrangement of flowers
Stephanandra incisa	Shrub	Cool Z 4-9	3 ft 5 ft 6 ft / 1 m 1.5 m 2 m	Decid	—	Autumn foliage	Shrub border, courtyard, rock garden, cut flowers	—	—
Stephanandra tanakae	Shrub	Cool Z 4-9	3 ft 4 ft 5 ft / 1 m 1.2 m 1.5 m	Decid	—	Autumn foliage; flowers (white, summer)	Shrub border, courtyard, rock garden, cut flowers	—	Suckers from base to form broad clump
Stewartia malacodendron	Tree	Cool Z 7-9	3 ft 6 ft 10 ft / 1 m 2 m 3 m	Decid	—	Flowers (white, summer); autumn foliage	Shrub border, lawn specimen, woodland garden	—	Camellia-like flowers with central bunch of yellow stamens (all stewartias)
Stewartia pseudocamellia	Tree	Cool Z 6-9	4 ft 8 ft 15 ft / 1.2 m 2.5 m 5 m	Decid	—	Flowers (white, late spring-early summer); autumn foliage; decorative fruit	Lawn specimen, woodland garden	—	Prefers semi-shade
Stewartia sinensis	Tree	Cool Z 6-9	4 ft 8 ft 15 ft / 1.2 m 2.5 m 5 m	Decid	—	Flowers (white, late spring-summer); autumn foliage; bark	Lawn specimen, woodland garden	—	—
Strelitzia nicolai	Shrub	Warm Z 10-11	4 ft 8 ft 15 ft / 1.2 m 2.5 m 5 m	Everg	—	Foliage; flowers (blue & white, summer)	Lawn specimen, courtyard, plaza	Dead foliage builds up	Flowers attract nectar-feeding birds
Strelitzia reginae	Shrub	Warm Z 10-11	2 ft 4 ft 5 ft / 0.6 m 1.2 m 1.5 m	Everg	—	Flowers (orange & blue, spring-summer); foliage	Shrub border, courtyard, plaza, cut flowers, conservatory	Clumps difficult to divide	Var. juncea has leaves with no blade, rush-like stalks
Streptosolen jamesonii	Shrub	Warm Z 9-11	3 ft 5 ft 6 ft / 1 m 1.5 m 2 m	Everg	—	Flowers (orange, most of year)	Shrub border, courtyard, conservatory, swimming pool	Can be short-lived	A yellow-flowered form is also grown
Styrax japonica	Tree	Cool Z 7-9	6 ft 12 ft 20 ft / 2 m 4 m 6 m	Decid	—	Flowers (white, late spring-early summer)	Lawn specimen, woodland garden	—	Pretty display of small white bells
Styrax obassia	Tree	Cool Z 6-9	6 ft 12 ft 20 ft / 2 m 4 m 6 m	Decid	—	Flowers (white, late spring-early summer); bark; autumn foliage	Lawn specimen, woodland garden	—	Large, pale leaves are an attractive feature
Sutherlandia frutescens	Shrub	Warm Z 8-10	2 ft 4 ft — / 0.6 m 1.2 m	Everg	Yes	Flowers (red, late winter-summer); decorative seed-pods	Shrub border, rock garden, courtyard, conservatory	Short-lived	Curious balloon-like pods, translucent when young
Swietenia macrophylla	Tree	Hot Z 10-12	10 ft 20 ft 40 ft / 3 m 6 m 12 m	Decid*	—	Foliage; stately habit	Timber, parks	—	One of the world's most renowned timbers (Honduras mahogany)
Swietenia mahagoni	Tree	Hot Z 11-12	10 ft 20 ft 30 ft / 3 m 6 m 9 m	Decid*	—	Foliage; decorative fruit	Timber, lawn specimen	—	More spreading habit than S. macrophylla, also an important timber
Syagrus romanzoffiana	Palm	Warm Z 10-11	8 ft 15 ft 30 ft / 2.5 m 5 m 9 m	Everg	Yes	Foliage; symmetrical form; flowers (cream, summer); decorative fruit	Lawn grouping, swimming pool, plaza, avenue	Dead fronds hang onto trunk	Fast-growing palm, popular for 'instant landscaping'
Symphoricarpos albus	Shrub	Cool Z 4-9	3 ft 5 ft 6 ft / 1 m 1.5 m 2 m	Decid	—	Decorative fruit	Shrub border, woodland garden, courtyard	—	Unusual pure white spongy berries, persist into winter
Symphoricarpos orbiculatus	Shrub	Cool Z 4-9	3 ft 5 ft 6 ft / 1 m 1.5 m 2 m	Decid	—	Decorative fruit	Shrub border, woodland garden, courtyard	—	Small pink berries persist into winter; tolerates urban pollution
Syncarpia glomulifera	Tree	Warm Z 9-11	10 ft 20 ft 40 ft / 3 m 6 m 12 m	Everg	—	Flowers (cream, spring-summer); bark	Lawn specimen, parks, streets, timber	Leaves disfigured by sooty mould	Extremely durable timber used for wharf piles in Australia
Syringa × hyacinthiflora	Shrub	Cool Z 6-9	3 ft 6 ft 8 ft / 1 m 2 m 2.5 m	Decid	—	Flowers (pink, mauve, lavender, spring)	Shrub border, lawn specimen, courtyard	—	S. oblata × vulgaris; not as fragrant as S. vulgaris cultivars
Syringa meyeri	Shrub	Cold Z 4-9	2 ft 3 ft 3 ft / 0.6 m 1 m 1 m	Decid	—	Flowers (purple-red, spring)	Shrub border, courtyard	—	—
Syringa patula	Shrub	Cold Z 4-9	2 ft 4 ft 5 ft / 0.6 m 1.2 m 1.5 m	Decid	—	Flowers (mauve & white, late spring)	Shrub border, courtyard, lawn specimen	—	Cultivar 'Miss Kim' has deeper flower colour
Syringa reflexa	Shrub	Cold Z 3-9	5 ft 8 ft 12 ft / 1.5 m 2.5 m 4 m	Decid	—	Flowers (deep pink, late spring)	Lawn specimen, shrub border, courtyard	—	Drooping clusters of tubular flowers with recurved petals
Syringa reticulata	Shrub	Cold Z 3-9	5 ft 12 ft 20 ft / 1.5 m 4 m 6 m	Decid	—	Flowers (white, fragrant, spring)	Lawn specimen, shrub border, parks, cut flowers	—	The tallest syringa, known to reach 30 ft (9 m) in height
Syringa vulgaris	Shrub	Cold Z 2-9	3 ft 6 ft 8 ft / 1 m 2 m 2.5 m	Decid	—	Flowers (white to pink, blue-mauve or purple, fragrant, late spring or summer)	Shrub border, lawn specimen, courtyard, cut flowers	Short-lived when grafted on privet stock	Numerous cultivars, varying in flowering period and fragrance
Syzygium jambos	Tree	Hot Z 10-12	8 ft 15 ft 25 ft / 2.5 m 5 m 8 m	Everg	—	Flowers (greenish-white, spring-autumn); edible fruit	Lawn specimen, parks	—	Fruit is aromatic as well as edible
Syzygium luehmannii	Tree	Warm Z 10-11	8 ft 15 ft 25 ft / 2.5m 5 m 8 m	Everg	—	Decorative fruit; pink new growths; flowers (white, summer)	Lawn specimen, parks, hedge	—	Profuse display of brilliant magenta fruit in summer

NAME	KIND	CLIMATE & ZONE	HEIGHT AT 5yrs	HEIGHT AT 10yrs	HEIGHT AT 20yrs	DECIDUOUS EVERGREEN	ARID CLIMATES	CHIEF ATTRACTIONS	USES	DRAWBACKS	COMMENTS
Syzygium paniculatum	Tree	Warm Z 10-11	8 ft 2.5m	15 ft 5 m	30 ft 9 m	Everg	—	Decorative fruit; flowers (white, late spring)	Lawn specimen, coastal planting, parks, streets	Fallen fruit litter pavements	Pendulous clusters of bright rose-purple fruit in late summer
Syzygium wilsonii	Tree	Hot Z 10-12	3 ft 1 m	5 ft 1.5 m	6 ft 2 m	Everg	—	Flowers (magenta, spring-summer); red new growths	Shrub border, courtyard, rainforest garden	—	Semi-scrambling habit, crimson flowers in large 'powder-puff' heads
Tabebuia avellanedae	Tree	Hot Z 11-12	8 ft 2.5m	15 ft 5 m	30 ft 9 m	Decid*	Yes	Flowers (rose-pink, spring)	Lawn specimen, parks, streets	—	Tree completely covered in blossom on leafless branches
Tabebuia chrysantha	Tree	Hot Z 11-12	6 ft 2 m	12 ft 4 m	20 ft 6 m	Decid*	—	Flowers (golden-yellow, spring)	Lawn specimen, parks, streets	—	One of the most brilliantly coloured tropical flowering trees
Tabebuia chrysotricha	Tree	Warm Z 10-11	6 ft 2 m	12 ft 4 m	20 ft 6 m	Decid*	Yes	Flowers (golden-yellow, spring)	Lawn specimen, parks, streets	—	The most cold tolerant tabebuia
Tabebuia heterophylla	Tree	Hot Z 11-12	6 ft 2 m	12 ft 4 m	20 ft 6 m	Decid*	Yes	Flowers (pink, spring)	Lawn specimen, parks, streets	—	—
Tabernaemontana divaricata	Shrub	Hot Z 11-12	3 ft 1 m	4 ft 1.2 m	6 ft 2 m	Everg	—	Flowers (white, fragrant, spring-autumn)	Courtyard, shrub border, container, conservatory	—	Gardenia-like shrub; fragrance is stronger in the evening
Taiwania cryptomerioides	Tree	Cool Z 8-10	8 ft 2.5m	15 ft 5 m	30 ft 9 m	Everg	—	Foliage; symmetrical form	Lawn specimen, parks	—	Cloosely related to Cryptomeria, more pendulous branches
Tamarindus indica	Tree	Hot Z 12	10 ft 3 m	20 ft 6 m	30 ft 9 m	Everg	Yes	Foliage; flowers (yellow, summer); decorative/edible fruit	Lawn specimen, parks, streets	Roots can be invasive	Sweet-sour pulp of pods used in cooking and for drinks
Tamarix aphylla	Tree	Warm Z 8-11	8 ft 2.5m	20 ft 6 m	30 ft 9 m	Everg	Yes	Foliage; dense canopy	Windbreak, shelter, avenues, soil stabilization	Can become a weed in hot dry climates	Atttractive fine, dense, cypress-like grey foliage
Tamarix chinensis	Shrub	Cool Z 7-10	6 ft 2 m	8 ft 2.5 m	12 ft 4 m	Decid	Yes	Flowers (pink, summer)	Shrub border, hedge, screen	—	Tiny pink flowers in large foamy sprays
Tamarix parviflora	Shrub	Cool Z 4-10	6 ft 2 m	8 ft 2.5 m	12 ft 4 m	Decid	Yes	Flowers (pink, spring)	Shrub border, hedge, screen	Gaunt, untidy appearance in winter	The common spring-flowering tamarisk; flowers on old wood
Tamarix ramosissima	Shrub	Cool Z 3-10	6 ft 2 m	8 ft 2.5 m	12 ft 4 m	Decid	Yes	Flowers (pink, late summer)	Shrub border, hedge, screen	—	Largest, showiest flower sprays of a tamarisk
Taxodium ascendens	Tree	Cool Z 4-10	8 ft 2.5m	15 ft 5 m	30 ft 9 m	Decid	—	Autumn foliage	Lawn specimen, edge of lake or stream, parks	—	Smaller, narrower tree than T. distichum
Taxodium distichum	Tree	Cool Z 4-10	8 ft 2.5m	15 ft 5 m	30 ft 9 m	Decid	—	Autumn foliage; stately habit	Lawn specimen, parks, streets, boggy areas	Fine fallen leaves can block drains	Trees in wet ground develop 'knees' (woody knobs from roots)
Taxodium mucronatum	Tree	Warm Z 9-11	8 ft 2.5m	20 ft 6 m	40 ft 12 m	Everg	—	Foliage; massive canopy	Parks, avenues, lake edges	—	Rapid growth, trunk achieves vast girth
Taxus baccata	Tree	Cool Z 4-9	3 ft 1 m	6 ft 2 m	15 ft 5 m	Everg	—	Foliage; decorative fruit	Lawn specimen, hedge, topiary, container	Foliage poisonous to livestock	Some cultivars are male, others female
Taxus cuspidata	Tree	Cool Z 3-9	3 ft 1 m	8 ft 2.5 m	20 ft 6 m	Everg	—	Foliage; decorative fruit	Lawn specimen, hedge, topiary, container	Foliage poisonous to livestock	Faster growing than T. baccata
Tecoma stans	Tree	Warm Z 10-12	8 ft 2.5m	15 ft 5 m	20 ft 6 m	Everg	Yes	Flowers (yellow, summer-autumn)	Lawn specimen, courtyard, plaza, streets	Can be short-lived	Easily grown in warm to hot climates, colourful flowers
Tecomaria capensis	Shrub	Warm Z 10-11	4 ft 1.2 m	8 ft 2.5 m	15 ft 5 m	Everg	Yes	Flowers (orange to scarlet, late summer-autumn)	Shrub border, hedge, courtyard	Suckers from roots	Scrambling shrub, dense foliage, vivid flowers
Tectona grandis	Tree	Hot Z 11-12	12 ft 4 m	25 ft 8 m	40 ft 12 m	Decid*	—	Foliage; flowers (bluish-white, summer)	Timber (teak), parks, avenues	Old flower panicles give untidy effect	Striking large leaves, especially on young trees; Asia's most famed timber
Telopea oreades	Tree	Warm Z 9	4 ft 1.2 m	8 ft 2.5 m	15 ft 5 m	Everg	—	Flowers (red, spring)	Shrub border, woodland garden, cut flowers	Prone to root rot	Smaller flower-heads than T. speciosissima; needs cool, humid environment
Telopea speciosissima	Shrub	Warm Z 9-10	3 ft 1 m	6 ft 2 m	10 ft 3 m	Everg	—	Flowers (red, spring)	Shrub border, courtyard, cut flowers	Prone to root rot	Spectacular large flower-head; floral emblem of New South Wales
Terminalia catappa	Tree	Hot Z 11-12	8 ft 2.5m	20 ft 6 m	30 ft 9 m	Everg	—	Foliage; edible nut	Coastal planting, parks, avenues	—	Often semi-deciduous, leaves turn red before falling
Ternstroemia gymnanthera	Tree	Cool Z 7-10	4 ft 1.2 m	8 ft 2.5 m	12 ft 4 m	Everg	—	Foliage; flowers (white, fragrant, late summer); decorative fruit	Shrub border, lawn specimen, courtyard	—	Camellia relative, but flowers tiny, foliage rather fleshy
Tetradium daniellii	Tree	Cool Z 8-9	6 ft 2 m	12 ft 4 m	25 ft 8 m	Decid	—	Flowers (white, fragrant, late summer); autumn foliage; decorative fruit	Lawn specimen, parks	—	Only female trees produce fruit
Tetrapanax papyrifer	Shrub	Warm Z 8-10	6 ft 2 m	10 ft 3 m	15 ft 5 m	Everg	—	Foliage; flowers (cream, autumn); decorative fruit	Shrub border, plaza	Spreads by long-running rhizomes	Rampant grower, huge pleated leaves with brownish 'scurf' when young
Theobroma cacao	Tree	Hot Z 12	6 ft 2 m	10 ft 3 m	15 ft 5 m	Everg	—	Beverage from seeds; large decorative pods	Plantations, lawn specimen, conservatory	—	Source of chocolate and cocoa; requires humid climate, shade
Thevetia peruviana	Shrub	Warm Z 10-12	4 ft 1.2 m	8 ft 2.5 m	12 ft 4 m	Everg	Yes	Flowers (pale orange or yellow, most of year)	Shrub border, lawn specimen, courtyard	Often short-lived; nuts highly poisonous	—
Thevetia thevetioides	Shrub	Hot Z 10-12	5 ft 1.5 m	10 ft 3 m	15 ft 5 m	Everg	Yes	Flowers (yellow, winter-summer)	Shrub border, lawn specimen, courtyard	Often short-lived; nuts poisonous	Larger, more vivid flowers than T. peruviana but more tender
Thryptomene calycina	Shrub	Warm Z 9-10	2 ft 0.6 m	3 ft 1 m	4 ft 1.2 m	Everg	—	Flowers (white, winter-spring)	Rock garden, shrub border, cut flowers	—	Frequent cutting of flowers maintains vigour

NAME	KIND	CLIMATE & ZONE	HEIGHT AT 5 yrs	10 yrs	20 yrs	DECIDUOUS EVERGREEN	ARID CLIMATES	CHIEF ATTRACTIONS	USES	DRAWBACKS	COMMENTS
Thryptomene saxicola	Shrub	Warm Z 9-10	2 ft 0.6 m	3 ft 1 m	4 ft 1.2 m	Everg	—	Flowers (pale pink, winter-spring)	Rock garden, shrub border, courtyard	—	Weeping branches make it less suitable for cut flowers
Thuja occidentalis	Tree	Cool Z 4-9	5 ft 1.5 m	10 ft 3 m	20 ft 6 m	Everg	—	Foliage; symmetrical form; winter colouring	Lawn specimen, parks	—	Cultivars (many dwarf) more widely grown than wild species
Thuja plicata	Tree	Cool Z 5-9	6 ft 2 m	12 ft 4 m	25 ft 8 m	Everg	—	Foliage; vigorous growth; symmetrical form	Timber (western red cedar); lawn specimen, parks	—	Foliage aromatic; one of America's most important timbers
Thujopsis dolabrata	Tree	Cool Z 4-9	3 ft 1 m	6 ft 2 m	12 ft 4 m	Everg	—	Foliage	Lawn specimen, screen	Slow-growing	Interesting fleshy foliage with bluish-white markings
Tibouchina granulosa	Tree	Warm Z 9-11	6 ft 2 m	12 ft 4 m	15 ft 5 m	Everg	—	Flowers (rose-purple or pink, autumn)	Lawn specimen, courtyard, shrub border	Prone to wind damage	Magnificent small flowering tree when well grown
Tibouchina lepidota	Tree	Warm Z 9-11	6 ft 2 m	12 ft 4 m	15 ft 5 m	Everg	—	Flowers (purple, late summer-early winter)	Lawn specimen, courtyard, shrub border, coastal planting	—	Sold in Australia as *Tibouchina* 'Alstonville'
Tibouchina urvilleana (semidecandra)	Tree	Warm Z 9-11	5 ft 1.5 m	8 ft 2.5 m	12 ft 4 m	Everg	—	Flowers (purple, summer-autumn)	Shrub border, courtyard, conservatory, indoor, espalier	Weak branches, prone to wind damage	Larger individual flowers, not massed like above tibouchinas
Tilia americana	Tree	Cool Z 2-9	10 ft 3 m	20 ft 6 m	40 ft 12 m	Decid	—	Foliage; flowers (cream, summer); bark	Parks, streets, timber	—	Taller-growing than European spp., rare outside North America
Tilia cordata	Tree	Cool Z 2-9	8 ft 2.5 m	15 ft 5 m	30 ft 9 m	Decid	—	Foliage; flowers (cream, fragrant, summer)	Lawn specimen, parks, streets, timber	—	Handsome, compact crown, smallish leaves
Tilia × europaea	Tree	Cool Z 3-9	8 ft 2.5m	15 ft 5 m	30 ft 9 m	Decid	—	Foliage; flowers (pale yellow, fragrant, early summer)	Lawn specimen, parks, streets, timber, beverage from flowers	Suckers from trunk base	Popular avenue tree in Europe
Tilia heterophylla	Tree	Cool Z 4-9	10 ft 3 m	20 ft 6 m	40 ft 12 m	Decid	—	Foliage	Timber, parks, streets	—	Leaves larger than most other *Tilia* spp., whitish beneath
Tilia platyphyllos	Tree	Cool Z 3-9	10 ft 3 m	20 ft 6 m	40 ft 12 m	Decid	—	Foliage; flowers (pale yellow, summer)	Avenues, parks	—	Handsome foliage, leaves dark green, bluish beneath
Tilia tomentosa	Tree	Cool Z 4-9	8 ft 2.5 m	15 ft 5 m	30 ft 9 m	Decid	—	Foliage; flowers (pale green, summer)	Lawn specimen	Nectar toxic to bees	Grown for the silvery leaf undersides; 'Petiolaris' has weeping branches
Tipuana tipu	Tree	Warm Z 9-11	12 ft 4 m	25 ft 8 m	40 ft 12 m	Everg	Yes	Flowers (yellow-orange, spring); decorative fruit; foliage	Parks, avenues, shade	—	Vigorous leguminous tree, may be deciduous in cooler climates
Tithonia diversifolia	Shrub	Warm Z 9-11	8 ft 2.5m	12 ft 4 m	15 ft 5 m	Everg	Yes	Flowers (yellow, late summer)	Shrub border, courtyard	Untidy weak stems	Resembles sunflower; can be cut back to ground after flowering
Toona ciliata (australis)	Tree	Warm Z 9-12	10 ft 3 m	20 ft 6 m	30 ft 9 m	Decid	—	Foliage; bark	Timber, parks, shade	Can be defoliated by cedar tip moth larvae	Australia's most famous timber, heavily exploited in 19th century
Toona (Cedrela) sinensis	Tree	Warm Z 7-11	6 ft 2 m	12 ft 4 m	20 ft 6 m	Decid	—	Spring foliage	Shrub border, courtyard, lawn specimen	Suckers from roots	Cultivar 'Flamingo' has striking pink spring foliage
Torreya californica	Tree	Cool Z 6-10	4 ft 1.2 m	8 ft 2.5 m	15 ft 5 m	Everg	—	Foliage	Lawn specimen	—	Yew-like conifer
Torreya nucifera	Tree	Cool Z 4-10	4 ft 1.2 m	8 ft 2.5 m	15 ft 5 m	Everg	—	Foliage; edible seeds; bark	Lawn specimen	—	Yew-like conifer; oily seeds eaten in Japan
Toxicodendron succedaneum (Rhus succedanea)	Tree	Warm Z 7-10	8 ft 2.5 m	12 ft 4 m	15 ft 5 m	Decid	Yes	Autumn foliage	Lawn specimen, shrub border	Severe allergic reaction may follow contact	Same genus as the notorious poison ivies of N America, causing similar problems
Trachycarpus fortunei	Palm	Cool Z 8-11	3 ft 1 m	6 ft 2 m	12 ft 4 m	Everg	Yes	Fan-shaped leaves; symmetrical form; flowers (yellow, spring); decorative fruit	Lawn grouping, shrub border, courtyard, parks	—	The only palm grown outdoors in cool-temperate regions, such as England
Trichilia emetica	Tree	Warm Z 10-11	8 ft 2.5m	15 ft 5 m	25 ft 8 m	Everg	—	Foliage; flowers (cream, fragrant, summer); decorative fruit	Lawn specimen, parks, streets, shade	—	Flowers attract nectar-feeding birds
Tristaniopsis (Tristania) laurina	Tree	Warm Z 9-11	8 ft 2.5 m	15 ft 5 m	25 ft 8 m	Everg	—	Bark; flowers (yellow, summer)	Lawn specimen, parks, streets, stream banks	—	Attractive smooth streaked bark; resists floods
Tsuga canadensis	Tree	Cold Z 2-9	6 ft 2 m	12 ft 4 m	20 ft 6 m	Everg	—	Foliage; dense canopy	Lawn specimen, parks, Christmas trees, topiary	—	Many cultivars exist, including dwarf & weeping forms
Tsuga caroliniana	Tree	Cool Z 4-9	6 ft 2 m	12 ft 4 m	25 ft 8 m	Everg	—	Foliage; bark	Lawn specimen, parks, Christmas trees	—	More upright, narrow form than *T. canadensis*
Tsuga chinensis	Tree	Cool Z 6-9	5 ft 1.5 m	10 ft 3 m	20 ft 6 m	Everg	—	Foliage; symmetrical form	Lawn specimen, bonsai, courtyard	—	Used in formal Japanese gardens
Tsuga heterophylla	Tree	Cold Z 4-9	8 ft 2.5m	15 ft 5 m	30 ft 9 m	Everg	—	Foliage; symmetrical form	Lawn specimen, timber	—	Tallest *Tsuga* sp., spire-like form
Tsuga mertensiana	Tree	Cold Z 4-9	5 ft 1.5 m	10 ft 3 m	20 ft 6 m	Everg	—	Foliage; decorative cones	Lawn specimen, parks, Christmas trees	Intolerant of urban conditions	Has larger cones than other *Tsuga* spp.
Ugni molinae (Myrtus ugni)	Shrub	Cool Z 8-10	5 ft 1.5 m	8 ft 2.5 m	12 ft 4 m	Everg	—	Flowers (white, spring); decorative/edible fruit	Shrub border, lawn specimen, hedge, screen	—	Small acid fruits make tasty jams & jellies
Ulmus americana	Tree	Cool Z 3-9	10 ft 3 m	25 ft 8 m	40 ft 12 m	Decid	—	Autumn foliage; bark; stately form	Parks, avenues, timber	Susceptible to Dutch elm disease	Little planted now because of disease

NAME	KIND	CLIMATE & ZONE	HEIGHT AT 5yrs	HEIGHT AT 10yrs	HEIGHT AT 20yrs	DECIDUOUS EVERGREEN	ARID CLIMATES	CHIEF ATTRACTIONS	USES	DRAWBACKS	COMMENTS
Ulmus glabra	Tree	Cool Z 3-10	10 ft 3 m	20 ft 6 m	30 ft 9 m	Decid	—	Autumn foliage; stately form	Lawn specimen, parks, avenues	Susceptible to Dutch elm disease	The golden 'Lutescens' and weeping 'Camperdownii' are widely grown cultivars
Ulmus × hollandica	Tree	Cool Z 4-10	10 ft 3 m	25 ft 8 m	40 ft 12 m	Decid	—	Autumn foliage; stately form	Parks, avenues, shade	Susceptible to Dutch elm disease	Includes several widely planted clones
Ulmus laevis	Tree	Cool Z 3-10	10 ft 3 m	20 ft 6 m	30 ft 9 m	Decid	—	Autumn foliage; vigorous growth	Parks, avenues, shade	—	Vigorous grower, dark green foliage
Ulmus minor	Tree	Cool Z 4-10	10 ft 3 m	25 ft 8 m	40 ft 12 m	Decid	—	Autumn foliage; vigorous growth	Parks, farms, shelter	Suckers profusely from roots	Variegated cultivar is the main ornamental form
Ulmus parvifolia	Tree	Warm Z 5-10	8 ft 2.5m	15 ft 5 m	25 ft 8 m	Decid	—	Bark; foliage	Lawn specimen, parks, courtyards, plazas	—	Almost evergreen in warmer climates; resistant to Dutch elm disease
Ulmus procera	Tree	Cool Z 4-9	10 ft 3 m	20 ft 6 m	30 ft 9 m	Decid	—	Autumn foliage; stately form	Lawn specimen, parks, avenues	Susceptible to Dutch elm disease	The best-loved tree of the English countryside
Ulmus pumila	Tree	Cool Z 3-9	10 ft 3 m	25 ft 8 m	30 ft 9 m	Decid	Yes	Autumn foliage; vigorous growth	Parks, streets, shade, erosion control	Branches brittle	Resistant to Dutch elm disease
Umbellularia californica	Tree	Warm Z 7-10	6 ft 2 m	12 ft 4 m	20 ft 6 m	Everg	—	Foliage; decorative fruit	Lawn specimen, shrub border	—	Crushed foliage very pungent, can cause temporary headache
Vaccinium arboreum	Shrub	Cool Z 7-10	5 ft 1.5 m	8 ft 2.5 m	10 ft 3 m	Decid	—	Autumn foliage; decorative fruit	Shrub border, woodland garden	—	Some forms may be evergreen
Vaccinium corymbosum	Shrub	Cool Z 2-9	4 ft 1.2 m	6 ft 2 m	6 ft 2 m	Decid	—	Edible fruit; flowers (white or pink, late spring); autumn foliage	Shrub border, kitchen garden, woodland garden	—	The chief parent species of the commercial blueberries
Vaccinium ovatum	Shrub	Cool Z 4-9	2 ft 0.6 m	3 ft 1 m	3 ft 1 m	Everg	—	Edible fruit; flowers (white or pink, early summer); foliage	Shrub border, cut foliage	—	—
Veitchia merrillii	Palm	Hot Z 11-12	5 ft 1.5 m	10 ft 3 m	20 ft 6 m	Everg	—	Foliage; symmetrical form; decorative fruit	Lawn grouping, courtyard, plaza	Juicy fruit litter pavement	Very elegant & colourful palm for tropics; single-stemmed
Vernicia (Aleurites) fordii	Tree	Warm Z 10-11	8 ft 2.5m	15 ft 5 m	20 ft 6 m	Decid	Yes	Flowers (cream & red, spring)	Oil from seeds, lawn specimen, courtyard	Seeds are poisonous (violent emetic)	Unsuccessful oil plantations in various countries; quite ornamental
Vestia lycioides	Shrub	Warm Z 9-11	3 ft 1 m	5 ft 1.5 m	6 ft 2 m	Everg	—	Flowers (yellow, spring-summer)	Shrub border, courtyard	Foliage smells unpleasant	Interesting tubular flowers
Viburnum × bodnantense	Shrub	Cool Z 6-9	3 ft 1 m	6 ft 2 m	10 ft 3 m	Decid	—	Flowers (pink & white, fragrant, autumn-early spring); autumn foliage	Shrub border, courtyard, woodland garden	—	Some cultivars have pinker flowers
Viburnum × burkwoodii	Shrub	Cool Z 6-9	3 ft 1 m	6 ft 2 m	8 ft 2.5 m	Everg	—	Flowers (white, fragrant, spring); autumn/winter foliage	Shrub border, courtyard, woodland garden	—	—
Viburnum carlesii	Shrub	Cool Z 3-9	2 ft 0.6 m	4 ft 1.2 m	5 ft 1.5 m	Decid	—	Flowers (pale pink, fragrant, spring); decorative fruit	Shrub border, courtyard, woodland garden	—	Deep pink buds contrast with pale or white open flowers
Viburnum davidii	Shrub	Cool Z 6-10	1 ft 0.3 m	2 ft 0.6 m	3 ft 1 m	Everg	—	Foliage; flowers (white, spring); decorative fruit	Courtyard, rock garden, groundcover, container	—	Very handsome foliage, compact growth habit
Viburnum dentatum	Shrub	Cool Z 2-9	6 ft 2 m	10 ft 3 m	12 ft 4 m	Decid	—	Autumn foliage; flowers (white, early summer); decorative fruit	Shrub border, informal hedge	—	—
Viburnum farreri (fragrans)	Shrub	Cool Z 5-9	4 ft 1.2 m	8 ft 2.5 m	8 ft 2.5 m	Decid	—	Flowers (white, fragrant, winter-early spring); autumn foliage	Shrub border, courtyard, woodland garden	—	One of the finest viburnums for cool climates
Viburnum lantana	Shrub	Cool Z 3-9	4 ft 1.2 m	8 ft 2.5 m	12 ft 4 m	Decid	Yes	Flowers (white, summer); decorative fruit; autumn foliage	Shrub border, hedge, woodland garden	—	—
Viburnum macrocephalum	Shrub	Cool Z 5-10	3 ft 1 m	6 ft 2 m	10 ft 3 m	Decid	—	Flowers (green & white, mid-spring-early summer)	Shrub border, courtyard	—	Semi-evergreen in warmer climates; the 'snowball' form is the one usually grown
Viburnum odoratissimum	Tree	Warm Z 8-11	4 ft 1.2 m	8 ft 2.5 m	15 ft 5 m	Everg	—	Foliage; flowers (white, fragrant, late spring); decorative fruit	Shrub border, lawn specimen, parks	Suckers from base of trunk	One of the few viburnums suitable for warm and hot climates
Viburnum opulus	Shrub	Cool Z 2-10	6 ft 2 m	10 ft 3 m	12 ft 4 m	Decid	—	Flowers (white, summer); decorative fruit; autumn foliage	Shrub border, woodland garden	Soft, weak stems	The 'snowball' form is the one mostly grown for flowers
Viburnum plicatum	Shrub	Cool Z 5-10	3 ft 1 m	8 ft 2.5 m	10 ft 3 m	Decid	—	Flowers (white, spring); decorative fruit; foliage	Shrub border, courtyard, woodland garden	—	Several cultivars popular including 'snowball' and pink-flowered forms
Viburnum prunifolium	Shrub	Cool Z 3-9	5 ft 1.5 m	10 ft 3 m	15 ft 5 m	Decid	—	Flowers (white, spring); autumn foliage; decorative fruit	Shrub border, hedge, screen	—	Root used medicinally in USA
Viburnum rhytidophyllum	Shrub	Cool Z 4-10	3 ft 1 m	6 ft 2 m	10 ft 3 m	Everg	—	Foliage; flowers (white, spring); decorative fruit	Shrub border, lawn specimen, courtyard	—	Very handsome foliage; needs several plants for good fruit display
Viburnum setigerum	Shrub	Cool Z 5-9	3 ft 1 m	6 ft 2 m	10 ft 3 m	Decid	—	Decorative fruit; autumn foliage; flowers (white, early summer)	Shrub border, lawn specimen, courtyard	—	Fine autumn display of fruit, bright yellow ripening red
Viburnum tinus	Shrub	Cool Z 6-10	4 ft 1.2 m	8 ft 2.5 m	12 ft 4 m	Everg	—	Flowers (white, late winter-spring); decorative fruit	Hedge, shrub border, coastal planting, courtyard	Scent of flowers somewhat unpleasant	Foliage has purple tones in winter
Virgilia oroboides	Tree	Warm Z 9-11	15 ft 5 m	25 ft 8 m	25 ft 8 m	Everg	—	Flowers (mauve-pink, early summer-autumn); vigorous growth	Courtyard, shrub border, lawn specimen, screen	May be short-lived	One of the fastest-growing small trees for warm areas

Reference Table

NAME	KIND	CLIMATE & ZONE	HEIGHT AT 5yrs / 10yrs / 20yrs	DECIDUOUS EVERGREEN	ARID CLIMATES	CHIEF ATTRACTIONS	USES	DRAWBACKS	COMMENTS
Vitex agnus-castus	Shrub	Cool Z 7-10	6 ft 2 m / 10 ft 3 m / 15 ft 5 m	Decid	Yes	Aromatic foliage; flowers (lavender, summer-autumn)	Shrub border, courtyard	Easily damaged by wind	Leaves once thought to induce chastity!
Vitex lucens	Tree	Warm Z 9-11	6 ft 2 m / 12 ft 4 m / 25 ft 8 m	Everg	Yes	Foliage; flowers (red or pink, winter); decorative fruit	Lawn specimen, parks, streets	—	One of New Zealand's most attractive broad-leaved trees
Vitex negundo	Shrub	Warm Z 6-11	6 ft 2 m / 12 ft 4 m / 20 ft 6 m	Everg	Yes	Aromatic foliage; flowers (mauve, fragrant, spring)	Shrub border, courtyard	—	Similar to V. agnus-castus
Vitex trifolia	Shrub	Warm Z 10-12	6 ft 2 m / 8 ft 2.5 m / 10 ft 3 m	Everg	Yes	Foliage; flowers (blue to purple, late spring-autumn)	Coastal planting, shrub border, hedge	Weak stems, easily damaged	Purple-leaved cultivar is the plant most commonly grown in gardens
Washingtonia filifera	Palm	Warm Z 9-11	4 ft 1.2 m / 8 ft 2.5 m / 15 ft 5 m	Everg	Yes	Foliage; symmetrical form	Avenues, parks, lawn grouping, plazas	Fire risk from dead fronds on trunk	Column-like trunk; thatch of dead leaves can be picturesque
Washingtonia robusta	Palm	Warm Z 10-11	4 ft 1.2 m / 10 ft 3 m / 20 ft 6 m	Everg	Yes	Foliage; symmetrical form	Avenues, parks, lawn grouping, plazas	Fire risk from dead fronds on trunk	Taller & faster-growing than W. filifera; transplantable at any size
Weigela 'Bristol Ruby'	Shrub	Cool Z 4-10	4 ft 1.2 m / 6 ft 2 m / 6 ft 2 m	Decid	—	Flowers (crimson, spring)	Shrub border, courtyard	—	Hybrid cultivar, very floriferous
Weigela florida	Shrub	Cool Z 4-10	6 ft 2 m / 8 ft 2.5 m / 10 ft 3 m	Decid	—	Flowers (white, pink, crimson, spring)	Shrub border, courtyard	—	Several cultivars popular, including variegated foliage
Weigela middendorfiana	Shrub	Cool Z 6-9	4 ft 1.2 m / 6 ft 2 m / 6 ft 2 m	Decid	—	Flowers (yellow-orange, spring)	Shrub border, courtyard, woodland garden	—	—
Westringia fruticosa (rosmariniformis)	Shrub	Warm Z 9-11	4 ft 1.2 m / 6 ft 2 m / 6 ft 2 m	Everg	—	Foliage; flowers (white, most of year)	Coastal planting, hedge, courtyard, plaza	May be short-lived	Fine greyish foliage, can be kept compact by trimming
Widdringtonia cupressoides	Tree	Warm Z 8-10	5 ft 1.5 m / 8 ft 2.5 m / 10 ft 3 m	Everg	—	Foliage	Lawn specimen, courtyard, shrub border	—	Cypress-like conifer, early foliage needle-like
Wodyetia bifurcata	Palm	Hot Z 10-12	6 ft 2 m / 12 ft 4 m / 25 ft 8 m	Everg	—	Foliage; symmetrical form; decorative fruit	Lawn grouping, courtyard, plaza, swimming pool	Large fruit may litter ground	Recently discovered but already popular in cultivation
Wollemia nobilis	Tree	Warm Z 9-10	4 ft 1.2 m / 8 ft 2.5 m / 15 ft 5 m	Everg	—	Foliage; symmetrical form	Lawn specimen, container	—	Recently discovered, one of the world's rarest and most remarkable trees
Xanthorrhoea glauca (australis)	Tree	Warm Z 9-11	3 ft 1 m / 4 ft 1.2 m / 6 ft 2 m	Everg	—	Foliage; symmetrical form	Lawn specimen, courtyard, rock garden, container	Slow-growing, difficult to transplant	Spear-like flower spikes only appear after many years
Xanthorrhoea malacophylla	Tree	Warm Z 10-11	3 ft 1 m / 4 ft 1.2 m / 6 ft 2 m	Everg	—	Foliage; symmetrical form	Lawn specimen, courtyard, rock garden, container	Slow-growing, difficult to transplant	Rare species, likes moist subtropical climate
Xanthorrhoea preissii	Tree	Warm Z 10-11	3 ft 1 m / 4 ft 1.2 m / 6 ft 2 m	Everg	—	Foliage; symmetrical form	Lawn specimen, courtyard, rock garden, container	Slow-growing, difficult to transplant	—
Xanthostemon chrysanthus	Tree	Hot Z 10-12	8 ft 2.5 m / 15 ft 5 m / 25 ft 8 m	Everg	—	Flowers (yellow, mainly winter); foliage	Lawn specimen, parks, streets, plazas	Lanky growth	Large yellow flower-heads, like Metrosideros
Xylomelum occidentale	Tree	Warm Z 9-11	6 ft 2 m / 12 ft 4 m / 20 ft 6 m	Everg	Yes	Decorative fruit; bark; foliage; flowers (cream, summer)	Lawn specimen, dried arrangements	Prone to root rot	Fruit a remarkable large woody follicle, pear-shaped
Yucca aloifolia	Shrub	Warm Z 9-12	2 ft 0.6 m / 4 ft 1.2 m / 8 ft 2.5 m	Everg	Yes	Foliage; symmetrical form; flowers (white, summer)	Courtyard, plaza, conservatory	Fierce spines on leaf tips	Fleshy sword-leaves; variegated cultivars popular
Yucca brevifolia	Tree	Warm Z 8-11	2 ft 0.6 m / 4 ft 1.2 m / 8 ft 2.5 m	Everg	Yes	Foliage; symmetrical form; flowers (white, spring)	Courtyard, plaza, desert garden	Slow-growing, very difficult	Rarely cultivated, strictly protected in the wild
Yucca elephantipes	Tree	Warm Z 9-12	3 ft 1 m / 6 ft 2 m / 12 ft 4 m	Everg	Yes	Foliage; symmetrical form; flowers (white, summer)	Courtyard, plaza, lawn specimen	—	Subtropical; one of the tallest, most vigorous yuccas
Zelkova carpinifolia	Tree	Cool Z 4-10	6 ft 2 m / 12 ft 4 m / 20 ft 6 m	Decid	—	Autumn foliage	Lawn specimen, parks, streets	—	Elm-like foliage, graceful habit
Zelkova serrata	Tree	Cool Z 3-10	6 ft 2 m / 12 ft 4 m / 25 ft 8 m	Decid	—	Autumn foliage; bark	Lawn specimen, parks, streets	—	Attractive dappled bark, elm-like foliage
Zieria buxijugum	Shrub	Warm Z 9-11	3 ft 1 m / 6 ft 2 m / —	Everg	—	Flowers (white, spring); foliage	Courtyard, woodland garden, container	Bruised leaves have rank odour	Graceful fine foliage
Zizyphus jujuba	Tree	Warm Z 9-11	8 ft 2.5 m / 15 ft 5 m / 25 ft 8 m	Decid	Yes	Edible fruit	Lawn specimen, courtyard, orchard	Fallen fruit litter pavements	Fruit (jujubes) are dried, pickled or candied in Asia

Index

Numbers in *italic* type refer to a photograph

Abelia 52
Abelia chinensis 52
Abelia floribunda 52
Abelia × grandiflora 52, *52*
Abelia × grandiflora 'Frances Mason' 52
Abelia schumannii 52, *52*
Abies 52–6
Abies alba 52, *52*
Abies amabilis 52, *53*
Abies balsamea 53
Abies balsamea 'Hudsonia' 53, *53*
Abies bracteata 53, *53*
Abies cephalonica 53, *53*
Abies concolor 53
Abies concolor 'Candicans' 53
Abies concolor 'Glauca' 53
Abies concolor var. *lowiana* 53, *53*
Abies delavayi 53
Abies delavayi var. *delavayi* 53
Abies delavayi var. *fabri* 53
Abies delavayi var. *faxoniana* 53
Abies delavayi var. *forrestii* 53
Abies delavayi var. *georgei* 53
Abies firma 54, *54*
Abies grandis 54, *54*
Abies homolepis 54
Abies homolepis 'Prostrata' 54, *54*
Abies koreana 54, *54*
Abies lasiocarpa 54, *54*
Abies lasiocarpa var. *arizonica* 54
Abies lasiocarpa 'Aurea' 54
Abies lasiocarpa 'Compacta' 54
Abies magnifica 54–5
Abies nordmanniana 55, *55*
Abies numidica 55, *55*
Abies pinsapo 55, *55*
Abies pinsapo 'Glauca' 55
Abies procera 55
Abies procera 'Glauca' 55, *55*
Abies spectabilis 56, *56*
Abies venusta see *Abies bracteata*
Abutilon 56–7
Abutilon × hybridum 56, *56*
Abutilon megapotamicum 56, *56*
Abutilon megapotamicum 'Variegatum' 56, *56*
Abutilon × suntense 57
Abutilon × suntense 'Jermyns' 57, *57*
Abutilon vitifolium 57
Abutilon vitifolium 'Album' 57, *57*
Abutilon vitifolium 'Veronica Tennant' 57
Acacia 57–61
Acacia acinacea 57, *57*
Acacia baileyana 57
Acacia baileyana 'Purpurea' 57
Acacia cultriformis 57, *57*
Acacia dealbata 58
Acacia decurrens 58, *58*
Acacia elata 58, *58*
Acacia harpophylla 58, *58*
Acacia karroo 58, *58*
Acacia koa 58
Acacia longifolia 58, *58*
Acacia mangium 59, *59*
Acacia mearnsii 59
Acacia melanoxylon 59, *59*
Acacia neriifolia 59, *59*
Acacia pendula 59, *59*
Acacia podalyriifolia 60, *60*
Acacia pravissima 60, *60*
Acacia pycnantha 60, *60*
Acacia sieberiana var. *woodii* 60
Acacia spectabilis 60, *60*
Acacia verticillata 61, *61*
Acacia xanthoploea 61, *61*
Acalypha 61
Acalypha hispida 61, *61*
Acalypha wilkesiana 61

Acalypha wilkesiana cultivar 61
Acalypha wilkesiana 'Godseffiana' 61
Acalypha wilkesiana 'Macafeeana' 61
Acalypha wilkesiana 'Macrophylla' 61
Acalypha wilkesiana 'Marginata' 61
Acer 62–8
Acer buergerianum 62, *62*
Acer campestre 62
Acer capillipes 62, *62*
Acer cappadocicum 62, *62*
Acer cappadocicum 'Rubrum' 62
Acer carpinifolium 62–3, *63*
Acer circinatum 63
Acer cissifolium 63, *63*
Acer davidii 63, *63*
Acer davidii subsp. *grosseri* see *Acer grosseri*
Acer davidii 'Serpentine' 63
Acer ginnala 64, *64*
Acer glabrum 64
Acer grandidentatum 64
Acer griseum 64, *64*
Acer grosseri 64, *65*
Acer grosseri var. *hersii* see *Acer grosseri*
Acer hersii see *Acer grosseri*
Acer hookeri 65, *65*
Acer japonicum 65, *65*
Acer japonicum 'Aconitifolium' 65
Acer macrophyllum 65, *65*
Acer maximowiczianum see *Acer nikoense*
Acer negundo 66, *66*
Acer negundo 'Aureo-marginatum' 66
Acer negundo 'Flamingo' 66
Acer negundo 'Variegatum' 66
Acer negundo 'Violaceum' 66
Acer nikoense 66
Acer palmatum 66, *66*
Acer palmatum 'Atrolineare' 66
Acer palmatum 'Atropurpureum' 66
Acer palmatum 'Dissectum' 66
Acer palmatum 'Dissectum Atropurpureum' 66
Acer palmatum 'Sangokaku' 66
Acer palmatum 'Senkaki' see *Acer palmatum* 'Sangokaku'
Acer pensylvanicum 67, *67*
Acer platanoides 67, *67*
Acer platanoides 'Crimson King' 67
Acer platanoides 'Drummondii' 67
Acer platanoides 'Faasen's Black' 67
Acer platanoides 'Schwedleri' 67
Acer pseudoplatanus 67, *67*
Acer pseudoplatanus 'Brilliantissimum' 67
Acer pseudoplatanus 'Erythrocarpum' 67
Acer pseudoplatanus 'Purpupeum' 67
Acer pseudoplatanus 'Variegatum' 67
Acer rubrum 68, *68*
Acer saccharinum 68, *68*
Acer saccharum 68, *68*
Acer saccharum subsp. *floridanum* 68
Acer saccharum subsp. *grandidentatum* 68
Acer saccharum subsp. *leucoderme* 68
Acer sikkimense see *Acer hookeri*
Acer truncatum 68, *68*
acerola (*Malpighia glabra*) 291, *291*
Acmena 68
Acmena smithii 68, *69*
Acokanthera 68–9
Acokanthera oblongifolia 69, *69*
Acokanthera oblongifolia 'Variegata' 69
acorn banksia (*Banksia prionotes*) 98
Acrocarpus 69
Acrocarpus fraxinifolius 69
Adansonia 69
Adansonia digitata 69, *69*
Adansonia gregorii 69, *69*
Adenandra 70
Adenandra uniflora 70, *70*
Adenium 70
Adenium obesum 70, *70*

Aeonium 70
Aeonium arboreum 70, *70*
Aesculus 70–2
Aesculus californica 71, *71*
Aesculus × carnea 71
Aesculus × carnea 'Briotii' 71
Aesculus flava 71, *71*
Aesculus glabra 71, *71*
Aesculus hippocastanum 72, *72*
Aesculus indica 72, *72*
Aesculus octandra see *Aesculus flava*
Aesculus parviflora 72, *72*
Aesculus pavia 72, *72*
Aesculus pavia 'Atrosanguinea' 72
Aesculus turbinata 72, *73*
African fern pine (*Afrocarpus gracilior*) 73, *73*
African hemp (*Sparrmania africana*) 406
African oil palm (*Elaeis guineensis*) 189, *189*
African tulip tree (*Spathodea campanulata*) 407, *407*
Afrocarpus 72–3
Afrocarpus falcatus 73
Afrocarpus gracilior 73, *73*
Agapetes 73
Agapetes serpens 73, *73*
Agapetes serpens 'Ludgvan Cross' 73, *73*
Agathis 73–4
Agathis australis 74, *74*
Agathis robusta 74, *74*
Agave 74
Agave americana 74
Agave americana 'Marginata' 74
Agave attenuata 74, *74*
Agonis 74
Agonis flexuosa 74, *75*
Agonis flexuosa 'Variegata' 74
Ailanthus 75
Ailanthus altissima 75, *75*
Ailanthus giraldi 75, *75*
Ailanthus glandulosa see *Ailanthus altissima*
alamillo (*Populus fremontii*) 351
Alaska blue willow (*Salix purpurea*) 394, *394*
Alaska cedar (*Chamaecyparis nootkatensis*) 144, *144*
alaternus (*Rhamnus alaternus*) 373
Alberta 75–6
Alberta magna 76, *76*
Albizia 76
Albizia julibrissin 76, *76*
Albizia lebbek 76
Aldenham crab (*Malus* 'Aldenhamensis') 292, *292*
alder (*Alnus*) 80–81
Alectryon 76
Alectryon excelsus 76, *76*
Aleppo pine (*Pinus halepensis*) 338, *338*
Aleurites 76–7
Aleurites moluccana 77, *77*
Alexandra palm (*Archontophoenix alexandrae*) 90, *90*
Alexandrian laurel (*Calophyllum inophyllum*) 120, *120*
Algerian fir (*Abies nimidica*) 55, *55*
aliso (*Platanus racemosa*) 346, *346*
Allamanda 77
Allamanda neriifolia 77, *77*
Alleghany serviceberry (*Amelanchier laevis*) 84
alligator juniper (*Juniperus deppeana* var. *pachyphlaea*) 261, *261*
Allocasuarina 77–9
Allocasuarina decaisneana 78, *78*
Allocasuarina littoralis 78, *78*
Allocasuarina luehmannii 78, *78*
Allocasuarina tessellata 78, *79*
Allocasuarina torulosa 78–9, *79*
Allocasuarina verticillata 79, *79*
Alloxylon 79–80
Alloxylon flammeum 79, *79*
Alloxylon pinnatum 80, *80*
allspice (*Calycanthus*) 120–1
Alnus 80–81

Alnus acuminata 80, *80*
Alnus cordata 80
Alnus firma 80, *80*
Alnus glutinosa 80–1, *80*
Alnus jorullensis see *Alnus acuminata*
Alnus nepalensis 81, *81*
Alnus orientalis 81, *81*
Alnus rubra 81, *81*
Aloe 81–2
Aloe candelabrum 81, *81*
Aloe plicatilis 82, *82*
Aloysia 82
Aloysia triphylla 82, *82*
alpine cider gum (*Eucalyptus gunnii*) 82
alpine mintbush (*Prostanthera cuneata*) 353, *353*
Alpinia 82
Alpinia zerumbet 82, *82*
Alpinia zerumbet 'Variegata' 82
Alyogyne 82–3
Alyogyne hakeifolia 82, *83*
Alyogyne huegelii 83, *83*
Amelanchier 83–4
Amelanchier alnifolia 83, *83*
Amelanchier arborea 83, *83*
Amelanchier canadensis see *Amelanchier arborea*
Amelanchier laevis 84
Amelanchier lamarckii 84, *84*
American aloe (*Agave americana*) 74
American arbor-vitae (*Thuja occidentalis*) 423, *423*
American aspen (*Populus tremuloides*) 352, *353*
American beech (*Fagus grandifolia*) 216, *216*
American black spruce (*Picea mariana*) 331
American chestnut (*Castanea dentata*) 131–2
American elder (*Sambucus canadensis*) 394, *394*
American elm (*Ulmus americana*) 432, *432*
American fringe tree (*Chionanthus virginicus*) 147, *147*
American hackberry (*Celtis occidentalis*) 137, *137*
American holly (*Ilex opaca*) 254, *255*
American hornbeam (*Carpinus caroliniana*) 128, *128*
American leatherwood (*Cyrilla*) 174
American linden (*Tilia americana*) 425, *425*
American persimmon (*Diospyros virginiana*) 182, *182*
American plane (*Platanus occidentalis*) 346
American red ash (*Fraxinus pennsylvanica*) 224, *224*
American sweet crab (*Malus coronaria*) 292
American walnut (*Juglans nigra*) 259, *259*
American white ash (*Fraxinus americana*) 223, *223*
American white oak (*Quercus alba*) 366, *367*
American yellow-wood (*Cladrastis lutea*) 152, *152*
Amherstia 84
Amherstia nobilis 84, *84*
Amphitecna 84
Amphitecna latifolia 84
Amur cork tree (*Phellodendron amurense*) 324, *324*
Amur maple (*Acer ginnala*) 64, *64*
Anacardium 84–5
Anacardium occidentale 84–5, *84*
anchor plant (*Colletia*) 156
Andromeda 85
Andromeda polifolia 85, *85*
angel's trumpet (*Brugmansia*) 107–8, *107*
Angophora 85
Angophora costata 85, *85*
Anisodontea 85
Anisodontea capensis 85, *85*

Anisodontea capensis 'African Queen' 85
annatto (*Bixa orellana*) 103, *103*
Annona 85–6
Annona muricata 86, *86*
Annona squamosa 85
Anopterus 86
Anopterus glandulosus 86, *86*
Antarctic beech (*Nothofagus moorei*) 312, *312*
apple (*Malus × domestica*) 292
apple gum (*Angophora*) 85
apricot (*Prunus armeniaca*) 357
Arabian coffee (*Coffea arabica*) 156, *156*
Aralia 86–7
Aralia chinensis 86, *86*
Aralia elata 86, *86*
Aralia japonica see *Fatsia japonica*
Aralia spinosa 86–7
Araucaria 87–8
Araucaria angustifolia 87, *87*
Araucaria araucana 87, *87*
Araucaria bidwillii 87, *87*
Araucaria cunninghamii 88, *88*
Araucaria heterophylla 88, *88*
arbor-vitae (*Thuja*) 423
arbutus (*Arbutus unedo*) 89, *89*
Arbutus 88–9
Arbutus andrachne 88
Arbutus × andrachnoides 88, *88*
Arbutus canariensis 88, *89*
Arbutus menziesii 89, *89*
Arbutus unedo 89, *89*
Archontophoenix 89–90
Archontophoenix alexandrae 90, *90*
Archontophoenix cunninghamiana 90, *90*
Arctostaphylos 90–1
Arctostaphylos hookeri 90, *90*
Arctostaphylos manzanita 90, *90, 91*
Arctostaphylos uva-ursi 91, *91*
Arctostaphylos uva-ursi 'Point Reyes' 91
Arecastrum romanzoffianum see Syagrus romanzoffiana
Argyle apple (*Eucalyptus cinerea*) 203
Argyrocytisus 91
Argyrocytisus buttandieri 91, *91*
Arizona ash (*Fraxinus velutina*) 224, *225*
Arnold hawthorn (*Crataegus arnoldiana*) 166, *167*
arolla pine (*Pinus cembra*) 337, *337*
Aronia 91–2
Aronia arbutifolia 91, *91*
Aronia melanocarpa 92, *92*
Artocarpus 92
Artocarpus altilis 92, *92*
Artocarpus heterophyllus 92, *92*
ash (*Fraxinus*) 222–4
Ashanti blood (*Mussaenda erythrophylla*) 306, *306*
Asian bell-flower (*Radermachera sinica*) 372, *372*
Asimina 92
Asimina triloba 92
asoka (*Saraca indica*) 395, *395*
aspen (*Populus tremula*) 352, *352*
athel tree (*Tamarix aphylla*) 417, *417*
Atherosperma 92
Atherosperma moschatum 92, *92*
Athrotaxis 92–3
Athrotaxis cupressoides 93
Athrotaxis selaginoides 93
Atlantic white cedar (*Chamaecyparis thyoides*) 145
Atlas cedar (*Cedrus atlantica*) 136, *136*
Aucuba 93
Aucuba japonica 93
Aucuba japonica 'Crotonifolia' 93, *93*
Aucuba japonica 'Variegata' 93
Australian baobab (*Adansonia gregorii*) 69, *69*
Australian boxthorn (*Bursaria spinosa*) 111, *111*

Index

Australian frangipani (*Hymenosporum flavum*) 249, *249*
Australian laurel (*Pittosporum rhombifolium*) 344–5, *344*
Australian pine (*Casuarina*) 132–3
Australian pine (*Casuarina equisetifolia*) 132–3, *133*
Australian red cedar (*Toona ciliata*) 427, *427*
Australian rhododendron (*Rhododendron lochiae*) 379, *379*
Australian rosella (*Hibiscus heterophyllus*) 244, *244*
Australian rosemary (*Westringia fruticosa*) 443, *443*
Australian teak (*Flindersia australis*) 220, *220*
Austrian briar (*Rosa foetida*) 386, *387*
Austrian pine (*Pinus nigra*) 340, *340*
Austrocedrus 93
Austrocedrus chilensis 93, *93*
Averrhoa 100
Averrhoa carambola 93, *93*
Avicennia 93–4
Avicennia marina 94, *94*
avocado (*Persea americana*) 323
Azadirachta 94
Azadirachta indica 94
Azalea see Rhododendron
'Azalea indica' (*Rhododendron simsii*) 380
Azara 94
Azara lanceolata 94
Azara microphylla 94, *94*
Azara microphylla 'Variegata' 94
Azara serrata 94, *94*
Azores bay (*Laurus azorica*) 271–2

Backhousia 96
Backhousia citriodora 96, *96*
bacurubu (*Schizolobium parahybum*) 397
Baeckea 96
Baeckea virgata 96, *96*
Bahamas pine (*Pinus caribaea* var. *bahamensis*) 336
bald cypress (*Taxodium distichum*) 418, *419*
balsam fir (*Abies balsamea*) 53
banana (*Musa* × *paradisiaca*) 306, *306*
banana shrub (*Michelia figo*) 303, *303*
Bangalow palm (*Archontophoenix cunninghamiana*) 90, *90*
Banksia 96–8
Banksia coccinea 97
Banksia 'Giant Candles' 97, *97*
Banksia integrifolia 97, *97*
Banksia lemanniana 97, *97*
Banksia marginata 98, *98*
Banksia menziesii 98
Banksia ornata 98, *98*
Banksia prionotes 98
Banksia serrata 98, *98*
Banksia spinulosa 'Birthday Candles' 97
Banks's grevillea (*Grevillea banksii*) 233, *233*
banyan (*Ficus benghalensis*) 218, *218*
baobab (*Adansonia*) 69
baobab (*Adansonia digitata*) 69, *69*
Barbados cherry (*Malpighia glabra*) 291, *291*
Barbados holly (*Malpighia coccigera*) 291, *291*
Barbados pride (*Caesalpinia pulcherrima*) 114, *114*
barberry (*Berberis*) 100–1
Barklya 98
Barklya syringifolia 98, *98*
Barleria 98–9
Barleria cristata 99, *99*
Barringtonia 99
Barringtonia asiatica 99, *99*
Bartlett pear (*Pyrus communis* 'Williams Bon Chrétien') 364
basket oak (*Quercus prinus*) 369

basswood (*Tilia americana*) 425, *425*
bats-wing coral tree (*Erythrina vespertilio*) 201
Bauera 99
Bauera rubioides 99, *99*
Bauhinia 99–100
Bauhinia × blakeana 99, *99*
Bauhinia galpinii 99
Bauhinia monandra 100, *100*
Bauhinia variegata 100, *100*
Bauhinia variegata 'Candida' 100
bay laurel (*Laurus nobilis*) 272, *272*
bay tree (*Laurus nobilis*) 272, *272*
bayberry (*Myrica cerifera*) 307, *307*
beach salvia (*Salvia africana-lutea*) 394, *394*
beach she-oak (*Casuarina equisetifolia*) 132–3, *133*
bead tree (*Melia azedarach*) 300
bearberry (*Arctostaphylos uva-ursi*) 91, *91*
bearberry (*Rhamnus purshiana*) 373
Beaucarnea 100
Beaucarnea recurvata 100, *100*
beauty bush (*Kolkwitzia*) 266
beauty-berry (*Callicarpa*) 116
beech (*Fagus*) 216
Bechtel crab (*Malus ioensis* 'Plena') 293
Beijing catalpa (*Catalpa bungei*) 133
Beilschmiedia 100
Beilschmiedia tarairi 100
bell heather (*Erica cinerea*) 193
bella sombra tree (*Phytolacca dioica*) 329, *329*
Benjamin bush (*Lindera benzoin*) 279
Berberis 100–1
Berberis darwinii 100, *101*
Berberis × ottawensis 101
Berberis × ottawensis 'Superba' 100, 101
Berberis × stenophylla see Berberis darwinii
Berberis × stenophylla 'Corallina Compacta' see Berberis darwinii
Berberis × stenophylla 'Crawley Gem' see Berberis darwinii
Berberis thunbergii 101
Berberis thunbergii 'Atropurpurea' 101
Berberis thunbergii 'Atropurpurea Nana' 101, *101*
Berberis thunbergii 'Keller's Surprise' 101
Berberis thunbergii 'Little Favourite' 101
Berberis vulgaris 101
Berberis wilsoniae 101, *101*
berrigan (*Pittosporum phyllireoides*) 344, *344*
be-still tree (*Thevetia thevetioides*) 422, *423*
Betula 101–3
Betula albosinensis 101
Betula alleghaniensis 101
Betula lenta 101, *101*
Betula lutea see Betula alleghaniensis
Betula nana 101
Betula nigra 102, *102*
Betula nigra 'Heritage' 102
Betula papyrifera 102, *102*
Betula pendula 102, *102*
Betula pendula 'Dalecarlica' 102
Betula pendula 'Youngii' 102
Betula platyphylla 102
Betula platyphylla var. *japonica* 102, 103
Betula populifolia 102
Betula pubescens 102–3, *103*
Betula utilis 103, *103*
Betula utilis var. *jacquemontii* 103
Bhutan cypress (*Cupressus torulosa*) 172, *172*
Bhutan pine (*Pinus wallichiana*) 343
big shellbark hickory (*Carya laciniosa*) 129, *129*
big tree (*Sequoiadendron giganteum*) 401, *401*

big-cone pine (*Pinus coulteri*) 337, *337*
bigleaf magnolia (*Magnolia macrophylla*) 288
bigleaf maple (*Acer macrophyllum*) 65, *65*
bigtooth maple (*Acer grandidentatum*) 64
Biota occidentalis see Platycladus
birch (*Betula*) 101–3
birchleaf mountain mahogany (*Cercocarpus betuloides* 142, *142*
bird flower (*Crotalaria agatiflora*) 168, *168*
bird lime tree (*Cordia dichotoma*) 158
bird lime tree (*Pisonia grandis*) 343
bird of paradise bush (*Caesalpinia gilliesii*) 114, *114*
bird-of-paradise flower (*Strelitzia reginae*) 410, *410*
bird's eye bush (*Ochna serrulata*) 314, *314*
bitou bush (*Chrysanthemoides monilifera*) 148, *148*
bitter orange (*Poncirus trifoliata*) 351, *351*
bitternut hickory (*Carya cordiformis*) 128, *128*
Bixa 103
Bixa orellana 103, *103*
black alder (*Alnus glutinosa*) 80–1, *80*
black alder (*Ilex verticillata*) 255, *255*
black bamboo (*Phyllostachys nigra*) 328, *329*
black beech (*Nothofagus solandri*) 312–13, *313*
black birch (*Betula lenta*) 101, *101*
black calabash (*Amphitecna latifolia*) 84
black cherry (*Prunus serotina*) 359, *359*
black chokeberry (*Aronia melanocarpa*) 92, *92*
black cottonwood (*Populus trichocarpa*) 352, *353*
black locust (*Robinia*) 384–5
black locust (*Robinia pseudoacacia*) 385
black mulberry (*Morus nigra*) 305, *305*
black oak (*Quercus velutina*) 370, *371*
black penda (*Xanthostemon chrysanthus*) 445, *445*
black poplar (*Populus nigra*) 352, *352*
black raspberry (*Rubus occidentalis*) 390, *390*
black sapote (*Diospyros digyna*) 182
black sassafras (*Atherosperma moschatum*) 92, *92*
black she-oak (*Allocasuarina littoralis*) 78, *78*
black tea-tree (*Melaleuca bracteata*) 297
black tupelo (*Nyssa sylvatica*) 314, *314*
black walnut (*Juglans nigra*) 259, *259*
blackberry (*Rubus*) 390
black-boy tree (*Xanthorrhoea*) 445–6
black-haw (*Viburnum prunifolium*) 439, *439*
blackleaf podocarp (*Podocarpus neriifolius*) 349
blackwattle (*Callicoma*) 116
blackwood (*Acacia melanoxylon*) 59, *59*
bleeding heart tree (*Omalanthus populifolius*) 316, *316*
blood-red tassel-flower (*Calliandra haematocephala*) 115, *115*
blue ash (*Fraxinus quadrangulata*) 224, *224*
blue beech (*Carpinus caroliniana*) 128, *128*

blue butterfly bush (*Clerodendrum ugandense*) 153, *153*
blue hibiscus (*Hibiscus syriacus*) 245, *245*
blue mintbush (*Prostanthera caerulea*) 353
blue palmetto (*Rhapidophyllum hystrix*) 374
blue plumbago (*Plumbago auriculata*) 347, *347*
blue strelitzia (*Strelitzia nicolai*) 410, *410*
blue sugarbush (*Protea neriifolia*) 356, *356*
blueberry (*Vaccinium*) 435–6
blueberry ash (*Elaeocarpus reticulatus*) 189
blueberry elder (*Sambucus caerulea*) 394
blushing bride (*Serruria florida*) 402, *402*
bo tree (*Ficus religiosa*) 219
boab (*Adansonia*) 69
bog myrtle (*Myrica gale*) 307
bog rosemary (*Andromeda*) 85
Bolusanthus 103–4
Bolusanthus speciosus 103–4, *104*
Bombax 104
Bombax ceiba 104
Bombax malabaricum see Bombax ceiba
boneseed (*Chrysanthemoides monilifera*) 148, *148*
boobialla (*Myoporum insulare*) 307
bopple nut (*Macadamia tetraphylla*) 286, *286*
Borassodendron 104
Borassodendron machadonis 104, *104*
boree (*Acacia pendula*) 59, *59*
Boronia 104
Boronia heterophylla 104, *104*
Boronia megastigma 104, *104*
Boronia megastigma 'Harlequin' 104, 104
Boronia megastigma 'Lutea' 104
Boronia pinnata 104, *104*
Boronia pinnata 'Spring White' 104
Bot River protea (*Protea compacta*) 354–5, *354*
bottle tree (*Adansonia gregorii*) 69, *69*
bottlebrush (*Callistemon*) 116–18
Bouvardia 104–5
Bouvardia 'Humboldtii' see Bouvardia longiflora
Bouvardia longiflora 105, *105*
box (*Buxus*) 112
box elder (*Acer negundo*) 66, *66*
box honeysuckle (*Lonicera nitida*) 283
box-elder maple (*Acer negundo*) 66, 66
Brabejum 105
Brabejum stellatifolium 105, *105*
bracelet honey-myrtle (*Melaleuca armillaris*) 297, *297*
Brachychiton 105
Brachychiton acerifolius 105, *105*
Brachychiton discolor 105, *105*
Brachychiton populneus 105, *105*
Brachyglottis 106
Brachyglottis greyii see Senecio greyii
Brachyglottis laxifolia see Senecio laxifolia
Brachyglottis repanda 106
Brachyglottis repanda 'Purpurea' 106, 106
Brachylaena 106
Brachylaena discolor 106, *106*
Bradford pear (*Pyrus calleryana* 'Bradford') 364
Brahea 106
Brahea armata 106, *106*
bramble (*Rubus*) 390
Brazilian bell-flower (*Abutilon megapotamicum*) 56, *56*
Brazilian ironwood (*Caesalpinia ferrea*) 114, *114*
Brazilian pepper tree (*Schinus terebinthifolia*) 397, *397*

Brazilian red cloak (*Megaskepasma erythrochlamys*) 296, *297*
bread tree (*Encephalartos altensteinii*) 190, *190*
breadfruit (*Artocarpus altilis*) 92, *92*
breath of heaven (*Coleonema*) 156
Brewer's weeping spruce (*Picea breweriana*) 330, *330*
Breynia 106–7
Breynia disticha 107, *107*
Breynia disticha 'Roseo-picta' 107
Breynia nivosa see Breynia disticha
Bribie Island pine (*Callitris columellaris*) 118, *118*
bridal heath (*Erica bauera*) 191, *192*
bridal wreath spiraea (*Spiraea prunifolia*) 408
brigalow (*Acacia harpophylla*) 58, *58*
bristlecone pine (*Pinus aristata*) 335, *335*
brittle gum (*Eucalyptus mannifera*) 206
broad-leaf drumsticks (*Isopogon anemonifolius*) 257, *257*
broad-leafed linden (*Tilia platyphyllos*) 426
broad-leafed paperbark (*Melaleuca quinquenervia*) 298–9, *299*
broad-leafed paperbark (*Melaleuca viridiflora*) 299
broad-leafed scribbly gum (*Eucalyptus haemastoma*) 206
broad-spined rose (*Rosa sericea* var. *pteracantha*) 388, *388*
broom (*Cytisus*) 174
broom (*Genista*) 230
broom cluster fig (*Ficus sur*) 220, 220
Broussonetia 107
Broussonetia papyrifera 107, *107*
brown birch (*Scolopia braunii*) 398, *398*
Brownea 107
Brownea × crawfordii see Brownea grandiceps
Brownea grandiceps 107
brown boronia (*Boronia megastigma*) 104, *104*
brown pine (*Podocarpus elatus*) 348, *348*
brown silky oak (*Darlingia darlingiana*) 177, *177*
brown tamarind (*Castanospora alphandii*) 132, *132*
Brugmansia 107–8, *107*
Brugmansia × candida 108, *108*
Brugmansia × candida 'Apricot' 108
Brugmansia × candida 'Plena' 108
Brugmansia sanguinea 108, *108*
Brugmansia suaveolens 108, *108*
Brugmansia suaveolens 'Plena' 108
Brugmansia versicolor see Brugmansia × candida 'Apricot'
Brunfelsia 108–9
Brunfelsia americana see Brunfelsia australis
Brunfelsia australis 108–9, *108*
Brunfelsia bonodora see Brunfelsia australis
Brunfelsia calycina see Brunfelsia pauciflora
Brunfelsia eximia see Brunfelsia pauciflora
Brunfelsia latifolia see Brunfelsia australis
Brunfelsia pauciflora 109, *109*
brush box (*Lophostemon confertus*) 283
brush cherry (*Syzygium*) 413–14
bruyère (*Erica arborea*) 192
Brya 109
Brya ebenus 109, *109*
buckeye (*Aesculus*) 70–2
Buckinghamia 109
Buckinghamia celsissima 109, *109*
buckthorn (*Rhamnus*) 373
Budda (*Eremophila mitchellii*) 192
Buddhist pine (*Podocarpus macrophyllus*) 349, *349*
Buddleia see Buddleja

Buddleja 109–10
Buddleja alternifolia 110, *110*
Buddleja davidii 110, *110*
Buddleja davidii 'Black Knight' 110
Buddleja davidii 'Royal Red' 110
Buddleja davidii 'White Bouquet' 110
Buddleja globosa 110, *111*
buffalo currant (*Ribes odoratum*) 383, *383*
bull oak (*Allocasuarina luehmannii*) 78, *78*
bull bay (*Magnolia grandiflora*) 288, *288*
bunya bunya (*Araucaria bidwillii*) 87, *87*
bunya pine (*Araucaria bidwillii*) 87, *87*
bur oak (*Quercus macrocarpa*) 368
Burchellia 110–11
Burchellia bubalina 110–11, *111*
burrawang (*Macrozamia communis*) 287, *287*
Bursaria 111
Bursaria spinosa 111, *111*
bush clover (*Lespedeza thunbergii*) 274, *274*
bush lavender (*Lavandula stoechas*) 273, *273*
bushman's poison (*Acokanthera oblongifolia*) 69, *69*
bush-tick berry (*Chrysanthemoides monilifera*) 148, *148*
Butea 111
Butea monosperma 111
Butia 111–12
Butia capitata 112, *112*
Butia eriospatha 112, *112*
butia palm (*Butia capitata*) 112, *112*
butterfly bush (*Buddleja davidii*) 110, *110*
butterfly palm (*Chrysalidocarpus lutescens*) 148, *148*
butternut (*Juglans cinerea*) 259
buttonwood (*Platanus occidentalis*) 346
Buxus 112
Buxus microphylla 112, *112*
Buxus microphylla var. *japonica* 112
Buxus microphylla var. *koreana* 112
Buxus microphylla var. *sinica* 112
Buxus sempervirens 112, *112*
Buxus sempervirens 'Argentea' 112
Buxus sempervirens 'Suffruticosa' 112

cabbage palm (*Livistona australis*) 282, *282*
cabbage palm (*Sabal palmetto*) 392, *392*
cabbage tree (*Cussonia paniculata*) 172, *172*
cabbage-tree (*Cordyline*) 158
cabbage-tree palm (*Livistona australis*) 282, *282*
cacao (*Theobroma cacao*) 422, *422*
Caesalpinia 114
Caesalpinia ferrea 114, *114*
Caesalpinia gilliesii 114, *114*
Caesalpinia pulcherrima 114, *114*
cajeput (*Melaleuca leucadendra*) 298
calabash (*Amphitecna*) 84
Calamus 114–15
Calamus australis 114–15, *114*
Calceolaria 115
Calceolaria integrifolia 115, *115*
calico bush (*Kalmia latifolia*) 264, *264*
California buckeye (*Aesculus californica*) 71, *71*
California buckthorn (*Rhamnus californica*) 373, *373*
California fan palm (*Washingtonia filifera*) 442, *442*
California holly (*Heteromeles arbutifolia*) 243, *243*
California laurel (*Umbellularia californica*) 434
California live oak (*Quercus agrifolia*) 367
California nutmeg (*Torreya californica*) 428, *428*

California privet (*Ligustrum ovalifolium*) 278
California redwood (*Sequoia sempervirens*) 400–1, *401*
Californian allspice (*Calycanthus occidentalis*) 121, *121*
Californian black oak (*Quercus kelloggii*) 368, *368*
Californian holly grape (*Mahonia repens*) 290–1, *291*
Californian lilac (*Ceanothus*) 134–5
Californian red fir (*Abies magnifica*) 54
callery pear (*Pyrus calleryana*) 364
Calliandra 115
Calliandra haematocephala 115, *115*
Calliandra portoricensis 115
Calliandra surinamensis 115, *115*
Calliandra tweedii 115, *115*
Callicarpa 116
Callicarpa americana 116, *116*
Callicarpa bodinieri 116
Callicarpa bodinieri var. *giraldii* 116
Callicarpa macrophylla 116, *116*
Callicoma 116
Callicoma serratifolia 116, *116*
Callistemon 116–18
Callistemon citrinus 117
Callistemon citrinus 'Alba' 117
Callistemon citrinus 'Burgundy' 117
Callistemon citrinus 'Endeavour' 117
Callistemon citrinus 'Mauve Mist' 117
Callistemon citrinus 'Reeves Pink' 117, *117*
Callistemon citrinus 'Splendens' 117
*Callistemon lineari*s 117, *117*
Callistemon linearis 'Pumila' 117
Callistemon phoeniceus 117, *117*
Callistemon salignus 117, *117*
Callistemon subulatus 118, *118*
Callistemon viminalis 118, *118*
Callistemon viminalis 'Captain Cook' 367
Callistemon viminalis 'Harkness' 118
Callitris 118
Callitris columellaris 118, *118*
Callitris glaucophylla 118, *119*
Callitris rhomboidea 118
Calluna 118–19
Calluna vulgaris 118–19, *119*
Calluna vulgaris 'H. E. Beale' 119
Calluna vulgaris 'Mair's Variety' 119
Calluna vulgaris 'Orange Queen' 119
Calocedrus 119
Calocedrus decurrens 119, *119*
Calodendrum 120
Calodendrum capense 120, *120*
Calophyllum 120
Calophyllum inophyllum 120, *120*
Calothamnus 120
Calothamnus quadrifidus 120, *120*
Calycanthus 120–1
Calycanthus floridus 121, *121*
Calycanthus occidentalis 121, *121*
Calytrix 121
Calytrix tetragona 121, *121*
Camellia 121–4
Camellia 'Cornish Snow' 122
Camellia granthamiana 122
Camellia japonica 122, *122*
Camellia japonica 'Bernice Perfection' 123
Camellia japonica 'Betty Sheffield' 122
Camellia japonica 'C. M. Hovey' 122
Camellia japonica 'Debutante' 122, *122*
Camellia japonica 'Hana Fuki' 123
Camellia japonica 'Nuccio's Gem' 123
Camellia reticulata 'Captain Rawes' 123
Camellia reticulata 'Dr Clifford Parks' 123, *123*
Camellia reticulata hybrids 123
Camellia reticulata 'Pavlova' 123, *123*
Camellia sasanqua 123, *123*
Camellia sasanqua 'Hiru' 123
Camellia sasanqua 'Jennifer Susan' 123

Camellia sasanqua 'Plantation Pink' 123
Camellia sinensis 124, *124*
Camellia × *williamsii* 124
Camellia × *williamsii* 'Caerhays' 124
Camellia × *williamsii* 'Donation' 124, *124*
camphor laurel (*Cinnamomum camphora*) 149, *149*
Camptotheca 124–5
Camptotheca acuminata 124–5, *124*
Cananga 125
Cananga odorata 125, *125*
Canarium indicum 125
Canary Island bay (*Laurus azorica*) 271–2
Canary Island palm (*Phoenix canariensis*) 325, *325*, *326*
Canary Island pine (*Pinus canariensis*) 336, *336*
Canary Island strawberry tree (*Arbutus canariensis*) 88, *89*
Canary oak (*Quercus canariensis*) 367, *367*
cancer bush (*Sutherlandia frutescens*) 411, *411*
candelabra aloe (*Aloe candelabrum*) 81, *81*
candle bush (*Senna alata*) 399, *399*
candlebark (*Eucalyptus rubida*) 208, *209*
candlenut tree (*Aleurites moluccana*) 77, *77*
candlewood (*Fouquieria splendens*) 222
cannonball tree (*Couroupita guianensis*) 166, *166*
canoe birch (*Betula papyrifera*) 102, *102*
Cantua 125
Cantua buxifolia 125, *125*
canyon live oak (*Quercus chrysolepis*) 367
Cape bush (*Ekebergia capensis*) 188, *188*
Cape chestnut (*Calodendrum capense*) 120, *120*
Cape chestnut (*Celtis africana*) 136–7
Cape gardenia (*Rothmannia capensis*) 389, *389*
Cape honeysuckle (*Tecomaria capensis*) 420, *420*
Cape jasmine (*Gardenia augusta*) 228
Cape Leeuwin wattle (*Paraserianthes lophantha*) 321, *321*
Cape lilac (*Virgilia oroboides*) 440, *440*
Caragana 125
Caragana arborescens 125, *125*
Caragana arborescens 'Pendula' 125
carambola (*Averrhoa carambola*) 93, *93*
carbeen (*Eucalyptus tessellaris*) 209
cardinal's hat (*Malvaviscus arboreus*) 294
Caribbean pine (*Pinus caribaea*) 336, *336*
Carica 125–6
Carica papaya 126, *126*
caricature plant (*Graptophyllum pictum*) 233
Carissa 126
Carissa macrocarpa 126, *126*
Carmichaelia 126–7
Carmichaelia arborea 126
Carmichaelia odorata 126–7, *126*
Carmichaelia williamsii 127
carmine cherry (*Prunus campanulata*) 357, *357*
Carnegiea 127
Carnegiea gigantea 127, *127*
carnival bush (*Ochna serrulata*) 314, *314*
carob (*Ceratonia siliqua*) 138, *138*
Carolina allspice (*Calycanthus floridus*) 121, *121*
Carolina hemlock (*Tsuga caroliniana*) 430, *430*

Carolina silverbell (*Halesia carolina*) 239, *239*
Carolina tea (*Ilex vomitoria*) 255
Carpenteria 127
Carpenteria californica 127, *127*
Carpinus 127–8
Carpinus betulus 127, *127*
Carpinus caroliniana 128, *128*
Carpinus japonica 128, *128*
Caribbean pine (*Pinus caribaea*) 336, *336*
Carya 128–9
Carya cordiformis 128, *128*
Carya glabra 128–9
Carya illinoinensis 129, *129*
Carya laciniosa 129, *129*
Carya ovata 129, *129*
Carya tomentosa 130, *130*
Caryota 130
Caryota mitis 130, *130*
Caryota no 130
Caryota urens 130, *130*
cascara sagrada (*Rhamnus purshiana*) 373
cashew (*Anacardium occidentale*) 84–5, *84*
Cassia 130–1; see also *Senna*
Cassia alata see *Senna alata*
Cassia bicapsularis see *Senna pendula*
Cassia fistula 130–1, *131*
Cassia javanica 131, *131*
Cassia multijuga see *Senna multijuga*
Cassia spectabilis see *Senna spectabilis*
Castanea 131
Castanea chrysophylla see *Chrysolepis chrysophylla*
Castanea dentata 131
Castanea sativa 131, *131*
Castanospermum 131–2
Castanospermum australe 131–2, *132*
Castanospermum australe 'Bean Ball' 132
Castanospermum australe 'Beany' 132
Castanospora 132
Castanospora alphandii 132, *132*
Casuarina 132–3
Casuarina cunninghamiana 132, *132*
Casuarina equisetifolia 132–3, *133*
Casuarina glauca 133, *133*
Catalina ironwood (*Lyonothamnus floribundus*) 284
Catalpa 133
Catalpa bignonioides 133, *133*
Catalpa bignonioides 'Aurea' 133
Catalpa bungei 133
Catalpa speciosa 133, *133*
Caucasian fir (*Abies nordmannia*) 55, *55*
Caucasian spruce (*Picea orientalis*) 332
Caucasian wingnut (*Pterocarya fraxinifolia*) 362
caustic bush (*Euphorbia tirucalli*) 212–13
Cavendishia 134
Cavendishia acuminata see *Cavendishia bracteata*
Cavendishia bracteata 134, *134*
Ceanothus 134–5
Ceanothus arboreus 134
Ceanothus griseus 134
Ceanothus griseus var. *horizontalis* 134, *134*
Ceanothus griseus var. *horizontalis* 'Hurricane Point' 134
Ceanothus griseus var. *horizontalis* 'Yankee Point' 134
Ceanothus impressus 134, *134*
Ceanothus papillosus 134, *134*
Ceanothus thyrsiflorus 134–5, *135*
Ceanothus × *veitchianus* 135
Cecropia 135
Cecropia palmata 135, *135*
cedar (*Cedrus*) 135–6
cedar of Goa (*Cupressus lusitanica*) 170, *171*
cedar of Lebanon (*Cedrus libani*) 136, *137*
cedar wattle (*Acacia elata*) 58, *58*

Cedrela 135
Cedrela mexicana 135, *135*
Cedrus 135–6
Cedrus atlantica 136, *136*
Cedrus atlantica 'Glauca' 136
Cedrus atlantica 'Glauca Pendula' 136, *136*
Cedrus brevifolia 136, *136*
Cedrus deodara 136, *136*
Cedrus deodara 'Aurea' 136
Cedrus libani 136, *137*
Ceiba 136
Ceiba pentandra 136, *137*
celery pine (*Phyllocladus aspleniifolius*) 328
Celtis 136
Celtis africana 136–7
Celtis australis 137
Celtis laevigata 137
Celtis mississippiensis see *Celtis laevigata*
Celtis occidentalis 137, *137*
Celtis sinensis 137, *137*
century plant (*Agave americana*) 74
Cephalotaxus 138
Cephalotaxus fortunei 138, *138*
Cephalotaxus harringtonia 138
Cephalotaxus harringtonia 'Chosen-maki' see *Cephalotaxus harringtonia* 'Fastigiata'
Cephalotaxus harringtonia var. *drupacea* 138
Cephalotaxus harringtonia 'Fastigiata' 138, *138*
Ceratonia 138
Ceratonia siliqua 138, *138*
Ceratopetalum 138–9
Ceratopetalum apetalum 138, *139*
Ceratopetalum gummiferum 138, *139*, *139*
Ceratopetalum gummiferum 'Albery's Red' 139
Ceratostigma 139
Ceratostigma willmottianum 139, *139*
Cercidiphyllum 139–40
Cercidiphyllum japonicum 139–40, *140*
Cercidiphyllum japonicum var. *magnificum* 140
Cercidiphyllum japonicum 'Pendulum' 140
Cercidiphyllum japonicum var. *sinense* 140
Cercidium 140
Cercidium floridum 140, *140*
Cercis 140–1
Cercis canadensis 141, *141*
Cercis occidentalis 141, *141*
Cercis siliquastrum 141, *141*
Cercis siliquastrum 'Alba' 141
Cercis siliquastrum 'Rubra' 141, *141*
Cercocarpus 141–2
Cercocarpus betuloides 142, *142*
Cestrum 142
Cestrum fasciculatum 142, *142*
Cestrum fasciculatum 'Newellii' 142, *142*
Cestrum nocturnum 142, *143*
Ceylon cinnamon (*Cinnamomum zeylanicum*) 149
Ceylon gooseberry (*Dovyalis hebecarpa*) 185
Chaenomeles 142–3
Chaenomeles sinensis see *Cydonia sinensis*
Chaenomeles speciosa 143, *143*
Chaenomeles speciosa 'Moerloosii' 143
Chaenomeles speciosa 'Nivalis' 143
Chaenomeles speciosa 'Rubra Grandiflora' 143
Chamaebatiaria 143
Chamaebatiaria millefolium 143, *143*
Chamaecyparis 143–5
Chamaecyparis funebris 143, *143*
Chamaecyparis lawsoniana 144
Chamaecyparis lawsoniana 'Allumii' 144
Chamaecyparis lawsoniana 'Erecta' 144

Chamaecyparis lawsoniana 'Fletcheri' 144
Chamaecyparis lawsoniana 'Lane' 144
Chamaecyparis lawsoniana 'Stewartii' 144
Chamaecyparis lawsoniana 'Winston Churchill' 144, *144*
Chamaecyparis nootkatensis 144, *144*
Chamaecyparis obtusa 144
Chamaecyparis obtusa 'Crippsii' 144
Chamaecyparis obtusa 'Nana Aurea' 144
Chamaecyparis obtusa 'Nana Gracilis' 144
Chamaecyparis obtusa 'Tetragona' 144
Chamaecyparis obtusa 'Tetragona Aurea' 144
Chamaecyparis pisifera 144–5
Chamaecyparis pisifera 'Boulevard' 144–5
Chamaecyparis pisifera 'Filifera Aurea' 144–5
Chamaecyparis pisifera, Plumosa group 144, *145*
Chamaecyparis pisifera 'Squarrosa' 144–5
Chamaecyparis pisifera 'Squarrosa Intermedia' 144
Chamaecyparis thyoides 145
Chamaecyparis thyoides 'Ericoides' 145
Chamaerops 145
Chamaerops humilis 145, *145*
Chamelaucium 145
Chamelaucium uncinatum 145, *145*
champak (*Michelia champaca*) 303
chaste tree (*Vitex agnus-castus*) 440
Cheal's weeping cherry (*Prunus serrulata* 'Kikushidare') 359
chequerboard juniper (*Juniperus deppeana* var. *pachyphlaea*) 261, *261*
chenille plant (*Acalypha hispida*) 61, *61*
chennar (*Platanus orientalis*) 346, *346*
cherry birch (*Betula lenta*) 101, *101*
cherry plum (*Prunus cerasifera*) 357, *357*
cherry-laurel (*Prunus laurocerasus*) 358, *358*
chestnut (*Castanea*) 131
chestnut-leafed oak (*Quercus castaneifolia*) 367, *367*
Chilean beech (*Nothofagus obliqua*) 312, *312*
Chilean cedar (*Austrocedrus chilensis*) 93, *93*
Chilean cranberry (*Ugni molinae*) 432, *432*
Chilean fire bush (*Embothrium coccineum*) 189–90
Chilean guava (*Ugni molinae*) 432, *432*
Chilean wine palm (*Jubaea chilensis*) 259, *259*
Chilopsis 146
Chilopsis linearis 146, *146*
Chimonanthus 146
Chimonanthus praecox 146, *146*
China doll (*Radermachera sinica*) 372, *372*
China fir (*Cunninghamia*) 169
China flower (*Adenandra uniflora*) 70, *70*
China rose (*Hibiscus rosa-sinensis*) 244, *245*
chinaberry (*Melia azedarach*) 300
chinar (*Platanus orientalis*) 346, *346*
Chinese anise (*Illicium anisatum*) 255, *255*
Chinese aralia (*Aralia chinensis*) 86, *86*
Chinese banyan (*Ficus microcarpa*) 219, *219*
Chinese cedar (*Cunninghamia*) 169
Chinese date (*Zizyphus jujuba*) 447, *447*

Chinese elm (*Ulmus parvifolia*) 433, *433*
Chinese evergreen azalea (*Rhododendron simsii*) 380
Chinese fan palm (*Livistona chinensis*) 282, *282*
Chinese fan palm (*Trachycarpus fortunei*) 428, *428*
Chinese flowering quince (*Chaenomeles speciosa*) 143, *143*
Chinese fringe tree (*Chionanthus retusus*) 146–7, *146*
Chinese hackberry (*Celtis sinensis*) 137, *137*
Chinese hat plant (*Holmskioldia sanguinea*) 247, *247*
Chinese hawthorn (*Photinia serrulata*) 327, *327*
Chinese hemlock (*Tsuga chinensis*) 430, *430*
Chinese holly (*Ilex cornuta*) 253, *253*
Chinese juniper (*Juniperus chinensis*) 260–1, *260*
Chinese lantern (*Abutilon × hybridum*) 56, *56*
Chinese larch (*Larix potaninii*) 271, *271*
Chinese necklace poplar (*Populus lasiocarpa*) 352, *352*
Chinese nettle tree (*Celtis sinensis*) 137, *137*
Chinese pistachio (*Pistacia chinensis*) 343, *343*
Chinese plum-yew (*Cephalotaxus fortunei*) 138, *138*
Chinese quince (*Cydonia sinensis*) 174, *174*
Chinese rowan (*Sorbus hupehensis*) 406, *406*
Chinese snowball tree (*Viburnum macrocephalum*) 438, *438*
Chinese sumac (*Rhus chinensis*) 382
Chinese swamp cypress (*Glyptostrobus pensilis*) 232, *232*
Chinese tallow tree (*Sapium sebiferum*) 395, *395*
Chinese tamarisk (*Tamarix chinensis*) 418
Chinese toon (*Toona sinensis*) 427
Chinese tulip tree (*Liriodendron chinense*) 280, *280*
Chinese weeping cypress (*Chamaecyparis funebris*) 143, *143*
Chinese witch hazel (*Hamamelis mollis*) 239, *239*
Chionanthus 146–7
Chionanthus retusus 146–7, *146*
Chionanthus virginicus 147, *147*
chinquapin (*Castanea*) 131
chir pine (*Pinus roxburghii*) 342, *342*
Choisya 147
Choisya ternata 147, *147*
chokeberry (*Aronia*) 91–2
Chorisia 147
Chorisia insignis 147, *147*
Chorisia speciosa 147, *147*
Christ thorn (*Paliurus spina-christi*) 321
Christmas berry (*Heteromeles arbutifolia*) 243, *243*
Christmas box (*Sarcococca*) 396
Christmas plant (*Euphorbia pulcherrima*) 212, *213*
Chrysalidocarpus 148
Chrysalidocarpus lutescens 148, *148*
Chrysanthemoides 148
Chrysanthemoides monilifera 148, *148*
Chrysanthemoides monilifera subsp. *monilifera* 148
Chrysanthemoides monilifera subsp. *rotundata* 148
Chrysobalanus 148
Chrysobalanus icaco 148
Chrysolepis 148

Chrysolepis chrysophylla 148
Chusan palm (*Trachycarpus fortunei*) 428, *428*
cigar flower (*Cuphea ignea*) 170, *171*
cigar-box cedar (*Cedrela*) 135
cigarette plant (*Cuphea ignea*) 170, *171*
Cinchona 148–9
Cinchona officinalis 149
Cinnamomum 149
Cinnamomum camphora 149, *149*
Cinnamomum zeylanicum 149
Cistus 149–50
Cistus albidus 149, *149*
Cistus ladanifer 150
Cistus ladanifer 'Albiflorus' 150
Cistus × lusitanicus 150, *150*
Cistus × lusitanicus 'Decumbens' 150
Cistus × pulverulentus 'Sunset' 149
Cistus × purpureus 150, *150*
Cistus × purpureus 'Betty Taudevin' 150
Cistus × purpureus 'Brilliancy' 150
Cistus salviifolius 150, *150*
Citharexylum 150–1
Citharexylum spinosum 150–1, *150*
Citrus 151–2
Citrus aurantifolia 151, *151*
Citrus limon 151, *151*
Citrus limon 'Eureka' 151
Citrus limon 'Lisbon' 151
Citrus limon 'Meyer' 151
Citrus paradisi 152
Citrus paradisi × Citrus reticulata 152, *152*
Citrus paradisi 'Golden Special' 152
Citrus paradisi 'Morrison's Seedless' 152
Citrus paradisi 'Ruby' 152
Citrus paradisi 'Wheeny' 152
Citrus sinensis 152, *152*
Citrus sinensis 'Joppa' 152
Citrus sinensis 'Ruby Blood' 152
Citrus sinensis 'Valencia' 152
Citrus sinensis 'Washington Navel' 152
Cladrastis 152
Cladrastis lutea 152, *152*
clammy locust (*Robinia viscosa*) 385
claret ash (*Fraxinus angustifolia* 'Raywood') 223
Clausena 152
Clausena lansium 152
Clerodendrum 152–3
Clerodendrum buchananii 153, *153*
Clerodendrum paniculatum 153, *153*
Clerodendrum trichotomum 153, *153*
Clerodendrum ugandense 153, *153*
Clerodendrum zambesiacum 153, *153*
Clethra 153–4
Clethra alnifolia 154
Clethra arborea 154, *154*
Clethra barbinervis 154, *154*
Clianthus 154
Clianthus puniceus 154, *154*
Clusia 154
Clusia rosea 154, *154*
cluster fishtail palm (*Caryota mitis*) 130, *130*
cluster pine (*Pinus pinaster*) 341, *341*
coach whip (*Fouquieria splendens*) 222
coachwood (*Ceratopetalum apetalum*) 138, *139*
coast banksia (*Banksia integrifolia*) 97, *97*
coast redwood (*Sequoia sempervirens*) 400–1, *401*
coast rosemary (*Westringia fruticosa*) 443, *443*
coast silver-leaf (*Brachylaena discolor*) 106, *106*
coast tea-tree (*Leptospermum laevigatum*) 274, *274*
coastal milkwood (*Sideroxylon*) 402
Coccoloba 155
Coccoloba uvifera 155
Cochlospermum 155

Cochlospermum fraseri 155, *155*
cockspur coral tree (*Erythrina crista-galli*) 198–9, *199*
cocky apple (*Planchonia careya*) 345, *345*
cocoa (*Theobroma cacao*) 422, *422*
coconut (*Cocos nucifera*) 155, *155*
coco-plum (*Chrysobalanus*) 148
Cocos 155
Cocos nucifera 155, *155*
cocos palm (*Syagrus romanzoffiana*) 411
Cocos plumosa see *Syagrus romanzoffiana*
cocus wood (*Brya ebenus*) 109, *109*
Codiaeum 155–6
Codiaeum variegatum 156
Coffea 156
Coffea arabica 156, *156*
coffee (*Coffea*) 156
coffeeberry (*Rhamnus californica*) 373, *373*
coffin fir (*Cunninghamia lanceolata*) 169, *169*
coffin juniper (*Juniperus recurva*) 262, *262*
coffin pine (*Cunninghamia lanceolata*) 169, *169*
Coleonema 156
Coleonema album 156
Coleonema pulchellum 156, *156*
Coleonema pulchellum 'Sunset Gold' 156, *156*
Coleonema pulchrum see *Coleonema pulchellum*
Colletia 156
Colletia cruciata 156
Colletia paradoxa see *Colletia cruciata*
Colorado blue spruce (*Picea pungens*) 333, *333*
Colorado white fir (*Abies concolor*) 53
Colvillea 156
Colvillea racemosa 156
Colville's glory (*Colvillea racemosa*) 156
Combretum 156–7
Combretum erythrophyllum 157
common alder (*Alnus glutinosa*) 80–1, *80*
common barberry (*Berberis vulgaris*) 101
common beech (*Fagus sylvatica*) 216, *216*
common box (*Buxus sempervirens*) 112, *112*
common broom (*Cytisus scoparius*) 174, *174*
common coral tree (*Erythrina lysistemon*) 200, *200*
common hornbeam (*Carpinus betulus*) 127, *127*
common jasmine (*Jasminum officinale*) 258
common juniper (*Juniperus communis*) 260, *261*
common laburnum (*Laburnum anagyroides*) 268, *269*
common lime tree (*Tilia × europaea*) 425
common mulberry see *Morus alba*
common oak (*Quercus robur*) 369, *369*
common pear (*Pyrus communis*) 364
common privet (*Ligustrum lucidum*) 278, *278*
common quince (*Cydonia oblonga*) 173, *173*
common spruce (*Picea abies*) 330, *330*
common walnut (*Juglans regia*) 260, *260*
common yew (*Taxus baccata*) 419
Confederate rose (*Hibiscus mutabilis*) 244, *244*
congoo mallee (*Eucalyptus dumosa*) 204, *204*
Convolvulus 157

Convolvulus cneorum 157, *157*
coolibah (*Eucalyptus microtheca*) 206–7
Cootamundra wattle (*Acacia baileyana*) 57
copey (*Clusia rosea*) 154, *154*
Coprosma 157
Coprosma brunnea 157, *157*
Coprosma repens 157, *157*
Coprosma repens 'Marble Queen' 157
Coprosma repens 'Picturata' 157
coquito palm (*Jubaea chilensis*) 259, *259*
coral gum (*Eucalyptus torquata*) 209, *209*
coral plant (*Jatropha multifida*) 258–9, *258*
coral tree (*Erythrina*) 197–201
coral tree (*Erythrina × sykesii*) 200–1, *200*
Cordia 157–8
Cordia dichotoma 158
Cordia sebestena 158, *158*
Cordyline 158
Cordyline australis 158, *158*
Cordyline australis 'Albertii' 158
Cordyline australis 'Purpurea' 158
Cordyline banksii 158, *158*
Cordyline fruticosa 158–9, *158*
Cordyline indivisa 158, *159*
Cordyline stricta 159, *159*
Cordyline terminalis see *Cordyline fruticosa*
cork oak (*Quercus suber*) 370, *371*
corkbark fir (*Abies lasiocarpa* var. *arizonica*) 54
corkscrew willow (*Salix matsudana* 'Tortuosa') 393, *393*
cornel (*Cornus*) 159–60
cornelian cherry (*Cornus mas*) 160, *160*
Cornish heath (*Erica vagans*) 196
Cornus 159–60
Cornus alba 159, *159*
Cornus alba 'Spaethii' 159
Cornus capitata 159
Cornus controversa 159, *159*
Cornus florida 159, *159*
Cornus florida 'Rubra' 159
Cornus kousa 160, *160*
Cornus kousa var. *chinensis* 160
Cornus mas 160, *160*
Cornus nuttallii 160
Cornus pumila 160, *161*
Corokia 160
Corokia buddleioides 160, *161*
Corokia cotoneaster 160
Correa 160–1
Correa alba 161, *161*
Correa lawrenciana 161, *161*
Correa pulchella 161, *161*
Corsican pine (*Pinus nigra* var. *maritima*) 340
Corylopsis 161–2
Corylopsis glabrescens 162, *162*
Corylopsis sinensis 162, *162*
Corylopsis sinensis forma *veitchiana* 162
Corylopsis spicata 162, *162*
Corylus 162–3
Corylus avellana 162–3, *162*
Corylus avellana 'Contorta' 163
Corylus maxima 163, *163*
Corylus maxima 'Purpurea' 163
Corynabutilon vitifolium see *Abutilon vitifolium*
Corypha 163
Corypha umbraculifera 163, *163*
cosmetic bark (*Murraya paniculata*) 305, *305*
Cotinus 163
Cotinus coggygria 163, *163*
Cotinus coggygria 'Purpureus' 163, *163*
Cotoneaster 164–6
Cotoneaster apiculatus 164, *164*
Cotoneaster conspicuus 164, *164*
Cotoneaster conspicuus 'Decorus' 164
Cotoneaster dammeri 164, *164*

Cotoneaster dammeri 'Radicans' 164
Cotoneaster franchetii 164, *165*
Cotoneaster frigidus 165
Cotoneaster glaucophyllus 165, *165*
Cotoneaster glaucophyllus var. *serotinus* 165
Cotoneaster horizontalis 165, *165*
Cotoneaster horizontalis var. *perpusillus* 165
Cotoneaster horizontalis 'Variegatus' 165
Cotoneaster 'Hybridus Pendulus' 165, *165*
Cotoneaster lacteus 165, *165*
Cotoneaster microphyllus 166, *166*
Cotoneaster microphyllus var. *cochleatus* 166
Cotoneaster microphyllus var. *thymifolius* 166
Cotoneaster multiflorus 166
Cotoneaster pannosus 166
Cotoneaster salicifolius 166, *166*
Cotoneaster serotinus see *Cotoneaster glaucophyllus*
cotton gum (*Nyssa aquatica*) 314
cotton palm (*Washingtonia filifera*) 442, *442*
cotton rose (*Hibiscus mutabilis*) 244, *244*
cottonwood (*Populus deltoides*) 352, *352*
cottonwood tree (*Hibiscus tiliaceus*) 246, *246*
coulter pine (*Pinus coulteri*) 337, *337*
Couroupita 166
Couroupita guianensis 166, *166*
cow's horn euphorbia (*Euphorbia grandicornis*) 212, *212*
cow's udder plant (*Solanum mammosum*) 403
crab apple (*Malus* 'Golden Hornet') 293, *293*
crab apple (*Malus sylvestris*) 294
crack willow (*Salix fragilis*) 393
cranberry (*Vaccinium*) 435–6
crane flower (*Strelitzia reginae*) 410, *410*
crape myrtle (*Lagerstroemia indica*) 269, *269*
crepe jasmine (*Tabernaemontana divaricata*) 416
Crataegus 166–7
Crataegus arnoldiana 166, *167*
Crataegus cordata see *Crataegus phaenopyrum*
Crataegus laciniata 167, *167*
Crataegus laevigata 167
Crataegus laevigata 'Paul's Scarlet' 167, *167*
Crataegus × *lavallei* 167
Crataegus monogyna 167, *167*
Crataegus orientalis see *Crataegus laciniata*
Crataegus phaenopyrum 167, *167*
Crataegus pubescens 168, *168*
Crateva 168
Crateva religiosa 168, *168*
crested wattle (*Paraserianthes lophantha*) 321, *321*
Crinodendron 168
Crinodendron hookerianum 168, *168*
Crinodendron patagua 168
cross berry (*Grewia occidentalis*) 235, *235*
cross-leafed heath (*Erica tetralix*) 196, *196*
Crotalaria 168
Crotalaria agatiflora 168, *168*
Crotalaria capensis 168, *168*
croton (*Codiaeum variegatum*) 156
crow's ash (*Flindersia australis*) 220, *220*
Crowea 168–9
Crowea exalata × *saligna* 169, *169*
Crowea saligna 169
crown bark (*Cinchona officinalis*) 149
Cryptomeria 169
Cryptomeria japonica 169, *169*

Cryptomeria japonica 'Araucarioides' 169
Cryptomeria japonica 'Elegans' 169
Cryptomeria japonica 'Globosa Nana' 169
Cryptomeria japonica var. *sinensis* 169
Cryptomeria japonica 'Vilmoriniana' 169
Cuban royal palm (*Roystonea regia*) 389–90, *389*
cucumber tree (*Magnolia acuminata*) 287, *287*
cumquat (*Fortunella japonica*) 221, *221*
Cunninghamia 169
Cunninghamia lanceolata 169, *169*
Cunonia 169
Cunonia capensis 169, *169*
Cupaniopsis 170
Cupaniopsis anacardioides 170, *170*
Cuphea 170
Cuphea ignea 170, *171*
Cuphea micropetala 170, *171*
× *Cupressocyparis* 170
× *Cupressocyparis leylandii* 170, *170*
× *Cupressocyparis leylandii* 'Haggerston Grey' 170
× *Cupressocyparis leylandii* 'Leighton Green' 170
× *Cupressocyparis leylandii* 'Naylor's Blue' 170
Cupressus 170–2
Cupressus arizonica var. *glabra* see *Cupressus glabra*
Cupressus cashmeriana 171, *171*
Cupressus duclouxiana 171, *171*
Cupressus funebris see *Chamaecyparis funebris*
Cupressus glabra 171, *171*
Cupressus lusitanica 170, *171*
Cupressus lusitanica var. *bethamii* 171
Cupressus macrocarpa 170, *171*
Cupressus macrocarpa 'Aurea' 171
Cupressus macrocarpa 'Aurea Saligna' 171
Cupressus macrocarpa 'Brunniana' 171
Cupressus macrocarpa 'Greenstead Magnificent' 171
Cupressus sempervirens 171
Cupressus sempervirens 'Horizontalis' 171
Cupressus sempervirens 'Stricta' 171
Cupressus sempervirens 'Swane's Golden' 171, *171*
Cupressus torulosa 172, *172*
currant (*Ribes*) 383–4
curry bush (*Hypericum revolutum*) 250, *250*
curry tree (*Murraya koenigii*) 305
Cussonia 172
Cussonia paniculata 172, *172*
Cussonia spicata 172, *172*
Cyathea 172
Cyathea cooperi 172
Cyathea dealbata 172, *173*
Cycas 172–3
Cycas armstrongii 173
Cycas circinalis 173
Cycas revoluta 173, *173*
Cydonia 173
Cydonia oblonga 173, *173*
Cydonia sinensis 174, *174*
cypress (*Cupressus*) 170–2
cypress-pine (*Callitris*) 118
Cyprus cedar (*Cedrus brevifolia*) 136, *136*
Cyrilla 174
Cyrilla racemiflora 174, *174*
Cytisus 174
Cytisus 'Burkwoodii' 174
Cytisus × *praecox* 174
Cytisus × *praecox* 'Allgold' 174
Cytisus × *praecox* 'Goldspear' 174
Cytisus scoparius 174, *174*

Daboecia 176
Daboecia azorica 176

Daboecia cantabrica 176, *176*
Daboecia cantabrica 'Alba' 176
Daboecia cantabrica 'Atropurpurea' 176
Daboecia × *scotica* see *Daboecia cantabrica*
Daboecia × *scotica* 'William Buchanan' see *Daboecia cantabrica*
Dacrydium 176
Dacrydium cupressinum 176, *176*
Dacrydium franklinii see *Lagarostrobos franklinii*
Dahurian larch (*Larix gmelinii*) 271, *271*
Daimyo oak (*Quercus dentata*) 368, *368*
Dais 176
Dais cotinifolia 176, *176*
daisy bush (*Olearia*) 315
Dalbergia 176–7
Dalbergia sissoo 176–7
Daphne 177
Daphne × *burkwoodii* 177, *177*
Daphne cneorum 177, *177*
Daphne genkwa 177, *177*
Daphne mezereum 177
Daphne odora 177, *177*
Daphne odora 'Alba' 177
Daphne odora 'Aureo-marginata' 177
Darlingia 177
Darlingia darlingiana 177, *177*
Darwin barberry (*Berberis darwini*) 100, *101*
Darwinia 178
Darwinia oxylepis 178, *178*
date (*Phoenix dactylifera*) 326, *326*
David's pine (*Pinus armandii*) 335, *335*
Davidia 178
Davidia involucrata 178, *178*
Davidia involucrata var. *vilmoriniana* 178
dawn redwood (*Metasequoia glyptostroboides*) 301, *301*
dead rat tree (*Adansonia gregorii*) 69, *69*
Delavayi's silver fir (*Abies delavayi*) 53
Delonix 178
Delonix regia 178, *179*
Denbrobenthamia fragifera see *Cornus capitata*
deodar (*Cedrus deodara*) 136, *136*
deodar cedar (*Cedrus deodara*) 136, *136*
desert ash (*Fraxinus angustifolia* subsp. *oxycarpa*) 223, *223*
desert banksia (*Banksia ornata*) 98, *98*
desert mahonia (*Mahonia fremontii*) 290
desert oak (*Allocasuarina decaisneana*) 78, *78*
desert rose (*Adenium obesum*) 70, *70*
desert willow (*Chilopsis linearis*) 146, *146*
Desfontainea 178–9
Desfontainea spinosa 179, *179*
Desmond mallee (*Eucalyptus desmondensis*) 204, *204*
Deutzia 179–80
Deutzia × *elegantissima* 179
Deutzia × *elegantissima* 'Elegantissima' 179
Deutzia × *elegantissima* 'Fasiculata' 179
Deutzia × *elegantissima* 'Rosealind' 179
Deutzia gracilis 179, *179*
Deutzia × *kalmiiflora* 179, *179*
Deutzia 'Nikko' see *Deutzia gracilis*
Deutzia × *rosea* 180, *180*
Deutzia × *rosea* 'Carminea' 180
Deutzia scabra 180, *180*
Deutzia scabra 'Candidissima' 180
Deutzia scabra 'Flore Pleno' 180
Deutzia scabra 'Pride of Rochester' 180

devil's walking-stick (*Aralia spinosa*) 86–7
Dicksonia 180–1
Dicksonia antarctica 180–1, *180*, *181*
Dicksonia fibrosa 181, *181*
Dicksonia squarrosa see *Dicksonia*
Dillenia 181
Dillenia alata 181, *181*
Dillenia indica 181, *181*
dinner-plate fig (*Ficus dammaropsis*) 218–19, *218*
Dioon 181–2
Dioon edule 182, *182*
diosma (*Coleonema*) 156
Diosma ericoides see *Coleonema album*
Diospyros 182
Diospyros digyna 182
Diospyros ebenum see *Diospyros*
Diospyros kaki 182, *182*
Diospyros virginiana 182, *182*
Dipelta 182–3
Dipelta floribunda 182, *183*
Disanthus 183
Disanthus cercidifolius 183, *183*
Dodonaea 183
Dodonaea boroniifolia 183, *183*
Dodonaea viscosa 183
Dodonaea viscosa 'Purpurea' 183, *183*
dog rose (*Bauera rubioides*) 99, *99*
dogwood (*Cornus*) 159–60
Dolichandrone 183
Dolichandrone heterophylla 183, *183*
Dombeya 183–4
Dombeya burgessiae 184, *184*
Dombeya × *cayeuxii* 184
Dombeya natalensis see *Dombeya tiliacea*
Dombeya rotundifolia 184, *184*
Dombeya tiliacea 184, *184*
dona flores (*Mussaenda philippica*) 306–7, *306*
Dorrigo waratah (*Alloxylon pinnatum*) 80, *80*
Doryanthes 184
Doryanthes excelsa 184, *185*
Douglas fir (*Pseudotsuga menziesii*) 361, *361*
dove tree (*Davidia*) 178
Dovyalis 184–5
Dovyalis caffra 185, *185*
Dovyalis hebecarpa 185
downy birch (*Betula pubescens*) 102–3, *103*
downy serviceberry (*Amelanchier arborea*) 83, *83*
Dracaena 185
Dracaena draco 185, *185*
Dracaena marginata 185
Dracaena marginata 'Tricolor' 185
dragon tree (*Dracaena draco*) 185, *185*
dragon's eye pine (*Pinus densiflora* 'Oculus-draconis') 338
dragon's-blood tree (*Dracaena draco*) 185, *185*
Drimys 185
Drimys winteri 185, *185*
drooping she-oak (*Allocasuarina verticillata*) 79, *79*
drumstick tree (*Moringa oleifera*) 304
drumsticks (*Isopogon*) 257
Duranta 186
Duranta erecta 186, *186*
Duranta erecta 'Alba' 186
Duranta erecta 'Variegata' 186
Duranta plumieri see *Duranta erecta*
Duranta repens see *Duranta erecta*
durian (*Durio zibethinus*) 186, *186*
Durio 186
Durio zibethinus 186, *186*
dusty daisy bush (*Olearia phlogopappa*) 315, *315*
dusty miller (*Senecio viravira*) 399, *399*
Dutch elm (*Ulmus* × *hollandica*) 433, *433*
Duvernoia 186

Duvernoia adhatodoides 186
dwarf Alberta spruce (*Picea glauca* 'Conica') 331, *331*
dwarf birch (*Betula nana*) 101
dwarf date palm (*Phoenix roebeleni*) 326, *326*
dwarf dogwood (*Cornus pumila*) 160, *161*
dwarf elm (*Ulmus pumila*) 434, *434*
dwarf erythrina (*Erythrina humeana*) 200, *200*
dwarf fothergilla (*Fothergilla gardenii*) 222, *222*
dwarf palmetto (*Sabal minor*) 392, *392*
dwarf poinciana (*Caesalpinia gilliesii*) 114, *114*
dwarf Russian almond (*Prunus tenella*) 359
dwarf Swiss mountain pine (*Pinus mugo* var. *pumilo*) 339
dyer's broom (*Genista tinctoria*) 230, *231*
dyer's greenwood (*Genista tinctoria*) 230, *231*

early tamarisk (*Tamarix parviflora*) 418, *418*
eastern hemlock (*Tsuga canadensis*) 429, *429*
eastern hop hornbeam (*Ostrya virginiana*) 318, *318*
eastern redbud (*Cercis canadensis*) 141, *141*
eastern white pine (*Pinus strobus*) 342, *342*
ebony (*Diospyros*) 182
Echium 188
Echium candicans see *Echium*
Echium fastuosum 188, *188*
Echium wildprettii see *Echium*
Edgworthia 188
Edgworthia chrysantha 188, *188*
Edgworthia chrysantha 'Red Dragon' 188, *188*
Edgworthia chrysantha 'Red Robin' 188, *188*
Edgworthia papyrifera see *Edgworthia chrysantha*
Ekebergia 188
Ekebergia capensis 188, *188*
Elaeagnus 188–9
Elaeagnus angustifolia 189
Elaeagnus pungens 189
Elaeagnus pungens 'Aurea' 189, *189*
Elaeagnus pungens 'Maculata' 189
Elaeagnus umbellata 189, *189*
Elaeis 189
Elaeis guineensis 189, *189*
Elaeocarpus 189
Elaeocarpus reticulatus 189
Elaeocarpus reticulatus 'Prima Donna' 189
elderberry (*Sambucus*) 394
elderberry (*Sambucus nigra*) 394, *394*
elephant apple (*Dillenia indica*) 181, *181*
elephant bush (*Portulacaria afra*) 353, *353*
elephant's food (*Portulacaria afra*) 353, *353*
elim heath (*Erica regia*) 195, *195*
elm (*Ulmus*) 432–4
Embothrium 189–90
Embothrium coccineum 189–90, *190*
Embothrium coccineum 'Norquinco Valley' 190
emu-bush (*Eremophila*) 192
Enallagma latifolia see *Amphitecna latifolia*
Encephalartos 190
Encephalartos altensteinii 190, *190*
Encephalartos friderici-guilielmi 190, *190*
Engelmann spruce (*Picea engelmannii*) 331, *331*
English elm (*Ulmus procera*) 433, *434*

English holly (Ilex aquifolium) 253, 253
English lavender (Lavandula angustifolia) 272
English oak (Quercus robur) 369, 369
English yew (Taxus baccata) 419
Enkianthus 190
Enkianthus campanulatus 190, 191
Enkianthus campanulatus var. palibinii 190
Enkianthus perulatus 190, 191
Epacris 190–1
Epacris impressa 191, 191
Epacris longiflora 191, 191
epaulette tree (Pterostyrax hispida) 362, 362
Ephedra 191–2
Ephedra distachya 191, 191
Ephedra viridis 192
Eremophila 192
Eremophila maculata 192, 192
Eremophila mitchellii 192
Eremophila polyclada 192, 192
Erica 192–6
Erica arborea 192
Erica arborea 'Alpina' 192, 192
Erica bauera 191, 192
Erica canaliculata 192
Erica carnea see Erica herbacea
Erica cerinthoides 192, 192
Erica cinerea 193
Erica cinerea 'Crimson King' 193, 193
Erica cinerea 'Kerry Cherry' 193, 193
Erica × darleyensis 'Darley Dale' 194
Erica × darleyensis 'George Rendall' 194
Erica × darleyensis 'Jack H. Brummage' 194
Erica erigena 194
Erica erigena 'Silver Bells' 194
Erica erigena 'W. T. Racklift' 194, 194
Erica grandiflora 194, 194
Erica herbacea 194
Erica herbacea 'Ruby Glow' 194
Erica herbacea 'Springwood Pink' 194
Erica herbacea 'Springwood White' 194, 194
Erica lusitanica 194–5, 195
Erica mammosa 195, 195
Erica mammosa 'Coccinea' 195, 195
Erica melanthera 195, 195
Erica regia 195, 195
Erica tetralix 196, 196
Erica vagans 196
Erica vagans 'St Keverne' 196
Erica × wilmorei 196
Erica × wilmorei 'Aurora' 196
Erica × wilmorei 'Linton's Red' 196
Erica × wilmorei 'Ruby Glow' 196
Eriobotrya 196
Eriobotrya japonica 196, 196
Eriostemon 210
Eriostemon australasius 196, 197
Eriostemon myoporoides 197
Eriostemon myoporoides 'Clearview Apple-blossom' 197
Eriostemon myoporoides 'Profusion' 197, 197
Ervatamia divaricata see Tabernaemontana divaricata
Erythrina 197–201
Erythrina acanthocarpa 197, 197
Erythrina × bidwillii 198, 198
Erythrina caffra 198, 198
Erythrina caffra 'Flavescens' 198, 198
Erythrina crista-galli 198–9, 199
Erythrina fusca 199, 199
Erythrina haerdii 199, 199
Erythrina humeana 200, 200
Erythrina indica see Erythrina × sykesii
Erythrina livingstoniana 200, 200
Erythrina lysistemon 200, 200
Erythrina × sykesii 200–1, 200

Erythrina variegata 201, 201; see also Erythrina × sykesii
Erythrina variegata 'Purcellii' 201, 201
Erythrina vespertilio 201
Escallonia 201–2
Escallonia bifida 201, 201
Escallonia 'Donard Beauty' 201
Escallonia 'Donard Star' 201, 201
Escallonia × exoniensis 201, 201
Escallonia montevidensis see Escallonia bifida
Escallonia 'Pride of Donard' 201
Escallonia rubra 202, 202
Escallonia rubra 'Apple Blossom' 202
Escallonia rubra var. macrantha 202
Eucalyptus 202–10
Eucalyptus brevifolia 202, 202
Eucalyptus caesia subsp. magna 202
Eucalyptus calophylla 202–3, 202
Eucalyptus calycogona 203
Eucalyptus camaldulensis 203, 203
Eucalyptus cinerea 203
Eucalyptus citriodora 203, 203
Eucalyptus cladocalyx 204, 204
Eucalyptus coolabah see Eucalyptus microtheca
Eucalyptus curtisii 204, 204
Eucalyptus desmondensis 204, 204
Eucalyptus diversicolor 204
Eucalyptus dumosa 204, 204
Eucalyptus elata 204–5
Eucalyptus eremophila 205
Eucalyptus erythrocorys 205, 205
Eucalyptus ficifolia 205, 205
Eucalyptus forrestiana 205
Eucalyptus globulus 205, 205
Eucalyptus gracilis 205, 205
Eucalyptus grandis 206, 206
Eucalyptus gunnii 206
Eucalyptus haemastoma 206
Eucalyptus leucoxylon 206
Eucalyptus leucoxylon 'Rosea' 206
Eucalyptus macrocarpa 206
Eucalyptus maculata 206, 206
Eucalyptus mannifera 206
Eucalyptus mannifera subsp. maculosa 206
Eucalyptus microtheca 206–7
Eucalyptus nicholii 207, 207
Eucalyptus papuana 207, 207
Eucalyptus pauciflora 207, 207
Eucalyptus pauciflora subsp. niphophila 207, 207
Eucalyptus perriniana 208, 208
Eucalyptus polyanthemos 208
Eucalyptus ptychocarpa 208, 208
Eucalyptus regnans 208–9, 208
Eucalyptus rubida 208, 209
Eucalyptus salmonophloia 209, 209
Eucalyptus sideroxylon 209, 209
Eucalyptus tereticornis 209, 209
Eucalyptus tessellaris 209
Eucalyptus torquata 209, 209
Eucalyptus woodwardii 210, 210
Eucommia 210
Eucommia ulmoides 210, 210
Eucryphia 210–11
Eucryphia cordifolia 210, 210
Eucryphia glutinosa 210
Eucryphia × intermedia 210–11
Eucryphia × intermedia 'Rostrevor' 210
Eucryphia lucida 211
Eucryphia lucida 'Leatherwood Cream' 211
Eucryphia lucida 'Pink Cream' 211
Eucryphia moorei 211, 211
Eucryphia × nymansensis 211, 211
Eucryphia × nymansensis 'Nymansay' 211
Eugenia 211; see also Acmena
Eugenia caryophyllus see Eugenia
Eugenia leuhamannii see Syzygium luehmannii
Eugenia paniculata see Syzygium paniculatum
Eugenia uniflora 211
Euonymus 211–12

Euonymus alatus 211, 211
Euonymus europaeus 212, 212
Euonymus japonicus 212, 212
Euonymus japonicus 'Albomarginatus' 212
Euonymus japonicus 'Microphyllus Variegatus' 212
Euonymus japonicus 'Ovatus Aureus' 212
Euphorbia 212–13
Euphorbia abyssinica 212
Euphorbia grandicornis 212, 212
Euphorbia pulcherrima 212, 213
Euphorbia tirucalli 212–13
European ash (Fraxinus excelsior) 223
European beech (Fagus sylvatica) 216, 216
European box (Buxus sempervirens) 112, 112
European elder (Sambucus nigra) 394, 394
European larch (Larix decidua) 270, 270
European linden (Tilia × europaea) 425
European plum (Prunus domestica) 357
European privet (Ligustrum vulgare) 278–9, 279
European silver fir (Abies alba) 52, 52
European spindle-tree (Euonymus europaeus) 212, 212
Euryops 213
Euryops chrysanthemoides 213, 213
Euryops pectinatus 213, 213
Euryops virgineus 213, 213
Euscaphis 214
Euscaphis japonica 214, 214
evergreen alder (Alnus acuminata) 80, 80
evergreen huckleberry (Vaccinium ovatum) 435, 435
Exochorda 214
Exochorda × macrantha 214, 214
Exochorda racemosa 214

Fagus 216
Fagus grandifolia 216, 216
Fagus orientalis 216
Fagus sylvatica 216, 216
Fagus sylvatica 'Aspleniifolia' 216
Fagus sylvatica 'Cuprea' 216
Fagus sylvatica 'Pendula' 216, 216
Fagus sylvatica 'Purpurea' 216, 216
Fagus sylvatica 'Rohannii' 216
false acacia (Robinia pseudoacacia) 385
false camellia (Stewartia pseudocamellia) 409, 409
false cypress (Chaemaecyparis) 143–4
false sandalwood (Eremophila mitchellii) 192
false spiraea (Sorbaria arborea) 404
fan aloe (Aloe plicatilis) 82, 82
fan flower (Scaevola) 396
farkleberry (Vaccinium arboreum) 435
Father David's maple (Acer davidii) 63, 63
Fatsia 217
Fatsia japonica 217, 217
feather duster palm (Rhopalostylis sapida) 382, 382
featherhead (Phylica pubescens) 327, 327
feather-leafed boronia (Boronia pinnata) 104, 104
feijoa (Feijoa sellowiana) 217, 217
Feijoa 217
Feijoa sellowiana 217, 217
fern leaf aralia (Polyscias filicifolia) 349
fernbush (Chamaebatiaria) 143
fetterbush (Leucothöe fontanesiana) 277
Ficus 217–20, 217
Ficus aspera 'Parcellii' 218, 218
Ficus benghalensis 218, 218
Ficus benjamina 218

Ficus benjamina 'Exotica' 218
Ficus benjamina 'Variegata' 218
Ficus carica 218, 218
Ficus dammaropsis 218–19, 218
Ficus elastica 219
Ficus elastica 'Decora' 219, 219
Ficus elastica 'Doescheri' 219
Ficus lyrata 219, 219
Ficus macrophylla 219, 219
Ficus microcarpa 219, 219
Ficus microcarpa var. hillii 219
Ficus religiosa 219
Ficus sur 220, 220
Ficus virens 220, 220
fiddlewood (Citharexylum spinosum) 150–1, 150
field elm (Ulmus minor) 433, 433
field maple (Acer campestre) 62
fig (Ficus) 217–20, 217
fig (Ficus carica) 218, 218
Fijian fire plant (Acalypha wilkesiana) 61
filbert (Corylus) 162–3
filbert (Corylus maxima) 163, 163
fir (Abies) 52–6
firebush (Hamelia patens) 240, 240
firethorn (Pyracantha) 363–4
firewheel pincushion (Leucospermum tottum) 277, 277
firewheel tree (Stenocarpus sinuatus) 408, 408
firewood banksia (Banksia menziesii) 98
Firmiana 220
Firmiana simplex 220, 220
fish-killer tree (Barringtonia asiatica) 99, 99
fishtail palm (Caryota) 130
five-corner (Averrhoa carambola) 93, 93
flamboyant tree (Delonix regia) 178, 179
flame azalea (Rhododendron calendulaceum) 376, 376
flame grevillea (Grevillea dimorpha) 233
flame kurrajong (Brachychiton acerifolius) 105, 105
flame of the forest (Butea monosperma) 111
flamegold tree (Koelreuteria elegans) 266
flaming sword (Fouquieria splendens) 222
flax-leafed paperbark (Melaleuca linarifolia) 298, 298
fleur-du-paradis (Delonix regia) 178, 179
Flindersia 220
Flindersia australis 220, 220
Flindersia maculosa 220
flooded gum (Eucalyptus grandis) 206, 206
Florida cherry (Eugenia uniflora) 211
Florida fishpoison tree (Piscidia piscipula) 343
floss-silk tree (Chorisia) 147
floss-silk tree (Chorisia speciosa) 147, 147
flowering ash (Fraxinus ornus) 223, 223
flowering banana (Musa ornata) 306, 306
flowering currant (Ribes sanguineum) 383, 383
flowering dogwood (Cornus florida) 159, 159
flowering maple (Abutilon) 56–7
flowering quince (Chaenomeles) 142–3
Fokienia 220–1
Fokienia hodginsii 220, 221
forest bell bush (Mackaya bella) 286, 286
forest elder (Nuxia floribunda) 313, 313
forest oak (Allocasuarina torulosa) 78–9, 79

forest red gum (Eucalyptus tereticornis) 209, 209
forest she-oak (Allocasuarina torulosa) 78–9, 79
Forsythia 221
Forsythia × intermedia 221, 221
Forsythia × intermedia 'Arnold Giant' 221
Forsythia × intermedia 'Beatrix Farrand' 221
Forsythia × intermedia 'Karl Sax' 221
Forsythia × intermedia 'Lynwood' 221
Forsythia × intermedia 'Spectabilis' 221
Forsythia suspensa 221, 221
Forsythia viridissima 221
Fortunella 221
Fortunella japonica 221, 221
Fothergilla 222
Fothergilla gardenii 222, 222
fountain tree (Spathodea campanulata) 407, 407
Fouquieria 222
Fouquieria splendens 222
four corners (Grewia occidentalis) 235, 235
foxtail palm (Wodyetia bifurcata) 443
fragrant sumac (Rhus aromatica) 382, 382
frangipani (Plumeria) 347–8
Franklin tree (Franklinia alatamaha) 222, 222
Franklinia 222
Franklinia alatamaha 222, 222
Fraxinus 222–4
Fraxinus americana 223, 223
Fraxinus americana var. juglandifolia 222
Fraxinus angustifolia 223
Fraxinus angustifolia subsp. oxycarpa 223, 223
Fraxinus angustifolia 'Raywood' 223
Fraxinus excelsior 223
Fraxinus excelsior 'Aurea' 223, 223
Fraxinus excelsior 'Jaspidea' see Fraxinus excelsior 'Aurea'
Fraxinus excelsior 'Pendula' 223
Fraxinus griffithii 223
Fraxinus latifolia 223, 224
Fraxinus ornus 223, 223
Fraxinus pennsylvanica 224, 224
Fraxinus quadrangulata 224, 224
Fraxinus uhdei 224, 224
Fraxinus uhdei 'Majestic Beauty' 224
Fraxinus uhdei 'Tomlinson' 224
Fraxinus velutina 224, 225
Fremont cottonwood (Populus fremontii) 351
fremontia (Fremontodendron) 224–5
Fremontodendron 224–5
Fremontodendron californicum 225, 225
Fremontodendron californicum 'California Glory' 225
French lavender (Lavandula dentata) 272, 272
French rose (Rosa gallica) 387, 387
fringe flower (Loropetalum chinense) 283, 283
fringe tree (Chionanthus) 146–7
fringe-myrtle (Calytrix) 121
frywood tree (Albizia lebbek) 76
Fuchsia 225–6, 226
Fuchsia arborescens 225, 225
Fuchsia denticulata 226, 226
Fuchsia excorticata 226
fuchsia gum (Eucalyptus forrestiana) 205
Fuchsia magellanica 226, 226
Fuchsia paniculata 226, 226
full-moon maple (Acer japonicum) 65, 65
funereal cypress (Cupressus sempervirens) 171

gamboge (Garcinia xanthochymus) 228, 228

Garcinia 228
Garcinia mangostana see Garcinia
Garcinia xanthochymus 228, 228
gardenia (Gardenia augusta) 228
Gardenia 228
Gardenia augusta 228
Gardenia augusta 'Florida' 228, 228
Gardenia augusta 'Magnifica' 228, 228
Gardenia augusta 'Radicans' 228, 228
Gardenia jasminoides see Gardinia augusta
Gardenia thunbergia 228, 228
garland flower (Daphne cneorum) 177, 177
Garrya 228–30
Garrya elliptica 229, 229
Garrya elliptica 'James Roof' 229
Gaultheria 229–30
Gaultheria fragrantissima 229, 229
Gaultheria mucronata 229
Gaultheria mucronata 'Bell's Seedling' 229
Gaultheria mucronata 'Mother of Pearl' 229
Gaultheria mucronata 'Mulberry Wine' 229
Gaultheria mucronata 'White Pearl' 229
Gaultheria shallon 229, 229
Gaultheria × wisleyensis 230, 230
gean (Prunus avium) 357
geiger tree (Cordia sebestena) 158, 158
Genista 230
Genista hispanica 230, 230
Genista lydia 230, 230
Genista × spachiana 230, 230
Genista tinctoria 230, 231
Genista tinctoria 'Plena' 230
Geraldton wax (Chamelaucium uncinatum) 145, 145
geranium-leaf aralia (Polyscias guilfoylei) 350
ghost gum (Eucalyptus papuana) 207, 207
giant fir (Abies grandis) 54, 54
giant fishtail palm (Caryota no) 130
giant protea (Protea cynaroides) 355, 355
giant saguaro (Carnegiea gigantea) 127, 127
giant sequoia (Sequoiadendron giganteum) 401, 401
giant timber bamboo (Phyllostachys bambusoides) 328, 328
Gilliam's bell (Darwinia cxylepis) 178, 178
ginger bush (Iboza riparia) 252, 252
ginger lily (Hedychium) 242
ginkgo (Ginkgo biloba) 231, 231
Ginkgo 230–1
Ginkgo biloba 231, 231
Ginkgo biloba 'Fastigiata' 231
Gippsland waratah (Telopea oreades) 420, 421
Gleditsia 231–2
Gleditsia aquatica 231
Gleditsia triacanthos 232, 232
Gleditsia triacanthos var. inermis 232, 232
Gleditsia triacanthos 'Ruby Lace' 232
Gleditsia triacanthos 'Sunburst' 232
Gliricidia 232
Gliricidia sepium 232
glory bush (Tibouchina) 424
Glyptostrobus 232
Glyptostrobus pensilis 232, 232
gold blossom tree (Barklya syringifolia) 98, 98
goldcup oak (Quercus chrysolepis) 367
gold-dust wattle (Acacia acinacea) 57, 57
golden ash (Fraxinus excelsior 'Aurea') 223, 223
golden bough (Nuytsia floribunda) 313, 313

golden cane palm (Chrysalidocarpus lutescens) 148, 148
golden chain tree (Laburnum) 268
golden chestnut (Chrysolepis chrysophylla) 148
golden currant (Ribes odoratum) 383, 383
golden dewdrop (Duranta) 186
golden larch (Pseudolarix amabilis) 360, 360
golden netbush (Pseuderanthemum reticulatum) 360, 360
golden oak (Quercus robur 'Concordia') 369
golden poplar (Populus nigra 'Aurea') 352
golden rain tree (Koelreuteria paniculata) 266, 266
golden salvia (Salvia africana-lutea) 394, 394
golden shower tree (Cassia fistula) 130–1, 131
golden trumpet tree (Tabebuia chrysantha) 416, 416
golden trumpet tree (Tabebuia chrysotricha) 416, 416
golden wattle (Acacia pycnantha) 60, 60
gooseberry (Ribes) 383–4
gooseberry (Ribes uva-crispa) 384, 384
Gordonia 232–3
Gordonia axillaris 233, 233
Gordonia lasianthus 233
Grampians thryptomene (Thryptomene calycina) 423, 423
grapefruit (Citrus paradisi) 152
Graptophyllum 233
Graptophyllum pictum 233
Graptophyllum pictum 'Purpureum Variegata' 233
Graptophyllum pictum 'Tricolor' 233
grass-tree (Xanthorrhoea) 445–6
grease nut (Hernandia bivalvis) 243
great laurel (Rhododendron maximum) 379
great white cherry (Prunus serrulata 'Tai Haku') 359
Grecian strawberry tree (Arbutus andrachne) 88
Greek fir (Abies cephalonica) 53, 53
green wattle (Acacia decurrens) 58, 58
Grevillea 233–5
Grevillea banksii 233, 233
Grevillea dimorpha 233
Grevillea fasciculata 234
Grevillea hilliana 234, 234
Grevillea 'Honey Gem' 234, 234
Grevillea juniperina 234, 234
Grevillea juniperina 'Molonglo' 234
Grevillea juniperina 'Pink Pearl' 234
Grevillea juniperina 'Poorinda Queen' 234
Grevillea juniperina 'Sulphurea' 234
Grevillea lanigera 234
Grevillea 'Ned Kelly' 234
Grevillea robusta 234, 234
Grevillea 'Robyn Gordon' 234, 235
Grevillea rosmarinifolia 235, 235
Grewia 235
Grewia occidentalis 235, 235
grey birch (Betula populifolia) 102
grey fig (Ficus virens) 220, 220
grey mangrove (Avicennia marina) 94, 94
grey-leafed euryops (Euryops pectinatus) 213, 213
grey-leafed honey myrtle (Melaleuca incana) 297, 297
Greyia 235
Greyia sutherlandii 235, 235
Griselinia 235–6
Griselinia littoralis 235, 235
Griselinia littoralis 'Dixon's Cream' 235
Griselinia littoralis 'Variegata' 235
Griselinia lucida 236, 236

Griselinia lucida 'Variegata' 236
Guatemala rhubarb (Jatropha multifida) 258–9, 258
guava (Psidium) 361–2
guelder rose (Viburnum opulus) 438, 438
Guiana chestnut (Pachira aquatica) 320, 320
guitar plant (Lomatia tinctoria) 282
gul mohr (Delonix regia) 178, 179
gumdigger's soap (Pomaderris kumeraho) 351, 351
gungurra (Eucalyptus caesia subsp. magna) 202
Gymea lily (Doryanthes excelsa) 184, 185
Gymnocladus 236
Gymnocladus dioica 236
Gymnostoma 236
Gymnostoma australianum 236, 236

hackberry (Celtis) 136
hairy hopbush (Dodonaea boroniifolia) 183, 183
Hakea 238–9
Hakea bucculenta 238
Hakea laurina 238, 238
Hakea microcarpa 238, 238
Hakea purpurea 238, 238
Hakea salicifolia 238
Hakea victoria 238–9, 238
hala screw pine (Pandanus tectorius) 321, 321
Halesia 239
Halesia carolina 239, 239
Halesia monticola 239
Halesia monticola var. vestita 'Rosea' 239
Hamamelis 239–40
Hamamelis × intermedia 239
Hamamelis × intermedia 'Arnold Primrose' 239
Hamamelis × intermedia 'Jelena' 239, 239
Hamamelis japonica 239, 239
Hamamelis mollis 239, 239
Hamamelis mollis 'Coombe Wood' 239
Hamamelis vernalis 240, 240
Hamamelis virginiana 240, 240
Hamelia 240
Hamelia patens 240, 240
handkerchief tree (Davidia) 178
hardy fuchsia (Fuchsia magellanica) 226, 226
Harpephyllum 240–1
Harpephyllum caffrum 241, 241
Hawaiian mahogany (Acacia koa) 58
hawthorn (Crataegus) 166–7
hawthorn (Crataegus monogyna) 167, 167
hazel (Corylus) 162–3
hazel (Corylus avellana) 162–3, 162
hazel pomaderris (Pomaderris aspera) 351
headache tree (Umbellularia californica) 434
heath (Erica) 192–6
heather (Calluna vulgaris) 118–19, 119
heavenly bamboo (Nandina domestica) 310, 310
Hebe 241–2
Hebe albicans 241, 241
Hebe armstrongii 241, 241
Hebe diosmifolia 241, 241
Hebe ochracea 242
Hebe ochracea 'James Stirling' 242, 242
Hebe odora 242, 242
Hebe salicifolia 242, 242
Hebe speciosa 242
Hebe speciosa 'Alicia Amherst' 242, 242
Hebe speciosa 'Variegata' 242
Hebe venustula 242, 242
hedge maple (Acer campestre) 62
hedgehog sage (Pycnostachys urticifolia) 363, 363

Hedychium 242
Hedychium coccineum 243; see also Hedychium
Hedychium gardnerianum 242
hemlock (Tsuga) 429
Henkel's yellowwood (Podocarpus henkelii) 348–9, 348
henna (Lawsonia inermis) 273
Hercules' club (Aralia spinosa) 86–7
Hernandia 242–3
Hernandia bivalvis 243
hesper palm (Brahea armata) 106, 106
Heteromeles 243
Heteromeles arbutifolia 243, 243
Hevea 243
Hevea brasiliensis 243, 243
Hibiscus 243–6
Hibiscus arnottianus 243, 243
Hibiscus arnottianus 'Wilder's White' 243
Hibiscus heterophyllus 244, 244
Hibiscus huegelii see Alyogyne huegelii
Hibiscus insularis 244, 244
Hibiscus mutabilis 244, 244
Hibiscus mutabilis 'Plena' 244, 244
Hibiscus rosa-sinensis 244, 245
Hibiscus rosa-sinensis, Hawaiian hybrids 244, 245
Hibiscus schizopetalus 245, 245
Hibiscus syriacus 245, 245
Hibiscus tiliaceus 246, 246
hickory (Carya) 128–9
higan cherry (Prunus subhirtella) 359
highbush blueberry (Vaccinium corymbosum) 435, 435
Highclere holly (Ilex × altaclarensis) 253
Himalayan birch (Betula utilis) 103, 103
Himalayan dogwood (Cornus capitata) 159
Himalayan longleaf pine (Pinus roxburghii) 342, 342
Himalayan strawberry tree (Cornus capitata) 159
Himalayan tree cotoneaster (Cotoneaster frigidus) 165
Himalayan white pine (Pinus wallichiana) 343
Hinoki cypress (Chamaecyparis obtusa) 144
Hippophae 246
Hippophae rhamnoides 246
Hoheria 246–7
Hoheria lyallii 246, 246
Hoheria populnea 246–7, 247
Hoheria sexstylosa 247, 247
holly (Ilex) 252–5
holly grape (Mahonia aquifolium) 290, 290
holly oak (Quercus ilex) 368, 368
holly osmanthus (Osmanthus heterophyllus) 318, 318
holly-leafed cherry (Prunus ilicifolia) 358, 358
hollywood juniper (Juniperus squamata) 262–3
holm oak (Quercus ilex) 368, 368
Holmskioldia 247
Holmskioldia sanguinea 247, 247
Honduran pine (Pinus caribaea var. hondurensis) 336
Honduras mahogany (Swietenia macrophylla) 411
honey locust (Gleditsia) 231–2
honey locust (Gleditsia triacanthos) 232, 232
honey protea (Protea repens) 356, 356
honey-myrtle (Melaleuca fulgens) 297
honeysuckle (Lonicera) 282
Hong Kong rose (Rhodoleia championii) 381, 381
hoop pine (Araucaria cunninghamii) 88, 88
hop hornbeam (Ostrya carpinifolia) 318

hopbush (Dodonaea) 183
hopbush (Dodonaea viscosa) 183
hop-tree (Ptelea trifoliata) 362, 362
hornbeam (Carpinus) 127–8
hornbeam maple (Acer carpinifolium) 62–3, 63
horoeka (Pseudopanax crassifolius) 361, 361
horse bean (Parkinsonia aculeata) 322, 322
horse-chestnut (Aesculus) 70–2
horse-chestnut (Aesculus hippocastanum) 72, 72
horseradish tree (Moringa oleifera) 304
hortensia (Hydrangea) 248–9
hortensia (Hydrangea macrophylla) 248, 248
houhere (Hoheria populnea) 246–7, 247
houpara (Pseudopanax lessonii) 361, 361
Hovenia 247
Hovenia dulcis 247, 247
Howea 247
Howea forsteriana 247
huon pine (Lagarostrobos franklinii) 269, 269
hupeh crab (Malus hupehensis) 293, 293
hybrid coral tree (Erythrina × bidwillii) 198, 198
hybrid Indian hawthorn (Rhaphiolepis × delacourii) 374
hybrid strawberry tree (Arbutus × andrachnoides) 88, 88
Hydrangea 248–9
Hydrangea aspera 248, 248
Hydrangea macrophylla 248, 248
Hydrangea macrophylla 'Blue Sky' 248, 248
Hydrangea paniculata 249, 249
Hydrangea paniculata 'Gandiflora' 249
Hydrangea quercifolia 249, 249
Hydrangea villosa see Hydrangea aspera
Hymenosporum 249
Hymenosporum flavum 249, 249
Hypericum 249–50
Hypericum beanii 249
Hypericum calycinum 249
Hypericum kouytchense 249
Hypericum monogynum 250, 250
Hypericum patulum 250
Hypericum patulum 'Hidcote' 250, 250
Hypericum patulum 'Rowallane' 250, 250
Hypericum revolutum 250, 250

Iboza 252
Iboza riparia 252, 252
icaco (Chrysobalanus) 148
Idesia 252
Idesia polycarpa 252, 252
Ilex 252–5
Ilex × altaclarensis 253
Ilex × altaclarensis 'Camelliifolia' 253
Ilex × altaclarensis 'Golden King' 253
Ilex aquifolium 253, 253
Ilex aquifolium 'Ferox' 253
Ilex aquifolium 'Ferox Argentea' 253, 253
Ilex aquifolium 'Golden Milkboy' 253
Ilex aquifolium 'J. C. van Tol' 253
Ilex aquifolium 'Silver Queen' 253
Ilex cornuta 253, 253
Ilex crenata 254, 254
Ilex crenata 'Convexa' 254
Ilex crenata 'Golden Gem' 254
Ilex crenata 'Schwoebel's Compact' 254
Ilex decidua 254, 254
Ilex glabra 254
Ilex glabra 'Compacta' 254, 254
Ilex glabra 'Ivory Queen' 254

Ilex glabra 'Nordic' 254
Ilex opaca 254, 255
Ilex paraguariensis 254–5
Ilex pernyi 255
Ilex serrata 255, 255
Ilex verticillata 255, 255
Ilex vomitoria 255
Illawarra flame-tree (*Brachychiton acerifolius*) 105, 105
Illicium 255–6
Illicium anisatum 255, 255
Illicium floridanum 256, 256
illyarie (*Eucalyptus erythrocorys*) 205, 205
incense cedar (*Calocedrus decurrens*) 119, 119
Indian almond (*Terminalia catappa*) 421, 421
Indian banyan (*Ficus benghalensis*) 218, 218
Indian bean tree (*Catalpa*) 133
Indian bean tree (*Catalpa bignioides*) 133, 133
Indian currant (*Symphoricarpos orbiculatus*) 412, 412
Indian hawthorn (*Raphiolepis*) 373–4
Indian hawthorn (*Raphiolepis indica*) 374, 374
Indian horse-chestnut (*Aesculus indica*) 72, 72
Indian laburnum (*Cassia fistula*) 130–1, 131
Indian laurel (*Calophyllum inophyllum*) 120, 120
India-rubber tree (*Ficus elastica*) 219
Indigofera 256
Indigofera decora 256, 256
inkberry (*Ilex glabra*) 254
interior live oak (*Quercus wislizenii*) 371, 371
Iochroma 256
Iochroma cyaneum 256, 256
Iochroma grandiflorum 256, 256
Iowa crab (*Malus ioensis*) 293
ipe roxo (*Tabebuia heptaphylla*) 416, 416
Irish yew (*Taxus baccata* 'Fastigiata') 419, 419
ironwood (*Ostrya virginiana*) 318, 318
Isopogon 257
Isopogon anemonifolius 257, 257
Italian alder (*Alnus cordata*) 80
Italian buckthorn (*Rhamnus alaternus*) 373
Italian lavender see *Lavandula stoechas*
Itea 257
Itea virginiana 257, 257
ivory curl tree (*Buckinghamia*) 109
Ixora 257
Ixora chinensis 257, 257
Ixora chinensis 'Lutea' 257
Ixora chinensis 'Prince of Orange' 257
Ixora coccinea 257, 257
Ixora 'Sunkist' 257

jaca (*Artocarpus heterophyllus*) 92, 92
Jacaranda 258
Jacaranda mimosifolia 258, 258
jackfruit (*Artocarpus heterophyllus*) 92, 92
jade plant (*Portulacaria afra*) 353, 353
Jamaica dogwood (*Piscidia piscipula*) 343
Jamaica ebony (*Brya ebenus* 109, 109)
Jamaican kino (*Coccoloba uvifera*) 155
Japanese alder (*Alnus firma*) 80, 80
Japanese angelica tree (*Aralia elata*) 86, 86
Japanese apricot (*Prunus mume*) 358
Japanese barberry (*Berberis thunbergii*) 101
Japanese black pine (*Pinus thunbergii*) 343, 343

Japanese box (*Buxus microphylla*) 112, 112
Japanese cedar (*Cryptomeria japonica*) 169, 169
Japanese crab (*Malus floribunda*) 293, 293
Japanese elm (*Zelkova serrata*) 447, 447
Japanese flowering cherry (*Prunus serrulata*) 359, 359
Japanese flowering dogwood (*Cornus kousa*) 160, 160
Japanese holly (*Ilex crenata*) 254, 254
Japanese hornbeam (*Carpinus japonica*) 128, 128
Japanese horse-chestnut (*Aesculus turbinata*) 72
Japanese larch (*Larix kaempferi*) 271, 271
Japanese maple (*Acer palmatum*) 66, 66
Japanese mock orange (*Pittosporum tobira*) 345
Japanese oak (*Quercus acutissima*) 366–7, 366
Japanese pear (*Pyrus pyrifolia*) 364
Japanese plum-yew (*Cephalotaxus harringtonia*) 138
Japanese privet (*Ligustrum japonicum*) 278
Japanese raisin tree (*Hovenia dulcis*) 247, 247
Japanese red pine (*Pinus densiflora*) 338, 338
Japanese rose (*Kerria japonica*) 265
Japanese rose (*Rosa rugosa*) 388, 388
Japanese rowan (*Sorbus commixta*) 405, 405
Japanese sago cycad (*Cycas revoluta*) 173, 173
Japanese shore juniper (*Juniperus conferta*) 261, 261
Japanese snowbell (*Styrax japonica*) 410, 410
Japanese snowdrop tree (*Styrax japonica*) 410, 410
Japanese umbrella pine (*Sciadopitys verticillata*) 398, 398
Japanese walnut (*Juglans ailantifolia*) 259, 259
Japanese white birch (*Betula platyphylla*) 102
Japanese white pine (*Pinus parviflora*) 340
Japanese witch hazel (*Hamamelis japonica*) 239, 239
Japanese yew (*Taxus cuspidata*) 419, 419
japonica (*Chaenomeles speciosa* 143, 143)
jasmine (*Jasminum*) 258
Jasminum 258
Jasminum mesnyi 258, 258
Jasminum nudiflorum see *Jasminum mesnyi*
Jasminum officinale 258
Jatropha 258–9
Jatropha integerrima 258
Jatropha multifida 258–9, 258
Jatropha pandurata see *Jatropha integerrima*
Jatropha pandurifolia see *Jatropha integerrima*
java willow (*Ficus virens*) 220, 220
Jeffrey pine (*Pinus jeffreyi*) 339, 339
jelly palm (*Butia capitata*) 112, 112
Jerusalem thorn (*Parkinsonia aculeata*) 322, 322
jessamine (*Cestrum*) 142
jojoba (*Simmondsia chinensis*) 402, 402
Joshua tree (*Yucca brevifolia*) 446
Jubaea 259
Jubaea chilensis 259, 259
Judas tree (*Cercis*) 140–1
Judas tree (*Cercis siliquastrum*) 141, 141
Juglans 259–60

Juglans ailantifolia 259, 259
Juglans cinerea 259
Juglans nigra 259, 259
Juglans regia 260, 260
Juglans regia 'Wilson's Wonder' 260
jujube (*Zizyphus jujuba*) 447, 447
juniper (*Juniperus*) 260–3
Juniperus 260-3
Juniperus chinensis 260–1, 260
Juniperus chinensis 'Kaizuka' 261, 261
Juniperus chinensis 'Pyramidalis' 261
Juniperus chinensis 'Variegata' 261
Juniperus communis 260, 261
Juniperus communis 'Compressa' 261
Juniperus communis 'Depressa Aurea' 261
Juniperus communis 'Hibernica' 261
Juniperus conferta 261, 261
Juniperus deppeana var. *pachyphlaea* 261, 261
Juniperus horizontalis 261; see also *Juniperus procumbens*
Juniperus horizontalis 'Bar Harbor' 261
Juniperus horizontalis 'Blue Chip' 261, 261
Juniperus horizontalis 'Douglasii' 261
Juniperus horizontalis 'Wiltonii' 261, 261
Juniperus × *media* 262
Juniperus × *media* 'Blaauw' 262
Juniperus × *media* 'Hetzii' 262
Juniperus × *media* 'Pfitzeriana' 262, 262
Juniperus × *media* 'Plumosa Aurea' 262
Juniperus monosperma 262, 262
Juniperus procumbens 262, 262
Juniperus procumbens 'Nana' 262
Juniperus recurva 262, 262
Juniperus recurva 'Coxii' 262
Juniperus rigida 262, 263
Juniperus sabina 262
Juniperus sabina 'Tamariscifolia' 262, 263
Juniperus scopulorum 262
Juniperus scopulorum 'Blue Heaven' 262
Juniperus scopulorum 'Repens' 262
Juniperus squamata 262–3
Juniperus squamata 'Blue Star' 263, 263
Juniperus virginiana 263, 263
Juniperus virginiana 'Glauca' 263
Juniperus virginiana 'Skyrocket' 263
Justicia 263
Justicia spicigera 263, 263

kaffir plum (*Harpephyllum caffrum*) 241, 241
kahili ginger (*Hedychium gardnerianum*) 242
kaka beak (*Clianthus puniceus*) 154, 154
Kalgan boronia (*Boronia heterophylla*) 104, 104
Kalmia 264
Kalmia angustifolia 264, 264
Kalmia latifolia 264, 264
Kalopanax 264
Kalopanax septemlobus 264, 264
kangaroo apple (*Solanum aviculare*) 403, 403
kanuka box (*Tristaniopsis laurina*) 429, 429
kaori (*Agathis*) 73–4
kapok (*Ceiba pentandra*) 136, 137
kapuka (*Griselinia littoralis*) 235, 235
karee (*Rhus lancea*) 382, 382
karo (*Pittosporum crassifolium*) 344, 344
karri (*Eucalyptus diversicolor*) 204
karroo thorn (*Acacia karroo*) 58, 58
Kashmir cypress (*Cupressus cashmeriana*) 171, 171
katsura tree (*Cercidiphyllum japonicum*) 139, 140, 140

kauri (*Agathis*) 73–4
kawa kawa (*Macropiper excelsum*) 286, 286
kawaka (*Libocedrus plumosa*) 278
kaya (*Torreya nucifera*) 428
kei apple (*Dovyalis caffra*) 185, 185
kentia palm (*Howea forsteriana*) 247
Kentucky coffee tree (*Gymnocladus dioica*) 236
Kermadec pohutukawa (*Metrosideros kermadecensis*) 302
Kerria 264–5
Kerria japonica 265
Kerria japonica 'Pleniflora' 265, 265
kiepersol (*Cussonia spicata*) 172, 172
Kigelia 265
Kigelia africana 265, 265
King Billy pine (*Athrotaxis selaginoides*) 93
king protea (*Protea cynaroides*) 355, 355
Kingia 265
Kingia australis 265, 265
kleindensuikerbos (*Protea aristata*) 354, 354
knife acacia (*Acacia cultriformis*) 57, 57
knife-leaf wattle (*Acacia cultriformis*) 57, 57
koa (*Acacia koa*) 58
Koelreuteria 265–6
Koelreuteria bipinnata 265, 265
Koelreuteria elegans 266
Koelreuteria paniculata 266, 266
kohuhu (*Pittosporum tenuifolium*) 345, 345
Kolkwitzia 266
Kolkwitzia amabilis 266, 266
Korean fir (*Abies koreana*) 54, 54
Korean lilac (*Syringa patula*) 412–13
Korean pine (*Pinus koraiensis*) 339, 339
Korean rowan (*Sorbus commixta*) 405, 405
Korean viburnum (*Viburnum carlesii*) 437, 437
kotukutuku (*Fuchsia excorticata*) 226
kowhai (*Sophora tetraptera*) 404, 404
kumarahou (*Pomaderris kumeraho*) 351, 351
Kunzea 266
Kunzea baxteri 266
Kunzea parvifolia 266, 266
kurrajong (*Brachychiton populneus*) 105, 105
kusamaki (*Podocarpus macrophyllus*) 349, 349

× *Laburnocytisus* 268
× *Laburnocytisus adamii* 268, 268
Laburnum 268–9, 268
Laburnum alpinum 268
Laburnum anagyroides 268, 269
Laburnum × *watereri* 'Vossii' 268, 269
lace shrub (*Stephanandra incisa*) 409, 409
lacebark (*Hoheria lyallii*) 246, 246
lacebark elm (*Ulmus parvifolia*) 433, 433
lacebark kurrajong (*Brachychiton discolor*) 105, 105
lacebark pine (*Pinus bungeana*) 336, 336
lacecap (*Hydrangea*) 248–9
ladies' eardrops (*Fuchsia magellanica*) 226, 226
lady flowers (*Mussaenda philippica*) 306–7, 306
lady of the night (*Cestrum nocturnum*) 142, 143
lady palm (*Rhapis*) 374
lady palm (*Rhapis excelsa*) 374
Lagarostrobos 269
Lagarostrobos franklinii 269, 269
Lagerstroemia 269–70

Lagerstroemia indica 269, 269
Lagerstroemia speciosa 270, 270
Lagerstroemia 'Eavesii' 269
Lagerstroemia 'Petite Snow' 269
Lagerstroemia 'Ruby Lace' 269
Lagunaria 270
Lagunaria patersonia 270, 270
lancewood (*Pseudopanax crassifolius*) 361, 361
larch (*Larix*) 270–1
large orange heath (*Erica grandiflora*) 194, 194
large-flowered yellow oleander (*Thevetia thevetioides*) 422, 423
Larix 270–1
Larix decidua 270, 270
Larix gmelinii 271, 271
Larix kaempferi 271, 271
Larix laricina 271
Larix potaninii 271, 271
lasiandra (*Tibouchina*) 424
late black wattle (*Acacia mearnsii*) 59
late tamarisk (*Tamarix ramosissima*) 418
laurel (*Laurus nobilis*) 272, 272
laurel cherry (*Prunus laurocerasus*) 358, 358
Laurus 271–2
Laurus azorica 271–2, 272
Laurus nobilis 272, 272
Laurus nobilis 'Aurea' 272, 272
laurustinus (*Viburnum tinus*) 439, 439
Lavalle hawthorn (*Crataegus* × *lavallei*) 167
Lavandula 272–3
Lavandula angustifolia 272
Lavandula angustifolia 'Hidcote' 272
Lavandula angustifolia 'Munstead' 272, 273
Lavandula dentata 272, 272
Lavandula latifolia 272–3
Lavandula stoechas 273, 273
Lawson cypress (*Chamaecyparis lawsoniana*) 144
Lawsonia 273
Lawsonia inermis 273
leadwort (*Plumbago*) 347
Leichhardt tree (*Nauclea orientalis*) 310, 310
lemon (*Citrus limon*) 151, 151
lemon-flowered gum (*Eucalyptus woodwardii*) 210, 210
lemon-scented gum (*Eucalyptus citriodora*) 203, 203
lemon-scented myrtle (*Backhousia citriodora*) 96, 96
lemon-scented tea-tree (*Leptospermum petersonii*) 274, 274
lemon-scented verbena (*Aloysia triphylla*) 82, 82
lemonwood (*Pittosporum eugenioides*) 344, 344
leopard tree (*Caesalpinia ferrea*) 114, 114
leopard tree (*Flindersia maculosa*) 220
Lepidozamia 273
Lepidozamia hopei see *Lepidozamia*
Lepidozamia peroffskyana 273, 273
Leptospermum 273–4
Leptospermum laevigatum 274, 274
Leptospermum petersonii 274, 274
Leptospermum scoparium 274, 274
Leptospermum scoparium 'Abundance' 274
Leptospermum scoparium 'Kiwi' 274
Leptospermum scoparium 'Pink Pixie' 274
Leptospermum scoparium 'Red Damask' 274, 274
Leptospermum scoparium 'Ruby Glow' 274, 274
Lespedeza 274
Lespedeza thunbergii 274, 274
Lespedeza thunbergii 'Alba' 274
Leucadendron 275–6

Leucadendron argenteum 275, 275
Leucadendron comosum 275
Leucadendron eucalyptifolium 275, 275
Leucadendron 'Safari Sunset' 276, 276
Leucadendron salignum 276
Leucadendron tinctum 276
Leucospermum 276–7
Leucospermum cordifolium 277, 277
Leucospermum erubescens 277, 277
Leucospermum 'Golden Star' see *Leucospermum tottum*
Leucospermum 'Red Sunset' see *Leucospermum cordifolium*
Leucospermum reflexum 277, 277
Leucospermum 'Scarlet Ribbons' 276; see also *Leucospermum tottum*
Leucospermum tottum 277, 277
Leucothöe 277
Leucothöe fontanesiana 277
Leucothöe fontanesiana 'Golden Rainbow' see *Leucothöe fontanesiana* 'Rainbow'
Leucothöe fontanesiana 'Rainbow' 277
Leyland cypress (× *Cupressocyparis leylandii*) 170, 170
Libocedrus 278
Libocedrus plumosa 278, 278
Ligustrum 278–9
Ligustrum japonicum 278
Ligustrum japonicum 'Rotundifolium' 278, 278
Ligustrum lucidum 278, 278
Ligustrum lucidum 'Tricolor' 278, 279
Ligustrum ovalifolium 278
Ligustrum ovalifolium 'Aureum' 278
Ligustrum vulgare 278–9, 279
lilac (*Syringa*) 412–13
lilac (*Syringa meyeri*) 412
lillypilly (*Acmena*) 68
lillypilly (*Acmena smithii*) 68, 69
lillypilly (*Syzygium*) 413–14
lily-of-the-valley shrub (*Pieris japonica*) 334
lily-of-the-valley tree (*Clethra arborea*) 154, 154
lime (*Citrus aurantifolia*) 151, 151
lime tree (*Tilia*) 424–6
linden (*Tilia*) 424–6
Lindera 279
Lindera benzoin 279
Lindera obtusiloba 279
ling (*Calluna vulgaris*) 118–19, 119
lipstick tree (*Bixa orellana*) 103, 103
liquidambar (*Liquidambar styraciflua*) 279
Liquidambar 279–80
Liquidambar formosana 279
Liquidambar orientalis 279, 279
Liquidambar styraciflua 280, 280
Liquidambar styraciflua 'Variegata' 280, 280
Liquidambar styraciflua 'Worplesdon' 280
Liriodendron 280–1
Liriodendron chinense 280, 280
Liriodendron tulipifera 281, 281
Liriodendron tulipifera 'Aureomarginatum' 281
Liriodendron tulipifera 'Fastigiatum' 281
Litchi 281
Litchi chinensis 281, 281
Lithocarpus 281
Lithocarpus densiflorus 281, 281
little shellbark hickory (*Carya ovata*) 129, 129
live oak (*Quercus virginiana*) 370–1, 371
Livistona 281–2
Livistona australis 282, 282
Livistona chinensis 282, 282
Lobelia 282
Lobelia keniensis 282, 282
loblolly bay (*Gordonia lasianthus*) 233

lodgepole pine (*Pinus contorta* var. *latifolia*) 337, 337
Lomatia 282
Lomatia ferruginea 282
Lomatia tinctoria 282
Lombardy poplar (*Populus nigra* 'Italica') 352
London plane (*Platanus* × *acerifolia*) 346, 346
longleaf pine (*Pinus palustris*) 340, 340
long-leaf waxflower (*Eriostemon myoporoides*) 197
Lonicera 282–3
Lonicera fragrantissima 282, 283
Lonicera ledebourii 283
Lonicera nitida 283
Lonicera nitida 'Aurea' 282, 283
Lonicera tatarica 282, 283
looking glass plant (*Coprosma repens*) 157, 157
Lophomyrtus 283
Lophomyrtus bullata 283
Lophomyrtus obcordata 283, 283
Lophomyrtus × *ralphii* 283
Lophomyrtus × *ralphii* 'Lilliput' 283
Lophomyrtus × *ralphii* 'Pixie' 283
Lophomyrtus × *ralphii* 'Purpurea' 283
Lophostemon 283
Lophostemon confertus 283
Lophostemon confertus 'Perth Gold' 283
Lophostemon confertus 'Variegata' 283
loquat (*Eriobotrya japonica*) 196, 196
Loropetalum 283
Loropetalum chinense 283, 283
lucky nut (*Thevetia peruviana*) 422, 422
Luculia 283–4
Luculia gratissima 284, 284
Luma 284
Luma apiculata 284, 284
lychee (*Litchi chinensis*) 281
Lycianthes rantonnei see *Solanum rantonnei*
Lyonothamnus 284
Lyonothamnus floribundus 284
Lyonothamnus floribundus subsp. *aspleniifolius* 284, 284

Macadamia 286
macadamia nut (*Macadamia tetraphylla*) 286, 286
Macadamia tetraphylla 286, 286
Macarthur palm (*Ptychosperma macarthurii*) 362, 362
Mackaya 286
Mackaya bella 286, 286
Maclura 286
Maclura pomifera 286
Macropiper 286
Macropiper excelsum 286, 286
Macrozamia 286–7
Macrozamia communis 287, 287
Macrozamia miquelii 287, 287
madake (*Phyllostachys bambusoides*) 328, 328
madre de cacao (*Gliricidia sepium*) 232
madrone (*Arbutus*) 88–9
madrone (*Arbutus menziesii*) 89, 89
magenta brush cherry (*Syzygium paniculatum*) 414
Magnolia 287–90
Magnolia acuminata 287, 287
Magnolia campbellii 288
Magnolia campbellii 'Alba' 288
Magnolia campbellii 'Charles Raffill' 288
Magnolia campbellii 'Lanarth' 288, 288
Magnolia campbellii 'Mollicomata' 288
Magnolia denudata 288, 288
Magnolia Freeman hybrids see *Magnolia grandiflora*
Magnolia grandiflora 288, 288

Magnolia grandiflora 'Exmouth' 288
Magnolia heptapeta see *Magnolia denudata*
Magnolia liliiflora 288, 288
Magnolia liliflora 'Nigra' 288
Magnolia × *loebneri* 288
Magnolia × *loebneri* 'Leonard Messel' 288
Magnolia × *loebneri* 'Merrill' 288
Magnolia macrophylla 288
Magnolia quinquepeta see *Magnolia liliiflora*
Magnolia × *soulangiana* 289, 289
Magnolia × *soulangiana* 'Alexandrina' 289
Magnolia × *soulangiana* 'Brozzoni' 289, 289
Magnolia × *soulangiana* 'Lennei' 289
Magnolia × *soulangiana* 'Lennei Alba' 289
Magnolia × *soulangiana* 'Rustica Rubra' 289
Magnolia sprengeri 'Diva' 289, 289
Magnolia stellata 289, 289
Magnolia stellata 'Waterlily' 289
Magnolia virginiana 290, 290
Magnolia wilsonii 290
mahogany (*Swietenia*) 411
mahogany pine (*Podocarpus totara*) 350, 350
Mahonia 290–1
Mahonia aquifolium 290, 290
Mahonia fremontii 290
Mahonia japonica 290
Mahonia lomariifolia 290, 290, 291
Mahonia repens 290–1, 291
maidenhair fern (*Ginkgo biloba*) 231, 231
Malesian rhododendrons see Vireya rhododendrons
Mallotus 291
Mallotus philippensis 291
mallow tree (*Stewartia malacodendron*) 409
Malpighia 291
Malpighia coccigera 291, 291
Malpighia glabra 291, 291
Malus 292–4, 292
Malus 'Aldenhamensis' 292, 292
Malus coronaria 292
Malus × *domestica* 292
Malus × *domestica* 'Delicious' 292, 292
Malus × *domestica* 'Jonathon' 292
Malus × *domestica* 'Starkspur Supreme Red Delicious' 292
Malus floribunda 293, 293
Malus 'Golden Hornet' 293, 293
Malus hupehensis 293, 293
Malus ioensis 293
Malus ioensis 'Plena' 293
Malus sargentii 294, 294
Malus sylvestris 294
Malus sylvestris 'Bittenfelder' 294
Malus toringoides 294, 294
Malvaviscus 294
Malvaviscus arboreus 294
Malvaviscus penduliflorus see *Malvaviscus arboreus*
Manchurian pear (*Pyrus ussuriensis*) 364, 364
Mangifera 295
Mangifera indica 295, 295
Mangifera indica 'Alphonso' 295, 295
mango (*Mangifera*) 295
mango (*Mangifera indica*) 295, 295
mangosteen (*Garcinia mangostana*) see Garcinia
mangrove hibiscus (*Hibiscus tiliaceus*) 246, 246
Manila palm (*Veitchia merrillii*) 435, 435
manna ash (*Fraxinus ornus*) 223, 223
manuka (*Leptospermum scoparium*) 274, 274
manzanita (*Arctostaphylos manzanita*) 90, 90, 91

maple (*Acer*) 62–8
maritime pine (*Pinus pinaster*) 341, 341
Marlborough rock daisy (*Pachystegia insignis*) 320, 320
marmalade bush (*Streptosolen jamesonii*) 410, 410
marri (*Eucalyptus calophylla*) 202–3, 202
mate (*Ilex paraguariensis*) 254–5
maul oak (*Quercus chrysolepis*) 367
may (*Crataegus*) 166–7
may (*Crataegus monogyna*) 167, 167
may (*Spiraea cantoniensis*) 407, 407
mayten (*Maytenus boaria*) 295, 295
Maytenus 295
Maytenus boaria 295, 295
mazzard (*Prunus avium*) 357
Mediterranean cypress (*Cupressus sempervirens*) 171
Mediterranean fan palm (*Chamaerops humilis*) 145, 145
medlar (*Mespilus germanica*) 300–1
megas (*Megaskepasma erythrochlamys*) 296, 296
Megaskepasma 296
Megaskepasma erythrochlamys 296, 296
Melaleuca 296–9
Melaleuca argentea 296, 296
Melaleuca armillaris 297, 297
Melaleuca bracteata 297
Melaleuca bracteata 'Golden Gem' 297
Melaleuca bracteata 'Revolution Gold' 297
Melaleuca bracteata 'Revolution Green' 297, 297
Melaleuca fulgens 297
Melaleuca incana 297, 297
Melaleuca leucadendra 298
Melaleuca linariifolia 298, 298
Melaleuca quinquenervia 298–9, 299
Melaleuca tamariscina 299
Melaleuca thymifolia 299, 299
Melaleuca viridiflora 299
Melastoma 300
Melastoma malabathricum 300
Melia 300
Melia azedarach 300
Melia azedarach form *australasica* 300, 300
Melia azedarach 'Umbraculiformis' 300
Mespilus 300–1
Mespilus germanica 300–1, 301
Mesua 301
Mesua nagassarium 301
Metasequoia 301
Metasequoia glyptostroboides 301, 301
Metrosideros 302
Metrosideros excelsa 302, 302
Metrosideros excelsa 'Variegata' 302
Metrosideros kermadecensis 302
Metrosideros kermadecensis 'Sunninghill' 302
Metrosideros kermadecensis 'Variegata' 302, 302
Metrosideros robusta 302, 302
Metrosideros umbellata 302, 302
Mexican alder (*Alnus acuminata*) 80, 80
Mexican bald cypress (*Taxodium mucronatum*) 419, 419
Mexican cypress (*Cupressus lusitanica*) 170, 171
Mexican daisy tree (*Montanoa bipinnatifida*) 304, 304
Mexican giant groundsel (*Senecio petasitis*) 399, 399
Mexican hawthorn (*Crataegus pubescens*) 168, 168
Mexican nut pine (*Pinus cembroides*) 337, 337
Mexican orange blossom (*Choisya ternata*) 147, 147
Mexican palo verde (*Parkinsonia aculeata*) 322, 322

Mexican piñon pine (*Pinus cembroides*) 337, 337
Mexican sunflower (*Tithonia diversifolia*) 427, 427
Mexican tree groundsel (*Senecio grandifolius*) 398, 398
Mexican washingtonia palm (*Washingtonia robusta*) 442, 442
Mexican white pine (*Pinus ayacahuite*) 335, 335
Mexican yellow pine (*Pinus patula*) 340–1, 341
mezereon (*Daphne mezereum*) 177
Michelia 302–3
Michelia champaca 303
Michelia doltsopa 303, 303
Michelia figo 303, 303
Michelia yunnanensis 303, 303
Mickey Mouse plant (*Ochna serrulata*) 314, 314
Microbiota 303
Microbiota decussa 303, 303
Midland hawthorn (*Crataegus laevigata*) 167
mignonette tree (*Lawsonia inermis*) 273
milkwort (*Polygala*) 350
Millettia 304
Millettia grandis 304, 304
mimosa (*Acacia dealbata*) 58
miniature umbrella tree (*Schefflera arboricola*) 397
mintbush (*Prostanthera*) 353–4
Mirbeck's oak (*Quercus canariensis*) 367, 367
miro (*Prumnopitys ferruginea*) 356, 356
mirror bush (*Coprosma repens*) 157, 157
mobcap (*Hydrangea*) 248–9
mock orange (*Murraya paniculata*) 305, 305
mock orange (*Philadelphus*) 324–5
mock thuja (*Thujopsis dolabrata*) 424, 424
mockernut hickory (*Carya tomentosa*) 130, 130
mohintli (*Justicia spicigera*) 263, 263
momi fir (*Abies firma*) 54, 54
Mongolian oak (*Quercus mongolica*) 368
monkey pod tree (*Samanea saman*) 394
monkey-pod tree (*Cassia fistula*) 130–1, 131
monkey puzzle pine (*Araucaria*) 87–8
monkey puzzle pine (*Araucaria araucana*) 87, 87
Montanoa 304
Montanoa bipinnatifida 304, 304
Monterey cypress (*Cupressus macrocarpa*) 170, 171
Monterey pine (*Pinus radiata*) 341, 341
Montezuma cypress (*Taxodium mucronatum*) 419, 419
moonbeam (*Tabernaemontana divaricata*) 416
mophead (*Hydrangea*) 248–9
mophead acacia (*Robinia pseudoacacia* 'Umbraculifera') 385
Moreton Bay ash (*Eucalyptus tessellaris*) 209
Moreton Bay chestnut (*Castanospermum australe*) 131–2, 132
Moreton Bay fig (*Ficus macrophylla*) 219, 219
Moringa 304
Moringa oleifera 304
Mormon tea (*Ephedra viridis*) 192
Morus 304–5
Morus alba 304, 305
Morus alba 'Pendula' 304, 305
Morus nigra 305, 305
Morus rubra 305, 305

mosaic fig (*Ficus aspera* 'Parcellii') 218, *218*
moschosma (*Iboza riparia*) 252, *252*
mottlecah (*Eucalyptus macrocarpa*) 206
Mt Atlas broom (*Argyrocytisus buttandieri*) 91, *91*
mountain ash (*Eucalyptus regnans*) 208–9, *208*
mountain ash (*Sorbus aucuparia*) 405, *405*
mountain cabbage tree (*Cordyline indivisa*) 158, *159*
mountain currant (*Ribes alpinum*) 383, *383*
mountain ebony (*Bauhinia variegata*) 100, *101*
mountain hemlock (*Tsuga mertensiana*) 430
mountain holly (*Olearia ilicifolia*) 315, *315*
mountain laurel (*Kalmia latifolia*) 264, *264*
mountain mahogany (*Cercocarpus*) 141–2
mountain pine (*Pinus mugo*) 339
mountain plum pine (*Podocarpus lawrencei*) 349, *349*
mountain silverbell (*Halesia monticola*) 239
mudan (*Paeonia suffruticosa*) 320, *321*
Mudgee wattle (*Acacia spectabilis*) 60, *60*
mugga (*Eucalyptus sideroxylon*) 209, *209*
mulberry (*Morus*) 304–5
Mundulea 305
Mundulea sericea 305
Murraya 305
Murraya koenigii 305
Murraya paniculata 305, *305*
Musa 306
Musa ornata 306, *306*
Musa × paradisiaca 306, *306*
musengera (*Afrocarpus gracilior*) 73, *73*
musk tree (*Olearia argophylla*) 315
Mussaenda 306–7
Mussaenda erythrophylla 306, *306*
Mussaenda philippica 306–7, *306*
Mussaenda philippica 'Dona Imelda' 306
Mussaenda philippica 'Dona Luz' 306
Mussaenda philippica 'Queen Sirikit' 306
Myoporum 307
Myoporum floribundum 307, *307*
Myoporum insulare 307
Myoporum laetum 307, *307*
myrabolan (*Prunus cerasifera*) 357, *357*
Myrica 307
Myrica cerifera 307, *307*
Myrica gale 307
Myristica 307–8
Myristica fragrans 308, *308*
Myroxylon 308
Myroxylon balsamum 308, *308*
myrtle beech (*Nothofagus cunninghamii*) 311, *311*
Myrtus 308
Myrtus communis 308, *308*
Myrtus communis 'Flore Pleno' 308, *308*
Myrtus communis 'Microphylla' 308, *308*
Myrtus communis 'Variegata' 308, *308*
Myrtus bullata see Lophomyrtus bullata
Myrtus luma see Luma apiculata

Nandina 310
Nandina domestica 310, *310*
Nandina domestica 'Firepower' 310
Nandina domestica 'Nana' 310, *310*
Nandina domestica 'Richmond' 310, *310*

narrow-leafed black peppermint (*Eucalyptus nicholii*) 207, *207*
Nashi pear (*Pyrus pyrifolia*) 364
Natal bottlebrush (*Greyia sutherlandii*) 235, *235*
Natal coral tree (*Erythrina humeana*) 200, *200*
Natal flame bush (*Alberta magna*) 76, *76*
Natal mahogany (*Trichilia emetica*) 428, *429*
Natal plum (*Carissa macrocarpa*) 126, *126*
Natal wedding flower (*Dombeya tiliacea*) 184, *184*
Natal yellowwood (*Podocarpus henkelii*) 348–9, *348*
native poplar (*Omalanthus populifolius*) 316, *316*
Nauclea 310
Nauclea orientalis 310, *310*
needle bush (*Hakea microcarpa*) 238, *238*
needle juniper (*Juniperus rigida*) 262
needle palm (*Rhapidophyllum hystrix*) 374
neem (*Azadirachta indica*) 94
negrohead beech (*Nothofagus moorei*) 312, *312*
Nelson mountain groundsel (*Senecio laxifolia*) 399
Neodypsis 310–11
Neodypsis decaryi 310–11, *311*
Nepal alder (*Alnus nepalensis*) 81, *81*
Nerium 311
Nerium oleander 311, *311*
Nerium oleander 'Album' 311, *311*
Nerium oleander 'Luteum Plenum' 311
Nerium oleander 'Mrs Fred Roeding' 311
Nerium oleander 'Punctatum' 311, *311*
Nerium oleander 'Splendens' 311
Nerium oleander 'Splendens Variegatum' 311
net bush (*Calothamnus*) 120
nettle tree (*Celtis*) 136
nettle tree (*Celtis australis*) 137
New South Wales Christmas bush (*Cerapetalum gummiferum*) 139, *139*
New Zealand cabbage tree (*Cordyline australis*) 158, *158*
New Zealand celery pine (*Phyllocladus trichomanoides*) 328, *328*
New Zealand Christmas tree (*Metrosideros excelsa*) 302, *302*
New Zealand kauri (*Agathis australis*) 74, *74*
New Zealand lacebark (*Hoheria populnea*) 246–7, *247*
New Zealand pink broom (*Notospartium carmichaeliae*) 313, *313*
New Zealand red pine (*Dacrydium cupressinum*) 176, *176*
New Zealand silver beech (*Nothofagus menziesii*) 312
New Zealand tree fuchsia (*Fuchsia excorticata*) 226
ngaio (*Myoporum laetum*) 307, *307*
night-scented jessamine (*Cestrum nocturnum*) 142, *143*
Nikau palm (*Rhopalostylis sapida*) 382, *382*
Nikko fir (*Abies homolepis*) 54
Nikko maple (*Acer nikoense*) 66
nim (*Azadirachta indica*) 94
nipple fruit (*Solanum mammosum*) 403
Noble fir (*Abies procera*) 55
Nootka cypress (*Chamaecyparis nootkatensis*) 144, *144*
Norfolk Island hibiscus (*Lagunaria patersonia*) 270
Norfolk Island pine (*Araucaria heterophylla*) 88, *88*

northern catalpa (*Catalpa speciosa*) 133, *133*
northern cottonwood (*Populus deltoides* var. *monilifera*) 352
northern rata (*Metrosideros robusta*) 302, *302*
northern red oak (*Quercus rubra*) 370
Norway maple (*Acer platanoides*) 67, *67*
Norway spruce (*Picea abies*) 330, *330*
Nothogagus 311–13
Nothofagus cunninghamii 311, *311*
Nothofagus menziesii 312
Nothofagus moorei 312, *312*
Nothofagus obliqua 312, *312*
Nothofagus procera 312
Nothofagus solandri 312–13, *312*
Notospartium 313
Notospartium carmichaeliae 313, *313*
Nuxia 313
Nuxia floribunda 313, *313*
Nuytsia 313
Nuytsia floribunda 313, *313*
Nyssa 314
Nyssa aquatica 314
Nyssa sylvatica 314, *314*

oak (*Quercus*) 366–71
oak-leafed hydrangea (*Hydrangea quercifolia*) 249, *249*
Ochna 314
Ochna serrulata 314, *314*
ocotillo (*Fouquieria*) 222
ocotillo (*Fouquieria splendens*) 222
Ohio buckeye (*Aesculus glabra*) 71, *71*
old man banksia (*Banksia serrata*) 98, *98*
Olea 314–15
Olea europaea 314–15, *314*
oleander (*Nerium*) 311
oleander (*Nerium oleander*) 311, *311*
oleander-leafed protea (*Protea neriifolia*) 356, *356*
Olearia 315
Olearia albida see Olearia 'Talbot de Malahide'
Olearia argophylla 315
Olearia avicenniifolia 315
Olearia ilicifolia 315, *315*
Olearia macrodonta 315, *315*
Olearia paniculata 315
Olearia phlogopappa 315, *315*
Olearia × scilloniensis 315, *315*
Olearia 'Talbot de Malahide' 315
Olearia traversii 315, *315*
oleaster (*Elaeagnus*) 188–9
oleaster (*Elaeagnus angustifolia*) 189
olive (*Olea europaea*) 314–15, *314*
Omalanthus 316
Omalanthus populifolius 316, *316*
ombu (*Phytolacca dioica*) 329, *329*
Oncoba 316
Oncoba spinosa 316, *316*
one-seed juniper (*Juniperus monosperma*) 262, *262*
Opuntia 316–17
Opuntia ficus-indica 316, *317*
Opuntia imbricata 317, *317*
Opuntia vulgaris 316
orange (*Citrus sinensis*) 152, *152*
orange firethorn (*Pyracantha angustifolia*) 363
orange jessamine (*Murraya paniculata*) 305, *305*
orchid tree (*Bauhinia variegata*) 100, *101*
Oregon ash (*Fraxinus latifolia*) 223, *224*
Oregon grape (*Mahonia aquifolium*) 290, *290*
Oregon maple (*Acer macrophyllum*) 65, *65*

Oregon pine (*Pseudotsuga menziesii*) 361, *361*
Oreocallis wickhamii see Alloxylon flammeum
oriental arbor-vitae (*Platycladus orientalis*) 347, *347*
oriental beech (*Fagus orientalis*) 216
oriental plane (*Platanus orientalis*) 346, *346*
oriental thorn (*Crataegus laciniata*) 167, *167*
ornamental ginger (*Alpinia*) 82
ornamental raspberry (*Rubus odoratus*) 390
Orphium 317
Orphium frutescens 317, *317*
osage orange (*Maclura pomifera*) 286
Osmanthus 317–18
Osmanthus delavayi 317, *317*
Osmanthus × fortunei 317, *317*
Osmanthus fragrans 317, *317*
Osmanthus heterophyllus 318, *318*
Ostrya 318
Ostrya carpinifolia 318
Ostrya virginiana 318, *318*
Otaheite gooseberry (*Phyllanthus acidus*) 328, *328*
Outeniqua yellowwood (*Afrocarpus falcatus*) 73
Ovens wattle (*Acacia pravissima*) 60, *60*
Oxydendrum 318
Oxydendrum arboreum 318, *318*
Oyster Bay pine (*Callitris rhomboidea*) 118
Ozark witch hazel (*Hamamelis vernalis*) 240, *240*

Pachira 320
Pachira aquatica 320, *320*
Pachystegia 320
Pachystegia insignis 320, *320*
Pacific dogwood (*Cornus nuttallii*) 160
Pacific fir (*Abies amabilis*) 52, *53*
Pacific fir (*Abies concolor*) 53, *53*
Paeonia 320–1
Paeonia lutea 320–1, *320*
Paeonia suffruticosa 320, *321*
pagoda flower (*Clerodendrum paniculatum*) 153, *153*
pagoda tree (*Sophora japonica*) 404, *404*
paintbrush (*Combretum erythrophyllum*) 157
palas tree (*Butea monosperma*) 111
Paliurus 321
Paliurus spina-christi 321
palmetto (*Sabal palmetto*) 392, *392*
palmetto palm (*Sabal*) 392
palo botella (*Chorisia insignis*) 147, *147*
palo verde (*Cercidium floridum*) 140, *140*
pandang (*Pandanus tectorius*) 321, *321*
Pandanus 321
Pandanus tectorius 321, *321*
papaya (*Carica*) 125–6
paper birch (*Betula papyrifera*) 102, *102*
paper bush (*Edgworthia chrysantha*) 188, *188*
paper mulberry (*Broussonetia*) 107
paper mulberry (*Broussonetia papyrifera*) 107, *107*
paperbark maple (*Acer griseum*) 64, *64*
Para rubber tree (*Hevea brasiliensis*) 243, *243*
Paraguay nightshade (*Solanum rantonnei*) 404, *404*
parana pine (*Araucaria angustifolia*) 87, *87*
Paraserianthes 321
Paraserianthes lophantha 321, *321*
parasol plant (*Holmskioldia sanguinea*) 247, *247*
parasol tree (*Firmiana simplex*) 220, *220*

Paris daisy (*Euryops chrysanthemoides*) 213, *213*
Parkinsonia 322
Parkinsonia aculeata 322, *322*
Parrotia 322
Parrotia persica 322, *322*
pau d'arco (*Tabebuia avellanedae*) 416
Paulownia 322–3
Paulownia fortunei 322–3, *323*
Paulownia imperialis see Paulownia tomentosa
Paulownia tomentosa 323, *323*
pawpaw (*Asimina triloba*) 92
paw-paw (*Carica*) 125–6
pea tree (*Caragana arborescens*) 125, *125*
peach (*Prunus persica*) 358, *358*
peach protea (*Protea grandiceps*) 355, *355*
peacock flower (*Caesalpinia pulcherrima*) 114, *114*
pear (*Pyrus*) 364
pearl acacia (*Acacia podalyriifolia*) 60, *60*
pearl bush (*Exochorda*) 214
pearl flower (*Leucothöe fontanesiana*) 277
pecan (*Carya*) 128–9
pedunculate oak (*Quercus robur*) 369, *369*
peegee hydrangea (*Hydrangea paniculata*) 249, *249*
peepul (*Ficus religiosa*) 219
Peltophorum 323
Peltophorum ferrugineum see Peltophorum pterocarpum
Peltophorum inerme see Peltophorum pterocarpum
Peltophorum pterocarpum 323, *323*
pencil cedar (*Juniperus virginiana*) 263, *263*
pencil euphorbia (*Euphorbia tirucalli*) 212–13
Pentapterygium serpens see Agapetes serpens
pepper tree (*Macropiper excelsum*) 286, *286*
pepper tree (*Schinus areira*) 397, *397*
peppercorn (*Schinus areira*) 397, *397*
peppermint tree (*Agonis flexuosa*) 74, *75*
peregrina (*Jatropha integerrima*) 258
Pernettya mucronata see Gaultheria mucronata
Perny's holly (*Ilex pernyi*) 255
Persea 323
Persea americana 323
Persea gratissima see Persea americana
Persian lilac (*Melia azedarach*) 300
Persian witch-hazel (*Parrotia persica*) 322, *322*
persimmon (*Diospyros*) 182
persimmon (*Diospyros kaki*) 182, *182*
persimmon (*Diospyros virginiana*) 182, *182*
Persoonia 324
Persoonia pinifolia 324, *324*
petticoat palm (*Washingtonia*) 442
Phellodendron 324
Phellodendron amurense 324, *324*
Philadelphus 324–5
Philadelphus coronarius 325
Philadelphus coronarius 'Aureus' 325
Philadelphus 'Lemoine' 325
Philadelphus lewisii 325, *325*
Philippines violet (*Barleria cristata*) 99, *99*
Phillip Island hibiscus (*Hibiscus insularis*) 244, *244*
Philodendron 325
Philodendron bipinnatifidum 325, *325*
Philodendron selloum see Philodendron bipinnatifidum
Phoenix 325–6

Phoenix canariensis 325, *325*, *326*
Phoenix dactylifera 326, *326*
Phoenix roebeleni 326, *326*
Photinia 326–7, *326*
Photinia × fraseri *326*, 327
Photinia × fraseri 'Red Robin' 327
Photinia × fraseri 'Robusta' 327
Photinia glabra 327
Photinia glabra 'Rubens' 327
Photinia serratifolia see *Photinia serrulata*
Photinia serrulata 327, *327*
Photinia villosa 327, *327*
Phylica 327
Phylica pubescens 327, *327*
Phyllanthus 327–8
Phyllanthus acidus 328, *328*
Phyllocladus 328
Phyllocladus aspleniifolius 328
Phyllocladus trichomanoides 328, *328*
Phyllostachys 328–9
Phyllostachys bambusoides 328, *328*
Phyllostachys bambusoides 'Castillonis' 328
Phyllostachys bambusoides 'Castillonis Inversa' 328
Phyllostachys bambusoides 'Holochrysa' 328
Phyllostachys nigra *328*, 329
Phyllostachys nigra var. *henonis* 329
Physocarpus 329
Physocarpus opulifolius 329, *329*
Physocarpus opulifolius 'Aureus' 329
Phytolacca 329
Phytolacca americana 329, *329*
Phytolacca dioica 329, *329*
piccabeen palm (*Archontophoenix cunninghamiana*) 90, *90*
Picea 330–4
Picea abies 330, *330*
Picea abies 'Maxwellii' 330
Picea abies 'Pumila Glauca' 330
Picea abies 'Pygmaea' 330, *330*
Picea abies 'Reflexa' 330
Picea breweriana 330, *330*
Picea engelmannii 331, *331*
Picea glauca 331
Picea glauca 'Conica' 331, *331*
Picea mariana 331
Picea mariana 'Nana' 331, *331*
Picea obovata 332, *332*
Picea omorika 332, *332*
Picea orientalis 332
Picea orientalis 'Atrovirens' 332
Picea pungens 333, *333*
Picea pungens 'Glauca' 333
Picea pungens 'Hoopsii' 333, *333*
Picea pungens 'Iseli Fastigiate' 333
Picea pungens 'Koester' 333
Picea pungens 'Moerheimii' 333
Picea pungens 'Royal Blue' 333, *333*
Picea sitchensis 333, *333*
Picea smithiana 334, *334*
Pieris 334
Pieris formosa 334
Pieris formosa var. *forrestii* 334, *334*
Pieris japonica 334
Pieris japonica 'Bert Chandler' 334
Pieris japonica 'Christmas Cheer' 334
Pieris japonica 'Flamingo' 334
Pieris japonica 'Purity' 334
Pieris japonica 'Variegata' 334
pigeon berry (*Duranta*) 186
pignut hickory (*Carya glabra*) 128–9
Pimelea 334–5
Pimelea ferruginea 334–5, *335*
pin oak (*Quercus palustris*) 368, *369*
pincushion (*Leucospermum*) 276
pincushion bush (*Hakea laurina*) 238, *238*
pine (*Pinus*) 335–43
pineapple guave (*Feijoa sellowiana*) 217, *217*
pineapple zamia (*Lepidozamia peroffskyana*) 273, *273*
pineleaf geebung (*Persoonia pinifolia*) 324, *324*
pink cedar (*Acrocarpus fraxinifolius*) 69
pink dombeya (*Dombeya burgessiae*) 184, *184*
pink shower (*Cassia javanica*) 131, *131*
pink tassel-flower (*Calliandra surinamensis*) 115, *115*
pink-tips (*Callistemon salignus*) 117, *117*
pinkwood (*Eucryphia moorei*) 211, *211*
Pinus 335–43
Pinus aristata 335, *335*
Pinus armandii 335, *335*
Pinus ayacahuite 335, *335*
Pinus bungeana 336, *336*
Pinus canariensis 336, *336*
Pinus caribaea 336, *336*; see also *Pinus elliottii*
Pinus caribaea var. *bahamensis* 336
Pinus caribaea var. *hondurensis* 336
Pinus cembra 337, *337*
Pinus cembroides 337, *337*
Pinus contorta var. *latifolia* 337, *337*
Pinus coulteri 337, *337*
Pinus densiflora 338, *338*
Pinus densiflora 'Oculus-draconis' 338
Pinus densiflora 'Umbraculifera' 338
Pinus elliottii 338, *338*
Pinus halepensis 338, *338*
Pinus jeffreyi 339, *339*
Pinus koraiensis 339, *339*
Pinus monophylla 339, *339*
Pinus monticola 339, *339*
Pinus mugo 339
Pinus mugo 'Aurea' 339
Pinus mugo 'Gnom' 339
Pinus mugo 'Mops' 339, *339*
Pinus mugo var. *pumilo* 339
Pinus nigra 340, *340*
Pinus nigra var. *maritima* 340
Pinus palustris 340, *340*
Pinus parviflora 340
Pinus parviflora 'Brevifolia' 340, *340*
Pinus parviflora 'Glauca' 340
Pinus patula 340–1, *341*
Pinus pinaster 341, *341*
Pinus pinea 341, *341*
Pinus ponderosa 341
Pinus radiata 341, *341*
Pinus roxburghii 342, *342*
Pinus strobus 342, *342*
Pinus strobus 'Fastigiata' 342, *342*
Pinus strobus 'Nana' 342
Pinus sylvestris 342–3, *343*
Pinus thunbergiana see *Pinus thunbergii*
Pinus thunbergii 343, *343*
Pinus wallichiana 343
Piscidia 343
Piscidia piscipula 343
Pisonia 343
Pisonia grandis 343
pistachio (*Pistacia vera*) 344
pistachio nut (*Pistacia vera*) 344
Pistacia 343–4
Pistacia chinensis 343, *343*
Pistacia vera 344
pistol bush (*Duvernoia adhatodoides*) 186
pitanga (*Eugenia uniflora*) 211
Pittosporum 344
Pittosporum crassifolium 344, *344*
Pittosporum crassifolium 'Variegatum' 344
Pittosporum eugenioides 344, *344*
Pittosporum eugenioides 'Variegatum' 344
Pittosporum phylliraeoides 344, *344*
Pittosporum rhombifolium 344–5, *344*
Pittosporum tenuifolium 345, *345*
Pittosporum tobira 345
Pittosporum tobira 'Variegatum' 345, *345*
Pittosporum tobira 'Wheeler's Dwarf' 345, *345*
Plagianthus 345
Plagianthus betulinus 345, *345*
Plagianthus divaricatus see *Plagianthus*
Planchonia 345
Planchonia careya 345, *345*
plane (*Platanus*) 346
plane-tree (*Platanus*) 346
plantain (*Musa × paradisiaca*) 306, *306*
Platanus 346
Platanus × acerifolia 346, *346*
Platanus occidentalis 346
Platanus occidentalis 'Digitata' 346
Platanus orientalis 346, *346*
Platanus racemosa 346, *346*
Platanus racemosa 'Wrightii' 346
Platycladus 346–7
Platycladus orientalis 347, *347*
Platycladus orientalis 'Aurea Nana' *347*
plum (*Prunus domestica*) 357
plum pine (*Podocarpus*) 348–50
plum pine (*Podocarpus elatus*) 348, *348*
plum yew (*Cephalotaxus*) 138
plum-fruited yew (*Prumnopitys elegans*) 356
Plumbago 347
Plumbago auriculata 347, *347*
Plumbago auriculata 'Alba' 347
Plumbago auriculata 'Royal Cape' 347, *347*
Plumbago capensis see *Plumbago auriculata*
plume-flower (*Justicia spicigera*) 263, *263*
Plumeria 347–8
Plumeria obtusa 348
Plumeria rubra 348, *348*
Plumeria rubra var. *acutifolia* 348, *348*
Plunkett mallee (*Eucalyptus curtisii*) 204, *204*
Podalyria 348
Podalyria calyptrata 348
Podocarpus 348–50
Podocarpus alpinus see *Podocarpus lawrencei*
Podocarpus elatus 348, *348*
Podocarpus falcatus see *Afrocarpus falcatus*
Podocarpus gracilior see *Afrocarpus gracilior*
Podocarpus henkelii 348–9, *348*
Podocarpus latifolius 349, *349*
Podocarpus lawrencei 349, *349*
Podocarpus macrophyllus 349, *349*
Podocarpus macrophyllus 'Maki' 349
Podocarpus neriifolius 349
Podocarpus salignus 349, *349*
Podocarpus totara 350, *350*
Podocarpus totara 'Aureus' 350
poet's jasmine (*Jasminum officinale*) 258
pohutukawa (*Metrosideros excelsa*) 302, *302*
poinciana (*Delonix regia*) 178, *179*
Poinciana gilliesii see *Caesalpinia gilliesii*
Poinciana pulcherrima see *Caesalpinia pulcherrima*
poinsettia (*Euphorbia pulcherrima*) 212, *213*
poison sumac (*Toxicodendron succedaneum*) 428, *428*
pokeberry (*Phytolacca*) 329
pokeweed (*Phytolacca*) 329
Polygala 350
Polygala myrtifolia 350, *350*
Polygala myrtifolia 'Grandiflora' 350, *350*
Polygala virgata 350, *350*
Polyscias 350
Polyscias filicifolia 350
Polyscias guilfoylei 350
Polyscias scutellaria 350
Pomaderris 350–1
Pomaderris aspera 351
Pomaderris kumeraho 351, *351*
pomegranate (*Punica granatum*) 362–3, *362*
pompon tree (*Dais cotinifolia*) 176, *176*
Poncirus 351
Poncirus trifoliata 351, *351*
pond cypress (*Taxodium ascendens*) 418–9, *418*
ponderosa pine (*Pinus ponderosa*) 341
ponga (*Cyathea dealbata*) 172, *173*
ponytail palm (*Beaucarnea recurvata*) 100, *100*
Populus 351–2
Populus alba 351
Populus alba 'Pyramidalis' 351, *351*
Populus alba 'Richardii' 351, *351*
Populus bolleana see *Populus alba*
Populus deltoides 352, *352*
Populus deltoides var. *monilifera* 352
Populus fremontii 352
Populus lasiocarpa 352, *352*
Populus nigra 352, *352*
Populus nigra 'Aurea' 352
Populus nigra 'Italica' 352
Populus tremula 352, *352*
Populus tremuloides 352, *353*
Populus trichocarpa 352, *353*
Populus yunnanensis 352
poro poro (*Solanum aviculare*) 403, *403*
Port Jackson pine (*Callitris rhomboidea*) 118
Port Orford cedar (*Chamaecyparis nootkatensis*) 144, *144*
Portugal heath (*Erica lusitanica*) 194–5, *195*
Portugal laurel (*Prunus lusitanica*) 358, *358*
Portulacaria 353
Portulacaria afra 353, *353*
Portulacaria afra 'Tricolor' 353
Portulacaria afra 'Variegata' 353
port-wine magnolia (*Michelia figo*) 303, *303*
possumhaw holly (*Ilex decidua*) 254, *254*
powderpuff lillypilly (*Syzygium wilsonii*) 414
powderpuff tree (*Calliandra haematocephala*) 115, *115*
powton (*Paulownia fortunei*) 322–3, *323*
prickly cycad (*Encephalartos altensteinii*) 190, *190*
prickly heath (*Gaultheria mucronata*) 229
prickly Moses (*Acacia verticillata*) 61, *61*
prickly pear (*Opuntia ficus-indica*) *316*, 317
pride of Bolivia (*Tipuana tipu*) 426, *426*
pride of China (*Koelreuteria bipinnata*) 265, *265*
pride-of-de-Kaap (*Bauhinia galpinii*) 99
pride of India (*Lagerstroemia indica*) 269, *269*
pride of India (*Melia azedarach*) 300
pride of Madeira (*Echium fastuosum*) 188, *188*
primrose jasmine (*Jasminum mesnyi*) 258, *258*
Prince Albert's yew (*Saxegothaea conspicua*) 396, *396*
princess flower (*Tibouchina urvilleana*) 424, *425*
princess tree (*Paulownia tomentosa*) 323, *323*
privet (*Ligustrum*) 278
Prostanthera 353–4
Prostanthera caerulea 353
Prostanthera cuneata 353, *353*
Prostanthera lasianthos 354, *354*
Prostanthera ovalifolia 354, *354*
Prostanthera rotundifolia 354
Protea 354–6
Protea aristata 354, *354*
Protea compacta 354–5, *354*
Protea cynaroides 355, *355*
Protea eximia 355, *355*
Protea eximia 'Sylvia' 355
Protea grandiceps 355, *355*
Protea longifolia 355
Protea neriifolia 356, *356*
Protea 'Pink Ice' *354*; see also *Protea*
Protea repens 356, *356*
Protea scolymocephala 356
provision tree (*Pachira aquatica*) 320, *320*
Prumnopitys 356
Prumnopitys elegans 356
Prumnopitys ferruginea 356, *356*
Prunus 356–60, *356*, *357*
Prunus armeniaca 357
Prunus avium 357
Prunus avium 'Plena' 357
Prunus × blireiana see *Prunus cerasifera*
Prunus campanulata 357, *357*
Prunus cerasifera 357, *357*
Prunus cerasifera 'Elvins' 357
Prunus cerasifera 'Nigra' 357
Prunus cerasifera 'Pissardii' 357
Prunus cerasoides 357, *357*
Prunus domestica 357
Prunus domestica 'Coe's Golden Drop' 357
Prunus ilicifolia 358, *358*
Prunus laurocerasus 358, *358*
Prunus lusitanica 358, *358*
Prunus mume 358
Prunus mume 'Albo-plena' 358
Prunus mume 'Beni-shidon' 358
Prunus mume 'Geisha' 358, *358*
Prunus mume 'Pendula' 358
Prunus persica 358, *358*
Prunus persica 'Alba Plena' 358
Prunus persica 'Klara Meyer' 358
Prunus persica 'Magnifica' 358
Prunus persica 'Versicolor' 358
Prunus sargentii 359, *359*
Prunus serotina 359, *359*
Prunus serrula 359, *359*
Prunus serrulata 359, *359*
Prunus serrulata 'Amanogawa' 359
Prunus serrulata 'Kanzan' 359
Prunus serrulata 'Kikushidare' 359
Prunus serrulata 'Mount Fuji' 359
Prunus serrulata 'Shiro-fugen' 359
Prunus serrulata 'Shirotae' 359, *359*
Prunus serrulata 'Tai Haku' 359
Prunus serrulata 'Ukon' 359
Prunus subhirtella 359
Prunus subhirtella 'Autumnalis' 359
Prunus subhirtella 'Pendula' 359, *359*
Prunus tenella 359
Prunus tenella 'Fire Hill' 359
Prunus × yedoensis 360, *360*
Prunus × yedoensis 'Ivensii' 360
Pseuderanthemum 360
Pseuderanthemum reticulatum 360, *360*
Pseudocydonia sinensis see *Cydonia sinensis*
Pseudolarix 360
Pseudolarix amabilis 360, *360*
Pseudolarix kaempferi see *Pseudolarix amabilis*
Pseudopanax 360–1
Pseudopanax crassifolius 361, *361*
Pseudopanax lessonii 361, *361*
Pseudotsuga 361
Pseudotsuga menziesii 361, *361*
Psidium 361–2
Psidium cattleianum 361, *361*
Psidium cattleianum var. *littorale* 361
Psidium cattleianum 'Lucidum' 361
Psidium guajava *241*, 362
Ptelea
Ptelea trifoliata 362, *362*
Pterocarya 362
Pterocarya fraxinifolia 362
Pterostyrax 362
Pterostyrax hispida 362, *362*
Ptychosperma 362
Ptychosperma macarthurii 362, *362*

pudding-pipe tree (*Cassia fistula*) 130–1, *131*
puka (*Griselinia lucida*) 236, *236*
Punica 362–3
Punica granatum 362–3, *362*
Punica granatum 'Nana' 363
Punica granatum 'Wonderful' 363
punk tree (*Melaleuca quinquenervia*) 298, *299*
punty (*Senna artemisioides*) 399, *399*
puriri (*Vitex lucens*) 440, *440*
purple anise (*Illicium floridanum*) 256, *256*
purple broom (*Polygala virgata*) 350, *350*
purple heath (*Erica canaliculata*) 192
purple mintbush (*Prostanthera ovalifolia*) 354, *354*
purple osier (*Salix purpurea*) 394, *394*
purple-leafed plum (*Prunus cerasifera*) 357, *357*
Puya 363
Puya alpestris see *Puya berteroniana*
Puya berteroniana 363, *363*
Pycnostachys 363
Pycnostachys urticifolia 363, *363*
Pyracantha 363–4
Pyracantha angustifolia 363
Pyracantha coccinea 363, *363*
Pyracantha coccinea 'Kasan' 363
Pyracantha coccinea 'Lalandei' 363, *363*
Pyracantha crenatoserrata 364
Pyrus 364
Pyrus calleryana 364
Pyrus calleryana 'Bradford' 364
Pyrus communis 364
Pyrus communis 'Beurre Bosc' 364, *364*
Pyrus communis 'Williams Bon Chrétien' 364
Pyrus pyrifolia 364
Pyrus salicifolia 364
Pyrus salicifolia 'Pendula' 364, *364*
Pyrus ussuriensis 364, *364*

quaking aspen (*Populus tremuloides*) 352, *353*
queen palm (*Syagrus romanzoffiana*) 411
queen's flower (*Lagerstroemia speciosa*) 270, *270*
Queensland black bean (*Castanospermum australe*) 131–2, *132*
Queensland kauri (*Agathis robusta*) 74, *74*
Queensland laurel (*Pittosporum rhombifolium*) 344–5, *344*
Queensland nut (*Macadamia tetraphylla*) 286, *286*
Queensland poplar (*Omalanthus populifolius*) 316, *316*
Queensland umbrella tree (*Schefflera actinophylla*) 397, *397*
Queensland wattle (*Acacia podalyriifolia*) 60, *60*
Quercus 366–71
Quercus acutissima 366–7, *366*
Quercus agrifolia 367
Quercus alba 366, *367*
Quercus bicolor 367, *367*
Quercus canariensis 367, *367*
Quercus castaneifolia 367, *367*
Quercus cerris 367, *367*
Quercus chrysolepis 367
Quercus coccinea 368
Quercus dentata 368, *368*
Quercus ilex 368, *368*
Quercus kelloggii 368, *368*
Quercus macrocarpa 368
Quercus mirbeckii see *Quercus canariensis*
Quercus mongolica 368
Quercus nigra 368, *369*
Quercus palustris 368, *369*

Quercus phellos 369, *369*
Quercus prinus 369
Quercus robur 369, *369*
Quercus robur 'Concordia' 369
Quercus robur 'Fastigiata' 369
Quercus rubra 370
Quercus rubra 'Aurea' 370, *370*
Quercus salicina 370, *370*
Quercus serrata see *Quercus acutissima*
Quercus shumardii 370, *370*
Quercus suber 370, *371*
Quercus velutina 370, *371*
Quercus virginiana 370–1, *371*
Quercus wislizenii 371, *371*
quillai (*Quillaja saponaria*) 371, *371*
Quillaja 371
Quillaja saponaria 371, *371*
quince (*Cydonia*) 173
quinine tree (*Cinchona*) 148–9
quinine tree (*Rauvolfia caffra*) 372, *372*

Radermachera 372
Radermachera sinica 372, *372*
radiata pine (*Pinus radiata*) 341, *341*
rain tree (*Samanea saman*) 394
Ramanas rose (*Rosa rugosa*) 388, *388*
rangiora (*Brachyglottis repanda*) 106
raspberry (*Rubus*) 390
raspberry (*Rubus idaeus*) 390, *390*
rat poison plant (*Hamelia*) 240
rattan (*Calamus*) 114–15
rauli (*Nothofagus procera*) 312
Rauvolfia 372
Rauvolfia caffra 372, *372*
Ravenala 372–3
Ravenala madagascariensis 372–3, *372*
ray-flowered protea (*Protea eximia*) 355, *355*
real yellowwood (*Podocarpus latifolius*) 349, *349*
red alder (*Alnus rubra*) 81, *81*
red alder (*Cunonia capensis*) 169, *169*
red angel's trumpet (*Brugmansia sanguinea*) 108, *108*
red ash (*Trichilia emetica*) 428, *429*
red boronia (*Boronia heterophylla*) 104, *104*
red box (*Eucalyptus polyanthemos*) 208
red buckeye (*Aesculus pavia*) 72, *72*
red chokeberry (*Aronia arbutifolia*) 91, *91*
red flag bush (*Mussaenda philippica*) 306–7, *306*
red horse-chestnut (*Aesculus* × *carnea*) 71
red ironbark (*Eucalyptus sideroxylon*) 209, *209*
red kamala (*Mallotus philippensis*) 291
red maple (*Acer rubrum*) 68, *68*
red mulberry (*Morus rubra*) 305, *305*
red poker (*Hakea bucculenta*) 238
red rose (*Rosa gallica*) 387, *387*
red signal heath (*Erica mammosa*) 195, *195*
red silk-cotton tree (*Bombax ceiba*) 104
red snakebark maple (*Acer capillipes*) 62, *62*
red sugarbush (*Protea grandiceps*) 355, *355*
red tassel-flower (*Calliandra tweedii*) 115, *115*
red turpentine (*Syncarpia glomulifera*) 412, *412*
red wax flower (*Crowea saligna*) 169
red-barked dogwood (*Cornus alba*) 159, *159*
redberry juniper (*Juniperus monosperma*) 262, *262*
redbud (*Cercis*) 140-1
red-centred hibiscus (*Alyogyne hakeifolia*) 82, *83*

redcurrant (*Ribes sativum*) 384, *384*
red-flowering gum (*Eucalyptus ficifolia*) 205, *205*
red-hot cat-tail (*Acalypha hispida*) 61, *61*
Reeves' spiraea (*Spiraea cantoniensis*) 407, *407*
Retama 373
Retama monosperma 373, *373*
Rhamnus 373
Rhamnus alaternus 373
Rhamnus alaternus 'Argenteo-variegata' 373, *373*
Rhamnus californica 373, *373*
Rhamnus purshiana 373
Rhaphiolepis 373–4
Rhaphiolepis × *delacourii* 374
Rhaphiolepis indica 374, *374*
Rhaphiolepis umbellata 374, *374*
Rhapidophyllum 374
Rhapidophyllum hystrix 374
Rhapis 374
Rhapis excelsa 374
rhapis palm (*Rhapis excelsa*) 374
Rhapis subtilis 374; see also *Rhapis excelsa*
Rhododendron 374–80
Rhododendron 'Alba Magna' 378; see also *Rhododendron* Indica azalea hybrids
Rhododendron arboreum 375, *375*
Rhododendron augustinii 376, *376*
Rhododendron aurigeranum × *macgregoriae* 380
Rhododendron 'Azuma-Kagami' see *Rhododendron* Kurume azalea hybrids
Rhododendron 'Bertina' 378; see also *Rhododendron* Indica azalea hybrids
Rhododendron 'Bow Bells' see *Rhododendron* Hardy hybrids
Rhododendron calendulaceum 376, *376*
Rhododendron catawbiense 376, *377*
Rhododendron 'Chinzan' see *Rhododendron* Satsuki and Gumpo azalea hybrids
Rhododendron 'Christo Ray' see *Rhododendron* Vireya hybrids
Rhododendron 'Cilpinense' 377; see also *Rhododendron* Hardy hybrids
Rhododendron cinnabarinum 377
Rhododendron 'Cocinea Speciosa' see *Rhododendron* Ghent azalea hybrids
Rhododendron 'Crest' see *Rhododendron* Hardy hybrids
Rhododendron 'Cynthia' see *Rhododendron* Hardy hybrids
Rhododendron 'Daviesii' see *Rhododendron* Ghent azalea hybrids
Rhododendron 'Daybreak' see *Rhododendron* Kurume azalea hybrids
Rhododendron decorum 376, *377*
Rhododendron degronianum 377
Rhododendron 'Flame' see *Rhododendron* Kurume azalea hybrids
Rhododendron 'Fragrantissimum' 377
Rhododendron Ghent azalea hybrids 377
Rhododendron 'Gilded Sunrise' see *Rhododendron* Vireya hybrids
Rhododendron griffithianum 377, *377*
Rhododendron 'Gunrei' see *Rhododendron* Satsuki and Gumpo azalea hybrids
Rhododendron Hardy hybrids 377, *377*
Rhododendron 'Hatsugiri' see *Rhododendron* Kurume azalea hybrids
Rhododendron 'Hinodegiri' 378; see also *Rhododendron* Kurume azalea hybrids

Rhododendron Indica azalea hybrids 378, *378*, *379*
Rhododendron 'Kirin' see *Rhododendron* Kurume azalea hybrids
Rhododendron kiusianum 378
Rhododendron Kurume azalea hybrids 375, *377*, 378–9
Rhododendron litiense 378, *379*
Rhododendron lochiae 379, *379*
Rhododendron macgregoriae 379
Rhododendron 'Madonna' see *Rhododendron* Kurume azalea hybrids
Rhododendron maximum 379
Rhododendron Mollis azalea hybrids 379, *379*
Rhododendron 'Mrs E. C. Stirling' 377; see also *Rhododendron* Hardy hybrids
Rhododendron 'Nacissiflora' see *Rhododendron* Ghent azalea hybrids
Rhododendron nuttallii 379, *379*
Rhododendron occidentale 380
Rhododendron occidentale 'Exquisita' 380, *380*
Rhododendron 'Osaraku' see *Rhododendron* Kurume azalea hybrids
Rhododendron 'Penelope' see *Rhododendron* Kurume azalea hybrids
Rhododendron 'Pink Pearl' see *Rhododendron* Kurume azalea hybrids
Rhododendron 'Pink Ray' see *Rhododendron* Vireya hybrids
Rhododendron ponticum 380, *380*
Rhododendron 'Salmonea' see *Rhododendron* Indica azalea hybrids
Rhododendron Satsuki and Gumpo azalea hybrids 380
Rhododendron schlippenbachii 380
Rhododendron 'Seikai' see *Rhododendron* Kurume azalea hybrids
Rhododendron 'Shugetsu' see *Rhododendron* Satsuki and Gumpo azalea hybrids
Rhododendron 'Simbu Sunset' see *Rhododendron* Vireya hybrids
Rhododendron simsii 380
Rhododendron sinogrande 380, *381*
Rhododendron 'Spek's Orange' see *Rhododendron* Mollis azalea hybrids
Rhododendron 'Splendens' see *Rhododendron* Indica azalea hybrids
Rhododendron 'Suetsumu' see *Rhododendron* Kurume azalea hybrids
Rhododendron Vireya hybrids 380, *380*, *381*
Rhododendron wardii see *Rhododendron litiense*
Rhodoleia 381
Rhodoleia championii 381, *381*
Rhodosphaera 381
Rhodosphaera rhodanthema 381, *381*
Rhopalostylis 381–2
Rhopalostylis sapida 382, *382*
Rhus 382–3
Rhus aromatica 382, *382*
Rhus chinensis 382
Rhus chinensis 'September Beauty' 382, *382*
Rhus lancea 382, *382*
Rhus pendulina 382–3, *383*
Rhus succedanea see *Toxicodendron succedaneum*
rhus tree (*Toxicodendron succedaneum*) 428, *428*
Rhus typhina 383, *383*
Rhus typhina 'Laciniata' 383
ribbonwood (*Hoheria sexstylosa*) 247, *247*

ribbonwood (*Plagianthus betulinus*) 345, *345*
riberry (*Syzygium luehmannii*) 414, *414*
Ribes 383–4
Ribes alpinum 383, *383*
Ribes fasciculatum 383
Ribes grossularia see *Ribes uva-crispa*
Ribes odoratum 383, *383*
Ribes sanguineum 383, *383*
Ribes sanguineum 'Brocklebankii' 383
Ribes sanguineum 'King Edward VII' 383
Ribes sanguineum 'Pulborough Scarlet' 383
Ribes sanguineum 'Tydeman's White' 383
Ribes sativum 384, *384*
Ribes uva-crispa 384, *384*
rice flower (*Pimelea*) 334–5
rice-paper plant (*Tetrapanax papyrifera*) 422, *422*
Richea 384
Richea pandanifolia 384
rimu (*Dacrydium cupressinum*) 176, *176*
ringworm senna (*Senna alata*) 399, *399*
river birch (*Betula nigra*) 102, *103*
river bushwillow (*Combretum erythrophyllum*) 157
river oak (*Casuarina cunninghamiana*) 132, *132*
river peppermint (*Eucalyptus elata*) 204–5
river red gum (*Eucalyptus camaldulensis*) 203, *203*
river resin bush (*Euryops virgineus*) 213, *213*
river rose (*Bauera rubioides*) 99, *99*
river she-oak (*Casuarina cunninghamiana*) 132, *132*
river tea-tree (*Melaleuca bracteata*) 297
Robinia 384–5
Robinia hispida 385
Robinia pseudoacacia 385
Robinia pseudoacacia 'Frisia' 384, *385*
Robinia pseudoacacia 'Tortuosa' 384, *385*
Robinia pseudoacacia 'Umbraculifera' 385
Robinia viscosa 385
roble (*Nothofagus obliqua*) 312, *312*
rock maple (*Acer glabrum*) 64
rock rose (*Cistus*) 149–50
rocket pincushion (*Leucospermum reflexum*) 277, *277*
Rocky Mountain maple (*Acer glabrum*) 64
Rocky Mountains juniper (*Juniperus scopulorum*) 262
Roldana petasitis see *Senecio petasitis*
Roman pine (*Pinus pinea*) 341, *341*
Rondeletia 385
Rondeletia amoena 385, *385*
Rosa 385–8
Rosa 'Carmenetta' see *Rosa glauca*
Rosa carolina 386, *386*
Rosa carolina 'Alba' 386
Rosa carolina 'Plena' 386
Rosa chinensis 386–7, *386*
Rosa foetida 386, *387*
Rosa foetida 'Bicolor' 387
Rosa foetida 'Persiana' 387
Rosa 'Fragrant Cloud' 386
Rosa gallica 387, *387*
Rosa gallica 'Officinalis' 387
Rosa gallica 'Versicolor' 387
Rosa 'Geranium' see *Rosa moyesii*
Rosa glauca 387, *387*
Rosa 'Intervilles' 385
Rosa moyesii 387, *387*
Rosa omeiensis var. *pteracantha* see *Rosa sericea* var. *pteracantha*
Rosa 'Pink Peace' 385
Rosa rubrifolia see *Rosa glauca*
Rosa rugosa 388, *388*

Rosa rugosa 'Alba' 388, *388*
Rosa sericea var. *pteracantha* 388, *388*
Rosa 'Sir Cedric Morris' see *Rosa glauca*
Rosa xanthina 388, *388*
Rosa xanthina 'Canary Bird' 388
rosary tree (*Melia azedarach*) 300
rose acacia (*Robinia hispida*) 385
rose apple (*Syzygium jambos*) 414, *414*
rose of Sharon (*Hibiscus syriacus*) 245, *245*
rose of Venezuela (*Brownea grandiceps*) 107
Rosebay rhododendron (*Rhododendron maximum*) 379
rosebud cherry (*Prunus subhirtella*) 359
rose-laurel (*Nerium*) 311
rosemary (*Rosmarinus officinalis*) 388–9, *389*
rosemary grevillea (*Grevillea rosmarinifolia*) 235, *235*
Rosmarinus 388–9
Rosmarinus officinalis 388–9, *389*
Rosmarinus officinalis 'Prostratus' 389
rotang (*Calamus*) 114–15
Rothmannia 389
Rothmannia capensis 389, *389*
Rothmannia globosa 389, *389*
round-leafed snow gum (*Eucalyptus perriniana*) 208, *208*
round-leafed mintbush (*Prostanthera rotundifolia*) 354
rowan (*Sorbus*) 405
rowan (*Sorbus aucuparia*) 405, *405*
royal hakea (*Hakea victoria*) 238–9, *238*
royal palm (*Roystonea*) 389–90
Roystonea 389–90
Roystonea regia 389–90, *389*
Rubus 390
Rubus idaeus 390, *390*
Rubus occidentalis 390, *390*
Rubus odoratus 390
rum cherry (*Prunus serotina*) 359, *359*
Russian elm (*Ulmus laevis*) 433
Russian olive (*Elaeagnus angustifolia*) 189
rust-bush (*Lomatia ferruginea*) 282
rusty-shield tree (*Peltophorum pterocarpum*) 323, *323*

Sabal 392
Sabal minor 392, *392*
Sabal palmetto 392, *392*
sacred bamboo (*Nandina domestica*) 310, *310*
sacred flower of the Incas (*Cantua*) 125
sage (*Salvia*) 394
sago cycad (*Cycas*) 172–3
St Dabeoc's heath (*Daboecia*) 176
St John's bread (*Ceratonia siliqua*) 138, *138*
St John's wort (*Hypericum*) 249–50
Salix 392–4
Salix alba 392, *392*
Salix alba 'Britzensis' 392
Salix alba var. *caerulea* 392
Salix alba 'Chrysostela' 392
Salix alba var. *sericea* 392
Salix apoda 392, *393*
Salix babylonica 393, *393*
Salix babylonica 'Annularis' see *Salix babylonica* 'Crispa'
Salix babylonica 'Crispa' 393
Salix × *chrysocoma* 393
Salix fragilis 393
Salix humboldtiana 393
Salix integra 393
Salix integra 'Alba Maculata' 393, *393*
Salix integra 'Hakuro-nishki' 393, *393*
Salix matsudana 'Tortuosa' 393, *393*
Salix purpurea 394, *394*
Salix chinensis see *Salix humboldtiana*
salmon gum (*Eucalyptus salmonophloia*) 209, *209*
Salvia 394
Salvia africana-lutea 394, *394*
Samanea 394
Samanea saman 394
Sambucus 394
Sambucus caerulea 394
Sambucus canadensis 394, *394*
Sambucus nigra 394, *394*
sand cypress-pine (*Callitris columellaris*) 118, *118*
sandalwood (*Santalum*) 394–5
Santa Lucia fir (*Abies bracteata*) 53, *53*
Santalum 394–5
Santalum acuminatum 395, *395*
Sapindus 395
Sapindus drummondii 395, *395*
Sapium 395
Sapium sebiferum 395, *395*
Saraca 395
Saraca indica 395, *395*
Sarcococca 396
Sarcococca hookeriana 396, *396*
Sarcococca hookeriana var. *hookeriana* 396
Sarcococca hookeriana 'Purple Stem' 396
Sarcococca ruscifolia 396, *396*
Sargent cherry (*Prunus sargentii*) 359, *359*
Sargent's crab apple (*Malus sargentii*) 294, *294*
Saskatoon serviceberry (*Amelanchier alnifolia*) 83, *83*
sassafras (*Sassafras albidum*) 396, *396*
Sassafras 396
Sassafras albidum 396, *396*
sausage tree (*Kigelia africana*) 265, *265*
Savana calabash (*Amphitecna latifolia*) 84
savin juniper (*Juniperus sabina*) 262
saw banksia (*Banksia serrata*) 98, *98*
saw palmetto (*Serenoa repens*) 401, *401*
Sawara cypress (*Chamaecyparis pisifera*) 144–5
sawtooth oak (*Quercus acutissima*) 366–7, *366*
Saxegothaea 396
Saxegothaea conspicua 396, *396*
Scaevola 396
Scaevola sericea 396, *396*
Scaevola taccada see *Scaevola sericea*
scaly tree fern (*Cyathea cooperi*) 172
scarlet banksia (*Banksia coccinea*) 97
scarlet bottlebrush (*Callistemon citrinus*) 117
scarlet bush (*Hamelia patens*) 240, *240*
scarlet heath (*Erica cerinthoides*) 192, *192*
scarlet oak (*Quercus coccinea*) 368
scarlet silky oak (*Alloxylon flammeum*) 79, *79*
scarlet-flowering gum (*Eucalyptus ficifolia*) 205, *205*
scented bouvardia (*Bouvardia longiflora*) 105, *105*
Schefflera 396–7
Schefflera actinophylla 397, *397*
Schefflera arboricola 397, *397*
Schefflera arboricola 'Renate' 397
Schinus 397
Schinus areira 397, *397*
Schinus molle see *Schinus areira*
Schinus terebinthifolia 397, *397*
Schizolobium 397
Schizolobium parahybum 397
Schotia 397–8
Schotia brachypetala 398, *398*
Sciadopitys 398
Sciadopitys verticillata 398, *398*
Scolopia 398

Scolopia braunii 398, *398*
Scotch broom (*Cytisus scoparius*) 174, *174*
Scotch elm (*Ulmus glabra*) 432, *433*
Scotch laburnum (*Laburnum alpinum*) 268
Scots pine (*Pinus sylvestris*) 342–3, *343*
screw pine (*Pandanus*) 321
scrub kurrajong (*Hibiscus heterophyllus*) 244, *244*
sea buckthorn (*Hippophae rhamnoides*) 246
sea grape (*Coccoloba uvifera*) 155
sea lettuce (*Scaevola sericea*) 396, *396*
Senecio 398–9
Senecio grandifolius 398, *398*
Senecio greyii 398, *399*
Senecio laxifolia 399
Senecio leucostachys see *Senecio viravira*
Senecio petasitis 399, *399*
Senecio viravira 399, *399*
Senna 399–400
Senna alata 399, *399*
Senna artemisioides 399, *399*
Senna didymobotrya 400, *400*
Senna multijuga 400, *400*
Senna pendula 400, *400*
Senna spectabilis 400, *400*
September bush (*Polygala myrtifolia*) 350, *350*
Sequoia 400–1
Sequoia sempervirens 400–1, *401*
Sequoia sempervirens 'Adpressa' 401
Sequoia sempervirens 'Aptos Blue' 401
Sequoia sempervirens 'Los Altos' 401
Sequoia sempervirens 'Santa Cruz' 401
Sequoiadendron 401
Sequoiadendron giganteum 401, *401*
Serbian spruce (*Picea omorika*) 332, *332*
Serenoa 401
Serenoa repens 401, *401*
Serruria 402
Serruria florida 402, *402*
Serruria 'Sugar'n'spice' see *Serruria florida*
service tree (*Sorbus domestica*) 405, *405*
serviceberry (*Amelanchier*) 83–4
shagbark hickory (*Carya ovata*) 129, *129*
shallon (*Gaultheria shallon*) 229, *229*
Shantung maple (*Acer truncatum*) 68, *68*
shaving brush tree (*Pachira aquatica*) 320, *320*
sheep laurel (*Kalmia angustifolia*) 264, *264*
shell ginger (*Alpinia zerumbet*) 82, *82*
she-oak (*Allocasuarina*) 77–9
she-oak (*Casuarina*) 132–3
shisham (*Dalbergia sissoo*) 176–7
shoe flower (*Hibiscus rosa-sinensis*) 244, *245*
shrubby allamanda (*Allamanda neriifolia*) 77, *77*
Shumard red oak (*Quercus shumardii*) 370, *370*
Siberian elm (*Ulmus pumila*) 434, *434*
Siberian spruce (*Picea obovata*) 332, *332*
Sideroxylon 402
Sideroxylon inerme 402, *402*
silk cotton (*Ceiba*) 136
silk rose (*Rhodoleia championii*) 381, *381*
silk tree (*Albizia julibrissin*) 76, *76*
silk-cotton tree (*Bombax*) 104
silk-tassel bush (*Garrya elliptica*) 229, *229*
silky oak (*Grevillea robusta*) 234, *234*

silver banksia (*Banksia marginata*) 98, *98*
silver birch (*Betula pendula*) 102, *102*
silver cassia (*Senna artemisioides*) 399, *399*
silver linden (*Tilia tomentosa*) 426
silver maple (*Acer saccharinum*) 68, *68*
silver oak (*Brachylaena discolor*) 106, *106*
silver pear (*Pyrus salicifolia*) 364
silver poplar (*Populus alba*) 351
silver princess gum (*Eucalyptus caesia* subsp. *magna*) 202
silver shrub (*Olearia argophylla*) 315
silver tree (*Leucadendron argenteum*) 275, *275*
silver tree fern (*Cyathea dealbata*) 172, *173*
silver wattle (*Acacia dealbata*) 58
silver wattle (*Acacia podalyriifolia*) 60, *60*
silver-leafed paperbark (*Melaleuca argentea*) 296, *296*
Simmondsia 402
Simmondsia chinensis 402, *402*
Singapore holly (*Malpighia coccigera*) 291, *291*
single-leaf piñon (*Pinus monophylla*) 339, *339*
Sir Lowry's Pass protea (*Protea longifolia*) 355
siris (*Ailanthus*) 75
sissoo (*Dalbergia sissoo*) 176–7
Sitka spruce (*Picea sitchensis*) 333, *333*
Skimmia 403
Skimmia japonica 403, *403*
skirted grass-tree (*Kingia*) 265
slash pine (*Pinus caribaea*) 336, *336*
slash pine (*Pinus elliottii*) 338, *338*
sleeping hibiscus (*Malvaviscus arboreus*) 294
slender palm lily (*Cordyline stricta*) 159, *159*
slimwood (*Fouquieria splendens*) 222
Sloanea 403
Sloanea woollsii 403, *403*
small-leafed lillypilly (*Syzygium luehmannii*) 414, *414*
small-leafed linden (*Tilia cordata*) 425, *425*
smoke bush (*Cotinus*) 163
smoke tree (*Cotinus*) 163
smoke tree (*Cotinus coggygria*) 163, *163*
smooth Arizona cypress (*Cupressus glabra*) 171, *171*
smooth-barked apple (*Angophora costata*) 85, *85*
smooth-leafed elm (*Ulmus minor*) 433, *433*
snakewood tree (*Cecropia palmata*) 135, *135*
snappy gum (*Eucalyptus brevifolia*) 202, *202*
snow bush (*Breynia disticha*) 107, *107*
snow gum (*Eucalyptus pauciflora*) 207, *207*
snow heath (*Erica herbacea*) 194
snowball tree (*Viburnum opulus*) 438, *438*
snowbell (*Styrax*) 410–11
snowberry (*Symphoricarpos albus*) 412
snowdrop tree (*Halesia carolina*) 239, *239*
snow-in-summer (*Melaleuca linarifolia*) 298, *298*
snowy mespilus (*Amelanchier*) 83–4
snowy mespilus (*Amelanchier lamarckii*) 84, *84*
soapbark tree (*Quillaja saponaria*) 371, *371*
soft tree fern (*Dicksonia antarctica*) 180–1, *180*, *181*
Solanum 403–4

Solanum aviculare 403, *403*
Solanum mammosum 403
Solanum rantonnei 404, *404*
Sophora 404
Sophora japonica 404, *404*
Sophora japonica 'Pendula' 404
Sophora microphylla 404
Sophora microphylla 'Golden Shower' 404
Sophora microphylla var. *longicarinata* 404
Sophora tetraptera 404, *404*
Sorbaria 404
Sorbaria arborea 404
Sorbus 405
Sorbus aria 405
Sorbus aria 'Aurea' 405
Sorbus aria 'Chrysophylla' 405
Sorbus aria 'Lutescens' 405
Sorbus aria 'Majestica' 405
Sorbus aucuparia 405, *405*
Sorbus aucuparia 'Aspleniifolia' 405
Sorbus aucuparia 'Edulis' 405
Sorbus aucuparia 'Pendula' 405
Sorbus aucuparia 'Xanthocarpa' 405
Sorbus chamaemespilus 405
Sorbus commixta 405, *405*
Sorbus domestica 405, *405*
Sorbus hupehensis 406, *406*
Sorbus 'Joseph Rock' 406
Sorbus megalocarpa 406, *406*
Sorbus pohuashanensis 406
Sorbus pohuashanensis 'Pagoda Red' 406, *406*
sorrel tree (*Oxydendrum arboreum*) 318, *318*
sorrowless tree (*Saraca indica*) 395, *395*
sour gum (*Nyssa sylvatica*) 314, *314*
soursop (*Annona muricata*) 86, *86*
sourwood (*Oxydendrum arboreum*) 318, *318*
South African cabbage tree (*Cussonia*) 172
South African coral tree (*Erythrina caffra*) 198, *198*
South African corkbush (*Mundulea sericea*) 305
South African ironwood (*Millettia grandis*) 304, *304*
South African pomegranate (*Burchellia bubalina*) 110–11, *111*
South African wild pear (*Dombeya rotundifolia*) 184, *184*
South American bottle tree (*Chorisia insignis*) 147, *147*
South American willow (*Salix humboldtiana*) 393
South Australian blue gum (*Eucalyptus leucoxylon*) 206
southern arrow-wood (*Viburnum dentatum*) 437, *437*
southern beech (*Nothofagus*) 311–12
southern catalpa (*Catalpa bignioides*) 133, *133*
southern magnolia (*Magnolia grandiflora*) 288, *288*
southern rata (*Metrosideros umbellata*) 302, *302*
southern sassafras (*Atherosperma moschatum*) 92, *92*
Spanish bayonet (*Yucca aloifolia*) 446, *446*
Spanish broom (*Genista hispanica*) 230, *230*
Spanish broom (*Spartium junceum*) 406, *406*
Spanish chestnut (*Castanea sativa*) 131, *131*
Spanish fir (*Abies pinsapo*) 55, *55*
Spanish lavender (*Lavandula stoechas*) 273, *273*
Sparrmania 406
Sparrmania africana 406
Sparrmania africana 'Flore Plena' 406, *406*
Spartium 406
Spartium junceum 406, *406*

Spathodea 407
Spathodea campanulata 407, *407*
spice bush (*Lindera benzoin*) 279
spicy jatropha (*Jatropha integerrima*) 258
spider flower (*Grevillea juniperina*) 234, *234*
spider flower (*Grevillea rosmarinifolia*) 235, *235*
spider tree (*Crateva religiosa*) 168, *168*
spike lavender (*Lavandula latifolia*) 272–3
spiked cabbage tree (*Cussonia spicata*) 172, *172*
spindle-tree (*Euonymus*) 211–12
spinning gum (*Eucalyptus perriniana*) 208, *208*
Spiraea 407
Spiraea cantoniensis 407, *407*
Spiraea douglasii 407
Spiraea japonica 407
Spiraea japonica 'Anthony Waterer' 407, *407*
Spiraea japonica 'Little Princess' 407
Spiraea japonica 'Nana' 407, *407*
Spiraea nipponica 408
Spiraea nipponica 'Snowmound' 408
Spiraea prunifolia 408
Spiraea prunifolia 'Plena' 408, *408*
Spiraea thunbergii 408
spoon bush (*Cunonia capensis*) 169, *169*
spotted emu-bush (*Eremophila maculata*) 192, *192*
spotted fig (*Ficus virens*) 220, *220*
spotted gum (*Eucalyptus maculata*) 206, *206*
spotted laurel (*Aucuba*) 93
spreading-leafed pine (*Pinus patula*) 340–1, *341*
spring bloodwood (*Eucalyptus ptychocarpa*) 208, *208*
spruce (*Picea*) 330–4
square-fruited mallee (*Eucalyptus calycogona*) 203
Stachyurus 408
Stachyurus chinensis see *Stachyurus*
Stachyurus praecox 408, *408*
stag's-horn sumac (*Rhus typhina*) 383, *383*
star fruit (*Averrhoa carambola*) 93, *93*
star gooseberry (*Phyllanthus acidus*) 328, *328*
star magnolia (*Magnolia stellata*) 289, *289*
Stenocarpus 408
Stenocarpus sinuatus 408, *408*
Stephanandra 408–9
Stephanandra incisa 409, *409*
Stephanandra incisa 'Crispa' 409
Stephanandra tanakae 409, *409*
Stewartia 409
Stewartia malacodendron 409
Stewartia pseudocamellia 409, *409*
Stewartia sinensis 409
sticky flower (*Orphium frutescens*) 317, *317*
stone pine (*Pinus pinea*) 341, *341*
straw tree fern (*Cyathea cooperi*) 172
strawberry guava (*Psidium cattleianum*) 361, *361*
strawberry tree (*Arbutus*) 88–9
strawberry tree (*Arbutus unedo*) 89, *89*
strelitzia (*Strelitzia reginae*) 410, *410*
Strelitzia 410
Strelitzia juncea see *Strelitzia reginae* var. *juncea*
Strelitzia nicolai 410, *410*
Strelitzia reginae 410, *410*
Strelitzia reginae var. *juncea* 410
Streptosolen 410
Streptosolen jamesonii 410, *410*
striped maple (*Acer pensylvanicum*) 67, *67*
Styrax 410–11
Styrax japonica 410, *410*

Styrax obassia 410–11, *411*
Stuartia see *Stewartia*
subalpine fir (*Abies lasiocarpa*) 54, *54*
sugar gum (*Eucalyptus cladocalyx*) 204, *204*
sugar maple (*Acer saccarum*) 68, *68*
sugarberry (*Celtis laevigata*) 137
sugarbush (*Protea repens*) 356, *356*
sugi (*Cryptomeria japonica*) 169, *169*
Surinam cherry (*Eugenia uniflora*) 211
Sutherlandia 411
Sutherlandia frutescens 411, *411*
swamp blueberry (*Vaccinium corymbosum*) 435, *435*
swamp chestnut oak (*Quercus prinus*) 369
swamp cypress (*Taxodium distichum*) 418, *419*
swamp cyrilla (*Cyrilla*) 174
swamp immortelle (*Erythrina fusca*) 199, *199*
swamp oak (*Casuarina glauca*) 133, *133*
swamp she-oak (*Casuarina glauca*) 133, *133*
swamp white oak (*Quercus bicolor*) 367, *367*
sweet bay (*Laurus nobilis*) 272, *272*
sweet bay (*Magnolia virginiana*) 290, *290*
sweet box (*Sarcococca*) 396
sweet buckeye (*Aesculus flava*) 71, *71*
sweet cherry (*Prunus avium*) 357
sweet chestnut (*Castanea sativa*) 131, *131*
sweet gale (*Myrica gale*) 307
sweet gum (*Liquidambar styraciflua*) 279
sweet olive (*Osmanthus fragrans*) 317, *317*
sweet osmanthus (*Osmanthus fragrans*) 317, *317*
sweet pepperbush (*Clethra alnifolia*) 154
sweet quandong (*Santalum acuminatum*) 395, *395*
sweet viburnum (*Viburnum odoratissimum*) 438, *438*
sweetpea bush (*Podalyria calyptrata*) 348
sweetsop (*Annona squamosa*) 85
sweetspire (*Itea virginica*) 257, *257*
Swietenia 411
Swietenia macrophylla 411
Swietenia mahagoni 411, *411*
Swiss mountain pine (*Pinus mugo*) 339
Swiss stone pine (*Pinus cembra*) 337, *337*
Syagrus 411
Syagrus romanzoffiana 411
sycamore (*Platanus*) 346
sycamore (*Platanus occidentalis*) 346
sycamore maple (*Acer pseudoplatanus*) 67, *67*
Sydney golden wattle (*Acacia longifolia*) 58, *58*
Sydney red gum (*Angophora costata*) 85, *85*
Symphoricarpos 411–12
Symphoricarpos albus 412
Symphoricarpos orbiculatus 412, *412*
Syncarpia 412
Syncarpia glomulifera 412, *412*
Syrian alder (*Alnus orientalis*) 81, *81*
syringa (*Philadelphus*) 324–5
Syringa 412–13
Syringa × *hyacinthiflora* 412
Syringa × *hyacinthiflora* 'Blue Hyacinth' 412
Syringa × *hyacinthiflora* 'Buffon' 412
Syringa × *hyacinthiflora* 'Clarke's Giant' 412
Syringa × *hyacinthiflora* 'Esther Staley' 412
Syringa meyeri 412

Syringa meyeri 'Palabin' 412, *412*
Syringa patula 412–13
Syringa patula 'Miss Kim' 412–13, *413*
Syringa reflexa 413
Syringa reticulata 413, *413*
Syringa vulgaris 413, *413*
Syringa vulgaris 'Aurea' 413
Syringa vulgaris 'Charles Joly' 413
Syringa vulgaris 'Edith Cavell' 413
Syringa vulgaris 'Katherine Havemeyer' 413
Syringa vulgaris 'Maréchal Foch' 413
Syringa vulgaris 'Mme F. Morel' 413, *413*
Syringa vulgaris 'President Lincoln' 413
Syringa vulgaris 'Primrose' 413
Syringa vulgaris 'Souvenir d'Alice Harding' 413
Syzygium 413–14
Syzygium jambos 414, *414*
Syzygium luehmannii 414, *414*
Syzygium paniculatum 414
Syzygium wilsonii 414

Tabebuia 416
Tabebuia avellanedae 416
Tabebuia chrysantha 416, *416*
Tabebuia chrysotricha 416, *416*
Tabebuia heptaphylla 416, *416*
Tabernaemontana 416
Tabernaemontana divaricata 416
Tabernaemontana divaricata 'Flore Pleno' 416
table dogwood (*Cornus controversa*) 159, *159*
Taiwan cherry (*Prunus campanulata*) 357, *357*
Taiwania 416–7
Taiwania cryptomerioides 416–7, *417*
talipot palm (*Corypha umbraculifera*) 163, *163*
tall baeckea (*Baeckea virgata*) 96, *96*
tall sand mallee (*Eucalyptus eremophila*) 205
tamarack (*Larix laricina*) 271, *271*
tamarind (*Tamarindus indica*) 417, *417*
Tamarindus 417
Tamarindus indica 417, *417*
Tamarix 417
Tamarix aphylla 417, *417*
Tamarix chinensis 418
Tamarix gallica see *Tamarix parviflora*
Tamarix parviflora 418, *418*
Tamarix pentandra see *Tamarix ramosissima*
Tamarix ramosissima 418
Tamarix ramosissima 'Pink Cascade' 418, *418*
tambookie thorn (*Erythrina acanthocarpa*) 197, *197*
tanbark oak (*Lithocarpus densiflorus*) 281
tanekaha (*Phyllocladus trichomanoides*) 328, *328*
tangelo (*Citrus paradisi* × *Citrus reticulata*) 152, *152*
Tanyosho pine (*Pinus densiflora* 'Umbraculifera') 338
taraire (*Beilschmiedia tarairi*) 100
tarata (*Pittosporum eugenioides*) 344, *344*
Tasmanian beech (*Nothofagus cunninghamii*) 311, *311*
Tasmanian blue gum (*Eucalyptus globulus*) 205, *205*
Tasmanian laurel (*Anopterus glandulosus*) 86, *86*
Tasmanian leatherwood (*Eucryphia lucida*) 211
Tasmanian myrtle (*Nothofagus cunninghamii*) 311, *311*
Tasmanian pencil pine (*Athrotaxis cupressoides*) 93
tatarian honeysuckle (*Lonicera tatarica*) 282, *283*

taupata (*Coprosma repens*) 157, *157*
Taxodium 418–9
Taxodium ascendens 418–9, *418*
Taxodium ascendens 'Nutans' 419
Taxodium distichum 418, *419*
Taxodium mucronatum 419, *419*
Taxus 419
Taxus baccata 419
Taxus baccata 'Aurea' 419
Taxus baccata 'Fastigiata' 419, *419*
Taxus baccata 'Repandens' 419, *419*
Taxus cuspidata 419, *419*
Taxus cuspidata 'Densiformis' 419
tea (*Camellia sinensis*) 124, *124*
teak (*Tectona*) 420
tea-tree (*Leptospermum*) 273
tea-tree (*Leptospermum scoparium*) 274, *274*
Tecoma 419–20
Tecoma stans 420, *420*
Tecomaria 420
Tecomaria capensis 420, *420*
Tecomaria capensis 'Aurea' 420
Tectona 420
Tectona grandis 420
Telanthophora grandifolius see *Senecio grandifolius*
Telopea 420–1
Telopea oreades 420, *421*
Telopea speciosissima 420, *421*
Telopea speciosissima 'Wirrimbirra White' 420, *421*
temple plant (*Crateva religiosa*) 168, *168*
temple plant (*Plumeria*) 347–8
Terminalia 421
Terminalia catappa 421, *421*
Ternstroemia 421
Ternstroemia gymnanthera 421, *421*
Tetradium 421–2
Tetradium daniellii 422, *422*
Tetrapanax 422
Tetrapanax papyrifera 422, *422*
Tetrapanax papyrifera 'Variegata' 422
Texas umbrella tree (*Melia azedarach* 'Umbraculiformis') 300
thatch palm (*Howea forsteriana*) 247
Theobroma 422
Theobroma cacao 422, *422*
Thevetia 422
Thevetia peruviana 422, *422*
Thevetia thevetioides 422, *423*
thimbleberry (*Rubus odoratus*) 390
thorn (*Crataegus*) 166–7
three-cornered palm (*Neodypsis decaryi*) 310–11, *311*
Thryptomene 422–3
Thryptomene calycina 423, *423*
Thryptomene saxicola 423, *423*
Thuja 423
Thuja occidentalis 423, *423*
Thuja occidentalis 'Ericoides' 423
Thuja occidentalis 'Lutea' 423
Thuja occidentalis 'Rheingold' 423
Thuja occidentalis 'Smaragd' 423, *423*
Thuja plicata 423, *423*
Thuja plicata 'Rogersii' 423
Thuja plicata 'Zebrina' 423, *424*
Thujopsis 424
Thujopsis dolabrata 424, *424*
Thujopsis dolabrata 'Nana' 424, *424*
Thujopsis dolabrata 'Variegata' 424
thunberg barberry (*Berberis thunbergii*) 101
ti (*Cordyline*) 158
ti (*Cordyline fruticosa*) 158–9, *158*
ti kouka (*Cordyline australis*) 158, *158*
ti ngahere (*Cordyline banksii*) 158, *158*
Tibetan cherry (*Prunus serrula*) 359, *359*
Tibouchina 424
Tibouchina granulosa 424, *424*
Tibouchina lepidota 424, *424*
Tibouchina lepidota 'Alstonville' 424

Tibouchina semidecandra see *Tibouchina urvilleana*
Tibouchina urvilleana 424, *425*
Tilia 424–6
Tilia americana 425, *425*
Tilia cordata 425, *425*
Tilia × *europaea* 425
Tilia × *europaea* 'Wratislaviensis' 425, *425*
Tilia heterophylla 426, *426*
Tilia platyphyllos 426
Tilia platyphyllos 'Rubra' 426, *426*
Tilia tomentosa 426
Tilia tomentosa 'Petiolaris' 426
tipu tree (*Tipuana tipu*) 426, *426*
Tipuana 426
Tipuana tipu 426, *426*
Tithonia 426–7
Tithonia diversifolia 427, *427*
titoki (*Alectryon excelsus*) 76, *76*
toddy palm (*Caryota urens*) 130, *130*
toii (*Cordyline indivisa*) 158, *159*
tolbos (*Leucadendron tinctum*) 276, *276*
tolu balsam (*Myroxylon balsamum*) 308, *308*
Toona 427
Toona australis see *Toona ciliata*
Toona ciliata 427, *427*
Toona sinensis 427
Toona sinensis 'Flamingo' 427, *427*
Torreya 427–8
Torreya californica 428, *428*
Torreya nucifera 428
totara (*Podocarpus totara*) 350, *350*
tower of jewels (*Echium fastuosum*) 188, *188*
Toxicodendron 428
Toxicodendron succedaneum 428, *428*
toyon (*Heteromeles arbutifolia*) 243, *243*
Trachycarpus 428
Trachycarpus fortunei 428, *428*
traveller's palm (*Ravenala madagascariensis*) 372–3, *372*
traveller's tree (*Ravenala madagascariensis*) 372–3, *372*
tree anemone (*Carpenteria californica*) 127, *127*
tree aralia (*Kalopanax*) 264
tree fern (*Dicksonia*) 180–1
tree fuchsia (*Fuchsia arborescens*) 225, *225*
tree fuchsia (*Schotia brachypetala*) 398, *398*
tree gardenia (*Rothmannia globosa*) 389, *389*
tree heath (*Erica arborea*) 192
tree heath (*Richea pandanifolia*) 384
tree huckleberry (*Vaccinium arboreum*) 435
tree marigold (*Tithonia diversifolia*) 427, *427*
tree of heaven (*Ailanthus*) 75
tree of heaven (*Ailanthus altissima*) 75, *75*
tree peony (*Paeonia suffruticosa*) 320, *321*
tree philodendron (*Philodendron bipinnatifidum*) 325, *325*
tree sparkleberry (*Vaccinium arboreum*) 435
tree waratah (*Alloxylon flammeum*) 79, *79*
tree wisteria (*Bolusanthus speciosus*) 103–4, *104*
tree-fern tree (*Schizolobium parahybum*) 397
tree-in-a-hurry (*Virgilia oroboides*) 440, *440*
Trichilia 428–9
Trichilia emetica 428, *429*
Tricuspidaria dependens see *Crinodendron patagua*
Tricuspidaria lanceolata see *Crinodendron hookerianum*
trifoliate orange (*Poncirus trifoliata*) 351
Tristaniopsis 429

Tristaniopsis laurina 429, *429*
Tristiana conferta see *Lophostemon confertus*
tropical almond (*Terminalia*) 421
true myrtle (*Myrtus communis*) 308, *308*
trumpet tree (*Tabebuia*) 416
Tsuga 429
Tsuga canadensis 429, *429*
Tsuga canadensis 'Pendula' 429, *429*
Tsuga caroliniana 430, *430*
Tsuga chinensis 430, *430*
Tsuga heterophylla 430, *430*
Tsuga mertensiana 430
tuckeroo (*Cupaniopsis anacardioides*) 170, *170*
tulip satinwood (*Rhodosphaera rhodanthema*) 381, *381*
tulip tree (*Liriodendron*) 280
tulip tree (*Liriodendron tulipifera*) 281, *281*
tupelo gum (*Nyssa aquatica*) 314
Turkey oak (*Quercus cerris*) 367, *367*
Turkish liquidambar (*Liquidambar orientalis*) 279, *279*
turpentine (*Syncarpia*) 412
twiggy heath-myrtle (*Baeckea virgata*) 96, *96*

Ugni 432
Ugni molinae 432, *432*
ulmo (*Eucryphia cordifolia*) 210, *210*
Ulmus 432–4
Ulmus americana 432, *432*
Ulmus carpinifolia see *Ulmus minor*
Ulmus glabra 432, *433*
Ulmus glabra 'Camperdownii' 433
Ulmus glabra 'Lutescens' 433
Ulmus × *hollandica* 433, *433*
Ulmus × *hollandica* 'Hollandica' 433
Ulmus × *hollandica* 'Jacqueline Hillier' 433
Ulmus × *hollandica* 'Purpurascens' 433
Ulmus × *hollandica* 'Vegeta' 433
Ulmus laevis 433
Ulmus minor 433, *433*
Ulmus minor 'Variegata' 433
Ulmus parvifolia 433, *433*
Ulmus procera 433, *433*
Ulmus procera 'Louis van Houtte' 433; see also *Ulmus glabra*
Ulmus pumila 434, *434*
Ulmus pumila 'Sapporo Autumn Gold' 434
Umbellularia 434
Umbellularia californica 434
umbrella pine (*Pinus pinea*) 341, *341*
umzimbeet (*Millettia grandis*) 304, *304*
Ussuri pear (*Pyrus ussuriensis*) 364, *364*

Vaccinium 435–6
Vaccinium arboreum 435
Vaccinium corymbosum 435, *435*
Vaccinium corymbosum 'Blue Ray' 435
Vaccinium ovatum 435, *435*
varnish tree (*Koelreuteria paniculata*) 266, *266*
Veitchia 435
Veitchia merrillii 435, *435*
velvet ash (*Fraxinus velutina*) 224, *225*
velvet geranium (*Senecio petasitis*) 399, *399*
Venetian sumac (*Cotinus coggygria*) 163, *163*
Vernicia 436
Vernicia fordii 436
veronica (*Hebe*) 241–2
Vestia 436
Vestia lycioides 436, *436*
Viburnum 436–9
Viburnum × *bodnantense* 436, *436*
Viburnum × *bodnantense* 'Dawn' 436

Viburnum × *bodnantense* 'Deben' 436
Viburnum × *burkwoodii* 437
Viburnum carlesii 437, *437*
Viburnum carlesii 'Aurora' 437
Viburnum carlesii 'Charis' 437
Viburnum carlesii 'Diana' 437
Viburnum davidii 437, *437*
Viburnum davidii 'Femina' 437
Viburnum dentatum 437, *437*
Viburnum farreri 437, *437*
Viburnum farreri 'Candidissimum' 437
Viburnum fragrans see *Viburnum farreri*
Viburnum lantana 438, *438*
Viburnum macrocephalum 438, *438*
Viburnum odoratissimum 438, *438*
Viburnum opulus 438, *438*
Viburnum opulus var. *americanum* 438, *438*
Viburnum opulus 'Compactum' 438
Viburnum opulus 'Sterile' 438
Viburnum opulus 'Xanthocarpum' 438
Viburnum plicatum 438–9
Viburnum plicatum 'Mariesii' 438
Viburnum plicatum 'Pink Beauty' 439, *439*
Viburnum plicatum var. *plicatum* 439
Viburnum prunifolium 439, *439*
Viburnum rhytidophyllum 439, *439*
Viburnum setigerum 439, *439*
Viburnum tinus 439, *439*
Viburnum trilobum see *Viburnum opulus*
Victorian Christmas bush (*Prostanthera lasianthos*) 354, *354*
Victorian waratah (*Telopea oreades*) 420, *421*
vine-leaf maple (*Acer cissifolium*) 63, *63*
violet kunzea (*Kunzea parvifolia*) 266, *266*
Vireya rhododendrons see *Rhododendron*
Virgilia 439–40
Virgilia capensis see *Virgilia oroboides*
Virgilia divaricata see *Virgilia*
Virgilia oroboides 440, *440*
Virginian witch hazel (*Hamamelis virginiana*) 240, *240*
Vitex 440
Vitex agnus-castus 440
Vitex lucens 440, *440*
Vitex negundo 440, *440*
Vitex trifolia 440
Vitex trifolia 'Purpurea' 440
Vitex trifolia 'Variegata' 440
voss laburnum (*Laburnum* × *watereri* 'Vossii') 268, 269

walnut (*Juglans*) 259–60
wampee (*Clausena lansium*) 152
waratah (*Telopea*) 420–1
waratah (*Telopea speciosissima*) 420, *421*
Warminster broom (*Cytisus* × *praecox*) 174
washington thorn (*Crataegus phaenopyrum*) 167, *167*
Washingtonia 442
Washingtonia filifera 442, *442*
washingtonia palm (*Washingtonia*) 442
Washingtonia robusta 442, *442*
water ash (*Ptelea trifoliata*) 362, *362*
water gum (*Tristaniopsis laurina*) 429, *429*
water locust (*Gleditsia aquatica*) 231
water oak (*Quercus nigra*) 368, *369*
water tupelo (*Nyssa aquatica*) 314
wattle (*Acacia*) 57–61
wax flowers (*Eriostemon*) 196–7
wax myrtle (*Myrica cerifera*) 307, *307*

wax plant (*Eriostemon australasius*) 196, *197*
wax tree (*Toxicodendron succedaneum*) 428, *428*
wayfarer tree (*Viburnum lantana*) 438, *438*
wedding bells (*Deutzia*) 179–80
wedding flower (*Dombeya*) 183–4
weeping boer-bean (*Schotia brachypetala*) 398, *398*
weeping boobialla (*Myoporum floribundum*) 307, *307*
weeping bottlebrush (*Callistemon viminalis*) 118, *118*
weeping fig (*Ficus benjamina*) 218
weeping fig (*Ficus microcarpa*) 219, *219*
weeping golden willow (*Salix* × *chrysocoma*) 393
weeping kowhai (*Sophora microphylla*) 404
weeping myall (*Acacia pendula*) 59, *59*
weeping paperbark (*Melaleuca leucadendra*) 298
weeping pittosporum (*Pittosporum phylliraeoides*) 344, *344*
weeping spruce (*Picea breweriana*) 330, *330*
weeping willow (*Salix babylonica*) 393
Weigela 442
Weigela 'Bristol Ruby' 442
Weigela florida 442
Weigela florida 'Variegata' 443, *442*
Weigela middendorffiana 443
West Himalayan spruce (*Picea smithiana*) 334, *334*
West Indian cherry (*Malpighia glabra*) 291, *291*
West Indian ebony (*Brya ebenus*) 109, *109*
West Indies mahogany (*Swietenia mahagoni*) 411, *411*
Western Australian Christmas tree (*Nuytsia floribunda*) 313, *313*
western balsam (*Populus trichocarpa*) 352, *353*
western hemlock (*Tsuga heterophylla*) 430, *430*
western red cedar (*Thuja plicata*) 423, *423*
western redbud (*Cercis occidentalis*) 141, *141*
western soapberry (*Sapindus drummondii*) 395, *395*
western spiraea (*Spiraea douglasii*) 407
western sycamore (*Platanus racemosa*) 346, *346*
western white pine (*Pinus monticola*) 339, *339*
western woody pear (*Xylomelum occidentale*) 445–6, *445*
western yellow pine (*Pinus ponderosa*) 341
Westringia 443
Westringia fruticosa 443, *443*
Westringia rosmariniformis see *Westringia fruticosa*
wheki-ponga (*Dicksonia fibrosa*) 181, *181*
white basswood (*Tilia heterophylla*) 426, *426*
white birch (*Betula pendula*) 102, *102*
white bottlebrush (*Callistemon salignus*) 117, *117*
white broom (*Retama monosperma*) 373, *373*
white cedar (*Melia azedarach*) 300
white correa (*Correa alba*) 161, *161*
white cypress-pine (*Callitris glaucophylla*) 118, *119*
white diosma (*Coleonema album*) 156
white elm (*Ulmus americana*) 432, *432*

white gardenia (*Gardenia thunbergia*) 228, *228*
white karee (*Rhus pendulina*) 382–3, *383*
white mulberry (*Morus alba*) 304, *305*
white oak (*Lagunaria patersonia*) 270, *270*
white poplar (*Populus alba*) 351
white siris (*Albizia lebbek*) 76
white spruce (*Picea glauca*) 331
white walnut (*Juglans cinerea*) 259
white willow (*Salix alba*) 392, *392*
white yiel-yiel (*Grevillea hilliana*) 234, *234*
whitebalm (*Sorbus*) 405
whitebeam (*Sorbus aria*) 405
white-haired cycad (*Encephalartos friderici-guilielmi*) 190, *190*
Widdringtonia 443
Widdringtonia cupressoides 443
wild almond (*Brabejum stellatifolium*) 105, *105*
wild apple (*Malus sylvestris*) 294
wild banana (*Strelitzia nicolai*) 410, *410*
wild cherry (*Prunus avium*) 357
wild China-tree (*Sapindus drummondii*) 395, *395*
wild coffee (*Polyscias guilfoylei*) 350
wild hollyhock (*Sparrmania africana*) 406
wild plum (*Harpephyllum caffrum*) 241, *241*
willow hakea (*Hakea salicifolia*) 238
willow (*Salix*) 392–4
willow oak (*Quercus phellos*) 369, *369*
willow pittosporum (*Pittosporum phylliraeoides*) 344, *344*
willowleaf podocarp (*Podocarpus salignus*) 349, *349*
willow-leafed pear (*Pyrus salicifolia*) 364
willow-myrtle (*Agonis flexuosa*) 74, *75*
Wilmore heath (*Erica* × *wilmorei*) 196
Wilson barberry (*Berberis wilsoniae*) 101, *101*
Wilson's magnolia (*Magnolia wilsonii*) 290
windmill palm (*Trachycarpus*) 428
winter hazel (*Corylopsis*) 161–2
winter heath (*Erica herbacea*) 194
winter honeysuckle (*Lonicera fragrantissima*) 282, *283*
winter jasmine (*Jasminum nudiflorum*) see *Jasminum mesnyi*
winterberry (*Ilex verticillata*) 255, *255*
winter's bark (*Drimys*) 185
wintersweet (*Acokanthera*) 69
wintersweet (*Acokanthera oblongifolia*) 69, *69*
wintersweet (*Chimonanthus*) 146
wire-netting bush (*Corokia cotoneaster*) 160
witch hazel (*Hamamelis*) 239
witch hazel (*Hamamelis* × *intermedia*) 239
Wodyetia 443
Wodyetia bifurcata 443
Wollemi pine (*Wollemia nobilis*) 443, *444*
Wollemia 443–4
Wollemia nobilis 443, *444*
woman's tongue tree (*Albizia lebbek*) 76
wonder tree (*Idesia polycarpa*) 252, *252*
woody pear (*Xylomelum*) 445–6
woolly grevillea (*Grevillea lanigera*) 234
wu tree (*Firmiana simplex*) 220, *220*
wych elm (*Ulmus glabra*) 432, *433*

Xanthorrhoea 444–5
Xanthorrhoea australis see *Xanthorrhoea glauca*
Xanthorrhoea glauca 445
Xanthorrhoea malacophylla 444, *445*
Xanthorrhoea preissii 445, *445*
Xanthostemon 445
Xanthostemon chrysanthus 445, *445*
Xylomelum 445–6
Xylomelum occidentale 445–6, *445*

yaupon (*Ilex vomitoria*) 255
Yeddo hawthorn (*Raphiolepis umbellata*) 374, *374*
yellow birch (*Betula alleghaniensis*) 101
yellow buckeye (*Aesculus flava*) 71, *71*
yellow carabeen (*Sloanea woollsii*) 403, *403*
yellow elder (*Tecoma stans*) 420, *420*
yellow flame tree (*Peltophorum pterocarpum*) 323, *323*
yellow guava (*Psidium guajava*) 362
yellow gum (*Eucalyptus leucoxylon*) 206
yellow jasmine (*Jasminum mesnyi*) 258, *258*
yellow kapok (*Cochlospermum fraseri*) 155, *155*
yellow oak (*Quercus velutina*) 370, *371*
yellow oleander (*Thevetia peruviana*) 422, *422*
yellow poinciana (*Peltophorum pterocarpum*) 323, *323*
yellow tree peony (*Paeonia lutea*) 320–1, *320*
yellow trumpet tree (*Tecoma stans*) 420, *420*
yellowbells (*Tecoma stans*) 420, *420*
yellow-bush (*Leucadendron comosum*) 275
yellow-wood (*Cladrastis*) 152
yellowwood (*Rhodosphaera rhodanthema*) 381, *381*
yesterday, today and tomorrow (*Brunfelsia australis*) 108–9, *108*
ylang ylang (*Cananga odorata*) 125, *125*
yorrell (*Eucalyptus gracilis*) 205, *205*
Yoshino cherry (*Prunus* × *yedoensis*) 360, *360*
Yucca 446
Yucca aloifolia 446, *446*
Yucca aloifolia 'Marginata' 446
Yucca aloifolia 'Tricolor' 446
Yucca aloifolia 'Variegata' 446, *446*
Yucca brevifolia 446
Yucca elephantipes 446, *446*
yulan magnolia (*Magnolia denudata*) 288, *288*
Yunnan firethorn (*Pyracantha crenatoserrata*) 364
Yunnan poplar (*Populus yunnanensis*) 352

zamia (*Macrozamia miquelii*) 287, *287*
Zelkova 446–7
Zelkova carpinifolia 446–7, *447*
Zelkova serrata 447, *447*
Zieria 447
Zieria buxijgum 447, *447*
Zizyphus 447
Zizyphus jujuba 447, *447*

© text Random House (Australia) Pty Ltd, 1996

© photographs Random House (Australia) Pty Ltd, 1996, except Wollemi pines photographs © Royal Botanic Gardens Sydney/ Jaime Plaza van Roon